A ROADMAP FOR SELECTING A STATISTICAL METHOD

Data Analysis Task	For Numerical Variables	For Categorical Variables
Describing a group or several groups	Ordered array, stem-and-leaf display, frequency distribution, relative frequency distribution, percentage distribution, cumulative percentage distribution, histogram, polygon, cumulative percentage polygon **(Sections 2.2, 2.4)** Mean, median, mode, quartiles, range, interquartile range, standard deviation, variance, coefficient of variation, skewness, kurtosis, boxplot, normal probability plot **(Sections 3.1, 3.2, 3.3, 6.3)**	Summary table, bar chart, pie chart, Pareto chart **(Sections 2.1 and 2.3)**
Inference about one group	Confidence interval estimate of the mean **(Sections 8.1 and 8.2)** t test for the mean **(Section 9.2)**	Confidence interval estimate of the proportion **(Section 8.3)** Z test for the proportion **(Section 9.4)**
Comparing two groups	Tests for the difference in the means of two independent populations **(Section 10.1)** Paired t test **(Section 10.2)** F test for the difference between two variances **(Section 10.4)**	Z test for the difference between two proportions **(Section 10.3)** Chi-square test for the difference between two proportions **(Section 11.1)**
Comparing more than two groups	One-way analysis of variance for comparing several means **(Section 10.5)**	Chi-square test for differences among more than two proportions **(Section 11.2)**
Analyzing the relationship between two variables	Scatter plot, time series plot **(Section 2.5)** Covariance, coefficient of correlation **(Section 3.5)** Simple linear regression **(Chapter 12)** t test of correlation **(Section 12.7)**	Contingency table, side-by-side bar chart, PivotTables **(Sections 2.1, 2.3, 2.6)** Chi-square test of independence **(Section 11.3)**
Analyzing the relationship between two or more variables	Multiple regression **(Chapter 13)**	Multidimensional contingency tables **(Section 2.6)**

Business Statistics
A First Course

SEVENTH EDITION

David M. Levine

Department of Statistics and Computer Information Systems

Zicklin School of Business, Baruch College, City University of New York

Kathryn A. Szabat

Department of Business Systems and Analytics

School of Business, La Salle University

David F. Stephan

Two Bridges Instructional Technology

PEARSON

Boston Columbus Hoboken Indianapolis New York San Francisco
Amsterdam Cape Town Dubai London Madrid Milan Munich Paris Montreal Toronto
Delhi Mexico City São Paulo Sydney Hong Kong Seoul Singapore Taipei Tokyo

Editorial Director: Chris Hoag
Editor in Chief: Deirdre Lynch
Acquisitions Editor: Suzanna Bainbridge
Editorial Assistant: Justin Billing
Program Manager: Chere Bemelmans
Project Manager: Sherry Berg
Program Management Team Lead: Marianne Stepanian
Project Management Team Lead: Peter Silvia
Media Producer: Jean Choe
TestGen Content Manager: John Flanagan
MathXL Content Developer: Bob Carroll

Marketing Manager: Erin Kelly
Marketing Assistant: Emma Sarconi
Senior Author Support/Technology Specialist: Joe Vetere
Rights and Permissions Project Manager: Diahanne Lucas Dowridge
Senior Procurement Specialist: Carol Melville
Associate Director of Design: Andrea Nix
Program Design Lead and Cover Design: Barbara Atkinson
Text Design, Production Coordination, Composition, and Illustrations: Lumina Datamatics
Cover Image: Pressmaster/Shutterstock

Library of Congress Cataloging-in-Publication Data

Levine, David M., 1946—
 Business statistics : a first course / David M. Levine, Baruch College City University, Kathryn A. Szabat, La Salle University, David F. Stephan, Instructional Technology.—7th edition.
  pages cm
  ISBN 978-0-321-97901-8
1. Commercial statistics. 2. Industrial management—Statistical methods. I. Szabat, Kathryn A. II. Stephan, David. III. Title.
  HF1017.B382 2016
  519.5—dc23

                                                          2014019092

1 2 3 4 5 6 7 8 9 10—CRK—18 17 16 15 14

www.pearsonhighered.com

ISBN-10: 0-321-97901-X
ISBN-13: 978-0-321-97901-8

To our spouses and children,
Marilyn, Sharyn, Mary, and Mark

---

and to our parents, in loving memory,
Lee, Reuben, Mary, William, Ruth, and Francis

About the Authors

Kathryn Szabat, David Levine, and David Stephan

David M. Levine, Kathryn A. Szabat, and David F. Stephan are all experienced business school educators committed to innovation and improving instruction in business statistics and related subjects.

David Levine, Professor Emeritus of Statistics and CIS at Baruch College, CUNY, is a nationally recognized innovator in statistics education for more than three decades. Levine has coauthored 14 books, including several business statistics textbooks; textbooks and professional titles that explain and explore quality management and the Six Sigma approach; and, with David Stephan, a trade paperback that explains statistical concepts to a general audience. Levine has presented or chaired numerous sessions about business education at leading conferences conducted by the Decision Sciences Institute (DSI) and the American Statistical Association, and he and his coauthors have been active participants in the annual DSI Making Statistics More Effective in Schools and Business (MSMESB) mini-conference. During his many years teaching at Baruch College, Levine was recognized for his contributions to teaching and curriculum development with the College's highest distinguished teaching honor. He earned B.B.A. and M.B.A. degrees from CCNY. and a Ph.D. in industrial engineering and operations research from New York University.

As Associate Professor and Chair of Business Systems and Analytics at La Salle University, **Kathryn Szabat** has transformed several business school majors into one interdisciplinary major that better supports careers in new and emerging disciplines of data analysis including analytics. Szabat strives to inspire, stimulate, challenge, and motivate students through innovation and curricular enhancements, and shares her coauthors' commitment to teaching excellence and the continual improvement of statistics presentations. Beyond the classroom she has provided statistical advice to numerous business, nonbusiness, and academic communities, with particular interest in the areas of education, medicine, and nonprofit capacity building. Her research activities have led to journal publications, chapters in scholarly books, and conference presentations. Szabat is a member of the American Statistical Association (ASA), DSI, Institute for Operation Research and Management Sciences (INFORMS), and DSI MSMESB. She received a B.S. from SUNY-Albany, an M.S. in statistics from the Wharton School of the University of Pennsylvania, and a Ph.D. degree in statistics, with a cognate in operations research, from the Wharton School of the University of Pennsylvania.

Advances in computing have always shaped **David Stephan's** professional life. As an undergraduate, he helped professors use statistics software that was considered advanced even though it could compute *only* several things discussed in Chapter 3, thereby gaining an early appreciation for the benefits of using software to solve problems (and perhaps positively influencing his grades). An early advocate of using computers to support instruction, he developed a prototype of a mainframe-based system that anticipated features found today in Pearson's MathXL and served as special assistant for computing to the Dean and Provost at Baruch College. In his many years teaching at Baruch, Stephan implemented the first computer-based *classroom*, helped redevelop the CIS curriculum, and, as part of a FIPSE project team, designed and implemented a multimedia learning environment. He was also nominated for teaching honors. Stephan has presented at the SEDSI conference and the DSI MSMESB mini-conferences, sometimes with his coauthors. Stephan earned a B.A. from Franklin & Marshall College and an M.S. from Baruch College, CUNY, and he studied instructional technology at Teachers College, Columbia University.

For all three coauthors, continuous improvement is a natural outcome of their curiosity about the world. Their varied backgrounds and many years of teaching experience have come together to shape this book in ways discussed in the Preface. To learn more about the coauthors, visit **authors .davidlevinestatistics.com**.

Brief Contents

Contents

3 Numerical Descriptive Measures   97

4 Basic Probability   142

5   Discrete Probability Distributions   176

6   The Normal Distribution   200

7   Sampling Distributions   226

8 Confidence Interval Estimation   248

9 Fundamentals of Hypothesis Testing: One-Sample Tests   284

10 Two-Sample Tests and One-Way ANOVA 323

11 Chi-Square Tests 387

12 Simple Linear Regression 414

Preface

The world of business statistics has grown larger, expanding into and combining with other disciplines. And, in a reprise of something that occurred a generation ago, new fields of study, this time with names such as informatics, data analytics, and decision science, have emerged.

This time of change makes what is taught in business statistics and how it is taught all the more critical. We, the coauthors, think about these changes as we seek ways to continuously improve the teaching of business statistics. We actively participate in Decision Sciences Institute (DSI), American Statistical Association (ASA), and Making Statistics More Effective in Schools and Business (MSMESB) conferences. We use the ASA's Guidelines for Assessment and Instruction (GAISE) reports and combine them with our experiences teaching business statistics to a diverse student body at several universities. We also benefit from the interests and efforts of our past coauthors, Mark Berenson and Timothy Krehbiel.

Our Educational Philosophy

When writing for introductory business statistics students, we are guided by these principles:

Help students see the relevance of statistics to their own careers by providing examples drawn from the functional areas in which they may be specializing. Students need to learn statistics in the context of the functional areas of business. We present each statistics topic in the context of areas such as accounting, finance, management, and marketing and explain the application of specific methods to business activities.

Emphasize interpretation and analysis of statistical results over calculation. We emphasize the interpretation of results, the evaluation of the assumptions, and the discussion of what should be done if the assumptions are violated. We believe that these activities are more important and will serve students better in the future than focusing on tedious hand calculations.

Give students ample practice in understanding how to apply statistics to business. We believe that both classroom examples and homework exercises should involve actual or realistic data, using small and large sets of data, to the extent possible.

Familiarize students with the use of spreadsheet and statistical software. We integrate spreadsheet and statistical software into all statistics topics to illustrate how this software assists business decision making. (Using software in this way also supports our second point about emphasizing interpretation over calculation).

Provide clear instructions to students for using spreadsheet and statistical software. We believe that providing such instructions facilitates learning and helps prevent minimizes the chance that learning software to the level necessary will distract from the learning of statistical concepts.

What's New and Innovative in This Edition?

This seventh edition of *Business Statistics: A First Course* contains these new and innovative features.

Getting Started: Important Things to Learn First   Created to help students get a jumpstart on the course, lessen any fear about learning statistics, and provide coverage of those things that would be helpful to know even before the first class of the term. "Getting Started" has been developed to be posted online or otherwise distributed before the first class section begins and is available for download as explained in Appendix C. Instructors teaching online or hybrid course sections may find this to be a particularly valuable tool to help organize the students in their section.

Student Tips   In-margin notes that reinforce hard-to-master concepts and provide quick study tips for mastering important details.

Discussion of Business Analytics   "Getting Started: Important Things to Learn First" quickly defines *business analytics* and *big data* and notes how these things are changing the face of statistics.

PHStat version 4   For Microsoft Excel users, this successor to the PHStat2 statistics add-in contains several new and enhanced procedures, is simpler to set up and run, and is compatible with both Microsoft Windows and (Mac) OS X Excel versions.

Additional Chapter Short Takes   Online PDF documents (available for download as explained in Appendix C) that supply additional insights or explanations to important statistical concepts or details about the results presented in this book.

Revised and Enhanced Content

This seventh edition of *Business Statistics: A First Course* contains the following revised and enhanced content.

New Continuing End-of-Chapter Cases   This edition features several new end-of-chapter cases. New and recurring throughout the book is a case that concerns the analysis of sales and marketing data for home fitness equipment (CardioGood Fitness), a case that concerns pricing decisions made by a retailer (Sure Value Convenience Stores), and the More Descriptive Choices Follow-Up case, which extends the use of the retirement funds sample first introduced in Chapter 2. Also recurring is the Clear Mountain State Student Surveys case, which uses data collected from surveys of undergraduate and graduate students to practice and reinforce statistical methods learned in various chapters. This case replaces end-of-chapter questions related to the student survey database in the previous edition. In addition, there is a new case in simple linear regression (Brynne Packaging).

Many New Applied Examples and Problems   Many of the applied examples throughout this book use new problems or revised data. Approximately 43% of the problems are new to this edition. The end-of-section and end-of-chapter problem sets contain many new problems that use data from *The Wall Street Journal*, *USA Today*, and other sources.

Revised Using Statistics Scenarios   Five chapters have new or revised Using Statistics scenarios.

Revised Making Best Use of This Book section   Included as part of Section GS.4 of "Getting Started: Important Things to Learn First," this section presents an overview of this book and checklist that helps students prepare for using Microsoft Excel or Minitab with this book.

Revised Software Appendices   These appendices review the foundational skills for using Microsoft Excel and Minitab, review the latest technical information, and, for Excel users, cover optional but useful skills for working with Excel.

Distinctive Features

This seventh edition of *Business Statistics: A First Course* continues the use of the following distinctive features.

Using Statistics Business Scenarios   Each chapter begins with a Using Statistics example that shows how statistics is used in the functional areas of business—accounting, finance, information systems, management, and marketing. Each scenario is used throughout the chapter to provide an applied context for the concepts. The chapter concludes with a Using Statistics, Revisited section that reinforces the statistical methods and applications discussed in each chapter.

Emphasis on Data Analysis and Interpretation of Excel and Minitab Results   Our focus emphasizes analyzing data by interpreting results while reducing emphasis on doing calculations. For example, in the coverage of tables and charts in Chapter 2, we help students interpret various charts and explain when to use each chart discussed. Our coverage of hypothesis testing in Chapters 9 through 11 and regression and multiple regression in Chapters 12 and 13 include extensive software results so that the p-value approach can be emphasized.

Pedagogical Aids   We use an active writing style, boxed numbered equations, set-off examples that reinforce learning concepts, student tips, problems divided into "Learning the Basics" and "Applying the Concepts," key equations, and key terms.

Digital Cases   In the Digital Cases, available for download as explained in Appendix C, learners must examine interactive PDF documents to sift through various claims and information to discover the data most relevant to a business case scenario. Learners then determine whether the conclusions and claims are supported by the data. In doing so, learners discover and learn how to identify common misuses of statistical information. (Instructional tips for using the Digital Cases and solutions to the Digital Cases are included in the Instructor's Solutions Manual.)

Answers   Most answers to the even-numbered exercises are included at the end of the book.

Flexibility Using Excel   For almost every statistical method discussed, students can use *In-Depth Excel* instructions to directly work with worksheet solution details *or* they can use either the *PHStat* instructions *or* the *Analysis ToolPak* instructions to automate the creation of those worksheet solutions.

PHStat   PHStat is the Pearson Education statistics add-in that includes more than 60 procedures that create Excel worksheets and charts. Unlike other add-ins, PHStat results are real worksheets that contain real Excel calculations (called formulas in Excel). You can examine the contents of worksheet solutions to learn the appropriate functions and calculations necessary to apply a particular statistical method. With most of these worksheet solutions, you can change worksheet data and immediately see how those changes affect the results.

Descriptive Statistics: boxplot, descriptive summary, dot scale diagram, frequency distribution, histogram and polygons, Pareto diagram, scatter plot, stem-and-leaf display, one-way tables and charts, and two-way tables and charts

Probability and probability distributions: simple and joint probabilities, normal probability plot, and binomial, and Poisson probability distributions

Sampling: sampling distributions simulation

Confidence interval estimation: for the mean, sigma unknown; for the mean, sigma known; and for the proportion

Sample size determination: for the mean and the proportion

One-sample tests: Z test for the mean, sigma known; t test for the mean, sigma unknown; and Z test for the proportion

Two-sample tests (unsummarized data): pooled-variance t test, separate-variance t test, paired t test, and F test for differences in two variances

Two-sample tests (summarized data): pooled-variance t test, separate-variance t test, paired t test, Z test for the differences in two means, F test for differences in two variances, chi-square test for differences in two proportions, and Z test for the difference in two proportions

Multiple-sample tests: chi-square test, Levene test, one-way ANOVA, and Tukey-Kramer procedure

Regression: simple linear regression, and multiple regression

Data preparation: stack and unstack data

Control charts: *p* chart, *c* chart, and *R* and *Xbar* charts.

To learn more about PHStat, see Appendix C.

Visual Explorations   The series of Excel workbooks that allow students to interactively explore important statistical concepts in the normal distribution, sampling distributions, and regression analysis. For the normal distribution, students see the effect of changes in the mean and standard deviation on the areas under the normal curve. For sampling distributions, students use simulation to explore the effect of sample size on a sampling distribution. For regression analysis, students fit a line of regression and observe how changes in the slope and intercept affect the goodness of fit. To learn more about Visual Explorations, see Appendix C.

Chapter-by-Chapter Changes Made for This Edition

Besides the new and innovative content described in "What's New and Innovative in This Edition?" the seventh edition of *Business Statistics: A First Course* contains the following specific changes to each chapter.

Getting Started: Important Things to Learn First   This all-new chapter includes new material on business analytics and introduces the DCOVA framework and a basic vocabulary of statistics, both of which were introduced in Chapter 1 of the sixth edition.

Chapter 1   Collecting data has been relocated to this chapter from Section 2.1. Sampling methods and types of survey errors have been relocated from Sections 7.1 and 7.2. There is a new subsection on data cleaning. The CardioGood Fitness and Clear Mountain State Surveys cases are included.

Chapter 2   Section 2.1, "Data Collection," has been moved to Chapter 1. The chapter uses a new data set that contains a sample of 316 mutual funds and a new set of restaurant cost data. The CardioGood Fitness, The Choice *Is* Yours Follow-up, and Clear Mountain State Surveys cases are included.

Chapter 3   For many examples, this chapter uses the new mutual funds data set that is introduced in Chapter 2. There is increased coverage of skewness and kurtosis. There is a new example on computing descriptive measures from a population using "Dogs of the Dow." The CardioGood Fitness, More Descriptive Choices Follow-up, and Clear Mountain State Surveys cases are included.

Chapter 4   The chapter example has been updated. There are new problems throughout the chapter. The CardioGood Fitness, The Choice *Is* Yours Follow-up, and Clear Mountain State Surveys cases are included.

Chapter 5   There are many new problems throughout the chapter. The notation used has been made more consistent.

Chapter 6   This chapter has an updated Using Statistics scenario and some new problems. The CardioGood Fitness, More Descriptive Choices Follow-up, and Clear Mountain State Surveys cases are included.

Chapter 7   Sections 7.1 and 7.2 have been moved to Chapter 1. An additional example of sampling distributions from a larger population has been included.

Chapter 8   This chapter includes an updated Using Statistics scenario and new examples and exercises throughout the chapter. The Sure Value Convenience Stores, CardioGood Fitness, More Descriptive Choices Follow-up, and Clear Mountain State Surveys cases are included. There is an online section on bootstrapping.

Chapter 9   This chapter includes additional coverage of the pitfalls of hypothesis testing. The Sure Value Convenience Stores case is included.

Chapter 10   This chapter has an updated Using Statistics scenario, a new example on the paired *t*-test on textbook prices, a new example on the *Z*-test for the difference between two proportions, and a new one-way ANOVA example on mobile electronics sales at a general merchandiser. The Sure Value Convenience Stores, CardioGood Fitness, More Descriptive Choices Follow-up, and Clear Mountain State Surveys cases are included. There is a new online section on Effect Size.

Chapter 11   The chapter includes many new problems. This chapter includes the Sure Value Convenience Stores, CardioGood Fitness, More Descriptive Choices Follow-up, and Clear Mountain State Surveys cases.

Chapter 12   The Using Statistics scenario has been updated and changed, with new data used throughout the chapter. This chapter includes the Brynne Packaging case.

Chapter 13   The chapter includes many new and revised problems.

Chapter 14   The "Statistical Applications in Quality Management" chapter has been renumbered as Chapter 14 and is available for download as explained in Appendix C.

Student and Instructor Resources

Student Solutions Manual, by Professor Pin Tian Ng of Northern Arizona University and accuracy checked by Annie Puciloski, provides detailed solutions to virtually all the even-numbered exercises and worked-out solutions to the self-test problems (ISBN-10: 0-321-99881-2; ISBN-13: 978-0-321-99881-1).

Online resources   The complete set of online resources are discussed fully in Appendix C

For adopting instructors, the following resources are among those available at the Instructor's Resource Center, located at **www.pearsonhighered.com/irc**.

Instructor's Solutions Manual, by Professor Pin Tian Ng of Northern Arizona University and accuracy checked by Annie Puciloski, includes solutions for end-of-section and end-of-chapter problems, answers to case questions where applicable, and teaching tips for each chapter.

Lecture PowerPoint Presentations, by Professor Patrick Schur of Miami University and accuracy checked by David Levine and Kathryn Szabat, are available for each chapter. The PowerPoint slides provide an instructor with individual lecture outlines to accompany the text. The slides include many of the figures and tables from the text. Instructors can use these lecture notes as is or can easily modify the notes to reflect specific presentation needs.

Test Bank, by Professor Pin Tian Ng of Northern Arizona University, contains true/false, multiple-choice, fill-in, and problem-solving questions based on the definitions, concepts, and ideas developed in each chapter of the text.

TestGen® (**www.pearsoned.com/testgen**) enables instructors to build, edit, print, and administer tests using a computerized bank of questions developed to cover all the objectives of the text. TestGen is algorithmically based, allowing instructors to create multiple but equivalent versions of the same question or test with the click of a button. Instructors can also modify test bank questions or add new questions. The software and test bank are available for download from Pearson Education's online catalog.

MathXL®

MathXL® for Statistics Online Course (access code required) MathXL® is the homework and assessment engine that runs MyStatLab. (MyStatLab is MathXL plus a learning management system.)

With *MathXL for Statistics*, instructors can:

- Create, edit, and assign online homework and tests using algorithmically generated exercises correlated at the objective level to the textbook.
- Create and assign their own online exercises and import TestGen tests for added flexibility.
- Maintain records of all student work, tracked in MathXL's online gradebook.

With *MathXL for Statistics*, students can:

- Take chapter tests in MathXL and receive personalized study plans and/or personalized homework assignments based on their test results.
- Use the study plan and/or the homework to link directly to tutorial exercises for the objectives they need to study.
- Access supplemental animations directly from selected exercises.
- Knowing that students often use external statistical software, we make it easy to copy our data sets, both from the eText and the MyStatLab questions, into StatCrunch™, Microsoft Excel, Minitab, and a variety of other software packages.

MathXL for Statistics is available to qualified adopters. For more information, visit **www.mathxl .com** or contact your Pearson representative.

MyStatLab™

MyStatLab™ Online Course (access code required) MyStatLab from Pearson is the world's leading online resource for teaching and learning statistics; integrating interactive homework, assessment, and media in a flexible, easy-to-use format. MyStatLab is a course management system that delivers **proven results** in helping individual students succeed.

- MyStatLab can be implemented successfully in any environment—lab-based, hybrid, fully online, traditional—and demonstrates the quantifiable difference that integrated usage has on student retention, subsequent success, and overall achievement.
- MyStatLab's comprehensive online gradebook automatically tracks students' results on tests, quizzes, homework, and in the study plan. Instructors can use the gradebook to provide positive feedback or intervene if students have trouble. Gradebook data can be easily exported to a variety of spreadsheet programs, such as Microsoft Excel.

MyStatLab provides **engaging experiences** that personalize, stimulate, and measure learning for each student. In addition to the resources below, each course includes a full interactive online version of the accompanying textbook.

- **Tutorial Exercises with Multimedia Learning Aids:** The homework and practice exercises in MyStatLab align with the exercises in the textbook, and most regenerate algorithmically to give students unlimited opportunity for practice and mastery. Exercises offer immediate helpful feedback, guided solutions, sample problems, animations, videos, statistical software tutorial videos and eText clips for extra help at point-of-use.
- **MyStatLab Accessibility:** MyStatLab is compatible with the JAWS screen reader, and enables multiple-choice and free-response problem-types to be read, and interacted with via keyboard controls and math notation input. MyStatLab also works with screen enlargers, including ZoomText, MAGic, and SuperNova. And all MyStatLab videos accompanying texts with copyright 2009 and later have closed captioning. More information on this functionality is available at http://mymathlab.com/accessibility.
- **StatTalk Videos:** Fun-loving statistician Andrew Vickers takes to the streets of Brooklyn, NY, to demonstrate important statistical concepts through interesting stories and real-life events. This series of 24 fun and engaging videos will help students actually understand statistical concepts. Available with an instructor's user guide and assessment questions.
- **Business Insight Videos:** 10 engaging videos show managers at top companies using statistics in their everyday work. Assignable question encourage discussion.
- **Additional Question Libraries:** In addition to algorithmically regenerated questions that are aligned with your textbook, MyStatLab courses come with two additional question libraries:
  - **450 exercises** in **Getting Ready for Statistics** cover the developmental math topics students need for the course. These can be assigned as a prerequisite to other assignments, if desired.
  - **1000 exercises** in the **Conceptual Question Library** require students to apply their statistical understanding.
- **StatCrunch™:** MyStatLab integrates the web-based statistical software, StatCrunch, within the online assessment platform so that students can easily analyze data sets from exercises and the text. In addition, MyStatLab includes access to **www.StatCrunch.com**, a vibrant online community where users can access tens of thousands of shared data sets, create and conduct online surveys, perform complex analyses using the powerful statistical software, and generate compelling reports.
- **Statistical Software Support and Integration:** We make it easy to copy our data sets, both from the eText and the MyStatLab questions, into software such as StatCrunch, Minitab, Excel, and more. Students have access to a variety of support tools—Technology Tutorial Videos, Technology Study Cards, and Technology Manuals for select titles—to learn how to effectively use statistical software.

And, MyStatLab comes from an **experienced partner** with educational expertise and an eye on the future.

- Knowing that you are using a Pearson product means knowing that you are using quality content. That means that our eTexts are accurate and our assessment tools work. It means we are committed to making MyMathLab as accessible as possible.
- Whether you are just getting started with MyStatLab, or have a question along the way, we're here to help you learn about our technologies and how to incorporate them into your course.

To learn more about how MyStatLab combines proven learning applications with powerful assessment, visit **www.mystatlab.com** or contact your Pearson representative.

StatCrunch™ StatCrunch is powerful web-based statistical software that allows users to perform complex analyses, share data sets, and generate compelling reports of their data. The vibrant online community offers tens of thousands of shared data sets for students to analyze.

Full access to StatCrunch is available with a MyStatLab kit, and StatCrunch is available by itself to qualified adopters. StatCrunch Mobile now available; just visit **www.statcrunch.com/mobile** from the browser on your smart phone or tablet. For more information, visit our website at **www.statcrunch.com**, or contact your Pearson representative.

A Note of Thanks

We thank the RAND Corporation and the American Society for Testing and Materials for their kind permission to publish various tables in Appendix E, and to the American Statistical Association for its permission to publish diagrams from the *American Statistician*.

Creating a new edition of a textbook is a team effort, and we would like to thank our Pearson Education editorial, marketing, and production teammates: Suzanna Bainbridge, Chere Bemelmans, Sherry Berg, Erin Kelly, Deirdre Lynch, Christine Stavrou, Jean Choe, Marianne Stepanian, and Joe Vetere. We also thank our statistical reader and accuracy checker Annie Puciloski for her diligence in checking our work and Nancy Kincade of Lumina Datamatics. Finally, we would like to thank our families for their patience, understanding, love, and assistance in making this book a reality.

Contact Us!

We invite you to email us at **authors@davidlevinestatistics.com** if you have a question or require clarification about the contents this book or if you have a suggestion for a future edition of this book. Please include "BSAFC7" in the subject line of your message. While we have strived to make this book as error-free as possible, we encourage you to also email us if you discover an error or have concern about the content in this book.

You can also visit us at **davidlevinestatistics.com**, where you will find additional information about us, this book, and our other textbooks and publications by the coauthors.

David M. Levine, Kathryn A. Szabat, and David F. Stephan

Important Things to Learn First

OBJECTIVES

That the preponderance of data makes learning statistics critically important

Statistics is a way of thinking that can lead to better decisions

How applying the DCOVA framework for statistics can help solve business problems

The significance of business analytics.

The opportunity business analytics represent for business students

How to prepare for using Microsoft Excel or Minitab with this book

USING STATISTICS

"You Cannot Escape from Data"

You hear the word *data* almost every day and may know that data are facts about the world. You might think about data as numbers, such as the poll results that show that 45% of the people polled believe the economy will improve during the next year. But data are more than just numerical facts. For example, every time you visit an online search engine, send or receive an email or text message, or post something to a social media site, you are creating and using data.

In this larger sense of *data*, you accept *as almost true* the premises of stories in which characters collect "lots of data" to uncover conspiracies, foretell disasters, or catch criminals. You might hear concerns about how a governmental agency might be collecting data to "spy" on you. You might even have heard how some businesses "mine" their data for profit. You may have realized that, in today's world, **you cannot escape from data.**

Although you cannot escape from data, you might choose to avoid data. If you avoid data, you must blindly accept other people's data summaries and that can expose you to fraud. (Recall financial scams that claimed great rewards that were totally fictitious.) If you avoid data, you must solely rely on "gut feelings" when making decisions—much less effective than using the rational processes you study in business courses. When you realize that avoiding data is not an option, you realize that knowing how to work with data effectively is an important skill. In identifying that skill, you have discovered that **you cannot escape learning statistics, the methods that allow you to work with data effectively.**

Angela Waye/Shutterstock

GS.1 Statistics: A Way of Thinking

Statistics are the methods that allow you to work with data effectively. These methods represent a way of thinking that can help you make better decisions. If you ever created a chart to summarize data or calculated values such as averages to summarize data, you have used statistics. But there's even more to statistics than these commonly taught techniques, as a quick review of the detailed table of contents shows.

The statistics that you have learned at a lower grade level most likely required you to perform mathematical calculations. In contrast, businesses today rely on software to perform those calculations faster and more accurately than you could do by hand. In any case, computation by software forms only part of one task of many when applying statistics. To best understand that statistics is a way of thinking, you need a framework that organizes the set of tasks that form statistics. One such framework is the **DCOVA framework.**

THE DCOVA FRAMEWORK

The tasks of DCOVA framework are:
- **Define** the data that you want to study to solve a problem or meet an objective.
- **Collect** the data from appropriate sources.
- **Organize** the data collected by developing tables.
- **Visualize** the data collected by developing charts.
- **Analyze** the data collected to reach conclusions and present those results.

The tasks **D**efine, **C**ollect, **O**rganize, **V**isualize, and **A**nalyze help you to apply statistics to business decision making. You must always do the first two tasks first to have meaningful results, but, in practice, the order of the other three can vary and sometimes are done concurrently. For example, certain ways of visualizing data help you to organize your data while performing preliminary analysis as well.

Using the DCOVA framework helps you to apply statistical methods to these four broad categories of business activities:

- Summarize and visualize business data
- Reach conclusions from those data
- Make reliable predictions about business activities
- Improve business processes

Throughout this book, and especially in the Using Statistics scenarios that begin the chapters, you will discover specific examples of how DCOVA helps you apply statistics. For example, in one chapter, you will learn how to demonstrate whether a marketing campaign has increased sales of a product, while in another you will learn how a television station can reduce unnecessary labor expenses.

GS.2 Data: What Is It?

Defining data as just "facts about the world," to quote the opening essay, can prove confusing as such facts could be singular, a value associated with something, or collective, a list of values associated with something. For example, "David Levine" is a singular fact, a coauthor of this book, whereas "David, Kathy, and David" is the *collective* list of authors of this book. Furthermore, if everything is data, how do you distinguish "David Levine" from "Business Statistics: A First Course," two very different facts (coauthor and title) about this book. Statisticians avoid this confusion by using a more specific definition of data and by defining a second word, *variable*.

In statistics, **data** are "the values associated with a trait or property that help distinguish the occurrences of something." For example, the names "David Levine" and "Kathryn Szabat" are data because they are both values that help distinguish one of the authors of this book from another. In this book, *data* is always plural to remind you that data are a collection, or set, of value*s*. While one could say that a single value, such as "David Levine," is a *datum*, the phrases *data point*, *observation*, *response*, and *single data value* are more typically encountered.

A trait or property of something with which values (data) are associated is called a **variable**. For example, you might define the variables "coauthor" and "title" if you were defining data about a set of textbooks.

Substituting the word characteristic for the phrase "trait or property" and using the phrase "an item or individual" instead of the vague "something" produces the definitions of *variable* and *data* that this book uses.

VARIABLE

A characteristic of an item or individual.

DATA

The set of individual values associated with a variable.

Think about characteristics that distinguish individuals in a human population. Name, height, weight, eye color, marital status, adjusted gross income, and place of residence are all characteristics of an individual. All of these traits are possible *variables* that describe people.

Defining a variable called author-name to be the first and last names of the authors of this text makes it clear that valid values would be "David Levine," "Kathryn Szabat," and "David Stephan" and not "Levine," "Szabat," and "Stephan." Be careful of cultural or other assumptions in definitions—for example, is "last name" a family name, as is common usage in North America, or an individual's own unique name, as is common usage in many Asian countries?

Statistics

Having defined *data*, you can define the subject of this book, **statistics** as the methods that help transform data into useful information for decision makers. Statistics allows you to determine whether your data represent information that could be used in making better decisions. Therefore, statistics helps you determine whether differences in the numbers are meaningful in a significant way or are due to chance. To illustrate, consider the following news reports about various data findings:

- **"Acceptable Online Ad Length Before Seeing Free Content"** (*USA Today*, February 16, 2012, p. 1B) A survey of 1,179 adults 18 and over reported that 54% thought that 15 seconds was an acceptable online ad length before seeing free content.
- **"6 New Facts About Facebook."** (Pew Research Center, **bit.ly/lkENZcA**, February 3, 2014) A survey reported that women were more likely than men to cite seeing photos or videos, sharing with many people at once, seeing entertaining or funny posts, learning about ways to help others, and receiving support from people in your network as reasons to use Facebook.
- **"Follow the Tweets"** (H. Rui, A. Whinston, and E. Winkler, *The Wall Street Journal*, November 30, 2009, p. R4) In this study, the authors found that the number of times a specific product was mentioned in comments in the Twitter social messaging service could be used to make accurate predictions of sales trends for that product.

Without statistics, you cannot determine whether the "numbers" in these stories represent useful information. Without statistics, you cannot validate claims such as the claim that the number of tweets can be used to predict the sales of certain products. And without statistics, you cannot see patterns that large amounts of data sometimes reveal.

When talking about statistics, you use the term **descriptive statistics** to refer to methods that primarily help summarize and present data. Counting physical objects in a kindergarten class may have been the first time you used a *descriptive* method. You use the term **inferential statistics** to refer to methods that use data collected from a small group to reach conclusions about a larger group. If you had formal statistics instruction in a lower grade, you were probably mostly taught descriptive methods, the focus of the early chapters of this book, and you may be unfamiliar with many of the inferential methods discussed in later chapters.

GS.3 The Changing Face of Statistics

The data from which the Using Statistics scenario notes you cannot "escape" has encouraged the increasing use of statistical methods that either did not exist, were not practical to do, or were not widely known in the past. These methods and changes in information and communications technologies that you may have studied in another course have helped to extend the application of statistics in business and make statistical knowledge more critical to business success. This is the changing face of statistics.

Business Analytics

Of all the recent changes that have made statistics more prominent and more important, the set of methods collectively known as **business analytics** best reflects this changing face of statistics. Business analytics combine traditional statistical methods with methods from management science and information systems to form an interdisciplinary tool that supports fact-based management decision making. Business analytics enables you to:

- Use statistical methods to analyze and explore data to uncover unforeseen relationships.
- Use management science methods to develop optimization models that support all levels of management, from strategic planning to daily operations.
- Use information systems methods to collect and process data sets of all sizes, including very large data sets that would otherwise be hard to examine efficiently.

Even if you have never heard of the term business analytics, you may be familiar with the application of these methods. Headlines about governmental agencies mining personal data to combat crime or terrorism, stories about how companies learn your secrets, including the example memorably summarized as "How Target Knows You're Pregnant" (a bit of an overstatement), or even discussions about how social media or streaming media companies recommend choices to their users or sell advertisements to display to particular users, all reflect this changing face of statistics.

"Big Data"

The data from which you cannot "escape" has taken new forms in recent years, including the form known as *big data*. **Big data** are the collections of data that cannot be easily browsed or analyzed using traditional methods.

Big data lacks a more precise operational definition, but using the term implies data that are being collected in huge volumes and at very fast rates (typically in near real-time) as well as data that takes a variety of forms other than the traditional structured forms such as data processing records, files, and tables. These attributes of "volume, velocity, and variety" (see reference 4) help distinguish "big data" from a set of data that happens to be "large" but that can be placed into a file that contains repeating records or rows that share the same arrangement or structure.

Big data presents opportunities to gain new management insights or extract value from the data resources of a business (see reference 7). Businesses gain these new insights or value through statistics, especially through the application of the newer methods of business analytics.

Integral Role of Software in Statistics

Section GS.1 notes that businesses rely on software to perform statistical calculations faster and more accurately than you could do by hand. Consistent to this observation, this book emphasizes the interpretation of statistical results generated by software over the hand calculation of those results. The book uses both Microsoft Excel and Minitab to generate those results and show in a larger way how software is integral to applying statistical methods to business decision making.

Both Excel and Minitab use *worksheets* to store data for analysis. **Worksheets** are tabular arrangements of data, in which the intersections of rows and columns form **cells**, boxes into which you make entries. In Minitab and Excel, you use columns of cells to enter the data for variables, using one column for each variable. Typically to use a statistical method in either program, you select one or more columns of data (one or more variables) and then apply the appropriate program function. This means the examples and problems found in this book use traditional structured data and not collections of data that could be considered big data. Not to worry, learning with structured data will allow you to master statistical principles that you can apply later when using big data.

> **Student Tip**
> The names of Excel and Minitab files that contain the data for examples and problems appear in this distinctive type face **Retirement Funds** throughout this book.

GS.4 Statistics: An Important Part of Your Business Education

The changing face of statistics means that statistics has become a very important part of your business education. In the current data-driven environment of business, you need general analytical skills that allow you to manipulate data, interpret analytical results, and incorporate results in a variety of decision-making applications, such as accounting, finance, HR management, marketing, strategy and planning, and supply chain management.

The decisions you make will be increasingly based on data and not on gut or intuition supported by personal experience. Data-guided practice is proving to be successful; studies have shown an increase in productivity, innovation, and competition for organizations that embrace business analytics. The use of data and data analysis to drive business decisions cannot be ignored. Having a well-balanced mix of technical skills—such as statistics, modeling, and basic information technology skills—and managerial skills—such as business acumen, problem-solving skills, and communication skills—will best prepare you for today's, and tomorrow's, workplace (see reference 1).

Business students once considered statistics to be merely a required course that contained content unrelated to their own majors. If you opened this book and had similar thoughts, you were overlooking the changing face of statistics. Use this book to better understand the implications of this change as you learn to use the DCOVA framework to apply statistical methods to the four categories of business activities listed in Section GS.1.

> **Student Tip**
> Don't worry if your course does not cover every section of every chapter. Introductory business statistics courses vary in terms of scope, length, and number of college credits earned. Your functional area of study or major may also affect what you learn.

Making Best Use of This Book

This book uses the DCOVA framework to organize and present its statistical content. To make best use of this book, first make sure you understand the DCOVA framework (see page 2). With that knowledge, you can group the chapters of this book as follows:

- Chapter 1: the **D**efine and **C**ollect tasks, the mandatory starting tasks for applying a statistical method.
- Chapters 2 and 3: the **O**rganize and **V**isualize tasks that help summarize and visualize business data (the first activity listed on page 2).
- Chapter 3 (again) and Chapters 4 through 11: the **A**nalyze task methods that use sample data to help reach conclusions about populations (the second activity listed on page 2).
- Chapters 12 and 13: the **A**nalyze task methods that help make reliable predictions (the third activity).
- Online Chapter 14: the **A**nalyze task methods that help you improve business processes (the fourth activity).

To get the most from every chapter, first read the opening Using Statistics scenarios. Each chapter's scenario always describes a business situation in which the methods about to be discussed in the chapter could be used to help resolve issues or problems that the scenario described. Scenarios are the source of many of the in-chapter examples used to discuss statistical methods. At the end of each chapter, a "revisited" section reviews how the chapter's statistical methods would help solve the issues and problems raised initially in the opening scenario.

Each chapter fully integrates Microsoft Excel and Minitab illustrations with its examples, reflecting the integral role that software plays in applying statistical methods to business decision making. Each chapter concludes with software guides (discussed separately below) that contain how-to instructions for using Excel or Minitab for the statistical topic the chapter discusses.

Each chapter also ends with a summary and a list of key equations and key terms that help you review what you have learned. "Checking Your Understanding" questions test your understanding of basic concepts and "Chapter Review Problems" allow you to practice what you have learned.

As you read through a chapter you will find pointers to supplemental material available online, end-of-section questions and problems as well as these recurring features:

- **Student Tips** that help clarify and reinforce significant details about particular statistical concepts (such as the tip that occurs on this page).
- **Visual Explorations** that allow you to interactively explore statistical concepts in Microsoft Excel.
- **"Think About This" essays** that further explore statistical concepts.

You can enhance your analytic and communication skills by making best use of the many case studies found in this book. The continuing case *Managing Ashland MultiComm Services* appears in most chapters and asks you to use your analytic skills to help solve problems managers of a residential telecommunications provider face. Cases unique to a chapter or a subset of chapters provide report-writing practice and additional problem-solving opportunities. The unique "Digital Cases" additionally challenge you to use statistical principles to sort through claims found in various documents to uncover which claims are well supported and which ones are dubious, at best.

Making Best Use of the Software Guides

Student Tip

If you need to review these skills, read **Basic Computing Skills**, a PDF file that you can download using instructions found in Appendix C.

To make best use of software guides, read the getting started information that appears later in this chapter for the program you will be using and complete the Table GS.1 checklist. The software how-to guides presume you already have awareness of basic computing concepts and skills such as mouse operations and interacting with windows and dialog boxes. Software guides use the following conventions in their instructions:

- Things to type and where to type them appear in boldface. (Enter **450** in **cell B5**.)
- Names of special keys are capitalized and in boldface. (Press **Enter**.)
- Targets of click or select operations appear in boldface. (Click **OK**. Select the **first 2-D Bar** gallery item.)
- When instructions require you to press more than one key at the same time, all keys are shown capitalized and in boldface and are joined together with the "+" symbol. (Press **Ctrl+C**. Press **Ctrl+Shift+Enter**. Press **Command+Enter**.)
- Consecutive menu or ribbon selections are shown capitalized, mixed case, and in boldface, joined together with the ➔ symbol. (Select **File ➔ New**. Select **Stat ➔ Tables ➔ Tally Individual Variables**.)
- Specific names of Excel and Minitab functions, worksheets, or files are shown capitalized, mixed case, and in boldface. (Open to the **DATA worksheet** of the **Retirement Funds workbook**.)
- Placeholder objects that express the general case of an instruction appear in italics and in boldface. Example: Use **AVERAGE(*cell range of variable*)** to compute the mean of a numerical variable.

Starting with Chapter 1, the section numbers of the software guides reflect their in-chapter counterparts. For example, guide sections EG1.1 and MG1.1 contain the Excel and Minitab instructions for Section 1.1 "Defining Variables."

TABLE GS.1

Checklist for Using Microsoft Excel or Minitab with This Book

❑ Read Appendix C to learn about the online resources you need to make best use of this book.

❑ Download the online resources that you will need to use this book, using the instructions in Appendix C.

❑ Check for and apply updates to the software that you plan to use. (See the Appendix Section D.1 instructions).

❑ If you plan to use PHStat, the Visual Explorations add-in workbooks, or the Analysis ToolPak with Microsoft Windows Excel, read the special instructions in Appendix D.

❑ Read Appendix G to learn answers to frequently asked questions (FAQs).

REFERENCES

1. Advani, D. "Preparing Students for the Jobs of the Future." *University Business* (2011), **bit.ly/1gNLTJm**.

2. Davenport, T., and J. Harris. *Competing on Analytics: The New Science of Winning*. Boston: Harvard Business School Press, 2007.

3. Davenport, T., J. Harris, and R. Morison. *Analytics at Work*. Boston: Harvard Business School Press, 2010.

4. Laney, D. *3D Data Management: Controlling Data Volume, Velocity, and Variety*. Stamford, CT: META Group. February 6, 2001.

5. Levine, D., and D. Stephan. "Teaching Introductory Business Statistics Using the DCOVA Framework." *Decision Sciences Journal of Innovative Education* 9 (Sept. 2011): 393–398.

6. Liberatore, M., and W. Luo. "The Analytics Movement." *Interfaces* 40 (2010): 313–324.

7. "What Is Big Data?" IBM Corporation, **www.ibm.com /big-data/us/en/**.

KEY TERMS

big data 4
cells 5
data 3
business analytics 4
DCOVA framework 2

descriptive statistics 4
inferential statistics 4
project 9
statistical package 9
statistics 3

templates 8
variable 3
workbook 8
worksheets 5

EXCEL GUIDE

EG.1 GETTING STARTED with MICROSOFT EXCEL

Microsoft Excel evolved from earlier applications that automated the preparation of accounting and financial worksheets. In Excel, worksheet cells can be individually formatted and contain either data values or programming-like statements called *formulas* (discussed fully in Appendix B). To make best use of Excel, businesses use worksheet solutions called **templates** that already contain formatted entries. Decision makers open such templates and make minor modifications, sometimes as simple as entering values into specific cells, to generate useful information.

Templates can be a single worksheet, but often are a set of worksheets that are stored in a **workbook**. This book uses a series of templates that collectively are called the Excel Guide workbooks. These workbooks typically contain one worksheet dedicated to computing and displaying the result, the worksheets that are pictured throughout this book, and at least one worksheet that stores the data being used by the results worksheet.

In this book, you can work with the templates in one of two ways. You can open the Excel Guide workbooks and make manual changes to its worksheets, similar to how an employee would open and use a business template. You can also use PHStat, the Pearson Education statistics add-in for Excel (discussed in Appendix C) that automates the retrieval and modification of these templates. Unless otherwise noted, using either method will result in results worksheets like the ones pictured in this book. If you choose to make manual changes to the Excel Guide workbooks, you will need to know how to edit formulas, alter worksheets, and correct charts, operations that are discussed in Appendix B. If you choose to use PHStat, you will need only the basic Microsoft Office skills of knowing how to enter data (discussed below), open and save files, print worksheets, and perform copy-and-paste and insert operations that are summarized at the start of Appendix B.

Occasionally, you will also find instructions for using the Data Analysis ToolPak, an add-in that comes with Microsoft Excel. Note that some templates have been designed to mimic the appearance of the worksheets created by ToolPak add-in procedures so that ToolPak users will see the same or similar results as template users. (However visually similar they may appear, ToolPak worksheets are formatted printed reports that are not templates and therefore cannot be reused with other data.)

The Excel Guide instructions work best with the current versions of Microsoft Windows Excel and (Mac) OS X Excel, including Excel 2011, Excel 2013, and Office 365 Excel. Versions occasionally vary and this book provides alternate instructions keyed to the version that varies when necessary. Starting with Excel 2010, Microsoft renamed, and in many cases revised, many of the statistical functions that formulas in this book's templates use. When a template uses one of these newer functions, an alternate template that uses the older function names will also be found in the workbook.

EG.2 ENTERING DATA

To enter data into a specific cell, move the cell pointer to that cell by using the cursor keys, moving the mouse pointer, or completing the proper touch operation. As you type an entry, the entry appears in the formula bar area that is located over the top of the worksheet. You complete your entry by pressing **Tab** or **Enter** or by clicking the checkmark button in the formula bar.

All "Excel data files" and most Excel Guide workbooks contain a **DATA worksheet** similar to the example shown below. Consistent to the rules first stated in Section GS.3, DATA worksheets use columns of cells to enter the data for variables, using one column for each variable and use the cell in the first row of a column to enter the name of variable for that column.

Use the DATA worksheets as models for worksheets you prepare to store the data for your variables. As you create your own "data" worksheets, never skip a row when entering data for a variable and try to avoid using numbers as row 1 variable headings. (If you must use a number for a heading, precede the number with an apostrophe.) Also, pay attention to special instructions in this book that discuss the entry order and arrangement of the columns for your variables. For some statistical methods, entering variables in a column order that Excel does not expect will lead to incorrect results.

> **Student Tip**
>
> All "Excel files" are *workbook* files, even those that contain a single worksheet, such as the Excel data files discussed in Appendix C. When instructions in this book use a workbook that contains two or more worksheets, the instructions identify the name of the worksheet that is the object of the instruction.

> When a results worksheet or other template uses at least one of the newer functions, the template workbook includes a worksheet with the prefix OLDER that users of Excel 2007 should use. (PHStat automatically switches to the older names if you are using Excel 2007.)

	A	B	C	D	E	F	G	H	I	J	K	L
1	Fund Number	Market Cap	Type	Assets	Turnover Ratio	Beta	SD	Risk	1YrReturn%	3YrReturn%	5YrReturn%	10YrReturn%
2	RF001	Large	Growth	309.90	12.21	1.15	18.72	Low	28.99	24.26	11.06	8.97
3	RF002	Large	Growth	23.30	0.00	2.19	35.72	High	33.40	22.72	-4.89	0.02
4	RF003	Large	Growth	141.50	147.00	2.24	36.69	High	33.98	21.91	1.53	12.55
5	RF004	Large	Growth	118.50	5.00	2.24	36.63	High	33.78	21.89	1.57	12.69
6	RF005	Large	Growth	575.30	121.00	0.89	14.56	Low	21.62	16.47	9.40	10.30

MINITAB GUIDE

MG.1 GETTING STARTED WITH MINITAB

Minitab is a **statistical package**, software developed specifically to perform a wide range of statistical analyses as accurately as possible. In Minitab, you enter data into a window that contains a worksheet, then select commands, and then see the results in other windows. The collection of all windows forms a **project** and you can save entire projects as **.mpj** project files or choose to save individual worksheets in **.mtw** worksheet files.

When you first open Minitab, you typically see a new project that contains a window with a blank worksheet and the Session window that records all commands you select and displays results. Pictured below is a project after a worksheet named DATA has been opened. Besides the slightly obscured DATA worksheet window and **Session** window, this figure also shows a **Project Manager** that summarizes the content of the current project. Note that all three windows appear *inside* the main Minitab window.

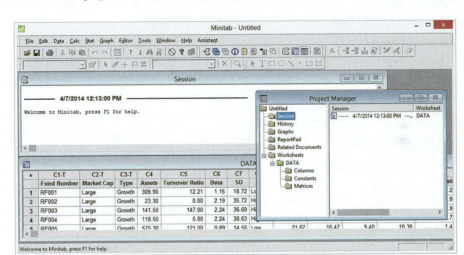

To make effective use of Minitab, you should be familiar with how to open and save Minitab worksheet and project files as well as how to insert worksheets in a project, and how to print parts of a project. These skills are summarized in Appendix B. Minitab Guide instructions work best with the current commercial and student versions of Minitab and note differences when they occur.

MG.2 ENTERING DATA

Minitab uses the standard business convention, expecting data for a variable to be entered into a column. In this book, data are entered in columns, left to right, starting with the first column. Column names take the form Cn, such that the first column is named C1, the second column is C2, and the tenth column is C10. Column names appear in the top border of a Minitab worksheet. Columns that contain non-numerical data have names that include "-T" (**C1-T**, **C2-T**, and **C3-T** in the DATA worksheet shown above). Columns that contain data that Minitab interprets as either dates or times have names that include "-D" (not seen in the DATA worksheet).

When entering data, you use the first, unnumbered and shaded row to enter variable names. You can then refer to the column by that name or its Cn name in Minitab procedures. If a variable name contains spaces or other special characters, such as **Market Cap**, Minitab will display that name in dialog boxes using a pair of single quotation marks (**'Market Cap'**). You must include those quotation marks any time you enter such a variable name in a dialog box.

To enter or edit data in a specific cell, either use the cursor keys to move the cell pointer to the cell or use your mouse to select the cell directly. Never skip a cell in numbered row when entering data because Minitab will interpret that skipped cell as a "missing value" (see Section 1.2).

Defining and Collecting Data

OBJECTIVES

Understand issues that arise when defining variables

How to define variables

How to collect data

Identify the different ways to collect a sample

Understand the types of survey errors

USING STATISTICS

Beginning of the End ... Or the End of the Beginning?

The past few years have been challenging for Good Tunes & More (GT&M), a business that traces its roots to Good Tunes, a store that exclusively sold music CDs and vinyl records.

GT&M first broadened its merchandise to include home entertainment and computer systems (the "More"), and then undertook an expansion to take advantage of prime locations left empty by bankrupt former competitors. Today, GT&M finds itself at a crossroads. Hoped-for increases in revenues that have failed to occur and declining profit margins due to the competitive pressures of online sellers have led management to reconsider the future of the business.

While some investors in the business have argued for an orderly retreat, closing stores and limiting the variety of merchandise, GT&M CEO Emma Levia has decided to "double down" and expand the business by purchasing Whitney Wireless, a successful three-store chain that sells smartphones and other mobile devices.

Levia foresees creating a brand new "A-to-Z" electronics retailer but first must establish a fair and reasonable price for the privately held Whitney Wireless. To do so, she has asked a group of analysts to identify the data that would be helpful in setting a price for the wireless business. As part of that group, you quickly realize that you need the data that would help to verify the contents of the wireless company's basic financial statements.

You focus on data associated with the company's profit and loss statement and quickly realize the need for sales and expense-related variables. You begin to

think about what the data for such variables would look like and how to collect those data. You realize that you are starting to apply the DCOVA framework to the objective of helping Levia acquire Whitney Wireless.

Tyler Olson/Shutterstock

When Emma Levia decides to purchase Whitney Wireless, she has defined a new goal or *business objective* for GT&M. Business objectives can arise from any level of management and can be as varied as the following:

- A marketing analyst needs to assess the effectiveness of a new online advertising campaign.
- A pharmaceutical company needs to determine whether a new drug is more effective than those currently in use.
- An operations manager wants to improve a manufacturing or service process.
- An auditor needs to review a company's financial transactions to determine whether the company is in compliance with generally accepted accounting principles.

Establishing an objective marks the *end* of a problem definition process. This end triggers the *new* process of identifying the correct data to support the objective. In the GT&M scenario, having decided to buy Whitney Wireless, Levia needs to identify the data that would be helpful in setting a price for the wireless business. This process of identifying the correct data triggers the start of applying the tasks of the DCOVA framework. In other words, the *end* of problem definition marks the *beginning* of applying statistics to business decision making.

Identifying the correct data to support a business objective is a two-part job that requires defining variables and collecting the data for those variables. These tasks are the first two tasks of the DCOVA framework first defined in Section GS.1 and which can be restated here as:

- **Define** the *variables* that you want to study to solve a problem or meet an objective.
- **Collect** the data *for those variables* from appropriate sources.

This chapter discusses these two tasks which must always be done before the **Organize**, **Visualize**, and **Analyze** tasks.

1.1 Defining Variables

Student Tip
Providing operational definitions for *concepts* is important, too, when writing a textbook! The end-of-chapter Key Terms gives you an index of operational definitions and the most fundamental definitions are presented in boxes such as the page 3 box that defines *variable* and *data*.

Defining variables at first may seem to be the simple process of making the list of things one needs to help solve a problem or meet an objective. However, consider the GT&M scenario. Most would quickly agree that *yearly sales* of Whitney Wireless would be part of the data needed to meet Levia's objective, but just placing "yearly sales" on a list could lead to confusion and miscommunication: Does this variable refer to sales per year for the entire chain or for individual stores? Does the variable refer to net or gross sales? Are the yearly sales values expressed in number of units or as currency amounts such as U.S. dollar sales?

These questions illustrate that for each variable of interest that you identify you must supply an **operational definition**, a universally accepted meaning that is clear to all associated with an analysis. Operational definitions should also *classify* the variable, as explained in the next section, and may include additional facts such as units of measures, allowed range of values, and definitions of specific variable values, depending on how the variable is classified.

Classifying Variables by Type

When you operationally define a variable, you must classify the variable as being either *categorical* or *numerical*. **Categorical variables** (also known as **qualitative variables**) take categories as their values. **Numerical variables** (also known as **quantitative variables**) have values that represent a counted or measured quantity. Classification also affects a variable's operational definition and getting the classification correct is important because certain statistical methods can be applied correctly to one type or the other, while other methods may need a specific mix of variable types.

Categorical variables can take the form of yes-and-no questions such as "Do you have a Twitter account?" (in which *yes* and *no* form the variable's two categories) or describe a trait or characteristic that has many categories such as undergraduate class standing (which might have the defined categories freshman, sophomore, junior, and senior). When defining a categorical variable, the list of permissible category values must be included and each category value should be defined, too, e.g., that a "freshman" is a student who has completed fewer than 32 credit hours. Overlooking these requirements can lead to confusion and incorrect data collection. In one famous example, when persons were asked by researchers to fill in a value for the categorical variable sex, many answered *yes* and not *male* or *female*, the values that the researchers intended. (Perhaps this is the reason that *gender* has replaced *sex* on many data collection forms—gender's operational definition is more self-apparent.)

The operational definitions of numerical variables are affected by whether the variable being defined is *discrete* or *continuous*. **Discrete variables** such as "number of items purchased" or "total amount paid" are numerical values that arise from a counting process. **Continuous variables** such as "time spent on checkout line" or "distance from home to store" have numerical values that arise from a measuring process and those values depend on the precision of the measuring instrument used. For example, "time spent on checkout line" might be 2, 2.1, 2.14, or 2.143 minutes, depending on the precision of the timing instrument being used. Units of measures and the level of precision should be part of the operational definitions of continuous variables, e.g., "tenths of a second" for "time spent on checkout line." The definitions of any numerical variable can include the allowed range of values, such as "must be greater than 0" for "number of items purchased."

When defining variables for survey collection (discussed in Section 1.2), thinking about the responses you seek helps classify variables as Table 1.1 demonstrates. Thinking about how a variable will be used to solve a problem or meet an objective can also be helpful when you define a variable. The variable age might be a numerical (discrete) variable in some cases or might be categorical with categories such as child, young adult, middle-aged, and retirement aged in other contexts.

> **LEARN MORE**
>
> Read the SHORT TAKES for Chapter 1 for more examples of classifying variables as either categorical or numerical.

TABLE 1.1

Identifying Types of Variables

Question	Responses	Variable Type
Do you have a Facebook profile?	☐ Yes ☐ No	Categorical
How many text messages have you sent in the past three days?	_____	Numerical (discrete)
How long did the mobile app update take to download?	_____ seconds	Numerical (continuous)

Problems for Section 1.1

LEARNING THE BASICS

1.1 Four different beverages are sold at a fast-food restaurant: soft drinks, tea, coffee, and bottled water. Explain why the type of beverage sold is an example of a categorical variable.

1.2 U.S. businesses are listed by size: small, medium, and large. Explain why business size is an example of a categorical variable.

1.3 The time it takes to download a video from the Internet is measured. Explain why the download time is a continuous numerical variable.

APPLYING THE CONCEPTS

✓ SELF Test **1.4** For each of the following variables, determine whether the variable is categorical or numerical. If the variable is numerical, determine whether the variable is discrete or continuous.
a. Number of cellphones in the household
b. Monthly data usage (in MB)
c. Number of text messages exchanged per month
d. Voice usage per month (in minutes)
e. Whether the cellphone is used for email

1.5 The following information is collected from students upon exiting the campus bookstore during the first week of classes.
a. Amount of time spent shopping in the bookstore
b. Number of textbooks purchased
c. Academic major
d. Gender

Classify each of these variables as categorical or numerical. If the variable is numerical, determine whether the variable is discrete or continuous.

1.6 For each of the following variables, determine whether the variable is categorical or numerical. If the variable is numerical, determine whether the variable is discrete or continuous.
a. Name of Internet service provider
b. Time, in hours, spent surfing the Internet per week
c. Whether the individual uses a mobile phone to connect to the Internet
d. Number of online purchases made in a month
e. Where the individual uses social networks to find sought-after information

1.7 For each of the following variables, determine whether the variable is categorical or numerical. If the variable is numerical, determine whether the variable is discrete or continuous.
a. Amount of money spent on clothing in the past month
b. Favorite department store
c. Most likely time period during which shopping for clothing takes place (weekday, weeknight, or weekend)
d. Number of pairs of shoes owned

1.8 Suppose the following information is collected from Robert Keeler on his application for a home mortgage loan at the Metro County Savings and Loan Association.
a. Monthly payments: $2,227
b. Number of jobs in past 10 years: 1
c. Annual family income: $96,000
d. Marital status: Married

Classify each of the responses by type of data.

1.9 One of the variables most often included in surveys is income. Sometimes the question is phrased "What is your income (in thousands of dollars)?" In other surveys, the respondent is asked to "Select the circle corresponding to your income level" and is given a number of income ranges to choose from.
a. In the first format, explain why income might be considered either discrete or continuous.
b. Which of these two formats would you prefer to use if you were conducting a survey? Why?

1.10 If two students score a 90 on the same examination, what arguments could be used to show that the underlying variable—test score—is continuous?

1.11 The director of market research at a large department store chain wanted to conduct a survey throughout a metropolitan area to determine the amount of time working women spend shopping for clothing in a typical month.
a. Indicate the type of data the director might want to collect.
b. Develop a first draft of the questionnaire needed in (a) by writing three categorical questions and three numerical questions that you feel would be appropriate for this survey.

1.2 Collecting Data

After defining the variables that you want to study, you can proceed with the data collection task. Collecting data is a critical task because if you collect data that are flawed by biases, ambiguities, or other types of errors, the results you will get from using such data with even the most sophisticated statistical methods will be suspect or in error. (For a famous example of flawed data collection leading to incorrect results, read the Think About This essay on page 21.)

Data collection consists of identifying data sources, deciding whether the data you collect will be from a population or a sample, cleaning your data, and sometimes recoding variables. The rest of this section explains these aspects of data collection.

Data Sources

You collect data from either primary or secondary data sources. You are using a **primary data source** if you collect your own data for analysis. You are using a **secondary data source** if the data for your analysis have been collected by someone else.

You collect data by using any of the following:

- Data distributed by an organization or individual
- The outcomes of a designed experiment
- The responses from a survey
- The results of conducting an observational study
- Data collected by ongoing business activities

Market research companies and trade associations distribute data pertaining to specific industries or markets. Investment services provide business and financial data on publicly listed companies. Syndicated services such as The Nielsen Company provide consumer research data to telecom and mobile media companies. Print and online media companies also distribute data that they may have collected themselves or may be republishing from other sources.

The outcomes of a designed experiment are a second data source. For example, a consumer electronics company might conduct an experiment that compares the sales of mobile electronics merchandise for different store locations. Note that developing a proper experimental design is mostly beyond the scope of this book, but Chapter 10 discusses some of the fundamental experimental design concepts.

Survey responses represent a third type of data source. People being surveyed are asked questions about their beliefs, attitudes, behaviors, and other characteristics. For example, people could be asked which store location for mobile electronics merchandise is preferable. (Such a survey could lead to data that differ from the data collected from the outcomes of the designed experiment of the previous paragraph.) Surveys can be affected by any of the four types of errors that are discussed in Section 1.4.

Observational study results are a fourth data source. A researcher collects data by directly observing a behavior, usually in a natural or neutral setting. Observational studies are a common tool for data collection in business. For example, market researchers use focus groups to elicit unstructured responses to open-ended questions posed by a moderator to a target audience. Observational studies are also commonly used to enhance teamwork or improve the quality of products and services.

Data collected by ongoing business activities are a fifth data source. Such data can be collected from operational and transactional systems that exist in both physical "bricks-and-mortar" and online settings but can also be gathered from secondary sources such as third-party social media networks and online apps and website services that collect tracking and usage data. For example, a bank might analyze a decade's worth of financial transaction data to identify patterns of fraud, and a marketer might use tracking data to determine the effectiveness of a website.

Sources for *big data* (see Section GS.3) tend to be a mix of primary and secondary sources of this last type. For example, a retailer interested in increasing sales might mine Facebook and Twitter accounts to identify sentiment about certain products or to pinpoint top influencers and then match those data to its own data collected during customer transactions.

LEARN MORE

Read the SHORT TAKES for Chapter 1 for a further discussion about data sources.

Populations and Samples

You collect your data from either a *population* or a *sample*. A **population** consists of all the items or individuals about which you want to reach conclusions. All the GT&M sales transactions for a specific year, all the full-time students enrolled in a college, and all the registered voters in Ohio are examples of populations. In Chapter 3, you will learn that when you analyze data from a population you compute **parameters**.

A **sample** is a portion of a population selected for analysis. The results of analyzing a sample are used to estimate characteristics of the entire population. From the three examples of populations just given, you could select a sample of 200 GT&M sales transactions randomly selected by an auditor for study, a sample of 50 full-time students selected for a marketing study, and a sample of 500 registered voters in Ohio contacted via telephone for a political poll. In each of these examples, the transactions or people in the sample represent a portion of the items or individuals that make up the population. In Chapter 3, you will learn that when you analyze data from a sample you compute *statistics*.

You collect data from a sample when any of the following applies:

Student Tip
To help remember the difference between a sample and a population, think of a pie. The entire *pie* represents the *population*, and the pie *slice* that you select is the *sample*.

- Selecting a sample is less time consuming than selecting every item in the population.
- Selecting a sample is less costly than selecting every item in the population.
- Analyzing a sample is less cumbersome and more practical than analyzing the entire population.

Structured Versus Unstructured Data

The data you collect may be formatted in a variety of ways, some of which add to the data collection task. For example, suppose that you wanted to collect electronic financial data about a sample of companies. That data might exist as tables of data, the contents of standardized documents such as fill-in-the-blank surveys, a continuous stream of data such as a stock ticker, or text messages or emails delivered from email systems or social media websites. Some of these forms, such as a set of text messages have very little or no repeating structure, are examples of **unstructured data.** Although unstructured data forms can form a part of a *big data* collection, collecting data in unstructured forms for the statistical methods discussed in this book requires conversion of the data to a structured form. For example, after collecting text messages, you could convert their contents to a structured form by defining a set of variables that might include a numerical variable that counts the number of words in the message and various categorical variables that help classify the content of the message.

Electronic Formats and Encodings

The same form of data can exist in more than one electronic format, with some formats more immediately usable than others. For example, a table of data might exist as a scanned image or as data in a worksheet file. The worksheet data could be immediately used in a statistical analysis, but the scanned image would need to be first converted to worksheet data using a character-scanning program that can recognize numbers in an image.

Data can also be encoded in more than one way, as you may have learned in an information systems course. Different encodings may affect the recorded precision of values for continuous variables and lead to values more imprecise or values that convey a false sense of precision, such as a time measurement that gets encoded in ten-thousandths of a second when the original measurement was only in tenths of a second. This changed precision can violate the operational definition of a continuous variable and sometimes affect results calculated.

Student Tip
While encoding issues go beyond the scope of this book, the Short Takes for Chapter 1 includes an experiment that you can perform in either Microsoft Excel or Minitab that illustrates how data encoding can affect the precision of values.

Data Cleaning

Whatever ways you choose to collect data, you may find irregularities in the values you collect such as undefined or impossible values. For a categorical variable, an undefined value would be a value that does not represent one of the categories defined for the variable. For a numerical variable, an impossible value would be a value that falls outside a defined range of possible values for the variable. For a numerical variable without a defined range of possible values, you might also find **outliers**, values that seem excessively different from most of the rest of the values. Such values may or may not be errors, but they demand a second review.

Values that are *missing* are another type of irregularity. A **missing value** is a value that was not able to be collected (and therefore not available to be analyzed). For example, you would record a nonresponse to a survey question as a missing value. You can represent missing values in Minitab by using an asterisk value for a numerical variable or by using a blank value for a categorical variable, and such values will be properly excluded from analysis. The more limited Excel has no special values that represent a missing value. When using Excel, you must find and then exclude missing values manually.

When you spot an irregularity in the data you have collected, you may have to "clean" the data. Although a full discussion of data cleaning is beyond the scope of this book (see reference 8), you can learn more about the ways you can use Excel or Minitab for data cleaning in the SHORT TAKES for Chapter 1.

Data cleaning will not be necessary when you use the (previously cleaned) data for the examples and problems in this book.

Recoding Variables

After you have collected data, you may discover that you need to reconsider the categories that you have defined for a categorical variable or that you need to transform a numerical variable into a categorical variable by assigning the individual numeric data values to one of several groups. In either case, you can define a **recoded variable** that supplements or replaces the original variable in your analysis.

For example, having already defined the variable undergraduate class standing with the categories freshmen, sophomore, junior, and senior, you realize that you are more interested in investigating the differences between lowerclassmen (defined as freshman or sophomore) and upperclassmen (junior or senior). You can create a new variable UpperLower and assign the value Upper if a student is a junior or senior and assign the value Lower if the student is a freshman or sophomore.

When recoding variables, be sure that the category definitions cause each data value to be placed in one and only one category, a property known as being **mutually exclusive**. Also ensure that the set of categories you create for the new, recoded variables include all the data values being recoded, a property known as being **collectively exhaustive**. If you are recoding a categorical variable, you can preserve one or more of the original categories, as long as your recodings are both mutually exclusive and collectively exhaustive.

When recoding numerical variables, pay particular attention to the operational definitions of the categories you create for the recoded variable, especially if the categories are not self-defining ranges. For example, while the recoded categories Under 12, 12–20, 21–34, 35–54, and 55 and Over are self-defining for age, the categories Child, Youth, Young Adult, Middle Aged, and Senior need their own operational definitions.

Problems for Section 1.2

APPLYING THE CONCEPTS

1.12 The Data and Story Library (DASL) is an online library of data files and stories that illustrate the use of basic statistical methods. Visit **lib.stat.cmu.edu/index.php**, click DASL, and explore a data set of interest to you. Which of the five sources of data best describes the sources of the data set you selected?

1.13 Visit the website of the Gallup organization at **www.gallup .com**. Read today's top story. What type of data source is the top story based on?

1.14 Visit the website of the Pew Research organization at **www .pewresearch.org**. Read today's top story. What type of data source is the top story based on?

1.15 Transportation engineers and planners want to address the dynamic properties of travel behavior by describing in detail the driving characteristics of drivers over the course of a month. What type of data collection source do you think the transportation engineers and planners should use?

1.16 Visit the opening page of the Statistics Portal "Statista" at (**statista.com**). Examine the "CHART OF THE DAY" panel on the page. What type of data source is the information presented here based on?

1.3 Types of Sampling Methods

When you collect data by selecting a sample, you begin by defining the **frame**. The frame is a complete or partial listing of the items that make up the population from which the sample will be selected. Inaccurate or biased results can occur if a frame excludes certain groups, or portions of the population. Using different frames to collect data can lead to different, even opposite, conclusions.

Using your frame, you select either a nonprobability sample or a probability sample. In a **nonprobability sample**, you select the items or individuals without knowing their probabilities of selection. In a **probability sample**, you select items based on known probabilities. Whenever possible, you should use a probability sample as such a sample will allow you to make inferences about the population being analyzed.

Nonprobability samples can have certain advantages, such as convenience, speed, and low cost. Such samples are typically used to obtain informal approximations or as small-scale initial or pilot analyses. However, because the theory of statistical inference depends on probability sampling, nonprobability samples *cannot be used* for statistical inference and this more than offsets those advantages in more formal analyses.

Figure 1.1 shows the subcategories of the two types of sampling. A nonprobability sample can be either a convenience sample or a judgment sample. To collect a **convenience sample**, you select items that are easy, inexpensive, or convenient to sample. For example, in a warehouse of stacked items, selecting only the items located on the tops of each stack and within easy reach would create a convenience sample. So, too, would be the responses to surveys that the websites of many companies offer visitors. While such surveys can provide large amounts of data quickly and inexpensively, the convenience samples selected from these responses will consist of self-selected website visitors. (Read the Think About This essay on page 21 for a related story.)

FIGURE 1.1

Types of samples

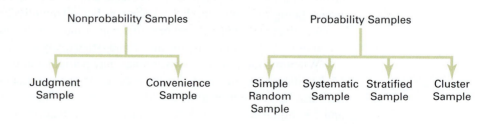

To collect a **judgment sample**, you collect the opinions of preselected experts in the subject matter. Although the experts may be well informed, you cannot generalize their results to the population.

The types of probability samples most commonly used include simple random, systematic, stratified, and cluster samples. These four types of probability samples vary in terms of cost, accuracy, and complexity, and they are the subject of the rest of this section.

Simple Random Sample

In a **simple random sample**, every item from a frame has the same chance of selection as every other item, and every sample of a fixed size has the same chance of selection as every other sample of that size. Simple random sampling is the most elementary random sampling technique. It forms the basis for the other random sampling techniques. However, simple random sampling has its disadvantages. Its results are often subject to more variation than other sampling methods. In addition, when the frame used is very large, carrying out a simple random sample may be time consuming and expensive.

With simple random sampling, you use n to represent the sample size and N to represent the frame size. You number every item in the frame from 1 to N. The chance that you will select any particular member of the frame on the first selection is $1/N$.

You select samples with replacement or without replacement. **Sampling with replacement** means that after you select an item, you return it to the frame, where it has the same probability of being selected again. Imagine that you have a fishbowl containing N business cards, one card for each person. On the first selection, you select the card for Grace Kim. You record pertinent information and replace the business card in the bowl. You then mix up the cards in the bowl and select a second card. On the second selection, Grace Kim has the same probability of being selected again, $1/N$. You repeat this process until you have selected the desired sample size, n.

Typically, you do not want the same item or individual to be selected again in a sample. **Sampling without replacement** means that once you select an item, you cannot select it again. The chance that you will select any particular item in the frame—for example, the business card for Grace Kim—on the first selection is $1/N$. The chance that you will select any card not previously chosen on the second selection is now 1 out of $N - 1$. This process continues until you have selected the desired sample of size n.

When creating a simple random sample, you should avoid the "fishbowl" method of selecting a sample because this method lacks the ability to thoroughly mix the cards and, therefore, randomly select a sample. You should use a more rigorous selection method.

LEARN MORE
Learn to use a table of random numbers to select a simple random sample in a Chapter 1 online section.

One such method is to use a **table of random numbers**, such as Table E.1 in Appendix E, for selecting the sample. A table of random numbers consists of a series of digits listed in a randomly generated sequence. To use a random number table for selecting a sample, you first need to assign code numbers to the individual items of the frame. Then you generate the random sample by reading the table of random numbers and selecting those individuals from the frame whose assigned code numbers match the digits found in the table. Because the number system uses 10 digits $(0, 1, 2, \ldots, 9)$, the chance that you will randomly generate any particular digit is equal to the probability of generating any other digit. This probability is 1 out of 10. Hence, if you generate a sequence of 800 digits, you would expect about 80 to be the digit 0, 80 to be the digit 1, and so on. Because every digit or sequence of digits in the table is random, the table can be read either horizontally or vertically. The margins of the table designate row numbers and column numbers. The digits themselves are grouped into sequences of five in order to make reading the table easier.

Systematic Sample

In a **systematic sample**, you partition the N items in the frame into n groups of k items, where

$$k = \frac{N}{n}$$

You round k to the nearest integer. To select a systematic sample, you choose the first item to be selected at random from the first k items in the frame. Then, you select the remaining $n - 1$ items by taking every kth item thereafter from the entire frame.

If the frame consists of a list of prenumbered checks, sales receipts, or invoices, taking a systematic sample is faster and easier than taking a simple random sample. A systematic sample is also a convenient mechanism for collecting data from membership directories, electoral registers, class rosters, and consecutive items coming off an assembly line.

To take a systematic sample of $n = 40$ from the population of $N = 800$ full-time employees, you partition the frame of 800 into 40 groups, each of which contains 20 employees. You then select a random number from the first 20 individuals and include every twentieth individual after the first selection in the sample. For example, if the first random number you select is 008, your subsequent selections are 028, 048, 068, 088, 108, . . . , 768, and 788.

Simple random sampling and systematic sampling are simpler than other, more sophisticated, probability sampling methods, but they generally require a larger sample size. In addition, systematic sampling is prone to selection bias that can occur when there is a pattern in the frame. To overcome the inefficiency of simple random sampling and the potential selection bias involved with systematic sampling, you can use either stratified sampling methods or cluster sampling methods.

Stratified Sample

LEARN MORE

Learn how to select a stratified sample in a Chapter 1 online section.

In a **stratified sample**, you first subdivide the N items in the frame into separate subpopulations, or **strata**. A stratum is defined by some common characteristic, such as gender or year in school. You select a simple random sample within each of the strata and combine the results from the separate simple random samples. Stratified sampling is more efficient than either simple random sampling or systematic sampling because you are ensured of the representation of items across the entire population. The homogeneity of items within each stratum provides greater precision in the estimates of underlying population parameters. In addition, stratified sampling enables you to reach conclusions about each strata in the frame. However, using a stratified sample requires that you can determine the variable(s) on which to base the stratification and can also be expensive to implement.

Cluster Sample

In a **cluster sample**, you divide the N items in the frame into clusters that contain several items. **Clusters** are often naturally occurring groups, such as counties, election districts, city blocks, households, or sales territories. You then take a random sample of one or more clusters and study all items in each selected cluster.

Cluster sampling is often more cost-effective than simple random sampling, particularly if the population is spread over a wide geographic region. However, cluster sampling often requires a larger sample size to produce results as precise as those from simple random sampling or stratified sampling. A detailed discussion of systematic sampling, stratified sampling, and cluster sampling procedures can be found in references 2, 4, and 5.

Problems for Section 1.3

LEARNING THE BASICS

1.17 For a population containing $N = 902$ individuals, what code number would you assign for
a. the first person on the list?
b. the fortieth person on the list?
c. the last person on the list?

1.18 For a population of $N = 902$, verify that by starting in row 05, column 01 of the table of random numbers (Table E.1), you need only six rows to select a sample of $N = 60$ *without* replacement.

1.19 Given a population of $N = 93$, starting in row 29, column 01 of the table of random numbers (Table E.1), and reading across the row, select a sample of $N = 15$
a. *without* replacement.
b. *with* replacement.

APPLYING THE CONCEPTS

1.20 For a study that consists of personal interviews with participants (rather than mail or phone surveys), explain why simple random sampling might be less practical than some other sampling methods.

1.21 You want to select a random sample of $n = 1$ from a population of three items (which are called A, B, and C). The rule for selecting the sample is as follows: Flip a coin; if it is heads, pick item A; if it is tails, flip the coin again; this time, if it is heads, choose B; if it is tails, choose C. Explain why this is a probability sample but not a simple random sample.

1.22 A population has four members (called A, B, C, and D). You would like to select a random sample of $n = 2$, which you decide to do in the following way: Flip a coin; if it is heads, the sample will be items A and B; if it is tails, the sample will be items C and D. Although this is a random sample, it is not a simple random sample. Explain why. (Compare the procedure described in Problem 1.21 with the procedure described in this problem.)

1.23 The registrar of a university with a population of $N = 4,000$ full-time students is asked by the president to conduct a survey to measure satisfaction with the quality of life on campus. The following table contains a breakdown of the 4,000 registered full-time students, by gender and class designation:

| GENDER | CLASS DESIGNATION | | | | |
	Fr.	So.	Jr.	Sr.	Total
Female	700	520	500	480	2,200
Male	560	460	400	380	1,800
Total	1,260	980	900	860	4,000

The registrar intends to take a probability sample of $n = 200$ students and project the results from the sample to the entire population of full-time students.
a. If the frame available from the registrar's files is an alphabetical listing of the names of all $N = 4,000$ registered full-time students, what type of sample could you take? Discuss.
b. What is the advantage of selecting a simple random sample in (a)?
c. What is the advantage of selecting a systematic sample in (a)?
d. If the frame available from the registrar's files is a list of the names of all $N = 4,000$ registered full-time students compiled from eight separate alphabetical lists, based on the gender and class designation breakdowns shown in the class designation table, what type of sample should you take? Discuss.
e. Suppose that each of the $N = 4,000$ registered full-time students lived in one of the 10 campus dormitories. Each dormitory accommodates 400 students. It is college policy to fully integrate students by gender and class designation in each dormitory. If the registrar is able to compile a listing of all students by dormitory, explain how you could take a cluster sample.

 SELF Test **1.24** Prenumbered sales invoices are kept in a sales journal. The invoices are numbered from 0001 to 5000.
a. Beginning in row 16, column 01, and proceeding horizontally in a table of random numbers (Table E.1), select a simple random sample of 50 invoice numbers.
b. Select a systematic sample of 50 invoice numbers. Use the random numbers in row 20, columns 05–07, as the starting point for your selection.
c. Are the invoices selected in (a) the same as those selected in (b)? Why or why not?

1.25 Suppose that 10,000 customers in a retailer's customer database are categorized by three customer types: 3,500 prospective buyers, 4,500 first time buyers, and 2,000 repeat (loyal) buyers. A sample of 1,000 customers is needed.
a. What type of sampling should you do? Why?
b. Explain how you would carry out the sampling according to the method stated in (a).
c. Why is the sampling in (a) not simple random sampling?

1.4 Types of Survey Errors

As you learned in Section 1.2, responses from a survey represent a source of data. Nearly every day, you read or hear about survey or opinion poll results in newspapers, on the Internet, or on radio or television. To identify surveys that lack objectivity or credibility, you must critically evaluate what you read and hear by examining the validity of the survey results. First, you must evaluate the purpose of the survey, why it was conducted, and for whom it was conducted.

The second step in evaluating the validity of a survey is to determine whether it was based on a probability or nonprobability sample (as discussed in Section 1.3). You need to remember that the only way to make valid statistical inferences from a sample to a population is by using a probability sample. Surveys that use nonprobability sampling methods are subject to serious biases that may make the results meaningless.

Even when surveys use probability sampling methods, they are subject to four types of potential survey errors:

- Coverage error
- Nonresponse error
- Sampling error
- Measurement error

Well-designed surveys reduce or minimize these four types of errors, often at considerable cost.

Coverage Error

The key to proper sample selection is having an adequate frame. **Coverage error** occurs if certain groups of items are excluded from the frame so that they have no chance of being selected in the sample or if items are included from outside the frame. Coverage error results in a **selection bias**. If the frame is inadequate because certain groups of items in the population were not properly included, any probability sample selected will provide only an estimate of the characteristics of the frame, not the *actual* population.

Nonresponse Error

Not everyone is willing to respond to a survey. **Nonresponse error** arises from failure to collect data on all items in the sample and results in a **nonresponse bias**. Because you cannot always assume that persons who do not respond to surveys are similar to those who do, you need to follow up on the nonresponses after a specified period of time. You should make several attempts to convince such individuals to complete the survey and possibly offer an incentive to participate. The follow-up responses are then compared to the initial responses in order to make valid inferences from the survey (see references 2, 4, and 5). The mode of response you use, such as face-to-face interview, telephone interview, paper questionnaire, or computerized questionnaire, affects the rate of response. Personal interviews and telephone interviews usually produce a higher response rate than do mail surveys—but at a higher cost.

Sampling Error

When conducting a probability sample, chance dictates which individuals or items will or will not be included in the sample. **Sampling error** reflects the variation, or "chance differences," from sample to sample, based on the probability of particular individuals or items being selected in the particular samples.

When you read about the results of surveys or polls in newspapers or on the Internet, there is often a statement regarding a margin of error, such as "the results of this poll are expected to be within ±4 percentage points of the actual value." This **margin of error** is the sampling error. You can reduce sampling error by using larger sample sizes. Of course, doing so increases the cost of conducting the survey.

Measurement Error

In the practice of good survey research, you design surveys with the intention of gathering meaningful and accurate information. Unfortunately, the survey results you get are often only a proxy for the ones you really desire. Unlike height or weight, certain information about behaviors and psychological states is impossible or impractical to obtain directly.

When surveys rely on self-reported information, the mode of data collection, the respondent to the survey, and or the survey itself can be possible sources of **measurement error**.

Satisficing, social desirability, reading ability, and/or interviewer effects can be dependent on the mode of data collection. The social desirability bias or cognitive/memory limitations of a respondent can affect the results. And vague questions, double-barreled questions that ask about multiple issues but require a single response, or questions that ask the respondent to report something that occurs over time but fail to clearly define the extent of time about which the question asks (the reference period) are some of the survey flaws that can cause errors.

To minimize measurement error, you need to standardize survey administration and respondent understanding of questions, but there are many barriers to this (see references 1, 3, and 10).

Ethical Issues About Surveys

Ethical considerations arise with respect to the four types of survey error. Coverage error can result in selection bias and becomes an ethical issue if particular groups or individuals are purposely excluded from the frame so that the survey results are more favorable to the survey's sponsor. Nonresponse error can lead to nonresponse bias and becomes an ethical issue if the sponsor knowingly designs the survey so that particular groups or individuals are less likely than others to respond. Sampling error becomes an ethical issue if the findings are purposely presented without reference to sample size and margin of error so that

THINK ABOUT THIS New Media Surveys/Old Sampling Problems

A software company executive decided to create a "customer experience improvement program" to record how customers use its products, with the goal of using the collected data to make product enhancements. An editor of a news website decides to create an instant poll to ask website visitors about important political issues. A marketer of products aimed at a specific demographic decides to use a social networking site to collect consumer feedback. What do these decisions have in common with a *dead-tree* publication that went out of business over 70 years ago?

By 1932, long before the Internet, "straw polls" conducted by the magazine *Literary Digest* had successfully predicted five U.S. presidential elections in a row. For the 1936 election, the magazine promised its largest poll ever and sent about 10 million ballots to people all across the country. After receiving and tabulating more than 2.3 million ballots, the *Digest* confidently proclaimed that Alf Landon would be an easy winner over Franklin D. Roosevelt. As things turned out, FDR won in a landslide, with Landon receiving the fewest electoral votes in U.S. history. The reputation of *Literary Digest* was ruined; the magazine would cease publication less than two years later.

The failure of the *Literary Digest* poll was a watershed event in the history of sample surveys

and polls. This failure refuted the notion that the larger the sample is, the better. (Remember this the next time someone complains about a political survey's "small" sample size.) The failure opened the door to new and more modern methods of sampling discussed in this chapter. Using the predecessors of those methods, George Gallup, the "Gallup" of the famous poll, and Elmo Roper, of the eponymous reports, both first gained widespread public notice for their correct "scientific" predictions of the 1936 election.

The failed *Literary Digest* poll became fodder for several postmortems, and the reason for the failure became almost an urban legend. Typically, the explanation is coverage error: The ballots were sent mostly to "rich people," and this created a frame that excluded poorer citizens (presumably more inclined to vote for the Democrat Roosevelt than the Republican Landon). However, later analyses suggest that this was not true; instead, low rates of response (2.3 million ballots represented less than 25% of the ballots distributed) and/or nonresponse error (Roosevelt voters were less likely to mail in a ballot than Landon voters) were significant reasons for the failure (see reference 9).

When Microsoft first revealed its Office Ribbon interface, a manager explained how Microsoft had applied data collected from its "Customer

Experience Improvement Program" to the user interface redesign. This led others to speculate that the data were biased toward beginners—who might be less likely to decline participation in the program—and that, in turn, had led Microsoft to create a user interface that ended up perplexing more experienced users. This was another case of nonresponse error!

The editor's instant poll mentioned earlier is targeted to the visitors of the news website, and the social network–based survey is aimed at "friends" of a product; such polls can also suffer from nonresponse errors. Often, marketers extol how much they "know" about survey respondents, thanks to data that can be collected from a social network community. But no amount of information about the respondents can tell marketers *who the nonrespondents are*. Therefore, new media surveys fall prey to the same old type of error that proved fatal to *Literary Digest* way back when.

Today, companies establish formal surveys based on probability sampling and go to great lengths—and spend large sums—to deal with coverage error, nonresponse error, sampling error, and measurement error. Instant polling and tell-a-friend surveys can be interesting and fun, but they are not replacements for the methods discussed in this chapter.

the sponsor can promote a viewpoint that might otherwise be inappropriate. Measurement error can become an ethical issue in one of three ways: (1) a survey sponsor chooses leading questions that guide the respondent in a particular direction; (2) an interviewer, through mannerisms and tone, purposely makes a respondent obligated to please the interviewer or otherwise guides the respondent in a particular direction; or (3) a respondent willfully provides false information.

Ethical issues also arise when the results of nonprobability samples are used to form conclusions about the entire population. When you use a nonprobability sampling method, you need to explain the sampling procedures and state that the results cannot be generalized beyond the sample.

Problems for Section 1.4

APPLYING THE CONCEPTS

1.26 A survey indicates that the vast majority of college students own their own personal computers. What information would you want to know before you accepted the results of this survey?

1.27 A simple random sample of $n = 300$ full-time employees is selected from a company list containing the names of all $N = 5,000$ full-time employees in order to evaluate job satisfaction.
a. Give an example of possible coverage error.
b. Give an example of possible nonresponse error.
c. Give an example of possible sampling error.
d. Give an example of possible measurement error.

1.28 The results of a 2013 Adobe Systems study on retail apps and buying habits reveal insights on perceptions and attitudes toward mobile shopping using retail apps and browsers, providing new direction for retailers to develop their digital publishing strategies (**adobe.ly/11gt8Rq**). Increased consumer interest in using shopping applications means retailers must adapt to meet the rising expectations for specialized mobile shopping experiences. The results indicate that tablet users (55%) are almost twice as likely as smartphone users (28%) to use their device to purchase products and services. The findings also reveal that retail and catalog apps are rapidly catching up to mobile browsers as a viable shopping channel: nearly half of all mobile shoppers are interested in using apps instead of a mobile browser (45% of tablet shoppers and 49% of smartphone shoppers). The research is based on an online survey with a sample of 1,003 consumers. Identify *potential* concerns with coverage, nonresponse, sampling, and measurement errors.

1.29 A recent PwC Supply Global Chain survey indicated that companies that acknowledge the supply chain as a strategic asset achieve 70% higher performance (**pwc.to/VaFpGz**). The "Leaders" in the survey point to next-generation supply chains, which are fast, flexible, and responsive. They are more concerned with skills that separate a company from the crowd: 51% say differentiating capabilities is the real key to success. What additional information would you want to know about the survey before you accepted the results of the study?

1.30 A recent survey points to a next generation of consumers seeking a more mobile TV experience. The 2013 KPMG International Consumer Media Behavior study found that while TV is still the most popular media activity with 88% of U.S. consumers watching TV, a relatively high proportion of U.S. consumers, 14%, now prefer to watch TV via their mobile device or tablet for greater flexibility (**bit.ly/Wb8Jv9**). What additional information would you want to know about the survey before you accepted the results of the study?

USING STATISTICS

Beginning of the End... Revisited

The analysts charged by GT&M CEO Emma Levia to identify, define, and collect the data that would be helpful in setting a price for Whitney Wireless have completed their task. The group has identified a number of variables to analyze. In the course of doing this work, the group realized that most of the variables to study would be discrete numerical variables based on data that (ac)counts the financials of the business. These data would mostly be from the primary source of the business itself, but some supplemental variables about economic conditions and other factors that might affect the long-term prospects of the business might come from a secondary data source, such as an economic agency.

Tyler Olson/Shutterstock

The group foresaw that examining several categorical variables related to the customers of both GT&M and Whitney Wireless would be necessary. The group discovered that the affinity ("shopper's card") programs of both firms had already collected demographic data of interest when customers enrolled in those programs. That primary source, when combined with secondary data gleaned from the social media networks to which the business belongs, might prove useful in getting a rough approximation of the profile of a typical customer that might be interested in doing business with an "A-to-Z" electronics retailer.

SUMMARY

In this chapter, you learned about the various types of variables used in business. In addition, you learned about different methods of collecting data, several statistical sampling methods, and issues involved in taking samples.

In the next two chapters, you will study a variety of tables and charts and descriptive measures that are used to present and analyze data.

REFERENCES

1. Biemer, P. B., R. M. Graves, L. E. Lyberg, A. Mathiowetz, and S. Sudman. *Measurement Errors in Surveys*. New York: Wiley Interscience, 2004.
2. Cochran, W. G. *Sampling Techniques*, 3rd ed. New York: Wiley, 1977.
3. Fowler, F. J. *Improving Survey Questions: Design and Evaluation*, *Applied Special Research Methods Series*, Vol. 38, Thousand Oaks, CA: Sage Publications, 1995.
4. Groves R. M., F. J. Fowler, M. P. Couper, J. M. Lepkowski, E. Singer, and R. Tourangeau. *Survey Methodology*, 2nd ed. New York: John Wiley, 2009.
5. Lohr, S. L. *Sampling Design and Analysis*, 2nd ed. Boston, MA: Brooks/Cole Cengage Learning, 2010.
6. *Microsoft Excel 2013*. Redmond, WA: Microsoft Corporation, 2012.
7. *Minitab Release 16*. State College, PA: Minitab, Inc., 2010.
8. Osbourne, J. *Best Practices in Data Cleaning*. Thousand Oaks, CA: Sage Publications, 2012.
9. Squire, P. "Why the 1936 *Literary Digest* Poll Failed." *Public Opinion Quarterly* 52 (1988): 125–133.
10. Sudman, S., N. M. Bradburn, and N. Schwarz. *Thinking About Answers: The Application of Cognitive Processes to Survey Methodology*. San Francisco, CA: Jossey-Bass, 1993.

KEY TERMS

categorical variable 11
cluster 18
cluster sample 18
collect 11
collectively exhaustive 15
continuous variable 12
convenience sample 16
coverage error 20
define 11
discrete variable 12
frame 16
judgment sample 17
margin of error 20
measurement error 20
missing value 15

mutually exclusive 15
nonprobability sample 16
nonresponse bias 20
nonresponse error 20
numerical variable 11
operational definition 11
outlier 15
parameter 14
population 14
primary data source 13
probability sample 16
qualitative variable 11
quantitative variable 11
recoded variable 15
sample 14

sampling error 20
sampling with replacement 17
sampling without replacement 17
secondary data source 13
selection bias 20
simple random sample 17
statistics 14
strata 18
stratified sample 18
systematic sample 18
table of random numbers 17
unstructured data 14

CHECKING YOUR UNDERSTANDING

1.31 What is the difference between a sample and a population?

1.32 What is the difference between a statistic and a parameter?

1.33 What is the difference between a categorical variable and a numerical variable?

1.34 What is the difference between a discrete numerical variable and a continuous numerical variable?

1.35 What is the difference between probability sampling and non-probability sampling?

CHAPTER REVIEW PROBLEMS

1.36 Visit the official website for either Excel (**www.office.microsoft.com/excel**) or Minitab (**www.minitab.com/products/minitab**). Read about the program you chose and then think about the ways the program could be useful in statistical analysis.

1.37 Results of a 2013 Adobe Systems study on retail apps and buying habits reveals insights on perceptions and attitudes toward mobile shopping using retail apps and browsers, providing new direction for retailers to develop their digital publishing strategies. Increased consumer interest in using shopping applications means retailers must adapt to meet the rising expectations for specialized mobile shopping experiences. The results indicate that tablet users (55%) are almost twice as likely as smartphone users (28%) to use their device to purchase products and services. The findings also reveal that retail and catalog apps are rapidly catching up to mobile browsers as a viable shopping channel: Nearly half of all mobile shoppers are interested in using apps instead of a mobile browser (45% of tablet shoppers and 49% of smartphone shoppers). The research is based on an online survey with a sample of 1,003 18–54 year olds who currently own a smartphone and/or tablet; it includes consumers who use and do not use these devices to shop (**adobe.ly/11gt8Rq**).
a. Describe the population of interest.
b. Describe the sample that was collected.
c. Describe a parameter of interest.
d. Describe the statistic used to estimate the parameter in (c).

1.38 The Gallup organization releases the results of recent polls at its website, **www.gallup.com**. Visit this site and read an article of interest.
a. Describe the population of interest.
b. Describe the sample that was collected.
c. Describe a parameter of interest.
d. Describe the statistic used to estimate the parameter in (c).

1.39 A recent PwC Supply Global Chain survey indicated that companies that acknowledge the supply chain as a strategic asset achieve 70% higher performance. The "Leaders" in the survey point to next-generation supply chains, which are fast, flexible, and responsive. They are more concerned with skills that separate a company from the crowd: 51% say differentiating capabilities is the real key to success (**pwc.to/VaFpGz**). The results are based on a survey of 503 supply chain executives in a wide range of industries representing a mix of company sizes from across three global regions: Asia, Europe, and the Americas.

a. Describe the population of interest.
b. Describe the sample that was collected.
c. Describe a parameter of interest.
d. Describe the statistic used to estimate the parameter in (c).

1.40 The Data and Story Library (DASL) is an online library of data files and stories that illustrate the use of basic statistical methods. Visit **lib.stat.cmu.edu/index.php**, click DASL, and explore a data set of interest to you.
a. Describe a variable in the data set you selected.
b. Is the variable categorical or numerical?
c. If the variable is numerical, is it discrete or continuous?

1.41 Download and examine the U.S. Census Bureau's "Business and Professional Classification Survey (SQ-CLASS)," available through the **Get Help with Your Form** link at **www.census.gov/econ/**.
a. Give an example of a categorical variable included in the survey.
b. Give an example of a numerical variable included in the survey.

1.42 Three professors examined awareness of four widely disseminated retirement rules among employees at the University of Utah. These rules provide simple answers to questions about retirement planning (R. N. Mayer, C. D. Zick, and M. Glaittle, "Public Awareness of Retirement Planning Rules of Thumb," *Journal of Personal Finance*, 2011 10(1), 12–35). At the time of the investigation, there were approximately 10,000 benefited employees, and 3,095 participated in the study. Demographic data collected on these 3,095 employees included gender, age (years), education level (years completed), marital status, household income ($), and employment category.
a. Describe the population of interest.
b. Describe the sample that was collected.
c. Indicate whether each of the demographic variables mentioned is categorical or numerical.

1.43 A manufacturer of cat food is planning to survey households in the United States to determine purchasing habits of cat owners. Among the variables to be collected are the following:
   i. The primary place of purchase for cat food
   ii. Whether dry or moist cat food is purchased
   iii. The number of cats living in the household
   iv. Whether any cat living in the household is pedigreed
a. For each of the four items listed, indicate whether the variable is categorical or numerical. If it is numerical, is it discrete or continuous?
b. Develop five categorical questions for the survey.
c. Develop five numerical questions for the survey.

CASES FOR CHAPTER 1

Managing Ashland MultiComm Services

Ashland MultiComm Services (AMS) provides high-quality communications networks in the Greater Ashland area. AMS traces its roots to Ashland Community Access Television (ACATV), a small company that redistributed the broadcast television signals from nearby major metropolitan areas but has evolved into a provider of a wide range of broadband services for residential customers.

AMS offers subscription-based services for digital cable video programming, local and long-distance telephone services, and high-speed Internet access. Recently, AMS has faced competition from other network providers that have expanded into the Ashland area. AMS has also seen decreases in the number of new digital cable installations and the rate of digital cable renewals.

AMS management believes that a combination of increased promotional expenditures, adjustment in subscription fees, and improved customer service will allow AMS to successfully face the competition from other network providers. However, AMS management worries about the possible effects that new Internet-based methods of program delivery may have had on their digital cable business. They decide that they need to conduct some research and organize a team of research specialists to examine the current status of the business and the marketplace in which it competes.

The managers suggest that the research team examine the company's own historical data for number of subscribers, revenues, and subscription renewal rates for the past few years. They direct the team to examine year-to-date data as well, as the managers suspect that some of the changes they have seen have been a relatively recent phenomena.

1. What type of data source would the company's own historical data be? Identify other possible data sources that the research team might use to examine the current marketplace for residential broadband services in a city such as Ashland.

2. What type of data collection techniques might the team employ?

3. In their suggestions and directions, the AMS managers have named a number of possible variables to study, but offered no operational definitions for those variables. What types of possible misunderstandings could arise if the team and managers do not first properly define each variable cited?

CardioGood Fitness

CardioGood Fitness is a developer of high-quality cardiovascular exercise equipment. Its products include treadmills, fitness bikes, elliptical machines, and e-glides. CardioGood Fitness looks to increase the sales of its treadmill products and has hired The AdRight Agency, a small advertising firm, to create and implement an advertising program. The AdRight Agency plans to identify particular market segments that are most likely to buy their clients' goods and services and then locates advertising outlets that will reach that market group. This activity includes collecting data on clients' actual sales and on the customers who make the purchases, with the goal of determining whether there is a distinct profile of the typical customer for a particular product or service. If a distinct profile emerges, efforts are made to match that profile to advertising outlets known to reflect the particular profile, thus targeting advertising directly to high-potential customers.

CardioGood Fitness sells three different lines of treadmills. The TM195 is an entry-level treadmill. It is as dependable as other models offered by CardioGood Fitness, but with fewer programs and features. It is suitable for individuals who thrive on minimal programming and the desire for simplicity to initiate their walk or hike. The TM195 sells for $1,500.

The middle-line TM498 adds to the features of the entry-level model two user programs and up to 15% elevation upgrade. The TM498 is suitable for individuals who are walkers at a transitional stage from walking to running or midlevel runners. The TM498 sells for $1,750.

The top-of-the-line TM798 is structurally larger and heavier and has more features than the other models. Its unique features include a bright blue backlit LCD console, quick speed and incline keys, a wireless heart rate monitor with a telemetric chest strap, remote speed and incline controls, and an anatomical figure that specifies which muscles are minimally and maximally activated. This model features a nonfolding platform base that is designed to handle rigorous, frequent running; the TM798 is therefore appealing to someone who is a power walker or a runner. The selling price is $2,500.

As a first step, the market research team at AdRight is assigned the task of identifying the profile of the typical customer for each treadmill product offered by CardioGood Fitness. The market research team decides to investigate whether there are differences across the product lines with respect to customer characteristics. The team decides to collect data on individuals who purchased a treadmill at a CardioGood Fitness retail store during the prior three months.

The team decides to use both business transactional data and the results of a personal profile survey that every purchaser completes as their sources of data. The team identifies the following customer variables to study: product purchased—TM195, TM498, or TM798; gender; age, in years; education, in years; relationship status, single or partnered; annual household income ($); mean number

of times the customer plans to use the treadmill each week; mean number of miles the customer expects to walk/run each week; and self-rated fitness on an 1-to-5 scale, where 1 is poor shape and 5 is excellent shape. For this set of variables:

1. Which variables in the survey are categorical?

2. Which variables in the survey are numerical?

3. Which variables are discrete numerical variables?

Clear Mountain State Student Surveys

1. The Student News Service at Clear Mountain State University (CMSU) has decided to gather data about the undergraduate students who attend CMSU. They create and distribute a survey of 14 questions and receive responses from 62 undergraduates (stored in `UndergradSurvey`). Download (see Appendix C) and review the survey document **CMUndergradSurvey .pdf**. For each question asked in the survey, determine whether the variable is categorical or numerical. If you determine that the variable is numerical, identify whether it is discrete or continuous.

2. The dean of students at CMSU has learned about the undergraduate survey and has decided to undertake a similar survey for graduate students at CMSU. She creates and distributes a survey of 14 questions and receives responses from 44 graduate students (stored in `GradSurvey`). Download (see Appendix C) and review the survey document **CMGradSurvey.pdf**. For each question asked in the survey, determine whether the variable is categorical or numerical. If you determine that the variable is numerical, identify whether it is discrete or continuous.

Learning with the Digital Cases

As you have already learned in this book, decision makers use statistical methods to help analyze data and communicate results. Every day, somewhere, someone misuses these techniques either by accident or intentional choice. Identifying and preventing such misuses of statistics is an important responsibility for all managers. The Digital Cases give you the practice you need to help develop the skills necessary for this important task.

Each chapter's Digital Case tests your understanding of how to apply an important statistical concept taught in the chapter. As in many business situations, not all of the information you encounter will be relevant to your task, and you may occasionally discover conflicting information that you have to resolve in order to complete the case.

To assist your learning, each Digital Case begins with a learning objective and a summary of the problem or issue at hand. Each case directs you to the information necessary to reach your own conclusions and to answer the case questions. Many cases, such as the sample case worked out next, extend a chapter's Using Statistics scenario. You can download digital case files for later use or retrieve them online from a MyStatLab course for this book, as explained in Appendix C.

To illustrate learning with a Digital Case, open the Digital Case file **WhitneyWireless.pdf** that contains summary information about the Whitney Wireless business. Recall from the Using Statistics scenario for this chapter that Good Tunes & More (GT&M) is a retailer seeking to expand by purchasing Whitney Wireless, a small chain that sells mobile media devices. Apparently, from the claim on the title page, this business is celebrating its "best sales year ever."

Review the **Who We Are**, **What We Do**, and **What We Plan to Do** sections on the second page. Do these sections contain any useful information? What *questions* does this passage raise? Did you notice that while many facts are presented, no data that would support the claim of "best sales year ever" are presented? And were those mobile "mobile-mobiles" used solely for promotion? Or did they generate any sales? Do you think that a talk-with-your-mouth-full event, however novel, would be a success?

Continue to the third page and the **Our Best Sales Year Ever!** section. How would you support such a claim? With a table of numbers? Remarks attributed to a knowledgeable source? Whitney Wireless has used a chart to present "two years ago" and "latest twelve months" sales data by category. Are there any problems with what the company has done? *Absolutely!*

First, note that there are no scales for the symbols used, so you cannot know what the actual sales volumes are. In fact, as you will learn in Section 2.7, charts that incorporate icons as shown on the third page are considered examples of *chartjunk* and would never be used by people seeking to properly visualize data. The use of chartjunk symbols creates the impression that unit sales data are being presented. If the data are unit sales, does such data best support the claim being made, or would something else, such as dollar volumes, be a better indicator of sales at the retailer?

For the moment, let's assume that unit sales are being visualized. What are you to make of the second row, in which the three icons on the right side are much wider than the three on the left? Does that row represent a newer (wider) model being sold or a greater sales volume? Examine the fourth row. Does that row represent a decline in sales or an increase? (Do two partial icons represent more than one whole icon?) As for the fifth row, what are we to think? Is a black icon worth more than a red icon or vice versa?

At least the third row seems to tell some sort of tale of increased sales, and the sixth row tells a tale of constant sales. But what is the "story" about the seventh row? There, the partial icon is so small that we have no idea what product category the icon represents.

Perhaps a more serious issue is those curious chart labels. "Latest twelve months" is ambiguous; it could include months from the current year as well as months from one year ago and therefore may not be an equivalent time period to "two years ago." But the business was established in 2001, and the claim being made is "best sales year ever," so why hasn't management included sales figures for *every* year?

Are the Whitney Wireless managers hiding something, or are they just unaware of the proper use of statistics? Either way, they have failed to properly organize and visualize their data and therefore have failed to communicate a vital aspect of their story.

In subsequent Digital Cases, you will be asked to provide this type of analysis, using the open-ended case questions as your guide. Not all the cases are as straightforward as this example, and some cases include perfectly appropriate applications of statistical methods.

CHAPTER 1 EXCEL GUIDE

EG1.1 DEFINING VARIABLES

Classifying Variables by Type

Microsoft Excel infers the variable type from the data you enter into a column. If Excel discovers a column that contains numbers, it treats the column as a numerical variable. If Excel discovers a column that contains words or alphanumeric entries, it treats the column as a non-numerical (categorical) variable.

This imperfect method works most of the time, especially if you make sure that the categories for your categorical variables are words or phrases such as "yes" and "no." However, because you cannot explicitly define the variable type, Excel can mistakenly offer or allow you to do nonsensical things such as using a statistical method that is designed for numerical variables on categorical variables. If you must use coded values such as 1, 2, or 3, enter them preceded with an apostrophe, as Excel treats all values that begin with an apostrophe as non-numerical data. (You can check whether a cell entry includes a leading apostrophe by selecting a cell and viewing the contents of the cell in the formula bar.)

EG1.2 COLLECTING DATA

Recoding Variables

Key Technique To recode a categorical variable, you first copy the original variable's column of data and then use the find-and-replace function on the copied data. To recode a numerical variable, enter a formula that returns a recoded value in a new column.

Example Using the **DATA worksheet** of the **Recoded workbook**, create the recoded variable UpperLower from the categorical variable Class and create the recoded Variable Dean's List from the numerical variable GPA.

In-Depth Excel Use the **RECODED worksheet** of the **Recoded workbook** as a model.

The worksheet already contains UpperLower, a recoded version of Class that uses the operational definitions on page 15, and Dean's List, a recoded version of GPA, in which the value No recodes all GPA values less than 3.3 and Yes recodes all values 3.3 or greater than 3.3. The **RECODED_FORMULAS worksheet** in the same workbook shows how formulas in column I use the IF function to recode GPA as the Dean's List variable.

These recoded variables were created by first opening to the **DATA worksheet** in the same workbook and then following these steps:

1. Right-click column **D** (right-click over the shaded "D" at the top of column D) and click **Copy** in the shortcut menu.
2. Right-click column **H** and click the **first choice** in the **Paste Options** gallery.
3. Enter **UpperLower** in cell **H1**.
4. Select column **H**. With column H selected, click **Home ➔ Find & Select ➔ Replace**.

In the Replace tab of the Find and Replace dialog box:

5. Enter **Senior** as **Find what**, **Upper** as **Replace with**, and then click **Replace All**.
6. Click **OK** to close the dialog box that reports the results of the replacement command.
7. Still in the Find and Replace dialog box, enter **Junior** as **Find what** (replacing **Senior**), and then click **Replace All**.
8. Click **OK** to close the dialog box that reports the results of the replacement command.
9. Still in the Find and Replace dialog box, enter **Sophomore** as **Find what**, **Lower** as **Replace with**, and then click **Replace All**.
10. Click **OK** to close the dialog box that reports the results of the replacement command.
11. Still in the Find and Replace dialog box, enter **Freshman** as **Find what** and then click **Replace All**.
12. Click **OK** to close the dialog box that reports the results of the replacement command.

(This creates the recoded variable UpperLower in column H.)

13. Enter **Dean's List** in cell **I1**.
14. Enter the formula =IF(G2 < 3.3, "No", "Yes") in cell **I2**.
15. Copy this formula down the column to the last row that contains student data (row 63).

(This creates the recoded variable Dean's List in column I.)

The RECODED worksheet uses the **IF** function (See Appendix F) to recode the numerical variable into two categories. Numerical variables can also be recoded into multiple categories by using the **VLOOKUP** function. Read the SHORT TAKES for Chapter 1 to learn more about this advanced recoding technique.

EG1.3 TYPES of SAMPLING METHODS

Simple Random Sample

Key Technique Use the **RANDBETWEEN(*smallest integer, largest integer*)** function to generate a random integer that can then be used to select an item from a frame.

Example 1 Create a simple random sample *with* replacement of size 40 from a population of 800 items.

In-Depth Excel Enter a formula that uses this function and then copy the formula down a column for as many rows as is necessary. For example, to create a simple random sample with replacement of size 40 from a population of 800 items, open to a new worksheet. Enter **Sample** in cell **A1** and enter the formula =RANDBETWEEN(1, 800) in cell **A2**. Then copy the formula down the column to cell **A41**.

Excel contains no functions to select a random sample *without* replacement. Such samples are most easily created using an add-in such as PHStat or the Analysis ToolPak, as described in the following paragraphs.

Analysis ToolPak Use **Sampling** to create a random sample *with replacement*.

For the example, open to the worksheet that contains the population of 800 items in column A and that contains a column heading in cell A1. Select **Data ➜ Data Analysis**. In the Data Analysis dialog box, select **Sampling** from the **Analysis Tools** list and then click **OK**. In the procedure's dialog box (shown below):

1. Enter **A1:A801** as the **Input Range** and check **Labels**.
2. Click **Random** and enter **40** as the **Number of Samples**.
3. Click **New Worksheet Ply** and then click **OK**.

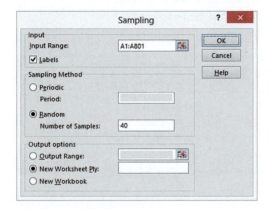

Example 2 Create a simple random sample *without* replacement of size 40 from a population of 800 items.

PHStat Use **Random Sample Generation**.
For the example, select **PHStat ➜ Sampling ➜ Random Sample Generation**. In the procedure's dialog box (shown in next column):

1. Enter **40** as the **Sample Size**.
2. Click **Generate list of random numbers** and enter **800** as the **Population Size**.
3. Enter a **Title** and click **OK**.

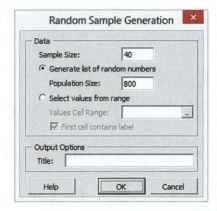

Unlike most other PHStat results worksheets, the worksheet created contains no formulas.

In-Depth Excel Use the **COMPUTE worksheet** of the **Random workbook** as a template.

The worksheet already contains 40 copies of the formula **=RANDBETWEEN(1, 800)** in column B. Because the **RANDBETWEEN** function samples *with* replacement as discussed at the start of this section, you may need to add additional copies of the formula in new column B rows until you have 40 unique values.

If your intended sample size is large, you may find it difficult to spot duplicates. Read the SHORT TAKES for Chapter 1 to learn more about an advanced technique that uses formulas to detect duplicate values.

CHAPTER 1 MINITAB GUIDE

MG1.1 DEFINING VARIABLES

Classifying Variables by Type

When Minitab adds a "-T" suffix to a column name, it is classifying the column as a categorical, or *text*, variable. When Minitab does not add a suffix, it is classifying the column as a numerical variable. (A column name with the "-D" suffix is a *date* variable, a special type of a numerical variable.)

Sometimes, Minitab will misclassify a variable, for example, mistaking a numerical variable for a categorical (text) variable. In such cases, select the column, then select **Data ➜ Change Data Type**, and then select one of the choices, for example, **Text to Numeric** for the case of when Minitab has mistaken a numerical variable as a categorical variable.

MG1.2 COLLECTING DATA

Recoding Variables

Use the **Replace** command to recode a categorical variable and **Calculator** to recode a numerical variable.

For example, to create the recoded variable UpperLower from the categorical variable Class (C4-T), open to the DATA worksheet of the Recode project and:

1. Select the **Class** column (**C4-T**).
2. Select **Editor ➜ Replace**.

In the Replace in Data Window dialog box:

3. Enter **Senior** as **Find what**, **Upper** as **Replace with**, and then click **Replace All**.
4. Click **OK** to close the dialog box that reports the results of the replacement command.

5. Still in the Find and Replace dialog box, enter **Junior** as **Find what** (replacing **Senior**), and then click **Replace All**.

6. Click **OK** to close the dialog box that reports the results of the replacement command.

7. Still in the Find and Replace dialog box, enter **Sophomore** as **Find what**, **Lower** as **Replace with**, and then click **Replace All**.

8. Click **OK** to close the dialog box that reports the results of the replacement command.

9. Still in the Find and Replace dialog box, enter **Freshman** as **Find what**, and then click **Replace All**.

10. Click **OK** to close the dialog box that reports the results of the replacement command.

To create the recoded variable Dean's List from the numerical variable GPA (C7), with the DATA worksheet of the Recode project still open:

1. Enter **Dean's List** as the name of the empty column **C8**.

2. Select **Calc → Calculator**.

In the Calculator dialog box (shown below):

3. Enter **C8** in the **Store result in variable** box.

4. Enter **IF(GPA < 3.3, "No", "Yes")** in the **Expression** box.

5. Click **OK**.

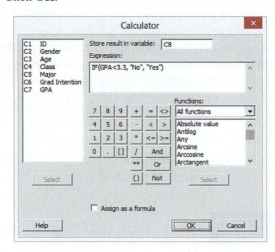

Variables can also be recoded into multiple categories by using the **Data → Code** command. Read the SHORT TAKES for Chapter 1 to learn more about this advanced recoding technique.

MG1.3 TYPES of SAMPLING METHODS

Simple Random Samples

Use **Sample From Columns**.

For example, to create a simple random sample with replacement of size 40 from a population of 800 items, first create the list of 800 employee numbers in column **C1**.

Select **Calc → Make Patterned Data → Simple Set of Numbers**. In the Simple Set of Numbers dialog box (shown below):

1. Enter **C1** in the **Store patterned data in** box.

2. Enter **1** in the **From first value** box.

3. Enter **800** in the **To last value** box.

4. Click **OK**.

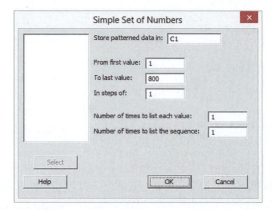

With the worksheet containing the column C1 list still open:

5. Select **Calc → Random Data → Sample from Columns**.

In the Sample From Columns dialog box (shown below):

6. Enter **40** in the **Number of rows to sample** box.

7. Enter **C1** in the **From columns** box.

8. Enter **C2** in the **Store samples in** box.

9. Click **OK**.

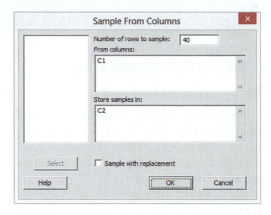

Organizing and Visualizing Variables

OBJECTIVES

Methods to organize variables

Methods to visualize variables

Methods to organize or visualize more than one variable at the same time

Principles of proper visualizations

USING STATISTICS

The Choice Is Yours

Even though he is still in his 20s, Tom Sanchez realizes that you can never start too early to save for retirement. Based on research he has already done, Sanchez seeks to contribute to his 401(k) retirement plan by investing in one or more retirement funds.

Meanwhile, the Choice *Is* Yours investment service has been thinking about being better prepared to counsel younger investors such as Sanchez about retirement funds. To pursue this business objective, a company task force has already selected 316 retirement funds that may prove appropriate for younger investors. You have been asked to define, collect, organize, and visualize data about these funds in ways that could assist prospective clients making decisions about the funds in which they will invest. As a starting point, you think about the facts about each fund that would help customers compare and contrast funds.

You decide to begin by defining the variables for key characteristics of each fund, such as each fund's past performance. You also decide to define variables such as the amount of assets that a fund manages and whether the goal of a fund is to invest in companies whose earnings are expected to substantially increase in future years (a "growth" fund) or invest in companies whose stock price is undervalued, priced low relative to their earnings potential (a "value" fund).

You collect data from appropriate sources and organize the data as a worksheet, placing each variable in its own column. As you think more about your task, you realize that 316 rows of data, one for each fund in the sample, would be hard for prospective clients to review easily.

Is there something else you can do? Can you organize and present these data to prospective clients in a more helpful and comprehensible manner?

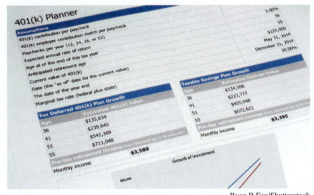

Ryan R Fox/Shutterstock

Placing data into a worksheet table represents the simplest case of the DCOVA Organize task. For many reasons, including the reasons noted in the Choice *Is* Yours scenario, you often need other methods to organize data, one of the subjects of this chapter.

When you organize data using the methods discussed in this chapter, you are creating tabular summaries of the variables that the data represent. These summaries provide insight about the variables, thereby facilitating decision making. For example, a summary that organized the retirement funds sample to help identify funds that were designed for growth and had a moderate risk might be useful for a prospective client such as Tom Sanchez.

Summaries can take visual forms and the methods that help visualize data are another subject of this chapter. Visual summaries can facilitate the rapid review of larger amounts of data as well as show patterns of the values associated with certain variables. For example, visualizing the ten-year rate of returns of funds along with the management fees charged by funds would help to identify the funds that would be charging you relatively little for a "good" rate of return as well as the funds whose management fees seem excessive given their rates of return.

Because both tabular and visual summaries can be useful, the DCOVA third and fourth tasks, **O**rganize and **V**isualize the variables, are often done in tandem or together. When so combined, the Organize and Visualize tasks can sometimes help jumpstart analysis by enabling a decision maker to reach preliminary conclusions about data that can be tested during the **A**nalyze task.

Because of this jumpstart effect, you will find yourself repeating some of the methods discussed in this chapter when, in later chapters, you will study methods that help analyze variables. Later chapters will discuss additional methods to organize and visualize data as Table 2.1 shows. In addition, Section 2.6 discusses the methods of multidimensional contingency tables, "PivotTables," and treemaps that summarize or visualize a mixed *set* of categorical and numerical variables.

Because the methods used to organize and visualize the data collected for categorical variables differ from the methods used to organize and visualize the data collected for numerical variables, this chapter discusses them in separate sections. You will always need to first determine the type of the variable, numerical or categorical, you seek to organize and visualize, in order to choose appropriate methods.

This chapter also contains a section on common errors that people make when visualizing variables. When learning methods to visualize variables, you should be aware of such possible errors because of the potential of such errors to mislead and misinform decision makers about the data you have collected.

LEARN MORE

Learn more about retirement funds and the variables used in the retirement funds sampled in this chapter in the **AllAboutRetirementFunds.pdf** online section.

TABLE 2.1

Organizing and Visualizing a Variable

Categorical Variable:
Summary table, contingency table (Section 2.1)
Bar chart, pie chart, Pareto chart, side-by-side bar chart (Section 2.3)
Numerical Variable:
Ordered array, frequency distribution, relative frequency distribution, percentage distribution, cumulative percentage distribution (Section 2.2)
Stem-and-leaf display, histogram, polygon, cumulative percentage polygon (Section 2.4)
Mean, median, mode, quartiles, range, interquartile range, standard deviation, variance, coefficient of variation, skewness, kurtosis (Sections 3.1, 3.2, and 3.3)
Boxplot (Section 3.3)
Normal probability plot (Section 6.3)
For *Two* Numerical Variable: Scatter plot, time-series plot (Section 2.5)

2.1 Organizing Categorical Variables

You organize categorical variables by tallying the values of a variable by categories and placing the results in tables. Typically, you construct a summary table to organize the data for a single categorical variable and you construct a contingency table to organize the data from two or more categorical variables.

The Summary Table

A **summary table** tallies the values as frequencies or percentages for each category. A summary table helps you see the differences among the categories by displaying the frequency, amount, or percentage of items in a set of categories in a separate column. Table 2.2 presents a summary table that tallies responses to a recent survey that asked young adults about the main reason that they shop online. From this table, stored in `Online Shopping`, you can conclude that 37% shop online mainly for better prices and convenience and that 29% shop online mainly to avoid holiday crowds and hassles.

TABLE 2.2

Main Reason Young Adults Shop Online

Reason	Percentage
Better prices	37%
Avoiding holiday crowds or hassles	29%
Convenience	18%
Better selection	13%
Ships directly	3%

Source: Data extracted and adapted from "Main Reason Young Adults Shop Online?" *USA Today*, December 5, 2012, p. 1A.

EXAMPLE 2.1

Summary Table of Levels of Risk of Retirement Funds

The sample of 316 retirement funds for the Choice *Is* Yours scenario (see page 31) includes the variable risk that has the defined categories Low, Average, and High. Construct a summary table of the retirement funds, categorized by risk.

SOLUTION From Table 2.3, you can see that about two-thirds of the funds have low risk. About 30% of the funds have average risk. Very few funds have high risk.

TABLE 2.3

Frequency and Percentage Summary Table of Risk Level for 316 Retirement Funds

Fund Risk Level	Number of Funds	Percentage of Funds
Low	212	67.09%
Average	91	28.80%
High	13	4.11%
Total	316	100.00%

The Contingency Table

A **contingency table** cross-tabulates, or tallies jointly, the values of two or more categorical variables, allowing you to study patterns that may exist between the variables. Tallies can be shown as a frequency, a percentage of the overall total, a percentage of the row total, or a percentage of the column total, depending on the type of contingency table you use. Each tally appears in its own **cell**, and there is a cell for each **joint response**, a unique combination of

Like worksheet cells, contingency table cells are the intersections of rows and columns, but unlike a worksheet, both the rows and the columns represent variables. To identify placement, the terms row variable and column variable are often used.

> **Student Tip**
> Remember, each joint response gets tallied into only one cell.

values for the variables being tallied. In the simplest contingency table, one that contains only two categorical variables, the joint responses appear in a table such that the tallies of one variable are located in the rows and the tallies of the other variable are located in the columns.

For the sample of 316 retirement funds for the Choice *Is* Yours scenario, you might create a contingency table to examine whether there is any pattern between the fund type variable and the risk level variable. Because fund type has the defined categories Growth and Value and the risk level has the categories Low, Average, and High, there are six possible joint responses for this table. You could create the table by hand tallying the joint responses for each of the retirement funds in the sample. For example, for the first fund listed in the sample you would add to the tally in the cell that is the intersection of the Growth row and the Low column because the first fund is of type Growth and risk level Low. However, using one of the automated methods for creating contingency tables found in Sections EG2.1 and MG2.1 of the Excel and Minitab Guides would be a better choice.

Table 2.4 presents the completed contingency table after all 316 funds have been tallied. This table shows that there are 143 retirement funds that have the fund type Growth and risk level Low. In summarizing all six joint responses, the table reveals that Growth and Low is the most frequent joint response in the sample of 316 retirement funds.

TABLE 2.4

Contingency Table Displaying Fund Type and Risk Level

	RISK LEVEL			
FUND TYPE	**Low**	**Average**	**High**	**Total**
Growth	143	74	10	227
Value	69	17	3	89
Total	212	91	13	316

Contingency tables that display cell values as a percentage of a total can help show patterns between variables. Table 2.5 shows a contingency table that displays values as a percentage of the Table 2.4 overall total (316), Table 2.6 shows a contingency table that displays values as a percentage of the Table 2.4 row totals (227 and 89), and Table 2.7 shows a contingency table that displays values as a percentage of the Table 2.4 column totals (212, 91, and 13).

TABLE 2.5

Contingency Table Displaying Fund Type and Risk Level, Based on Percentage of Overall Total

	RISK LEVEL			
FUND TYPE	**Low**	**Average**	**High**	**Total**
Growth	45.25%	23.42%	3.16%	71.84%
Value	21.84%	5.38%	0.95%	28.16%
Total	67.09%	28.80%	4.11%	100.00%

TABLE 2.6

Contingency Table Displaying Fund Type and Risk Level, Based on Percentage of Row Total

	RISK LEVEL			
FUND TYPE	**Low**	**Average**	**High**	**Total**
Growth	63.00%	32.60%	4.41%	100.00%
Value	77.53%	19.10%	3.37%	100.00%
Total	67.09%	28.80%	4.11%	100.00%

TABLE 2.7

Contingency Table
Displaying Fund Type
and Risk Level, Based
on Percentage of
Column Total

	RISK LEVEL			
FUND TYPE	**Low**	**Average**	**High**	**Total**
Growth	67.45%	81.32%	76.92%	71.84%
Value	32.55%	18.68%	23.08%	28.16%
Total	100.00%	100.00%	100.00%	100.00%

Table 2.5 shows that 71.84% of the funds sampled are growth funds, 28.16% are value funds, and 45.25% are growth funds that have low risk. Table 2.6 shows that 63% of the growth funds have low risk, while 77.53% of the value funds have low risk. Table 2.7 shows that of the funds that have low risk, 67.45% are growth funds. From Tables 2.5 through 2.7, you see that growth funds are less likely than value funds to have low risk.

Problems for Section 2.1

LEARNING THE BASICS

2.1 A categorical variable has three categories, with the following frequencies of occurrence:

Category	Frequency
A	13
B	28
C	9

a. Compute the percentage of values in each category.
b. What conclusions can you reach concerning the categories?

2.2 The following data represent the responses to two questions asked in a survey of 40 college students majoring in business: What is your gender? (M = male; F = female) and What is your major? (A = Accounting; C = Computer Information Systems; M = Marketing):

Gender:	M	M	M	F	M	F	F	M	F	M
Major:	A	C	C	M	A	C	A	A	C	C

Gender:	F	M	M	M	M	F	F	M	F	F
Major:	A	A	A	M	C	M	A	A	A	C

Gender:	M	M	M	M	F	M	F	F	M	M
Major:	C	C	A	A	M	M	C	A	A	A

Gender:	F	M	M	M	M	F	M	F	M	M
Major:	C	C	A	A	A	A	C	C	A	C

a. Tally the data into a contingency table where the two rows represent the gender categories and the three columns represent the academic major categories.
b. Construct contingency tables based on percentages of all 40 student responses, based on row percentages and based on column percentages.

APPLYING THE CONCEPTS

2.3 The following table, stored in **Smartphone Sales**, represents the annual market share of smartphones, by type, for the years 2011, 2012, and 2013.

Type	2011	2012	2013
Android	47%	66%	78%
iOS	19%	19%	16%
Microsoft	2%	3%	3%
Blackberry	11%	5%	2%
Other OS	21%	7%	1%

Source: Data extracted from **gartner.com/newsroom/id/2665715** and **www.gartner.com/resId=2334916**.

a. What conclusions can you reach about the market for smartphones in 2011, 2012, and 2013?
b. What differences are there in the market for smartphones in 2011, 2012, and 2013?

2.4 The **Edmunds.com** NHTSA Complaints Activity Report contains consumer vehicle complaint submissions by automaker, brand, and category (data extracted from **edmu.in/Ybmpuz**). The following table, stored in **Automaker1**, represents complaints received by automaker for January 2013.

Automaker	Number
American Honda	169
Chrysler LLC	439
Ford Motor Company	440
General Motors	551
Nissan Motors Corporation	467
Toyota Motor Sales	332
Other	516

a. Compute the percentage of complaints for each automaker.
b. What conclusions can you reach about the complaints for the different automakers?

The following table, stored in **Automaker2**, represents complaints received by category for January 2013.

Category	Number
Airbags and seatbelts	201
Body and glass	182
Brakes	163
Fuel/emission/exhaust system	240
Interior electronics/hardware	279
Powertrain	1,148
Steering	397
Tires and wheels	71

c. Compute the percentage of complaints for each category.
d. What conclusions can you reach about the complaints for different categories?

2.5 The 2013 Mortimer Spinks and Computer Weekly Technology Survey reflects the views of technology and digital experts across the United Kingdom (**bit.ly/WS4jg3**). Respondents were asked, "What is the most important factor influencing the success of a tech start-up?" Assume the following results:

Most Important Factor	Frequency
Leadership	400
Marketing	346
Product	464
Technology	86

a. Compute the percentage of values for each factor.
b. What conclusions can you reach concerning factors influencing successful tech start-ups?

 2.6 The following table represents world oil production in millions of barrels a day in 2013:

Region	Oil Production (millions of barrels a day)
Iran	2.69
Saudi Arabia	9.58
Other OPEC countries	17.93
Non-OPEC countries	51.99

Source: **opec.org**, accessed February 2014.

a. Compute the percentage of values in each category.
b. What conclusions can you reach concerning the production of oil in 2013?

2.7 Visier's Survey of Employers explores how North American organizations are solving the challenges of delivering workforce analytics. Employers were asked what would help them be successful with human resources metrics and reports. The responses (stored in **Needs**) were as follows:

Needs	Frequency
Easier-to-use analytic tools	127
Faster access to data	41
Improved ability to present and interpret data	123
Improved ability to plan actions	33
Improved ability to predict impacts of my actions	49
Improved relationships to the business line organizations	37

Source: Data extracted from **bit.ly/1fmPZrQ**.

a. Compute the percentage of values for each response need.
b. What conclusions can you reach concerning needs for employer success with human resources metrics and reports?

2.8 A survey of 1,085 adults asked "Do you enjoy shopping for clothing for yourself?" The results indicated that 51% of the females enjoyed shopping for clothing for themselves as compared to 44% of the males. (Data extracted from "Split Decision on Clothes Shopping," *USA Today*, January 28, 2011, p. 1B.) The sample sizes of males and females were not provided. Suppose that the results were as shown in the following table:

	GENDER		
ENJOY SHOPPING	**Male**	**Female**	**Total**
Yes	238	276	514
No	304	267	571
Total	542	543	1,085

a. Construct contingency tables based on total percentages, row percentages, and column percentages.
b. What conclusions can you reach from these analyses?

2.9 A study of Kickstarter projects showed that 54.2% were successful, that is, achieved its goal and raised at least the targeted goal amount. In an effort to identify network dynamics that influences success, projects were subdivided into projects of owners who had backed other projects before, during or after creating their project (owners with backing history) and projects of owners without backing history. The results are as follows:

	PROJECT OWNER'S BACKING HISTORY		
Project Outcome	**Backing History**	**No Backing History**	**Total**
Successful	17,667	19,202	36,869
Not successful	10,921	20,267	31,188
Total	28,588	39,469	68,057

Source: Data extracted from Zvilichovsky et al., "Playing Both Sides of the Market: Success and Reciprocity on Crowdfunding Platforms," **bit.ly/OoyhqZ**.

a. Construct contingency tables based on total percentages, row percentages, and column percentages.

b. Which type of percentage—row, column, or total—do you think is most informative for these data? Explain.

c. What conclusions concerning the pattern of successful Kickstarter projects can you reach?

2.10 Do social recommendations increase ad effectiveness? A study of online video viewers compared viewers who arrived at an advertising video for a particular brand by following a social media recommendation link to viewers who arrived at the same video by web browsing. Data were collected on whether the viewer could correctly recall the brand being advertised after seeing the video. The results were:

ARRIVAL METHOD	CORRECTLY RECALLED THE BRAND	
	Yes	No
Recommendation	407	150
Browsing	193	91

Source: Data extracted from "Social Ad Effectiveness: An Unruly White Paper," **www.unrulymedia.com**, January 2012, p. 3.

What do these results tell you about social recommendations?

2.2 Organizing Numerical Variables

You organize numerical variables by creating ordered arrays of one or more variables. This section uses the numerical variable meal cost, which represents the cost of a meal at a restaurant, as the basis for its examples. Because the meal cost data has been collected from a sample of 100 restaurants that can be further categorized by their locations as either "city" or "suburban" restaurants, the variable meal cost raises the common question about how data should be organized in a worksheet when a numerical variable represents data from more than one group. This question is answered at the end of this section, after ordered arrays and distributions are first discussed.

The Ordered Array

An **ordered array** arranges the values of a numerical variable in rank order, from the smallest value to the largest value. An ordered array helps you get a better sense of the range of values in your data and is particularly useful when you have more than a few values. For example, financial analysts reviewing travel and entertainment costs might have the business objective of determining whether meal costs at city restaurants differ from meal costs at suburban restaurants. They collect data from a sample of 50 city restaurants and from a sample of 50 suburban restaurants for the cost of one meal (in $). Table 2.8A shows the unordered data (stored in Restaurants). The lack of ordering prevents you from reaching any quick conclusions about meal costs.

TABLE 2.8A

Meal Cost at 50 City Restaurants and 50 Suburban Restaurants

City Restaurant Meal Costs

33 26 43 32 44 44 50 42 44 36 61 50 51 50 76 53 44 77 57 43 29 34 77 50 74
56 67 57 66 80 68 42 48 60 35 45 32 25 74 43 39 55 65 35 61 37 54 41 33 27

Suburban Restaurant Meal Costs

47 48 35 59 44 51 37 36 43 52 34 38 51 34 51 34 51 56 26 34 34 44 40 54
41 50 71 60 37 27 34 48 39 44 41 37 47 67 68 49 29 33 39 39 28 46 70 60 52

In contrast, Table 2.8B, the ordered array version of the same data, enables you to quickly see that the cost of a meal at the city restaurants is between $25 and $80 and that the cost of a meal at the suburban restaurants is between $26 and $71.

TABLE 2.8B

Ordered Arrays of Meal Costs at 50 City Restaurants and 50 Suburban Restaurants

City Restaurant Meal Cost

25 26 27 29 32 32 33 33 34 35 35 36 37 39 41 42 42 43 43 43 44 44 44 44 45
48 50 50 50 50 51 53 54 55 56 57 57 60 61 61 65 66 67 68 74 74 76 77 77 80

Suburban Restaurant Meal Cost

26 27 28 29 31 33 34 34 34 34 34 34 35 36 37 37 37 38 39 39 39 40 41 41 43
44 44 44 46 47 47 48 48 49 50 51 51 51 51 52 52 54 56 59 60 60 67 68 70 71

When a variable contains a large number of values, reaching conclusions from an ordered array can be difficult. In such cases, creating one of the distributions discussed in the following pages would be a better choice.

The Frequency Distribution

A **frequency distribution** tallies the values of a numerical variable into a set of numerically ordered **classes**. Each class groups a mutually exclusive range of values, called a **class interval**. Each value can be assigned to only one class, and every value must be contained in one of the class intervals.

To create a useful frequency distribution, you must consider how many classes would be appropriate for your data as well as determine a suitable *width* for each class interval. In general, a frequency distribution should have at least 5 and no more than 15 classes because having too few or too many classes provides little new information. To determine the **class interval width** (see Equation[2.1]), you subtract the lowest value from the highest value and divide that result by the number of classes you want the frequency distribution to have.

DETERMINING THE CLASS INTERVAL WIDTH

$$\text{Interval width} = \frac{\text{highest value} - \text{lowest value}}{\text{number of classes}} \tag{2.1}$$

For the city restaurant meal cost data shown in Tables 2.8A and 2.8B, between 5 and 10 classes are acceptable, given the size (50) of that sample. From the city restaurant meal costs ordered array in Table 2.8B, the difference between the highest value of $80 and the lowest value of $25 is $55. Using Equation (2.1), you approximate the class interval width as follows:

$$\frac{55}{10} = 5.5$$

This result suggests that you should choose an interval width of $5.50. However, your width should always be an amount that simplifies the reading and interpretation of the frequency distribution. In this example, such an amount would be either $5 or $10, and you should choose $10, which creates 7 classes, and not $5, which creates 13 classes, too many for the sample size of 50.

Because each value can appear in only one class, you must establish proper and clearly defined **class boundaries** for each class. For example, if you chose $10 as the class interval for the restaurant data, you would need to establish boundaries that would include all the values and simplify the reading and interpretation of the frequency distribution. Because the cost of a city restaurant meal varies from $25 to $80, establishing the first class interval as $20 to less than $30, the second as $30 to less than $40, and so on, until the last class interval is $80 to less than $90, would meet the requirements. Table 2.9 contains frequency distributions of the cost per meal for the 50 city restaurants and the 50 suburban restaurants using these class intervals.

TABLE 2.9

Frequency Distributions of the Meal Costs for 50 City Restaurants and 50 Suburban Restaurants

Meal Cost ($)	City Frequency	Suburban Frequency
20 but less than 30	4	4
30 but less than 40	10	17
40 but less than 50	12	13
50 but less than 60	11	10
60 but less than 70	7	4
70 but less than 80	5	2
80 but less than 90	1	0
Total	50	50

The frequency distribution allows you to reach some preliminary conclusions about the data. For example, Table 2.9 shows that the cost of city restaurant meals is concentrated between $30 and $60, as is the cost of suburban restaurant meals. However, many more meals at suburban restaurants cost between $30 and $40 than at city restaurants.

For some charts discussed later in this chapter, class intervals are identified by their **class midpoints**, the values that are halfway between the lower and upper boundaries of each class. For the frequency distributions shown in Table 2.9, the class midpoints are $25, $35, $45, $55, $65, $75, and $85. Note that well-chosen class intervals lead to class midpoints that are simple to read and interpret, as in this example.

If the data you have collected do not contain a large number of values, different sets of class intervals can create different impressions of the data. Such perceived changes will diminish as you collect more data. Likewise, choosing different lower and upper class boundaries can also affect impressions.

> **Student Tip**
> The total of the frequency column must always equal the number of values.

EXAMPLE 2.2

Frequency Distributions of the One-Year Return Percentages for Growth and Value Funds

As a member of the company task force in The Choice *Is* Yours scenario (see page 31), you are examining the sample of 316 retirement funds stored in `Retirement Funds`. You want to compare the numerical variable 1YrReturn%, the one-year percentage return of a fund, for the two subgroups that are defined by the categorical variable Type (Growth and Value). You construct separate frequency distributions for the growth funds and the value funds.

SOLUTION The one-year percentage returns for both the growth and value funds are concentrated between 10 and 20 (see Table 2.10).

TABLE 2.10

Frequency Distributions of the One-Year Return Percentage for Growth and Value Funds

One-Year Return Percentage	Growth Frequency	Value Frequency
−15 but less than −10	1	0
−10 but less than −5	0	0
−5 but less than 0	0	0
0 but less than 5	6	2
5 but less than 10	23	12
10 but less than 15	104	29
15 but less than 20	75	37
20 but less than 25	12	8
25 but less than 30	3	1
30 but less than 35	3	0
Total	227	89

In the solution for Example 2.2, the total frequency is different for each group (227 and 89). When such totals differ among the groups being compared, you cannot compare the distributions directly as was done in Table 2.9 because of the chance that the table will be misinterpreted. For example, the frequencies for the class interval "5 but less than 10" for growth and "10 but less than 15" for value look similar—23 and 29—but represent two very different parts of a whole: 23 out of 227 and 29 out of 89, or about 10% and 33%, respectively. When the total frequency differs among the groups being compared, you construct either a relative frequency distribution or a percentage distribution.

Classes and Excel Bins

Microsoft Excel requires that you implement your set of classes as a set of Excel **bins**. While bins and classes are both ranges of values, bins do not have explicitly stated intervals.

You establish bins by creating a column that contains a list of bin numbers arranged in ascending order. Each bin number explicitly states the upper boundary of its bin. Bins' lower boundaries are defined implicitly: A bin's lower boundary is the first value greater than the previous bin number. For the column of bin numbers 4.99, 9.99, and 14.99, the second bin has the explicit upper boundary of 9.99 and has the implicit lower boundary of "values greater than 4.99." Compare this to a class interval, which defines both the lower and upper boundaries of the class, such as in "*0* (lower) but *less than 5* (upper)."

Because the first bin number does not have a "previous" bin number, the first bin always has negative infinity as its lower boundary. A common workaround to this problem, used in the examples throughout this book (and in PHStat, too), is to define an extra bin, using a bin number that is slightly lower than the lower boundary value of the first class. This extra bin number, appearing first, will allow the now-second bin number to better approximate the first class, though at the cost of adding an unwanted bin to the results.

In this chapter, Tables 2.9 through 2.13 use class groupings in the form "*valueA* but less than *valueB*." You can translate class groupings in this form into nearly equivalent bins by creating a list of bin numbers that are slightly lower than each *valueB* that appears in the class groupings. For example, the Table 2.10 classes on page 39 could be translated into nearly equivalent bins by using this bin number list: −15.01 (the extra bin number is slightly lower than the first lower boundary value −15), −10.01 (slightly less than −10, −5.01, −0.01, 4.99, 9.99, 14.99, 19.99, 24.99, 29.99, and 34.99.

For class groupings in the form "all values from *valueA* to *valueB*," such as the set 0.0 through 4.9, 5.0 through 9.9, 10.0 through 14.9, and 15.0 through 19.9, you can approximate each class grouping by choosing a bin number slightly more than each *valueB*, as in this list of bin numbers: −0.01 (the extra bin number), 4.99 (slightly more than 4.9), 9.99, 14.99, and 19.99.

The Relative Frequency Distribution and the Percentage Distribution

Relative frequency and percentage distributions present tallies in ways other than as frequencies. A **relative frequency distribution** presents the relative frequency, or proportion, of the total for each group that each class represents. A **percentage distribution** presents the percentage of the total for each group that each class represents. When you compare two or more groups, knowing the proportion (or percentage) of the total for each group is more useful than knowing the frequency for each group, as Table 2.11 demonstrates. Compare this table to Table 2.9 on page 38, which displays frequencies. Table 2.11 organizes the meal cost data in a manner that facilitates comparisons.

TABLE 2.11

Relative Frequency Distributions and Percentage Distributions of the Meal Costs at City and Suburban Restaurants

| | CITY | | SUBURBAN | |
MEAL COST ($)	Relative Frequency	Percentage	Relative Frequency	Percentage
20 but less than 30	0.08	8.0%	0.08	8.0%
30 but less than 40	0.20	20.0%	0.34	34.0%
40 but less than 50	0.24	24.0%	0.26	26.0%
50 but less than 60	0.22	22.0%	0.20	20.0%
60 but less than 70	0.14	14.0%	0.08	8.0%
70 but less than 80	0.10	10.0%	0.04	4.0%
80 but less than 90	0.02	2.0%	0.00	0.0%
Total	1.00	100.0%	1.00	100.0%

The **proportion**, or **relative frequency**, in each group is equal to the number of *values* in each class divided by the total number of values. The percentage in each group is its proportion multiplied by 100%.

COMPUTING THE PROPORTION OR RELATIVE FREQUENCY

The proportion, or relative frequency, is the number of *values* in each class divided by the total number of values:

$$\text{Proportion} = \text{relative frequency} = \frac{\text{number of values in each class}}{\text{total number of values}} \qquad (2.2)$$

If there are 80 values and the frequency in a certain class is 20, the proportion of values in that class is

$$\frac{20}{80} = 0.25$$

and the percentage is

$$0.25 \times 100\% = 25\%$$

You construct a relative frequency distribution by first determining the relative frequency in each class. For example, in Table 2.9 on page 38, there are 50 city restaurants, and the cost per meal at 11 of these restaurants is between $50 and $60. Therefore, as shown in Table 2.11, the proportion (or relative frequency) of meals that cost between $50 and $60 at city restaurants is

$$\frac{11}{50} = 0.22$$

> **Student Tip**
> The total of the relative frequency column must always be 1.00. The total of the percentage column must always be 100.

You construct a percentage distribution by multiplying each proportion (or relative frequency) by 100%. Thus, the proportion of meals at city restaurants that cost between $50 and $60 is 11 divided by 50, or 0.22, and the percentage is 22%. Table 2.11 on page 40 presents the relative frequency distribution and percentage distribution of the cost of meals at city and suburban restaurants.

From Table 2.11, you conclude that meal cost is slightly more at city restaurants than at suburban restaurants. You note that 14% of the city restaurant meals cost between $60 and $70 as compared to 8% of the suburban restaurant meals and that 20% of the city restaurant meals cost between $30 and $40 as compared to 34% of the suburban restaurant meals.

EXAMPLE 2.3

Relative Frequency Distributions and Percentage Distributions of the One-Year Return Percentage for Growth and Value Funds

As a member of the company task force in The Choice *Is* Yours scenario (see page 31), you want to properly compare the one-year return percentages for the growth and value retirement funds. You construct relative frequency distributions and percentage distributions for these funds.

SOLUTION From Table 2.12, you conclude that the one-year return percentage for the growth funds is lower than the one-year return percentage for the value funds. For example, 45.81% of the growth funds have returns between 10 and 15, while 32.58% of the value funds have returns between 10 and 15. Of the growth funds, 33.04% have returns between 15 and 20 as compared to 41.57% of the value funds.

TABLE 2.12

Relative Frequency Distributions and Percentage Distributions of the One-Year Return Percentage for Growth and Value Funds

ONE-YEAR RETURN PERCENTAGE	GROWTH		VALUE	
	Relative Frequency	Percentage	Relative Frequency	Percentage
−15 but less than −10	0.0044	0.44	0.0000	0.00
−10 but less than −5	0.0000	0.00	0.0000	0.00
−5 but less than 0	0.0000	0.00	0.000	0.00
0 but less than 5	0.0264	2.64	0.0225	2.25
5 but less than 10	0.1013	10.13	0.1348	13.48
10 but less than 15	0.4581	45.81	0.3258	32.58
15 but less than 20	0.3304	33.04	0.4157	41.57
20 but less than 25	0.0529	5.29	0.0899	8.99
25 but less than 30	0.0132	1.32	0.0112	1.12
30 but less than 35	0.0132	1.32	0.0000	0.00
Total	1.0000	100.00	1.0000	100.00

The Cumulative Distribution

The **cumulative percentage distribution** provides a way of presenting information about the percentage of values that are less than a specific amount. You use a percentage distribution as the basis to construct a cumulative percentage distribution.

For example, you might want to know what percentage of the city restaurant meals cost less than $40 or what percentage cost less than $50. Starting with the Table 2.11 meal cost percentage distribution for city restaurants on page 40, you combine the percentages of individual class intervals to form the cumulative percentage distribution. Table 2.13 presents the necessary calculations. From this table, you see that none (0%) of the meals cost less than $20, 8% of meals cost less than $30, 28% of meals cost less than $40 (because 20% of the meals cost between $30 and $40), and so on, until all 100% of the meals cost less than $90.

TABLE 2.13

Developing the Cumulative Percentage Distribution for City Restaurant Meal Costs

From Table 2.11:		Percentage (%) of Meal Costs That Are Less Than the Class Interval Lower Boundary
Class Interval	Percentage (%)	
20 but less than 30	8	0 (there are no meals that cost less than 20)
30 but less than 40	20	8 = 0 + 8
40 but less than 50	24	28 = 8 + 20
50 but less than 60	22	52 = 8 + 20 + 24
60 but less than 70	14	74 = 8 + 20 + 24 + 22
70 but less than 80	10	88 = 8 + 20 + 24 + 22 + 14
80 but less than 90	2	98 = 8 + 20 + 24 + 22 + 14 + 10
90 but less than 100	0	100 = 8 + 20 + 24 + 22 + 14 + 10 + 2

Table 2.14 is the cumulative percentage distribution for meal costs that uses cumulative calculations for the city restaurants (shown in Table 2.13) as well as cumulative calculations for the suburban restaurants (which are not shown). The cumulative distribution shows that the cost of suburban restaurant meals is lower than the cost of meals in city restaurants. This distribution shows that 42% of the suburban restaurant meals cost less than $40 as compared to 28% of the meals at city restaurants; 68% of the suburban restaurant meals cost less than $50, but only 52% of the city restaurant meals do; and 88% of the suburban restaurant meals cost less than $60 as compared to 74% of such meals at the city restaurants.

TABLE 2.14

Cumulative
Percentage
Distributions of
the Meal Costs for
City and Suburban
Restaurants

Meal Cost ($)	Percentage of City Restaurants Meals That Cost Less Than Indicated Amount	Percentage of Suburban Restaurants Meals That Cost Less Than Indicated Amount
20	0	0
30	8	8
40	28	42
50	52	68
60	74	88
70	88	96
80	98	100
90	100	100
100	100	100

Unlike in other distributions, the rows of a cumulative distribution do not correspond to class intervals. (Recall that class intervals are mutually *exclusive*. The rows of cumulative distributions are not: the next row "down" *includes* all of the rows above it.) To identify a row, you use the lower class boundaries from the class intervals of the percentage distribution as is done in Table 2.14.

EXAMPLE 2.4

Cumulative Percentage Distributions of the One-Year Return Percentage for Growth and Value Funds

As a member of the company task force in The Choice *Is* Yours scenario (see page 31), you want to continue comparing the one-year return percentages for the growth and value retirement funds. You construct cumulative percentage distributions for the growth and value funds.

SOLUTION The cumulative distribution in Table 2.15 indicates that returns are lower for the growth funds than for the value funds. The table shows that 59.03% of the growth funds and 48.31% of the value funds have returns below 15%. The table also reveals that 92.07% of the growth funds have returns below 20 as compared to 89.89% of the value funds.

TABLE 2.15

Cumulative
Percentage
Distributions of the
One-Year Return
Percentages for
Growth and Value
Funds

One-Year Return Percentages	Growth Percentage Less Than Indicated Value	Value Percentage Less Than Indicated Value
−15	0.00	0.00
−10	0.44	0.00
−5	0.44	0.00
0	0.44	0.00
5	3.08	2.25
10	13.22	15.73
15	59.03	48.31
20	92.07	89.89
25	97.36	98.88
30	98.68	100.00
35	100.00	100.00

Stacked and Unstacked Data

When data for a numerical variable have been collected for more than one group, you can enter those data in a worksheet as either *unstacked* or *stacked* data.

In an **unstacked** format, you create separate numerical variables for each group. For example, if you entered the meal cost data used in the examples in this section in unstacked format, you would create two numerical variables—city meal cost and suburban meal cost—enter the top data in Table 2.8A on page 37 as the city meal cost data, and enter the bottom data in Table 2.8A as the suburban meal cost data.

In a **stacked** format, you pair a numerical variable that contains all of the values with a second, separate categorical variable that contains values that identify to which group each numerical value belongs. For example, if you entered the meal cost data used in the examples in this section in stacked format, you would create a meal cost numerical variable to hold the 100 meal cost values shown in Table 2.8A and create a second location (categorical) variable that would take the value "City" or "Suburban," depending upon whether a particular value came from a city or suburban restaurant (the top half or bottom half of Table 2.8A).

Sometimes a particular procedure in a data analysis program will require data to be either stacked (or unstacked), and instructions in the Excel and Minitab Guides note such requirements when they arise. (Both PHStat and Minitab have commands that allow you to automate the stacking or unstacking of data as discussed in the Excel and Minitab Guides for this chapter.) Otherwise, it makes little difference whether your data are stacked or unstacked. However, if you have multiple numerical variables that represent data from the same set of groups, stacking your data will be the more efficient choice. For this reason, the DATA worksheet in **Restaurants** contains the numerical variable Cost and the categorical variable Location to store the meal cost data for the sample of 100 restaurants as stacked data.

Problems for Section 2.2

LEARNING THE BASICS

2.11 Construct an ordered array, given the following data from a sample of $n = 7$ midterm exam scores in accounting:

$$68 \quad 94 \quad 63 \quad 75 \quad 71 \quad 88 \quad 64$$

2.12 Construct an ordered array, given the following data from a sample of midterm exam scores in marketing:

$$88 \quad 78 \quad 78 \quad 73 \quad 91 \quad 78 \quad 85$$

2.13 In November 2013, the National Small Business Association (NSBA) surveyed small business owners with fewer than 500 employees. The purpose of the study was to gain insight into how America's small businesses are dealing with rising health care costs, what kind of benefits they offer, and how the Affordable Care Act (ACA) is impacting their business. Small business owners were asked if they offered a health benefits plan to their employees that included fitness programs and/or gym memberships, and if so, what portion (%) of the employee's cost for the plan the business paid. The following frequency distribution was formed to summarize the *portion of plan cost paid* for 70 small businesses who offer this health-related benefit to employees:

Portion of Plan Cost Paid (%)	Frequency
less than 1%	17
1% to 20%	7
21% to 50%	7
51% to 75%	4
76% to 100%	35

Source: Data extracted from "NSBA 2014 Small Business Health Care Survey," **bit.ly/NaQwzb**.

a. What percentage of small businesses pays less than 21% of the employee monthly health-care premium?
b. What percentage of small businesses pays between 21% and 75% of the employee monthly health-care premium?
c. What percentage of small businesses pays more than 75% of the employee monthly health-care premium?

2.14 Data were collected on the Facebook website about the most "liked" fast food brands. The data values (the number of "likes" for each fast food brand) for the brands named ranged from 1.0 million to 29.2 million.
a. If these values are grouped into six class intervals, indicate the class boundaries.
b. What class interval width did you choose?
c. What are the six class midpoints?

APPLYING THE CONCEPTS

2.15 The file **NBACost2013** contains the total cost ($) for four average-priced tickets, two beers, four soft drinks, four hot dogs, two game programs, two adult-sized caps, and one parking space at each of the 30 National Basketball Association arenas during the 2013–2014 season. These costs were:

240.04 434.96 382.00 203.06 456.60 271.74 321.18 319.10
262.40 324.08 336.05 227.36 395.20 542.00 212.16 472.20
309.30 273.98 208.48 659.92 295.40 263.10 266.40 344.92
308.18 268.28 338.00 321.63 280.98 249.22

Source: Data extracted "NBA FCI 13-14 Fan Cost Experience," **bit.ly/1nnu9rf**.

a. Organize these costs as an ordered array.
b. Construct a frequency distribution and a percentage distribution for these costs.
c. Around which class grouping, if any, are the costs of attending a basketball game concentrated? Explain.

✓ **SELF** **2.16** The file Utility contains the following data about
Test the cost of electricity (in $) during July 2014 for a random
sample of 50 one-bedroom apartments in a large city.

```
 96  171  202  178  147  102  153  197  127   82
157  185   90  116  172  111  148  213  130  165
141  149  206  175  123  128  144  168  109  167
 95  163  150  154  130  143  187  166  139  149
108  119  183  151  114  135  191  137  129  158
```

a. Construct a frequency distribution and a percentage distribution that have class intervals with the upper class boundaries $99, $119, and so on.
b. Construct a cumulative percentage distribution.
c. Around what amount does the monthly electricity cost seem to be concentrated?

2.17 How much time do commuters living in or near cities spend waiting in traffic, and how much does this waiting cost them per year? The file Congestion contains the time spent waiting in traffic and the yearly cost associated with that waiting for commuters in 31 U.S. cities. (Source: Data extracted from "The High Cost of Congestion," *Time*, October 17, 2011, p. 18.) For both the time spent waiting in traffic and the yearly cost associated with that waiting data,
a. Construct a frequency distribution and a percentage distribution.
b. Construct a cumulative percentage distribution.
c. What conclusions can you reach concerning the time Americans living in or near cities spend sitting in traffic?
d. What conclusions can you reach concerning the time and cost of waiting in traffic per year?

2.18 How do the average credit scores of people living in different American cities differ? The data in Credit Scores is an ordered array of the average credit scores of 143 American cities. (Data extracted from **usat.ly/109hZAR**.)
a. Construct a frequency distribution and a percentage distribution.
b. Construct a cumulative percentage distribution.
c. What conclusions can you reach concerning the average credit scores of people living in different American cities?

2.19 One operation of a mill is to cut pieces of steel into parts that will later be used as the frame for front seats in an automobile. The steel is cut with a diamond saw and requires the resulting parts to be within ±0.005 inch of the length specified by the automobile company. Data are collected from a sample of 100 steel parts and stored in Steel. The measurement reported is the difference in inches between the actual length of the steel part, as measured by a laser measurement device, and the specified length of the steel part. For example, the first value, −0.002, represents a steel part that is 0.002 inch shorter than the specified length.
a. Construct a frequency distribution and a percentage distribution.
b. Construct a cumulative percentage distribution.
c. Is the steel mill doing a good job meeting the requirements set by the automobile company? Explain.

2.20 A manufacturing company produces steel housings for electrical equipment. The main component part of the housing is a steel trough that is made out of a 14-gauge steel coil. It is produced using a 250-ton progressive punch press with a wipe-down operation that puts two 90-degree forms in the flat steel to make the trough. The distance from one side of the form to the other is critical because of weatherproofing in outdoor applications. The company requires that the width of the trough be between 8.31 inches and 8.61 inches. The widths of the troughs, in inches, collected from a sample of 49 troughs and stored in Trough, are:

```
8.312  8.343  8.317  8.383  8.348  8.410  8.351  8.373
8.481  8.422  8.476  8.382  8.484  8.403  8.414  8.419
8.385  8.465  8.498  8.447  8.436  8.413  8.489  8.414
8.481  8.415  8.479  8.429  8.458  8.462  8.460  8.444
8.429  8.460  8.412  8.420  8.410  8.405  8.323  8.420
8.396  8.447  8.405  8.439  8.411  8.427  8.420  8.498
8.409
```

a. Construct a frequency distribution and a percentage distribution.
b. Construct a cumulative percentage distribution.
c. What can you conclude about the number of troughs that will meet the company's requirements of troughs being between 8.31 and 8.61 inches wide?

2.21 The manufacturing company in Problem 2.20 also produces electric insulators. If the insulators break when in use, a short circuit is likely to occur. To test the strength of the insulators, destructive testing in high-powered labs is carried out to determine how much *force* is required to break the insulators. Force is measured by observing how many pounds must be applied to the insulator before it breaks. The force measurements, collected from a sample of 30 insulators and stored in Force, are:

```
1,870  1,728  1,656  1,610  1,634  1,784  1,522  1,696
1,592  1,662  1,866  1,764  1,734  1,662  1,734  1,774
1,550  1,756  1,762  1,866  1,820  1,744  1,788  1,688
1,810  1,752  1,680  1,810  1,652  1,736
```

a. Construct a frequency distribution and a percentage distribution.
b. Construct a cumulative percentage distribution.
c. What can you conclude about the strength of the insulators if the company requires a force measurement of at least 1,500 pounds before the insulator breaks?

2.22 The file Bulbs contains the life (in hours) of a sample of forty 20-watt compact fluorescent light bulbs produced by Manufacturer A and a sample of forty 20-watt compact fluorescent light bulbs produced by Manufacturer B.
a. Construct a frequency distribution and a percentage distribution for each manufacturer, using the following class interval widths for each distribution:

Manufacturer A: 6,500 but less than 7,500, 7,500 but less than 8,500, and so on.
Manufacturer B: 7,500 but less than 8,500, 8,500 but less than 9,500, and so on.

b. Construct cumulative percentage distributions.
c. Which bulbs have a longer life—those from Manufacturer A or Manufacturer B? Explain.

2.23 The file Drink contains the following data for the amount of soft drink (in liters) in a sample of fifty 2-liter bottles:

2.109 2.086 2.066 2.075 2.065 2.057 2.052 2.044 2.036 2.038
2.031 2.029 2.025 2.029 2.023 2.020 2.015 2.014 2.013 2.014
2.012 2.012 2.012 2.010 2.005 2.003 1.999 1.996 1.997 1.992
1.994 1.986 1.984 1.981 1.973 1.975 1.971 1.969 1.966 1.967
1.963 1.957 1.951 1.951 1.947 1.941 1.941 1.938 1.908 1.894

a. Construct a cumulative percentage distribution.
b. On the basis of the results of (a), does the amount of soft drink filled in the bottles concentrate around specific values?

2.3 Visualizing Categorical Variables

The chart you use to visualize the data for a single categorical variable depends on whether you seek to emphasize how categories directly compare to each other (bar chart) or how categories form parts of a whole (pie chart), or whether you have data that are concentrated in only a few of your categories (Pareto chart). To visualize the data for two categorical variables, you use a side-by-side bar chart.

The Bar Chart

A **bar chart** visualizes a categorical variable as a series of bars, with each bar representing the tallies for a single category. In a bar chart, the length of each bar represents either the frequency or percentage of values for a category and each bar is separated by space, called a gap.

The left illustration in Figure 2.1 displays the bar chart for the Table 2.2 summary table on page 33 that tallies responses to a recent survey that asked young adults the main reason they shop online. Reviewing Figure 2.1, you see that respondents are most likely to say because of better prices, followed by avoiding holiday crowds or hassles. Very few respondents mentioned ships directly.

FIGURE 2.1

Excel bar chart (left) and pie chart (right) for reasons for shopping online

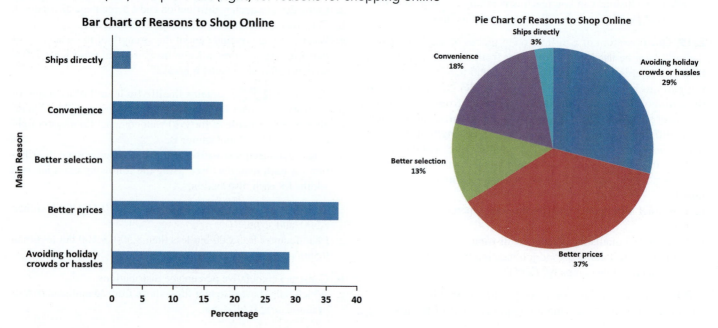

EXAMPLE 2.5

Bar Chart of Levels of Risk of Retirement Funds

As a member of the company task force in The Choice *Is* Yours scenario (see page 31), you want to first construct a bar chart of the risk of the funds that is based on Table 2.3 on page 33 and then interpret the results.

SOLUTION Reviewing Figure 2.2, you see that low risk is the largest category, followed by average risk. Very few of the funds have high risk.

FIGURE 2.2

Excel bar chart of the levels of risk of retirement funds

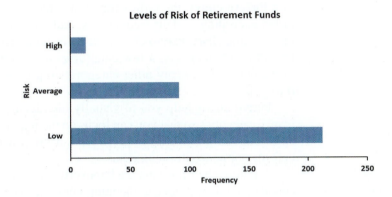

The Pie Chart

A **pie chart** uses parts of a circle to represent the tallies of each category. The size of each part, or pie slice, varies according to the percentage in each category. For example, in Table 2.2 on page 33, 37% of the respondents stated that they shop online mainly because of better prices. To represent this category as a pie slice, you multiply 37% by the 360 degrees that makes up a circle to get a pie slice that takes up 133.2 degrees of the 360 degrees of the circle, as shown in Figure 2.1 on page 46. From the Figure 2.1 pie chart, you can see that the second largest slice is avoiding holiday crowd and hassles, which contains 29% of the pie.

EXAMPLE 2.6

Pie Chart of Levels of Risk of Retirement Funds

As a member of the company task force in The Choice *Is* Yours scenario (see page 31), you want to visualize the risk level of the funds by constructing a pie chart based on Table 2.3 (see page 33) for the risk variable and then interpret the results.

SOLUTION Reviewing Figure 2.3, you see that more than two-thirds of the funds are low risk, about 30% are average risk, and only about 4% are high risk.

FIGURE 2.3

Excel pie chart of the risk of retirement funds

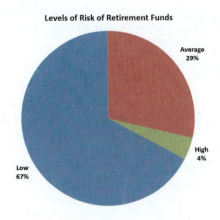

Today, some assert that pie charts should never be used. Others argue that they offer an easily comprehended way to visualize parts of a whole. All commentators agree that variations such as 3D perspective pies and "exploded" pie charts, in which one or more slices are pulled away from the center of a pie, should not be used because of the visual distortions they introduce.

The Pareto Chart

In a **Pareto chart**, the tallies for each category are plotted as vertical bars in descending order, according to their frequencies, and are combined with a cumulative percentage line on the same chart. Pareto charts get their name from the **Pareto principle**, the observation that in many data sets, a few categories of a categorical variable represent the majority of the data, while many other categories represent a relatively small, or trivial, amount of the data.

Pareto charts help you to visually identify the "vital few" categories from the "trivial many" categories so that you can focus on the important categories. Pareto charts are also powerful tools for prioritizing improvement efforts, such as when data are collected that identify defective or nonconforming items.

The informal "80/20" rule, which states that often 80% of results are from 20% of some thing, such as "80% of the work is done by 20% of the employees," derives from the Pareto principle.

A Pareto chart presents the bars vertically, along with a cumulative percentage line. The cumulative line is plotted at the midpoint of each category, at a height equal to the cumulative percentage. In order for a Pareto chart to include all categories, even those with few defects, in some situations, you need to include a category labeled Other or Miscellaneous. If you include such a category, you place the bar that represents that category at the far end (to the right) of the X axis.

Using Pareto charts can be an effective way to visualize data for many studies that seek causes for an observed phenomenon. For example, consider a bank study team that wants to enhance the user experience of automated teller machines (ATMs). During this study, the team identifies incomplete ATM transactions as a significant issue and decides to collect data about the causes of such transactions. Using the bank's own processing systems as a primary data source, causes of incomplete transactions are collected, stored in ATM Transactions, and then organized in the Table 2.16 summary table.

TABLE 2.16

Summary Table of Causes of Incomplete ATM Transactions

Cause	Frequency	Percentage
ATM malfunctions	32	4.42%
ATM out of cash	28	3.87%
Invalid amount requested	23	3.18%
Lack of funds in account	19	2.62%
Card unreadable	234	32.32%
Warped card jammed	365	50.41%
Wrong keystroke	23	3.18%
Total	724	100.00%

Source: Data extracted from A. Bhalla, "Don't Misuse the Pareto Principle," *Six Sigma Forum Magazine*, May 2009, pp. 15–18.

To separate out the "vital few" causes from the "trivial many" causes, the bank study team creates the Table 2.17 summary table, in which the causes of incomplete transactions appear in descending order by frequency, as required for constructing a Pareto chart. The table includes the percentages and cumulative percentages for the reordered causes, which the team then uses to construct the Pareto chart shown in Figure 2.4. In Figure 2.4, the vertical axis on the left represents the percentage due to each cause and the vertical axis on the right represents the cumulative percentage.

TABLE 2.17

Ordered Summary Table of Causes of Incomplete ATM Transactions

Cause	Frequency	Percentage	Cumulative Percentage
Warped card jammed	365	50.41%	50.41%
Card unreadable	234	32.32%	82.73%
ATM malfunctions	32	4.42%	87.15%
ATM out of cash	28	3.87%	91.02%
Invalid amount requested	23	3.18%	94.20%
Wrong keystroke	23	3.18%	97.38%
Lack of funds in account	19	2.62%	100.00%
Total	724	100.00%	

FIGURE 2.4

Minitab Pareto chart of incomplete ATM transactions

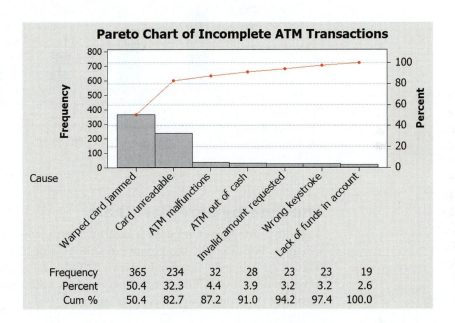

Pareto Chart of Incomplete ATM Transactions

	Warped card jammed	Card unreadable	ATM malfunctions	ATM out of cash	Invalid amount requested	Wrong keystroke	Lack of funds in account
Frequency	365	234	32	28	23	23	19
Percent	50.4	32.3	4.4	3.9	3.2	3.2	2.6
Cum %	50.4	82.7	87.2	91.0	94.2	97.4	100.0

Because the categories in a Pareto chart are ordered by decreasing frequency of occurrence, the team can quickly see which causes contribute the most to the problem of incomplete transactions. (Those causes would be the "vital few," and figuring out ways to avoid such causes would be, presumably, a starting point for improving the user experience of ATMs.) By following the cumulative percentage line in Figure 2.4, you see that the first two causes, warped card jammed (50.44%) and card unreadable (32.3%), account for 82.7% of the incomplete transactions. Attempts to reduce incomplete ATM transactions due to warped or unreadable cards should produce the greatest payoff.

EXAMPLE 2.7

Pareto Chart of the Main Reason for Shopping Online

Construct a Pareto chart from Table 2.2 (see page 33), which summarizes the main reason young adults shop online.

SOLUTION First, create a new table from Table 2.2 in which the categories are ordered by descending frequency and columns for percentages and cumulative percentages for the ordered categories are included (not shown). From that table, create the Pareto chart in Figure 2.5.

From Figure 2.5, you see that better prices and avoiding holiday crowds and hassles accounted for 66% of the responses and better prices, avoiding holiday crowds and hassles, convenience, and better selection accounted for 97% of the responses.

FIGURE 2.5

Excel Pareto chart of the main reason for shopping online

The Side-by-Side Bar Chart

A **side-by-side bar chart** uses sets of bars to show the joint responses from two categorical variables. For example, the Figure 2.6 side-by-side chart visualizes the data for the levels of risk for growth and value funds shown in Table 2.4 on page 34. In Figure 2.6, you see that a substantial portion of the growth funds and the value funds have low risk. However, a larger portion of the growth funds have average risk.

FIGURE 2.6

Side-by-side bar chart of fund type and risk level

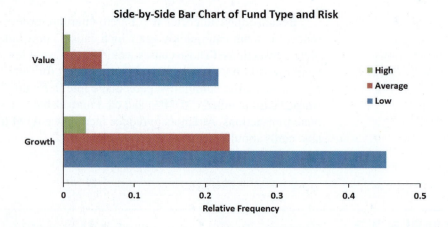

Problems for Section 2.3

APPLYING THE CONCEPTS

2.24 An online survey of CFA Institute members was conducted to gather feedback on market sentiment, performance, and market integrity issues in October 2013. Members were asked to indicate the most needed action to improve investor trust and market integrity. The survey results were as follows:

Most Needed Action	Percentage (%)
Improved regulation and oversight of global systemic risk	29%
Improved transparency of financial reporting and other corporate disclosures	21%
Improved corporate governance practices	17%
Improved enforcement of existing laws and regulations	16%
Improved market trading rules on transparency and frequency of trades	11%
Improved auditing practices and standards	6%

Source: Data extracted from **cfa.is/PxR8Bh.html**.

a. Construct a bar chart, a pie chart, and a Pareto chart.
b. Which graphical method do you think is best for portraying these data?
c. What conclusions can you reach concerning the most needed action to improve investor trust and market integrity?

2.25 What do college students do with their time? A survey of 3,000 traditional-age students was taken, with the results as follows:

Activity	Percentage
Attending class/lab	9%
Sleeping	24%
Socializing, recreation, other	51%
Studying	7%
Working, volunteering, student clubs	9%

Source: Data extracted from M. Marklein, "First Two Years of College Wasted?" *USA Today*, January 18, 2011, p. 3A.

a. Construct a bar chart, a pie chart, and a Pareto chart.
b. Which graphical method do you think is best for portraying these data?
c. What conclusions can you reach concerning what college students do with their time?

2.26 The Energy Information Administration reported the following sources of electricity in the United States in 2013:

Source of Electricity	Percentage
Coal	39%
Hydro and renewables	13%
Natural gas	27%
Nuclear power	19%
Other	2%

Source: Energy Information Administration, 2014.

a. Construct a Pareto chart.
b. What percentage of power is derived from coal, nuclear power, or natural gas?

c. Construct a pie chart.
d. For these data, do you prefer using a Pareto chart or a pie chart? Why?

2.27 The **Edmunds.com** NHTSA Complaints Activity Report contains consumer vehicle complaint submissions by automaker, brand, and category (data extracted from **edmu.in/Ybmpuz**.) The following tables, stored in `Automaker1` and `Automaker2`, represent complaints received by automaker and complaints received by category for January 2013.

Automaker	Number
American Honda	169
Chrysler LLC	439
Ford Motor Company	440
General Motors	551
Nissan Motors Corporation	467
Toyota Motor Sales	332
Other	516

a. Construct a bar chart and a pie chart for the complaints received by automaker.
b. Which graphical method do you think is best for portraying these data?

Category	Number
Airbags and seatbelts	201
Body and glass	182
Brakes	63
Fuel/emission/exhaust system	240
Interior electronics/hardware	279
Powertrain	1,148
Steering	397
Tires and wheels	71

c. Construct a Pareto chart for the categories of complaints.
d. Discuss the "vital few" and "trivial many" reasons for the categories of complaints.

2.28 The following table indicates the percentage of residential electricity consumption in the United States, in a recent year organized by type of use.

Type of Use	Percentage %
Cooking	2%
Cooling	15%
Electronics	9%
Heating	15%
Lighting	13%
Refrigeration	10%
Water heating	10%
Wet cleaning	3%
Other	23%

Source: Department of Energy

a. Construct a bar chart, a pie chart, and a Pareto chart.

b. Which graphical method do you think is best for portraying these data?

c. What conclusions can you reach concerning residential electricity consumption in the United States?

2.29 Visier's Survey of Employers explores how North American organizations are solving the challenges of delivering workforce analytics. Employers were asked what would help them be successful with human resources metrics and reports. The responses were as follows (stored in Needs):

Needs	Frequency
Easier-to-use analytic tools	127
Faster access to data	41
Improved ability to present and interpret data	123
Improved ability to plan actions	33
Improved ability to predict impacts of my actions	49
Improved relationships to the business line organizations	37

Source: Data extracted from **bit.ly/1fmPZrQ**.

a. Construct a bar chart and a pie chart.

b. What conclusions can you reach concerning needs for employer success with human resource metrics and reports?

2.30 A survey of 1,085 adults asked "Do you enjoy shopping for clothing for yourself?" The results indicated that 51% of the females enjoyed shopping for clothing for themselves as compared to 44% of the males. (Data extracted from "Split Decision on Clothes Shopping," *USA Today*, January 28, 2011, p. 1B.) The sample sizes of males and females were not provided. Suppose that the results were as shown in the following table:

ENJOY SHOPPING FOR CLOTHING	GENDER		
	Male	Female	Total
Yes	238	276	514
No	304	267	571
Total	542	543	1,085

a. Construct a side-by-side bar chart of enjoying shopping and gender.

b. What conclusions can you reach from this chart?

2.31 A study of Kickstarter projects showed that 54.2% were successful, that is, achieved its goal and raised at least the targeted goal amount. In an effort to identify network dynamics that influences success, projects were subdivided into projects of owners who had backed other projects before, during or after creating their project (owners with backing history), and projects of owners without backing history. The results are as follows:

PROJECT OUTCOME	PROJECT OWNER'S BACKING HISTORY		
	Backing History	No Backing History	Total
Successful	17,667	19,202	36,869
Not successful	10,921	20,267	31,188
Total	28,588	39,469	68,057

Source: Data extracted from Zvilichovsky et al., "Playing Both Sides of the Market: Success and Reciprocity on Crowdfunding Platforms," **bit.ly/OoyhqZ**.

a. Construct a side-by-side bar chart of project outcome and project owner's backing history.

b. What conclusions concerning the pattern of successful Kickstarter projects can you reach?

2.32 Do social recommendations increase ad effectiveness? A study of online video viewers compared viewers who arrived at an advertising video for a particular brand by following a social media recommendation link to viewers who arrived at the same video by web browsing. Data were collected on whether the viewer could correctly recall the brand being advertised after seeing the video. The results were as follows:

ARRIVAL METHOD	CORRECTLY RECALLED THE BRAND	
	Yes	No
Recommendation	407	150
Browsing	193	91

Source: Data extracted from "Social Ad Effectiveness: An Unruly White Paper," **www.unrulymedia.com**, January 2012, p. 3.

a. Construct a side-by-side bar chart of the arrival method and whether the brand was promptly recalled.

b. What do these results tell you about the arrival method and brand recall?

2.4 Visualizing Numerical Variables

You visualize the data for a numerical variable through a variety of techniques that show the distribution of values. These techniques include the stem-and-leaf display, the histogram, the percentage polygon, and the cumulative percentage polygon (ogive), all discussed in this section, as well as the boxplot, which requires descriptive summary measures, as explained in Section 3.3.

The Stem-and-Leaf Display

A **stem-and-leaf display** visualizes data by presenting the data as one or more row-wise *stems* that represent a range of values. In turn, each stem has one or more *leaves* that branch out to the right of their stem and represent the values found in that stem. For stems with more than one leaf, the leaves are arranged in ascending order.

Stem-and-leaf displays allow you to see how the data are distributed and where concentrations of data exist. Leaves typically present the last significant digit of each value, but sometimes you round values. For example, suppose you collect the following meal costs (in $) for 15 classmates who had lunch at a fast-food restaurant (stored in FastFood):

7.42 6.29 5.83 6.50 8.34 9.51 7.10 6.80 5.90 4.89 6.50 5.52 7.90 8.30 9.60

To construct the stem-and-leaf display, you use whole dollar amounts as the stems and round the cents to one decimal place to use as the leaves. For the first value, 7.42, the stem would be 7 and its leaf would be 4. For the second value, 6.29, the stem would be 6 and its leaf 3. The completed stem-and-leaf display for these data is

4	9
5	589
6	3558
7	149
8	33
9	56

> **Student Tip**
> If you turn a stem-and-leaf display sideways, the display looks like a histogram.

EXAMPLE 2.8

Stem-and-Leaf Display of the One-Year Return Percentage for the Value Funds

As a member of the company task force in The Choice *Is* Yours scenario (see page 31), you want to study the past performance of the value funds. One measure of past performance is the numerical variable 1YrReturn%, the one-year return percentage. Using the data from the 89 value funds, you want to visualize this variable as a stem-and-leaf display.

SOLUTION Figure 2.7 illustrates the stem-and-leaf display of the one-year return percentage for value funds.

FIGURE 2.7

Minitab stem-and-leaf display of the one-year return percentage for value funds

Using Excel with PHStat will create an equivalent display that contains a different set of stems.

```
Stem-and-Leaf Display: 1YrReturn%_Value

Stem-and-leaf of 1YrReturn%_Value   N  = 89
Leaf Unit = 1.0

   1     0   1
   1     0
   3     0   45
   7     0   6667
  14     0   8899999
  22     1   00001111
  36     1   22233333333333
 (19)    1   4444444555555555555
  34     1   66666666667777
  20     1   88889999999
   9     2   00001
   4     2   222
   1     2
   1     2
   1     2   8
```

Figure 2.7 allows you to conclude:

- The lowest one-year return was approximately 1.
- The highest one-year return was 28.
- The one-year returns were concentrated between 12 and 19.
- Very few of the one-year returns were above 21.
- The distribution of the one-year return appears to be bell-shaped.

The Histogram

A **histogram** visualizes data as a vertical bar chart in which each bar represents a class interval from a frequency or percentage distribution. In a histogram, you display the numerical variable along the horizontal (*X*) axis and use the vertical (*Y*) axis to represent either the frequency or the percentage of values per class interval. There are never any gaps between adjacent bars in a histogram.

Figure 2.8 visualizes the data of Table 2.9 on page 38, meal costs at city and suburban restaurants, as a pair of frequency histograms. The histogram for city restaurants shows that the cost of meals is concentrated between approximately $30 and $60. Only one meal at city restaurants cost more than $80. The histogram for suburban restaurants shows that the cost of meals is also concentrated between $30 and $60. However, many more meals at suburban restaurants cost between $30 and $40 than at city restaurants. Very few meals at suburban restaurants cost more than $70.

FIGURE 2.8

Minitab frequency histograms for meal costs at city and suburban restaurants

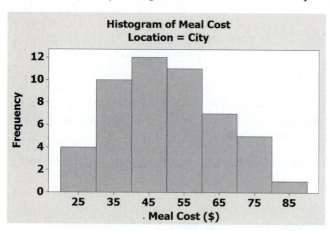
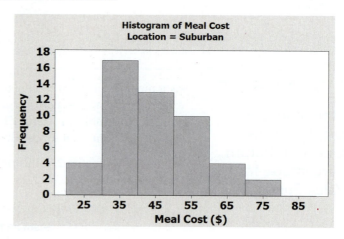

EXAMPLE 2.9

Histograms of the One-Year Return Percentages for the Growth and Value Funds

As a member of the company task force in The Choice *Is* Yours scenario (see page 31), you seek to compare the past performance of the growth funds and the value funds, using the one-year return percentage variable. Using the data from the sample of 316 funds, you construct histograms for the growth and the value funds to create a visual comparison.

SOLUTION Figure 2.9 displays frequency histograms for the one-year return percentages for the growth and value funds.

Reviewing the histograms in Figure 2.9 leads you to conclude that the returns were lower for the growth funds than for value funds. The return for both the growth funds and the value funds is concentrated between 10 and 20, but the return for the value funds is more concentrated between 15 and 20 while the return for the growth funds is more concentrated between 10 and 15.

(continued)

FIGURE 2.9

Excel frequency histograms for the one-year return percentages for the growth and value funds

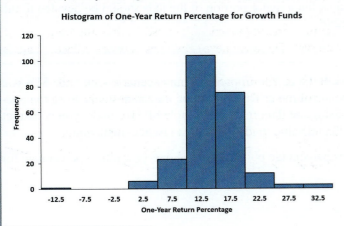

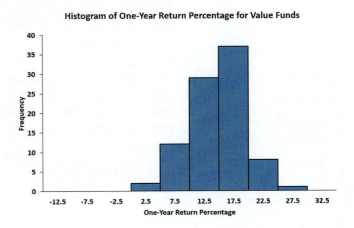

The Percentage Polygon

When using a categorical variable to divide the data of a numerical variable into two or more groups, you visualize data by constructing a **percentage polygon**. This chart uses the midpoints of each class interval to represent the data of each class and then plots the midpoints, at their respective class percentages, as points on a line along the *X* axis. While you can construct two or more histograms, as was done in Figures 2.8 and 2.9, a percentage polygon allows you to make a direct comparison that is easier to interpret. (You cannot, of course, combine two histograms into one chart as bars from the two groups would overlap and obscure data.)

Figure 2.10 displays percentage polygons for the cost of meals at city and suburban restaurants. Compare this figure to the pair of histograms in Figure 2.8 on page 54. Reviewing the polygons in Figure 2.10 allows you to make the same observations as were made when examining Figure 2.8, including the fact that while city restaurant meal costs are both concentrated between $30 and $60, suburban restaurants have a much higher concentration between $30 and $40. However, unlike the pair of histograms, the polygons allow you to more easily identify which class intervals have similar percentages for the two groups and which do not.

The polygons in Figure 2.10 have points whose values on the *X* axis represent the midpoint of the class interval. For example, look at the points plotted at *X* = 35 ($35). The point for meal costs at city restaurants (the lower one) show that 20% of the meals cost between $30 and $40, while the point for the meal costs at suburban restaurants (the higher one) shows that 34% of meals at these restaurants cost between $30 and $40.

FIGURE 2.10

Minitab percentage polygons of meal costs for city and suburban restaurants

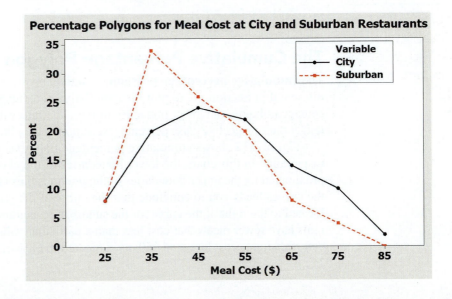

When you construct polygons or histograms, the vertical (Y) axis should include zero to avoid distorting the character of the data. The horizontal (X) axis does not need to show the zero point for the numerical variable, but a major portion of the axis should be devoted to the entire range of values for the variable.

EXAMPLE 2.10

Percentage Polygons of the One-Year Return Percentage for the Growth and Value Funds

FIGURE 2.11

Excel percentage polygons of the one-year return percentages for the growth and value funds

As a member of the company task force in The Choice *Is* Yours scenario (see page 31), you seek to compare the past performance of the growth funds and the value funds using the one-year return percentage variable. Using the data from the sample of 316 funds, you construct percentage polygons for the growth and value funds to create a visual comparison.

SOLUTION Figure 2.11 displays percentage polygons of the one-year return percentage for the growth and value funds.

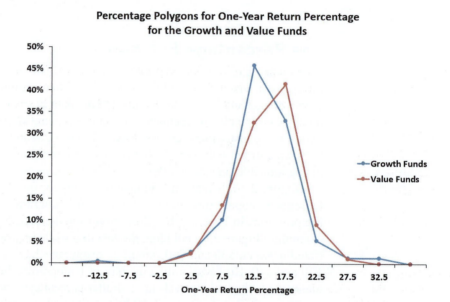

Figure 2.11 shows that the value funds polygon is to the right of the growth funds polygon. This allows you to conclude that the one-year return percentage is higher for value funds than for growth funds. The polygons also show that the return for value funds is concentrated between 15 and 20, and the return for the growth funds is concentrated between 10 and 15.

The Cumulative Percentage Polygon (Ogive)

The **cumulative percentage polygon**, or **ogive**, uses the cumulative percentage distribution discussed in Section 2.2 to plot the cumulative percentages along the Y axis. Unlike the percentage polygon, the lower boundary of the class interval for the numerical variable are plotted, at their respective class percentages, as points on a line along the X axis.

Figure 2.12 shows cumulative percentage polygons of meal costs for city and suburban restaurants. In this chart, the lower boundaries of the class intervals (20, 30, 40, etc.) are approximated by the upper boundaries of the previous bins (19.99, 29.99, 39.99, etc.). Reviewing the curves leads you to conclude that the curve of the cost of meals at the city restaurants is located to the right of the curve for the suburban restaurants. This indicates that the city restaurants have fewer meals that cost less than a particular value. For example, 52% of the meals at city restaurants cost less than $50, as compared to 68% of the meals at suburban restaurants.

FIGURE 2.12

Minitab cumulative percentage polygons of meal costs for city and suburban restaurants

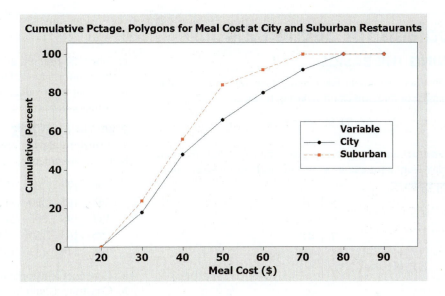

EXAMPLE 2.11

Cumulative Percentage Polygons of the One-Year Return Percentages for the Growth and Value Funds

As a member of the company task force in The Choice *Is* Yours scenario (see page 31), you seek to compare the past performance of the growth funds and the value funds using the one-year return percentage variable. Using the data from the sample of 316 funds, you construct cumulative percentage polygons for the growth and the value funds.

SOLUTION Figure 2.13 displays cumulative percentage polygons of the one-year return percentages for the growth and value funds.

FIGURE 2.13

Excel cumulative percentage polygons of the one-year return percentages for the growth and value funds

In Microsoft Excel, you approximate the lower boundary by using the upper boundary of the previous bin.

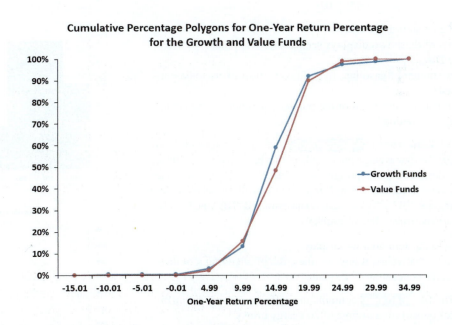

The cumulative percentage polygons in Figure 2.13 show that the curve for the one-year return percentage for the growth funds is located slightly to the left of the curve for the value funds. This allows you to conclude that the growth funds have fewer one-year return percentages that are higher than a particular value. For example, 59.03% of the growth funds had one-year return percentages below 15, as compared to 48.31% of the value funds. You can conclude that, in general, the value funds slightly outperformed the growth funds in their one-year returns.

Problems for Section 2.4

LEARNING THE BASICS

2.33 Construct a stem-and-leaf display, given the following data from a sample of midterm exam scores in finance:

54 69 98 93 53 74

2.34 Construct an ordered array, given the following stem-and-leaf display from a sample of $n = 7$ midterm exam scores in information systems:

5	0
6	
7	446
8	19
9	2

APPLYING THE CONCEPTS

2.35 The following is a stem-and-leaf display representing the amount of gasoline purchased, in gallons (with leaves in tenths of gallons), for a sample of 25 cars that use a particular service station on the New Jersey Turnpike:

9	147
10	02238
11	125566777
12	223489
13	02

a. Construct an ordered array.
b. Which of these two displays seems to provide more information? Discuss.
c. What amount of gasoline (in gallons) is most likely to be purchased?
d. Is there a concentration of the purchase amounts in the center of the distribution?

✓ SELF Test **2.36** The file **NBACost2013** contains the total cost (in $) for four average-priced tickets, two beers, four soft drinks, four hot dogs, two game programs, two adult-sized caps, and one parking space at each of the 30 National Basketball Association arenas during the 2013–2014 season. (Data extracted "NBA FCI 13-14 Fan Cost Experience," **bit.ly/1nnu9rf**.)

a. Construct a stem-and-leaf display.
b. Around what value, if any, are the costs of attending a basketball game concentrated? Explain.

2.37 The file **Caffeine** contains the caffeine content (in milligrams per ounce) for a sample of 26 energy drinks:

3.2	1.5	4.6	8.9	7.1	9.0	9.4	31.2	10.0	10.1
9.9	11.5	11.8	11.7	13.8	14.0	16.1	74.5	10.8	26.3
17.7	113.3	32.5	14.0	91.6	127.4				

Source: Data extracted from "The Buzz on Energy-Drink Caffeine," *Consumer Reports,* December 2012.

a. Construct an ordered array.
b. Construct a stem-and-leaf display.

c. Does the ordered array or the stem-and-leaf display provide more information? Discuss.
d. Around what value, if any, is the amount of caffeine in energy drinks concentrated? Explain.

2.38 The file **Utility** contains the following data about the cost of electricity during July 2014 for a random sample of 50 one-bedroom apartments in a large city:

96	171	202	178	147	102	153	197	127	82
157	185	90	116	172	111	148	213	130	165
141	149	206	175	123	128	144	168	109	167
95	163	150	154	130	143	187	166	139	149
108	119	183	151	114	135	191	137	129	158

a. Construct a histogram and a percentage polygon.
b. Construct a cumulative percentage polygon.
c. Around what amount does the monthly electricity cost seem to be concentrated?

2.39 As player salaries have increased, the cost of attending baseball games has increased dramatically. The following histogram and cumulative percentage polygon visualizes the total cost (in $) for four tickets, two beers, four soft drinks, four hot dogs, two game programs, two baseball caps, and parking for one vehicle at each of the 30 Major League Baseball parks during the 2012 season that is stored in **BBCost2012**.

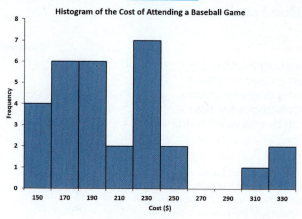

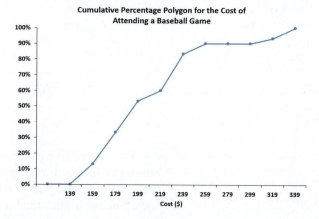

What conclusions can you reach concerning the cost of attending a baseball game at different ballparks?

2.40 The following histogram and cumulative percentage polygon visualize the data about the property taxes per capita($) for the 50 states and the District of Columbia, stored in **Property Taxes** .

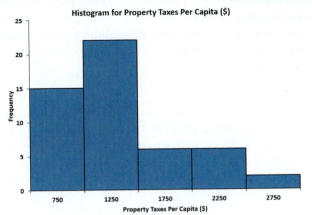

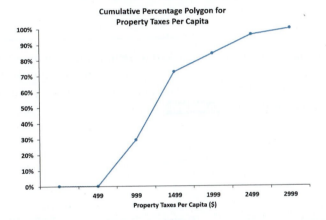

What conclusions can you reach concerning the property taxes per capita?

2.41 How much time do Americans living in or near cities spend waiting in traffic, and how much does waiting in traffic cost them per year? The data in the file **Congestion** include this cost for 31 cities. (Source: Data extracted from "The High Cost of Congestion," *Time*, October 17, 2011, p. 18.) For the time Americans living in or near cities spend waiting in traffic and the cost of waiting in traffic per year,
a. Construct a percentage histogram.
b. Construct a cumulative percentage polygon.
c. What conclusions can you reach concerning the time Americans living in or near cities spend waiting in traffic?
d. What conclusions can you reach concerning the cost of waiting in traffic per year?

2.42 How do the average credit scores of people living in various cities differ? The file **Credit Scores** contains an ordered array of the average credit scores of 143 American cities. (Data extracted from **usat.ly/17a1fA6**.)
a. Construct a percentage histogram.
b. Construct a cumulative percentage polygon.
c. What conclusions can you reach concerning the average credit scores of people living in different American cities?

2.43 One operation of a mill is to cut pieces of steel into parts that will later be used as the frame for front seats in an automobile. The steel is cut with a diamond saw and requires the resulting parts to be within ± 0.005 inch of the length specified by the automobile company. The data are collected from a sample of 100 steel parts and stored in **Steel** . The measurement reported is the difference in inches between the actual length of the steel part, as measured by a laser measurement device, and the specified length of the steel part. For example, the first value, −0.002, represents a steel part that is 0.002 inch shorter than the specified length.
a. Construct a percentage histogram.
b. Is the steel mill doing a good job meeting the requirements set by the automobile company? Explain.

2.44 A manufacturing company produces steel housings for electrical equipment. The main component part of the housing is a steel trough that is made out of a 14-gauge steel coil. It is produced using a 250-ton progressive punch press with a wipe-down operation that puts two 90-degree forms in the flat steel to make the trough. The distance from one side of the form to the other is critical because of weatherproofing in outdoor applications. The company requires that the width of the trough be between 8.31 inches and 8.61 inches. The widths of the troughs, in inches, collected from a sample of 49 troughs, are stored in **Trough** .
a. Construct a percentage histogram and a percentage polygon.
b. Plot a cumulative percentage polygon.
c. What can you conclude about the number of troughs that will meet the company's requirements of troughs being between 8.31 and 8.61 inches wide?

2.45 The manufacturing company in Problem 2.44 also produces electric insulators. If the insulators break when in use, a short circuit is likely to occur. To test the strength of the insulators, destructive testing in high-powered labs is carried out to determine how much *force* is required to break the insulators. Force is measured by observing how many pounds must be applied to the insulator before it breaks. The force measurements, collected from a sample of 30 insulators, are stored in **Force** .
a. Construct a percentage histogram and a percentage polygon.
b. Construct a cumulative percentage polygon.
c. What can you conclude about the strengths of the insulators if the company requires a force measurement of at least 1,500 pounds before the insulator breaks?

2.46 The file **Bulbs** contains the life (in hours) of a sample of forty 20-watt compact fluorescent light bulbs produced by Manufacturer A and a sample of forty 20-watt compact fluorescent light bulbs produced by Manufacturer B.

Use the following class interval widths for each distribution:

Manufacturer A: 6,500 but less than 7,500, 7,500 but less than 8,500, and so on.
Manufacturer B: 7,500 but less than 8,500, 8,500 but less than 9,500, and so on.

a. Construct percentage histograms on separate graphs and plot the percentage polygons on one graph.
b. Plot cumulative percentage polygons on one graph.
c. Which manufacturer has bulbs with a longer life—Manufacturer A or Manufacturer B? Explain.

2.47 The data stored in **Drink** represents the amount of soft drink in a sample of fifty 2-liter bottles.
a. Construct a histogram and a percentage polygon.
b. Construct a cumulative percentage polygon.
c. On the basis of the results in (a) and (b), does the amount of soft drink filled in the bottles concentrate around specific values?

2.5 Visualizing Two Numerical Variables

Visualizing two numerical variables together can reveal possible relationships between two variables and serve as a basis for applying the methods discussed in Chapters 12 and 13. To visualize two numerical variables, you construct a scatter plot. For the special case in which one of the two variables represents the passage of time, you construct a time-series plot.

The Scatter Plot

A **scatter plot** explores the possible relationship between two numerical variables by plotting the values of one numerical variable on the horizontal, or X, axis and the values of a second numerical variable on the vertical, or Y, axis. For example, a marketing analyst could study the effectiveness of advertising by comparing advertising expenses and sales revenues of 50 stores by using the X axis to represent advertising expenses and the Y axis to represent sales revenues.

EXAMPLE 2.12

Scatter Plot for NBA Investment Analysis

Suppose that you are an investment analyst who has been asked to review the valuations of the 30 NBA professional basketball teams. You seek to know if the value of a team reflects its revenues. You collect revenue and valuation data (both in $millions) for all 30 NBA teams, organize the data as Table 2.18, and store the data in NBAValues.

TABLE 2.18

Revenues and Values for NBA Teams

Team Code	Revenue ($millions)	Value ($millions)	Team Code	Revenue ($millions)	Value ($millions)	Team Code	Revenue ($millions)	Value ($millions)
ATL	119	425	HOU	191	775	OKC	144	590
BOS	169	875	IND	121	475	ORL	139	560
BKN	190	780	LAC	128	575	PHI	117	469
CHA	115	410	LAL	295	1,350	PHX	137	565
CHI	195	1,000	MEM	126	453	POR	140	587
CLE	145	515	MIA	188	770	SAC	115	550
DAL	162	765	MIL	109	405	SAS	167	660
DEN	124	495	MIN	116	430	TOR	149	520
DET	139	450	NOH	116	420	UTA	131	525
GSW	160	750	NYK	287	1,400	WAS	122	485

Source: Data extracted from **www.forbes.com/nba-valuations**.

To quickly visualize a possible relationship between team revenues and valuations, you construct a scatter plot as shown in Figure 2.14, in which you plot the revenues on the X axis and the value of the team on the Y axis.

SOLUTION From Figure 2.14, you see that there appears to be a strong increasing (positive) relationship between revenues and the value of a team. In other words, teams that generate a smaller amount of revenues have a lower value, while teams that generate higher revenues have a higher value. This relationship has been highlighted by the addition of a linear regression prediction line that will be discussed in Chapter 12.

(continued)

FIGURE 2.14

Scatter plot of revenue and value for NBA teams

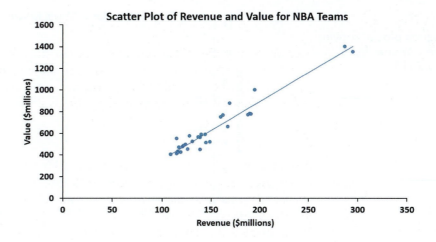

Scatter Plot of Revenue and Value for NBA Teams

LEARN MORE

Read the SHORT TAKES for Chapter 2 for an example that illustrates a negative relationship.

Other pairs of variables may have a decreasing (negative) relationship in which one variable decreases as the other increases. In other situations, there may be a weak or no relationship between the variables.

The Time-Series Plot

A **time-series plot** plots the values of a numerical variable on the Y axis and plots the time period associated with each numerical value on the X axis. A time-series plot can help you visualize trends in data that occur over time.

EXAMPLE 2.13

Time-Series Plot for Movie Revenues

As an investment analyst who specializes in the entertainment industry, you are interested in discovering any long-term trends in movie revenues. You collect the annual revenues (in $billions) for movies released from 1995 to 2013, and organize the data as Table 2.19, and store the data in Movie Revenues.

To see if there is a trend over time, you construct the time-series plot shown in Figure 2.15.

TABLE 2.19

Movie Revenues (in $billions) from 1995 to 2013

Year	Revenue ($billions)	Year	Revenue ($billions)	Year	Revenue ($billions)
1995	5.29	2002	9.19	2008	9.95
1996	5.59	2003	9.35	2009	10.65
1997	6.51	2004	9.11	2010	10.54
1998	6.78	2005	8.95	2011	10.19
1999	7.30	2006	9.25	2012	10.83
2000	7.48	2007	9.63	2013	9.77
2001	8.13				

Source: Data extracted from **www.the-numbers.com/market**, February 12, 2014.

SOLUTION From Figure 2.15, you see that there was a steady increase in the revenue of movies between 1995 and 2003, a leveling off from 2003 to 2006, followed by a further increase from 2007 to 2009, followed by another leveling off from 2010 to 2012, and then a decline in 2013 back to the level below the revenue in 2008. During that time, the revenue increased from under $6 billion in 1995 to more than $10 billion in 2009 to 2012.

FIGURE 2.15

Time-series plot of movie revenue per year from 1995 to 2013

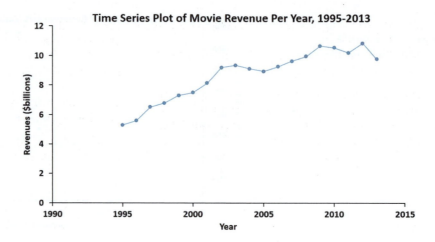

Problems for Section 2.5

LEARNING THE BASICS

2.48 The following is a set of data from a sample of $n = 11$ items:

X: 7 5 8 3 6 0 2 4 9 5 8
Y: 1 5 4 9 8 0 6 2 7 5 4

a. Construct a scatter plot.
b. Is there a relationship between X and Y? Explain.

2.49 The following is a series of annual sales (in $millions) over an 11-year period (2003 to 2013):

Year: 2003 2004 2005 2006 2007 2008 2009 2010 2011 2012 2013
Sales: 13.0 17.0 19.0 20.0 20.5 20.5 20.5 20.0 19.0 17.0 13.0

a. Construct a time-series plot.
b. Does there appear to be any change in annual sales over time? Explain.

APPLYING THE CONCEPTS

✓ SELF Test **2.50** Movie companies need to predict the gross receipts of individual movies once a movie has debuted. The following results, stored in **PotterMovies**, are the first weekend gross, the U.S. gross, and the worldwide gross (in $millions) of the eight Harry Potter movies:

Title	First Weekend ($millions)	U.S. Gross ($millions)	Worldwide Gross ($millions)
Sorcerer's Stone	90.295	317.558	976.458
Chamber of Secrets	88.357	261.988	878.988
Prisoner of Azkaban	93.687	249.539	795.539
Goblet of Fire	102.335	290.013	896.013
Order of the Phoenix	77.108	292.005	938.469
Half-Blood Prince	77.836	301.460	934.601
Deathly Hallows Part I	125.017	295.001	955.417
Deathly Hallows Part II	169.189	381.011	1,328.111

Source: Data extracted from **www.the-numbers.com/interactive /comp-HarryPotter.php**.

a. Construct a scatter plot with first weekend gross on the X axis and U.S. gross on the Y axis.
b. Construct a scatter plot with first weekend gross on the X axis and worldwide gross on the Y axis.
c. What can you say about the relationship between first weekend gross and U.S. gross and first weekend gross and worldwide gross?

2.51 Data were collected on the typical cost of dining at American-cuisine restaurants within a 1-mile walking distance of a hotel located in a large city. The file **Bundle** contains the typical cost (a per transaction cost in $) as well as a Bundle score, a measure of overall popularity and customer loyalty, for each of 40 selected restaurants. (Data extracted from **www.bundle.com** via the link **on-msn.com/MnlBxo**.)

a. Construct a scatter plot with Bundle score on the X axis and typical cost on the Y axis.
b. What conclusions can you reach about the relationship between Bundle score and typical cost?

2.52 College football is big business, with coaches' pay and revenues in millions of dollars. The file **College Football** contains the coaches' total pay and net revenue for college football at 105 schools (Data extracted from "College Football Coaches Continue to See Salary Explosion," *USA Today*, November 20, 2012, p. 1C.)

a. Do you think schools with higher net revenues also have higher coaches' pay?
b. Construct a scatter plot with net revenue on the X axis and coaches' pay on the Y axis.
c. Does the scatter plot confirm or contradict your answer to (a)?

2.53 A Pew Research Center survey found that social networking is popular in many nations around the world. The file **Global SocialMedia** contains the level of social media networking (measured as the percentage of individuals polled who use social networking sites) and the GDP at purchasing power parity (PPP) per capita for each of 24 selected countries. (Data extracted from "Emerging Nations Embrace Internet, Mobile Technology," **bit. ly/1mg8Nvc**.)

a. Construct a scatterplot with GDP (PPP) per capita on the X axis and social media usage on the Y axis.
b. What conclusions can your reach about the relationship between GDP and social media usage?

2.54 How have stocks performed in the past? The following table presents the data stored in **Stock Performance** and shows the performance of a broad measure of stocks (by percentage) for each decade from the 1830s through the 2000s:

Decade	Performance (%)
1830s	2.8
1840s	12.8
1850s	6.6
1860s	12.5
1870s	7.5
1880s	6.0
1890s	5.5
1900s	10.9
1910s	2.2
1920s	13.3
1930s	−2.2
1940s	9.6
1950s	18.2
1960s	8.3
1970s	6.6
1980s	16.6
1990s	17.6
2000s*	−0.5

*Through December 15, 2009.

Source: Data extracted from T. Lauricella, "Investors Hope the '10s Beat the '00s," *The Wall Street Journal*, December 21, 2009, pp. C1, C2.

a. Construct a time-series plot of the stock performance from the 1830s to the 2000s.
b. Does there appear to be any pattern in the data?

2.55 The data in **NewHomeSales** represent number and median sales price of new single-family houses sold in the United States recorded at the end of each month from January 2000 through December 2013. (Data extracted from **www.census.gov**, February 28, 2014.)
a. Construct a time-series plot of new home sales prices.
b. What pattern, if any, is present in the data?

2.56 The file **Movie Attendance** contains the yearly movie attendance (in billions) from 2001 through 2013:

Year	Attendance (billions)
2001	1.44
2002	1.58
2003	1.55
2004	1.47
2005	1.39
2006	1.41
2007	1.40
2008	1.39
2009	1.42
2010	1.34
2011	1.28
2012	1.36
2013	1.15

Source: Data extracted from **the-numbers.com/market**.

a. Construct a time-series plot for the movie attendance (in billions).
b. What pattern, if any, is present in the data?

2.57 The file **Audits** contains the number of audits of corporations with assets of more than $250 million conducted by the Internal Revenue Service between 2001 and 2013. (Data extracted from **www.irs.gov**.)
a. Construct a time-series plot.
b. What pattern, if any, is present in the data?

2.6 Organizing and Visualizing a Set of Variables

So far the methods discussed in this chapter apply to either a single categorical or numerical variable or the special case of two numerical variables. Methods also exist to organize and visualize multiple categorical or numerical variables or a mixed set of categorical and numerical variables. While any number of variables could be used with these methods, using more than three or four variables at once will usually produce results that can be hard to interpret.

Methods that work with a set of variables can help you to discover patterns and relationships that simpler tables and charts would fail to make apparent. However, in summarizing variables in a way to facilitate the discovery of patterns and relationships, these methods can sometimes be less precise than the simpler methods already discussed in this chapter. Because of this trade-off, the methods in this section are typically used to reach preliminary conclusions about the set of variables being analyzed and are used to complement, not replace, the methods discussed in Sections 2.1 through 2.5.

Multidimensional Contingency Tables

A **multidimensional contingency table** tallies the responses of three or more categorical variables. In Excel, you construct a table called a **PivotTable** that allows you to interactively change the level of summarization and the arrangement and formatting of the variables. In Minitab, you create a noninteractive table to which specialized statistical and graphing procedures (beyond the scope of this book to discuss) can be applied to analyze and visualize multidimensional data. For the case of three categorical variables, each cell in the table contains the tallies of the third variable, organized by the subgroups represented by the row and column variables.

For example, return to the Table 2.5 contingency table on page 34 that jointly tallies the type and risk variables for the sample of 316 retirement funds as percentages of the overall total (shown a second time at left in Figure 2.16 below). This table shows, among other things, that there are many more growth funds of low risk than of average or high risk.

FIGURE 2.16

PivotTables for the retirement funds sample showing percentages of overall total that each subgroup represents

Type	Risk			
	Low	Average	High	Grand Total
Growth	45.25%	23.42%	3.16%	71.84%
Value	21.84%	5.38%	0.95%	28.16%
Grand Total	67.09%	28.80%	4.11%	100.00%

Type	Risk			
	Low	Average	High	Grand Total
Growth	45.25%	23.42%	3.16%	71.84%
Large	28.48%	3.16%	0.95%	32.59%
Mid-Cap	11.71%	11.08%	0.00%	22.78%
Small	5.06%	9.18%	2.22%	16.46%
Value	21.84%	5.38%	0.95%	28.16%
Large	14.24%	1.27%	0.32%	15.82%
Mid-Cap	4.75%	1.27%	0.00%	6.01%
Small	2.85%	2.85%	0.63%	6.33%
Grand Total	67.09%	28.80%	4.11%	100.00%

Adding a third categorical variable, the market cap with the categories Small, Mid-Cap, and Large, creates the multidimensional contingency table shown at right in Figure 2.16. This second PivotTable reveals the following patterns that cannot be seen in the first table:

- **For the growth funds, the pattern of risk differs depending on the market cap of the fund.** Large-cap funds are most likely to have low risk and are very unlikely to have high risk. Mid-cap funds are equally likely to have low or average risk. Small-cap funds are most likely to have average risk and are less likely to have high risk.
- **The value funds show a pattern of risk that is different from the pattern seen in the growth funds.** Mid-cap funds are more likely to have low risk. Almost all of large value funds are low risk, and the small value funds are equally likely to have low or average risk.

These results reveal that market cap is an example of a **lurking variable**, a variable that is affecting the results of the other variables. The relationship between the fund type and the level of risk is clearly affected by the market cap of the retirement fund.

Adding Numerical Variables Multidimensional contingency tables can also include a numerical variable. When you add a numerical variable to a multidimensional analysis, you use other variables (categorical or variables that represent units of time) as the row and column variables to form the groups by which the numerical variable will be summarized.

You typically summarize numerical variables using one of the numerical descriptive statistics discussed in Sections 3.1 and 3.2. For example, Figure 2.17 presents the multidimensional contingency table that computes the mean, or average, 10-year return percentage for each of the groups formed by the type, risk, and market-cap categorical variables.

FIGURE 2.17

PivotTable of fund type, risk, market cap, showing the mean 10-year return percentage

Mean 10YrReturn%	Risk			
Type	Low	Average	High	Grand Total
Growth	7.13	8.17	6.65	7.45
Value	6.69	8.11	6.22	6.95
Grand Total	6.99	8.16	6.55	7.31

Mean 10YrReturn%	Risk			
Type	Low	Average	High	Grand Total
Growth	7.13	8.17	6.65	7.45
Large	6.37	7.16	8.42	6.51
Mid-Cap	8.36	8.65		8.50
Small	8.59	7.94	5.89	7.86
Value	6.69	8.11	6.22	6.95
Large	5.81	7.01	4.03	5.87
Mid-Cap	7.87	8.23		7.94
Small	9.15	8.55	7.32	8.70
Grand Total	6.99	8.16	6.55	7.31

The left table in Figure 2.17 has the market cap categories collapsed, or hidden from view. This table highlights that the value funds with low or high risk have a lower mean 10-year return percentage than the growth funds with those risk levels. The right table, with the market cap categories expanded, uncovers several patterns including that growth funds with large market capitalizations and high risk were among the best performers, but that large value funds with high risk were the subgroup with the poorest performance. (Because there are no mid-cap funds with high risk, no mean can be computed for this group and therefore the cells that represent these subgroups are blank.)

Data Discovery

The two tables in Figure 2.17 also illustrate **data discovery**. Data discovery are methods that enable you to perform preliminary analyses by manipulating interactive summarizations. Data discovery methods can be used to take a closer look at historical or status data or to quickly review data for unusual values. Data discovery also allows you to add or remove variables or statistics to uncover new patterns in the data, something done to the Figure 2.16 tables to produce the Figure 2.17 tables. In these ways, data discovery realizes the earlier promise of executive information systems to give decision makers the tools of data exploration and presentation.

In its simplest form, data discovery involves **drill-down**, the revealing of the data that underlies a higher-level summary. In Figure 2.17, when you expand the market cap categories, you are drilling down one level. Drill-down can proceed all the way "down" to the unsummarized data. For example, Figure 2.18 shows the details about all of the small market cap value funds that have low risk, the group with the 9.15% mean 10-year return in the table at right in Figure 2.17.

FIGURE 2.18

Results of drilling down to the details about small market cap value funds that have low risk

	A	B	C	D	E	F	G	H	I	J	K	L	M	N
1	Fund Number	Market Cap	Type	Assets	Turnover Ratio	Beta	SD	Risk	1YrReturn%	3YrReturn%	5YrReturn%	10YrReturn%	Expense Ratio	Star Rating
2	RF316	Small	Value	71.30	14.00	0.84	13.79	Low	4.83	7.12	4.41	9.80	1.27	Four
3	RF310	Small	Value	664.50	68.00	0.71	11.68	Low	8.87	9.63	11.35	11.51	1.46	Five
4	RF308	Small	Value	48.30	14.60	0.94	17.02	Low	11.79	10.40	-2.27	4.27	1.66	Two
5	RF306	Small	Value	40.90	28.00	1.16	18.97	Low	12.49	11.08	5.11	8.76	1.60	Three
6	RF304	Small	Value	73.30	32.00	1.15	18.69	Low	22.54	11.76	6.27	10.15	1.61	Three
7	RF303	Small	Value	103.20	16.78	1.05	17.41	Low	16.54	12.09	7.31	8.29	1.51	Four
8	RF302	Small	Value	1837.60	16.04	1.20	1.92	Low	13.78	12.11	4.91	10.10	1.38	Four
9	RF300	Small	Value	1980.30	27.00	1.14	18.80	Low	20.13	13.13	6.63	9.63	1.13	Four
10	RF298	Small	Value	127.80	89.00	0.95	15.90	Low	7.35	14.69	3.09	9.86	1.50	Four

Some data discovery methods are primarily visual. A **treemap** visualizes the comparison of two or more variables using the size and color of rectangles to represent values. When used with one or more categorical variables, a treemap forms a multilevel hierarchy or *tree* that can uncover patterns among numerical variables.

Figure 2.19 presents a treemap that visualizes the numerical variables assets (size) and 10-year return percentage (color) for the growth and value funds in the retirement funds sample that have small market capitalizations and low risk. The treemap suggests the preliminary conclusions that the best 10-year returns (represented by darkest color) are associated with "middle-sized" funds and that the worst returns (lightest color) tend to be associated with smaller-sized funds. As noted at the beginning of this section, a treemap in suggesting these patterns trades off the precise detail of the data. (Compare the value funds visualization at the right in Figure 2.19 with the detailed table of Figure 2.18.)

Other data discovery methods provide you with a set of controls that allow you to select sets of variables or ask questions of the data. Read the SHORT TAKES for Chapter 2 to learn about the Microsoft Excel slicer feature for an example of this type of method.

FIGURE 2.19

Treemap of assets and 10-year return percentage for small market cap retirement funds with low risk by fund type

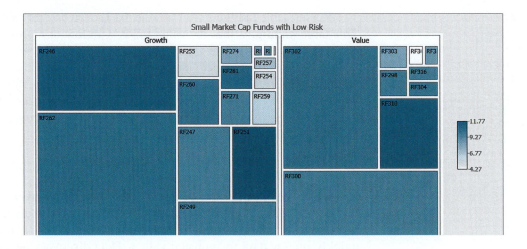

Problems for Section 2.6

APPLYING THE CONCEPTS

2.58 Using the sample of retirement funds stored in `RetirementFunds`:

a. Construct a table that tallies type, market cap, and rating.

b. What conclusions can you reach concerning differences among the types of retirement funds (growth and value), based on market cap (small, mid-cap, and large) and the rating (one, two, three, four, and five)?

2.59 Using the sample of retirement funds stored in `RetirementFunds`:

a. Construct a table that tallies market cap, risk, and rating.

b. What conclusions can you reach concerning differences among the funds based on market cap (small, mid-cap, and large), risk (low, average, and high), and the rating (one, two, three, four, and five)?

2.60 Using the sample of retirement funds stored in `RetirementFunds`:

a. Construct a table that tallies type, risk, and rating.

b. What conclusions can you reach concerning differences among the types of retirement funds (growth and value), based on the risk (low, average, and high), and the rating (one, two, three, four, and five)?

2.61 Using the sample of retirement funds stored in `RetirementFunds`:

a. Construct a table that tallies type, market cap, risk, and rating.

b. What conclusions can you reach concerning differences among the types of funds based on market cap (small, mid-cap, and large), based on type (growth and value), risk (low, average, and high), and rating (one, two, three, four, and five)?

2.62 The value of a National Basketball Association (NBA) franchise has increased dramatically over the past few years. The value of a franchise varies based on the size of the city in which the team is located, the amount of revenue it receives, and the success of the team. The file `NBAValues` contains the value of each team and the change in value in the past year. (Data extracted from **www .forbes.com/nba-valuations**.):

a. Construct a treemap that visualizes the values of the NBA teams (size) and the one year changes in value (color).

b. What conclusions can you reach concerning the value of NBA teams and the one year change in value?

2.63 The annual ranking of the FT Global 500 2013 provides a snapshot of the world's largest companies. The companies are ranked by market capitalization—the greater the stock market value of a company, the higher the ranking. The market capitalizations (in $billions) and the 52-week change in market capitalizations (in %) for companies in the Automobile & Parts, Financial Services, Health Care Equipment & Services, and Software & Computer Services sectors are stored in `FTGlobal500`. (Data extracted from **ft.com/intl/indepth/ft500**.)

a. Construct a treemap that presents each company's market capitalization (size) and the 52-week change in market capitalization (color) grouped by sector and country.

b. Which sector seems to have the best gains in the market capitalizations of its companies? Which sectors seem to have the worst gains (or greatest losses)?

c. Construct a treemap that presents the each company's market capitalization (size) and the 52-week change in market capitalization (color) grouped by country.

d. What comparison can be more easily made with the treemap constructed in (c) compared to the treemap constructed in (a).

2.64 Your task as a member of the International Strategic Management Team in your company is to investigate the potential for entry into a foreign market. As part of your initial investigation, you must provide an assessment of the economies of countries in the Americas and the Asia and Pacific regions. The file `DoingBusiness` contains the 2012 GDPs per capita for these countries as well as the number of Internet users in 2011 (per 100 people) and the number of mobile cellular subscriptions in 2011 (per 100 people). (Data extracted from data.worldbank.org.)

a. Construct a treemap of the GDPs per capita (size) and their number of Internet users in 2011 (per 100 people) (color) for each country grouped by region.

b. Construct a treemap of the GDPs per capita (size) and their number of mobile cellular subscriptions in 2011 (per 100 people) (color) for each country grouped by region.

c. What patterns to these data do the two treemaps suggest? Are the patterns in the two treemaps similar or different? Explain.

2.65 Sales of automobiles in the United States fluctuate from month to month and year to year. The file **AutoSales** contains the sales for various automakers in July 2013 and the percentage change from June 2013 sales. (Data extracted from "How the Auto Industry Fared in July," **nyti.ms/1nnlCV2**.)

a. Construct a treemap of the sales of autos and the change in sales from June 2013.

b. What conclusions can you reach concerning the sales of autos and the change in sales from June 2013?

2.66 Using the sample of retirement funds stored in **RetirementFunds**:

a. Construct a table that tallies type, market cap, and rating.

b. Drill down to examine the large-cap growth funds with a rating of three. How many funds are there? What conclusions can you reach about these funds?

2.67 Using the sample of retirement funds stored in **RetirementFunds**:

a. Construct a table that tallies market cap, risk, and rating.

b. Drill down to examine the large cap funds that are high risk with a rating of three. How many funds are there? What conclusions can you reach about these funds?

2.68 Using the sample of retirement funds stored in **RetirementFunds**:

a. Construct a table that tallies type, risk, and rating.

b. Drill down to examine the growth funds with high risk with a rating of three. How many funds are there? What conclusions can you reach about these funds?

2.69 Using the sample of retirement funds stored in **RetirementFunds**:

a. Construct a table that tallies type, market cap, and risk.

b. Drill down to examine the large cap growth funds with high risk. How many funds are there? What conclusions can you reach about these funds?

2.7 The Challenge in Organizing and Visualizing Variables

Organizing and visualizing variables can provide useful summaries that can jumpstart the analysis of the variables. However, you must be mindful of the limits of others to be able to perceive and comprehend your results as well as the presentation issues that can undercut the usefulness of the methods discussed in this chapter. You can too easily create summaries that obscure the data or create false impressions that would lead to misleading or unproductive analysis. The challenge in organizing and visualizing variables is to avoid these complications.

Obscuring Data

Management specialists have long known that information overload, presenting too many details, can obscure data and hamper decision making (see Reference 3). Both tabular summaries and visualizations can suffer from this problem. For example, consider the Figure 2.20 side-by-side bar chart that shows percentages of the overall total for subgroups formed from combinations of fund type, market cap, risk, and star rating. While this chart highlights that there are more large-cap retirement funds with low risk and a three-star rating than any other combination of risk and star rating, other details about the retirement funds sample are less obvious. The overly complex legend obscures as well, even for people who do not suffer from color perception problems.

FIGURE 2.20

Side-by-side bar chart for the retirement funds sample showing percentage of overall total for fund type, market cap, risk, and star rating

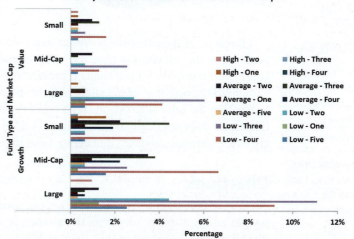

Creating False Impressions

As you organize and visualize variables, you must be careful not to create false impressions that could affect preliminary conclusions about the data. Selective summarizations and improperly constructed visualizations often create false impressions.

A *selective summarization* is the presentation of only part of the data that have been collected. Frequently, selective summarization occurs when data collected over a long period of time are summarized as percentage changes for a shorter period. For example, Table 2.20 (left) presents the one-year difference in sales of seven auto industry companies for the month of April. The selective summarization tells a different story, particularly for company G, than does Table 2.20 (right), which shows the year-to-year differences for a three-year period that included the 2008 economic downturn.

TABLE 2.20

Left: One-Year
Percentage Change
in Year-to-Year Sales
for the Month of April;
Right: Percentage
Change for Three
Consecutive Years

Company	Change from Prior Year	Company	Change from Prior Year		
			Year 1	Year 2	Year 3
A	+7.2	A	−22.6	−33.2	+7.2
B	+24.4	B	−4.5	−41.9	+24.4
C	+24.9	C	−18.5	−31.5	+24.9
D	+24.8	D	−29.4	−48.1	+24.8
E	+12.5	E	−1.9	−25.3	+12.5
F	+35.1	F	−1.6	−37.8	+35.1
G	+29.7	G	+7.4	−13.6	+29.7

Improperly constructed charts can also create false impressions. Figure 2.21 shows two pie charts that display the market shares of companies in two industries. How quickly did you notice that both pie charts summarize identical data?

FIGURE 2.21

Market shares of
companies in "two"
industries

*If you want to verify that the
two pie charts visualize the
same data, open the **TwoPies
worksheet** in the **Challenging
workbook or** (Minitab) **project**.*

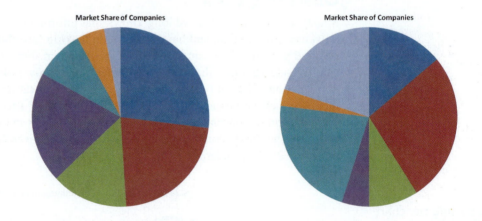

Market Share of Companies   Market Share of Companies

Student Tip

When using pie charts,
pie slices should be
ordered from the largest
to the smallest slice and
pie charts meant for
comparison should be
colored in the same way.

Because of their relative positions and colorings, many people will perceive the dark blue pie slice on the left chart to have a smaller market share than the dark red pie chart on the right chart even though both pie slices represent the company that has 27% market share. In this case, both the ordering of pie slices and the different colorings of the two pie charts contribute to creating the false impression. With other types of charts, improperly scaled axes or a Y axis that either does not begin at the origin or is a "broken" axis that is missing intermediate values are other common mistakes that create false impressions.

Chartjunk

Seeking to construct a visualization that can more effectively convey an important point, some people add decorative elements to enhance or replace the simple bar and line shapes of the visualizations discussed in this chapter. While judicious use of such elements may aid in the memorability of a chart (see Reference 1), most often such elements either obscure the data or, worse, create a false impression of the data. Such elements are called **chartjunk**.

Figure 2.22 visualizes the market share for selected soft drink brands. The chartjunk version fails to convey any more information than a simple bar or pie chart would, and the soft drink bottle tops included on the chart obscure and distort the data. The side-by-side bar chart at right shows how the market shares as represented by the height of the "fizzy" elements overstate the actual market shares of the five lesser brands, using the height of the first bottle and fizz to represent 20%.

FIGURE 2.22

Two visualizations of market share of soft drinks

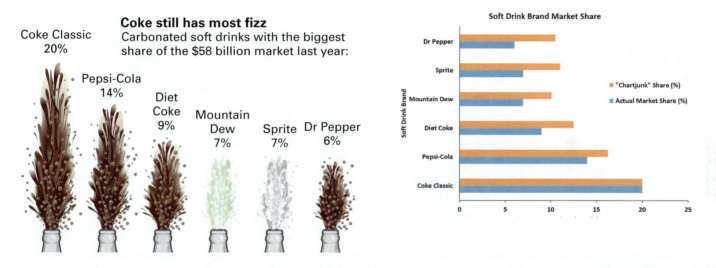

Source: Left illustration adapted from Anne B. Carey and Sam Ward, "Coke Still Has Most Fizz," *USA Today*, May 10, 2000, p. 1B.

Figure 2.23 visualizes Australian wine exports to the United States for four years. The chartjunk version on the left uses wine glasses in a histogram-like display in lieu of a proper time-series plot, such as the one shown on the right. Because the years between measurements are not equally spaced, the four wine glasses create a false impression about the ever-increasing trend in wine exports. The wine glasses also distort the data by using an object with a three-dimensional volume. (While the height of wine in the 1997 glass is a bit more than six times the height of the 1989 glass, the volume of that filled 1997 wine glass would be much more than the almost empty 1989 glass.)

FIGURE 2.23

Two visualizations of Australian wine exports to the United States, in millions of gallons

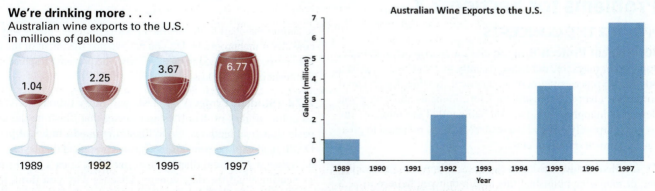

Left illustration adapted from S. Watterson, "Liquid Gold—Australians Are Changing the World of Wine. Even the French Seem Grateful," *Time*, November 22, 1999, p. 68.

Figure 2.24 presents another visual used in the same magazine article. This visualization suffers from a number of mistakes that are common ways of creating chartjunk unintentionally. The grapevine with its leaves and bunch of grapes adds to the clutter of decoration without conveying any useful information. The chart inaccurately shows the 1949–1950 measurement (135,326 acres) at a *higher* point on the Y axis than other, larger values, e.g., the 1969–1970 measurement, 150,300 acres. The inconsistent scale of the X axis distorts the time variable. (Note that the last two measurements, eight years apart, are drawn about as far apart as the 30-year gap between 1959 and 1989.) All of these errors create a very wrong impression that obscures the important trend of accelerating growth of land planted in the 1990s.

FIGURE 2.24

Visualization of the amount of land planted with grapes for the wine industry

Adapted from S. Watterson, "Liquid Gold—Australians Are Changing the World of Wine. Even the French Seem Grateful," *Time*, November 22, 1999, pp. 68–69.

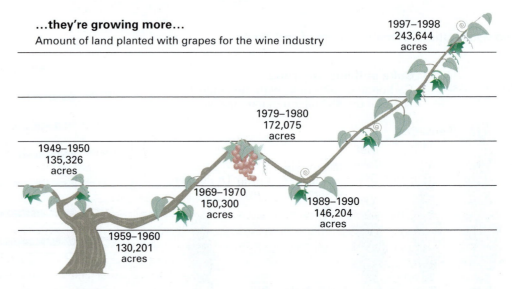

...they're growing more...
Amount of land planted with grapes for the wine industry

1997–1998
243,644
acres

1979–1980
172,075
acres

1949–1950
135,326
acres

1969–1970
150,300
acres

1989–1990
146,204
acres

1959–1960
130,201
acres

Best Practices for Constructing Visualizations

To avoid distortions and to create a visualization that best conveys the data, use the following guidelines:

- Use the simplest possible visualization
- Include a title
- Label all axes
- Include a scale for each axis if the chart contains axes
- Begin the scale for a vertical axis at zero
- Use a constant scale

- Avoid 3D effects
- Avoid chartjunk

When using Microsoft Excel, beware of such types of distortions. Excel can construct charts in which the vertical axis does not begin at zero and may tempt you to restyle simple charts in an inappropriate manner or may tempt you to use uncommon chart choices such as doughnut, radar, surface, bubble, cone, and pyramid charts. You should resist these temptations as they will often result in a visualization that obscures the data or creates a false impression or both.

Problems for Section 2.7

APPLYING THE CONCEPTS

2.70 (Student Project) Bring to class a chart from a website, newspaper, or magazine published recently that you believe to be a poorly drawn representation of a numerical variable. Be prepared to submit the chart to the instructor with comments about why you believe it is inappropriate. Do you believe that the intent of the chart is to purposely mislead the reader? Also, be prepared to present and comment on this in class.

2.71 (Student Project) Bring to class a chart from a website, newspaper, or magazine published this month that you believe to be a poorly drawn representation of a categorical variable. Be prepared

to submit the chart to the instructor with comments about why you consider it inappropriate. Do you believe that the intent of the chart is to purposely mislead the reader? Also, be prepared to present and comment on this in class.

2.72 (Student Project) The Data and Story Library (DASL) is an online library of data files and stories that illustrate the use of basic statistical methods. Go to **lib.stat.cmu.edu/index.php**, click DASL, and explore some of the various graphical displays.

a. Select a graphical display that you think does a good job revealing what the data convey. Discuss why you think it is a good graphical display.

b. Select a graphical display that you think needs a lot of improvement. Discuss why you think that it is a poorly constructed graphical display.

2.73 Examine the following visualization, adapted from one that appeared in a post in a digital marketing blog.

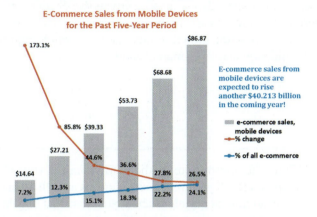

a. Describe at least one good feature of this visual display.
b. Describe at least one bad feature of this visual display.
c. Redraw the graph, using the guidelines above.

2.74 Examine the following visualization, adapted from one that appeared in the post "Who Are the Comic Book Fans on Facebook?" on February 2, 2013, as reported by **graphicspolicy .com**.

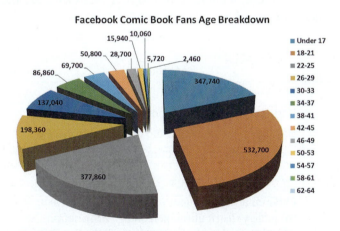

a. Describe at least one good feature of this visual display.
b. Describe at least one bad feature of this visual display.
c. Redraw the graph, using the best practices given on page 70.

2.75 Examine the following visualization, adapted from a management consulting white paper.

a. Describe at least one good feature of this visual display.
b. Describe at least one bad feature of this visual display.
c. Redraw the graph, using the guidelines given on page 70.

2.76 Professor Deanna Oxender Burgess of Florida Gulf Coast University conducted research on annual reports of corporations (see D. Rosato, "Worried About the Numbers? How About the Charts?" The *New York Times*, September 15, 2002, p. B7). Burgess found that even slight distortions in a chart changed readers' perception of the information. Using online or library sources, select a corporation and study its most recent annual report. Find at least one chart in the report that you think needs improvement and develop an improved version of the chart. Explain why you believe the improved chart is better than the one included in the annual report.

2.77 Figure 2.1 shows a bar chart and a pie chart for the main reason young adults shop online (see page 46).
a. Create an exploded pie chart, a doughnut chart, a cone chart, or a pyramid chart that shows the main reason young adults shop online.
b. Which graphs do you prefer—the bar chart or pie chart or the exploded pie chart, doughnut chart, cone chart, and pyramid chart? Explain.

2.78 Figures 2.2 and 2.3 show a bar chart and a pie chart for the risk level for the retirement fund data (see page 47).
a. Create an exploded pie chart, a doughnut chart, a cone chart, and a pyramid chart that shows the risk level of retirement funds.
b. Which graphs do you prefer—the bar chart or pie chart or the exploded pie chart, doughnut chart, cone chart, and pyramid chart? Explain.

USING STATISTICS
The Choice *Is* Yours, Revisited

In the Using Statistics scenario, you were hired by the Choice *Is* Yours investment company to assist clients who seek to invest in retirement funds. A sample of 316 retirement funds was selected, and information on the funds and past performance history was recorded. For each of the 316 funds, data were collected on 13 variables. With so much information, visualizing all these numbers required the use of properly selected graphical displays.

From bar charts and pie charts, you were able to see that about two-thirds of the funds were classified as having low risk, about 30% had average risk, and about 4% had high risk. Contingency

Dmitriy Shironosov/Shutterstock

tables of the fund type and risk revealed that more of the value funds have low risk as compared to average or high. After constructing histograms and percentage polygons of the one-year returns, you were able to conclude that the one-year return was slightly higher for the value funds than for the growth funds. The return for both the growth and value funds is concentrated between 10 and 20, the return for the growth funds is more concentrated between 10 and 15, and the return for the value funds is more concentrated between 15 and 20.

From a multidimensional contingency table, you discovered more complex relationships; for example, for the growth funds, the pattern of risk differs depending on the market cap of the fund.

With these insights, you can inform your clients about how the different funds performed. Of course, the past performance of a fund does not guarantee its future performance. You might also want to analyze the differences in return in the past 3 years, in the past 5 years, and the past 10 years to see how the growth funds, the value funds, and the small, mid-cap, and large market cap funds performed.

SUMMARY

Organizing and visualizing data are the third and fourth tasks of the DCOVA framework. How you accomplish these tasks varies by the type of variable, categorical or numerical, as well as the number of variables you seek to organize and visualize at the same time. Table 2.21 summarizes the appropriate methods to do these tasks.

Using the appropriate methods to organize and visualize your data allows you to reach preliminary conclusions about the data. In several different chapter examples, tables and charts helped you reach conclusions about the main reason that young adults shop online and about the cost of restaurant meals in a city and its suburbs; they also provided some insights about the sample of retirement funds in The Choice *Is* Yours scenario.

Using the appropriate methods to visualize your data may help you reach preliminary conclusions as well as cause you to ask additional questions about your data that may lead to further analysis at a later time. If used improperly, methods to organize and visualize the variables can obscure data or create false impressions, as Section 2.7 discusses.

Methods to organize and visualize data help summarize data. For numerical variables, there are many additional ways to summarize data that involve computing sample statistics or population parameters. The most common examples of these, *numerical descriptive measures*, are the subject of Chapter 3.

TABLE 2.21

Organizing and Visualizing Data

Type of Variable	Methods
Categorical variables	
Organize	Summary table, contingency table (Section 2.1)
Visualize one variable	Bar chart, pie chart, Pareto chart (Section 2.3)
Visualize two variables	Side-by-side chart (Section 2.3)
Numerical variables	
Organize	Ordered array, frequency distribution, relative frequency distribution, percentage distribution, cumulative percentage distribution (Section 2.2)
Visualize one variable	Stem-and-leaf display, histogram, percentage polygon, cumulative percentage polygon (ogive) (Section 2.4)
Visualize two variables	Scatter plot, time-series plot (Section 2.5)
Many variables together	
Organize	Multidimensional tables, treemap (Section 2.6)

REFERENCES

1. Batemen, S., R. Mandryk, C. Gutwin, A. Genest, D. McDine, and C. Brooks. "Useful Junk? The Effects of Visual Embellishment on Comprehension and Memorability of Charts." April 10, 2010, **www.hci.usask.ca/uploads/173-pap0297 -bateman.pdf**.

2. Few, S. *Displaying Data for At-a-Glance Monitoring*, Second ed. Burlingame, CA: Analytics Press, 2013.

3. Gross, B. *The Managing of Organizations: The Administrative Struggle, Vols. I & II*. New York: The Free Press of Glencoe, 1964.

4. Huff, D. *How to Lie with Statistics*. New York: Norton, 1954.

5. *Microsoft Excel 2013*. Redmond, WA: Microsoft Corporation, 2012.

6. *Minitab Release 16*. State College, PA: Minitab, 2010.

7. Tufte, E. R. *Beautiful Evidence*. Cheshire, CT: Graphics Press, 2006.

8. Tufte, E. R. *Envisioning Information*. Cheshire, CT: Graphics Press, 1990.

9. Tufte, E. R. *The Visual Display of Quantitative Information*, 2nd ed. Cheshire, CT: Graphics Press, 2002.

10. Tufte, E. R. *Visual Explanations*. Cheshire, CT: Graphics Press, 1997.

11. Wainer, H. *Visual Revelations: Graphical Tales of Fate and Deception from Napoleon Bonaparte to Ross Perot*. New York: Copernicus/Springer-Verlag, 1997.

KEY EQUATIONS

Determining the Class Interval Width

$$\text{Interval width} = \frac{\text{highest value} - \text{lowest value}}{\text{number of classes}} \quad (2.1)$$

Computing the Proportion or Relative Frequency

$$\text{Proportion} = \text{relative frequency} = \frac{\text{number of values in each class}}{\text{total number of values}} \quad (2.2)$$

KEY TERMS

bar chart 46
bins 40
cell 33
chartjunk 69
class boundaries 38
class interval 38
class interval width 38
class midpoints 39
classes 38
contingency table 33
cumulative percentage distribution 42
cumulative percentage polygon (ogive) 56
data discovery 65

drill-down 65
frequency distribution 38
histogram 54
joint response 33
lurking variables 64
multidimensional contingency table 64
ogive (cumulative percentage polygon) 56
ordered array 37
Pareto chart 48
Pareto principle 48
percentage distribution 40
percentage polygon 55
pie chart 47

PivotTable 64
proportion 40
relative frequency 40
relative frequency distribution 40
scatter plot 60
side-by-side bar chart 50
stacked 44
stem-and-leaf display 52
summary table 33
time-series plot 61
treemap 65
unstacked 44

CHECKING YOUR UNDERSTANDING

2.79 How do histograms and polygons differ in construction and use?

2.80 Why would you construct a summary table?

2.81 What are the advantages and disadvantages of using a bar chart, a pie chart, and a Pareto chart?

2.82 Compare and contrast the bar chart for categorical data with the histogram for numerical data.

2.83 What is the difference between a time-series plot and a scatter plot?

2.84 Why is it said that the main feature of a Pareto chart is its ability to separate the "vital few" from the "trivial many"?

2.85 What are the three different ways to break down the percentages in a contingency table?

2.86 How can a multidimensional table differ from a two-variable contingency table?

2.87 What type of insights can you gain from a contingency table that contains three variables that you cannot gain from a contingency table that contains two variables?

CHAPTER REVIEW PROBLEMS

2.88 The following summary, table, presents the breakdown of the price of a new college textbook:

Revenue Category	Percentage (%)	
Publisher	64.8	
Manufacturing costs		32.3
Marketing and promotion		15.4
Administrative costs and taxes		10.0
After-tax profit		7.1
Bookstore	22.4	
Employee salaries and benefits		11.3
Operations		6.6
Pretax profit		4.5
Author	11.6	
Freight	1.2	

Source: Data extracted from T. Lewin, "When Books Break the Bank," The *New York Times*, September 16, 2003, pp. B1, B4.

a. Using the four categories of publisher, bookstore, author, and freight, construct a bar chart, a pie chart, and a Pareto chart.
b. Using the four subcategories of publisher and three subcategories of bookstore, along with the author and freight categories, construct a Pareto chart.
c. Based on the results of (a) and (b), what conclusions can you reach concerning who gets the revenue from the sales of new college textbooks? Does any of these results surprise you? Explain.

2.89 The following table represents the market share (in number of movies, gross in millions of dollars, and millions of tickets sold) of each type of movie in 2013:

Type	Number	Gross ($millions)	Tickets (millions)
Original screenplay	365	4,468.0	547.6
Based on fiction book/short story	77	2,083.8	255.4
Based on comic/ graphic novel	15	1,399.9	171.6
Based on real-life events	210	934.4	114.5
Based on factual book/article	11	407.0	49.9
Based on folk tale/ fairy tale	7	398.3	48.8
Based on TV	5	345.9	42.4
Remake	12	142.8	17.5
Based on short film	3	173.9	21.3
Spin-off	2	256.4	31.4

Source: Data extracted from **www.the-numbers.com/market/2013/summary**.

a. Construct a bar chart, a pie chart, and a Pareto chart for the number of movies, gross (in $millions), and number of tickets sold (in millions).
b. What conclusions can you reach about the market shares of the different types of movies in 2013?

2.90 A survey was completed by senior-level marketers on marketer expectations and perspectives going into the next year for such things as marketing spending levels, media usage, and new business activities. Marketers were asked about how they are most often finding out about new marketing agencies for hire and the value they are placing on marketing agencies that specialize in their industry. The results are presented in the tables below:

Most Often Ways to Find out About New Marketing Agencies	Percentage (%)
Calls/emails from agencies	32%
Social outreach	6%
Searching on Google, Bing	7%
Referrals from friends, colleagues	48%
Agency search consultants	7%

Source: Data extracted from "2014 RSW/US New Year Outlook Report," **bit.ly/1fVZTj5**.

a. Construct a bar chart, a pie chart, and a Pareto chart.
b. Which graphical method do you think is best for portraying these data?

Importance of Marketing Agency Specializing in Marketer's Industry	Percentage (%)
Very important	43%
Somewhat important	45%
Not at all important	12%

Source: Data extracted from "2014 RSW/US New Year Outlook Report," **bit.ly/1fVZTj5**.

c. Construct a bar chart, a pie chart, and a Pareto chart.
d. Which graphical method do you think is best for portraying these data?
e. Based on both summaries above, what conclusions can you reach concerning marketers' perspective on new marketing agencies?

2.91 The owner of a restaurant that serves Continental-style entrées has the business objective of learning more about the patterns of patron demand during the Friday-to-Sunday weekend time period. Data were collected from 630 customers on the type of entrée ordered and organized in the following table (and stored in **Entree**):

Type of Entrée	Number Served
Beef	187
Chicken	103
Mixed	30
Duck	25
Fish	122
Pasta	63
Shellfish	74
Veal	26
Total	630

a. Construct a percentage summary table for the types of entrées ordered.
b. Construct a bar chart, a pie chart, and a Pareto chart for the types of entrées ordered.

c. Do you prefer using a Pareto chart or a pie chart for these data? Why?

d. What conclusions can the restaurant owner reach concerning demand for different types of entrées?

2.92 Suppose that the owner of the restaurant in Problem 2.91 also wants to study the demand for dessert during the same time period. She decides that in addition to studying whether a dessert was ordered, she will also study the gender of the individual and whether a beef entrée was ordered. Data were collected from 630 customers and organized in the following contingency tables:

	GENDER		
DESSERT ORDERED	**Male**	**Female**	**Total**
Yes	50	96	146
No	250	234	484
Total	300	330	630

	BEEF ENTRÉE		
DESSERT ORDERED	**Yes**	**No**	**Total**
Yes	74	68	142
No	123	365	488
Total	197	433	630

a. For each of the two contingency tables, construct contingency tables of row percentages, column percentages, and total percentages.

b. Which type of percentage (row, column, or total) do you think is most informative for each gender? For beef entrée? Explain.

c. What conclusions concerning the pattern of dessert ordering can the restaurant owner reach?

2.93 The following data represent the pounds per capita of fresh food and packaged food consumed in the United States, Japan, and Russia in a recent year:

	COUNTRY		
FRESH FOOD	**United States**	**Japan**	**Russia**
Eggs, nuts, and beans	88	94	88
Fruit	124	126	88
Meat and seafood	197	146	125
Vegetables	194	278	335
PACKAGED FOOD			
Bakery goods	108	53	144
Dairy products	298	147	127
Pasta	12	32	16
Processed, frozen, dried, and chilled food, and ready-to-eat meals	183	251	70
Sauces, dressings, and condiments	63	75	49
Snacks and candy	47	19	24
Soup and canned food	77	17	25

Source: Data extracted from H. Fairfield, "Factory Food," *The New York Times*, April 4, 2010, p. BU5.

a. For the United States, Japan, and Russia, construct a bar chart, a pie chart, and a Pareto chart for different types of fresh foods consumed.

b. For the United States, Japan, and Russia, construct a bar chart, a pie chart, and a Pareto chart for different types of packaged foods consumed.

c. What conclusions can you reach concerning differences between the United States, Japan, and Russia in the fresh foods and packaged foods consumed?

2.94 The Air Travel Consumer Report, a monthly product of the Department of Transportation's Office of Aviation Enforcement and Proceedings (OAEP), is designed to assist consumers with information on the quality of services provided by airlines. The report includes a summary of consumer complaints by industry group and by complaint category. A breakdown of 1,114 December 2013 consumer complaints based on industry group is given in the following table:

Industry Group	Number of Consumer Complaints
Airlines	992
Travel agents	94
Tour operators	1
Miscellaneous	27
Industry total	1,114

Source: Data extracted from "The Travel Consumer Report," Office of Aviation Enforcement and Proceedings, February 2014.

a. Construct a Pareto chart for the number of complaints by industry group. What industry group accounts for most of the complaints?

The 992 consumer complaints against airlines fall into one of two groups: complaints against U.S. airlines and complaints against foreign airlines. The following table summarizes these 992 complaints by complaint type:

Complaint Category	Complaints Against U.S. Airlines	Complaints Against Foreign Airlines
Flight problems	263	41
Oversales	38	5
Reservation/ticketing/ boarding	98	41
Fares	23	4
Refunds	48	24
Baggage	147	56
Customer service	92	30
Disability	38	8
Advertising	8	0
Discrimination	6	3
Animals	0	0
Other	14	5
Total	775	217

b. Construct pie charts to display the percentage of complaints by type against U.S. airlines and foreign airlines.

c. Construct a Pareto chart for the complaint categories against U.S. airlines. Does a certain complaint category account for most of the complaints?

d. Construct a Pareto chart for the complaint categories against foreign airlines. Does a certain complaint category account for most of the complaints?

2.95 One of the major measures of the quality of service provided by an organization is the speed with which the organization responds to customer complaints. A large family-held department store selling furniture and flooring, including carpet, had undergone a major expansion in the past several years. In particular, the flooring department had expanded from 2 installation crews to an installation supervisor, a measurer, and 15 installation crews. A business objective of the company was to reduce the time between when the complaint is received and when it is resolved. During a recent year, the company received 50 complaints concerning carpet installation. The number of days between the receipt of the complaint and the resolution of the complaint for the 50 complaints, stored in Furniture , are:

54	5	35	137	31	27	152	2	123	81	74	27
11	19	126	110	110	29	61	35	94	31	26	5
12	4	165	32	29	28	29	26	25	1	14	13
13	10	5	27	4	52	30	22	36	26	20	23
33	68										

a. Construct a frequency distribution and a percentage distribution.
b. Construct a histogram and a percentage polygon.
c. Construct a cumulative percentage distribution and plot a cumulative percentage polygon (ogive).
d. On the basis of the results of (a) through (c), if you had to tell the president of the company how long a customer should expect to wait to have a complaint resolved, what would you say? Explain.

2.96 The file DomesticBeer contains the percentage alcohol, number of calories per 12 ounces, and number of carbohydrates (in grams) per 12 ounces for 156 of the best selling domestic beers in the United States.

Source: Data extracted from **www.beer100.com/beercalories. htm,** March 12, 2014.

a. Construct a percentage histogram for percentage alcohol, number of calories per 12 ounces, and number of carbohydrates (in grams) per 12 ounces.
b. Construct three scatter plots: percentage alcohol versus calories, percentage alcohol versus carbohydrates, and calories versus carbohydrates.
c. Discuss what you learn from studying the graphs in (a) and (b).

2.97 The file CigaretteTax contains the state cigarette tax ($) for each state as of January 1, 2014.
a. Construct an ordered array.
b. Plot a percentage histogram.
c. What conclusions can you reach about the differences in the state cigarette tax between the states?

2.98 The file CDRate contains the yields for one-year certificates of deposit (CDs) and a five-year CDs for 22 banks in the United States, as of March 12, 2014.

Source: Data extracted and compiled from **www.Bankrate.com,** March 12, 2014.

a. Construct a stem-and-leaf display for one-year CDs and five-year CDs.
b. Construct a scatter plot of one-year CDs versus five-year CDs.
c. What is the relationship between the one-year CD rate and the five-year CD rate?

2.99 The file CEO-Compensation includes the total compensation (in $millions) for CEOs of 170 large public companies and the investment return in 2012. (Data extracted from "CEO Pay Skyrockets as Economy, Stocks Recover," *USA Today*, March 27, 2013, p. B1.) For total compensation:
a. Construct a frequency distribution and a percentage distribution.
b. Construct a histogram and a percentage polygon.
c. Construct a cumulative percentage distribution and plot a cumulative percentage polygon (ogive).
d. Based on (a) through (c), what conclusions can you reach concerning CEO compensation in 2012?
e. Construct a scatter plot of total compensation and investment return in 2012.
f. What is the relationship between the total compensation and investment return in 2012?

2.100 Studies conducted by a manufacturer of Boston and Vermont asphalt shingles have shown product weight to be a major factor in customers' perception of quality. Moreover, the weight represents the amount of raw materials being used and is therefore very important to the company from a cost standpoint. The last stage of the assembly line packages the shingles before the packages are placed on wooden pallets. The variable of interest is the weight in pounds of the pallet, which for most brands holds 16 squares of shingles. The company expects pallets of its Boston brand-name shingles to weigh at least 3,050 pounds but less than 3,260 pounds. For the company's Vermont brand-name shingles, pallets should weigh at least 3,600 pounds but less than 3,800. Data, collected from a sample of 368 pallets of Boston shingles and 330 pallets of Vermont shingles, are stored in Pallet .
a. For the Boston shingles, construct a frequency distribution and a percentage distribution having eight class intervals, using 3,015, 3,050, 3,085, 3,120, 3,155, 3,190, 3,225, 3,260, and 3,295 as the class boundaries.
b. For the Vermont shingles, construct a frequency distribution and a percentage distribution having seven class intervals, using 3,550, 3,600, 3,650, 3,700, 3,750, 3,800, 3,850, and 3,900 as the class boundaries.
c. Construct percentage histograms for the Boston and Vermont shingles.
d. Comment on the distribution of pallet weights for the Boston and Vermont shingles. Be sure to identify the percentages of pallets that are underweight and overweight.

2.101 What was the average price of a room at two-star, three-star, and four-star hotels around the world during the first half of 2013? The file HotelPrices contains the prices in English pounds, (about US$1.52 as of July 2013). (Data extracted from "Hotel Price Index," **press .hotels.com/content/blogs.dir/13/files/2013/09/HPI_UK.pdf.**) Complete the following for the two-star, three-star, and four-star hotels:
a. Construct a frequency distribution and a percentage distribution.
b. Construct a histogram and a percentage polygon.
c. Construct a cumulative percentage distribution and plot a cumulative percentage polygon (ogive).
d. What conclusions can you reach about the cost of two-star, three-star, and four-star hotels?
e. Construct separate scatter plots of the cost of two-star hotels versus three-star hotels, two-star hotels versus four-star hotels, and three-star hotels versus four-star hotels.
f. What conclusions can you reach about the relationship of the price of two-star, three-star, and four-star hotels?

2.102 The file **Protein** contains calorie and cholesterol information for popular protein foods (fresh red meats, poultry, and fish).

Source: U.S. Department of Agriculture.

a. Construct a percentage histogram for the number of calories.
b. Construct a percentage histogram for the amount of cholesterol.
c. What conclusions can you reach from your analyses in (a) and (b)?

2.103 The file **Natural Gas** contains the monthly average wellhead and residential prices for natural gas (dollars per thousand cubic feet) in the United States from January 1, 2008, to January 1, 2013. (Data extracted from "U.S. Natural Gas Prices," **1.usa.gov/qHDWNz**, March 1, 2013.) For the wellhead price and the residential price:
a. Construct a time-series plot.
b. What pattern, if any, is present in the data?
c. Construct a scatter plot of the wellhead price and the residential price.
d. What conclusion can you reach about the relationship between the wellhead price and the residential price?

2.104 The following data (stored in **Drink**) represent the amount of soft drink in a sample of 50 consecutively filled 2-liter bottles. The results are listed horizontally in the order of being filled:

2.109 2.086 2.066 2.075 2.065 2.057 2.052 2.044 2.036 2.038
2.031 2.029 2.025 2.029 2.023 2.020 2.015 2.014 2.013 2.014
2.012 2.012 2.012 2.010 2.005 2.003 1.999 1.996 1.997 1.992
1.994 1.986 1.984 1.981 1.973 1.975 1.971 1.969 1.966 1.967
1.963 1.957 1.951 1.951 1.947 1.941 1.941 1.938 1.908 1.894

a. Construct a time-series plot for the amount of soft drink on the *Y* axis and the bottle number (going consecutively from 1 to 50) on the *X* axis.
b. What pattern, if any, is present in these data?
c. If you had to make a prediction about the amount of soft drink filled in the next bottle, what would you predict?
d. Based on the results of (a) through (c), explain why it is important to construct a time-series plot and not just a histogram, as was done in Problem 2.47 on page 59.

2.105 The file **Currency** contains the exchange rates of the Canadian dollar, the Japanese yen, and the English pound from 1980 to 2013, where the Canadian dollar, the Japanese yen, and the English pound are expressed in units per U.S. dollar.
a. Construct time-series plots for the yearly closing values of the Canadian dollar, the Japanese yen, and the English pound.
b. Explain any patterns present in the plots.
c. Write a short summary of your findings.
d. Construct separate scatter plots of the value of the Canadian dollar versus the Japanese yen, the Canadian dollar versus the English pound, and the Japanese yen versus the English pound.
e. What conclusions can you reach concerning the value of the Canadian dollar, Japanese yen, and English pound in terms of the U.S. dollar?

2.106 A/B testing is a method used by businesses to test different designs and formats of a web page to determine if a new web page is more effective than a current web page. Web designers tested a new call to action button on its web page. Every visitor to the web page was randomly shown either the original call-to-action button (the control) or the new variation. The metric used to measure success was the download rate: the number of people who downloaded the file divided by the number of people who saw that particular call-to-action button. Results of the experiment yielded the following:

Variations	Downloads	Visitors
Original call to action button	351	3,642
New call to action button	485	3,556

a. Compute the percentage of downloads for the original call-to-action button and the new call-to-action button.
b. Construct a bar chart of the percentage of downloads for the original call-to-action button and the new call-to-action button.
c. What conclusions can you reach concerning the original call-to-action button and the new call-to-action button?

Web designers tested a new web design on its web page. Every visitor to the web page was randomly shown either the original web design (the control) or the new variation. The metric used to measure success was the download rate: the number of people who downloaded the file divided by the number of people who saw that particular web design. Results of the experiment yielded the following:

Variations	Downloads	Visitors
Original web design	305	3,427
New web design	353	3,751

d. Compute the percentage of downloads for the original web design and the new web design.
e. Construct a bar chart of the percentage of downloads for the original web design and the new web design.
f. What conclusions can you reach concerning the original web design and the new web design?
g. Compare your conclusions in (f) with those in (c).

Web designers now tested two factors simultaneously—the call-to-action button and the new web design. Every visitor to the web page was randomly shown one of the following:

Old call to action button with original web design
New call to action button with original web design
Old call to action button with new web design
New call to action button with new web design

Again, the metric used to measure success was the download rate: the number of people who downloaded the file divided by the number of people who saw that particular call-to-action button and web design. Results of the experiment yielded the following:

Call to Action Button	Web Design	Downloaded	Declined	Total
Original	Original	83	917	1,000
New	Original	137	863	1,000
Original	New	95	905	1,000
New	New	170	830	1,000
Total		485	3,515	4,000

h. Compute the percentage of downloads for each combination of call-to-action button and web design.

i. What conclusions can you reach concerning the original call to action button and the new call to action button and the original web design and the new web design?

j. Compare your conclusions in (i) with those in (c) and (g).

2.107 (Class Project) Have each student in the class respond to the question "Which carbonated soft drink do you most prefer?" so that the instructor can tally the results into a summary table.

a. Convert the data to percentages and construct a Pareto chart.

b. Analyze the findings.

2.108 (Class Project) Cross-classify each student in the class by gender (male, female) and current employment status (yes, no), so that the instructor can tally the results.

a. Construct a table with either row or column percentages, depending on which you think is more informative.

b. What would you conclude from this study?

c. What other variables would you want to know regarding employment in order to enhance your findings?

REPORT WRITING EXERCISES

2.109 Referring to the results from Problem 2.100 on page 76 concerning the weights of Boston and Vermont shingles, write a report that evaluates whether the weights of the pallets of the two types of shingles are what the company expects. Be sure to incorporate tables and charts into the report.

CASES FOR CHAPTER 2

Managing Ashland MultiComm Services

Recently, Ashland MultiComm Services has been criticized for its inadequate customer service in responding to questions and problems about its telephone, cable television, and Internet services. Senior management has established a task force charged with the business objective of improving customer service. In response to this charge, the task force collected data about the types of customer service errors, the cost of customer service errors, and the cost of wrong billing errors. It found the following data:

Types of Customer Service Errors

Type of Errors	Frequency
Incorrect accessory	27
Incorrect address	42
Incorrect contact phone	31
Invalid wiring	9
On-demand programming error	14
Subscription not ordered	8
Suspension error	15
Termination error	22
Website access error	30
Wrong billing	137
Wrong end date	17
Wrong number of connections	19
Wrong price quoted	20
Wrong start date	24
Wrong subscription type	33
Total	448

Cost of Customer Service Errors in the Past Year

Type of Errors	Cost ($ thousands)
Incorrect accessory	17.3
Incorrect address	62.4
Incorrect contact phone	21.3
Invalid wiring	40.8
On-demand programming errors	38.8
Subscription not ordered	20.3
Suspension error	46.8
Termination error	50.9
Website access errors	60.7
Wrong billing	121.7
Wrong end date	40.9
Wrong number of connections	28.1
Wrong price quoted	50.3
Wrong start date	40.8
Wrong subscription type	60.1
Total	701.2

Type and Cost of Wrong Billing Errors

Type of Wrong Billing Errors	Cost ($ thousands)
Declined or held transactions	7.6
Incorrect account number	104.3
Invalid verification	9.8
Total	121.7

1. Review these data (stored in **AMS2-1**). Identify the variables that are important in describing the customer service problems. For each variable you identify, construct the graphical representation you think is most appropriate and explain your choice. Also, suggest what other information concerning the different types of errors would be useful to examine. Offer possible courses of action for either the task force or management to take that would support the goal of improving customer service.

2. As a follow-up activity, the task force decides to collect data to study the pattern of calls to the help desk (stored in **AMS2-2**). Analyze these data and present your conclusions in a report.

Digital Case

In the Using Statistics scenario, you were asked to gather information to help make wise investment choices. Sources for such information include brokerage firms, investment counselors, and other financial services firms. Apply your knowledge about the proper use of tables and charts in this Digital Case about the claims of foresight and excellence by an Ashland-area financial services firm.

Open **EndRunGuide.pdf**, which contains the EndRun Financial Services "Guide to Investing." Review the guide, paying close attention to the company's investment claims and supporting data and then answer the following.

1. How does the presentation of the general information about EndRun in this guide affect your perception of the business?

2. Is EndRun's claim about having more winners than losers a fair and accurate reflection of the quality of its investment service? If you do not think that the claim is a fair and accurate one, provide an alternate presentation that you think is fair and accurate.

3. Review the discussion about EndRun's "Big Eight Difference" and then open and examine the attached sample of mutual funds. Are there any other relevant data from that file that could have been included in the Big Eight table? How would the new data alter your perception of EndRun's claims?

4. EndRun is proud that all Big Eight funds have gained in value over the past five years. Do you agree that EndRun should be proud of its selections? Why or why not?

CardioGood Fitness

The market research team at AdRight is assigned the task to identify the profile of the typical customer for each treadmill product offered by CardioGood Fitness. The market research team decides to investigate whether there are differences across the product lines with respect to customer characteristics. The team decides to collect data on individuals who purchased a treadmill at a CardioGood Fitness retail store during the prior three months. The data are stored in the `CardioGood Fitness` file. The team identifies the following customer variables to study: product purchased, TM195, TM498, or TM798; gender; age, in years; education, in years; relationship status, single or partnered; annual

household income ($); average number of times the customer plans to use the treadmill each week; average number of miles the customer expects to walk/run each week; and self-rated fitness on an 1-to-5 ordinal scale, where 1 is poor shape and 5 is excellent shape.

1. Create a customer profile for each CardioGood Fitness treadmill product line by developing appropriate tables and charts.

2. Write a report to be presented to the management of CardioGood Fitness detailing your findings.

The Choice *Is* Yours Follow-Up

Follow up the Using Statistics Revisited section on page 71 by analyzing the differences in 3-year return percentages, 5-year return percentages, and 10-year return percentages for the sample of 316 retirement funds stored in `Retirement Funds`. In your analysis, examine differences between the growth and value funds as well as the differences among the small, mid-cap, and large market cap funds.

Clear Mountain State Student Surveys

1. The student news service at Clear Mountain State University (CMSU) has decided to gather data about the undergraduate students that attend CMSU. They create and distribute a survey of 14 questions and receive responses from 62 undergraduates (stored in `UndergradSurvey`). For each question asked in the survey, construct all the appropriate tables and charts and write a report summarizing your conclusions.

2. The dean of students at CMSU has learned about the undergraduate survey and has decided to undertake a similar survey for graduate students at CMSU. She creates and distributes a survey of 14 questions and receives responses from 44 graduate students (stored in `GradSurvey`). For each question asked in the survey, construct all the appropriate tables and charts and write a report summarizing your conclusions.

CHAPTER 2 EXCEL GUIDE

EG2.1 ORGANIZING CATEGORICAL VARIABLES

The Summary Table

Key Technique Use the PivotTable feature to create a summary table for untallied data.

Example Create a frequency and percentage summary table similar to Table 2.3 on page 33.

PHStat Use **One-Way Tables & Charts**.

For the example, open to the **DATA worksheet** of the **Retirement Funds workbook**. Select **PHStat → Descriptive Statistics → One-Way Tables & Charts**. In the procedure's dialog box (shown below):

1. Click **Raw Categorical Data** (because the worksheet contains untallied data).
2. Enter **H1:H317** as the **Raw Data Cell Range** and check **First cell contains label**.
3. Enter a **Title**, check **Percentage Column**, and click **OK**.

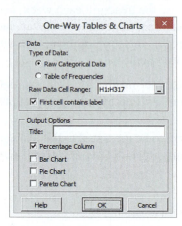

PHStat creates a PivotTable summary table on a new worksheet. For data that have already been tallied into categories, click **Table of Frequencies** in step 1.

In the PivotTable, risk categories appear in alphabetical order and not in the order low, average, and high as would normally be expected. To change to the expected order, use steps 14 and 15 of the *In-Depth Excel* instructions but change all references to cell A6 to cell A7 and drop the Low label over cell A5, not cell A4.

In-Depth Excel (untallied data) Use the **Summary Table workbook** as a model.

For the example, open to the **DATA worksheet** of the **Retirement Funds workbook** and select **Insert → PivotTable**. In the Create PivotTable dialog box (shown at top in right column):

1. Click **Select a table or range** and enter **H1:H317** as the **Table/Range** cell range.

2. Click **New Worksheet** and then click **OK**.

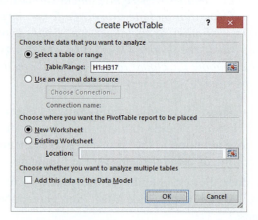

In the Excel 2013 PivotTable Fields task pane (shown below) or in the similar PivotTable Field List task pane in other Excels:

3. Drag **Risk** in the **Choose fields to add to report** box and drop it in the **ROWS** (or **Row Labels**) box.
4. **Drag Risk** in the **Choose fields to add to report** box a second time and drop it in the **Σ Values** box. This second label changes to **Count of Risk to** indicate that a count, or tally, of the risk categories will be displayed in the Pivot-Table.

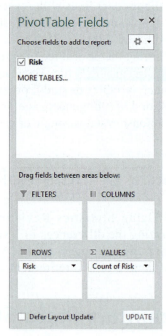

In the PivotTable being created:

5. Enter **Risk** in cell **A3** to replace the heading Row Labels.
6. Right-click cell **A3** and then click **PivotTable Options** in the shortcut menu that appears.

In the PivotTable Options dialog box (shown below):

7. Click the **Layout & Format** tab.
8. Check **For empty cells show** and enter **0** as its value. Leave all other settings unchanged.
9. Click **OK** to complete the PivotTable.

To add a column for the percentage frequency:

10. Enter **Percentage** in cell **C3**. Enter the formula $= B4/B\$7$ in cell **C4** and copy it down through **row 7**.
11. Select cell range **C4:C7**, right-click, and select **Format Cells** in the shortcut menu.
12. In the **Number** tab of the Format Cells dialog box, select **Percentage** as the **Category** and click **OK**.
13. Adjust the worksheet formatting, if appropriate (see Appendix B) and enter a title in cell **A1**.

In the PivotTable, risk categories appear in alphabetical order and not in the order low, average, and high, as would normally be expected. To change to the expected order:

14. Click the **Low** label in cell **A6** to highlight cell A6. Move the mouse pointer to the top edge of the cell until the mouse pointer changes to a four-way arrow.
15. Drag the **Low** label and drop the label over cell **A4**. The risk categories now appear in the order Low, Average, and High in the summary table.

In-Depth Excel (tallied data) Use the **SUMMARY_ SIMPLE worksheet** of the **Summary Table workbook** as a model for creating a summary table.

The Contingency Table

Key Technique Use the PivotTable feature to create a contingency table for untallied data.

Example Construct a contingency table displaying fund type and risk level similar to Table 2.4 on page 34.

PHStat (untallied data) Use **Two-Way Tables & Charts**. For the example, open to the **DATA worksheet** of the **Retirement Funds workbook**. Select **PHStat → Descriptive Statistics → Two-Way Tables & Charts**. In the procedure's dialog box (shown below):

1. Enter **C1:C317** as the **Row Variable Cell Range**.
2. Enter **H1:H317** as the **Column Variable Cell Range**.
3. Check **First cell in each range contains label**.
4. Enter a **Title** and click **OK**.

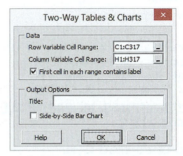

In the PivotTable, risk categories appear in alphabetical order and not in the order low, average, and high as would normally be expected. To change the expected order, use steps 14 and 15 of the *In-Depth Excel* instructions in the left column.

In-Depth Excel (untallied data) Use the **Contingency Table workbook** as a model.
For the example, open to the **DATA worksheet** of the **Retirement Funds workbook**. Select **Insert → PivotTable**. In the Create PivotTable dialog box:

1. Click **Select a table or range** and enter **A1:N317** as the **Table/Range** cell range.
2. Click **New Worksheet** and then click **OK**.

In the PivotTable Fields (called the PivotTable Field List in some Excel versions) task pane:

3. Drag **Type** from **Choose fields to add to report** and drop it in the **ROWS** (or **Row Labels**) box.
4. Drag **Risk** from **Choose fields to add to report** and drop it in the **COLUMNS** (or **Column Labels**) box.
5. Drag **Type** from **Choose fields to add to report** a second time and drop it in the **Σ VALUES** box. (**Type** changes to **Count of Type**.)

In the PivotTable being created:

6. Select cell **A3** and enter a **space character** to clear the label **Count of Type**.
7. Enter **Type** in cell **A4** to replace the heading Row Labels.
8. Enter **Risk** in cell **B3** to replace the heading Column Labels.
9. Click the **Low** label in cell **D4** to highlight cell D4. Move the mouse pointer to the left edge of the cell until the mouse pointer changes to a four-way arrow.
10. Drag the **Low** label to the left and drop the label when an I-beam appears between columns A and B. The Low label appears in B4 and column B now contains the low risk tallies.

11. Right-click over the PivotTable and then click **PivotTable Options** in the shortcut menu that appears.

In the PivotTable Options dialog box:

12. Click the **Layout & Format** tab.
13. Check **For empty cells show** and enter **0** as its value. Leave all other settings unchanged.
14. Click the **Total & Filters** tab.
15. Check **Show grand totals for columns** and **Show grand totals for rows**.
16. Click **OK** to complete the table.

In-Depth Excel (tallied data) Use the **CONTINGENCY_ SIMPLE** worksheet of the **Contingency Table workbook** as a model for creating a contingency table.

EG2.2 ORGANIZING NUMERICAL VARIABLES

Stacked and Unstacked Data

PHStat Use **Stack Data** or **Unstack Data**.
For example, to unstack the 3YrReturn% variable by the Type variable in the retirement funds sample, open to the **DATA worksheet** of the **Retirement Funds workbook**. Select **Data Preparation → Unstack Data**. In that procedure's dialog box, enter **C1:C317** (the Type variable cell range) as the **Grouping Variable Cell Range** and enter **J1:J317** (the 3YrReturn% variable cell range) as the **Stacked Data Cell Range**. Check **First cells in both ranges contain label** and click **OK**. The unstacked data appear on a new worksheet.

The Ordered Array

In-Depth Excel To create an ordered array, first select the numerical variable to be sorted. Then select **Home → Sort & Filter** (in the Editing group) and in the drop-down menu click **Sort Smallest to Largest**. (You will see **Sort A to Z** as the first drop-down choice if you did not select a cell range of *numerical* data.)

The Frequency Distribution

Key Technique Establish bins (see *Classes and Excel Bins* on page 40) and then use the **FREQUENCY**(*untallied data cell range, bins cell range*) array function to tally data.

Example Create a frequency, percentage, and cumulative percentage distribution for the restaurant meal cost data that contain the information found in Tables 2.9, 2.11, and 2.14, in Section 2.2.

PHStat (untallied data) Use **Frequency Distribution**. (Use **Histogram & Polygons**, discussed in Section EG2.4, if you plan to construct a histogram or polygon in addition to a frequency distribution.) For the example, open to the **DATA worksheet** of the **Restaurants workbook**. This worksheet contains the meal cost data in stacked format in column G and a set of bin numbers

appropriate for those data in column H. Select **PHStat → Descriptive Statistics → Frequency Distribution**. In the procedure's dialog box (shown below):

1. Enter **G1:G101** as the **Variable Cell Range**, enter **I1:I9** as the **Bins Cell Range**, and check **First cell in each range contains label**.
2. Click **Multiple Groups - Stacked** and enter **A1:A101** as the **Grouping Variable Cell Range**. (The cell range A1:A101 contains the Location variable.)
3. Enter a **Title** and click **OK**.

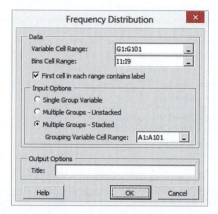

Click **Single Group Variable** in step 2 if constructing a distribution from a single group of untallied data. Click **Multiple Groups - Unstacked** in step 2 if the **Variable Cell Range** contains two or more columns of unstacked, untallied data.

Frequency distributions for the two groups appear on separate worksheets. To display the information for the two groups on one worksheet, select the cell range **B3:D11** on one of the worksheets. Right-click that range and click **Copy** in the shortcut menu. Open to the other worksheet. In that other worksheet, right-click cell **E3** and click **Paste Special** in the shortcut menu. In the Paste Special dialog box, click **Values and numbers format** and click **OK**. Adjust the worksheet title as necessary. (Learn more about the Paste Special command in Appendix B.)

In-Depth Excel (untallied data) Use the **Distributions workbook** as a model.
For the example, open to the **UNSTACKED worksheet** of the **Restaurants workbook**. This worksheet contains the meal cost data unstacked in columns A and B and a set of bin numbers appropriate for those data in column D. Then:

1. Right-click the **UNSTACKED** sheet tab and click **Insert** in the shortcut menu.
2. In the **General** tab of the Insert dialog box, click **Worksheet** and then click **OK**.

In the new worksheet:

3. Enter a title in cell **A1**, **Bins** in cell **A3**, and **Frequency** in cell **B3**.
4. Copy the bin number list in the cell range **D2:D9** of the **UNSTACKED worksheet** and paste this list into cell **A4** of the new worksheet.
5. Select the cell range **B4:B12** that will hold the array formula.

6. Type, but do not press the **Enter** or **Tab** key, the formula **=FREQUENCY(UNSTACKED!$A$1:$A$51, $A$4:$A$11)**. Then, while holding down the **Ctrl** and **Shift** keys, press the **Enter** key to enter the array formula into the cell range **B4:B12**. (Learn more about array formulas in Appendix B.)

7. Adjust the worksheet formatting as necessary.

Note that in step 6, you enter the cell range as **UNSTACKED! $A$1:$A$51** and not as **$A$1:$A$51** because the untallied data are located on another (the UNSTACKED) worksheet. (Learn more about referring to data on another worksheet, as well as the significance of entering the cell range as **$A$1:$A$51** and not as **A1:A51**, in Appendix B.)

Steps 1 through 7 construct a frequency distribution for the meal costs at city restaurants. To construct a frequency distribution for the meal costs at suburban restaurants, repeat steps 1 through 7 but in step 6 type **=FREQUENCY(UNSTACKED!$B$1:$B$51, $A$4:$A$11)** as the array formula.

To display the distributions for the two groups on one worksheet, select the cell range **B3:B11** on one of the worksheets. Right-click that range and click **Copy** in the shortcut menu. Open to the other worksheet. In that other worksheet, right-click cell **C3** and click **Paste Special** in the shortcut menu. In the Paste Special dialog box, click **Values and numbers format** and click **OK**. Adjust the worksheet title as necessary. (Learn more about the Paste Special command in Appendix B.)

Analysis ToolPak (untallied data) Use **Histogram**.

For the example, open to the **UNSTACKED worksheet** of the **Restaurants workbook**. This worksheet contains the meal cost data unstacked in columns A and B and a set of bin numbers appropriate for those data in column D. Then:

1. Select **Data → Data Analysis**. In the Data Analysis dialog box, select **Histogram** from the **Analysis Tools** list and then click **OK**.

In the Histogram dialog box (shown below):

2. Enter **A1:A51** as the **Input Range** and enter **D1:D9** as the **Bin Range**. (If you leave **Bin Range** blank, the procedure creates a set of bins that will not be as well formed as the ones you can specify.)

3. Check **Labels** and click **New Worksheet Ply**.

4. Click **OK** to create the frequency distribution on a new worksheet.

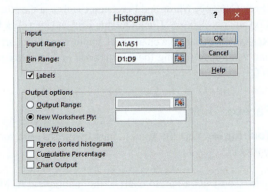

In the new worksheet:

5. Select **row 1**. Right-click this row and click **Insert** in the shortcut menu. Repeat. (This creates two blank rows at the top of the worksheet.)

6. Enter a title in cell **A1**.

The ToolPak creates a frequency distribution that contains an improper bin labeled **More**. Correct this error by using these general instructions:

7. Manually add the frequency count of the **More** row to the frequency count of the preceding row. (For the example, the More row contains a zero for the frequency, so the frequency of the preceding row does not change.)

8. Select the worksheet row (for this example, row 12) that contains the **More** row.

9. Right-click that row and click **Delete** in the shortcut menu.

Steps 1 through 9 construct a frequency distribution for the meal costs at city restaurants. To construct a frequency distribution for the meal costs at suburban restaurants, repeat these nine steps but in step 6 enter **B1:B51** as the **Input Range.**

The Relative Frequency, Percentage, and Cumulative Distributions

Key Technique Add columns that contain formulas for the relative frequency or percentage and cumulative percentage to a previously constructed frequency distribution.

Example Create a distribution that includes the relative frequency or percentage as well as the cumulative percentage information found in Tables 2.11 (relative frequency and percentage) and 2.14 (cumulative percentage) in Section 2.2 for the restaurant meal cost data.

PHStat (untallied data) Use **Frequency Distribution**.

For the example, use the *PHStat* instructions in "The Frequency Distribution" to construct a frequency distribution. Note that the frequency distribution constructed by PHStat also includes columns for the percentages and cumulative percentages. To change the column of percentages to a column of relative frequencies, reformat that column. For example, open to the new worksheet that contains the city restaurant frequency distribution and:

1. Select the cell range **C4:C11**, right-click, and select **Format Cells** from the shortcut menu.

2. In the **Number** tab of the Format Cells dialog box, select **Number** as the **Category** and click **OK**.

Then repeat these two steps for the new worksheet that contains the suburban restaurant frequency distribution.

In-Depth Excel (untallied data) Use the **Distributions workbook** as a model.

For the example, first construct a frequency distribution created using the *In-Depth Excel* instructions in "The Frequency

Distribution." Open to the new worksheet that contains the frequency distribution for the city restaurants and:

1. Enter **Percentage** in cell **C3** and **Cumulative Pctage** in cell **D3**.
2. Enter **=B4/SUM($B$4:$B$11)** in cell **C4** and copy this formula down through **row 11**.
3. Enter **=C4** in cell **D4**.
4. Enter **=C5 + D4** in cell **D5** and copy this formula down through row **11**.
5. Select the cell range **C4:D11**, right-click, and click **Format Cells** in the shortcut menu.
6. In the **Number** tab of the Format Cells dialog box, click **Percentage** in the **Category** list and click **OK**.

Then open to the worksheet that contains the frequency distribution for the suburban restaurants and repeat steps 1 through 6.

If you want column C to display relative frequencies instead of percentages, enter **Rel. Frequencies** in cell **C3**. Select the cell range **C4:C12**, right-click, and click **Format Cells** in the shortcut menu. In the **Number** tab of the Format Cells dialog box, click **Number** in the **Category** list and click **OK**.

Analysis ToolPak Use **Histogram** and then modify the worksheet created.

For the example, first construct the frequency distributions using the *Analysis ToolPak* instructions in "The Frequency Distribution." Then use the *In-Depth Excel* instructions to modify those distributions.

EG2.3 VISUALIZING CATEGORICAL VARIABLES

Many of the *In-Depth Excel* instructions in the rest of this Excel Guide refer to the following labeled Charts group illustration.

The Bar Chart and the Pie Chart

Key Technique Use the Excel bar or pie chart feature. If the variable to be visualized is untallied, first construct a summary table (see the Section EG2.1 "The Summary Table" instructions).

Example Construct a bar or pie chart from a summary table similar to Table 2.3 on page 33.

PHStat Use **One-Way Tables & Charts**.
For the example, use the Section EG2.1 "The Summary Table" *PHStat* instructions, but in step 3, check either **Bar Chart** or **Pie Chart** (or both) in addition to entering a **Title**, checking **Percentage Column**, and clicking **OK**.

In-Depth Excel Use the **Summary Table workbook** as a model.
For the example, open to the **OneWayTable worksheet** of the **Summary Table workbook**. (The PivotTable in this worksheet

was constructed using the Section EG2.1 "The Summary Table" instructions.) To construct a bar chart:

1. Select cell range **A4:B6**. (Begin your selection at cell B6 and not at cell A4, as you would normally do.)
2. In Excel 2013, select **Insert**, then the **Bar icon** in the **Charts group** (#2 in the Charts group illustration), and then select the **first 2-D Bar** gallery item (**Clustered Bar**). In other Excels, select **Insert ➔ Bar** and then select the **first 2-D Bar** gallery item (**Clustered Bar**).
3. Right-click the **Risk** drop-down button in the chart and click **Hide All Field Buttons on Chart**.
4. (Excel 2013) Select **Design ➔ Add Chart Element ➔ Axis Titles ➔ Primary Horizontal**.
   (Other Excels) Select **Layout ➔ Axis Titles ➔ Primary Horizontal Axis Title ➔ Title Below Axis**. Select the words "Axis Title" in the chart and enter the title **Frequency**.
5. Relocate the chart to a chart sheet and turn off the chart legend and gridlines by using the instructions in Appendix Section B.6.

Although not the case with the example, sometimes the horizontal-axis scale of a bar chart will not begin at 0. If this occurs, right-click the horizontal (value) axis in the bar chart and click **Format Axis** in the shortcut menu. In the Excel 2013 Format Axis task pane, click **Axis Options**. In the Axis Options, enter **0** in the **Minimum** box and then close the pane. In other Excels, in the Format Axis dialog box, click **Axis Options** in the left pane. In the Axis Options right pane, click the first **Fixed** option button (for Minimum), enter **0** in its box, and then click **Close**.

To construct a pie chart, replace steps 2, 4, and 5 with these steps:

2. In Excel 2013, select **Insert**, then the **Pie icon** (#4 in the Step 4 illustration), and then select the **first 2-D Pie** gallery item (**Pie**). In other Excels, select **Insert ➔ Pie** and then select the **first 2-D Pie** gallery item (**Pie**).
4. (Excel 2013) Select **Design ➔ Add Chart Element ➔ Data Labels ➔ More Data Label Options**. In the Format Data Labels task pane, click **Label Options**. In the Label Options, check **Category Name** and **Percentage**, clear the other Label Contains check boxes, and click **Outside End**. (To see the Label Options, you may have to first click the chart [fourth] icon near the top of the task pane.) Then, close the task pane.
   (Other Excels) Select **Layout ➔ Data Labels ➔ More Data Label Options**. In the Format Data Labels dialog box, click **Label Options** in the left pane. In the Label Options right pane, check **Category Name** and **Percentage** and clear the other Label Contains check boxes. Click **Outside End** and then click **Close**.
5. Relocate the chart to a chart sheet and turn off the chart legend and gridlines by using the instructions in Appendix Section B.6.

The Pareto Chart

Key Technique Use the Excel chart feature with a modified summary table.

Example Construct a Pareto chart of the incomplete ATM transactions equivalent to Figure 2.4 on page 49.

PHStat Use **One-Way Tables & Charts**.
For the example, open to the **DATA worksheet** of the **ATM Transactions workbook**. Select **PHStat → Descriptive Statistics → One-Way Tables & Charts**. In the procedure's dialog box:

1. Click **Table of Frequencies** (because the worksheet contains tallied data).
2. Enter **A1:B8** as the **Freq. Table Cell Range** and check **First cell contains label**.
3. Enter a **Title**, check **Pareto Chart**, and click **OK**.

In-Depth Excel Use the **Pareto workbook** as a model.
For the example, open to the **ATMTable worksheet** of the **ATM Transactions workbook**. Begin by sorting the modified table by decreasing order of frequency:

1. Select row **11** (the Total row), right-click, and click **Hide** in the shortcut menu. (This prevents the total row from getting sorted.)
2. Select cell **B4** (the first frequency), right-click, and select **Sort → Sort Largest to Smallest**.
3. Select rows **10** and **12** (there is no row 11 visible), right-click, and click **Unhide** in the shortcut menu to restore row 11.

Next, add a column for cumulative percentage:

4. Enter **Cumulative Pct.** in cell **D3**. Enter **=C4** in cell **D4**. Enter **=D4 + C5** in cell **D5** and copy this formula down through **row 10**.
5. Adjust the formatting of column D as necessary.

Next, create the Pareto chart:

6. Select the cell range **A3:A10** and while holding down the **Ctrl** key also select the cell range **C3:D10**.
7. In Excel 2013, select **Insert**, then the **Column icon** (#1 in the illustration on page 85), and select the **first 2-D Column** gallery item (**Clustered Column**). In other Excels, select **Insert → Column** and select the **first 2-D Column** gallery item (**Clustered Column**).
8. Select **Format**. In the **Current Selection** group, select **Series "Cumulative Pct."** from the drop-down list and then click **Format Selection**.
9. (Excel 2013) In the Format Data Series task pane, click **Series Options**. In the Series Options, click **Secondary Axis**, and then close the task pane. (To see the Series Options, you may have to first click the chart [third] icon near the top of the task pane.)
   (**Other Excels**) In the Format Data Series dialog box, click **Series Options** in the left pane, and in the **Series Options** right pane, click **Secondary Axis**. Click **Close**.
10. With the cumulative percentage series still selected in the Current Selection group, select **Design → Change Chart Type**. In Excel 2013, in the Change Chart Type dialog box, click **Combo** in the **All Charts** tab. In the **Cumulative Pct.** drop-down list, select the **fourth Line** gallery item (**Line with Markers**). Then, check **Secondary Axis** for the Cumulative Pct. and click **OK**. In other Excels, in the Change Chart Type dialog box, select the **fourth Line** gallery item (**Line with Markers**) and click **OK**.

Next, set the maximum value of the primary and secondary (left and right) *Y* axis scales to 100%. For each *Y* axis:

11. Right-click on the axis and click **Format Axis** in the shortcut menu.
12. (**Excel 2013**) In the Format Axis task pane, click **Axis Options.** In the Axis Options, enter **1** in the **Maximum** box. Click **Tick Marks** and select **Outside** from the **Major** type drop-down list. Then, close the Format Axis pane. (To see the Axis Options, you may have to first click the chart [fourth] icon near the top of the task pane.)
    (**Other Excels**) In the Format Axis dialog box, click **Axis Options** in the left pane, and in the **Axis Options** right pane, click the **Fixed** option button for Maximum, enter **1** in its box, and click **Close**.
13. Relocate the chart to a chart sheet, turn off the chart legend and gridlines, and add chart and axis titles by using the instructions in Appendix Section B.6.

If you use a PivotTable as a summary table, replace steps 1 through 6 with these steps:

1. Add a percentage column in column C. (See the Section EG2.1 "The Summary Table" instructions, Steps 10 through 13.)
2. Add a cumulative percentage column in column D. Enter **Cumulative Pctage** in cell **D3**. Enter **=C4** in cell **D4**. Enter **=C5 + D4** in cell **D5**, and copy the formula down through all the rows in the PivotTable.
3. Select the total row, right-click, and click **Hide** in the shortcut menu. (This prevents the total row from getting sorted.)
4. Right-click the cell that contains the first frequency (typically this will be cell **B4**).
5. Right-click and select **Sort → Sort Largest to Smallest**.
6. Select the cell range of only the percentage and cumulative percentage columns (the equivalent of the cell range C3:D10 in the example).

The Pareto chart constructed from a PivotTable using these modified steps will not have proper labels for the categories. To add the correct labels, right-click over the chart and click **Select Data** in the shortcut menu. In the Select Data Source dialog box, click **Edit** that appears under **Horizontal (Category) Axis Labels**. In the Axis Labels dialog box, drag the mouse to *select* the cell range (**A4:A10** in the example) to enter that cell range. Do *not* type the cell range in the **Axis label range** box as you would otherwise do for the reasons explained in Appendix Section B.7. Click **OK** in this dialog box and then click **OK** in the original dialog box.

The Side-by-Side Chart

Key Technique Use an Excel bar chart that is based on a contingency table.

Example Construct a side-by-side chart that displays the fund type and risk level, similar to Figure 2.6 on page 50.

PHStat Use **Two-Way Tables & Charts**.
For the example, use the Section EG2.1 "The Contingency Table" *PHStat* instructions on page 81, but in step 4, check **Side-by-Side Bar Chart** in addition to entering a **Title** and clicking **OK**.

In-Depth Excel Use the **Contingency Table workbook** as a model.

For the example, open to the **TwoWayTable worksheet** of the **Contingency Table workbook** and:

1. Select cell **A3** (or any other cell inside the PivotTable).
2. Select **Insert → Bar** and select the **first 2-D Bar** gallery item (**Clustered Bar**).
3. Right-click the **Risk** drop-down button in the chart and click **Hide All Field Buttons on Chart**.
4. Relocate the chart to a chart sheet, turn off the gridlines, and add chart and axis titles by using the instructions in Appendix Section B.6.

When creating a chart from a contingency table that is not a PivotTable, select the cell range of the contingency table, including row and column headings, but excluding the total row and total column, as step 1.

If you need to switch the row and column variables in a side-by-side chart, right-click the chart and then click **Select Data** in the shortcut menu. In the Select Data Source dialog box, click **Switch Row/Column** and then click **OK**. (In Excel 2007, if the chart is based on a PivotTable, the **Switch Row/Column** as that button will be disabled. In that case, you need to change the Pivot-Table to change the chart.)

EG2.4 VISUALIZING NUMERICAL VARIABLES

The Stem-and-Leaf Display

Key Technique Enter leaves as a string of digits that begin with the ' (apostrophe) character.

Example Construct a stem-and-leaf display of the one-year return percentage for the value retirement funds, similar to Figure 2.7 on page 53.

PHStat Use the **Stem-and-Leaf Display**.

For the example, open to the **UNSTACKED worksheet** of the **Retirement Funds workbook**. Select **PHStat → Descriptive Statistics → Stem-and-Leaf Display**. In the procedure's dialog box (shown in the next column):

1. Enter **B1:B90** as the **Variable Cell Range** and check **First cell contains label**.
2. Click **Set stem unit as** and enter **10** in its box.
3. Enter a **Title** and click **OK**.

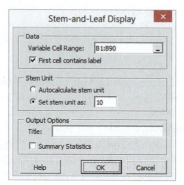

When creating other displays, use the **Set stem unit as** option sparingly and only if **Autocalculate stem unit** creates a display that has too few or too many stems. (Any stem unit you specify must be a power of 10.)

In-Depth Excel Use the **Stem-and-leaf workbook** as a model. Manually construct the stems and leaves on a new worksheet to create a stem-and-leaf display. Adjust the column width of the column that holds the leaves as necessary.

The Histogram

Key Technique Modify an Excel column chart.

Example Construct histograms for the one-year return percentages for the growth and value retirement funds, similar to Figure 2.9 on page 55.

PHStat Use **Histogram & Polygons**.

For the example, open to the **DATA worksheet** of the **Retirement Funds workbook**. Select **PHStat → Descriptive Statistics → Histogram & Polygons**. In the procedure's dialog box (shown below):

1. Enter **I1:I317** as the **Variable Cell Range**, **P1:P12** as the **Bins Cell Range**, **Q1:Q11** as the **Midpoints Cell Range**, and check **First cell in each range contains label**.
2. Click **Multiple Groups - Stacked** and enter **C1:C317** as the **Grouping Variable Cell Range**. (In the DATA worksheet, the one-year return percentages for both types of retirement funds are stacked, or placed in a single column. The column C values allow PHStat to separate the returns for growth funds from the returns for the value funds.)
3. Enter a **Title**, check **Histogram**, and click **OK**.

PHStat inserts two new worksheets, each of which contains a frequency distribution and a histogram. To relocate the histograms to their own chart sheets, use the instructions in Appendix Section B.6.

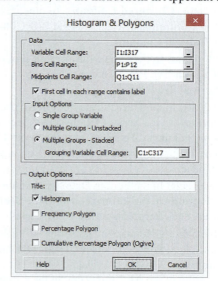

As explained in Section 2.2, you cannot define an explicit lower boundary for the first bin, so the first bin can never have a midpoint. Therefore, the **Midpoints Cell Range** you enter must have one fewer cell than the **Bins Cell Range**. PHStat associates the first midpoint with the second bin and uses—as the label for the first bin.

The example uses the workaround discussed in "Classes and Excel Bins" on page 40. When you use this workaround, the histogram bar labeled—will *always* be a zero bar. Appendix Section B.8 explains how you can delete this unnecessary bar from the histogram, as was done for the examples shown in Section 2.4.

In-Depth Excel Use the **Histogram workbook** as a model. For the example, first construct frequency distributions for the growth and value funds. Open to the **UNSTACKED worksheet** of the **Retirement Funds workbook**. This worksheet contains the retirement funds data unstacked in columns A and B and a set of bin numbers and midpoints appropriate for those variables in columns D and E. Then:

1. Right-click the **UNSTACKED** sheet tab and click **Insert** in the shortcut menu.
2. In the **General** tab of the Insert dialog box, click **Worksheet** and then click **OK**.

In the new worksheet,

3. Enter a title in cell **A1**, **Bins** in cell **A3**, **Frequency** in cell **B3**, and **Midpoints** in cell **C3**.
4. Copy the bin number list in the cell range **D2:D12** of the **UNSTACKED worksheet** and paste this list into cell **A4** of the new worksheet.
5. Enter **'--** in cell **C4**. Copy the midpoints list in the cell range **E2:E11** of the **UNSTACKED worksheet** and paste this list into cell **C5** of the new worksheet.
6. Select the cell range **B4:B14** that will hold the array formula.
7. Type, but do not press the **Enter** or **Tab** key, the formula =FREQUENCY(UNSTACKED!$A$2:$A$228, $A$4: $A$14). Then, while holding down the **Ctrl** and **Shift** keys, press the **Enter** key to enter the array formula into the cell range **B4:B14**.
8. Adjust the worksheet formatting as necessary.

Steps 1 through 8 construct a frequency distribution for the growth retirement funds. To construct a frequency distribution for the value retirement funds, repeat steps 1 through 8 but in step 7 type =FREQUENCY(UNSTACKED!$B$1:$B$90, $A$4: $A$14) as the array formula.

Having constructed the two frequency distributions, continue by constructing the two histograms. Open to the worksheet that contains the frequency distribution for the growth funds and:

1. Select the cell range **B3:B14** (the cell range of the frequencies).
2. In Excel 2013, select **Insert**, then the **Column icon** in the **Charts group** (#3 in the illustration on page 84), and then select the **first 2-D Column** gallery item (**Clustered Column**). In other Excels, select **Insert → Column** and select the **first 2-D Column** gallery item (**Clustered Column**).
3. Right-click the chart and click **Select Data** in the shortcut menu.

In the Select Data Source dialog box:

4. Click **Edit** under the **Horizontal (Categories) Axis Labels** heading.
5. In the Axis Labels dialog box, drag the mouse to *select* the cell range **C4:C14** (containing the midpoints) to enter that

cell range. Do not type this cell range in the Axis label range box as you would otherwise do for the reasons explained in Appendix Section B.7. Click **OK** in this dialog box and then click **OK** (in the Select Data Source dialog box).

In the chart:

6. Right-click inside a bar and click **Format Data Series** in the shortcut menu.
7. (Excel 2013) In the Format Data Series task pane, click **Series Options**. In the Series Options, click **Series Options,** enter **0** in the **Gap Width** box, and then close the task pane. (To see the Series Options, you may have to first click the chart [third] icon near the top of the task pane.)
   (Other Excels) In the Format Data Series dialog box, click **Series Options** in the left pane, and in the Series Options right pane, change the **Gap Width** slider to **No Gap**. Click **Close**.
8. Relocate the chart to a chart sheet, turn off the chart legend and gridlines, add axis titles, and modify the chart title by using the instructions in Appendix Section B.6.

This example uses the workaround discussed in "Classes and Excel Bins" on page 40. When you use this workaround, the histogram bar labeled—will *always* be a zero bar. Appendix Section B.8 explains how you can delete this unnecessary bar from the histogram, as was done for the examples shown in Section 2.4.

Analysis ToolPak Use **Histogram**. For the example, open to the **UNSTACKED worksheet** of the **Retirement Funds workbook** and:

1. Select **Data → Data Analysis**. In the Data Analysis dialog box, select **Histogram** from the **Analysis Tools** list and then click **OK**.

In the Histogram dialog box:

2. Enter **A1:A228** as the **Input Range** and enter **D1:D12** as the **Bin Range**.
3. Check **Labels**, click **New Worksheet Ply**, and check **Chart Output**.
4. Click **OK** to create the frequency distribution and histogram on a new worksheet.

In the new worksheet:

5. Follow steps 5 through 9 of the *Analysis ToolPak* instructions in "The Frequency Distribution" on page 83.

These steps construct a frequency distribution and histogram for the growth funds. To construct a frequency distribution and histogram for the value funds, repeat the nine steps but in step 2 enter **B1:B90** as the **Input Range**. You will need to correct several formatting errors that Excel makes to the histograms it constructs. For each histogram:

1. Right-click inside a bar and click **Format Data Series** in the shortcut menu.
2. (Excel 2013) In the Format Data Series task pane, click **Series Options**. In the Series Options, click **Series Options,** enter **0** in the **Gap Width** box, and then close the task pane. (To see the Series Options, you may have to first click the chart [third] icon near the top of the task pane.)

(Other Excels) In the Format Data Series dialog box, click **Series Options** in the left pane, and in the Series Options right pane, change the **Gap Width** slider to **No Gap**. Click **Close**.

Histogram bars are labeled by bin numbers. To change the labeling to midpoints, open to each of the new worksheets and:

3. Enter **Midpoints** in cell **C1** and **'--** in cell **C2**. Copy the cell range **E2:E11** of the **UNSTACKED worksheet** and paste this list into cell **C5** of the new worksheet.
4. Right-click the histogram and click **Select Data**.
5. In the Select Data Source dialog box, click **Edit** under the **Horizontal (Categories) Axis Labels** heading.
6. In the Axis Labels dialog box, drag the mouse to select the cell range **C2:C12** to enter that cell range. Do not type this cell range in the Axis label range box as you would otherwise do for the reasons explained in Appendix Section B.7. Click **OK** in this dialog box and then click **OK** (in the Select Data Source dialog box).
7. Relocate the chart to a chart sheet, turn off the chart legend, and modify the chart title by using the instructions in Appendix Section B.6.

This example uses the workaround discussed on page 40, "Classes and Excel Bins." Appendix Section B.8 explains how you can delete this unnecessary bar from the histogram, as was done for the examples shown in Section 2.4.

The Percentage Polygon and the Cumulative Percentage Polygon (Ogive)

Key Technique Modify an Excel line chart that is based on a frequency distribution.

Example Construct percentage polygons and cumulative percentage polygons for the one-year return percentages for the growth and value retirement funds, similar to Figure 2.11 on page 56 and equivalent to Figure 2.12 on page 57.

PHStat Use **Histogram & Polygons**.
For the example, use the *PHStat* instructions for creating a histogram on page 86 but in step 3 of those instructions, also check **Percentage Polygon** and **Cumulative Percentage Polygon (Ogive)** before clicking **OK**.

In-Depth Excel Use the **Polygons workbook** as a model.
For the example, open to the **UNSTACKED worksheet** of the **Retirement Funds workbook** and follow steps 1 through 8 to construct a frequency distribution for the growth retirement funds. Repeat steps 1 through 8 but in step 7 type the array formula =**FREQUENCY(UNSTACKED!$B$1:$B$90, $A$4: $A$14)** to construct a frequency distribution for the value funds. Open to the worksheet that contains the growth funds frequency distribution and:

1. Select column C. Right-click and click **Insert** in the shortcut menu. Right-click and click **Insert** in the shortcut menu a second time. (The worksheet contains new, blank columns C and D and the midpoints column is now column E.)
2. Enter **Percentage** in cell **C3** and **Cumulative Pctage.** in cell **D3**.

3. Enter = **B4/SUM($B$4:$B$14)** in cell **C4** and copy this formula down through **row 14**.
4. Enter = **C4** in cell **D4**.
5. Enter = **C5 + D4** in cell **D5** and copy this formula down through row **14**.
6. Select the cell range **C4:D14**, right-click, and click **Format Cells** in the shortcut menu.
7. In the **Number** tab of the Format Cells dialog box, click **Percentage** in the **Category** list and click **OK**.

Open to the worksheet that contains the value funds frequency distribution and repeat steps 1 through 7. To construct the percentage polygons, open to the worksheet that contains the growth funds distribution and:

1. Select cell range **C4:C14**.
2. In Excel 2013, select **Insert**, then select the **Line icon** in the **Charts group** (#4 in the illustration on page 84), and then select the **fourth 2-D Line** gallery item (**Line with Markers**). In other Excels, select **Insert → Line** and select the **fourth 2-D Line** gallery item (**Line with Markers**).
3. Right-click the chart and click **Select Data** in the shortcut menu.

In the Select Data Source dialog box:

4. Click **Edit** under the **Legend Entries (Series)** heading. In the Edit Series dialog box, enter the *formula* =**"Growth Funds"** as the **Series name** and click **OK**.
5. Click **Edit** under the **Horizontal (Categories) Axis Labels** heading. In the Axis Labels dialog box, drag the mouse to select the cell range **E4:E14** to enter that cell range. Do not type this cell range in the Axis label range box as you would otherwise do for the reasons explained in Appendix Section B.7.
6. Click **OK** in this dialog box and then click **OK** (in the Select Data Source dialog box).

Back in the chart:

7. Relocate the chart to a chart sheet, turn off the chart gridlines, add axis titles, and modify the chart title by using the instructions in Appendix Section B.6.

In the new chart sheet:

8. Right-click the chart and click **Select Data** in the shortcut menu.
9. In the Select Data Source dialog box, click **Add**.

In the Edit Series dialog box:

10. Enter the formula =**"Value Funds"** as the **Series name** and press **Tab**.
11. With the current value in **Series values** highlighted, click the worksheet tab for the worksheet that contains the value funds distribution.
12. Drag the mouse to select the cell range **C4:C14** to enter that cell range as the **Series values**. Do not type this cell range in the Series values box as you would otherwise do, for the reasons explained in Appendix Section B.7.
13. Click **OK**. Back in the Select Data Source dialog box, click **OK**.

To construct the cumulative percentage polygons, open to the worksheet that contains the growth funds distribution and repeat steps 1 through 13 but replace steps 1, 5, and 12 with these steps:

1. Select the cell range **D4:D14**.
5. Click **Edit** under the **Horizontal (Categories) Axis Labels** heading. In the Axis Labels dialog box, drag the mouse to select the cell range **A4:A14** to enter that cell range.
12. Drag the mouse to select the cell range **D4:D14** to enter that cell range as the **Series values**.

If the *Y* axis of the cumulative percentage polygon extends past 100%, right-click the axis and click **Format Axis** in the short-cut menu. In the Excel 2013 Format Axis task pane, click **Axis Options**. In the Axis Options, enter **0** in the **Minimum** box and then close the pane. In other Excels, you set this value in the Format Axis dialog box. Click **Axis Options** in the left pane, and in the Axis Options right pane, click the first **Fixed** option button (for Minimum), enter **0** in its box, and then click **Close**.

EG2.5 VISUALIZING TWO NUMERICAL VARIABLES

The Scatter Plot

Key Technique Use the Excel scatter chart.

Example Construct a scatter plot of revenue and value for NBA teams, similar to Figure 2.14 on page 61.

PHStat Use **Scatter Plot**.
For the example, open to the **DATA worksheet** of the **NBAValues workbook**. Select **PHStat → Descriptive Statistics → Scatter Plot**. In the procedure's dialog box (shown below):

1. Enter **D1:D31** as the **Y Variable Cell Range**.
2. Enter **C1:C31** as the **X Variable Cell Range**.
3. Check **First cells in each range contains label**.
4. Enter a **Title** and click **OK**.

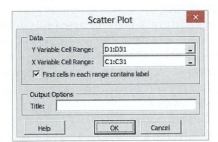

To add a superimposed line like the one shown in Figure 2.14, click the chart and use step 3 of the *In-Depth Excel* instructions.

In-Depth Excel Use the **Scatter Plot workbook** as a model. For the example, open to the **DATA worksheet** of the **NBAValues workbook** and:

1. Select the cell range **C1:D31.**
2. In Excel 2013, select **Insert**, then the **Scatter (X,Y) icon** in the **Charts group** (#5 in the illustration on page 84), and then select the **first Scatter** gallery item (**Scatter**). In other Excels,

select **Insert → Scatter** and select the **first Scatter** gallery item (**Scatter with only Markers**).
3. In Excel 2013, select **Design → Add Chart Element → Trendline → Linear**. In other Excels, select **Layout → Trendline → Linear Trendline**.
4. Relocate the chart to a chart sheet, turn off the chart legend and gridlines, add axis titles, and modify the chart title by using the instructions in Appendix Section B.6.

When constructing Excel scatter charts with other variables, make sure that the *X* variable column precedes (is to the left of) the *Y* variable column. (If the worksheet is arranged *Y* then *X*, cut and paste so that the *Y* variable column appears to the right of the *X* variable column.)

The Time-Series Plot

Key Technique Use the Excel scatter chart.

Example Construct a time-series plot of movie revenue per year from 1995 to 2012, similar to Figure 2.15 on page 62.

In-Depth Excel Use the **Time Series workbook** as a model. For the example, open to the **DATA worksheet** of the **Movie Revenues workbook** and:

1. Select the cell range **A1:B19**.
2. In Excel 2013, select **Insert**, then select the **Scatter (X, Y) icon** in the **Charts group** (#5 in the illustration on page 84), and then select the **fourth Scatter** gallery item (**Scatter with Straight Lines and Markers**). In other Excels, select **Insert → Scatter** and select the **fourth Scatter** gallery item (**Scatter with Straight Lines and Markers**).
3. Relocate the chart to a chart sheet, turn off the chart legend and gridlines, add axis titles, and modify the chart title by using the instructions in Appendix Section B.6.

When constructing time-series charts with other variables, make sure that the *X* variable column precedes (is to the left of) the *Y* variable column. (If the worksheet is arranged *Y* then *X*, cut and paste so that the *Y* variable column appears to the right of the *X* variable column.)

EG2.6 ORGANIZING AND VISUALIZING A SET OF VARIABLES

Multidimensional Contingency Tables

Key Technique Use the Excel PivotTable feature.

Example Construct a PivotTable showing percentage of overall total for fund type, risk, and market cap for the retirement funds sample, similar to the one shown at the right in Figure 2.16 on page 64.

In-Depth Excel Use the **MCT workbook** as a model. For the example, open to the **DATA worksheet** of the **Retirement Funds workbook** and:

1. Select **Insert → PivotTable**.

In the Create PivotTable dialog box:

2. Click **Select a table or range** and enter **A1:N317** as the **Table/Range**.
3. Click **New Worksheet** and then click **OK**.

Excel inserts a new worksheet and displays the PivotTable Field List pane. The worksheet contains a graphical representation of a PivotTable that will change as you work inside the PivotTable Field List (or PivotTable Fields) task pane. In that pane (partially shown below):

4. Drag **Type** in the **Choose fields to add to report** box and drop it in the **ROWS** (or **Row Labels**) box.
5. Drag **Market Cap** in the **Choose fields to add to report** box and drop it in the **ROWS** (or **Row Labels**) box.
6. Drag **Risk** in the **Choose fields to add to report** box and drop it in the **COLUMNS** (or **Column Labels**) box.
7. Drag **Type** in the **Choose fields to add to report** box a second time and drop it in the **Σ VALUES** box. The dropped label changes to **Count of Type**.
8. Click (not right-click) the dropped label **Count of Type** and click **Value Field Settings** in the shortcut menu.

In the Value Field Settings dialog box:

9. Click the **Show Values As** tab and select **% of Grand Total** from the **Show values as** drop-down list (shown below).
10. Click **OK**.

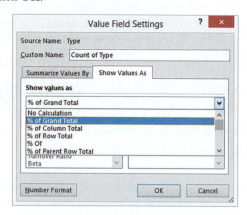

In the PivotTable:

11. Enter a title in cell **A1**.
12. Enter a **space character** in cell **A3** to replace the value "Count of Type."
13. Follow steps 8 and 9 of the *In-Depth Excel* "The Contingency Table" instructions on page 82 to relocate the Low column from column D to column B.

If the PivotTable you construct does not contain a row and column for the grand totals as the PivotTables in Figure 2.16 contain, follow steps 10 through 15 of the *In-Depth Excel*, "The Contingency Table" instructions to include the grand totals.

Adding a Numerical Variable to a Multidimensional Contingency Table

Key Technique Alter the contents of the Σ Values box in the PivotTable Field List pane.

Example Construct a PivotTable of fund type, risk, and market cap, showing the mean three-year return percentage for the retirement funds sample, similar to the one shown in Figure 2.17 on page 64.

In-Depth Excel Use the **MCT workbook** as a model.
For the example, first construct the PivotTable showing percentage of overall total for fund type, risk, and market cap for the retirement funds sample using the 13-step instructions of the "Multidimensional Contingency Table" *In-Depth Excel* instructions that begins on the previous page. Then continue with these steps:

14. If the PivotTable Field List pane is not visible, right-click cell **A3** and click **Show Field List** in the shortcut menu.

In the PivotTable Field List pane:

15. Drag the **blank label** (initially labeled **Count of Type** after step 7) in the **Σ VALUES** box and drop it outside the pane to delete this label. The PivotTable changes and all of the percentages disappear.
16. Drag **10YrReturn%** in the **Choose fields to add to report** box and drop it in the **Σ VALUES** box. The dropped label changes to **Sum of 10YrReturn%**
17. Click **Sum of 10YrReturn%** and click **Value Field Settings** in the shortcut menu. In the Value Field Settings dialog box (shown below):
18. Click the **Summarize Values By** tab and select **Average** from the list. The **Custom Name** changes to **Average of 10YrReturn%**.
19. Click **OK**.

In the PivotTable:

20. Select cell range **B5:E13**, right-click, and click **Format Cells** in the shortcut menu. In the Number tab of the Format Cells dialog box, click **Number**, set the **Decimal places** to **2**, and click **OK**.

Treemap

In-Depth Excel Use the **Treemap App** (requires being signed in to the Microsoft Office Store and Excel 2011, Excel 2013, or Office 365).

For example, to construct the Figure 2.19 treemap on page 66 that summarizes the small market cap funds with low risk, open to the **SmallLowDATA worksheet** of the **Retirement Funds workbook** and:

1. Select **Insert → Apps for Office** and click **Treemap** in the Apps for Office gallery. (If **Treemap** is not listed, the Treemap App has not been installed.)

In the Treemap panel:

2. Click **Name list** and in the Select Data dialog box enter **C2:B26** and click **OK**. A treemap begins to take shape in the Treemap panel.

3. Click **Size** and in the Select Data dialog box enter **E2:E26** and click **OK**.
4. Click **Color** (under **Size**) and in the Select Data dialog box enter **M2:M26** and click **OK**.
5. Enter a title in the **Title** box.

If the treemap displayed does not use the red-to-blue spectrum, click the **color icon** (under Title) and click the red-to-blue (third) spectrum.

If you use an Excel version older than Excel 2011 (or a newer version not signed into the Microsoft Office Store), open to the **Data worksheet** of the **Treemap workbook** to view a non-modifiable version of the Figure 2.19 treemap.

CHAPTER 2 MINITAB GUIDE

MG2.1 ORGANIZING CATEGORICAL VARIABLES

The Summary Table

Use **Tally Individual Variables** to create a summary table. For example, to create a summary table similar to Table 2.3 on page 33, open to the **Retirement Funds worksheet**. Select **Stat → Tables → Tally Individual Variables**. In the procedure's dialog box (shown at below):

1. Double-click **C8 Risk** in the variables list to add **Risk** to the **Variables** box.
2. Check **Counts** and **Percents**.
3. Click **OK**.

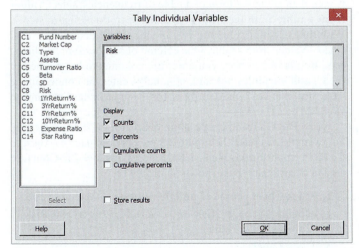

The Contingency Table

Use **Cross Tabulation and Chi-Square** to create a contingency table. For example, to create a contingency table similar to Table 2.4 on page 34, open to the **Retirement Funds worksheet**. Select

Stat → Tables → Cross Tabulation and Chi-Square. In the procedure's dialog box (shown below):

1. Enter **Type** in the **For rows** box.
2. Enter **Risk** in the **For columns** box
3. Check **Counts**.
4. Click **OK**.

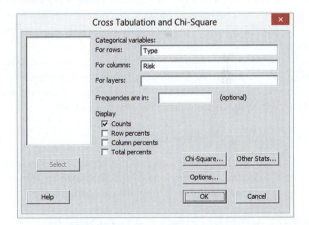

To create the other types of contingency tables shown in Tables 2.5 through 2.7, check **Row percents, Column percents**, or **Total percents**, respectively, in step 3.

MG2.2 ORGANIZING NUMERICAL VARIABLES

Stacked and Unstacked Data

Use **Stack** or **Unstack Columns** to rearrange data. For example, to unstack the **1YrReturn%** variable in column C9 of the **Retirement Funds worksheet** by fund type, open to that worksheet. Select **Data → Unstack Columns**. In the procedure's dialog box (shown on page 92):

1. Double-click **C9 1YrReturn%** in the variables list to add **'1YrReturn%'** to the **Unstack the data in** box and press **Tab**.

2. Double-click **C3 Type** in the variables list to add **Type** to the **Using subscripts in** box.
3. Click **After last column in use**.
4. Check **Name the columns containing the unstacked data**.
5. Check **OK**.

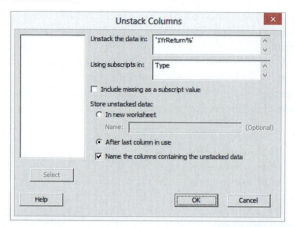

Minitab inserts two new columns, **1YrReturn%_Growth** and **1YrReturn%_Value**, the names of which you can edit.

To stack columns, select **Data → Stack → Columns**. In the Stack Columns dialog box, add the names of columns that contain the data to be stacked to the **Stack the following columns** box and then click either **New worksheet** or **Column of current worksheet** as the place to store the stacked data.

The Ordered Array

Use **Sort** to create an ordered array. Select **Data → Sort** and in the Sort dialog box (not shown), double-click a column name in the variables list to add it to the **Sort column(s)** box and then press **Tab**. Double-click the same column name in the variables list to add it to the first **By column** box. Click either **New worksheet**, **Original column(s)**, or **Column(s) of current worksheet**. (If you choose the third option, also enter the name of the column in which to place the ordered data in the box). Click **OK**.

The Frequency Distribution

There are no Minitab commands that use classes that you specify to create frequency distributions of the type seen in Tables 2.9 through 2.12. (See also "The Histogram" in Section MG2.4.)

MG2.3 VISUALIZING CATEGORICAL VARIABLES

The Bar Chart and the Pie Chart

Use **Bar Chart** to create a bar chart from a summary table and use **Pie Chart** to create a pie chart from a summary table. For example, to create the Figure 2.2 bar chart on page 47, open to the **Retirement Funds worksheet**. Select **Graph → Bar Chart**. In the procedure's dialog box (shown first in right column):

1. Select **Counts of unique values** from the **Bars represent** drop-down list.
2. In the gallery of choices, click **Simple**.

3. Click **OK**.

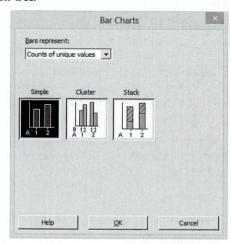

In the Bar Chart - Counts of unique values, Simple dialog box (shown below):

4. Double-click **C8 Risk** in the variables list to add **Risk** to **Categorical variables**.
5. Click **OK**.

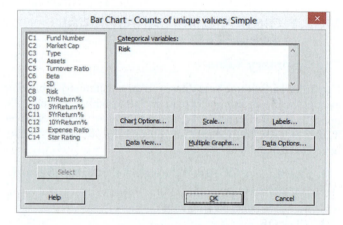

If your data are in the form of a table of frequencies, select **Values from a table** from the **Bars represent** drop-down list in step 1. With this selection, clicking **OK** in step 3 will display the "Bar Chart - Values from a table, One column of values, Simple" dialog box. In this dialog box, you enter the columns to be graphed in the **Graph variables** box and, optionally, enter the column in the worksheet that holds the categories for the table in the **Categorical variable** box.

Use **Pie Chart** to create a pie chart from a summary table. For example, to create the Figure 2.3 pie chart on page 47, open to the **Retirement Funds worksheet**. Select **Graph → Pie Chart**. In the Pie Chart dialog box (shown on page 93):

1. Click **Chart counts of unique values** and then press **Tab**.
2. Double-click **C8 Risk** in the variables list to add **Risk** to **Categorical variables**.
3. Click **Labels**.

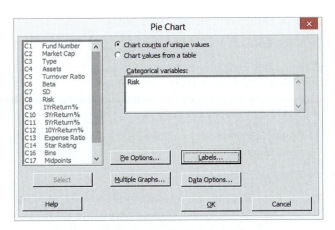

In the Pie Chart - Labels dialog box (shown below):

4. Click the **Slice Labels** tab.
5. Check **Category name** and **Percent**.
6. Click **OK** to return to the original dialog box.

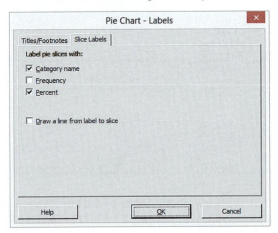

Back in the original Pie Chart dialog box:

7. Click **OK**.

The Pareto Chart

Use **Pareto Chart** to create a Pareto chart. For example, to create the Figure 2.4 Pareto chart on page 49, open to the **ATM Transactions worksheet**. Select **Stat → Quality Tools → Pareto Chart**. In the procedure's dialog box (shown below):

1. Double-click **C1 Cause** in the variables list to add **Cause** to the **Defects or attribute data in** box.
2. Double-click **C2 Frequency** in the variables list to add **Frequency** to the **Frequencies in** box.
3. Click **Do not combine**.
4. Click **OK**.

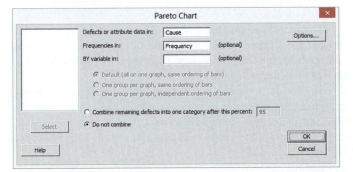

The Side-by-Side Chart

Use **Bar Chart** to create a side-by-side chart. For example, to create the Figure 2.6 side-by-side chart on page 50, open to the **Retirement Funds worksheet**. Select **Graph → Bar Chart**. In the Bar Charts dialog box:

1. Select **Counts of unique values** from the **Bars represent** drop-down list.
2. In the gallery of choices, click **Cluster**.
3. Click **OK**.

In the "Bar Chart - Counts of unique values, Cluster" dialog box (shown below):

4. Double-click **C3 Type** and **C8 Risk** in the variables list to add **Type** and **Risk** to the **Categorical variables (2–4, outermost first)** box.
5. Click **OK**.

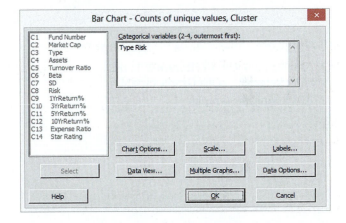

MG2.4 VISUALIZING NUMERICAL VARIABLES

The Stem-and-Leaf Display

Use **Stem-and-Leaf** to create a stem-and-leaf display. For example, to create the Figure 2.7 stem-and-leaf display on page 53, open to the **Unstacked1YrReturn Funds worksheet**. Select **Graph → Stem-and-Leaf**. In the procedure's dialog box (shown on page 94):

1. Double-click **C2 1YrReturn%_Value** in the variables list to add **'1YrReturn%_Value'** in the **Graph variables** box.
2. Click **OK**.

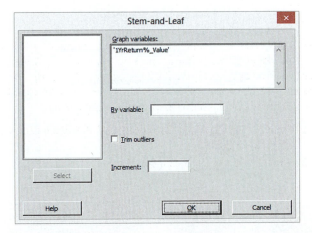

The Histogram

Use **Histogram** to create a histogram. For example, to create the pair of histograms shown in Figure 2.9 on page 55, open to the **Retirement Funds worksheet**. Select **Graph ➔ Histogram**. In the Histograms dialog box (shown below):

1. Click **Simple** and then click **OK**.

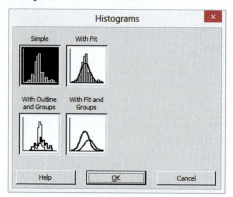

In the Histogram - Simple dialog box (shown below):

2. Double-click **C9 1YrReturn%** in the variables list to add **'1YrReturn%'** in the **Graph variables** box.
3. Click **Multiple Graphs**.

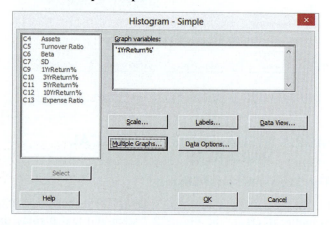

In the Histogram - Multiple Graphs dialog box (shown below):

4. In the **Multiple Variables** tab (not shown), click **On separate graphs** and then click the **By Variables** tab.
5. In the **By Variables** tab (shown below), enter **Type** in the **By variables in groups on separate graphs** box.
6. Click **OK**.

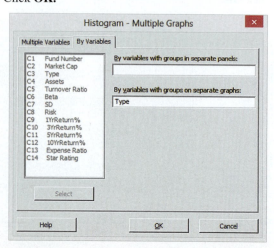

Back in the Histogram - Simple dialog box:

7. Click **OK**.

The histograms created use classes that differ from the classes used in Figure 2.9 (and in Table 2.10 on page 39) and do not use the midpoints shown in Figure 2.9. To better match the histograms shown in Figure 2.9, for each histogram:

8. Right-click the *X* axis and then click **Edit X Scale** from the shortcut menu.

In the Edit Scale dialog box:

9. Click the **Binning** tab (shown below). Click **Cutpoint** (as the **Interval Type**) and **Midpoint/Cutpoint positions** and enter **-15 -10 -5 0 5 10 15 20 25 30 35** in the box (with a space after each value).

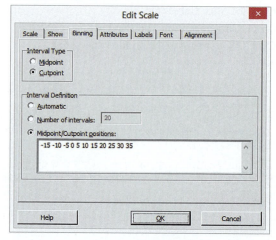

10. Click the **Scale** tab (shown below). Click **Position of ticks** and enter **-12.5 -7.5 -2.5 2.5 7.5 12.5 17.5 22.5 27.5 32.5** in the box (with a space after each value).
11. Click **OK**.

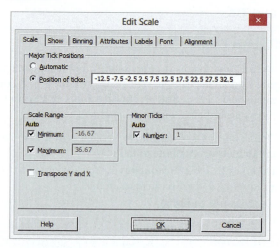

To create the histogram of the one-year return percentage variable for all funds in the retirement fund sample, repeat steps 1 through 11, but in step 5 delete **Type** from the **By variables in groups on separate graphs** box.

To modify the histogram bars, double-click over the histogram bars and make the appropriate entries and selections in the Edit Bars dialog box. To modify an axis, double-click the axis and make the appropriate entries and selections in the Edit Scale dialog box.

The Percentage Polygon

Use **Histogram** to create a percentage polygon. For example, to create the pair of percentage polygons shown in Figure 2.11 on page 56, open to the **Unstacked 1YrReturn worksheet**. Select **Graph → Histogram**. In the Histograms dialog box:

1. Click **Simple** and then click **OK**.

In the Histogram - Simple dialog box:

2. Double-click **C1 1YrReturn%_Growth** in the variables list to add **'1YrReturn%_Growth'** in the **Graph variables** box.
3. Double-click **C2 1YrReturn%_Value** in the variables list to add **'1YrReturn%_Value'** in the **Graph variables** box.
4. Click **Scale.**

In the Histogram - Scale dialog box:

5. Click the **Y-Scale Type** tab. Click **Percent**, clear **Accumulate values across bins**, and then click **OK.**

Back again in the Histogram - Simple dialog box:

6. Click **Data View**.

In the Histogram - Data View dialog box:

7. Click the **Data Display** tab. Check **Symbols** and clear all of the other check boxes.
8. Click the **Smoother** tab and then click **Lowness** and enter **0** as the **Degree of smoothing** and **1** as the **Number of steps**.
9. Click **OK**.

Back again in the Histogram - Simple dialog box:

10. Click **OK** to create the polygons.

The percentage polygons created do not use the classes and midpoints shown in Figure 2.11. To better match the polygons shown in Figure 2.11:

11. Right-click the *X* axis and then click **Edit X Scale** from the shortcut menu.

In the Edit Scale dialog box:

12. Click the **Binning** tab. Click **Cutpoint** as the **Interval Type** and **Midpoint/Cutpoint positions** and enter **-15 -10 -5 0 5 10 15 20 25 30 35** in the box (with a space after each value).
13. Click the **Scale** tab. Click **Position of ticks** and enter **-12.5 -7.5 -2.5 2.5 7.5 12.5 17.5 22.5 27.5 32.5** in the box (with a space after each value).
14. Click **OK**.

The Cumulative Percentage Polygon (Ogive)

Modify the "The Percentage Polygon" instructions to create a cumulative percentage polygon. Replace steps 5 and 12 with the following steps:

5. Click the **Y-Scale Type** tab. Click **Percent**, check **Accumulate values across bins**, and then click **OK.**
12. Click the **Binning** tab. Click **Midpoint** as the **Interval Type** and **Midpoint/Cutpoint positions** and enter **-15 -10 -5 0 5 10 15 20 25 30 35** in the box (with a space after each value).

MG2.5 VISUALIZING TWO NUMERICAL VARIABLES

The Scatter Plot

Use **Scatterplot** to create a scatter plot. For example, to create a scatter plot similar to the one shown in Figure 2.14 on page 61, open to the **NBAValues worksheet**. Select **Graph → Scatterplot**. In the Scatterplots dialog box:

1. Click **With Regression** and then click **OK**.

In the Scatterplot - With Regression dialog box (shown below):

2. Double-click **C4 Current Value** in the variables list to enter **'Current Value'** in the **row 1 Y variables** cell.
3. Enter **Revenue** in the **row 1 X variables** cell.
4. Click **OK**.

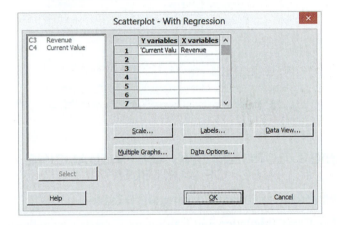

The Time-Series Plot

Use **Time Series Plot** to create a time-series plot. For example, to create the Figure 2.15 time-series plot on page 62, open to the **Movie Revenues worksheet** and select **Graph → Time Series Plot**. In the Time Series Plots dialog box:

1. Click **Simple** and then click **OK**.

In the Time Series Plot - Simple dialog box (shown below):

2. Double-click **C2 Revenues** in the variables list to add **Revenues** in the **Series** box.
3. Click **Time/Scale**.

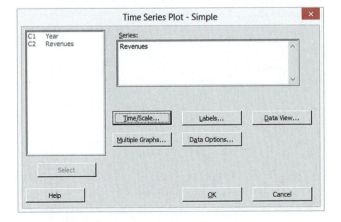

In the Time Series Plot - Time/Scale dialog box (shown below):

4. Click **Stamp** and then press **Tab**.
5. Double-click **C1 Year** in the variables list to add **Year** in the **Stamp columns (1-3, innermost first)** box.
6. Click **OK**.

Back in the Time Series Plot - Simple dialog box:

7. Click **OK**.

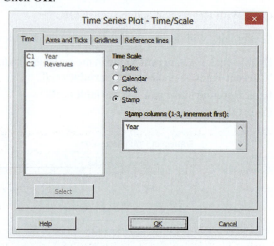

MG2.6 ORGANIZING AND VISUALIZING A SET OF VARIABLES

Multidimensional Contingency Tables

Use **Cross Tabulation and Chi-Square** to create a multidimensional contingency table. For example, to create a table similar to the Figure 2.16 fund type, market cap, and risk table on page 64, open to the **Retirement Funds worksheet**. Select **Stat → Tables → Cross Tabulation and Chi-Square**. In the procedure's dialog box:

1. Double-click **C3 Type** in the variables list to add **Type** to the **For rows** box.
2. Double-click **C2 Market Cap** in the variables list to add **'Market Cap'** to the **For rows** box and then press **Tab.**
3. Double-click **C8 Risk** in the variables list to add **Risk** to the **For columns** box.
4. Check **Counts**.
5. Click **OK**.

To display the cell values as percentages, as was done in Figure 2.1, check **Total percents** instead of **Counts** in step 4.

Adding a Numerical Variable to a Multidimensional Contingency Table

Use **Descriptive Statistics** to create a multidimensional contingency table that contains a numerical variable.

For example, to create the Figure 2.17 table of fund type, risk, and market cap, showing the mean ten-year return percentage for the retirement funds samples, similar to the one shown in Example 3.9 on page 111, open to the **Retirement Funds worksheet.** Select **Stat → Tables → Descriptive Statistics**. In the Table of Descriptive Statistics dialog box (shown below):

1. Double-click **C3 Type** in the variables list to add **Type** to the **For rows** box.
2. Double-click **C2 Market Cap** in the variables list to add **'Market Cap'** to the **For rows** box and then press **Tab**.
3. Double-click **C8 Risk** in the variables list to add **Risk** to the **For columns** box.
4. Click **Associated Variables**.

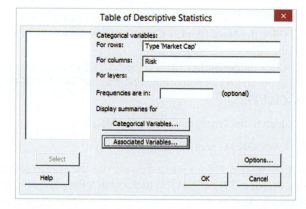

In the Descriptive Statistics - Summaries for Associated Variables dialog box (not shown):

5. Double-click **C12 10YrReturn%** in the variables list to add **'10YrReturn%'** to the **Associated variables** box.
6. Check **Means**.
7. Click **OK**.

Back in Table of Descriptive Statistics dialog box:

8. Click **OK**.

Numerical Descriptive Measures

OBJECTIVES

Describe the properties of central tendency, variation, and shape in numerical variables

Construct and interpret a boxplot

Compute descriptive summary measures for a population

Compute the covariance and the coefficient of correlation

USING STATISTICS

More Descriptive Choices

As a member of a Choice *Is* Yours investment service task force, you helped organize and visualize the variables found in a sample of 316 retirement funds. Now, several weeks later, prospective clients are asking for more information on which they can base their investment decisions. In particular, they would like to compare the results of an individual retirement fund to the results of similar funds.

For example, while the earlier work your team did shows how the one-year return percentages are distributed, prospective clients would like to know how the value for a particular mid-cap growth fund compares to the one-year returns of all mid-cap growth funds. They also seek to understand the variation among the returns. Are all the values relatively similar? And does any variable have outlier values that are either extremely small or extremely large?

While doing a complete search of the retirement funds data could lead to answers to the preceding questions, you wonder if there are better ways than extensive searching to uncover those answers. You also wonder if there are other ways of being more *descriptive* about the sample of funds—providing answers to questions not yet raised by prospective clients. If you can help the Choice *Is* Yours investment service provide such answers, prospective clients will be better able to evaluate the retirement funds that your firm features.

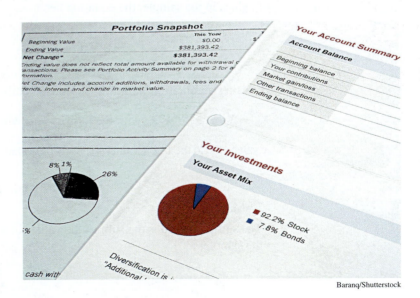

Baranq/Shutterstock

T he prospective clients in the More Descriptive Choices scenario have begun asking questions about numerical variables such as how the one-year return percentages vary among the individual funds that comprise the sample of 316 retirement funds. When describing numerical variables, the summarizing methods discussed in Chapter 2 are only the starting point. You also need to apply methods that help describe the central tendency, variation, and shape of such variables.

Central tendency is the extent to which the values of a numerical variable group around a typical, or central, value. Variation measures the amount of dispersion, or scattering, away from a central value that the values of a numerical variable show. The shape of a variable is the pattern of the distribution of values from the lowest value to the highest value.

This chapter discusses ways you can compute these numerical descriptive measures as you begin to analyze your data within the DCOVA framework. The chapter also talks about the covariance and the coefficient of correlation, measures that can help show the strength of the association between two numerical variables. Computing the descriptive measures discussed in this chapter would be one way to help prospective clients of the Choice *Is* Yours service find the answers they seek.

3.1 Central Tendency

Most variables show a distinct tendency to group around a central value. When people talk about an "average value" or the "middle value" or the "most frequent value," they are talking informally about the mean, median, and mode—three measures of central tendency.

The Mean

The **arithmetic mean** (typically referred to as the **mean**) is the most common measure of central tendency. The mean can suggest a typical or central value and serves as a "balance point" in a set of data, similar to the fulcrum on a seesaw. The mean is the only common measure in which all the values play an equal role. You compute the mean by adding together all the values and then dividing that sum by the number of values in the data set.

The symbol $\overline{X}$, called *X-bar*, is used to represent the mean of a sample. For a sample containing n values, the equation for the mean of a sample is written as

$$\overline{X} = \frac{\text{sum of the values}}{\text{number of values}}$$

Using the series $X_1, X_2, \ldots, X_n$ to represent the set of n values and n to represent the number of values in the sample, the equation becomes

$$\overline{X} = \frac{X_1 + X_2 + \cdots + X_n}{n}$$

By using summation notation (discussed fully in Appendix A), you replace the numerator $X_1 + X_2 + \cdots + X_n$ with the term $\sum_{i=1}^{n} X_i$, which means sum all the X_i values from the first X value, X_1, to the last X value, X_n, to form Equation (3.1), a formal definition of the sample mean.

SAMPLE MEAN

The **sample mean** is the sum of the values in a sample divided by the number of values in the sample:

$$\overline{X} = \frac{\sum_{i=1}^{n} X_i}{n} \tag{3.1}$$

where

$$\overline{X} = \text{sample mean}$$
$$n = \text{number of values or sample size}$$
$$X_i = i\text{th value of the variable } X$$

$$\sum_{i=1}^{n} X_i = \text{summation of all } X_i \text{ values in the sample}$$

Because all the values play an equal role, a mean is greatly affected by any value that is very different from the others. When you have such extreme values, you should avoid using the mean as a measure of central tendency.

For example, if you knew the typical time it takes you to get ready in the morning, you might be able to arrive at your first destination every day in a more timely manner. Using the DCOVA framework, you first define the time to get ready as the time from when you get out of bed to when you leave your home, rounded to the nearest minute. Then, you collect the times for 10 consecutive workdays and organize and store them in **Times** .

Using the collected data, you compute the mean to discover the "typical" time it takes for you to get ready. For these data:

Day:	1	2	3	4	5	6	7	8	9	10
Time (minutes):	39	29	43	52	39	44	40	31	44	35

the mean time is 39.6 minutes, computed as follows:

$$\overline{X} = \frac{\text{sum of the values}}{\text{number of values}}$$

$$\overline{X} = \frac{\sum_{i=1}^{n} X_i}{n}$$

$$\overline{X} = \frac{39 + 29 + 43 + 52 + 39 + 44 + 40 + 31 + 44 + 35}{10}$$

$$= \frac{396}{10} = 39.6$$

Even though no individual day in the sample had a value of 39.6 minutes, allotting this amount of time to get ready in the morning would be a reasonable decision to make. The mean is a good measure of central tendency in this case because the data set does not contain any exceptionally small or large values.

To illustrate how the mean can be greatly affected by any value that is very different from the others, imagine that on Day 3, a set of unusual circumstances delayed you getting ready by an extra hour, so that the time for that day was 103 minutes. This extreme value causes the mean to rise to 45.6 minutes, as follows:

$$\overline{X} = \frac{\text{sum of the values}}{\text{number of values}}$$

$$\overline{X} = \frac{\sum_{i=1}^{n} X_i}{n}$$

$$\overline{X} = \frac{39 + 29 + 103 + 52 + 39 + 44 + 40 + 31 + 44 + 35}{10}$$

$$\overline{X} = \frac{456}{10} = 45.6$$

The one extreme value has increased the mean by 6 minutes. The extreme value also moved the position of the mean relative to all the values. The original mean, 39.6 minutes, had a middle, or *central*, position among the data values: 5 of the times were less than that mean and 5 were greater than that mean. In contrast, the mean using the extreme value is greater than 9 of the 10 times, making the new mean a poor measure of central tendency.

EXAMPLE 3.1

The Mean Calories in Cereals

Nutritional data about a sample of seven breakfast cereals (stored in Cereals) includes the number of calories per serving:

Cereal	Calories
Kellogg's All Bran	80
Kellogg's Corn Flakes	100
Wheaties	100
Nature's Path Organic Multigrain Flakes	110
Kellogg's Rice Krispies	130
Post Shredded Wheat Vanilla Almond	190
Kellogg's Mini Wheats	200

Compute the mean number of calories in these breakfast cereals.

SOLUTION The mean number of calories is 130, computed as follows:

$$\overline{X} = \frac{\text{sum of the values}}{\text{number of values}}$$

$$\overline{X} = \frac{\sum_{i=1}^{n} X_i}{n}$$

$$= \frac{910}{7} = 130$$

The Median

The **median** is the middle value in an ordered array of data that has been ranked from smallest to largest. Half the values are smaller than or equal to the median, and half the values are larger than or equal to the median. The median is not affected by extreme values, so you can use the median when extreme values are present.

To compute the median for a set of data, you first rank the values from smallest to largest and then use Equation (3.2) to compute the rank of the value that is the median.

MEDIAN

$$\text{Median} = \frac{n + 1}{2} \text{ ranked value} \tag{3.2}$$

You compute the median by following one of two rules:

- **Rule 1**   If the data set contains an *odd* number of values, the median is the measurement associated with the middle-ranked value.
- **Rule 2**   If the data set contains an *even* number of values, the median is the measurement associated with the average of the two middle-ranked values.

To further analyze the sample of 10 times to get ready in the morning, you can compute the median. To do so, you rank the daily times as follows:

Ranked values:	29	31	35	39	39	40	43	44	44	52
Ranks:	1	2	3	4	5	6	7	8	9	10

↑
Median = 39.5

> **Student Tip**
> Remember that you must rank the values in order from the smallest to the largest to compute the median.

Because the result of dividing $n + 1$ by 2 for this sample of 10 is $(10 + 1)/2 = 5.5$, you must use Rule 2 and average the measurements associated with the fifth and sixth ranked values, 39 and 40. Therefore, the median is 39.5. The median of 39.5 means that for half the days, the time to get ready is less than or equal to 39.5 minutes, and for half the days, the time to get ready is greater than or equal to 39.5 minutes. In this case, the median time to get ready of 39.5 minutes is very close to the mean time to get ready of 39.6 minutes.

EXAMPLE 3.2

Computing the Median from an Odd-Sized Sample

Nutritional data about a sample of seven breakfast cereals (stored in **Cereals**) includes the number of calories per serving (see Example 3.1 on page 100). Compute the median number of calories in breakfast cereals.

SOLUTION Because the result of dividing $n + 1$ by 2 for this sample of seven is $(7 + 1)/2 = 4$, using Rule 1, the median is the measurement associated with the fourth-ranked value. The number of calories per serving values are ranked from the smallest to the largest:

Ranked values:	80	100	100	110	130	190	200
Ranks:	1	2	3	4	5	6	7

↑
Median = 110

The median number of calories is 110. Half the breakfast cereals have equal to or less than 110 calories per serving, and half the breakfast cereals have equal to or more than 110 calories.

The Mode

The **mode** is the value that appears most frequently. Like the median and unlike the mean, extreme values do not affect the mode. For a particular variable, there can be several modes or no mode at all. For example, for the sample of 10 times to get ready in the morning:

29   31   35   39   39   40   43   44   44   52

there are two modes, 39 minutes and 44 minutes, because each of these values occurs twice. However, for this sample of seven smartphone prices offered by a cellphone provider (stored in **Smartphones**):

20   80   150   200   230   280   370

there is no mode. None of the values is "most typical" because each value appears the same number of times (once) in the data set.

EXAMPLE 3.3

Determining the Mode

A systems manager in charge of a company's network keeps track of the number of server failures that occur in a day. Determine the mode for the following data, which represent the number of server failures per day for the past two weeks:

$$1 \quad 3 \quad 0 \quad 3 \quad 26 \quad 2 \quad 7 \quad 4 \quad 0 \quad 2 \quad 3 \quad 3 \quad 6 \quad 3$$

SOLUTION The ordered array for these data is

$$0 \quad 0 \quad 1 \quad 2 \quad 2 \quad 3 \quad 3 \quad 3 \quad 3 \quad 3 \quad 4 \quad 6 \quad 7 \quad 26$$

Because 3 occurs five times, more times than any other value, the mode is 3. Thus, the systems manager can say that the most common occurrence is having three server failures in a day. For this data set, the median is also equal to 3, and the mean is equal to 4.5. The value 26 is an extreme value. For these data, the median and the mode are better measures of central tendency than the mean.

3.2 Variation and Shape

In addition to central tendency, every variable can be characterized by its variation and shape. Variation measures the **spread**, or **dispersion**, of the values. One simple measure of variation is the range, the difference between the largest and smallest values. More commonly used in statistics are the standard deviation and variance, two measures explained later in this section. The shape of a variable represents a pattern of all the values, from the lowest to highest value. As you will learn later in this section, many variables have a pattern that looks approximately like a bell, with a peak of values somewhere in the middle.

The Range

The **range** is the difference between the largest and smallest value and is the simplest descriptive measure of variation for a numerical variable.

RANGE

The range is equal to the largest value minus the smallest value.

$$\text{Range} = X_{\text{largest}} - X_{\text{smallest}} \qquad (3.3)$$

To further analyze the sample of 10 times to get ready in the morning, you can compute the range. To do so, you rank the data from smallest to largest:

$$29 \quad 31 \quad 35 \quad 39 \quad 39 \quad 40 \quad 43 \quad 44 \quad 44 \quad 52$$

Using Equation (3.3), the range is $52 - 29 = 23$ minutes. The range of 23 minutes indicates that the largest difference between any two days in the time to get ready in the morning is 23 minutes.

EXAMPLE 3.4

Computing
the Range in the
Calories in Cereals

Nutritional data about a sample of seven breakfast cereals (stored in **Cereals**) includes the number of calories per serving (see Example 3.1 on page 100). Compute the range of the number of calories for the cereals.

SOLUTION Ranked from smallest to largest, the calories for the seven cereals are

$$80 \quad 100 \quad 100 \quad 110 \quad 130 \quad 190 \quad 200$$

Therefore, using Equation (3.3), the range $= 200 - 80 = 120$. The largest difference in the number of calories between any two cereals is 120.

The range measures the *total spread* in the set of data. Although the range is a simple measure of the total variation of the variable, it does not take into account *how* the values are distributed between the smallest and largest values. In other words, the range does not indicate whether the values are evenly distributed, clustered near the middle, or clustered near one or both extremes. Thus, using the range as a measure of variation when at least one value is an extreme value is misleading.

The Variance and the Standard Deviation

Being a simple measure of variation, the range does not consider how the values distribute or cluster between the extremes. Two commonly used measures of variation that account for how all the values are distributed are the **variance** and the **standard deviation**. These statistics measure the "average" scatter around the mean—how larger values fluctuate above it and how smaller values fluctuate below it.

A simple measure of variation around the mean might take the difference between each value and the mean and then sum these differences. However, if you did that, you would find that these differences sum to zero because the mean is the balance point for *every* numerical variable. A measure of variation that *differs* from one data set to another *squares* the difference between each value and the mean and then sums these squared differences. The sum of these squared differences, known as the **sum of squares (SS)**, is then used to compute the sample variance (S^2) and the sample standard deviation (S).

The **sample variance** (S^2) is the sum of squares divided by the sample size minus 1. The **sample standard deviation** (S) is the square root of the sample variance. Because this sum of squares will always be nonnegative according to the rules of algebra, *neither the variance nor the standard deviation can ever be negative*. For virtually all variables, the variance and standard deviation will be a positive value. Both of these statistics will be zero only if every value in the sample is the same value (i.e., the values show no variation).

For a sample containing n values, $X_1, X_2, X_3, \ldots, X_n$, the sample variance (S^2) is

$$S^2 = \frac{(X_1 - \overline{X})^2 + (X_2 - \overline{X})^2 + \cdots + (X_n - \overline{X})^2}{n - 1}$$

Equations (3.4) and (3.5) define the sample variance and sample standard deviation using summation notation. The term $\sum_{i=1}^{n}(X_i - \overline{X})^2$ represents the sum of squares.

SAMPLE VARIANCE

The sample variance is the sum of the squared differences around the mean divided by the sample size minus 1:

$$S^2 = \frac{\sum\limits_{i=1}^{n}(X_i - \overline{X})^2}{n - 1} \tag{3.4}$$

where

$$\overline{X} = \text{sample mean}$$
$$n = \text{sample size}$$
$$X_i = i\text{th value of the variable } X$$

$$\sum\limits_{i=1}^{n}(X_i - \overline{X})^2 = \text{summation of all the squared differences between the } X_i \text{ values and } \overline{X}$$

SAMPLE STANDARD DEVIATION

The sample standard deviation is the square root of the sum of the squared differences around the mean divided by the sample size minus 1:

$$S = \sqrt{S^2} = \sqrt{\frac{\sum\limits_{i=1}^{n}(X_i - \overline{X})^2}{n - 1}} \tag{3.5}$$

Note that in both equations, the sum of squares is divided by the sample size minus 1, $n - 1$. The value is used for reasons related to statistical inference and the properties of sampling distributions, a topic discussed in Section 7.2. For now, observe that the difference between dividing by n and by $n - 1$ becomes smaller as the sample size increases.

In practice, you will most likely use the sample standard deviation as the measure of variation. Unlike the sample variance, a squared quantity, the standard deviation will always be a number expressed in the same units as the original sample data. For almost all sets of data, the majority of the values in a sample will be within an interval of plus and minus 1 standard deviation above and below the mean. Therefore, knowledge of the mean and the standard deviation usually helps define where at least the majority of the data values are clustering.

To hand-compute the sample variance, S^2, and the sample standard deviation, S:

1. Compute the difference between each value and the mean.
2. Square each difference.
3. Sum the squared differences.
4. Divide this total by $n - 1$ to compute the sample variance.
5. Take the square root of the sample variance to compute the sample standard deviation.

Student Tip
Remember, neither the variance nor the standard deviation can ever be negative.

To further analyze the sample of 10 times to get ready in the morning, Table 3.1 shows the first four steps for calculating the variance and standard deviation with a mean ($\overline{X}$) equal to 39.6. (Computing the mean is explained on page 99.) The second column of Table 3.1 shows step 1. The third column of Table 3.1 shows step 2. The sum of the squared differences (step 3) is shown at the bottom of Table 3.1. This total is then divided by $10 - 1 = 9$ to compute the variance (step 4).

TABLE 3.1

Computing the
Variance of the
Getting-Ready Times

	Time (X)	Step 1: $(X_i - \overline{X})$	Step 2: $(X_i - \overline{X})^2$
	39	−0.60	0.36
	29	−10.60	112.36
	43	3.40	11.56
	52	12.40	153.76
$n = 10$	39	−0.60	0.36
$\overline{X} = 39.6$	44	4.40	19.36
	40	0.40	0.16
	31	−8.60	73.96
	44	4.40	19.36
	35	−4.60	21.16
		Step 3: Sum	412.40
		Step 4: Divide by $(n - 1)$	45.82

You can also compute the variance by substituting values for the terms in Equation (3.4):

$$S^2 = \frac{\sum\limits_{i=1}^{n}(X_i - \overline{X})^2}{n - 1}$$

$$= \frac{(39 - 39.6)^2 + (29 - 39.6)^2 + \cdots + (35 - 39.6)^2}{10 - 1}$$

$$= \frac{412.4}{9}$$

$$= 45.82$$

Because the variance is in squared units (in squared minutes, for these data), to compute the standard deviation, you take the square root of the variance. Using Equation (3.5) on page 104, the sample standard deviation, S, is

$$S = \sqrt{S^2} = \sqrt{\frac{\sum\limits_{i=1}^{n}(X_i - \overline{X})^2}{n - 1}} = \sqrt{45.82} = 6.77$$

This indicates that the getting-ready times in this sample are clustering within 6.77 minutes around the mean of 39.6 minutes (i.e., clustering between $\overline{X} - 1S = 32.83$ and $\overline{X} + 1S = 46.37$). In fact, 7 out of 10 getting-ready times lie within this interval.

Using the second column of Table 3.1, you can also compute the sum of the differences between each value and the mean to be zero. For any set of data, this sum will always be zero:

$$\sum_{i=1}^{n}(X_i - \overline{X}) = 0 \text{ for all sets of data}$$

This property is one of the reasons that the mean is used as the most common measure of central tendency.

Z Scores

The **Z score** of a value is the difference between that value and the mean, divided by the standard deviation. A Z score of 0 indicates that the value is the same as the mean. If a Z score is a positive or negative number, it indicates whether the value is above or below the mean and by how many standard deviations.

Z scores help identify **outliers**, the values that seem excessively different from most of the rest of the values (see Section 1.2). Values that are very different from the mean will have either very small (negative) Z scores or very large (positive) Z scores. As a general rule, a Z score that is less than −3.0 or greater than +3.0 indicates an outlier value.

Z SCORE

The Z score for a value is equal to the difference between the value and the mean, divided by the standard deviation:

$$Z = \frac{X - \overline{X}}{S} \qquad (3.7)$$

To further analyze the sample of 10 times to get ready in the morning, you can compute the Z scores. Because the mean is 39.6 minutes, the standard deviation is 6.77 minutes, and the time to get ready on the first day is 39.0 minutes, you compute the Z score for Day 1 by using Equation (3.7):

$$Z = \frac{X - \overline{X}}{S}$$
$$= \frac{39.0 - 39.6}{6.77}$$
$$= -0.09$$

The Z score of −0.09 for the first day indicates that the time to get ready on that day is very close to the mean. Table 3.3 presents the Z scores for all 10 days.

TABLE 3.3

Z Scores for the 10 Getting-Ready Times

	Time (X)	Z Score
	39	−0.09
	29	−1.57
	43	0.50
	52	1.83
$\overline{X} = 39.6$	39	−0.09
$S = 6.77$	44	0.65
	40	0.06
	31	−1.27
	44	0.65
	35	−0.68

The largest Z score is 1.83 for Day 4, on which the time to get ready was 52 minutes. The lowest Z score is −1.57 for Day 2, on which the time to get ready was 29 minutes. Because none of the Z scores are less than −3.0 or greater then +3.0, you conclude that the getting-ready times include no apparent outliers.

EXAMPLE 3.7

Computing the Z Scores of the Number of Calories in Cereals

Nutritional data about a sample of seven breakfast cereals (stored in **Cereals**) includes the number of calories per serving (see Example 3.1 on page 100). Compute the Z scores of the calories in breakfast cereals.

SOLUTION Table 3.4 presents the Z scores of the calories for the cereals. The largest Z score is 1.49, for a cereal with 200 calories. The lowest Z score is -1.07, for a cereal with 80 calories. There are no apparent outliers in these data because none of the Z scores are less than -3.0 or greater than $+3.0$.

TABLE 3.4

Z Scores of the Number of Calories in Cereals

	Calories	Z Scores
	80	-1.07
	100	-0.64
	100	-0.64
$\overline{X} = 130$	110	-0.43
$S = 46.9042$	130	0.00
	190	1.28
	200	1.49

Shape: Skewness

Skewness measures the extent to which the data values are not **symmetrical** around the mean. The three possibilities are:

- **Mean < median:** negative, or **left-skewed distribution**
- **Mean = median:** **symmetrical distribution** (zero skewness)
- **Mean > median:** positive, or **right-skewed distribution**

In a *symmetrical* distribution, the values below the mean are distributed in exactly the same way as the values above the mean, and the skewness is zero. In a **skewed** distribution, there is an imbalance of data values below and above the mean, and the skewness is a nonzero value (less than zero for a left-skewed distribution, greater than zero for a right-skewed distribution). Figure 3.1 visualizes these possibilities.

FIGURE 3.1

The shapes of three data distributions

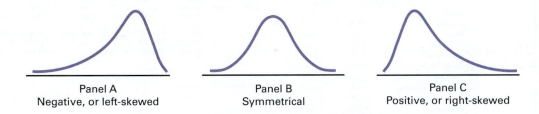

Panel A	Panel B	Panel C
Negative, or left-skewed	Symmetrical	Positive, or right-skewed

Panel A displays a left-skewed distribution. In a left-skewed distribution, most of the values are in the upper portion of the distribution. Some extremely small values cause the long tail and distortion to the left and cause the mean to be less than the median. Because the skewness statistic for such a distribution will be less than zero, some use the term *negative skew* to describe this distribution.

Panel B displays a symmetrical distribution. In a symmetrical distribution, values are equally distributed in the upper and lower portions of the distribution. This equality causes the portion of the curve below the mean to be the mirror image of the portion of the curve above the mean and makes the mean equal to the median.

Panel C displays a right-skewed distribution. In a right-skewed distribution, most of the values are in the lower portion of the distribution. Some extremely large values cause the long tail and distortion to the right and cause the mean to be more than median. Because the skewness statistic for such a distribution will be greater than zero, some use the term *positive skew* to describe this distribution.

Shape: Kurtosis

Kurtosis measures the peakedness of the curve of the distribution—that is, how sharply the curve rises approaching the center of the distribution. Kurtosis compares the shape of the peak to the shape of the peak of a bell-shaped normal distribution (see Chapter 6), which, by definition, has a kurtosis of zero.[1] A distribution that has a sharper-rising center peak than the peak of a normal distribution has *positive* kurtosis, a kurtosis value that is greater than zero, and is called **lepokurtic**. A distribution that has a slower-rising (flatter) center peak than the peak of a normal distribution has *negative* kurtosis, a kurtosis value that is less than zero, and is called **platykurtic**. A lepokurtic distribution has a higher concentration of values near the mean of the distribution compared to a normal distribution, while a platykurtic distribution has a lower concentration compared to a normal distribution.

In affecting the shape of the central peak, the relative concentration of values near the mean also affects the ends, or *tails*, of the curve of a distribution. A lepokurtic distribution has *fatter* tails, many more values in the tails, than a normal distribution has. If decision making about a set of data mistakenly assumes a normal distribution, when, in fact, the data forms a lepokurtic distribution, then that decision making will underestimate the occurrence of extreme values (values that are very different from the mean). Such an observation has been a basis for several explanations about the unanticipated reverses and collapses that financial markets have experienced in the recent past. (See reference 5 for an example of such an explanation.)

[1]Several different operational definitions exist for kurtosis. The definition here, used by both Excel and Minitab, is sometimes called *excess kurtosis* to distinguish it from other definitions. Read the SHORT TAKES for Chapter 3 to learn how Excel calculates kurtosis (and skewness).

EXAMPLE 3.8

Descriptive Statistics for Growth and Value Funds

In the More Descriptive Choices scenario, you are interested in comparing the past performance of the growth and value funds from a sample of 316 funds. One measure of past performance is the one-year return percentage variable. Compute descriptive statistics for the growth and value funds.

SOLUTION Figure 3.2 presents descriptive summary measures for the two types of funds. The results include the mean, median, mode, minimum, maximum, range, variance, standard deviation, coefficient of variation, skewness, kurtosis, count (the sample size), and standard error. The standard error, discussed in Section 7.2, is the standard deviation divided by the square root of the sample size.

FIGURE 3.2

Excel and Minitab Descriptive statistics for the one-year return percentages for the growth and value funds

	A	B	C
1	Descriptive Statistics for the 1YrReturn% Variable		
2			
3		Growth	Value
4	Mean	14.28	14.70
5	Median	14.18	15.30
6	Mode	16.95	19.09
7	Minimum	-11.28	1.67
8	Maximum	33.98	28.27
9	Range	45.26	26.6
10	Variance	25.0413	19.9369
11	Standard Deviation	5.0041	4.4651
12	Coeff. of Variation	35.05%	30.38%
13	Skewness	0.2039	-0.2083
14	Kurtosis	5.1479	0.6684
15	Count	227	89
16	Standard Error	0.3321	0.4733

Descriptive Statistics: 1YrReturn%

Variable	Type	Total Count	Mean	StDev	Variance	CoefVar	Minimum	Q1
1YrReturn%	Growth	227	14.278	5.004	25.041	35.05	-11.280	11.780
	Value	89	14.698	4.465	19.937	30.38	1.670	12.165

Variable	Type	Median	Q3	Maximum	Range	IQR		Mode
1YrReturn%	Growth	14.180	16.640	33.980	45.260	4.860		16.95
	Value	15.300	17.225	28.270	26.600	5.060	13.83, 15.3,	19.09

Variable	Type	N for Mode	Skewness	Kurtosis
1YrReturn%	Growth	3	0.20	5.15
	Value	2	-0.21	0.67

In examining the results, you see that there are some differences in the one-year return for the growth and value funds. The growth funds had a mean one-year return of 14.28 and a median return of 14.18. This compares to a mean of 14.70 and a median of 15.30 for the value funds. The medians indicate that half of the growth funds had one-year returns of 14.18 or better, and half the value funds had one-year returns of 15.30 or better. You conclude that the value funds had a slightly higher return than the growth funds.

The growth funds had a higher standard deviation than the value funds (5.0041, as compared to 4.4651). Both the growth funds and the value funds showed very little skewness, as the skewness of the growth funds was 0.2039 and the skewness of the value funds was −0.2083. The kurtosis of the growth funds was very positive, indicating a distribution that was much more peaked than a normal distribution. The kurtosis of the value funds was slightly positive indicating a distribution that did not depart markedly from a normal distribution.

EXAMPLE 3.9

Descriptive Statistics Using Multidimensional Contingency Tables

Continuing with the More Descriptive Choices scenario, you wish to explore the effects of each combination of type, market cap, and risk on measures of past performance. One measure of past performance is the three-year return percentage. Compute the mean three-year return percentage for each combination of type, market cap, and risk.

SOLUTION Compute the mean for each combination by adding the numerical variable three-year return percentage to a multidimensional contingency table. The Excel and Minitab results are:

Average of 3YrReturn%	Risk			
Type	Low	Average	High	Grand Total
Growth	10.65	10.20	11.88	10.56
Large	9.56	8.83	22.17	9.86
Mid-Cap	12.10	10.28		11.21
Small	13.41	10.58	7.47	11.03
Value	9.49	10.24	9.30	9.63
Large	8.76	6.94	6.70	8.57
Mid-Cap	10.56	11.65		10.79
Small	11.33	11.08	10.61	11.15
Grand Total	10.27	10.21	11.29	10.29

Tabulated statistics: Type, Market Cap, Risk

Rows: Type / Market Cap   Columns: Risk

		Average	High	Low	All
Growth					
	Large	8.83	22.17	9.56	9.86
		10	3	90	103
	Mid-Cap	10.28	*	12.10	11.21
		35	0	37	72
	Small	10.58	7.47	13.41	11.03
		29	7	16	52
Value					
	Large	6.94	6.70	8.76	8.57
		4	1	45	50
	Mid-Cap	11.65	*	10.56	10.79
		4	0	15	19
	Small	11.08	10.61	11.33	11.15
		9	2	9	20
All					
	All	10.21	11.29	10.27	10.29
		91	13	212	316

Cell Contents: 3YrReturn% : Mean
                                 Count

Analyzing each combination of type, market cap, and risk reveals patterns that would not be seen if the mean of the three-year return percentage had been computed for only the growth and value funds (similar to what is done in Example 3.8). Empty cells (Excel) and starred cells (Minitab), such as those for mid-cap growth funds with high risk, represent combinations that do not exist in the sample of 316 funds.

Problems for Sections 3.1 and 3.2

LEARNING THE BASICS

3.1 The following set of data is from a sample of $n = 5$:

$$7\ 4\ 9\ 8\ 2$$

a. Compute the mean, median, and mode.
b. Compute the range, variance, standard deviation, and coefficient of variation.
c. Compute the Z scores. Are there any outliers?
d. Describe the shape of the data set.

3.2 The following set of data is from a sample of $n = 6$:

$$7\ 4\ 9\ 7\ 3\ 12$$

a. Compute the mean, median, and mode.
b. Compute the range, variance, standard deviation, and coefficient of variation.
c. Compute the Z scores. Are there any outliers?
d. Describe the shape of the data set.

3.3 The following set of data is from a sample of $n = 7$:

$$12\ 7\ 4\ 9\ 0\ 7\ 3$$

a. Compute the mean, median, and mode.
b. Compute the range, variance, standard deviation, and coefficient of variation.
c. Compute the Z scores. Are there any outliers?
d. Describe the shape of the data set.

3.4 The following set of data is from a sample of $n = 5$:

$$7\ -5\ -8\ 7\ 9$$

a. Compute the mean, median, and mode.
b. Compute the range, variance, standard deviation, and coefficient of variation.
c. Compute the Z scores. Are there any outliers?
d. Describe the shape of the data set.

APPLYING THE CONCEPTS

3.5 *Wired*, a magazine that delivers a glimpse into the future of business, culture, innovation, and science, reported the following summary for the household incomes of its two types of subscribers, the print reader and the digital reader.

Audience	Median
Wired reader	$93,437
Wired.com user	91,769
Source: Data extracted from "*Wired* 2014 Media Kit," **www.condenast.com/brands/wired/media-kit**.	

Interpret the median household income for the *Wired* readers and the Wired.com users.

3.6 The operations manager of a plant that manufactures tires wants to compare the actual inner diameters of two grades of tires, each of which is expected to be 575 millimeters. A sample of five tires of each grade was selected, and the results representing the inner diameters of the tires, ranked from smallest to largest, are as follows:

Grade X	Grade Y
568 570 575 578 584	573 574 575 577 578

a. For each of the two grades of tires, compute the mean, median, and standard deviation.
b. Which grade of tire is providing better quality? Explain.
c. What would be the effect on your answers in (a) and (b) if the last value for grade *Y* was 588 instead of 578? Explain.

3.7 According to the U.S. Census Bureau (**census.gov**), in 2013, the median sales price of new houses was $265,900 and the mean sales price was $322,100.
a. Interpret the median sales price.
b. Interpret the mean sales price.
c. Discuss the shape of the distribution of the price of new houses.

✓ SELF Test **3.8** The file MobileLoyalty contains spending on products ($) during a three-month period by a sample of 15 customers receiving incentives through a mobile loyalty program.

55.35 22.90 67.50 46.10 57.45 108.25 50.75 35.20
78.30 50.65 63.00 59.70 41.55 56.65 52.60

a. Compute the mean and median.
b. Compute the variance, standard deviation, range, and coefficient of variation.
c. Are the data skewed? If so, how?
d. Based on the results of (a) through (c), what conclusions can you reach concerning spending on products by customers receiving incentives through a mobile loyalty program?

3.9 The file Sedans contains the overall miles per gallon (MPG) of 2014 midsized sedans:

38 26 30 26 25 27 24 22 27 32 39
26 24 24 23 24 25 31 26 37 22 33

Source: Data extracted from "Which Car Is Right for You," *Consumer Reports*, April 2014, pp. 40–41.

a. Compute the mean, median, and mode.
b. Compute the variance, standard deviation, range, coefficient of variation, and Z scores.
c. Are the data skewed? If so, how?
d. Compare the results of (a) through (c) to those of Problem 3.10 (a) through (c) that refer to the miles per gallon of small SUVs.

3.10 The file SUV contains the overall miles per gallon (MPG) of 2014 small SUVs:

26 22 23 21 25 24 22 26 25 22
21 21 22 22 23 24 23 22 21 22

Source: Data extracted from "Which Car Is Right for You," *Consumer Reports*, April 2014, pp. 60–61.

a. Compute the mean, median, and mode.
b. Compute the variance, standard deviation, range, coefficient of variation, and Z scores.
c. Are the data skewed? If so, how?
d. Compare the results of (a) through (c) to those of Problem 3.9 (a) through (c) that refer to the MPG of midsized sedans.

3.11 The file AccountingPartners contains the number of partners in a cohort of rising accounting firms that have been tagged as "firms to watch." The firms have the following numbers of partners:

17 23 19 23 18 17 23 16 34 10 14 30 14 33 26 17 19 22
20 27 33 25 12 26 13 30 13 13 33 21 17 12 10 14 12

Source: Data extracted from **bit.ly/ODuzd3**.

a. Compute the mean, median, and mode.
b. Compute the variance, standard deviation, range, coefficient of variation, and Z scores. Are there any outliers? Explain.
c. Are the data skewed? If so, how?
d. Based on the results of (a) through (c), what conclusions can you reach concerning the number of partners in rising accounting firms?

3.12 The file MarketPenetration contains Facebook penetration values (the percentage of the country population who are Facebook users) for 22 of the world's largest economies:

56 57 43 55 42 35 7 25 42 17 43
6 31 28 59 20 27 36 45 80 57 56

Source: Data extracted from **slidesha.re/ODv6vG**.

a. Compute the mean, median, and mode.
b. Compute the variance, standard deviation, range, coefficient of variation, and Z scores. Are there any outliers? Explain.
c. Are the data skewed? If so, how?
d. Based on the results of (a) through (c), what conclusions can you reach concerning Facebook's market penetration?

3.13 Is there a difference in the variation of the yields of different types of investments? The file CD Rate contains the yields for one-year certificates of deposit (CDs) and five-year CDs for 22 banks in the United States, as of March 12, 2014.

Source: Data extracted from **www.Bankrate.com**, March 12, 2014.

a. For one-year and five-year CDs, separately compute the variance, standard deviation, range, and coefficient of variation.
b. Based on the results of (a), do one-year CDs or five-year CDs have more variation in the yields offered? Explain.

3.14 The file [HotelAway] contains the average room price (in US$) paid by various nationalities while traveling abroad (away from their home country) in 2013:

179   173   175   173   164   143   153   155

Source: Data extracted from **http://bit.ly/1pdFkOG**.

a. Compute the mean, median, and mode.
b. Compute the range, variance, and standard deviation.
c. Based on the results of (a) and (b), what conclusions can you reach concerning the room price (in US$) in 2013?

3.15 A bank branch located in a commercial district of a city has the business objective of developing an improved process for serving customers during the noon-to-1:00 P.M. lunch period. The waiting time, in minutes, is defined as the time the customer enters the line to when he or she reaches the teller window. Data collected from a sample of 15 customers during this hour are stored in [Bank1]:

4.21   5.55   3.02   5.13   4.77   2.34   3.54   3.20
4.50   6.10   0.38   5.12   6.46   6.19   3.79

a. Compute the mean and median.
b. Compute the variance, standard deviation, range, coefficient of variation, and Z scores. Are there any outliers? Explain.
c. Are the data skewed? If so, how?
d. As a customer walks into the branch office during the lunch hour, she asks the branch manager how long she can expect to wait. The branch manager replies, "Almost certainly less than five minutes." On the basis of the results of (a) through (c), evaluate the accuracy of this statement.

3.16 Suppose that another bank branch, located in a residential area, is also concerned with the noon-to-1:00 P.M. lunch hour. The waiting time, in minutes, collected from a sample of 15 customers during this hour, are stored in [Bank2]:

9.66   5.90   8.02   5.79   8.73   3.82   8.01   8.35
10.49   6.68   5.64   4.08   6.17   9.91   5.47

a. Compute the mean and median.
b. Compute the variance, standard deviation, range, coefficient of variation, and Z scores. Are there any outliers? Explain.
c. Are the data skewed? If so, how?
d. As a customer walks into the branch office during the lunch hour, he asks the branch manager how long he can expect to wait. The branch manager replies, "Almost certainly less than five minutes." On the basis of the results of (a) through (c), evaluate the accuracy of this statement.

3.17 Using the one-year return percentage variable in [Retirement Funds]:
a. Construct a table that computes the mean for each combination of type, market cap, and risk.
b. Construct a table that computes the standard deviation for each combination of type, market cap, and risk.
c. What conclusions can you reach concerning differences among the types of retirement funds (growth and value), based on market cap (small, mid-cap, and large) and the risk (low, average, and high)?

3.18 Using the one-year return percentage variable in [Retirement Funds]:
a. Construct a table that computes the mean for each combination of type, market cap, and rating.
b. Construct a table that computes the standard deviation for each combination of type, market cap, and rating.
c. What conclusions can you reach concerning differences among the types of retirement funds (growth and value), based on market cap (small, mid-cap, and large) and the rating (one, two, three, four, and five)?

3.19 Using the one-year return percentage variable in [Retirement Funds]:
a. Construct a table that computes the mean for each combination of market cap, risk, and rating.
b. Construct a table that computes the standard deviation for each combination of market cap, risk, and rating.
c. What conclusions can you reach concerning differences based on the market cap (small, mid-cap, and large), risk (low, average, and high), and rating (one, two, three, four, and five)?

3.20 Using the one-year return percentage variable in [Retirement Funds]:
a. Construct a table that computes the mean for each combination of type, risk, and rating.
b. Construct a table that computes the standard deviation for each combination of type, risk, and rating.
c. What conclusions can you reach concerning differences among the types of retirement funds (growth and value), based on the risk (low, average, and high) and the rating (one, two, three, four, and five)?

3.3 Exploring Numerical Data

Sections 3.1 and 3.2 discuss measures of central tendency, variation, and shape. You can also visualize the distribution of the values for a numerical variable by computing the quartiles and the five-number summary and constructing a boxplot.

Quartiles

Quartiles split the values into four equal parts—the **first quartile (Q_1)** divides the smallest 25.0% of the values from the other 75.0% that are larger. The **second quartile (Q_2)** is the median; 50.0% of the values are smaller than or equal to the median, and 50.0% are larger than or equal to the median. The **third quartile (Q_3)** divides the smallest 75.0% of the values from the largest 25.0%. Equations (3.8) and (3.9) define the first and third quartiles.

Student Tip
The methods of this section are commonly used in **exploratory data analysis.**

FIRST QUARTILE, Q_1

25.0% of the values are smaller than or equal to Q_1, the first quartile, and 75.0% are larger than or equal to the first quartile, Q_1:

$$Q_1 = \frac{n + 1}{4} \text{ ranked value} \qquad (3.8)$$

THIRD QUARTILE, Q_3

75.0% of the values are smaller than or equal to the third quartile, Q_3, and 25.0% are larger than or equal to the third quartile, Q_3:

$$Q_3 = \frac{3(n + 1)}{4} \text{ ranked value} \qquad (3.9)$$

Student Tip
As is the case when you compute the median, you must rank the values in order from smallest to largest before computing the quartiles.

Use the following rules to compute the quartiles from a set of ranked values:

- **Rule 1**   If the ranked value is a whole number, the quartile is equal to the measurement that corresponds to that ranked value. For example, if the sample size $n = 7$, the first quartile, Q_1, is equal to the measurement associated with the $(7 + 1)/4 =$ second ranked value.
- **Rule 2**   If the ranked value is a fractional half (2.5, 4.5, etc.), the quartile is equal to the measurement that corresponds to the average of the measurements corresponding to the two ranked values involved. For example, if the sample size $n = 9$, the first quartile, Q_1, is equal to the $(9 + 1)/4 = 2.5$ ranked value, halfway between the second ranked value and the third ranked value.
- **Rule 3**   If the ranked value is neither a whole number nor a fractional half, you round the result to the nearest integer and select the measurement corresponding to that ranked value. For example, if the sample size $n = 10$, the first quartile, Q_1, is equal to the $(10 + 1)/4 = 2.75$ ranked value. Round 2.75 to 3 and use the third ranked value.

To further analyze the sample of 10 times to get ready in the morning, you can compute the quartiles. To do so, you rank the data from smallest to largest:

Ranked values:	29	31	35	39	39	40	43	44	44	52
Ranks:	1	2	3	4	5	6	7	8	9	10

The first quartile is the $(n + 1)/4 = (10 + 1)/4 = 2.75$ ranked value. Using Rule 3, you round up to the third ranked value. The third ranked value for the getting-ready data is 35 minutes. You interpret the first quartile of 35 to mean that on 25% of the days, the time to get ready is less than or equal to 35 minutes, and on 75% of the days, the time to get ready is greater than or equal to 35 minutes.

The third quartile is the $3(n + 1)/4 = 3(10 + 1)/4 = 8.25$ ranked value. Using Rule 3 for quartiles, you round this down to the eighth ranked value. The eighth ranked value is 44 minutes. Thus, on 75% of the days, the time to get ready is less than or equal to 44 minutes, and on 25% of the days, the time to get ready is greater than or equal to 44 minutes.

Percentiles   Related to quartiles are **percentiles** that split a variable into 100 equal parts. By this definition, the first quartile is equivalent to the 25th percentile, the second quartile to the 50th percentile, and the third quartile to the 75th percentile. Learn more about percentiles in the SHORT TAKES for Chapter 3.

EXAMPLE 3.10

Computing the Quartiles

Nutritional data about a sample of seven breakfast cereals (stored in **Cereals**) includes the number of calories per serving (see Example 3.1 on page 100). Compute the first quartile (Q_1) and third quartile (Q_3) of the number of calories for the cereals.

SOLUTION   Ranked from smallest to largest, the numbers of calories for the seven cereals are as follows:

Ranked values:	80	100	100	110	130	190	200
Ranks:	1	2	3	4	5	6	7

For these data

$$Q_1 = \frac{(n+1)}{4} \text{ ranked value}$$

$$= \frac{7+1}{4} \text{ ranked value} = \text{2nd ranked value}$$

Therefore, using Rule 1, Q_1 is the second ranked value. Because the second ranked value is 100, the first quartile, Q_1, is 100.

To compute the third quartile, Q_3,

$$Q_3 = \frac{3(n+1)}{4} \text{ ranked value}$$

$$= \frac{3(7+1)}{4} \text{ ranked value} = \text{6th ranked value}$$

Therefore, using Rule 1, Q_3 is the sixth ranked value. Because the sixth ranked value is 190, Q_3 is 190.

The first quartile of 100 indicates that 25% of the cereals contain 100 calories or fewer per serving and 75% contain 100 or more calories. The third quartile of 190 indicates that 75% of the cereals contain 190 calories or fewer per serving and 25% contain 190 or more calories.

The Interquartile Range

The **interquartile range** (also called the **midspread**) measures the difference in the center of a distribution between the third and first quartiles.

INTERQUARTILE RANGE

The interquartile range is the difference between the third quartile and the first quartile:

$$\text{Interquartile range} = Q_3 - Q_1 \qquad\qquad \textbf{(3.10)}$$

The interquartile range measures the spread in the middle 50% of the values. Therefore, it is not influenced by extreme values. To further analyze the sample of 10 times to get ready in the morning, you can compute the interquartile range. You first order the data as follows:

$$29 \quad 31 \quad 35 \quad 39 \quad 39 \quad 40 \quad 43 \quad 44 \quad 44 \quad 52$$

You use Equation (3.10) and the earlier results on page 114, $Q_1 = 35$ and $Q_3 = 44$:

$$\text{Interquartile range} = 44 - 35 = 9 \text{ minutes}$$

Therefore, the interquartile range in the time to get ready is 9 minutes. The interval 35 to 44 is often referred to as the *middle fifty*.

EXAMPLE 3.11

Computing the Interquartile Range for the Number of Calories in Cereals

Nutritional data about a sample of seven breakfast cereals (stored in [Cereals]) includes the number of calories per serving (see Example 3.1 on page 100). Compute the interquartile range of the number of calories in cereals.

SOLUTION Ranked from smallest to largest, the numbers of calories for the seven cereals are as follows:

$$80 \quad 100 \quad 100 \quad 110 \quad 130 \quad 190 \quad 200$$

Using Equation (3.10) and the earlier results from Example 3.10 on page 115, $Q_1 = 100$ and $Q_3 = 190$:

$$\text{Interquartile range} = 190 - 100 = 90$$

Therefore, the interquartile range of the number of calories in cereals is 90 calories.

Because the interquartile range does not consider any value smaller than Q_1 or larger than Q_3, it cannot be affected by extreme values. Descriptive statistics such as the median, Q_1, Q_3, and the interquartile range, which are not influenced by extreme values, are called **resistant measures**.

The Five-Number Summary

The **five-number summary** for a variable consists of the smallest value (X_{smallest}), the first quartile, the median, the third quartile, and the largest value (X_{largest}).

FIVE-NUMBER SUMMARY

$$X_{\text{smallest}} \quad Q_1 \quad \text{Median} \quad Q_3 \quad X_{\text{largest}}$$

The five-number summary provides a way to determine the shape of the distribution for a set of data. Table 3.5 explains how relationships among these five statistics help to identify the shape of the distribution.

TABLE 3.5

Relationships Among the Five-Number Summary and the Type of Distribution

COMPARISON	TYPE OF DISTRIBUTION		
	Left-Skewed	**Symmetrical**	**Right-Skewed**
The distance from X_{smallest} to the median versus the distance from the median to X_{largest}.	The distance from X_{smallest} to the median is greater than the distance from the median to X_{largest}.	The two distances are the same.	The distance from X_{smallest} to the median is less than the distance from the median to X_{largest}.
The distance from X_{smallest} to Q_1 versus the distance from Q_3 to X_{largest}.	The distance from X_{smallest} to Q_1 is greater than the distance from Q_3 to X_{largest}.	The two distances are the same.	The distance from X_{smallest} to Q_1 is less than the distance from Q_3 to X_{largest}.
The distance from Q_1 to the median versus the distance from the median to Q_3.	The distance from Q_1 to the median is greater than the distance from the median to Q_3.	The two distances are the same.	The distance from Q_1 to the median is less than the distance from the median to Q_3.

To further analyze the sample of 10 times to get ready in the morning, you can compute the five-number summary. For these data, the smallest value is 29 minutes, and the largest value is 52 minutes (see page 101). Calculations done on pages 101 and 114 show that the median = 39.5, $Q_1 = 35$, and $Q_3 = 44$. Therefore, the five-number summary is as follows:

$$29 \quad 35 \quad 39.5 \quad 44 \quad 52$$

The distance from $X_{smallest}$ to the median $(39.5 - 29 = 10.5)$ is slightly less than the distance from the median to $X_{largest}$ $(52 - 39.5 = 12.5)$. The distance from $X_{smallest}$ to Q_1 $(35 - 29 = 6)$ is slightly less than the distance from Q_3 to $X_{largest}$ $(52 - 44 = 8)$. The distance from Q_1 to the median $(39.5 - 35 = 4.5)$ is the same as the distance from the median to $Q_3(44 - 39.5 = 4.5)$. Therefore, the getting-ready times are slightly right-skewed.

EXAMPLE 3.12

Computing the Five-Number Summary of the Number of Calories in Cereals

Nutritional data about a sample of seven breakfast cereals (stored in Cereals) includes the number of calories per serving (see Example 3.1 on page 101). Compute the five-number summary of the number of calories in cereals.

SOLUTION From previous computations for the number of calories in cereals (see pages 101 and 115), you know that the median = 110, $Q_1 = 100$, and $Q_3 = 190$.

In addition, the smallest value in the data set is 80, and the largest value is 200. Therefore, the five-number summary is as follows:

$$80 \quad 100 \quad 110 \quad 190 \quad 200$$

The three comparisons listed in Table 3.5 are used to evaluate skewness. The distance from $X_{smallest}$ to the median $(110 - 80 = 30)$ is less than the distance $(200 - 110 = 90)$ from the median to $X_{largest}$. The distance from $X_{smallest}$ to Q_1 $(100 - 80 = 20)$ is greater than the distance from Q_3 to $X_{largest}$ $(200 - 190 = 10)$. The distance from Q_1 to the median $(110 - 100 = 10)$ is less than the distance from the median to Q_3 $(190 - 110 = 80)$. Two comparisons indicate a right-skewed distribution, whereas the other indicates a left-skewed distribution. Therefore, given the small sample size and the conflicting results, the shape cannot be clearly determined.

The Boxplot

The **boxplot** uses a five-number summary to visualize the shape of the distribution for a variable. Figure 3.3 contains a boxplot for the sample of 10 times to get ready in the morning.

FIGURE 3.3

Boxplot for the getting-ready times

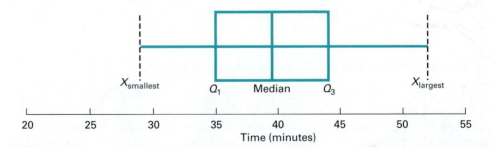

The vertical line drawn within the box represents the median. The vertical line at the left side of the box represents the location of Q_1, and the vertical line at the right side of the box represents the location of Q_3. Thus, the box contains the middle 50% of the values. The lower 25% of the data are represented by a line connecting the left side of the box to the location of the smallest value, $X_{smallest}$. Similarly, the upper 25% of the data are represented by a line connecting the right side of the box to $X_{largest}$.

The Figure 3.3 boxplot for the getting-ready times shows a slight right-skewness: The distance between the median and the highest value is slightly greater than the distance between the lowest value and the median, and the right tail is slightly longer than the left tail.

EXAMPLE 3.13

Boxplots of the
One-Year Returns
for the Growth and
Value Funds

In the More Descriptive Choices scenario, you are interested in comparing the past performance of the growth and value funds from a sample of 316 funds. One measure of past performance is the one-year return percentage variable. Construct the boxplots for this variable for the growth and value funds.

SOLUTION Figure 3.4 contains the boxplots for the one-year return percentages for the growth and value funds. The five-number summary for the growth funds associated with these boxplots is $X_{\text{smallest}} = -11.28$, $Q_1 = 11.78$, median $= 14.18$, $Q_3 = 16.64$, and $X_{\text{largest}} = 33.98$. The five-number summary for the value funds associated with these boxplots is $X_{\text{smallest}} = 1.67$, $Q_1 = 12.17$, median $= 15.3$, $Q_3 = 17.23$, and $X_{\text{largest}} = 28.27$.

FIGURE 3.4

Excel and Minitab boxplots for the one-year return percentage variable

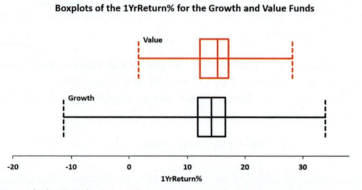

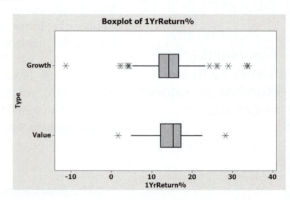

The lines, or whiskers, in the Minitab plots each extend 1.5 times the interquartile range from the boxes. Values beyond these ranges Minitab considers to be outliers, and plots them as asterisks.

The median return, the quartiles, and the minimum returns are higher for the value funds than for the growth funds. Both the growth and value funds are somewhat symmetrical, but the growth funds have a much larger range. These results are consistent with the statistics computed in Figure 3.2 on page 110.

Figure 3.5 demonstrates the relationship between the boxplot and the density curve for four different types of distributions. The area under each density curve is split into quartiles corresponding to the five-number summary for the boxplot.

The distributions in Panels A and D of Figure 3.5 are symmetrical. In these distributions, the mean and median are equal. In addition, the length of the left tail is equal to the length of the right tail, and the median line divides the box in half.

FIGURE 3.5

Boxplots and corresponding density curves for four distributions

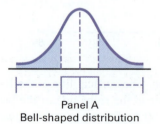

Panel A
Bell-shaped distribution

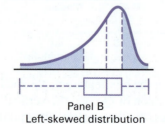

Panel B
Left-skewed distribution

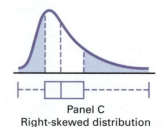

Panel C
Right-skewed distribution

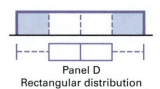

Panel D
Rectangular distribution

The distribution in Panel B of Figure 3.5 is left-skewed. The few small values distort the mean toward the left tail. For this left-skewed distribution, there is a heavy clustering of values at the high end of the scale (i.e., the right side); 75% of all values are found between the left edge of the box (Q_1) and the end of the right tail (X_{largest}). There is a long left tail that contains the smallest 25% of the values, demonstrating the lack of symmetry in this data set.

The distribution in Panel C of Figure 3.5 is right-skewed. The concentration of values is on the low end of the scale (i.e., the left side of the boxplot). Here, 75% of all values are found between the beginning of the left tail and the right edge of the box (Q_3). There is a long right tail that contains the largest 25% of the values, demonstrating the lack of symmetry in this data set.

Problems for Section 3.3

LEARNING THE BASICS

3.21 The following is a set of data from a sample of $n = 7$:

$$12 \quad 7 \quad 4 \quad 9 \quad 0 \quad 7 \quad 3$$

a. Compute the first quartile (Q_1), the third quartile (Q_3), and the interquartile range.
b. List the five-number summary.
c. Construct a boxplot and describe its shape.
d. Compare your answer in (c) with that from Problem 3.3 (d) on page 111. Discuss.

3.22 The following is a set of data from a sample of $n = 6$:

$$7 \quad 4 \quad 9 \quad 7 \quad 3 \quad 12$$

a. Compute the first quartile (Q_1), the third quartile (Q_3), and the interquartile range.
b. List the five-number summary.
c. Construct a boxplot and describe its shape.
d. Compare your answer in (c) with that from Problem 3.2 (d) on page 111. Discuss.

3.23 The following is a set of data from a sample of $n = 5$:

$$7 \quad 4 \quad 9 \quad 8 \quad 2$$

a. Compute the first quartile (Q_1), the third quartile (Q_3), and the interquartile range.
b. List the five-number summary.
c. Construct a boxplot and describe its shape.
d. Compare your answer in (c) with that from Problem 3.1 (d) on page 111. Discuss.

3.24 The following is a set of data from a sample of $n = 5$:

$$7 \quad -5 \quad -8 \quad 7 \quad 9$$

a. Compute the first quartile (Q_1), the third quartile (Q_3), and the interquartile range.
b. List the five-number summary.
c. Construct a boxplot and describe its shape.
d. Compare your answer in (c) with that from Problem 3.4 (d) on page 111. Discuss.

APPLYING THE CONCEPTS

3.25 The file **AccountingPartners** contains the number of partners in a cohort of rising accounting firms that have been tagged as "firms to watch." The firms have the following numbers of partners:

17 23 19 23 18 17 23 16 34 10 14 30 14 33 26 17 19 22
20 27 33 25 12 26 13 30 13 13 33 21 17 12 10 14 12

Source: Data extracted from **bit.ly/ODuzd3**.

a. Compute the first quartile (Q_1), the third quartile (Q_3), and the interquartile range.
b. List the five-number summary.
c. Construct a boxplot and describe its shape.

3.26 The file **MarketPenetration** contains Facebook penetration values (the percentage of the country population that are Facebook users) for 22 of the world's largest economies:

56 57 43 55 42 35 7 25 42 17 43
 6 31 28 59 20 27 36 45 80 57 56

Source: Data extracted from **slidesha.re/ODv6vG**.

a. Compute the first quartile (Q_1), the third quartile (Q_3), and the interquartile range.
b. List the five-number summary.
c. Construct a boxplot and describe its shape.

3.27 The file **HotelAway** contains the average room price (in US$) paid by various nationalities while traveling abroad (away from their home country) in 2013:

179   173   175   173   164   143   153   155

Source: Data extracted from **http://bit.ly/1pdFkOG**.

a. Compute the first quartile (Q_1), the third quartile (Q_3), and the interquartile range.
b. List the five-number summary.
c. Construct a boxplot and describe its shape.

3.28 The file **SUV** contains the overall MPG of 2014 small SUVs:

26 22 23 21 25 24 22 26 25 22
21 21 22 22 23 24 23 22 21 22

Source: Data extracted from "Which Car Is Right for You," *Consumer Reports*, April 2014, pp. 60–61.

a. Compute the first quartile (Q_1), the third quartile (Q_3), and the interquartile range.
b. List the five-number summary.
c. Construct a boxplot and describe its shape.

3.29 The file **CD Rate** contains the yields for one-year CDs and five-year CDs, for 22 banks in the United States, as of March 12, 2014.

Source: Data extracted from **www.Bankrate.com**, March 12, 2014.

For each type of account:
a. Compute the first quartile (Q_1), the third quartile (Q_3), and the interquartile range.
b. List the five-number summary.
c. Construct a boxplot and describe its shape.

3.30 A bank branch located in a commercial district of a city has the business objective of developing an improved process for serving customers during the noon-to-1:00 P.M. lunch period. The waiting time, in minutes, is defined as the time the customer enters the line to when he or she reaches the teller window. Data are collected from a sample of 15 customers during this hour. The file **Bank1** contains the results, which are listed below:

4.21   5.55   3.02   5.13   4.77   2.34   3.54   3.20
4.50   6.10   0.38   5.12   6.46   6.19   3.79

Another bank branch, located in a residential area, is also concerned with the noon-to-1:00 P.M. lunch hour. The waiting times,

in minutes, collected from a sample of 15 customers during this hour, are contained in the file **Bank2** and listed here:

9.66   5.90   8.02   5.79   8.73   3.82   8.01   8.35
10.49   6.68   5.64   4.08   6.17   9.91   5.47

a. List the five-number summaries of the waiting times at the two bank branches.
b. Construct boxplots and describe the shapes of the distributions for the two bank branches.
c. What similarities and differences are there in the distributions of the waiting times at the two bank branches?

3.4 Numerical Descriptive Measures for a Population

Sections 3.1 and 3.2 discuss the statistics that can be computed to describe the properties of central tendency and variation for a sample. When you collect data from an entire population (see Section 1.2), you compute and analyze population *parameters* for these properties, including the population mean, population variance, and population standard deviation.

To help illustrate these parameters, consider the population of stocks for the 10 companies in the Dow Jones Industrial Average (DJIA) that form the "Dogs of the Dow," the 10 stocks in the DJIA whose dividend is the highest fraction of their price in the previous year. (An alternative investment scheme popularized by Michael O'Higgins uses these "dogs.") Table 3.6 contains the 2013 one-year returns (excluding dividends) for the 10 "Dow Dog" stocks of 2012. These data, stored in **DowDogs**, will be used to illustrate the population parameters discussed in this section.

TABLE 3.6

One-Year Return for the "Dogs of the Dow"

Stock	One-Year Return	Stock	One-Year Return
AT&T	4.3	DuPont	44.4
Verizon	13.6	Johnson & Johnson	30.7
Merck	22.3	Intel	25.9
Pfizer	22.1	Hewlett-Packard	96.4
General Electric	33.5	McDonald's	10.0

Source: Data extracted from **dogsofthedow.com**.

The Population Mean

The **population mean** is the sum of the values in the population divided by the population size, N. This parameter, represented by the Greek lowercase letter mu, μ, serves as a measure of central tendency. Equation (3.11) defines the population mean.

POPULATION MEAN

The population mean is the sum of the values in the population divided by the population size, N.

$$\mu = \frac{\sum_{i=1}^{N} X_i}{N} \tag{3.11}$$

where

μ = population mean

X_i = ith value of the variable X

$\sum_{i=1}^{N} X_i$ = summation of all X_i values in the population

N = number of values in the population

To compute the mean one-year return for the population of "Dow Dog" stocks in Table 3.6, use Equation (3.11):

$$\mu = \frac{\sum_{i=1}^{N} X_i}{N}$$

$$= \frac{4.3 + 13.6 + 22.3 + 22.1 + 33.5 + 44.4 + 30.7 + 25.9 + 96.4 + 10.0}{10}$$

$$= \frac{303.2}{10} = 30.32$$

Thus, the mean one-year return for the "Dow Dog" stocks is 30.32.

The Population Variance and Standard Deviation

The population variance and the population standard deviation parameters measure variation in a population. The **population variance** is the sum of the squared differences around the population mean divided by the population size, N, and the **population standard deviation** is the square root of the population variance. In practice, you will most likely use the population standard deviation because, unlike the population variance, the standard deviation will always be a number expressed in the same units as the original population data.

The lowercase Greek letter sigma, σ, represents the population standard deviation, and sigma squared, σ^2, represents the population variance. Equations (3.12) and (3.13) define these parameters. The denominators for the right-side terms in these equations use N and not the $(n - 1)$ term that is found in Equations (3.4) and (3.5) on page 104 that define the sample variance and standard deviation.

POPULATION VARIANCE

$$\sigma^2 = \frac{\sum_{i=1}^{N} (X_i - \mu)^2}{N} \tag{3.12}$$

where

$$\mu = \text{population mean}$$
$$X_i = i\text{th value of the variable } X$$

$$\sum_{i=1}^{N} (X_i - \mu)^2 = \text{summation of all the squared differences between the } X_i \text{ values and } \mu$$

POPULATION STANDARD DEVIATION

$$\sigma = \sqrt{\frac{\sum_{i=1}^{N} (X_i - \mu)^2}{N}} \tag{3.13}$$

To compute the population variance for the data of Table 3.6, you use Equation (3.12):

$$\sigma^2 = \frac{\sum_{i=1}^{N}(X_i - \mu)^2}{N}$$

$$= \frac{677.0404 + 279.5584 + 64.3204 + 67.5684 + 10.1124 + 198.2464 + 0.1444 + 19.5364 + 4{,}366.5664 + 412.9024}{10}$$

$$= \frac{6{,}095.996}{10} = 609.5996$$

From Equation (3.13), the population sample standard deviation is

$$\sigma = \sqrt{\sigma^2} = \sqrt{\frac{\sum_{i=1}^{N}(X_i - \mu)^2}{N}} = \sqrt{\frac{6{,}095.996}{10}} = 24.6901$$

Therefore, the typical percentage return differs from the mean of 30.32 by approximately 24.6901. This large amount of variation suggests that the "Dow Dog" stocks produce results that differ greatly.

The Empirical Rule

In most data sets, a large portion of the values tend to cluster somewhere near the mean. In right-skewed data sets, this clustering occurs to the left of the mean—that is, at a value less than the mean. In left-skewed data sets, the values tend to cluster to the right of the mean—that is, greater than the mean. In symmetrical data sets, where the median and mean are the same, the values often tend to cluster around the median and mean, producing a bell-shaped normal distribution (discussed in Chapter 6).

The **empirical rule** states that for population data that form a normal distribution, the following are true:

- Approximately 68% of the values are within ± 1 standard deviation from the mean.
- Approximately 95% of the values are within ± 2 standard deviations from the mean.
- Approximately 99.7% of the values are within ± 3 standard deviations from the mean.

The empirical rule helps you examine variability in a population as well as identify outliers. The empirical rule implies that in a normal distribution, only about 1 out of 20 values will be beyond 2 standard deviations from the mean in either direction. As a general rule, you can consider values not found in the interval $\mu \pm 2\sigma$ as potential outliers. The rule also implies that only about 3 in 1,000 will be beyond 3 standard deviations from the mean. Therefore, values not found in the interval $\mu \pm 3\sigma$ are almost always considered outliers.

EXAMPLE 3.14

Using the Empirical Rule

A population of 2-liter bottles of cola is known to have a mean fill-weight of 2.06 liters and a standard deviation of 0.02 liter. The population is known to be bell-shaped. Describe the distribution of fill-weights. Is it very likely that a bottle will contain less than 2 liters of cola?

SOLUTION

$$\mu \pm \sigma = 2.06 \pm 0.02 = (2.04, 2.08)$$
$$\mu \pm 2\sigma = 2.06 \pm 2(0.02) = (2.02, 2.10)$$
$$\mu \pm 3\sigma = 2.06 \pm 3(0.02) = (2.00, 2.12)$$

(Continued)

Using the empirical rule, you can see that approximately 68% of the bottles will contain between 2.04 and 2.08 liters, approximately 95% will contain between 2.02 and 2.10 liters, and approximately 99.7% will contain between 2.00 and 2.12 liters. Therefore, it is highly unlikely that a bottle will contain less than 2 liters.

The Chebyshev Rule

For heavily skewed sets of data and data sets that do not appear to be normally distributed, you should use the Chebyshev rule instead of the empirical rule. The **Chebyshev rule** (see reference 2) states that for any data set, regardless of shape, the percentage of values that are found within distances of k standard deviations from the mean must be at least

$$\left(1 - \frac{1}{k^2}\right) \times 100\%$$

You can use this rule for any value of k greater than 1. For example, consider $k = 2$. The Chebyshev rule states that at least $[1 - (1/2)^2] \times 100\% = 75\%$ of the values must be found within ± 2 standard deviations of the mean.

The Chebyshev rule is very general and applies to any distribution. The rule indicates *at least* what percentage of the values fall within a given distance from the mean. However, if the data set is approximately bell-shaped, the empirical rule will more accurately reflect the greater concentration of data close to the mean. Table 3.7 compares the Chebyshev and empirical rules.

TABLE 3.7

How Data Vary
Around the Mean

Section EG3.4 describes the **VE-Variability workbook** *that allows you to use Excel to explore the empirical and Chebyshev rules.*

	% of Values Found in Intervals Around the Mean	
Interval	**Chebyshev (any distribution)**	**Empirical Rule (normal distribution)**
$(\mu - \sigma, \mu + \sigma)$	At least 0%	Approximately 68%
$(\mu - 2\sigma, \mu + 2\sigma)$	At least 75%	Approximately 95%
$(\mu - 3\sigma, \mu + 3\sigma)$	At least 88.89%	Approximately 99.7%

EXAMPLE 3.15

Using the
Chebyshev Rule

As in Example 3.14, a population of 2-liter bottles of cola is known to have a mean fill-weight of 2.06 liter and a standard deviation of 0.02 liter. However, the shape of the population is unknown, and you cannot assume that it is bell-shaped. Describe the distribution of fill-weights. Is it very likely that a bottle will contain less than 2 liters of cola?

SOLUTION

$$\mu \pm \sigma = 2.06 \pm 0.02 = (2.04, 2.08)$$
$$\mu \pm 2\sigma = 2.06 \pm 2(0.02) = (2.02, 2.10)$$
$$\mu \pm 3\sigma = 2.06 \pm 3(0.02) = (2.00, 2.12)$$

Because the distribution may be skewed, you cannot use the empirical rule. Using the Chebyshev rule, you cannot say anything about the percentage of bottles containing between 2.04 and 2.08 liters. You can state that at least 75% of the bottles will contain between 2.02 and 2.10 liters and at least 88.89% will contain between 2.00 and 2.12 liters. Therefore, between 0 and 11.11% of the bottles will contain less than 2 liters.

You can use these two rules to understand how data are distributed around the mean when you have sample data. With each rule, you use the value you computed for $\overline{X}$ in place of μ and the value you computed for S in place of σ. The results you compute using the sample statistics are *approximations* because you used sample statistics $(\overline{X}, S)$ and not population parameters (μ, σ).

Problems for Section 3.4

LEARNING THE BASICS

3.31 The following is a set of data for a population with $N = 10$:

$$7 \quad 5 \quad 11 \quad 8 \quad 3 \quad 6 \quad 2 \quad 1 \quad 9 \quad 8$$

a. Compute the population mean.
b. Compute the population standard deviation.

3.32 The following is a set of data for a population with $N = 10$:

$$7 \quad 5 \quad 6 \quad 6 \quad 6 \quad 4 \quad 8 \quad 6 \quad 9 \quad 3$$

a. Compute the population mean.
b. Compute the population standard deviation.

APPLYING THE CONCEPTS

3.33 The file **RadioShack** contains the number of RadioShack stores located in each of the 50 U.S. states and the District of Columbia, as of December 31, 2013:

65	20	76	53	565	82	68	18	12	309	127
24	28	197	122	68	56	75	81	33	99	115
155	81	47	97	28	33	40	36	156	41	342
139	9	203	59	70	232	20	69	22	88	408
41	16	144	111	36	101	19				

Source: Data extracted from "RadioShack closing up to 1,100 stores," *USA Today*, March 6, 2014, p. 1B.

a. Compute the mean, variance, and standard deviation for this population.
b. What percentage of the 50 states have RadioShack stores within ± 1, ± 2, or ± 3 standard deviations of the mean?
c. Compare your findings with what would be expected on the basis of the empirical rule. Are you surprised at the results in (b)?

3.34 Consider a population of 1,024 mutual funds that primarily invest in large companies. You have determined that μ, the mean one-year total percentage return achieved by all the funds, is 8.20 and that σ, the standard deviation, is 2.75.

a. According to the empirical rule, what percentage of these funds is expected to be within ± 1 standard deviation of the mean?

b. According to the empirical rule, what percentage of these funds is expected to be within ± 2 standard deviations of the mean?
c. According to the Chebyshev rule, what percentage of these funds is expected to be within ± 1, ± 2, or ± 3 standard deviations of the mean?
d. According to the Chebyshev rule, at least 93.75% of these funds are expected to have one-year total returns between what two amounts?

3.35 The file **CigaretteTax** contains the state cigarette tax (in \$) for each of the 50 states as of January 1, 2014.
a. Compute the population mean and population standard deviation for the state cigarette tax.
b. Interpret the parameters in (a).

SELF Test **3.36** The file **Energy** contains the per capita energy consumption, in kilowatt-hours, for each of the 50 states and the District of Columbia during a recent year.
a. Compute the mean, variance, and standard deviation for the population.
b. What proportion of these states has per capita energy consumption within ± 1 standard deviation of the mean, within ± 2 standard deviations of the mean, and within ± 3 standard deviations of the mean?
c. Compare your findings with what would be expected based on the empirical rule. Are you surprised at the results in (b)?
d. Repeat (a) through (c) with the District of Columbia removed. How have the results changed?

3.37 Thirty companies comprise the DJIA. Just how big are these companies? One common method for measuring the size of a company is to use its market capitalization, which is computed by multiplying the number of stock shares by the price of a share of stock. On March 14, 2014, the market capitalization of these companies ranged from Traveler's \$29.1 billion to ExxonMobil's \$403.9 billion. The entire population of market capitalization values is stored in **DowMarketCap**.

Source: Data extracted from **money.cnn.com**, March 14, 2014.

a. Compute the mean and standard deviation of the market capitalization for this population of 30 companies.
b. Interpret the parameters computed in (a).

3.5 The Covariance and the Coefficient of Correlation

In Section 2.5, you used scatter plots to visually examine the relationship between two numerical variables. This section presents two measures of the relationship between two numerical variables: the covariance and the coefficient of correlation.

The Covariance

The **covariance** measures the strength of the linear relationship between two numerical variables (X and Y). Equation (3.14) defines the **sample covariance**, and Example 3.16 illustrates its use.

SAMPLE COVARIANCE

$$\text{cov}(X, Y) = \frac{\sum_{i=1}^{n}(X_i - \overline{X})(Y_i - \overline{Y})}{n - 1} \tag{3.14}$$

EXAMPLE 3.16

Computing the Sample Covariance

In Example 2.12 on page 60, you used the NBA team revenue and value data from Table 2.18 (stored in NBAValues) to construct a scatter plot that showed the relationship between those two variables. Now, you want to measure the association between the annual revenue and value of a team by determining the sample covariance.

SOLUTION Figure 3.6 contains two worksheets that together compute the covariance using the Table 2.18 data on page 60.

FIGURE 3.6

Excel data and covariance worksheets for the revenue and value for the 30 NBA teams

	A	B	C	D
1	Revenue	Value	(X-XBar)	(Y-YBar)
2	119	425	-32.8667	-209.3000
3	169	875	17.1333	240.7000
4	190	780	38.1333	145.7000
5	115	410	-36.8667	-224.3000
6	195	1000	43.1333	365.7000
7	145	515	-6.8667	-119.3000
8	162	765	10.1333	130.7000
9	124	495	-27.8667	-139.3000
10	139	450	-12.8667	-184.3000
11	160	750	8.1333	115.7000
12	191	775	39.1333	140.7000
13	121	475	-30.8667	-159.3000
14	128	575	-23.8667	-59.3000
15	295	1350	143.1333	715.7000
16	126	453	-25.8667	-181.3000

	A	B	C	D
1	Revenue	Value	(X-XBar)	(Y-YBar)
17	188	770	36.1333	135.7000
18	109	405	-42.8667	-229.3000
19	116	430	-35.8667	-204.3000
20	116	420	-35.8667	-214.3000
21	287	1400	135.1333	765.7000
22	144	590	-7.8667	-44.3000
23	139	560	-12.8667	-74.3000
24	117	469	-34.8667	-165.3000
25	137	565	-14.8667	-69.3000
26	140	587	-11.8667	-47.3000
27	115	550	-36.8667	-84.3000
28	167	660	15.1333	25.7000
29	149	520	-2.8667	-114.3000
30	131	525	-20.8667	-109.3000
31	122	485	-29.8667	-149.3000

	A	B	
1	Covariance Analysis of Revenue and Value		
2			
3	Intermediate Calculations		
4	XBar	151.8667	=AVERAGE(DATA!A:A)
5	YBar	634.3000	=AVERAGE(DATA!B:B)
6	Σ(X-XBar)(Y-YBar)	321350.2000	=SUMPRODUCT(DATA!C:C, DATA!D:D)
7	n-1	29	=COUNT(DATA!A:A) - 1
8			
9	Covariance	11081.0414	=COVARIANCE.S(DATA!A:A, DATA!B:B)

In Figure 3.6, the covariance worksheet illustration includes a list of formulas to the right of the cells in which they occur, a style used throughout the rest of this book.

From the result in cell B9 of the covariance worksheet, or by using Equation (3.14) directly (shown below), you determine that the covariance is 11,081.0414:

$$\text{cov}(X, Y) = \frac{321,350.2}{30 - 1}$$

$$= 11,081.0414$$

The covariance has a major flaw as a measure of the linear relationship between two numerical variables. Because the covariance can have any value, you cannot use it to determine the relative strength of the relationship. In Example 3.16, you cannot tell whether the value 11,081.0414 indicates a strong relationship or a weak relationship between revenue and value. To better determine the relative strength of the relationship, you need to compute the coefficient of correlation.

The Coefficient of Correlation

The **coefficient of correlation** measures the relative strength of a linear relationship between two numerical variables. The values of the coefficient of correlation range from -1 for a perfect negative correlation to $+1$ for a perfect positive correlation. *Perfect* in this case means that if the points were plotted on a scatter plot, all the points could be connected with a straight line.

When dealing with population data for two numerical variables, the Greek letter ρ (*rho*) is used as the symbol for the coefficient of correlation. Figure 3.7 illustrates three different types of association between two variables.

FIGURE 3.7

Types of association between variables

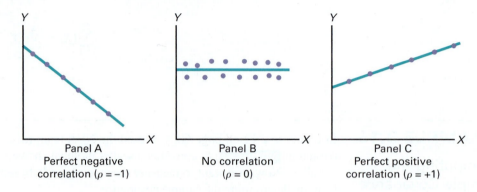

Panel A	Panel B	Panel C
Perfect negative correlation ($\rho = -1$)	No correlation ($\rho = 0$)	Perfect positive correlation ($\rho = +1$)

In Panel A of Figure 3.7, there is a perfect negative linear relationship between X and Y. Thus, the coefficient of correlation, ρ, equals -1, and when X increases, Y decreases in a perfectly predictable manner. Panel B shows a situation in which there is no relationship between X and Y. In this case, the coefficient of correlation, ρ, equals 0, and as X increases, there is no tendency for Y to increase or decrease. Panel C illustrates a perfect positive relationship where ρ equals $+1$. In this case, Y increases in a perfectly predictable manner when X increases.

Correlation alone cannot prove that there is a causation effect—that is, that the change in the value of one variable caused the change in the other variable. A strong correlation can be produced by chance; by the effect of a **lurking variable**, a third variable not considered in the calculation of the correlation; or by a cause-and-effect relationship. You would need to perform additional analysis to determine which of these three situations actually produced the correlation. Therefore, you can say that *causation implies correlation, but correlation alone does not imply causation.*

Equation (3.15) defines the **sample coefficient of correlation (r)**.

SAMPLE COEFFICIENT OF CORRELATION

$$r = \frac{\text{cov}(X, Y)}{S_X S_Y} \tag{3.15}$$

where

$$\text{cov}(X, Y) = \frac{\sum_{i=1}^{n} (X_i - \bar{X})(Y_i - \bar{Y})}{n - 1}$$

$$S_X = \sqrt{\frac{\sum_{i=1}^{n} (X_i - \bar{X})^2}{n - 1}}$$

$$S_Y = \sqrt{\frac{\sum_{i=1}^{n} (Y_i - \bar{Y})^2}{n - 1}}$$

When you have sample data, you can compute the sample coefficient of correlation, r. When using sample data, you are unlikely to have a sample coefficient of correlation of exactly $+1, 0$, or -1. Figure 3.8 presents scatter plots along with their respective sample coefficients of correlation, r, for six data sets, each of which contains 100 X and Y values.

FIGURE 3.8

Six scatter plots and their sample coefficients of correlation, r

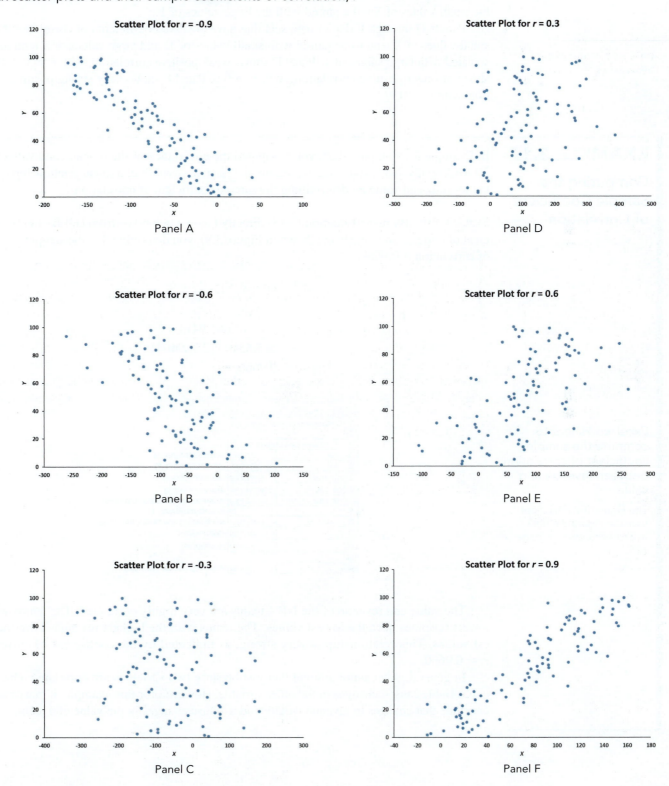

In Panel A, the coefficient of correlation, r, is -0.9. You can see that for small values of X, there is a very strong tendency for Y to be large. Likewise, the large values of X tend to be paired with small values of Y. The data do not all fall on a straight line, so the association between X and Y cannot be described as perfect. The data in Panel B have a coefficient of correlation equal to -0.6, and the small values of X tend to be paired with large values of Y. The linear relationship between X and Y in Panel B is not as strong as that in Panel A. Thus, the coefficient of correlation in Panel B is not as negative as that in Panel A. In Panel C, the linear relationship between X and Y is very weak, $r = -0.3$, and there is only a slight tendency for the small values of X to be paired with the large values of Y.

Panels D through F depict data sets that have positive coefficients of correlation because small values of X tend to be paired with small values of Y, and large values of X tend to be associated with large values of Y. Panel D shows weak positive correlation, with $r = 0.3$. Panel E shows stronger positive correlation, with $r = 0.6$. Panel F shows very strong positive correlation, with $r = 0.9$.

EXAMPLE 3.17

Computing the Sample Coefficient of Correlation

In Example 3.16 on page 125, you computed the covariance of the revenue and value for the 30 NBA teams. Now, you want to measure the relative strength of a linear relationship between the revenue and value by determining the sample coefficient of correlation.

SOLUTION By using Equation (3.15) directly (shown below) or from cell B14 in the coefficient of correlation worksheet (shown in Figure 3.9), you determine that the sample coefficient of correlation is 0.9660:

$$r = \frac{\text{cov}(X, Y)}{S_X S_Y}$$

$$= \frac{11{,}081.0414}{(45.5319)\,(251.9404)}$$

$$= 0.9660$$

FIGURE 3.9

Excel worksheet to compute the sample coefficient of correlation between revenue and value

The Figure 3.9 worksheet uses the Figure 3.6 data worksheet shown on page 125.

	A	B
1	Coefficient of Correlation Analysis	
2		
3	Intermediate Calculations	
4	XBar	151.8667 =AVERAGE(DATA!A:A)
5	YBar	634.3000 =AVERAGE(DATA!B:B)
6	$\Sigma(X-XBar)^2$	60121.4667 =DEVSQ(DATA!A:A)
7	$\Sigma(Y-YBar)^2$	1840744.3000 =DEVSQ(DATA!B:B)
8	$\Sigma(X-XBar)(Y-YBar)$	321350.2000 =SUMPRODUCT(DATA!C:C, DATA!D:D)
9	$n-1$	29 =COUNT(DATA!A:A) - 1
10	Covariance	11081.0414 =COVARIANCE.S(DATA!A:A, DATA!B:B)
11	S_X	45.5319 =SQRT(B6/B9)
12	S_Y	251.9404 =SQRT(B7/B9)
13		
14	r	0.9660 =CORREL(DATA!A:A, DATA!B:B)

The value and revenue of the NBA teams are very highly correlated. The teams with the lowest revenues have the lowest values. The teams with the highest revenues have the highest values. This relationship is very strong, as indicated by the coefficient of correlation, $r = 0.9660$.

In general, you cannot assume that just because two variables are correlated, changes in one variable caused changes in the other variable. However, for this example, it makes sense to conclude that changes in revenue would tend to cause changes in the value of a team.

In summary, the coefficient of correlation indicates the linear relationship, or association, between two numerical variables. When the coefficient of correlation gets closer to $+1$ or -1, the linear relationship between the two variables is stronger. When the coefficient of correlation is near 0, little or no linear relationship exists. The sign of the coefficient of correlation indicates whether the data are positively correlated (i.e., the larger values of X are typically paired with the larger values of Y) or negatively correlated (i.e., the larger values of X are typically paired with the smaller values of Y). The existence of a strong correlation does not imply a causation effect. It only indicates the tendencies present in the data.

Problems for Section 3.5

LEARNING THE BASICS

3.38 The following is a set of data from a sample of $n = 11$ items:

X	7	5	8	3	6	10	12	4	9	15	18
Y	21	15	24	9	18	30	36	12	27	45	54

a. Compute the covariance.
b. Compute the coefficient of correlation.
c. How strong is the relationship between X and Y? Explain.

APPLYING THE CONCEPTS

3.39 A study of 483 first-year college women suggests a link between media usage such as texting, chatting on cell phones, and posting status updates on Facebook, and grade point average. Students reporting a higher use of media had lower grade point averages than students reporting a lower use of media. (Source: Walsh et al., "Female College Students' Media Use and Academic Outcomes," *Emerging Adulthood*, 2013.)

a. Does the study suggest that use of media and grade point average are positively correlated or negatively correlated?
b. Do you think that there might be a cause-and-effect relationship between use of media and grade point average? Explain.

 3.40 The file **Cereals** lists the calories and sugar, in grams, in one serving of seven breakfast cereals:

Cereal	Calories	Sugar
Kellogg's All Bran	80	6
Kellogg's Corn Flakes	100	2
Wheaties	100	4
Nature's Path Organic Multigrain Flakes	110	4
Kellogg's Rice Krispies	130	4
Post Shredded Wheat Vanilla Almond	190	11
Kellogg's Mini Wheats	200	10

a. Compute the covariance.
b. Compute the coefficient of correlation.
c. Which do you think is more valuable in expressing the relationship between calories and sugar—the covariance or the coefficient of correlation? Explain.
d. Based on (a) and (b), what conclusions can you reach about the relationship between calories and sugar?

3.41 Movie companies need to predict the gross receipts of individual movies once a movie has debuted. The data, shown in the next column and stored in **PotterMovies**, are the first weekend gross, the U.S. gross, and the worldwide gross (in $ millions) of the eight Harry Potter movies:

a. Compute the covariance between first weekend gross and U.S. gross, first weekend gross and worldwide gross, and U.S. gross and worldwide gross.
b. Compute the coefficient of correlation between first weekend gross and U.S. gross, first weekend gross and worldwide gross, and U.S. gross and worldwide gross.

Title	First Weekend	U.S. Gross	Worldwide Gross
Sorcerer's Stone	90.295	317.558	976.458
Chamber of Secrets	88.357	261.988	878.988
Prisoner of Azkaban	93.687	249.539	795.539
Goblet of Fire	102.335	290.013	896.013
Order of the Phoenix	77.108	292.005	938.469
Half-Blood Prince	77.836	301.460	934.601
Deathly Hallows Part 1	125.017	295.001	955.417
Deathly Hallows Part 2	169.189	381.011	1,328.111

Source: Data extracted from **www.the-numbers.com/interactive/comp-HarryPotter.php**.

c. Which do you think is more valuable in expressing the relationship between first weekend gross, U.S. gross, and worldwide gross—the covariance or the coefficient of correlation? Explain.
d. Based on (a) and (b), what conclusions can you reach about the relationship between first weekend gross, U.S. gross, and worldwide gross?

3.42 College football is big business, with coaches' total pay and revenues, in millions of dollars. The file **College Football** contains the coaches' pay and revenues for college football at 105 of the 124 schools that are part of the Division I Football Bowl Subdivision.

Source: Data extracted from "College Football Coaches Continue to See Salary Explosion," *USA Today*, November 20, 2012.

a. Compute the covariance.
b. Compute the coefficient of correlation.
c. Based on (a) and (b), what conclusions can you reach about the relationship between coaches' total pay and revenues?

3.43 A Pew Research Center survey found that social networking is popular in many nations around the world. The file **GlobalSocialMedia** contains the level of social media networking (measured as the percentage of individuals polled who use social networking sites) and the GDP at purchasing power parity (PPP) per capita for each of 24 emerging and developing countries. (Data extracted from Pew Research Center, "Emerging Nations Embrace Internet, Mobile Technology," **bit.ly/1mg8Nvc**.)

a. Compute the covariance.
b. Compute the coefficient of correlation.
c. Based on (a) and (b), what conclusions can you reach about the relationship between the GDP and social media use?

3.6 Descriptive Statistics: Pitfalls and Ethical Issues

This chapter describes how a set of numerical data can be characterized by the statistics that measure the properties of central tendency, variation, and shape. In business, descriptive statistics such as the ones discussed in this chapter are frequently included in summary reports that are prepared periodically.

The volume of information available from online, broadcast, or print media has produced much skepticism in the minds of many about the objectivity of data. When you are reading information that contains descriptive statistics, you should keep in mind the quip often attributed to the famous nineteenth-century British statesman Benjamin Disraeli: "There are three kinds of lies: lies, damned lies, and statistics."

For example, in examining statistics, you need to compare the mean and the median. Are they similar, or are they very different? Or is only the mean provided? The answers to these questions will help you determine whether the data are skewed or symmetrical and whether the median might be a better measure of central tendency than the mean. In addition, you should look to see whether the standard deviation or interquartile range for a very skewed set of data has been included in the statistics provided. Without this, it is impossible to determine the amount of variation that exists in the data.

Ethical considerations arise when you are deciding what results to include in a report. You should document both good and bad results. In addition, in all presentations, you need to report results in a fair, objective, and neutral manner. Unethical behavior occurs when you selectively fail to report pertinent findings that are detrimental to the support of a particular position.

USING STATISTICS

More Descriptive Choices, Revisited

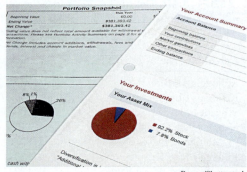

Baranq/Shutterstock

In the More Descriptive Choices scenario, you were hired by the Choice *Is* Yours investment company to assist investors interested in stock mutual funds. A sample of 316 stock mutual funds included 227 growth funds and 89 value funds. By comparing these two categories, you were able to provide investors with valuable insights.

The one-year returns for both the growth funds and the value funds were symmetrical, as indicated by the boxplots (see Figure 3.4 on page 118). The descriptive statistics (see Figure 3.2 on page 110) allowed you to compare the central tendency, variability, and shape of the returns of the growth funds and the value funds. The mean indicated that the growth funds returned a mean of 14.28, and the median indicated that half of the growth funds had returns of 14.18 or more. The value funds' central tendencies were slightly higher than those of the growth funds—they had a mean of 14.70, and half the funds had one-year returns above 15.30. The growth funds showed slightly more variability than the value funds, with a standard deviation of 5.0041 as compared to 4.4651. The kurtosis of growth funds was very positive, indicating a distribution that was much more peaked than a normal distribution. Although past performance is no assurance of future performance, the value funds slightly outperformed the growth funds in 2012. (You can examine other variables in **Retirement Funds** to see if the value funds outperformed the growth funds for the 3-year period 2010–2012, for the 5-year period 2008–2012 and for the 10-year period 2003–2012.)

SUMMARY

In this chapter and the previous chapter, you studied descriptive statistics—how you can organize data through tables, visualize data through charts, and how you can use various statistics to help analyze the data and reach conclusions. In Chapter 2, you organized data by constructing summary tables and visualized data by constructing bar and pie charts, histograms, and other charts. In this chapter, you learned how descriptive statistics such as the mean, median, quartiles, range, and standard deviation describe the characteristics of central tendency, variability, and shape. In addition, you constructed boxplots to visualize the distribution of the data. You also learned how the coefficient of correlation describes the relationship between two numerical variables. All the methods of this chapter are summarized in Table 3.8.

You also learned several concepts about variation in data that will prove useful in later chapters. These concepts are:

- The greater the spread or dispersion of the data, the larger the range, variance, and standard deviation.
- The smaller the spread or dispersion of the data, the smaller the range, variance, and standard deviation.
- If the values are all the same (no variation in the data), the range, variance, and standard deviation will all equal zero.
- Measures of variation (the range, variance, and standard deviation) are never negative.

In the next chapter, the basic principles of probability are presented in order to bridge the gap between the subject of descriptive statistics and the subject of inferential statistics.

TABLE 3.8

Chapter 3 Descriptive Statistics Methods

Type of Analysis	Methods
Central tendency	Mean, median, mode (Section 3.1)
Variation and shape	Quartiles, range, interquartile range, variance, standard deviation, coefficient of variation, Z scores, boxplot (Sections 3.2 through 3.4)
Describing the relationship between two numerical variables	Covariance, coefficient of correlation (Section 3.5)

REFERENCES

1. Booker, J., and L. Ticknor. "A Brief Overview of Kurtosis." **www.osti.gov/bridge/purl.cover.jsp?purl=/677174-zdulqk/ webviewable/677174.pdf**.
2. Kendall, M. G., A. Stuart, and J. K. Ord. *Kendall's Advanced Theory of Statistics*, *Volume 1: Distribution Theory*, 6th ed. New York: Oxford University Press, 1994.
3. *Microsoft Excel 2013*. Redmond, WA: Microsoft Corporation, 2012.
4. *Minitab Release 16*. State College, PA: Minitab, Inc., 2010.
5. Taleb, N. *The Black Swan*, 2nd ed. New York: Random House, 2010.

KEY EQUATIONS

Sample Mean

$$\overline{X} = \frac{\sum_{i=1}^{n} X_i}{n} \qquad (3.1)$$

Median

$$\text{Median} = \frac{n+1}{2} \text{ ranked value} \qquad (3.2)$$

Range

$$\text{Range} = X_{\text{largest}} - X_{\text{smallest}} \qquad (3.3)$$

Sample Variance

$$S^2 = \frac{\sum_{i=1}^{n} (X_i - \overline{X})^2}{n-1} \qquad (3.4)$$

Sample Standard Deviation

$$S = \sqrt{S^2} = \sqrt{\frac{\sum\limits_{i=1}^{n}(X_i - \overline{X})^2}{n-1}} \tag{3.5}$$

Coefficient of Variation

$$CV = \left(\frac{S}{\overline{X}}\right)100\% \tag{3.6}$$

Z Score

$$Z = \frac{X - \overline{X}}{S} \tag{3.7}$$

First Quartile, Q_1

$$Q_1 = \frac{n+1}{4} \text{ ranked value} \tag{3.8}$$

Third Quartile, Q_3

$$Q_3 = \frac{3(n+1)}{4} \text{ ranked value} \tag{3.9}$$

Interquartile Range

$$\text{Interquartile range} = Q_3 - Q_1 \tag{3.10}$$

Population Mean

$$\mu = \frac{\sum\limits_{i=1}^{N} X_i}{N} \tag{3.11}$$

Population Variance

$$\sigma^2 = \frac{\sum\limits_{i=1}^{N}(X_i - \mu)^2}{N} \tag{3.12}$$

Population Standard Deviation

$$\sigma = \sqrt{\frac{\sum\limits_{i=1}^{N}(X_i - \mu)^2}{N}} \tag{3.13}$$

Sample Covariance

$$\text{cov}(X, Y) = \frac{\sum\limits_{i=1}^{n}(X_i - \overline{X})(Y_i - \overline{Y})}{n-1} \tag{3.14}$$

Sample Coefficient of Correlation

$$r = \frac{\text{cov}(X, Y)}{S_X S_Y} \tag{3.15}$$

KEY TERMS

arithmetic mean (mean) 98
boxplot 117
central tendency 98
Chebyshev rule 123
coefficient of correlation 126
coefficient of variation (CV) 107
covariance 125
dispersion (spread) 102
empirical rule 122
five-number summary 116
interquartile range (midspread) 115
kurtosis 110
left-skewed 109
lepokurtic 110
lurking variable 126
mean (arithmetic mean) 98

median 100
midspread (interquartile range) 115
mode 101
outliers 108
percentiles 114
platykurtic 110
population mean 120
population standard deviation 121
population variance 121
Q_1: first quartile 113
Q_2: second quartile 113
Q_3: third quartile 113
quartiles 113
range 102
resistant measure 116
right-skewed 109

sample coefficient of correlation (r) 126
sample covariance 125
sample mean 98
sample standard deviation (S) 103
sample variance (S^2) 103
shape 98
skewed 109
skewness 109
spread (dispersion) 102
standard deviation 103
sum of squares (SS) 103
symmetrical 109
variance 103
variation 98
Z score 108

CHECKING YOUR UNDERSTANDING

3.44 What are the properties of a set of numerical data?

3.45 What is meant by the property of central tendency?

3.46 What are the differences among the mean, median, and mode, and what are the advantages and disadvantages of each?

3.47 How do you interpret the first quartile, median, and third quartile?

3.48 What is meant by the property of variation?

3.49 What does the Z score measure?

3.50 What are the differences among the various measures of variation, such as the range, interquartile range, variance, standard deviation, and coefficient of variation, and what are the advantages and disadvantages of each?

3.51 How does the empirical rule help explain the ways in which the values in a set of numerical data cluster and distribute?

3.52 How do the empirical rule and the Chebyshev rule differ?

3.53 What is meant by the property of shape?

3.54 What is the difference between skewness and kurtosis?

3.55 How do the covariance and the coefficient of correlation differ?

3.56 How do the boxplots for the variously shaped distributions differ?

CHAPTER REVIEW PROBLEMS

3.57 The American Society for Quality (ASQ) conducted a salary survey of all its members. ASQ members work in all areas of manufacturing and service-related institutions, with a common theme of an interest in quality. Manager and quality engineer were the most frequently reported job titles among the valid responses. Master Black Belt, a person who takes a leadership role as the keeper of the Six Sigma process (see Section 14.6) and Green Belt, someone who works on Six Sigma projects part time, were among the other job titles cited. Descriptive statistics concerning salaries for these four titles are given in the following table:

Job Title	Sample Size	Minimum	Maximum	Standard Deviation	Mean	Median
Green Belt	39	45,000	140,000	21,272	73,045	67,045
Manager	1,517	27,000	306,000	28,700	92,740	90,000
Quality Engineer	964	29,000	180,000	21,793	79,621	77,000
Master Black Belt	75	58,000	200,000	32,328	119,274	116,750

Source: Data extracted from M. Hansen, "QP Salary Survey," *Quality Progress*, December 2013, p. 31.

Compare the salaries of Green Belts, managers, quality engineers, and Master Black Belts.

3.58 In certain states, savings banks are permitted to sell life insurance. The approval process consists of underwriting, which includes a review of the application, a medical information bureau check, possible requests for additional medical information and medical exams, and a policy compilation stage, in which the policy pages are generated and sent to the bank for delivery. The ability to deliver approved policies to customers in a timely manner is critical to the profitability of this service to the bank. Using the Define, Collect, Organize, Visualize, and Analyze steps first discussed on page 2, you define the variable of interest as the total processing time in days. You collect the data by selecting a random sample of 27 approved policies during a period of one month. You organize the data collected in a worksheet and store them in **Insurance** :

```
73  19  16  64  28  28  31  90  60  56  31  56  22  18
45  48  17  17  17  91  92  63  50  51  69  16  17
```

a. Compute the mean, median, first quartile, and third quartile.
b. Compute the range, interquartile range, variance, standard deviation, and coefficient of variation.

c. Construct a boxplot. Are the data skewed? If so, how?
d. What would you tell a customer who enters the bank to purchase this type of insurance policy and asks how long the approval process takes?

3.59 One of the major measures of the quality of service provided by an organization is the speed with which it responds to customer complaints. A large family-held department store selling furniture and flooring, including carpet, had undergone a major expansion in the past several years. In particular, the flooring department had expanded from 2 installation crews to an installation supervisor, a measurer, and 15 installation crews. The business objective of the company was to reduce the time between when a complaint is received and when it is resolved. During a recent year, the company received 50 complaints concerning carpet installation. The data from the 50 complaints, organized in **Furniture** , represent the number of days between the receipt of a complaint and the resolution of the complaint:

```
54    5   35  137   31   27  152    2  123   81   74   27   11
19  126  110  110   29   61   35   94   31   26    5   12    4
165   32   29   28   29   26   25    1   14   13   13   10    5
27    4   52   30   22   36   26   20   23   33   68
```

a. Compute the mean, median, first quartile, and third quartile.
b. Compute the range, interquartile range, variance, standard deviation, and coefficient of variation.
c. Construct a boxplot. Are the data skewed? If so, how?
d. On the basis of the results of (a) through (c), if you had to tell the president of the company how long a customer should expect to wait to have a complaint resolved, what would you say? Explain.

3.60 A manufacturing company produces steel housings for electrical equipment. The main component part of the housing is a steel trough that is made of a 14-gauge steel coil. It is produced using a 250-ton progressive punch press with a wipe-down operation and two 90-degree forms placed in the flat steel to make the trough. The distance from one side of the form to the other is critical because of weatherproofing in outdoor applications. The company requires that the width of the trough be between 8.31 inches and 8.61 inches. Data are collected from a sample of 49 troughs and stored in **Trough** , which contains these widths of the troughs, in inches:

```
8.312  8.343  8.317  8.383  8.348  8.410  8.351  8.373  8.481  8.422
8.476  8.382  8.484  8.403  8.414  8.419  8.385  8.465  8.498  8.447
8.436  8.413  8.489  8.414  8.481  8.415  8.479  8.429  8.458  8.462
8.460  8.444  8.429  8.460  8.412  8.420  8.410  8.405  8.323  8.420
8.396  8.447  8.405  8.439  8.411  8.427  8.420  8.498  8.409
```

a. Compute the mean, median, range, and standard deviation for the width. Interpret these measures of central tendency and variability.
b. List the five-number summary.
c. Construct a boxplot and describe its shape.
d. What can you conclude about the number of troughs that will meet the company's requirement of troughs being between 8.31 and 8.61 inches wide?

3.61 The manufacturing company in Problem 3.60 also produces electric insulators. If the insulators break when in use, a short circuit is likely to occur. To test the strength of the insulators, destructive testing is carried out to determine how much force is required to break the insulators. Force is measured by observing how many pounds must be applied to an insulator before it breaks. Data are collected from a sample of 30 insulators. The file **Force** contains the strengths, as follows:

1,870 1,728 1,656 1,610 1,634 1,784 1,523 1,696 1,592 1,662
1,866 1,764 1,734 1,662 1,734 1,774 1,550 1,756 1,762 1,866
1,820 1,744 1,788 1,688 1,810 1,752 1,680 1,810 1,652 1,736

a. Compute the mean, median, range, and standard deviation for the force needed to break the insulators.
b. Interpret the measures of central tendency and variability in (a).
c. Construct a boxplot and describe its shape.
d. What can you conclude about the strength of the insulators if the company requires a force of at least 1,500 pounds before breakage?

3.62 Data were collected on the typical cost of dining at American-cuisine restaurants within a 1-mile walking distance of a hotel located in a large city. The file **Bundle** contains the typical cost (a per transaction cost in $) as well as a Bundle score, a measure of overall popularity and customer loyalty, for each of 40 selected restaurants. (Data extracted from www.bundle.com via the link **on-msn.com/MnlBxo**.)
a. For each variable, compute the mean, median, first quartile, and third quartile.
b. For each variable, compute the range, interquartile range, variance, standard deviation, and coefficient of variation.
c. For each variable, construct a boxplot. Are the data skewed? If so, how?
d. Compute the coefficient of correlation between Bundle score and typical cost.
e. What conclusions can you reach concerning Bundle score and typical cost?

3.63 A quality characteristic of interest for a tea-bag-filling process is the weight of the tea in the individual bags. If the bags are underfilled, two problems arise. First, customers may not be able to brew the tea to be as strong as they wish. Second, the company may be in violation of the truth-in-labeling laws. For this product, the label weight on the package indicates that, on average, there are 5.5 grams of tea in a bag. If the mean amount of tea in a bag exceeds the label weight, the company is giving away product. Getting an exact amount of tea in a bag is problematic because of variation in the temperature and humidity inside the factory, differences in the density of the tea, and the extremely fast filling operation of the machine (approximately 170 bags per minute). The file **Teabags** contains these weights, in grams, of a sample of 50 tea bags produced in one hour by a single machine:

5.65 5.44 5.42 5.40 5.53 5.34 5.54 5.45 5.52 5.41
5.57 5.40 5.53 5.54 5.55 5.62 5.56 5.46 5.44 5.51

5.47 5.40 5.47 5.61 5.53 5.32 5.67 5.29 5.49 5.55
5.77 5.57 5.42 5.58 5.58 5.50 5.32 5.50 5.53 5.58
5.61 5.45 5.44 5.25 5.56 5.63 5.50 5.57 5.67 5.36

a. Compute the mean, median, first quartile, and third quartile.
b. Compute the range, interquartile range, variance, standard deviation, and coefficient of variation.
c. Interpret the measures of central tendency and variation within the context of this problem. Why should the company producing the tea bags be concerned about the central tendency and variation?
d. Construct a boxplot. Are the data skewed? If so, how?
e. Is the company meeting the requirement set forth on the label that, on average, there are 5.5 grams of tea in a bag? If you were in charge of this process, what changes, if any, would you try to make concerning the distribution of weights in the individual bags?

3.64 The manufacturer of Boston and Vermont asphalt shingles provides its customers with a 20-year warranty on most of its products. To determine whether a shingle will last as long as the warranty period, accelerated-life testing is conducted at the manufacturing plant. Accelerated-life testing exposes a shingle to the stresses it would be subject to in a lifetime of normal use via an experiment in a laboratory setting that takes only a few minutes to conduct. In this test, a shingle is repeatedly scraped with a brush for a short period of time, and the shingle granules removed by the brushing are weighed (in grams). Shingles that experience low amounts of granule loss are expected to last longer in normal use than shingles that experience high amounts of granule loss. In this situation, a shingle should experience no more than 0.8 gram of granule loss if it is expected to last the length of the warranty period. The file **Granule** contains a sample of 170 measurements made on the company's Boston shingles and 140 measurements made on Vermont shingles.
a. List the five-number summaries for the Boston shingles and for the Vermont shingles.
b. Construct side-by-side boxplots for the two brands of shingles and describe the shapes of the distributions.
c. Comment on the ability of each type of shingle to achieve a granule loss of 0.8 gram or less.

3.65 The file **Restaurants** contains the cost per meal and the ratings of 50 city and 50 suburban restaurants on their food, décor, and service (and their summated ratings). (Data extracted from *Zagat Survey 2013 New York City Restaurants* and *Zagat Survey 2012–2013 Long Island Restaurants*.) Complete the following for the urban and suburban restaurants:
a. Construct the five-number summary of the cost of a meal.
b. Construct a boxplot of the cost of a meal. What is the shape of the distribution?
c. Compute and interpret the correlation coefficient of the summated rating and the cost of a meal.
d. What conclusions can you reach about the cost of a meal at city and suburban restaurants?

3.66 The file **Protein** contains calories, protein, and cholesterol of popular protein foods (fresh red meats, poultry, and fish).
Source: U.S. Department of Agriculture.
a. Compute the correlation coefficient between calories and protein.
b. Compute the correlation coefficient between calories and cholesterol.
c. Compute the correlation coefficient between protein and cholesterol.
d. Based on the results of (a) through (c), what conclusions can you reach concerning calories, protein, and cholesterol?

3.67 The file HotelPrices contains the prices in British pounds (about US$1.52 as of July 2013) of a room at two-star, three-star, and four-star hotels in cities around the world in 2013. (Data extracted from **press.hotels.com/content/blogs.dir/13 /files/2013/09/HPI_UK.pdf**.) Complete the following for two-star, three-star, and four-star hotels:

a. Compute the mean, median, first quartile, and third quartile.

b. Compute the range, interquartile range, variance, standard deviation, and coefficient of variation.

c. Interpret the measures of central tendency and variation within the context of this problem.

d. Construct a boxplot. Are the data skewed? If so, how?

e. Compute the covariance between the average price at two-star and three-star hotels, between two-star and four-star hotels, and between three-star and four-star hotels.

f. Compute the coefficient of correlation between the average price at two-star and three-star hotels, between two-star and four-star hotels, and between three-star and four-star hotels.

g. Which do you think is more valuable in expressing the relationship between the average price of a room at two-star, three-star, and four-star hotels—the covariance or the coefficient of correlation? Explain.

h. Based on (f), what conclusions can you reach about the relationship between the average price of a room at two-star, three-star, and four-star hotels?

3.68 The file PropertyTaxes contains the property taxes per capita for the 50 states and the District of Columbia.

a. Compute the mean, median, first quartile, and third quartile.

b. Compute the range, interquartile range, variance, standard deviation, and coefficient of variation.

c. Construct a boxplot. Are the data skewed? If so, how?

d. Based on the results of (a) through (c), what conclusions can you reach concerning property taxes per capita for each state and the District of Columbia?

3.69 Have you wondered how Internet download speed varies around the globe? The file DownloadSpeed contains the mean download speed Mbps for various countries. (Data extracted from **www.netindex.com/download/allcountries/**.)

a. Compute the mean, median, first quartile, and third quartile.

b. Compute the range, interquartile range, variance, standard deviation, and coefficient of variation.

c. Construct a boxplot. Are the data skewed? If so, how?

d. Based on the results of (a) through (c), what conclusions can you reach concerning the download speed around the globe?

3.70 311 is Chicago's web and phone portal for government information and nonemergency services. 311 serves as a comprehensive one-stop shop for residents, visitors, and business owners; therefore, it is critical that 311 representatives answer calls and respond to requests in a timely and accurate fashion. The target response time for answering 311 calls is 45 seconds. Agent abandonment rate is one of several call center metrics tracked by 311 officials. This metric tracks the percentage of callers who hang up after the target response time of 45 seconds has elapsed. The file 311CallCenter contains the agent abandonment rate for 22 weeks of call center operation during the 7:00 A.M.–3:00 P.M. shift.

a. Compute the mean, median, first quartile, and third quartile.

b. Compute the range, interquartile range, variance, standard deviation, and coefficient of variation.

c. Construct a boxplot. Are the data skewed? If so, how?

d. Compute the correlation coefficient between day and agent abandonment rate.

e. Based on the results of (a) through (c), what conclusions might you reach concerning 311 call center performance operation?

3.71 How much time do Americans living in or near cities spend waiting in traffic, and how much does waiting in traffic cost them per year? The file Congestion includes this cost for 31 cities. (Source: Data extracted from "The High Cost of Congestion," *Time*, October 17, 2011, p. 18.) For the time Americans living in or near cities spend waiting in traffic and the cost of waiting in traffic per year:

a. Compute the mean, median, first quartile, and third quartile.

b. Compute the range, interquartile range, variance, standard deviation, and coefficient of variation.

c. Construct a boxplot. Are the data skewed? If so, how?

d. Compute the correlation coefficient between the time spent sitting in traffic and the cost of sitting in traffic.

e. Based on the results of (a) through (c), what conclusions might you reach concerning the time spent waiting in traffic and the cost of waiting in traffic.

3.72 How do the average credit scores of people living in various American cities differ? The file Credit Scores is an ordered array of the average credit scores of people living in 143 American cities. (Data extracted from **usat.ly/17a1fA6**)

a. Compute the mean, median, first quartile, and third quartile.

b. Compute the range, interquartile range, variance, standard deviation, and coefficient of variation.

c. Construct a boxplot. Are the data skewed? If so, how?

d. Based on the results of (a) through (c), what conclusions might you reach concerning the average credit scores of people living in various American cities?

3.73 You are planning to study for your statistics examination with a group of classmates, one of whom you particularly want to impress. This individual has volunteered to use Microsoft Excel to generate the needed summary information, tables, and charts for a data set that contains several numerical and categorical variables assigned by the instructor for study purposes. This person comes over to you with the printout and exclaims, "I've got it all—the means, the medians, the standard deviations, the boxplots, the pie charts—for all our variables. The problem is, some of the output looks weird—like the boxplots for gender and for major and the pie charts for grade point average and for height. Also, I can't understand why Professor Szabat said we can't get the descriptive stats for some of the variables; I got them for everything! See, the mean for height is 68.23, the mean for grade point average is 2.76, the mean for gender is 1.50, the mean for major is 4.33." What is your reply?

REPORT WRITING EXERCISES

3.74 The file DomesticBeer contains the percentage alcohol, number of calories per 12 ounces, and number of carbohydrates (in grams) per 12 ounces for 156 of the best-selling domestic beers in the United States. (Data extracted from **bit.ly/17H3Ct**, March 12, 2014.) Write a report that includes a complete descriptive evaluation of each of the numerical variables—percentage of alcohol, number of calories per 12 ounces, and number of carbohydrates (in grams) per 12 ounces. Append to your report all appropriate tables, charts, and numerical descriptive measures.

CASES FOR CHAPTER 3

Managing Ashland MultiComm Services

For what variable in the Chapter 2 "Managing Ashland MultiComm Services" case (see page 78) are numerical descriptive measures needed?

1. For the variable you identify, compute the appropriate numerical descriptive measures and construct a boxplot.

2. For the variable you identify, construct a graphical display. What conclusions can you reach from this other plot that cannot be made from the boxplot?

3. Summarize your findings in a report that can be included with the task force's study.

Digital Case

Apply your knowledge about the proper use of numerical descriptive measures in this continuing Digital Case from Chapter 2.

Open **EndRunGuide.pdf**, the EndRun Financial Services "Guide to Investing." Reexamine EndRun's supporting data for the "More Winners Than Losers" and "The Big Eight Difference" and then answer the following:

1. Can descriptive measures be computed for any variables? How would such summary statistics support EndRun's

claims? How would those summary statistics affect your perception of EndRun's record?

2. Evaluate the methods EndRun used to summarize the results presented on the "Customer Survey Results" page. Is there anything you would do differently to summarize these results?

3. Note that the last question of the survey has fewer responses than the other questions. What factors may have limited the number of responses to that question?

CardioGood Fitness

Return to the CardioGood Fitness case first presented on page 78. Using the data stored in **CardioGoodFitness** :

1. Compute descriptive statistics to create a customer profile for each CardioGood Fitness treadmill product line.

2. Write a report to be presented to the management of CardioGood Fitness, detailing your findings.

More Descriptive Choices Follow-up

Follow up the Using Statistics Revisited section on page 130 by computing descriptive statistics to analyze the differences in 3-year return percentages, 5-year return percentages, and 10-year return percentages for the sample of 316 retirement

funds stored in **Retirement Funds** . In your analysis, examine differences between the growth and value funds as well as the differences among the small, mid-cap, and large market cap funds.

Clear Mountain State Student Surveys

1. The student news service at Clear Mountain State University (CMSU) has decided to gather data about the undergraduate students who attend CMSU. They create and distribute a survey of 14 questions and receive responses from 62 undergraduates (stored in **UndergradSurvey**). For each numerical variable included in the survey, compute all the appropriate descriptive statistics and write a report summarizing your conclusions.

2. The dean of students at CMSU has learned about the undergraduate survey and has decided to undertake a similar survey for graduate students at CMSU. She creates and distributes a survey of 14 questions and receives responses from 44 graduate students (stored in **GradSurvey**). For each numerical variable included in the survey, compute all the appropriate descriptive statistic and write a report summarizing your conclusions.

CHAPTER 3 EXCEL GUIDE

EG3.1 CENTRAL TENDENCY

The Mean, Median, and Mode

Key Technique Use the **AVERAGE(*variable cell range*)**, **MEDIAN(*variable cell range*),** and **MODE(*variable cell range*)** functions to compute these measures.

Example Compute the mean, median, and mode for the sample of getting-ready times introduced in Section 3.1.

PHStat Use **Descriptive Summary**.
For the example, open to the **DATA worksheet** of the **Times workbook.** Select **PHStat → Descriptive Statistics → Descriptive Summary**. In the procedure's dialog box (shown below):

1. Enter **A1:A11** as the **Raw Data Cell Range** and check **First cell contains label**.
2. Click **Single Group Variable**.
3. Enter a **Title** and click **OK**.

PHStat inserts a new worksheet that contains various measures of central tendency, variation, and shape discussed in Sections 3.1 and 3.2. This worksheet is similar to the CompleteStatistics worksheet of the Descriptive workbook.

In-Depth Excel Use the **CentralTendency worksheet** of the **Descriptive workbook** as a model.
For the example, open the **Times workbook** and insert a new worksheet (see Section B.1) and:

1. Enter a title in cell **A1**.
2. Enter **Get-Ready Times** in cell **B3**, **Mean** in cell **A4**, **Median** in cell **A5**, and **Mode** in cell **A6**.
3. Enter the formula **=AVERAGE(DATA!A:A)** in cell **B4**, the formula **=MEDIAN(DATA!A:A)** in cell **B5**, and the formula **=MODE(DATA!A:A)** in cell **B6**.

For these functions, the *variable cell range* includes the name of the DATA worksheet because the data being summarized appears on the separate DATA worksheet.

Analysis ToolPak Use **Descriptive Statistics.**
For the example, open to the **DATA worksheet** of the **Times workbook** and:

1. Select **Data → Data Analysis**.
2. In the Data Analysis dialog box, select **Descriptive Statistics** from the **Analysis Tools** list and then click **OK**.

In the Descriptive Statistics dialog box (shown below):

3. Enter **A1:A11** as the **Input Range**. Click **Columns** and check **Labels in first row**.
4. Click **New Worksheet Ply** and check **Summary statistics**, **Kth Largest**, and **Kth Smallest**.
5. Click **OK**.

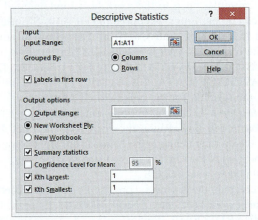

The ToolPak inserts a new worksheet that contains various measures of central tendency, variation, and shape discussed in Sections 3.1 and 3.2.

EG3.2 VARIATION and SHAPE

The Range

Key Technique Use the **MIN(*variable cell range*)** and **MAX(*variable cell range*)** functions to help compute the range.

Example Compute the range for the sample of getting-ready times first introduced in Section 3.1.

PHStat Use **Descriptive Summary** (see Section EG3.1).

In-Depth Excel Use the **Range worksheet** of the **Descriptive workbook** as a model.
For the example, open the worksheet implemented for the example in the *In-Depth Excel* "The Mean, Median, and Mode" instructions.
Enter **Minimum** in cell **A7**, **Maximum** in cell **A8**, and **Range** in cell **A9**. Enter the formula **=MIN(DATA!A:A)** in cell **B7**, the formula **=MAX(DATA!A:A)** in cell **B8**, and the formula **=B8 − B7** in cell **B9**.

The Variance, Standard Deviation, Coefficient of Variation, and Z Scores

Key Technique Use the **VAR.S**(*variable cell range*) and **STDEV.S**(*variable cell range*) functions to compute the sample variation and the sample standard deviation, respectively. Use the AVERAGE and STDEV.S functions for the coefficient of variation. Use the **STANDARDIZE**(*value, mean, standard deviation*) function to compute Z scores.

Example Compute the variance, standard deviation, coefficient of variation, and Z scores for the sample of getting-ready times first introduced in Section 3.1.

PHStat Use **Descriptive Summary** (see Section EG3.1).

In-Depth Excel Use the **Variation** and **ZScores worksheets** of the **Descriptive workbook** as models.
For the example, open to the worksheet implemented for the earlier examples. Enter **Variance** in cell **A10**, **Standard Deviation** in cell **A11**, and **Coeff. of Variation** in cell **A12**. Enter the formula **=VAR.S(DATA!A:A)** in cell **B10**, the formula **=STDEV.S(DATA!A:A)** in cell **B11**, and the formula **=B11/AVERAGE(DATA!A:A)** in cell **B12**. If you previously entered the formula for the mean in cell A4 using the Section EG3.1 *In-Depth Excel* instructions, enter the simpler formula **=B11/B4** in cell **B12**. Right-click cell **B12** and click **Format Cells** in the shortcut menu. In the **Number** tab of the Format Cells dialog box, click **Percentage** in the **Category** list, enter **2** as the **Decimal places**, and click **OK**.
   To compute the Z scores, copy the DATA worksheet. In the new, copied worksheet, enter **Z Score** in cell **B1**. Enter the formula **=STANDARDIZE(A2, Variation!$B$4, Variation!$B$11)** in cell **B2** and copy the formula down through row **11**. If you use an Excel version older than Excel 2010, enter **Variation_OLDER!$B$4** and **Variation_OLDER!$B$11** as the cell references in the formula.

Analysis ToolPak Use **Descriptive Statistics** (see Section EG3.1). This procedure does not compute Z scores.

Shape: Skewness and Kurtosis

Key Technique Use the **SKEW**(*variable cell range*) and the **KURT**(*variable cell range*) functions to compute these measures.

Example Compute the skewness and kurtosis for the sample of getting-ready times first introduced in Section 3.1.

PHStat Use **Descriptive Summary** (see Section EG3.1).

In-Depth Excel Use the **Shape worksheet** of the **Descriptive workbook** as a model.
For the example, open to the worksheet implemented for the earlier examples. Enter **Skewness** in cell **A13** and **Kurtosis** in cell **A14**. Enter the formula **=SKEW(DATA!A:A)** in cell **B13** and the formula **=KURT(DATA!A:A)** in cell **B14**. Then format cells B13 and B14 for four decimal places.

Analysis ToolPak Use **Descriptive Statistics** (see Section EG3.1).

EG3.3 EXPLORING NUMERICAL DATA

Quartiles

Key Technique Use the MEDIAN, COUNT, SMALL, INT, FLOOR, and CEILING functions in combination with the IF decision-making function to compute the quartiles. To apply the rules of Section 3.3, avoid using any of the Excel quartile functions to compute the first and third quartiles.

Example Compute the quartiles for the sample of getting-ready times first introduced in Section 3.1.

PHStat Use **Boxplot** (discussed later on this page).

In-Depth Excel Use the **COMPUTE worksheet** of the **Quartiles workbook** as a model.
For the example, the COMPUTE worksheet already computes the quartiles for the getting-ready times. To compute the quartiles for another set of data, paste the data into **column A** of the **DATA worksheet**, overwriting the existing getting-ready times.
   Open to the **COMPUTE_FORMULAS worksheet** to examine the formulas and read the SHORT TAKES for Chapter 3 for an extended discussion of the formulas in the worksheet.
   The workbook uses the older **QUARTILE**(*variable cell range, quartile number*) function and not the newer QUARTILE .EXC function for reasons explained in Appendix Section F.3. Both the older and newer functions use rules that differ from the Section 3.3 rules to compute quartiles. To compare the results using these newer functions, open to the **COMPARE worksheet**.

The Interquartile Range

Key Technique Use a formula to subtract the first quartile from the third quartile.

Example Compute the interquartile range for the sample of getting-ready times first introduced in Section 3.1.

In-Depth Excel Use the **COMPUTE worksheet** of the **Quartiles workbook** (introduced in the previous section) as a model. For the example, the interquartile range is already computed in cell B19 using the formula **=B18 − B16**.

The Five-Number Summary and the Boxplot

Key Technique Plot a series of line segments on the same chart to construct a boxplot. (Excel chart types do not include boxplots.)

Example Compute the five-number summary and construct the boxplots of the one-year return percentage variable for the growth and value funds used in Example 3.13 on page 118.

PHStat Use **Boxplot**.
For the example, open to the **DATA worksheet** of the **Retirement Funds workbook**. Select **PHStat → Descriptive Statistics → Boxplot**. In the procedure's dialog box (shown on page 139):

1. Enter **I1:I317** as the **Raw Data Cell Range** and check **First cell contains label**.
2. Click **Multiple Groups - Stacked** and enter **C1:C317** as the **Grouping Variable Cell Range**.

3. Enter a **Title**, check **Five-Number Summary**, and click **OK**.

The boxplot appears on its own chart sheet, separate from the worksheet that contains the five-number summary.

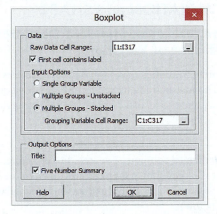

In-Depth Excel Use the worksheets of the **Boxplot workbook** as templates.

For the example, use the **PLOT_DATA worksheet** which already shows the five-number summary and boxplot for the value funds. To compute the five-number summary and construct a boxplot for the growth funds, copy the growth funds from **column A** of the **UNSTACKED worksheet** of the **Retirement Funds workbook** and paste into **column A** of the **DATA worksheet** of the **Boxplot workbook**.

For other problems, use the **PLOT_SUMMARY worksheet** as the template if the five-number summary has already been determined; otherwise, paste your unsummarized data into column A of the DATA worksheet and use the PLOT_DATA worksheet as was done for the example.

The worksheets creatively misuse Excel line charting features to construct a boxplot. Read the SHORT TAKES for Chapter 3 for an explanation of this "misuse."

EG3.4 NUMERICAL DESCRIPTIVE MEASURES for a POPULATION

The Population Mean, Population Variance, and Population Standard Deviation

Key Technique Use **AVERAGE(***variable cell range***)**, **VAR.P(***variable cell range***)**, and **STDEV.P(***variable cell range***)** to compute these measures.

Example Compute the population mean, population variance, and population standard deviation for the "Dow Dogs" population data of Table 3.6 on page 120.

In-Depth Excel Use the **Parameters workbook** as a model. For the example, the **COMPUTE worksheet** of the **Parameters workbook** already computes the three population parameters for the "Dow Dogs." If you use an Excel version older than Excel 2010, use the COMPUTE_OLDER worksheet.

The Empirical Rule and the Chebyshev Rule

Use the **COMPUTE worksheet** of the **VE-Variability workbook** to explore the effects of changing the mean and standard deviation on the ranges associated with ± 1 standard deviation, ± 2 standard deviations, and ± 3 standard deviations from the mean. Change the mean in cell **B4** and the standard deviation in cell **B5** and then note the updated results in rows 9 through 11.

EG3.5 THE COVARIANCE and the COEFFICIENT of CORRELATION

The Covariance

Key Technique Use the **COVARIANCE.S(***variable 1 cell range***, ***variable 2 cell range***)** function to compute this measure.

Example Compute the sample covariance for the NBA team revenue and value shown in Figure 3.6 on page 125.

In-Depth Excel Use the **Covariance workbook** as a model. For the example, the revenue and value have already been placed in columns A and B of the DATA worksheet and the COMPUTE worksheet displays the computed covariance in cell B9. For other problems, paste the data for two variables into columns A and B of the DATA worksheet, overwriting the revenue and value data.

Read the SHORT TAKES for Chapter 3 for an explanation of the formulas found in the DATA and COMPUTE worksheets. If you use an Excel version older than Excel 2010, use the COMPUTE_OLDER worksheet that computes the covariance without using the COVARIANCE.S function that was introduced in Excel 2010.

The Coefficient of Correlation

Key Technique Use the **CORREL(***variable 1 cell range***, ***variable 2 cell range***)** function to compute this measure.

Example Compute the coefficient of correlation for the NBA team revenue and value data of Example 3.17 on page 128.

In-Depth Excel Use the **Correlation workbook** as a model. For the example, the revenue and value have already been placed in columns A and B of the DATA worksheet and the COMPUTE worksheet displays the coefficient of correlation in cell B14. For other problems, paste the data for two variables into columns A and B of the DATA worksheet, overwriting the revenue and value data.

The COMPUTE worksheet that uses the COVARIANCE.S function to compute the covariance (see the previous section) and also uses the DEVSQ, COUNT, and SUMPRODUCT functions discussed in Appendix F. Open to the **COMPUTE_FORMULAS worksheet** to examine the use of all these functions.

CHAPTER 3 MINITAB GUIDE

MG3.1 CENTRAL TENDENCY

The Mean, Median, and Mode

Use **Descriptive Statistics** to compute the mean, the median, the mode, and selected measures of variation and shape. For example, to create results similar to Figure 3.2 on page 110 that presents descriptive statistics of the one-year return percentage variable for the growth and value funds, open to the **Retirement Funds** worksheet. Select **Stat → Basic Statistics → Display Descriptive Statistics**. In the Display Descriptive Statistics dialog box (shown below):

1. Double-click **C9 1YrReturn%** in the variables list to add **'1YrReturn%'** to the **Variables** box and then press **Tab**.
2. Double-click **C3 Type** in the variables list to add **Type** to the **By variables (optional)** box.
3. Click **Statistics**.

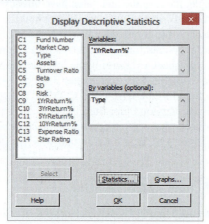

In the Display Descriptive Statistics - Statistics dialog box (shown below):

4. Check **Mean**, **Standard deviation**, **Variance**, **Coefficient of variation**, **First quartile**, **Median**, **Third quartile**, **Interquartile range**, **Mode**, **Minimum**, **Maximum**, **Range**, **Skewness**, **Kurtosis**, and **N total**.
5. Click **OK**.

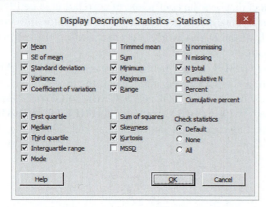

6. Back in the Display Descriptive Statistics dialog box, click **OK**.

MG3.2 VARIATION and SHAPE

The Range, Variance, Standard Deviation, and Coefficient of Variation

Use **Descriptive Statistics** to compute these measures of variation and shape. The instructions in Section MG3.1 for computing the mean, median, and mode also compute these measures.

Z Scores

Use **Standardize** to compute Z scores. For example, to compute the Table 3.4 Z scores shown on page 109, open to the **CEREALS** worksheet. Select **Calc → Standardize**. In the Standardize dialog box (shown below):

1. Double-click **C2 Calories** in the variables list to add **Calories** to the **Input column(s)** box and press **Tab**.
2. Enter **C5** in the **Store results in** box. (C5 is the first empty column on the worksheet and the Z scores will be placed in column C5.)
3. Click **Subtract mean and divide by standard deviation**.
4. Click **OK**.
5. In the new column C5, enter **Z Scores** as the name of the column.

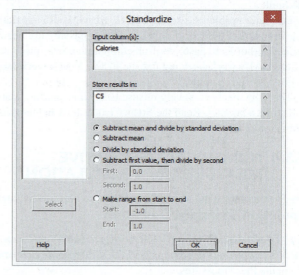

Shape

Use **Descriptive Statistics** to compute skewness and kurtosis. The instructions in Section MG3.1 for computing the mean, median, and mode also compute these measures.

MG3.3 EXPLORING NUMERICAL DATA

Quartiles, the Interquartile Range, and the Five-Number Summary

Use **Descriptive Statistics** to compute these measures. The instructions in Section MG3.1 for computing the mean, median, and mode also compute these measures.

The Boxplot

Use **Boxplot**.

For example, to create the Figure 3.4 boxplots on page 118, open to the **Retirement Funds worksheet**. Select **Graph → Boxplot**. In the Boxplots dialog box:

1. Click **With Groups** in the **One Y gallery** and then click **OK**.

   In the Boxplot-One Y, With Groups dialog box (shown below):

2. Double-click **C9 1YrReturn%** in the variables list to add **'1YrReturn%'** to the **Graph variables** box and then press **Tab**.

3. Double-click **C3 Type** in the variables list to add **Type** in the **Categorical variables** box.

4. Click **OK**.

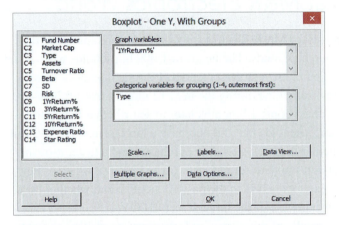

In the boxplot created, pausing the mouse pointer over the boxplot reveals a number of measures, including the quartiles. For problems that involve single-group data, click **Simple** in the **One Y gallery** in step 1.

To rotate the boxplots 90 degrees (as was done in Figure 3.4), replace step 4 with these steps 4 through 6:

4. Click **Scale**.

5. In the **Axes and Ticks** tab of the Boxplot–Scale dialog box, check **Transpose value and category scales** and click **OK**.

6. Back in the Boxplot-One Y, With Groups dialog box, click **OK**.

MG3.4 NUMERICAL DESCRIPTIVE MEASURES for a POPULATION

The Population Mean, Population Variance, and Population Standard Deviation

Minitab does not contain commands that compute these population parameters directly.

The Empirical Rule and the Chebyshev Rule

Manually compute the values needed to apply these rules using the statistics computed in the Section MG3.1 instructions.

MG3.5 THE COVARIANCE and the COEFFICIENT of CORRELATION

The Covariance

Use **Covariance**.

For example, to compute the covariance for Example 3.16 on page 125, open to the **NBAValues worksheet**. Select **Stat → Basic Statistics → Covariance**. In the Covariance dialog box (shown below):

1. Double-click **C3 Revenue** in the variables list to add **Revenue** to the **Variables** box.

2. Double-click **C4 Current Value** in the variables list to add **'Current Value'** to the **Variables** box.

3. Click **OK**.

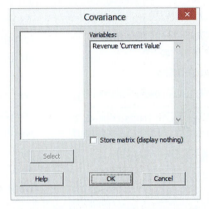

In the table of numbers produced, the covariance is the number that appears in the cell position that is the intersection of the two variables (the lower-left cell).

The Coefficient of Correlation

Use **Correlation**.

For example, to compute the coefficient of correlation for Example 3.17 on page 128, open to the **NBAValues worksheet**. Select **Stat → Basic Statistics → Correlation**. In the Correlation dialog box (shown below):

1. Double-click **C3 Revenue** in the variables list to add **Revenue** to the **Variables** box.

2. Double-click **C4 Current Value** in the variables list to add **'Current Value'** to the **Variables** box.

3. Click **OK**.

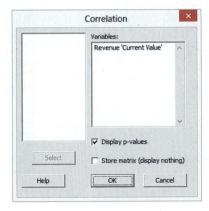

4

Basic Probability

OBJECTIVES

Understand basic probability concepts

Understand conditional probability

Use Bayes' theorem to revise probabilities

Learn various counting rules

USING STATISTICS

Possibilities at M&R Electronics World

As the marketing manager for M&R Electronics World, you are analyzing the results of an intent-to-purchase study. The heads of 1,000 households were asked about their intentions to purchase a large-screen HDTV (one that has a screen size of at least 50 inches) sometime during the next 12 months. As a follow-up, you plan to survey the same people 12 months later to see whether they purchased a television. For households that did purchase a large-screen HDTV, you would like to know whether the television they purchased had a faster refresh rate (240 Hz or higher) or a standard refresh rate (60 or 120 Hz), whether they also purchased a streaming media box in the past 12 months, and whether they were satisfied with their purchase of the large-screen HDTV.

You plan to use the results of this survey to form a new marketing strategy that will enhance sales and better target those households likely to purchase multiple or more expensive products. What questions can you ask in this survey? How can you express the relationships among the various intent-to-purchase responses of individual households?

Shock/Fotolia

T he principles of probability help bridge the worlds of descriptive statistics and inferential statistics. Probability principles are the foundation for the probability distribution, the concept of mathematical expectation, and the binomial and Poisson distributions, topics that are discussed in Chapter 5. In this chapter, you will learn about probability to answer questions such as the following:

- What is the probability that a household is planning to purchase a large-screen HDTV in the next year?
- What is the probability that a household will actually purchase a large-screen HDTV?
- What is the probability that a household is planning to purchase a large-screen HDTV and actually purchases the television?
- Given that the household is planning to purchase a large-screen HDTV, what is the probability that the purchase is made?
- Does knowledge of whether a household *plans* to purchase the television change the likelihood of predicting whether the household *will* purchase the television?
- What is the probability that a household that purchases a large-screen HDTV will purchase a television with a faster refresh rate?
- What is the probability that a household that purchases a large-screen HDTV with a faster refresh rate will also purchase a streaming media box?
- What is the probability that a household that purchases a large-screen HDTV will be satisfied with the purchase?

With answers to questions such as these, you can begin to form a marketing strategy. You can consider whether to target households that have indicated an intent to purchase or to focus on selling televisions that have faster refresh rates or both. You can also explore whether households that purchase large-screen HDTVs with faster refresh rates can be easily persuaded to also purchase streaming media boxes.

4.1 Basic Probability Concepts

What is meant by the word *probability*? A **probability** is the numerical value representing the chance, likelihood, or possibility that a particular event will occur, such as the price of a stock increasing, a rainy day, a defective product, or the outcome five dots in a single toss of a die. In all these instances, the probability involved is a proportion or fraction whose value ranges between 0 and 1, inclusive. An event that has no chance of occurring (the **impossible event**) has a probability of 0. An event that is sure to occur (the **certain event**) has a probability of 1.

There are three types of probability:

- *A priori*
- Empirical
- Subjective

In the simplest case, where each outcome is equally likely, the chance of occurrence of the event is defined in Equation (4.1).

PROBABILITY OF OCCURRENCE

$$\text{Probability of occurrence} = \frac{X}{T} \qquad (4.1)$$

where

X = number of ways in which the event occurs
T = total number of possible outcomes

In *a priori* **probability**, the probability of an occurrence is based on prior knowledge of the process involved. Consider a standard deck of cards that has 26 red cards and 26 black cards. The probability of selecting a black card is $26/52 = 0.50$ because there are $X = 26$ black cards and $T = 52$ total cards. What does this probability mean? If each card is replaced after it is selected, does it mean that 1 out of the next 2 cards selected will be black? No, because you cannot say for certain what will happen on the next several selections. However, you can say that in the long run, if this selection process is continually repeated, the proportion of black cards selected will approach 0.50. Example 4.1 shows another example of computing an *a priori* probability.

EXAMPLE 4.1 Finding *A Priori* Probabilities	A standard six-sided die has six faces. Each face of the die contains either one, two, three, four, five, or six dots. If you roll a die, what is the probability that you will get a face with five dots? **SOLUTION** Each face is equally likely to occur. Because there are six faces, the probability of getting a face with five dots is 1/6.

The preceding examples use the *a priori* probability approach because the number of ways the event occurs and the total number of possible outcomes are known from the composition of the deck of cards or the faces of the die.

In the **empirical probability** approach, the probabilities are based on observed data, not on prior knowledge of a process. Surveys are often used to generate empirical probabilities. Examples of this type of probability are the proportion of individuals in the Using Statistics scenario who actually purchase large-screen HDTVs, the proportion of registered voters who prefer a certain political candidate, and the proportion of students who have part-time jobs. For example, if you take a survey of students, and 60% state that they have part-time jobs, then there is a 0.60 probability that an individual student has a part-time job.

The third approach to probability, **subjective probability**, differs from the other two approaches because subjective probability differs from person to person. For example, the development team for a new product may assign a probability of 0.60 to the chance of success for the product, while the president of the company may be less optimistic and assign a probability of 0.30. The assignment of subjective probabilities to various outcomes is usually based on a combination of an individual's past experience, personal opinion, and analysis of a particular situation. Subjective probability is especially useful in making decisions in situations in which you cannot use *a priori* probability or empirical probability.

Events and Sample Spaces

The basic elements of probability theory are the individual outcomes of a variable under study. You need the following definitions to understand probabilities.

> **Student Tip**
> Events are represented by letters of the alphabet.

> EVENT
>
> Each possible outcome of a variable is referred to as an **event**.
> A **simple event** is described by a single characteristic.

For example, when you toss a coin, the two possible outcomes are heads and tails. Each of these represents a simple event. When you roll a standard six-sided die in which the six faces of the die contain either one, two, three, four, five, or six dots, there are six possible simple events. An event can be any one of these simple events, a set of them, or a subset of all of them. For example, the event of an *even number of dots* consists of three simple events (i.e., two, four, or six dots).

⬤ **Student Tip**
The key word when describing a joint event is *and*.

JOINT EVENT

A **joint event** is an event that has two or more characteristics.

Getting two heads when you toss a coin twice is an example of a joint event because it consists of heads on the first toss and heads on the second toss.

COMPLEMENT

The **complement** of event A (represented by the symbol A') includes all events that are not part of A.

The complement of a head is a tail because that is the only event that is not a head. The complement of five dots on a die is not getting five dots. Not getting five dots consists of getting one, two, three, four, or six dots.

SAMPLE SPACE

The collection of all the possible events is called the **sample space**.

The sample space for tossing a coin consists of heads and tails. The sample space when rolling a die consists of one, two, three, four, five, and six dots. Example 4.2 demonstrates events and sample spaces.

EXAMPLE 4.2

Events and Sample Spaces

The Using Statistics scenario on page 142 concerns M&R Electronics World. Table 4.1 presents the results of the sample of 1,000 households in terms of purchase behavior for large-screen HDTVs.

TABLE 4.1

Purchase Behavior for Large-screen HDTVs

PLANNED TO PURCHASE	ACTUALLY PURCHASED		
	Yes	No	Total
Yes	200	50	250
No	100	650	750
Total	300	700	1,000

What is the sample space? Give examples of simple events and joint events.

SOLUTION The sample space consists of the 1,000 respondents. Simple events are "planned to purchase," "did not plan to purchase," "purchased," and "did not purchase." The complement of the event "planned to purchase" is "did not plan to purchase." The event "planned to purchase and actually purchased" is a joint event because in this joint event, the respondent must plan to purchase the television *and* actually purchase it.

Contingency Tables and Venn Diagrams

There are several ways in which you can view a particular sample space. One way involves using a **contingency table** (see Section 2.1) such as the one displayed in Table 4.1. You get the values in the cells of the table by subdividing the sample space of 1,000 households according to whether someone planned to purchase and actually purchased a large-screen HDTV. For example, 200 of the respondents planned to purchase a large-screen HDTV and subsequently did purchase the large-screen HDTV.

A second way to present the sample space is by using a **Venn diagram**. This diagram graphically represents the various events as "unions" and "intersections" of circles. Figure 4.1 presents a typical Venn diagram for a two-variable situation, with each variable having only two events (A and A', B and B'). The circle on the left (the red one) represents all events that are part of A.

FIGURE 4.1

Venn diagram for events A and B

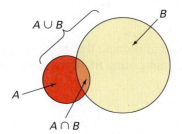

FIGURE 4.2

Venn diagram for the M&R Electronics World example

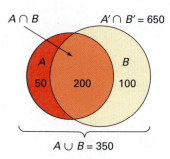

The circle on the right (the yellow one) represents all events that are part of B. The area contained within circle A and circle B (center area) is the intersection of A and B (written as $A \cap B$), since it is part of A and also part of B. The total area of the two circles is the union of A and B (written as $A \cup B$) and contains all outcomes that are just part of event A, just part of event B, or part of both A and B. The area in the diagram outside of $A \cup B$ contains outcomes that are neither part of A nor part of B.

You must define A and B in order to develop a Venn diagram. You can define either event as A or B, as long as you are consistent in evaluating the various events. For the large-screen HDTV example, you can define the events as follows:

A = planned to purchase B = actually purchased
A' = did not plan to purchase B' = did not actually purchase

In drawing the Venn diagram (see Figure 4.2), you must first determine the value of the intersection of A and B so that the sample space can be divided into its parts. $A \cap B$ consists of all 200 households who planned to purchase and actually purchased a large-screen HDTV. The remainder of event A (planned to purchase) consists of the 50 households who planned to purchase a large-screen HDTV but did not actually purchase one. The remainder of event B (actually purchased) consists of the 100 households who did not plan to purchase a large-screen HDTV but actually purchased one. The remaining 650 households represent those who neither planned to purchase nor actually purchased a large-screen HDTV.

Simple Probability

Now you can answer some of the questions posed in the Using Statistics scenario. Because the results are based on data collected in a survey (refer to Table 4.1), you can use the empirical probability approach.

As stated previously, the most fundamental rule for probabilities is that they range in value from 0 to 1. An impossible event has a probability of 0, and an event that is certain to occur has a probability of 1.

Simple probability refers to the probability of occurrence of a simple event, $P(A)$. A simple probability in the Using Statistics scenario is the probability of planning to purchase a large-screen HDTV. How can you determine the probability of selecting a household that planned to purchase a large-screen HDTV? Using Equation (4.1) on page 143:

$$\text{Probability of occurrence} = \frac{X}{T}$$

$$P(\text{Planned to purchase}) = \frac{\text{Number who planned to purchase}}{\text{Total number of households}}$$

$$= \frac{250}{1,000} = 0.25$$

Thus, there is a 0.25 (or 25%) chance that a household planned to purchase a large-screen HDTV.

Example 4.3 illustrates another application of simple probability.

EXAMPLE 4.3

Computing the Probability That the Large-Screen HDTV Purchased Had a Faster Refresh Rate

In the Using Statistics follow-up survey, additional questions were asked of the 300 households that actually purchased large-screen HDTVs. Table 4.2 indicates the consumers' responses to whether the television purchased had a faster refresh rate and whether they also purchased a streaming media box in the past 12 months.

Find the probability that if a household that purchased a large-screen HDTV is randomly selected, the television purchased had a faster refresh rate.

TABLE 4.2

Purchase Behavior Regarding Purchasing a Faster Refresh Rate Television and a Streaming Media Box

REFRESH RATE OF TELEVISION PURCHASED	STREAMING MEDIA BOX		
	Yes	No	Total
Faster	38	42	80
Standard	70	150	220
Total	108	192	300

SOLUTION Using the following definitions:

A = purchased a television with a faster refresh rate

A' = purchased a television with a standard refresh rate

B = purchased a streaming media box

B' = did not purchase a streaming media box

$$P(\text{Faster refresh rate}) = \frac{\text{Number of faster refresh rate televisions purchased}}{\text{Total number of televisions}}$$

$$= \frac{80}{300} = 0.267$$

There is a 26.7% chance that a randomly selected large-screen HDTV purchased has a faster refresh rate.

Joint Probability

Whereas simple probability refers to the probability of occurrence of simple events, **joint probability** refers to the probability of an occurrence involving two or more events. An example of joint probability is the probability that you will get heads on the first toss of a coin and heads on the second toss of a coin.

In Table 4.1 on page 145, the group of individuals who planned to purchase and actually purchased a large-screen HDTV consist only of the outcomes in the single cell "yes—planned to purchase *and* yes—actually purchased." Because this group consists of 200 households, the probability of picking a household that planned to purchase *and* actually purchased a large-screen HDTV is

$$P(\text{Planned to purchase } and \text{ actually purchased}) = \frac{\text{Planned to purchase } and \text{ actually purchased}}{\text{Total number of respondents}}$$

$$= \frac{200}{1,000} = 0.20$$

Example 4.4 also demonstrates how to determine joint probability.

EXAMPLE 4.4

Determining the Joint Probability That a Household Purchased a Large-Screen HDTV with a Faster Refresh Rate and Purchased a Streaming Media Box

In Table 4.2 on page 147, the purchases are cross-classified as having a faster refresh rate or having a standard refresh rate and whether the household purchased a streaming media box. Find the probability that a randomly selected household that purchased a large-screen HDTV also purchased a television that had a faster refresh rate and purchased a streaming media box.

SOLUTION Using Equation (4.1) on page 143,

$$P\left(\begin{array}{l}\text{Television with a faster refresh}\\ \text{rate } and \text{ streaming media box}\end{array}\right) = \frac{\begin{array}{l}\text{Number that purchased a television with a faster}\\ \text{refresh rate } and \text{ purchased a streaming media box}\end{array}}{\text{Total number of large-screen HDTV purchasers}}$$

$$= \frac{38}{300} = 0.127$$

Therefore, there is a 12.7% chance that a randomly selected household that purchased a large-screen HDTV purchased a television that had a faster refresh rate and purchased a streaming media box.

Marginal Probability

The **marginal probability** of an event consists of a set of joint probabilities. You can determine the marginal probability of a particular event by using the concept of joint probability just discussed. For example, if B consists of two events, B_1 and B_2, then $P(A)$, the probability of event A, consists of the joint probability of event A occurring with event B_1 and the joint probability of event A occurring with event B_2. You use Equation (4.2) to compute marginal probabilities.

MARGINAL PROBABILITY

$$P(A) = P(A \text{ and } B_1) + P(A \text{ and } B_2) + \cdots + P(A \text{ and } B_k) \qquad \textbf{(4.2)}$$

where $B_1, B_2, \ldots, B_k$ are k mutually exclusive and collectively exhaustive events, defined as follows:

Two events are **mutually exclusive** if both the events cannot occur simultaneously.
A set of events is **collectively exhaustive** if one of the events must occur.

Heads and tails in a coin toss are mutually exclusive events. The result of a coin toss cannot simultaneously be a head and a tail. Heads and tails in a coin toss are also collectively exhaustive events. One of them must occur. If heads does not occur, tails must occur. If tails does not occur, heads must occur. Being male and being female are mutually exclusive and collectively exhaustive events. No person is both (the two are mutually exclusive), and everyone is one or the other (the two are collectively exhaustive).

You can use Equation (4.2) to compute the marginal probability of "planned to purchase" a large-screen HDTV:

$$P(\text{Planned to purchase}) = P(\text{Planned to purchase } and \text{ purchased})$$
$$+ \; P(\text{Planned to purchase } and \text{ did not purchase})$$
$$= \frac{200}{1,000} + \frac{50}{1,000}$$
$$= \frac{250}{1,000} = 0.25$$

You get the same result if you add the number of outcomes that make up the simple event "planned to purchase."

General Addition Rule

Student Tip
The key word when using the addition rule is *or*.

How do you find the probability of event "*A or B*"? You need to consider the occurrence of either event *A* or event *B* or both *A* and *B*. For example, how can you determine the probability that a household planned to purchase *or* actually purchased a large-screen HDTV?

The event "planned to purchase *or* actually purchased" includes all households that planned to purchase and all households that actually purchased a large-screen HDTV. You examine each cell of the contingency table (Table 4.1 on page 145) to determine whether it is part of this event. From Table 4.1, the cell "planned to purchase *and* did not actually purchase" is part of the event because it includes respondents who planned to purchase. The cell "did not plan to purchase *and* actually purchased" is included because it contains respondents who actually purchased. Finally, the cell "planned to purchase *and* actually purchased" has both characteristics of interest. Therefore, one way to calculate the probability of "planned to purchase *or* actually purchased" is

$$P(\text{Planned to purchase } or \text{ actually purchased}) = P(\text{Planned to purchase } and \text{ did not actually}$$
$$\text{purchase}) + P(\text{Did not plan to}$$
$$\text{purchase } and \text{ actually purchased}) +$$
$$P(\text{Planned to purchase } and \text{ actually purchased})$$
$$= \frac{50}{1,000} + \frac{100}{1,000} + \frac{200}{1,000}$$
$$= \frac{350}{1,000} = 0.35$$

Often, it is easier to determine *P(A or B)*, the probability of the event *A or B*, by using the **general addition rule**, defined in Equation (4.3).

GENERAL ADDITION RULE

The probability of *A or B* is equal to the probability of *A* plus the probability of *B* minus the probability of *A and B*.

$$P(A \text{ } or \text{ } B) = P(A) + P(B) - P(A \text{ } and \text{ } B) \tag{4.3}$$

Applying Equation (4.3) to the previous example produces the following result:

$$P(\text{Planned to purchase } or \text{ actually purchased}) = P(\text{Planned to purchase})$$
$$+ P(\text{Actually purchased}) - P(\text{Planned to purchase } and \text{ actually purchased})$$

$$= \frac{250}{1,000} + \frac{300}{1,000} - \frac{200}{1,000}$$

$$= \frac{350}{1,000} = 0.35$$

The general addition rule consists of taking the probability of A and adding it to the probability of B and then subtracting the probability of the joint event A *and* B from this total because the joint event has already been included in computing both the probability of A and the probability of B. Referring to Table 4.1 on page 145, if the outcomes of the event "planned to purchase" are added to those of the event "actually purchased," the joint event "planned to purchase *and* actually purchased" has been included in each of these simple events. Therefore, because this joint event has been included twice, you must subtract it to compute the correct result. Example 4.5 illustrates another application of the general addition rule.

EXAMPLE 4.5

Using the General Addition Rule for the Households That Purchased Large-Screen HDTVs

In Example 4.3 on page 147, the purchases were cross-classified in Table 4.2 as televisions that had a faster refresh rate or televisions that had a standard refresh rate and whether the household purchased a streaming media box. Find the probability that among households that purchased a large-screen HDTV, they purchased a television that had a faster refresh rate or purchased a streaming media box.

SOLUTION Using Equation (4.3),

$$P(\text{Television had a faster refresh} = P(\text{Television had a faster refresh rate})$$
$$\text{rate } or \text{ purchased a streaming media box}) \quad + P(\text{purchased a streaming media box})$$
$$- P(\text{Television had a faster refresh}$$
$$\text{rate } and \text{ purchased a streaming media box})$$

$$= \frac{80}{300} + \frac{108}{300} - \frac{38}{300}$$

$$= \frac{150}{300} = 0.50$$

Therefore, of households that purchased a large-screen HDTV, there is a 50% chance that a randomly selected household purchased a television that had a faster refresh rate or purchased a streaming media box.

Problems for Section 4.1

LEARNING THE BASICS

4.1 Two coins are tossed.
a. Give an example of a simple event.
b. Give an example of a joint event.
c. What is the complement of a head on the first toss?
d. What does the sample space consist of?

4.2 An urn contains 12 red balls and 8 white balls. One ball is to be selected from the urn.
a. Give an example of a simple event.
b. What is the complement of a red ball?
c. What does the sample space consist of?

4.3 Consider the following contingency table:

	B	B'
A	10	20
A'	20	40

What is the probability of event
a. A?
b. A'?
c. A and B?
d. A or B?

4.4 Consider the following contingency table:

	B	B'
A	10	30
A'	25	35

What is the probability of event
a. A'?
b. A and B?
c. A' and B'?
d. A' or B'?

APPLYING THE CONCEPTS

4.5 For each of the following, indicate whether the type of probability involved is an example of *a priori* probability, empirical probability, or subjective probability.
a. The next toss of a fair coin will land on heads.
b. Italy will win soccer's World Cup the next time the competition is held.
c. The sum of the faces of two dice will be seven.
d. The train taking a commuter to work will be more than 10 minutes late.

4.6 For each of the following, state whether the events created are mutually exclusive and whether they are collectively exhaustive.
a. Undergraduate business students were asked whether they were sophomores or juniors.
b. Each respondent was classified by the type of car he or she drives: sedan, SUV, American, European, Asian, or none.
c. People were asked, "Do you currently live in (i) an apartment or (ii) a house?"
d. A product was classified as defective or not defective.

4.7 Which of the following events occur with a probability of zero? For each, state why or why not.
a. A company is listed on the New York Stock Exchange and NASDAQ.
b. A consumer owns a smartphone and a tablet.
c. A cellphone is a Motorola and a Samsung.
d. An automobile is a Toyota and was manufactured in the United States.

4.8 Do males or females feel more tense or stressed out at work? A survey of employed adults conducted online by Harris Interactive on behalf of the American Psychological Association revealed the following:

	FELT TENSE OR STRESSED OUT AT WORK	
GENDER	**Yes**	**No**
Male	244	495
Female	282	480

Source: Data extracted from "The 2013 Work and Well-Being Survey," American Psychological Association and Harris Interactive, March 2013, p. 5, **bit.ly/11JGcPf**.

a. Give an example of a simple event.
b. Give an example of a joint event.
c. What is the complement of "Felt tense or stressed out at work"?
d. Why is "Male and felt tense or stressed out at work" a joint event?

4.9 Referring to the contingency table in Problem 4.8, if an employed adult is selected at random, what is the probability that
a. the employed adult felt tense or stressed out at work?
b. the employed adult was a male who felt tense or stressed out at work?
c. the employed adult was a male *or* felt tense or stressed out at work?
d. Explain the difference in the results in (b) and (c).

4.10 How will marketers change their social media use in the near future? A survey by Social Media Examiner reported that 78% of B2B marketers (marketers that focus primarily on attracting businesses) plan to increase their use of LinkedIn, as compared to 54% of B2C marketers (marketers that primarily target consumers). The survey was based on 1,331 B2B marketers and 1,694 B2C marketers. The following table summarizes the results:

INCREASE USE OF LINKEDIN?	BUSINESS FOCUS		
	B2B	**B2C**	**Total**
Yes	1,038	915	1,953
No	293	779	1,072
Total	1,331	1,694	3,025

Source: Data extracted from "2013 Social Media Marketing Industry Report," May 2013, **bit.ly/1g5vMQN**.

a. Give an example of a simple event.
b. Give an example of a joint event.
c. What is the complement of a marketer who plans to increase use of LinkedIn?
d. Why is a marketer who plans to increase use of LinkedIn and is a B2C marketer a joint event?

4.11 Referring to the contingency table in Problem 4.10, if a marketer is selected at random, what is the probability that
a. he or she plans to increase use of LinkedIn?
b. he or she is a B2C marketer?
c. he or she plans to increase use of LinkedIn *or* is a B2C marketer?
d. Explain the difference in the results in (b) and (c).

✓ SELF Test **4.12** What business and technical skills are critical for today's business intelligence/analytics and information management professionals? As part of InformationWeek's 2013 U.S. IT Salary Survey, business intelligence/analytics and information management professionals, both staff and managers, were asked to indicate what business and technical skills are critical to their job. The list of business and technical skills included *Analyzing Data*. The following table summarizes the responses to this skill:

| ANALYZING DATA | PROFESSIONAL POSITION | | |
	Staff	Management	Total
Critical	4,374	3,633	8,007
Not critical	3,436	2,631	6,067
Total	7,810	6,264	14,074

Source: Data extracted from "IT Salaries Show Slow Growth," *InformationWeek Reports*, April 2013, p. 40, **ubm.io/1ewjKT5**.

If a professional is selected at random, what is the probability that he or she

a. indicates analyzing data as critical to his or her job?
b. is a manager?
c. indicates analyzing data as critical to his or her job *or* is a manager?
d. Explain the difference in the results in (b) and (c).

4.13 Do Americans prefer Coke or Pepsi? A survey was conducted by Public Policy Polling (PPP) in 2013; the results were as follows:

| PREFERENCE | GENDER | | |
	Female	Male	Total
Coke	120	95	215
Pepsi	95	80	175
Neither/Unsure	65	45	110
Total	280	220	500

Source: Data extracted from "Public Policy Polling," Report 2013, **bit.ly/YKXfzN**.

If an American is selected at random, what is the probability that he or she

a. prefers Pepsi?
b. is male *and* prefers Pepsi?
c. is male *or* prefers Pepsi?
d. Explain the difference in the results in (b) and (c).

4.14 A survey of 1,085 adults asked, "Do you enjoy shopping for clothing for yourself?" The results (data extracted from "Split Decision on Clothes Shopping," *USA Today*, January 28, 2011, p. 1B) indicated that 51% of the females enjoyed shopping for clothing for themselves as compared to 44% of the males. The sample sizes of males and females were not provided. Suppose that the results indicated that of 542 males, 238 answered yes. Of 543 females, 276 answered yes. Construct a contingency table to evaluate the probabilities. What is the probability that a respondent chosen at random

a. enjoys shopping for clothing for himself or herself?
b. is a female *and* enjoys shopping for clothing for herself?
c. is a female *or* is a person who enjoys shopping for clothing?
d. is a male *or* a female?

4.15 Each year, ratings are compiled concerning the performance of new cars during the first 90 days of use. Suppose that the cars have been categorized according to whether a car needs warranty-related repair (yes or no) and the country in which the company manufacturing a car is based (United States or not United States). Based on the data collected, the probability that the new car needs a warranty repair is 0.04, the probability that the car was manufactured by a U.S.-based company is 0.60, and the probability that the new car needs a warranty repair *and* was manufactured by a U.S.-based company is 0.025. Construct a contingency table to evaluate the probabilities of a warranty-related repair. What is the probability that a new car selected at random

a. needs a warranty repair?
b. needs a warranty repair *and* was manufactured by a U.S.-based company?
c. needs a warranty repair *or* was manufactured by a U.S.-based company?
d. needs a warranty repair *or* was not manufactured by a U.S.-based company?

4.2 Conditional Probability

Each example in Section 4.1 involves finding the probability of an event when sampling from the entire sample space. How do you determine the probability of an event if you know certain information about the events involved?

Computing Conditional Probabilities

Conditional probability refers to the probability of event *A*, given information about the occurrence of another event, *B*.

CONDITIONAL PROBABILITY

The probability of A given B is equal to the probability of A *and* B divided by the probability of B.

$$P(A|B) = \frac{P(A \text{ and } B)}{P(B)} \tag{4.4a}$$

The probability of B given A is equal to the probability of A *and* B divided by the probability of A.

$$P(B|A) = \frac{P(A \text{ and } B)}{P(A)} \tag{4.4b}$$

where

$$P(A \text{ and } B) = \text{joint probability of } A \text{ and } B$$
$$P(A) = \text{marginal probability of } A$$
$$P(B) = \text{marginal probability of } B$$

> **Student Tip**
> The variable that is *given* goes in the denominator of Equation (4.4). Since you were given planned to purchase, planned to purchase is in the denominator.

Referring to the Using Statistics scenario involving the purchase of large-screen HDTVs, suppose you were told that a household planned to purchase a large-screen HDTV. Now, what is the probability that the household actually purchased the television?

In this example, the objective is to find $P(\text{Actually purchased} | \text{Planned to purchase})$. Here you are given the information that the household planned to purchase the large-screen HDTV. Therefore, the sample space does not consist of all 1,000 households in the survey. It consists of only those households that planned to purchase the large-screen HDTV. Of 250 such households, 200 actually purchased the large-screen HDTV. Therefore, based on Table 4.1 on page 145, the probability that a household actually purchased the large-screen HDTV given that they planned to purchase is

$$P(\text{Actually purchased} | \text{Planned to purchase}) = \frac{\text{Planned to purchase } and \text{ actually purchased}}{\text{Planned to purchase}}$$

$$= \frac{200}{250} = 0.80$$

You can also use Equation (4.4b) to compute this result:

$$P(B|A) = \frac{P(A \text{ and } B)}{P(A)}$$

where

$$A = \text{planned to purchase}$$
$$B = \text{actually purchased}$$

then

$$P(\text{Actually purchased} | \text{Planned to purchase}) = \frac{200/1,000}{250/1,000}$$

$$= \frac{200}{250} = 0.80$$

Example 4.6 further illustrates conditional probability.

EXAMPLE 4.6

Finding the Conditional Probability of Purchasing a Streaming Media Box

Table 4.2 on page 147 is a contingency table for whether a household purchased a television with a faster refresh rate and whether the household purchased a streaming media box. If a household purchased a television with a faster refresh rate, what is the probability that it also purchased a streaming media box?

SOLUTION Because you know that the household purchased a television with a faster refresh rate, the sample space is reduced to 80 households. Of these 80 households, 38 also purchased a streaming media box. Therefore, the probability that a household purchased a streaming media box, given that the household purchased a television with a faster refresh rate, is

$$P(\text{Purchased streaming media box} \mid \text{Purchased television with faster refresh rate}) = \frac{\text{Number purchasing television with faster refresh rate } and \text{ streaming media box}}{\text{Number purchasing television with faster refresh rate}}$$

$$= \frac{38}{80} = 0.475$$

If you use Equation (4.4b) on page 153:

A = purchased a television with a faster refresh rate

B = purchased a streaming media box

then

$$P(B \mid A) = \frac{P(A \text{ and } B)}{P(A)} = \frac{38/300}{80/300} = 0.475$$

Therefore, given that the household purchased a television with a faster refresh rate, there is a 47.5% chance that the household also purchased a streaming media box. You can compare this conditional probability to the marginal probability of purchasing a streaming media box, which is $108/300 = 0.36$, or 36%. These results tell you that households that purchased televisions with a faster refresh rate are more likely to purchase a streaming media box than are households that purchased large-screen HDTVs that have a standard refresh rate.

Decision Trees

In Table 4.1 on page 145, households are classified according to whether they planned to purchase and whether they actually purchased large-screen HDTVs. A **decision tree** is an alternative to the contingency table. Figure 4.3 represents the decision tree for this example.

FIGURE 4.3

Decision tree for planned to purchase and actually purchased

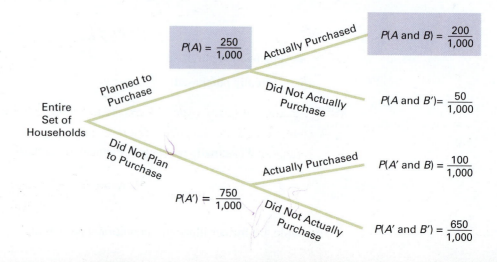

In Figure 4.3, beginning at the left with the entire set of households, there are two "branches" for whether or not the household planned to purchase a large-screen HDTV. Each of these branches has two subbranches, corresponding to whether the household actually purchased or did not actually purchase the large-screen HDTV. The probabilities at the end of the initial branches represent the marginal probabilities of A and A'. The probabilities at the end of each of the four subbranches represent the joint probability for each combination of events A and B. You compute the conditional probability by dividing the joint probability by the appropriate marginal probability.

For example, to compute the probability that the household actually purchased, given that the household planned to purchase the large-screen HDTV, you take P(Planned to purchase *and* actually purchased) and divide by P(Planned to purchase). From Figure 4.3,

$$P(\text{Actually purchased} \mid \text{Planned to purchase}) = \frac{200/1{,}000}{250/1{,}000}$$

$$= \frac{200}{250} = 0.80$$

Example 4.7 illustrates how to construct a decision tree.

EXAMPLE 4.7

Constructing the Decision Tree for the Households That Purchased Large-Screen HDTVs

Using the cross-classified data in Table 4.2 on page 147, construct the decision tree. Use the decision tree to find the probability that a household purchased a streaming media box, given that the household purchased a television with a faster refresh rate.

SOLUTION The decision tree for purchased a streaming media box and a television with a faster refresh rate is displayed in Figure 4.4.

FIGURE 4.4

Decision tree for purchased a television with a faster refresh rate and a streaming media box

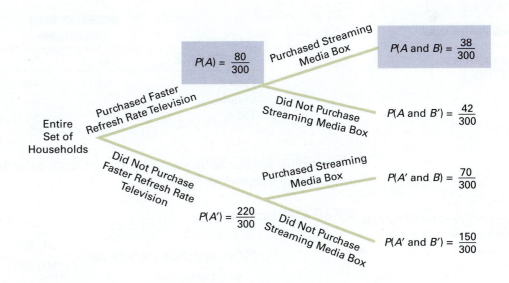

Using Equation (4.4b) on page 153 and the following definitions,

A = purchased a television with a faster refresh rate

B = purchased a streaming media box

$$P(B \mid A) = \frac{P(A \text{ and } B)}{P(A)} = \frac{38/300}{80/300} = 0.475$$

Independence

In the example concerning the purchase of large-screen HDTVs, the conditional probability is $200/250 = 0.80$ that the selected household actually purchased the large-screen HDTV, given that the household planned to purchase. The simple probability of selecting a household that actually purchased is $300/1,000 = 0.30$. This result shows that the prior knowledge that the household planned to purchase affected the probability that the household actually purchased the television. In other words, the outcome of one event is *dependent* on the outcome of a second event.

When the outcome of one event does *not* affect the probability of occurrence of another event, the events are said to be independent. **Independence** can be determined by using Equation (4.5).

INDEPENDENCE

Two events, A and B, are independent if and only if

$$P(A \mid B) = P(A) \qquad \text{(4.5)}$$

where

$$P(A \mid B) = \text{conditional probability of } A \text{ given } B$$
$$P(A) = \text{marginal probability of } A$$

Example 4.8 demonstrates the use of Equation (4.5).

EXAMPLE 4.8

Determining Independence

In the follow-up survey of the 300 households that actually purchased large-screen HDTVs, the households were asked if they were satisfied with their purchases. Table 4.3 cross-classifies the responses to the satisfaction question with the responses to whether the television had a faster refresh rate.

TABLE 4.3

Satisfaction with Purchase of Large-Screen HDTVs

TELEVISION REFRESH RATE	SATISFIED WITH PURCHASE?		
	Yes	No	Total
Faster	64	16	80
Standard	176	44	220
Total	240	60	300

Determine whether being satisfied with the purchase and the refresh rate of the television purchased are independent.

SOLUTION For these data,

$$P(\text{Satisfied} \mid \text{Faster refresh rate}) = \frac{64/300}{80/300} = \frac{64}{80} = 0.80$$

which is equal to

$$P(\text{Satisfied}) = \frac{240}{300} = 0.80$$

Thus, being satisfied with the purchase and the refresh rate of the television purchased are independent. Knowledge of one event does not affect the probability of the other event.

Multiplication Rules

The **general multiplication rule** is derived using Equation (4.4a) on page 154:

$$P(A \mid B) = \frac{P(A \text{ and } B)}{P(B)}$$

and solving for the joint probability $P(A \text{ and } B)$.

GENERAL MULTIPLICATION RULE

The probability of A and B is equal to the probability of A given B times the probability of B.

$$P(A \text{ and } B) = P(A \mid B)P(B) \qquad \textbf{(4.6)}$$

Example 4.9 demonstrates the use of the general multiplication rule.

EXAMPLE 4.9

Using the General Multiplication Rule

Consider the 80 households that purchased televisions that had a faster refresh rate. In Table 4.3 on page 156, you see that 64 households are satisfied with their purchase, and 16 households are dissatisfied. Suppose 2 households are randomly selected from the 80 households. Find the probability that both households are satisfied with their purchase.

SOLUTION Here you can use the multiplication rule in the following way. If

$$A = \text{second household selected is satisfied}$$
$$B = \text{first household selected is satisfied}$$

then, using Equation (4.6),

$$P(A \text{ and } B) = P(A \mid B)P(B)$$

   The probability that the first household is satisfied with the purchase is $64/80$. However, the probability that the second household is also satisfied with the purchase depends on the result of the first selection. If the first household is not returned to the sample after the satisfaction level is determined (i.e., sampling without replacement), the number of households remaining is 79. If the first household is satisfied, the probability that the second is also satisfied is $63/79$ because 63 satisfied households remain in the sample. Therefore,

$$P(A \text{ and } B) = \left(\frac{63}{79}\right)\left(\frac{64}{80}\right) = 0.6380$$

There is a 63.80% chance that both of the households sampled will be satisfied with their purchase.

   The **multiplication rule for independent events** is derived by substituting $P(A)$ for $P(A \mid B)$ in Equation (4.6).

MULTIPLICATION RULE FOR INDEPENDENT EVENTS

If A and B are independent, the probability of A and B is equal to the probability of A times the probability of B.

$$P(A \text{ and } B) = P(A)P(B) \qquad \textbf{(4.7)}$$

If this rule holds for two events, A and B, then A and B are independent. Therefore, there are two ways to determine independence:

1. Events A and B are independent if, and only if, $P(A|B) = P(A)$.
2. Events A and B are independent if, and only if, $P(A \text{ and } B) = P(A)P(B)$.

Marginal Probability Using the General Multiplication Rule

In Section 4.1, marginal probability was defined using Equation (4.2) on page 148. You can state the equation for marginal probability by using the general multiplication rule. If

$$P(A) = P(A \text{ and } B_1) + P(A \text{ and } B_2) + \cdots + P(A \text{ and } B_k)$$

then, using the general multiplication rule, Equation (4.8) defines the marginal probability.

MARGINAL PROBABILITY USING THE GENERAL MULTIPLICATION RULE

$$P(A) = P(A|B_1)P(B_1) + P(A|B_2)P(B_2) + \cdots + P(A|B_k)P(B_k) \qquad \textbf{(4.8)}$$

where $B_1, B_2, \ldots, B_k$ are k mutually exclusive and collectively exhaustive events.

To illustrate Equation (4.8), refer to Table 4.1 on page 145. Let

$$P(A) = \text{probability of planned to purchase}$$
$$P(B_1) = \text{probability of actually purchased}$$
$$P(B_2) = \text{probability of did not actually purchase}$$

Then, using Equation (4.8), the probability of planned to purchase is

$$P(A) = P(A|B_1)P(B_1) + P(A|B_2)P(B_2)$$
$$= \left(\frac{200}{300}\right)\left(\frac{300}{1,000}\right) + \left(\frac{50}{700}\right)\left(\frac{700}{1,000}\right)$$
$$= \frac{200}{1,000} + \frac{50}{1,000} = \frac{250}{1,000} = 0.25$$

Problems for Section 4.2

LEARNING THE BASICS

4.16 Consider the following contingency table:

	B	B'
A	10	20
A'	20	40

What is the probability of
a. $A|B$?
b. $A|B'$?
c. $A'|B'$?
d. Are events A and B independent?

4.17 Consider the following contingency table:

	B	B'
A	10	30
A'	25	35

What is the probability of
a. $A|B$?
b. $A'|B'$?
c. $A|B'$?
d. Are events A and B independent?

4.18 If $P(A \text{ and } B) = 0.4$ and $P(B) = 0.8$, find $P(A|B)$.

4.19 If $P(A) = 0.7, P(B) = 0.6$, and A and B are independent, find $P(A \text{ and } B)$.

4.20 If $P(A) = 0.3, P(B) = 0.4$, and $P(A \text{ and } B) = 0.2$, are A and B independent?

APPLYING THE CONCEPTS

4.21 Do males or females feel more tense or stressed out at work? A survey of employed adults conducted online by Harris Interactive on behalf of the American Psychological Association revealed the following:

	FELT TENSE OR STRESSED OUT AT WORK	
GENDER	Yes	No
Male	244	495
Female	282	480

Source: Data extracted from "The 2013 Work and Well-Being Survey," American Psychological Association and Harris Interactive, March 2013, p. 5, **bit.ly/11JGcPf**.

a. Given that the employed adult felt tense or stressed out at work, what is the probability that the employed adult was a male?
b. Given that the employed adult is male, what is the probability that he felt tense or stressed out at work?
c. Explain the difference in the results in (a) and (b).
d. Is feeling tense or stressed out at work and gender independent?

4.22 How will marketers change their social media use in the near future? A survey by Social Media Examiner of B2B marketers (marketers that focus primarily on attracting businesses) and B2C marketers (marketers that primarily target consumers) was based on 1,331 B2B marketers and 1,694 B2C marketers. The following table summarizes the results:

INCREASE USE OF LINKEDIN?	BUSINESS FOCUS		
	B2B	B2C	Total
Yes	1,038	915	1,953
No	293	779	1,072
Total	1,331	1,694	3,025

Source: Data extracted from "2013 Social Media Marketing Industry Report," May 2013, **bit.ly/1g5vMQN**.

a. Suppose you know that the marketer is a B2B marketer. What is the probability that he or she plans to increase use of LinkedIn?
b. Suppose you know that the marketer is a B2C marketer. What is the probability that he or she plans to increase use of LinkedIn?
c. Are the two events, increase use of LinkedIn and business focus, independent? Explain.

4.23 Do Americans prefer Coke or Pepsi? A survey was conducted by Public Policy Polling (PPP) in 2013; the results were as follows:

	GENDER		
PREFERENCE	Female	Male	Total
Coke	120	95	215
Pepsi	95	80	175
Neither/Unsure	65	45	110
Total	280	220	500

Source: Data extracted from "Public Policy Polling" Report 2013, **bit.ly/YKXfzN**.

a. Given that an American is a male, what is the probability that he prefers Pepsi?
b. Given that an American is a female, what is the probability that she prefers Pepsi?
c. Is preference independent of gender? Explain.

SELF Test **4.24** What business and technical skills are critical for today's business intelligence/analytics and information management professionals? As part of InformationWeek's 2013 U.S. IT Salary Survey, business intelligence/analytics and information management professionals, both staff and managers, were asked to indicate what business and technical skills are critical to their job. The list of business and technical skills included *Analyzing Data*. The following table summarizes the responses to this skill:

ANALYZING DATA	PROFESSIONAL POSITION		
	Staff	Management	Total
Critical	4,374	3,633	8,007
Not critical	3,436	2,631	6,067
Total	7,810	6,264	14,074

Source: Data extracted from "IT Salaries Show Slow Growth," *InformationWeek Reports*, April 2013, p. 40, **ubm.io/1ewjKT5**.

a. Given that a professional is staff, what is the probability that the professional indicates analyzing data as critical to his or her job?
b. Given that a professional is staff, what is the probability that the professional does not indicate analyzing data as critical to his or her job?
c. Given that a professional is a manager, what is the probability that the professional indicates analyzing data as critical to his or her job?
d. Given that a professional is a manager, what is the probability that the professional does not indicate analyzing data as critical to his or her job?

4.25 A survey of 1,085 adults asked, "Do you enjoy shopping for clothing for yourself?" The results (data extracted from "Split Decision on Clothes Shopping," *USA Today*, January 28, 2011, p. 1B) indicated that 51% of the females enjoyed shopping for clothing for themselves as compared to 44% of the males. The sample sizes of males and females were not provided. Suppose that the results were as shown in the following table:

ENJOYS SHOPPING FOR CLOTHING	GENDER		
	Male	Female	Total
Yes	238	276	514
No	304	267	571
Total	542	543	1,085

a. Suppose that the respondent chosen is a female. What is the probability that she does not enjoy shopping for clothing?
b. Suppose that the respondent chosen enjoys shopping for clothing. What is the probability that the individual is a male?
c. Are enjoying shopping for clothing and the gender of the individual independent? Explain.

4.26 Each year, ratings are compiled concerning the performance of new cars during the first 90 days of use. Suppose that the cars have been categorized according to whether a car needs warranty-related repair (yes or no) and the country in which the company manufacturing a car is based (United States or not United States). Based on the data collected, the probability that the new car needs a warranty repair is 0.04, the probability that the car is manufactured by a U.S.-based company is 0.60, and the probability that the new car needs a warranty repair *and* was manufactured by a U.S.-based company is 0.025.

a. Suppose you know that a company based in the United States manufactured a particular car. What is the probability that the car needs a warranty repair?
b. Suppose you know that a company based in the United States did not manufacture a particular car. What is the probability that the car needs a warranty repair?
c. Are need for a warranty repair and location of the company manufacturing the car independent?

4.27 In 41 of the 63 years from 1950 through 2013 (in 2011 there was virtually no change), the S&P 500 finished higher after the first five days of trading. In 36 out of 41 years, the S&P 500 finished higher for the year. Is a good first week a good omen for the upcoming year? The following table gives the first-week and annual performance over this 63-year period:

FIRST WEEK	S&P 500'S ANNUAL PERFORMANCE	
	Higher	Lower
Higher	36	5
Lower	11	11

a. If a year is selected at random, what is the probability that the S&P 500 finished higher for the year?
b. Given that the S&P 500 finished higher after the first five days of trading, what is the probability that it finished higher for the year?
c. Are the two events "first-week performance" and "annual performance" independent? Explain.
d. Look up the performance after the first five days of 2014 and the 2014 annual performance of the S&P 500 at **finance.yahoo.com**. Comment on the results.

4.28 A standard deck of cards is being used to play a game. There are four suits (hearts, diamonds, clubs, and spades), each having 13 faces (ace, 2, 3, 4, 5, 6, 7, 8, 9, 10, jack, queen, and king), making a total of 52 cards. This complete deck is thoroughly mixed, and you will receive the first 2 cards from the deck, without replacement (the first card is not returned to the deck after it is selected).

a. What is the probability that both cards are queens?
b. What is the probability that the first card is a 10 and the second card is a 5 or 6?
c. If you were sampling with replacement (the first card is returned to the deck after it is selected), what would be the answer in (a)?
d. In the game of blackjack, the face cards (jack, queen, king) count as 10 points, and the ace counts as either 1 or 11 points. All other cards are counted at their face value. Blackjack is achieved if 2 cards total 21 points. What is the probability of getting blackjack in this problem?

4.29 A box of nine iPhone 5C cellphones (the iPhone "for the colorful") contains two yellow cellphones and seven green cellphones.

a. If two cellphones are randomly selected from the box, without replacement (the first cellphone is not returned to the box after it is selected), what is the probability that both cellphones selected will be green?
b. If two cellphones are randomly selected from the box, without replacement (the first cellphone is not returned to the box after it is selected), what is the probability that there will be one yellow cellphone and one green cellphone selected?
c. If three cellphones are selected, with replacement (the cellphones are returned to the box after they are selected), what is the probability that all three will be yellow?
d. If you were sampling with replacement (the first cellphone is returned to the box after it is selected), what would be the answers to (a) and (b)?

4.3 Bayes' Theorem

Bayes' theorem is used to revise previously calculated probabilities based on new information. Developed by Thomas Bayes in the eighteenth century (see references 1, 2, 3, and 8), Bayes' theorem is an extension of what you previously learned about conditional probability.

You can apply Bayes' theorem to the situation in which M&R Electronics World is considering marketing a new model of televisions. In the past, 40% of the new-model televisions have been successful, and 60% have been unsuccessful. Before introducing the new-model television, the marketing research department conducts an extensive study and releases a report, either favorable or unfavorable. In the past, 80% of the successful new-model television(s) had received favorable market research reports, and 30% of the unsuccessful new-model television(s) had received favorable reports. For the new model of television under consideration, the marketing research department has issued a favorable report. What is the probability that the television will be successful?

Bayes' theorem is developed from the definition of conditional probability. To find the conditional probability of B given A, consider Equation (4.4b) (originally presented on page 154 and shown again below):

$$P(B|A) = \frac{P(A \text{ and } B)}{P(A)} = \frac{P(A|B)P(B)}{P(A)}$$

Bayes' theorem is derived by substituting Equation (4.8) on page 158 for $P(A)$ in the denominator of Equation (4.4b).

BAYES' THEOREM

$$P(B_i|A) = \frac{P(A|B_i)P(B_i)}{P(A|B_1)P(B_1) + P(A|B_2)P(B_2) + \cdots + P(A|B_k)P(B_k)} \qquad (4.9)$$

where B_i is the ith event out of k mutually exclusive and collectively exhaustive events.

To use Equation (4.9) for the television-marketing example, let

event S = successful television   event F = favorable report
event S' = unsuccessful television   event F' = unfavorable report

and

$$P(S) = 0.40 \quad P(F|S) = 0.80$$
$$P(S') = 0.60 \quad P(F|S') = 0.30$$

Then, using Equation (4.9),

$$P(S|F) = \frac{P(F|S)P(S)}{P(F|S)P(S) + P(F|S')P(S')}$$
$$= \frac{(0.80)(0.40)}{(0.80)(0.40) + (0.30)(0.60)}$$
$$= \frac{0.32}{0.32 + 0.18} = \frac{0.32}{0.50}$$
$$= 0.64$$

The probability of a successful television, given that a favorable report was received, is 0.64. Thus, the probability of an unsuccessful television, given that a favorable report was received, is $1 - 0.64 = 0.36$.

Table 4.4 summarizes the computation of the probabilities, and Figure 4.5 presents the decision tree.

TABLE 4.4

Bayes' Theorem
Computations for the
Television-Marketing
Example

Event S_i	Prior Probability $P(S_i)$	Conditional Probability $P(F \mid S_i)$	Joint Probability $P(F \mid S_i) P(S_i)$	Revised Probability $P(S_i \mid F)$
S = successful television	0.40	0.80	0.32	$P(S \mid F) = 0.32/0.50$ $= 0.64$
S' = unsuccessful television	0.60	0.30	$\dfrac{0.18}{0.50}$	$P(S' \mid F) = 0.18/0.50$ $= 0.36$

FIGURE 4.5

Decision tree for
marketing a new
television

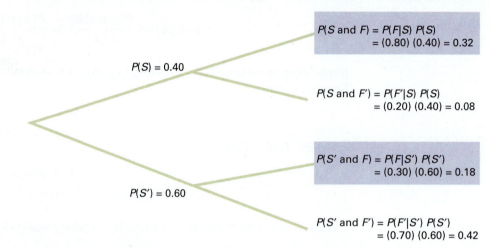

$P(S \text{ and } F) = P(F \mid S) P(S)$
$= (0.80)(0.40) = 0.32$

$P(S \text{ and } F') = P(F' \mid S) P(S)$
$= (0.20)(0.40) = 0.08$

$P(S) = 0.40$

$P(S' \text{ and } F) = P(F \mid S') P(S')$
$= (0.30)(0.60) = 0.18$

$P(S') = 0.60$

$P(S' \text{ and } F') = P(F' \mid S') P(S')$
$= (0.70)(0.60) = 0.42$

Example 4.10 applies Bayes' theorem to a medical diagnosis problem.

EXAMPLE 4.10

Using Bayes' Theorem in a Medical Diagnosis Problem

The probability that a person has a certain disease is 0.03. Medical diagnostic tests are available to determine whether the person actually has the disease. If the disease is actually present, the probability that the medical diagnostic test will give a positive result (indicating that the disease is present) is 0.90. If the disease is not actually present, the probability of a positive test result (indicating that the disease is present) is 0.02. Suppose that the medical diagnostic test has given a positive result (indicating that the disease is present). What is the probability that the disease is actually present? What is the probability of a positive test result?

SOLUTION Let

$$\text{event } D = \text{has disease} \qquad \text{event } T = \text{test is positive}$$
$$\text{event } D' = \text{does not have disease} \qquad \text{event } T' = \text{test is negative}$$

and

$$P(D) = 0.03 \quad P(T \mid D) = 0.90$$
$$P(D') = 0.97 \quad P(T \mid D') = 0.02$$

Using Equation (4.9) on page 161,

$$P(D \mid T) = \frac{P(T \mid D)P(D)}{P(T \mid D)P(D) + P(T \mid D')P(D')}$$

$$= \frac{(0.90)(0.03)}{(0.90)(0.03) + (0.02)(0.97)}$$

$$= \frac{0.0270}{0.0270 + 0.0194} = \frac{0.0270}{0.0464}$$

$$= 0.582$$

(continued)

The probability that the disease is actually present, given that a positive result has occurred (indicating that the disease is present), is 0.582. Table 4.5 summarizes the computation of the probabilities, and Figure 4.6 presents the decision tree. The denominator in Bayes' theorem represents $P(T)$, the probability of a positive test result, which in this case is 0.0464, or 4.64%.

TABLE 4.5

Bayes' Theorem Computations for the Medical Diagnosis Problem

Event D_i	Prior Probability $P(D_i)$	Conditional Probability $P(T \mid D_i)$	Joint Probability $P(T \mid D_i)P(D_i)$	Revised Probability $P(D_i \mid T)$
D = has disease	0.03	0.90	0.0270	$P(D \mid T) = 0.0270/0.0464$ $= 0.582$
D' = does not have disease	0.97	0.02	$\dfrac{0.0194}{0.0464}$	$P(D' \mid T) = 0.0194/0.0464$ $= 0.418$

FIGURE 4.6

Decision tree for a medical diagnosis problem

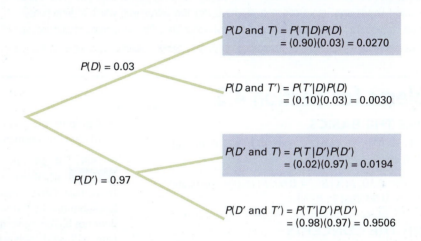

$P(D) = 0.03$

$P(D \text{ and } T) = P(T \mid D)P(D)$
$= (0.90)(0.03) = 0.0270$

$P(D \text{ and } T') = P(T' \mid D)P(D)$
$= (0.10)(0.03) = 0.0030$

$P(D') = 0.97$

$P(D' \text{ and } T) = P(T \mid D')P(D')$
$= (0.02)(0.97) = 0.0194$

$P(D' \text{ and } T') = P(T' \mid D')P(D')$
$= (0.98)(0.97) = 0.9506$

THINK ABOUT THIS | # Divine Providence and Spam

Would you ever guess that the essays *Divine Benevolence: Or, An Attempt to Prove That the Principal End of the Divine Providence and Government Is the Happiness of His Creatures* and *An Essay Towards Solving a Problem in the Doctrine of Chances* were written by the same person? Probably not, and in doing so, you illustrate a modern-day application of Bayesian statistics: spam, or junk mail filters.

In not guessing correctly, you probably looked at the words in the titles of the essays and concluded that they were talking about two different things. An implicit rule you used was that word frequencies vary by subject matter. A statistics essay would very likely contain the word *statistics* as well as words such as *chance*, *problem*, and *solving*. An eighteenth-century essay about theology and religion would be more likely to contain the uppercase forms of *Divine* and *Providence*.

Likewise, there are words you would guess to be very unlikely to appear in either book, such as technical terms from finance, and words that are most likely to appear in both—common words

such as *a*, *and*, and *the*. That words would be either likely or unlikely suggests an application of probability theory. Of course, likely and unlikely are fuzzy concepts, and we might occasionally misclassify an essay if we kept things too simple, such as relying solely on the occurrence of the words *Divine* and *Providence*.

For example, a profile of the late Harris Milstead, better known as *Divine*, the star of *Hairspray* and other films, visiting Providence (Rhode Island), would most certainly not be an essay about theology. But if we widened the number of words we examined and found such words as *movie* or the name John Waters (Divine's director in many films), we probably would quickly realize the essay had something to do with twentieth-century cinema and little to do with theology and religion.

We can use a similar process to try to classify a new email message in your in-box as either spam or a legitimate message (called "ham," in this context). We would first need to add to your email program a "spam filter" that has the ability to track word frequencies associated with spam and

ham messages as you identify them on a day-to-day basis. This would allow the filter to constantly update the prior probabilities necessary to use Bayes' theorem. With these probabilities, the filter can ask, "What is the probability that an email is spam, given the presence of a certain word?"

Applying the terms of Equation (4.9) on page 161, such a Bayesian spam filter would multiply the probability of finding the word in a spam email, $P(A \mid B)$, by the probability that the email is spam, $P(B)$, and then divide by the probability of finding the word in an email, the denominator in Equation (4.9). Bayesian spam filters also use shortcuts by focusing on a small set of words that have a high probability of being found in a spam message as well as on a small set of other words that have a low probability of being found in a spam message.

As spammers (people who send junk email) learned of such new filters, they tried to outfox them. Having learned that Bayesian filters might be assigning a high $P(A \mid B)$ value to words commonly found in spam, such as Viagra, spammers thought they could fool the filter by misspelling the word as Vi@gr@ or V1agra. What they overlooked was that the misspelled variants were even *more likely* to be found in a spam message than the original word. Thus, the misspelled variants made the job of spotting spam *easier* for the Bayesian filters.

Other spammers tried to fool the filters by adding "good" words, words that would have a low probability of being found in a spam message, or "rare" words, words not frequently encountered in any message. But these spammers overlooked the fact that the conditional probabilities are constantly updated and that words once considered "good" would be soon discarded from the good list by the filter as their $P(A|B)$, value increased. Likewise, as "rare" words grew more common in spam and yet stayed rare in ham, such words

acted like the misspelled variants that others had tried earlier.

Even then, and perhaps after reading about Bayesian statistics, spammers thought that they could "break" Bayesian filters by inserting random words in their messages. Those random words would affect the filter by causing it to see many words whose $P(A|B)$, value would be low. The Bayesian filter would begin to label many spam messages as ham and end up being of no practical use. Spammers again overlooked that conditional probabilities are constantly updated.

Other spammers decided to eliminate all or most of the words in their messages and replace them with graphics so that Bayesian filters would have very few words with which to form conditional probabilities. But this approach failed, too, as

Bayesian filters were rewritten to consider things other than words in a message. After all, Bayes' theorem concerns *events*, and "graphics present with no text" is as valid an event as "some word, *X*, present in a message." Other future tricks will ultimately fail for the same reason. (By the way, spam filters use non-Bayesian techniques as well, which makes spammers' lives even more difficult.)

Bayesian spam filters are an example of the unexpected way that applications of statistics can show up in your daily life. You will discover more examples as you read the rest of this book. By the way, the author of the two essays mentioned earlier was Thomas Bayes, who is a lot more famous for the second essay than the first essay, a failed attempt to use mathematics and logic to prove the existence of God.

Problems for Section 4.3

LEARNING THE BASICS

4.30 If $P(B) = 0.05$, $P(A|B) = 0.80$, $P(B') = 0.95$, and $P(A|B') = 0.40$, find $P(B|A)$.

4.31 If $P(B) = 0.30$, $P(A|B) = 0.60$, $P(B') = 0.70$, and and $P(A|B') = 0.50$, find $P(B|A)$.

APPLYING THE CONCEPTS

4.32 In Example 4.10 on page 163, suppose that the probability that a medical diagnostic test will give a positive result if the disease is not present is reduced from 0.02 to 0.01.
a. If the medical diagnostic test has given a positive result (indicating that the disease is present), what is the probability that the disease is actually present?
b. If the medical diagnostic test has given a negative result (indicating that the disease is not present), what is the probability that the disease is not present?

4.33 A banking executive is studying the role of trust in creating customer advocates, and how valuable trust is to the overall banking relationship. Based on study results, the executive has determined that 44% of banking customers have *complete trust* in their primary financial institution, 49% of banking customers have *moderate trust* in their primary financial institution, and 7% have *minimal* or *no trust* in their primary financial institution. Of the banking customers that have *complete trust* in their primary financial institution, 68% are very likely to recommend their primary financial institution; of the banking customers that have *moderate trust* in their primary financial institution, 20% are very likely to recommend their primary financial institution; and of the banking customers that have *minimal* or *no trust* in their primary financial institution, 3% are very likely to recommend their primary financial institution. (Data extracted from "Global Consumer Banking Survey-2014," **bit.ly/1gwJJuT**.)
a. Compute the probability that if the banking customer indicates he or she is very likely to recommend his or her primary financial institution, the banking customer also has *complete trust* in his or her primary financial institution.

b. Compute the probability that the banking customer is very likely to recommend his or her primary financial institution.

 4.34 Olive Construction Company is determining whether it should submit a bid for a new shopping center. In the past, Olive's main competitor, Base Construction Company, has submitted bids 70% of the time. If Base Construction Company does not bid on a job, the probability that Olive Construction Company will get the job is 0.50. If Base Construction Company bids on a job, the probability that Olive Construction Company will get the job is 0.25.
a. If Olive Construction Company gets the job, what is the probability that Base Construction Company did not bid?
b. What is the probability that Olive Construction Company will get the job?

4.35 According to a report by The Kauffman Foundation and LegalZoom, 35% of new businesses in 2013 were started by women and 65% of new businesses in 2013 were started by men. Twenty percent of 2013 new businesses started by women had revenues of $50,000 and above, whereas 24% of 2013 new businesses started by men had revenues of $50,000 and above.
a. If a new business started in 2013 is selected at random and the new business had revenues of $50,000 and above, what is the probability that the new business was started by a woman?
b. If a new business started in 2013 is selected at random, what is the probability that the new business had revenues of $50,000 and above?

4.36 The editor of a textbook publishing company is trying to decide whether to publish a proposed business statistics textbook. Information on previous textbooks published indicates that 10% are huge successes, 20% are modest successes, 40% break-even, and 30% are losers. However, before a publishing decision is made, the book will be reviewed. In the past, 99% of the huge successes received favorable reviews, 70% of the moderate successes received favorable reviews, 40% of the break-even books received favorable reviews, and 20% of the losers received favorable reviews.

a. If the proposed textbook receives a favorable review, how should the editor revise the probabilities of the various outcomes to take this information into account?

b. What proportion of textbooks receive favorable reviews?

4.37 A municipal bond service has three rating categories (A, B, and C). Suppose that in the past year, of the municipal bonds issued throughout the United States, 70% were rated A, 20% were rated B, and 10% were rated C. Of the municipal bonds rated A, 50%

were issued by cities, 40% by suburbs, and 10% by rural areas. Of the municipal bonds rated B, 60% were issued by cities, 20% by suburbs, and 20% by rural areas. Of the municipal bonds rated C, 90% were issued by cities, 5% by suburbs, and 5% by rural areas.

a. If a new municipal bond is to be issued by a city, what is the probability that it will receive an A rating?

b. What proportion of municipal bonds are issued by cities?

c. What proportion of municipal bonds are issued by suburbs?

4.4 Counting Rules

In Equation (4.1) on page 143, the probability of occurrence of an outcome was defined as the number of ways the outcome occurs, divided by the total number of possible outcomes. Often, there are a large number of possible outcomes, and determining the exact number can be difficult. In such circumstances, rules have been developed for counting the number of possible outcomes. This section presents five different counting rules.

Counting Rule 1   Counting rule 1 determines the number of possible outcomes for a set of mutually exclusive and collectively exhaustive events.

COUNTING RULE 1

If any one of k different mutually exclusive and collectively exhaustive events can occur on each of n trials, the number of possible outcomes is equal to

$$k^n \tag{4.10}$$

For example, using Equation (4.10), the number of different possible outcomes from tossing a two-sided coin five times is $2^5 = 2 \times 2 \times 2 \times 2 \times 2 = 32$.

EXAMPLE 4.11

Rolling a Die Twice

Suppose you roll a die twice. How many different possible outcomes can occur?

SOLUTION If a six-sided die is rolled twice, using Equation (4.10), the number of different outcomes is $6^2 = 36$.

Counting Rule 2   The second counting rule is a more general version of the first counting rule and allows the number of possible events to differ from trial to trial.

COUNTING RULE 2

If there are k_1 events on the first trial, k_2 events on the second trial, . . . , and k_n events on the nth trial, then the number of possible outcomes is

$$(k_1)(k_2) \ldots (k_n) \tag{4.11}$$

For example, a state motor vehicle department would like to know how many license plate numbers are available if a license plate number consists of three letters followed by three numbers (0 through 9). Using Equation (4.11), if a license plate number consists of three letters followed by three numbers, the total number of possible outcomes is $(26)(26)(26)(10)(10)(10) = 17,576,000$.

EXAMPLE 4.12

Determining the Number of Different Dinners

A restaurant menu has a price-fixed complete dinner that consists of an appetizer, an entrée, a beverage, and a dessert. You have a choice of 5 appetizers, 10 entrées, 3 beverages, and 6 desserts. Determine the total number of possible dinners.

SOLUTION Using Equation (4.11), the total number of possible dinners is $(5)(10)(3)(6) = 900$.

Counting Rule 3 The third counting rule involves computing the number of ways that a set of items can be arranged in order.

> COUNTING RULE 3
>
> The number of ways that all n items can be arranged in order is
>
> $$n! = (n)(n-1)\ldots(1) \tag{4.12}$$
>
> where $n!$ is called n factorial, and $0!$ is defined as 1.

EXAMPLE 4.13

Using Counting Rule 3

If a set of six books is to be placed on a shelf, in how many ways can the six books be arranged?

SOLUTION To begin, you must realize that any of the six books could occupy the first position on the shelf. Once the first position is filled, there are five books to choose from in filling the second position. You continue this assignment procedure until all the positions are occupied. The number of ways that you can arrange six books is

$$n! = 6! = (6)(5)(4)(3)(2)(1) = 720$$

Counting Rule 4 In many instances you need to know the number of ways in which a subset of an entire group of items can be arranged in *order*. Each possible arrangement is called a **permutation**.

> **Student Tip**
> Both permutations and combinations assume that you are sampling without replacement.

> COUNTING RULE 4: PERMUTATIONS
>
> The number of ways of arranging x objects selected from n objects in order is
>
> $$_nP_x = \frac{n!}{(n-x)!} \tag{4.13}$$
>
> where
>
> n = total number of objects
> x = number of objects to be arranged
> $n!$ = n factorial = $n(n-1)\ldots(1)$
> P = symbol for permutations[1]

[1] On many scientific calculators, there is a button labeled nPr that allows you to compute permutations. The symbol r is used instead of x.

EXAMPLE 4.14

Using Counting Rule 4

Modifying Example 4.13, if you have six books, but there is room for only four books on the shelf, in how many ways can you arrange these books on the shelf?

SOLUTION Using Equation (4.13), the number of ordered arrangements of four books selected from six books is equal to

$$_nP_x = \frac{n!}{(n-x)!} = \frac{6!}{(6-4)!} = \frac{(6)(5)(4)(3)(2)(1)}{(2)(1)} = 360$$

Counting Rule 5   In many situations, you are not interested in the *order* of the outcomes but only in the number of ways that x items can be selected from n items, *irrespective of order*. Each possible selection is called a **combination**.

> ### COUNTING RULE 5: COMBINATIONS
>
> The number of ways of selecting x objects from n objects, irrespective of order, is equal to
>
> $$_nC_x = \frac{n!}{x!(n-x)!} \qquad (4.14)$$
>
> where
>
> n = total number of objects
> x = number of objects to be arranged
> $n!$ = n factorial = $n(n-1)\ldots(1)$
> C = symbol for combinations[2]

[2]On many scientific calculators, there is a button labeled nCr that allows you to compute combinations. The symbol r is used instead of x.

If you compare this rule to counting rule 4, you see that it differs only in the inclusion of a term $x!$ in the denominator. When permutations were used, all of the arrangements of the x objects are distinguishable. With combinations, the $x!$ possible arrangements of objects are irrelevant.

EXAMPLE 4.15

Using Counting Rule 5

Modifying Example 4.14, if the order of the books on the shelf is irrelevant, in how many ways can you arrange these books on the shelf?

SOLUTION Using Equation (4.14), the number of combinations of four books selected from six books is equal to

$$_nC_x = \frac{n!}{x!(n-x)!} = \frac{6!}{4!(6-4)!} = \frac{(6)(5)(4)(3)(2)(1)}{(4)(3)(2)(1)(2)(1)} = 15$$

Problems for Section 4.4

APPLYING THE CONCEPTS

SELF Test **4.38** If there are 10 multiple-choice questions on an exam, each having three possible answers, how many different sequences of answers are there?

4.39 A lock on a bank vault consists of three dials, each with 30 positions. In order for the vault to open, each of the three dials must be in the correct position.
a. How many different possible dial combinations are there for this lock?

b. What is the probability that if you randomly select a position on each dial, you will be able to open the bank vault?

c. Explain why "dial combinations" are not mathematical combinations expressed by Equation (4.14).

4.40 a. If a coin is tossed seven times, how many different outcomes are possible?

b. If a die is tossed seven times, how many different outcomes are possible?

c. Discuss the differences in your answers to (a) and (b).

4.41 A particular brand of women's jeans is available in seven different sizes, three different colors, and three different styles. How many different women's jeans does the store manager need to order to have one pair of each type?

4.42 You would like to "build-your-own-burger" at a fast-food restaurant. There are five different breads, seven different cheeses, four different cold toppings, and five different sauces on the menu. If you want to include one choice from each of these ingredient categories, how many different burgers can you build?

4.43 A team is being formed that includes four different people. There are four different positions on the teams. How many different ways are there to assign the four people to the four positions?

4.44 In Major League Baseball, there are five teams in the Eastern Division of the National League: Atlanta, Florida, New York, Philadelphia, and Washington. How many different orders of finish are there for these five teams? (Assume that there are no ties in the standings.) Do you believe that all these orders are equally likely? Discuss.

4.45 Referring to Problem 4.44, how many different orders of finish are possible for the first four positions?

4.46 A gardener has six rows available in his vegetable garden to place tomatoes, eggplant, peppers, cucumbers, beans, and lettuce. Each vegetable will be allowed one and only one row. How many ways are there to position these vegetables in this garden?

4.47 How many different ways can a senior project manager and an associate project manager be selected for an analytics project if there are eight data scientists available?

4.48 Four members of a group of 10 people are to be selected to a team. How many ways are there to select these four members?

4.49 A student has seven books that she would like to place in her backpack. However, there is room for only four books. Regardless of the arrangement, how many ways are there of placing four books into the backpack?

4.50 A daily lottery is conducted in which 2 winning numbers are selected out of 100 numbers. How many different combinations of winning numbers are possible?

4.51 There are 15 exercise bikes in a fitness store showroom. The fitness store owner wishes to select three of them to display at a fitness expo. How many ways can a group of three be selected?

4.5 Ethical Issues and Probability

Ethical issues can arise when any statements related to probability are presented to the public, particularly when these statements are part of an advertising campaign for a product or service. Unfortunately, many people are not comfortable with numerical concepts (see reference 7) and tend to misinterpret the meaning of the probability. In some instances, the misinterpretation is not intentional, but in other cases, advertisements may unethically try to mislead potential customers.

One example of a potentially unethical application of probability relates to advertisements for state lotteries. When purchasing a lottery ticket, the customer selects a set of numbers (such as 6) from a larger list of numbers (such as 54). Although virtually all participants know that they are unlikely to win the lottery, they also have very little idea of how unlikely it is for them to select all 6 winning numbers from the list of 54 numbers. They have even less of an idea of the probability of not selecting any winning numbers.

Given this background, you might consider a recent commercial for a state lottery that stated, "We won't stop until we have made everyone a millionaire" to be deceptive and possibly unethical. Do you think the state has any intention of ever stopping the lottery, given the fact that the state relies on it to bring millions of dollars into its treasury? Is it possible that the lottery can make everyone a millionaire? Is it ethical to suggest that the purpose of the lottery is to make everyone a millionaire?

Another example of a potentially unethical application of probability relates to an investment newsletter promising a 90% probability of a 20% annual return on investment. To make the claim in the newsletter an ethical one, the investment service needs to (a) explain the basis on which this probability estimate rests, (b) provide the probability statement in another format, such as 9 chances in 10, and (c) explain what happens to the investment in the 10% of the cases in which a 20% return is not achieved (e.g., is the entire investment lost?).

These are serious ethical issues. If you were going to write an advertisement for the state lottery that ethically describes the probability of winning a certain prize, what would you say? If you were going to write an advertisement for the investment newsletter that ethically states the probability of a 20% return on an investment, what would you say?

USING STATISTICS
Possibilities at M&R Electronics World, Revisited

Shock/Fotolia

As the marketing manager for M&R Electronics World, you analyzed the survey results of an intent-to-purchase study. This study asked the heads of 1,000 households about their intentions to purchase a large-screen HDTV sometime during the next 12 months, and as a follow-up, M&R surveyed the same people 12 months later to see whether such a television was purchased. In addition, for households purchasing large-screen HDTVs, the survey asked whether the television they purchased had a faster refresh rate, whether they also purchased a streaming media box in the past 12 months, and whether they were satisfied with their purchase of the large-screen HDTV.

By analyzing the results of these surveys, you were able to uncover many pieces of valuable information that will help you plan a marketing strategy to enhance sales and better target those households likely to purchase multiple or more expensive products. Whereas only 30% of the households actually purchased a large-screen HDTV, if a household indicated that it planned to purchase a large-screen HDTV in the next 12 months, there was an 80% chance that the household actually made the purchase. Thus the marketing strategy should target those households that have indicated an intention to purchase.

You determined that for households that purchased a television that had a faster refresh rate, there was a 47.5% chance that the household also purchased a streaming media box. You then compared this conditional probability to the marginal probability of purchasing a streaming media box, which was 36%. Thus, households that purchased televisions that had a faster refresh rate are more likely to purchase a streaming media box than are households that purchased large-screen HDTVs that have a standard refresh rate.

You were also able to apply Bayes' theorem to M&R Electronics World's market research reports. The reports investigate a potential new television model prior to its scheduled release. If a favorable report was received, then there was a 64% chance that the new television model would be successful. However, if an unfavorable report was received, there is only a 16% chance that the model would be successful. Therefore, the marketing strategy of M&R needs to pay close attention to whether a report's conclusion is favorable or unfavorable.

SUMMARY

This chapter began by developing the basic concepts of probability. You learned that probability is a numeric value from 0 to 1 that represents the chance, likelihood, or possibility that a particular event will occur. In addition to simple probability, you learned about conditional probabilities and independent events. Bayes' theorem was used to revise previously calculated probabilities based on new information. Throughout the chapter, contingency tables and decision trees were used to display information. You also learned about several counting rules. In the next chapter, important discrete probability distributions including the binomial and Poisson distributions are developed.

REFERENCES

1. Anderson-Cook, C. M. "Unraveling Bayes' Theorem." *Quality Progress*, March 2014, p. 52–54.
2. Bellhouse, D. R. "The Reverend Thomas Bayes, FRS: A Biography to Celebrate the Tercentenary of His Birth." *Statistical Science*, 19 (2004), 3–43.
3. Hooper, W. "Probing Probabilities." *Quality Progress*, March 2014, pp. 18–22.
4. Lowd, D., and C. Meek. "Good Word Attacks on Statistical Spam Filters." Presented at the Second Conference on Email and Anti-Spam, 2005.
5. *Microsoft Excel 2013*. Redmond, WA: Microsoft Corp., 2012.
6. *Minitab Release 16*. State College, PA: Minitab, Inc, 2010.
7. Paulos, J. A. *Innumeracy*. New York: Hill and Wang, 1988.
8. Silberman, S. "The Quest for Meaning," *Wired 8.02*, February 2000.
9. Zeller, T. "The Fight Against V1@gra (and Other Spam)." *The New York Times*, May 21, 2006, pp. B1, B6.

KEY EQUATIONS

Probability of Occurrence

$$\text{Probability of occurrence} = \frac{X}{T} \qquad (4.1)$$

Marginal Probability

$$P(A) = P(A \text{ and } B_1) + P(A \text{ and } B_2) \\ + \cdots + P(A \text{ and } B_k) \qquad (4.2)$$

General Addition Rule

$$P(A \text{ or } B) = P(A) + P(B) - P(A \text{ and } B) \qquad (4.3)$$

Conditional Probability

$$P(A \mid B) = \frac{P(A \text{ and } B)}{P(B)} \qquad (4.4a)$$

$$P(B \mid A) = \frac{P(A \text{ and } B)}{P(A)} \qquad (4.4b)$$

Independence

$$P(A \mid B) = P(A) \qquad (4.5)$$

General Multiplication Rule

$$P(A \text{ and } B) = P(A \mid B)P(B) \qquad (4.6)$$

Multiplication Rule for Independent Events

$$P(A \text{ and } B) = P(A)P(B) \qquad (4.7)$$

Marginal Probability Using the General Multiplication Rule

$$P(A) = P(A \mid B_1)P(B_1) + P(A \mid B_2)P(B_2) \\ + \cdots + P(A \mid B_k)P(B_k) \qquad (4.8)$$

Bayes' Theorem

$$P(B_i \mid A) = \\ \frac{P(A \mid B_i)P(B_i)}{P(A \mid B_1)P(B_1) + P(A \mid B_2)P(B_2) + \cdots + P(A \mid B_k)P(B_k)} \qquad (4.9)$$

Counting Rule 1

$$k^n \qquad (4.10)$$

Counting Rule 2

$$(k_1)(k_2) \ldots (k_n) \qquad (4.11)$$

Counting Rule 3

$$n! = (n)(n - 1) \ldots (1) \qquad (4.12)$$

Counting Rule 4: Permutations

$$_nP_x = \frac{n!}{(n - x)!} \qquad (4.13)$$

Counting Rule 5: Combinations

$$_nC_x = \frac{n!}{x!(n - x)!} \qquad (4.14)$$

KEY TERMS

CHECKING YOUR UNDERSTANDING

4.52 What are the differences between *a priori* probability, empirical probability, and subjective probability?

4.53 What is the difference between a simple event and a joint event?

4.54 How can you use the general addition rule to find the probability of occurrence of event *A* or *B*?

4.55 What is the difference between mutually exclusive events and collectively exhaustive events?

4.56 How does conditional probability relate to the concept of independence?

4.57 How does the multiplication rule differ for events that are and are not independent?

4.58 How can you use Bayes' theorem to revise probabilities in light of new information?

4.59 In Bayes' theorem, how does the prior probability differ from the revised probability?

CHAPTER REVIEW PROBLEMS

4.60 A survey by the Health Research Institute at PricewaterhouseCoopers LLP indicated that 80% of "young invincibles" (those aged 18 to 24) are likely to share health information through social media, as compared to 45% of "baby boomers" (those aged 45 to 64).

Source: Data extracted from "Social Media 'Likes' Healthcare: From Marketing to Social Business," Health Research Institute, April 2012, p. 8.

Suppose that the survey was based on 500 respondents from each of the two groups.
a. Construct a contingency table.
b. Give an example of a simple event and a joint event.
c. What is the probability that a randomly selected respondent is likely to share health information through social media?
d. What is the probability that a randomly selected respondent is likely to share health information through social media *and* is in the 45- to 64-year-old group?
e. Are the events "age group" and "likely to share health information through social media" independent? Explain.

4.61 SHL Americas provides a unique, global perspective of how talent is measured in its Global Assessment Trends Report. The report presents the results of an online survey conducted in late 2012 with HR professionals from companies headquartered throughout the world. The authors were interested in examining differences between respondents in *emerging economies* and those in *established economies* to provide relevant information for readers who may be creating assessment programs for organizations with global reach; one area of focus was on HR professionals' response to two statements: "My organization views HR as a strategic function" and "My organization uses talent information to make business decisions." The results are as follows:

	ORGANIZATION VIEWS HR AS A STRATEGIC FUNCTION		
ECONOMY	**Yes**	**No**	**Total**
Established	171	78	249
Emerging	222	121	343
Total	393	199	592

	ORGANIZATION USES INFORMATION ABOUT TALENT TO MAKE BUSINESS DECISIONS		
ECONOMY	**Yes**	**No**	**Total**
Established	122	127	249
Emerging	130	213	343
Total	252	340	592

What is the probability that a randomly chosen HR professional
a. is from an established economy?
b. is from an established economy *or* agrees to the statement "My organization uses information about talent to make business decisions?"
c. does not agree with the statement "My organization views HR as a strategic function" *and* is from an emerging economy?
d. does not agree with the statement "My organization views HR as a strategic function" *or* is from an emerging economy?
e. Suppose the randomly chosen HR professional does not agree with the statement "My organization views HR as a strategic function." What is the probability that the HR professional is from an emerging economy?
f. Are "My organization views HR as a strategic function" and the type of economy independent?
g. Is "My organization uses information about talent to make business decisions" independent of the type of economy?

4.62 The 2012 Restaurant Industry Forecast takes a closer look at today's consumers. Based on a 2011 National Restaurant Association survey, consumers are divided into three segments (optimistic, cautious, and hunkered-down) based on their financial situation, current spending behavior, and economic outlook. Suppose the results, based on a sample of 100 males and 100 females, were as follows:

	GENDER		
CONSUMER SEGMENT	**Male**	**Female**	**Total**
Optimistic	26	16	42
Cautious	41	43	84
Hunkered-down	33	41	74
Total	100	100	200

Source: Data extracted from "The 2012 Restaurant Industry Forecast," National Restaurant Association, 2012, p. 12, **restaurant.org/research/forecast**.

If a consumer is selected at random, what is the probability that he or she

a. is classified as cautious?

b. is classified as optimistic or cautious?

c. is a male *or* is classified as hunkered-down?

d. is a male *and* is classified as hunkered-down?

e. Given that the consumer selected is a female, what is the probability that she is classified as optimistic?

4.63 Content Marketing Institute provides insights on the content marketing habits of nonprofit professionals representing a broad range of nonprofit agencies and organizations. A survey of nonprofit marketers conducted by the Content Marketing Institute indicated that 26% of nonprofit marketers rated themselves *highly* in terms of use of content marketing effectiveness. Furthermore, of the nonprofit marketers who rated themselves *highly* in terms of use of content marketing effectiveness, 63% reported having a documented content strategy. Of the nonprofit marketers who did not rate themselves *highly* in terms of use of content marketing effectiveness, 21% reported having a documented content strategy. (Data extracted from *2014 Nonprofit Content Marketing*, **bit.ly/ KrCLvl.**)

If a nonprofit marketer is known to have a documented content strategy, what is the probability that the nonprofit marketer rates himself or herself *highly* in terms of use of content marketing effectiveness?

4.64 The CMO Council and SAS set out to better understand the key challenges, opportunities, and requirements that both chief marketing officers (CMOs) and chief information officers (CIOs) were facing in their journey to develop a more customer-centric enterprise. The following findings are from an online audit of 237 senior marketers and 210 senior IT executives. (Data extracted from "Big Data's Biggest Role: Aligning the CMO & CIO," March 2013, **bit.ly/11z7uKW.**)

EXECUTIVE GROUP	BIG DATA IS CRITICAL TO EXECUTING A CUSTOMER-CENTRIC PROGRAM		
	Yes	No	Total
Marketing	95	142	237
IT	107	103	210
Total	202	245	447

EXECUTIVE GROUP	FUNCTIONAL SILOS BLOCK AGGREGATION OF CUSTOMER DATA THROUGHOUT THE ORGANIZATION		
	Yes	No	Total
Marketing	122	115	237
IT	95	115	210
Total	217	230	447

a. What is the probability that a randomly selected executive identifies Big Data as critical to executing a customer-centric program?

b. Given that a randomly selected executive is a senior marketing executive, what is the probability that the executive identifies Big Data as critical to executing a customer-centric program?

c. Given that a randomly selected executive is a senior IT executive, what is the probability that the executive identifies Big Data as critical to executing a customer-centric program?

d. What is the probability that a randomly selected executive identifies that functional silos block aggregation of customer data throughout the organization?

e. Given that a randomly selected executive is a senior marketing executive, what is the probability that the executive identifies that functional silos block aggregation of customer data throughout the organization?

f. Given that a randomly selected executive is a senior IT executive, what is the probability that the executive identifies that functional silos block aggregation of customer data throughout the organization?

g. Comment on the results in (a) through (f).

4.65 A 2013 Sage North America survey examined the "financial literacy" of small business owners. The study found that 23% of small business owners indicated concern about income tax compliance for their business; 41% of small business owners use accounting software, given that the small business owner indicated concern about income tax compliance for his or her business. Given that a small business owner did not indicate concern about income tax compliance for his or her business, 58% of small business owners use accounting software. (Data extracted from "Sage Financial Capability Survey: What Small Business Owners Don't Understand Could Be Holding Them Back," April 17, 2013, **http://bit.ly/Z3FAqx.**)

a. Use Bayes' theorem to find the probability that a small business owner uses accounting software, given that the small business owner indicated concern about income tax compliance for his or her business.

b. Compare the result in (a) to the probability that a small business owner uses accounting software and comment on whether small business owners who are concerned about income tax compliance for their business are generally more likely to use accounting software than small business owners who are not concerned about income tax compliance for their business.

CASES FOR CHAPTER 4

Digital Case

Apply your knowledge about contingency tables and the proper application of simple and joint probabilities in this continuing Digital Case from Chapter 3.

Open **EndRunGuide.pdf**, the EndRun Financial Services "Guide to Investing," and read the information about the Guaranteed Investment Package (GIP). Read the claims and examine the supporting data. Then answer the following questions:

1. How accurate is the claim of the probability of success for EndRun's GIP? In what ways is the claim misleading? How would you calculate and state the probability of having an annual rate of return not less than 15%?

2. Using the table found under the "Show Me the Winning Probabilities" subhead, compute the proper probabilities for the group of investors. What mistake was made in reporting the 7% probability claim?

3. Are there any probability calculations that would be appropriate for rating an investment service? Why or why not?

CardioGood Fitness

1. For each CardioGood Fitness treadmill product line (see the `CardioGoodFitness` file), construct two-way contingency tables of gender, education in years, relationship status, and self-rated fitness. (There will be a total of six tables for each treadmill product.)

2. For each table you construct, compute all conditional and marginal probabilities.

3. Write a report detailing your findings to be presented to the management of CardioGood Fitness.

The Choice *Is* Yours Follow-Up

1. Follow up the "Using Statistics: The Choice *Is* Yours, Revisited" on page 71 by constructing contingency tables of market cap and type, market cap and risk, market cap and rating, type and risk, type and rating, and risk and rating for the sample of 316 retirement funds stored in `Retirement Funds`.

2. For each table you construct, compute all conditional and marginal probabilities.

3. Write a report summarizing your conclusions.

Clear Mountain State Student Surveys

The Student News Service at Clear Mountain State University (CMSU) has decided to gather data about the undergraduate students that attend CMSU. CMSU creates and distributes a survey of 14 questions and receive responses from 62 undergraduates (stored in `UndergradSurvey`).

1. For these data, construct contingency tables of gender and major, gender and graduate school intention, gender and employment status, gender and computer preference, class and graduate school intention, class and employment status, major and graduate school intention, major and employment status, and major and computer preference.

   a. For each of these contingency tables, compute all the conditional and marginal probabilities.

   b. Write a report summarizing your conclusions.

2. The CMSU Dean of Students has learned about the undergraduate survey and has decided to undertake a similar survey for graduate students at Clear Mountain State. She creates and distributes a survey of 14 questions and receives responses from 44 graduate students (stored in `GradSurvey`). Construct contingency tables of gender and graduate major, gender and undergraduate major, gender and employment status, gender and computer preference, graduate major and undergraduate major, graduate major and employment status, and graduate major and computer preference.

   a. For each of these contingency tables, compute all the conditional and marginal probabilities.

   b. Write a report summarizing your conclusions.

CHAPTER 4 EXCEL GUIDE

EG4.1 BASIC PROBABILITY CONCEPTS

Simple Probability, Joint Probability, and the General Addition Rule

Key Technique Use Excel arithmetic formulas.

Example Compute simple and joint probabilities for the Table 4.1 purchase behavior data on page 145.

PHStat2 Use **Simple & Joint Probabilities**.
For the example, select **PHStat → Probability & Prob. Distributions → Simple & Joint Probabilities**. In the new template, similar to the worksheet shown below, fill in the **Sample Space** area with the data.

In-Depth Excel Use the **COMPUTE worksheet** of the **Probabilities workbook** as a template.
The worksheet (shown below) already contains the Table 4.1 purchase behavior data. For other problems, change the sample space table entries in the cell ranges **C3:D4** and **A5:D6**.

	A	B	C	D	E
1	Probabilities				
2					
3	Sample Space		Actually Purchased		
4			Yes	No	Totals
5	Planned to Purchase	Yes	200	50	250
6		No	100	650	750
7		Totals	300	700	1000
8					
9	Simple Probabilities				
10	P(Yes)		0.25	=E5/E7	
11	P(No)		0.75	=E6/E7	
12	P(Yes)		0.30	=C7/E7	
13	P(No)		0.70	=D7/E7	
14					
15	Joint Probabilities				
16	P(Yes and Yes)		0.20	=C5/E7	
17	P(Yes and No)		0.05	=D5/E7	
18	P(No and Yes)		0.10	=C6/E7	
19	P(No and No)		0.65	=D6/E7	
20					
21	Addition Rule				
22	P(Yes or Yes)		0.35	=H16 + H18 - H22	
23	P(Yes or No)		0.90	=H16 + H19 - H23	
24	P(No or Yes)		0.95	=H17 + H18 - H24	
25	P(No or No)		0.80	=H17 + H19 - H25	

Read the SHORT TAKES for Chapter 4 for an explanation of the formulas found in the COMPUTE worksheet (shown in the **COMPUTE_FORMULAS worksheet**).

EG4.2 CONDITIONAL PROBABILITY

There is no Excel material for this section.

EG4.3 BAYES' THEOREM

Key Technique Use Excel arithmetic formulas.

Example Apply Bayes' theorem to the television marketing example in Section 4.3.

In-Depth Excel Use the **COMPUTE worksheet** of the **Bayes workbook** as a template.

The worksheet (shown below) already contains the probabilities for the Section 4.3 example. For other problems, change those probabilities in the cell range **B5:C6**.

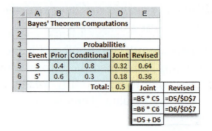

Open to the **COMPUTE_FORMULAS worksheet** to examine the arithmetic formulas that compute the probabilities, which are also shown as an inset to the worksheet.

EG4.4 COUNTING RULES

Counting Rule 1

In-Depth Excel Use the **POWER(k, n)** worksheet function in a cell formula to compute the number of outcomes given k events and n trials.
For example, the formula **=POWER(6, 2)** computes the answer for Example 4.11 on page 166.

Counting Rule 2

In-Depth Excel Use a formula that takes the product of successive **POWER(k, n)** functions to solve problems related to counting rule 2.
For example, the formula **=POWER(26, 3) * POWER(10, 3)** computes the answer for the state motor vehicle department example on page 166.

Counting Rule 3

In-Depth Excel Use the **FACT(n)** worksheet function in a cell formula to compute how many ways n items can be arranged.
For example, the formula **=FACT(6)** computes 6!

Counting Rule 4

In-Depth Excel Use the **PERMUT(n, x)** worksheet function in a cell formula to compute the number of ways of arranging x objects selected from n objects in order.
For example, the formula **= PERMUT(6, 4)** computes the answer for Example 4.14 on page 168.

Counting Rule 5

In-Depth Excel Use the **COMBIN(n, x)** worksheet function in a cell formula to compute the number of ways of arranging x objects selected from n objects, irrespective of order.
For example, the formula **=COMBIN(6, 4)** computes the answer for Example 4.15 on page 168.

CHAPTER 4 MINITAB GUIDE

MG4.1 BASIC PROBABILITY CONCEPTS

There is no Minitab material for this section.

MG4.2 CONDITIONAL PROBABILITY

There is no Minitab material for this section.

MG4.3 BAYES' THEOREM

There is no Minitab material for this section.

MG4.4 COUNTING RULES

Use **Calculator** to apply the counting rules. Select **Calc ➜ Calculator**. In the Calculator dialog box (shown below):

1. Enter the column name of an empty column in the **Store result in variable** box and then press **Tab**.
2. Build the appropriate expression (as discussed later in this section) in the **Expression** box. To apply counting rules 3 through 5, select **Arithmetic** from the **Functions** drop-down list to facilitate the function selection.
3. Click **OK**.

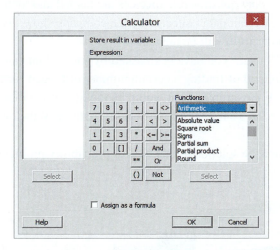

If you have previously used the Calculator during your Minitab session, you may have to clear the contents of the Expression box by selecting the contents and pressing **Del** before you begin step 2.

Counting Rule 1

Enter an expression that uses the exponential operator **. For example, the expression **6 ** 2** computes the answer for Example 4.11 on page 165.

Counting Rule 2

Enter an expression that uses the exponential operator **. For example, the expression **26 ** 3 * 10 ** 3** computes the answer for the state motor vehicle department example on page 165.

Counting Rule 3

Enter an expression that uses the **FACTORIAL(*n*)** function to compute how many ways *n* items can be arranged. For example, the expression **FACTORIAL(6)** computes 6!

Counting Rule 4

Enter an expression that uses the **PERMUTATIONS(*n*, *x*)** function to compute the number of ways of arranging *x* objects selected from *n* objects in order. For example, the expression **PERMUTATIONS(6, 4)** computes the answer for Example 4.14 on page 167.

Counting Rule 5

Enter an expression that uses the **COMBINATIONS(*n*, *x*)** function to compute the number of ways of arranging *x* objects selected from *n* objects, irrespective of order. For example, the expression **COMBINATIONS(6, 4)** computes the answer for Example 4.15 on page 167.

Discrete Probability Distributions

OBJECTIVES

Learn the properties of a probability distribution

Compute the expected value and variance of a probability distribution

Compute probabilities from the binomial and Poisson, distributions

Use the binomial and Poisson, distributions to solve business problems

USING STATISTICS

Events of Interest at Ricknel Home Centers

Like most other large businesses, Ricknel Home Centers, LLC, a regional home improvement chain, uses an accounting information system (AIS) to manage its accounting and financial data. The Ricknel AIS collects, organizes, stores, analyzes, and distributes financial information to decision makers both inside and outside the firm.

One important function of the Ricknel AIS is to continuously audit accounting information, looking for errors or incomplete or improbable information. For example, when customers submit orders online, the Ricknel AIS reviews the orders for possible mistakes. Any questionable invoices are tagged and included in a daily *exceptions report*. Recent data collected by the company show that the likelihood is 0.10 that an order form will be tagged.

As a member of the AIS team, you have been asked by Ricknel management to determine the likelihood of finding a certain number of tagged forms in a sample of a specific size. For example, what would be the likelihood that none of the order forms are tagged in a sample of four forms? That one of the order forms is tagged?

How could you determine the solution to this type of probability problem?

Sebastian Kaulitzki/Shutterstock

This chapter introduces you to the concept and characteristics of probability distributions. You will learn how the binomial and Poisson distributions can be applied to help solve business problems. In the Rickel Home Centers scenario, you could use a *probability distribution* as a mathematical model, or small-scale representation, that approximates the process. By using such an approximation, you could make inferences about the actual order process including the likelihood of finding a certain number of tagged forms in a sample.

5.1 The Probability Distribution for a Discrete Variable

Recall from Section 1.1 that *numerical* variables are variables that have values that represent quantities, such as the cost of a restaurant meal or the number of social media sites to which you belong. Some numerical variables are *discrete*, having numerical values that arise from a counting process, while others are *continuous*, having numerical values that arise from a measuring process (e.g., the one-year return of growth and value funds that were the subject of the Using Statistics scenario in Chapters 2 and 3). This chapter deals with probability distributions that represent a discrete numerical variable, such as the number of social media sites to which you belong.

> **PROBABILITY DISTRIBUTION FOR A DISCRETE VARIABLE**
> A **probability distribution for a discrete variable** is a mutually exclusive list of all the possible numerical outcomes along with the probability of occurrence of each outcome.

For example, Table 5.1 gives the distribution of the number of interruptions per day in a large computer network. The list in Table 5.1 is collectively exhaustive because all possible outcomes are included. Thus, the probabilities sum to 1. Figure 5.1 is a graphical representation of Table 5.1.

TABLE 5.1

Probability Distribution of the Number of Interruptions per Day

Interruptions per Day	Probability
0	0.35
1	0.25
2	0.20
3	0.10
4	0.05
5	0.05

FIGURE 5.1

Probability distribution of the number of interruptions per day

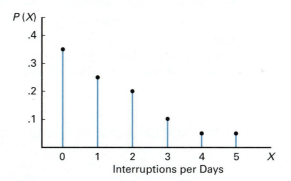

Expected Value of a Discrete Variable

The **expected value** of a discrete variable is the mean, μ, of its probability distribution. To calculate the expected value, you multiply each possible outcome, x_i, by its corresponding probability, $P(X = x_i)$, and then sum these products.

EXPECTED VALUE, μ, OF A DISCRETE VARIABLE

$$\mu = E(X) = \sum_{i=1}^{N} x_i P(X = x_i) \tag{5.1}$$

where

$$x_i = \text{the } i\text{th value of the discrete variable } X$$
$$P(X = x_i) = \text{probability of occurrence of the } i\text{th value of } X$$

For the probability distribution of the number of interruptions per day in a large computer network (Table 5.1), the expected value is computed as follows, using Equation (5.1), and is also shown in Table 5.2:

$$\mu = E(X) = \sum_{i=1}^{N} x_i P(X = x_i)$$
$$= (0)(0.35) + (1)(0.25) + (2)(0.20) + (3)(0.10) + (4)(0.05) + (5)(0.05)$$
$$= 0 + 0.25 + 0.40 + 0.30 + 0.20 + 0.25$$
$$= 1.40$$

TABLE 5.2

Computing the Expected Value of the Number of Interruptions per Day

Interruptions per Day (x_i)	$P(X = x_i)$	$x_i P(X = x_i)$
0	0.35	$(0)(0.35) = 0.00$
1	0.25	$(1)(0.25) = 0.25$
2	0.20	$(2)(0.20) = 0.40$
3	0.10	$(3)(0.10) = 0.30$
4	0.05	$(4)(0.05) = 0.20$
5	0.05	$(5)(0.05) = 0.25$
	1.00	$\mu = E(X) = 1.40$

The expected value is 1.40. The expected value of 1.40 interruptions per day is not a possible result because the actual number of interruptions on a given day must be an integer value. The expected value represents the *mean* number of interruptions on a given day.

Variance and Standard Deviation of a Discrete Variable

You compute the variance of a probability distribution by multiplying each possible squared difference $[x_i - E(X)]^2$ by its corresponding probability, $P(X = x_i)$, and then summing the resulting products. Equation (5.2) defines the **variance of a discrete variable**, and Equation (5.3) defines the **standard deviation of a discrete variable**.

VARIANCE OF A DISCRETE VARIABLE

$$\sigma^2 = \sum_{i=1}^{N} [x_i - E(X)]^2 P(X = x_i) \tag{5.2}$$

where

$$x_i = \text{the } i\text{th value of the discrete variable } X$$
$$P(X = x_i) = \text{probability of occurrence of the } i\text{th value of } X$$

STANDARD DEVIATION OF A DISCRETE VARIABLE

$$\sigma = \sqrt{\sigma^2} = \sqrt{\sum_{i=1}^{N}[x_i - E(X)]^2 P(X = x_i)} \qquad (5.3)$$

The variance and the standard deviation of the number of interruptions per day are computed as follows and in Table 5.3, using Equations (5.2) and (5.3):

$$\sigma^2 = \sum_{i=1}^{N}[x_i - E(X)]^2 P(X = x_i)$$

$$= (0 - 1.4)^2(0.35) + (1 - 1.4)^2(0.25) + (2 - 1.4)^2(0.20) + (3 - 1.4)^2(0.10)$$
$$+ (4 - 1.4)^2(0.05) + (5 - 1.4)^2(0.05)$$

$$= 0.686 + 0.040 + 0.072 + 0.256 + 0.338 + 0.648$$

$$= 2.04$$

and

$$\sigma = \sqrt{\sigma^2} = \sqrt{2.04} = 1.4283$$

TABLE 5.3

Computing the Variance and Standard Deviation of the Number of Interruptions per Day

Interruptions per Day (x_i)	$P(X = x_i)$	$x_i P(X = x_i)$	$[x_i - E(X)]^2$	$[x_i - E(X)]^2 P(X = x_i)$
0	0.35	0.00	$(0 - 1.4)^2 = 1.96$	$(1.96)(0.35) = 0.686$
1	0.25	0.25	$(1 - 1.4)^2 = 0.16$	$(0.16)(0.25) = 0.040$
2	0.20	0.40	$(2 - 1.4)^2 = 0.36$	$(0.36)(0.20) = 0.072$
3	0.10	0.30	$(3 - 1.4)^2 = 2.56$	$(2.56)(0.10) = 0.256$
4	0.05	0.20	$(4 - 1.4)^2 = 6.76$	$(6.76)(0.05) = 0.338$
5	0.05	0.25	$(5 - 1.4)^2 = 12.96$	$(12.96)(0.05) = 0.648$
	1.00	$\mu = E(X) = 1.40$		$\sigma^2 = 2.04$
				$\sigma = \sqrt{\sigma^2} = 1.4283$

Thus, the mean number of interruptions per day is 1.4, the variance is 2.04, and the standard deviation is approximately 1.43 interruptions per day.

Problems for Section 5.1

LEARNING THE BASICS

5.1 Given the following probability distributions:

Distribution A		Distribution B	
x_i	$P(X = x_i)$	x_i	$P(X = x_i)$
0	0.50	0	0.05
1	0.20	1	0.10
2	0.15	2	0.15
3	0.10	3	0.20
4	0.05	4	0.50

a. Compute the expected value for each distribution.
b. Compute the standard deviation for each distribution.
c. Compare the results of distributions A and B.

APPLYING THE CONCEPTS

✓ **SELF** **5.2** The following table contains the probability distri-
Test bution for the number of traffic accidents daily in a small town:

Number of Accidents Daily (X)	$P(X = x_i)$
0	0.10
1	0.20
2	0.45
3	0.15
4	0.05
5	0.05

a. Compute the mean number of accidents per day.
b. Compute the standard deviation.

5.3 Recently, a regional automobile dealership sent out fliers to perspective customers indicating that they had already won one of three different prizes: an automobile valued at $25,000, a $100 gas card, or a $5 Walmart shopping card. To claim his or her prize, a prospective customer needed to present the flier at the dealership's showroom. The fine print on the back of the flier listed the probabilities of winning. The chance of winning the car was 1 out of 31,478, the chance of winning the gas card was 1 out of 31,478, and the chance of winning the shopping card was 31,476 out of 31,478.
a. How many fliers do you think the automobile dealership sent out?
b. Using your answer to (a) and the probabilities listed on the flier, what is the expected value of the prize won by a prospective customer receiving a flier?
c. Using your answer to (a) and the probabilities listed on the flier, what is the standard deviation of the value of the prize won by a prospective customer receiving a flier?
d. Do you think this is an effective promotion? Why or why not?

5.4 In the carnival game Under-or-Over-Seven, a pair of fair dice is rolled once, and the resulting sum determines whether the player wins or loses his or her bet. For example, the player can bet $1 that the sum will be under 7—that is, 2, 3, 4, 5, or 6. For this bet, the player wins $1 if the result is under 7 and loses $1 if the outcome equals or is greater than 7. Similarly, the player can bet $1 that the sum will be over 7—that is, 8, 9, 10, 11, or 12. Here, the player wins $1 if the result is over 7 but loses $1 if the result is 7 or under. A third method of play is to bet $1 on the outcome 7. For this bet, the player wins $4 if the result of the roll is 7 and loses $1 otherwise.
a. Construct the probability distribution representing the different outcomes that are possible for a $1 bet on under 7.
b. Construct the probability distribution representing the different outcomes that are possible for a $1 bet on over 7.
c. Construct the probability distribution representing the different outcomes that are possible for a $1 bet on 7.
d. Show that the expected long-run profit (or loss) to the player is the same, no matter which method of play is used.

5.5 The number of arrivals per minute at a bank located in the central business district of a large city was recorded over a period of 200 minutes, with the following results:

Arrivals	Frequency
0	14
1	31
2	47
3	41
4	29
5	21
6	10
7	5
8	2

a. Compute the expected number of arrivals per minute.
b. Compute the standard deviation.

5.6 The manager of the commercial mortgage department of a large bank has collected data during the past two years concerning the number of commercial mortgages approved per week. The results from these two years (104 weeks) are as follows:

Number of Commercial Mortgages Approved	Frequency
0	13
1	25
2	32
3	17
4	9
5	6
6	1
7	1

a. Compute the expected number of mortgages approved per week.
b. Compute the standard deviation.

5.7 You are trying to develop a strategy for investing in two different stocks. The anticipated annual return for a $1,000 investment in each stock under four different economic conditions has the following probability distribution:

Probability	Economic Condition	Returns Stock X	Returns Stock Y
0.1	Recession	−50	−100
0.3	Slow growth	20	50
0.4	Moderate growth	100	130
0.2	Fast growth	150	200

Compute the
a. expected return for stock X and for stock Y.
b. standard deviation for stock X and for stock Y.
c. Would you invest in stock X or stock Y? Explain.

5.8 You plan to invest $1,000 in a corporate bond fund or in a common stock fund. The following table presents the annual return (per $1,000) of each of these investments under various economic conditions and the probability that each of those economic conditions will occur. Compute the

Probability	Economic Condition	Corporate Bond Fund	Common Stock Fund
0.01	Extreme recession	−200	−999
0.09	Recession	−70	−300
0.15	Stagnation	30	−100
0.35	Slow growth	80	100
0.30	Moderate growth	100	150
0.10	High growth	120	350

a. expected return for the corporate bond fund and for the common stock fund.
b. standard deviation for the corporate bond fund and for the common stock fund.
c. Would you invest in the corporate bond fund or the common stock fund? Explain.
d. If you chose to invest in the common stock fund in (c), what do you think about the possibility of losing $999 of every $1,000 invested if there is an extreme recession?

5.2 Binomial Distribution

This is the first of two sections that considers mathematical models. A **mathematical model** is a mathematical expression that represents a variable of interest. When a mathematical model exists, you can compute the exact probability of occurrence of any particular value of the variable. For discrete variables, the mathematical model is a **probability distribution function**.

The **binomial distribution** is an important mathematical model used in many business situations. You use the binomial distribution when the discrete variable is the number of events of interest in a sample of n observations. The binomial distribution has four important properties.

> **Student Tip**
> Do not confuse this use of the Greek letter pi, π, to represent the probability of an event of interest with the constant that is the ratio of the circumference to a diameter of a circle—approximately 3.14159.

PROPERTIES OF THE BINOMIAL DISTRIBUTION

- The sample consists of a fixed number of observations, n.
- Each observation is classified into one of two mutually exclusive and collectively exhaustive categories.
- The probability of an observation being classified as the event of interest, π, is constant from observation to observation. Thus, the probability of an observation being classified as not being the event of interest, $1 - \pi$, is constant over all observations.
- The value of any observation is independent of the value of any other observation.

Returning to the Ricknel Home Improvement scenario presented on page 176 concerning the accounting information system, suppose the event of interest is defined as a tagged order form. You want to determine the number of tagged order forms in a given sample of orders.

What results can occur? If the sample contains four orders, there could be none, one, two, three, or four tagged order forms. No other value can occur because the number of tagged order forms cannot be more than the sample size, n, and cannot be less than zero. Therefore, the range of the binomial variable is from 0 to n.

Suppose that you observe the following result in a sample of four orders:

First Order	Second Order	Third Order	Fourth Order
Tagged	Tagged	Not tagged	Tagged

What is the probability of having three tagged order forms in a sample of four orders in this particular sequence? Because the historical probability of a tagged order is 0.10, the probability that each order occurs in the sequence is

First Order	Second Order	Third Order	Fourth Order
$\pi = 0.10$	$\pi = 0.10$	$1 - \pi = 0.90$	$\pi = 0.10$

Each outcome is independent of the others because the order forms were selected from an extremely large or practically infinite population and each order form could only be selected once. Therefore, the probability of having this particular sequence is

$$
\begin{aligned}
\pi\pi(1 - \pi)\pi &= \pi^3(1 - \pi)^1 \\
&= (0.10)^3(0.90)^1 \\
&= (0.10)(0.10)(0.10)(0.90) \\
&= 0.0009
\end{aligned}
$$

This result indicates only the probability of three tagged order forms (events of interest) from a sample of four order forms in a *specific sequence*. To find the number of ways of selecting x objects from n objects, *irrespective of sequence*, you use the **rule of combinations** (see Section 4.4) given in Equation (5.4).

[1] On many scientific calculators, there is a button labeled $_nC_r$ that allows you to compute the number of combinations. On these calculators, the symbol r is used instead of x.

COMBINATIONS

The number of combinations of selecting x objects[1] out of n objects is given by

$$
_nC_x = \frac{n!}{x!(n - x)!} \tag{5.4}
$$

where

$n! = (n)(n - 1) \cdots (1)$ is called n factorial. By definition, $0! = 1$.

With $n = 4$ and $x = 3$, there are

$$
_nC_x = \frac{n!}{x!(n - x)!} = \frac{4!}{3!(4 - 3)!} = \frac{4 \times 3 \times 2 \times 1}{(3 \times 2 \times 1)(1)} = 4
$$

such sequences. The four possible sequences are

Sequence 1 = (*tagged, tagged, tagged, not tagged*), with probability
$$\pi\pi\pi(1 - \pi) = \pi^3(1 - \pi)^1 = 0.0009$$

Sequence 2 = (*tagged, tagged, not tagged, tagged*), with probability
$$\pi\pi(1 - \pi)\pi = \pi^3(1 - \pi)^1 = 0.0009$$

Sequence 3 = (*tagged, not tagged, tagged, tagged*), with probability
$$\pi(1 - \pi)\pi\pi = \pi^3(1 - \pi)^1 = 0.0009$$

Sequence 4 = (*not tagged, tagged, tagged, tagged*), with probability
$$(1 - \pi)\pi\pi\pi = \pi^3(1 - \pi)^1 = 0.0009$$

Therefore, the probability of three tagged order forms is equal to

(number of possible sequences) $\times$ (probability of a particular sequence)
$$= (4) \times (0.0009) = 0.0036$$

You can make a similar, intuitive derivation for the other possible values of the variable—zero, one, two, and four tagged order forms. However, as n, the sample size, gets large, the computations involved in using this intuitive approach become time-consuming. Equation (5.5) is the mathematical model that provides a general formula for computing any probability from the binomial distribution with the number of events of interest, x, given n and π.

BINOMIAL DISTRIBUTION

$$P(X = x \mid n, \pi) = \frac{n!}{x!(n-x)!} \pi^x (1-\pi)^{n-x} \tag{5.5}$$

where

$P(X = x \mid n, \pi)$ = probability that $X = x$ events of interest, given n and π

n = number of observations

π = probability of an event of interest

$1 - \pi$ = probability of not having an event of interest

x = number of events of interest in the sample $(X = 0, 1, 2, \dots, n)$

$\dfrac{n!}{x!(n-x)!}$ = number of combinations of x events of interest out of n observations

Equation (5.5) restates what was intuitively derived previously. The binomial variable X can have any integer value x from 0 through n. In Equation (5.5), the product

$$\pi^x (1-\pi)^{n-x}$$

represents the probability of exactly x events of interest from n observations in a *particular sequence*.

The term

$$\frac{n!}{x!(n-x)!}$$

is the number of *combinations* of the x events of interest from the n observations possible. Hence, given the number of observations, n, and the probability of an event of interest, π, the probability of x events of interest is

$$P(X = x \mid n, \pi) = \text{(number of combinations)} \times \text{(probability of a particular combination)}$$

$$= \frac{n!}{x!(n-x)!} \pi^x (1-\pi)^{n-x}$$

Example 5.1 illustrates the use of Equation (5.5). Examples 5.2 and 5.3 show the computations for other values of X.

EXAMPLE 5.1

Determining
$P(X = 3)$, Given
$n = 4$ and $\pi = 0.1$

If the likelihood of a tagged order form is 0.1, what is the probability that there are three tagged order forms in the sample of four?

SOLUTION Using Equation (5.5), the probability of three tagged orders from a sample of four is

$$
\begin{aligned}
P(X = 3 \,|\, n = 4, \pi = 0.1) &= \frac{4!}{3!(4-3)!}(0.1)^3(1-0.1)^{4-3} \\
&= \frac{4!}{3!(1)!}(0.1)^3(0.9)^1 \\
&= 4(0.1)(0.1)(0.1)(0.9) = 0.0036
\end{aligned}
$$

EXAMPLE 5.2

Determining
$P(X \geq 3)$, Given
$n = 4$ and $\pi = 0.1$

If the likelihood of a tagged order form is 0.1, what is the probability that there are three or more (i.e., at least three) tagged order forms in the sample of four?

SOLUTION In Example 5.1, you found that the probability of *exactly* three tagged order forms from a sample of four is 0.0036. To compute the probability of *at least* three tagged order forms, you need to add the probability of three tagged order forms to the probability of four tagged order forms. The probability of four tagged order forms is

> **Student Tip**
> Another way of saying
> "three or more" is "at
> least three."

$$
\begin{aligned}
P(X = 4 \,|\, n = 4, \pi = 0.1) &= \frac{4!}{4!(4-4)!}(0.1)^4(1-0.1)^{4-4} \\
&= \frac{4!}{4!(0)!}(0.1)^4(0.9)^0 \\
&= 1(0.1)(0.1)(0.1)(0.1)(1) = 0.0001
\end{aligned}
$$

Thus, the probability of at least three tagged order forms is

$$
\begin{aligned}
P(X \geq 3) &= P(X = 3) + P(X = 4) \\
&= 0.0036 + 0.0001 \\
&= 0.0037
\end{aligned}
$$

There is a 0.37% chance that there will be at least three tagged order forms in a sample of four.

EXAMPLE 5.3

Determining
$P(X < 3)$, Given
$n = 4$ and $\pi = 0.1$

If the likelihood of a tagged order form is 0.1, what is the probability that there are less than three tagged order forms in the sample of four?

SOLUTION The probability that there are less than three tagged order forms is

$$
P(X < 3) = P(X = 0) + P(X = 1) + P(X = 2)
$$

Using Equation (5.5) on page 183, these probabilities are

$$
P(X = 0 \,|\, n = 4, \pi = 0.1) = \frac{4!}{0!(4-0)!}(0.1)^0(1-0.1)^{4-0} = 0.6561
$$

$$P(X = 1 \,|\, n = 4, \pi = 0.1) = \frac{4!}{1!(4-1)!}(0.1)^1(1 - 0.1)^{4-1} = 0.2916$$

$$P(X = 2 \,|\, n = 4, \pi = 0.1) = \frac{4!}{2!(4-2)!}(0.1)^2(1 - 0.1)^{4-2} = 0.0486$$

Therefore, $P(X < 3) = 0.6561 + 0.2916 + 0.0486 = 0.9963$. $P(X < 3)$ could also be calculated from its complement, $P(X \geq 3)$, as follows:

$$P(X < 3) = 1 - P(X \geq 3)$$
$$= 1 - 0.0037 = 0.9963$$

Computing binomial probabilities become tedious as n gets large. Figure 5.2 shows how Excel and Minitab can compute binomial probabilities for you. You can also look up binomial probabilities in a table of probabilities.

FIGURE 5.2
Excel and Minitab results for computing binomial probabilities with $n = 4$ and $\pi = 0.1$

	A	B	
1	**Binomial Probabilities**		
2			
3	**Data**		
4	Sample size	4	
5	Probability of an event of interest	0.1	
6			
7	**Statistics**		
8	Mean	0.4	=B4 * B5
9	Variance	0.36	=B8 * (1 - B5)
10	Standard deviation	0.6	=SQRT(B9)
11			
12	**Binomial Probabilities Table**		
13		X	P(X)	
14		0	0.6561	=BINOM.DIST(A14, $B$4, $B$5, FALSE)
15		1	0.2916	=BINOM.DIST(A15, $B$4, $B$5, FALSE)
16		2	0.0486	=BINOM.DIST(A16, $B$4, $B$5, FALSE)
17		3	0.0036	=BINOM.DIST(A17, $B$4, $B$5, FALSE)
18		4	0.0001	=BINOM.DIST(A18, $B$4, $B$5, FALSE)

Cumulative Distribution Function

Binomial with n = 4 and p = 0.1

x	P(X <= x)
0	0.6561
1	0.9477
2	0.9963
3	0.9999
4	1.0000

LEARN MORE
The **Binomial Table** **online topic** contains both a binomial probabilities table and a cumulative binomial probabilities table and explains how to use these tables to compute binomial and cumulative binomial probabilities.

The shape of a binomial probability distribution depends on the values of n and π. Whenever $\pi = 0.5$, the binomial distribution is symmetrical, regardless of how large or small the value of n. When $\pi \neq 0.5$, the distribution is skewed. The closer π is to 0.5 and the larger the number of observations, n, the less skewed the distribution becomes. For example, the distribution of the number of tagged order forms is highly right-skewed because $\pi = 0.1$ and $n = 4$ (see Figure 5.3).

FIGURE 5.3
Histogram of the binomial probability with $n = 4$ and $\pi = 0.1$

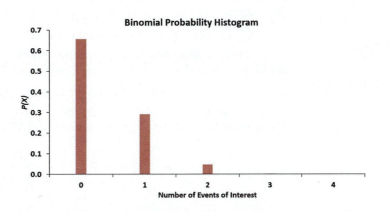

Observe from Figure 5.3 that unlike the histogram for continuous variables in Section 2.4, the bars for the values are very thin, and there is a large gap between each pair of values. That is because the histogram represents a discrete variable. (Theoretically, the bars should have no width. They should be vertical lines.)

The mean (or expected value) of the binomial distribution is equal to the product of n and π. Instead of using Equation (5.1) on page 178 to compute the mean of the probability distribution, you can use Equation (5.6) to compute the mean for variables that follow the binomial distribution.

MEAN OF THE BINOMIAL DISTRIBUTION

The mean, μ, of the binomial distribution is equal to the sample size, n, multiplied by the probability of an event of interest, π.

$$\mu = E(X) = n\pi \tag{5.6}$$

On the average, over the long run, you theoretically expect $\mu = E(X) = n\pi = (4)(0.1) = 0.4$ tagged order form in a sample of four orders.

The standard deviation of the binomial distribution can be calculated using Equation (5.7).

STANDARD DEVIATION OF THE BINOMIAL DISTRIBUTION

$$\sigma = \sqrt{\sigma^2} = \sqrt{Var(X)} = \sqrt{n\pi(1 - \pi)} \tag{5.7}$$

The standard deviation of the number of tagged order forms is

$$\sigma = \sqrt{4(0.1)(0.9)} = 0.60$$

You get the same result if you use Equation (5.3) on page 179.

Example 5.4 applies the binomial distribution to service at a fast-food restaurant.

EXAMPLE 5.4

Computing Binomial Probabilities for Service at a Fast-Food Restaurant

Accuracy in taking orders at a drive-through window is important for fast-food chains. Periodically, *QSR Magazine* publishes "The Drive-Thru Performance Study: Order Accuracy" that measures the percentage of orders that are filled correctly. In a recent month, the percentage of orders filled correctly at Wendy's was approximately 86.8%. Suppose that you go to the drive-through window at Wendy's and place an order. Two friends of yours independently place orders at the drive-through window at the same Wendy's. What are the probabilities that all three, that none of the three, and that at least two of the three orders will be filled correctly? What are the mean and standard deviation of the binomial distribution for the number of orders filled correctly?

SOLUTION Because there are three orders and the probability of a correct order is 0.868, $n = 3$, and $\pi = 0.868$, using Equation (5.5) on page 183,

$$P(X = 3 \mid n = 3, \pi = 0.868) = \frac{3!}{3!(3-3)!}(0.868)^3(1 - 0.868)^{3-3}$$

$$= \frac{3!}{3!(3-3)!}(0.868)^3(0.132)^0$$

$$= 1(0.868)(0.868)(0.868)(1) = 0.6540$$

$$P(X = 0 \mid n = 3, \pi = 0.868) = \frac{3!}{0!(3-0)!}(0.868)^0(1-0.868)^{3-0}$$

$$= \frac{3!}{0!(3-0)!}(0.868)^0(0.132)^3$$

$$= 1(1)(0.132)(0.132)(0.132) = 0.0023$$

$$P(X = 2 \mid n = 3, \pi = 0.868) = \frac{3!}{2!(3-2)!}(0.868)^2(1-0.868)^{3-2}$$

$$= \frac{3!}{2!(3-2)!}(0.868)^2(0.132)^1$$

$$= 3(0.868)(0.868)(0.132) = 0.2984$$

$$P(X \geq 2) = P(X = 2) + P(X = 3)$$
$$= 0.2984 + 0.6540$$
$$= 0.9524$$

Using Equations (5.6) and (5.7),

$$\mu = E(X) = n\pi = 3(0.868) = 2.604$$

$$\sigma = \sqrt{\sigma^2} = \sqrt{Var(X)} = \sqrt{n\pi(1-\pi)}$$

$$= \sqrt{3(0.868)(0.132)}$$

$$= \sqrt{0.3437} = 0.5863$$

The mean number of orders filled correctly in a sample of three orders is 2.604, and the standard deviation is 0.5863. The probability that all three orders are filled correctly is 0.6540, or 65.4%. The probability that none of the orders are filled correctly is 0.0023 (0.23%). The probability that at least two orders are filled correctly is 0.9524 (95.24%).

Problems for Section 5.2

LEARNING THE BASICS

5.9 Determine the following:
a. For $n = 4$ and $\pi = 0.12$, what is $P(X = 0)$?
b. For $n = 10$ and $\pi = 0.40$, what is $P(X = 9)$?
c. For $n = 10$ and $\pi = 0.50$, what is $P(X = 8)$?
d. For $n = 6$ and $\pi = 0.83$, what is $P(X = 5)$?

5.10 Determine the mean and standard deviation of the variable X in each of the following binomial distributions:
a. $n = 4$ and $\pi = 0.10$
b. $n = 4$ and $\pi = 0.40$
c. $n = 5$ and $\pi = 0.80$
d. $n = 3$ and $\pi = 0.50$

APPLYING THE CONCEPTS

5.11 The increase or decrease in the price of a stock between the beginning and the end of a trading day is assumed to be an equally likely random event. What is the probability that a stock will show an increase in its closing price on five consecutive days?

5.12 A recent Pew Research survey reported that 48% of 18- to 29-year-olds in the United States own tablets. (Data extracted from "Tablet and E-Reader Ownership," **bit.ly/1gEwogC**). Using the binomial distribution, what is the probability that in the next six 18- to 29-year-olds surveyed,
a. four will own a tablet?
b. all six will own a tablet?
c. at least four will own a tablet?
d. What are the mean and standard deviation of the number of 18- to 29-year-olds who will own a tablet in a survey of six?
e. What assumptions do you need to make in (a) through (c)?

5.13 A student is taking a multiple-choice exam in which each question has four choices. Assume that the student has no knowledge of the correct answers to any of the questions. She has decided on a strategy in which she will place four balls (marked $A, B, C,$ and D) into a box. She randomly selects one ball for each question and replaces the ball in the box. The marking on the ball will determine her answer to the question. There are five multiple-choice questions on the exam. What is the probability that she will get

a. five questions correct?
b. at least four questions correct?
c. no questions correct?
d. no more than two questions correct?

5.14 A manufacturing company regularly conducts quality control checks at specified periods on the products it manufactures. Historically, the failure rate for LED light bulbs that the company manufactures is 5%. Suppose a random sample of 10 LED light bulbs is selected. What is the probability that

a. none of the LED light bulbs are defective?
b. exactly one of the LED light bulbs is defective?
c. two or fewer of the LED light bulbs are defective?
d. three or more of the LED light bulbs are defective?

5.15 Past records indicate that the probability of online retail orders that turn out to be fraudulent is 0.08. Suppose that, on a given day, 20 online retail orders are placed. Assume that the number of online retail orders that turn out to be fraudulent is distributed as a binomial random variable.

a. What are the mean and standard deviation of the number of online retail orders that turn out to be fraudulent?
b. What is the probability that zero online retail orders will turn out to be fraudulent?

c. What is the probability that one online retail order will turn out to be fraudulent?
d. What is the probability that two or more online retail orders will turn out to be fraudulent?

 5.16 In Example 5.4 on page 186, you and two friends decided to go to Wendy's. Now, suppose that instead you go to Burger King, which recently filled approximately 82.3% of orders correctly. What is the probability that

a. all three orders will be filled correctly?
b. none of the three will be filled correctly?
c. at least two of the three will be filled correctly?
d. What are the mean and standard deviation of the binomial distribution used in (a) through (c)? Interpret these values.

5.17 In Example 5.4 on page 186, you and two friends decided to go to Wendy's. Now, suppose that instead you go to McDonald's, which recently filled approximately 88.3% of the orders correctly. What is the probability that

a. all three orders will be filled correctly?
b. none of the three will be filled correctly?
c. at least two of the three will be filled correctly?
d. What are the mean and standard deviation of the binomial distribution used in (a) through (c)? Interpret these values.
e. Compare the result of (a) through (d) with those of Burger King in Problem 5.16 and Wendy's in Example 5.4 on page 186.

5.3 Poisson Distribution

Many studies are based on counts of the occurrences of a particular event in a given interval of time or space (often referred to as an *area of opportunity*). In such an **area of opportunity** there can be more than one occurrence of an event. The Poisson distribution can be used to compute probabilities in such situations. Examples of variables that follow the Poisson distribution are the surface defects on a new refrigerator, the number of network failures in a day, the number of people arriving at a bank, and the number of fleas on the body of a dog. You can use the **Poisson distribution** to calculate probabilities in situations such as these if the following properties hold:

- You are interested in counting the number of times a particular event occurs in a given area of opportunity. The area of opportunity is defined by time, length, surface area, and so forth.
- The probability that an event occurs in a given area of opportunity is the same for all the areas of opportunity.
- The number of events that occur in one area of opportunity is independent of the number of events that occur in any other area of opportunity.
- The probability that two or more events will occur in an area of opportunity approaches zero as the area of opportunity becomes smaller.

Consider the number of customers arriving during the lunch hour at a bank located in the central business district in a large city. You are interested in the number of customers who arrive each minute. Does this situation match the four properties of the Poisson distribution given earlier?

First, the *event* of interest is a customer arriving, and the *given area of opportunity* is defined as a one-minute interval. Will zero customers arrive, one customer arrive, two customers arrive, and so on? Second, it is reasonable to assume that the probability that a customer arrives during a particular one-minute interval is the same as the probability for all the other one-minute intervals. Third, the arrival of one customer in any one-minute interval has no effect on (i.e., is independent of) the arrival of any other customer in any other one-minute interval. Finally, the probability that two or more customers will arrive in a given time period approaches zero as the time interval becomes small. For example, the probability is virtually zero that two customers will arrive in a time interval of 0.01 second. Thus, you can use the Poisson distribution to determine probabilities involving the number of customers arriving at the bank in a one-minute time interval during the lunch hour.

The Poisson distribution has one characteristic, called λ (the Greek lowercase letter *lambda*), which is the mean or expected number of events per unit. The variance of a Poisson distribution is also equal to λ, and the standard deviation is equal to $\sqrt{\lambda}$. The number of events, X, of the Poisson variable ranges from 0 to infinity (∞).

Equation (5.8) is the mathematical expression for the Poisson distribution for computing the probability of $X = x$ events, given that λ events are expected.

POISSON DISTRIBUTION

$$P(X = x \mid \lambda) = \frac{e^{-\lambda}\lambda^{x}}{x!} \tag{5.8}$$

where

$P(X = x \mid \lambda)$ = probability that $X = x$ events in an area of opportunity given λ

λ = expected number of events per unit

e = mathematical constant approximated by 2.71828

x = number of events $(x = 0, 1, 2, \ldots)$

To illustrate an application of the Poisson distribution, suppose that the mean number of customers who arrive per minute at the bank during the noon-to-1 P.M. hour is equal to 3.0. What is the probability that in a given minute, exactly two customers will arrive? And what is the probability that more than two customers will arrive in a given minute?

Using Equation (5.8) and $\lambda = 3$, the probability that in a given minute exactly two customers will arrive is

$$P(X = 2 \mid \lambda = 3) = \frac{e^{-3.0}(3.0)^{2}}{2!} = \frac{9}{(2.71828)^{3}(2)} = 0.2240$$

To determine the probability that in any given minute more than two customers will arrive,

$$P(X > 2) = P(X = 3) + P(X = 4) + \cdots$$

Because in a probability distribution, all the probabilities must sum to 1, the terms on the right side of the equation $P(X > 2)$ also represent the complement of the probability that X is less than or equal to 2 [i.e., $1 - P(X \le 2)$]. Thus,

$$P(X > 2) = 1 - P(X \le 2) = 1 - [P(X = 0) + P(X = 1) + P(X = 2)]$$

Now, using Equation (5.8),

$$P(X > 2) = 1 - \left[\frac{e^{-3.0}(3.0)^{0}}{0!} + \frac{e^{-3.0}(3.0)^{1}}{1!} + \frac{e^{-3.0}(3.0)^{2}}{2!} \right]$$

$$= 1 - [0.0498 + 0.1494 + 0.2240]$$

$$= 1 - 0.4232 = 0.5768$$

Thus, there is a 57.68% chance that more than two customers will arrive in the same minute.

Computing Poisson probabilities can be tedious. Figure 5.4 shows how Excel and Minitab can compute Poisson probabilities for you. You can also look up Poisson probabilities in a table of probabilities.

FIGURE 5.4

Excel and Minitab results for computing Poisson probabilities with $\lambda = 3$

	A	B	C	D	E
1	**Poisson Probabilities**				
2					
3		Data			
4	Mean/Expected number of events of interest:				3
5					
6	**Poisson Probabilities Table**				
7	**x**	**P(X)**			
8	0	0.0498	=POISSON.DIST(A8, $E$4, FALSE)		
9	1	0.1494	=POISSON.DIST(A9, $E$4, FALSE)		
10	2	0.2240	=POISSON.DIST(A10, $E$4, FALSE)		
11	3	0.2240	=POISSON.DIST(A11, $E$4, FALSE)		
12	4	0.1680	=POISSON.DIST(A12, $E$4, FALSE)		
13	5	0.1008	=POISSON.DIST(A13, $E$4, FALSE)		
14	6	0.0504	=POISSON.DIST(A14, $E$4, FALSE)		
15	7	0.0216	=POISSON.DIST(A15, $E$4, FALSE)		
16	8	0.0081	=POISSON.DIST(A16, $E$4, FALSE)		
17	9	0.0027	=POISSON.DIST(A17, $E$4, FALSE)		
18	10	0.0008	=POISSON.DIST(A18, $E$4, FALSE)		
19	11	0.0002	=POISSON.DIST(A19, $E$4, FALSE)		
20	12	0.0001	=POISSON.DIST(A20, $E$4, FALSE)		
21	13	0.0000	=POISSON.DIST(A21, $E$4, FALSE)		
22	14	0.0000	=POISSON.DIST(A22, $E$4, FALSE)		
23	15	0.0000	=POISSON.DIST(A23, $E$4, FALSE)		

Probability Density Function

Poisson with mean = 3

x	P(X = x)
0	0.049787
1	0.149361
2	0.224042
3	0.224042
4	0.168031
5	0.100819
6	0.050409
7	0.021604
8	0.008102
9	0.002701
10	0.000810
11	0.000221
12	0.000055
13	0.000013
14	0.000003
15	0.000001

> **LEARN MORE**
> The **Poisson Table online topic** contains a table of Poisson probabilities and explains how to use the table to compute Poisson probabilities.

EXAMPLE 5.5

Computing Poisson Probabilities

The number of work-related injuries per month in a manufacturing plant is known to follow a Poisson distribution, with a mean of 2.5 work-related injuries a month. What is the probability that in a given month, no work-related injuries occur? That at least one work-related injury occurs?

SOLUTION Using Equation (5.8) on page 189 with $\lambda = 2.5$ (or Excel, Minitab, or a Poisson table lookup), the probability that in a given month no work-related injuries occur is

$$P(X = 0 \mid \lambda = 2.5) = \frac{e^{-2.5}(2.5)^0}{0!} = \frac{1}{(2.71828)^{2.5}(1)} = 0.0821$$

The probability that there will be no work-related injuries in a given month is 0.0821, or 8.21%. Thus,

$$P(X \geq 1) = 1 - P(X = 0)$$
$$= 1 - 0.0821$$
$$= 0.9179$$

The probability that there will be at least one work-related injury is 0.9179, or 91.79%.

Problems for Section 5.3

LEARNING THE BASICS

5.18 Assume a Poisson distribution.
a. If $\lambda = 2.5$, find $P(X = 2)$.
b. If $\lambda = 8.0$, find $P(X = 8)$.
c. If $\lambda = 0.5$, find $P(X = 1)$.
d. If $\lambda = 3.7$, find $P(X = 0)$.

5.19 Assume a Poisson distribution.
a. If $\lambda = 2.0$, find $P(X \geq 2)$.
b. If $\lambda = 8.0$, find $P(X \geq 3)$.

c. If $\lambda = 0.5$, find $P(X \leq 1)$.
d. If $\lambda = 4.0$, find $P(X \geq 1)$.
e. If $\lambda = 5.0$, find $P(X \leq 3)$.

5.20 Assume a Poisson distribution with $\lambda = 5.0$. What is the probability that
a. $X = 1$?
b. $X < 1$?
c. $X > 1$?
d. $X \leq 1$?

APPLYING THE CONCEPTS

5.21 Assume that the number of new visitors to a website in one hour is distributed as a Poisson variable. The mean number of new visitors to the website is 4.0 per hour. What is the probability that in any given hour

a. zero new visitors will arrive at the website?

b. exactly one new visitor will arrive at the website?

c. two or more new visitors will arrive at the website?

d. fewer than three new visitors will arrive at the website?

✓ SELF Test **5.22** The quality control manager of Marilyn's Cookies is inspecting a batch of chocolate-chip cookies that has just been baked. If the production process is in control, the mean number of chocolate-chip parts per cookie is 6.0. What is the probability that in any particular cookie being inspected

a. fewer than five chocolate-chip parts will be found?

b. exactly five chocolate-chip parts will be found?

c. five or more chocolate-chip parts will be found?

d. either four or five chocolate-chip parts will be found?

5.23 Refer to Problem 5.22. How many cookies in a batch of 100 should the manager expect to discard if company policy requires that all chocolate-chip cookies sold have at least four chocolate-chip parts?

5.24 The U.S. Department of Transportation maintains statistics for mishandled bags per 1,000 airline passengers. In October 2013, Delta mishandled 1.55 bags per 1,000 passengers. What is the probability that in the next 1,000 passengers, Delta will have

a. no mishandled bags?

b. at least one mishandled bag?

c. at least two mishandled bags?

5.25 The U.S. Department of Transportation maintains statistics for involuntary denial of boarding. In July–September 2013, the American Airlines rate of involuntarily denying boarding was 0.45 per 10,000 passengers. What is the probability that in the next 10,000 passengers, there will be

a. no one involuntarily denied boarding?

b. at least one person involuntarily denied boarding?

c. at least two persons involuntarily denied boarding?

5.26 The Consumer Financial Protection Bureau's consumer response team hears directly from consumers about the challenges they face in the marketplace, brings their concerns to the attention of financial institutions, and assists in addressing their complaints. The consumer response team accepts complaints related to mortgages, bank accounts and services, private student loans, other consumer loans, and credit reporting. An analysis of complaints over time indicates that the mean number of credit reporting complaints registered by consumers is 2.70 per day. (Source: *Consumer Response: A Snapshot of Complaints Received*, **1.usa.gov/WZ9N8Q**.) Assume that the number of credit reporting complaints registered by consumers is distributed as a Poisson random variable. What is the probability that on a given day

a. no credit reporting complaints will be registered by consumers?

b. exactly one credit reporting complaint will be registered by consumers?

c. more than one credit reporting complaint will be registered by consumers?

d. fewer than two credit reporting complaints will be registered by consumers?

5.27 J.D. Power and Associates calculates and publishes various statistics concerning car quality. The dependability score measures problems experienced during the past 12 months by original owners of three-year-old vehicles (those that were introduced for the 2010 model year). For these models of cars, Ford had 1.27 problems per car and Toyota had 1.12 problems per car. (Data extracted from "2013 U.S. Vehicle Dependability Study," J.D. Power and Associates, February 13, 2013, **bit.ly/101aR9l**.) Let X be equal to the number of problems with a three-year-old Ford.

a. What assumptions must be made in order for X to be distributed as a Poisson random variable? Are these assumptions reasonable?

Making the assumptions as in (a), if you purchased a Ford in the 2010 model year, what is the probability that in the past 12 months, the car had

b. zero problems?

c. two or fewer problems?

d. Give an operational definition for *problem*. Why is the operational definition important in interpreting the initial quality score?

5.28 Refer to Problem 5.27. If you purchased a Toyota in the 2010 model year, what is the probability that in the past 12 months the car had

a. zero problems?

b. two or fewer problems?

c. Compare your answers in (a) and (b) to those for the Ford in Problem 5.27 (b) and (c).

5.29 Refer to Problem 5.27. Another press release reported that for 2011 model cars, Ford had 1.40 problems per car and Toyota had 1.14 problems per car. (Data extracted from J. B. Healey, "Used Cars Get Less Reliable," *USA Today*, February 13, 2014, p. 2B.) If you purchased a 2011 Ford, what is the probability that in the past 12 months the car had

a. zero problems?

b. two or fewer problems?

c. Compare your answers in (a) and (b) to those for the 2010 model year Ford in Problem 5.27 (b) and (c).

5.30 Refer to Problem 5.29. If you purchased a 2011 Toyota, what is the probability that in the past 12 months, the car had

a. zero problems?

b. two or fewer problems?

c. Compare your answers in (a) and (b) to those for the 2010 model year Toyota in Problem 5.28 (a) and (b).

5.31 A toll-free phone number is available from 9 A.M. to 9 P.M. for your customers to register complaints about a product purchased from your company. Past history indicates that an average of 0.8 calls is received per minute.

a. What properties must be true about the situation described here in order to use the Poisson distribution to calculate probabilities concerning the number of phone calls received in a one-minute period?

Assuming that this situation matches the properties discussed in (a), what is the probability that during a one-minute period

b. zero phone calls will be received?

c. three or more phone calls will be received?

d. What is the maximum number of phone calls that will be received in a one-minute period 99.99% of the time?

Sebastian Kaulitzki/Shutterstock

USING STATISTICS

Events of Interest at Ricknel Home Centers, Revisited

In the Ricknel Home Improvement scenario at the beginning of this chapter, you were an accountant for the Ricknel Home Improvement Company. The company's accounting information system automatically reviews order forms from online customers for possible mistakes. Any questionable invoices are tagged and included in a daily exceptions report. Knowing that the probability that an order will be tagged is 0.10, you were able to use the binomial distribution to determine the chance of finding a certain number of tagged forms in a sample of size four. There was a 65.6% chance that none of the forms would be tagged, a 29.2% chance that one would be tagged, and a 5.2% chance that two or more would be tagged. You were also able to determine that, on average, you would expect 0.4 form to be tagged, and the standard deviation of the number of tagged order forms would be 0.6. Now that you have learned the mechanics of using the binomial distribution for a known probability of 0.10 and a sample size of four, you will be able to apply the same approach to any given probability and sample size. Thus, you will be able to make inferences about the online ordering process and, more importantly, evaluate any changes or proposed changes to the process.

SUMMARY

In this chapter, you have studied the probability distribution for a discrete variable and two important discrete probability distributions: the binomial and Poisson distributions. In the next chapter, you will study the normal distribution.

Use the following to help decide what probability distribution to use for a particular situation:

- If there is a fixed number of observations, n, each of which is classified as an event of interest or not an event of interest, use the binomial distribution.
- If there is an area of opportunity, use the Poisson distribution.

REFERENCES

1. Levine, D. M., P. Ramsey, and R. Smidt. *Applied Statistics for Engineers and Scientists Using Microsoft Excel and Minitab.* Upper Saddle River, NJ: Prentice Hall, 2001.

2. *Microsoft Excel 2013.* Redmond, WA: Microsoft Corp., 2012.
3. *Minitab Release 16.* State College, PA: Minitab, Inc., 2010.

KEY EQUATIONS

Expected Value, μ, of a Discrete Variable

$$\mu = E(X) = \sum_{i=1}^{N} x_i P(X = x_i) \tag{5.1}$$

Variance of a Discrete Variable

$$\sigma^2 = \sum_{i=1}^{N} [x_i - E(X)]^2 P(X = x_i) \tag{5.2}$$

Standard Deviation of a Discrete Variable

$$\sigma = \sqrt{\sigma^2} = \sqrt{\sum_{i=1}^{N} [x_i - E(X)]^2 P(X = x_i)} \tag{5.3}$$

Combinations

$$_nC_x = \frac{n!}{x!(n-x)!} \tag{5.4}$$

Binomial Distribution

$$P(X = x \,|\, n, \pi) = \frac{n!}{x!(n - x)!} \pi^x (1 - \pi)^{n-x} \qquad \textbf{(5.5)}$$

Mean of the Binomial Distribution

$$\mu = E(X) = n\pi \qquad \textbf{(5.6)}$$

Standard Deviation of the Binomial Distribution

$$\sigma = \sqrt{\sigma^2} = \sqrt{\text{Var}(X)} = \sqrt{n\pi(1 - \pi)} \qquad \textbf{(5.7)}$$

Poisson Distribution

$$P(X = x \,|\, \lambda) = \frac{e^{-\lambda} \lambda^x}{x!} \qquad \textbf{(5.8)}$$

KEY TERMS

area of opportunity 188
binomial distribution 181
expected value 177
mathematical model 181

Poisson distribution 188
probability distribution for a discrete
   variable 177
probability distribution function 181

rule of combinations 182
standard deviation of a discrete
   variable 178
variance of a discrete variable 178

CHECKING YOUR UNDERSTANDING

5.32 What is the meaning of the expected value of a random variable?

5.33 What are the four properties that must be present in order to use the binomial distribution?

5.34 What are the four properties that must be present in order to use the Poisson distribution?

CHAPTER REVIEW PROBLEMS

5.35 Darwin Head, a 35-year-old sawmill worker, won $1 million and a Chevrolet Malibu Hybrid by scoring 15 goals within 24 seconds at the Vancouver Canucks National Hockey League game (B. Ziemer, "Darwin Evolves into an Instant Millionaire," *Vancouver Sun*, February 28, 2008, p. 1). Head said he would use the money to pay off his mortgage and provide for his children, and he had no plans to quit his job. The contest was part of the Chevrolet Malibu Million Dollar Shootout, sponsored by General Motors Canadian Division. Did GM-Canada risk the $1 million? No! GM-Canada purchased event insurance from a company specializing in promotions at sporting events such as a half-court basketball shot or a hole-in-one giveaway at the local charity golf outing. The event insurance company estimates the probability of a contestant winning the contest, and for a modest charge, insures the event. The promoters pay the insurance premium but take on no added risk as the insurance company will make the large payout in the unlikely event that a contestant wins. To see how it works, suppose that the insurance company estimates that the probability a contestant would win a million-dollar shootout is 0.001 and that the insurance company charges $4,000.

a. Calculate the expected value of the profit made by the insurance company.

b. Many call this kind of situation a win–win opportunity for the insurance company and the promoter. Do you agree? Explain.

5.36 Between 1896—when the Dow Jones index was created—and 2013, the index rose in 66% of the years. (Sources: M. Hulbert, "What the Past Can't Tell Investors," *The New York Times*, January 3, 2010, p. BU2 and **bit.ly/100zwvT**.) Based on this information, and assuming a binomial distribution, what do you think is the probability that the stock market will rise

a. next year?

b. the year after next?

c. in four of the next five years?

d. in none of the next five years?

e. For this situation, what assumption of the binomial distribution might not be valid?

5.37 Smartphone adoption among American teens has increased substantially, and mobile access to the Internet is pervasive. One in four teenagers are "cell mostly" Internet users—that is, they *mostly go online using their phone* and not using some other device such as a desktop or laptop computer. (Source: *Teens and Technology 2013*, Pew Research Center, **bit.ly/101ciF1**.)

If a sample of 10 American teens is selected, what is the probability that

a. 4 are "cell mostly" Internet users?

b. at least 4 are "cell mostly" Internet users?

c. at most 8 are "cell mostly" Internet users?

d. If you selected the sample in a particular geographical area and found that none of the 10 respondents are "cell mostly" Internet users, what conclusions might you reach about whether the percentage of "cell mostly" Internet users in this area was 25%?

5.38 One theory concerning the Dow Jones Industrial Average is that it is likely to increase during U.S. presidential election years. From 1964 through 2012, the Dow Jones Industrial Average increased in 10 of the 13 U.S. presidential election years. Assuming that this indicator is a random event with no predictive value, you would expect that the indicator would be correct 50% of the time.

a. What is the probability of the Dow Jones Industrial Average increasing in 10 or more of the 13 U.S. presidential election years if the probability of an increase in the Dow Jones Industrial Average is 0.50?

b. What is the probability that the Dow Jones Industrial Average will increase in 10 or more of the 13 U.S. presidential election years if the probability of an increase in the Dow Jones Industrial Average in any year is 0.75?

5.39 Medical billing errors and fraud are on the rise. According to the MBAA website, 8 out of 10 times, the medical bills that you get are not right. (Source: "Accurate Medical Billing," **bit.ly/1lHKIu3**, April 2, 2014.) If a sample of 10 medical bills is selected, what is the probability that

a. 0 medical bills will contain errors?

b. exactly 5 medical bills will contain errors?

c. more than 5 medical bills will contain errors?

d. What are the mean and standard deviation of the probability distribution?

5.40 Refer to Problem 5.39. Suppose that a quality improvement initiative has reduced the percentage of medical bills containing errors to 40%. If a sample of 10 medical bills is selected, what is the probability that

a. 0 medical bills will contain errors?

b. exactly 5 medical bills will contain errors?

c. more than 5 medical bills contain errors?

d. What are the mean and standard deviation of the probability distribution?

e. Compare the results of (a) through (c) to those of Problem 5.39 (a) through (c).

5.41 Social log-ins involve recommending or sharing an article that you read online. According to Janrain, in the fourth quarter of 2013, 35% signed in via Facebook compared with 35% for Google. (Source: "Social Login Trends Across the Web for Q4 2013," **bit.ly/1jmLXRr**.) If a sample of 10 social log-ins is selected, what is the probability that

a. more than 5 signed in using Facebook?

b. more than 5 signed in using Google?

c. none signed in using Facebook?

d. What assumptions did you have to make to answer (a) through (c)?

5.42 The Consumer Financial Protection Bureau's consumer response team hears directly from consumers about the challenges they face in the marketplace, brings their concerns to the attention of financial institutions, and assists in addressing their complaints. Consumer response accepts complaints related to mortgages, bank accounts and services, private student loans, other consumer loans, and credit reporting. Of the consumers who registered a bank account and service complaint, 45% cited "account management" as the type of complaint; these complaints are related to opening, closing, or managing the account and address issues, such as confusing marketing, denial, fees, statements, and joint accounts. (Source: *Consumer Response Annual Report*, **1.usa.gov/1kjpS2k**.)

Consider a sample of 20 consumers who registered bank account and service complaints. Use the binomial model to answer the following questions:

a. What is the expected value, or mean, of the binomial distribution?

b. What is the standard deviation of the binomial distribution?

c. What is the probability that 10 of the 20 consumers cited "account management" as the type of complaint?

d. What is the probability that no more than 5 of the consumers cited "account management" as the type of complaint?

e. What is the probability that 5 or more of the consumers cited "account management" as the type of complaint?

5.43 Refer to Problem 5.42. In the same time period, 25% of the consumers registering a bank account and service compliant cited "deposit and withdrawal" as the type of complaint; these are issues such as transaction holds and unauthorized transactions.

a. What is the expected value, or mean, of the binomial distribution?

b. What is the standard deviation of the binomial distribution?

c. What is the probability that none of the 20 consumers cited "deposit and withdrawal" as the type of complaint?

d. What is the probability that no more than 2 of the consumers cited "deposit and withdrawal" as the type of complaint?

e. What is the probability that 3 or more of the consumers cited "deposit and withdrawal" as the type of complaint?

5.44 One theory concerning the S&P 500 Index is that if it increases during the first five trading days of the year, it is likely to increase during the entire year. From 1950 through 2013, the S&P 500 Index had these early gains in 41 years (in 2011 there was virtually no change). In 36 of these 41 years, the S&P 500 Index increased for the entire year. Assuming that this indicator is a random event with no predictive value, you would expect that the indicator would be correct 50% of the time. What is the probability of the S&P 500 Index increasing in 36 or more years if the true probability of an increase in the S&P 500 Index is

a. 0.50?

b. 0.70?

c. 0.90?

d. Based on the results of (a) through (c), what do you think is the probability that the S&P 500 Index will increase if there is an early gain in the first five trading days of the year? Explain.

5.45 *Spurious correlation* refers to the apparent relationship between variables that either have no true relationship or are related to other variables that have not been measured. One widely publicized stock market indicator in the United States that is an example of spurious correlation is the relationship between the winner of the National Football League Super Bowl and the performance of the Dow Jones Industrial Average in that year. The "indicator" states that when a team that existed before the National Football League merged with the American Football League wins the Super Bowl, the Dow Jones Industrial Average will increase in that year. (Of course, any correlation between these is spurious as one thing has absolutely nothing to do with the other!) Since the first Super Bowl was held in 1967 through 2013, the indicator has been correct 37 out of 47 times. Assuming that this indicator is a random event with no predictive value, you would expect that the indicator would be correct 50% of the time.

a. What is the probability that the indicator would be correct 37 or more times in 47 years?

b. What does this tell you about the usefulness of this indicator?

5.46 The United Auto Courts Reports blog notes that the National Insurance Crime Bureau says that Miami-Dade, Broward, and Palm Beach counties account for a substantial number of questionable insurance claims referred to investigators. Assume that the number of questionable insurance claims referred to investigators by Miami-Dade, Broward, and Palm Beach counties is distributed as a Poisson random variable with a mean of 7 per day.

a. What assumptions need to be made so that the number of questionable insurance claims referred to investigators by Miami-Dade, Broward, and Palm Beach counties is distributed as a Poisson random variable?

Making the assumptions given in (a), what is the probability that

b. 5 questionable insurance claims will be referred to investigators by Miami-Dade, Broward, and Palm Beach counties in a day?

c. 10 or fewer questionable insurance claims will be referred to investigators by Miami-Dade, Broward, and Palm Beach counties in a day?

d. 11 or more questionable insurance claims will be referred to investigators by Miami-Dade, Broward, and Palm Beach counties in a day?

CASES FOR CHAPTER 5

Managing Ashland MultiComm Services

The Ashland MultiComm Services (AMS) marketing department wants to increase subscriptions for its *3-For-All* telephone, cable, and Internet combined service. AMS marketing has been conducting an aggressive direct-marketing campaign that includes postal and electronic mailings and telephone solicitations. Feedback from these efforts indicates that including premium channels in this combined service is a very important factor for both current and prospective subscribers. After several brainstorming sessions, the marketing department has decided to add premium cable channels as a no-cost benefit of subscribing to the *3-For-All* service.

The research director, Mona Fields, is planning to conduct a survey among prospective customers to determine how many premium channels need to be added to the *3-For-All* service in order to generate a subscription to the service. Based on past campaigns and on industry-wide data, she estimates the following:

Number of Free Premium Channels	Probability of Subscriptions
0	0.02
1	0.04
2	0.06
3	0.07
4	0.08
5	0.085

1. If a sample of 50 prospective customers is selected and no free premium channels are included in the *3-For-All* service offer, given past results, what is the probability that

a. fewer than 3 customers will subscribe to the *3-For-All* service offer?

b. 0 customers or 1 customer will subscribe to the *3-For-All* service offer?

c. more than 4 customers will subscribe to the *3-For-All* service offer?

d. Suppose that in the actual survey of 50 prospective customers, 4 customers subscribe to the *3-For-All* service offer. What does this tell you about the previous estimate of the proportion of customers who would subscribe to the *3-For-All* service offer?

2. Instead of offering no premium free channels as in Problem 1, suppose that two free premium channels are included in the *3-For-All* service offer. Given past results, what is the probability that

a. fewer than 3 customers will subscribe to the *3-For-All* service offer?

b. 0 customers or 1 customer will subscribe to the *3-For-All* service offer?

c. more than 4 customers will subscribe to the *3-For-All* service offer?

d. Compare the results of (a) through (c) to those of **1**.

e. Suppose that in the actual survey of 50 prospective customers, 6 customers subscribe to the *3-For-All* service offer. What does this tell you about the previous estimate of the proportion of customers who would subscribe to the *3-For-All* service offer?

f. What do the results in (e) tell you about the effect of offering free premium channels on the likelihood of obtaining subscriptions to the *3-For-All* service?

3. Suppose that additional surveys of 50 prospective customers were conducted in which the number of free premium channels was varied. The results were as follows:

Number of Free Premium Channels	Number of Subscriptions
1	5
3	6
4	6
5	7

How many free premium channels should the research director recommend for inclusion in the *3-For-All* service? Explain.

Digital Case

Apply your knowledge about expected value in this continuing Digital Case from Chapters 3 and 4.

Open **BullsAndBears.pdf**, a marketing brochure from EndRun Financial Services. Read the claims and examine the supporting data. Then answer the following:

1. Are there any "catches" about the claims the brochure makes for the rate of return of Happy Bull and Worried Bear funds?

2. What subjective data influence the rate-of-return analyses of these funds? Could EndRun be accused of making false and misleading statements? Why or why not?

3. The expected-return analysis seems to show that the Worried Bear fund has a greater expected return than the Happy Bull fund. Should a rational investor never invest in the Happy Bull fund? Why or why not?

CHAPTER 5 EXCEL GUIDE

EG5.1 The PROBABILITY DISTRIBUTION for a DISCRETE VARIABLE

Key Technique Use the **SUMPRODUCT(*cell range 1, cell range 2*)** function (see Appendix F) to compute the expected value and variance.

Example Compute the expected value, variance, and standard deviation for the number of interruptions per day data of Table 5.1 on page 177.

In-Depth Excel Use the **Discrete Variable workbook** as a model. For the example, open to the **DATA worksheet** of the **Discrete Variable workbook**. The worksheet already contains the entries needed to compute the expected value, variance, and standard deviation (shown in the COMPUTE worksheet) for the example.

For other problems, modify the DATA worksheet. Enter the probability distribution data into columns A and B and, if necessary, extend columns C through E, first selecting cell range C7:E7 and then copying that cell range down as many rows as necessary. If the probability distribution has fewer than six outcomes, select the rows that contain the extra, unwanted outcomes, right-click, and then click **Delete** in the shortcut menu.

Read the SHORT TAKES for Chapter 5 for an explanation of the formulas found in the worksheets.

EG5.2 BINOMIAL DISTRIBUTION

Key Technique Use the **BINOM.DIST(*number of events of interest, sample size, probability of an event of interest*, FALSE)** function.

Example Compute the binomial probabilities for $n = 4$ and $\pi = 0.1$, as is done in Figure 5.2 on page 185.

PHStat Use **Binomial**.
For the example, select **PHStat → Probability & Prob. Distributions → Binomial**. In the procedure's dialog box (shown below):

1. Enter **4** as the **Sample Size**.
2. Enter **0.1** as the **Prob. of an Event of Interest**.
3. Enter **0** as the **Outcomes From** value and enter **4** as the (Outcomes) **To** value.
4. Enter a **Title**, check **Histogram**, and click **OK**.

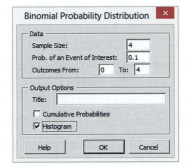

Check **Cumulative Probabilities** before clicking **OK** in step 4 to have the procedure include columns for $P(\leq X), P(<X), P(>X)$, and $P(\geq X)$ in the binomial probabilities table.

In-Depth Excel Use the **Binomial workbook** as a template and model.

For the example, open to the **COMPUTE worksheet** of the **Binomial workbook**, shown in Figure 5.2 on page 185. The worksheet already contains the entries needed for the example. For other problems, change the sample size in cell B4 and the probability of an event of interest in cell B5. If necessary, extend the binomial probabilities table by first selecting cell range A18:B18 and then copying that cell range down as many rows as necessary. To construct a histogram of the probability distribution, use the Appendix Section B.9 instructions.

Read the SHORT TAKES for Chapter 5 for an explanation of the CUMULATIVE worksheet, which computes cumulative probabilities, and the worksheets to use with versions older than Excel 2010.

EG5.3 POISSON DISTRIBUTION

Key Technique Use the **POISSON.DIST(*number of events of interest, the average or expected number of events of interest,* FALSE)** function.

Example Compute the Poisson probabilities for the customer arrival problem in which $\lambda = 3$, as is done in Figure 5.4 on page 190.

PHStat Use **Poisson**.
For the example, select **PHStat → Probability & Prob. Distributions → Poisson**. In this procedure's dialog box (shown below):

1. Enter **3** as the **Mean/Expected No. of Events of Interest**.
2. Enter a **Title** and click **OK**.

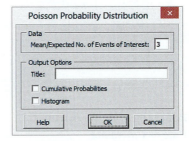

Check **Cumulative Probabilities** before clicking **OK** in step 2 to have the procedure include columns for $P(\leq X), P(<X), P(>X)$, and $P(\geq X)$ in the Poisson probabilities table. Check **Histogram** to construct a histogram of the Poisson probability distribution.

In-Depth Excel Use the **Poisson workbook** as a template.
For the example, open to the **COMPUTE worksheet** of the **Poisson workbook**, shown in Figure 5.4 on page 190. The worksheet already contains the entries for the example. For other problems, change the mean or expected number of events of interest in cell E4. To construct a histogram of the probability distribution, use the Appendix Section B.9 instructions.

Read the SHORT TAKES for Chapter 5 for an explanation of the CUMULATIVE worksheet, which computes cumulative probabilities, and the worksheets to use with versions older than Excel 2010.

CHAPTER 5 MINITAB GUIDE

MG5.1 The PROBABILITY DISTRIBUTION for a DISCRETE VARIABLE

Expected Value of a Discrete Variable

Use **Calculator** to compute the expected value of a discrete variable.

For example, to compute the expected value for the number of interruptions per day of Table 5.1 on page 177, open to the **Table_5.1 worksheet**. Select **Calc → Calculator**. In the Calculator dialog box (shown below):

1. Enter **C3** in the **Store result in variable** box and then press **Tab**. (C3 is the first empty column on the worksheet.)
2. Double-click **C1 X** in the variables list to add **X** to the **Expression** box.
3. Click ***** on the simulated keypad to add ***** to the **Expression** box.
4. Double-click **C2 P(X)** in the variables list to form the expression **X * 'P(X)'** in the **Expression** box.
5. Check **Assign as a formula**.
6. Click **OK**.

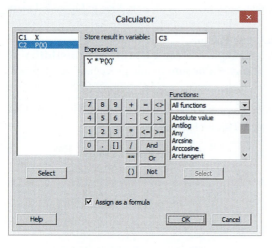

7. Enter **X*P(X)** as the name for **column C3**.
8. Reselect **Calc → Calculator**.

In the Calculator dialog box:

9. Enter **C4** in the **Store result in variable** box and then press **Tab**. (C4 is the first empty column on the worksheet.)
10. Enter **SUM(C3)** in the **Expression** box.
11. If necessary, clear **Assign as a formula**.
12. Click **OK**.

MG5.2 BINOMIAL DISTRIBUTION

Use **Binomial** to compute binomial probabilities.
For example, to compute these probabilities for the Section 5.2 tagged orders example on page 182, open to a new, blank worksheet and:

1. Enter **X** as the name of **column C1**.
2. Enter the values **0** through **4** in **column C1**, starting with row 1.
3. Enter **P(X)** as the name of **column C2**.
4. Select **Calc → Probability Distributions → Binomial**.

In the Binomial Distribution dialog box (shown below):

5. Click **Probability** (to compute the probabilities of exactly X events of interest for all values of X).
6. Enter **4** (the sample size) in the **Number of trials** box.
7. Enter **0.1** in the **Event probability** box.
8. Click **Input column**, enter **C1** in its box, and press **Tab**.
9. Enter **C2** in the first **Optional storage** box.
10. Click **OK**.

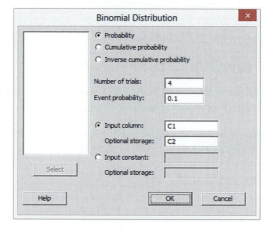

Skip step 9 to create the results shown in Figure 5.2 on page 185.

MG5.3 POISSON DISTRIBUTION

Use **Poisson** to compute Poisson probabilities.
For example, to compute these probabilities for the Section 5.3 bank customer arrivals example on page 189, open to a new, blank worksheet and:

1. Enter **X** as the name of **column C1**.
2. Enter the values **0** through **15** in **column C1**, starting with row 1.
3. Enter **P(X)** as the name of **column C2**.
4. Select **Calc → Probability Distributions → Poisson**.

In the Poisson Distribution dialog box (shown on page 199):

5. Click **Probability** (to compute the probabilities of exactly X events of interest for all values of X).
6. Enter **3** in the **Mean** box.

7. Click **Input column**, enter **C1** in its box, and press **Tab**.

8. Enter **C2** in the first **Optional storage** box.

9. Click **OK**.

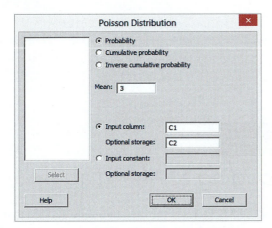

Skip step 8 to create the results shown in Figure 5.4 on page 190.

The Normal Distribution

OBJECTIVES

Compute probabilities from the normal distribution

Use the normal distribution to solve business problems

Use the normal probability plot to determine whether a set of data is approximately normally distributed

USING STATISTICS

Normal Downloading at MyTVLab

You are a project manager for the MyTVLab website, an online service that streams movies and episodes from broadcast and cable TV series and that allows users to upload and share original videos. To attract and retain visitors to the website, you need to ensure that users can quickly download the exclusive-content daily videos.

To check how fast a video downloads, you open a web browser on a computer at the corporate offices of MyTVLab, load the MyTVLab home page, download the first website-exclusive video, and measure the download time. Download time—the amount of time in seconds, that passes from first clicking a download link until the video is ready to play—is a function of both the streaming media technology used and the number of simultaneous users of the website. Past data indicate that the mean download time is 7 seconds and that the standard deviation is 2 seconds. Approximately two-thirds of the download times are between 5 and 9 seconds, and about 95% of the download times are between 3 and 11 seconds. In other words, the download times are distributed as a bell-shaped curve, with a clustering around the mean of 7 seconds. How could you use this information to answer questions about the download times of the first video?

I n Chapter 5, accounting managers at Ricknel Home Centers wanted to be able to answer questions about the number of tagged items in a given sample size. As a MyTVLab project manager, you face a different task—one that involves a continuous measurement because a download time could be any value and not just a whole number. How can you answer questions, such as the following, about this *continuous numerical variable*:

- What proportion of the video downloads take more than 9 seconds?
- How many seconds elapse before 10% of the downloads are complete?
- How many seconds elapse before 99% of the downloads are complete?
- How would enhancing the streaming media technology used affect the answers to these questions?

As in Chapter 5, you can use a probability distribution as a model. Reading this chapter will help you learn about characteristics of continuous probability distributions and how to use the normal distribution to solve business problems.

6.1 Continuous Probability Distributions

A **probability density function** is a mathematical expression that defines the distribution of the values for a continuous variable. Figure 6.1 graphically displays three probability density functions.

FIGURE 6.1

Three continuous probability distributions

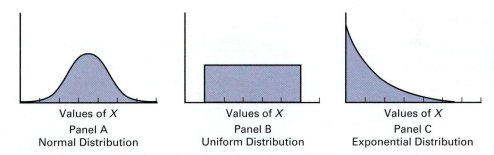

Panel A depicts a **normal distribution**. The normal distribution is symmetrical and bell-shaped, implying that most observed values tend to cluster around the mean, which, due to the distribution's symmetrical shape, is equal to the median. Although the values in a normal distribution can range from negative infinity to positive infinity, the shape of the distribution makes it very unlikely that extremely large or extremely small values will occur.

Panel B shows a **uniform distribution** where the values are equally distributed in the range between the smallest value and the largest value. Sometimes referred to as the *rectangular distribution*, the uniform distribution is symmetrical, and therefore the mean equals the median.

Panel C illustrates an **exponential distribution**. This distribution is skewed to the right, making the mean larger than the median. The range for an exponential distribution is zero to positive infinity, but the distribution's shape makes it unlikely that extremely large values will occur.

6.2 The Normal Distribution

The normal distribution (also known as the *Gaussian distribution*) is the most common continuous distribution used in statistics. The normal distribution is vitally important in statistics for three main reasons:

- Numerous continuous variables common in business have distributions that closely resemble the normal distribution.
- The normal distribution can be used to approximate various discrete probability distributions.
- The normal distribution provides the basis for *classical statistical inference* because of its relationship to the *Central Limit Theorem* (which is discussed in Section 7.2).

The normal distribution is represented by the classic bell shape shown in Panel A of Figure 6.1. In the normal distribution, you can calculate the probability that values occur within certain ranges or intervals. However, because probability for continuous variables is measured as an area under the curve, the probability of a *particular value* from a continuous distribution such as the normal distribution is zero. As an example, time (in seconds) is measured and not counted. Therefore, you can determine the probability that the download time for a video on a web browser is between 7 and 10 seconds, or the probability that the download time is between 8 and 9 seconds, or the probability that the download time is between 7.99 and 8.01 seconds. However, the probability that the download time is *exactly* 8 seconds is zero.

The normal distribution has several important theoretical properties:

- It is symmetrical, and its mean and median are therefore equal.
- It is bell-shaped in appearance.
- Its interquartile range is equal to 1.33 standard deviations. Thus, the middle 50% of the values are contained within an interval of two-thirds of a standard deviation below the mean and two-thirds of a standard deviation above the mean.
- It has an infinite range $(-\infty < X < \infty)$.

In practice, many variables have distributions that closely resemble the theoretical properties of the normal distribution. The data in Table 6.1 represent the amount of soft drink in 10,000 1-liter bottles filled on a recent day. The continuous variable of interest, the amount of soft drink filled, can be approximated by the normal distribution. The measurements of the amount of soft drink in the 10,000 bottles cluster in the interval 1.05 to 1.055 liters and distribute symmetrically around that grouping, forming a bell-shaped pattern.

TABLE 6.1

Amount of Fill in 10,000 Bottles of a Soft Drink

Amount of Fill (liters)	Relative Frequency
< 1.025	48/10,000 = 0.0048
1.025 < 1.030	122/10,000 = 0.0122
1.030 < 1.035	325/10,000 = 0.0325
1.035 < 1.040	695/10,000 = 0.0695
1.040 < 1.045	1,198/10,000 = 0.1198
1.045 < 1.050	1,664/10,000 = 0.1664
1.050 < 1.055	1,896/10,000 = 0.1896
1.055 < 1.060	1,664/10,000 = 0.1664
1.060 < 1.065	1,198/10,000 = 0.1198
1.065 < 1.070	695/10,000 = 0.0695
1.070 < 1.075	325/10,000 = 0.0325
1.075 < 1.080	122/10,000 = 0.0122
1.080 or above	48/10,000 = 0.0048
Total	1.0000

Figure 6.2 shows the relative frequency histogram and polygon for the distribution of the amount filled in 10,000 bottles.

FIGURE 6.2

Relative frequency histogram and polygon of the amount filled in 10,000 bottles of a soft drink

Source: Data are taken from Table 6.1.

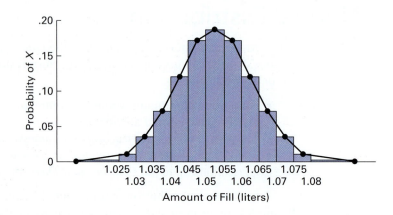

For these data, the first three theoretical properties of the normal distribution are approximately satisfied. However, the fourth one, having an infinite range, is not. The amount filled in a bottle cannot possibly be zero or below, nor can a bottle be filled beyond its capacity. From Table 6.1, you see that only 48 out of every 10,000 bottles filled are expected to contain 1.08 liters or more, and an equal number are expected to contain less than 1.025 liters.

The symbol $f(X)$ is used to represent a probability density function. The **probability density function for the normal distribution** is given in Equation (6.1).

NORMAL PROBABILITY DENSITY FUNCTION

$$f(X) = \frac{1}{\sqrt{2\pi}\sigma} e^{-(1/2)[(X-\mu)/\sigma]^2}$$

(6.1)

where

e = mathematical constant approximated by 2.71828
π = mathematical constant approximated by 3.14159
μ = mean
σ = standard deviation
X = any value of the continuous variable, where $-\infty < X < \infty$

> **Student Tip**
> There is a different normal distribution for each combination of the mean, μ, and the standard deviation, σ.

Although Equation (6.1) may look complicated, the probabilities of the variable X are dependent only on the mean, μ, and the standard deviation, σ, the two parameters of the normal distribution, because e and π are mathematical constants. There is a different normal distribution for each combination of the mean μ and the standard deviation σ. Figure 6.3 illustrates this principle. The distributions labeled A and B have the same mean (μ) but have different standard deviations. Distributions A and C have the same standard deviation (σ) but have different means. Distributions B and C have different values for both μ and σ.

FIGURE 6.3
Three normal distributions

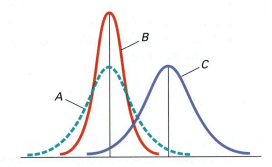

Computing Normal Probabilities

To compute normal probabilities, you first convert a normally distributed variable, X, to a **standardized normal variable**, Z, using the **transformation formula**, shown in Equation (6.2). Applying this formula allows you to look up values in a normal probability table and avoid the tedious and complex computations that Equation (6.1) would otherwise require.

Z TRANSFORMATION FORMULA

The Z value is equal to the difference between X and the mean, μ, divided by the standard deviation, σ.

$$Z = \frac{X - \mu}{\sigma}$$

(6.2)

The transformation formula computes a Z value that expresses the difference of the X value from the mean, μ, in standard deviation units (see Section 3.2 on page 108) called *standardized units*. While a variable, X, has mean, μ, and standard deviation, σ, the standardized variable, Z, always has mean $\mu = 0$ and standard deviation $\sigma = 1$.

Then you can determine the probabilities by using Table E.2, the **cumulative standardized normal distribution**. For example, recall from the Using Statistics scenario on page 200 that past data indicate that the time to download a video is normally distributed, with a mean $\mu = 7$ seconds and a standard deviation $\sigma = 2$ seconds. From Figure 6.4, you see that every measurement X has a corresponding standardized measurement Z, computed from Equation (6.2), the transformation formula.

FIGURE 6.4

Transformation of scales

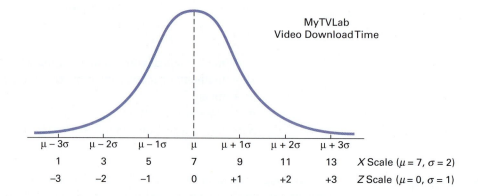

Therefore, a download time of 9 seconds is equivalent to 1 standardized unit (1 standard deviation) above the mean because

$$Z = \frac{9 - 7}{2} = +1$$

A download time of 1 second is equivalent to -3 standardized units (3 standard deviations) below the mean because

$$Z = \frac{1 - 7}{2} = -3$$

In Figure 6.4, the standard deviation is the unit of measurement. In other words, a time of 9 seconds is 2 seconds (1 standard deviation) higher, or *slower*, than the mean time of 7 seconds. Similarly, a time of 1 second is 6 seconds (3 standard deviations) lower, or *faster*, than the mean time.

To further illustrate the transformation formula, suppose that another website has a download time for a video that is normally distributed, with a mean $\mu = 4$ seconds and a standard deviation $\sigma = 1$ second. Figure 6.5 on page 205 shows this distribution.

Comparing these results with those of the MyTVLab website, you see that a download time of 5 seconds is 1 standard deviation above the mean download time because

$$Z = \frac{5 - 4}{1} = +1$$

FIGURE 6.5

A different transformation of scales

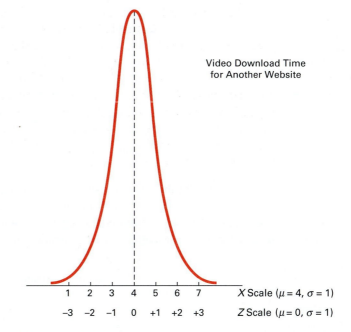

Video Download Time
for Another Website

| | 1 | 2 | 3 | 4 | 5 | 6 | 7 | X Scale ($\mu = 4$, $\sigma = 1$) |
| | -3 | -2 | -1 | 0 | +1 | +2 | +3 | Z Scale ($\mu = 0$, $\sigma = 1$) |

A time of 1 second is 3 standard deviations below the mean download time because

$$Z = \frac{1 - 4}{1} = -3$$

With the Z value computed, you look up the normal probability using a table of values from the cumulative standardized normal distribution, such as Table E.2 in Appendix E. Suppose you wanted to find the probability that the download time for the MyTVLab website is less than 9 seconds. Recall from page 204 that transforming $X = 9$ to standardized Z units, given a mean $\mu = 7$ seconds and a standard deviation $\sigma = 2$ seconds, leads to a Z value of $+1.00$.

With this value, you use Table E.2 to find the cumulative area under the normal curve less than (to the left of) $Z = +1.00$. To read the probability or area under the curve less than $Z = +1.00$, you scan down the Z column in Table E.2 until you locate the Z value of interest (in 10ths) in the Z row for 1.0. Next, you read across this row until you intersect the column that contains the 100ths place of the Z value. Therefore, in the body of the table, the probability for $Z = 1.00$ corresponds to the intersection of the row $Z = 1.0$ with the column $Z = .00$. Table 6.2, which reproduces a portion of Table E.2, shows this intersection. The probability listed at the intersection is 0.8413, which means that there is an 84.13% chance that the download time will be less than 9 seconds. Figure 6.6 on page 206 graphically shows this probability.

Student Tip

Remember that when dealing with a continuous distribution such as the normal, the word *area* has the same meaning as *probability*.

TABLE 6.2

Finding a Cumulative Area Under the Normal Curve

				Cumulative Probabilities						
Z	.00	.01	.02	.03	.04	.05	.06	.07	.08	.09
0.0	.5000	.5040	.5080	.5120	.5160	.5199	.5239	.5279	.5319	.5359
0.1	.5398	.5438	.5478	.5517	.5557	.5596	.5636	.5675	.5714	.5753
0.2	.5793	.5832	.5871	.5910	.5948	.5987	.6026	.6064	.6103	.6141
0.3	.6179	.6217	.6255	.6293	.6331	.6368	.6406	.6443	.6480	.6517
0.4	.6554	.6591	.6628	.6664	.6700	.6736	.6772	.6808	.6844	.6879
0.5	.6915	.6950	.6985	.7019	.7054	.7088	.7123	.7157	.7190	.7224
0.6	.7257	.7291	.7324	.7357	.7389	.7422	.7454	.7486	.7518	.7549
0.7	.7580	.7612	.7642	.7673	.7704	.7734	.7764	.7794	.7823	.7852
0.8	.7881	.7910	.7939	.7967	.7995	.8023	.8051	.8078	.8106	.8133
0.9	.8159	.8186	.8212	.8238	.8264	.8289	.8315	.8340	.8365	.8389
1.0	.8413	.8438	.8461	.8485	.8508	.8531	.8554	.8577	.8599	.8621

Source: Extracted from Table E.2.

FIGURE 6.6

Determining the area less than Z from a cumulative standardized normal distribution

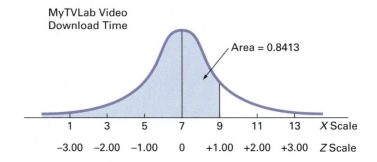

MyTVLab Video Download Time

Area = 0.8413

| 1 | 3 | 5 | 7 | 9 | 11 | 13 | X Scale |

–3.00 –2.00 –1.00 0 +1.00 +2.00 +3.00 Z Scale

However, for the other website, you see that a time of 5 seconds is 1 standardized unit above the mean time of 4 seconds. Thus, the probability that the download time will be less than 5 seconds is also 0.8413. Figure 6.7 shows that regardless of the value of the mean, μ, and standard deviation, σ, of a normally distributed variable, Equation (6.2) can transform the X value to a Z value.

FIGURE 6.7

Demonstrating a transformation of scales for corresponding cumulative portions under two normal curves

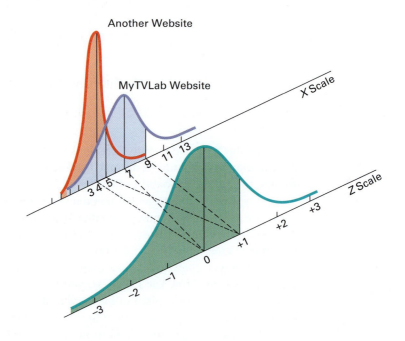

Another Website

MyTVLab Website

X Scale

Z Scale

> **Student Tip**
> You will find it very helpful when computing probabilities under the normal curve if you draw a normal curve and then enter the values for the mean and X below the curve and shade the desired area to be determined under the curve.

Now that you have learned to use Table E.2 with Equation (6.2), you can answer many questions related to the MyTVLab video download, using the normal distribution.

EXAMPLE 6.1

Finding $P(X > 9)$

What is the probability that the video download time for the MyTVLab website will be more than 9 seconds?

SOLUTION The probability that the download time will be less than 9 seconds is 0.8413 (see Figure 6.6 above). Thus, the probability that the download time will be more than 9 seconds is the *complement* of less than 9 seconds, $1 - 0.8413 = 0.1587$. Figure 6.8 illustrates this result.

FIGURE 6.8

Finding $P(X > 9)$

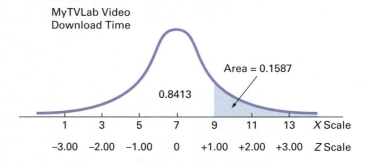

MyTVLab Video Download Time

Area = 0.1587

0.8413

| 1 | 3 | 5 | 7 | 9 | 11 | 13 | X Scale |

–3.00 –2.00 –1.00 0 +1.00 +2.00 +3.00 Z Scale

EXAMPLE 6.2

Finding $P(X < 7$ or $X > 9)$

What is the probability that the video download time for the MyTVLab website will be less than 7 seconds or more than 9 seconds?

SOLUTION To find this probability, you separately calculate the probability of a download time less than 7 seconds and the probability of a download time greater than 9 seconds and then add these two probabilities together. Figure 6.9 illustrates this result.

FIGURE 6.9

Finding $P(X < 7$ or $X > 9)$

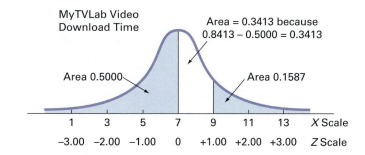

Because the mean is 7 seconds, and because the mean is equal to the median in a normal distribution, 50% of download times are under 7 seconds. From Example 6.1, you know that the probability that the download time is greater than 9 seconds is 0.1587. Therefore, the probability that a download time is under 7 or over 9 seconds, $P(X < 7$ or $X > 9)$, is $0.5000 + 0.1587 = 0.6587$.

EXAMPLE 6.3

Finding $P(5 < X < 9)$

What is the probability that video download time for the MyTVLab website will be between 5 and 9 seconds—that is, $P(5 < X < 9)$?

SOLUTION In Figure 6.10, you can see that the area of interest is located between two values, 5 and 9.

FIGURE 6.10

Finding $P(5 < X < 9)$

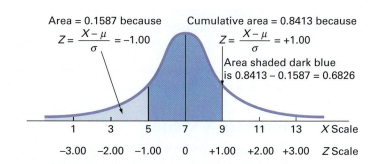

In Example 6.1 on page 206, you already found that the area under the normal curve less than 9 seconds is 0.8413. To find the area under the normal curve less than 5 seconds,

$$Z = \frac{5 - 7}{2} = -1.00$$

Using Table E.2, you look up $Z = -1.00$ and find 0.1587. Therefore, the probability that the download time will be between 5 and 9 seconds is $0.8413 - 0.1587 = 0.6826$, as displayed in Figure 6.10.

The result of Example 6.3 enables you to state that for any normal distribution, 68.26% of the values are within ±1 standard deviation of the mean. From Figure 6.11, you can see that 95.44% of the values are within ±2 standard deviations of the mean. Thus, 95.44% of the download times are between 3 and 11 seconds. From Figure 6.12, you can see that 99.73% of the values are within ±3 standard deviations above or below the mean.

FIGURE 6.11

Finding $P(3 < X < 11)$

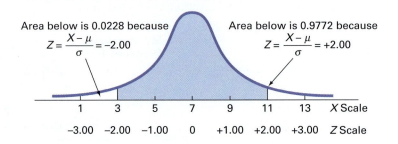

FIGURE 6.12

Finding $P(1 < X < 13)$

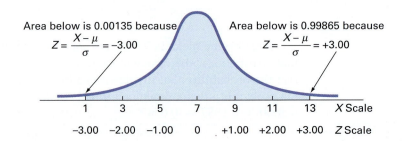

Thus, 99.73% of the download times are between 1 and 13 seconds. Therefore, it is unlikely (0.0027, or only 27 in 10,000) that a download time will be so fast or so slow that it will take less than 1 second or more than 13 seconds. In general, you can use 6σ (i.e., 3 standard deviations below the mean to 3 standard deviations above the mean) as a practical approximation of the range for normally distributed data.

Figures 6.10, 6.11, and 6.12 illustrate that for any normal distribution,

- Approximately 68.26% of the values fall within ±1 standard deviation of the mean
- Approximately 95.44% of the values fall within ±2 standard deviations of the mean
- Approximately 99.73% of the values fall within ±3 standard deviations of the mean

This result is the justification for the empirical rule presented on page 122. The accuracy of the empirical rule increases the closer the variable follows the normal distribution.

Finding X Values

Examples 6.1 through 6.3 require you to use the normal distribution Table E.2 to find an area under the normal curve that corresponds to a specific X value. For other situations, you may need to do the reverse: Find the X value that corresponds to a specific area. In general, you use Equation (6.3) for finding an X value.

FINDING AN X VALUE ASSOCIATED WITH A KNOWN PROBABILITY

The X value is equal to the mean, μ, plus the product of the Z value and the standard deviation, σ.

$$X = \mu + Z\sigma \qquad\qquad (6.3)$$

To find a *particular* value associated with a known probability, follow these steps:

- Sketch the normal curve and then place the values for the mean and X on the X and Z scales.
- Find the cumulative area less than X.
- Shade the area of interest.
- Using Table E.2, determine the Z value corresponding to the area under the normal curve less than X.
- Using Equation (6.3), solve for X:

$$X = \mu + Z\sigma$$

Examples 6.4 and 6.5 illustrate this technique.

EXAMPLE 6.4

Finding the X Value for a Cumulative Probability of 0.10

How much time (in seconds) will elapse before the fastest 10% of the downloads of a MyTVLab video are complete?

SOLUTION Because 10% of the videos are expected to download in under X seconds, the area under the normal curve less than this value is 0.1000. Using the body of Table E.2, you search for the area or probability of 0.1000. The closest result is 0.1003, as shown in Table 6.3 (which is extracted from Table E.2).

TABLE 6.3

Finding a Z Value Corresponding to a Particular Cumulative Area (0.10) Under the Normal Curve

| | | | | | Cumulative Probabilities | | | | |
Z	.00	.01	.02	.03	.04	.05	.06	.07	.08	.09
⋮	⋮	⋮	⋮	⋮	⋮	⋮	⋮	⋮	⋮	⋮
−1.5	.0668	.0655	.0643	.0630	.0618	.0606	.0594	.0582	.0571	.0559
−1.4	.0808	.0793	.0778	.0764	.0749	.0735	.0721	.0708	.0694	.0681
−1.3	.0968	.0951	.0934	.0918	.0901	.0885	.0869	.0853	.0838	.0823
−1.2	.1151	.1131	.1112	.1093	.1075	.1056	.1038	.1020	.1003	.0985

Source: Extracted from Table E.2.

Working from this area to the margins of the table, you find that the Z value corresponding to the particular Z row (−1.2) and Z column (.08) is −1.28 (see Figure 6.13).

FIGURE 6.13

Finding Z to determine X

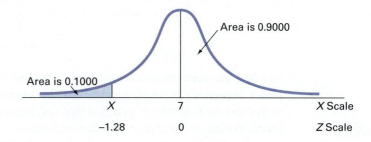

Once you find Z, you use Equation (6.3) on page 208 to determine the X value. Substituting $\mu = 7$, $\sigma = 2$, and $Z = -1.28$,

$$X = \mu + Z\sigma$$
$$X = 7 + (-1.28)(2) = 4.44 \text{ seconds}$$

Thus, 10% of the download times are 4.44 seconds or less.

EXAMPLE 6.5

Finding the X Values That Include 95% of the Download Times

What are the lower and upper values of X, symmetrically distributed around the mean, that include 95% of the download times for a video at the MyTVLab website?

SOLUTION First, you need to find the lower value of X (called X_L). Then, you find the upper value of X (called X_U). Because 95% of the values are between X_L and X_U, and because X_L and X_U are equally distant from the mean, 2.5% of the values are below X_L (see Figure 6.14).

FIGURE 6.14

Finding Z to determine X_L

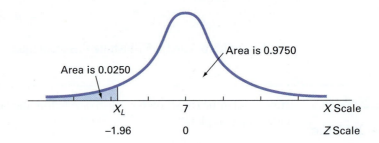

Although X_L is not known, you can find the corresponding Z value because the area under the normal curve less than this Z is 0.0250. Using the body of Table 6.4, you search for the probability 0.0250.

TABLE 6.4

Finding a Z Value Corresponding to a Cumulative Area of 0.025 Under the Normal Curve

					Cumulative Area					
Z	**.00**	**.01**	**.02**	**.03**	**.04**	**.05**	**.06**	**.07**	**.08**	**.09**
⋮	⋮	⋮	⋮	⋮	⋮	⋮	⋮	⋮	⋮	⋮
−2.0	.0228	.0222	.0217	.0212	.0207	.0202	.0197	.0192	.0188	.0183
−1.9	.0287	.0281	.0274	.0268	.0262	.0256	.0250	.0244	.0239	.0233
−1.8	.0359	.0351	.0344	.0336	.0329	.0232	.0314	.0307	.0301	.0294

Source: Extracted from Table E.2.

Working from the body of the table to the margins of the table, you see that the Z value corresponding to the particular Z row (−1.9) and Z column (.06) is −1.96.

Once you find Z, the final step is to use Equation (6.3) on page 208 as follows:

$$X = \mu + Z\sigma$$
$$= 7 + (-1.96)(2)$$
$$= 7 - 3.92$$
$$= 3.08 \text{ seconds}$$

You use a similar process to find X_U. Because only 2.5% of the video downloads take longer than X_U seconds, 97.5% of the video downloads take less than X_U seconds. From the symmetry of the normal distribution, you find that the desired Z value, as shown in Figure 6.15, is +1.96 (because Z lies to the right of the standardized mean of 0). You can also extract this Z value from Table 6.5. You can see that 0.975 is the area under the normal curve less than the Z value of +1.96.

FIGURE 6.15

Finding Z to determine X_U

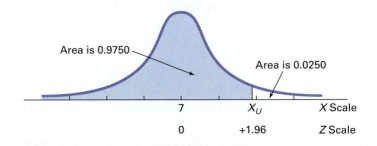

TABLE 6.5

Finding a Z Value Corresponding to a Cumulative Area of 0.975 Under the Normal Curve

					Cumulative Area					
Z	**.00**	**.01**	**.02**	**.03**	**.04**	**.05**	**.06**	**.07**	**.08**	**.09**
⋮	⋮	⋮	⋮	⋮	⋮	⋮	⋮	⋮	⋮	⋮
+1.8	.9641	.9649	.9656	.9664	.9671	.9678	.9686	.9693	.9699	.9706
+1.9	.9713	.9719	.9726	.9732	.9738	.9744	.9750	.9756	.9761	.9767
+2.0	.9772	.9778	.9783	.9788	.9793	.9798	.9803	.9808	.9812	.9817

Source: Extracted from Table E.2.

Using Equation (6.3) on page 208,

$$X = \mu + Z\sigma$$
$$= 7 + (+1.96)(2)$$
$$= 7 + 3.92$$
$$= 10.92 \text{ seconds}$$

Therefore, 95% of the download times are between 3.08 and 10.92 seconds.

Instead of looking up cumulative probabilities in a table, you can use Excel or Minitab to compute normal probabilities. Figure 6.16 displays an Excel worksheet that computes normal probabilities and finds X values for problems similar to Examples 6.1 through 6.5. Figure 6.17 shows Minitab results for Examples 6.1 and 6.4. (You need to subtract the results in the left part of the figure from 1.0 to obtain the answer to Example 6.1.)

FIGURE 6.16

Excel worksheet for computing normal probabilities and finding X values (shown in two parts)

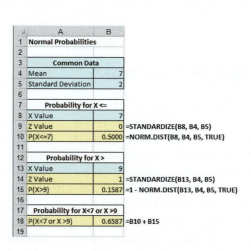

FIGURE 6.17

Minitab results for Examples 6.1 and 6.4

Cumulative Distribution Function

Normal with mean = 7 and standard deviation = 2

```
x    P( X <= x )
9    0.841345
```

Inverse Cumulative Distribution Function

Normal with mean = 7 and standard deviation = 2

```
P( X <= x )        x
0.1    4.43690
```

VISUAL EXPLORATIONS   Exploring the Normal Distribution

Open the **VE-Normal Distribution add-in workbook** to explore the normal distribution. (See Appendix C to learn more about using this workbook.) When this workbook opens properly, it adds a Normal Distribution menu in the Add-ins tab.

To explore the effects of changing the mean and standard deviation on the area under a normal distribution curve workbook, select **Add-ins → Normal Distribution → Probability Density Function**. The add-in displays a normal curve for the MyTVLab website download example and a floating control panel (shown at top right). Use the control panel spinner buttons to change the values for the mean, standard deviation, and *X* value and then note the effects of these changes on the probability of *X* < value and the corresponding shaded area under the curve. To see the normal curve labeled with *Z* values, click **Z Values**. Click the **Reset** button to reset the control panel values. Click **Finish** to finish exploring.

To create shaded areas under the curve for problems similar to Examples 6.2 and 6.3, select **Add-ins → Normal Distribution → Areas**. In the Areas dialog box (shown at bottom right), enter values, select an Area Option, and click **OK**. The add-in creates a normal distribution curve with areas that are shaded according to the values you entered.

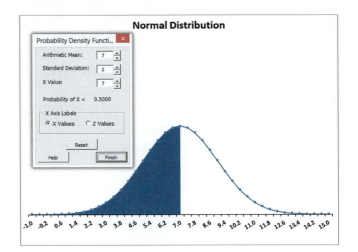

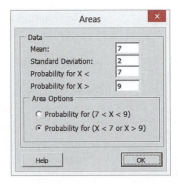

THINK ABOUT THIS   What Is Normal?

Ironically, the statistician who popularized the use of "normal" to describe the distribution discussed in Section 6.2 was someone who saw the distribution as anything but the everyday, anticipated occurrence that the adjective *normal* usually suggests.

Starting with an 1894 paper, Karl Pearson argued that measurements of phenomena do not naturally, or "normally," conform to the classic bell shape. While this principle underlies much of statistics today, Pearson's point of view was radical to contemporaries who saw the world as standardized and normal. Pearson changed minds by showing that some populations are naturally *skewed* (coining that term in passing), and he helped put to rest the notion that the normal distribution underlies all phenomena.

Today, people still make the type of mistake that Pearson refuted. As a student, you are probably familiar with discussions about grade inflation,

a real phenomenon at many schools. But have you ever realized that a "proof" of this inflation—that there are "too few" low grades because grades are skewed toward A's and B's—wrongly implies that grades should be "normally" distributed? Because college students represent small *nonrandom* samples, there are plenty of reasons to suspect that the distribution of grades would not be "normal."

Misunderstandings about the normal distribution have occurred both in business and in the public sector through the years. These misunderstandings have caused a number of business blunders and have sparked several public policy debates, including the causes of the collapse of large financial institutions in 2008. According to one theory, the investment banking industry's application of the normal distribution to assess risk may have contributed to the global collapse (see

"A Finer Formula for Assessing Risks," *The New York Times*, May 11, 2010, p. B2 and reference 8). Using the normal distribution led these banks to overestimate the probability of having stable market conditions and underestimate the chance of unusually large market losses.

According to this theory, the use of other distributions that have less area in the middle of their curves, and, therefore, more in the "tails" that represent unusual market outcomes, may have led to less serious losses.

As you study this chapter, make sure you understand the assumptions that must hold for the proper use of the "normal" distribution, assumptions that were not explicitly verified by the investment bankers. And, most importantly, always remember that the name *normal distribution* does not mean normal in the everyday sense of the word.

Problems for Section 6.2

LEARNING THE BASICS

6.1 Given a standardized normal distribution (with a mean of 0 and a standard deviation of 1, as in Table E.2), what is the probability that
a. Z is less than 1.57?
b. Z is greater than 1.84?
c. Z is between 1.57 and 1.84?
d. Z is less than 1.57 or greater than 1.84?

6.2 Given a standardized normal distribution (with a mean of 0 and a standard deviation of 1, as in Table E.2), what is the probability that
a. Z is between -1.57 and 1.84?
b. Z is less than -1.57 or greater than 1.84?
c. What is the value of Z if only 2.5 percent of all possible Z values are larger?
d. Between what two values of Z (symmetrically distributed around the mean) will 68.26 percent of all possible Z values be contained?

6.3 Given a standardized normal distribution (with a mean of 0 and a standard deviation of 1, as in Table E.2), what is the probability that
a. Z is less than 1.08?
b. Z is greater than -0.21?
c. Z is less than -0.21 or greater than the mean?
d. Z is less than -0.21 or greater than 1.08?

6.4 Given a standardized normal distribution (with a mean of 0 and a standard deviation of 1, as in Table E.2), determine the following probabilities:
a. $P(Z > 1.08)$
b. $P(Z < -0.21)$
c. $P(-1.96 < Z < -0.21)$
d. What is the value of Z if only 15.87 percent of all possible Z values are larger?

6.5 Given a normal distribution with $\mu = 100$ and $\sigma = 10$, what is the probability that
a. $X > 75$?
b. $X < 70$?
c. $X < 80$ or $X > 110$?
d. Between what two X values (symmetrically distributed around the mean) are eighty percent of the values?

6.6 Given a normal distribution with $\mu = 50$ and $\sigma = 4$, what is the probability that
a. $X > 43$?
b. $X < 42$?
c. Five percent of the values are less than what X value?
d. Between what two X values (symmetrically distributed around the mean) are sixty percent of the values?

APPLYING THE CONCEPTS

6.7 According to the "Bottled Water Trends for 2014" report (**bit .ly/1gx5ub8**), the U.S. per capita consumption of bottled water in 2013 was 31.8 gallons. Assume that the per capita consumption of bottled water in the United States is approximately normally distributed with a mean of 31.8 gallons and a standard deviation of 10 gallons.
a. What is the probability that someone in the United States consumed more than 32 gallons of bottled water in 2013?

b. What is the probability that someone in the United States consumed between 10 and 20 gallons of bottled water in 2013?
c. What is the probability that someone in the United States consumed less than 10 gallons of bottled water in 2013?
d. Ninety-nine percent of the people in the United States consumed less than how many gallons of bottled water?

✓ SELF Test **6.8** Toby's Trucking Company determined that the distance traveled per truck per year is normally distributed, with a mean of 50 thousand miles and a standard deviation of 12 thousand miles.
a. What proportion of trucks can be expected to travel between 34 and 50 thousand miles in a year?
b. What percentage of trucks can be expected to travel either less than 30 or more than 60 thousand miles in a year?
c. How many miles will be traveled by at least eighty percent of the trucks?
d. What are your answers to (a) through (c) if the standard deviation is 10 thousand miles?

6.9 Consumers spent an average of $14.99 on a meal at a restaurant in 2013. (Data extracted from **bit.ly/1hObH22**.) Assume that the amount spent on a restaurant meal is normally distributed and that the standard deviation is $2.
a. What is the probability that a randomly selected person spent more than $15?
b. What is the probability that a randomly selected person spent between $10 and $12?
c. Between what two values will the middle Ninety-five percent of the amounts spent fall?

6.10 A set of final examination grades in an introductory statistics course is normally distributed, with a mean of 73 and a standard deviation of 8.
a. What is the probability that a student scored below 91 on this exam?
b. What is the probability that a student scored between 65 and 89?
c. The probability is five percent that a student taking the test scores higher than what grade?
d. If the professor grades on a curve (i.e., gives As to the top ten percent of the class, regardless of the score), are you better off with a grade of 81 on this exam or a grade of 68 on a different exam, where the mean is 62 and the standard deviation is 3? Show your answer statistically and explain.

6.11 A Nielsen study indicates that 18- to 24- year olds spend a mean of 135 minutes watching video on their smartphones per month. (Data extracted **bit.ly/1hF3BP2**.) Assume that the amount of time watching video on a smartphone per month is normally distributed and that the standard deviation is 15 minutes.
a. What is the probability that an 18- to 24-year-old spends less than 112 minutes watching video on his or her smartphone per month?
b. What is the probability that an 18- to 24-year-old spends between 112 and 158 minutes watching video on his or her smartphone per month?
c. What is the probability that an 18- to 24-year-old spends more than 158 minutes watching video on his or her smartphone per month?
d. One percent of all 18- to 24-year-olds will spend less than how many minutes watching video on his or her smartphone per month?

6.12 According to a speical issue of *Beverage Digest* (**bit. ly/1e9ORS3**), the U.S. per capita consumption of soft drinks in 2013 was 42.2 gallons. Assume that the per capita consumption of soft drinks in the United States is approximately normally distributed with a mean of 42.2 gallons and a standard deviation of 13 gallons.

a. What is the probability that someone in the United States consumed more than 60 gallons of soft drinks in 2013?

b. What is the probability that someone in the United States consumed between 15 and 30 gallons of soft drinks in 2013?

c. What is the probability that someone in the United States consumed less than 15 gallons of soft drinks in 2013?

d. Ninety-nine percent of the people in the United States consumed less than how many gallons of soft drinks?

6.13 Many manufacturing problems involve the matching of machine parts, such as shafts that fit into a valve hole. A particular design requires a shaft with a diameter of 22.000 mm, but shafts with diameters between 21.990 mm and 22.010 mm are acceptable. Suppose that the manufacturing process yields shafts with diameters normally distributed, with a mean of 22.002 mm and a standard deviation of 0.005 mm. For this process, what is

a. the proportion of shafts with a diameter between 21.99 mm and 22.00 mm?

b. the probability that a shaft is acceptable?

c. the diameter that will be exceeded by only two percent of the shafts?

d. What would be your answers in (a) through (c) if the standard deviation of the shaft diameters were 0.004 mm?

6.3 Evaluating Normality

As first stated in Section 6.2, the normal distribution has several important theoretical properties:

- It is symmetrical; thus, the mean and median are equal.
- It is bell-shaped; thus, the empirical rule applies.
- The interquartile range equals 1.33 standard deviations.
- The range is approximately equal to 6 standard deviations.

As Section 6.2 notes, many continuous variables used in business closely follow a normal distribution. To determine whether a set of data can be approximated by the normal distribution, you either compare the characteristics of the data with the theoretical properties of the normal distribution or construct a normal probability plot.

Comparing Data Characteristics to Theoretical Properties

Many continuous variables have characteristics that approximate theoretical properties. However, other continuous variables are often neither normally distributed nor approximately normally distributed. For such variables, the descriptive characteristics of the data are inconsistent with the properties of a normal distribution. One approach you can use to determine whether a variable follows a normal distribution is to compare the observed characteristics of the variable with what would be expected if the variable followed a normal distribution. To do so, you can

- Construct charts and observe their appearance. For small- or moderate-sized data sets, create a stem-and-leaf display or a boxplot. For large data sets, in addition, plot a histogram or polygon.
- Compute descriptive statistics and compare these statistics with the theoretical properties of the normal distribution. Compare the mean and median. Is the interquartile range approximately 1.33 times the standard deviation? Is the range approximately 6 times the standard deviation?
- Evaluate how the values are distributed. Determine whether approximately two-thirds of the values lie between the mean and ± 1 standard deviation. Determine whether approximately four-fifths of the values lie between the mean and ± 1.28 standard deviations. Determine whether approximately 19 out of every 20 values lie between the mean and ± 2 standard deviations.

For example, you can use these techniques to determine whether the one-year returns discussed in Chapters 2 and 3 (stored in **Retirement Funds**) follow a normal distribution.

Table 6.6 presents the descriptive statistics and the five-number summary for the one-year return percentage variable. Figure 6.18 presents the Excel and Minitab boxplots for the one-year return percentages.

TABLE 6.6

Descriptive Statistics and Five-Number Summary for the One-Year Return Percentages

Descriptive Statistics for 1YrReturn%		Five-Number Summary	
Mean	14.40	Minimum	−11.28
Median	14.48	First quartile	11.80
Mode	14.50	Median	14.48
Minimum	−11.28	Third quartile	16.81
Maximum	33.98	Maximum	33.98
Range	45.26		
Variance	23.57		
Standard deviation	4.86		
Coeff. of variation	33.72%		
Skewness	0.1036		
Kurtosis	4.2511		
Count	316		
Standard error	0.27		

FIGURE 6.18

Excel and Minitab boxplots for the one-year return percentages

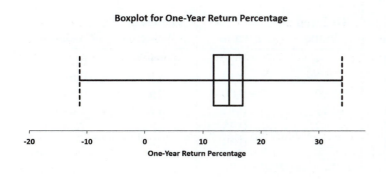

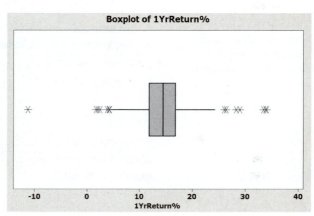

From Table 6.6, Figure 6.18, and from an ordered array of the returns (not shown here), you can make the following statements about the one-year returns:

- The mean of 14.40 is approximately the same as the median of 14.48. (In a normal distribution, the mean and median are equal.)
- The boxplot is slightly left-skewed. (The normal distribution is symmetrical.)
- The interquartile range of 5.01 is approximately 1.03 standard deviations. (In a normal distribution, the interquartile range is 1.33 standard deviations.)
- The range of 45.26 is equal to 9.32 standard deviations. (In a normal distribution, the range is approximately 6 standard deviations.)
- 76.27% of the returns are within ± 1 standard deviation of the mean. (In a normal distribution, 68.26% of the values lie within ± 1 standard deviation of the mean.)
- 85.13% of the returns are within ± 1.28 standard deviations of the mean. (In a normal distribution, 80% of the values lie within ± 1.28 standard deviations of the mean.)
- 94.94% of the returns are within ± 2 standard deviations of the mean. (In a normal distribution, 95.44% of the values lie within ± 2 standard deviations of the mean.)
- The skewness statistic is 0.1036 and the kurtosis statistic is 4.2511. (In a normal distribution, each of these statistics equals zero.)

Based on these statements and the criteria given on page 214, you can conclude that the one-year returns are slightly skewed and have somewhat more values within ±1 standard deviation of the mean than expected. The range is higher than what would be expected in a normal distribution, but this is mostly due to the single outlier at −11.28. The skewness is very slightly positive, and the kurtosis indicates a distribution that is much more peaked than a normal distribution. Thus, you can conclude that the data characteristics of the one-year returns differ somewhat from the theoretical properties of a normal distribution.

Constructing the Normal Probability Plot

A **normal probability plot** is a visual display that helps you evaluate whether the data are normally distributed. One common plot is called the **quantile–quantile plot**. To create this plot, you first transform each ordered value to a Z value. For example, if you have a sample of $n = 19$, the Z value for the smallest value corresponds to a cumulative area of

$$\frac{1}{n + 1} = \frac{1}{19 + 1} = \frac{1}{20} = 0.05$$

The Z value for a cumulative area of 0.05 (from Table E.2) is −1.65. Table 6.7 illustrates the entire set of Z values for a sample of $n = 19$.

TABLE 6.7

Ordered Values and Corresponding Z Values for a Sample of $n = 19$

Ordered Value	Z Value	Ordered Value	Z Value	Ordered Value	Z Value
1	−1.65	8	−0.25	14	0.52
2	−1.28	9	−0.13	15	0.67
3	−1.04	10	−0.00	16	0.84
4	−0.84	11	0.13	17	1.04
5	−0.67	12	0.25	18	1.28
6	−0.52	13	0.39	19	1.65
7	−0.39				

In a quantile–quantile plot, the Z values are plotted on the X axis, and the corresponding values of the variable are plotted on the Y axis. If the data are normally distributed, the values will plot along an approximately straight line. Figure 6.19 illustrates the typical shape of the quantile–quantile normal probability plot for a left-skewed distribution (Panel A), a normal distribution (Panel B), and a right-skewed distribution (Panel C). If the data are left-skewed, the curve will rise more rapidly at first and then level off. If the data are normally distributed, the points will plot along an approximately straight line. If the data are right-skewed, the data will rise more slowly at first and then rise at a faster rate for higher values of the variable being plotted.

FIGURE 6.19

Normal probability plots for a left-skewed distribution, a normal distribution, and a right-skewed distribution

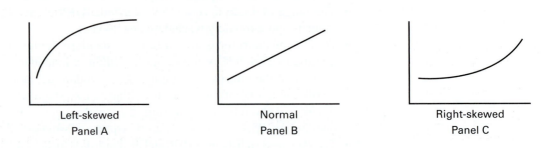

Left-skewed   Normal   Right-skewed
Panel A   Panel B   Panel C

Figure 6.20 shows Excel (quantile–quantile) and Minitab normal probability plots for the one-year returns. The Excel quantile–quantile plot shows a single extremely low value followed by the bulk of the points that approximately follow a straight line except for a few high values.

FIGURE 6.20

Excel (quantile–quantile) and Minitab normal probability plots for the one-year returns

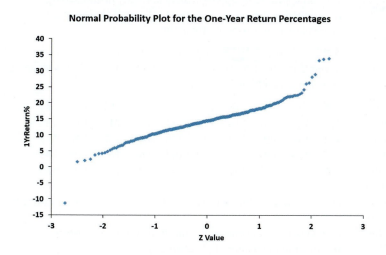
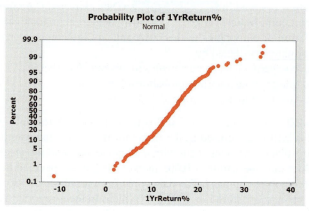

The Minitab normal probability plot has the one-year return percentage variable on the X axis and the cumulative percentage for a normal distribution on the Y axis. As with a quantile–quantile plot, the points will plot along an approximately straight line if the data are normally distributed. However, if the data are right-skewed, the curve will rise more rapidly at first and then level off. If the data are left-skewed, the data will rise more slowly at first and then rise at a faster rate for higher values of the variable being plotted. Observe that although the bulk of the points on the normal probability plot approximately follow a straight line, there are several high values that depart from a straight line, indicating a distribution that differs somewhat from a normal distribution.

Problems for Section 6.3

LEARNING THE BASICS

6.14 Show that for a sample of $n = 39$, the smallest and largest Z values are -1.96 and $+1.96$, and the middle (i.e., 20th) Z value is 0.00.

6.15 For a sample of $n = 6$, list the six Z values.

APPLYING THE CONCEPTS

 6.16 The file **SUV** contains the overall miles per gallon (MPG) of 2014 small SUVs ($n = 20$):

26 22 23 21 25 24 22 26 25 22
21 21 22 22 23 24 23 22 21 22

Source: Data extracted from "Which Car Is Right for You," *Consumer Reports*, April 2014, pp. 60–61.

Decide whether the data appear to be approximately normally distributed by
a. comparing data characteristics to theoretical properties.
b. constructing a normal probability plot.

6.17 As player salaries have increased, the cost of attending basketball games has increased dramatically. The file **NBACost2013** contains the cost of four averaged-priced tickets, two beers, four soft drinks, four hot dogs, two game programs, two adult-sized caps, and one parking space at each of the 30 National Basketball Association arenas during the 2013–2014 season. These costs were

240.04	434.96	382.00	203.06	456.60	271.74
321.18	319.10	262.40	324.08	336.05	227.36
395.20	542.00	212.16	472.20	309.30	273.98
208.48	659.92	295.40	263.10	266.40	344.92
308.18	268.28	338.00	321.63	280.98	249.22

Source: Data extracted "NBA FCI 13-14 Fan Cost Experience," **bit.ly/1nnu9rf**.

Decide whether the data appear to be approximately normally distributed by
a. comparing data characteristics to theoretical properties.
b. constructing a normal probability plot.

6.18 The file **Property Taxes** contains the property taxes per capita for the 50 states and the District of Columbia. Decide whether the data appear to be approximately normally distributed by
a. comparing data characteristics to theoretical properties.
b. constructing a normal probability plot.

6.19 Thirty companies comprise the DJIA. How big are these companies? One common method for measuring the size of a company is to use its market capitalization, which is computed by multiplying the number of stock shares by the price of a share of stock. On March 14, 2014, the market capitalization of these companies ranged from Traveler's $29.1 billion to ExxonMobil's $403.9 billion. The entire population of market capitalization values is stored in DowMarketCap . (Data extracted from **money .cnn.com**, March 14, 2014.) Decide whether the market capitalization of companies in the DJIA appears to be approximately normally distributed by

a. comparing data characteristics to theoretical properties.

b. constructing a normal probability plot.

c. constructing a histogram.

6.20 One operation of a mill is to cut pieces of steel into parts that will later be used as the frame for front seats in an automotive plant. The steel is cut with a diamond saw, and the resulting parts must be within ± 0.005 inch of the length specified by the automobile company. The data come from a sample of 100 steel parts and are stored in Steel . The measurement reported is the difference, in inches, between the actual length of the steel part, as measured by a laser measurement device, and the specified length of the steel part. Determine whether the data appear to be approximately normally distributed by

a. comparing data characteristics to theoretical properties.

b. constructing a normal probability plot.

6.21 The file CD Rate contains the yields for a one-year certificate of deposit (CD) and a five-year CD for 22 banks in the United States, as of March 12, 2014. (Data extracted from **www.Bankrate .com**, March 12, 2014.) For each type of investment, decide whether the data appear to be approximately normally distributed by

a. comparing data characteristics to theoretical properties.

b. constructing a normal probability plot.

6.22 The file Utility contains the electricity costs, in dollars, during July 2014 for a random sample of 50 one-bedroom apartments in a large city:

96	171	202	178	147	102	153	197	127	82
157	185	90	116	172	111	148	213	130	165
141	149	206	175	123	128	144	168	109	167
95	163	150	154	130	143	187	166	139	149
108	119	183	151	114	135	191	137	129	158

Decide whether the data appear to be approximately normally distributed by

a. comparing data characteristics to theoretical properties.

b. constructing a normal probability plot.

USING STATISTICS

Normal Downloading at MyTVLab, Revisited

In the Normal Downloading at MyTVLab scenario, you were a project manager for an online social media and video website. You sought to ensure that a video could be downloaded quickly by visitors to the website. By running experiments in the corporate offices, you determined that the amount of time, in seconds, that passes from clicking a download link until a video is fully displayed is a bell-shaped distribution with a mean download time of 7 seconds and standard deviation of 2 seconds. Using the normal distribution, you were able to calculate that approximately 84% of the download times are 9 seconds or less, and 95% of the download times are between 3.08 and 10.92 seconds.

Now that you understand how to compute probabilities from the normal distribution, you can evaluate download times of a video using different website designs. For example, if the standard deviation remained at 2 seconds, lowering the mean to 6 seconds would shift the entire distribution lower by

Cloki/Shutterstock

1 second. Thus, approximately 84% of the download times would be 8 seconds or less, and 95% of the download times would be between 2.08 and 9.92 seconds. Another change that could reduce long download times would be reducing the variation. For example, consider the case where the mean remained at the original 7 seconds but the standard deviation was reduced to 1 second. Again, approximately 84% of the download times would be 8 seconds or less, and 95% of the download times would be between 5.04 and 8.96 seconds.

SUMMARY

In this and the previous chapter, you have learned about mathematical models called probability distributions and how they can be used to solve business problems. In Chapter 5, you used discrete probability distributions in situations where the values come from a counting process such as the number of social media sites to which you belong or the number of tagged order forms in a report generated by an accounting information system. In this chapter, you learned about continuous probability distributions where the values come from a measuring process such as your height or the download time of a video.

Continuous probability distributions come in various shapes, but the most common and most important in business is the normal distribution. The normal distribution is symmetrical; thus, its mean and median are equal. It is also bell-shaped, and approximately 68.26% of its values are within ± 1 standard deviation of the mean, approximately 95.44% of its values are within ± 2 standard deviations of the mean, and approximately 99.73% of its values are within ± 3 standard deviations of the mean. Although many variables in business are closely approximated by the normal distribution, do not think that all variables can be approximated by the normal distribution.

In Section 6.3, you learned about various methods for evaluating normality in order to determine whether the normal distribution is a reasonable mathematical model to use in specific situations. Chapter 7 uses the normal distribution to develop the subject of statistical inference.

REFERENCES

1. Gunter, B. "Q-Q Plots." *Quality Progress* (February 1994): 81–86.
2. Levine, D. M., P. Ramsey, and R. Smidt. *Applied Statistics for Engineers and Scientists Using Microsoft Excel and Minitab*. Upper Saddle River, NJ: Prentice Hall, 2001.
3. *Microsoft Excel 2013*. Redmond, WA: Microsoft Corp., 2012.
4. Miller, J. "Earliest Known Uses of Some of the Words of Mathematics." **jeff560.tripod.com/mathword.html**.
5. *Minitab Release 16*. State College, PA: Minitab, Inc., 2010.
6. Pearl, R. "Karl Pearson, 1857–1936." *Journal of the American Statistical Association*, 31 (1936): 653–664.
7. Pearson, E. S. "Some Incidents in the Early History of Biometry and Statistics, 1890–94." *Biometrika* 52 (1965): 3–18.
8. Taleb, N. *The Black Swan*, 2nd ed. New York: Random House, 2010.
9. Walker, H. "The Contributions of Karl Pearson." *Journal of the American Statistical Association* 53 (1958): 11–22.

KEY EQUATIONS

Normal Probability Density Function

$$f(X) = \frac{1}{\sqrt{2\pi}\sigma}e^{-(1/2)[(X-\mu)/\sigma]^2} \qquad (6.1)$$

Z Transformation Formula

$$Z = \frac{X - \mu}{\sigma} \qquad (6.2)$$

Finding an X Value Associated with a Known Probability

$$X = \mu + Z\sigma \qquad (6.3)$$

KEY TERMS

cumulative standardized normal distribution 204
exponential distribution 201
normal distribution 201
normal probability plot 216

probability density function 201
probability density function for the normal distribution 203
quantile–quantile plot 216

standardized normal variable 203
transformation formula 203
uniform distribution 201

CHECKING YOUR UNDERSTANDING

6.23 Why is only one normal distribution table such as Table E.2 needed to find any probability under the normal curve?

6.24 How do you find the area between two values under the normal curve?

6.25 How do you find the X value that corresponds to a given percentile of the normal distribution?

6.26 What are some of the distinguishing properties of a normal distribution?

6.27 How does the shape of the normal distribution differ from the shapes of the uniform and exponential distributions?

6.28 How can you use the normal probability plot to evaluate whether a set of data is normally distributed?

CHAPTER REVIEW PROBLEMS

6.29 An industrial sewing machine uses ball bearings that are targeted to have a diameter of 0.75 inch. The lower and upper specification limits under which the ball bearings can operate are 0.74 inch and 0.76 inch, respectively. Past experience has indicated that the actual diameter of the ball bearings is approximately normally distributed, with a mean of 0.753 inch and a standard deviation of 0.004 inch. What is the probability that a ball bearing is
a. between the target and the actual mean?
b. between the lower specification limit and the target?
c. above the upper specification limit?
d. below the lower specification limit?
e. Of all the ball bearings, 93% of the diameters are greater than what value?

6.30 The fill amount in 2-liter soft drink bottles is normally distributed, with a mean of 2.0 liters and a standard deviation of 0.05 liter. If bottles contain less than 95% of the listed net content (1.90 liters, in this case), the manufacturer may be subject to penalty by the state office of consumer affairs. Bottles that have a net content above 2.10 liters may cause excess spillage upon opening. What proportion of the bottles will contain
a. between 1.90 and 2.0 liters?
b. between 1.90 and 2.10 liters?
c. below 1.90 liters or above 2.10 liters?
d. At least how much soft drink is contained in 99% of the bottles?
e. Ninety-nine percent of the bottles contain an amount that is between which two values (symmetrically distributed) around the mean?

6.31 In an effort to reduce the number of bottles that contain less than 1.90 liters, the bottler in Problem 6.30 sets the filling machine so that the mean is 2.02 liters. Under these circumstances, what are your answers in Problem 6.30 (a) through (e)?

6.32 An Ipsos MediaCT study indicates that mobile device owners who used their mobile device while shopping for consumer electronics spent an average of $1,539 on consumer electronics in the past six months. (Data extracted from **iab.net/showrooming**.) Assume that the amount spent on consumer electronics in the last six months is normally distributed and that the standard deviation is $500.
a. What is the probability that a mobile device owner who used his or her mobile device while shopping for consumer electronics spent less than $1,000 on consumer electronics?
b. What is the probability that a mobile device owner who used his or her mobile device while shopping for consumer electronics spent between $2,500 and $3,000 on consumer electronics?

c. Ninety percent of the amounts spent on consumer electronics by mobile device owners who used their mobile device while shopping for consumer electronics are less than what value?
d. Eighty percent of the amounts spent on consumer electronics by mobile device owners who used their mobile device while shopping for consumer electronics are between what two values symmetrically distributed around the mean?

6.33 The file **DomesticBeer** contains the percentage alcohol, number of calories per 12 ounces, and number of carbohydrates (in grams) per 12 ounces for 156 of the best-selling domestic beers in the United States. Determine whether each of these variables appears to be approximately normally distributed. Support your decision through the use of appropriate statistics and graphs. (Data extracted from **www.Beer100.com**, March 12, 2014.)

6.34 The evening manager of a restaurant was very concerned about the length of time some customers were waiting in line to be seated. She also had some concern about the seating times—that is, the length of time between when a customer is seated and the time he or she leaves the restaurant. Over the course of one week, 100 customers (no more than 1 per party) were randomly selected, and their waiting and seating times (in minutes) were recorded in **Wait**.
a. Think about your favorite restaurant. Do you think waiting times more closely resemble a uniform, an exponential, or a normal distribution?
b. Again, think about your favorite restaurant. Do you think seating times more closely resemble a uniform, an exponential, or a normal distribution?
c. Construct a histogram and a normal probability plot of the waiting times. Do you think these waiting times more closely resemble a uniform, an exponential, or a normal distribution?
d. Construct a histogram and a normal probability plot of the seating times. Do you think these seating times more closely resemble a uniform, an exponential, or a normal distribution?

6.35 The major stock market indexes had strong results in 2013. The mean one-year return for stocks in the S&P 500, a group of 500 very large companies, was +29.6%. The mean one-year return for the NASDAQ, a group of 3,200 small and medium-sized companies, was +38.3%. Historically, the one-year returns are approximately normally distributed, the standard deviation in the S&P 500 is approximately 20%, and the standard deviation in the NASDAQ is approximately 30%.

a. What is the probability that a stock in the S&P 500 gained value in 2013?

b. What is the probability that a stock in the S&P 500 gained 10% or more in 2013?

c. What is the probability that a stock in the S&P 500 lost 20% or more in 2013?

d. What is the probability that a stock in the S&P 500 lost 30% or more in 2013?

e. Repeat (a) through (d) for a stock in the NASDAQ.

f. Write a short summary on your findings. Be sure to include a discussion of the risks associated with a large standard deviation.

6.36 Interns report that when deciding on where to work, career growth, salary and compensation, location and commute, and company culture and values are important factors to them. According to the Glassdoor blog's "25 Highest Paying Companies for Interns 2014," **bit.ly/1gx6vjx**, the mean monthly pay of interns at Intel is $4,648. Suppose that the intern monthly pay is normally distributed, with a standard deviation of $400. What is the probability that the monthly pay of an intern at Intel is

a. less than $4,500?

b. between $4,300 and $4,700?

c. above $5,200?

d. Ninety-nine percent of the intern monthly pays are higher than what value?

e. Ninety-five percent of the intern monthly pays are between what two values, symmetrically distributed around the mean?

6.37 According to the same Glassdoor blog report mentioned in the previous question, the mean monthly pay for interns at Facebook is $6,213. Suppose that the intern monthly pay is normally distributed, with a standard deviation of $500. What is the probability that the monthly pay of an intern at Facebook is

a. less than $4,500?

b. between $4,300 and $4,700?

c. above $5,200?

d. Ninety-nine percent of the intern monthly pays are higher than what value?

e. Ninety-five percent of the intern monthly pays are between what two values, symmetrically distributed around the mean?

f. Compare the results for the Intel interns computed in Problem 6.36 to those of the Facebook interns.

6.38 (Class Project) One theory about the daily changes in the closing price of stock is that these changes follow a *random walk*—that is, these daily events are independent of each other and move upward or downward in a random manner—and can be approximated by a normal distribution. To test this theory, use either a newspaper or the Internet to select one company traded on the NYSE, one company traded on the American Stock Exchange, and one company traded on the NASDAQ and then do the following:

1. Record the daily closing stock price of each of these companies for six consecutive weeks (so that you have 30 values per company).

2. Compute the daily changes in the closing stock price of each of these companies for six consecutive weeks (so that you have 30 values per company).

Note: The random-walk theory pertains to the daily changes in the closing stock price, not the daily closing stock price.

For each of your six data sets, decide whether the data are approximately normally distributed by

a. constructing the stem-and-leaf display, histogram or polygon, and boxplot.

b. comparing data characteristics to theoretical properties.

c. constructing a normal probability plot.

d. Discuss the results of (a) through (c). What can you say about your three stocks with respect to daily closing prices and daily changes in closing prices? Which, if any, of the data sets are approximately normally distributed?

CASES FOR CHAPTER 6

Managing Ashland MultiComm Services

The AMS technical services department has embarked on a quality improvement effort. Its first project relates to maintaining the target upload speed for its Internet service subscribers. Upload speeds are measured on a standard scale in which the target value is 1.0. Data collected over the past year indicate that the upload speed is approximately normally distributed, with a mean of 1.005 and a standard deviation of 0.10. Each day, one upload speed is measured. The upload speed is considered acceptable if the measurement on the standard scale is between 0.95 and 1.05.

1. Assuming that the distribution has not changed from what it was in the past year, what is the probability that the upload speed is

a. less than 1.0?

b. between 0.95 and 1.0?

c. between 1.0 and 1.05?

d. less than 0.95 or greater than 1.05?

2. The objective of the operations team is to reduce the probability that the upload speed is below 1.0. Should the team focus on process improvement that increases the mean upload speed to 1.05 or on process improvement that reduces the standard deviation of the upload speed to 0.075? Explain.

Digital Case

Apply your knowledge about the normal distribution in this Digital Case, which extends the Using Statistics scenario from this chapter.

To satisfy concerns of potential customers, the management of MyTVLab has undertaken a research project to learn how much time it takes users to load a complex video features page. The research team has collected data and has made some claims based on the assertion that the data follow a normal distribution.

Open **MTL_QRTStudy.pdf**, which documents the work of a quality response team at MyTVLab. Read the internal report that documents the work of the team and their conclusions. Then answer the following:

1. Can the collected data be approximated by the normal distribution?
2. Review and evaluate the conclusions made by the MyTVLab research team. Which conclusions are correct? Which ones are incorrect?
3. If MyTVLab could improve the mean time by 5 seconds, how would the probabilities change?

CardioGood Fitness

Return to the CardioGood Fitness case (stored in **CardioGood Fitness**) first presented on page 79.

1. For each CardioGood Fitness treadmill product line, determine whether the age, income, usage, and the number of miles the customer expects to walk/run each week can be approximated by the normal distribution.

2. Write a report to be presented to the management of CardioGood Fitness, detailing your findings.

More Descriptive Choices Follow-up

Follow up the More Descriptive Choices Revisited Using Statistics scenario on page 136 by constructing normal probability plots for the 3-year return percentages, 5-year return percentages, and 10-year return percentages for the sample of 316 retirement funds stored in **Retirement Funds**. In your analysis, examine differences between the growth and value funds as well as the differences among the small, mid-cap, and large market cap funds.

Clear Mountain State Student Surveys

1. The Student News Service at Clear Mountain State University (CMSU) has decided to gather data about the undergraduate students who attend CMSU. They create and distribute a survey of 14 questions and receive responses from 62 undergraduates (stored in **UndergradSurvey**). For each numerical variable in the survey, decide whether the variable is approximately normally distributed by
   a. comparing data characteristics to theoretical properties.
   b. constructing a normal probability plot.
   c. writing a report summarizing your conclusions.

2. The dean of students at CMSU has learned about the undergraduate survey and has decided to undertake a similar survey for graduate students at CMSU. She creates and distributes a survey of 14 questions and receives responses from 44 graduate students (stored in **GradSurvey**). For each numerical variable in the survey, decide whether the variable is approximately normally distributed by
   a. comparing data characteristics to theoretical properties.
   b. constructing a normal probability plot.
   c. writing a report summarizing your conclusions.

CHAPTER 6 EXCEL GUIDE

EG6.1 CONTINUOUS PROBABILITY DISTRIBUTIONS

There are no Excel Guide instructions for this section.

EG6.2 The NORMAL DISTRIBUTION

Key Technique Use the **NORM.DIST(*X value*, *mean*, *standard deviation*, True)** function to compute normal probabilities and use the **NORM.S.INV(*percentage*)** function and the STANDARDIZE function (see Section EG3.2) to compute the Z value.

Example Compute the normal probabilities for Examples 6.1 through 6.3 on pages 206 and 207 and the X and Z values for Examples 6.4 and 6.5 on pages 209 and 210.

PHStat Use **Normal**.
For the example, select **PHStat → Probability & Prob. Distributions → Normal**. In this procedure's dialog box (shown below):

1. Enter **7** as the **Mean** and **2** as the **Standard Deviation**.
2. Check **Probability for: X <=** and enter **7** in its box.
3. Check **Probability for: X >** and enter **9** in its box.
4. Check **Probability for range** and enter **5** in the first box and **9** in the second box.
5. Check **X for Cumulative Percentage** and enter **10** in its box.
6. Check **X Values for Percentage** and enter **95** in its box.
7. Enter a **Title** and click **OK**.

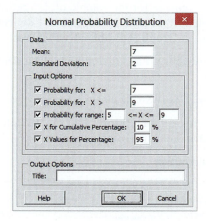

In-Depth Excel Use the **COMPUTE worksheet** of the **Normal workbook** as a template.
The worksheet already contains the data for solving the problems in Examples 6.1 through 6.5. For other problems, change the values for the **Mean**, **Standard Deviation**, **X Value**, **From X Value**, **To X Value**, **Cumulative Percentage**, and/or **Percentage**.

Read the SHORT TAKES for Chapter 6 for an explanation of the formulas found in the COMPUTE worksheet (shown in the **COMPUTE_FORMULAS worksheet**). If you use an Excel version older than Excel 2010, use the COMPUTE_OLDER worksheet.

EG6.3 EVALUATING NORMALITY

Comparing Data Characteristics to Theoretical Properties

Use the Sections EG3.1 through EG3.3 instructions to compare data characteristics to theoretical properties.

Constructing the Normal Probability Plot

Key Technique Use an Excel Scatter (X, Y) chart with Z values computed using the NORM.S.INV function.

Example Construct the normal probability plot for the one-year return percentages for the sample of 316 retirement funds that is shown in Figure 6.20 on page 217.

PHStat Use **Normal Probability Plot**.
For the example, open to the **DATA worksheet** of the **Retirement Funds workbook**. Select **PHStat → Probability & Prob. Distributions → Normal Probability Plot**. In the procedure's dialog box (shown below):

1. Enter **I1:I317** as the **Variable Cell Range**.
2. Check **First cell contains label**.
3. Enter a **Title** and click **OK**.

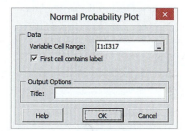

In addition to the chart sheet containing the normal probability plot, the procedure creates a plot data worksheet identical to the PlotData worksheet discussed in the *In-Depth Excel* instructions.

In-Depth Excel Use the worksheets of the **NPP workbook** as templates.
The **NormalPlot chart sheet** displays a normal probability plot using the rank, the proportion, the Z value, and the variable found in the **PLOT_DATA worksheet**. The PLOT_DATA worksheet already contains the one-year return percentages for the example. To construct a plot for a different variable, paste the *sorted* values for that variable in **column D** of the **PLOT_DATA worksheet**. Adjust the number of ranks in **column A** and the divisor in the formulas in **column B** to compute cumulative percentages to reflect the quantity $n + 1$ (317 for the example). (Column C formulas use the NORM.S.INV function to compute the Z values for those cumulative percentages.)

If you have fewer than 316 values, delete rows from the bottom up. If you have more than 316 values, select row 317, right-click, click **Insert** in the shortcut menu, and copy down the formulas in columns B and C to the new rows. To create your own normal probability plot for the 1YrReturn% variable, open to the PLOT_DATA worksheet and select the cell range **C1:D317**. Then select **Insert → Scatter** and select the **first Scatter** gallery item (that shows only points and is labeled with **Scatter** or **Scatter with only Markers**). Relocate the chart to a chart sheet, turn off

the chart legend and gridlines, add axis titles, and modify the chart title by using the instructions in Appendix Section B.6.

If you use an Excel version older than Excel 2010, use the PLOT_OLDER worksheet and the NormalPlot_OLDER chart sheet.

CHAPTER 6 MINITAB GUIDE

MG6.1 CONTINUOUS PROBABILITY DISTRIBUTIONS

There are no Minitab Guide instructions for this section.

MG6.2 The NORMAL DISTRIBUTION

Use **Normal**.
For example, to compute the normal probability for Example 6.1 on page 206, open to a new worksheet. Enter **X Value** as the name of column **C1** and enter **9** in the row 1 cell of that column. Select **Calc → Probability Distributions → Normal**. In the Normal Distribution dialog box (shown below):

1. Click **Cumulative probability**.
2. Enter **7** in the **Mean** box.
3. Enter **2** in the **Standard deviation** box.
4. Click **Input column** and enter **C1** in its box and press **Tab**.
5. Enter **C2** in the first **Optional storage** box.
6. Click **OK**.

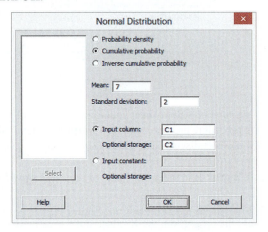

Minitab places in the row 1 cell of column C2 the probability for a download time that is *less than* 9 seconds with $\mu = 7$ and $\sigma = 2$. To compute the Example 6.1 probability for a download time that is *greater than* 9 seconds, select **Calc → Calculator**. Enter C3 in the Store result in variable box, enter $1 - C2$ in the Expression box, and click OK. The probability appears in row 1 of column C3.

To compute the normal probability for Example 6.4 on page 209, open to a new worksheet. Enter **Cumulative Percentage** as the name of column **C1** and enter **0.1** in the row 1 cell of that column. Select **Calc → Probability Distributions → Normal**. In the Normal Distribution dialog box:

1. Click **Inverse cumulative probability**.
2. Enter **7** in the **Mean** box.

3. Enter **2** in the **Standard deviation** box.
4. Click **Input column** and enter **C1** in its box and press **Tab**.
5. Enter **C2** in the first **Optional storage** box.
6. Click **OK**.

Minitab displays the Example 6.4 *Z* value corresponding to a cumulative area of 0.10. Skip step 5 in either set of instructions to create the results shown in Figure 6.17 on page 211.

MG6.3 EVALUATING NORMALITY

Comparing Data Characteristics to Theoretical Properties

Use instructions in Sections MG3.1 through MG3.3 to compare data characteristics to theoretical properties.

Constructing the Normal Probability Plot

Use **Probability Plot**.
For example, to construct the normal probability plot for the one-year return percentage for the sample of 316 retirement funds shown in Figure 6.20 on page 217, open to the **Retirement Funds worksheet**. Select **Graph → Probability Plot** and:

1. In the Probability Plots dialog box, click **Single** and then click **OK**.

In the Probability Plot - Single dialog box (shown below):

2. Double-click **C9 1YrReturn%** in the variables list to add **'1YrReturn%'** to the **Graph variables** box.

3. Click **Distribution**.

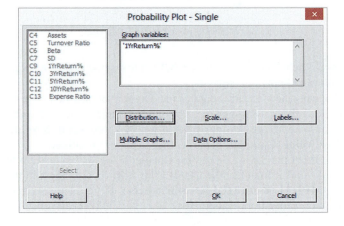

In the Probability Plot - Distribution dialog box (shown below):

4. Click the **Distribution** tab and select **Normal** from the **Distribution** drop-down list.

5. Click the **Data Display** tab. Click **Symbols only**. If the **Show confidence interval** check box is not disabled (as shown below), clear this check box.

6. Click **OK**.

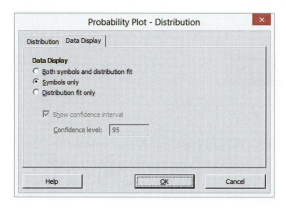

7. Back in the Probability Plot - Single dialog box, click **Scale**.

8. Click the **Gridlines** tab. Clear all check boxes and then click **OK**.

9. Back in the Probability Plot - Single dialog box, click **OK**.

Sampling Distributions

OBJECTIVES

Learn about the concept of the sampling distribution

Compute probabilities related to the sample mean and the sample proportion

Understand the importance of the Central Limit Theorem

USING STATISTICS

Sampling Oxford Cereals

The automated production line at the Oxford Cereals main plant fills thousands of boxes of cereal during each shift. As the plant operations manager, you are responsible for monitoring the amount of cereal placed in each box. To be consistent with package labeling, boxes should contain a mean of 368 grams of cereal. Because of the speed of the process, the cereal weight varies from box to box, causing some boxes to be underfilled and others to be overfilled. If the automated process fails to work as intended, the mean weight in the boxes could vary too much from the label weight of 368 grams to be acceptable.

Because weighing every single box is too time-consuming, costly, and inefficient, you must take a sample of boxes. For each sample you select, you plan to weigh the individual boxes and calculate a sample mean. You need to determine the probability that such a sample mean could have been randomly selected from a population whose mean is 368 grams. Based on your analysis, you will have to decide whether to maintain, alter, or shut down the cereal-filling process.

Corbis

I n Chapter 6, you used the normal distribution to study the distribution of video download times from the MyTVLab website. In this chapter, you need to make a decision about a cereal-filling process, based on the weights of a sample of cereal boxes packaged at Oxford Cereals. You will learn about sampling distributions and how to use them to solve business problems.

7.1 Sampling Distributions

In many applications, you want to make inferences that are based on statistics calculated from samples to estimate the values of population parameters. In the next two sections, you will learn about how the sample mean (a statistic) is used to estimate the population mean (a parameter) and how the sample proportion (a statistic) is used to estimate the population proportion (a parameter). Your main concern when making a statistical inference is reaching conclusions about a population, *not* about a sample. For example, a political pollster is interested in the sample results only as a way of estimating the actual proportion of the votes that each candidate will receive from the population of voters. Likewise, as plant operations manager for Oxford Cereals, you are only interested in using the mean weight calculated from a sample of cereal boxes to estimate the mean weight of a population of boxes.

In practice, you select a single random sample of a predetermined size from the population. Hypothetically, to use the sample statistic to estimate the population parameter, you could examine *every* possible sample of a given size that could occur. A **sampling distribution** is the distribution of the results if you actually selected all possible samples. The single result you obtain in practice is just one of the results in the sampling distribution.

7.2 Sampling Distribution of the Mean

In Chapter 3, several measures of central tendency, including the mean, median, and mode, were discussed. For several reasons, the mean is the most widely used measure of central tendency, and the sample mean is often used to estimate the population mean. The **sampling distribution of the mean** is the distribution of all possible sample means if you select all possible samples of a given size.

The Unbiased Property of the Sample Mean

LEARN MORE

Learn more about the unbiased property of the sample mean in the SHORT TAKES for Chapter 7.

The sample mean is **unbiased** because the mean of all the possible sample means (of a given sample size, n) is equal to the population mean, μ. A simple example concerning a population of four administrative assistants demonstrates this property. Each assistant is asked to apply the same set of updates to a human resources database. Table 7.1 presents the number of errors made by each of the administrative assistants. This population distribution is shown in Figure 7.1.

TABLE 7.1

Number of Errors Made by Each of Four Administrative Assistants

Administrative Assistant	Number of Errors
Ann	$X_1 = 3$
Bob	$X_2 = 2$
Carla	$X_3 = 1$
Dave	$X_4 = 4$

FIGURE 7.1

Number of errors made by a population of four administrative assistants

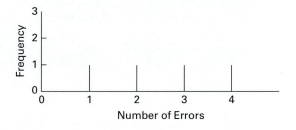

When you have data from a population, you compute the population mean by using Equation (7.1), and you compute the population standard deviation, σ, by using Equation (7.2).

Recall from Section 3.4 that the population mean is the sum of the values in the population divided by the population size, N.

POPULATION MEAN

$$\mu = \frac{\sum_{i=1}^{N} X_i}{N} \tag{7.1}$$

POPULATION STANDARD DEVIATION

$$\sigma = \sqrt{\frac{\sum_{i=1}^{N} (X_i - \mu)^2}{N}} \tag{7.2}$$

For the data of Table 7.1,

$$\mu = \frac{3 + 2 + 1 + 4}{4} = 2.5 \text{ errors}$$

and

$$\sigma = \sqrt{\frac{(3 - 2.5)^2 + (2 - 2.5)^2 + (1 - 2.5)^2 + (4 - 2.5)^2}{4}} = 1.12 \text{ errors}$$

If you select samples of two administrative assistants *with* replacement from this population, there are 16 possible samples ($N^n = 4^2 = 16$). Table 7.2 lists the 16 possible sample outcomes. If you average all 16 of these sample means, the mean of these values is equal to 2.5, which is also the mean of the population, μ.

TABLE 7.2

All 16 Samples of $n = 2$ Administrative Assistants from a Population of $N = 4$ Administrative Assistants When Sampling with Replacement

Sample	Administrative Assistants	Sample Outcomes	Sample Mean
1	Ann, Ann	3, 3	$\overline{X}_1 = 3$
2	Ann, Bob	3, 2	$\overline{X}_2 = 2.5$
3	Ann, Carla	3, 1	$\overline{X}_3 = 2$
4	Ann, Dave	3, 4	$\overline{X}_4 = 3.5$
5	Bob, Ann	2, 3	$\overline{X}_5 = 2.5$
6	Bob, Bob	2, 2	$\overline{X}_6 = 2$
7	Bob, Carla	2, 1	$\overline{X}_7 = 1.5$
8	Bob, Dave	2, 4	$\overline{X}_8 = 3$
9	Carla, Ann	1, 3	$\overline{X}_9 = 2$
10	Carla, Bob	1, 2	$\overline{X}_{10} = 1.5$
11	Carla, Carla	1, 1	$\overline{X}_{11} = 1$
12	Carla, Dave	1, 4	$\overline{X}_{12} = 2.5$
13	Dave, Ann	4, 3	$\overline{X}_{13} = 3.5$
14	Dave, Bob	4, 2	$\overline{X}_{14} = 3$
15	Dave, Carla	4, 1	$\overline{X}_{15} = 2.5$
16	Dave, Dave	4, 4	$\overline{X}_{16} = 4$
			$\mu_{\overline{X}} = 2.5$

Because the mean of the 16 sample means is equal to the population mean, the sample mean is an unbiased estimator of the population mean. Therefore, although you do not know how close the sample mean of any particular sample selected is to the population mean, you are assured that the mean of all the possible sample means that could have been selected is equal to the population mean.

Standard Error of the Mean

Figure 7.2 illustrates the variation in the sample means when selecting all 16 possible samples.

FIGURE 7.2

Sampling distribution of the mean, based on all possible samples containing two administrative assistants

Source: Data are from Table 7.2.

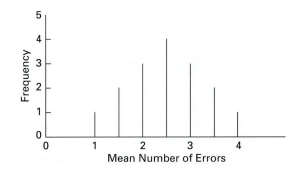

In this small example, although the sample means vary from sample to sample, depending on which two administrative assistants are selected, the sample means do not vary as much as the individual values in the population. That the sample means are less variable than the individual values in the population follows directly from the fact that each sample mean averages together all the values in the sample. A population consists of individual outcomes that can take on a wide range of values, from extremely small to extremely large. However, if a sample contains an extreme value, although this value will have an effect on the sample mean, the effect is reduced because the value is averaged with all the other values in the sample. As the sample size increases, the effect of a single extreme value becomes smaller because it is averaged with more values.

The value of the standard deviation of all possible sample means, called the **standard error of the mean**, expresses how the sample means vary from sample to sample. As the sample size increases, the standard error of the mean decreases by a factor equal to the square root of the sample size. Equation (7.3) defines the standard error of the mean when sampling *with* replacement or sampling *without* replacement from large or infinite populations.

> **Student Tip**
> Remember, the standard error of the mean measures variation among the means not the individual values.

STANDARD ERROR OF THE MEAN

The standard error of the mean, $\sigma_{\bar{X}}$, is equal to the standard deviation in the population, σ, divided by the square root of the sample size, n.

$$\sigma_{\bar{X}} = \frac{\sigma}{\sqrt{n}}$$

(7.3)

Example 7.1 computes the standard error of the mean when the sample selected without replacement contains less than 5% of the entire population.

EXAMPLE 7.1

Computing the Standard Error of the Mean

Returning to the cereal-filling process described in the Using Statistics scenario on page 226, if you randomly select a sample of 25 boxes without replacement from the thousands of boxes filled during a shift, the sample contains a very small portion of the population. Given that the standard deviation of the cereal-filling process is 15 grams, compute the standard error of the mean.

SOLUTION Using Equation (7.3) with $n = 25$ and $\sigma = 15$ the standard error of the mean is

$$\sigma_{\bar{X}} = \frac{\sigma}{\sqrt{n}} = \frac{15}{\sqrt{25}} = \frac{15}{5} = 3$$

The variation in the sample means for samples of $n = 25$ is much less than the variation in the individual boxes of cereal (i.e., $\sigma_{\bar{X}} = 3$, while $\sigma = 15$).

Sampling from Normally Distributed Populations

Now that the concept of a sampling distribution has been introduced and the standard error of the mean has been defined, what distribution will the sample mean, $\bar{X}$, follow? If you are sampling from a population that is normally distributed with mean μ and standard deviation σ, then regardless of the sample size, n, the sampling distribution of the mean is normally distributed, with mean $\mu_{\bar{X}} = \mu$, and standard error of the mean $\sigma_{\bar{X}} = \sigma/\sqrt{n}$.

In the simplest case, if you take samples of size $n = 1$, each possible sample mean is a single value from the population because

$$\bar{X} = \frac{\sum\limits_{i=1}^{n} X_i}{n} = \frac{X_1}{1} = X_1$$

Therefore, if the population is normally distributed, with mean μ and standard deviation σ, the sampling distribution $\bar{X}$ for samples of $n = 1$ must also follow the normal distribution, with mean $\mu_{\bar{X}} = \mu$ and standard error of the mean $\sigma_{\bar{X}} = \sigma/\sqrt{1} = \sigma$. In addition, as the sample size increases, the sampling distribution of the mean still follows a normal distribution, with $\mu_{\bar{X}} = \mu$, but the standard error of the mean decreases so that a larger proportion of sample means are closer to the population mean. Figure 7.3 illustrates this reduction in variability.

FIGURE 7.3

Sampling distributions of the mean from 500 samples of sizes $n = 1, 2, 4, 8, 16,$ and 32 selected from a normal population

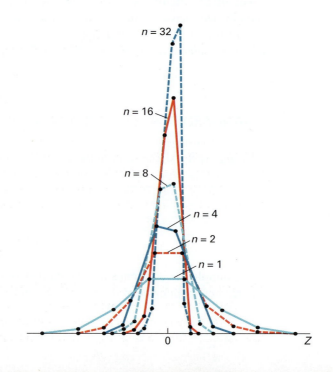

[1]Remember that "only" 500 samples out of an infinite number of samples have been selected, so that the sampling distributions shown are only approximations of the population distribution.

Note that 500 samples of size 1, 2, 4, 8, 16, and 32 were randomly selected from a normally distributed population. From the polygons in Figure 7.3, you can see that, although the sampling distribution of the mean is approximately[1] normal for each sample size, the sample means are distributed more tightly around the population mean as the sample size increases.

To further examine the concept of the sampling distribution of the mean, consider the Using Statistics scenario described on page 226. The packaging equipment that is filling 368-gram boxes of cereal is set so that the amount of cereal in a box is normally distributed, with a mean of 368 grams. From past experience, you know the population standard deviation for this filling process is 15 grams.

If you randomly select a sample of 25 boxes from the many thousands that are filled in a day and the mean weight is computed for this sample, what type of result could you expect? For example, do you think that the sample mean could be 368 grams? 200 grams? 365 grams?

The sample acts as a miniature representation of the population, so if the values in the population are normally distributed, the values in the sample should be approximately normally distributed. Thus, if the population mean is 368 grams, the sample mean has a good chance of being close to 368 grams.

How can you determine the probability that the sample of 25 boxes will have a mean below 365 grams? From the normal distribution (Section 6.2), you know that you can find the area below any value X by converting to standardized Z values:

$$Z = \frac{X - \mu}{\sigma}$$

In the examples in Section 6.2, you studied how any single value, X, differs from the population mean. Now, in this example, you want to study how a sample mean, $\overline{X}$, differs from the population mean. Substituting $\overline{X}$ for X, $\mu_{\overline{X}}$ for μ, and $\sigma_{\overline{X}}$ for σ in the equation above results in Equation (7.4).

FINDING Z FOR THE SAMPLING DISTRIBUTION OF THE MEAN

The Z value is equal to the difference between the sample mean, $\overline{X}$, and the population mean, μ, divided by the standard error of the mean, $\sigma_{\overline{X}}$.

$$Z = \frac{\overline{X} - \mu_{\overline{X}}}{\sigma_{\overline{X}}} = \frac{\overline{X} - \mu}{\frac{\sigma}{\sqrt{n}}} \tag{7.4}$$

To find the area below 365 grams, from Equation (7.4),

$$Z = \frac{\overline{X} - \mu_{\overline{X}}}{\sigma_{\overline{X}}} = \frac{365 - 368}{\frac{15}{\sqrt{25}}} = \frac{-3}{3} = -1.00$$

The area corresponding to $Z = -1.00$ in Table E.2 is 0.1587. Therefore, 15.87% of all the possible samples of 25 boxes have a sample mean below 365 grams.

The preceding statement is not the same as saying that a certain percentage of *individual* boxes will contain less than 365 grams of cereal. You compute that percentage as follows:

$$Z = \frac{X - \mu}{\sigma} = \frac{365 - 368}{15} = \frac{-3}{15} = -0.20$$

The area corresponding to $Z = -0.20$ in Table E.2 is 0.4207. Therefore, 42.07% of the *individual* boxes are expected to contain less than 365 grams. Comparing these results, you see that many more *individual boxes* than *sample means* are below 365 grams. This result is explained by the fact that each sample consists of 25 different values, some small and some large. The averaging process dilutes the importance of any individual value, particularly when the sample size is large. Therefore, the chance that the sample mean of 25 boxes is very different from the population mean is less than the chance that a *single* box is very different from the population mean.

Examples 7.2 and 7.3 show how these results are affected by using different sample sizes.

EXAMPLE 7.2

The Effect of Sample Size, *n*, on the Computation of $\sigma_{\bar{X}}$

How is the standard error of the mean affected by increasing the sample size from 25 to 100 boxes?

SOLUTION If $n = 100$ boxes, then using Equation (7.3) on page 229,

$$\sigma_{\bar{X}} = \frac{\sigma}{\sqrt{n}} = \frac{15}{\sqrt{100}} = \frac{15}{10} = 1.5$$

The fourfold increase in the sample size from 25 to 100 reduces the standard error of the mean by half—from 3 grams to 1.5 grams. This demonstrates that taking a larger sample results in less variability in the sample means from sample to sample.

EXAMPLE 7.3

The Effect of Sample Size, *n*, on the Clustering of Means in the Sampling Distribution

If you select a sample of 100 boxes, what is the probability that the sample mean is below 365 grams?

SOLUTION Using Equation (7.4) on page 231,

$$Z = \frac{\bar{X} - \mu_{\bar{X}}}{\sigma_{\bar{X}}} = \frac{365 - 368}{\dfrac{15}{\sqrt{100}}} = \frac{-3}{1.5} = -2.00$$

From Table E.2, the area less than $Z = -2.00$ is 0.0228. Therefore, 2.28% of the samples of 100 boxes have means below 365 grams, as compared with 15.87% for samples of 25 boxes.

Sometimes you need to find the interval that contains a specific proportion of the sample means. To do so, you determine a distance below and above the population mean containing a specific area of the normal curve. From Equation (7.4) on page 231,

$$Z = \frac{\bar{X} - \mu}{\dfrac{\sigma}{\sqrt{n}}}$$

Solving for $\bar{X}$ results in Equation (7.5).

FINDING $\bar{X}$ FOR THE SAMPLING DISTRIBUTION OF THE MEAN

$$\bar{X} = \mu + Z\frac{\sigma}{\sqrt{n}} \tag{7.5}$$

Example 7.4 illustrates the use of Equation (7.5).

EXAMPLE 7.4

Determining the Interval That Includes a Fixed Proportion of the Sample Means

In the cereal-filling example, find an interval symmetrically distributed around the population mean that will include 95% of the sample means, based on samples of 25 boxes.

SOLUTION If 95% of the sample means are in the interval, then 5% are outside the interval. Divide the 5% into two equal parts of 2.5%. The value of Z in Table E.2 corresponding to an area of 0.0250 in the lower tail of the normal curve is -1.96, and the value of Z corresponding to a cumulative area of 0.9750 (i.e., 0.0250 in the upper tail of the normal curve) is $+1.96$.

The lower value of $\overline{X}$ (called $\overline{X}_L$) and the upper value of $\overline{X}$ (called $\overline{X}_U$) are found by using Equation (7.5):

$$\overline{X}_L = 368 + (-1.96)\frac{15}{\sqrt{25}} = 368 - 5.88 = 362.12$$

$$\overline{X}_U = 368 + (1.96)\frac{15}{\sqrt{25}} = 368 + 5.88 = 373.88$$

Therefore, 95% of all sample means, based on samples of 25 boxes, are between 362.12 and 373.88 grams.

Sampling from Non-normally Distributed Populations—The Central Limit Theorem

So far in this section, only the sampling distribution of the mean for a normally distributed population has been considered. However, for many analyses, you will either be able to know that the population is not normally distributed or conclude that it would be unrealistic to assume that the population is normally distributed. An important theorem in statistics, the **Central Limit Theorem**, deals with these situations.

THE CENTRAL LIMIT THEOREM

As the sample size (the number of values in each sample) gets *large enough*, the sampling distribution of the mean is approximately normally distributed. This is true regardless of the shape of the distribution of the individual values in the population.

What sample size is *large enough*? As a general rule, statisticians have found that for many population distributions, when the sample size is at least 30, the sampling distribution of the mean is approximately normal. However, you can apply the Central Limit Theorem for even smaller sample sizes if the population distribution is approximately bell-shaped. In the case in which the distribution of a variable is extremely skewed or has more than one mode, you may need sample sizes larger than 30 to ensure normality in the sampling distribution of the mean.

Figure 7.4 illustrates that the Central Limit Theorem applies to all types of populations, regardless of their shape. In the figure, the effects of increasing sample size are shown for these populations:

- A normally distributed population (left column)
- A uniformly distributed population in which the values are evenly distributed between the smallest and largest values (middle column)
- An exponentially distributed population in which the values are heavily skewed to the right (right column)

FIGURE 7.4

Sampling distribution of the mean for samples of $n = 2, 5$, and 30, for three different populations

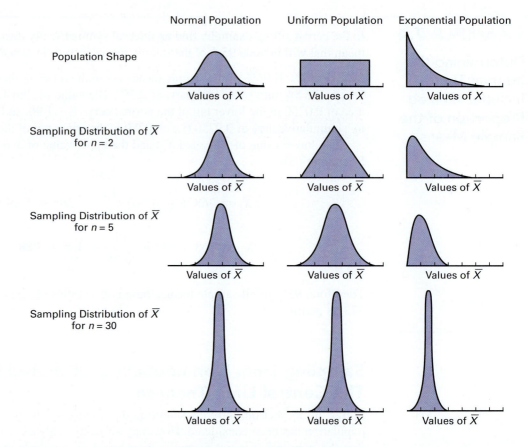

Note: The mean of each of the three sampling distributions shown in a column is equal to the mean of that column's population because the sample mean is an unbiased estimator of the population mean.

For the normally distributed population, the sampling distribution of the mean is always normally distributed, too. However, as the sample size increases, the variability of the sample means decreases resulting in a narrowing of the width of the graph.

For the other two populations, a *central limiting* effect causes the sample means to become more similar and the shape of the graphs to become more like a normal distribution. This effect happens initially more slowly for the heavily skewed exponential distribution than for the uniform distribution, but when the sample size is increased to 30, the sampling distributions of these two populations converge to the shape of the sampling distribution of the normal population.

Using the results from the normal, uniform, and exponential distributions, you can reach the following conclusions regarding the Central Limit Theorem:

- For most distributions, regardless of the shape of the population, the sampling distribution of the mean is approximately normally distributed if samples of at least size 30 are selected.
- If the distribution of the population is fairly symmetrical, the sampling distribution of the mean is approximately normal for samples as small as size 5.
- If the population is normally distributed, the sampling distribution of the mean is normally distributed, regardless of the sample size.

The Central Limit Theorem is of crucial importance in using statistical inference to reach conclusions about a population. It allows you to make inferences about the population mean without having to know the specific shape of the population distribution. Example 7.5 illustrates a sampling distribution for a skewed population.

EXAMPLE 7.5

Constructing a Sampling Distribution for a Skewed Population

Figure 7.5 shows the distribution of the time it takes to fill orders at a fast-food chain drive-through lane. Note that the probability distribution table is unlike Table 7.1 (page 227), which presents a population in which each value is equally likely to occur.

FIGURE 7.5

Probability distribution and histogram of the service time (in minutes) at a fast-food chain drive-through lane

Service Time (minutes)	Probability
1	0.10
2	0.40
3	0.20
4	0.15
5	0.10
6	0.05

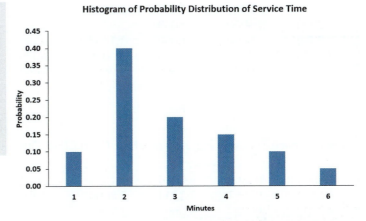

Histogram of Probability Distribution of Service Time

Using Equation (5.1) on page 178, the population mean is computed as 2.9 minutes. Using Equation (5.3) on page 179, the population standard deviation is computed as 1.34. Select 100 samples of $n = 2$, $n = 15$, and $n = 30$. What conclusions can you reach about the sampling distribution of the service time (in minutes) at the fast-food chain drive-through lane?

SOLUTION Table 7.3 represents the mean service time (in minutes) at the fast-food chain drive-through lane for 100 different random samples of $n = 2$. The mean of these 100 sample means is 2.825 minutes, and the standard error of the mean is 0.883.

TABLE 7.3

Mean Service Times (in minutes) at a Fast-Food Chain Drive-Through Lane for 100 Different Random Samples of $n = 2$

3.5	2.5	3	3.5	4	3	2.5	2	2	2.5
3	3	2.5	2.5	2	2.5	2.5	2	3.5	1.5
2	3	2.5	3	3	2	3.5	3.5	2.5	2
4.5	3.5	4	2	2	4	3.5	2.5	2.5	3.5
3.5	3.5	2	1.5	2.5	2	3.5	3.5	2.5	2.5
2.5	3	3	3.5	2	3.5	2	1.5	5.5	2.5
3.5	3	3	2	1.5	3	2.5	2.5	2.5	2.5
3.5	1.5	6	2	1.5	2.5	3.5	2	3.5	5
2.5	3.5	4.5	3.5	3.5	2	4	2	3	3
4.5	1.5	2.5	2	2.5	2.5	2	2	2	4

Table 7.4 represents the mean service time (in minutes) at the fast-food chain drive-through lane for 100 different random samples of $n = 15$. The mean of these 100 sample means is 2.9313 minutes, and the standard error of the mean is 0.3458.

Table 7.5 represents the mean service time (in minutes) at the fast-food chain drive-through lane for 100 different random samples of $n = 30$. The mean of these 100 sample means is 2.9527 minutes, and the standard error of the mean is 0.2701.

(Continued)

TABLE 7.4

Mean Service Times (in minutes) at a Fast-Food Chain Drive-Through Lane for 100 Different Random Samples of $n = 15$

3.5333	2.8667	3.1333	3.6000	2.5333	2.8000	2.8667	3.1333	3.2667	3.3333
3.0000	3.3333	2.7333	2.6000	2.8667	3.0667	2.1333	2.5333	2.8000	3.1333
2.8000	2.7333	2.6000	3.1333	2.8667	3.4667	2.9333	2.8000	2.2000	3.0000
2.9333	2.6000	2.6000	3.1333	3.1333	3.1333	2.5333	3.0667	3.9333	2.8000
3.0000	2.7333	2.6000	2.4667	3.2000	2.4667	3.2000	2.9333	2.8667	3.4667
2.6667	3.0000	3.1333	3.1333	2.7333	2.7333	3.3333	3.4000	3.2000	3.0000
3.2000	3.0000	2.6000	2.9333	3.0667	2.8667	2.2667	2.5333	2.7333	2.2667
2.8000	2.8000	2.6000	3.1333	2.9333	3.0667	3.6667	2.6667	2.8667	2.6667
3.0000	3.4000	2.7333	3.6000	2.6000	2.7333	3.3333	2.6000	2.8667	2.8000
3.7333	2.9333	3.0667	2.6667	2.8667	2.2667	2.7333	2.8667	3.5333	3.2000

TABLE 7.5

Mean Service Times (in minutes) at a Fast-Food Chain Drive-Through Lane for 100 Different Random Samples of $n = 30$

3.0000	3.3667	3.0000	3.1333	2.8667	2.8333	3.2667	2.9000	2.7000	3.2000
3.2333	2.7667	3.2333	2.8000	3.4000	3.0333	2.8667	3.0000	3.1333	3.4000
2.3000	3.0000	3.0667	2.9667	3.0333	2.4000	2.8667	2.8000	2.5000	2.7000
2.7000	2.9000	2.8333	3.3000	3.1333	2.8667	2.6667	2.6000	3.2333	2.8667
2.7667	2.9333	2.5667	2.5333	3.0333	3.2333	3.0667	2.9667	2.4000	3.3000
2.8000	3.0667	3.2000	2.9667	2.9667	3.2333	3.3667	2.9000	3.0333	3.1333
3.3333	2.8667	2.8333	3.0667	3.3667	3.0667	3.0667	3.2000	3.1667	3.3667
3.0333	3.1667	2.4667	3.0000	2.6333	2.6667	2.9667	3.1333	2.8000	2.8333
2.9333	2.7000	3.0333	2.7333	2.6667	2.6333	3.1333	3.0667	2.5333	3.3333
3.1000	2.5667	2.9000	3.9333	2.9000	2.7000	2.7333	2.8000	2.6667	2.8333

Figure 7.6 Panels A through C show histograms of the mean service time (in minutes) at the fast-food chain drive-through lane for the three sets of 100 different random samples shown in Tables 7.3 through 7.5. Panel A, the histogram for the mean service time for 100 different random samples of $n = 2$, shows a skewed distribution, but a distribution that is not as skewed as the population distribution of service times shown in Figure 7.5.

Panel B, the histogram for the mean service time for 100 different random samples of $n = 15$, shows a somewhat symmetrical distribution that contains a concentration of values in the center of the distribution. Panel C, the histogram for the mean service time for 100 different

FIGURE 7.6

Histograms of the mean service time (in minutes) at the fast-food chain drive-through lane of 100 different random samples of $n = 2$ (Panel A, left), 100 different random samples of $n = 15$ (Panel B, right), and 100 different random samples of $n = 30$ (Panel C, next page)

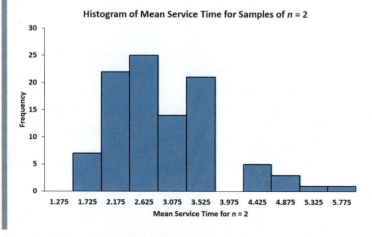

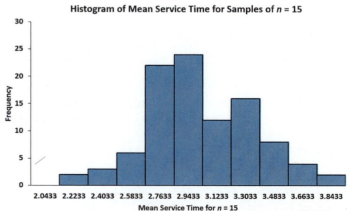

FIGURE 7.6
(continued)

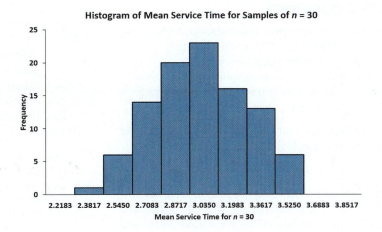

random samples of $n = 30$, shows a distribution that appears to be approximately bell-shaped with a concentration of values in the center of the distribution. The progression of the histograms from a skewed population toward a bell-shaped distribution as the sample size increases is consistent with the Central Limit Theorem.

VISUAL EXPLORATIONS | Exploring Sampling Distributions

Open the **VE-Sampling Distribution add-in workbook** to observe the effects of simulated rolls on the frequency distribution of the sum of two dice. (For Excel technical requirements, review Appendix Section D.4.) When this workbook opens properly, it adds a Sampling Distribution menu to the Add-ins tab (Apple menu in Excel 2011).

To observe the effects of simulated throws on the frequency distribution of the sum of the two dice, select **Sampling Distribution → Two Dice Simulation**. In the Sampling Distribution dialog box, enter the **Number of rolls per tally** and click **Tally**. Click **Finish** when done.

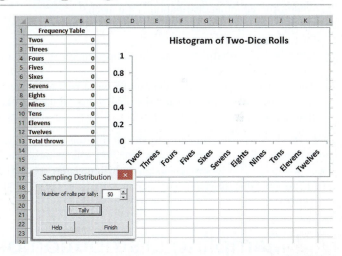

Problems for Section 7.2

LEARNING THE BASICS

7.1 Given a normal distribution with $\mu = 100$ and $\sigma = 10$, if you select a sample of $n = 25$, what is the probability that $\overline{X}$ is
a. less than 95?
b. between 95 and 97.5?
c. above 102.2?
d. There is a 65% chance that $\overline{X}$ is above what value?

7.2 Given a normal distribution with $\mu = 50$ and $\sigma = 5$, if you select a sample of $n = 100$, what is the probability that $\overline{X}$ is
a. less than 47?
b. between 47 and 49.5?
c. above 51.1?
d. There is a 35% chance that $\overline{X}$ is above what value?

APPLYING THE CONCEPTS

7.3 For each of the following three populations, indicate what the sampling distribution for samples of 25 would consist of:
a. Customer receipts for a supermarket for a year.
b. Insurance payouts in a particular geographical area in a year.
c. Call center logs of inbound calls tracking handling time for a credit card company during the year.

7.4 The following data represent the number of days absent per year in a population of six employees of a small company:

$$1 \quad 3 \quad 6 \quad 7 \quad 9 \quad 10$$

a. Assuming that you sample without replacement, select all possible samples of $n = 2$ and construct the sampling distribution of the mean. Compute the mean of all the sample means and also compute the population mean. Are they equal? What is this property called?
b. Repeat (a) for all possible samples of $n = 3$.
c. Compare the shape of the sampling distribution of the mean in (a) and (b). Which sampling distribution has less variability? Why?
d. Assuming that you sample with replacement, repeat (a) through (c) and compare the results. Which sampling distributions have the least variability—those in (a) or (b)? Why?

7.5 The diameter of a brand of tennis balls is approximately normally distributed, with a mean of 2.63 inches and a standard deviation of 0.03 inch. If you select a random sample of nine tennis balls,
a. what is the sampling distribution of the mean?
b. what is the probability that the sample mean is less than 2.61 inches?
c. what is the probability that the sample mean is between 2.62 and 2.64 inches?
d. The probability is 60% that the sample mean will be between what two values symmetrically distributed around the population mean?

7.6 The U.S. Census Bureau announced that the median sales price of new houses sold in 2013 was $265,900, and the mean sales price was $322,100 (**www.census.gov/newhomesales**, March 1, 2014). Assume that the standard deviation of the prices is $90,000.

a. If you select samples of $n = 4$, describe the shape of the sampling distribution of $\overline{X}$.
b. If you select samples of $n = 100$, describe the shape of the sampling distribution of $\overline{X}$.
c. If you select a random sample of $n = 100$, what is the probability that the sample mean will be less than $346,000?
d. If you select a random sample of $n = 100$, what is the probability that the sample mean will be between 326,000 and 341,000?

7.7 According to a social media blog, time spent on Tumblr, a microblogging platform and social networking website, has a mean of 20 minutes per visit. (Source: "2014: The year of Tumblr," **bit.ly/QwM8ga**.) Assume that time spent on Tumblr per visit is normally distributed and that the standard deviation is 5 minutes. If you select a random sample of 25 visits,
a. what is the probability that the sample mean is between 19.5 and 20.5 minutes?
b. what is the probability that the sample mean is between 19 and 20 minutes?
c. If you select a random sample of 100 visits, what is the probability that the sample mean is between 19.5 and 20.5 minutes?
d. Explain the difference in the results of (a) and (c).

✓ **SELF Test** **7.8** Today, full-time college students report spending a mean of 27 hours per week on academic activities, both inside and outside the classroom. (Source: "A Challenge to College Students for 2013: Don't Waste Your 6,570," *Huffington Post*, January 29, 2013, **huff.to/13dNtuT**.) Assume the standard deviation of time spent on academic activities is 4 hours. If you select a random sample of 16 full-time college students,
a. what is the probability that the mean time spent on academic activities is at least 26 hours per week?
b. there is an 85% chance that the sample mean is less than how many hours per week?
c. What assumption must you make in order to solve (a) and (b)?
d. If you select a random sample of 64 full-time college students, there is an 85% chance that the sample mean is less than how many hours per week?

7.3 Sampling Distribution of the Proportion

> **Student Tip**
> Do not confuse this use of the Greek letter pi, π, to represent the population proportion with the mathematical constant that uses the same letter to represent the ratio of the circumference to a diameter of a circle—approximately 3.14159.

Consider a categorical variable that has only two categories, such as the customer prefers your brand or the customer prefers the competitor's brand. You are interested in the proportion of items belonging to one of the categories—for example, the proportion of customers that prefer your brand. The population proportion, represented by π, is the proportion of items in the entire population with the characteristic of interest. The sample proportion, represented by p, is the proportion of items in the sample with the characteristic of interest. The sample proportion, a statistic, is used to estimate the population proportion, a parameter. To calculate the sample proportion, you assign one of two possible values, 1 or 0, to represent the presence or absence of the characteristic. You then sum all the 1 and 0 values and divide by n, the sample size. For example, if, in a sample of five customers, three preferred your brand and two did not, you have three 1s and two 0s. Summing the three 1s and two 0s and dividing by the sample size of 5 results in a sample proportion of 0.60.

SAMPLE PROPORTION

$$p = \frac{X}{n} = \frac{\text{Number of items having the characteristic of interest}}{\text{Sample size}} \tag{7.6}$$

Student Tip
Remember that the sample proportion cannot be negative and also cannot be greater than 1.0.

The sample proportion, p, will be between 0 and 1. If all items have the characteristic, you assign each a score of 1, and p is equal to 1. If half the items have the characteristic, you assign half a score of 1 and assign the other half a score of 0, and p is equal to 0.5. If none of the items have the characteristic, you assign each a score of 0, and p is equal to 0.

In Section 7.2, you learned that the sample mean, $\overline{X}$, is an unbiased estimator of the population mean, μ. Similarly, the statistic p is an unbiased estimator of the population proportion, π. By analogy to the sampling distribution of the mean, whose standard error is $\sigma_{\overline{X}} = \dfrac{\sigma}{\sqrt{n}}$, the **standard error of the proportion**, σ_p, is given in Equation (7.7).

STANDARD ERROR OF THE PROPORTION

$$\sigma_p = \sqrt{\frac{\pi(1 - \pi)}{n}} \tag{7.7}$$

The **sampling distribution of the proportion** follows the binomial distribution, as discussed in Section 5.2, when sampling with replacement (or without replacement from extremely large populations). However, you can use the normal distribution to approximate the binomial distribution when $n\pi$ and $n(1 - \pi)$ are each at least 5. In most cases in which inferences are made about the population proportion, the sample size is substantial enough to meet the conditions for using the normal approximation (see reference 1). Therefore, in many instances, you can use the normal distribution to estimate the sampling distribution of the proportion.

Substituting p for $\overline{X}$, π for μ, and $\sqrt{\dfrac{\pi(1 - \pi)}{n}}$ for $\dfrac{\sigma}{\sqrt{n}}$ in Equation (7.4) on page 231 results in Equation (7.8).

FINDING Z FOR THE SAMPLING DISTRIBUTION OF THE PROPORTION

$$Z = \frac{p - \pi}{\sqrt{\dfrac{\pi(1 - \pi)}{n}}} \tag{7.8}$$

To illustrate the sampling distribution of the proportion, a recent survey ("Can You Stop Thinking About Work on Your Vacation?" *USA Today Snapshots*, October 5, 2011, p. 1A) reported that 32% of adults are unable to stop thinking about work while on vacation. Suppose that you select a random sample of 200 vacationers who have booked tours from a certain tour company, and you want to determine the probability that more than 40% of the vacationers are unable to stop thinking about work while on vacation. Because $n\pi = 200(0.32) = 64 > 5$ and $n(1 - \pi) = 200(1 - 0.32) = 136 > 5$, the sample size is large enough to assume that the sampling distribution of the proportion is approximately normally distributed. Then, using the survey percentage of 32% as the population proportion, you can calculate the probability that more than 40% of the sample of vacationers are unable to stop thinking about work while on vacation by using Equation (7.8):

$$Z = \frac{p - \pi}{\sqrt{\dfrac{\pi(1 - \pi)}{n}}}$$

$$= \frac{0.40 - 0.32}{\sqrt{\dfrac{(0.32)(0.68)}{200}}} = \frac{0.08}{\sqrt{\dfrac{0.2176}{200}}} = \frac{0.08}{0.0330}$$

$$= 2.42$$

Using Table E.2, the area under the normal curve greater than 2.42 is 0.0078. Therefore, if the population proportion is 0.32, the probability is 0.78% that more than 40% of the 200 vacationers in the sample will be unable to stop thinking about work while on vacation.

Problems for Section 7.3

LEARNING THE BASICS

7.9 In a random sample of 64 people, 48 are classified as "successful."
a. Determine the sample proportion, p, of "successful" people.
b. If the population proportion is 0.70, determine the standard error of the proportion.

7.10 A random sample of 50 households was selected for a phone (landline and cellphone) survey. The key question asked was, "Do you or any member of your household own an Apple product (iPhone, iPod, iPad, or Mac computer)?" Of the 50 respondents, 20 said yes and 30 said no.
a. Determine the sample proportion, p, of households that own an Apple product.
b. If the population proportion is 0.45, determine the standard error of the proportion.

7.11 The following data represent the responses (Y for yes and N for no) from a sample of 40 college students to the question "Do you currently own shares in any stocks?"

```
N N Y N N Y N Y N Y N N N Y N Y Y N N N Y
N Y N N N N Y N N Y Y N N N Y N N Y N N
```

a. Determine the sample proportion, p, of college students who own shares of stock.
b. If the population proportion is 0.30, determine the standard error of the proportion.

APPLYING THE CONCEPTS

SELF Test **7.12** A political pollster is conducting an analysis of sample results in order to make predictions on election night. Assuming a two-candidate election, if a specific candidate receives at least 55% of the vote in the sample, that candidate will be forecast as the winner of the election. If you select a random sample of 100 voters, what is the probability that a candidate will be forecast as the winner when

a. the population percentage of her vote is 50.1%?
b. the population percentage of her vote is 60%?
c. the population percentage of her vote is 49% (and she will actually lose the election)?
d. If the sample size is increased to 400, what are your answers to (a) through (c)? Discuss.

7.13 You plan to conduct a marketing experiment in which students are to taste one of two different brands of soft drink. Their task is to correctly identify the brand tasted. You select a random sample of 200 students and assume that the students have no ability to distinguish between the two brands. (Hint: If an individual has no ability to distinguish between the two soft drinks, then the two brands are equally likely to be selected.)
a. What is the probability that the sample will have between 50% and 60% of the identifications correct?
b. The probability is 90% that the sample percentage is contained within what symmetrical limits of the population percentage?
c. What is the probability that the sample percentage of correct identifications is greater than 65%?
d. Which is more likely to occur—more than 60% correct identifications in the sample of 200 or more than 55% correct identifications in a sample of 1,000? Explain.

7.14 Accenture's *Defining Success* global research study found that the majority of today's working women would prefer a better work–life balance to an increased salary. One of the most important contributors to work–life balance identified by the survey was "flexibility," with 80% of women saying that having a flexible work schedule is either very important or extremely important to their career success. (Source: **bit.ly/17IM8gq**.) Suppose you select a sample of 100 working women.
a. What is the probability that in the sample fewer than 85% say that having a flexible work schedule is either very important or extremely important to their career success?
b. What is the probability that in the sample between 75% and 85% say that having a flexible work schedule is either very important or extremely important to their career success?

c. What is the probability that in the sample more than 82% say that having a flexible work schedule is either very important or extremely important to their career success?

d. If a sample of 400 is taken, how does this change your answers to (a) through (c)?

7.15 The goal of corporate sustainability is to manage the environmental, economic, and social effects of a corporation's operations so it is profitable over the long term while acting in a responsible manner toward society. A Hill + Knowlton Strategies survey found that 57% of U.S. respondents are more likely to buy stock in a U.S. corporation, or shop at its stores, if it is making an effort to publicly talk about how it is becoming more sustainable. (Source: "Sustainability," **bit.ly/10A2Snl**.) Suppose you select a sample of 100 U.S. respondents.

a. What is the probability that in the sample, fewer than 57% are more likely to buy stock in a U.S. corporation, or shop at its stores, if it is making an effort to publicly talk about how it is becoming more sustainable?

b. What is the probability that in the sample, between 52% and 62% are more likely to buy stock in a U.S. corporation, or shop at its stores, if it is making an effort to publicly talk about how it is becoming more sustainable?

c. What is the probability that in the sample, more than 62% are more likely to buy stock in a U.S. corporation, or shop at its stores, if it is making an effort to publicly talk about how it is becoming more sustainable?

d. If a sample of 400 is taken, how does this change your answers to (a) through (c)?

7.16 According to *GMI Ratings' 2013 Women on Boards Report*, the percentage of women on U.S. boards has increased marginally in 2009–2012 and now stands at 14%, well below the values for Nordic countries and France. A number of initiatives are underway in an effort to increase the representation. For example, a network of investors, corporate leaders, and other advocates, known as the 30% coalition, is seeking to raise the proportion of female directors to that number (30%) by 2015. This study also reports that 15% of U.S. companies have three or more female board directors. (Data extracted from **bit.ly/13oSFem**.) If you select a random sample of 200 U.S. companies,

a. what is the probability that the sample will have between 12% and 18% U.S. companies that have three or more female board directors?

b. the probability is 90% that the sample percentage of U.S. companies having three or more female board directors will be contained within what symmetrical limits of the population percentage?

c. the probability is 95% that the sample percentage of U.S. companies having three or more female board directors will be contained within what symmetrical limits of the population percentage?

7.17 The Chartered Financial Analyst (CFA) Institute reported that 49% of its U.S. members indicate that lack of ethical culture within financial firms has contributed the most to the lack of trust in the financial industry. (Source: "Global Market Sentiment Survey 2014," **cfa.is/Psk5O3**.) Suppose that you select a sample of 100 CFA members.

a. What is the probability that the sample percentage indicating that lack of ethical culture within financial firms has contributed the most to the lack of trust in the financial industry will be between 48% and 53%?

b. The probability is 90% that the sample percentage will be contained within what symmetrical limits of the population percentage?

c. The probability is 95% that the sample percentage will be contained within what symmetrical limits of the population percentage?

d. Suppose you selected a sample of 400 CFA members. How does this change your answers in (a) through (c)?

7.18 A Pew Research Center project on the state of news media showed that digital video consumption is growing and digital news video consumption is growing with it. According to Pew Research data, 36% of U.S. adults watch news videos. (Source: "The State of the News Media 2014," **bit.ly/1ielXR7**.)

a. Suppose that you take a sample of 100 U.S. adults. If the population proportion of U.S. adults who watch news videos is 0.36, what is the probability that fewer than 30% in your sample will watch news videos?

b. Suppose that you take a sample of 400 U.S. adults. If the population proportion of U.S. adults who watch news videos is 0.36, what is the probability that fewer than 30% in your sample will watch news videos?

c. Discuss the effect of sample size on the sampling distribution of the proportion in general and the effect on the probabilities in (a) and (b).

Because the population mean, μ (equal to 368), is included within the interval, this sample results in a correct statement about μ (see Figure 8.1).

FIGURE 8.1

Confidence interval estimates for five different samples of $n = 25$ taken from a population where $\mu = 368$ and $\sigma = 15$

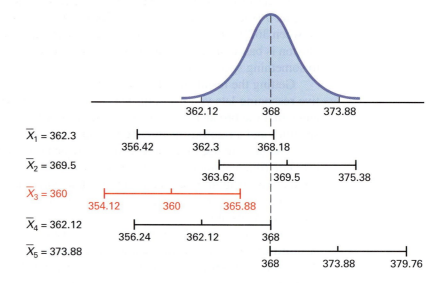

To continue this hypothetical example, suppose that for a different sample of $n = 25$ boxes, the mean is 369.5. The interval developed from this sample is

$$369.5 \pm (1.96)(15)/(\sqrt{25})$$

or 369.5 ± 5.88. The estimate is

$$363.62 \le \mu \le 375.38$$

Because the population mean, μ (equal to 368), is also included within this interval, this statement about μ is correct.

Now, before you begin to think that correct statements about μ are always made by developing a confidence interval estimate, suppose a third hypothetical sample of $n = 25$ boxes is selected and the sample mean is equal to 360 grams. The interval developed here is $360 \pm (1.96)(15)/(\sqrt{25})$, or 360 ± 5.88. In this case, the estimate of μ is

$$354.12 \le \mu \le 365.88$$

This estimate is *not* a correct statement because the population mean, μ, is not included in the interval developed from this sample (see Figure 8.1). Thus, for some samples, the interval estimate for μ is correct, but for others it is incorrect. In practice, only one sample is selected, and because the population mean is unknown, you cannot determine whether the interval estimate is correct. To resolve this, you need to determine the proportion of samples producing intervals that result in correct statements about the population mean, μ. To do this, consider two other hypothetical samples: the case in which $\overline{X} = 362.12$ grams and the case in which $\overline{X} = 373.88$ grams. If $\overline{X} = 362.12$, the interval is $362.12 \pm (1.96)(15)/(\sqrt{25})$, or 362.12 ± 5.88. This leads to the following interval:

$$356.24 \le \mu \le 368.00$$

Because the population mean of 368 is at the upper limit of the interval, the statement is correct (see Figure 8.1).

When $\overline{X} = 373.88$, the interval is $373.88 \pm (1.96)(15)/(\sqrt{25})$, or 373.88 ± 5.88. The interval estimate for the mean is

$$368.00 \le \mu \le 379.76$$

In this case, because the population mean of 368 is included at the lower limit of the interval, the statement is correct.

In Figure 8.1, you see that when the sample mean falls somewhere between 362.12 and 373.88 grams, the population mean is included *somewhere* within the interval. In Example 7.4 on page 233, you found that 95% of the sample means are between 362.12 and 373.88 grams. Therefore, 95% of all samples of $n = 25$ boxes have sample means that will result in intervals that include the population mean.

Because, in practice, you select only one sample of size n, and μ is unknown, you never know for sure whether your specific interval includes the population mean. However, if you take all possible samples of n and compute their 95% confidence intervals, 95% of the intervals will include the population mean, and only 5% of them will not. In other words, you have 95% confidence that the population mean is somewhere in your interval.

Consider once again the first sample discussed in this section. A sample of $n = 25$ boxes had a sample mean of 362.3 grams. The interval constructed to estimate μ is

$$362.3 \pm (1.96)(15)/(\sqrt{25})$$
$$362.3 \pm 5.88$$
$$356.42 \leq \mu \leq 368.18$$

The interval from 356.42 to 368.18 is referred to as a *95% confidence interval*. The following contains an interpretation of the interval that most business professionals will understand. (For a technical discussion of different ways to interpret confidence intervals, see reference 4.)

"I am 95% confident that the mean amount of cereal in the population of boxes is somewhere between 356.42 and 368.18 grams."

To help you understand the meaning of the confidence interval, consider the order-filling process at a website. Filling orders consists of several steps, including receiving an order, picking the parts of the order, checking the order, packing, and shipping the order. The file **Order** contains the time, in minutes, to fill orders for a population of $N = 200$ orders on a recent day. Although in practice the population characteristics are rarely known, for this population of orders, the mean, μ, is known to be equal to 69.637 minutes; the standard deviation, σ, is known to be equal to 10.411 minutes; and the population is normally distributed. To illustrate how the sample mean and sample standard deviation can vary from one sample to another, 20 different samples of $n = 10$ were selected from the population of 200 orders, and the sample mean and sample standard deviation (and other statistics) were calculated for each sample. Figure 8.2 shows these results.

FIGURE 8.2

Sample statistics and 95% confidence intervals for 20 samples of $n = 10$ randomly selected from the population of $N = 200$ orders

Sample	n	Mean	Std Dev	Minimum	Median	Maximum	Range	95% Conf. Int.
S01	10	74.15	13.39	56.10	76.85	97.70	41.60	(67.70, 80.60)
S02	10	61.10	10.60	46.80	61.35	79.50	32.70	(54.65, 67.55)
S03	10	74.36	6.50	62.50	74.50	84.00	21.50	(67.91, 80.81)
S04	10	70.40	12.80	47.20	70.95	84.00	36.80	(63.95, 76.85)
S05	10	62.18	10.85	47.10	59.70	84.00	36.90	(55.73, 68.63)
S06	10	67.03	9.68	51.10	69.60	83.30	32.20	(60.58, 73.48)
S07	10	69.03	8.81	56.60	68.85	83.70	27.10	(62.58, 75.48)
S08	10	72.30	11.52	54.20	71.35	87.00	32.80	(65.85, 78.75)
S09	10	68.18	14.10	50.10	69.95	86.20	36.10	(61.73, 74.63)
S10	10	66.67	9.08	57.10	64.65	86.10	29.00	(60.22, 73.12)
S11	10	72.42	9.76	59.60	74.65	86.10	26.50	(65.97, 78.87)
S12	10	76.26	11.69	50.10	80.60	87.00	36.90	(69.81, 82.71)
S13	10	65.74	12.11	47.10	62.15	86.10	39.00	(59.29, 72.19)
S14	10	69.99	10.97	51.00	73.40	84.60	33.60	(63.54, 76.44)
S15	10	75.76	8.60	61.10	75.05	87.80	26.70	(69.31, 82.21)
S16	10	67.94	9.19	56.70	67.70	87.80	31.10	(61.49, 74.39)
S17	10	71.05	10.48	50.10	71.15	86.20	36.10	(64.60, 77.50)
S18	10	71.68	7.96	55.60	72.35	82.60	27.00	(65.23, 78.13)
S19	10	70.97	9.83	54.40	70.05	84.00	30.20	(64.52, 77.42)
S20	10	74.48	8.80	62.00	76.25	85.70	23.70	(68.03, 80.93)

From Figure 8.2, you can see the following:

- The sample statistics differ from sample to sample. The sample means vary from 61.10 to 76.26 minutes, the sample standard deviations vary from 6.50 to 14.10 minutes, the sample medians vary from 59.70 to 80.60 minutes, and the sample ranges vary from 21.50 to 41.60 minutes.
- Some of the sample means are greater than the population mean of 69.637 minutes, and some of the sample means are less than the population mean.
- Some of the sample standard deviations are greater than the population standard deviation of 10.411 minutes, and some of the sample standard deviations are less than the population standard deviation.
- The variation in the sample ranges is much more than the variation in the sample standard deviations.

The variation of sample statistics from sample to sample is called *sampling error*. **Sampling error** is the variation that occurs due to selecting a single sample from the population. The size of the sampling error is primarily based on the amount of variation in the population and on the sample size. Large samples have less sampling error than small samples, but large samples cost more to select.

The last column of Figure 8.2 contains 95% confidence interval estimates of the population mean order-filling time, based on the results of those 20 samples of $n = 10$. Begin by examining the first sample selected. The sample mean is 74.15 minutes, and the interval estimate for the population mean is 67.70 to 80.60 minutes. In a typical study, you would not know for sure whether this interval estimate is correct because you rarely know the value of the population mean. However, for this example *concerning the order-filling times*, the population mean is known to be 69.637 minutes. If you examine the interval 67.70 to 80.60 minutes, you see that the population mean of 69.637 minutes is located *between* these lower and upper limits. Thus, the first sample provides a correct estimate of the population mean in the form of an interval estimate. Looking over the other 19 samples, you see that similar results occur for all the other samples *except* for samples 2, 5, and 12. For each of the intervals generated (other than samples 2, 5, and 12), the population mean of 69.637 minutes is located *somewhere* within the interval.

For sample 2, the sample mean is 61.10 minutes, and the interval is 54.65 to 67.55 minutes; for sample 5, the sample mean is 62.18, and the interval is between 55.73 and 68.63; for sample 12, the sample mean is 76.26, and the interval is between 69.81 and 82.71 minutes. The population mean of 69.637 minutes is *not* located within any of these intervals, and the estimate of the population mean made using these intervals is incorrect. Although 3 of the 20 intervals did not include the population mean, if you had selected all the possible samples of $n = 10$ from a population of $N = 200$, 95% of the intervals would include the population mean.

In some situations, you might want a higher degree of confidence of including the population mean within the interval (such as 99%). In other cases, you might accept less confidence (such as 90%) of correctly estimating the population mean. In general, the **level of confidence** is symbolized by $(1 - \alpha) \times 100\%$, where α is the proportion in the tails of the distribution that is outside the confidence interval. The proportion in the upper tail of the distribution is $\alpha/2$, and the proportion in the lower tail of the distribution is $\alpha/2$. You use Equation (8.1) to construct a $(1 - \alpha) \times 100\%$ confidence interval estimate for the mean with σ known.

CONFIDENCE INTERVAL FOR THE MEAN (σ KNOWN)

$$\bar{X} \pm Z_{\alpha/2}\frac{\sigma}{\sqrt{n}}$$

or

$$\bar{X} - Z_{\alpha/2}\frac{\sigma}{\sqrt{n}} \leq \mu \leq \bar{X} + Z_{\alpha/2}\frac{\sigma}{\sqrt{n}} \qquad (8.1)$$

where

$Z_{\alpha/2}$ is the value corresponding to an upper-tail probability of $\alpha/2$ from the standardized normal distribution (i.e., a cumulative area of $1 - \alpha/2$).

The value of $Z_{\alpha/2}$ needed for constructing a confidence interval is called the **critical value** for the distribution. 95% confidence corresponds to an α value of 0.05. The critical Z value corresponding to a cumulative area of 0.975 is 1.96 because there is 0.025 in the upper tail of the distribution, and the cumulative area less than $Z = 1.96$ is 0.975.

There is a different critical value for each level of confidence, $1 - \alpha$. A level of confidence of 95% leads to a Z value of 1.96 (see Figure 8.3). 99% confidence corresponds to an α value of 0.01. The Z value is approximately 2.58 because the upper-tail area is 0.005 and the cumulative area less than $Z = 2.58$ is 0.995 (see Figure 8.4).

FIGURE 8.3

Normal curve for determining the Z value needed for 95% confidence

FIGURE 8.4

Normal curve for determining the Z value needed for 99% confidence

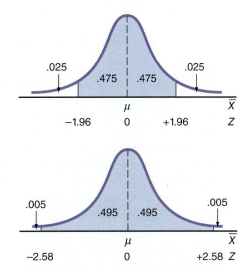

Now that various levels of confidence have been considered, why not make the confidence level as close to 100% as possible? Before doing so, you need to realize that any increase in the level of confidence is achieved only by widening (and making less precise) the confidence interval. There is no "free lunch" here. You would have more confidence that the population mean is within a broader range of values; however, this might make the interpretation of the confidence interval less useful. The trade-off between the width of the confidence interval and the level of confidence is discussed in greater depth in the context of determining the sample size in Section 8.4. Example 8.1 illustrates the application of the confidence interval estimate.

EXAMPLE 8.1

Estimating the Mean Paper Length with 95% Confidence

A paper manufacturer has a production process that operates continuously throughout an entire production shift. The paper is expected to have a mean length of 11 inches, and the standard deviation of the length is 0.02 inch. At periodic intervals, a sample is selected to determine whether the mean paper length is still equal to 11 inches or whether something has gone wrong in the production process to change the length of the paper produced. You select a random sample of 100 sheets, and the mean paper length is 10.998 inches. Construct a 95% confidence interval estimate for the population mean paper length.

SOLUTION Using Equation (8.1) on page 253, with $Z_{\alpha/2} = 1.96$ for 95% confidence,

$$\bar{X} \pm Z_{\alpha/2}\frac{\sigma}{\sqrt{n}} = 10.998 \pm (1.96)\frac{0.02}{\sqrt{100}}$$

$$= 10.998 \pm 0.0039$$

$$10.9941 \leq \mu \leq 11.0019$$

Thus, with 95% confidence, you conclude that the population mean is between 10.9941 and 11.0019 inches. Because the interval includes 11, the value indicating that the production process is working properly, you have no reason to believe that anything is wrong with the production process.

Example 8.2 illustrates the effect of using a 99% confidence interval.

EXAMPLE 8.2

Estimating the Mean Paper Length with 99% Confidence

Construct a 99% confidence interval estimate for the population mean paper length.

SOLUTION Using Equation (8.1) on page 252, with $Z_{\alpha/2} = 2.58$ for 99% confidence,

$$\bar{X} \pm Z_{\alpha/2}\frac{\sigma}{\sqrt{n}} = 10.998 \pm (2.58)\frac{0.02}{\sqrt{100}}$$

$$= 10.998 \pm 0.00516$$

$$10.9928 \le \mu \le 11.0032$$

Once again, because 11 is included within this wider interval, you have no reason to believe that anything is wrong with the production process.

As discussed in Section 7.2, the sampling distribution of the sample mean, $\bar{X}$, is normally distributed if the population for your characteristic of interest, X, follows a normal distribution. And if the population of X does not follow a normal distribution, the Central Limit Theorem almost always ensures that $\bar{X}$ is approximately normally distributed when n is large. However, when dealing with a small sample size and a population that does not follow a normal distribution, the sampling distribution of $\bar{X}$ is not normally distributed, and therefore the confidence interval discussed in this section is inappropriate. In practice, however, as long as the sample size is large enough and the population is not very skewed, you can use the confidence interval defined in Equation (8.1) to estimate the population mean when σ is known. To assess the assumption of normality, you can evaluate the shape of the sample data by constructing a histogram, stem-and-leaf display, boxplot, or normal probability plot.

> **Student Tip**
> Because understanding the confidence interval concept is very important when reading the rest of this book, review this section carefully to understand the underlying concept—even if you never have a practical reason to use the confidence interval estimate of the mean (σ known) method.

Can You Ever Know the Population Standard Deviation?

To solve Equation (8.1), you must know the value for σ, the population standard deviation. To know σ implies that you know all the values in the entire population. (How else would you know the value of this population parameter?) If you knew all the values in the entire population, you could directly compute the population mean. There would be no need to use the *inductive* reasoning of inferential statistics to *estimate* the population mean. In other words, if you know σ, you really do not have a need to use Equation (8.1) to construct a confidence interval estimate of the mean (σ known).

More significantly, in virtually all real-world business situations, you would never know the standard deviation of the population. In business situations, populations are often too large to examine all the values. So why study the confidence interval estimate of the mean (σ known) at all? This method serves as an important introduction to the concept of a confidence interval because it uses the normal distribution, which has already been thoroughly discussed in Chapters 6 and 7. In the next section, you will see that constructing a confidence interval estimate when σ is not known requires another distribution (the t distribution) not previously mentioned in this book.

Problems for Section 8.1

LEARNING THE BASICS

8.1 If $\bar{X} = 85$, $\sigma = 8$, and $n = 64$, construct a 95% confidence interval estimate for the population mean, μ.

8.2 If $\bar{X} = 125$, $\sigma = 24$, and $n = 36$, construct a 99% confidence interval estimate for the population mean, μ.

8.3 Why is it not possible in Example 8.1 on page 253 to have 100% confidence? Explain.

8.4 Is it true in Example 8.1 on page 253 that you do not know for sure whether the population mean is between 10.9941 and 11.0019 inches? Explain.

APPLYING THE CONCEPTS

8.5 A market researcher selects a simple random sample of $n = 100$ Twitter users from a population of over 100 million Twitter registered users. After analyzing the sample, she states that she has 95% confidence that the mean time spent on the site per day is between 15 and 57 minutes. Explain the meaning of this statement.

8.6 Suppose that you are going to collect a set of data, either from an entire population or from a random sample taken from that population.
a. Which statistical measure would you compute first: the mean or the standard deviation? Explain.
b. What does your answer to (a) tell you about the "practicality" of using the confidence interval estimate formula given in Equation (8.1)?

8.7 Consider the confidence interval estimate discussed in Problem 8.5. Suppose the population mean time spent on the site is 36 minutes a day. Is the confidence interval estimate stated in Problem 8.5 correct? Explain.

8.8 You are working as an assistant to the dean of institutional research at your university. The dean wants to survey members of the alumni association who obtained their baccalaureate degrees five years ago to learn what their starting salaries were in their first full-time job after receiving their degrees. A sample of 100 alumni is to be randomly selected from the list of 2,500 graduates in that class. If the dean's goal is to construct a 95% confidence interval estimate for the population mean starting salary, why is it not possible that you will be able to use Equation (8.1) on page 252 for this purpose? Explain.

8.9 A bottled water distributor wants to estimate the amount of water contained in 1-gallon bottles purchased from a nationally known water bottling company. The water bottling company's specifications state that the standard deviation of the amount of water is equal to 0.02 gallon. A random sample of 50 bottles is selected, and the sample mean amount of water per 1-gallon bottle is 0.995 gallon.
a. Construct a 99% confidence interval estimate for the population mean amount of water included in a 1-gallon bottle.
b. On the basis of these results, do you think that the distributor has a right to complain to the water bottling company? Why?
c. Must you assume that the population amount of water per bottle is normally distributed here? Explain.
d. Construct a 95% confidence interval estimate. How does this change your answer to (b)?

✓ **SELF Test** **8.10** The operations manager at a compact fluorescent light bulb (CFL) factory needs to estimate the mean life of a large shipment of CFLs. The manufacturer's specifications are that the standard deviation is 1,000 hours. A random sample of 64 CFLs indicated a sample mean life of 7,500 hours.
a. Construct a 95% confidence interval estimate for the population mean life of compact fluorescent light bulbs in this shipment.
b. Do you think that the manufacturer has the right to state that the compact fluorescent light bulbs have a mean life of 8,000 hours? Explain.
c. Must you assume that the population compact fluorescent light bulb life is normally distributed? Explain.
d. Suppose that the standard deviation changes to 800 hours. What are your answers in (a) and (b)?

8.2 Confidence Interval Estimate for the Mean (σ Unknown)

In the previous section, you learned that in most business situations, you do not know σ, the population standard deviation. This section discusses a method of constructing a confidence interval estimate of μ that uses the sample statistic S as an estimate of the population parameter σ.

Student's *t* Distribution

At the start of the twentieth century, William S. Gosset was working at Guinness in Ireland, trying to help brew better beer less expensively (see reference 5). As he had only small samples to study, he needed to find a way to make inferences about means without having to know σ. Writing under the pen name "Student,"[1] Gosset solved this problem by developing what today is known as the **Student's *t* distribution**, or the *t* distribution.

If the variable X is normally distributed, then the following statistic:

$$t = \frac{\overline{X} - \mu}{\frac{S}{\sqrt{n}}}$$

[1]Guinness considered all research conducted to be proprietary and a trade secret. The firm prohibited its employees from publishing their results. Gosset circumvented this ban by using the pen name "Student" to publish his findings.

has a *t* distribution with $n - 1$ **degrees of freedom**. This expression has the same form as the Z statistic in Equation (7.4) on page 231, except that S is used to estimate the unknown σ.

Properties of the *t* Distribution

The *t* distribution is very similar in appearance to the standardized normal distribution. Both distributions are symmetrical and bell-shaped, with the mean and the median equal to zero. However, because *S* is used to estimate the unknown σ, the values of *t* are more variable than those for *Z*. Therefore, the *t* distribution has more area in the tails and less in the center than does the standardized normal distribution (see Figure 8.5).

FIGURE 8.5

Standardized normal distribution and *t* distribution for 5 degrees of freedom

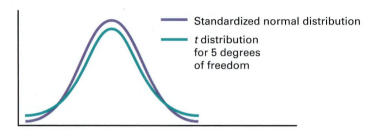

The degrees of freedom, $n - 1$, are directly related to the sample size, *n*. The concept of *degrees of freedom* is discussed further on page 257. As the sample size and degrees of freedom increase, *S* becomes a better estimate of σ, and the *t* distribution gradually approaches the standardized normal distribution, until the two are virtually identical. With a sample size of about 120 or more, *S* estimates σ closely enough so that there is little difference between the *t* and *Z* distributions.

As stated earlier, the *t* distribution assumes that the variable *X* is normally distributed. In practice, however, when the sample size is large enough and the population is not very skewed, in most cases you can use the *t* distribution to estimate the population mean when σ is unknown. When dealing with a small sample size and a skewed population distribution, the confidence interval estimate may not provide a valid estimate of the population mean. To assess the assumption of normality, you can evaluate the shape of the sample data by constructing a histogram, stem-and-leaf display, boxplot, or normal probability plot. However, the ability of any of these graphs to help you evaluate normality is limited when you have a small sample size.

You find the critical values of *t* for the appropriate degrees of freedom from the table of the *t* distribution (see Table E.3). The columns of the table present the most commonly used cumulative probabilities and corresponding upper-tail areas. The rows of the table represent the degrees of freedom. The critical *t* values are found in the cells of the table. For example, with 99 degrees of freedom, if you want 95% confidence, you find the appropriate value of *t*, as shown in Table 8.1. The 95% confidence level means that 2.5% of the values (an area of

TABLE 8.1

Determining the Critical Value from the *t* Table for an Area of 0.025 in Each Tail with 99 Degrees of Freedom

	Cumulative Probabilities					
	.75	.90	.95	.975	.99	.995
	Upper-Tail Areas					
Degrees of Freedom	.25	.10	.05	.025	.01	.005
1	1.0000	3.0777	6.3138	12.7062	31.8207	63.6574
2	0.8165	1.8856	2.9200	4.3027	6.9646	9.9248
3	0.7649	1.6377	2.3534	3.1824	4.5407	5.8409
4	0.7407	1.5332	2.1318	2.7764	3.7469	4.6041
5	0.7267	1.4759	2.0150	2.5706	3.3649	4.0322
⋮	⋮	⋮	⋮	⋮	⋮	⋮
96	0.6771	1.2904	1.6609	1.9850	2.3658	2.6280
97	0.6770	1.2903	1.6607	1.9847	2.3654	2.6275
98	0.6770	1.2902	1.6606	1.9845	2.3650	2.6269
99	0.6770	1.2902	1.6604	1.9842	2.3646	2.6264
100	0.6770	1.2901	1.6602	1.9840	2.3642	2.6259

Source: Extracted from Table E.3.

0.025) are in each tail of the distribution. Looking in the column for a cumulative probability of 0.975 and an upper-tail area of 0.025 in the row corresponding to 99 degrees of freedom gives you a critical value for t of 1.9842 (see Figure 8.6). Because t is a symmetrical distribution with a mean of 0, if the upper-tail value is $+1.9842$, the value for the lower-tail area (lower 0.025) is -1.9842. A t value of -1.9842 means that the probability that t is less than -1.9842 is 0.025, or 2.5%.

FIGURE 8.6

t distribution with 99 degrees of freedom

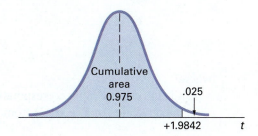

Note that for a 95% confidence interval, you will always have a cumulative probability of 0.975 and an upper-tail area of 0.025. Similarly, for a 99% confidence interval, you will have 0.995 and 0.005, and for a 90% confidence interval you will have 0.95 and 0.05.

The Concept of Degrees of Freedom

In Chapter 3, you learned that the numerator of the sample variance, S^2 [see Equation (3.4) on page 104], requires the computation of the sum of squares around the sample mean:

$$\sum_{i=1}^{n} (X_i - \overline{X})^2$$

In order to compute S^2, you first need to know $\overline{X}$. Therefore, only $n - 1$ of the sample values are free to vary. This means that you have $n - 1$ degrees of freedom. For example, suppose a sample of five values has a mean of 20. How many values do you need to know before you can determine the remainder of the values? The fact that $n = 5$ and $\overline{X} = 20$ also tells you that

$$\sum_{i=1}^{n} X_i = 100$$

because

$$\frac{\sum_{i=1}^{n} X_i}{n} = \overline{X}$$

Thus, when you know four of the values, the fifth one is *not* free to vary because the sum must be 100. For example, if four of the values are 18, 24, 19, and 16, the fifth value must be 23, so that the sum is 100.

The Confidence Interval Statement

Equation (8.2) defines the $(1 - \alpha) \times 100\%$ confidence interval estimate for the mean with σ unknown.

CONFIDENCE INTERVAL FOR THE MEAN (σ UNKNOWN)

$$\overline{X} \pm t_{\alpha/2}\frac{S}{\sqrt{n}}$$

or

$$\overline{X} - t_{\alpha/2}\frac{S}{\sqrt{n}} \leq \mu \leq \overline{X} + t_{\alpha/2}\frac{S}{\sqrt{n}} \tag{8.2}$$

where

$t_{\alpha/2}$ is the critical value corresponding to an upper-tail probability of $\alpha/2$ (i.e., a cumulative area of $1 - \alpha/2$) from the t distribution with $n - 1$ degrees of freedom.

To illustrate the application of the confidence interval estimate for the mean when the standard deviation is unknown, recall the Ricknel Home Centers scenario presented on page 248. Using the DCOVA steps first discussed on page 2, you define the variable of interest as the dollar amount listed on the sales invoices for the month. Your business objective is to estimate the mean dollar amount. Then you collect the data by selecting a sample of 100 sales invoices from the population of sales invoices during the month. Once you have collected the data, you organize the data in a worksheet. You can construct various graphs (not shown here) to better visualize the distribution of the dollar amounts. To analyze the data, you compute the sample mean of the 100 sales invoices to be equal to $110.27 and the sample standard deviation to be equal to $28.95. For 95% confidence, the critical value from the t distribution (as shown in Table 8.1 on page 256) is 1.9842. Using Equation (8.2),

$$\overline{X} \pm t_{\alpha/2}\frac{S}{\sqrt{n}}$$

$$= 110.27 \pm (1.9842)\frac{28.95}{\sqrt{100}}$$

$$= 110.27 \pm 5.74$$

$$104.53 \leq \mu \leq 116.01$$

Figure 8.7 presents this confidence interval estimate of the mean dollar amount as computed by Excel and Minitab.

FIGURE 8.7

Excel and Minitab results for the confidence interval estimate for the mean sales invoice amount worksheet for the Ricknel Home Centers example

	A	B	
1	Confidence Interval Estimate for the Mean		
2			
3	Data		
4	Sample Standard Deviation	28.95	
5	Sample Mean	110.27	
6	Sample Size	100	
7	Confidence Level	95%	
8			
9	Intermediate Calculations		
10	Standard Error of the Mean	2.895	=B4/SQRT(B6)
11	Degrees of Freedom	99	=B6 - 1
12	t Value	1.9842	=T.INV.2T(1 - B7, B11)
13	Interval Half Width	5.7443	=B12 * B10
14			
15	Confidence Interval		
16	Interval Lower Limit	104.53	=B5 - B13
17	Interval Upper Limit	116.01	=B5 + B13

One-Sample T

N	Mean	StDev	SE Mean	95% CI
100	110.27	28.95	2.90	(104.53, 116.01)

Thus, with 95% confidence, you conclude that the mean amount of all the sales invoices is between $104.53 and $116.01. The 95% confidence level indicates that if you selected all possible samples of 100 (something that is never done in practice), 95% of the intervals developed would include the population mean somewhere within the interval. The validity of this confidence interval estimate depends on the assumption of normality for the distribution of the amount of the sales invoices. With a sample of 100, the normality assumption is not overly restrictive, and the use of the *t* distribution is likely appropriate. Example 8.3 further illustrates how you construct the confidence interval for a mean when the population standard deviation is unknown.

EXAMPLE 8.3 Estimating the Mean Processing Time of Life Insurance Applications	An insurance company has the business objective of reducing the amount of time it takes to approve applications for life insurance. The approval process consists of underwriting, which includes a review of the application, a medical information bureau check, possible requests for additional medical information and medical exams, and a policy compilation stage in which the policy pages are generated and sent for delivery. Using the DCOVA steps first discussed on page 2, you define the variable of interest as the total processing time in days. You collect the data by selecting a random sample of 27 approved policies during a period of one month. You organize the data collected in a worksheet. Table 8.2 lists the total processing time, in days, which are stored in **Insurance**. To analyze the data, you need to construct a 95% confidence interval estimate for the population mean processing time.

TABLE 8.2

Processing Time for Life Insurance Applications

73	19	16	64	28	28	31	90	60	56	31	56	22	18
45	48	17	17	17	91	92	63	50	51	69	16	17	

SOLUTION To visualize the data, you construct a boxplot of the processing time, as displayed in Figure 8.8, and a normal probability plot, as shown in Figure 8.9. To analyze the data, you construct the confidence interval estimate shown in Figure 8.10.

FIGURE 8.8

Excel and Minitab boxplots for the processing time for life insurance applications

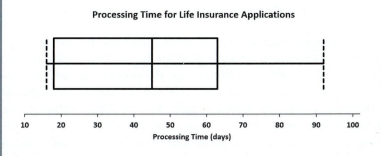
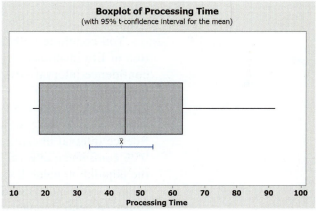

FIGURE 8.9

Excel and Minitab normal probability plots for the processing time for life insurance applications

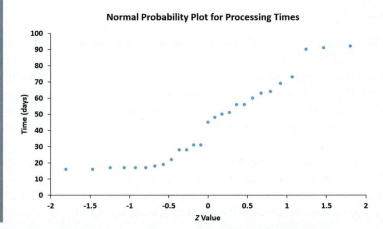
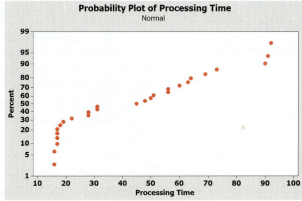

FIGURE 8.10

Excel and Minitab confidence interval estimates for the mean processing time worksheet for life insurance applications

	A	B
1	Processing Time for Life Insurance Applications	
2		
3	Data	
4	Sample Standard Deviation	25.28
5	Sample Mean	43.89
6	Sample Size	27
7	Confidence Level	95%
8		
9	Intermediate Calculations	
10	Standard Error of the Mean	4.8651
11	Degrees of Freedom	26
12	t Value	2.0555
13	Interval Half Width	10.0004
14		
15	Confidence Interval	
16	Interval Lower Limit	33.89
17	Interval Upper Limit	53.89

One-Sample T: Time

Variable	N	Mean	StDev	SE Mean	95% CI
Time	27	43.89	25.28	4.87	(33.89, 53.89)

Figure 8.10 shows that the sample mean is $\overline{X} = 43.89$ days and the sample standard deviation is $S = 25.28$ days. Using Equation (8.2) on page 259 to construct the confidence interval, you need to determine the critical value from the t table, using the row for 26 degrees of freedom. For 95% confidence, you use the column corresponding to an upper-tail area of 0.025 and a cumulative probability of 0.975. From Table E.3, you see that $t_{\alpha/2} = 2.0555$. Thus, using $\overline{X} = 43.89$, $S = 25.28$, $n = 27$, and $t_{\alpha/2} = 2.0555$,

$$\overline{X} \pm t_{\alpha/2}\frac{S}{\sqrt{n}}$$

$$= 43.89 \pm (2.0555)\frac{25.28}{\sqrt{27}}$$

$$= 43.89 \pm 10.00$$

$$33.89 \le \mu \le 53.89$$

You conclude with 95% confidence that the mean processing time for the population of life insurance applications is between 33.89 and 53.89 days. The validity of this confidence interval estimate depends on the assumption that the processing time is normally distributed. From the boxplot displayed in Figure 8.8 and the normal probability plot shown in Figure 8.9, the processing time appears right-skewed. Thus, although the sample size is close to 30, you would have some concern about the validity of this confidence interval in estimating the population mean processing time. The concern is that a 95% confidence interval based on a small sample from a skewed distribution will contain the population mean less than 95% of the time in repeated sampling. In the case of small sample sizes and skewed distributions, you might consider the sample median as an estimate of central tendency and construct a confidence interval for the population median (see reference 2).

The interpretation of the confidence interval when σ is unknown is the same as when σ is known. To illustrate the fact that the confidence interval for the mean varies more when σ is unknown, return to the example concerning the order-filling times discussed in Section 8.1 on pages 251 and 252. Suppose that, in this case, you do *not* know the population standard deviation and instead use the sample standard deviation to construct the confidence interval estimate of the mean. Figure 8.11 shows the results for each of 20 samples of $n = 10$ orders.

FIGURE 8.11

Confidence interval estimates of the mean for 20 samples of $n = 10$ randomly selected from the population of $N = 200$ orders with σ unknown

Sample	N	Mean	Std Dev	SE Mean	95% Conf. Int.
S01	10	71.64	7.58	2.40	(66.22, 77.06)
S02	10	67.22	10.95	3.46	(59.39, 75.05)
S03	10	67.97	14.83	4.69	(57.36, 78.58)
S04	10	73.90	10.59	3.35	(66.33, 81.47)
S05	10	67.11	11.12	3.52	(59.15, 75.07)
S06	10	68.12	10.83	3.43	(60.37, 75.87)
S07	10	65.80	10.85	3.43	(58.03, 73.57)
S08	10	77.58	11.04	3.49	(69.68, 85.48)
S09	10	66.69	11.45	3.62	(58.50, 74.88)
S10	10	62.55	8.58	2.71	(56.41, 68.69)
S11	10	71.12	12.82	4.05	(61.95, 80.29)
S12	10	70.55	10.52	3.33	(63.02, 78.08)
S13	10	65.51	8.16	2.58	(59.67, 71.35)
S14	10	64.90	7.55	2.39	(59.50, 70.30)
S15	10	66.22	11.21	3.54	(58.20, 74.24)
S16	10	70.43	10.21	3.23	(63.12, 77.74)
S17	10	72.04	6.25	1.96	(67.57, 76.51)
S18	10	73.91	11.29	3.57	(65.83, 81.99)
S19	10	71.49	9.76	3.09	(64.51, 78.47)
S20	10	70.15	10.84	3.43	(62.39, 77.91)

In Figure 8.11, observe that the standard deviation of the samples varies from 6.25 (sample 17) to 14.83 (sample 3). Thus, the width of the confidence interval developed varies from 8.94 in sample 17 to 21.22 in sample 3. Because you know that the population mean order time $\mu = 69.637$ minutes, you can see that the interval for sample $8\,(69.68 - 85.48)$ and the interval for sample $10\,(56.41 - 68.69)$ do not correctly estimate the population mean. All the other intervals correctly estimate the population mean. Once again, remember that in practice you select only one sample, and you are unable to know for sure whether your one sample provides a confidence interval that includes the population mean.

Problems for Section 8.2

LEARNING THE BASICS

8.11 If $\overline{X} = 75, S = 24$, and $n = 36$, and assuming that the population is normally distributed, construct a 95% confidence interval estimate for the population mean, μ.

8.12 Determine the critical value of t in each of the following circumstances:
a. $1 - \alpha = 0.95, n = 10$
b. $1 - \alpha = 0.99, n = 10$
c. $1 - \alpha = 0.95, n = 32$
d. $1 - \alpha = 0.95, n = 65$
e. $1 - \alpha = 0.90, n = 16$

8.13 Assuming that the population is normally distributed, construct a 95% confidence interval estimate for the population mean for each of the following samples:

Sample A: 1 1 1 1 8 8 8 8

Sample B: 1 2 3 4 5 6 7 8

Explain why these two samples produce different confidence intervals even though they have the same mean and range.

8.14 Assuming that the population is normally distributed, construct a 95% confidence interval for the population mean, based on the following sample of size $n = 7$:

1 2 3 4 5 6 20

Change the value of 20 to 7 and recalculate the confidence interval. Using these results, describe the effect of an outlier (i.e., an extreme value) on the confidence interval.

APPLYING THE CONCEPTS

8.15 A marketing researcher wants to estimate the mean savings ($) realized by shoppers who showroom. Showrooming is the practice of inspecting products in retail stores and then purchasing the products online at a lower price. A random sample of 100 shoppers who recently purchased a consumer electronics item online after making a visit to a retail store yielded a mean savings of $58 and a standard deviation of $55.
a. Construct a 95% confidence interval estimate for the mean savings for all showroomers who purchased a consumer electronics item.
b. Suppose the owners of a consumer electronics retailer wants to estimate the total value of lost sales attributed to the next 1,000 showroomers that enter their retail store. How are the results in (a) useful in assisting the consumer electronics retailer in their estimation?

✓ SELF Test **8.16** A survey of nonprofit organizations showed that online fundraising has increased in the past year. Based on a random sample of 55 nonprofits, the mean one-time gift donation in the past year was $75, with a standard deviation of $9.
a. Construct a 95% confidence interval estimate for the population mean one-time gift donation.
b. Interpret the interval constructed in (a).

8.17 The U.S. Department of Transportation requires tire manufacturers to provide tire performance information on the sidewall of a tire to better inform prospective customers as they make purchasing decisions. One very important measure of tire performance is the tread wear index, which indicates the tire's resistance to tread wear compared with a tire graded with a base of 100.

A tire with a grade of 200 should last twice as long, on average, as a tire graded with a base of 100. A consumer organization wants to estimate the actual tread wear index of a brand name of tires that claims "graded 200" on the sidewall of the tire. A random sample of $n = 18$ indicates a sample mean tread wear index of 195.3 and a sample standard deviation of 21.4.

a. Assuming that the population of tread wear indexes is normally distributed, construct a 95% confidence interval estimate for the population mean tread wear index for tires produced by this manufacturer under this brand name.

b. Do you think that the consumer organization should accuse the manufacturer of producing tires that do not meet the performance information provided on the sidewall of the tire? Explain.

c. Explain why an observed tread wear index of 210 for a particular tire is not unusual, even though it is outside the confidence interval developed in (a).

8.18 The file **FastFood** contains the amount that a sample of 15 customers spent for lunch ($) at a fast-food restaurant:

   7.42 6.29 5.83 6.50 8.34 9.51 7.10 6.80 5.90
   4.89 6.50 5.52 7.90 8.30 9.60

a. Construct a 95% confidence interval estimate for the population mean amount spent for lunch ($) at a fast-food restaurant, assuming a normal distribution.

b. Interpret the interval constructed in (a).

8.19 The file **Sedans** contains the overall miles per gallon (MPG) of 2014 midsized sedans:

   38 26 30 26 25 27 24 22 27 32 39
   26 24 24 23 24 25 31 26 37 22 33

Source: Data extracted from "Which Car Is Right for You," *Consumer Reports,* April 2014, pp. 40–41.

a. Construct a 95% confidence interval estimate for the population mean MPG of 2014 midsized sedans, assuming a normal distribution.

b. Interpret the interval constructed in (a).

c. Compare the results in (a) to those in Problem 8.20(a).

8.20 The file **SUV** contains the overall MPG of 2014 small SUVs:

   26 22 23 21 25 24 22 26 25 22
   21 21 22 22 23 24 23 22 21 22

Source: Data extracted from "Which Car Is Right for You," *Consumer Reports,* April 2014, pp. 60–61.

a. Construct a 95% confidence interval estimate for the population mean MPG of 2014 small SUVs, assuming a normal distribution.

b. Interpret the interval constructed in (a).

c. Compare the results in (a) to those in Problem 8.19(a).

8.21 Is there a difference in the yields of different types of investments? The file **CDRate** contains the yields for a one-year certificate of deposit (CD) and a five-year CD for 22 banks in the United States as of March 12, 2014. (Data extracted from **www.Bankrate.com**, March 12, 2014.)

a. Construct a 95% confidence interval estimate for the mean yield of one-year CDs.

b. Construct a 95% confidence interval estimate for the mean yield of five-year CDs.

c. Compare the results of (a) and (b).

8.22 One of the major measures of the quality of service provided by any organization is the speed with which the organization responds to customer complaints. A large family-held department store selling furniture and flooring, including carpet, had undergone a major expansion in the past several years. In particular, the flooring department had expanded from 2 installation crews to an installation supervisor, a measurer, and 15 installation crews. The store had the business objective of improving its response to complaints. The variable of interest was defined as the number of days between when the complaint was made and when it was resolved. Data were collected from 50 complaints that were made in the past year. The data, stored in **Furniture**, are as follows:

   54 5 35 137   31 27 152   2 123 81 74 27
   11 19 126 110 110 29   61 35   94 31 26 5
   12 4 165 32 29 28   29 26 25 1 14 13
   13 10   5 27   4 52 30 22 36 26 20 23
   33 68

a. Construct a 95% confidence interval estimate for the population mean number of days between the receipt of a complaint and the resolution of the complaint.

b. What assumption must you make about the population distribution in order to construct the confidence interval estimate in (a)?

c. Do you think that the assumption needed in order to construct the confidence interval estimate in (a) is valid? Explain.

d. What effect might your conclusion in (c) have on the validity of the results in (a)?

8.23 A manufacturing company produces electric insulators. You define the variable of interest as the strength of the insulators. If the insulators break when in use, a short circuit is likely. To test the strength of the insulators, you carry out destructive testing to determine how much force is required to break the insulators. You measure force by observing how many pounds are applied to the insulator before it breaks. You collect the force data for 30 insulators selected for the experiment and organize and store these data in **Force**:

   1,870 1,728 1,656 1,610 1,634 1,784 1,522 1,696
   1,592 1,662 1,866 1,764 1,734 1,662 1,734 1,774
   1,550 1,756 1,762 1,866 1,820 1,744 1,788 1,688
   1,810 1,752 1,680 1,810 1,652 1,736

a. Construct a 95% confidence interval estimate for the population mean force.

b. What assumption must you make about the population distribution in order to construct the confidence interval estimate in (a)?

c. Do you think that the assumption needed in order to construct the confidence interval estimate in (a) is valid? Explain.

8.24 The file **Market Penetration** contains Facebook penetration values (the percentage of the country population that are Facebook users) for 22 of the world's largest economies:

   56 57 43 55 42 35   7 25 42 17 43
    6 31 28 59 20 27 36 45 80 57 56

Source: Data extracted from **slidesha.re/ODv6vG**.

a. Construct a 95% confidence interval estimate for the population mean Facebook penetration.

b. What assumption do you need to make about the population to construct the interval in (a)?

c. Given the data presented, do you think the assumption needed in (a) is valid? Explain.

8.25 One operation of a mill is to cut pieces of steel into parts that are used in the frame for front seats in an automobile. The steel is cut with a diamond saw, and the resulting parts must be cut to be within ±0.005 inch of the length specified by the automobile company. The measurement reported from a sample of 100 steel parts (stored in **Steel**) is the difference, in inches, between the actual length of the steel part, as measured by a laser

measurement device, and the specified length of the steel part. For example, the first observation, −0.002, represents a steel part that is 0.002 inch shorter than the specified length.

a. Construct a 95% confidence interval estimate for the population mean difference between the actual length of the steel part and the specified length of the steel part.

b. What assumption must you make about the population distribution in order to construct the confidence interval estimate in (a)?

c. Do you think that the assumption needed in order to construct the confidence interval estimate in (a) is valid? Explain.

d. Compare the conclusions reached in (a) with those of Problem 2.43 on page 59.

8.3 Confidence Interval Estimate for the Proportion

The concept of a confidence interval also applies to categorical data. With categorical data, you want to estimate the proportion of items in a population having a certain characteristic of interest. The unknown population proportion is represented by the Greek letter π. The point estimate for π is the sample proportion, $p = X/n$, where n is the sample size and X is the number of items in the sample having the characteristic of interest. Equation (8.3) defines the confidence interval estimate for the population proportion.

> ### CONFIDENCE INTERVAL ESTIMATE FOR THE PROPORTION
>
> $$p \pm Z_{\alpha/2}\sqrt{\frac{p(1-p)}{n}}$$
>
> or
>
> $$p - Z_{\alpha/2}\sqrt{\frac{p(1-p)}{n}} \le \pi \le p + Z_{\alpha/2}\sqrt{\frac{p(1-p)}{n}} \tag{8.3}$$
>
> where
>
> $$p = \text{sample proportion} = \frac{X}{n} = \frac{\text{Number of items having the characteristic}}{\text{sample size}}$$
>
> π = population proportion
>
> $Z_{\alpha/2}$ = critical value from the standardized normal distribution
>
> n = sample size
>
> Note: To use this equation for the confidence interval, the sample size n must be large enough to ensure that both X and $n - X$ are greater than 5.

You can use the confidence interval estimate for the proportion defined in Equation (8.3) to estimate the proportion of sales invoices that contain errors (see the Ricknel Home Centers scenario on page 248). Using the DCOVA steps, you define the variable of interest as whether the invoice contains errors (yes or no). Then, you collect the data from a sample of 100 sales invoices. The results, which you organize and store in a worksheet, show that 10 invoices contain errors. To analyze the data, you compute, for these data, $p = X/n = 10/100 = 0.10$. Since both $X = 10$ and $n - X = 100 - 10 = 90$ are > 5, using Equation (8.3) and $Z_{\alpha/2} = 1.96$, for 95% confidence,

$$p \pm Z_{\alpha/2}\sqrt{\frac{p(1-p)}{n}}$$

$$= 0.10 \pm (1.96)\sqrt{\frac{(0.10)(0.90)}{100}}$$

$$= 0.10 \pm (1.96)(0.03)$$

$$= 0.10 \pm 0.0588$$

$$0.0412 \leq \pi \leq 0.1588$$

Therefore, you have 95% confidence that the population proportion of all sales invoices containing errors is between 0.0412 and 0.1588. This means that you estimate that between 4.12% and 15.88% of all the sales invoices contain errors. Figure 8.12 shows a confidence interval estimate for this example.

FIGURE 8.12

Excel and Minitab confidence interval estimates for the proportion of sales invoices that contain errors worksheet

Test and CI for One Proportion

Sample	X	N	Sample p	95% CI
1	10	100	0.100000	(0.041201, 0.158799)

Using the normal approximation.

	A	B
1	Proportion of In-Error Sales Invoices	
2		
3	Data	
4	Sample Size	100
5	Number of Successes	10
6	Confidence Level	95%
7		
8	Intermediate Calculations	
9	Sample Proportion	0.1
10	Z Value	-1.9600
11	Standard Error of the Proportion	0.03
12	Interval Half Width	0.0588
13		
14	Confidence Interval	
15	Interval Lower Limit	0.0412
16	Interval Upper Limit	0.1588

Example 8.4 illustrates another application of a confidence interval estimate for the proportion.

EXAMPLE 8.4

Estimating the Proportion of Nonconforming Newspapers Printed

The operations manager at a large newspaper wants to estimate the proportion of newspapers printed that have a nonconforming attribute. Using the DCOVA steps, you define the variable of interest as whether the newspaper has excessive rub-off, improper page setup, missing pages, or duplicate pages. You collect the data by selecting a random sample of $n = 200$ newspapers from all the newspapers printed during a single day. You organize the results in a worksheet, which shows that 35 newspapers contain some type of nonconformance. To analyze the data, you need to construct and interpret a 90% confidence interval estimate for the proportion of newspapers printed during the day that have a nonconforming attribute.

SOLUTION Using Equation (8.3),

$$p = \frac{X}{n} = \frac{35}{200} = 0.175, \text{ and with a 90\% level of confidence } Z_{\alpha/2} = 1.645$$

$$p \pm Z_{\alpha/2}\sqrt{\frac{p(1-p)}{n}}$$

$$= 0.175 \pm (1.645)\sqrt{\frac{(0.175)(0.825)}{200}}$$

$$= 0.175 \pm (1.645)(0.0269)$$

$$= 0.175 \pm 0.0442$$

$$0.1308 \leq \pi \leq 0.2192$$

You conclude with 90% confidence that the population proportion of all newspapers printed that day with nonconformities is between 0.1308 and 0.2192. This means you estimate that between 13.08% and 21.92% of the newspapers printed on that day have some type of nonconformance.

Equation (8.3) contains a *Z* statistic because you can use the normal distribution to approximate the binomial distribution when the sample size is sufficiently large. In Example 8.4, the confidence interval using *Z* provides an excellent approximation for the population proportion because both *X* and *n* − *X* are greater than 5. However, if you do not have a sufficiently large sample size, you should use the binomial distribution rather than Equation (8.3) (see references 1, 3, and 9). The exact confidence intervals for various sample sizes and proportions of items of interest have been tabulated by Fisher and Yates (reference 3) and can also be computed using Minitab.

Problems for Section 8.3

LEARNING THE BASICS

8.26 If *n* = 200 and *X* = 50, construct a 95% confidence interval estimate for the population proportion.

8.27 If *n* = 400 and *X* = 25, construct a 99% confidence interval estimate for the population proportion.

APPLYING THE CONCEPTS

✓SELF **8.28** A cellphone provider has the business objective **Test** of wanting to estimate the proportion of subscribers who would upgrade to a new cellphone with improved features if it were made available at a substantially reduced cost. Data are collected from a random sample of 500 subscribers. The results indicate that 135 of the subscribers would upgrade to a new cellphone at a reduced cost.

a. Construct a 99% confidence interval estimate for the population proportion of subscribers that would upgrade to a new cellphone at a reduced cost.

b. How would the manager in charge of promotional programs use the results in (a)?

8.29 In a survey of 529 travelers, 386 said that location was very important and 323 said that room quality was very important in choosing a hotel. (Source: C. Jones, "Top Reason for Picking a Hotel? It's Where It's At," *USA Today*, April 28, 2014, p. 3B.)

a. Construct a 95% confidence interval estimate for the population proportion of travelers who said that location was very important for choosing a hotel.

b. Construct a 95% confidence interval estimate for the population proportion of travelers who said that room quality was very important in choosing a hotel.

c. Write a short summary of the information derived from (a) and (b).

8.30 Are you likely to purchase an item promoted by a celebrity on a social media site? According to a Brand Republic survey, 26% of social media users have made such a purchase (Source: "Celebrity endorsement on social media," **bit.ly/1o4yNHa**.)

a. Suppose that the survey had a sample size of *n* = 1,000. Construct a 95% confidence interval estimate for the population proportion of social media users that have purchased an item promoted by a celebrity on a social media site.

b. Based on (a), can you claim that more than a quarter of all social media users have purchased an item promoted by a celebrity on a social media site?

c. Repeat parts (a) and (b), assuming that the survey had a sample size of *n* = 10,000.

d. Discuss the effect of sample size on confidence interval estimation.

8.31 In a survey of 239 organizations, 75 responded that "the need for collaboration among increasing number of locations" is a business driver that led them to implement cloud solutions. Cloud solutions enable more effective employee communication and higher decision maker visibility into real-time data. (Source: *The Benefits of Cloud ERP: It's About Transforming Your Business,* Aberdeen Group, available at **bit.ly/1meEC3D**.)

Construct a 95% confidence interval estimate for the population proportion of organizations that indicated "the need for collaboration among increasing number of locations" as a business driver for cloud solution implementation.

8.32 In a Pew Research Center survey of 960 Facebook users, 452 cited "seeing photos or videos" as a major reason why they use Facebook, while 298 cited "keeping up with news and current events" as a major reason why they use Facebook. (Source: "6 new facts about Facebook," **bit.ly/1lAmkv5**.)

a. Construct a 95% confidence interval estimate for the population proportion of Facebook users who cite "seeing photos or videos" as a major reason for why they use Facebook.

b. Construct a 95% confidence interval estimate for the population proportion of Facebook users who cite "keeping up with news and current events" as a major reason why they use Facebook.

c. Compare the results of (a) and (b).

8.33 What are the global trends that technology CEOs believe will transform their business? According to a PwC white paper, 105 of 117 technology CEOs from around the world responded that technological advances will transform their business and 42 responded that resource scarcity and climate change will transform their business. (Source: *Fit for the Future: 17th Annual Global CEO Survey,* available at **pwc.to/PRQZYr**.)

a. Construct a 95% confidence interval estimate for the population proportion of tech CEOs who indicate technological advances as one of the global trends that will transform their business.

b. Construct a 95% confidence interval estimate for the population proportion of tech CEOs who indicate resource scarcity and climate change as one of the global trends that will transform their business.

c. Interpret the intervals in (a) and (b).

8.4 Determining Sample Size

In each confidence interval developed so far in this chapter, the sample size was reported along with the results, with little discussion of the width of the resulting confidence interval. In the business world, sample sizes are determined prior to data collection to ensure that the confidence interval is narrow enough to be useful in making decisions. Determining the proper sample size is a complicated procedure, subject to the constraints of budget, time, and the amount of acceptable sampling error. In the Ricknel Home Centers scenario, if you want to estimate the mean dollar amount of the sales invoices, you must determine in advance how large a sampling error to allow in estimating the population mean. You must also determine, in advance, the level of confidence (i.e., 90%, 95%, or 99%) to use in estimating the population parameter.

Sample Size Determination for the Mean

To develop an equation for determining the appropriate sample size needed when constructing a confidence interval estimate for the mean, recall Equation (8.1) on page 252:

$$\overline{X} \pm Z_{\alpha/2} \frac{\sigma}{\sqrt{n}}$$

[2] In this context, some statisticians refer to e as the **margin of error**.

The amount added to or subtracted from $\overline{X}$ is equal to half the width of the interval. This quantity represents the amount of imprecision in the estimate that results from sampling error.[2] The sampling error, e, is defined as

$$e = Z_{\alpha/2} \frac{\sigma}{\sqrt{n}}$$

Solving for n gives the sample size needed to construct the appropriate confidence interval estimate for the mean. "Appropriate" means that the resulting interval will have an acceptable amount of sampling error.

SAMPLE SIZE DETERMINATION FOR THE MEAN

The sample size, n, is equal to the product of the $Z_{\alpha/2}$ value squared and the standard deviation, σ, squared, divided by the square of the sampling error, e.

$$n = \frac{Z_{\alpha/2}^2 \, \sigma^2}{e^2} \qquad\qquad (8.4)$$

To compute the sample size, you must know three quantities:

- The desired confidence level, which determines the value of $Z_{\alpha/2}$, the critical value from the standardized normal distribution[3]
- The acceptable sampling error, e
- The standard deviation, σ

[3] You use Z instead of t because, to determine the critical value of t, you need to know the sample size, but you do not know it yet. For most studies, the sample size needed is large enough that the standardized normal distribution is a good approximation of the t distribution.

In some business-to-business relationships that require estimation of important parameters, legal contracts specify acceptable levels of sampling error and the confidence level required. For companies in the food and drug sectors, government regulations often specify sampling errors and confidence levels. In general, however, it is usually not easy to specify the three quantities needed to determine the sample size. How can you determine the level of confidence and sampling error? Typically, these questions are answered only by a subject matter expert (i.e., an individual very familiar with the variables under study). Although 95% is the most common confidence level used, if more confidence is desired, then 99% might be more appropriate; if less confidence is deemed acceptable, then 90% might be used. For the sampling error, you should think not of how much sampling error you would like to have (you really do not want any error) but of how much you can tolerate when reaching conclusions from the confidence interval.

In addition to specifying the confidence level and the sampling error, you need an estimate of the standard deviation. Unfortunately, you rarely know the population standard deviation, σ. In some instances, you can estimate the standard deviation from past data. In other situations, you can make an educated guess by taking into account the range and distribution of the variable. For example, if you assume a normal distribution, the range is approximately equal to 6σ (i.e., $\pm 3\sigma$ around the mean) so that you estimate σ as the range divided by 6. If you cannot estimate σ in this way, you can conduct a small-scale study and estimate the standard deviation from the resulting data.

To explore how to determine the sample size needed for estimating the population mean, consider again the audit at Ricknel Home Centers. In Section 8.2, you selected a sample of 100 sales invoices and constructed a 95% confidence interval estimate for the population mean sales invoice amount. How was this sample size determined? Should you have selected a different sample size?

Suppose that, after consulting with company officials, you determine that a sampling error of no more than $\pm \$5$ is desired, along with 95% confidence. Past data indicate that the standard deviation of the sales amount is approximately $25. Thus, $e = \$5, \sigma = \$25$, and $Z_{\alpha/2} = 1.96$ (for 95% confidence). Using Equation (8.4),

$$n = \frac{Z_{\alpha/2}^2 \sigma^2}{e^2} = \frac{(1.96)^2(25)^2}{(5)^2}$$
$$= 96.04$$

Because the general rule is to slightly oversatisfy the criteria by rounding the sample size up to the next whole integer, you should select a sample of size 97. Thus, the sample of size $n = 100$ used on page 258 is slightly more than what is necessary to satisfy the needs of the company, based on the estimated standard deviation, desired confidence level, and sampling error. Because the calculated sample standard deviation is slightly higher than expected, $28.95 compared to $25.00, the confidence interval is slightly wider than desired. Figure 8.13 shows a worksheet for determining the sample size.

FIGURE 8.13

Excel worksheet for determining the sample size for estimating the mean sales invoice amount for the Ricknel Home Centers example

	A	B	
1	For the Mean Sales Invoice Amount		
2			
3	Data		
4	Population Standard Deviation	25	
5	Sampling Error	5	
6	Confidence Level	95%	
7			
8	Intemediate Calculations		
9	Z Value	-1.9600	=NORM.S.INV((1 - B6)/2)
10	Calculated Sample Size	96.0365	=((B9 * B4)/B5)^2
11			
12	Result		
13	Sample Size Needed	97	=ROUNDUP(B10, 0)

Example 8.5 illustrates another application of determining the sample size needed to develop a confidence interval estimate for the mean.

EXAMPLE 8.5

Determining the Sample Size for the Mean

Returning to Example 8.3 on page 259, suppose you want to estimate, with 95% confidence, the population mean processing time to within ± 4 days. On the basis of a study conducted the previous year, you believe that the standard deviation is 25 days. Determine the sample size needed.

SOLUTION Using Equation (8.4) on page 266 and $e = 4$, $\sigma = 25$, and $Z_{\alpha/2} = 1.96$ for 95% confidence,

$$n = \frac{Z_{\alpha/2}^2 \sigma^2}{e^2} = \frac{(1.96)^2(25)^2}{(4)^2}$$

$$= 150.06$$

Therefore, you should select a sample of 151 applications because the general rule for determining sample size is to always round up to the next integer value in order to slightly oversatisfy the criteria desired. An actual sampling error slightly larger than 4 will result if the sample standard deviation calculated in this sample of 151 is greater than 25 and slightly smaller if the sample standard deviation is less than 25.

Sample Size Determination for the Proportion

So far in this section, you have learned how to determine the sample size needed for estimating the population mean. Now suppose that you want to determine the sample size necessary for estimating a population proportion.

To determine the sample size needed to estimate a population proportion, π, you use a method similar to the method for a population mean. Recall that in developing the sample size for a confidence interval for the mean, the sampling error is defined by

$$e = Z_{\alpha/2} \frac{\sigma}{\sqrt{n}}$$

When estimating a proportion, you replace σ with $\sqrt{\pi(1 - \pi)}$. Thus, the sampling error is

$$e = Z_{\alpha/2} \sqrt{\frac{\pi(1 - \pi)}{n}}$$

Solving for n, you have the sample size necessary to develop a confidence interval estimate for a proportion.

SAMPLE SIZE DETERMINATION FOR THE PROPORTION

The sample size n is equal to the product of $Z_{\alpha/2}$ squared, the population proportion, π, and 1 minus the population proportion, π, divided by the square of the sampling error, e.

$$n = \frac{Z_{\alpha/2}^2 \pi(1 - \pi)}{e^2} \tag{8.5}$$

To determine the sample size, you must know three quantities:

- The desired confidence level, which determines the value of $Z_{\alpha/2}$, the critical value from the standardized normal distribution
- The acceptable sampling error (or margin of error), e
- The population proportion, π

In practice, selecting these quantities requires some planning. Once you determine the desired level of confidence, you can find the appropriate $Z_{\alpha/2}$ value from the standardized normal distribution. The sampling error, e, indicates the amount of error that you are willing to tolerate in estimating the population proportion. The third quantity, π, is actually the population parameter that you want to estimate! Thus, how do you state a value for what you are trying to determine?

Here you have two alternatives. In many situations, you may have past information or relevant experience that provides an educated estimate of π. If you do not have past information or relevant experience, you can try to provide a value for π that would never *underestimate* the sample size needed. Referring to Equation (8.5), you can see that the quantity $\pi(1 - \pi)$ appears in the numerator. Thus, you need to determine the value of π that will make the quantity $\pi(1 - \pi)$ as large as possible. When $\pi = 0.5$, the product $\pi(1 - \pi)$ achieves its maximum value. To show this result, consider the following values of π, along with the accompanying products of $\pi(1 - \pi)$:

When $\pi = 0.9$, then $\pi(1 - \pi) = (0.9)(0.1) = 0.09$.

When $\pi = 0.7$, then $\pi(1 - \pi) = (0.7)(0.3) = 0.21$.

When $\pi = 0.5$, then $\pi(1 - \pi) = (0.5)(0.5) = 0.25$.

When $\pi = 0.3$, then $\pi(1 - \pi) = (0.3)(0.7) = 0.21$.

When $\pi = 0.1$, then $\pi(1 - \pi) = (0.1)(0.9) = 0.09$.

Therefore, when you have no prior knowledge or estimate for the population proportion, π, you should use $\pi = 0.5$ for determining the sample size. Using $\pi = 0.5$ produces the largest possible sample size and results in the narrowest and most precise confidence interval. This increased precision comes at the cost of spending more time and money for an increased sample size. Also, note that if you use $\pi = 0.5$ and the proportion is different from 0.5, you will overestimate the sample size needed, because you will get a confidence interval narrower than originally intended.

Returning to the Ricknel Home Centers scenario on page 248, suppose that the auditing procedures require you to have 95% confidence in estimating the population proportion of sales invoices with errors to within ± 0.07. The results from past months indicate that the largest proportion has been no more than 0.15. Thus, using Equation (8.5) with $e = 0.07$, $\pi = 0.15$, and $Z_{\alpha/2} = 1.96$ for 95% confidence,

$$n = \frac{Z_{\alpha/2}^2 \pi(1 - \pi)}{e^2}$$

$$= \frac{(1.96)^2(0.15)(0.85)}{(0.07)^2}$$

$$= 99.96$$

Because the general rule is to round the sample size up to the next whole integer to slightly oversatisfy the criteria, a sample size of 100 is needed. Thus, the sample size needed to satisfy the requirements of the company, based on the estimated proportion, desired confidence level, and sampling error, is equal to the sample size taken on page 263. The actual confidence interval is narrower than required because the sample proportion is 0.10, whereas 0.15 was used for π in Equation (8.5). Figure 8.14 shows a worksheet for determining the sample size.

FIGURE 8.14

Excel worksheet for determining sample size for estimating the proportion of in-error sales invoices for Ricknel Home Centers

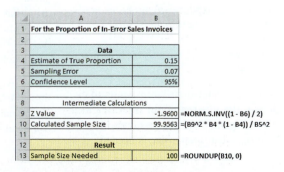

	A	B
1	For the Proportion of In-Error Sales Invoices	
2		
3	Data	
4	Estimate of True Proportion	0.15
5	Sampling Error	0.07
6	Confidence Level	95%
7		
8	Intermediate Calculations	
9	Z Value	-1.9600 =NORM.S.INV((1 - B6) / 2)
10	Calculated Sample Size	99.9563 =(B9^2 * B4 * (1 - B4)) / B5^2
11		
12	Result	
13	Sample Size Needed	100 =ROUNDUP(B10, 0)

Example 8.6 provides another application of determining the sample size for estimating the population proportion.

EXAMPLE 8.6

Determining the Sample Size for the Population Proportion

You want to have 90% confidence of estimating the proportion of office workers who respond to email within an hour to within ± 0.05. Because you have not previously undertaken such a study, there is no information available from past data. Determine the sample size needed.

SOLUTION Because no information is available from past data, assume that $\pi = 0.50$. Using Equation (8.5) on page 269 and $e = 0.05$, $\pi = 0.50$, and $Z_{\alpha/2} = 1.645$ for 90% confidence,

$$n = \frac{Z_{\alpha/2}^2 \pi(1 - \pi)}{e^2}$$

$$= \frac{(1.645)^2(0.50)(0.50)}{(0.05)^2}$$

$$= 270.6$$

Therefore, you need a sample of 271 office workers to estimate the population proportion to within ± 0.05 with 90% confidence.

Problems for Section 8.4

LEARNING THE BASICS

8.34 If you want to be 95% confident of estimating the population mean to within a sampling error of ± 5 and the standard deviation is assumed to be 15, what sample size is required?

8.35 If you want to be 99% confident of estimating the population mean to within a sampling error of ± 20 and the standard deviation is assumed to be 100, what sample size is required?

8.36 If you want to be 99% confident of estimating the population proportion to within a sampling error of ± 0.04, what sample size is needed?

8.37 If you want to be 95% confident of estimating the population proportion to within a sampling error of ± 0.02 and there is historical evidence that the population proportion is approximately 0.40, what sample size is needed?

APPLYING THE CONCEPTS

√SELF Test **8.38** A survey is planned to determine the mean annual family medical expenses of employees of a large company. The management of the company wishes to be 95% confident that the sample mean is correct to within $\pm \$50$ of the population mean annual family medical expenses. A previous study indicates that the standard deviation is approximately $400.
a. How large a sample is necessary?
b. If management wants to be correct to within $\pm \$25$, how many employees need to be selected?

8.39 If the manager of a bottled water distributor wants to estimate, with 95% confidence, the mean amount of water in a 1-gallon bottle to within ± 0.004 gallon and also assumes that the standard deviation is 0.02 gallon, what sample size is needed?

8.40 If a light bulb manufacturing company wants to estimate, with 95% confidence, the mean life of compact fluorescent light bulbs to within ± 200 hours and also assumes that the population standard deviation is 1,000 hours, how many compact fluorescent light bulbs need to be selected?

8.41 If the inspection division of a county weights and measures department wants to estimate the mean amount of soft-drink fill in 2-liter bottles to within ± 0.01 liter with 95% confidence and also assumes that the standard deviation is 0.05 liter, what sample size is needed?

8.42 An advertising executive wants to estimate the mean weekly amount of time consumers spend watching traditional television daily. Based on previous studies, the standard deviation is assumed to be 20 minutes. The executive wants to estimate, with 99% confidence, the mean weekly amount of time to within ± 5 minutes.
a. What sample size is needed?
b. If 95% confidence is desired, how many consumers need to be selected?

8.43 An advertising executive wants to estimate the mean amount of time that consumers spend with digital media daily. From past studies, the standard deviation is estimated as 45 minutes.
a. What sample size is needed if the executive wants to be 90% confident of being correct to within ± 5 minutes?
b. If 99% confidence is desired, how many consumers need to be selected?

8.44 A growing niche in the restaurant business is gourmet-casual breakfast, lunch, and brunch. Chains in this group include EggSpectation and Panera Bread. Suppose that the mean per-person check for breakfast at EggSpectation is approximately $14.50.

a. Assuming a standard deviation of $2.00, what sample size is needed to estimate, with 95% confidence, the mean per-person check for EggSpectation to within $\pm\$0.25$?

b. Assuming a standard deviation of $2.50, what sample size is needed to estimate, with 95% confidence, the mean per-person check for EggSpectation to within $\pm\$0.25$?

c. Assuming a standard deviation of $3.00, what sample size is needed to estimate, with 95% confidence, the mean per-person check for EggSpectation to within $\pm\$0.25$?

d. Discuss the effect of variation on the sample size needed.

8.45 What advertising medium gives a brand the most credibility in influencing brand decisions? According to an Adroit Digital survey, 35% of Millennials point to TV. (Source: "U.S. Millennials: TV is Most Influential Advertising Medium," *MC Marketing Charts*, March 20, 2014.)

a. To conduct a follow-up study that would provide 95% confidence that the point estimate is correct to within ±0.04 of the population proportion, how large a sample size is required?

b. To conduct a follow-up study that would provide 99% confidence that the point estimate is correct to within ±0.04 of the population proportion, how many people need to be sampled?

c. To conduct a follow-up study that would provide 95% confidence that the point estimate is correct to within ±0.02 of the population proportion, how large a sample size is required?

d. To conduct a follow-up study that would provide 99% confidence that the point estimate is correct to within ±0.02 of the population proportion, how many people need to be sampled?

e. Discuss the effects on sample size requirements of changing the desired confidence level and the acceptable sampling error.

8.46 A Nielsen Mobile Shopping Report looks at how consumers are using mobile devices throughout their purchase journey. In response to a survey question about shopping, 27% of tablet owners said they use mobile devices for payment, 21% said they use such devices to make social media comments about their purchases, and 10% said they use such devices to retrieve mobile coupons. (Source: "Mobile Ticks All the Shopping Boxes," **bit.ly/1hfKC8K.**)

Suppose the results are based on a survey of 300 tablet owners. Construct a 95% confidence interval estimate of the population proportion of tablet owners who said they use their mobile device while shopping

a. for payment.

b. to make social media comments about their purchases.

c. to retrieve mobile coupons.

d. You have been asked to update the results of this study. Determine the sample size necessary to estimate, with 95% confidence, the population proportions in (a) through (c) to within ±0.02.

8.47 In a study of 413 nonprofits nationwide, 83 indicated that turnover has been the biggest employment challenge at their organization. (Source: Nonprofit HR, *2014 Nonprofit Employment Practices Survey*, available at **bit.ly/1mfy2tJ.**)

a. Construct a 95% confidence interval for the population proportion of nonprofits that indicate turnover as the biggest employment challenge at their organization.

b. Interpret the interval constructed in (a).

c. If you wanted to conduct a follow-up study to estimate the population proportion of nonprofits that indicate turnover as the biggest employment challenge at their organization to within ±0.01 with 95% confidence, how many nonprofits would you survey?

8.48 According to a study released by The Financial Brand, an online publication focusing on branding issues and advice affecting retail banks and credit unions, 68% of financial institutions use churn rate (attrition) to gauge the effectiveness of their marketing efforts. (Source: "2014 State of Bank & Credit Union Marketing," **bit.ly/1np8FVx.**)

a. If you conduct a follow-up study to estimate the population proportion of financial institutions that use churn rate to gauge the effectiveness of their marketing efforts, would you use a π of 0.68 or 0.50 in the sample size formula?

b. Using your answer in (a), find the sample size necessary to estimate, with 95% confidence, the population proportion to within ±0.03.

8.49 What prevents consumers from sharing data with retailers? A recent ClickFox Consumer Behavior Survey (**bit.ly/1fAfJAI**) found that 32% of consumers responded "breaches of consumer data."

a. To conduct a follow-up study that would provide 99% confidence that the point estimate is correct to within ±0.03 of the population proportion, how many consumers need to be sampled?

b. To conduct a follow-up study that would provide 99% confidence that the point estimate is correct to within ±0.05 of the population proportion, how many consumers need to be sampled?

c. Compare the results of (a) and (b).

8.5 Confidence Interval Estimation and Ethical Issues

The selection of samples and the inferences that accompany them raise several ethical issues. The major ethical issue concerns whether confidence interval estimates accompany point estimates. Failure to include a confidence interval estimate might mislead the user of the results into thinking that the point estimate is all that is needed to predict the population characteristic with certainty. Confidence interval limits (typically set at 95%), the sample size used, and an interpretation of the meaning of the confidence interval in terms that a person untrained in statistics can understand should always accompany point estimates.

When media outlets publicize the results of a political poll, they often overlook including this type of information. Sometimes, the results of a poll include the sampling error, but the sampling error is often presented in fine print or as an afterthought to the story being reported.

A fully ethical presentation of poll results would give equal prominence to the confidence levels, sample size, sampling error, and confidence limits of the poll.

When you prepare your own point estimates, always state the interval estimate in a *prominent* place and include a brief explanation of the meaning of the confidence interval. In addition, make sure you highlight the sample size and sampling error.

8.6 Bootstrapping

The confidence interval estimation procedures discussed in this chapter make assumptions that are often not valid, especially for small samples. Bootstrapping, the selection of an initial sample and repeated sampling from that initial sample, provides an alternative approach that does not rely on those assumptions. The **Section 8.6 online topic** explains this alternative technique.

USING STATISTICS

Getting Estimates at Ricknel Home Centers, Revisited

Mangostock/Shutterstock

In the Ricknel Home Centers scenario, you were an accountant for a distributor of home improvement supplies in the northeastern United States. You were responsible for the accuracy of the integrated inventory management and sales information system. You used confidence interval estimation techniques to draw conclusions about the population of all records from a relatively small sample collected during an audit.

At the end of the month, you collected a random sample of 100 sales invoices and made the following inferences:

- With 95% confidence, you concluded that the mean amount of all the sales invoices is between $104.53 and $116.01.

- With 95% confidence, you concluded that between 4.12% and 15.88% of all the sales invoices contain errors.

These estimates provide an interval of values that you believe contain the true population parameters. If these intervals are too wide (i.e., the sampling error is too large) for the types of decisions Ricknel Home Centers needs to make, you will need to take a larger sample. You can use the sample size formulas in Section 8.4 to determine the number of sales invoices to sample to ensure that the size of the sampling error is acceptable.

SUMMARY

This chapter discusses confidence intervals for estimating the characteristics of a population, along with how you can determine the necessary sample size. You learned how to apply these methods to numerical and categorical data. Table 8.3 provides a list of topics covered in this chapter.

To determine what equation to use for a particular situation, you need to answer these questions:

- Are you constructing a confidence interval, or are you determining sample size?
- Do you have a numerical variable, or do you have a categorical variable?

The next three chapters develop a hypothesis-testing approach to making decisions about population parameters.

TABLE 8.3

Summary of Topics in Chapter 8

TYPE OF ANALYSIS	TYPE OF DATA	
	Numerical	Categorical
Confidence interval for a population parameter	Confidence interval estimate for the mean (Sections 8.1 and 8.2)	Confidence interval estimate for the proportion (Section 8.3)
Determining sample size	Sample size determination for the mean (Section 8.4)	Sample size determination for the proportion (Section 8.4)

REFERENCES

1. Cochran, W. G. *Sampling Techniques*, 3rd ed. New York: Wiley, 1977.
2. Daniel, W. W. *Applied Nonparametric Statistics*, 2nd ed. Boston: PWS Kent, 1990.
3. Fisher, R. A., and F. Yates. *Statistical Tables for Biological, Agricultural and Medical Research*, 5th ed. Edinburgh: Oliver & Boyd, 1957.
4. Hahn, G., and W. Meeker. *Statistical Intervals: A Guide for Practitioners*. New York: John Wiley and Sons, Inc., 1991.
5. Kirk, R. E., ed. *Statistical Issues: A Reader for the Behavioral Sciences*. Belmont, CA: Wadsworth, 1972.
6. Larsen, R. L., and M. L. Marx. *An Introduction to Mathematical Statistics and Its Applications*, 5th ed. Upper Saddle River, NJ: Prentice Hall, 2012.
7. *Microsoft Excel 2013*. Redmond, WA: Microsoft Corp., 2012.
8. *Minitab Release 16*. State College, PA: Minitab, Inc., 2010.
9. Snedecor, G. W., and W. G. Cochran. *Statistical Methods*, 7th ed. Ames, IA: Iowa State University Press, 1980.

KEY EQUATIONS

Confidence Interval for the Mean (σ Known)

$$\overline{X} \pm Z_{\alpha/2}\frac{\sigma}{\sqrt{n}}$$

or

$$\overline{X} - Z_{\alpha/2}\frac{\sigma}{\sqrt{n}} \leq \mu \leq \overline{X} + Z_{\alpha/2}\frac{\sigma}{\sqrt{n}} \tag{8.1}$$

Confidence Interval for the Mean (σ Unknown)

$$\overline{X} \pm t_{\alpha/2}\frac{S}{\sqrt{n}}$$

or

$$\overline{X} - t_{\alpha/2}\frac{S}{\sqrt{n}} \leq \mu \leq \overline{X} + t_{\alpha/2}\frac{S}{\sqrt{n}} \tag{8.2}$$

Confidence Interval Estimate for the Proportion

$$p \pm Z_{\alpha/2}\sqrt{\frac{p(1-p)}{n}}$$

or

$$p - Z_{\alpha/2}\sqrt{\frac{p(1-p)}{n}} \leq \pi \leq p + Z_{\alpha/2}\sqrt{\frac{p(1-p)}{n}} \tag{8.3}$$

Sample Size Determination for the Mean

$$n = \frac{Z_{\alpha/2}^2 \sigma^2}{e^2} \tag{8.4}$$

Sample Size Determination for the Proportion

$$n = \frac{Z_{\alpha/2}^2 \pi(1-\pi)}{e^2} \tag{8.5}$$

KEY TERMS

confidence interval estimate 249	level of confidence 252	sampling error 252
critical value 253	margin of error 266	Student's t distribution 255
degrees of freedom 255	point estimate 249	

CHECKING YOUR UNDERSTANDING

8.50 Why can you never really have 100% confidence of correctly estimating the population characteristic of interest?

8.51 When should you use the t distribution to develop the confidence interval estimate for the mean?

8.52 Why is it true that for a given sample size, n, an increase in confidence is achieved by widening (and making less precise) the confidence interval?

8.53 Why is the sample size needed to determine the proportion smaller when the population proportion is 0.20 than when the population proportion is 0.50?

CHAPTER REVIEW PROBLEMS

8.54 The Pew Internet Project survey of 1,006 American adults found the following:

> 906 have a cell phone
> 584 have a smartphone
> 322 have an ebook reader
> 423 have a tablet computer

Source: "Device Ownership Over Time," **bit.ly/1fvWYrL**.

a. Construct 95% confidence interval estimates for the population proportion of the electronic devices adults own.
b. What conclusions can you reach concerning what electronic devices adults have?

8.55 What proposals for dealing with energy and the environment do Americans favor? Gallup conducted a survey of 1,048 adults, ages 18+ in all 50 U.S. states and the District of Columbia and found the following:

> Spending more government money on developing solar and wind power: 702
> Setting higher emissions and pollutions standards for business and industry: 681
> Setting stricter standards on the use of techniques to extract natural gas from the earth: 608
> Expanding the use of nuclear power: 493

Source: "Americans Still Favor Energy Conservation Over Production," **bit.ly/1iLhkn2**.

a. Construct a 95% confidence interval estimate for the population proportion of each proposal Americans favor for dealing with energy and the environment.
b. What conclusions can you reach concerning proposals Americans favor for dealing with energy and the environment?

8.56 A market researcher for a consumer electronics company wants to study the media viewing behavior of residents of a particular area. A random sample of 40 respondents is selected, and each respondent is instructed to keep a detailed record of time spent engaged viewing content across all screens (traditional TV, DVD/Blu-ray, game console, Internet on a computer, video on a computer, video on a mobile phone) in a particular week. The results are as follows:

- Content viewing time per week: $\overline{X} = 41$ hours, $S = 3.5$ hours.
- 30 respondents have high definition (HD) on at least one television set.

a. Construct a 95% confidence interval estimate for the mean content viewing time per week in this area.
b. Construct a 95% confidence interval estimate for the population proportion of residents who have HD on at least one television set.

Suppose that the market researcher wants to take another survey in a different location. Answer these questions:

c. What sample size is required to be 95% confident of estimating the population mean content viewing time to within ± 2 hours assuming that the population standard deviation is equal to 5 hours?
d. How many respondents need to be selected to be 95% confident of being within ± 0.06 of the population proportion who have HD on at least one television set if no previous estimate is available?
e. Based on (c) and (d), how many respondents should the market researcher select if a single survey is being conducted?

8.57 An information technology (IT) consulting firm specializing in health care solutions wants to study communication deficiencies in the health care industry. A random sample of 70 health care clinicians reveals the following:

- Time wasted in a day due to outdated communication technologies: $\overline{X} = 45$ minutes, $S = 10$ minutes.
- Thirty-six health care clinicians cite inefficiency of pagers as the reason for the wasted time.

a. Construct a 99% confidence interval estimate for the population mean time wasted in a day due to outdated communication technologies.
b. Construct a 95% confidence interval estimate for the population proportion of health care clinicians who cite inefficiency of pagers as the reason for the wasted time.

8.58 The human resource (HR) director of a large corporation wishes to study absenteeism among its mid-level managers at its central office during the year. A random sample of 25 mid-level managers reveals the following:

- Absenteeism: $\overline{X} = 6.2$ days, $S = 7.3$ days.
- 13 mid-level managers cite stress as a cause of absence.

a. Construct a 95% confidence interval estimate for the mean number of absences for mid-level managers during the year.
b. Construct a 95% confidence interval estimate for the population proportion of mid-level managers who cite stress as a cause of absence.

Suppose that the HR director wishes to administer a survey in one of its regional offices. Answer these questions:

c. What sample size is needed to have 95% confidence in estimating the population mean absenteeism to within ± 1.5 days if the population standard deviation is estimated to be 8 days?
d. How many mid-level managers need to be selected to have 90% confidence in estimating the population proportion of mid-level managers who cite stress as a cause of absence to within ± 0.075 if no previous estimate is available?
e. Based on (c) and (d), what sample size is needed if a single survey is being conducted?

8.59 A national association devoted to HR and workplace programs, practices, and training wants to study HR department practices and employee turnover of its member organizations. HR professionals and organization executives focus on turnover not only because it has significant cost implications but also because it affects overall business performance. A survey is designed to estimate the proportion of member organizations that have both talent and development programs in place to drive human-capital management as well as the member organizations' mean annual employee turnover rate (the ratio of the number of employees that left an organization in a given time period to the average number of employees in the organization during the given time period). A random sample of 100 member organizations reveals the following:

- Annual turnover rate: $\overline{X} = 8.1\%$, $S = 1.5\%$.
- Thirty member organizations have both talent and development programs in place to drive human-capital management.

a. Construct a 95% confidence interval estimate for the population mean annual turnover rate of member organizations.

b. Construct a 95% confidence interval estimate for the population proportion of member organizations that have both talent and development programs in place to drive human-capital management.

c. What sample size is needed to have 99% confidence of estimating the population mean annual employee turnover rate to within $\pm 1.5\%$?

d. How many member organizations need to be selected to have 90% confidence of estimating the population proportion of organizations that have both talent and development programs in place to drive human-capital management to within ± 0.045?

8.60 The financial impact of IT systems downtime is a concern of plant operations management today. A survey of manufacturers examined the satisfaction level with the reliability and availability of their manufacturing IT applications. The variables of focus are whether the manufacturer experienced downtime in the past year that affected one or more manufacturing IT applications, the number of downtime incidents that occurred in the past year, and the approximate cost of a typical downtime incident. The results from a sample of 200 manufacturers are as follows:

- Sixty-two experienced downtime this year that affected one or more manufacturing applications.
- Number of downtime incidents: $\overline{X} = 3.5, S = 2.0$
- Cost of downtime incidents: $\overline{X} = \$18,000, S = \$3,000$.

a. Construct a 90% confidence interval estimate for the population proportion of manufacturers who experienced downtime in the past year that affected one or more manufacturing IT applications.

b. Construct a 95% confidence interval estimate for the population mean number of downtime incidents experienced by manufacturers in the past year.

c. Construct a 95% confidence interval estimate for the population mean cost of downtime incidents.

8.61 The branch manager of an outlet (Store 1) of a nationwide chain of pet supply stores wants to study characteristics of her customers. In particular, she decides to focus on two variables: the amount of money spent by customers and whether the customers own only one dog, only one cat, or more than one dog and/or cat. The results from a sample of 70 customers are as follows:

- Amount of money spent: $\overline{X} = \$21.34, S = \$9.22$.
- Thirty-seven customers own only a dog.
- Twenty-six customers own only a cat.
- Seven customers own more than one dog and/or cat.

a. Construct a 95% confidence interval estimate for the population mean amount spent in the pet supply store.

b. Construct a 90% confidence interval estimate for the population proportion of customers who own only a cat.

The branch manager of another outlet (Store 2) wishes to conduct a similar survey in his store. The manager does not have access to the information generated by the manager of Store 1. Answer the following questions:

c. What sample size is needed to have 95% confidence of estimating the population mean amount spent in this store to within $\pm \$1.50$ if the standard deviation is estimated to be $\$10$?

d. How many customers need to be selected to have 90% confidence of estimating the population proportion of customers who own only a cat to within ± 0.045?

e. Based on your answers to (c) and (d), how large a sample should the manager take?

8.62 Scarlett and Heather, the owners of an upscale restaurant in Dayton, Ohio, want to study the dining characteristics of their customers. They decide to focus on two variables: the amount of money spent by customers and whether customers order dessert. The results from a sample of 60 customers are as follows:

- Amount spent: $\overline{X} = \$38.54, S = \$7.26$.
- Eighteen customers purchased dessert.

a. Construct a 95% confidence interval estimate for the population mean amount spent per customer in the restaurant.

b. Construct a 90% confidence interval estimate for the population proportion of customers who purchase dessert.

Jeanine, the owner of a competing restaurant, wants to conduct a similar survey in her restaurant. Jeanine does not have access to the information that Scarlett and Heather have obtained from the survey they conducted. Answer the following questions:

c. What sample size is needed to have 95% confidence of estimating the population mean amount spent in her restaurant to within $\pm \$1.50$, assuming that the standard deviation is estimated to be $\$8$?

d. How many customers need to be selected to have 90% confidence of estimating the population proportion of customers who purchase dessert to within ± 0.04?

e. Based on your answers to (c) and (d), how large a sample should Jeanine take?

8.63 The manufacturer of Ice Melt claims that its product will melt snow and ice at temperatures as low as $0°$ Fahrenheit. A representative for a large chain of hardware stores is interested in testing this claim. The chain purchases a large shipment of 5-pound bags for distribution. The representative wants to know, with 95% confidence and within ± 0.05, what proportion of bags of Ice Melt perform the job as claimed by the manufacturer.

a. How many bags does the representative need to test? What assumption should be made concerning the population proportion? (This is called *destructive testing*; i.e., the product being tested is destroyed by the test and is then unavailable to be sold.)

b. Suppose that the representative tests 50 bags, and 42 of them do the job as claimed. Construct a 95% confidence interval estimate for the population proportion that will do the job as claimed.

c. How can the representative use the results of (b) to determine whether to sell the Ice Melt product?

8.64 Claims fraud (illegitimate claims) and buildup (exaggerated loss amounts) continue to be major issues of concern among automobile insurance companies. Fraud is defined as specific material misrepresentation of the facts of a loss; buildup is defined as the inflation of an otherwise legitimate claim. A recent study examined auto injury claims closed with payment under private passenger coverages. Detailed data on injury, medical treatment, claimed losses, and total payments, as well as claim-handling techniques, were collected. In addition, auditors were asked to review the claim files to indicate whether specific elements of fraud or buildup appeared in the claim and, in the case of buildup, to specify the amount of excess payment. The file **InsuranceClaims** contains data for 90 randomly selected auto injury claims. The following variables are included: CLAIM—Claim ID; BUILDUP—1 if buildup indicated, 0 if not; and EXCESSPAYMENT—excess payment amount, in dollars.

a. Construct a 95% confidence interval for the population proportion of all auto injury files that have exaggerated loss amounts.
b. Construct a 95% confidence interval for the population mean dollar excess payment amount.

8.65 A quality characteristic of interest for a tea-bag-filling process is the weight of the tea in the individual bags. In this example, the label weight on the package indicates that the mean amount is 5.5 grams of tea in a bag. If the bags are underfilled, two problems arise. First, customers may not be able to brew the tea to be as strong as they wish. Second, the company may be in violation of the truth-in-labeling laws. On the other hand, if the mean amount of tea in a bag exceeds the label weight, the company is giving away product. Getting an exact amount of tea in a bag is problematic because of variation in the temperature and humidity inside the factory, differences in the density of the tea, and the extremely fast filling operation of the machine (approximately 170 bags per minute). The following data (stored in Teabags) are the weights, in grams, of a sample of 50 tea bags produced in one hour by a single machine:

```
5.65  5.44  5.42  5.40  5.53  5.34  5.54  5.45  5.52  5.41
5.57  5.40  5.53  5.54  5.55  5.62  5.56  5.46  5.44  5.51
5.47  5.40  5.47  5.61  5.53  5.32  5.67  5.29  5.49  5.55
5.77  5.57  5.42  5.58  5.58  5.50  5.32  5.50  5.53  5.58
5.61  5.45  5.44  5.25  5.56  5.63  5.50  5.57  5.67  5.36
```

a. Construct a 99% confidence interval estimate for the population mean weight of the tea bags.
b. Is the company meeting the requirement set forth on the label that the mean amount of tea in a bag is 5.5 grams?
c. Do you think the assumption needed to construct the confidence interval estimate in (a) is valid?

8.66 A manufacturing company produces steel housings for electrical equipment. The main component part of the housing is a steel trough that is made from a 14-gauge steel coil. It is produced using a 250-ton progressive punch press with a wipe-down operation that puts two 90-degree forms in the flat steel to make the trough. The distance from one side of the form to the other is critical because of weatherproofing in outdoor applications. The widths (in inches), shown below and stored in Trough , are from a sample of 49 troughs:

```
8.312  8.343  8.317  8.383  8.348  8.410  8.351  8.373  8.481
8.422  8.476  8.382  8.484  8.403  8.414  8.419  8.385  8.465
8.498  8.447  8.436  8.413  8.489  8.414  8.481  8.415  8.479
8.429  8.458  8.462  8.460  8.444  8.429  8.460  8.412  8.420
8.410  8.405  8.323  8.420  8.396  8.447  8.405  8.439  8.411
8.427  8.420  8.498  8.409
```

a. Construct a 95% confidence interval estimate for the mean width of the troughs.
b. Interpret the interval developed in (a).
c. Do you think the assumption needed to construct the confidence interval estimate in (a) is valid?

8.67 The manufacturer of Boston and Vermont asphalt shingles knows that product weight is a major factor in a customer's perception of quality. The last stage of the assembly line packages the shingles before they are placed on wooden pallets. Once a pallet is full (a pallet for most brands holds 16 squares of shingles), it is weighed, and the measurement is recorded. The file Pallet contains the weight (in pounds) from a sample of 368 pallets of Boston shingles and 330 pallets of Vermont shingles.
a. For the Boston shingles, construct a 95% confidence interval estimate for the mean weight.
b. For the Vermont shingles, construct a 95% confidence interval estimate for the mean weight.
c. Do you think the assumption needed to construct the confidence interval estimates in (a) and (b) is valid?
d. Based on the results of (a) and (b), what conclusions can you reach concerning the mean weight of the Boston and Vermont shingles?

8.68 The manufacturer of Boston and Vermont asphalt shingles provides its customers with a 20-year warranty on most of its products. To determine whether a shingle will last the entire warranty period, accelerated-life testing is conducted at the manufacturing plant. Accelerated-life testing exposes the shingle to the stresses it would be subject to in a lifetime of normal use via a laboratory experiment that takes only a few minutes to conduct. In this test, a shingle is repeatedly scraped with a brush for a short period of time, and the shingle granules removed by the brushing are weighed (in grams). Shingles that experience low amounts of granule loss are expected to last longer in normal use than shingles that experience high amounts of granule loss. In this situation, a shingle should experience no more than 0.8 grams of granule loss if it is expected to last the length of the warranty period. The file Granule contains a sample of 170 measurements made on the company's Boston shingles and 140 measurements made on Vermont shingles.
a. For the Boston shingles, construct a 95% confidence interval estimate for the mean granule loss.
b. For the Vermont shingles, construct a 95% confidence interval estimate for the mean granule loss.
c. Do you think the assumption needed to construct the confidence interval estimates in (a) and (b) is valid?
d. Based on the results of (a) and (b), what conclusions can you reach concerning the mean granule loss of the Boston and Vermont shingles?

REPORT WRITING EXERCISE

8.69 Referring to the results in Problem 8.66 concerning the width of a steel trough, write a report that summarizes your conclusions.

CASES FOR CHAPTER 8

Managing Ashland MultiComm Services

The marketing department has been considering ways to increase the number of new subscriptions to the *3-For-All* cable/phone/Internet service. Following the suggestion of Assistant Manager Lauren Adler, the department staff designed a survey to help determine various characteristics of households who subscribe to cable television service from Ashland. The survey consists of the following 10 questions:

1. Does your household subscribe to telephone service from Ashland?
   (1) Yes   (2) No

2. Does your household subscribe to Internet service from Ashland?
   (1) Yes   (2) No

3. What type of cable television service do you have?
   (1) Basic   (2) Enhanced
   (If Basic, skip to question 5.)

4. How often do you watch the cable television stations that are only available with enhanced service?
   (1) Every day   (2) Most days
   (3) Occasionally or never

5. How often do you watch premium or on-demand services that require an extra fee?
   (1) Almost every day   (2) Several times a week
   (3) Rarely   (4) Never

6. Which method did you use to obtain your current AMS subscription?
   (1) AMS toll-free phone number
   (2) AMS website
   (3) Direct mail reply card
   (4) Good Tunes & More promotion
   (5) Other

7. Would you consider subscribing to the *3-For-All* cable/phone/Internet service for a trial period if a discount were offered?
   (1) Yes   (2) No
   (If no, skip to question 9.)

8. If purchased separately, cable, Internet, and phone services would currently cost $24.99 per week. How much would you be willing to pay per week for the *3-For-All* cable/phone/Internet service?

9. Does your household use another provider of telephone service?
   (1) Yes   (2) No

10. AMS may distribute Ashland Gold Cards that would provide discounts at selected Ashland-area restaurants for subscribers who agree to a two-year subscription contract to the *3-For-All* service. Would being eligible to receive a Gold Card cause you to agree to the two-year term?
    (1) Yes   (2) No

Of the 500 households selected that subscribe to cable television service from Ashland, 82 households either refused to participate, could not be contacted after repeated attempts, or had telephone numbers that were not in service. The summary results for the 418 households that were contacted are as follows:

Household Has AMS Telephone Service	Frequency
Yes	83
No	335

Household Has AMS Internet Service	Frequency
Yes	262
No	156

Type of Cable Service	Frequency
Basic	164
Enhanced	254

Watches Enhanced Programming	Frequency
Every day	50
Most days	144
Occasionally or never	60

Watches Premium or On-Demand Services	Frequency
Almost every day	14
Several times a week	35
Almost never	313
Never	56

Method Used to Obtain Current AMS Subscription	Frequency
Toll-free phone number	230
AMS website	106
Direct mail	46
Good Tunes & More	10
Other	26

Would Consider Discounted Trial Offer	Frequency
Yes	40
No	378

Trial Weekly Rate ($) Willing to Pay (stored in AMS8 **)**

23.00 20.00 22.75 20.00 20.00 24.50 17.50 22.25 18.00 21.00
18.25 21.00 18.50 20.75 21.25 22.25 22.75 21.75 19.50 20.75
16.75 19.00 22.25 21.00 16.75 19.00 22.25 21.00 19.50 22.75
23.50 19.50 21.75 22.00 24.00 23.25 19.50 20.75 18.25 21.50

Uses Another Phone Service Provider	Frequency
Yes	354
No	64

Gold Card Leads to Two-Year Agreement	Frequency
Yes	38
No	380

Analyze the results of the survey of Ashland households that receive AMS cable television service. Write a report that discusses the marketing implications of the survey results for Ashland MultiComm Services.

Digital Case

Apply your knowledge about confidence interval estimation in this Digital Case, which extends the MyTVLab Digital Case from Chapter 6.

Among its other features, the MyTVLab website allows customers to purchase MyTVLab LifeStyles merchandise online. To handle payment processing, the management of MyTVLab has contracted with the following firms:

- **PayAFriend (PAF)**—This is an online payment system with which customers and businesses such as MyTVLab register in order to exchange payments in a secure and convenient manner, without the need for a credit card.
- **Continental Banking Company (Conbanco)**—This processing services provider allows MyTVLab customers to pay for merchandise using nationally recognized credit cards issued by a financial institution.

To reduce costs, management is considering eliminating one of these two payment systems. However, Lorraine Hildick of the sales department suspects that customers use the two forms of payment in unequal numbers and that customers display different buying behaviors when using the two forms of payment. Therefore, she would like to first determine the following:

- The proportion of customers using PAF and the proportion of customers using a credit card to pay for their purchases.
- The mean purchase amount when using PAF and the mean purchase amount when using a credit card.

Assist Ms. Hildick by preparing an appropriate analysis. Open **PaymentsSample.pdf**, read Ms. Hildick's comments, and use her random sample of 50 transactions as the basis for your analysis. Summarize your findings to determine whether Ms. Hildick's conjectures about MyTVLab LifeStyle customer purchasing behaviors are correct. If you want the sampling error to be no more than $3 when estimating the mean purchase amount, is Ms. Hildick's sample large enough to perform a valid analysis?

Sure Value Convenience Stores

You work in the corporate office for a nationwide convenience store franchise that operates nearly 10,000 stores. The per-store daily customer count has been steady, at 900, for some time (i.e., the mean number of customers in a store in one day is 900). To increase the customer count, the franchise is considering cutting coffee prices. The 12-ounce size will now be $0.59 instead of $0.99, and the 16-ounce size will be $0.69 instead of $1.19. Even with this reduction in price, the franchise will have a 40% gross margin on coffee. To test the new initiative, the franchise has reduced coffee prices in a sample of 34 stores, where customer counts have been running almost exactly at the national average of 900. After four weeks, the sample stores stabilize at a mean customer count of 974 and a standard deviation of 96. This increase seems like a substantial amount to you, but it also seems like a pretty small sample. Is there some way to get a feel for what the mean per-store count in all the stores will be if you cut coffee prices nationwide? Do you think reducing coffee prices is a good strategy for increasing the mean customer count?

CardioGood Fitness

Return to the CardioGood Fitness case first presented on page 25. Using the data stored in `CardioGood Fitness`:

1. Construct 95% confidence interval estimates to create a customer profile for each CardioGood Fitness treadmill product line.

2. Write a report to be presented to the management of CardioGood Fitness detailing your findings.

More Descriptive Choices Follow-Up

Follow up the More Descriptive Choices, Revisited Using Statistics scenario on page 136 by constructing 95% confidence intervals estimates of the three-year return percentages, five-year return percentages, and ten-year return percentages for the sample of growth and value funds and for the small, mid-cap, and large market cap funds (stored in `Retirement Funds`). In your analysis, examine differences between the growth and value funds as well as the differences among the small, mid-cap, and large market cap funds.

Clear Mountain State Student Surveys

1. The Student News Service at Clear Mountain State University (CMSU) has decided to gather data about the undergraduate students that attend CMSU. They create and distribute a survey of 14 questions and receive responses from 62 undergraduates (stored in `UndergradSurvey`). For each variable included in the survey, construct a 95% confidence interval estimate for the population characteristic and write a report summarizing your conclusions.

2. The Dean of Students at CMSU has learned about the undergraduate survey and has decided to undertake a similar survey for graduate students at CMSU. She creates and distributes a survey of 14 questions and receives responses from 44 graduate students (stored in `GradSurvey`). For each variable included in the survey, construct a 95% confidence interval estimate for the population characteristic and write a report summarizing your conclusions.

CHAPTER 8 EXCEL GUIDE

EG8.1 CONFIDENCE INTERVAL ESTIMATE for the MEAN (σ KNOWN)

Key Technique Use the **NORM.S.INV(*cumulative percentage*)** to compute the Z value for one-half of the $(1 - \alpha)$ value and use the **CONFIDENCE(1 − *confidence level*, *population standard deviation*, *sample size*)** function to compute the half-width of a confidence interval.

Example Compute the confidence interval estimate for the mean for the Example 8.1 mean paper length problem on page 253.

PHStat Use **Estimate for the Mean, sigma known.** For the example, select **PHStat → Confidence Intervals → Estimate for the Mean, sigma known.** In the procedure's dialog box (shown below):

1. Enter **0.02** as the **Population Standard Deviation**.
2. Enter **95** as the **Confidence Level** percentage.
3. Click **Sample Statistics Known** and enter **100** as the **Sample Size** and **10.998** as the **Sample Mean**.
4. Enter a **Title** and click **OK**.

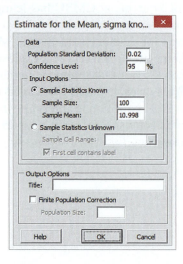

When using unsummarized data, click **Sample Statistics Unknown** and enter the **Sample Cell Range** in step 3.

In-Depth Excel Use the **COMPUTE worksheet** of the **CIE sigma known workbook** as a template.
The worksheet already contains the data for the example. For other problems, change the **Population Standard Deviation, Sample Mean, Sample Size,** and **Confidence Level** values in cells B4 through B7. If you use an Excel version older than Excel 2010, use these instructions with the COMPUTE_OLDER worksheet.

EG8.2 CONFIDENCE INTERVAL ESTIMATE for the MEAN (σ UNKNOWN)

Key Technique Use the **T.INV.2T(1 − *confidence level*, *degrees of freedom*)** function to determine the critical value from the *t* distribution.

Example Compute the Figure 8.7 confidence interval estimate for the mean sales invoice amount shown on page 258.

PHStat Use **Estimate for the Mean, sigma unknown.** For the example, select **PHStat → Confidence Intervals → Estimate for the Mean, sigma unknown.** In the procedure's dialog box (shown below):

1. Enter **95** as the **Confidence Level** percentage.
2. Click **Sample Statistics Known** and enter **100** as the **Sample Size**, **110.27** as the **Sample Mean**, and **28.95** as the **Sample Std. Deviation**.
3. Enter a **Title** and click **OK**.

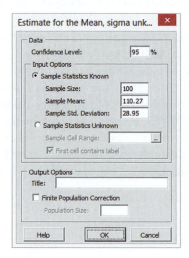

When using unsummarized data, click **Sample Statistics Unknown** and enter the **Sample Cell Range** in step 2.

In-Depth Excel Use the **COMPUTE worksheet** of the **CIE sigma unknown workbook** as a template.
The worksheet already contains the data for solving the example. For other problems, change the **Sample Standard Deviation, Sample Mean, Sample Size,** and **Confidence Level** values in cells B4 through B7. If you use an Excel version older than Excel 2010, use these instructions with the COMPUTE_OLDER worksheet.

EG8.3 CONFIDENCE INTERVAL ESTIMATE for the PROPORTION

Key Technique Use the **NORM.S.INV((1 − *confidence level*)/2)** function to compute the *Z* value.

Example Compute the Figure 8.12 confidence interval estimate for the proportion of in-error sales invoices shown on page 264.

PHStat Use **Estimate for the Proportion**.
For the example, select **PHStat → Confidence Intervals → Estimate for the Proportion**. In the procedure's dialog box (shown below):

1. Enter **100** as the **Sample Size**.
2. Enter **10** as the **Number of Successes**.
3. Enter **95** as the **Confidence Level** percentage.
4. Enter a **Title** and click **OK**.

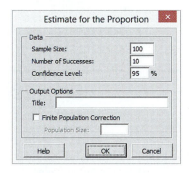

In-Depth Excel Use the **COMPUTE worksheet** of the **CIE Proportion workbook** as a template.
The worksheet contains the data for the example. Note that the formula **= SQRT(*sample proportion* * (1 − *sample proportion*)/*sample size*)** computes the standard error of the proportion in cell B11.

To compute confidence interval estimates for other problems, change the **Sample Size**, **Number of Successes**, and **Confidence Level** values in cells B4 through B6. If you use an Excel version older than Excel 2010, use these instructions with the COMPUTE_OLDER worksheet.

EG8.4 DETERMINING SAMPLE SIZE

Sample Size Determination for the Mean

Key Technique Use the **NORM.S.INV((1 − *confidence level*)/2)** function to compute the *Z* value and use the **ROUNDUP(*calculated sample size*, 0)** function to round up the computed sample size to the next higher integer.

Example Determine the sample size for the mean sales invoice amount example that is shown in Figure 8.13 on page 267.

PHStat Use **Determination for the Mean**.
For the example, select **PHStat → Sample Size → Determination for the Mean**. In the procedure's dialog box (shown at top right):

1. Enter **25** as the **Population Standard Deviation**.
2. Enter **5** as the **Sampling Error**.

3. Enter **95** as the **Confidence Level** percentage.
4. Enter a **Title** and click **OK**.

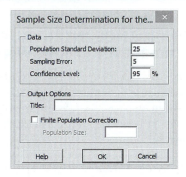

In-Depth Excel Use the **COMPUTE worksheet** of the **Sample Size Mean workbook** as a template.
The worksheet already contains the data for the example. For other problems, change the **Population Standard Deviation**, **Sampling Error**, and **Confidence Level** values in cells B4 through B6. If you use an Excel version older than Excel 2010, use these instructions with the COMPUTE_OLDER worksheet.

Sample Size Determination for the Proportion

Key Technique Use the **NORM.S.INV** and **ROUNDUP** functions (see previous section) to help determine the sample size needed for estimating the proportion.

Example Determine the sample size for the proportion of in-error sales invoices example that is shown in Figure 8.14 on page 269.

PHStat Use **Determination for the Proportion**.
For the example, select **PHStat → Sample Size → Determination for the Proportion**. In the procedure's dialog box (shown below):

1. Enter **0.15** as the **Estimate of True Proportion**.
2. Enter **0.07** as the **Sampling Error**.
3. Enter **95** as the **Confidence Level** percentage.
4. Enter a **Title** and click **OK**.

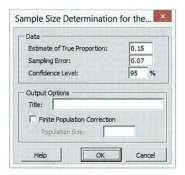

In-Depth Excel Use the **COMPUTE worksheet** of the **Sample Size Proportion workbook** as a template.
The worksheet already contains the data for the example. To compute confidence interval estimates for other problems, change the **Estimate of True Proportion**, **Sampling Error**, and **Confidence Level** in cells B4 through B6. If you use an Excel version older than Excel 2010, use these instructions with the COMPUTE_OLDER worksheet.

CHAPTER 8 MINITAB GUIDE

MG8.1 CONFIDENCE INTERVAL ESTIMATE for the MEAN (σ KNOWN)

Use **1-Sample Z**.

For example, to compute the estimate for the Example 8.1 mean paper length problem on page 253, select **Stat → Basic Statistics → 1-Sample Z.** In the 1-Sample Z (Test and Confidence Interval) dialog box (shown below):

1. Click **Summarized data**.
2. Enter **100** in the **Sample size** box and **10.998** in the **Mean** box.
3. Enter **0.02** in the **Standard deviation** box.
4. Click **Options**.

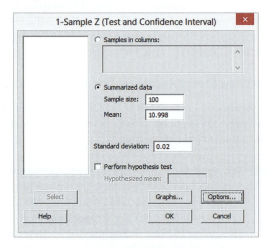

In the 1-Sample Z - Options dialog box (shown below):

5. Enter **95.0** in the **Confidence level** box.
6. Select **not equal** from the **Alternative** drop-down list.
7. Click **OK**.

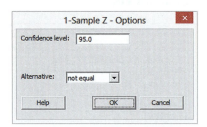

8. Back in the original dialog box, click **OK**.

When using unsummarized data, click **Samples in columns** in step 1 and, in step 2, enter the name of the column that contains the data in the **Samples in columns** box.

MG8.2 CONFIDENCE INTERVAL ESTIMATE for the MEAN (σ UNKNOWN)

Use **1-Sample t**.

For example, to compute the Figure 8.7 estimate for the mean sales invoice amount on page 258, select **Stat → Basic Statistics**

→ 1-Sample t. In the 1-Sample t (Test and Confidence Interval) dialog box (shown below):

1. Click **Summarized data**.
2. Enter **100** in the **Sample size** box, **110.27** in the **Mean** box, and **28.95** in the **Standard deviation** box.
3. Click **Options**.

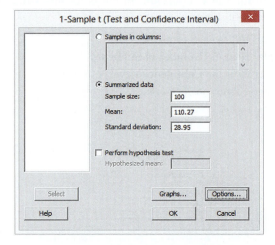

In the 1-Sample t - Options dialog box (similar to the 1-Sample Z - Options dialog box shown in left column:

4. Enter **95.0** in the **Confidence level** box.
5. Select **not equal** from the **Alternative** drop-down list.
6. Click **OK**.
7. Back in the original dialog box, click **OK**.

When using unsummarized data, click **Samples in columns** in step 1 and, in step 2, enter the name of the column that contains the data. To create a boxplot of the type shown in Figure 8.9 on page 259, replace step 7 with these steps 7 through 9:

7. Back in the original dialog box, click **Graphs**.
8. In the 1-Sample t - Graphs dialog box, check **Boxplot of data** and then click **OK**.
9. Back in the original dialog box, click **OK**.

MG8.3 CONFIDENCE INTERVAL ESTIMATE for the PROPORTION

Use **1 Proportion**.

For example, to compute the Figure 8.12 estimate for the proportion of in-error sales invoices on page 264, select **Stat → Basic Statistics → 1 Proportion**. In the 1 Proportion dialog box (shown on page 283):

1. Click **Summarized data**.
2. Enter **10** in the **Number of events** box and **100** in the **Number of trials** box.
3. Click **Options**.

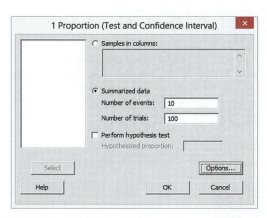

In the 1 Proportion - Options dialog box (shown below):

4. Enter **95.0** in the **Confidence level** box.
5. Select **not equal** from the **Alternative** drop-down list.
6. Check **Use test and interval based on normal distribution**.
7. Click **OK** (to return to the previous dialog box).

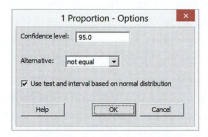

8. Back in the original dialog box, click **OK**.

When using unsummarized data, click **Samples in columns** in step 1 and, in step 2, enter the name of the column that contains the data.

MG8.4 DETERMINING SAMPLE SIZE

Minitab version 16 includes Sample Size for Estimation that computes the sample size needed for estimating the mean or the proportion.

To use this new command, select **Stat → Power and Sample Size → Sample Size for Estimation** and in the procedure's dialog box select a parameter from the Parameter drop-down list, complete the entries, and click OK. Because this comment is not included in Minitab Student 14, the command is not demonstrated or further discussed in this book. (Results using the Minitab 16 command will vary slightly from the Excel results shown in this chapter.)

Fundamentals of Hypothesis Testing: One-Sample Tests

CONTENTS

OBJECTIVES

Learn the basic principles of hypothesis testing

How to use hypothesis testing to test a mean or proportion

Identify the assumptions of each hypothesis-testing procedure, how to evaluate them, and the consequences if they are seriously violated

Become aware of the pitfalls and ethical issues involved in hypothesis testing

How to avoid the pitfalls involved in hypothesis testing

USING STATISTICS

Significant Testing at Oxford Cereals

As in Chapter 7, you again find yourself as plant operations manager for Oxford Cereals. Among other responsibilities, you are responsible for monitoring the amount in each cereal box filled. Company specifications require a mean weight of 368 grams per box. You must adjust the cereal-filling process when the mean fill-weight in the population of boxes differs from 368 grams. Adjusting the process requires shutting down the cereal production line temporarily, so you do not want to make unnecessary adjustments.

What decision-making method can you use to decide if the cereal-filling process needs to be adjusted? You decide to begin by selecting a random sample of 25 cereal boxes and weighing each box. From the weights collected, you compute a sample mean. How could that sample mean be used to help decide whether adjustment is necessary?

Peter Close/Shutterstock

I n Chapter 7, you learned methods to determine whether the value of a sample mean is consistent with a known population mean. In this Oxford Cereals scenario, you seek to use a sample mean to validate a claim about the population mean, a somewhat different problem. For this type of situation, you use the inferential method known as **hypothesis testing**. Hypothesis testing requires that you state a claim unambiguously. In this scenario, the claim is that the population mean is 368 grams. You examine a sample statistic to see if it better supports the stated claim, called the *null hypothesis*, or the mutually exclusive alternative hypothesis (for this scenario, that the population mean is not 368 grams).

In this chapter, you will learn several applications of hypothesis testing. You will learn how to make inferences about a population parameter by *analyzing differences* between the results observed, the sample statistic, and the results you would expect to get if an underlying hypothesis were actually true. For the Oxford Cereals scenario, hypothesis testing allows you to infer one of the following:

- The mean weight of the cereal boxes in the sample is a value consistent with what you would expect if the mean of the entire population of cereal boxes were 368 grams.
- The population mean is not equal to 368 grams because the sample mean is significantly different from 368 grams.

9.1 Fundamentals of Hypothesis-Testing Methodology

Hypothesis testing typically begins with a theory, a claim, or an assertion about a particular parameter of a population. For example, your initial hypothesis in the cereal example is that the process is working properly, so the mean fill is 368 grams, and no corrective action is needed.

The Null and Alternative Hypotheses

The hypothesis that the population parameter is equal to the company specification is referred to as the null hypothesis. A **null hypothesis** is often one of status quo and is identified by the symbol H_0. Here the null hypothesis is that the filling process is working properly, and therefore the mean fill is the 368-gram specification provided by Oxford Cereals. This is stated as

$$H_0 : \mu = 368$$

Even though information is available only from the sample, the null hypothesis is stated in terms of the population parameter because your focus is on the population of all cereal boxes. You use the sample statistic to make inferences about the entire filling process. One inference may be that the results observed from the sample data indicate that the null hypothesis is false. If the null hypothesis is considered false, something else must be true.

Whenever a null hypothesis is specified, an alternative hypothesis is also specified, and it must be true if the null hypothesis is false. The **alternative hypothesis**, H_1, is the opposite of the null hypothesis, H_0. This is stated in the cereal example as

$$H_1 : \mu \neq 368$$

The alternative hypothesis represents the conclusion reached by rejecting the null hypothesis. In many research situations, the alternative hypothesis serves as the hypothesis that is the focus of the research being conducted. The null hypothesis is rejected when there is sufficient evidence from the sample data that the null hypothesis is false. In the cereal example, if the weights of the sampled boxes are sufficiently above or below the expected 368-gram mean specified by Oxford Cereals, you reject the null hypothesis in favor of the alternative hypothesis that the mean fill is different from 368 grams. You stop production and take whatever action is necessary to correct the problem. If the null hypothesis is not rejected, you should continue to believe that the process is working correctly and that no corrective action is necessary. In this second circumstance, you have not proven that the process is working correctly.

> **Student Tip**
> Remember, hypothesis testing reaches conclusions about parameters, not statistics.

Rather, you have failed to prove that it is working incorrectly, and therefore you continue your belief (although unproven) in the null hypothesis.

In hypothesis testing, you reject the null hypothesis when the sample evidence suggests that it is far more likely that the alternative hypothesis is true. However, failure to reject the null hypothesis is not proof that it is true. You can never prove that the null hypothesis is correct because the decision is based only on the sample information, not on the entire population. Therefore, if you fail to reject the null hypothesis, you can only conclude that there is insufficient evidence to warrant its rejection. The following key points summarize the null and alternative hypotheses:

- The null hypothesis, H_0, represents the current belief in a situation.
- The alternative hypothesis, H_1, is the opposite of the null hypothesis and represents a research claim or specific inference you would like to prove.
- If you reject the null hypothesis, you have statistical proof that the alternative hypothesis is correct.
- If you do not reject the null hypothesis, you have failed to prove the alternative hypothesis. The failure to prove the alternative hypothesis, however, does not mean that you have proven the null hypothesis.
- The null hypothesis, H_0, always refers to a specified value of the population parameter (such as μ), not a sample statistic (such as $\overline{X}$).
- The statement of the null hypothesis always contains an equal sign regarding the specified value of the population parameter (e.g., $H_0 : \mu = 368$ grams).
- The statement of the alternative hypothesis never contains an equal sign regarding the specified value of the population parameter (e.g., $H_1 : \mu \neq 368$ grams).

EXAMPLE 9.1

The Null and Alternative Hypotheses

You are the manager of a fast-food restaurant. You want to determine whether the waiting time to place an order has changed in the past month from its previous population mean value of 4.5 minutes. State the null and alternative hypotheses.

SOLUTION The null hypothesis is that the population mean has not changed from its previous value of 4.5 minutes. This is stated as

$$H_0 : \mu = 4.5$$

The alternative hypothesis is the opposite of the null hypothesis. Because the null hypothesis is that the population mean is 4.5 minutes, the alternative hypothesis is that the population mean is not 4.5 minutes. This is stated as

$$H_1 : \mu \neq 4.5$$

The Critical Value of the Test Statistic

Hypothesis testing uses sample data to determine how likely it is that the null hypothesis is true. In the Oxford Cereal Company scenario, the null hypothesis is that the mean amount of cereal per box in the entire filling process is 368 grams (the population parameter specified by the company). You select a sample of boxes from the filling process, weigh each box, and compute the sample mean $\overline{X}$. This sample statistic is an estimate of the corresponding parameter, the population mean, μ. Even if the null hypothesis is true, the sample statistic $\overline{X}$ is likely to differ from the value of the parameter (the population mean, μ) because of variation due to sampling.

You do expect the sample statistic to be close to the population parameter if the null hypothesis is true. If the sample statistic is close to the population parameter, you have insufficient evidence to reject the null hypothesis. For example, if the sample mean is 367.9 grams, you might conclude that the population mean has not changed (i.e., $\mu = 368$) because a sample mean of 367.9 grams is very close to the hypothesized value of 368 grams. Intuitively, you think that it is likely that you could get a sample mean of 367.9 grams from a population whose mean is 368.

However, if there is a large difference between the value of the sample statistic and the hypothesized value of the population parameter, you might conclude that the null hypothesis is false. For example, if the sample mean is 320 grams, you might conclude that the population mean is not 368 grams (i.e., $\mu \neq 368$) because the sample mean is very far from the hypothesized value of 368 grams. In such a case, you might conclude that it is very unlikely to get a sample mean of 320 grams if the population mean is really 368 grams. Therefore, it is more logical to conclude that the population mean is not equal to 368 grams. Here you reject the null hypothesis.

However, the decision-making process is not always so clear-cut. Determining what is "very close" and what is "very different" is arbitrary without clear definitions. Hypothesis-testing methodology provides clear definitions for evaluating differences. Furthermore, it enables you to quantify the decision-making process by computing the probability of getting a certain sample result if the null hypothesis is true. You calculate this probability by determining the sampling distribution for the sample statistic of interest (e.g., the sample mean) and then computing the particular **test statistic** based on the given sample result. Because the sampling distribution for the test statistic often follows a well-known statistical distribution, such as the standardized normal distribution or t distribution, you can use these distributions to help determine whether the null hypothesis is true.

Student Tip
Every test statistic follows a specific sampling distribution.

Regions of Rejection and Nonrejection

The sampling distribution of the test statistic is divided into two regions, a **region of rejection** (sometimes called the critical region) and a **region of nonrejection** (see Figure 9.1). If the test statistic falls into the region of nonrejection, you do not reject the null hypothesis. In the Oxford Cereals scenario, you conclude that there is insufficient evidence that the population mean fill is different from 368 grams. If the test statistic falls into the rejection region, you reject the null hypothesis. In this case, you conclude that the population mean is not 368 grams.

FIGURE 9.1

Regions of rejection and nonrejection in hypothesis testing

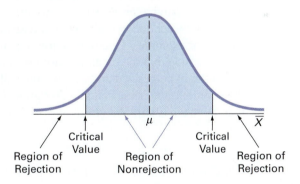

The region of rejection consists of the values of the test statistic that are unlikely to occur if the null hypothesis is true. These values are much more likely to occur if the null hypothesis is false. Therefore, if a value of the test statistic falls into this rejection region, you reject the null hypothesis because that value is unlikely if the null hypothesis is true.

To make a decision concerning the null hypothesis, you first determine the **critical value** of the test statistic. The critical value divides the nonrejection region from the rejection region. Determining the critical value depends on the size of the rejection region. The size of the rejection region is directly related to the risks involved in using only sample evidence to make decisions about a population parameter.

Risks in Decision Making Using Hypothesis Testing

Using hypothesis testing involves the risk of reaching an incorrect conclusion. You might wrongly reject a true null hypothesis, H_0, or, conversely, you might wrongly *not* reject a false null hypothesis, H_0. These types of risk are called Type I and Type II errors.

TYPE I AND TYPE II ERRORS

A **Type I error** occurs if you reject the null hypothesis, H_0, when it is true and should not be rejected. A Type I error is a "false alarm." The probability of a Type I error occurring is α.

A **Type II error** occurs if you do not reject the null hypothesis, H_0, when it is false and should be rejected. A Type II error represents a "missed opportunity" to take some corrective action. The probability of a Type II error occurring is β.

In the Oxford Cereals scenario, you would make a Type I error if you concluded that the population mean fill is *not* 368 grams when it *is* 368 grams. This error causes you to needlessly adjust the filling process (the "false alarm") even though the process is working properly. In the same scenario, you would make a Type II error if you concluded that the population mean fill *is* 368 grams when it is *not* 368 grams. In this case, you would allow the process to continue without adjustment, even though an adjustment is needed (the "missed opportunity").

Traditionally, you control the Type I error by determining the risk level, α (the lowercase Greek letter *alpha*), that you are willing to have of rejecting the null hypothesis when it is true. This risk, or probability, of committing a Type I error is called the *level of significance* (α). Because you specify the level of significance before you perform the hypothesis test, you directly control the risk of committing a Type I error. Traditionally, you select a level of 0.01, 0.05, or 0.10. The choice of a particular risk level for making a Type I error depends on the cost of making a Type I error. After you specify the value for α, you can then determine the critical values that divide the rejection and nonrejection regions. You know the size of the rejection region because α is the probability of rejection when the null hypothesis is true. From this, you can then determine the critical value or values that divide the rejection and nonrejection regions.

The probability of committing a Type II error is called the β *risk*. Unlike the Type I error, which you control through the selection of α, the probability of making a Type II error depends on the difference between the hypothesized and actual values of the population parameter. Because large differences are easier to find than small ones, if the difference between the hypothesized and actual values of the population parameter is large, β is small. For example, if the population mean is 330 grams, there is a small chance (β) that you will conclude that the mean has not changed from 368 grams. However, if the difference between the hypothesized and actual values of the parameter is small, β is large. For example, if the population mean is actually 367 grams, there is a large chance (β) that you will conclude that the mean is still 368 grams.

PROBABILITY OF TYPE I AND TYPE II ERRORS

The **level of significance (α)** of a statistical test is the probability of committing a Type I error.

The **β risk** is the probability of committing a Type II error.

The complement of the probability of a Type I error, $(1 - \alpha)$, is called the *confidence coefficient*. The confidence coefficient is the probability that you will not reject the null hypothesis, H_0, when it is true and should not be rejected. In the Oxford Cereals scenario, the confidence coefficient measures the probability of concluding that the population mean fill is 368 grams when it is actually 368 grams.

The complement of the probability of a Type II error, $(1 - \beta)$, is called the *power of a statistical test*. The power of a statistical test is the probability that you will reject the null hypothesis when it is false and should be rejected. In the Oxford Cereals scenario, the power of the test is the probability that you will correctly conclude that the mean fill amount is not 368 grams when it actually is not 368 grams.

COMPLEMENTS OF TYPE I AND TYPE II ERRORS

The **confidence coefficient**, $(1 - \alpha)$, is the probability that you will not reject the null hypothesis, H_0, when it is true and should not be rejected.

The **power of a statistical test**, $(1 - \beta)$, is the probability that you will reject the null hypothesis when it is false and should be rejected.

Table 9.1 illustrates the results of the two possible decisions (do not reject H_0 or reject H_0) that you can make in any hypothesis test. You can make a correct decision or make one of two types of errors.

TABLE 9.1

Hypothesis Testing and Decision Making

	ACTUAL SITUATION	
STATISTICAL DECISION	H_0 **True**	H_0 **False**
Do not reject H_0	Correct decision Confidence $= (1 - \alpha)$	Type II error $P(\text{Type II error}) = \beta$
Reject H_0	Type I error $P(\text{Type I error}) = \alpha$	Correct decision Power $= (1 - \beta)$

One way to reduce the probability of making a Type II error is by increasing the sample size. Large samples generally permit you to detect even very small differences between the hypothesized values and the actual population parameters. For a given level of α, increasing the sample size decreases β and therefore increases the power of the statistical test to detect that the null hypothesis, H_0, is false.

However, there is always a limit to your resources, and this affects the decision of how large a sample you can select. For any given sample size, you must consider the trade-offs between the two possible types of errors. Because you can directly control the risk of a Type I error, you can reduce this risk by selecting a smaller value for α. For example, if the negative consequences associated with making a Type I error are substantial, you could select $\alpha = 0.01$ instead of 0.05. However, when you decrease α, you increase β, so reducing the risk of a Type I error results in an increased risk of a Type II error. However, to reduce β, you could select a larger value for α. Therefore, if it is important to try to avoid a Type II error, you can select α of 0.05 or 0.10 instead of 0.01.

In the Oxford Cereals scenario, the risk of a Type I error occurring involves concluding that the mean fill amount has changed from the hypothesized 368 grams when it actually has not changed. The risk of a Type II error occurring involves concluding that the mean fill amount has not changed from the hypothesized 368 grams when it actually has changed. The choice of reasonable values for α and β depends on the costs inherent in each type of error. For example, if it is very costly to change the cereal-filling process, you would want to be very confident that a change is needed before making any changes. In this case, the risk of a Type I error occurring is more important, and you would choose a small α. However, if you want to be very certain of detecting changes from a mean of 368 grams, the risk of a Type II error occurring is more important, and you would choose a higher level of α.

Now that you have been introduced to hypothesis testing, recall that in the Oxford Cereals scenario on page 284, the business problem facing Oxford Cereals is to determine if the mean fill-weight in the population of boxes in the cereal-filling process differs from 368 grams. To make this determination, you select a random sample of 25 boxes, weigh each box, compute the sample mean, $\overline{X}$, and then evaluate the difference between this sample statistic and the hypothesized population parameter by comparing the sample mean weight (in grams) to the expected population mean of 368 grams specified by the company. The null and alternative hypotheses are:

$$H_0 : \mu = 368$$
$$H_1 : \mu \neq 368$$

Z Test for the Mean (σ Known)

When the standard deviation, σ, is known (which rarely occurs), you use the **Z test for the mean** if the population is normally distributed. If the population is not normally distributed, you can still use the Z test if the sample size is large enough for the Central Limit Theorem to take effect (see Section 7.2). Equation (9.1) defines the Z_{STAT} test statistic for determining the difference between the sample mean, $\overline{X}$, and the population mean, μ, when the standard deviation, σ, is known.

Z TEST FOR THE MEAN (σ KNOWN)

$$Z_{STAT} = \frac{\overline{X} - \mu}{\dfrac{\sigma}{\sqrt{n}}} \qquad (9.1)$$

In Equation (9.1), the numerator measures the difference between the observed sample mean, $\overline{X}$, and the hypothesized mean, μ. The denominator is the standard error of the mean, so Z_{STAT} represents the difference between $\overline{X}$ and μ in standard error units.

Hypothesis Testing Using the Critical Value Approach

The critical value approach compares the value of the computed Z_{STAT} test statistic from Equation (9.1) to critical values that divide the normal distribution into regions of rejection and nonrejection. The critical values are expressed as standardized Z values that are determined by the level of significance.

For example, if you use a level of significance of 0.05, the size of the rejection region is 0.05. Because the null hypothesis contains an equal sign and the alternative hypothesis contains a not equal sign, you have a **two-tail test** in which the rejection region is divided into the two tails of the distribution, with two equal parts of 0.025 in each tail. For this two-tail test, a rejection region of 0.025 in each tail of the normal distribution results in a cumulative area of 0.025 below the lower critical value and a cumulative area of 0.975 $(1 - 0.025)$ below the upper critical value (which leaves an area of 0.025 in the upper tail). According to the cumulative standardized normal distribution table (Table E.2), the critical values that divide the rejection and nonrejection regions are -1.96 and $+1.96$. Figure 9.2 illustrates that if the mean is actually 368 grams, as H_0 claims, the values of the Z_{STAT} test statistic have a standardized normal distribution centered at $Z = 0$ (which corresponds to an $\overline{X}$ value of 368 grams). Values of Z_{STAT} greater than $+1.96$ and less than -1.96 indicate that $\overline{X}$ is sufficiently different from the hypothesized $\mu = 368$ that it is unlikely that such an $\overline{X}$ value would occur if H_0 were true.

> **Student Tip**
>
> Remember, first you determine the level of significance. This enables you to then determine the critical value. A different level of significance leads to a different critical value.

FIGURE 9.2

Testing a hypothesis about the mean (σ known) at the 0.05 level of significance

> **Student Tip**
>
> In a two-tail test, there is a rejection region in each tail of the distribution.

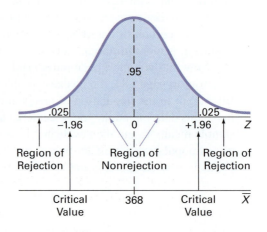

Region of Rejection	Region of Nonrejection	Region of Rejection
Critical Value	368	Critical Value

Therefore, the decision rule is

$$\text{Reject } H_0 \text{ if } Z_{STAT} > +1.96$$
$$\text{or if } Z_{STAT} < -1.96;$$
$$\text{otherwise, do not reject } H_0.$$

Suppose that the sample of 25 cereal boxes indicates a sample mean, $\overline{X}$, of 372.5 grams, and the population standard deviation, σ, is 15 grams. Using Equation (9.1) on page 290,

$$Z_{STAT} = \frac{\overline{X} - \mu}{\dfrac{\sigma}{\sqrt{n}}} - \frac{372.5 - 368}{\dfrac{15}{\sqrt{25}}} = +1.50$$

Student Tip
Remember, the decision rule always concerns H_0. Either you reject H_0 or you do not reject H_0.

Because $Z_{STAT} = +1.50$ is greater than -1.96 and less than $+1.96$, you do not reject H_0 (see Figure 9.3).

You continue to believe that the mean fill amount is 368 grams. To take into account the possibility of a Type II error, you state the conclusion as "there is insufficient evidence that the mean fill is different from 368 grams."

FIGURE 9.3

Testing a hypothesis about the mean cereal weight (σ known) at the 0.05 level of significance

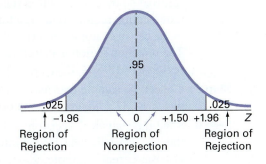

Exhibit 9.1 summarizes the critical value approach to hypothesis testing. Steps 1 and 2 are part of the Define task, step 5 combines the Collect and Organize tasks, and steps 3, 4, and 6 involve the Visualize and Analyze tasks of the DCOVA framework first introduced on page 2. Examples 9.2 and 9.3 apply the critical value approach to hypothesis testing to Oxford Cereals and to a fast-food restaurant.

EXHIBIT 9.1

The Critical Value Approach to Hypothesis Testing

Step 1 State the null hypothesis, H_0, and the alternative hypothesis, H_1.

Step 2 Choose the level of significance, α, and the sample size, n. The level of significance is based on the relative importance of the risks of committing Type I and Type II errors in the problem.

Step 3 Determine the appropriate test statistic and sampling distribution.

Step 4 Determine the critical values that divide the rejection and nonrejection regions.

Step 5 Collect the sample data, organize the results, and compute the value of the test statistic.

Step 6 Make the statistical decision, determine whether the assumptions are valid, and state the managerial conclusion in the context of the theory, claim, or assertion being tested. If the test statistic falls into the nonrejection region, you do not reject the null hypothesis. If the test statistic falls into the rejection region, you reject the null hypothesis.

EXAMPLE 9.2

Applying the Critical Value Approach to Hypothesis Testing at Oxford Cereals

State the critical value approach to hypothesis testing at Oxford Cereals.

SOLUTION

Step 1 State the null and alternative hypotheses. The null hypothesis, H_0, is always stated as a mathematical expression, using population parameters. In testing whether the mean fill is 368 grams, the null hypothesis states that μ equals 368. The alternative hypothesis, H_1, is also stated as a mathematical expression, using population parameters. Therefore, the alternative hypothesis states that μ is not equal to 368 grams.

Step 2 Choose the level of significance and the sample size. You choose the level of significance, α, according to the relative importance of the risks of committing Type I and Type II errors in the problem. The smaller the value of α, the less risk there is of making a Type I error. In this example, making a Type I error means that you conclude that the population mean is not 368 grams when it is 368 grams. Thus, you will take corrective action on the filling process even though the process is working properly. Here, $\alpha = 0.05$ is selected. The sample size, n, is 25.

Step 3 Select the appropriate test statistic. Because σ is known from information about the filling process, you use the normal distribution and the Z_{STAT} test statistic.

Step 4 Determine the rejection region. Critical values for the appropriate test statistic are selected so that the rejection region contains a total area of α when H_0 is true and the nonrejection region contains a total area of $1 - \alpha$ when H_0 is true. Because $\alpha = 0.05$ in the cereal example, the critical values of the Z_{STAT} test statistic are -1.96 and $+1.96$. The rejection region is therefore $Z_{STAT} < -1.96$ or $Z_{STAT} > +1.96$. The nonrejection region is $-1.96 \leq Z_{STAT} \leq +1.96$.

Step 5 Collect the sample data and compute the value of the test statistic. In the cereal example, $\overline{X} = 372.5$, and the value of the test statistic is $Z_{STAT} = +1.50$.

Step 6 State the statistical decision and the managerial conclusion. First, determine whether the test statistic has fallen into the rejection region or the nonrejection region. For the cereal example, $Z_{STAT} = +1.50$ is in the region of nonrejection because $-1.96 \leq Z_{STAT} = +1.50 \leq +1.96$. Because the test statistic falls into the nonrejection region, the statistical decision is to not reject the null hypothesis, H_0. The managerial conclusion is that insufficient evidence exists to prove that the mean fill is different from 368 grams. No corrective action on the filling process is needed.

EXAMPLE 9.3

Testing and Rejecting a Null Hypothesis

You are the manager of a fast-food restaurant. The business problem is to determine whether the population mean waiting time to place an order has changed in the past month from its previous population mean value of 4.5 minutes. From past experience, you can assume that the population is normally distributed, with a population standard deviation of 1.2 minutes. You select a sample of 25 orders during a one-hour period. The sample mean is 5.1 minutes. Use the six-step approach listed in Exhibit 9.1 on page 291 to determine whether there is evidence at the 0.05 level of significance that the population mean waiting time to place an order has changed in the past month from its previous population mean value of 4.5 minutes.

SOLUTION

Step 1 The null hypothesis is that the population mean has not changed from its previous value of 4.5 minutes:

$$H_0 : \mu = 4.5$$

The alternative hypothesis is the opposite of the null hypothesis. Because the null hypothesis is that the population mean is 4.5 minutes, the alternative hypothesis is that the population mean is not 4.5 minutes:

$$H_1 : \mu \neq 4.5$$

Step 2 You have selected a sample of $n = 25$. The level of significance is 0.05 (i.e., $\alpha = 0.05$).

Step 3 Because σ is assumed to be known, you use the normal distribution and the Z_{STAT} test statistic.

Step 4 Because $\alpha = 0.05$, the critical values of the Z_{STAT} test statistic are -1.96 and $+1.96$. The rejection region is $Z_{STAT} < -1.96$ or $Z_{STAT} > +1.96$. The nonrejection region is $-1.96 \leq Z_{STAT} \leq +1.96$.

Step 5 You collect the sample data and compute $\overline{X} = 5.1$. Using Equation (9.1) on page 290, you compute the test statistic:

$$Z_{STAT} = \frac{\overline{X} - \mu}{\dfrac{\sigma}{\sqrt{n}}} = \frac{5.1 - 4.5}{\dfrac{1.2}{\sqrt{25}}} = +2.50$$

Step 6 Because $Z_{STAT} = +2.50 > +1.96$, you reject the null hypothesis. You conclude that there is evidence that the population mean waiting time to place an order has changed from its previous value of 4.5 minutes. The mean waiting time for customers is longer now than it was last month. As the manager, you would now want to determine how waiting time could be reduced to improve service.

Hypothesis Testing Using the *p*-Value Approach

The **p-value** is the probability of getting a test statistic equal to or more extreme than the sample result, given that the null hypothesis, H_0, is true. The *p*-value is also known as the *observed level of significance*. Using the *p*-value to determine rejection and nonrejection is another approach to hypothesis testing.

The decision rules for rejecting H_0 in the *p*-value approach are

- If the *p*-value is greater than or equal to α, do not reject the null hypothesis.
- If the *p*-value is less than α, reject the null hypothesis.

Many people confuse these rules, mistakenly believing that a high *p*-value is reason for rejection. You can avoid this confusion by remembering the following:

If the *p*-value is low, then H_0 must go.

To understand the *p*-value approach, consider the Oxford Cereals scenario. You tested whether the mean fill was equal to 368 grams. The test statistic resulted in a Z_{STAT} value of $+1.50$ and you did not reject the null hypothesis because $+1.50$ was less than the upper critical value of $+1.96$ and greater than the lower critical value of -1.96.

To use the *p*-value approach for the *two-tail test*, you find the probability that the test statistic Z_{STAT} is equal to or *more extreme than* 1.50 standard error units from the center of a standardized normal distribution. In other words, you need to compute the probability that the Z_{STAT} value is greater than $+1.50$ along with the probability that the Z_{STAT} value is less than -1.50. Table E.2 shows that the probability of a Z_{STAT} value below -1.50 is 0.0668. The probability of a value below $+1.50$ is 0.9332, and the probability of a value above $+1.50$ is $1 - 0.9332 = 0.0668$. Therefore, the *p*-value for this two-tail test is $0.0668 + 0.0668 = 0.1336$ (see Figure 9.4). Thus, the probability of a test statistic equal to or more extreme than the sample result is 0.1336. Because 0.1336 is greater than $\alpha = 0.05$, you do not reject the null hypothesis.

FIGURE 9.4

Finding a *p*-value for a
two-tail test

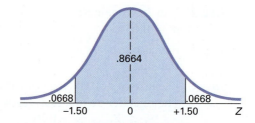

In this example, the observed sample mean is 372.5 grams, 4.5 grams above the hypothesized value, and the *p*-value is 0.1336. Thus, if the population mean is 368 grams, there is a 13.36% chance that the sample mean differs from 368 grams by at least 4.5 grams (i.e., is $\geq$ 372.5 grams or $\leq$ 363.5 grams). Therefore, even though 372.5 grams is above the hypothesized value of 368 grams, a result as extreme as or more extreme than 372.5 grams is not highly unlikely when the population mean is 368 grams.

Unless you are dealing with a test statistic that follows the normal distribution, you will only be able to approximate the *p*-value from the tables of the distribution. However, Excel and Minitab can compute the *p*-value for any hypothesis test, and this allows you to substitute the *p*-value approach for the critical value approach when you conduct hypothesis testing.

Figure 9.5 displays the Excel and Minitab results for the cereal-filling example discussed beginning on page 290.

FIGURE 9.5

Excel and Minitab results
for the *Z* test for the
mean (σ known) for the
cereal-filling example

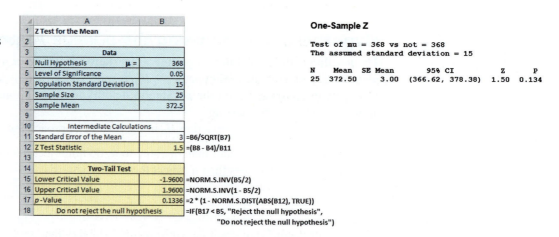

Exhibit 9.2 summarizes the *p*-value approach to hypothesis testing. Example 9.4 applies the *p*-value approach to the fast-food restaurant example.

EXHIBIT 9.2

The *p*-Value Approach to Hypothesis Testing

Step 1   State the null hypothesis, H_0, and the alternative hypothesis, H_1.

Step 2   Choose the level of significance, α, and the sample size, *n*. The level of significance is based on the relative importance of the risks of committing Type I and Type II errors in the problem.

Step 3   Determine the appropriate test statistic and the sampling distribution.

Step 4   Collect the sample data, compute the value of the test statistic, and compute the *p*-value.

Step 5   Make the statistical decision and state the managerial conclusion in the context of the theory, claim, or assertion being tested. If the *p*-value is greater than or equal to α, do not reject the null hypothesis. If the *p*-value is less than α, reject the null hypothesis.

EXAMPLE 9.4

Testing and Rejecting a Null Hypothesis Using the *p*-Value Approach

You are the manager of a fast-food restaurant. The business problem is to determine whether the population mean waiting time to place an order has changed in the past month from its previous value of 4.5 minutes. From past experience, you can assume that the population standard deviation is 1.2 minutes and the population waiting time is normally distributed. You select a sample of 25 orders during a one-hour period. The sample mean is 5.1 minutes. Use the five-step *p*-value approach of Exhibit 9.2 to determine whether there is evidence that the population mean waiting time to place an order has changed in the past month from its previous population mean value of 4.5 minutes.

SOLUTION

Step 1 The null hypothesis is that the population mean has not changed from its previous value of 4.5 minutes:

$$H_0 : \mu = 4.5$$

The alternative hypothesis is the opposite of the null hypothesis. Because the null hypothesis is that the population mean is 4.5 minutes, the alternative hypothesis is that the population mean is not 4.5 minutes:

$$H_1 : \mu \neq 4.5$$

Step 2 You have selected a sample of $n = 25$ and you have chosen a 0.05 level of significance (i.e., $\alpha = 0.05$).

Step 3 Select the appropriate test statistic. Because σ is assumed known, you use the normal distribution and the Z_{STAT} test statistic.

Step 4 You collect the sample data and compute $\overline{X} = 5.1$. Using Equation (9.1) on page 290, you compute the test statistic as follows:

$$Z_{STAT} = \frac{\overline{X} - \mu}{\dfrac{\sigma}{\sqrt{n}}} = \frac{5.1 - 4.5}{\dfrac{1.2}{\sqrt{25}}} = +2.50$$

To find the probability of getting a Z_{STAT} test statistic that is equal to or more extreme than 2.50 standard error units from the center of a standardized normal distribution, you compute the probability of a Z_{STAT} value greater than +2.50 along with the probability of a Z_{STAT} value less than −2.50. From Table E.2, the probability of a Z_{STAT} value below −2.50 is 0.0062. The probability of a value below +2.50 is 0.9938. Therefore, the probability of a value above +2.50 is $1 - 0.9938 = 0.0062$. Thus, the *p*-value for this two-tail test is $0.0062 + 0.0062 = 0.0124$.

Step 5 Because the *p*-value $= 0.0124 < \alpha = 0.05$, you reject the null hypothesis. You conclude that there is evidence that the population mean waiting time to place an order has changed from its previous population mean value of 4.5 minutes. The mean waiting time for customers is longer now than it was last month.

A Connection Between Confidence Interval Estimation and Hypothesis Testing

This chapter and Chapter 8 discuss confidence interval estimation and hypothesis testing, the two major elements of statistical inference. Although confidence interval estimation and hypothesis testing share the same conceptual foundation, they are used for different purposes. In Chapter 8, confidence intervals estimated parameters. In this chapter, hypothesis testing makes decisions about specified values of population parameters. Hypothesis tests are used when trying to determine whether a parameter is less than, more than, or not equal to a specified value. Proper interpretation of a confidence interval, however, can also indicate whether a parameter is less than, more than, or not equal to a specified value. For example, in this section, you tested whether the population mean fill amount was different from 368 grams by using Equation (9.1) on page 290:

$$Z_{STAT} = \frac{\overline{X} - \mu}{\frac{\sigma}{\sqrt{n}}}$$

Instead of testing the null hypothesis that $\mu = 368$ grams, you can reach the same conclusion by constructing a confidence interval estimate of μ. If the hypothesized value of $\mu = 368$ is contained within the interval, you do not reject the null hypothesis because 368 would not be considered an unusual value. However, if the hypothesized value does not fall into the interval, you reject the null hypothesis because $\mu = 368$ grams is then considered an unusual value. Using Equation (8.1) on page 252 and the following results:

$$n = 25, \overline{X} = 372.5 \text{ grams}, \sigma = 15 \text{ grams}$$

for a confidence level of 95% (i.e., $\alpha = 0.05$),

$$\overline{X} \pm Z_{\alpha/2} \frac{\sigma}{\sqrt{n}}$$

$$372.5 \pm (1.96) \frac{15}{\sqrt{25}}$$

$$372.5 \pm 5.88$$

so that

$$366.62 \le \mu \le 378.38$$

Because the interval includes the hypothesized value of 368 grams, you do not reject the null hypothesis. There is insufficient evidence that the mean fill amount for the entire filling process is not 368 grams. You reached the same decision by using a two-tail hypothesis test.

Can You Ever Know the Population Standard Deviation?

The end of Section 8.1 on page 254 discussed how learning a confidence interval estimation method that required knowing σ, the population standard deviation, served as an effective introduction to the concept of a confidence interval. That section then revealed that you would be unlikely to use that procedure for most practical applications for several reasons.

Likewise, for most practical applications, you are unlikely to use a hypothesis-testing method that requires knowing σ. If you knew the population standard deviation, you would also know the population mean and would not need to form a hypothesis about the mean

and then test that hypothesis. So why study a hypothesis test of the mean, which requires that σ is known? Using such a test makes it much easier to explain the fundamentals of hypothesis testing. With a known population standard deviation, you can use the normal distribution and compute p-values using the tables of the normal distribution.

Because it is important that you understand the concept of hypothesis testing when reading the rest of this book, review this section carefully—even if you anticipate never having a practical reason to use the test represented in Equation (9.1).

Problems for Section 9.1

LEARNING THE BASICS

9.1 If you use a 0.05 level of significance in a two-tail hypothesis test, what decision will you make if $Z_{STAT} = -0.76$?

9.2 If you use a 0.05 level of significance in a two-tail hypothesis test, what decision will you make if $Z_{STAT} = +2.21$?

9.3 If you use a 0.10 level of significance in a two-tail hypothesis test, what is your decision rule for rejecting a null hypothesis that the population mean equals 500 if you use the Z test?

9.4 If you use a 0.01 level of significance in a two-tail hypothesis test, what is your decision rule for rejecting $H_0 : \mu = 12.5$ if you use the Z test?

9.5 What is your decision in Problem 9.4 if $Z_{STAT} = -2.61$?

9.6 What is the *p*-value if, in a two-tail hypothesis test, $Z_{STAT} = +2.00$?

9.7 In Problem 9.6, what is your statistical decision if you test the null hypothesis at the 0.10 level of significance?

9.8 What is the *p*-value if, in a two-tail hypothesis test, $Z_{STAT} = -1.38$?

APPLYING THE CONCEPTS

9.9 In the U.S. legal system, a defendant is presumed innocent until proven guilty. Consider a null hypothesis, H_0, that a defendant is innocent, and an alternative hypothesis, H_1, that the defendant is guilty. A jury has two possible decisions: Convict the defendant (i.e., reject the null hypothesis) or do not convict the defendant (i.e., do not reject the null hypothesis). Explain the meaning of the risks of committing either a Type I or Type II error in this example.

9.10 Suppose the defendant in Problem 9.9 is presumed guilty until proven innocent. How do the null and alternative hypotheses differ from those in Problem 9.9? What are the meanings of the risks of committing either a Type I or Type II error here?

9.11 Many consumer groups feel that the U.S. Food and Drug Administration (FDA) drug approval process is too easy and, as a result, too many drugs are approved that are later found to be unsafe. On the other hand, a number of industry lobbyists have pushed for a more lenient approval process so that pharmaceutical companies can get new drugs approved more easily and quickly. Consider a null hypothesis that a new, unapproved drug is unsafe and an alternative hypothesis that a new, unapproved drug is safe.
a. Explain the risks of committing a Type I or Type II error.
b. Which type of error are the consumer groups trying to avoid? Explain.
c. Which type of error are the industry lobbyists trying to avoid? Explain.
d. How would it be possible to lower the chances of both Type I and Type II errors?

9.12 As a result of complaints from both students and faculty about lateness, the registrar at a large university is ready to undertake a study to determine whether the scheduled break between classes should be changed. Until now, the registrar has believed that there should be 20 minutes between scheduled classes. State the null hypothesis, H_0, and the alternative hypothesis, H_1.

9.13 Do business seniors at your school prepare for class more than, less than, or about the same as business seniors at other schools? The National Survey of Student Engagement (NSSE) found that business seniors spent a mean of 14 hours per week preparing for class. (*Source: A Fresh Look at Student Engagement Annual Results 2013,* available at **bit.ly/1j3Ob7N**.)
a. State the null and alternative hypotheses to try to prove that the mean number of hours preparing for class by business seniors at your school is different from the 14-hour-per-week benchmark reported by the NSSE.
b. What is a Type I error for your test?
c. What is a Type II error for your test?

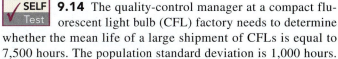 **9.14** The quality-control manager at a compact fluorescent light bulb (CFL) factory needs to determine whether the mean life of a large shipment of CFLs is equal to 7,500 hours. The population standard deviation is 1,000 hours. A random sample of 64 CFLs indicates a sample mean life of 7,250 hours.
a. At the 0.05 level of significance, is there evidence that the mean life is different from 7,500 hours?
b. Compute the *p*-value and interpret its meaning.
c. Construct a 95% confidence interval estimate of the population mean life of the CFLs.
d. Compare the results of (a) and (c). What conclusions do you reach?

9.15 Suppose that in Problem 9.14, the standard deviation is 1,200 hours.
a. Repeat (a) through (d) of Problem 9.14, assuming a standard deviation of 1,200 hours.
b. Compare the results of (a) to those of Problem 9.14.

9.16 A bottled water distributor wants to determine whether the mean amount of water contained in 1-gallon bottles purchased from a nationally known water bottling company is actually 1 gallon. You know from the water bottling company specifications that the standard deviation of the amount of water per bottle is 0.02 gallon. You select a random sample of 50 bottles, and the mean amount of water per 1-gallon bottle is 0.995 gallon.
a. Is there evidence that the mean amount is different from 1.0 gallon? (Use $\alpha = 0.01$.)
b. Compute the *p*-value and interpret its meaning.
c. Construct a 99% confidence interval estimate of the population mean amount of water per bottle.
d. Compare the results of (a) and (c). What conclusions do you reach?

9.17 Suppose that in Problem 9.16, the standard deviation is 0.012 gallon.
a. Repeat (a) through (d) of Problem 9.16, assuming a standard deviation of 0.012 gallon.
b. Compare the results of (a) to those of Problem 9.16.

9.2 *t* Test of Hypothesis for the Mean (σ Unknown)

In virtually all hypothesis-testing situations concerning the population mean, μ, you do not know the population standard deviation, σ. However, you will always be able to know the sample standard deviation, S. If you assume that the population is normally distributed, then the sampling distribution of the mean will follow a *t* distribution with $n - 1$ degrees of freedom and you can use the ***t* test for the mean**. If the population is not normally distributed, you can still use the *t* test if the population is not too skewed and the sample size is not too small. Equation (9.2) defines the test statistic for determining the difference between the sample mean, $\overline{X}$, and the population mean, μ, when using the sample standard deviation, S.

t TEST FOR THE MEAN (σ UNKNOWN)

$$t_{STAT} = \frac{\overline{X} - \mu}{\dfrac{S}{\sqrt{n}}} \qquad (9.2)$$

where the t_{STAT} test statistic follows a t distribution having $n - 1$ degrees of freedom.

To illustrate the use of the t test for the mean, return to the Chapter 8 Ricknel Home Centers scenario on page 248. The business objective is to determine whether the mean amount per sales invoice is unchanged from the $120 of the past five years. As an accountant for the company, you need to determine whether this amount has changed. In other words, the hypothesis test is used to try to determine whether the mean amount per sales invoice is increasing or decreasing.

The Critical Value Approach

To perform this two-tail hypothesis test, you use the six-step method listed in Exhibit 9.1 on page 291.

Step 1   You define the following hypotheses:

$$H_0 : \mu = 120$$
$$H_1 : \mu \neq 120$$

Student Tip
Remember, the null hypothesis uses an equal sign and the alternative hypothesis *never* uses an equal sign.

The alternative hypothesis contains the statement you are trying to prove. If the null hypothesis is rejected, then there is statistical evidence that the population mean amount per sales invoice is no longer $120. If the statistical conclusion is "do not reject H_0," then you will conclude that there is insufficient evidence to prove that the mean amount differs from the long-term mean of $120.

Step 2   You collect the data from a sample of $n = 12$ sales invoices. You decide to use $\alpha = 0.05$.

Step 3   Because σ is unknown, you use the t distribution and the t_{STAT} test statistic. You must assume that the population of sales invoices is approximately normally distributed in order to use the t distribution because the sample size is only 12. This assumption is discussed on page 300.

Step 4   For a given sample size, n, the test statistic t_{STAT} follows a t distribution with $n - 1$ degrees of freedom. The critical values of the t distribution with $12 - 1 = 11$ degrees of freedom are found in Table E.3, as illustrated in Table 9.2 and Figure 9.6. The alternative hypothesis, $H_1 : \mu \neq 120$, has two tails. The area in the rejection region of the t distribution's left (lower) tail is 0.025, and the area in the rejection region of the t distribution's right (upper) tail is also 0.025.

From the t table as given in Table E.3, a portion of which is shown in Table 9.2, the critical values are ± 2.2010. The decision rule is

Student Tip
Since this is a two-tail test, the level of significance, $\alpha = 0.05$, is divided into two equal 0.025 parts, in each of the two tails of the distribution.

$$\text{Reject } H_0 \text{ if } t_{STAT} < -2.2010$$
$$\text{or if } t_{STAT} > +2.2010;$$
$$\text{otherwise, do not reject } H_0.$$

TABLE 9.2

Determining the Critical Value from the *t* Table for an Area of 0.025 in Each Tail, with 11 Degrees of Freedom

Degrees of Freedom	Cumulative Probabilities					
	.75	.90	.95	.975	.99	.995
	Upper-Tail Areas					
	.25	.10	.05	.025	.01	.005
1	1.0000	3.0777	6.3138	12.7062	31.8207	63.6574
2	0.8165	1.8856	2.9200	4.3027	6.9646	9.9248
3	0.7649	1.6377	2.3534	3.1824	4.5407	5.8409
4	0.7407	1.5332	2.1318	2.7764	3.7469	4.6041
5	0.7267	1.4759	2.0150	2.5706	3.3649	4.0322
6	0.7176	1.4398	1.9432	2.4469	3.1427	3.7074
7	0.7111	1.4149	1.8946	2.3646	2.9980	3.4995
8	0.7064	1.3968	1.8595	2.3060	2.8965	3.3554
9	0.7027	1.3830	1.8331	2.2622	2.8214	3.2498
10	0.6998	1.3722	1.8125	2.2281	2.7638	3.1693
11	0.6974	1.3634	1.7959	2.2010	2.7181	3.1058

Source: Extracted from Table E.3.

FIGURE 9.6

Testing a hypothesis about the mean (σ unknown) at the 0.05 level of significance with 11 degrees of freedom

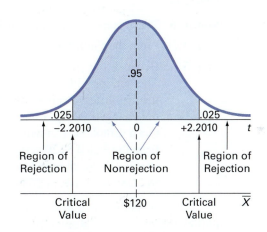

Step 5   You organize and store the data from a random sample of 12 sales invoices in **Invoices** :

| 108.98 | 152.22 | 111.45 | 110.59 | 127.46 | 107.26 |
| 93.32 | 91.97 | 111.56 | 75.71 | 128.58 | 135.11 |

Using Equations (3.1) and (3.5) on pages 98 and 104,

$$\overline{X} = \$112.85 \text{ and } S = \$20.80$$

From Equation (9.2) on page 298,

$$t_{STAT} = \frac{\overline{X} - \mu}{\dfrac{S}{\sqrt{n}}} = \frac{112.85 - 120}{\dfrac{20.80}{\sqrt{12}}} = -1.1908$$

Step 6   Because $-2.2010 < t_{STAT} = -1.1908 < 2.2010$, you do not reject H_0. You have insufficient evidence to conclude that the mean amount per sales invoice differs from $120. The audit suggests that the mean amount per invoice has not changed.

Figure 9.7 shows the results for this test of hypothesis, as computed by Excel and Minitab.

FIGURE 9.7

Excel and Minitab
results for the *t* test of
sales invoices

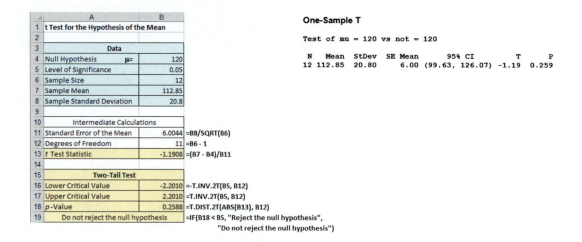

The *p*-Value Approach

To perform this two-tail hypothesis test, you use the five-step method listed in Exhibit 9.2 on page 294.

Step 1–3 These steps are the same as in the critical value approach discussed on page 298.

Step 4 From the Figure 9.7 results, $t_{STAT} = -1.19$ and the *p*-value $= 0.2588$

Step 5 Because the *p*-value of 0.2588 is greater than $\alpha = 0.05$, you do not reject H_0. The data provide insufficient evidence to conclude that the mean amount per sales invoice differs from \$120. The audit suggests that the mean amount per invoice has not changed. The *p*-value indicates that if the null hypothesis is true, the probability that a sample of 12 invoices could have a sample mean that differs by \$7.15 or more from the stated \$120 is 0.2588. In other words, if the mean amount per sales invoice is truly \$120, then there is a 25.88% chance of observing a sample mean below \$112.85 or above \$127.15.

In the preceding example, it is incorrect to state that there is a 25.88% chance that the null hypothesis is true. Remember that the *p*-value is a conditional probability, calculated by *assuming* that the null hypothesis is true. In general, it is proper to state the following:

> If the null hypothesis is true, there is a (*p*-value) $\times$ 100% chance of observing a test statistic at least as contradictory to the null hypothesis as the sample result.

Checking the Normality Assumption

You use the *t* test when the population standard deviation, σ, is not known and is estimated using the sample standard deviation, S. To use the *t* test, you assume that the data represent a random sample from a population that is normally distributed. In practice, as long as the sample size is not very small and the population is not very skewed, the *t* distribution provides a good approximation of the sampling distribution of the mean when σ is unknown.

There are several ways to evaluate the normality assumption necessary for using the *t* test. You can examine how closely the sample statistics match the normal distribution's theoretical properties. You can also construct a histogram, stem-and-leaf display, boxplot, or normal probability plot to visualize the distribution of the sales invoice amounts. For details on evaluating normality, see Section 6.3.

Figures 9.8 and 9.9 show the descriptive statistics, boxplot, and normal probability plot for the sales invoice data.

FIGURE 9.8

Excel and Minitab descriptive statistics and boxplots for the sales invoice data

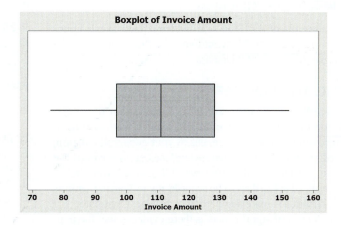

Invoice Amount	
Mean	112.8508
Median	111.02
Mode	#N/A
Minimum	75.71
Maximum	152.22
Range	76.51
Variance	432.5565
Standard Deviation	20.7980
Coeff. of Variation	18.43%
Skewness	0.1336
Kurtosis	0.1727
Count	12
Standard Error	6.0039

FIGURE 9.9

Excel and Minitab normal probability plots for the sales invoice data

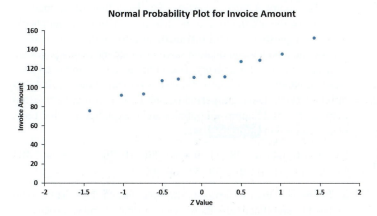

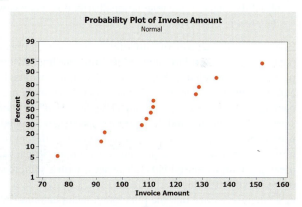

The mean is very close to the median, and the points on the normal probability plot appear to be increasing approximately in a straight line. The boxplot appears to be approximately symmetrical. Thus, you can assume that the population of sales invoices is approximately normally distributed. The normality assumption is valid, and therefore the auditor's results are valid.

The *t* test is a **robust** test. A robust test does not lose power if the shape of the population departs somewhat from a normal distribution, particularly when the sample size is large enough to enable the test statistic *t* to follow the *t* distribution. However, you can reach erroneous conclusions and can lose statistical power if you use the *t* test incorrectly. If the sample size, *n*, is small (i.e., less than 30) and you cannot easily make the assumption that the underlying population is at least approximately normally distributed, then *nonparametric* testing procedures are more appropriate (see references 2 and 3).

Problems for Section 9.2

LEARNING THE BASICS

9.18 If, in a sample of $n = 16$ selected from a normal population, $\overline{X} = 56$ and $S = 12$, what is the value of t_{STAT} if you are testing the null hypothesis $H_0: \mu = 50$?

9.19 In Problem 9.18, how many degrees of freedom does the *t* test have?

9.20 In Problems 9.18 and 9.19, what are the critical values of *t* if the level of significance, α, is 0.05 and the alternative hypothesis, H_1, is $\mu \neq 50$?

9.21 In Problems 9.18, 9.19, and 9.20, what is your statistical decision if the alternative hypothesis, H_1, is $\mu \neq 50$?

9.22 If, in a sample of $n = 16$ selected from a left-skewed population, $\bar{X} = 65$, and $S = 21$, would you use the t test to test the null hypothesis $H_0 : \mu = 60$? Discuss.

9.23 If, in a sample of $n = 160$ selected from a left-skewed population, $\bar{X} = 65$, and $S = 21$, would you use the t test to test the null hypothesis $H_0 : \mu = 60$? Discuss.

APPLYING THE CONCEPTS

✓**SELF** **9.24** You are the manager of a restaurant for a fast-
Test food franchise. Last month, the mean waiting time at the drive-through window for branches in your geographic region, as measured from the time a customer places an order until the time the customer receives the order, was 3.7 minutes. You select a random sample of 64 orders. The sample mean waiting time is 3.57 minutes, with a sample standard deviation of 0.8 minute.
a. At the 0.05 level of significance, is there evidence that the population mean waiting time is different from 3.7 minutes?
b. Because the sample size is 64, do you need to be concerned about the shape of the population distribution when conducting the t test in (a)? Explain.

9.25 A manufacturer of chocolate candies uses machines to package candies as they move along a filling line. Although the packages are labeled as 8 ounces, the company wants the packages to contain a mean of 8.17 ounces so that virtually none of the packages contain less than 8 ounces. A sample of 50 packages is selected periodically, and the packaging process is stopped if there is evidence that the mean amount packaged is different from 8.17 ounces. Suppose that in a particular sample of 50 packages, the mean amount dispensed is 8.159 ounces, with a sample standard deviation of 0.051 ounce.
a. Is there evidence that the population mean amount is different from 8.17 ounces? (Use a 0.05 level of significance.)
b. Determine the p-value and interpret its meaning.

9.26 A marketing researcher wants to estimate the mean savings ($) realized by shoppers who showroom. Showrooming is the practice of inspecting products in retail stores and then purchasing the products online at a lower price. A random sample of 100 shoppers who recently purchased a consumer electronics item online after making a visit to a retail store yielded a mean savings of $58 and a standard deviation of $55.
a. Is there evidence that the population mean savings for all showroomers who purchased a consumer electronics item is different from $50? (Use a 0.05 level of significance.)
b. Determine the p-value and interpret its meaning.

9.27 The U.S. Department of Transportation requires tire manufacturers to provide performance information on tire sidewalls to help prospective buyers make their purchasing decisions. One very important piece of information is the tread wear index, which indicates the tire's resistance to tread wear. A tire with a grade of 200 should last twice as long, on average, as a tire with a grade of 100.

A consumer organization wants to test the actual tread wear index of a brand name of tires that claims "graded 200" on the sidewall of the tire. A random sample of $n = 18$ indicates a sample mean tread wear index of 195.3 and a sample standard deviation of 21.4.

a. Is there evidence that the population mean tread wear index is different from 200? (Use a 0.05 level of significance.)
b. Determine the p-value and interpret its meaning.

9.28 The file **FastFood** contains the amount that a sample of fifteen customers spent for lunch ($) at a fast-food restaurant:

7.42 6.29 5.83 6.50 8.34 9.51 7.10 6.80 5.90
4.89 6.50 5.52 7.90 8.30 9.60

a. At the 0.05 level of significance, is there evidence that the mean amount spent for lunch is different from $6.50?
b. Determine the p-value in (a) and interpret its meaning.
c. What assumption must you make about the population distribution in order to conduct the t test in (a) and (b)?
d. Because the sample size is 15, do you need to be concerned about the shape of the population distribution when conducting the t test in (a)? Explain.

9.29 An insurance company has the business objective of reducing the amount of time it takes to approve applications for life insurance. The approval process consists of underwriting, which includes a review of the application, a medical information bureau check, possible requests for additional medical information and medical exams, and a policy compilation stage in which the policy pages are generated and sent for delivery. The ability to deliver approved policies to customers in a timely manner is critical to the profitability of this service. During a period of one month, you collect a random sample of 27 approved policies and the total processing time, in days, stored in **Insurance**, are:

73 19 16 64 28 28 31 90 60 56 31 56 22 18 45 48
17 17 17 91 92 63 50 51 69 16 17

a. In the past, the mean processing time was 45 days. At the 0.05 level of significance, is there evidence that the mean processing time has changed from 45 days?
b. What assumption about the population distribution is needed in order to conduct the t test in (a)?
c. Construct a boxplot or a normal probability plot to evaluate the assumption made in (b).
d. Do you think that the assumption needed in order to conduct the t test in (a) is valid? Explain.

9.30 The following data (in **Drink**) represent the amount of soft drink filled in a sample of 50 consecutive 2-liter bottles. The results, listed horizontally in the order of being filled, were:

2.109 2.086 2.066 2.075 2.065 2.057 2.052 2.044
2.036 2.038 2.031 2.029 2.025 2.029 2.023 2.020
2.015 2.014 2.013 2.014 2.012 2.012 2.012 2.010
2.005 2.003 1.999 1.996 1.997 1.992 1.994 1.986
1.984 1.981 1.973 1.975 1.971 1.969 1.966 1.967
1.963 1.957 1.951 1.951 1.947 1.941 1.941 1.938
1.908 1.894

a. At the 0.05 level of significance, is there evidence that the mean amount of soft drink filled is different from 2.0 liters?
b. Determine the p-value in (a) and interpret its meaning.

c. In (a), you assumed that the distribution of the amount of soft drink filled was normally distributed. Evaluate this assumption by constructing a boxplot or a normal probability plot.

d. Do you think that the assumption needed in order to conduct the *t* test in (a) is valid? Explain.

e. Examine the values of the 50 bottles in their sequential order, as given in the problem. Does there appear to be a pattern to the results? If so, what impact might this pattern have on the validity of the results in (a)?

9.31 One of the major measures of the quality of service provided by any organization is the speed with which it responds to customer complaints. A large family-held department store selling furniture and flooring, including carpet, had undergone a major expansion in the past several years. In particular, the flooring department had expanded from 2 installation crews to an installation supervisor, a measurer, and 15 installation crews. The store had the business objective of improving its response to complaints. The variable of interest was defined as the number of days between when the complaint was made and when it was resolved. Data were collected from 50 complaints that were made in the past year. These data, stored in **Furniture** , are:

```
54   5   35  137   31  27  152   2  123  81  74  27
11  19  126  110  110  29   61  35   94  31  26   5
12   4  165   32   29  28   29  26   25   1  14  13
13  10    5   27    4  52   30  22   36  26  20  23
33  68
```

a. The installation supervisor claims that the mean number of days between the receipt of a complaint and the resolution of the complaint is 20 days. At the 0.05 level of significance, is there evidence that the claim is not true (i.e., the mean number of days is different from 20)?

b. What assumption about the population distribution is needed in order to conduct the *t* test in (a)?

c. Construct a boxplot or a normal probability plot to evaluate the assumption made in (b).

d. Do you think that the assumption needed in order to conduct the *t* test in (a) is valid? Explain.

9.32 A manufacturing company produces steel housings for electrical equipment. The main component part of the housing is a steel trough that is made out of a 14-gauge steel coil. It is produced using a 250-ton progressive punch press with a wipe-down operation that puts two 90-degree forms in the flat steel to make the trough. The distance from one side of the form to the other is critical because of weatherproofing in outdoor applications. The company requires that the width of the trough be between 8.31 inches and 8.61 inches. The file **Trough** contains the widths of the troughs, in inches, for a sample of $n = 49$:

```
8.312 8.343 8.317 8.383 8.348 8.410 8.351 8.373 8.481 8.422
8.476 8.382 8.484 8.403 8.414 8.419 8.385 8.465 8.498 8.447
8.436 8.413 8.489 8.414 8.481 8.415 8.479 8.429 8.458 8.462
8.460 8.444 8.429 8.460 8.412 8.420 8.410 8.405 8.323 8.420
8.396 8.447 8.405 8.439 8.411 8.427 8.420 8.498 8.409
```

a. At the 0.05 level of significance, is there evidence that the mean width of the troughs is different from 8.46 inches?

b. What assumption about the population distribution is needed in order to conduct the *t* test in (a)?

c. Evaluate the assumption made in (b).

d. Do you think that the assumption needed in order to conduct the *t* test in (a) is valid? Explain.

9.33 One operation of a steel mill is to cut pieces of steel into parts that are used in the frame for front seats in an automobile. The steel is cut with a diamond saw and requires the resulting parts must be cut to be within ± 0.005 inch of the length specified by the automobile company. The file **Steel** contains a sample of 100 steel parts. The measurement reported is the difference, in inches, between the actual length of the steel part, as measured by a laser measurement device, and the specified length of the steel part. For example, a value of -0.002 represents a steel part that is 0.002 inch shorter than the specified length.

a. At the 0.05 level of significance, is there evidence that the mean difference is different from 0.0 inches?

b. Construct a 95% confidence interval estimate of the population mean. Interpret this interval.

c. Compare the conclusions reached in (a) and (b).

d. Because $n = 100$, do you have to be concerned about the normality assumption needed for the *t* test and *t* interval?

9.34 In Problem 3.63 on page 134, you were introduced to a tea-bag-filling operation. An important quality characteristic of interest for this process is the weight of the tea in the individual bags. The file **Teabags** contains an ordered array of the weight, in grams, of a sample of 50 tea bags produced during an 8-hour shift.

a. Is there evidence that the mean amount of tea per bag is different from 5.5 grams? (Use $\alpha = 0.01$.)

b. Construct a 99% confidence interval estimate of the population mean amount of tea per bag. Interpret this interval.

c. Compare the conclusions reached in (a) and (b).

9.35 Experian Marketing Services reported that the typical American spends a mean of 144 minutes (2.4 hours) per day accessing the Internet via a mobile device. (Source: *The 2014 Digital Marketer*, available at **ex.pn/1kXJjfX**.) In order to test the validity of this statement, you select a sample of 30 friends and family. The results for the time spent per day accessing the Internet via mobile device (in minutes) are stored in **InternetMobileTime** .

a. Is there evidence that the population mean time spent per day accessing the Internet via mobile device is different from 144 minutes? Use the *p*-value approach and a level of significance of 0.05.

b. What assumption about the population distribution is needed in order to conduct the *t* test in (a)?

c. Make a list of the various ways you could evaluate the assumption noted in (b).

d. Evaluate the assumption noted in (b) and determine whether the test in (a) is valid.

9.3 One-Tail Tests

The examples of hypothesis testing in Sections 9.1 and 9.2 are called two-tail tests because the rejection region is divided into the two tails of the sampling distribution of the mean. In contrast, some hypothesis tests are one-tail tests because they require an alternative hypothesis that focuses on a *particular direction*.

One example of a one-tail hypothesis test would test whether the population mean is *less than* a specified value. One such situation involves the business problem concerning the service time at the drive-through window of a fast-food restaurant. According to *QSR* magazine, the speed with which customers are served is of critical importance to the success of the service (see **bit.ly/WoJpTT**). In one past study, an audit of McDonald's drive-throughs had a mean service time of 188.83 seconds, which was slower than the drive-throughs of several other fast-food chains. Suppose that McDonald's began a quality improvement effort to reduce the service time by deploying an improved drive-through service process in a sample of 25 stores. Because McDonald's would want to institute the new process in all of its stores only if the test sample saw a *decreased* drive-through time, the entire rejection region is located in the lower tail of the distribution.

The Critical Value Approach

You wish to determine whether the new drive-through process has a mean that is less than 188.83 seconds. To perform this one-tail hypothesis test, you use the six-step method listed in Exhibit 9.1 on page 291:

Step 1 You define the null and alternative hypotheses:

$$H_0 : \mu \geq 188.83$$

$$H_1 : \mu < 188.83$$

> **Student Tip**
>
> The rejection region matches the direction of the alternative hypothesis. If the alternative hypothesis contains a $<$ sign, the rejection region is in the lower tail. If the alternative hypothesis contains a $>$ sign, the rejection region is in the upper tail.

The alternative hypothesis contains the statement for which you are trying to find evidence. If the conclusion of the test is "reject H_0," there is statistical evidence that the mean drive-through time is less than the drive-through time in the old process. This would be reason to change the drive-through process for the entire population of stores. If the conclusion of the test is "do not reject H_0," then there is insufficient evidence that the mean drive-through time in the new process is significantly less than the drive-through time in the old process. If this occurs, there would be insufficient reason to institute the new drive-through process in the population of stores.

Step 2 You collect the data by selecting a sample of $n = 25$ stores. You decide to use $\alpha = 0.05$.

Step 3 Because σ is unknown, you use the t distribution and the t_{STAT} test statistic. You need to assume that the drive-through time is normally distributed because a sample of only 25 drive-through times is selected.

Step 4 The rejection region is entirely contained in the lower tail of the sampling distribution of the mean because you want to reject H_0 only when the sample mean is significantly less than 188.83 seconds. When the entire rejection region is contained in one tail of the sampling distribution of the test statistic, the test is called a **one-tail test**, or **directional test**. If the alternative hypothesis includes the *less than* sign, the critical value of t is negative. As shown in Table 9.3 and Figure 9.10, because the entire rejection region is in the lower tail of the t distribution and contains an area of 0.05, due to the symmetry of the t distribution, the critical value of the t test statistic with $25 - 1 = 24$ degrees of freedom is -1.7109.

The decision rule is

$$\text{Reject } H_0 \text{ if } t_{STAT} < -1.7109;$$

$$\text{otherwise, do not reject } H_0.$$

TABLE 9.3

Determining the Critical Value from the *t* Table for an Area of 0.05 in the Lower Tail, with 24 Degrees of Freedom

	Cumulative Probabilities					
	.75	.90	.95	.975	.99	.995
Degrees of Freedom	Upper-Tail Areas					
	.25	.10	.05	.025	.01	.005
1	1.0000	3.0777	6.3138	12.7062	31.8207	63.6574
2	0.8165	1.8856	2.9200	4.3027	6.9646	9.9248
3	0.7649	1.6377	2.3534	3.1824	4.5407	5.8409
⋮	⋮	⋮	⋮	⋮	⋮	⋮
23	0.6853	1.3195	1.7139	2.0687	2.4999	2.8073
24	0.6848	1.3178	1.7109	2.0639	2.4922	2.7969
25	0.6844	1.3163	1.7081	2.0595	2.4851	2.7874

Source: Extracted from Table E.3.

FIGURE 9.10

One-tail test of hypothesis for a mean (σ unknown) at the 0.05 level of significance

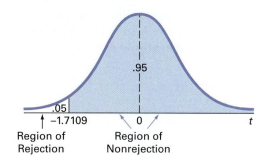

Step 5 From the sample of 25 stores you selected, you find that the sample mean service time at the drive-through equals 170.8 seconds and the sample standard deviation equals 21.3 seconds. Using $n = 25, \overline{X} = 170.8, S = 21.3$, and Equation (9.2) on page 298,

$$t_{STAT} = \frac{\overline{X} - \mu}{\dfrac{S}{\sqrt{n}}} = \frac{170.8 - 188.83}{\dfrac{21.3}{\sqrt{25}}} = -4.2324$$

Step 6 Because $t_{STAT} = -4.2324 < -1.7109$, you reject the null hypothesis (see Figure 9.10). You conclude that the mean service time at the drive-through is less than 188.83 seconds. There is sufficient evidence to change the drive-through process for the entire population of stores.

The *p*-Value Approach

Use the five steps listed in Exhibit 9.2 on page 294 to illustrate the *t* test for the drive-through time study using the *p*-value approach:

Step 1–3 These steps are the same as was used in the critical value approach on page 304.

Step 4 $t_{STAT} = -4.2324$ (see step 5 of the critical value approach). Because the alternative hypothesis indicates a rejection region entirely in the lower tail of the sampling distribution, to compute the *p*-value, you need to find the probability that the t_{STAT} test statistic will be less than -4.2324. Figure 9.11 shows that the *p*-value is 0.0001 (displayed as 0.000 in Minitab).

FIGURE 9.11

Excel and Minitab *t* test results for the drive-through time study

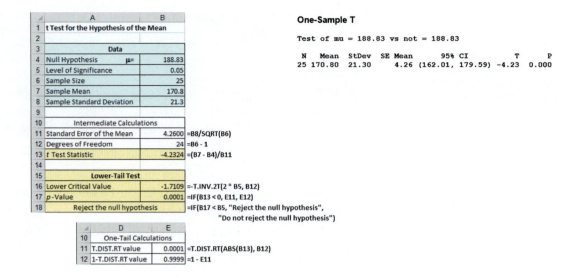

Step 5   The *p*-value of 0.0001 is less than $\alpha = 0.05$ (see Figure 9.12). You reject H_0 and conclude that the mean service time at the drive-through is less than 188.83 seconds. There is sufficient evidence to change the drive-through process for the entire population of stores.

FIGURE 9.12

Determining the *p*-value for a one-tail test

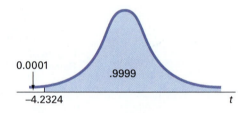

Example 9.5 illustrates a one-tail test in which the rejection region is in the upper tail.

EXAMPLE 9.5

A One-Tail Test for the Mean

A company that manufactures chocolate bars is particularly concerned that the mean weight of a chocolate bar is not greater than 6.03 ounces. A sample of 50 chocolate bars is selected; the sample mean is 6.034 ounces, and the sample standard deviation is 0.02 ounce. Using the $\alpha = 0.01$ level of significance, is there evidence that the population mean weight of the chocolate bars is greater than 6.03 ounces?

SOLUTION   Using the critical value approach, listed in Exhibit 9.1 on page 291,

Step 1   First, you define the null and alternative hypotheses:

$$H_0 : \mu \leq 6.03$$

$$H_1 : \mu > 6.03$$

Step 2   You collect the data from a sample of $n = 50$. You decide to use $\alpha = 0.01$.

Step 3   Because σ is unknown, you use the *t* distribution and the t_{STAT} test statistic.

Step 4   The rejection region is entirely contained in the upper tail of the sampling distribution of the mean because you want to reject H_0 only when the sample mean is significantly greater than 6.03 ounces. Because the entire rejection region is in the upper tail of the *t* distribution and contains an area of 0.01, the critical value of the *t* distribution with $50 - 1 = 49$ degrees of freedom is 2.4049 (see Table E.3).

The decision rule is

$$\text{Reject } H_0 \text{ if } t_{STAT} > 2.4049;$$

$$\text{otherwise, do not reject } H_0.$$

Step 5 From your sample of 50 chocolate bars, you find that the sample mean weight is 6.034 ounces, and the sample standard deviation is 0.02 ounces. Using $n = 50, \overline{X} = 6.034, S = 0.02$, and Equation (9.2) on page 298,

$$t_{STAT} = \frac{\overline{X} - \mu}{\dfrac{S}{\sqrt{n}}} = \frac{6.034 - 6.03}{\dfrac{0.02}{\sqrt{50}}} = 1.414$$

Step 6 Because $t_{STAT} = 1.414 < 2.4049$ or the p-value (from Excel) is $0.0818 > 0.01$, you do not reject the null hypothesis. There is insufficient evidence to conclude that the population mean weight is greater than 6.03 ounces.

To perform one-tail tests of hypotheses, you must properly formulate H_0 and H_1. A summary of the null and alternative hypotheses for one-tail tests is as follows:

- The null hypothesis, H_0, represents the status quo or the current belief in a situation.
- The alternative hypothesis, H_1, is the opposite of the null hypothesis and represents a research claim or specific inference you would like to prove.
- If you reject the null hypothesis, you have statistical proof that the alternative hypothesis is correct.
- If you do not reject the null hypothesis, you have failed to prove the alternative hypothesis. The failure to prove the alternative hypothesis, however, does not mean that you have proven the null hypothesis.
- The null hypothesis always refers to a specified value of the *population parameter* (such as μ), not to a *sample statistic* (such as $\overline{X}$).
- The statement of the null hypothesis *always* contains an equal sign regarding the specified value of the parameter (e.g., $H_0 : \mu \geq 188.83$).
- The statement of the alternative hypothesis *never* contains an equal sign regarding the specified value of the parameter (e.g., $H_1 : \mu < 188.83$).

Problems for Section 9.3

LEARNING THE BASICS

9.36 In a one-tail hypothesis test where you reject H_0 only in the *upper* tail, what is the p-value if $Z_{STAT} = +2.00$?

9.37 In Problem 9.36, what is your statistical decision if you test the null hypothesis at the 0.05 level of significance?

9.38 In a one-tail hypothesis test where you reject H_0 only in the *lower* tail, what is the p-value if $Z_{STAT} = -1.38$?

9.39 In Problem 9.38, what is your statistical decision if you test the null hypothesis at the 0.01 level of significance?

9.40 In a one-tail hypothesis test where you reject H_0 only in the *lower* tail, what is the p-value if $Z_{STAT} = +1.38$?

9.41 In Problem 9.40, what is the statistical decision if you test the null hypothesis at the 0.01 level of significance?

9.42 In a one-tail hypothesis test where you reject H_0 only in the *upper* tail, what is the critical value of the t-test statistic with 10 degrees of freedom at the 0.01 level of significance?

9.43 In Problem 9.42, what is your statistical decision if $t_{STAT} = +2.39$?

9.44 In a one-tail hypothesis test where you reject H_0 only in the *lower* tail, what is the critical value of the t_{STAT} test statistic with 20 degrees of freedom at the 0.01 level of significance?

9.45 In Problem 9.44, what is your statistical decision if $t_{STAT} = -1.15$?

APPLYING THE CONCEPTS

9.46 The Los Angeles County Metropolitan Transportation Authority has set a bus mechanical reliability goal of 3,900 bus miles. Bus mechanical reliability is measured specifically as the number of bus miles between mechanical road calls. Suppose a sample of 100 buses resulted in a sample mean of 3,975 bus miles and a sample standard deviation of 275 bus miles.

a. Is there evidence that the population mean bus miles is greater than 3,900 bus miles? (Use a 0.05 level of significance.)
b. Determine the p-value and interpret its meaning.

9.47 *CarMD* reports that the cost of repairing a hybrid vehicle is falling even while typical repairs on conventional vehicles are getting more expensive. The most common hybrid repair, replacing the hybrid inverter assembly, had a mean repair cost of $2,826 in 2013. (Data extracted from *2014 CarMD Vehicle Health Index*, available at **corp.carmd.com**.) Industry experts suspect that the cost will continue to decrease given the increase in the number of technicians who have gained expertise on fixing gas–electric engines in recent months. Suppose a sample of 100 hybrid inverter assembly repairs completed in the last month was selected. The sample mean repair cost was $2,700 with the sample standard deviation of $500.

a. Is there evidence that the population mean cost is less than $2,826? (Use a 0.05 level of significance.)

b. Determine the *p*-value and interpret its meaning.

✓ SELF **9.48** A quality improvement project was conducted
✓ Test with the objective of improving the wait time in a county health department (CHD) Adult Primary Care Unit (APCU). The evaluation plan included *waiting room time* as one key waiting time process measure. Waiting room time was defined as the time elapsed between requesting that the patient be seated in the waiting room and the time he or she was called to be placed in an exam room. Suppose that, initially, a targeted wait time goal of 25 minutes was set. After implementing an improvement framework and process, the quality improvement team collected data on a sample of 355 patients. In this sample, the mean wait time was 23.05 minutes, with a standard deviation of 16.83 minutes. (Data extracted from M. Michael, S. D. Schaffer, P. L. Egan, B. B. Little, and P. S. Pritchard, "Improving Wait Times and Patient Satisfaction in Primary Care," *Journal for Healthcare Quality*, 2013, 35(2), pp. 50–60.)

a. If you test the null hypothesis at the 0.01 level of significance, is there evidence that the population mean wait time is less than 25 minutes?

b. Interpret the meaning of the *p*-value in this problem.

9.49 You are the manager of a restaurant that delivers pizza to college dormitory rooms. You have just changed your delivery process in an effort to reduce the mean time between the order and completion of delivery from the current 25 minutes. A sample of 36 orders using the new delivery process yields a sample mean of 22.4 minutes and a sample standard deviation of 6 minutes.

a. Using the six-step critical value approach, at the 0.05 level of significance, is there evidence that the population mean delivery time has been reduced below the previous population mean value of 25 minutes?

b. At the 0.05 level of significance, use the five-step *p*-value approach.

c. Interpret the meaning of the *p*-value in (b).

d. Compare your conclusions in (a) and (b).

9.50 A survey of nonprofit organizations showed that online fundraising has increased in the past year. Based on a random sample of 55 nonprofit organizations, the mean one-time gift donation in the past year was $75, with a standard deviation of $9.

a. If you test the null hypothesis at the 0.01 level of significance, is there evidence that the mean one-time gift donation is greater than $70?

b. Interpret the meaning of the *p*-value in this problem.

9.51 The population mean waiting time to check out of a supermarket has been 4 minutes. Recently, in an effort to reduce the waiting time, the supermarket has experimented with a system in which infrared cameras use body heat and in-store software to determine how many lanes should be opened. A sample of 100 customers was selected, and their mean waiting time to check out was 3.25 minutes, with a sample standard deviation of 2.7 minutes.

a. At the 0.05 level of significance, using the critical value approach to hypothesis testing, is there evidence that the population mean waiting time to check out is less than 4 minutes?

b. At the 0.05 level of significance, using the *p*-value approach to hypothesis testing, is there evidence that the population mean waiting time to check out is less than 4 minutes?

c. Interpret the meaning of the *p*-value in this problem.

d. Compare your conclusions in (a) and (b).

9.4 Z Test of Hypothesis for the Proportion

In some situations, you want to test a hypothesis about the proportion of events of interest in the population, π, rather than test the population mean. To begin, you select a random sample and compute the **sample proportion**, $p = X/n$. You then compare the value of this statistic to the hypothesized value of the parameter, π, in order to decide whether to reject the null hypothesis.

If the number of events of interest (X) and the number of events that are not of interest ($n - X$) are each at least five, the sampling distribution of a proportion approximately follows a normal distribution, and you can use the **Z test for the proportion**. Equation (9.3) defines this hypothesis test for the difference between the sample proportion, p, and the hypothesized population proportion, π.

> **Student Tip**
> Do not confuse this use of the Greek letter pi, π, to represent the population proportion with the mathematical constant that uses the same letter to represent the ratio of the circumference to a diameter of a circle—approximately 3.14159.

Z TEST FOR THE PROPORTION

$$Z_{STAT} = \frac{p - \pi}{\sqrt{\dfrac{\pi(1 - \pi)}{n}}} \tag{9.3}$$

where

$$p = \text{sample proportion} = \frac{X}{n} = \frac{\text{number of events of interest in the sample}}{\text{sample size}}$$

$$\pi = \text{hypothesized proportion of events of interest in the population}$$

The Z_{STAT} test statistic approximately follows a standardized normal distribution when X and $(n - X)$ are each at least 5.

Alternatively, by multiplying the numerator and denominator by n, you can write the Z_{STAT} test statistic in terms of the number of events of interest, X, as shown in Equation (9.4).

Z TEST FOR THE PROPORTION IN TERMS OF THE NUMBER OF EVENTS OF INTEREST

$$Z_{STAT} = \frac{X - n\pi}{\sqrt{n\pi(1 - \pi)}}$$

(9.4)

The Critical Value Approach

In a survey of 792 Internet users, 681 said that they had taken steps to remove or mask their digital footprints. (Source: E. Dwoskin, "Give Me Back My Privacy," *The Wall Street Journal*, March 24, 2014, p. R2.) Suppose that a survey conducted in the previous year indicated that 80% of Internet users said that they had taken steps to remove or mask their digital footprints. Is there evidence that the proportion of Internet users who said that they had taken steps to remove or mask their digital footprints has changed from the previous year? To investigate this question, the null and alternative hypotheses are as follows:

$H_0 : \pi = 0.80$ (i.e., the proportion of Internet users who said that they had taken steps to re-move or mask their digital footprints has not changed from the previous year)

$H_1 : \pi \neq 0.80$ (i.e., the proportion of Internet users who said that they had taken steps to remove or mask their digital footprints has changed from the previous year)

Because you are interested in determining whether the population proportion of Internet users who said that they had taken steps to remove or mask their digital footprints has changed from 0.80 in the previous year, you use a two-tail test. If you select the $\alpha = 0.05$ level of significance, the rejection and nonrejection regions are set up as in Figure 9.13, and the decision rule is

Reject H_0 if $Z_{STAT} < -1.96$ or if $Z_{STAT} > +1.96$;

otherwise, do not reject H_0.

FIGURE 9.13

Two-tail test of hypothesis for the proportion at the 0.05 level of significance

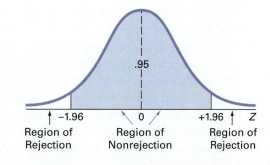

.95

| ↑ −1.96 | ↘ 0 ↗ | +1.96 ↑ | *Z* |

Region of Rejection   Region of Nonrejection   Region of Rejection

Because 681 of the 792 Internet users said that they had taken steps to remove or mask their digital footprints,

$$p = \frac{681}{792} = 0.8598$$

Since $X = 681$ and $n - X = 111$, each > 5, using Equation (9.3),

$$Z_{STAT} = \frac{p - \pi}{\sqrt{\dfrac{\pi(1 - \pi)}{n}}} = \frac{0.8598 - 0.80}{\sqrt{\dfrac{0.80(1 - 0.80)}{792}}} = \frac{0.0598}{0.0142} = 4.2107$$

or, using Equation (9.4),

$$Z_{STAT} = \frac{X - n\pi}{\sqrt{n\pi(1 - \pi)}} = \frac{681 - (792)(0.80)}{\sqrt{792(0.80)(0.20)}} = \frac{47.4}{11.257} = 4.2107$$

Because $Z_{STAT} = 4.2107 > 1.96$, you reject H_0. There is evidence that the population proportion of all Internet users who said that they had taken steps to remove or mask their digital footprints has changed from 0.80 in the previous year. Figure 9.14 presents the Excel and Minitab results for these data.

FIGURE 9.14

Excel and Minitab results for the Z test for whether the proportion of Internet users who said that they had taken steps to remove or mask their digital footprints has changed from 0.80 in the previous year

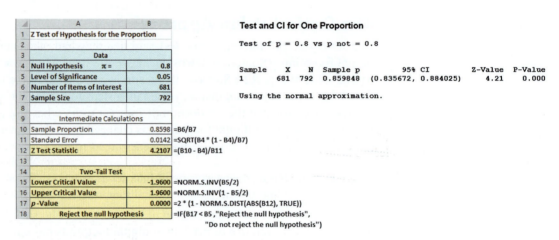

The p-Value Approach

As an alternative to the critical value approach, you can compute the p-value. For this two-tail test in which the rejection region is located in the lower tail and the upper tail, you need to find the area below a Z value of -4.2107 and above a Z value of $+4.2107$. Figure 9.14 reports a p-value of 0.0000. Because this value is less than the selected level of significance ($\alpha = 0.05$), you reject the null hypothesis.

Example 9.6 illustrates a one-tail test for a proportion.

EXAMPLE 9.6

Testing a Hypothesis for a Proportion

In addition to the business problem of the speed of service at the drive-through, fast-food chains want to fill orders correctly. The same audit that reported that McDonald's had a drive-through service time of 188.83 seconds also reported that McDonald's filled 90.9% of its drive-through orders correctly. Suppose that McDonald's begins a quality improvement effort to ensure that orders at the drive-through are filled correctly. The business problem is defined as determining whether the new process can increase the percentage of orders filled correctly. Data are collected from a sample of 400 orders using the new process. The results indicate that

378 orders were filled correctly. At the 0.01 level of significance, can you conclude that the new process has increased the proportion of orders filled correctly?

SOLUTION The null and alternative hypotheses are

$$H_0 : \pi \leq 0.909 \text{ (i.e., the population proportion of orders filled correctly using the new process is less than or equal to 0.909)}$$

$$H_1 : \pi > 0.909 \text{ (i.e., the population proportion of orders filled correctly using the new process is greater than 0.909)}$$

Since $X = 378$ and $n - X = 22$, both > 5, using Equation (9.3) on page 308,

$$p = \frac{X}{n} = \frac{378}{400} = 0.945$$

$$Z_{STAT} = \frac{p - \pi}{\sqrt{\dfrac{\pi(1 - \pi)}{n}}} = \frac{0.945 - 0.909}{\sqrt{\dfrac{0.909(1 - 0.909)}{400}}} = \frac{0.036}{0.0144} = 2.5034$$

The *p*-value (computed by Excel) for $Z_{STAT} > 2.5034$ is 0.0062.

Using the critical value approach, you reject H_0 if $Z_{STAT} > 2.33$. Using the *p*-value approach, you reject H_0 if the *p*-value < 0.01. Because $Z_{STAT} = 2.5034 > 2.33$ or the *p*-value $= 0.0062 < 0.01$, you reject H_0. You have evidence that the new process has increased the proportion of correct orders above 0.909 or 90.9%.

Problems for Section 9.4

LEARNING THE BASICS

9.52 If, in a random sample of 400 items, 88 are defective, what is the sample proportion of defective items?

9.53 In Problem 9.52, if the null hypothesis is that 20% of the items in the population are defective, what is the value of Z_{STAT}?

9.54 In Problems 9.52 and 9.53, suppose you are testing the null hypothesis $H_0 : \pi = 0.20$ against the two-tail alternative hypothesis $H_1 : \pi \neq 0.20$ and you choose the level of significance $\alpha = 0.05$. What is your statistical decision?

APPLYING THE CONCEPTS

9.55 According to a recent National Association of Colleges and Employers (NACE) report, 48% of college student internships are unpaid. (Source: "Just 38 Percent of Unpaid Internships Were Subject to FLSA Guidelines," **bit.ly/Rx76M8**.) A recent survey of 60 college interns at a local university found that 30 had unpaid internships.
a. Use the five-step *p*-value approach to hypothesis testing and a 0.05 level of significance to determine whether the proportion of college interns that had unpaid internships is different from 0.48.
b. Assume that the study found that 37 of the 60 college interns had unpaid internships and repeat (a). Are the conclusions the same?

9.56 The worldwide market share for the Mozilla Firefox web browser was 17% in a recent month. (Data extracted from **netmarketshare.com**.) Suppose that you decide to select a sample

of 100 students at your university and you find that 22 use the Mozilla Firefox web browser.
a. Use the five-step *p*-value approach to try to determine whether there is evidence that the market share for the Mozilla Firefox web browser at your university is greater than the worldwide market share of 17%. (Use the 0.05 level of significance.)
b. Suppose that the sample size is $n = 400$, and you find that 22% of the sample of students at your university (88 out of 400) use the Mozilla Firefox web browser. Use the five-step *p*-value approach to try to determine whether there is evidence that the market share for the Mozilla Firefox web browser at your university is greater than the worldwide market share of 17%. (Use the 0.05 level of significance.)
c. Discuss the effect that sample size has on hypothesis testing.
d. What do you think are your chances of rejecting any null hypothesis concerning a population proportion if a sample size of $n = 20$ is used?

9.57 One of the issues facing organizations is increasing diversity throughout an organization. One of the ways to evaluate an organization's success at increasing diversity is to compare the percentage of employees in the organization in a particular position with a specific background to the percentage in a particular position with that specific background in the general workforce. Recently, a large academic medical center determined that 9 of 17 employees in a particular position were female, whereas 55% of the employees for this position in the general workforce were female. At the 0.05 level of significance, is there evidence that the proportion of females in this position at this medical center is different from what would be expected in the general workforce?

9.58 How do professionals stay on top of their careers? Of 935 surveyed U.S. LinkedIn members, 543 reported that they engaged in professional networking within the last month. (Source: LinkedIn Talent Solutions, *Talent Trends 2014*, available at **linkd.in/Rx7o5T**.) At the 0.05 level of significance, is there evidence that the proportion of all LinkedIn members who engaged in professional networking within the last month is different from 52%?

9.59 A cellphone provider has the business objective of wanting to determine the proportion of subscribers who would upgrade to a new cellphone with improved features if it were made available at a substantially reduced cost. Data are collected from a random sample of 500 subscribers. The results indicate that 135 of the subscribers would upgrade to a new cellphone at a reduced cost.

a. At the 0.05 level of significance, is there evidence that more than 20% of the customers would upgrade to a new cellphone at a reduced cost?

b. How would the manager in charge of promotional programs concerning residential customers use the results in (a)?

9.60 Actuation Consulting and Enterprise Agility recently conducted a global survey of product teams with the goal of better understanding the dynamics of product team performance and uncovering the practices that make these teams successful. One of the survey findings was that 37% of organizations have a coherent business strategy that they stick to and effectively communicate. (Source: *The Study of Product Team Performance, 2013,* available at **bit.ly/1ja3ndA**.) Suppose another study is conducted to check the validity of this result, with the goal of proving that the percentage is less than 37%.

a. State the null and research hypotheses.

b. A sample of 100 organizations is selected, and results indicate that 34 organizations have a coherent business strategy that they stick to and effectively communicate. Use either the six-step critical value hypothesis testing approach or the five-step *p*-value approach to determine at the 0.05 level of significance whether there is evidence that the percentage is less than 37%.

9.5 Potential Hypothesis-Testing Pitfalls and Ethical Issues

To this point, you have studied the fundamental concepts of hypothesis testing. You have used hypothesis testing to analyze differences between sample statistics and hypothesized population parameters in order to make business decisions concerning the underlying population characteristics. You have also learned how to evaluate the risks involved in making these decisions.

When planning to carry out a hypothesis test based on a survey, research study, or designed experiment, you must ask several questions to ensure that you use proper methodology. You need to raise and answer questions such as the following in the planning stage:

- What is the goal of the survey, study, or experiment? How can you translate the goal into a null hypothesis and an alternative hypothesis?
- Is the hypothesis test a two-tail test or one-tail test?
- Can you select a random sample from the underlying population of interest?
- What types of data will you collect in the sample? Are the variables numerical or categorical?
- At what level of significance should you conduct the hypothesis test?
- Is the intended sample size large enough to achieve the desired power of the test for the level of significance chosen?
- What statistical test procedure should you use and why?
- What conclusions and interpretations can you reach from the results of the hypothesis test?

Failing to consider these questions early in the planning process can lead to biased or incomplete results. Proper planning can help ensure that the statistical study will provide objective information needed to make good business decisions.

Statistical Significance Versus Practical Significance

You need to make a distinction between the existence of a statistically significant result and its practical significance in a field of application. Sometimes, due to a very large sample size, you may get a result that is statistically significant but has little practical significance.

For example, suppose that prior to a national marketing campaign focusing on a series of expensive television commercials, you believe that the proportion of people who recognize your brand is 0.30. At the completion of the campaign, a survey of 20,000 people indicates that 6,168 recognized your brand. A one-tail test trying to prove that the proportion is now greater than 0.30 results in a p-value of 0.0047, and the correct statistical conclusion is that the proportion of consumers recognizing your brand name has now increased. Was the campaign successful? The result of the hypothesis test indicates a statistically significant increase in brand awareness, but is this increase practically important? The population proportion is now estimated at $6,168/20,000 = 0.3084 = 0.3084$ or 30.84%. This increase is less than 1% more than the hypothesized value of 30%. Did the large expenses associated with the marketing campaign produce a result with a meaningful increase in brand awareness? Because of the minimal real-world impact that an increase of less than 1% has on the overall marketing strategy and the huge expenses associated with the marketing campaign, you should conclude that the campaign was not successful. On the other hand, if the campaign increased brand awareness from 30% to 50%, you would be inclined to conclude that the campaign was successful.

Statistical *Insignificance* Versus Importance

In contrast to the issue of the practical significance of a statistically significant result is the situation in which an important result may not be statistically significant. In a recent case (see reference 1), the U.S. Supreme Court ruled that companies cannot rely solely on whether the result of a study is significant when determining what they communicate to investors. In some situations (see reference 6), the lack of a large enough sample size may result in a nonsignificant result when in fact an important difference does exist. A study that compared male and female entrepreneurship rates globally and within Massachusetts found a significant difference globally but not within Massachusetts, even though the entrepreneurship rates for females and for males in the two geographic areas were similar (8.8% for males in Massachusetts as compared to 8.4% globally; 5% for females in both geographic areas). The difference was due to the fact that the global sample size was 20 times larger than the Massachusetts sample size.

Reporting of Findings

In conducting research, you should document both good and bad results. You should not just report the results of hypothesis tests that show statistical significance but omit those for which there is insufficient evidence in the findings. In instances in which there is insufficient evidence to reject H_0, you must make it clear that this does not prove that the null hypothesis is true. What the result indicates is that with the sample size used, there is not enough information to *disprove* the null hypothesis.

Ethical Issues

You need to distinguish between poor research methodology and unethical behavior. Ethical considerations arise when the hypothesis-testing process is manipulated. Some of the areas where ethical issues can arise include the use of human subjects in experiments, the data collection method, the type of test (one-tail or two-tail test), the choice of the level of significance, the cleansing and discarding of data, and the failure to report pertinent findings.

USING STATISTICS

Significant Testing at Oxford Cereals, Revisited

Shutterstock

As the plant operations manager for Oxford Cereals, you were responsible for the cereal-filling process. It was your responsibility to adjust the process when the mean fill-weight in the population of boxes deviated from the company specification of 368 grams. You chose to conduct a hypothesis test.

You determined that the null hypothesis should be that the population mean fill was 368 grams. If the mean weight of the sampled boxes was sufficiently above or below the expected 368-gram mean specified by Oxford Cereals, you would reject the null hypothesis in favor of the alternative hypothesis that the mean fill was different from 368 grams. If this happened, you would stop production and take whatever action was necessary to correct the problem. If the null hypothesis was not rejected, you would continue to believe in the status quo—that the process was working correctly—and therefore take no corrective action.

Before proceeding, you considered the risks involved with hypothesis tests. If you rejected a true null hypothesis, you would make a Type I error and conclude that the population mean fill was not 368 when it actually was 368 grams. This error would result in adjusting the filling process even though the process was working properly. If you did not reject a false null hypothesis, you would make a Type II error and conclude that the population mean fill was 368 grams when it actually was not 368 grams. Here, you would allow the process to continue without adjustment even though the process was not working properly.

After collecting a random sample of 25 cereal boxes, you used either the six-step critical value approach or the five-step p-value approach to hypothesis testing. Because the test statistic fell into the nonrejection region, you did not reject the null hypothesis. You concluded that there was insufficient evidence to prove that the mean fill differed from 368 grams. No corrective action on the filling process was needed.

SUMMARY

This chapter presented the foundation of hypothesis testing. You learned how to perform tests on the population mean and on the population proportion. The chapter developed both the critical value approach and the p-value approach to hypothesis testing.

In deciding which test to use, you should ask the following question: Does the test involve a numerical variable or a categorical variable? If the test involves a numerical variable, you use the t test for the mean. If the test involves a categorical variable, you use the Z test for the proportion. Table 9.4 lists the hypothesis tests covered in the chapter.

TABLE 9.4

Summary of Topics in Chapter 9

	TYPE OF DATA	
TYPE OF ANALYSIS	**Numerical**	**Categorical**
Hypothesis test concerning a single parameter	Z test of hypothesis for the mean (Section 9.1) t test of hypothesis for the mean (Section 9.2)	Z test of hypothesis for the proportion (Section 9.4)

REFERENCES

1. Bialik, C. "Making a Stat Less Significant." *The Wall Street Journal*, April 2, 2011, A5.
2. Bradley, J. V. *Distribution-Free Statistical Tests*. Upper Saddle River, NJ: Prentice Hall, 1968.
3. Daniel, W. *Applied Nonparametric Statistics*, 2nd ed. Boston: Houghton Mifflin, 1990.
4. *Microsoft Excel 2013*. Redmond, WA: Microsoft Corp., 2012.
5. *Minitab Release 16*. State College, PA: Minitab, Inc., 2010.
6. Seaman, J., and E. Allen. "Not Significant, But Important?" *Quality Progress*, August 2011, 57–59.

KEY EQUATIONS

Z Test for the Mean (σ Known)

$$Z_{STAT} = \frac{\overline{X} - \mu}{\dfrac{\sigma}{\sqrt{n}}} \qquad (9.1)$$

t Test for the Mean (σ Unknown)

$$t_{STAT} = \frac{\overline{X} - \mu}{\dfrac{S}{\sqrt{n}}} \qquad (9.2)$$

Z Test for the Proportion

$$Z_{STAT} = \frac{p - \pi}{\sqrt{\dfrac{\pi(1 - \pi)}{n}}} \qquad (9.3)$$

Z Test for the Proportion in Terms of the Number of Events of Interest

$$Z_{STAT} = \frac{X - n\pi}{\sqrt{n\pi(1 - \pi)}} \qquad (9.4)$$

KEY TERMS

alternative hypothesis (H_1) 285
β risk 288
confidence coefficient 289
critical value 287
directional test 304
hypothesis testing 285
level of significance (α) 288
null hypothesis (H_0) 285

one-tail test 304
p-value 293
power of a statistical test 289
region of nonrejection 287
region of rejection 287
robust 301
sample proportion 308
t test for the mean 297

test statistic 287
two-tail test 290
Type I error 288
Type II error 288
Z test for the mean 290
Z test for the proportion 308

CHECKING YOUR UNDERSTANDING

9.61 What is the difference between a null hypothesis, H_0, and an alternative hypothesis, H_1?

9.62 What is the difference between a Type I error and a Type II error?

9.63 What is meant by the power of a test?

9.64 What is the difference between a one-tail test and a two-tail test?

9.65 What is meant by a p-value?

9.66 How can a confidence interval estimate for the population mean provide conclusions for the corresponding two-tail hypothesis test for the population mean?

9.67 What is the six-step critical value approach to hypothesis testing?

9.68 What is the five-step p-value approach to hypothesis testing?

CHAPTER REVIEW PROBLEMS

9.69 In hypothesis testing, the common level of significance is $\alpha = 0.05$. Some might argue for a level of significance greater than 0.05. Suppose that web designers tested the proportion of potential web page visitors with a preference for a new web design over the existing web design. The null hypothesis was that the population proportion of web page visitors preferring the new design was 0.50, and the alternative hypothesis was that it was not equal to 0.50. The p-value for the test was 0.20.

a. State, in statistical terms, the null and alternative hypotheses for this example.

b. Explain the risks associated with Type I and Type II errors in this case.

c. What would be the consequences if you rejected the null hypothesis for a p-value of 0.20?

d. What might be an argument for raising the value of α?

e. What would you do in this situation?

f. What is your answer in (e) if the p-value equals 0.12? What if it equals 0.06?

9.70 Financial institutions utilize prediction models to predict bankruptcy. One such model is the Altman Z-score model, which uses multiple corporate income and balance sheet values to measure the financial health of a company. If the model predicts a low Z-score value, the firm is in financial stress and is predicted to go bankrupt within the next two years. If the model predicts a moderate or high Z-score value, the firm is financially healthy and is predicted to be a non-bankrupt firm (see **pages.stern.nyu.edu/~ealtman/Zscores.pdf**). This decision-making procedure can be expressed in the hypothesis-testing framework. The null hypothesis is that a firm is predicted to be a non-bankrupt firm. The alternative hypothesis is that the firm is predicted to be a bankrupt firm.

a. Explain the risks associated with committing a Type I error in this case.
b. Explain the risks associated with committing a Type II error in this case.
c. Which type of error do you think executives want to avoid? Explain.
d. How would changes in the model affect the probabilities of committing Type I and Type II errors?

9.71 Salesforce ExactTarget Marketing Cloud conducted a study of U.S. consumers that included 205 tablet owners. The study found that 134 tablet owners use their tablet while watching TV at least once per day. (Source: "New Mobile Tracking & Survey Data: 2014 Mobile Behavior Report," **bit.ly/1odMZ3D**.) The authors of the report imply that the survey proves that more than half of all tablet owners use their tablet while watching TV at least once per day.

a. Use the five-step p-value approach to hypothesis testing and a 0.05 level of significance to try to prove that more than half of all tablet owners use their tablet while watching TV at least once per day.
b. Based on your result in (a), is the claim implied by the authors valid?
c. Suppose the study found that 105 tablet owners use their tablet while watching TV at least once per day. Repeat parts (a) and (b).
d. Compare the results of (b) and (c).

9.72 The owner of a specialty coffee shop wants to study coffee purchasing habits of customers at her shop. She selects a random sample of 60 customers during a certain week, with the following results:

- The amount spent was $\overline{X} = \$7.25, S = \$1.75$.
- Thirty-one customers say they "definitely will" recommend the specialty coffee shop to family and friends.

a. At the 0.05 level of significance, is there evidence that the population mean amount spent was different from $6.50?
b. Determine the p-value in (a).
c. At the 0.05 level of significance, is there evidence that more than 50% of all the customers say they "definitely will" recommend the specialty coffee shop to family and friends?
d. What is your answer to (a) if the sample mean equals $6.25?
e. What is your answer to (c) if 39 customers say they "definitely will" recommend the specialty coffee shop to family and friends?

9.73 An auditor for a government agency was assigned the task of evaluating reimbursement for office visits to physicians paid by Medicare. The audit was conducted on a sample of 75 reimbursements, with the following results:

- In 12 of the office visits, there was an incorrect amount of reimbursement.
- The amount of reimbursement was $\overline{X} = \$93.70, S = \$34.55$.

a. At the 0.05 level of significance, is there evidence that the population mean reimbursement was less than $100?
b. At the 0.05 level of significance, is there evidence that the proportion of incorrect reimbursements in the population was greater than 0.10?
c. Discuss the underlying assumptions of the test used in (a).
d. What is your answer to (a) if the sample mean equals $90?

e. What is your answer to (b) if 15 office visits had incorrect reimbursements?

9.74 A bank branch located in a commercial district of a city has the business objective of improving the process for serving customers during the noon-to-1:00 P.M. lunch period. The waiting time (defined as the time the customer enters the line until he or she reaches the teller window) of a random sample of 15 customers is collected, and the results are organized and stored in **Bank1**. These data are:

4.21 5.55 3.02 5.13 4.77 2.34 3.54 3.20
4.50 6.10 0.38 5.12 6.46 6.19 3.79

a. At the 0.05 level of significance, is there evidence that the population mean waiting time is less than 5 minutes?
b. What assumption about the population distribution is needed in order to conduct the t test in (a)?
c. Construct a boxplot or a normal probability plot to evaluate the assumption made in (b).
d. Do you think that the assumption needed in order to conduct the t test in (a) is valid? Explain.
e. As a customer walks into the branch office during the lunch hour, she asks the branch manager how long she can expect to wait. The branch manager replies, "Almost certainly not longer than 5 minutes." On the basis of the results of (a), evaluate this statement.

9.75 A manufacturing company produces electrical insulators. If the insulators break when in use, a short circuit is likely to occur. To test the strength of the insulators, destructive testing is carried out to determine how much force is required to break the insulators. Force is measured by observing the number of pounds of force applied to the insulator before it breaks. The following data (stored in **Force**) are from 30 insulators subjected to this testing:

1,870 1,728 1,656 1,610 1,634 1,784 1,522 1,696 1,592 1,662
1,866 1,764 1,734 1,662 1,734 1,774 1,550 1,756 1,762 1,866
1,820 1,744 1,788 1,688 1,810 1,752 1,680 1,810 1,652 1,736

a. At the 0.05 level of significance, is there evidence that the population mean force required to break the insulator is greater than 1,500 pounds?
b. What assumption about the population distribution is needed in order to conduct the t test in (a)?
c. Construct a histogram, boxplot, or normal probability plot to evaluate the assumption made in (b).
d. Do you think that the assumption needed in order to conduct the t test in (a) is valid? Explain.

9.76 An important quality characteristic used by the manufacturer of Boston and Vermont asphalt shingles is the amount of moisture the shingles contain when they are packaged. Customers may feel that they have purchased a product lacking in quality if they find moisture and wet shingles inside the packaging. In some cases, excessive moisture can cause the granules attached to the shingles for texture and coloring purposes to fall off the shingles, resulting in appearance problems. To monitor the amount of moisture present, the company conducts moisture tests. A shingle is weighed and then dried. The shingle is then reweighed, and, based on the amount of moisture taken out of the product, the pounds of moisture per 100 square feet are calculated. The company would like to show that the mean moisture content is less than 0.35 pound per 100 square feet. The file **Moisture** includes 36 measurements (in pounds per 100 square feet) for Boston shingles and 31 for Vermont shingles.

a. For the Boston shingles, is there evidence at the 0.05 level of significance that the population mean moisture content is less than 0.35 pound per 100 square feet?

b. Interpret the meaning of the *p*-value in (a).

c. For the Vermont shingles, is there evidence at the 0.05 level of significance that the population mean moisture content is less than 0.35 pound per 100 square feet?

d. Interpret the meaning of the *p*-value in (c).

e. What assumption about the population distribution is needed in order to conduct the *t* tests in (a) and (c)?

f. Construct histograms, boxplots, or normal probability plots to evaluate the assumption made in (a) and (c).

g. Do you think that the assumption needed in order to conduct the *t* tests in (a) and (c) is valid? Explain.

9.77 Studies conducted by the manufacturer of Boston and Vermont asphalt shingles have shown product weight to be a major factor in the customer's perception of quality. Moreover, the weight represents the amount of raw materials being used and is therefore very important to the company from a cost standpoint. The last stage of the assembly line packages the shingles before the packages are placed on wooden pallets. Once a pallet is full (a pallet for most brands holds 16 squares of shingles), it is weighed, and the measurement is recorded. The file **Pallet** contains the weight (in pounds) from a sample of 368 pallets of Boston shingles and 330 pallets of Vermont shingles.

a. For the Boston shingles, is there evidence at the 0.05 level of significance that the population mean weight is different from 3,150 pounds?

b. Interpret the meaning of the *p*-value in (a).

c. For the Vermont shingles, is there evidence at the 0.05 level of significance that the population mean weight is different from 3,700 pounds?

d. Interpret the meaning of the *p*-value in (c).

e. In (a) through (d), do you have to be concerned with the normality assumption? Explain.

9.78 The manufacturer of Boston and Vermont asphalt shingles provides its customers with a 20-year warranty on most of its products. To determine whether a shingle will last through the warranty period, accelerated-life testing is conducted at the manufacturing plant. Accelerated-life testing exposes the shingle to the stresses it would be subject to in a lifetime of normal use in a laboratory setting via an experiment that takes only a few minutes to conduct. In this test, a shingle is repeatedly scraped with a brush for a short period of time, and the shingle granules removed by the brushing are weighed (in grams). Shingles that experience low amounts of granule loss are expected to last longer in normal use than shingles that experience high amounts of granule loss. The file **Granule** contains a sample of 170 measurements made on the company's Boston shingles and 140 measurements made on Vermont shingles.

a. For the Boston shingles, is there evidence at the 0.05 level of significance that the population mean granule loss is different from 0.30 grams?

b. Interpret the meaning of the *p*-value in (a).

c. For the Vermont shingles, is there evidence at the 0.05 level of significance that the population mean granule loss is different from 0.30 grams?

d. Interpret the meaning of the *p*-value in (c).

e. In (a) through (d), do you have to be concerned with the normality assumption? Explain.

REPORT WRITING EXERCISE

9.79 Referring to the results of Problems 9.76 through 9.78 concerning Boston and Vermont shingles, write a report that evaluates the moisture level, weight, and granule loss of the two types of shingles.

CASES FOR CHAPTER 9

Managing Ashland MultiComm Services

Continuing its monitoring of the upload speed first described in the Chapter 6 Managing Ashland MultiComm Services case on page 221, the technical operations department wants to ensure that the mean target upload speed for all Internet service subscribers is at least 0.97 on a standard scale in which the target value is 1.0. Each day, upload speed was measured 50 times, with the following results (stored in **AMS9**).

0.854	1.023	1.005	1.030	1.219	0.977	1.044	0.778	1.122	1.114
1.091	1.086	1.141	0.931	0.723	0.934	1.060	1.047	0.800	0.889
1.012	0.695	0.869	0.734	1.131	0.993	0.762	0.814	1.108	0.805
1.223	1.024	0.884	0.799	0.870	0.898	0.621	0.818	1.113	1.286
1.052	0.678	1.162	0.808	1.012	0.859	0.951	1.112	1.003	0.972

1. Compute the sample statistics and determine whether there is evidence that the population mean upload speed is less than 0.97.

2. Write a memo to management that summarizes your conclusions.

Digital Case

Apply your knowledge about hypothesis testing in this Digital Case, which continues the cereal-fill-packaging dispute first discussed in the Digital Case from Chapter 7.

In response to the negative statements made by the Concerned Consumers About Cereal Cheaters (CCACC) in the Chapter 7 Digital Case, Oxford Cereals recently conducted an experiment concerning cereal packaging. The company claims that the results of the experiment refute the CCACC allegations that Oxford Cereals has been cheating consumers by packaging cereals at less than labeled weights.

Open **OxfordCurrentNews.pdf**, a portfolio of current news releases from Oxford Cereals. Review the relevant press releases and supporting documents. Then answer the following questions:

1. Are the results of the experiment valid? Why or why not? If you were conducting the experiment, is there anything you would change?

2. Do the results support the claim that Oxford Cereals is not cheating its customers?

3. Is the claim of the Oxford Cereals CEO that many cereal boxes contain *more* than 368 grams surprising? Is it true?

4. Could there ever be a circumstance in which the results of the Oxford Cereals experiment *and* the CCACC's results are both correct? Explain.

Sure Value Convenience Stores

You work in the corporate office for a nationwide convenience store franchise that operates nearly 10,000 stores. The per-store daily customer count (i.e., the mean number of customers in a store in one day) has been steady, at 900, for some time. To increase the customer count, the chain is considering cutting prices for coffee beverages. The small size will now be $0.59 instead of $0.99, and the medium size will be $0.69 instead of $1.19. Even with this reduction in price, the chain will have a 40% gross margin on coffee.

To test the new initiative, the chain has reduced coffee prices in a sample of 34 stores, where customer counts have been running almost exactly at the national average of 900. After four weeks, the stores sampled stabilize at a mean customer count of 974 and a standard deviation of 96. This increase seems like a substantial amount to you, but it also seems like a pretty small sample. Is there statistical evidence that reducing coffee prices is a good strategy for increasing the mean customer count? Be prepared to explain your conclusion.

CHAPTER 9 EXCEL GUIDE

EG9.1 FUNDAMENTALS of HYPOTHESIS-TESTING METHODOLOGY

Key Technique Use the **NORM.S.INV** function to compute the lower and upper critical values and use **NORM.S.DIST** (*absolute value of the Z test statistic*, **True**) as part of a formula to compute the *p*-value. Use an **IF** function (see Appendix Section F.4) to determine whether to display a rejection or nonrejection message.

Example Perform the Figure 9.5 two-tail *Z* test for the mean for the cereal-filling example shown on page 294.

PHStat Use **Z Test for the Mean, sigma known**.
For the example, select **PHStat → One-Sample Tests → Z Test for the Mean, sigma known**. In the procedure's dialog box (shown below):

1. Enter **368** as the **Null Hypothesis**.
2. Enter **0.05** as the **Level of Significance**.
3. Enter **15** as the **Population Standard Deviation**.
4. Click **Sample Statistics Known** and enter **25** as the **Sample Size** and **372.5** as the **Sample Mean**.
5. Click **Two-Tail Test**.
6. Enter a **Title** and click **OK**.

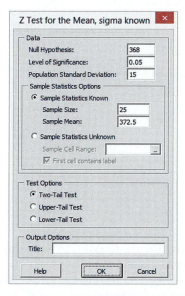

When using unsummarized data, click **Sample Statistics Unknown** in step 4 and enter the cell range of the unsummarized data as the **Sample Cell Range**.

In-Depth Excel Use the **COMPUTE worksheet** of the **Z Mean workbook** as a template.
The worksheet already contains the data for the example. For other problems, change the null hypothesis, level of significance, population standard deviation, sample size, and sample mean values in cells B4 through B8 as necessary.

Read the SHORT TAKES for Chapter 9 for an explanation of the formulas found in the COMPUTE worksheet. If you use an Excel version older than Excel 2010, use the COMPUTE_OLDER worksheet.

EG9.2 *t* TEST of HYPOTHESIS for the MEAN (σ UNKNOWN)

Key Technique Use the **T.INV.2T**(*level of significance*, *degrees of freedom*) function to compute the lower and upper critical values and use **T.DIST.2T**(*absolute value of the t test statistic*, *degrees of freedom*) to compute the *p*-value. Use an **IF** function (see Appendix Section F.4) to determine whether to display a rejection or nonrejection message.

Example Perform the Figure 9.7 two-tail *t* test for the mean for the sales invoices example shown on page 300.

PHStat Use **t Test for the Mean, sigma unknown**.
For the example, select **PHStat → One-Sample Tests → t Test for the Mean, sigma unknown**. In the procedure's dialog box (shown below):

1. Enter **120** as the **Null Hypothesis**.
2. Enter **0.05** as the **Level of Significance**.
3. Click **Sample Statistics Known** and enter **12** as the **Sample Size**, **112.85** as the **Sample Mean**, and **20.8** as the **Sample Standard Deviation**.
4. Click **Two-Tail Test**.
5. Enter a **Title** and click **OK**.

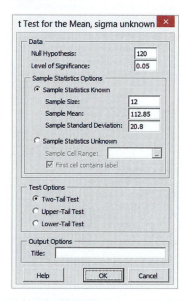

When using unsummarized data, click **Sample Statistics Unknown** in step 3 and enter the cell range of the unsummarized data as the **Sample Cell Range**.

In-Depth Excel Use the **COMPUTE worksheet** of the **T mean workbook**, as a template.

The worksheet already contains the data for the example. For other problems, change the values in cells B4 through B8 as necessary.

Read the SHORT TAKES for Chapter 9 for an explanation of the formulas found in the COMPUTE worksheet. If you use an Excel version older than Excel 2010, use the COMPUTE_OLDER worksheet.

EG9.3 ONE-TAIL TESTS

Key Technique Use the functions discussed in Section EG9.1 and EG9.2 to perform one-tail tests. For the *t* test of the mean, use **T.DIST.RT(*absolute value of the t test statistic*, *degrees of freedom*)** to help compute *p*-values. (See Appendix Section F.4.)

Example Perform the Figure 9.11 lower-tail *t* test for the mean for the drive-through time study example shown on page 306.

PHStat Click either **Lower-Tail Test** or **Upper-Tail Test** in the procedure dialog boxes discussed in Sections EG9.1 and EG9.2 to perform a one-tail test.

For the example, select **PHStat → One-Sample Tests → t Test for the Mean, sigma unknown**. In the procedure's dialog box (shown below):

1. Enter **188.83** as the **Null Hypothesis**.
2. Enter **0.05** as the **Level of Significance**.
3. Click **Sample Statistics Known** and enter **25** as the **Sample Size**, **170.8** as the **Sample Mean**, and **21.3** as the **Sample Standard Deviation**.
4. Click **Lower-Tail Test**.
5. Enter a **Title** and click **OK**.

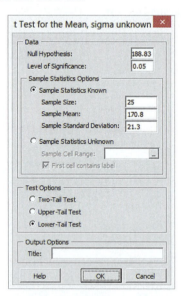

In-Depth Excel Use the **COMPUTE_LOWER worksheet** or the **COMPUTE_UPPER worksheet** of the **Z Mean workbook** or the **T mean workbook** as templates.

For the example, open to the **COMPUTE_LOWER worksheet** of the **T mean workbook**.

Read the SHORT TAKES for Chapter 9 for an explanation of the formulas found in the worksheets. If you use an Excel version older than Excel 2010, use the COMPUTE_OLDER worksheet.

EG9.4 Z TEST of HYPOTHESIS for the PROPORTION

Key Technique Use the **NORM.S.INV** function to compute the lower and upper critical values and use **NORM.S.DIST(*absolute value of the Z test statistic*, True)** as part of a formula to compute the *p*-value. Use an **IF** function (see Appendix Section F.4) to determine whether to display a rejection or nonrejection message.

Example Perform the Figure 9.14 two-tail *Z* test for the proportion of Internet users who said that they had taken steps to remove or mask their digital footprints shown on page 310.

PHStat Use **Z Test for the Proportion**.

For the example, select **PHStat → One-Sample Tests → Z Test for the Proportion**. In the procedure's dialog box (shown below):

1. Enter **0.8** as the **Null Hypothesis**.
2. Enter **0.05** as the **Level of Significance**.
3. Enter **681** as the **Number of Items of Interest**.
4. Enter **792** as the **Sample Size**.
5. Click **Two-Tail Test**.
6. Enter a **Title** and click **OK**.

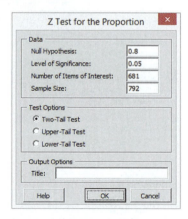

In-Depth Excel Use the **COMPUTE worksheet** of the **Z Proportion workbook** as a template.

The worksheet already contains the data for the example. For other problems, change the null hypothesis, level of significance, population standard deviation, sample size, and sample mean values in cells B4 through B7 as necessary.

Read the SHORT TAKES for Chapter 9 for an explanation of the formulas found in the COMPUTE worksheet. Use the **COMPUTE_LOWER** or **COMPUTE_UPPER worksheets** as templates for performing one-tail tests. If you use an Excel version older than Excel 2010, use the COMPUTE_OLDER worksheet.

CHAPTER 9 MINITAB GUIDE

MG9.1 FUNDAMENTALS of HYPOTHESIS-TESTING METHODOLOGY

Use **1-Sample Z** to perform the Z test for the mean when σ is known. For example, to perform the two-tail Z test for the Figure 9.5 cereal-filling example on page 294, select **Stat → Basic Statistics → 1-Sample Z**. In the 1-Sample Z (Test and Confidence Interval) dialog box (shown below):

1. Click **Summarized data**.
2. Enter **25** in the **Sample size** box and **372.5** in the **Mean** box.
3. Enter **15** in the **Standard deviation** box.
4. Check **Perform hypothesis test** and enter **368** in the **Hypothesized mean** box.
5. Click **Options**.

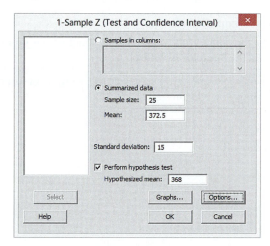

In the 1-Sample Z - Options dialog box:

6. Enter **95.0** in the **Confidence level** box.
7. Select **not equal** from the **Alternative** drop-down list.
8. Click **OK**.
9. Back in the original dialog box, click **OK**.

When using unsummarized data, open the worksheet that contains the data and replace steps 1 and 2 with these steps:

1. Click **Samples in columns**.
2. Enter the name of the column containing the unsummarized data in the **Samples in column** box.

MG9.2 t TEST of HYPOTHESIS for the MEAN (σ UNKNOWN)

Use **1-Sample t** to perform the t test for the mean when σ is unknown.
For example, to perform the t test for the Figure 9.7 sales invoice example on page 300, select **Stat → Basic Statistics → 1-Sample t**.

In the 1-Sample t (Test and Confidence Interval) dialog box (shown below):

1. Click **Summarized data**.
2. Enter **12** in the **Sample size** box, **112.85** in the **Mean** box, and **20.8** in the **Standard deviation** box.
3. Check **Perform hypothesis test** and enter **120** in the **Hypothesized mean** box.
4. Click **Options**.

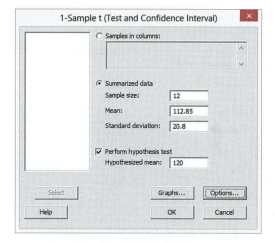

In the 1-Sample t - Options dialog box:

5. Enter **95.0** in the **Confidence level** box.
6. Select **not equal** from the **Alternative** drop-down list.
7. Click **OK**.
8. Back in the original dialog box, click **OK**.

When using unsummarized data, open the worksheet that contains the data and replace steps 1 and 2 with these steps:

1. Click **Samples in columns**.
2. Enter the name of the column containing the unsummarized data in the **Samples in column** box.

To create a boxplot of the unsummarized data, replace step 8 with the following steps 8 through 10:

8. Back in the original dialog box, click **Graphs**.
9. In the 1-Sample t - Graphs dialog box, check **Boxplot of data** and then click **OK**.
10. Back in the original dialog box, click **OK**.

MG9.3 ONE-TAIL TESTS

To perform a one-tail test for **1-Sample Z**, select **less than** or **greater than** from the drop-down list in step 7 of the Section MG9.1 instructions.

To perform a one-tail test for **1-Sample t**, select **less than** or **greater than** from the drop-down list in step 6 of the Section MG9.2 instructions.

MG9.4 Z TEST of HYPOTHESIS for the PROPORTION

Use **1 Proportion**.

For example, to perform the Figure 9.14 Z test for the proportion of Internet users who said that they had taken steps to remove or mask their digital footprints on page 310, select **Stat → Basic Statistics → 1 Proportion**. In the 1 Proportion (Test and Confidence Interval) dialog box (shown below):

1. Click **Summarized data**.

2. Enter **681** in the **Number of events** box and **792** in the **Number of trials** box.

3. Check **Perform hypothesis test** and enter **0.8** in the **Hypothesized proportion** box.

4. Click **Options**.

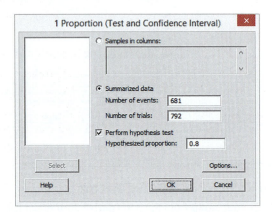

In the 1-Proportion - Options dialog box (shown below):

5. Enter **95.0** in the **Confidence level** box.

6. Select **not equal** from the **Alternative** drop-down list.

7. Check **Use test and interval based on normal distribution**.

8. Click **OK**.

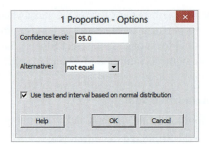

9. Back in the original dialog box, click **OK**.

When using unsummarized data, open the worksheet that contains the data and replace steps 1 and 2 with these steps:

1. Click **Samples in columns**.

2. Enter the name of the column containing the unsummarized data in the **Samples in column** box.

To perform a one-tail test, select **less than** or **greater than** from the drop-down list in step 6.

CHAPTER 10

Two-Sample Tests and One-Way ANOVA

OBJECTIVES

Compare the means of two independent populations

Compare the means of two related populations

Compare the proportions of two independent populations

Compare the variances of two independent populations

Compare the means of more than two populations

USING STATISTICS

For North Fork, Are There Different Means to the Ends?

To what extent does the location of products affect sales in a supermarket? As a North Fork Beverages sales manager, you are negotiating with the management of FoodPlace Supermarkets for the location of displays for the new HandMade Real Citrus Cola. FoodPlace Supermarkets has offered you two different end-aisle display areas to feature your new cola: one near the produce department and the other at the front of the aisle that contains other beverage products. These ends of aisle, or end-caps, have different costs, and you would like to compare the effectiveness of the produce end-cap to the beverage end-cap.

To test the comparative effectiveness of the two end-caps, FoodPlace agrees to a pilot study. You will be able to select 20 stores from the supermarket chain that experience similar storewide sales volumes. You then randomly assign 10 of the 20 stores to sample 1 and 10 other stores to sample 2. In the sample 1 stores, you will place the new cola in the beverage end-cap, while in the sample 2 stores you will place the new cola in the produce end-cap. At the end of one week, the sales of the new cola will be recorded. How can you determine whether the sales of the new cola using beverage end-caps are different from the sales of the new cola using produce end-caps? How can you decide if the variability in new cola sales from store to store is different for the two types of displays? How could you use the answers to these questions to improve sales of your new HandMade Real Citrus Cola?

Fotolia

323

I n Chapter 9, you learned several hypothesis-testing procedures commonly used to test a single sample of data selected from a single population. In this chapter, you learn how to extend hypothesis testing to **two-sample tests** that compare statistics from samples selected from *two* populations. In the North Fork Beverages scenario one such test would be "Are the mean weekly sales of the new cola when using the beverage end-cap location (one population) different from the mean weekly sales of the new cola when using the produce end-cap location (a second population)?"

10.1 Comparing the Means of Two Independent Populations

In Sections 8.1 and 9.1, you learned that in almost all cases, you would not know the standard deviation of the population under study. Likewise, when you take a random sample from each of two independent populations, you almost always do not know the standard deviation of either population. In addition, when using a two-sample test that compares the means of samples selected from two populations, you must establish whether the assumption that the variances in the two populations are equal holds. The statistical method used to test whether the means of each population are different depends on whether the assumption holds or not.

> **Student Tip**
> Whichever population is defined as population 1 in the null and alternative hypotheses must be defined as population 1 in Equation (10.1). Whichever population is defined as population 2 in the null and alternative hypotheses must be defined as population 2 in Equation (10.1).

Pooled-Variance t Test for the Difference Between Two Means

If you assume that the random samples are independently selected from two populations and that the populations are normally distributed and have equal variances, you can use a **pooled-variance t test** to determine whether there is a significant difference between the means. If the populations do not differ greatly from a normal distribution, you can still use the pooled-variance t test, especially if the sample sizes are large enough (typically ≥ 30 for each sample).

Using subscripts to distinguish between the population mean of the first population, μ_1, and the population mean of the second population, μ_2, the null hypothesis of no difference in the means of two independent populations can be stated as

$$H_0: \mu_1 = \mu_2 \quad \text{or} \quad \mu_1 - \mu_2 = 0$$

and the alternative hypothesis, that the means are different, can be stated as

$$H_1: \mu_1 \neq \mu_2 \quad \text{or} \quad \mu_1 - \mu_2 \neq 0$$

[1]When the two sample sizes are equal (i.e., $n_1 = n_2$), the equation for the pooled variance can be simplified to

$$S_p^2 = \frac{S_1^2 + S_2^2}{2}$$

To test the null hypothesis, you use the pooled-variance t test statistic t_{STAT} shown in Equation (10.1). The pooled-variance t test gets its name from the fact that the test statistic pools, or combines, the two sample variances S_1^2 and S_2^2 to compute S_p^2, the best estimate of the variance common to both populations, under the assumption that the two population variances are equal.[1]

POOLED-VARIANCE t TEST FOR THE DIFFERENCE BETWEEN TWO MEANS

$$t_{STAT} = \frac{(\overline{X}_1 - \overline{X}_2) - (\mu_1 - \mu_2)}{\sqrt{S_p^2\left(\dfrac{1}{n_1} + \dfrac{1}{n_2}\right)}} \tag{10.1}$$

where

$$S_p^2 = \frac{(n_1 - 1)S_1^2 + (n_2 - 1)S_2^2}{(n_1 - 1) + (n_2 - 1)}$$

and S_p^2 = pooled variance

$\overline{X}_1$ = mean of the sample taken from population 1

(continued)

$$S_1^2 = \text{variance of the sample taken from population 1}$$
$$n_1 = \text{size of the sample taken from population 1}$$
$$\overline{X}_2 = \text{mean of the sample taken from population 2}$$
$$S_2^2 = \text{variance of the sample taken from population 2}$$
$$n_2 = \text{size of the sample taken from population 2}$$

The t_{STAT} test statistic follows a t distribution with $n_1 + n_2 - 2$ degrees of freedom.

For a given level of significance, α, in a two-tail test, you reject the null hypothesis if the computed t_{STAT} test statistic is greater than the upper-tail critical value from the t distribution or if the computed t_{STAT} test statistic is less than the lower-tail critical value from the t distribution. Figure 10.1 displays the regions of rejection.

FIGURE 10.1

Regions of rejection and nonrejection for the pooled-variance t test for the difference between the means (two-tail test)

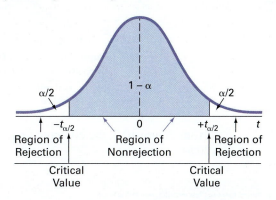

In a one-tail test in which the rejection region is in the lower tail, you reject the null hypothesis if the computed t_{STAT} test statistic is less than the lower-tail critical value from the t distribution. In a one-tail test in which the rejection region is in the upper tail, you reject the null hypothesis if the computed t_{STAT} test statistic is greater than the upper-tail critical value from the t distribution.

To demonstrate the pooled-variance t test, return to the North Fork Beverages scenario on page 323. Using the DCOVA problem-solving approach, you define the business objective as determining whether there is a difference in the mean weekly sales of the new cola when using the beverage end-cap location and when using the produce end-cap location. There are two populations of interest. The first population is the set of all possible weekly sales of the new cola if all the FoodPlace Supermarkets used the beverage end-cap location. The second population is the set of all possible weekly sales of the new cola if all the FoodPlace Supermarkets used the produce end-cap location. You collect the data from a sample of 10 FoodPlace Supermarkets that have been assigned a beverage end-cap location and another sample of 10 FoodPlace Supermarkets that have been assigned a produce end-cap location. You organize and store the results in Cola. Table 10.1 contains the new cola sales (in number of cases) for the two samples.

> **Student Tip**
> When *lower* or *less than* is used in an example, you have a lower-tail test. When *upper* or *more than* is used in an example, you have an upper-tail test. When *different* or *the same as* is used in an example, you have a two-tail test.

TABLE 10.1

Comparing New Cola Weekly Sales from Two Different End-Cap Locations (in number of cases)

DISPLAY LOCATION									
Beverage End-Cap					**Produce End-Cap**				
22	34	52	62	30	52	71	76	54	67
40	64	84	56	59	83	66	90	77	84

The null and alternative hypotheses are

$$H_0: \mu_1 = \mu_2 \quad \text{or} \quad \mu_1 - \mu_2 = 0$$

$$H_1: \mu_1 \neq \mu_2 \quad \text{or} \quad \mu_1 - \mu_2 \neq 0$$

Assuming that the samples are from normal populations having equal variances, you can use the pooled-variance t test. The t_{STAT} test statistic follows a t distribution with

$10 + 10 - 2 = 18$ degrees of freedom. Using an $\alpha = 0.05$ level of significance, you divide the rejection region into the two tails for this two-tail test (i.e., two equal parts of 0.025 each). Table E.3 shows that the critical values for this two-tail test are $+2.1009$ and -2.1009. As shown in Figure 10.2, the decision rule is

$$\text{Reject } H_0 \text{ if } t_{STAT} > +2.1009$$

$$\text{or if } t_{STAT} < -2.1009;$$

$$\text{otherwise, do not reject } H_0.$$

FIGURE 10.2

Two-tail test of hypothesis for the difference between the means at the 0.05 level of significance with 18 degrees of freedom

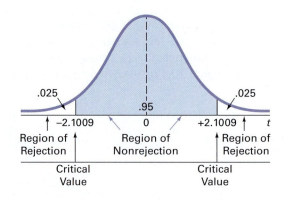

From Figure 10.3, the computed t_{STAT} test statistic for this test is -3.0446 and the p-value is 0.0070.

FIGURE 10.3

Excel and Minitab pooled-variance t test results for the two end-cap locations data

⬜	A	B
1	**Pooled-Variance t Test for Differences in Two Means**	
2	(assumes equal population variances)	
3	**Data**	
4	Hypothesized Difference	0
5	Level of Significance	0.05
6	**Population 1 Sample**	
7	Sample Size	10 =COUNT(DATACOPY!$A:$A)
8	Sample Mean	50.3 =AVERAGE(DATACOPY!$A:$A)
9	Sample Standard Deviation	18.7264 =STDEV.S(DATACOPY!$A:$A)
10	**Population 2 Sample**	
11	Sample Size	10 =COUNT(DATACOPY!$B:$B)
12	Sample Mean	72 =AVERAGE(DATACOPY!$B:$B)
13	Sample Standard Deviation	12.5433 =STDEV.S(DATACOPY!$B:$B)
14		
15	**Intermediate Calculations**	
16	Population 1 Sample Degrees of Freedom	9 =B7 - 1
17	Population 2 Sample Degrees of Freedom	9 =B11 - 1
18	Total Degrees of Freedom	18 =B16 + B17
19	Pooled Variance	254.0056 =((B16 * B9^2) + (B17 * B13^2))/B18
20	Standard Error	7.1275 =SQRT(B19 * (1/B7 + 1/B11))
21	Difference in Sample Means	-21.7 =B8 - B12
22	*t* Test Statistic	-3.0446 =(B21 - B4)/B20
23		
24	**Two-Tail Test**	
25	Lower Critical Value	-2.1009 =-(T.INV.2T(B5, B18))
26	Upper Critical Value	2.1009 =T.INV.2T(B5, B18)
27	*p-Value*	0.0070 =T.DIST.2T(ABS(B22), B18)
28	Reject the null hypothesis	=IF(B27 < B5, "Reject the null hypothesis", "Do not reject the null hypothesis")

```
Two-Sample T-Test and CI: Beverage, Produce

Two-sample T for Beverage vs Produce

              N    Mean   StDev   SE Mean
Beverage     10    50.3    18.7       5.9
Produce      10    72.0    12.5       4.0

Difference = mu (Beverage) - mu (Produce)
Estimate for difference:  -21.70
95% CI for difference:  (-36.67, -6.73)
T-Test of difference = 0 (vs not =):
          T-Value = -3.04  P-Value = 0.007  DF = 18
Both use Pooled StDev = 15.9376
```

Using Equation (10.1) on page 324 and the descriptive statistics provided in Figure 10.3,

$$t_{STAT} = \frac{(\overline{X}_1 - \overline{X}_2) - (\mu_1 - \mu_2)}{\sqrt{S_p^2 \left(\dfrac{1}{n_1} + \dfrac{1}{n_2} \right)}}$$

where

$$S_p^2 = \frac{(n_1 - 1)S_1^2 + (n_2 - 1)S_2^2}{(n_1 - 1) + (n_2 - 1)}$$

$$= \frac{9(18.7264)^2 + 9(12.5433)^2}{9 + 9} = 254.0056$$

Therefore,

$$t_{STAT} = \frac{(50.3 - 72.0) - 0.0}{\sqrt{254.0056\left(\dfrac{1}{10} + \dfrac{1}{10}\right)}} = \frac{-21.7}{\sqrt{50.801}} = -3.0446$$

You reject the null hypothesis because $t_{STAT} = -3.0446 < -2.1009$ and the p-value is 0.0070. In other words, the probability that $t_{STAT} > 3.0446$ or $t_{STAT} < -3.0446$ is equal to 0.0070. This p-value indicates that if the population means are equal, the probability of observing a difference in the two sample means this large or larger is only 0.0070. Because the p-value is less than $\alpha = 0.05$, there is sufficient evidence to reject the null hypothesis. You can conclude that the mean sales are different for the beverage end-cap and produce end-cap locations. Because the t_{STAT} statistic is negative, you can conclude that the mean sales are lower for the beverage end-cap location (and, therefore, higher for the produce end-cap location).

In testing for the difference between the means, you assume that the populations are normally distributed, with equal variances. For situations in which the two populations have equal variances, the pooled-variance t test is **robust** (i.e., not sensitive) to moderate departures from the assumption of normality, provided that the sample sizes are large. In such situations, you can use the pooled-variance t test without serious effects on its power. However, if you cannot assume that both populations are normally distributed, you have two choices. You can use a nonparametric procedure, such as the Wilcoxon rank sum test (see references 1 and 2), that does not depend on the assumption of normality for the two populations, or you can use a normalizing transformation (see reference 10) on each of the outcomes and then use the pooled-variance t test.

To check the assumption of normality in each of the two populations, you can construct a boxplot of the sales for the two display locations shown in Figure 10.4. For these two small samples, there appears to be only moderate departure from normality, so the assumption of normality needed for the t test is not seriously violated.

FIGURE 10.4
Excel and Minitab boxplots for beverage and produce end-cap sales

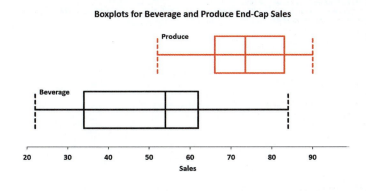
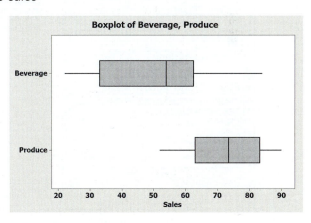

Example 10.1 provides another application of the pooled-variance t test.

EXAMPLE 10.1

Testing for the Difference in the Mean Delivery Times

You and some friends have decided to test the validity of an advertisement by a local pizza restaurant, which says it delivers to the dormitories faster than a local branch of a national chain. Both the local pizza restaurant and national chain are located across the street from your college campus. You define the variable of interest as the delivery time, in minutes, from the time the pizza is ordered to when it is delivered. You collect the data by ordering 10 pizzas from the local pizza restaurant and 10 pizzas from the national chain at different times. You organize and store the data in **PizzaTime**. Table 10.2 shows the delivery times.

(continued)

TABLE 10.2

Delivery Times (in minutes) for a Local Pizza Restaurant and a National Pizza Chain

Local		Chain	
16.8	18.1	22.0	19.5
11.7	14.1	15.2	17.0
15.6	21.8	18.7	19.5
16.7	13.9	15.6	16.5
17.5	20.8	20.8	24.0

At the 0.05 level of significance, is there evidence that the mean delivery time for the local pizza restaurant is less than the mean delivery time for the national pizza chain?

SOLUTION Because you want to know whether the mean is *lower* for the local pizza restaurant than for the national pizza chain, you have a one-tail test with the following null and alternative hypotheses:

$H_0: \mu_1 \geq \mu_2$ (The mean delivery time for the local pizza restaurant is equal to or greater than the mean delivery time for the national pizza chain.)

$H_1: \mu_1 < \mu_2$ (The mean delivery time for the local pizza restaurant is less than the mean delivery time for the national pizza chain.)

Figure 10.5 displays the results for the pooled-variance t test for these data.

FIGURE 10.5

Excel and Minitab pooled-variance t test results for the pizza delivery time data

	A	B
1	Pooled-Variance t Test for Differences in Two Means	
2	(assumes equal population variances)	
3	**Data**	
4	Hypothesized Difference	0
5	Level of Significance	0.05
6	**Population 1 Sample**	
7	Sample Size	10
8	Sample Mean	16.7
9	Sample Standard Deviation	3.0955
10	**Population 2 Sample**	
11	Sample Size	10
12	Sample Mean	18.88
13	Sample Standard Deviation	2.8662
14		
15	**Intermediate Calculations**	
16	Population 1 Sample Degrees of Freedom	9
17	Population 2 Sample Degrees of Freedom	9
18	Total Degrees of Freedom	18
19	Pooled Variance	8.8986
20	Standard Error	1.3341
21	Difference in Sample Means	-2.18
22	t Test Statistic	-1.6341
23		
24	**Lower-Tail Test**	
25	Lower Critical Value	-1.7341
26	p-Value	0.0598
27	Do not reject the null hypothesis	

```
Two-Sample T-Test and CI: Local, Chain

Two-sample T for Local vs Chain

          N    Mean   StDev   SE Mean
Local    10   16.70   3.10      0.98
Chain    10   18.88   2.87      0.91

Difference = mu (Local) - mu (Chain)
Estimate for difference:  -2.18
95% CI for difference:  (-4.98, 0.62)
T-Test of difference = 0 (vs not =): T-Value = -1.63 P-Value = 0.120 DF = 18
Both use Pooled StDev = 2.9831
```

To illustrate the computations, using Equation (10.1) on page 324,

$$t_{STAT} = \frac{(\overline{X}_1 - \overline{X}_2) - (\mu_1 - \mu_2)}{\sqrt{S_p^2\left(\dfrac{1}{n_1} + \dfrac{1}{n_2}\right)}}$$

where

$$S_p^2 = \frac{(n_1 - 1)S_1^2 + (n_2 - 1)S_2^2}{(n_1 - 1) + (n_2 - 1)}$$

$$= \frac{9(3.0955)^2 + 9(2.8662)^2}{9 + 9} = 8.8986$$

Therefore,

$$t_{STAT} = \frac{(16.7 - 18.88) - 0.0}{\sqrt{8.8986\left(\dfrac{1}{10} + \dfrac{1}{10}\right)}} = \frac{-2.18}{\sqrt{1.7797}} = -1.6341$$

You do not reject the null hypothesis because $t_{STAT} = -1.6341 > -1.7341$. The p-value (as computed in Figure 10.5) is 0.0598. This p-value indicates that the probability that $t_{STAT} < -1.6341$ is equal to 0.0598. In other words, if the population means are equal, the probability that the sample mean delivery time for the local pizza restaurant is at least 2.18 minutes faster than the national chain is 0.0598. Because the p-value is greater than $\alpha = 0.05$, there is insufficient evidence to reject the null hypothesis. Based on these results, there is insufficient evidence for the local pizza restaurant to make the advertising claim that it has a faster delivery time.

Confidence Interval Estimate for the Difference Between Two Means

Instead of, or in addition to, testing for the difference between the means of two independent populations, you can use Equation (10.2) to develop a confidence interval estimate of the difference in the means.

CONFIDENCE INTERVAL ESTIMATE FOR THE DIFFERENCE BETWEEN THE MEANS OF TWO INDEPENDENT POPULATIONS

$$(\overline{X}_1 - \overline{X}_2) \pm t_{\alpha/2}\sqrt{S_p^2\left(\frac{1}{n_1} + \frac{1}{n_2}\right)} \tag{10.2}$$

or

$$(\overline{X}_1 - \overline{X}_2) - t_{\alpha/2}\sqrt{S_p^2\left(\frac{1}{n_1} + \frac{1}{n_2}\right)} \leq \mu_1 - \mu_2 \leq (\overline{X}_1 - \overline{X}_2) + t_{\alpha/2}\sqrt{S_p^2\left(\frac{1}{n_1} + \frac{1}{n_2}\right)}$$

where $t_{\alpha/2}$ is the critical value of the t distribution, with $n_1 + n_2 - 2$ degrees of freedom, for an area of $\alpha/2$ in the upper tail.

For the sample statistics pertaining to the two end-cap locations reported in Figure 10.3 on page 326, using 95% confidence, and Equation (10.2),

$$\overline{X}_1 = 50.3,\, n_1 = 10,\, \overline{X}_2 = 72.0,\, n_2 = 10,\, S_p^2 = 254.0056,\, \text{and with } 10 + 10 - 2$$
$$= 18 \text{ degrees of freedom, } t_{0.025} = 2.1009$$

$$(50.3 - 72.0) \pm (2.1009)\sqrt{254.0056\left(\frac{1}{10} + \frac{1}{10}\right)}$$
$$-21.7 \pm (2.1009)(7.1275)$$
$$-21.7 \pm 14.97$$
$$-36.67 \leq \mu_1 - \mu_2 \leq -6.73$$

Therefore, you are 95% confident that the difference in mean sales between the beverage and produce end-cap locations is between -36.67 cases of cola and -6.73 cases of cola. In other words, you can estimate, with 95% confidence, that the produce end-cap location sells, on average, 6.73 to 36.67 cases more than the beverage end-cap location. From a hypothesis-testing perspective, using a two-tail test at the 0.05 level of significance, because the interval does not include zero, you reject the null hypothesis of no difference between the means of the two populations.

t Test for the Difference Between Two Means, Assuming Unequal Variances

If you can assume that the two independent populations are normally distributed but cannot assume that they have equal variances, you cannot pool the two sample variances into the common estimate S_p^2 and therefore cannot use the pooled-variance *t* test. Instead, you use the **separate-variance *t* test** developed by Satterthwaite that uses the two separate sample variances (see reference 9).

Figure 10.6 displays the separate-variance *t* test results for the end-cap display location data. Observe that the test statistic $t_{STAT} = -3.0446$ and the *p*-value is $0.0082 < 0.05$. Thus, the results for the separate-variance *t* test are nearly the same as those of the pooled-variance *t* test.

FIGURE 10.6

Excel and Minitab separate-variance *t* test results for the sales data for the two end-caps

	A	B	
1	Separate-Variances *t* Test		
2	(assumes unequal population variances)		
3	**Data**		
4	Hypothesized Difference	0	
5	Level of Significance	0.05	
6	**Population 1 Sample**		
7	Sample Size	10	=COUNT(DATACOPY!$A:$A)
8	Sample Mean	50.3	=AVERAGE(DATACOPY!$A:$A)
9	Sample Standard Deviation	18.7264	=STDEV.S(DATACOPY!$A:$A)
10	**Population 2 Sample**		
11	Sample Size	10	=COUNT(DATACOPY!$B:$B)
12	Sample Mean	72	=AVERAGE(DATACOPY!$B:$B)
13	Sample Standard Deviation	12.5433	=STDEV.S(DATACOPY!$B:$B)
14			
15	**Intermediate Calculations**		
16	Pop. 1 Sample Variance	350.6778	=B9^2
17	Pop. 2 Sample Variance	157.3333	=B13^2
18	Pop. 1 Sample Var./Sample Size	35.0678	=B16/B7
19	Pop. 2 Sample Var./Sample Size	15.7333	=B17/B11
20	Numerator of Degrees of Freedom	2580.7529	=(B18 + B19)^2
21	Denominator of Degrees of Freedom	164.1430	=(B18^2)/(B7 - 1) + (B19^2)/(B11 - 1)
22	Total Degrees of Freedom	15.7226	=B20/B21
23	Degrees of Freedom	15	=INT(B22)
24	Separate Variance Denominator	7.1275	=SQRT(B18 + B19)
25	Difference in Sample Means	-21.7	=B8 - B12
26	*t* Test Statistic	-3.0446	=(B25 - B4)/B24
27			
28	**Two-Tail Test**		
29	Lower Critical Value	-2.1314	=-(T.INV.2T(B5, B23))
30	Upper Critical Value	2.1314	=T.INV.2T(B5, B23)
31	*p*-Value	0.0082	=T.DIST.2T(ABS(B26),B23) - B4
32	Reject the null hypothesis		=IF(B31 < B5,"Reject the null hypothesis", "Do not reject the null hypothesis")

```
Two-Sample T-Test and CI: Beverage, Produce

Two-sample T for Beverage vs Produce

            N   Mean   StDev   SE Mean
Beverage   10   50.3    18.7       5.9
Produce    10   72.0    12.5       4.0

Difference = mu (Beverage) - mu (Produce)
Estimate for difference:  -21.70
95% CI for difference:  (-36.89, -6.51)
T-Test of difference = 0 (vs not =):
          T-Value = -3.04  P-Value = 0.008  DF = 15
```

Do People Really Do This?

Some question whether decision makers really use confirmatory methods, such as hypothesis testing, in this emerging era of big data. The following real case study, contributed by a former student of a colleague of the authors, reveals a role that confirmatory methods still play in business as well as answering another question: "Do businesses really monitor their customer service calls for quality assurance purposes as they sometime claim?"

In her first full-time job at a financial services company, a student was asked to improve a training program for new hires at a call center that handled customer questions about outstanding loans. For feedback and evaluation, she planned to randomly select phone calls received by each new employee and rate the employee on 10 aspects of the call, including whether the employee maintained a pleasant tone with the customer. When she presented her plan to her boss for approval, her boss wanted proof that her new training program would improve customer service. The boss, quoting a famous statistician, said "In God we trust; all others must bring data." Faced with this request, she called her business statistics professor. "Hello, Professor, you'll never believe why I called. I work for a large company, and in the project I am currently working on, I have to put some of the statistics you taught us to work! Can you help?" Together they formulated this test:

- Randomly assign the 60 most recent hires to two training programs. Assign half to the preexisting training program and the other half to the new training program.

- At the end of the first month, compare the mean score for the 30 employees in the new training program against the mean score for the 30 employees in the preexisting training program.

She listened as her professor explained, "What you are trying to show is that the mean score from the new training program is higher than the mean score from the current program. You can make the null hypothesis that the means are equal and see if you can reject it in favor of the alternative that the mean score from the new program is higher."

"Or, as you used to say, 'if the *p*-value is low, H_0 must go!'—yes, I do remember!" she replied. Her professor chuckled and added, "If you can reject H_0 you will have the evidence to present to your boss." She thanked him for his help and got back to work, with the newfound confidence that she would be able to successfully apply the *t* test that compares the means of two independent populations.

The assumption of equality of population variances had no appreciable effect on the results. Sometimes, however, the results from the pooled-variance and separate-variance t tests conflict because the assumption of equal variances is violated. Therefore, it is important that you evaluate the assumptions and use those results as a guide in selecting a test procedure. In Section 10.4, the F test for the ratio of two variances is used to determine whether there is evidence of a difference in the two population variances. The results of that test can help you decide which of the t tests—pooled-variance or separate-variance—is more appropriate.

Problems for Section 10.1

LEARNING THE BASICS

10.1 If you have samples of $n_1 = 12$ and $n_2 = 15$, in performing the pooled-variance t test, how many degrees of freedom do you have?

10.2 Assume that you have a sample of $n_1 = 8$, with the sample mean $\overline{X}_1 = 42$, and a sample standard deviation $S_1 = 4$, and you have an independent sample of $n_2 = 15$ from another population with a sample mean of $\overline{X}_2 = 34$ and a sample standard deviation $S_2 = 5$.
a. What is the value of the pooled-variance t_{STAT} test statistic for testing $H_0: \mu_1 = \mu_2$?
b. In finding the critical value, how many degrees of freedom are there?
c. Using the level of significance $\alpha = 0.01$, what is the critical value for a one-tail test of the hypothesis $H_0: \mu_1 \le \mu_2$ against the alternative, $H_1: \mu_1 > \mu_2$?
d. What is your statistical decision?

10.3 What assumptions about the two populations are necessary in Problem 10.2?

10.4 Referring to Problem 10.2, construct a 95% confidence interval estimate of the population mean difference between μ_1 and μ_2.

10.5 Referring to Problem 10.2, if $n_1 = 5$ and $n_2 = 4$, how many degrees of freedom do you have?

10.6 Referring to Problem 10.2, if $n_1 = 5$ and $n_2 = 4$, at the 0.01 level of significance, is there evidence that $\mu_1 > \mu_2$?

APPLYING THE CONCEPTS

10.7 When people make estimates, they are influenced by anchors to their estimates. A study was conducted in which students were asked to estimate the number of calories in a cheeseburger. One group was asked to do this after thinking about a calorie-laden cheesecake. A second group was asked to do this after thinking about an organic fruit salad. The mean number of calories estimated in a cheeseburger was 780 for the group that thought about the cheesecake and 1,041 for the group that thought about the organic fruit salad. (Data extracted from "Drilling Down, Sizing Up a Cheeseburger's Caloric Heft," *The New York Times*, October 4, 2010, p. B2.) Suppose that the study was based on a sample of 20 people who thought about the cheeseburger first and 20 people who thought about the organic fruit salad first, and the standard deviation of the number of calories in the cheeseburger was 128 for the people who thought about the cheesecake first and 140 for the people who thought about the organic fruit salad first.
a. State the null and alternative hypotheses if you want to determine whether the mean estimated number of calories in the cheeseburger is lower for the people who thought about the cheesecake first than for the people who thought about the organic fruit salad first.
b. In the context of this study, what is the meaning of the Type I error?

c. In the context of this study, what is the meaning of the Type II error?
d. At the 0.01 level of significance, is there evidence that the mean estimated number of calories in the cheeseburger is lower for the people who thought about the cheesecake first than for the people who thought about the organic fruit salad first?

10.8 A recent study (data extracted from E. J. Boyland et al., "Food Choice and Overconsumption: Effect of a Premium Sports Celebrity Endorser," *Journal of Pediatrics*, March 13, 2013, **bit.ly/16NR4Bi**) found that 51 children who watched a commercial for Walker Crisps (potato chips) featuring a long-standing sports celebrity endorser ate a mean of 36 grams of Walker Crisps as compared to a mean of 25 grams of Walker Crisps for 41 children who watched a commercial for an alternative food snack. Suppose that the sample standard deviation for the children who watched the sports celebrity–endorsed Walker Crisps commercial was 21.4 grams and the sample standard deviation for the children who watched the alternative food snack commercial was 12.8 grams.
a. Assuming that the population variances are equal and $\alpha = 0.05$, is there evidence that the mean amount of Walker Crisps eaten was significantly higher for the children who watched the sports celebrity–endorsed Walker Crisps commercial?
b. Assuming that the population variances are equal, construct a 95% confidence interval estimate of the difference between the mean amount of Walker Crisps eaten by children who watched the sports celebrity–endorsed Walker Crisps commercial and children who watched the alternative food snack commercial.
c. Compare and discuss the results of (a) and (b).

10.9 A problem with a phone line that prevents a customer from receiving or making calls is upsetting to both the customer and the telecommunications company. The file **Phone** contains samples of 20 problems reported to two different offices of a telecommunications company and the time to clear these problems (in minutes) from the customers' lines:

Central Office I Time to Clear Problems (minutes)

1.48	1.75	0.78	2.85	0.52	1.60	4.15	3.97	1.48	3.10
1.02	0.53	0.93	1.60	0.80	1.05	6.32	3.93	5.45	0.97

Central Office II Time to Clear Problems (minutes)

7.55	3.75	0.10	1.10	0.60	0.52	3.30	2.10	0.58	4.02
3.75	0.65	1.92	0.60	1.53	4.23	0.08	1.48	1.65	0.72

a. Assuming that the population variances from both offices are equal, is there evidence of a difference in the mean waiting time between the two offices? (Use $\alpha = 0.05$.)
b. Find the p-value in (a) and interpret its meaning.
c. What other assumption is necessary in (a)?

d. Assuming that the population variances from both offices are equal, construct and interpret a 95% confidence interval estimate of the difference between the population means in the two offices.

✓ SELF 10.10 *Accounting Today* identified the top accounting Test firms in 10 geographic regions across the United States. All 10 regions reported growth in 2013. The Southeast and Gulf Coast regions reported growth of 4.7% and 13.86%, respectively. A characteristic description of the accounting firms in the Southeast and Gulf Coast regions included the number of partners in the firm. The file **AccountingPartners2** contains the number of partners. (Data extracted from **bit.ly/ODuzd3**.)

a. At the 0.05 level of significance, is there evidence of a difference between Southeast region accounting firms and Gulf Coast accounting firms with respect to the mean number of partners?

b. Determine the *p*-value and interpret its meaning.

c. What assumptions do you have to make about the two populations in order to justify the use of the *t* test?

10.11 An important feature of tablets is battery life, the number of hours before the battery needs to be recharged. The file **Tablets** contains the battery life of 12 WiFi-only and 7 3G/4G/WiFi 9- through 12-inch tablets. (Data extracted from "Ratings and recommendations: Tablets," *Consumer Reports*, August 2013, p. 24.)

a. Assuming that the population variances from both types of tablets are equal, is there evidence of a difference in the mean battery life between the two types of tablets? (Use $\alpha = 0.05$.)

b. Determine the *p*-value in (a) and interpret its meaning.

c. Assuming that the population variances from both types of tablets are equal, construct and interpret a 95% confidence interval estimate of the difference between the population mean battery life of the two types of tablets.

10.12 A bank with a branch located in a commercial district of a city has the business objective of developing an improved process for serving customers during the noon-to-1 P.M. lunch period. Management decides to first study the waiting time in the current process. The waiting time is defined as the number of minutes that elapses from when the customer enters the line until he or she reaches the teller window. Data are collected from a random sample of 15 customers and stored in **Bank1**. These data are:

```
4.21  5.55  3.02  5.13  4.77  2.34  3.54  3.20
4.50  6.10  0.38  5.12  6.46  6.19  3.79
```

Suppose that another branch, located in a residential area, is also concerned with improving the process of serving customers in the noon-to-1 P.M. lunch period. Data are collected from a random sample of 15 customers and stored in **Bank2**. These data are:

```
9.66   5.90  8.02  5.79  8.73  3.82  8.01  8.35
10.49  6.68  5.64  4.08  6.17  9.91  5.47
```

a. Assuming that the population variances from both banks are equal, is there evidence of a difference in the mean waiting time between the two branches? (Use $\alpha = 0.05$.)

b. Determine the *p*-value in (a) and interpret its meaning.

c. In addition to equal variances, what other assumption is necessary in (a)?

d. Construct and interpret a 95% confidence interval estimate of the difference between the population means in the two branches.

10.13 Repeat Problem 10.12 (a), assuming that the population variances in the two branches are not equal. Compare these results with those of Problem 10.12 (a).

10.14 As a member of the international strategic management team in your company, you are assigned the task of exploring potential foreign market entry. As part of your initial investigation, you want to know if there is a difference between developed markets and emerging markets with respect to the time required to start a business. You select 15 developed countries and 15 emerging countries. The time required to start a business, defined as the number of days needed to complete the procedures to legally operate a business in these countries, is stored in **ForeignMarket**. (Data extracted from **data.worldbank.org**.)

a. Assuming that the population variances for developed countries and emerging countries are equal, is there evidence of a difference in the mean time required to start a business between developed countries and emerging countries? (Use $\alpha = 0.05$.)

b. Determine the *p*-value in (a) and interpret its meaning.

c. In addition to equal variances, what other assumption is necessary in (a)?

d. Construct a 95% confidence interval estimate of the difference between the population means of developed countries and emerging countries.

10.15 Repeat Problem 10.14 (a), assuming that the population variances from developed and emerging countries are not equal. Compare these results with those of Problem 10.14 (a).

10.16 Experian Marketing Services reported that the typical American spends 2.4 hours (144 minutes) per day accessing the Internet via a mobile device. (Source: *The 2014 Digital Marketer*, available at **ex.pn/1kXJjfX**.) You wonder if males and females spend differing amounts of time per day accessing the Internet through a mobile device.

You select a sample of 60 friends and family (30 males and 30 females), collect times spent per day accessing the Internet through a mobile device (in minutes), and store the data collected in **InternetMobileTime2**.

a. Assuming that the variances in the population of times spent per day accessing the Internet via a mobile device are equal, is there evidence of a difference between males and females in the mean time spent per day accessing the Internet via a mobile device? (Use a 0.05 level of significance.)

b. In addition to equal variances, what other assumption is necessary in (a)?

10.17 Brand valuations are critical to CEOs, financial and marketing executives, security analysts, institutional investors, and others who depend on well-researched, reliable information needed for assessments, and comparisons in decision making. Millward Brown Optimor has developed the BrandZ Top 100 Most Valuable Global Brands for WPP, the world's largest communications services group. Unlike other studies, the BrandZ Top 100 Most Valuable Global Brands fuses consumer measures of brand equity with financial measures to place a financial value on brands. The file **BrandZTechFin** contains the brand values for two sectors in the BrandZ Top 100 Most Valuable Global Brands for 2014: the technology sector and the financial institutions sector. (Data extracted from **bit.ly/18OL5Mu**.)

a. Assuming that the population variances are equal, is there evidence of a difference between the technology sector and the financial institutions sector with respect to mean brand value? (Use $\alpha = .05$.)

b. Repeat (a), assuming that the population variances are not equal.

c. Compare the results of (a) and (b).

10.2 Comparing the Means of Two Related Populations

The hypothesis-testing procedures presented in Section 10.1 enable you to examine differences between the means of two *independent* populations. In this section, you will learn about a procedure for examining the mean difference between two populations when you collect sample data from populations that are related—that is, when results of the first population are *not* independent of the results of the second population.

There are two situations that involve related data: when you take repeated measurements from the same set of items or individuals or when you match items or individuals according to some characteristic. In either situation, you are interested in the *difference between the two related values* rather than the *individual values* themselves.

When you take **repeated measurements** on the same items or individuals, you assume that the same items or individuals will behave alike if treated alike. Your objective is to show that any differences between two measurements of the same items or individuals are due to different treatments that have been applied to the items or individuals. For example, when performing a taste-testing experiment comparing two beverages, you can use each person in the sample as his or her own control so that you can have *repeated measurements* on the same individual.

Another example of repeated measurements involves the pricing of the same goods from two different vendors. For example, have you ever wondered whether new textbook prices at a local college bookstore are different from the prices offered at a major online retailer? You could take two independent samples—that is, select two different sets of textbooks—and then use the hypothesis tests discussed in Section 10.1.

However, by random chance, the first sample may have many large-format hardcover textbooks and the second sample may have many small trade paperback books. This would imply that the first set of textbooks will always be more expensive than the second set of textbooks, regardless of where they are purchased. This observation means that using the Section 10.1 tests would not be a good choice. The better choice would be to use two related samples—that is, to determine the price of the *same* sample of textbooks at both the local bookstore and the online retailer.

The second situation that involves related data between populations is when you have **matched samples**. Here items or individuals are paired together according to some characteristic of interest. For example, in test marketing a product in two different advertising campaigns, a sample of test markets can be *matched* on the basis of the test-market population size and/or demographic variables. By accounting for the differences in test-market population size and/or demographic variables, you are better able to measure the effects of the two different advertising campaigns.

Regardless of whether you have matched samples or repeated measurements, the objective is to study the difference between two measurements by reducing the effect of the variability that is due to the items or individuals themselves. Table 10.3 shows the differences between the individual values for two related populations. To read this table, let $X_{11}, X_{12}, \ldots, X_{1n}$ represent the n values from the first sample. And let $X_{21}, X_{22}, \ldots, X_{2n}$ represent either the corresponding n matched values from a second sample or the corresponding n repeated measurements from the initial sample. Then $D_1, D_2, \ldots, D_n$ will represent the corresponding set of n *difference scores* such that

$$D_1 = X_{11} - X_{21}, D_2 = X_{12} - X_{22}, \ldots, \text{and } D_n = X_{1n} - X_{2n}.$$

To test for the mean difference between two related populations, you treat the difference scores, each D_i, as values from a single sample.

TABLE 10.3

Determining the
Difference Between
Two Related Samples

	SAMPLE		
VALUE	1	2	DIFFERENCE
1	X_{11}	X_{21}	$D_1 = X_{11} - X_{21}$
2	X_{12}	X_{22}	$D_2 = X_{12} - X_{22}$
$\vdots$	$\vdots$	$\vdots$	$\vdots$
i	X_{1i}	X_{2i}	$D_i = X_{1i} - X_{2i}$
$\vdots$	$\vdots$	$\vdots$	$\vdots$
n	X_{1n}	X_{2n}	$D_n = X_{1n} - X_{2n}$

☞ Student Tip
Which sample you define
as group 1 will determine
whether you will be doing
a lower-tail test or an
upper-tail test if you are
conducting a one-tail test.

Paired t Test

If you assume that the difference scores are randomly and independently selected from a population that is normally distributed, you can use the **paired t test for the mean difference** in related populations to determine whether there is a significant population mean difference. As with the one-sample t test developed in Section 9.2 [see Equation (9.2) on page 298], the paired t test statistic follows the t distribution with $n - 1$ degrees of freedom. Although the paired t test assumes that the population is normally distributed, since this test is robust, you can use this test as long as the sample size is not very small and the population is not highly skewed.

To test the null hypothesis that there is no difference in the means of two related populations:

$$H_0: \mu_D = 0 \; (\text{where } \mu_D = \mu_1 - \mu_2)$$

against the alternative that the means are not the same:

$$H_1: \mu_D \neq 0$$

you compute the t_{STAT} test statistic using Equation (10.3).

PAIRED t TEST FOR THE MEAN DIFFERENCE

$$t_{STAT} = \frac{\overline{D} - \mu_D}{\frac{S_D}{\sqrt{n}}} \tag{10.3}$$

where

$$\mu_D = \text{hypothesized mean difference}$$

$$\overline{D} = \frac{\sum\limits_{i=1}^{n} D_i}{n}$$

$$S_D = \sqrt{\frac{\sum\limits_{i=1}^{n} (D_i - \overline{D})^2}{n - 1}}$$

The t_{STAT} test statistic follows a t distribution with $n - 1$ degrees of freedom.

For a two-tail test with a given level of significance, α, you reject the null hypothesis if the computed t_{STAT} test statistic is greater than the upper-tail critical value $t_{\alpha/2}$ from the t distribution, or, if the computed t_{STAT} test statistic is less than the lower-tail critical value $-t_{\alpha/2}$, from the t distribution. The decision rule is

$$\text{Reject } H_0 \text{ if } t_{STAT} > t_{\alpha/2}$$

$$\text{or if } t_{STAT} < -t_{\alpha/2};$$

$$\text{otherwise, do not reject } H_0.$$

You can use the paired t test for the mean difference to investigate a question raised earlier in this section: Are new textbook prices at a local college bookstore different from the prices offered at a major online retailer?

In this repeated-measurements experiment, you use one set of textbooks. For each textbook, you determine the price at the local bookstore and the price at the online retailer. By determining the two prices for the same textbooks, you can reduce the variability in the prices compared with what would occur if you used two independent sets of textbooks. This approach focuses on the differences between the prices of the same textbooks offered by the two retailers.

You collect data by conducting an experiment from a sample of $n = 16$ textbooks used primarily in business school courses during a recent semester at a local college. You determine the college bookstore price and the online price (which includes shipping costs, if any). You organize and store the data in **BookPrices**. Table 10.4 shows the results. Notice that each row of the table shows the bookstore price and online retailer price for a specific book.

TABLE 10.4

Prices of Textbooks at the College Bookstore and at the Online Retailer

Author	Title	Bookstore	Online
Bade	*Foundations of Microeconomics* 6/e	200.00	121.49
Brigham	*Financial Management* 13/e	304.00	235.88
Clauretie	*Real Estate Finance: Theory and Practice*	179.35	107.61
Foner	*Give Me Liberty!* (*Brief*) Vol. 2 3/e	72.00	59.99
Garrison	*Managerial Accounting*	277.15	146.99
Grewal	*M: Marketing* 3/e	73.75	63.49
Hill	*Global Business Today*	171.65	138.99
Lafore	*Object-Oriented Programming in C++*	65.00	42.26
Lank	*Modern Real Estate Practice* 11/e	47.45	65.99
Meyer	*Entrepreneurship*	106.00	37.83
Mitchell	*Public Affairs in the Nation and New York*	55.95	102.99
Pindyck	*Microeconomics* 8/e	224.40	144.99
Robbins	*Organizational Behavior* 15/e	223.20	179.39
Ross	*Fundamentals of Corporate Finance* 9/e	250.65	191.49
Schneier	*New York Politics: Tale of Two States*	34.95	28.66
Wilson	*American Government: The Essentials* 12/e	172.65	108.49

Your objective is to determine whether there is any difference between the mean textbook price at the college bookstore and at the online retailer. In other words, is there evidence that the mean price is different between the two textbook sellers? Thus, the null and alternative hypotheses are

H_0: $\mu_D = 0$ (There is no difference in the mean price between the college bookstore and the online retailer.)

H_1: $\mu_D \neq 0$ (There is a difference in the mean price between the college bookstore and the online retailer.)

Choosing the level of significance $\alpha = 0.05$ and assuming that the differences are normally distributed, you use the paired t test [Equation (10.3)]. For a sample of $n = 16$ textbooks, there are $n - 1 = 15$ degrees of freedom. Using Table E.3, the decision rule is

$$\text{Reject } H_0 \text{ if } t_{STAT} > 2.1314$$

$$\text{or if } t_{STAT} < -2.1314;$$

$$\text{otherwise, do not reject } H_0.$$

For the $n = 16$ differences (see Table 10.4), the sample mean difference is

$$\overline{D} = \frac{\sum\limits_{i=1}^{n} D_i}{n} = \frac{681.62}{16} = 42.6013$$

and

$$S_D = \sqrt{\frac{\sum\limits_{i=1}^{n}(D_i - \overline{D})^2}{n - 1}} = 43.797$$

From Equation (10.3) on page 334,

$$t_{STAT} = \frac{\overline{D} - \mu_D}{\dfrac{S_D}{\sqrt{n}}} = \frac{42.6013 - 0}{\dfrac{43.797}{\sqrt{16}}} = 3.8908$$

Because $t_{STAT} = 3.8908 > 2.1314$, you reject the null hypothesis, H_0 (see Figure 10.7). There is evidence of a difference in the mean price of textbooks purchased at the college bookstore and the online retailer. You can conclude that the mean price is higher at the college bookstore than at the online retailer.

FIGURE 10.7

Two-tail paired t test at the 0.05 level of significance with 15 degrees of freedom

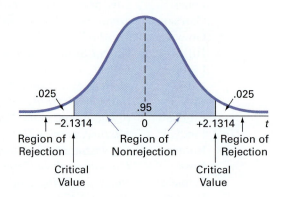

Figure 10.8 presents the results for this example, computing both the t test statistic and the p-value. Because the p-value $= 0.0014 < \alpha = 0.05$, you reject H_0. The p-value indicates that if the two sources for textbooks have the same population mean price, the probability that one source would have a sample mean \$42.60 more than the other is 0.0014. Because this probability is less than $\alpha = 0.05$, you conclude that there is evidence to reject the null hypothesis.

To evaluate the validity of the assumption of normality, you construct a boxplot of the differences, as shown in Figure 10.9.

The Figure 10.9 boxplots show approximate symmetry and look similar to the boxplot for the normal distribution displayed in Figure 3.5 on page 118. Thus, the distribution of textbook price differences does not greatly contradict the underlying assumption of normality. If a boxplot, histogram, or normal probability plot reveals that the assumption of underlying normality in the population is severely violated, then the t test may be inappropriate, especially if the

FIGURE 10.8
Excel and Minitab paired *t* test results for the textbook price data

	A	B
1	Paired *t* Test	
2		
3	**Data**	
4	Hypothesized Mean Diff.	0
5	Level of Significance	0.05
6		
7	**Intermediate Calculations**	
8	Sample Size	16 =COUNT(PtCalcsOld!$A:$A)
9	DBar	42.6013 =AVERAGE(PtCalcsOld!$C:$C)
10	degrees of freedom	15 =B8 - 1
11	S_D	43.7970 =SQRT(DEVSQ(PtCalcsOld!C:C)/B10)
12	Standard Error	10.9493 =B11/SQRT(B8)
13	*t* Test Statistic	3.8908 =(B9 - B4)/B12
14		
15	**Two-Tailed Test**	
16	Lower Critical Value	-2.1314 =-T.INV.2T(B5, B10)
17	Upper Critical Value	2.1314 =T.INV.2T(B5, B10)
18	*p*-Value	0.0014 =T.DIST.2T(ABS(B13), B10)
19	Reject the null hypothesis	=IF(B18 < B5, "Reject the null hypothesis", "Do not reject the null hypothesis")

```
Paired T-Test and CI: Bookstore, Online

Paired T for Bookstore - Online

              N    Mean   StDev   SE Mean
Bookstore    16   153.6    89.0     22.2
Online       16   111.0    60.0     15.0
Difference   16    42.6    43.8     10.9

95% CI for mean difference: (19.3, 65.9)
T-Test of mean difference = 0 (vs not = 0): T-Value = 3.89 P-Value = 0.001
```

FIGURE 10.9
Excel and Minitab boxplots for the textbook price differences

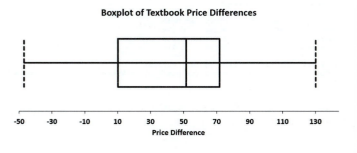
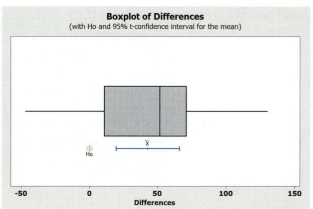

sample size is small. If you believe that the *t* test is inappropriate, you can use either a *nonparametric* procedure that does not make the assumption of underlying normality (see references 1 and 2) or make a data transformation (see reference 10) and then check the assumptions again to determine whether you should use the *t* test.

EXAMPLE 10.2

Paired *t* Test of Pizza Delivery Times

Recall from Example 10.1 on page 327 that a local pizza restaurant situated across the street from your college campus advertises that it delivers to the dormitories faster than the local branch of a national pizza chain. In order to determine whether this advertisement is valid, you and some friends decided to order 10 pizzas from the local pizza restaurant and 10 pizzas from the national chain. In fact, each time you ordered a pizza from the local pizza restaurant, at the same time, your friends ordered a pizza from the national pizza chain. Thus, you have matched samples. For each of the 10 times that pizzas were ordered, you have one measurement from the local pizza restaurant and one from the national chain. At the 0.05 level of significance, is the mean delivery time for the local pizza restaurant less than the mean delivery time for the national pizza chain?

(continued)

SOLUTION Use the paired t test to analyze the Table 10.5 data (stored in PizzaTime). Figure 10.10 shows the paired t test results for the pizza delivery data.

TABLE 10.5

Delivery Times for Local Pizza Restaurant and National Pizza Chain

Time	Local	Chain	Difference
1	16.8	22.0	−5.2
2	11.7	15.2	−3.5
3	15.6	18.7	−3.1
4	16.7	15.6	1.1
5	17.5	20.8	−3.3
6	18.1	19.5	−1.4
7	14.1	17.0	−2.9
8	21.8	19.5	2.3
9	13.9	16.5	−2.6
10	20.8	24.0	−3.2
			−21.8

FIGURE 10.10

Excel and Minitab paired t test results for the pizza delivery data

	A	B
1	Paired *t* Test	
2		
3	**Data**	
4	Hypothesized Mean Diff.	0
5	Level of significance	0.05
6		
7	**Intermediate Calculations**	
8	Sample Size	10
9	DBar	-2.1800
10	degrees of freedom	9
11	S_D	2.2641
12	Standard Error	0.7160
13	*t* Test Statistic	-3.0448
14		
15	**Lower-Tail Test**	
16	Lower Critical Value	-1.8331
17	*p*-Value	0.0070
18	Reject the null hypothesis	

```
Paired T-Test and CI: Local, Chain

Paired T for Local - Chain

              N     Mean   StDev   SE Mean
Local         10   16.700   3.096    0.979
Chain         10   18.880   2.866    0.906
Difference    10   -2.180   2.264    0.716

% CI for mean difference: (-3.800, -0.560)
T-Test of mean difference = 0 (vs not = 0): T-Value = -3.04   P-Value = 0.014
```

The null and alternative hypotheses are

H_0: $\mu_D \geq 0$ (Mean difference in the delivery time between the local pizza restaurant and the national pizza chain is greater than or equal to 0.)

H_1: $\mu_D < 0$ (Mean difference in the delivery time between the local pizza restaurant and the national pizza chain is less than 0.)

Choosing the level of significance $\alpha = 0.05$ and assuming that the differences are normally distributed, you use the paired t test [Equation (10.3) on page 334]. For a sample of $n = 10$ delivery times, there are $n - 1 = 9$ degrees of freedom. Using Table E.3, the decision rule is

$$\text{Reject } H_0 \text{ if } t_{STAT} < -t_{0.05} = -1.8331;$$

$$\text{otherwise, do not reject } H_0.$$

To illustrate the computations, for $n = 10$ differences (see Table 10.5), the sample mean difference is

$$\bar{D} = \frac{\sum_{i=1}^{n} D_i}{n} = \frac{-21.8}{10} = -2.18$$

and the sample standard deviation of the difference is

$$S_D = \sqrt{\frac{\sum_{i=1}^{n}(D_i - \overline{D})^2}{n-1}} = 2.2641$$

From Equation (10.3) on page 334,

$$t_{STAT} = \frac{\overline{D} - \mu_D}{\dfrac{S_D}{\sqrt{n}}} = \frac{-2.18 - 0}{\dfrac{2.2641}{\sqrt{10}}} = -3.0448$$

Because $t_{STAT} = -3.0448$ is less than -1.8331, you reject the null hypothesis, H_0 (the p-value is $0.0070 < 0.05$). There is evidence that the mean delivery time is lower for the local pizza restaurant than for the national pizza chain.

This conclusion differs from the conclusion you reached on page 329 for Example 10.1 when you used the pooled-variance t test for these data. By pairing the delivery times, you are able to focus on the differences between the two pizza delivery services and not the variability created by ordering pizzas at different times of day. The paired t test is a more powerful statistical procedure that reduces the variability in the delivery time because you are controlling for the time of day the pizza was ordered.

Confidence Interval Estimate for the Mean Difference

Instead of, or in addition to, testing for the mean difference between two related populations, you can use Equation (10.4) to construct a confidence interval estimate for the population mean difference.

CONFIDENCE INTERVAL ESTIMATE FOR THE MEAN DIFFERENCE

$$\overline{D} \pm t_{\alpha/2}\frac{S_D}{\sqrt{n}} \tag{10.4}$$

or

$$\overline{D} - t_{\alpha/2}\frac{S_D}{\sqrt{n}} \leq \mu_D \leq \overline{D} + t_{\alpha/2}\frac{S_D}{\sqrt{n}}$$

where $t_{\alpha/2}$ is the critical value of the t distribution, with $n - 1$ degrees of freedom, for an area of $\alpha/2$ in the upper tail.

Recall the example comparing textbook prices on page 335. Using Equation (10.4), $\overline{D} = 42.6013$, $S_D = 43.797$, $n = 16$, and $t_{\alpha/2} = 2.1314$ (for 95% confidence and $n - 1 = 15$ degrees of freedom),

$$42.6013 \pm (2.1314)\frac{43.797}{\sqrt{16}}$$

$$42.6013 \pm 23.3373$$

$$19.264 \leq \mu_D \leq 65.9386$$

Thus, with 95% confidence, you estimate that the population mean difference in textbook prices between the college bookstore and the online retailer is between \$19.26 and \$65.94.

Because the interval estimate does not contain zero, using the 0.05 level of significance and a two-tail test, you can conclude that there is evidence of a difference in the mean prices of textbooks at the college bookstore and the online retailer. Since both the lower and upper limits of the confidence interval are above 0, you can conclude that the mean price is higher at the college bookstore than the online retailer.

Problems for Section 10.2

LEARNING THE BASICS

10.18 An experimental design for a paired t test has 20 pairs of identical twins. How many degrees of freedom are there in this t test?

10.19 Fifteen volunteers are recruited to participate in an experiment. A measurement is made (such as blood pressure) before each volunteer is asked to read a particularly upsetting passage from a book and after each volunteer reads the passage from the book. In the analysis of the data collected from this experiment, how many degrees of freedom are there in the test?

APPLYING THE CONCEPTS

✓ SELF Test **10.20** Nine experts rated two brands of Colombian coffee in a taste-testing experiment. A rating on a 7-point scale (1 = extremely unpleasing, 7 = extremely pleasing) is given for each of four characteristics: taste, aroma, richness, and acidity. The following data stored in Coffee contain the ratings accumulated over all four characteristics:

	BRAND	
EXPERT	A	B
C.C.	24	26
S.E.	27	27
E.G.	19	22
B.L.	24	27
C.M.	22	25
C.N.	26	27
G.N.	27	26
R.M.	25	27
P.V.	22	23

a. At the 0.05 level of significance, is there evidence of a difference in the mean ratings between the two brands?
b. What assumption is necessary about the population distribution in order to perform this test?
c. Determine the p-value in (a) and interpret its meaning.
d. Construct and interpret a 95% confidence interval estimate of the difference in the mean ratings between the two brands.

10.21 How do the ratings of TV and Internet services compare? The file Telecom contains the rating of 14 different providers.

(Data extracted from "Ratings: TV, Phone, and Internet Services," *Consumer Reports*, May 2014, pp. 28–29.)
a. At the 0.05 level of significance, is there evidence of a difference in the mean service rating between TV and Internet services?
b. What assumption is necessary about the population distribution in order to perform this test?
c. Use a graphical method to evaluate the validity of the assumption in (a).
d. Construct and interpret a 95% confidence interval estimate of the difference in the mean service rating between TV and Internet services.

10.22 Super Target versus Walmart: Who has the lowest prices? Given Walmart's slogan "Save Money—Live Better," you suspect that Walmart does. The prices of 33 foods were compared (data extracted from "Supermarket Showdown," *The Palm Beach Post*, February 13, 2011, pp. 1F, 2F) and the results are stored in TargetWalmart .
a. At the 0.05 level of significance, is there evidence that the mean price of items is higher at Super Target than at Walmart?
b. What assumption is necessary about the population distribution in order to perform this test?
c. Find the p-value in (a) and interpret its meaning.

10.23 What motivates employees? The Great Place to Work Institute evaluated nonfinancial factors both globally and in the United States. (Data extracted from L. Petrecca, "Tech Companies Top List of 'Great Workplaces,'" *USA Today*, October 31, 2011, p. 7B.) The results, which indicate the importance rating of each factor, are stored in Motivation .
a. At the 0.05 level of significance, is there evidence of a difference in the mean rating between global and U.S. employees?
b. What assumption is necessary about the population distribution in order to perform this test?
c. Use a graphical method to evaluate the validity of the assumption in (b).

10.24 Multiple myeloma, or blood plasma cancer, is characterized by increased blood vessel formulation (angiogenesis) in the bone marrow that is a predictive factor in survival. One treatment approach used for multiple myeloma is stem cell transplantation with the patient's own stem cells. The data stored in Myeloma , and shown on page 341 represent the bone marrow microvessel density for patients who had a complete response to the stem cell transplant (as measured by blood and urine tests). The measurements were taken immediately prior to the stem cell transplant and at the time the complete response was determined.

Patient	Before	After
1	158	284
2	189	214
3	202	101
4	353	227
5	416	290
6	426	176
7	441	290

Data extracted from S. V. Rajkumar, R. Fonseca, T. E. Witzig, M. A. Gertz, and P. R. Greipp, "Bone Marrow Angiogenesis in Patients Achieving Complete Response After Stem Cell Transplantation for Multiple Myeloma," *Leukemia* 13 (1999): 469–472.

a. At the 0.05 level of significance, is there evidence that the mean bone marrow microvessel density is higher before the stem cell transplant than after the stem cell transplant?
b. Interpret the meaning of the *p*-value in (a).
c. Construct and interpret a 95% confidence interval estimate of the mean difference in bone marrow microvessel density before and after the stem cell transplant.

d. What assumption is necessary about the population distribution in order to perform the test in (a)?

10.25 To assess the effectiveness of a cola video ad, a random sample of 38 individuals from a target audience was selected to participate in a copy test. Participants viewed two ads, one of which was the ad being tested. Participants then answered a series of questions about how much they liked the ads. An adindex measure was created and stored in Adindex ; the higher the adindex value, the more likeable the ad. Compute descriptive statistics and perform a paired *t* test. State your findings and conclusions in a report. (Use the 0.05 level of significance.)

10.26 The file Concrete1 contains the compressive strength, in thousands of pounds per square inch (psi), of 40 samples of concrete taken two and seven days after pouring. (Data extracted from O. Carrillo-Gamboa and R. F. Gunst, "Measurement-Error-Model Collinearities," *Technometrics*, 34 (1992): 454–464.)
a. At the 0.01 level of significance, is there evidence that the mean strength is lower at two days than at seven days?
b. What assumption is necessary about the population distribution in order to perform this test?
c. Find the *p*-value in (a) and interpret its meaning.

10.3 Comparing the Proportions of Two Independent Populations

Often, you need to make comparisons and analyze differences between two population proportions. You can perform a test for the difference between two proportions selected from independent populations by using two different methods. This section presents a procedure whose test statistic, Z_{STAT}, is approximated by a standardized normal distribution. In Section 11.1, a procedure whose test statistic, χ^2_{STAT}, is approximated by a chi-square distribution is used. As explained in the latter section, the results from these two tests are equivalent.

Z Test for the Difference Between Two Proportions

In evaluating differences between two population proportions, you can use a **Z test for the difference between two proportions**. The Z_{STAT} test statistic is based on the difference between two sample proportions $(p_1 - p_2)$. This test statistic, given in Equation (10.5), approximately follows a standardized normal distribution for large enough sample sizes.

Z TEST FOR THE DIFFERENCE BETWEEN TWO PROPORTIONS

$$Z_{STAT} = \frac{(p_1 - p_2) - (\pi_1 - \pi_2)}{\sqrt{\bar{p}(1 - \bar{p})\left(\frac{1}{n_1} + \frac{1}{n_2}\right)}} \qquad (10.5)$$

where

$$\bar{p} = \frac{X_1 + X_2}{n_1 + n_2} \qquad p_1 = \frac{X_1}{n_1} \qquad p_2 = \frac{X_2}{n_2}$$

(continued)

and

p_1 = proportion of items of interest in sample 1

X_1 = number of items of interest in sample 1

n_1 = sample size of sample 1

π_1 = proportion of items of interest in population 1

p_2 = proportion of items of interest in sample 2

X_2 = number of items of interest in sample 2

n_2 = sample size of sample 2

π_2 = proportion of items of interest in population 2

$\bar{p}$ = pooled estimate of the population proportion of items of interest

The Z_{STAT} test statistic approximately follows a standardized normal distribution.

The null hypothesis in the Z test for the difference between two proportions states that the two population proportions are equal ($\pi_1 = \pi_2$). Because the pooled estimate for the population proportion is based on the null hypothesis, you combine, or pool, the two sample proportions to compute $\bar{p}$, an overall estimate of the common population proportion. This estimate is equal to the number of items of interest in the two samples ($X_1 + X_2$) divided by the total sample size from the two samples ($n_1 + n_2$).

As shown in the following table, you can use this Z test for the difference between population proportions to determine whether there is a difference in the proportion of items of interest in the two populations (two-tail test) or whether one population has a higher proportion of items of interest than the other population (one-tail test):

Two-Tail Test	One-Tail Test	One-Tail Test
$H_0: \pi_1 = \pi_2$	$H_0: \pi_1 \geq \pi_2$	$H_0: \pi_1 \leq \pi_2$
$H_1: \pi_1 \neq \pi_2$	$H_1: \pi_1 < \pi_2$	$H_1: \pi_1 > \pi_2$

where

π_1 = proportion of items of interest in population 1

π_2 = proportion of items of interest in population 2

To test the null hypothesis that there is no difference between the proportions of two independent populations:

$$H_0: \pi_1 = \pi_2$$

against the alternative that the two population proportions are not the same:

$$H_1: \pi_1 \neq \pi_2$$

you use the Z_{STAT} test statistic, given by Equation (10.5). For a given level of significance, α, you reject the null hypothesis if the computed Z_{STAT} test statistic is greater than the upper-tail critical value from the standardized normal distribution or if the computed Z_{STAT} test statistic is less than the lower-tail critical value from the standardized normal distribution.

To illustrate the use of the Z test for the equality of two proportions, suppose that you are the manager of T.C. Resort Properties, a collection of five upscale resort hotels located on two tropical islands. On one of the islands, T.C. Resort Properties has two hotels, the Beachcomber and the Windsurfer. Using the DCOVA problem-solving approach, you have defined the business objective as improving the return rate of guests at the Beachcomber and the Windsurfer hotels. On the survey completed by hotel guests upon or after their departure, one question asked is whether the guest is likely to return to the hotel. Responses to this and other questions were collected from 227 guests at the Beachcomber and 262 guests at the Windsurfer. The results for this question indicated that 163 of 227 guests at the Beachcomber responded yes, they were likely to return to the hotel and 154 of 262 guests at the Windsurfer responded yes, they were likely to return to the hotel. At the 0.05 level of significance, is there evidence of a significant difference in guest satisfaction (as measured by the likelihood to return to the hotel) between the two hotels?

The null and alternative hypotheses are

$$H_0: \pi_1 = \pi_2 \quad \text{or} \quad \pi_1 - \pi_2 = 0$$
$$H_1: \pi_1 \neq \pi_2 \quad \text{or} \quad \pi_1 - \pi_2 \neq 0$$

Using the 0.05 level of significance, the critical values are -1.96 and $+1.96$ (see Figure 10.11), and the decision rule is

$$\text{Reject } H_0 \text{ if } Z_{STAT} < -1.96$$
$$\text{or if } Z_{STAT} > +1.96;$$
$$\text{otherwise, do not reject } H_0.$$

Using Equation (10.5) on page 341,

$$Z_{STAT} = \frac{(p_1 - p_2) - (\pi_1 - \pi_2)}{\sqrt{\bar{p}(1 - \bar{p})\left(\dfrac{1}{n_1} + \dfrac{1}{n_2}\right)}}$$

FIGURE 10.11

Regions of rejection and nonrejection when testing a hypothesis for the difference between two proportions at the 0.05 level of significance

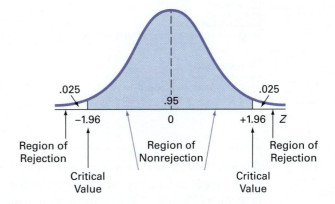

where

$$p_1 = \frac{X_1}{n_1} = \frac{163}{227} = 0.7181 \quad p_2 = \frac{X_2}{n_2} = \frac{154}{262} = 0.5878$$

and

$$\bar{p} = \frac{X_1 + X_2}{n_1 + n_2} = \frac{163 + 154}{227 + 262} = \frac{317}{489} = 0.6483$$

so that

$$Z_{STAT} = \frac{(0.7181 - 0.5878) - (0)}{\sqrt{0.6483(1 - 0.6483)\left(\dfrac{1}{227} + \dfrac{1}{262}\right)}}$$

$$= \frac{0.1303}{\sqrt{(0.228)(0.0082)}}$$

$$= \frac{0.1303}{\sqrt{0.00187}}$$

$$= \frac{0.1303}{0.0432} = +3.0088$$

Using the 0.05 level of significance, you reject the null hypothesis because $Z_{STAT} = +3.0088 > +1.96$. The p-value is 0.0026 (computed using Table E.2 or from Figure 10.12) and indicates that if the null hypothesis is true, the probability that a Z_{STAT} test statistic is less than -3.0088 is 0.0013, and, similarly, the probability that a Z_{STAT} test statistic is greater than $+3.0088$ is 0.0013. Thus, for this two-tail test, the p-value is $0.0013 + 0.0013 = 0.0026$. Because $0.0026 < \alpha = 0.05$, you reject the null hypothesis. There is evidence to conclude that the two hotels are significantly different with respect to guest satisfaction; a greater proportion of guests are willing to return to the Beachcomber than to the Windsurfer.

FIGURE 10.12

Excel and Minitab Z test results for the difference between two proportions for the hotel guest satisfaction problem

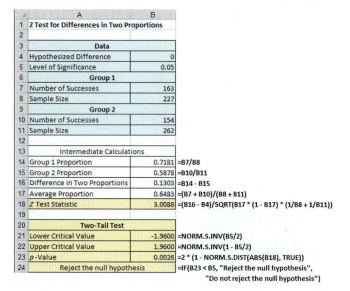

Test and CI for Two Proportions

Sample	X	N	Sample p
1	163	227	0.718062
2	154	262	0.587786

Difference = p (1) – p (2)
Estimate for difference: 0.130275
95% CI for difference: (0.0467379, 0.213813)
Test for difference = 0 (vs not = 0): Z = 3.01   P-Value = 0.003

Fisher's exact test: P-Value = 0.003

EXAMPLE 10.3

Testing for the Difference Between Two Proportions

Are men less likely than women to say that a major reason they use Facebook is to share with many people at once? A survey reported that 42% of men (193 out of 459 sampled) and 50% of women (250 out of 501 sampled) said that a major reason they use Facebook is to share with many people at once. (Source: "6 new facts about Facebook," **bit.ly/1kENZcA**.)

SOLUTION Because you want to know whether there is evidence that the proportion of men who say that a major reason they use Facebook is to share with many people at once is *less* than the proportion of women who say that a major reason they use Facebook is to share with many people at once, you have a one-tail test. The null and alternative hypotheses are

$H_0: \pi_1 \geq \pi_2$ (The proportion of men who say that a major reason they use Facebook is to share with many people at once is greater than or equal to the proportion of women who say that a major reason they use Facebook is to share with many people at once.)

$H_1: \pi_1 < \pi_2$ (The proportion of men who say that a major reason they use Facebook is to share with many people at once is less than the proportion of women who say that a major reason they use Facebook is to share with many people at once.)

Using the 0.05 level of significance, for the one-tail test in the lower tail, the critical value is $+1.645$. The decision rule is

Reject H_0 if $Z_{STAT} < -1.645$;

otherwise, do not reject H_0.

(*continued*)

Using Equation (10.5) on page 341,

$$Z_{STAT} = \frac{(p_1 - p_2) - (\pi_1 - \pi_2)}{\sqrt{\bar{p}(1 - \bar{p})\left(\dfrac{1}{n_1} + \dfrac{1}{n_2}\right)}}$$

where

$$p_1 = \frac{X_1}{n_1} = \frac{193}{459} = 0.4205 \quad p_2 = \frac{X_2}{n_2} = \frac{250}{501} = 0.4990$$

and

$$\bar{p} = \frac{X_1 + X_2}{n_1 + n_2} = \frac{193 + 250}{459 + 501} = \frac{443}{960} = 0.4615$$

so that

$$Z_{STAT} = \frac{(0.4205 - 0.4990) - (0)}{\sqrt{0.4615(1 - 0.4615)\left(\dfrac{1}{459} + \dfrac{1}{501}\right)}}$$

$$= \frac{-0.0785}{\sqrt{(0.2485)(0.0042)}}$$

$$= \frac{-0.0785}{\sqrt{0.0010437}}$$

$$= \frac{-0.0785}{0.0322} = -2.4379$$

Using the 0.05 level of significance, you reject the null hypothesis because $Z_{STAT} = -2.4379$ < -1.645. The p-value is 0.0148. Therefore, if the null hypothesis is true, the probability that a Z_{STAT} test statistic is less than -2.4379 is 0.0148 (which is less than $\alpha = 0.05$). You conclude that there is evidence that the proportion of men who say that a major reason they use Facebook is to share with many people at once is less than the proportion of women who say that a major reason they use Facebook is to share with many people at once.

Confidence Interval Estimate for the Difference Between Two Proportions

Instead of, or in addition to, testing for the difference between the proportions of two independent populations, you can construct a confidence interval estimate for the difference between the two proportions using Equation (10.6).

CONFIDENCE INTERVAL ESTIMATE FOR THE DIFFERENCE
BETWEEN TWO PROPORTIONS

$$(p_1 - p_2) \pm Z_{\alpha/2}\sqrt{\frac{p_1(1 - p_1)}{n_1} + \frac{p_2(1 - p_2)}{n_2}} \qquad \textbf{(10.6)}$$

or

$$(p_1 - p_2) - Z_{\alpha/2}\sqrt{\frac{p_1(1 - p_1)}{n_1} + \frac{p_2(1 - p_2)}{n_2}} \le (\pi_1 - \pi_2)$$

$$\le (p_1 - p_2) + Z_{\alpha/2}\sqrt{\frac{p_1(1 - p_1)}{n_1} + \frac{p_2(1 - p_2)}{n_2}}$$

FIGURE 10.13
Excel and Minitab *F* test results for the two end-cap locations data

	A	B
1	F Test for Differences in Two Variances	
2		
3	**Data**	
4	Level of Significance	0.05
5	**Larger-Variance Sample**	
6	Sample Size	10 =COUNT(DATACOPY!$A:$A)
7	Sample Variance	350.6778 =VAR.S(DATACOPY!$A:$A)
8	**Smaller-Variance Sample**	
9	Sample Size	10 =COUNT(DATACOPY!$B:$B)
10	Sample Variance	157.3333 =VAR.S(DATACOPY!$B:$B)
11		
12	**Intermediate Calculations**	
13	F Test Statistic	2.2289 =B7/B10
14	Population 1 Sample Degrees of Freedom	9 =B6 - 1
15	Population 2 Sample Degrees of Freedom	9 =B9 - 1
16		
17	**Two-Tail Test**	
18	Upper Critical Value	4.0260 =F.INV.RT(B4/2, B14, B15)
19	p-Value	0.2482 =2 * F.DIST.RT(B13, B14, B15)
20	Do not reject the null hypothesis	=IF(B19 < B4, "Reject the null hypothesis", "Do not reject the null hypothesis")

```
Alternative hypothesis   Sigma(Beverage) / Sigma(Produce) not = 1
Significance level       Alpha = 0.05

Statistics
Variable    N    StDev   Variance
Beverage   10   18.726   350.678
Produce    10   12.543   157.333

Ratio of standard deviations = 1.493
Ratio of variances = 2.229

95% Confidence Intervals

                            CI for
Distribution   CI for StDev   Variance
of Data          Ratio         Ratio
Normal        (0.744, 2.996)  (0.554, 8.973)
Continuous    (0.664, 3.082)  (0.441, 9.497)

Tests
                                        Test
Method                        DF1  DF2  Statistic  P-Value
F Test (normal)                 9    9    2.23      0.248
Levene's Test (any continuous)  1   18    1.27      0.275
```

EXAMPLE 10.4

A One-Tail Test for the Difference Between Two Variances

Waiting time is a critical issue at fast-food chains, which not only want to minimize the mean service time but also want to minimize the variation in the service time from customer to customer. One fast-food chain carried out a study to measure the variability in the waiting time (defined as the time in minutes from when an order was completed to when it was delivered to the customer) at lunch and breakfast at one of the chain's stores. The results were as follows:

$$\text{Lunch: } n_1 = 25 \; S_1^2 = 4.4$$

$$\text{Breakfast: } n_2 = 21 \; S_2^2 = 1.9$$

At the 0.05 level of significance, is there evidence that there is more variability in the service time at lunch than at breakfast? Assume that the population service times are normally distributed.

SOLUTION The null and alternative hypotheses are

$$H_0: \sigma_L^2 \leq \sigma_B^2$$
$$H_1: \sigma_L^2 > \sigma_B^2$$

The F_{STAT} test statistic is given by Equation (10.7) on page 348:

$$F_{STAT} = \frac{S_1^2}{S_2^2}$$

You use Table E.5 to find the upper critical value of the F distribution. With $n_1 - 1 = 25 - 1 = 24$ degrees of freedom in the numerator, $n_2 - 1 = 21 - 1 = 20$ degrees of freedom in the denominator, and $\alpha = 0.05$, the upper-tail critical value, $F_{0.05}$, is 2.08. The decision rule is

$$\text{Reject } H_0 \text{ if } F_{STAT} > 2.08;$$

otherwise, do not reject H_0.

(continued)

From Equation (10.7) on page 348,

$$F_{STAT} = \frac{S_1^2}{S_2^2}$$

$$= \frac{4.4}{1.9} = 2.3158$$

Because $F_{STAT} = 2.3158 > 2.08$, you reject H_0. Using a 0.05 level of significance, you conclude that there is evidence that there is more variability in the service time at lunch than at breakfast.

Problems for Section 10.4

LEARNING THE BASICS

10.36 Determine the upper-tail critical values of F in each of the following two-tail tests.
a. $\alpha = 0.10, n_1 = 16, n_2 = 21$
b. $\alpha = 0.05, n_1 = 16, n_2 = 21$
c. $\alpha = 0.01, n_1 = 16, n_2 = 21$

10.37 Determine the upper-tail critical value of F in each of the following one-tail tests.
a. $\alpha = 0.05, n_1 = 16, n_2 = 21$
b. $\alpha = 0.01, n_1 = 16, n_2 = 21$

10.38 The following information is available for two samples selected from independent normally distributed populations:

$$\text{Population A: } n_1 = 25 \quad S_1^2 = 16$$

$$\text{Population B: } n_2 = 25 \quad S_2^2 = 25$$

a. Which sample variance do you place in the numerator of F_{STAT}?
b. What is the value of F_{STAT}?

10.39 The following information is available for two samples selected from independent normally distributed populations:

$$\text{Population A: } n_1 = 25 \quad S_1^2 = 161.9$$

$$\text{Population B: } n_2 = 25 \quad S_2^2 = 133.7$$

What is the value of F_{STAT} if you are testing the null hypothesis $H_0: \sigma_1^2 = \sigma_2^2$?

10.40 In Problem 10.39, how many degrees of freedom are there in the numerator and denominator of the F test?

10.41 In Problems 10.39 and 10.40, what is the upper-tail critical value for F if the level of significance, α, is 0.05 and the alternative hypothesis is $H_1: \sigma_1^2 \neq \sigma_2^2$?

10.42 In Problems 10.39 through 10.41, what is your statistical decision?

10.43 The following information is available for two samples selected from independent but very right-skewed populations:

$$\text{Population A: } n_1 = 16 \quad S_1^2 = 47.3$$

$$\text{Population B: } n_2 = 13 \quad S_2^2 = 36.4$$

Should you use the F test to test the null hypothesis of equality of variances? Discuss.

10.44 In Problem 10.43, assume that two samples are selected from independent normally distributed populations.
a. At the 0.05 level of significance, is there evidence of a difference between σ_1^2 and σ_2^2?
b. Suppose that you want to perform a one-tail test. At the 0.05 level of significance, what is the upper-tail critical value of F to determine whether there is evidence that $\sigma_1^2 > \sigma_2^2$? What is your statistical decision?

APPLYING THE CONCEPTS

10.45 A problem with a telephone line that prevents a customer from receiving or making calls is upsetting to both the customer and the telecommunications company. The file **Phone** contains samples of 20 problems reported to two different offices of a telecommunications company and the time to clear these problems (in minutes) from the customers' lines.
a. At the 0.05 level of significance, is there evidence of a difference in the variability of the time to clear problems between the two central offices?
b. Determine the p-value in (a) and interpret its meaning.
c. What assumption do you need to make in (a) about the two populations in order to justify your use of the F test?
d. Based on the results of (a) and (b), which t test defined in Section 10.1 should you use to compare the mean time to clear problems in the two central offices?

✓ SELF Test **10.46** *Accounting Today* identified the top accounting firms in 10 geographic regions across the United States. All 10 regions reported growth in 2013. The Southeast and Gulf Coast regions reported growth of 4.7% and 13.86%, respectively. A characteristic description of the accounting firms in the Southeast and Gulf Coast regions included the number of partners in the firm. The file **AccountingPartners2** contains the number of partners. (Data extracted from **bit.ly/ODuzd3**.)
a. At the 0.05 level of significance, is there evidence of a difference in the variability in numbers of partners for Southeast region accounting firms and Gulf Coast accounting firms?
b. Determine the p-value in (a) and interpret its meaning.
c. What assumption do you have to make about the two populations in order to justify the use of the F test?

d. Based on (a) and (b), which *t* test defined in Section 10.1 should you use to test whether there is a significant difference in the mean number of partners for Southeast region accounting firms and Gulf Coast accounting firms?

10.47 A bank with a branch located in a commercial district of a city has the business objective of improving the process for serving customers during the noon-to-1 P.M. lunch period. To do so, the waiting time (defined as the number of minutes that elapses from when the customer enters the line until he or she reaches the teller window) needs to be shortened to increase customer satisfaction. A random sample of 15 customers is selected and the waiting times are collected and stored in **Bank1** . These data are:

4.21   5.55   3.02   5.13   4.77   2.34   3.54   3.20
4.50   6.10   0.38   5.12   6.46   6.19   3.79

Suppose that another branch, located in a residential area, is also concerned with the noon-to-1 P.M. lunch period. A random sample of 15 customers is selected and the waiting times are collected and stored in **Bank2** . These data are:

9.66   5.90   8.02   5.79   8.73   3.82   8.01   8.35
10.49   6.68   5.64   4.08   6.17   9.91   5.47

a. Is there evidence of a difference in the variability of the waiting time between the two branches? (Use $\alpha = 0.05$.)
b. Determine the *p*-value in (a) and interpret its meaning.
c. What assumption about the population distribution of each bank is necessary in (a)? Is the assumption valid for these data?
d. Based on the results of (a), is it appropriate to use the pooled-variance *t* test to compare the means of the two branches?

10.48 An important feature of tablets is battery life, the number of hours before the battery needs to be recharged. The file **Tablets** contains the battery life of 12 WiFi-only and 7 3G/4G/WiFi 9- through 12-inch tablets. (Data extracted from "Ratings and recommendations: Tablets," *Consumer Reports*, August 2013, p. 24.)

a. Is there evidence of a difference in the variability of the battery life between the two types of tablets? (Use $\alpha = 0.05$.)
b. Determine the *p*-value in (a) and interpret its meaning.
c. What assumption about the population distribution of the two types of tablets is necessary in (a)? Is the assumption valid for these data?
d. Based on the results of (a), which *t* test defined in Section 10.1 should you use to compare the mean battery life of the two types of tablets?

10.49 Experian Marketing Services reported that the typical American spends 144 minutes (2.4 hours) per day accessing the Internet through a mobile device. (Source: *The 2014 Digital Marketer*, available at **ex.pn/1kXJjfX**.) You wonder if males and females spend differing amounts of time per day accessing the Internet through a mobile device.

You select a sample of 60 friends and family (30 males and 30 females), collect times spent per day accessing the Internet through a mobile device (in minutes), and store the data collected in **InternetMobileTime2** .

a. Using a 0.05 level of significance, is there evidence of a difference in the variances of time spent per day accessing the Internet via mobile device between males and females?
b. On the basis of the results in (a), which *t* test defined in Section 10.1 should you use to compare the means of males and females? Discuss.

10.50 Is there a difference in the variation of the yield of five-year certificates of deposit (CDs) in different cities? The file **FiveYearCDRate** contains the yields for a five-year CD for ten banks in New York and eight banks in Los Angeles, as of April 19, 2014. (Data extracted from **www.Bankrate.com**, April 19, 2014.) At the 0.05 level of significance, is there evidence of a difference in the variance of the yield of five-year CDs in the two cities? Assume that the population yields are normally distributed.

10.5 One-Way ANOVA

Section 10.1 through 10.4 discuss hypothesis-testing methods that allow you to reach conclusions about differences between two populations. **Analysis of variance**, known by the acronym **ANOVA**, are methods that allow you to compare *multiple* populations, or **groups**. Unlike the hypothesis-testing methods discussed previously, in ANOVA, you take samples from each group to examine the effects of differences among two or more groups. The criteria that distinguishes the groups are called **factors**, or sometimes the factors of interest. Factors contain **levels** which are analogous to the categories of a categorical variable.

In the simplest method, **one-way ANOVA**, also known as the *completely randomized design*, you examine only one factor and the levels provide the basis for dividing the variable under study into groups. One-way ANOVA is a two-part process. You first determine if there is a significant difference among the group means. If you reject the null hypothesis that there is no difference among the means, you continue with a second method that seeks to identify the groups whose means are significantly different from the other group means.

In one-way ANOVA, you **partition** the total variation into variation that is due to differences among the groups and variation that is due to differences within the groups (see Figure 10.14). The **within-group variation (*SSW*)** measures random variation. The **among-group** variation (*SSA*) measures differences from group to group. The symbol *n* represents the number of values in all groups and the symbol *c* represents the number of groups.

FIGURE 10.14

Partitioning the total variation in a completely randomized design

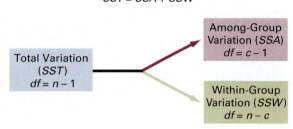

Partitioning the Total Variation
$SST = SSA + SSW$

If using Excel, always organize multiple-sample data as unstacked data, one column per group. (Some Minitab procedures work best with stacked data.) For more information about unstacked (and stacked) data, see page 44.

Assuming that the *c* groups represent populations whose values are randomly and independently selected, follow a normal distribution, and have equal variances, the null hypothesis of no differences in the population means:

$$H_0: \mu_1 = \mu_2 = \cdots = \mu_c$$

is tested against the alternative that not all the *c* population means are equal:

$$H_1: \text{Not all } \mu_j \text{ are equal (where } j = 1, 2, \ldots, c).$$

The alternative hypothesis, H_1, can also be stated as "at least one population mean is different from the other population means."

To perform an ANOVA test of equality of population means, you subdivide the total variation in the values into two parts—that which is due to variation among the groups and that which is due to variation within the groups. The **total variation** is represented by the **sum of squares total (*SST*)**. Because the population means of the *c* groups are assumed to be equal under the null hypothesis, you compute the total variation among all the values by summing the squared differences between each individual value and the **grand mean, $\overline{\overline{X}}$**. The grand mean is the mean of all the values in all the groups combined. Equation (10.8) shows the computation of the total variation.

TOTAL VARIATION IN ONE-WAY ANOVA

$$SST = \sum_{j=1}^{c} \sum_{i=1}^{n_j} (X_{ij} - \overline{\overline{X}})^2 \tag{10.8}$$

where

$$\overline{\overline{X}} = \frac{\sum_{j=1}^{c} \sum_{i=1}^{n_j} X_{ij}}{n} = \text{grand mean}$$

$X_{ij} = i$th value in group j

n_j = number of values in group j

n = total number of values in all groups combined
(that is, $n = n_1 + n_2 + \cdots + n_c$)

c = number of groups

Student Tip

A sum of squares (*SS*) cannot be negative.

You compute the among-group variation, usually called the **sum of squares among groups (*SSA*)**, by summing the squared differences between the sample mean of each group, $\overline{X}_j$, and the grand mean, $\overline{\overline{X}}$, weighted by the sample size, n_j, in each group. Equation (10.9) shows the computation of the among-group variation.

AMONG-GROUP VARIATION IN ONE-WAY ANOVA

$$SSA = \sum_{j=1}^{c} n_j (\overline{X}_j - \overline{\overline{X}})^2 \qquad (10.9)$$

where

c = number of groups
n_j = number of values in group j
$\overline{X}_j$ = sample mean of group j
$\overline{\overline{X}}$ = grand mean

The within-group variation, usually called the **sum of squares within groups (SSW)**, measures the difference between each value and the mean of its own group and sums the squares of these differences over all groups. Equation (10.10) shows the computation of the within-group variation.

WITHIN-GROUP VARIATION IN ONE-WAY ANOVA

$$SSW = \sum_{j=1}^{c} \sum_{i=1}^{n_j} (X_{ij} - \overline{X}_j)^2 \qquad (10.10)$$

where

X_{ij} = ith value in group j
$\overline{X}_j$ = sample mean of group j

Because you are comparing c groups, there are $c - 1$ degrees of freedom associated with the sum of squares among groups. Because each of the c groups contributes $n_j - 1$ degrees of freedom, there are $n - c$ degrees of freedom associated with the sum of squares within groups. In addition, there are $n - 1$ degrees of freedom associated with the sum of squares total because you are comparing each value, X_{ij}, to the grand mean, $\overline{\overline{X}}$, based on all n values.

If you divide each of these sums of squares by its respective degrees of freedom, you have three variances. In ANOVA, these three variances are called the **mean squares** and the three mean squares are defined as MSA (mean square among), MSW (mean square within), and MST (mean square total).

👉 **Student Tip**
Because the mean square is equal to the sum of squares divided by the degrees of freedom, a mean square can never be negative.

MEAN SQUARES IN ONE-WAY ANOVA

$$MSA = \frac{SSA}{c - 1} \qquad (10.11a)$$

$$MSW = \frac{SSW}{n - c} \qquad (10.11b)$$

$$MST = \frac{SST}{n - 1} \qquad (10.11c)$$

F Test for Differences Among More Than Two Means

To determine if there is a significant difference among the group means, you use the F test for differences among more than two means. If the null hypothesis is true and there are no differences among the c group means, MSA, MSW, and MST, will provide estimates of the overall variance in the population. Thus, to test the null hypothesis:

$$H_0: \mu_1 = \mu_2 = \cdots = \mu_c$$

against the alternative:

$$H_1: \text{Not all } \mu_j \text{ are equal (where } j = 1, 2, \ldots, c)$$

you compute the one-way ANOVA F_{STAT} test statistic as the ratio of MSA to MSW, as in Equation (10.12).

ONE-WAY ANOVA F_{STAT} TEST STATISTIC

$$F_{STAT} = \frac{MSA}{MSW} \tag{10.12}$$

The F_{STAT} test statistic follows an F distribution, with $c - 1$ degrees of freedom in the numerator and $n - c$ degrees of freedom in the denominator.

The test statistic compares mean squares (the variances) because the one-way ANOVA reaches conclusions about possible differences among the means of c groups by examining variances. For a given level of significance, α, you reject the null hypothesis if the F_{STAT} test statistic computed in Equation (10.12) is greater than the upper-tail critical value, F_α, from the F distribution with $c - 1$ degrees of freedom in the numerator and $n - c$ in the denominator (see Table E.5). Thus, as shown in Figure 10.15, the decision rule is

$$\text{Reject } H_0 \text{ if } F_{STAT} > F_\alpha;$$

$$\text{otherwise, do not reject } H_0.$$

FIGURE 10.15

Regions of rejection and nonrejection when using ANOVA

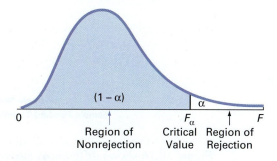

If the null hypothesis is true, the computed F_{STAT} test statistic is expected to be approximately equal to 1 because both the numerator and denominator mean square terms are estimating the overall variance in the population. If H_0 is false (and there are differences in the group means), the computed F_{STAT} test statistic is expected to be larger than 1 because the numerator, MSA, is estimating the differences among groups in addition to the overall variability in the values, while the denominator, MSW, is measuring only the overall variability in the values. Therefore, you reject the null hypothesis at a selected level of significance, α, only if the computed F_{STAT} test statistic is *greater than* F_α, the upper-tail critical value of the F distribution having $c - 1$ and $n - c$ degrees of freedom.

Table 10.7 presents the **ANOVA summary table** that is typically used to summarize the results of a one-way ANOVA. The table includes entries for the sources of variation (among groups, within groups, and total), the degrees of freedom, the sums of squares, the mean squares (the variances), and the computed F_{STAT} test statistic. The table may also include the p-value, the probability of having an F_{STAT} value as large as or larger than the one computed, given that the null hypothesis is true. The p-value allows you to reach conclusions about the null hypothesis without needing to refer to a table of critical values of the F distribution. If the p-value is less than the chosen level of significance, α, you reject the null hypothesis.

TABLE 10.7

ANOVA Summary Table

Source	Degrees of Freedom	Sum of Squares	Mean Square (Variance)	F
Among groups	$c - 1$	SSA	$MSA = \dfrac{SSA}{c - 1}$	$F_{STAT} = \dfrac{MSA}{MSW}$
Within groups	$n - c$	SSW	$MSW = \dfrac{SSW}{n - c}$	
Total	$n - 1$	SST		

Student Tip

In ordinary English, you could characterize this sales experiment as asking the question "How much of a *factor* is in-store location in determining mobile electronics sales?" echoing the sense of factor as defined in this section.

To illustrate the one-way ANOVA F test, suppose you were the manager of a general merchandiser looking for ways of increasing sales of mobile electronics items. You decide to experiment with the placement of such items in a store. You devise an experiment to compare sales at the current location in aisle 5 ("in-aisle") with sales at three other locations: at the front of the store near weekly specials ("front"), in an end-of-aisle special kiosk display ("end-cap"), or adjacent to the Expert Counter that is staffed with specially trained salespeople ("expert"). You decide to conduct a one-way ANOVA in which these four in-store locations in-aisle, front, kiosk, and expert are the *levels* of the *factor* in-store location.

To test the comparative effectiveness of the four in-store locations, you conduct a 60-day experiment at 20 same-sized stores that have similar storewide net sales. You randomly assign five stores to use the in-aisle location, five stores to use the front location, five stores to use the end-cap kiosk, and five stores to use the expert location to form the four groups. At the end of the experiment, you organize the mobile electronics sales data by group and store the data in unstacked format in Mobile Electronics . Figure 10.16 presents that unstacked data, along with the sample mean and the sample standard deviation for each group.

FIGURE 10.16

Mobile electronic sales ($000), sample means, and sample standard deviations for four different in-store locations

	In-aisle	Front	Kiosk	Expert
	30.06	32.22	30.78	30.33
	29.96	31.47	30.91	30.29
	30.19	32.13	30.79	30.25
	29.96	31.86	30.95	30.25
	29.74	32.29	31.13	30.55
Sample Mean	29.982	31.994	30.912	30.334
Sample Standard Deviation	0.165	0.335	0.143	0.125

Figure 10.16 shows differences among the sample means for the mobile electronics sales for the four in-store locations. For the original in-aisle location, mean sales were $29.982 thousands, whereas mean sales at the three new locations varied from $30.334 thousands ("expert" location) to $30.912 thousands ("kiosk" location) to $31.994 thousands ("front" location).

Differences in the mobile electronic sales for the four in-store locations can also be presented visually. In Figure 10.17, the Minitab cell means plot displays the four sample means and connects the sample means with a straight line. In the same figure, the Excel scatter plot presents the mobile electronics sales at each store in each group, permitting you to observe differences *within* each location as well as among the four locations. (In this example, because the difference within each group is slight, the points for each group overlap and blur together.)

FIGURE 10.17

Excel scatter plot and Minitab main effects plot of mobile electronics sales for four in-store locations

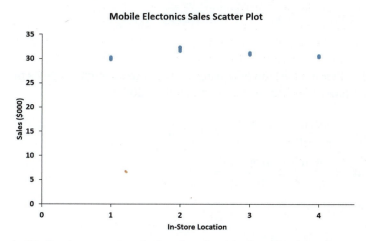

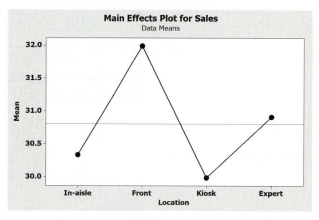

In the Excel scatter plot, the locations in-aisle, front, kiosk, and expert were relabeled 1, 2, 3, and 4 in order to use the scatter plot chart type.

> **Student Tip**
>
> If the sample sizes in each group were larger, you could construct stem-and-leaf displays, boxplots, and normal probability plots as additional ways of visualizing the sales data.

Having observed that the four sample means appear to be different, you use the *F* test for differences among more than two means to determine if these sample means are sufficiently different to conclude that the *population* means are not all equal. The null hypothesis states that there is no difference in the mean sales among the four in-store locations:

$$H_0: \mu_1 = \mu_2 = \mu_3 = \mu_4$$

The alternative hypothesis states that at least one of the in-store location mean sales differs from the other means:

$$H_1: \text{Not all the means are equal.}$$

To construct the ANOVA summary table, you first compute the sample means in each group (see Figure 10.16 on page 356). Then you compute the grand mean by summing all 20 values and dividing by the total number of values:

$$\overline{\overline{X}} = \frac{\sum_{j=1}^{c} \sum_{j=1}^{n_j} X_{ij}}{n} = \frac{616.12}{20} = 30.806$$

Then, using Equations (10.8) through (10.10) on pages 353–354, you compute the sum of squares:

$$SSA = \sum_{j=1}^{c} n_j (\overline{X}_j - \overline{\overline{X}})^2 = (5)(29.982 - 30.806)^2 + (5)(31.994 - 30.806)^2$$
$$+ (5)(30.912 - 30.806)^2 + (5)(30.334 - 30.806)^2$$
$$= 11.6217$$

$$SSW = \sum_{j=1}^{c} \sum_{i=1}^{n_j} (X_{ij} - \overline{X}_j)^2$$
$$= (30.06 - 29.982)^2 + \cdots + (29.74 - 29.982)^2 + (32.22 - 31.994)^2 + \cdots$$
$$+ (32.29 - 31.994)^2 + (30.78 - 30.912)^2 + \cdots + (31.13 - 30.912)^2$$
$$+ (30.33 - 30.334)^2 + \cdots + (30.55 - 30.334)^2$$
$$= 0.7026$$

$$SST = \sum_{j=1}^{c} \sum_{i=1}^{n_j} (X_{ij} - \overline{\overline{X}})^2$$
$$= (30.06 - 30.806)^2 + (29.96 - 30.806)^2 + \cdots + (30.55 - 30.806)^2$$
$$= 12.3243$$

You compute the mean squares by dividing the sum of squares by the corresponding degrees of freedom [see Equation (10.11) on page 354]. Because $c = 4$ and $n = 20$,

$$MSA = \frac{SSA}{c-1} = \frac{11.6217}{4-1} = 3.8739$$

$$MSW = \frac{SSW}{n-c} = \frac{0.7026}{20-4} = 0.0439$$

so that using Equation (10.12) on page 355,

$$F_{STAT} = \frac{MSA}{MSW} = \frac{3.8739}{0.0439} = 88.2186$$

Because you are trying to determine whether MSA is greater than MSW, you only reject H_0 if F_{STAT} is greater than the upper critical value of F. For a selected level of significance, α, you find the upper-tail critical value, F_α, from the F distribution using Table E.5. A portion of Table E.5 is presented in Table 10.8. In the in-store location sales experiment, there are 3 degrees of freedom in the numerator and 16 degrees of freedom in the denominator. F_α, the upper-tail critical value at the 0.05 level of significance, is 3.24.

TABLE 10.8

Finding the Critical Value of *F* with 3 and 16 Degrees of Freedom at the 0.05 Level of Significance

	Cumulative Probabilities = 0.95								
	Upper-Tail Area = 0.05								
	Numerator df_1								
Denominator df_2	1	2	3	4	5	6	7	8	9
⋮	⋮	⋮	⋮	⋮	⋮	⋮	⋮	⋮	⋮
11	4.84	3.98	3.59	3.36	3.20	3.09	3.01	2.95	2.90
12	4.75	3.89	3.49	3.26	3.11	3.00	2.91	2.85	2.80
13	4.67	3.81	3.41	3.18	3.03	2.92	2.83	2.77	2.71
14	4.60	3.74	3.34	3.11	2.96	2.85	2.76	2.70	2.65
15	4.54	3.68	3.29	3.06	2.90	2.79	2.71	2.64	2.59
16	4.49	3.63	3.24	3.01	2.85	2.74	2.66	2.59	2.54

Source: Extracted from Table E.5.

Because $F_{STAT} = 88.2186$ is greater than $F_\alpha = 3.24$, you reject the null hypothesis (see Figure 10.18). You conclude that there is a significant difference in the mean sales for the four in-store locations.

FIGURE 10.18

Regions of rejection and nonrejection for the one-way ANOVA at the 0.05 level of significance, with 3 and 16 degrees of freedom

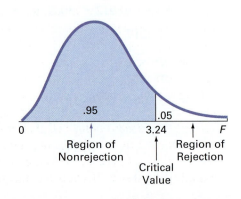

Figure 10.19 shows the ANOVA results for the in-store location sales experiment, including the *p*-value. In Figure 10.19, what Table 10.7 (see page 356) labels Among Groups is labeled Between Groups in the Excel worksheet. Minitab labels Among Groups as Factor and Within Groups as Error.

FIGURE 10.19

Excel and Minitab ANOVA results for the in-store location sales experiment

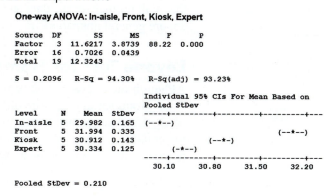

The formulas in the Excel results worksheet are not shown in Figure 10.19 but are discussed in Section EG10.5 and the SHORT TAKES for Chapter 10.

The *p*-value, or probability of getting a computed F_{STAT} statistic of 88.2186 or larger when the null hypothesis is true, is 0.0000. Because this *p*-value is less than the specified α of 0.05, you reject the null hypothesis. The *p*-value of 0.0000 indicates that there is a 0.00% chance of observing differences this large or larger if the population means for the four in-store locations are all equal. After performing the one-way ANOVA and finding a significant difference among the in-store locations, you still do not know *which* in-store locations differ. All you know is that there is sufficient evidence to state that the population means are not all the same. In other words, one or more population means are significantly different. Before proceeding to determine which in-store locations differ, you check to see if the assumptions of ANOVA hold.

One-Way ANOVA *F* Test Assumptions

To use the one-way ANOVA *F* test, you must make three assumptions about your data:

- **Randomness and independence** of the samples selected
- **Normality** of the *c* groups from which the samples are selected
- **Homogeneity of variance** (the variances of the *c* groups are equal)

Most critical of all is the first assumption. The validity of any experiment depends on random sampling and/or the randomization process. To avoid biases in the outcomes, you need to select random samples from the *c* groups or use the randomization process to randomly assign the items to the *c* levels of the factor. Selecting a random sample or randomly assigning the levels ensures that a value from one group is independent of any other value in the experiment. Departures from this assumption can seriously affect inferences from the ANOVA. These problems are discussed more thoroughly in references 3 and 10.

As for the second assumption, **normality**, the one-way ANOVA *F* test is fairly robust against departures from the normal distribution. As long as the distributions are not extremely different from a normal distribution, the level of significance of the ANOVA *F* test is usually not greatly affected, particularly for large samples. You can assess the normality of each of the *c* samples by constructing a normal probability plot or a boxplot.

As for the third assumption, **homogeneity of variance**, if you have equal sample sizes in each group, inferences based on the *F* distribution are not seriously affected by unequal variances. However, if you have unequal sample sizes, unequal variances can have a serious effect on inferences from the ANOVA procedure. Thus, when possible, you should have equal sample sizes in all groups. You can use the Levene test for homogeneity of variance discussed below, to test whether the variances of the c groups are equal.

When only the normality assumption is violated, you can use the Kruskal-Wallis rank test, a nonparametric procedure (see references 1 and 2). When only the homogeneity-of-variance assumption is violated, you can use procedures similar to those used in the separate-variance t test of Section 10.1 (see references 1 and 2). When both the normality and homogeneity-of-variance assumptions have been violated, you need to use an appropriate data transformation that both normalizes the data and reduces the differences in variances (see reference 10) or use a more general nonparametric procedure (see reference 1).

Levene Test for Homogeneity of Variance

Although the one-way ANOVA F test is relatively robust with respect to the assumption of equal group variances, large differences in the group variances can seriously affect the level of significance and the power of the F test. One powerful yet simple procedure for testing the equality of the variances is the modified **Levene test** (see reference 5). To test for the homogeneity of variance, you use the following null hypothesis:

$$H_0: \sigma_1^2 = \sigma_2^2 = \cdots = \sigma_c^2$$

against the alternative hypothesis:

$$H_1: \text{Not all } \sigma_j^2 \text{ are equal } (j = 1, 2, 3, \ldots, c)$$

> **Student Tip**
> Remember when performing the Levene test that you are conducting a one-way ANOVA on the absolute differences from the median in each group, not on the actual values themselves.

To test the null hypothesis of equal variances, you first compute the absolute value of the difference between each value and the median of the group. Then you perform a one-way ANOVA on these *absolute differences*. Most statisticians suggest using a level of significance of $\alpha = 0.05$ when performing the ANOVA. To illustrate the modified Levene test, return to the Figure 10.16 data and summary statistics on page 356 for the in-store location sales experiment. Table 10.9 summarizes the absolute differences from the median of each location.

TABLE 10.9

Absolute Differences from the Median Sales for Four Locations

In-Aisle (Median = 29.96)	Front (Median = 32.13)	Kiosk (Median = 30.91)	Expert (Median = 30.29)
$\|30.06 - 29.96\| = 0.10$	$\|32.22 - 32.13\| = 0.09$	$\|30.78 - 30.91\| = 0.13$	$\|30.33 - 30.29\| = 0.04$
$\|29.96 - 29.96\| = 0.00$	$\|31.47 - 32.13\| = 0.66$	$\|30.91 - 30.91\| = 0.00$	$\|30.29 - 30.29\| = 0.00$
$\|30.19 - 29.96\| = 0.23$	$\|32.13 - 32.13\| = 0.00$	$\|30.79 - 30.91\| = 0.12$	$\|30.25 - 30.29\| = 0.04$
$\|29.96 - 29.96\| = 0.00$	$\|31.86 - 32.13\| = 0.27$	$\|30.95 - 30.91\| = 0.04$	$\|30.25 - 30.29\| = 0.04$
$\|29.74 - 29.96\| = 0.22$	$\|32.29 - 32.13\| = 0.16$	$\|31.13 - 30.91\| = 0.22$	$\|30.55 - 30.29\| = 0.26$

Using the absolute differences given in Table 10.9, you perform a one-way ANOVA (see Figure 10.20).

From the Figure 10.20 results, observe that $F_{STAT} = 1.0556$. (The Excel worksheet labels this value F and Minitab labels the value Test statstic.) Because $F_{STAT} = 1.0556 < 3.2389$ (or the p-value $= 0.3953 > 0.05$), you do not reject H_0. There is insufficient evidence of a significant difference among the four variances. In other words, it is reasonable to assume that the

FIGURE 10.20

Excel and Minitab Levene test results for the absolute differences for the in-store location sales experiment

	A	B	C	D	E	F	G
1	ANOVA: Levene Test						
2							
3	SUMMARY						
4	*Groups*	*Count*	*Sum*	*Average*	*Variance*		
5	In-aisle	5	0.55	0.11	0.0127		
6	Front	5	1.18	0.236	0.06593		
7	Kiosk	5	0.51	0.102	0.00732		
8	Expert	5	0.38	0.076	0.01088		
9							
10							
11	ANOVA						
12	*Source of Variation*	*SS*	*df*	*MS*	*F*	*P-value*	*F crit*
13	Between Groups	0.07666	3	0.0256	1.0556	0.3953	3.2389
14	Within Groups	0.38732	16	0.0242			
15							
16	Total	0.46398	19				
17						*Level of significance*	0.05

Test for Equal Variances: Sales versus Location

Levene's Test (Any Continuous Distribution)
Test statistic = 1.06, p-value = 0.395

four in-store locations have an equal amount of variability in sales. Therefore, the homogeneity-of-variance assumption for the ANOVA procedure is justified.

Example 10.5 illustrates another example of the one-way ANOVA.

Student Tip

You have an α level of risk in the entire set of comparisons not just a single comparison.

Multiple Comparisons: The Tukey-Kramer Procedure

In the mobile electronics sales experiment example, the one-way ANOVA F test determined that there was a difference among the four in-store sales locations. Having verified that the assumptions were valid, the next step in one-way ANOVA analysis would be to construct **multiple comparisons** to test the null hypothesis that the differences in the means of all pairs of in-store locations are equal to 0.

Although many methods could be used to determine which of the c means are significantly different (see references 3 and 4), one commonly used method is the **Tukey-Kramer multiple comparisons procedure for one-way ANOVA**. This procedure enables you to simultaneously make comparisons between *all* pairs of groups. The procedure consists of the following four steps:

1. Compute the absolute mean differences, $|\bar{X}_j - \bar{X}_{j'}|$ (where j refers to group j, j' refers to group j', and $j \neq j'$), among all pairs of sample means [$c(c - 1)/2$ pairs].
2. Compute the **critical range** for the Tukey-Kramer procedure, using Equation (10.13). If the sample sizes differ, compute a critical range for each pairwise comparison of sample means.

CRITICAL RANGE FOR THE TUKEY-KRAMER PROCEDURE

$$\text{Critical range} = Q_\alpha \sqrt{\frac{MSW}{2}\left(\frac{1}{n_j} + \frac{1}{n_{j'}}\right)}$$

(10.13)

where

n_j = the sample size in group j

$n_{j'}$ = the sample size in group j'

Q_α = the upper-tail critical value from a **Studentized range distribution** having c degrees of freedom in the numerator and $n - c$ degrees of freedom in the denominator.

Student Tip

Table E.7 contains the critical values for the Studentized range distribution.

3. Compare each of the $c(c - 1)/2$ pairs of means against its corresponding critical range. Declare a specific pair significantly different if the absolute difference in the sample means, $|\bar{X}_j - \bar{X}_{j'}|$, is greater than the critical range.
4. Interpret the results.

In the mobile electronics sales example, there are four in-store locations. Thus, there are $4(4 - 1)/2 = 6$ pairwise comparisons. To apply the Tukey-Kramer multiple comparisons procedure, you first compute the absolute mean differences for all six pairwise comparisons:

1. $|\bar{X}_1 - \bar{X}_2| = |29.982 - 31.994| = 2.012$
2. $|\bar{X}_1 - \bar{X}_3| = |29.982 - 30.912| = 0.930$
3. $|\bar{X}_1 - \bar{X}_4| = |29.982 - 30.334| = 0.352$
4. $|\bar{X}_2 - \bar{X}_3| = |31.994 - 30.912| = 1.082$
5. $|\bar{X}_2 - \bar{X}_4| = |31.994 - 30.334| = 1.660$
6. $|\bar{X}_3 - \bar{X}_4| = |30.912 - 30.334| = 0.578$

You then compute only one critical range because the sample sizes in the four groups are equal. (Had the sample sizes in some of the groups been different, you would compute several critical ranges.) From the ANOVA summary table (Figure 10.19 on page 359), $MSW = 0.0439$ and $n_j = n_{j'} = 5$. From Table E.7, for $\alpha = 0.05$, $c = 4$, and $n - c = 20 - 4 = 16$, Q_α, the upper-tail critical value of the test statistic, is 4.05 (see Table 10.10).

TABLE 10.10

Finding the Studentized Range, Q_α, Statistic for $\alpha = 0.05$, with 4 and 16 Degrees of Freedom

			Cumulative Probabilities = 0.95 Upper-Tail Area = 0.05 Numerator df_1					
Denominator df_2	2	3	4	5	6	7	8	9
⋮	⋮	⋮	⋮	⋮	⋮	⋮	⋮	⋮
11	3.11	3.82	4.26	4.57	4.82	5.03	5.20	5.35
12	3.08	3.77	4.20	4.51	4.75	4.95	5.12	5.27
13	3.06	3.73	4.15	4.45	4.69	4.88	5.05	5.19
14	3.03	3.70	4.11	4.41	4.64	4.83	4.99	5.13
15	3.01	3.67	4.08	4.37	4.60	4.78	4.94	5.08
16	3.00	3.65	4.05	4.33	4.56	4.74	4.90	5.03

Source: Extracted from Table E.7.

From Equation (10.13),

$$\text{Critical range} = 4.05\sqrt{\left(\frac{0.0439}{2}\right)\left(\frac{1}{5} + \frac{1}{5}\right)} = 0.3795$$

Because the absolute mean difference for five pairs (1, 2, 4, 5, and 6) is greater than 0.3795, you can conclude that there is a significant difference between the mobile electronic sales means of those pairs. Because the absolute mean difference for pair 3 (in-aisle and expert locations) is 0.352, which is less than 0.3795, you conclude that there is no evidence of a difference in the means of those two locations. These results allow you to estimate that the population mean sales for mobile electronics items will be higher at the front location than any other location *and* that the population mean sales for mobile electronics items at kiosk locations will be higher when compared to either the in-aisle or expert locations.

Figure 10.21 presents the Excel and Minitab results for the Tukey-Kramer procedure for the mobile electronics sales in-store location experiment. Note that by using $\alpha = 0.05$, you are able to make all six of the comparisons with an overall error rate of only 5%.

FIGURE 10.21

Excel and Minitab Tukey-Kramer procedure results for the in-store location sales experiment

	A	B	C	D	E	F	G	H	I
1	Tukey Kramer Multiple Comparisons								
2									
3		Sample	Sample			Absolute	Std. Error	Critical	
4	Group	Mean	Size		Comparison	Difference	of Difference	Range	Results
5	1: In-aisle	29.982	5		Group 1 to Group 2	2.012	0.0937	0.3795	Means are different
6	2: Front	31.994	5		Group 1 to Group 3	0.93	0.0937	0.3795	Means are different
7	3: Kiosk	30.912	5		Group 1 to Group 4	0.352	0.0937	0.3795	Means are not different
8	4: Expert	30.334	5		Group 2 to Group 3	1.082	0.0937	0.3795	Means are different
9					Group 2 to Group 4	1.66	0.0937	0.3795	Means are different
10	Other Data				Group 3 to Group 4	0.578	0.0937	0.3795	Means are different
11	Level of significance	0.05							
12	Numerator d.f.	4							
13	Denominator d.f.	16							
14	MSW	0.043913							
15	Q Statistic	4.05							

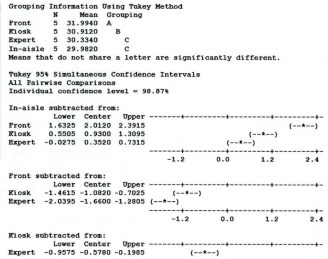

```
Grouping Information Using Tukey Method
          N    Mean   Grouping
Front     5  31.9940  A
Kiosk     5  30.9120  B
Expert    5  30.3340    C
In-aisle  5  29.9820    C
Means that do not share a letter are significantly different.

Tukey 95% Simultaneous Confidence Intervals
All Pairwise Comparisons
Individual confidence level = 98.87%

In-aisle subtracted from:
          Lower   Center   Upper  -------+---------+---------+---------+-
Front    1.6325   2.0120  2.3915                               (--*--)
Kiosk    0.5505   0.9300  1.3095                      (--*--)
Expert  -0.0275   0.3520  0.7315                 (--*--)
                                  -------+---------+---------+---------+-
                                      -1.2      0.0       1.2       2.4

Front subtracted from:
          Lower   Center   Upper  -------+---------+---------+---------+-
Kiosk   -1.4615  -1.0820 -0.7025     (--*--)
Expert  -2.0395  -1.6600 -1.2805 (--*--)
                                  -------+---------+---------+---------+-
                                      -1.2      0.0       1.2       2.4

Kiosk subtracted from:
          Lower   Center   Upper  -------+---------+---------+---------+-
Expert  -0.9575  -0.5780 -0.1985           (--*--)
                                  -------+---------+---------+---------+-
                                      -1.2      0.0       1.2       2.4
```

The formulas in the Excel results worksheet are not shown in Figure 10.21 but are discussed in Section EG10.5 and the SHORT TAKES for Chapter 10.

The Figure 10.21 Excel results follow the steps used on pages 361–362 for evaluating the comparisons. The Minitab results show the comparisons in terms of interval estimates. Each interval is computed. Any interval that does not include 0 is considered significant. Thus all the comparisons are significant except for the comparison of in-aisle to expert store location. The interval for that comparison includes 0 since the lower limit is -0.0275 and the upper limit is 0.7315.

EXAMPLE 10.5

ANOVA of the Speed of Drive-Through Service at Fast-Food Chains

For fast-food restaurants, the drive-through window is an important revenue source. The chain that offers the fastest service is likely to attract additional customers. Each year *QSR Magazine*, **www.qsrmagazine.com**, publishes its results of a survey of drive-through service times (from menu board to departure) at fast-food chains. In a recent year, the mean time was 129.75 seconds for Wendy's, 149.69 seconds for Taco Bell, 201.33 seconds for Burger King, 188.83 seconds for McDonald's, and 190.06 seconds for Chick-fil-A. Suppose the study was based on 20 customers for each fast-food chain. At the 0.05 level of significance, is there evidence of a difference in the mean drive-through service times of the five chains?

Table 10.11 contains the ANOVA table for this problem.

TABLE 10.11

ANOVA Summary Table of Drive-Through Service Times at Fast-Food Chains

Source	Degrees of Freedom	Sum of Squares	Mean Squares	F	*p*-value
Among chains	4	75,048.74	18,762.185	143.66	0.0000
Within chains	95	12,407.00	130.60		

SOLUTION

$H_0: \mu_1 = \mu_2 = \mu_3 = \mu_4 = \mu_5$ where 1 = Wendy's, 2 = Taco Bell, 3 = Burger King,

$$4 = \text{McDonald's}, 5 = \text{Chick-fil-A}$$

H_1: Not all μ_j are equal   where $j = 1, 2, 3, 4, 5$

Decision rule: If the *p*-value < 0.05, reject H_0. Because the *p*-value is 0.0000, which is less than $\alpha = 0.05$, reject H_0. You have sufficient evidence to conclude that the mean drive-through times of the five chains are not all equal.

(continued)

To determine which of the means are significantly different from one another, use the Tukey-Kramer procedure [Equation (10.13) on page 361] to establish the critical range:

Critical value of Q with 5 and 95 degrees of freedom ≈ 3.92

$$\text{Critical range} = Q_\alpha \sqrt{\left(\frac{MSW}{2}\right)\left(\frac{1}{n_j} + \frac{1}{n_{j'}}\right)} = (3.92)\sqrt{\left(\frac{130.6}{2}\right)\left(\frac{1}{20} + \frac{1}{20}\right)}$$

$$= 10.02$$

Any observed difference greater than 10.02 is considered significant. The mean drive-through service times are different between Wendy's (mean of 129.75 seconds) and Taco Bell, Burger King, McDonald's, and Chick-fil-A and also between Taco Bell (mean of 149.69) and Burger King, McDonald's, and Chick-fil-A. In addition, the mean drive-through service time is different between Burger King and McDonald's, and between Burger King and Chick-fil-A. Thus, with 95% confidence, you can conclude that the estimated population mean drive-through service time is faster for Wendy's than for Taco Bell. In addition, the population mean service time for Wendy's and for Taco Bell is faster than those of Burger King, McDonald's, and Chick-fil-A. Also, the population mean drive-through service time for Burger King is slower than for McDonald's and for Chick-Fil-A.

Problems for Section 10.5

LEARNING THE BASICS

10.51 An experiment has a single factor with five groups and seven values in each group.
a. How many degrees of freedom are there in determining the among-group variation?
b. How many degrees of freedom are there in determining the within-group variation?
c. How many degrees of freedom are there in determining the total variation?

10.52 You are working with the same experiment as in Problem 10.51.
a. If $SSA = 60$ and $SST = 210$, what is SSW?
b. What is MSA?
c. What is MSW?
d. What is the value of F_{STAT}?

10.53 You are working with the same experiment as in Problems 10.51 and 10.52.
a. Construct the ANOVA summary table and fill in all values in the table.
b. At the 0.05 level of significance, what is the upper-tail critical value from the F distribution?
c. State the decision rule for testing the null hypothesis that all five groups have equal population means.
d. What is your statistical decision?

10.54 Consider an experiment with three groups, with seven values in each.
a. How many degrees of freedom are there in determining the among-group variation?
b. How many degrees of freedom are there in determining the within-group variation?

c. How many degrees of freedom are there in determining the total variation?

10.55 Consider an experiment with four groups, with eight values in each. For the ANOVA summary table below, fill in all the missing results:

Source	Degrees of Freedom	Sum of Squares	Mean Square (Variance)	F
Among groups	$c - 1 = ?$	$SSA = ?$	$MSA = 80$	$F_{STAT} = ?$
Within groups	$n - c = ?$	$SSW = 560$	$MSW = ?$	
Total	$n - 1 = ?$	$SST = ?$		

10.56 You are working with the same experiment as in Problem 10.55.
a. At the 0.05 level of significance, state the decision rule for testing the null hypothesis that all four groups have equal population means.
b. What is your statistical decision?
c. At the 0.05 level of significance, what is the upper-tail critical value from the Studentized range distribution?
d. To perform the Tukey-Kramer procedure, what is the critical range?

APPLYING THE CONCEPTS

10.57 *Accounting Today* identified the top accounting firms in 10 geographic regions across the United States. All 10 regions reported growth in 2013, including the Capital, Great Lakes, Mid-Atlantic, and New England regions which reported combined growths of 2.06%, 16.58%, 8.31%, and 9.49%, respectively. A characteristic description of the accounting firms in the Capital, Great Lakes, Mid-Atlantic, and New England regions included the number of partners in the firm.

The file **AccountingPartners4** contains the number of partners. (Data extracted from **bit.ly/ODuzd3**.)

a. At the 0.05 level of significance, is there evidence of a difference among the Capital, Great Lakes, Mid-Atlantic, and New England region accounting firms with respect to the mean number of partners?

b. If the results in (a) indicate that it is appropriate to do so, use the Tukey-Kramer procedure to determine which regions differ in the mean number of partners. Discuss your findings.

✓ SELF Test **10.58** The more costly and time consuming it is to export and import, the more difficult it is for local companies to be competitive and to reach international markets. As part of an initial investigation exploring foreign market entry, 10 countries were selected from each of four global regions. The cost associated with importing a standardized cargo of goods by sea transport in these countries (in US$ per container) is stored in **ForeignMarket2**. (Data extracted from **doingbusiness.org/data**.)

a. At the 0.05 level of significance, is there evidence of a difference in the mean cost of importing across the four global regions?

b. If appropriate, determine which global regions differ in mean cost of importing.

c. At the 0.05 level of significance, is there evidence of a difference in the variation in cost of importing among the four global regions?

d. Which global region(s) should you consider for foreign market entry? Explain.

10.59 A hospital conducted a study of the waiting time in its emergency room. The hospital has a main campus and three satellite locations. Management had a business objective of reducing waiting time for emergency room cases that did not require immediate attention. To study this, a random sample of 15 emergency room cases that did not require immediate attention at each location were selected on a particular day, and the waiting times (measured from check-in to when the patient was called into the clinic area) were collected and stored in **ERWaiting**.

a. At the 0.05 level of significance, is there evidence of a difference in the mean waiting times in the four locations?

b. If appropriate, determine which locations differ in mean waiting time.

c. At the 0.05 level of significance, is there evidence of a difference in the variation in waiting time among the four locations?

10.60 A manufacturer of pens has hired an advertising agency to develop an advertising campaign for the upcoming holiday season. To prepare for this project, the research director decides to initiate a study of the effect of advertising on product perception. An experiment is designed to compare five different advertisements. Advertisement *A* greatly undersells the pen's characteristics. Advertisement *B* slightly undersells the pen's characteristics. Advertisement *C* slightly oversells the pen's characteristics. Advertisement *D* greatly oversells the pen's characteristics. Advertisement *E* attempts to correctly state the pen's characteristics. A sample of 30 adult respondents, taken from a larger focus group, is randomly assigned to the five advertisements (so that there are 6 respondents to each advertisement). After reading the advertisement and developing a sense of "product expectation," all respondents unknowingly receive the same pen to evaluate. The respondents are permitted to test the pen and the plausibility of the advertising copy. The respondents are then asked to rate the pen from 1 to 7 (lowest to highest) on the product characteristic scales of appearance, durability, and writing performance. The *combined* scores of three ratings (appearance, durability, and writing performance) for the 30 respondents, stored in **Pen**, are as follows:

A	B	C	D	E
15	16	8	5	12
18	17	7	6	19
17	21	10	13	18
19	16	15	11	12
19	19	14	9	17
20	17	14	10	14

a. At the 0.05 level of significance, is there evidence of a difference in the mean rating of the pens following exposure to five advertisements?

b. If appropriate, determine which advertisements differ in mean ratings.

c. At the 0.05 level of significance, is there evidence of a difference in the variation in ratings among the five advertisements?

d. Which advertisement(s) should you use, and which advertisement(s) should you avoid? Explain.

10.61 *QSR* magazine reports on the largest quick serve and fast casual restaurants in the United States. Do the various market segments (burger, chicken, sandwich, and pizza) differ in their mean sales per unit? The file **FastFoodChain** contains the mean sales in a recent year. (Data extracted **bit.ly/1mw56xA**.)

a. At the 0.05 level of significance, is there evidence of a difference in the mean U.S. mean sales per unit ($ thousands) among the food segments?

b. At the 0.05 level of significance, is there a difference in the variation in U.S. average sales per unit ($ thousands) among the food segments?

c. What effect does your result in (b) have on the validity of the results in (a)?

10.62 Researchers conducted a study to determine whether graduates with an academic background in the discipline of leadership studies were better equipped with essential soft skills required to be successful in contemporary organizations than students with no leadership education and/or students with a certificate in leadership. The Teams Skills Questionnaire was used to capture students' self-reported ratings of their soft skills. The researchers found the following:

Source	Degrees of Freedom	Sum of Squares	Mean Squares	F
Among groups	2	1.879		
Within groups	297	31.865		
Total	299	33.744		

Group	N	Mean
No coursework in leadership	109	3.290
Certificate in leadership	90	3.362
Degree in leadership	102	3.471

Source: Data Extracted from C. Brungardt, "The Intersection Between Soft Skill Development and Leadership Education," *Journal of Leadership Education*, 10 (Winter 2011): 1–22.

a. Complete the ANOVA summary table.
b. At the 0.05 level of significance, is there evidence of a difference in the mean soft-skill score reported by different groups?
c. If the results in (b) indicate that it is appropriate, use the Tukey-Kramer procedure to determine which groups differ in mean soft-skill score. Discuss your findings.

10.63 A pet food company has a business objective of expanding its product line beyond its current kidney- and shrimp-based cat foods. The company developed two new products, one based on chicken liver and the other based on salmon. The company conducted an experiment to compare the two new products with its two existing ones, as well as a generic beef-based product sold at a supermarket chain.

For the experiment, a sample of 50 cats from the population at a local animal shelter was selected. Ten cats were randomly assigned to each of the five products being tested. Each of the cats was then presented with 3 ounces of the selected food in a dish at feeding time. The researchers defined the variable to be measured as the number of ounces of food that the cat consumed within a 10-minute time interval that began when the filled dish was presented. The results for this experiment are summarized in the table at top right and stored in `CatFood`.
a. At the 0.05 level of significance, is there evidence of a difference in the mean amount of food eaten among the various products?
b. If appropriate, determine which products appear to differ significantly in the mean amount of food eaten.
c. At the 0.05 level of significance, is there evidence of a difference in the variation in the amount of food eaten among the various products?
d. What should the pet food company conclude? Fully describe the pet food company's options with respect to the products.

Kidney	Shrimp	Chicken Liver	Salmon	Beef
2.37	2.26	2.29	1.79	2.09
2.62	2.69	2.23	2.33	1.87
2.31	2.25	2.41	1.96	1.67
2.47	2.45	2.68	2.05	1.64
2.59	2.34	2.25	2.26	2.16
2.62	2.37	2.17	2.24	1.75
2.34	2.22	2.37	1.96	1.18
2.47	2.56	2.26	1.58	1.92
2.45	2.36	2.45	2.18	1.32
2.32	2.59	2.57	1.93	1.94

10.64 A sporting goods manufacturing company wanted to compare the distance traveled by golf balls produced using four different designs. Ten balls were manufactured with each design and were brought to the local golf course for the club professional to test. The order in which the balls were hit with the same club from the first tee was randomized so that the pro did not know which type of ball was being hit. All 40 balls were hit in a short period of time, during which the environmental conditions were essentially the same. The results (distance traveled in yards) for the four designs are stored in `Golfball` and shown in the following table:

Design 1	Design 2	Design 3	Design 4
206.32	217.08	226.77	230.55
207.94	221.43	224.79	227.95
206.19	218.04	229.75	231.84
204.45	224.13	228.51	224.87
209.65	211.82	221.44	229.49
203.81	213.90	223.85	231.10
206.75	221.28	223.97	221.53
205.68	229.43	234.30	235.45
204.49	213.54	219.50	228.35
210.86	214.51	233.00	225.09

a. At the 0.05 level of significance, is there evidence of a difference in the mean distances traveled by the golf balls with different designs?
b. If the results in (a) indicate that it is appropriate to do so, use the Tukey-Kramer procedure to determine which designs differ in mean distances.
c. What assumptions are necessary in (a)?
d. At the 0.05 level of significance, is there evidence of a difference in the variation of the distances traveled by the golf balls with different designs?
e. What golf ball design should the manufacturing manager choose? Explain.

10.6 Effect Size

Section 9.5 discusses the issue of the practical significance of a statistically significant test and explains that when a very large sample is selected, a statistically significant result can be of limited importance. The **Section 10.6 online topic** shows how to measure the effect size of a statistical test.

USING STATISTICS

For North Fork, Are There Different Means to the Ends? Revisited

In the North Fork Beverages scenario, you were a regional sales manager for North Fork Beverages. You compared the sales volume of your new HandMade Citrus Cola when the product was featured in the beverage aisle end-cap to the sales volume when the product was featured in the end-cap by the produce department. An experiment was performed in which 10 stores used the beverage end-cap location and 10 stores used the produce end-cap location. Using a *t* test for the difference between two means, you were able to conclude that the mean sales using the produce end-cap location are higher than the mean sales for the beverage end-cap location. A confidence interval allowed you to infer with 95% confidence that population mean amount sold at the produce

end-cap location was between 6.73 and 36.67 cases more than the beverage end-cap location. You also performed the *F* test for the difference between two variances to see if the store-to-store variability in sales in stores using the produce end-cap location differed from the store-to-store variability in sales in stores using the beverage end-cap location. You concluded that there was no significant difference in the variability of the sales of cola for the two display locations. As a regional sales manager, you decide to lease the produce end-cap location in all FoodPlace Supermarkets during your next sales promotional period.

SUMMARY

In this chapter, you were introduced to a variety of tests for two or more samples. For situations in which the samples are independent, you learned statistical test procedures for analyzing possible differences between means, proportions, and variances. In addition, you learned a test procedure that is frequently used when analyzing differences between the means of two related samples. Remember that you need to select the test that is most appropriate for a given set of conditions and to critically investigate the validity of the assumptions underlying each of the hypothesis-testing procedures.

Table 10.12 provides a list of topics covered in this chapter. The roadmap in Figure 10.22 illustrates the steps needed in determining which two-sample test of hypothesis to use. The following are the questions you need to consider:

1. What type of variables do you have? If you are dealing with categorical variables, use the *Z* test for the difference between two proportions. (This test assumes independent samples.)

2. If you have a numerical variable, determine whether you have independent samples or related samples. If you have related samples, and you can assume approximate normality, use the paired *t* test.

3. If you have independent samples, is your focus on variability or central tendency? If the focus is on variability, and you can assume approximate normality, use the *F* test.

4. If your focus is central tendency and you can assume approximate normality, determine whether you can assume that the variances of the two populations are equal. (This assumption can be tested using the *F* test.)

5. If you can assume that the two populations have equal variances, use the pooled-variance *t* test. If you cannot assume that the two populations have equal variances, use the separate-variance *t* test.

6. If you have more than two independent samples, you can use the one-way ANOVA.)

TABLE 10.12

Summary of Topics in Chapter 10

TYPE OF ANALYSIS	TYPES OF DATA	
	Numerical	**Categorical**
Compare two populations	*t* tests for the difference in the means of two independent populations (Section 10.1)	*Z* test for the difference between two proportions (Section 10.3)
	Paired *t* test (Section 10.2)	
	F test for the difference between two variances (Section 10.4)	
Compare more than two populations	One-way ANOVA (Section 10.5)	

FIGURE 10.22

Roadmap for selecting
a test of hypothesis for
two or more samples

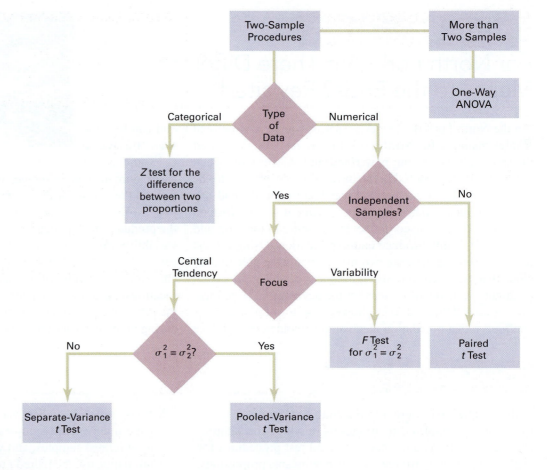

REFERENCES

1. Conover, W. J. *Practical Nonparametric Statistics*, 3rd ed. New York: Wiley, 2000.

2. Daniel, W. *Applied Nonparametric Statistics*, 2nd ed. Boston: Houghton Mifflin, 1990.

3. Hicks, C. R., and K. V. *Turner. Fundamental Concepts in the Design of Experiments,* 5th ed. New York: Oxford University Press, 1999.

4. Kutner, M. H., J. Neter, C. Nachtsheim, and W. Li. *Applied Linear Statistical Models,* 5th ed. New York: McGraw-Hill-Irwin, 2005.

5. Levine, D. M. *Statistics for Six Sigma Green Belts*. Upper Saddle River, NJ: Financial Times/Prentice Hall, 2006.

6. *Microsoft Excel 2013*. Redmond, WA: Microsoft Corp., 2012.

7. *Minitab Release 16* State College, PA: Minitab, 2010.

8. Montgomery, D. M. *Design and Analysis of Experiments*, 6th ed. New York: Wiley, 2005.

9. Satterthwaite, F. E. "An Approximate Distribution of Estimates of Variance Components." *Biometrics Bulletin*, 2(1946): 110–114.

10. Snedecor, G. W., and W. G. Cochran. *Statistical Methods*, 8th ed. Ames, IA: Iowa State University Press, 1989.

KEY EQUATIONS

Pooled-Variance *t* Test for the Difference Between Two Means

$$t_{STAT} = \frac{(\overline{X}_1 - \overline{X}_2) - (\mu_1 - \mu_2)}{\sqrt{S_p^2 \left(\frac{1}{n_1} + \frac{1}{n_2}\right)}} \tag{10.1}$$

Confidence Interval Estimate for the Difference Between the Means of Two Independent Populations

$$(\overline{X}_1 - \overline{X}_2) \pm t_{\alpha/2} \sqrt{S_p^2 \left(\frac{1}{n_1} + \frac{1}{n_2}\right)} \tag{10.2}$$

or

$$(\overline{X}_1 - \overline{X}_2) - t_{\alpha/2}\sqrt{S_p^2\left(\frac{1}{n_1} + \frac{1}{n_2}\right)} \le \mu_1 - \mu_2$$
$$\le (\overline{X}_1 - \overline{X}_2) + t_{\alpha/2}\sqrt{S_p^2\left(\frac{1}{n_1} + \frac{1}{n_2}\right)}$$

Paired *t* Test for the Mean Difference

$$t_{STAT} = \frac{\overline{D} - \mu_D}{\frac{S_D}{\sqrt{n}}} \tag{10.3}$$

Confidence Interval Estimate for the Mean Difference

$$\overline{D} \pm t_{\alpha/2}\frac{S_D}{\sqrt{n}} \tag{10.4}$$

or

$$\overline{D} - t_{\alpha/2}\frac{S_D}{\sqrt{n}} \le \mu_D \le \overline{D} + t_{\alpha/2}\frac{S_D}{\sqrt{n}}$$

Z Test for the Difference Between Two Proportions

$$Z_{STAT} = \frac{(p_1 - p_2) - (\pi_1 - \pi_2)}{\sqrt{\overline{p}(1 - \overline{p})\left(\frac{1}{n_1} + \frac{1}{n_2}\right)}} \tag{10.5}$$

Confidence Interval Estimate for the Difference Between Two Proportions

$$(p_1 - p_2) \pm Z_{\alpha/2}\sqrt{\left(\frac{p_1(1 - p_1)}{n_1} + \frac{p_2(1 - p_2)}{n_2}\right)} \tag{10.6}$$

or

$$(p_1 - p_2) - Z_{\alpha/2}\sqrt{\frac{p_1(1 - p_1)}{n_1} + \frac{p_2(1 - p_2)}{n_2}} \le (\pi_1 - \pi_2)$$

$$\le (p_1 - p_2) + Z_{\alpha/2}\sqrt{\frac{p_1(1 - p_1)}{n_1} + \frac{p_2(1 - p_2)}{n_2}}$$

F Test Statistic for Testing the Ratio of Two Variances

$$F_{STAT} = \frac{S_1^2}{S_2^2} \tag{10.7}$$

Total Variation in One-Way ANOVA

$$SST = \sum_{j=1}^{c}\sum_{i=1}^{n_j}(X_{ij} - \overline{\overline{X}})^2 \tag{10.8}$$

Among-Group Variation in One-Way ANOVA

$$SSA = \sum_{j=1}^{c}n_j(\overline{X}_j - \overline{\overline{X}})^2 \tag{10.9}$$

Within-Group Variation in One-Way ANOVA

$$SSW = \sum_{j=1}^{c}\sum_{i=1}^{n_j}(X_{ij} - \overline{X}_j)^2 \tag{10.10}$$

Mean Squares in One-Way ANOVA

$$MSA = \frac{SSA}{c - 1} \tag{10.11a}$$

$$MSW = \frac{SSW}{n - c} \tag{10.11b}$$

$$MST = \frac{SST}{n - 1} \tag{10.11c}$$

One-Way ANOVA F_{STAT} Test Statistic

$$F_{STAT} = \frac{MSA}{MSW} \tag{10.12}$$

Critical Range for the Tukey-Kramer Procedure

$$\text{Critical range} = Q_\alpha\sqrt{\frac{MSW}{2}\left(\frac{1}{n_j} + \frac{1}{n_{j'}}\right)} \tag{10.13}$$

KEY TERMS

CHECKING YOUR UNDERSTANDING

10.65 What are some of the criteria used in the selection of a particular hypothesis-testing procedure?

10.66 Under what conditions should you use the pooled-variance *t* test to examine possible differences in the means of two independent populations?

10.67 Under what conditions should you use the *F* test to examine possible differences in the variances of two independent populations?

10.68 What is the distinction between two independent populations and two related populations?

10.69 What is the distinction between repeated measurements and matched items?

10.70 When you have two independent populations, explain the similarities and differences between the test of hypothesis for the difference between the means and the confidence interval estimate for the difference between the means.

10.71 Under what conditions should you use the paired *t* test for the mean difference between two related populations?

10.72 In a one-way ANOVA, what is the difference between the among-groups variance *MSA* and the within-groups variance *MSW*?

10.73 What are the assumptions of ANOVA?

10.74 Under what conditions should you use the one-way ANOVA *F* test to examine possible differences among the means of *c* independent populations?

10.75 What is the difference between the one-way ANOVA *F* test and the Levene test?

CHAPTER REVIEW PROBLEMS

10.76 The American Society for Quality (ASQ) conducted a salary survey of all its members. ASQ members work in all areas of manufacturing and service-related institutions, with a common theme of an interest in quality. Two job titles are black belt and green belt. (See Section 14.6 for a description of these titles in a Six Sigma quality improvement initiative.) Descriptive statistics concerning salaries for these two job titles are given in the following table:

Job Title	Sample Size	Mean	Standard Deviation
Black belt	128	93,123	21,186
Green belt	39	73,045	21,272

Source: Data extracted from "QP Salary Survey," *Quality Progress*, December 2013, p. 17.

a. Using a 0.05 level of significance, is there a difference in the variability of salaries between black belts and green belts?
b. Based on the result of (a), which *t* test defined in Section 10.1 is appropriate for comparing mean salaries?
c. Using a 0.05 level of significance, is the mean salary of black belts greater than the mean salary of green belts?

10.77 Do male and female students study the same amount per week? In a recent year, 58 sophomore business students were surveyed at a large university that has more than 1,000 sophomore business students each year. The file **StudyTime** contains the gender and the number of hours spent studying in a typical week for the sampled students.
a. At the 0.05 level of significance, is there a difference in the variance of the study time for male students and female students?
b. Using the results of (a), which *t* test is appropriate for comparing the mean study time for male and female students?

c. At the 0.05 level of significance, conduct the test selected in (b).
d. Write a short summary of your findings.

10.78 Do males and females differ in the amount of time they talk on the phone and the number of text messages they send? A study reported that women spent a mean of 818 minutes per month talking as compared to 716 minutes per month for men. (Data extracted from "Women Talk and Text More," *USA Today*, February 1, 2011, p. 1A.) The sample sizes were not reported. Suppose that the sample sizes were 100 each for women and men and that the standard deviation for women was 125 minutes per month as compared to 100 minutes per month for men.
a. Using a 0.01 level of significance, is there evidence of a difference in the variances of the amount of time spent talking between women and men?
b. To test for a difference in the mean talking time of women and men, is it most appropriate to use the pooled-variance *t* test or the separate-variance *t* test? Use the most appropriate test to determine if there is a difference in the amount of time spent talking on the phone between women and men.

The article also reported that women sent a mean of 716 text messages per month compared to 555 per month for men. Suppose that the standard deviation for women was 150 text messages per month compared to 125 text messages per month for men.
c. Using a 0.01 level of significance, is there evidence of a difference in the variances of the number of text messages sent per month by women and men?
d. Based on the results of (c), use the most appropriate test to determine, at the 0.01 level of significance, whether there is evidence of a difference in the mean number of text messages sent per month by women and men.

10.79 The file **Restaurants** contains the ratings for food, décor, service, and the price per person for a sample of 50 restaurants located in a city and 50 restaurants located in a suburb. Completely analyze the differences between city and suburban restaurants for the variables food rating, décor rating, service rating, and cost per person, using $\alpha = 0.05$.

Source: Data extracted from *Zagat Survey 2013 New York City Restaurants* and *Zagat Survey 2012–2013 Long Island Restaurants*.

10.80 A computer information systems professor is interested in studying the amount of time it takes students enrolled in the Introduction to Computers course to write a program in VB.NET. The professor hires you to analyze the following results (in minutes), stored in **VB**, from a random sample of nine students:

10 13 9 15 12 13 11 13 12

a. At the 0.05 level of significance, is there evidence that the population mean time is greater than 10 minutes? What will you tell the professor?
b. Suppose that the professor, when checking her results, realizes that the fourth student needed 51 minutes rather than the recorded 15 minutes to write the VB.NET program. At the 0.05 level of significance, reanalyze the question posed in (a), using the revised data. What will you tell the professor now?
c. The professor is perplexed by these paradoxical results and requests an explanation from you regarding the justification for the difference in your findings in (a) and (b). Discuss.
d. A few days later, the professor calls to tell you that the dilemma is completely resolved. The original number 15 (the fourth data value) was correct, and therefore your findings in (a) are being used in the article she is writing for a computer journal. Now she wants to hire you to compare the results from that group of Introduction to Computers students against those from a sample of 11 computer majors in order to determine whether there is evidence that computer majors can write a VB.NET program in less time than introductory students. For the computer majors, the sample mean is 8.5 minutes, and the sample standard deviation is 2.0 minutes. At the 0.05 level of significance, completely analyze these data. What will you tell the professor?
e. A few days later, the professor calls again to tell you that a reviewer of her article wants her to include the *p*-value for the "correct" result in (a). In addition, the professor inquires about an unequal-variances problem, which the reviewer wants her to discuss in her article. In your own words, discuss the concept of *p*-value and also describe the unequal-variances problem. Then, determine the *p*-value in (a) and discuss whether the unequal-variances problem had any meaning in the professor's study.

10.81 Do Pinterest shoppers and Facebook shoppers differ with respect to spending behavior? A study of browser-based shopping sessions reported that Pinterest shoppers spent a mean of $153 per order and Facebook shoppers spent a mean of $85 per order. (Data extracted from **bit.ly/14wG1YI**.) Suppose that the study consisted of 500 Pinterest shoppers and 500 Facebook shoppers, and the standard deviation of the order value was $150 for Pinterest shoppers and $80 for Facebook shoppers. Assume a level of significance of 0.05.
a. Is there evidence of a difference in the variances of the order values between Pinterest shoppers and Facebook shoppers?
b. Is there evidence of a difference in the mean order value between Pinterest shoppers and Facebook shoppers?
c. Construct a 95% confidence interval estimate for the difference in mean order value between Pinterest shoppers and Facebook shoppers.

10.82 The lengths of life (in hours) of a sample of 40 20-watt compact fluorescent light bulbs produced by manufacturer A and a sample of 40 20-watt compact fluorescent light bulbs produced by manufacturer B are stored in **Bulbs**. Completely analyze the differences between the lengths of life of the compact fluorescent light bulbs produced by the two manufacturers. (Use $\alpha = 0.05$.)

10.83 A hotel manager looks to enhance the initial impressions that hotel guests have when they check in. Contributing to initial impressions is the time it takes to deliver a guest's luggage to the room after check-in. A random sample of 20 deliveries on a particular day were selected in Wing A of the hotel, and a random sample of 20 deliveries were selected in Wing B. The results are stored in **Luggage**. Analyze the data and determine whether there is a difference between the mean delivery times in the two wings of the hotel. (Use $\alpha = 0.05$.)

10.84 The owner of a restaurant that serves Continental-style entrées has the business objective of learning more about the patterns of patron demand during the Friday-to-Sunday weekend time period. She decided to study the demand for dessert during this time period. In addition to studying whether a dessert was ordered, she will study the gender of the individual and whether a beef entrée was ordered. Data were collected from 630 customers and organized in the following contingency tables:

	GENDER		
DESSERT ORDERED	**Male**	**Female**	**Total**
Yes	50	96	146
No	250	234	484
Total	300	330	630

	BEEF ENTRÉE		
DESSERT ORDERED	**Yes**	**No**	**Total**
Yes	74	68	142
No	123	365	488
Total	197	433	630

a. At the 0.05 level of significance, is there evidence of a difference between males and females in the proportion who order dessert?
b. At the 0.05 level of significance, is there evidence of a difference in the proportion who order dessert based on whether a beef entrée has been ordered?

10.85 The manufacturer of Boston and Vermont asphalt shingles knows that product weight is a major factor in the customer's perception of quality. Moreover, the weight represents the amount of raw materials being used and is therefore very important to the company from a cost standpoint. The last stage of the assembly line packages the shingles before they are placed on wooden pallets. Once a pallet is full (a pallet for most brands holds 16 squares of shingles), it is weighed, and the measurement is recorded. The file **Pallet** contains the weight (in pounds) from a sample of 368 pallets of Boston shingles and 330 pallets of Vermont shingles. Completely analyze the differences in the weights of the Boston and Vermont shingles, using $\alpha = 0.05$.

10.86 The manufacturer of Boston and Vermont asphalt shingles provides its customers with a 20-year warranty on most of its products. To determine whether a shingle will last as long as the warranty period, the manufacturer conducts accelerated-life testing. Accelerated-life testing exposes the shingle to the stresses it would be subject to in a lifetime of normal use in a laboratory setting via an experiment that takes only a few minutes to conduct. In this test, a shingle is repeatedly scraped with a brush for a short period of time, and the shingle granules removed by the brushing are weighed (in grams). Shingles that experience low amounts of granule loss are expected to last longer in normal use than shingles that experience high amounts of granule loss. In this situation, a shingle should experience no more than 0.8 grams of granule loss if it is expected to last the length of the warranty period. The file Granule contains a sample of 170 measurements made on the company's Boston shingles and 140 measurements made on Vermont shingles. Completely analyze the differences in the granule loss of the Boston and Vermont shingles, using $\alpha = 0.05$.

10.87 There are a very large number of mutual funds from which an investor can choose. Each mutual fund has its own mix of different types of investments. The data in BestFunds1 present the one-year return for the 10 best short-term bond funds and the 10 best long-term bond funds, according to the *U.S. News & World Report*. (Data extracted from **money.usnews.com/mutual-funds**.) Analyze the data and determine whether any differences exist between short-term and long-term bond funds. (Use the 0.05 level of significance.)

10.88 An investor can choose from a very large number of mutual funds. Each mutual fund has its own mix of different types of investments. The data in BestFunds2 present the one-year return for the 10 best short-term bond, long-term bond, and world bond funds, according to the *U.S. News & World Report*. (Data extracted from **money.usnews.com/mutual-funds**.) Analyze the data and determine whether any differences exist in the one-year return between short-term, long-term, and world bond funds. (Use the 0.05 level of significance.)

10.89 An investor can choose from a very large number of mutual funds. Each mutual fund has its own mix of different types of investments. The data in BestFunds3 present the one-year return for the 10 best small cap growth, mid-cap growth, and large cap growth funds, according to the *U.S. News & World Report*. (Data extracted from **money.usnews.com/mutual-funds**.) Analyze the data and determine whether any differences exist in the one-year return between small cap growth, mid-cap growth, and large cap growth funds. (Use the 0.05 level of significance.)

REPORT WRITING EXERCISE

10.90 Referring to the results of Problems 10.85 and 10.86 concerning the weight and granule loss of Boston and Vermont shingles, write a report that summarizes your conclusions.

CASES FOR CHAPTER 10

Managing Ashland MultiComm Services

Part 1 AMS communicates with customers who subscribe to cable television services through a special secured email system that sends messages about service changes, new features, and billing information to in-home digital set-top boxes for later display. To enhance customer service, the operations department established the business objective of reducing the amount of time to fully update each subscriber's set of messages. The department selected two candidate messaging systems and conducted an experiment in which 30 randomly chosen cable subscribers were assigned one of the two systems (15 assigned to each system). Update times were measured, and the results are organized in Table AMS10.1 and stored in AMS10-1.

1. Analyze the data in Table AMS10.1 and write a report to the computer operations department that indicates your findings. Include an appendix in which you discuss the reason you selected a particular statistical test to compare the two independent groups of callers.

TABLE AMS10.1

Update Times (in seconds) for Two Different Email Interfaces

Email Interface 1	Email Interface 2
4.13	3.71
3.75	3.89
3.93	4.22
3.74	4.57
3.36	4.24
3.85	3.90
3.26	4.09
3.73	4.05
4.06	4.07
3.33	3.80
3.96	4.36
3.57	4.38
3.13	3.49
3.68	3.57
3.63	4.74

2. Suppose that instead of the research design described in the case, there were only 15 subscribers sampled, and the update process for each subscriber email was measured for each of the two messaging systems. Suppose that the results were organized in Table AMS10.1—making each row in the table a pair of values for an individual subscriber. Using these suppositions, reanalyze the Table AMS10.1 data and write a report for presentation to the team that indicates your findings.

Part 2 The computer operations department had a business objective of reducing the amount of time to fully update each subscriber's set of messages in a special secured email system. An experiment was conducted in which 24 subscribers were selected and three different messaging systems were used. Eight subscribers were assigned to each system, and the update times were measured. The results, stored in **AMS10-2**, are presented in Table AMS10.2.

TABLE AMS10.2

Update Times (in seconds) for Three Different Systems

System 1	System 2	System 3
38.8	41.8	32.9
42.1	36.4	36.1
45.2	39.1	39.2
34.8	28.7	29.3
48.3	36.4	41.9
37.8	36.1	31.7
41.1	35.8	35.2
43.6	33.7	38.1

3. Analyze the data in Table AMS10.2 and write a report to the computer operations department that indicates your findings. Include an appendix in which you discuss the reason you selected a particular statistical test to compare the three email interfaces.

Digital Case

Apply your knowledge about hypothesis testing in this Digital Case, which continues the cereal-fill packaging dispute Digital Case from Chapters 7 and 9.

Part 1 Even after the recent public experiment about cereal box weights, Consumers Concerned About Cereal Cheaters (CCACC) remains convinced that Oxford Cereals has misled the public. The group has created and circulated **MoreCheating.pdf**, a document in which it claims that cereal boxes produced at Plant Number 2 in Springville weigh less than the claimed mean of 368 grams. Review this document and then answer the following questions:

1. Do the CCACC's results prove that there is a statistically significant difference in the mean weights of cereal boxes produced at Plant Numbers 1 and 2?

2. Perform the appropriate analysis to test the CCACC's hypothesis. What conclusions can you reach based on the data?

Part 2 *Apply your knowledge about ANOVA in this part, which continues the cereal-fill packaging dispute Digital Case.*

After reviewing the CCACC's **MoreCheating.pdf** document, Oxford Cereals has released **SecondAnalysis.pdf**, a press kit that Oxford Cereals has assembled to refute the claim that it is guilty of using selective data. Review the Oxford Cereals press kit and then answer the following questions.

3. Does Oxford Cereals have a legitimate argument? Why or why not?

4. Assuming that the samples Oxford Cereals has posted were randomly selected, perform the appropriate analysis to resolve the ongoing weight dispute.

5. What conclusions can you reach from your results? If you were called as an expert witness, would you support the claims of the CCACC or the claims of Oxford Cereals? Explain.

Sure Value Convenience Stores

Part 1 You continue to work in the corporate office for a nationwide convenience store franchise that operates nearly 10,000 stores. The per-store daily customer count (i.e., the mean number of customers in a store in one day) has been steady, at 900, for some time. To increase the customer count, the chain is considering cutting prices for coffee beverages. The small size will now be either $0.59 or $0.79

instead of $0.99. Even with this reduction in price, the chain will have a 40% gross margin on coffee.

The question to be determined is how much to cut prices to increase the daily customer count without reducing the gross margin on coffee sales too much. The chain decides to carry out an experiment in a sample of 30 stores where customer counts have been running almost exactly at the national average of 900. In 15 of the stores, the price of a small coffee will now be $0.59 instead of $0.99, and in 15 other stores, the price of a small coffee will now be $0.79. After four weeks, the 15 stores that priced the small coffee at $0.59 had a mean daily customer count of 964 and a standard deviation of 88, and the 15 stores that priced the small coffee at $0.79 had a mean daily customer count of 941 and a standard deviation of 76. Analyze these data (using the 0.05 level of significance) and answer the following questions.

1. Does reducing the price of a small coffee to either $0.59 or $0.79 increase the mean per-store daily customer count?

2. If reducing the price of a small coffee to either $0.59 or $0.79 increases the mean per-store daily customer count, is there any difference in the mean per-store daily customer count between stores in which a small coffee was priced at $0.59 and stores in which a small coffee was priced at $0.79?

3. What price do you recommend for a small coffee?

Part 2 As you continue to work in the corporate office for a nationwide convenience store franchise that operates nearly 10,000 stores, you decide to carry out an experiment in a sample of 24 stores where customer counts have been running almost exactly at the national average of 900. In 6 of the stores, the price of a small coffee will now be $0.59, in 6 stores the price of a small coffee will now be $0.69, in 6 stores the price of a small coffee will now be $0.79, and in 6 stores, the price of a small coffee will now be $0.89. After four weeks of selling the coffee at the new price, the daily customer counts in the stores were recorded and stored in **CoffeeSales**.

4. Analyze the data and determine whether there is evidence of a difference in the daily customer count, based on the price of a small coffee.

5. If appropriate, determine which mean prices differ in daily customer counts.

6. What price do you recommend for a small coffee?

CardioGood Fitness

Return to the CardioGood Fitness case first presented on page 25. Using the data stored in **CardioGood Fitness**:

1. Determine whether differences exist between males and females in their age in years, education in years, annual household income ($), mean number of times the customer plans to use the treadmill each week, and mean number of miles the customer expects to walk or run each week.

2. Determine whether differences exist between customers based on the product purchased (TM195, TM498, TM798) in their age in years, education in years, annual household income ($), mean number of times the customer plans to use the treadmill each week, and mean number of miles the customer expects to walk or run each week.

3. Write a report to be presented to the management of CardioGood Fitness detailing your findings.

More Descriptive Choices Follow-Up

Follow up the Using Statistics scenario "More Descriptive Choices, Revisited" on page 136.

1. Determine whether there is a difference in the 3-year return percentage, 5-year return percentages, and 10-year return percentages of the growth and value funds (stored in **Retirement Funds**).

2. Determine whether there is a difference between the small, mid-cap, and large market cap funds in the three-year return percentages, five-year return percentages, and ten-year return percentages (stored in **Retirement Funds**).

Clear Mountain State Student Surveys

1. The Student News Service at Clear Mountain State University (CMSU) has decided to gather data about the undergraduate students that attend CMSU. It creates and distributes a survey of 14 questions and receives responses from 62 undergraduates (stored in **UndergradSurvey**).

a. At the 0.05 level of significance, is there evidence of a difference between males and females in grade point average, expected starting salary, number of social networking sites registered for, age, spending on textbooks and supplies, text messages sent in a week, and the wealth needed to feel rich?

b. At the 0.05 level of significance, is there evidence of a difference between students who plan to go to graduate school and those who do not plan to go to graduate school in grade point average, expected starting salary, number of social networking sites registered for, age, spending on textbooks and supplies, text messages sent in a week, and the wealth needed to feel rich?

c. At the 0.05 level of significance, is there evidence of a difference based on academic major in expected starting salary, number of social networking sites registered for, age, spending on textbooks and supplies, text messages sent in a week, and the wealth needed to feel rich?

d. At the 0.05 level of significance, is there evidence of a difference based on graduate school intention in grade point average, expected starting salary, number of social networking sites registered for, age, spending on textbooks and supplies, text messages sent in a week, and the wealth needed to feel rich?

2. The dean of students at CMSU has learned about the undergraduate survey and has decided to undertake a similar survey for graduate students at Clear Mountain State. She creates and distributes a survey of 14 questions and receives responses from 44 graduate students (stored in GradSurvey). For these data, at the 0.05 level of significance.

a. Is there evidence of a difference between males and females in age, undergraduate grade point average, graduate grade point average, expected salary upon graduation, spending on textbooks and supplies, text messages sent in a week, and the wealth needed to feel rich?

b. Is there evidence of a difference based on undergraduate major in age, undergraduate grade point average, graduate grade point average, expected salary upon graduation, spending on textbooks and supplies, text messages sent in a week, and the wealth needed to feel rich?

c. Is there evidence of a difference based on graduate major in age, undergraduate grade point average, graduate grade point average, expected salary upon graduation, spending on textbooks and supplies, text messages sent in a week, and the wealth needed to feel rich?

d. Is there evidence of a difference based on employment status in age, undergraduate grade point average, graduate grade point average, expected salary upon graduation, spending on textbooks and supplies, text messages sent in a week, and the wealth needed to feel rich?

CHAPTER 10 EXCEL GUIDE

EG10.1 COMPARING the MEANS of TWO INDEPENDENT POPULATIONS

Pooled-Variance *t* Test for the Difference Between Two Means

Key Technique Use the **T.INV.2T**(*level of significance, degrees of freedom*) function to compute the lower and upper critical values and use the **T.DIST.2T**(*absolute value of the t test statistic, degrees of freedom*) to compute the *p*-value.

Example Perform the Figure 10.3 pooled-variance *t* test for the two end-cap locations data shown on page 326.

PHStat Use **Pooled-Variance t Test**.

For the example, open to the **DATA worksheet** of the **Cola workbook**. Select **PHStat → Two-Sample Tests (Unsummarized Data) → Pooled-Variance t Test**. In the procedure's dialog box (shown below):

1. Enter **0** as the **Hypothesized Difference**.
2. Enter **0.05** as the **Level of Significance**.
3. Enter **A1:A11** as the **Population 1 Sample Cell Range**.
4. Enter **B1:B11** as the **Population 2 Sample Cell Range**.
5. Check **First cells in both ranges contain label**.
6. Click **Two-Tail Test**.
7. Enter a **Title** and click **OK**.

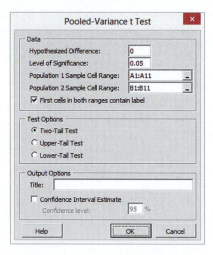

When using summarized data, select **PHStat → Two-Sample Tests (Summarized Data) → Pooled-Variance t Test**. In that procedure's dialog box, enter the hypothesized difference and level of significance, as well as the sample size, sample mean, and sample standard deviation for each sample.

In-Depth Excel Use the **COMPUTE worksheet** of the **Pooled-Variance T workbook** as a template.

The worksheet already contains the data and formulas to use the unsummarized data for the example. For other problems, use this worksheet with either unsummarized or summarized data. For unsummarized data, paste the data in columns A and B in the **DATACOPY worksheet** and keep the COMPUTE worksheet formulas that compute the sample size, sample mean, and sample standard deviation in the cell range B7:B13. For summarized data, replace the formulas in the cell range B7:B13 with the sample statistics and ignore the DATACOPY worksheet.

Use the **COMPUTE_LOWER** or **COMPUTE_UPPER** worksheets in the same workbook as templates for performing one-tail pooled-variance *t* tests with either unsummarized or summarized data. If you use an Excel version older than Excel 2010, use the COMPUTE_OLDER worksheet as a template for both the two-tail and one-tail tests.

Analysis ToolPak Use **t-Test: Two-Sample Assuming Equal Variances**.

For the example, open to the **DATA worksheet** of the **Cola workbook** and:

1. Select **Data → Data Analysis**.
2. In the Data Analysis dialog box, select **t-Test: Two-Sample Assuming Equal Variances** from the **Analysis Tools** list and then click **OK**.

In the procedure's dialog box (shown below):

3. Enter **A1:A11** as the **Variable 1 Range**.
4. Enter **B1:B11** as the **Variable 2 Range**.
5. Enter **0** as the **Hypothesized Mean Difference**.
6. Check **Labels** and enter **0.05** as **Alpha**.
7. Click **New Worksheet Ply**.
8. Click **OK**.

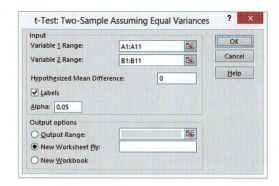

Results (shown below) appear in a new worksheet that contains both two-tail and one-tail test critical values and *p*-values. Unlike the results shown in Figure 10.3, only the positive (upper) critical value is listed for the two-tail test.

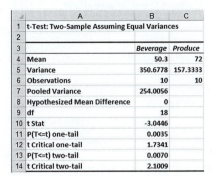

	A	B	C
1	t-Test: Two-Sample Assuming Equal Variances		
2			
3		Beverage	Produce
4	Mean	50.3	72
5	Variance	350.6778	157.3333
6	Observations	10	10
7	Pooled Variance	254.0056	
8	Hypothesized Mean Difference	0	
9	df	18	
10	t Stat	-3.0446	
11	P(T<=t) one-tail	0.0035	
12	t Critical one-tail	1.7341	
13	P(T<=t) two-tail	0.0070	
14	t Critical two-tail	2.1009	

Confidence Interval Estimate for the Difference Between Two Means

PHStat Modify the *PHStat* instructions for the pooled-variance *t* test. In step 7, check **Confidence Interval Estimate** and enter a **Confidence Level** in its box, in addition to entering a **Title** and clicking **OK**.

In-Depth Excel Use the *In-Depth Excel* instructions for the pooled-variance *t* test. The Pooled-Variance T workbook worksheets include a confidence interval estimate for the difference between two means in the cell range D3:E16.

t Test for the Difference Between Two Means, Assuming Unequal Variances

Key Technique Use the **T.INV.2T(***level of significance, degrees of freedom***)** function to compute the lower and upper critical values and use the **T.DIST.2T(***absolute value of the t test statistic, degrees of freedom***)** to compute the *p*-value.

Example Perform the Figure 10.6 separate-variance *t* test for the two end-cap locations data shown on page 330.

PHStat Use **Separate-Variance t Test**.
For the example, open to the **DATA worksheet** of the **Cola workbook**. Select **PHStat → Two-Sample Tests (Unsummarized Data) → Separate-Variance t Test**. In the procedure's dialog box (shown in the right column):

1. Enter **0** as the **Hypothesized Difference**.
2. Enter **0.05** as the **Level of Significance**.
3. Enter **A1:A11** as the **Population 1 Sample Cell Range**.
4. Enter **B1:B11** as the **Population 2 Sample Cell Range**.
5. Check **First cells in both ranges contain label**.
6. Click **Two-Tail Test**.
7. Enter a **Title** and click **OK**.

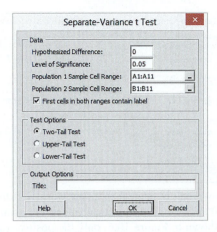

When using summarized data, select **PHStat → Two-Sample Tests (Summarized Data) → Separate-Variance t Test**. In that procedure's dialog box, enter the hypothesized difference and the level of significance, as well as the sample size, sample mean, and sample standard deviation for each group.

In-Depth Excel Use the **COMPUTE worksheet** of the **Separate-Variance T workbook** as a template.
The worksheet already contains the data and formulas to use the unsummarized data for the example. For other problems, use the COMPUTE worksheet with either unsummarized or summarized data. For unsummarized data, paste the data in columns A and B in the **DATACOPY worksheet** and keep the COMPUTE worksheet formulas that compute the sample size, sample mean, and sample standard deviation in the cell range B7:B13. For summarized data, replace those formulas in the cell range B7:B13 with the sample statistics and ignore the DATACOPY worksheet.

Use the **COMPUTE_LOWER** or **COMPUTE_UPPER worksheets** in the same workbook as templates for performing one-tail pooled-variance *t* tests with either unsummarized or summarized data. If you use an Excel version older than Excel 2010, use the COMPUTE_OLDER worksheet as a template for both the two-tail and one-tail tests.

Analysis ToolPak Use **t-Test: Two-Sample Assuming Unequal Variances**.
For the example, open to the **DATA worksheet** of the **Cola workbook** and:

1. Select **Data → Data Analysis**.
2. In the Data Analysis dialog box, select **t-Test: Two-Sample Assuming Unequal Variances** from the **Analysis Tools** list and then click **OK**.

In the procedure's dialog box (shown on page 378):

3. Enter **A1:A11** as the **Variable 1 Range**.
4. Enter **B1:B11** as the **Variable 2 Range**.
5. Enter **0** as the **Hypothesized Mean Difference**.
6. Check **Labels** and enter **0.05** as **Alpha**.
7. Click **New Worksheet Ply**.
8. Click **OK**.

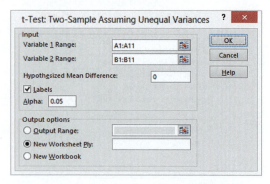

Results (shown below) appear in a new worksheet that contains both two-tail and one-tail test critical values and *p*-values. Unlike the results shown in Figure 10.6, only the positive (upper) critical value is listed for the two-tail test. Because the Analysis ToolPak uses table lookups to approximate the critical values and the *p*-value, the results will differ slightly from the values shown in Figure 10.6.

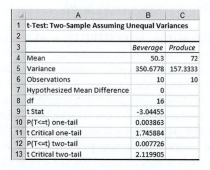

	A	B	C
1	t-Test: Two-Sample Assuming Unequal Variances		
2			
3		*Beverage*	*Produce*
4	Mean	50.3	72
5	Variance	350.6778	157.3333
6	Observations	10	10
7	Hypothesized Mean Difference	0	
8	df	16	
9	t Stat	-3.04455	
10	P(T<=t) one-tail	0.003863	
11	t Critical one-tail	1.745884	
12	P(T<=t) two-tail	0.007726	
13	t Critical two-tail	2.119905	

EG10.2 COMPARING the MEANS of TWO RELATED POPULATIONS

Paired *t* Test

Key Technique Use the **T.INV.2T**(*level of significance, degrees of freedom*) function to compute the lower and upper critical values and use the **T.DIST.2T**(*absolute value of the t test statistic, degrees of freedom*) to compute the *p*-value.

Example Perform the Figure 10.8 paired *t* test for the textbook price data shown on page 337.

PHStat Use **Paired t Test**.
For the example, open to the **DATA worksheet** of the **Book-Prices workbook**. Select **PHStat → Two-Sample Tests (Unsummarized Data) → Paired t Test**. In the procedure's dialog box (shown in the right column):

1. Enter **0** as the **Hypothesized Mean Difference**.
2. Enter **0.05** as the **Level of Significance**.
3. Enter **C1:C17** as the **Population 1 Sample Cell Range**.
4. Enter **D1:D17** as the **Population 2 Sample Cell Range**.
5. Check **First cells in both ranges contain label**.
6. Click **Two-Tail Test**.
7. Enter a **Title** and click **OK**.

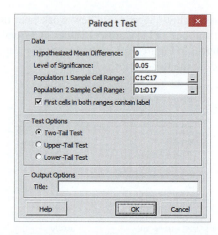

The procedure creates two worksheets, one of which is similar to the PtCalcs worksheet discussed in the following *In-Depth Excel* section. When using summarized data, select **PHStat → Two-Sample Tests (Summarized Data) → Paired t Test**. In that procedure's dialog box, enter the hypothesized mean difference, the level of significance, and the differences cell range.

In-Depth Excel Use the **COMPUTE** and **PtCalcs worksheets** of the **Paired T workbook** as a template.
The COMPUTE and supporting PtCalcs worksheets already contain the textbook price data for the example. The PtCalcs worksheet also computes the differences that allow the COMPUTE worksheet to compute the S_D in cell B11.

For other problems, paste the unsummarized data into columns A and B of the PtCalcs worksheet. For sample sizes greater than 16, select cell C17 and copy the formula in that cell down through the last data row. For sample sizes less than 16, delete the column C formulas for which there are no column A and B values. If you know the sample size, $\overline{D}$, and S_D values, you can ignore the PtCalcs worksheet and enter the values in cells B8, B9, and B11 of the COMPUTE worksheet, overwriting the formulas that those cells contain.

Use the similar **COMPUTE_LOWER** and **COMPUTE_UPPER worksheets** in the same workbook as templates for performing one-tail tests. If you use an Excel version older than Excel 2010, use the COMPUTE_OLDER worksheet as a template for both the two-tail and one-tail tests.

Analysis ToolPak Use **t-Test: Paired Two Sample for Means**. For the example, open to the **DATA worksheet** of the **BookPrices workbook** and:

1. Select **Data → Data Analysis**.
2. In the Data Analysis dialog box, select **t-Test: Paired Two Sample for Means** from the **Analysis Tools** list and then click **OK**.

In the procedure's dialog box (shown on page 379):

3. Enter **C1:C17** as the **Variable 1 Range**.
4. Enter **D1:D17** as the **Variable 2 Range**.
5. Enter **0** as the **Hypothesized Mean Difference**.
6. Check **Labels** and enter **0.05** as **Alpha**.
7. Click **New Worksheet Ply**.
8. Click **OK**.

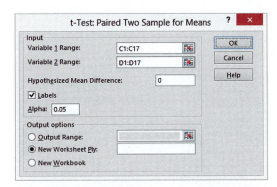

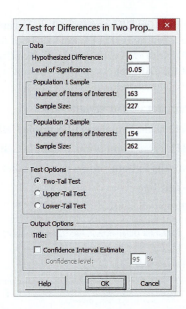

Results (shown below) appear in a new worksheet that contains both two-tail and one-tail test critical values and *p*-values. Unlike in Figure 10.8, only the positive (upper) critical value is listed for the two-tail test.

	A	B	C
1	t-Test: Paired Two Sample for Means		
2			
3		Bookstore	Online
4	Mean	153.6344	111.0331
5	Variance	7913.0962	3594.7263
6	Observations	16	16
7	Pearson Correlation	0.8990	
8	Hypothesized Mean Difference	0	
9	df	15	
10	t Stat	3.8908	
11	P(T<=t) one-tail	0.0007	
12	t Critical one-tail	1.7531	
13	P(T<=t) two-tail	0.0014	
14	t Critical two-tail	2.1314	

EG10.3 COMPARING the PROPORTIONS of TWO INDEPENDENT POPULATIONS

Z Test for the Difference Between Two Proportions

Key Technique Use the **NORM.S.INV** (*percentage*) function to compute the critical values and use the **NORM.S.DIST** (*absolute value of the Z test statistic*, **True**) function to compute the *p*-value.

Example Perform the Figure 10.12 Z test for the hotel guest satisfaction survey shown on page 344.

PHStat Use **Z Test for Differences in Two Proportions**. For the example, select **PHStat → Two-Sample Tests (Summarized Data) → Z Test for Differences in Two Proportions**. In the procedure's dialog box (shown in the right column):

1. Enter **0** as the **Hypothesized Difference**.
2. Enter **0.05** as the **Level of Significance**.
3. For the Population 1 Sample, enter **163** as the **Number of Items of Interest** and **227** as the **Sample Size**.
4. For the Population 2 Sample, enter **154** as the **Number of Items of Interest** and **262** as the **Sample Size**.
5. Click **Two-Tail Test**.
6. Enter a **Title** and click **OK**.

In-Depth Excel Use the **COMPUTE worksheet** of the **Z Two Proportions workbook** as a template.

The worksheet already contains data for the hotel guest satisfaction survey. For other problems, change the hypothesized difference, the level of significance, and the number of items of interest and sample size for each group in the cell range B4:B11.

Use the similar **COMPUTE_LOWER** and **COMPUTE_UPPER worksheets** in the same workbook as templates for performing one-tail Z tests for the difference between two proportions. If you use an Excel version older than Excel 2010, use the COMPUTE_OLDER worksheet as a template for both the two-tail and one-tail tests.

Confidence Interval Estimate for the Difference Between Two Proportions

PHStat Modify the *PHStat* instructions for the Z test for the difference between two proportions. In step 6, also check **Confidence Interval Estimate** and enter a **Confidence Level** in its box, in addition to entering a **Title** and clicking **OK**.

In-Depth Excel Use the *In-Depth Excel* instructions for the Z test for the difference between two proportions. The Z Two Proportions workbook worksheets include a confidence interval estimate for the difference between two means in the cell range D3:E16.

EG10.4 *F* TEST for the RATIO of TWO VARIANCES

Key Technique Use the **F.INV.RT**(*level of significance / 2, population 1 sample degrees of freedom, population 2 sample degrees of freedom*) function to compute the upper critical value and use the **F.DIST.RT**(*F test statistic, population 1 sample degrees of freedom, population 2 sample degrees of freedom*) function to compute the *p*-values.

Example Perform the Figure 10.13 *F* test for the ratio of two variances for the two end-cap locations data shown on page 350.

PHStat Use **F Test for Differences in Two Variances**.
For the example, open to the **DATA worksheet** of the **Cola workbook**. Select **PHStat → Two-Sample Tests (Unsummarized Data) → F Test for Differences in Two Variances**. In the procedure's dialog box (shown below):

1. Enter **0.05** as the **Level of Significance**.
2. Enter **A1:A11** as the **Population 1 Sample Cell Range**.
3. Enter **B1:B11** as the **Population 2 Sample Cell Range**.
4. Check **First cells in both ranges contain label**.
5. Click **Two-Tail Test**.
6. Enter a **Title** and click **OK**.

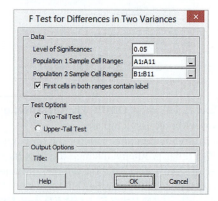

When using summarized data, select **PHStat → Two-Sample Tests (Summarized Data) → F Test for Differences in Two Variances**. In that procedure's dialog box, enter the level of significance and the sample size and sample variance for each sample.

In-Depth Excel Use the **COMPUTE worksheet** of the **F Two Variances workbook** as a template.
The worksheet already contains the data and formulas for using the unsummarized data for the example. For unsummarized data, paste the data in columns A and B in the **DATACOPY worksheet** and keep the COMPUTE worksheet formulas that compute the sample size and sample variance for the two samples in cell range B4:B10. For summarized data, replace the COMPUTE worksheet formulas in cell ranges B4:B10 with the sample statistics and ignore the DATACOPY worksheet.

Use the similar **COMPUTE_UPPER worksheet** in the same workbook as a template for performing the upper-tail test. If you use an Excel version older than Excel 2010, use the COMPUTE_OLDER worksheet as a template for both the two-tail and upper-tail tests.

Analysis ToolPak Use **F-Test Two-Sample for Variances**.
For the example, open to the **DATA worksheet** of the **Cola workbook** and:

1. Select **Data → Data Analysis**.
2. In the Data Analysis dialog box, select **F-Test Two-Sample for Variances** from the **Analysis Tools** list and then click **OK**.

In the procedure's dialog box (shown in the right column):

3. Enter **A1:A11** as the **Variable 1 Range** and enter **B1:B11** as the **Variable 2 Range**.
4. Check **Labels** and enter **0.05** as **Alpha**.

5. Click **New Worksheet Ply**.
6. Click **OK**.

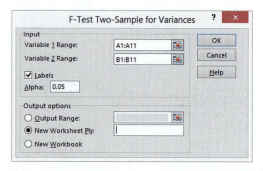

Results (shown below) appear in a new worksheet and include only the one-tail test *p*-value (0.1241), which must be doubled for the two-tail test shown in Figure 10.13 on page 350.

	A	B	C
1	F-Test Two-Sample for Variances		
2			
3		*Beverage*	*Produce*
4	Mean	50.3	72
5	Variance	350.6778	157.3333
6	Observations	10	10
7	df	9	9
8	F	2.2289	
9	P(F<=f) one-tail	0.1241	
10	F Critical one-tail	3.1789	

EG10.5 ONE-WAY ANOVA

Analyzing Variation in One-Way ANOVA

Key Technique Use the Section EG2.5 instructions to construct scatter plots using stacked data. If necessary, change the levels of the factor to consecutive integers beginning with 1, as was done for the in-store location sales experiment data in Figure 10.17 on page 357.

F Test for Differences Among More Than Two Means

Key Technique Use the **DEVSQ** (*cell range of data of all groups*) function to compute *SST* and use an expression in the form *SST* – **DEVSQ** (*group 1 data cell range*) – **DEVSQ** (*group 2 data cell range*) ... – **DEVSQ** (*group n data cell range*) to compute *SSA*.

Example Perform the Figure 10.19 one-way ANOVA for the in-store location sales experiment shown on page 359.

PHStat Use **One-Way ANOVA**.
For the example, open to the **DATA worksheet** of the **Mobile Electronics workbook**. Select **PHStat → Multiple-Sample Tests → One-Way ANOVA**. In the procedure's dialog box (shown on page 381):

1. Enter **0.05** as the **Level of Significance**.
2. Enter **A1:D6** as the **Group Data Cell Range**.
3. Check **First cells contain label**.
4. Enter a **Title**, clear the **Tukey-Kramer Procedure** check box, and click **OK**.

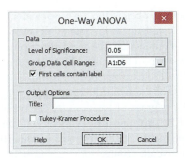

In addition to the worksheet shown in Figure 10.19, this procedure creates an **ASFData worksheet** to hold the data used for the test. See the following *In-Depth Excel* section for a complete description of this worksheet.

In-Depth Excel
Use the **COMPUTE worksheet** of the **One-Way ANOVA workbook** as a template.

The COMPUTE worksheet, and the supporting ASFData worksheet, already contains the data for the example. Modifying the One-Way ANOVA workbook for use with other problems is more difficult than modifications discussed in the previous Excel Guides. To modify the workbook:

1. Paste the data for the problem into the **ASFData worksheet**, overwriting the in-store locations sales experiment data.

In the COMPUTE worksheet (see Figure 10.19):

2. Edit the *SST* formula **= DEVSQ(ASFData!A1:D6)** in cell B16 to use the cell range of the new data just pasted into the ASFData worksheet.

3. Edit the cell B13 *SSA* formula so there are as many **DEVSQ(*group column cell range*)** terms as there are groups.

4. Change the level of significance in cell G17, if necessary.

5. If the problem contains three groups, select **row 8**, right-click, and select **Delete** from the shortcut menu.

   If the problem contains more than four groups, select **row 8**, right-click, and click **Insert** from the shortcut menu. Repeat this step as many times as necessary.

6. If you inserted new rows, enter (not copy) the formulas for those rows, using the formulas in row 7 as models.

7. Adjust table formatting as necessary.

   Read the SHORT TAKES for Chapter 10 for an explanation of the formulas found in the COMPUTE worksheet (shown in the **COMPUTE_FORMULAS worksheet**). If you use an Excel version older than Excel 2010, use the COMPUTE_OLDER worksheet.

Analysis ToolPak
Use **Anova: Single Factor**.

For the example, open to the **DATA worksheet** of the **Mobile Electronics workbook** and:

1. Select **Data → Data Analysis**.

2. In the Data Analysis dialog box, select **Anova: Single Factor** from the **Analysis Tools** list and then click **OK**.

In the procedure's dialog box (shown in the right column):

3. Enter **A1:D6** as the **Input Range**.

4. Click **Columns**, check **Labels in First Row**, and enter **0.05** as **Alpha**.

5. Click **New Worksheet Ply**.

6. Click **OK**.

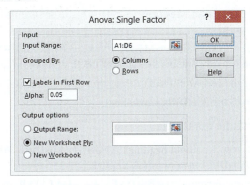

The Analysis ToolPak creates a worksheet that does not use formulas but is similar in layout to the Figure 10.19 worksheet on page 359.

Levene Test for Homogeneity of Variance

Key Technique Use the techniques for performing a one-way ANOVA.

Example Perform the Figure 10.20 Levene test for the in-store location sales experiment shown on page 361.

PHStat
Use **Levene Test**.

For the example, open to the **DATA worksheet** of the **Mobile Electronics workbook**. Select **PHStat → Multiple-Sample Tests → Levene Test**. In the procedure's dialog box (shown below):

1. Enter **0.05** as the **Level of Significance**.

2. Enter **A1:D6** as the **Sample Data Cell Range**.

3. Check **First cells contain label**.

4. Enter a **Title** and click **OK**.

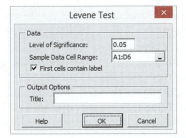

The procedure creates a worksheet that performs the Table 10.9 absolute differences computations (see page 360) as well as the Figure 10.20 worksheet. See the following *In-Depth Excel* section for a description of these worksheets.

In-Depth Excel
Use the **COMPUTE worksheet** of the **Levene workbook** as a template.

The COMPUTE worksheet and the supporting AbsDiffs and DATA worksheets already contain the data for the example.

For other problems in which the absolute differences are already known, paste the absolute differences into the AbsDiffs worksheet. Otherwise, paste the problem data into the DATA worksheet, add formulas to compute the median for each group, and adjust the AbsDiffs worksheet as necessary. For example, for the in-store location sales experiment, the following steps 1 through 7 were done with the workbook open to the DATA worksheet:

1. Enter the label **Medians** in **cell A7**, the first empty cell in column A.

2. Enter the formula **=MEDIAN(A2:A6)** in **cell A8**. (Cell range A2:A6 contains the data for the first group, in-aisle.)

3. Copy the cell A8 formula across through column D.

4. Open to the **AbsDiffs worksheet**.

In the AbsDiffs worksheet:

5. Enter row 1 column headings **AbsDiff1**, **AbsDiff2**, **AbsDiff3**, and **AbsDiff4** in columns A through D.

6. Enter the formula **=ABS(DATA!A2 – DATA!A8)** in cell A2. Copy this formula down through row 6.

7. Copy the formulas now in cell range A2:A6 across through column D. Absolute differences now appear in the cell range A2:D6.

If you use an Excel version older than Excel 2010, use the COMPUTE_OLDER worksheet.

Analysis ToolPak Use **Anova: Single Factor** with absolute difference data to perform the Levene test. If the absolute differences have not already been computed, use steps 1 through 7 of the preceding *In-Depth Excel* instructions to compute them.

Multiple Comparisons: The Tukey-Kramer Procedure

Key Technique Use formulas to compute the absolute mean differences and use the **IF** function to compare pairs of means.

Example Perform the Figure 10.21 Tukey-Kramer procedure for the in-store location sales experiment shown on page 363.

PHStat Use the *PHStat* instructions for the one-way ANOVA *F* test to perform the Tukey-Kramer procedure, *checking* **Tukey-Kramer Procedure** instead in step 4. The procedure creates a worksheet identical to the one shown in Figure 10.21 on page 363 and discussed in the following *In-Depth Excel* section. To complete the worksheet, enter the Studentized range *Q* statistic (use Table E.7) for the level of significance and the numerator and denominator degrees of freedom that are given in the worksheet.

In-Depth Excel To perform the Tukey-Kramer procedure, first use the *In-Depth Excel* instructions for the one-way ANOVA *F* test and then use the appropriate "**TK**" **worksheet** in the **One-Way ANOVA workbook**.

For the example, open to the **TK4 worksheet** that already has the value of the *Q* statistic (4.05) entered in cell B15.

The TK worksheets can be used for problems using three (**TK3**), four (**TK4**), five (**TK5**), six (**TK6**), or seven (**TK7**) groups. Use Table E.7 to look up the proper value of the Studentized range *Q* statistic for the level of significance and the numerator and denominator degrees of freedom for the problem. When you use either the **TK5**, **TK6**, and **TK7** worksheets, you must also enter the name, sample mean, and sample size for the fifth and, if applicable, sixth and seventh groups.

Read the SHORT TAKES for Chapter 10 for an explanation of the formulas found in the COMPUTE worksheet (shown in the **COMPUTE_FORMULAS worksheet**). If you use an Excel version older than Excel 2010, use the TK4_OLDER worksheet.

Analysis ToolPak Modify the previous *In-Depth Excel* instructions to perform the Tukey-Kramer procedure in conjunction with using the **Anova: Single Factor** procedure. Transfer selected values from the Analysis ToolPak results worksheet to one of the TK worksheets in the **One-Way ANOVA workbook.** For example, to perform the Figure 10.21 Tukey-Kramer procedure for the in-store location sales experiment on page 363:

1. Use the **Anova: Single Factor** procedure, as described earlier in this section, to create a worksheet that contains ANOVA results for the in-store locations experiment.

2. Record the name, **sample size** (in the **Count** column), and **sample mean** (in the **Average** column) of each group. Also record the *MSW* value, found in the cell that is the intersection of the **MS** column and **Within Groups** row, and the **denominator degrees of freedom**, found in the cell that is the intersection of the **df** column and **Within Groups** row.

3. Open to the **TK4 worksheet** of the **One-Way ANOVA workbook**.

In the TK4 worksheet:

4. Overwrite the formulas in cell range A5:C8 by entering the name, sample mean, and sample size of each group into that range.

5. Enter **0.05** as the **Level of significance** in cell B11.

6. Enter **4** as the **Numerator d.f.** (equal to the number of groups) in cell B12.

7. Enter **16** as the **Denominator d.f** in cell B13.

8. Enter **0.0439** as the **MSW** in cell B14.

9. Enter **4.05** as the **Q Statistic** in cell B15. (Look up the Studentized range *Q* statistic using Table E.7.)

CHAPTER 10 MINITAB GUIDE

MG10.1 COMPARING the MEANS of TWO INDEPENDENT POPULATIONS

Pooled-Variance *t* Test for the Difference Between Two Means

Use **2-Sample t**.

For example, to perform the Figure 10.3 pooled-variance *t* test for the two end-cap locations shown on page 326, open to the **Cola worksheet**. Select **Stat → Basic Statistics → 2-Sample t**. In the 2-Sample t (Test and Confidence Interval) dialog box (shown below):

1. Click **Samples in different columns** and press **Tab**.
2. Double-click **C1 Beverage** in the variables list to add **Beverage** to the **First** box.
3. Double-click **C2 Produce** in the variables list to add **Produce** to the **Second** box.
4. Check **Assume equal variances**.
5. Click **Options**.

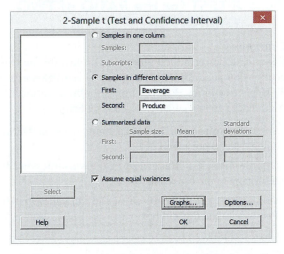

In the 2-Sample t-Options dialog box (not shown):

6. Enter **95.0** in the **Confidence level** box.
7. Select **not equal** from the **Alternative** drop-down list.
8. Click **OK**.
9. Back in the original dialog box, click **OK**.

For stacked data, use these replacement steps 1 through 3:

1. Click **Samples in one column**.
2. Enter the name of the column that contains the measurement in the **Samples** box.
3. Enter the name of the column that contains the sample names in the **Subscripts** box.

To create a boxplot for the analysis, replace step 9 with the following steps 9 through 11:

9. Back in the original dialog box, click **Graphs**.
10. In the 2-Sample t-Graphs dialog box (not shown), check **Boxplots of data** and then click **OK**.
11. Back in the original dialog box, click **OK**.

For a one-tail test, select **less than** or **greater than** in step 7.

Confidence Interval Estimate for the Difference Between Two Means

Use the instructions for the pooled-variance *t* test, which computes a confidence interval estimate as part of the analysis.

t Test for the Difference Between Two Means, Assuming Unequal Variances

Use the instructions for the pooled-variance *t* test with this replacement step 4:

4. Clear **Assume equal variances.**

MG10.2 COMPARING the MEANS of TWO RELATED POPULATIONS

Paired *t* Test

Use **Paired t**.

For example, to perform the Figure 10.8 paired *t* test for the textbook price data on page 337, open to the **BookPrices worksheet**. Select **Stat → Basic Statistics → Paired t**. In the Paired *t* (Test and Confidence Interval) dialog box (shown below):

1. Click **Samples in columns** and press **Tab**.
2. Double-click **C3 Bookstore** in the variables list to enter **Bookstore** in the **First sample** box.
3. Double-click **C4 Online** in the variables list to enter **Online** in the **Second sample** box.
4. Click **Options**.

In the Paired t-Options dialog box (not shown):

5. Enter **95.0** in the **Confidence level** box.

6. Select **not equal** from the **Alternative** drop-down list.

7. Click **OK**.

8. Back in the original dialog box, click **OK**.

To create a boxplot, replace step 8 with the following steps 8 through 10:

8. Back in the original dialog box, click **Graphs**.

9. In the Paired t-Graphs dialog box (not shown), check **Boxplots of data** and then click **OK**.

10. Back in the original dialog box, click **OK**.

For a one-tail test, select **less than** or **greater than** in step 6.

Confidence Interval Estimate for the Mean Difference

Use the instructions for the paired *t* test, which computes a confidence interval estimate as part of the analysis.

MG10.3 COMPARING the PROPORTIONS of TWO INDEPENDENT POPULATIONS

Z Test for the Difference Between Two Proportions

Use **2 Proportions**.
For example, to perform the Figure 10.12 *Z* test for the hotel guest satisfaction survey on page 344, select **Stat → Basic Statistics → 2 Proportions**. In the 2 Proportions (Test and Confidence Interval) dialog box (shown below):

1. Click **Summarized data**.

2. In the **First** row, enter **163** in the **Events** box and **227** in the **Trials** box.

3. In the **Second** row, enter **154** in the **Events** box and **262** in the **Trials** box.

4. Click **Options**.

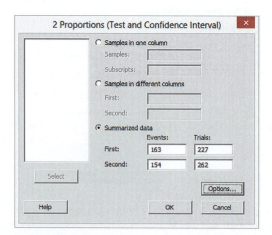

In the 2 Proportions - Options dialog box (shown in the right column):

5. Enter **95.0** in the **Confidence level** box.

6. Enter **0.0** in the **Test difference** box.

7. Select **not equal** from the **Alternative** drop-down list.

8. Check **Use pooled estimate of p for test**.

9. Click **OK**.

10. Back in the 2 Proportions (Test and Confidence Interval) dialog box, click **OK**.

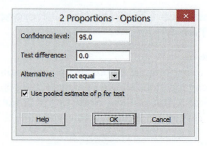

Confidence Interval Estimate for the Difference Between Two Proportions

Use the instructions for the *Z* test for the difference between two proportions, which computes a confidence interval estimate as part of the analysis.

MG10.4 *F* TEST for the RATIO of TWO VARIANCES

Use **2 Variances**.
For example, to perform the Figure 10.13 *F* test for the two end-cap locations on page 350, open to the **COLA worksheet**. Select **Stat → Basic Statistics → 2 Variances**. In the 2 Variances (Test and Confidence Interval) dialog box (shown below):

1. Select **Samples in different columns** from the **Data** drop-down list and press **Tab**.

2. Double-click **C1 Beverage** in the variables list to add **Beverage** to the **First** box.

3. Double-click **C2 Produce** in the variables list to add **Produce** to the **Second** box.

4. Click **Graphs**.

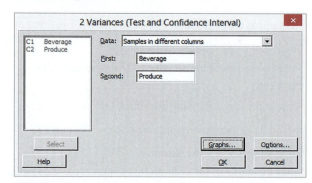

In the 2 Variances - Graphs dialog box (not shown):

5. Clear all check boxes.

6. Click **OK**.

7. Back in the 2 Variances (Test and Confidence Interval) dialog box, click **OK**.

For summarized data, select **Sample standard deviations** or **Sample variances** in step 1 and enter the sample size and the sample statistics for the two variables in lieu of steps 2 and 3. For stacked data, use these replacement steps 1 through 3:

1. Select **Samples in one column** from the **Data** drop-down list.
2. Enter the name of the column that contains the measurement in the **Samples** box.
3. Enter the name of the column that contains the sample names in the **Subscripts** box.

If you use an older version of Minitab, you will see a 2 Variances dialog box instead of the 2 Variances (Test and Confidence Interval) dialog box. This older dialog box is similar, and you click either **Samples in different columns** or **Summarized data** and then make entries similar to the ones listed in this section. The results created will differ slightly from the results shown in Figure 10.13.

MG10.5 ONE-WAY ANOVA

Analyzing Variation in One-Way ANOVA

Use **Main Effects Plot** (requires stacked data).
For example, to construct the Figure 10.17 main effects plot for the in-store location sales experiment on page 357, open to the **Mobile Electronics Stacked** worksheet. Select **Stat → ANOVA → Main Effects Plot**. In the Main Effects Plot dialog box (shown below):

1. Double-click **C2 Sales** in the variables list to add **Sales** to the **Responses** box and press **Tab**.
2. Double-click **C1 Location** in the variables list to add **Location** to the **Factors** box.
3. Click **OK**.

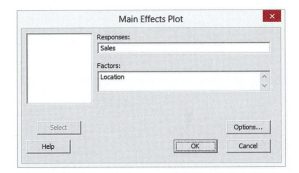

In step 2, if the column entered in the Factors box contains a text variable, as it does in the example, Minitab will sort the factor levels alphabetically. To present levels in a different order, as was done in Figure 10.17, right-click one of the factor levels in the chart and click **Edit X Scale** from the shortcut menu. In the Edit Scale dialog box, click **Specified**, type the factor levels in the desired order separated by spaces, and click **OK**.

F Test for Differences Among More Than Two Means

Use **One-Way (Unstacked)** or **One-Way** (for stacked data). In Minitab 17, use **One-Way**.
For example, to perform the Figure 10.19 one-way ANOVA for the in-store location sales experiment on page 359, open to the **Mobile Electronics** worksheet. Select **Stat → ANOVA → One-**

Way (Unstacked). In the One-Way Analysis of Variance dialog box (shown below):

1. Enter **C1-C4** in the **Responses (in separate columns)** box.
2. Enter **95.0** in the **Confidence level** box.
3. Click **Comparisons**.

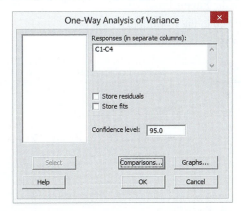

In the One-Way Multiple Comparisons dialog box (shown below):

4. Clear all check boxes.
5. Click **OK**.

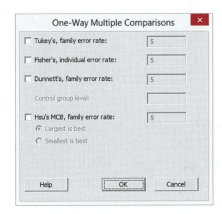

6. Back in the original dialog box, click **Graphs**.

In the One-Way Analysis of Variance - Graphs dialog box (not shown):

7. Check **Boxplots of data**.
8. Click **OK**.
9. Back in the original dialog box, click **OK**.

When using stacked data (or when using Minitab 17), select **Stat → ANOVA → One-Way** and in step 1 enter the name of the column that contains the variable of interest in the **Response** box and enter the name of the column that contains the factor names in the **Factor** box.

Levene Test for Homogeneity of Variance

Use **Test for Equal Variances** (requires stacked data).
For example, to perform the Figure 10.20 Levene test for the in-store location sales experiment on page 361, open to the **Mobile Electronics Stacked** worksheet, which contains the data of the Mobile Electronics worksheet in stacked order. Select **Stat →**

ANOVA → Test for Equal Variances. In the Test for Equal Variances dialog box (shown below):

1. Double-click **C2 Sales** in the variables list to add **Sales** to the **Response** box

2. Double-click **C1 Location** in the variables list to add **Location** to the **Factor** box.

3. Enter **95.0** in the **Confidence level** box.

4. Click **OK**.

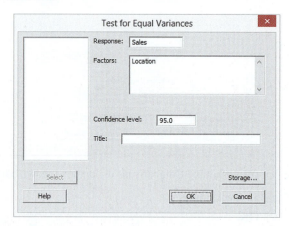

The Levene test results shown in Figure 10.20 on page 361 appear last in the results this procedure creates.

Multiple Comparisons: The Tukey-Kramer Procedure

Use the *F* Test for Differences Among More Than Two Means instructions to perform the Tukey-Kramer procedure, replacing step 4 with:

4. Check **Tukey's, family error rate** and enter **5** in its box. (A family error rate of 5 produces comparisons with an overall confidence level of 95%.)

CHAPTER 11

Chi-Square Tests

CONTENTS

OBJECTIVE

Learn when to use the chi-square test for contingency tables

Avoiding Guesswork About Resort Guests

You are the manager of T.C. Resort Properties, a collection of five upscale hotels located on two tropical islands. Guests who are satisfied with the quality of services during their stay are more likely to return on a future vacation and to recommend the hotel to friends and relatives. You have defined the business objective as improving the percentage of guests who choose to return to the hotels later. To assess the quality of services being provided by your hotels, your staff encourages guests to complete a satisfaction survey when they check out or via email after they check out.

You need to analyze the data from these surveys to determine the overall satisfaction with the services provided, the likelihood that the guests will return to the hotel, and the reasons some guests indicate that they will not return. For example, on one island, T.C. Resort Properties operates the Beachcomber and Windsurfer hotels. Is the perceived quality at the Beachcomber Hotel the same as at the Windsurfer Hotel? If there is a difference, how can you use this information to improve the overall quality of service at T.C. Resort Properties? Furthermore, if guests indicate that they are not planning to return, what are the most common reasons cited for this decision? Are the reasons cited unique to a certain hotel or common to all hotels operated by T.C. Resort Properties?

Maturos1812/Shutterstock

I n the preceding two chapters, you used hypothesis-testing procedures to analyze both numerical and categorical data. Chapter 9 presented some one-sample tests and Chapter 10 developed several two-sample tests and discussed the one-way analysis of variance (ANOVA). This chapter extends hypothesis testing to analyze differences between population *proportions* based on two or more samples and to test the hypothesis of independence in the joint responses to two categorical variables.

11.1 Chi-Square Test for the Difference Between Two Proportions

In Section 10.3, you studied the Z test for the difference between two proportions. In this section, the differences between two proportions are examined from a different perspective. The hypothesis-testing procedure uses a test statistic, whose sampling distribution is approximated by a chi-square (χ^2) distribution. The results of this χ^2 test are equivalent to those of the Z test described in Section 10.3.

If you are interested in comparing the counts of categorical responses between two independent groups, you can develop a **two-way contingency table** to display the frequency of occurrence of items of interest and items not of interest for each group. (Contingency tables were first discussed in Section 2.1, and in Chapter 4, contingency tables were used to define and study probability.)

To illustrate a contingency table, return to the Using Statistics scenario concerning T.C. Resort Properties. On one of the islands, T.C. Resort Properties has two hotels (the Beachcomber and the Windsurfer). You collect data from customer satisfaction surveys and focus on the responses to the single question "Are you likely to choose this hotel again?" You organize the results of the survey and determine that 163 of 227 guests at the Beachcomber responded yes to "Are you likely to choose this hotel again?" and 154 of 262 guests at the Windsurfer responded yes to "Are you likely to choose this hotel again?" You want to analyze the results to determine whether, at the 0.05 level of significance, there is evidence of a significant difference in guest satisfaction (as measured by likelihood to return to the hotel) between the two hotels.

The contingency table displayed in Table 11.1, which has two rows and two columns, is called a **2 $\times$ 2 contingency table**. The cells in the table indicate the frequency for each row-and-column combination.

TABLE 11.1

Layout of a 2 $\times$ 2 Contingency Table

	COLUMN VARIABLE		
ROW VARIABLE	**Group 1**	**Group 2**	**Totals**
Items of interest	X_1	X_2	X
Items not of interest	$n_1 - X_1$	$n_2 - X_2$	$n - X$
Totals	n_1	n_2	n

where

$$X_1 = \text{number of items of interest in group 1}$$
$$X_2 = \text{number of items of interest in group 2}$$
$$n_1 - X_1 = \text{number of items that are not of interest in group 1}$$
$$n_2 - X_2 = \text{number of items that are not of interest in group 2}$$
$$X = X_1 + X_2, \text{the total number of items of interest}$$
$$n - X = (n_1 - X_1) + (n_2 - X_2), \text{the total number of items that are not of interest}$$

$$n_1 = \text{sample size in group 1}$$
$$n_2 = \text{sample size in group 2}$$
$$n = n_1 + n_2 = \text{total sample size}$$

Table 11.2 is the contingency table for the hotel guest satisfaction study. The contingency table has two rows, indicating whether the guests would return to the hotel or would not return to the hotel, and two columns, one for each hotel. The cells in the table indicate the frequency of each row-and-column combination. The row totals indicate the number of guests who would return to the hotel and the number of guests who would not return to the hotel. The column totals are the sample sizes for each hotel location.

TABLE 11.2

2 × 2 Contingency Table for the Hotel Guest Satisfaction Survey

CHOOSE HOTEL AGAIN?	HOTEL Beachcomber	Windsurfer	Total
Yes	163	154	317
No	64	108	172
Total	227	262	489

To test whether the population proportion of guests who would return to the Beachcomber, π_1, is equal to the population proportion of guests who would return to the Windsurfer, π_2, you can use the **chi-square (χ^2) test for the difference between two proportions**. To test the null hypothesis that there is no difference between the two population proportions:

$$H_0: \pi_1 = \pi_2$$

against the alternative that the two population proportions are not the same:

$$H_1: \pi_1 \neq \pi_2$$

you use the χ^2_{STAT} test statistic, shown in Equation (11.1) whose sampling distribution follows the chi-square distribution.

Student Tip

Do not confuse this use of the Greek letter pi, π, to represent the population proportion with the mathematical constant that uses the same letter to represent the ratio of the circumference to a diameter of a circle—approximately 3.14159.

Student Tip

You are computing the squared difference between f_o and f_e. Therefore, unlike the Z_{STAT} and t_{STAT} test statistics, the χ^2_{STAT} test statistic can never be negative.

χ^2 TEST FOR THE DIFFERENCE BETWEEN TWO PROPORTIONS

The χ^2_{STAT} test statistic is equal to the squared difference between the observed and expected frequencies, divided by the expected frequency in each cell of the table, summed over all cells of the table.

$$\chi^2_{STAT} = \sum_{\text{all cells}} \frac{(f_o - f_e)^2}{f_e} \qquad (11.1)$$

where

$f_o =$ **observed frequency** in a particular cell of a contingency table

$f_e =$ **expected frequency** in a particular cell if the null hypothesis is true

The χ^2_{STAT} test statistic approximately follows a chi-square distribution with 1 degree of freedom.[1]

[1]In general, the degrees of freedom in a contingency table are equal to (number of rows −1) multiplied by (number of columns −1).

To compute the expected frequency, f_e, in any cell, you need to understand that if the null hypothesis is true, the proportion of items of interest in the two populations will be equal. In such situations, the sample proportions you compute from each of the two groups would differ from each other only by chance. Each would provide an estimate of the common population parameter, π. A statistic that combines these two separate estimates together into one overall estimate of the population parameter provides more information than either of the two separate estimates could provide by itself. This statistic, given by the symbol $\bar{p}$, represents the estimated overall proportion of items of interest for the two groups combined (i.e., the total number of items of interest divided by the total sample size). The complement of $\bar{p}$, $1 - \bar{p}$, represents the estimated overall proportion of items that are not of interest in the two groups. Using the notation presented in Table 11.1 on page 388, Equation (11.2) defines $\bar{p}$.

COMPUTING THE ESTIMATED OVERALL PROPORTION FOR TWO GROUPS

$$\bar{p} = \frac{X_1 + X_2}{n_1 + n_2} = \frac{X}{n} \tag{11.2}$$

To compute the expected frequency, f_e, for cells that involve items of interest (i.e., the cells in the first row in the contingency table), you multiply the sample size (or column total) for a group by $\bar{p}$. To compute the expected frequency, f_e, for cells that involve items that are not of interest (i.e., the cells in the second row in the contingency table), you multiply the sample size (or column total) for a group by $1 - \bar{p}$.

The sampling distribution of the χ^2_{STAT} test statistic shown in Equation (11.1) on page 389 approximately follows a **chi-square (χ^2) distribution** (see Table E.4) with 1 degree of freedom. Using a level of significance α, you reject the null hypothesis if the computed χ^2_{STAT} test statistic is greater than χ^2_α, the upper-tail critical value from the χ^2 distribution with 1 degree of freedom. Thus, the decision rule is

Reject H_0 if $\chi^2_{STAT} > \chi^2_\alpha$;

otherwise, do not reject H_0.

Figure 11.1 illustrates the decision rule.

FIGURE 11.1

Regions of rejection and nonrejection when using the chi-square test for the difference between two proportions, with level of significance α

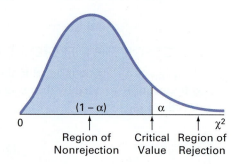

If the null hypothesis is true, the computed χ^2_{STAT} test statistic should be close to zero because the squared difference between what is actually observed in each cell, f_o, and what is theoretically expected, f_e, should be very small. If H_0 is false, then there are differences in the population proportions, and the computed χ^2_{STAT} test statistic is expected to be large. However, what is a large difference in a cell is relative. Because you are dividing by the expected frequencies, the same actual difference between f_o and f_e from a cell with a small number of expected frequencies contributes more to the χ^2_{STAT} test statistic than a cell with a large number of expected frequencies.

To illustrate the use of the chi-square test for the difference between two proportions, return to the Using Statistics scenario concerning T.C. Resort Properties on page 387 and the corresponding contingency table displayed in Table 11.2 on page 389. The null hypothesis

$(H_0: \pi_1 = \pi_2)$ states that there is no difference between the proportion of guests who are likely to choose either of these hotels again. To begin,

$$\bar{p} = \frac{X_1 + X_2}{n_1 + n_2} = \frac{163 + 154}{227 + 262} = \frac{317}{489} = 0.6483$$

$\bar{p}$ is the estimate of the common parameter π, the population proportion of guests who are likely to choose either of these hotels again if the null hypothesis is true. The estimated proportion of guests who are *not* likely to choose these hotels again is the complement of $\bar{p}$, $1 - 0.6483 = 0.3517$. Multiplying these two proportions by the sample size for the Beachcomber Hotel gives the number of guests expected to choose the Beachcomber again and the number not expected to choose this hotel again. In a similar manner, multiplying the two proportions by the Windsurfer Hotel's sample size yields the corresponding expected frequencies for that group.

EXAMPLE 11.1

Computing the Expected Frequencies

Compute the expected frequencies for each of the four cells of Table 11.2 on page 389.

SOLUTION

Yes—Beachcomber: $\bar{p} = 0.6483$ and $n_1 = 227$, so $f_e = 147.16$

Yes—Windsurfer: $\bar{p} = 0.6483$ and $n_2 = 262$, so $f_e = 169.84$

No—Beachcomber: $1 - \bar{p} = 0.3517$ and $n_1 = 227$, so $f_e = 79.84$

No—Windsurfer: $1 - \bar{p} = 0.3517$ and $n_2 = 262$, so $f_e = 92.16$

Table 11.3 presents these expected frequencies next to the corresponding observed frequencies.

TABLE 11.3

Comparing the Observed (f_o) and Expected (f_e) Frequencies

| | HOTEL | | | | |
| | Beachcomber | | Windsurfer | | |
CHOOSE HOTEL AGAIN?	**Observed**	**Expected**	**Observed**	**Expected**	**Total**
Yes	163	147.16	154	169.84	317
No	64	79.84	108	92.16	172
Total	227	227.00	262	262.00	489

To test the null hypothesis that the population proportions are equal:

$$H_0: \pi_1 = \pi_2$$

against the alternative that the population proportions are not equal:

$$H_1: \pi_1 \neq \pi_2$$

you use the observed and expected frequencies from Table 11.3 to compute the χ^2_{STAT} test statistic given by Equation (11.1) on page 389. Table 11.4 presents these calculations.

TABLE 11.4

Computing the χ^2_{STAT} Test Statistic for the Hotel Guest Satisfaction Survey

f_o	f_e	$(f_o - f_e)$	$(f_o - f_e)^2$	$(f_o - f_e)^2/f_e$
163	147.16	15.84	250.91	1.71
154	169.84	−15.84	250.91	1.48
64	79.84	−15.84	250.91	3.14
108	92.16	15.84	250.91	2.72
				9.05

The chi-square (χ^2) distribution is a right-skewed distribution whose shape depends solely on the number of degrees of freedom. You find the critical value for the χ^2 test from Table E.4, a portion of which is presented in Table 11.5.

TABLE 11.5

Finding the Critical Value from the Chi-Square Distribution with 1 Degree of Freedom, Using the 0.05 Level of Significance

	Cumulative Probabilities						
	.005	.01	...	.95	.975	.99	.995
	Upper-Tail Area						
Degrees of Freedom	.995	.99	...	.05	.025	.01	.005
1			...	3.841	5.024	6.635	7.879
2	0.010	0.020	...	5.991	7.378	9.210	10.597
3	0.072	0.115	...	7.815	9.348	11.345	12.838
4	0.207	0.297	...	9.488	11.143	13.277	14.860
5	0.412	0.554	...	11.071	12.833	15.086	16.750

The values in Table 11.5 refer to selected upper-tail areas of the χ^2 distribution. A 2×2 contingency table has 1 degree of freedom because there are two rows and two columns. [The degrees of freedom are equal to the (number of rows -1)(number of columns -1).] Using $\alpha = 0.05$, with 1 degree of freedom, the critical value of χ^2 from Table 11.5 is 3.841. You reject H_0 if the computed χ^2_{STAT} test statistic is greater than 3.841 (see Figure 11.2). Because $\chi^2_{STAT} = 9.05 > 3.841$, you reject H_0. You conclude that the proportion of guests who would return to the Beachcomber is different from the proportion of guests who would return to the Windsurfer.

FIGURE 11.2

Regions of rejection and nonrejection when finding the χ^2 critical value with 1 degree of freedom, at the 0.05 level of significance

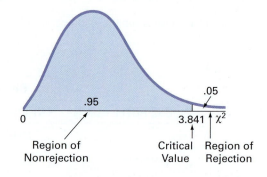

Figure 11.3 shows the Excel and Minitab results for the Table 11.2 guest satisfaction contingency table on page 389.

FIGURE 11.3

Excel and Minitab results of the chi-square test for the two-hotel guest satisfaction survey

	A	B	C	D	E	F	G
1	Chi-Square Test						
2							
3		Observed Frequencies					
4			Hotel			Calculations	
5	Choose Again?	Beachcomber	Windsurfer	Total		fo-fe	
6	Yes	163	154	317		15.8446	-15.8446
7	No	64	108	172		-15.8446	15.8446
8	Total	227	262	489			
9							
10		Expected Frequencies					
11			Hotel				
12	Choose Again?	Beachcomber	Windsurfer	Total		(fo-fe)^2/fe	
13	Yes	147.1554	169.8446	317		1.7060	1.4781
14	No	79.8446	92.1554	172		3.1442	2.7242
15	Total	227	262	489			
16							
17		Data					
18	Level of Significance	0.05					
19	Number of Rows	2					
20	Number of Columns	2					
21	Degrees of Freedom	1	=(B19 - 1) * (B20 - 1)				
22							
23		Results					
24	Critical Value	3.8415	=CHISQ.INV.RT(B18, B21)				
25	Chi-Square Test Statistic	9.0526	=SUM(F13:G14)				
26	p-Value	0.0026	=CHISQ.DIST.RT(B25, B21)				
27	Reject the null hypothesis		=IF(B26 < B18, "Reject the null hypothesis",				
28			"Do not reject the null hypothesis")				
29	Expected frequency assumption						
30	is met.		=IF(OR(B13 < 5, C13 < 5, B14 < 5, C14 < 5),				
			" is violated.", " is met.")				

Chi-Square Test: Beachcomber, Windsurfer

Expected counts are printed below observed counts
Chi-Square contributions are printed below expected counts

	Beachcomber	Windsurfer	Total
1	163	154	317
	147.16	169.84	
	1.706	1.478	
2	64	108	172
	79.84	92.16	
	3.144	2.724	
Total	227	262	489

Chi-Sq = 9.053, DF = 1, P-Value = 0.003

These results include the expected frequencies, χ^2_{STAT}, degrees of freedom, and p-value. The computed χ^2_{STAT} test statistic is 9.0526, which is greater than the critical value of 3.8415 (or the p-value $= 0.0026 < 0.05$), so you reject the null hypothesis that there is no difference in guest satisfaction between the two hotels. The p-value, equal to 0.0026, is the probability of observing sample proportions as different as or more different from the actual difference between the Beachcomber and Windsurfer $(0.718 - 0.588 = 0.13)$ observed in the sample data, if the population proportions for the Beachcomber and Windsurfer hotels are equal. Thus, there is strong evidence to conclude that the two hotels are significantly different with respect to guest satisfaction, as measured by whether a guest is likely to return to the hotel again. From Table 11.3 on page 391 you can see that a greater proportion of guests are likely to return to the Beachcomber than to the Windsurfer.

For the χ^2 test to give accurate results for a 2×2 table, you must assume that each expected frequency is at least 5. If this assumption is not satisfied, you can use alternative procedures, such as Fisher's exact test (see references 1, 2, and 4).

In the hotel guest satisfaction survey, both the Z test based on the standardized normal distribution (see Section 10.3) and the χ^2 test based on the chi-square distribution lead to the same conclusion. You can explain this result by the interrelationship between the standardized normal distribution and a chi-square distribution with 1 degree of freedom. For such situations, the χ^2_{STAT} test statistic is the square of the Z_{STAT} test statistic.

For example, in the guest satisfaction study, the computed Z_{STAT} test statistic is $+3.0088$, and the computed χ^2_{STAT} test statistic is 9.0526. Except for rounding differences, this 9.0526 value is the square of $+3.0088$ [i.e., $(+3.0088)^2 \cong 9.0526$]. Also, if you compare the critical values of the test statistics from the two distributions, at the 0.05 level of significance, the χ^2 value of 3.841 with 1 degree of freedom is the square of the Z value of ± 1.96. Furthermore, the p-values for both tests are equal. Therefore, when testing the null hypothesis of equality of proportions:

$$H_0: \pi_1 = \pi_2$$

against the alternative that the population proportions are not equal:

$$H_1: \pi_1 \neq \pi_2$$

the Z test and the χ^2 test are equivalent. If you are interested in determining whether there is evidence of a *directional* difference, such as $\pi_1 > \pi_2$, you must use the Z test, with the entire rejection region located in one tail of the standardized normal distribution.

In Section 11.2, the χ^2 test is extended to make comparisons and evaluate differences between the proportions among more than two groups. However, you cannot use the Z test if there are more than two groups.

Problems for Section 11.1

LEARNING THE BASICS

11.1 Determine the critical value of χ^2 with 1 degree of freedom in each of the following circumstances:
a. $\alpha = 0.01$
b. $\alpha = 0.005$
c. $\alpha = 0.10$

11.2 Determine the critical value of χ^2 with 1 degree of freedom in each of the following circumstances:
a. $\alpha = 0.05$
b. $\alpha = 0.025$
c. $\alpha = 0.01$

11.3 Use the following contingency table:

	A	B	Total
1	20	30	50
2	30	45	75
Total	50	75	125

a. Compute the expected frequency for each cell.
b. Compare the observed and expected frequencies for each cell.
c. Compute χ^2_{STAT}. Is it significant at $\alpha = 0.05$?

Using the level of significance α, you reject the null hypothesis if the computed χ^2_{STAT} test statistic is greater than χ^2_α, the upper-tail critical value from a chi-square distribution with $c - 1$ degrees of freedom. Therefore, the decision rule is

$$\text{Reject } H_0 \text{ if } \chi^2_{STAT} > \chi^2_\alpha;$$

$$\text{otherwise, do not reject } H_0.$$

Figure 11.4 illustrates this decision rule.

FIGURE 11.4

Regions of rejection and nonrejection when testing for differences among c proportions using the χ^2 test

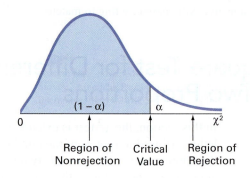

To illustrate the χ^2 test for equality of proportions when there are more than two groups, return to the Using Statistics scenario on page 387 concerning T.C. Resort Properties. Once again, you define the business objective as improving the quality of service, but this time, you are comparing three hotels located on a different island. Data are collected from customer satisfaction surveys at these three hotels. You organize the responses into the contingency table shown in Table 11.6.

TABLE 11.6

2 × 3 Contingency Table for Guest Satisfaction Survey

| | HOTEL | | | |
CHOOSE HOTEL AGAIN?	Golden Palm	Palm Royale	Palm Princess	Total
Yes	128	199	186	513
No	88	33	66	187
Total	216	232	252	700

Because the null hypothesis states that there are no differences among the three hotels in the proportion of guests who would likely return again, you use Equation (11.3) to calculate an estimate of π, the population proportion of guests who would likely return again:

$$\bar{p} = \frac{X_1 + X_2 + \cdots + X_c}{n_1 + n_2 + \cdots + n_c} = \frac{X}{n}$$

$$= \frac{(128 + 199 + 186)}{(216 + 232 + 252)} = \frac{513}{700}$$

$$= 0.733$$

The estimated overall proportion of guests who would *not* be likely to return again is the complement, $(1 - \bar{p})$, or 0.267. Multiplying these two proportions by the sample size for each hotel yields the expected number of guests who would and would not likely return.

EXAMPLE 11.2

Computing the Expected Frequencies

Compute the expected frequencies for each of the six cells in Table 11.6.

SOLUTION

Yes—Golden Palm: $\bar{p} = 0.733$ and $n_1 = 216$, so $f_e = 158.30$

Yes—Palm Royale: $\bar{p} = 0.733$ and $n_2 = 232$, so $f_e = 170.02$

Yes—Palm Princess: $\bar{p} = 0.733$ and $n_3 = 252$, so $f_e = 184.68$

No—Golden Palm: $1 - \bar{p} = 0.267$ and $n_1 = 216$, so $f_e = 57.70$

No—Palm Royale: $1 - \bar{p} = 0.267$ and $n_2 = 232$, so $f_e = 61.98$

No—Palm Princess: $1 - \bar{p} = 0.267$ and $n_3 = 252$, so $f_e = 67.32$

Table 11.7 presents these expected frequencies.

TABLE 11.7

Contingency Table of Expected Frequencies from a Guest Satisfaction Survey of Three Hotels

	HOTEL			
CHOOSE HOTEL AGAIN?	**Golden Palm**	**Palm Royale**	**Palm Princess**	**Total**
Yes	158.30	170.02	184.68	513
No	57.70	61.98	67.32	187
Total	216.00	232.00	252.00	700

To test the null hypothesis that the proportions are equal:

$$H_0: \pi_1 = \pi_2 = \pi_3$$

against the alternative that not all three proportions are equal:

$$H_1: \text{Not all } \pi_j \text{ are equal (where } j = 1, 2, 3)$$

you use the observed frequencies from Table 11.6 and the expected frequencies from Table 11.7 to compute the χ^2_{STAT} test statistic [given by Equation (11.1) on page 389]. Table 11.8 presents the calculations.

TABLE 11.8

Computing the χ^2_{STAT} Test Statistic for the Three-Hotel Guest Satisfaction Survey

f_o	f_e	$(f_o - f_e)$	$(f_o - f_e)^2$	$(f_o - f_e)^2/f_e$
128	158.30	-30.30	918.09	5.80
199	170.02	28.98	839.84	4.94
186	184.68	1.32	1.74	0.01
88	57.70	30.30	918.09	15.91
33	61.98	-28.98	839.84	13.55
66	67.32	-1.32	1.74	0.02
				40.23

You use Table E.4 to find the critical value of the χ^2 test statistic. In the guest satisfaction survey, because there are three hotels, there are $(2 - 1)(3 - 1) = 2$ degrees of freedom. Using $\alpha = 0.05$, the χ^2 critical value with 2 degrees of freedom is 5.991 (see Figure 11.5).

FIGURE 11.5

Regions of rejection and nonrejection when testing for differences in three proportions at the 0.05 level of significance, with 2 degrees of freedom

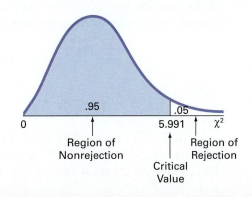

Because the computed χ^2_{STAT} test statistic is 40.23, which is greater than this critical value, you reject the null hypothesis. Figure 11.6 shows the Excel and Minitab results for this problem. These results also report the p-value. Because the p-value is 0.0000, less than $\alpha = 0.05$, you reject the null hypothesis. Further, this p-value indicates that there is virtually no chance that there will be differences this large or larger among the three sample proportions, if the population proportions for the three hotels are equal. Thus, there is sufficient evidence to conclude that the hotel properties are different with respect to the proportion of guests who are likely to return.

FIGURE 11.6

Excel and Minitab chi-square test results for the three-hotel guest satisfaction survey

For the χ^2 test to give accurate results when dealing with $2 \times c$ contingency tables, all expected frequencies must be large. The definition of "large" has led to research among statisticians. Some statisticians (see reference 5) have found that the test gives accurate results as long as all expected frequencies are at least 0.5. Other statisticians, more conservative in their approach, believe that no more than 20% of the cells should contain expected frequencies less than 5, and no cells should have expected frequencies less than 1 (see reference 3). As a reasonable compromise between these points of view, to ensure the validity of the test, you should make sure that each expected frequency is at least 1. To do this, you may need to collapse two or more low-expected-frequency categories into one category in the contingency table before performing the test. If combining categories is undesirable, you can use one of the available alternative procedures (see references 1, 2, and 6).

Problems for Section 11.2

LEARNING THE BASICS

11.11 Consider a contingency table with two rows and five columns.

a. How many degrees of freedom are there in the contingency table?
b. Determine the critical value for $\alpha = 0.05$.
c. Determine the critical value for $\alpha = 0.01$.

11.12 Use the following contingency table:

	A	B	C	Total
1	10	30	50	90
2	40	45	50	135
Total	50	75	100	225

a. Compute the expected frequency for each cell.
b. Compute χ^2_{STAT}. Is it significant at $\alpha = 0.05$?

11.13 Use the following contingency table:

	A	B	C	Total
1	20	30	25	75
2	30	20	25	75
Total	50	50	50	150

a. Compute the expected frequency for each cell.
b. Compute χ^2_{STAT}. Is it significant at $\alpha = 0.05$?

APPLYING THE CONCEPTS

11.14 How common is online personal data theft? A survey of internet users found that 15% of the 18- to 29-year-olds, 20% of the 30- to 49-year-olds, 20% of the 50- to 64-year-olds, and 13% of the 65+-year-olds have had important personal information stolen. (Data extracted from *How Common is Online Personal Data Theft?* available at **bit.ly/1rKlqRW**.) Suppose the survey was based on 200 Internet users in each of the four age groups: 18–29, 30–49, 50–64, and 65+.

a. At the 0.05 level of significance, is there evidence of a difference among the age groups in the proportion of internet users who have had important personal information stolen?
b. Determine the *p*-value in (a) and interpret its meaning.

11.15 A digital CEO is one of five behaviors important to raising an organization's Digital IQ. A survey of business and IT executives found that 80% of automotive executives, 70% of financial services executives, 82% of health care executives, 59% of retail & consumer executives, and 76% of technology executives say their CEOs are active champions of using digital technology to achieve strategy. (Data extracted from *PwC's 2014 Global Digital IQ Survey*, available at **pwc.to/1tGKCVa**.)

Suppose these results were based on 500 business and IT executives in each of the five industries: automotive, financial services, health care, retail & consumer, and technology.

a. At the 0.05 level of significance, is there evidence of a difference among the industries with respect to the proportion of executives that say their CEOs are active champions of using digital technology to achieve strategy?
b. Compute the *p*-value and interpret its meaning.

11.16 Most companies consider Big Data analytics **SELF Test** critical to success. However, is there a difference among small (<100 employees), mid-sized (100–999 employees), and large (1,000+ employees) companies in the proportion of companies that have already deployed Big Data projects? A study showed the results for the different company sizes. (Data extracted from *2014 Big Data Outlook: Big Data Is Transformative—Where Is Your Company?* available at: **bit.ly/1o8kaEo**.)

HAVE ALREADY DEPLOYED BIG DATA PROJECTS	COMPANY SIZE		
	Small	**Mid-Sized**	**Large**
Yes	9%	37%	26%
No	91%	63%	74%

Assume that 200 decision makers involved in Big Data purchases within each company size were surveyed.

a. At the 0.05 level of significance, is there evidence of a difference among companies of different sizes with respect to the proportion of companies that have already deployed Big Data projects?
b. Determine the *p*-value in (a) and interpret its meaning.

11.17 Repeat (a) and (b) of Problem 11.16, assuming that only 50 decision makers involved in Big Data purchases for each company size were surveyed. Discuss the implications of sample size on the χ^2 test for differences among more than two populations.

11.18 Most marketers at mid-size companies feel overwhelmed by the number of technology vendor relationships they must manage. A study by DNN based on samples of 57 companies with 50–99 employees, 93 companies with 100–499 employees, 69 companies with 500–999 employees, and 81 companies with 1,000–5,000 employees reported that 19 of the companies with 50–99 employees, 44 of the companies with 100–499 employees, 43 of the companies with 500–999 employees, and 61 of the companies with 1,000–5,000 employees are working simultaneously with five or more vendors. (Data extracted from *Marketing Got Complicated: Challenges (and Opportunities) for Marketers at Mid-Sized Companies*, **bit.ly/S6PIOj**.)

a. Is there evidence of a significant difference among companies of different sizes with respect to the proportion that are working simultaneously with five or more vendors ? (Use $\alpha = 0.05$).
b. Determine the *p*-value and interpret its meaning.

11.19 The GMI Ratings' 2013 Women on Boards Survey showed that progress on most measures of female board representation continues to be slow. The study reported that 68 of 101 (67%) of French companies sampled, 148 of 212 (70%) of Australian companies sampled, 28 of 30 (93%) of Norwegian companies sampled, 31 of 58 (53%) of Singaporean companies, and 96 of 145 (66%) of Canadian companies sampled have at least one female director on their boards. (Data extracted from *GMI Ratings' 2013 Woman on Boards Survey*, **http://bit.ly/1jPXYc4**.)

a. Is there evidence of a significant difference among the countries with respect to the proportion of companies that have at least one female director on their boards? (Use $\alpha = 0.05$).
b. Determine the *p*-value and interpret its meaning.

11.3 Chi-Square Test of Independence

In Sections 11.1 and 11.2, you used the χ^2 test to evaluate potential differences among population proportions. For a contingency table that has r rows and c columns, you can generalize the χ^2 test as a *test of independence* for two categorical variables.

For a test of independence, the null and alternative hypotheses follow:

H_0: The two categorical variables are independent (i.e., there is no relationship between them).

H_1: The two categorical variables are dependent (i.e., there is a relationship between them).

Once again, you use Equation (11.1) on page 389 to compute the test statistic:

$$\chi^2_{STAT} = \sum_{all\ cells} \frac{(f_o - f_e)^2}{f_e}$$

You reject the null hypothesis at the α level of significance if the computed value of the χ^2_{STAT} test statistic is greater than χ^2_α, the upper-tail critical value from a chi-square distribution with $(r-1)(c-1)$ degrees of freedom (see Figure 11.7).

FIGURE 11.7

Regions of rejection and nonrejection when testing for independence in an $r \times c$ contingency table, using the χ^2 test

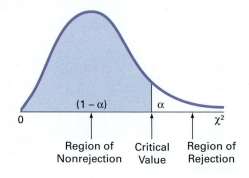

Thus, the decision rule is

$$\text{Reject } H_0 \text{ if } \chi^2_{STAT} > \chi^2_\alpha;$$

otherwise, do not reject H_0.

> **Student Tip**
> Remember that *independence* means no relationship, so you do not reject the null hypothesis. *Dependence* means there is a relationship, so you reject the null hypothesis.

The **chi-square (χ^2) test of independence** is similar to the χ^2 test for equality of proportions. The test statistics and the decision rules are the same, but the null and alternative hypotheses and conclusions are different. For example, in the guest satisfaction survey of Sections 11.1 and 11.2, there is evidence of a significant difference between the hotels with respect to the proportion of guests who would return. From a different viewpoint, you could conclude that there is a significant relationship between the hotels and the likelihood that a guest would return. However, the two types of tests differ in how the samples are selected.

In a test for equality of proportions, there is one factor of interest, with two or more levels. These levels represent samples selected from independent populations. The categorical responses in each group or level are classified into two categories, such as *an item of interest* and *not an item of interest*. The objective is to make comparisons and evaluate differences between the proportions of the *items of interest* among the various levels. However, in a test for independence, there are two factors of interest, each of which has two or more levels. You select one sample and tally the joint responses to the two categorical variables into the cells of a contingency table.

To illustrate the χ^2 test for independence, suppose that, in the three-hotel guest satisfaction survey, respondents who stated that they were not likely to return also indicated the primary reason for their unwillingness to return. Table 11.9 presents the resulting 4 × 3 contingency table.

From Table 11.9, the primary reasons for not planning to return were price, 67 respondents; location, 60; room accommodation, 31; and some other reason, 29. In Table 11.6 on page 396, there were 88 guests at the Golden Palm, 33 guests at the Palm Royale, and 66 guests at the Palm Princess who were not planning to return.

TABLE 11.9

Contingency Table of Primary Reason for Not Returning and Hotel

PRIMARY REASON FOR NOT RETURNING	HOTEL			
	Golden Palm	Palm Royale	Palm Princess	Total
Price	23	7	37	67
Location	39	13	8	60
Room accommodation	13	5	13	31
Other	13	8	8	29
Total	88	33	66	187

The observed frequencies in the cells of the 4×3 contingency table represent the joint tallies of the sampled guests with respect to primary reason for not returning and the hotel where they stayed. The null and alternative hypotheses are

H_0: There is no relationship between the primary reason for not returning and the hotel.

H_1: There is a relationship between the primary reason for not returning and the hotel.

To test this null hypothesis of independence against the alternative that there is a relationship between the two categorical variables, you use Equation (11.1) on page 389 to compute the test statistic:

$$\chi^2_{STAT} = \sum_{all\ cells} \frac{(f_o - f_e)^2}{f_e}$$

where

f_o = observed frequency in a particular cell of the $r \times c$ contingency table

f_e = expected frequency in a particular cell if the null hypothesis of independence is true

To compute the expected frequency, f_e, in any cell, you use the multiplication rule for independent events discussed on page 157 [see Equation (4.7)]. For example, under the null hypothesis of independence, the probability of responses expected in the upper-left-corner cell representing primary reason of price for the Golden Palm is the product of the two separate probabilities $P(\text{Price})$ and $P(\text{Golden Palm})$. Here, the proportion of reasons that are due to price, $P(\text{Price})$, is $67/187 = 0.3583$, and the proportion of all responses from the Golden Palm, $P(\text{Golden Palm})$, is $88/187 = 0.4706$. If the null hypothesis is true, then the primary reason for not returning and the hotel are independent:

$$P(\text{Price } and \text{ Golden Palm}) = P(\text{Price}) \times P(\text{Golden Palm})$$
$$= (0.3583) \times (0.4706)$$
$$= 0.1686$$

The expected frequency is the product of the overall sample size, n, and this probability, $187 \times 0.1686 = 31.53$. The f_e values for the remaining cells are shown in Table 11.10.

TABLE 11.10

Contingency Table of Expected Frequencies of Primary Reason for Not Returning with Hotel

PRIMARY REASON FOR NOT RETURNING	HOTEL			
	Golden Palm	Palm Royale	Palm Princess	Total
Price	31.53	11.82	23.65	67
Location	28.24	10.59	21.18	60
Room accommodation	14.59	5.47	10.94	31
Other	13.65	5.12	10.24	29
Total	88.00	33.00	66.00	187

You can also compute the expected frequency by taking the product of the row total and column total for a cell and dividing this product by the overall sample size, as Equation (11.4) shows.

COMPUTING THE EXPECTED FREQUENCY

The expected frequency in a cell is the product of its row total and column total, divided by the overall sample size.

$$f_e = \frac{\text{Row total} \times \text{Column total}}{n} \tag{11.4}$$

where

$$\text{Row total} = \text{sum of the frequencies in the row}$$
$$\text{Column total} = \text{sum of the frequencies in the column}$$
$$n = \text{overall sample size}$$

This alternate method results in simpler computations. For example, using Equation (11.4) for the upper-left-corner cell (price for the Golden Palm),

$$f_e = \frac{\text{Row total} \times \text{Column total}}{n} = \frac{(67)(88)}{187} = 31.53$$

and for the lower-right-corner cell (other reason for the Palm Princess),

$$f_e = \frac{\text{Row total} \times \text{Column total}}{n} = \frac{(29)(66)}{187} = 10.24$$

To perform the test of independence, you use the χ^2_{STAT} test statistic shown in Equation (11.1) on page 389. The sampling distribution of the χ^2_{STAT} test statistic approximately follows a chi-square distribution, with degrees of freedom equal to the number of rows in the contingency table minus 1, multiplied by the number of columns in the table minus 1:

$$\text{Degrees of freedom} = (r-1)(c-1)$$
$$= (4-1)(3-1) = 6$$

Table 11.11 presents the computations for the χ^2_{STAT} test statistic.

TABLE 11.11

Computing the χ^2_{STAT} Test Statistic for the Test of Independence

Cell	f_o	f_e	$(f_o - f_e)$	$(f_o - f_e)^2$	$(f_o - f_e)^2/f_e$
Price/Golden Palm	23	31.53	−8.53	72.76	2.31
Price/Palm Royale	7	11.82	−4.82	23.23	1.97
Price/Palm Princess	37	23.65	13.35	178.22	7.54
Location/Golden Palm	39	28.24	10.76	115.78	4.10
Location/Palm Royale	13	10.59	2.41	5.81	0.55
Location/Palm Princess	8	21.18	−13.18	173.71	8.20
Room/Golden Palm	13	14.59	−1.59	2.53	0.17
Room/Palm Royale	5	5.47	−0.47	0.22	0.04
Room/Palm Princess	13	10.94	2.06	4.24	0.39
Other/Golden Palm	13	13.65	−0.65	0.42	0.03
Other/Palm Royale	8	5.12	2.88	8.29	1.62
Other/Palm Princess	8	10.24	−2.24	5.02	0.49
					27.41

Using the $\alpha = 0.05$ level of significance, the upper-tail critical value from the chi-square distribution with 6 degrees of freedom is 12.592 (see Table E.4). Because $\chi^2_{STAT} = 27.41 > 12.592$, you reject the null hypothesis of independence (see Figure 11.8).

FIGURE 11.8

Regions of rejection and nonrejection when testing for independence in the three hotel guest satisfaction survey example at the 0.05 level of significance, with 6 degrees of freedom

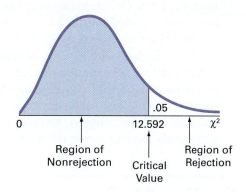

Figure 11.9 shows the Excel and Minitab results for this test, which are identical when rounded to three decimal places. Because $\chi^2_{STAT} = 27.410 > 12.592$, you reject the null hypothesis of independence. Using the p-value approach, you reject the null hypothesis of independence because the p-value $= 0.000 < 0.05$. The p-value indicates that there is virtually no chance of having a relationship this strong or stronger between the hotel and the primary reasons for not returning in a sample, if the primary reasons for not returning are independent of the specific hotels in the entire population. Thus, there is strong evidence of a relationship between the primary reason for not returning and the hotel.

FIGURE 11.9

Excel and Minitab chi-square test results for the Table 11.9 primary reason for not returning to hotel data

	A	B	C	D	E
1	Chi-Square Test of Independence				
2					
3		**Observed Frequencies**			
4			Hotel		
5	Reason for Not Returning	Golden Palm	Palm Royale	Palm Princess	Total
6	Price	23	7	37	67
7	Location	39	13	8	60
8	Room accommodation	13	5	13	31
9	Other	13	8	8	29
10	Total	88	33	66	187
11					
12		**Expected Frequencies**			
13			Hotel		
14	Reason for Not Returning	Golden Palm	Palm Royale	Palm Princess	Total
15	Price	31.5294	11.8235	23.6471	67
16	Location	28.2353	10.5882	21.1765	60
17	Room accommodation	14.5882	5.4706	10.9412	31
18	Other	13.6471	5.1176	10.2353	29
19	Total	88	33	66	187
20					
21		**Data**			
22	Level of Significance	0.05			
23	Number of Rows	4			
24	Number of Columns	3			
25	Degrees of Freedom	6	=(B23 - 1) * (B24 - 1)		
26					
27		**Results**			
28	Critical Value	12.5916	=CHISQ.INV.RT(B22, B25)		
29	Chi-Square Test Statistic	27.4104	=SUM(G15:I18)		
30	p-Value	0.0001	=CHISQ.DIST.RT(B29, B25)		
31	Reject the null hypothesis		=IF(B30 < B22, "Reject the null hypothesis",		
32			"Do not reject the null hypothesis")		
33	Expected frequency assumption				
34	is met.		=IF(OR(B15 < 1, C15 < 1, D15 < 1, B16 < 1, C16 < 1, D16 < 1,		
			B17 < 1, C17 < 1, D17 < 1, B18 < 1, C18 < 1, D18 < 1),		
			" is violated.", " is met.")		

Chi-Square Test: Golden Palm, Palm Royale, Palm Princess

Expected counts are printed below observed counts
Chi-Square contributions are printed
below expected counts

	Golden Palm	Palm Royale	Palm Princess	Total
1	23	7	37	67
	31.53	11.82	23.65	
	2.307	1.968	7.540	
2	39	13	8	60
	28.24	10.59	21.18	
	4.104	0.549	8.199	
3	13	5	13	31
	14.59	5.47	10.94	
	0.173	0.040	0.387	
4	13	8	8	29
	13.65	5.12	10.24	
	0.031	1.623	0.488	
Total	88	33	66	187

Chi-Sq = 27.410, DF = 6, P-Value = 0.000

Examination of the observed and expected frequencies (see Table 11.11 above on page 402) reveals that price is underrepresented as a reason for not returning to the Golden Palm (i.e., $f_o = 23$ and $f_e = 31.53$) but is overrepresented at the Palm Princess. Guests are more satisfied with the price at the Golden Palm than at the Palm Princess. Location is overrepresented as a reason for not returning to the Golden Palm but greatly underrepresented at the Palm Princess. Thus, guests are much more satisfied with the location of the Palm Princess than with that of the Golden Palm.

To ensure accurate results, all expected frequencies need to be large in order to use the χ^2 test when dealing with $r \times c$ contingency tables. As in the case of $2 \times c$ contingency tables in Section 11.2, all expected frequencies should be at least 1. For contingency tables in which one or more expected frequencies are less than 1, you can use the chi-square test after collapsing two or more low-frequency rows into one row (or collapsing two or more low-frequency columns into one column). Merging rows or columns usually results in expected frequencies sufficiently large to ensure the accuracy of the χ^2 test.

Problems for Section 11 .3

LEARNING THE BASICS

11.20 If a contingency table has three rows and four columns, how many degrees of freedom are there for the χ^2 test of independence?

11.21 When performing a χ^2 test of independence in a contingency table with r rows and c columns, determine the upper-tail critical value of the test statistic in each of the following circumstances:
a. $\alpha = 0.05, r = 4$ rows, $c = 5$ columns
b. $\alpha = 0.01, r = 4$ rows, $c = 5$ columns
c. $\alpha = 0.01, r = 4$ rows, $c = 6$ columns
d. $\alpha = 0.01, r = 3$ rows, $c = 6$ columns
e. $\alpha = 0.01, r = 6$ rows, $c = 3$ columns

APPLYING THE CONCEPTS

11.22 The owner of a restaurant serving Continental-style entrées has the business objective of learning more about the patterns of patron demand during the Friday-to-Sunday weekend time period. Data were collected from 630 customers on the type of entrée ordered and the type of dessert ordered and organized into the following table:

TYPE OF DESSERT	TYPE OF ENTRÉE				
	Beef	Poultry	Fish	Pasta	Total
Ice cream	13	8	12	14	47
Cake	98	12	29	6	145
Fruit	8	10	6	2	26
None	124	98	149	41	412
Total	243	128	196	63	630

At the 0.05 level of significance, is there evidence of a relationship between type of dessert and type of entrée?

11.23 Is there a generation gap in the type of music that people listen to? The following table represents the type of favorite music for a sample of 1,000 respondents classified according to their age group:

	AGE				
FAVORITE TYPE	16–29	30–49	50–64	65 and over	Total
Rock	71	62	51	27	211
Rap or hip-hop	40	21	7	3	71
Rhythm and blues	48	46	46	40	180
Country	43	53	59	79	234
Classical	22	28	33	46	129
Jazz	18	26	36	43	123
Salsa	8	14	18	12	52
Total	250	250	250	250	1,000

At the 0.05 level of significance, is there evidence of a relationship between favorite type of music and age group?

SELF Test **11.24** How many airline loyalty programs do non-business travelers belong to? A study by Parago, Inc., revealed the following results:

NUMBER OF LOYALTY PROGRAMS	AGE						
	18–22	23–29	30–39	40–49	50–59	60+	Total
0	78	113	79	74	88	88	520
1	36	50	41	48	69	82	326
2–3	12	34	36	48	52	85	267
4–5	4	4	6	7	13	25	59
6+	0	0	3	0	2	3	8
Total	130	201	165	177	224	283	1,180

Source: The Great American Vacation Study, **parago.com/travel-study**.

At the 0.01 level of significance, is there evidence of a significant relationship between number of airline loyalty programs and age?

11.25 Where people look for news is different for various age groups. A study indicated where different age groups primarily get their news:

MEDIA	AGE GROUP		
	Under 36	36–50	50 +
Local TV	107	119	133
National TV	73	102	127
Radio	75	97	109
Local newspaper	52	79	107
Internet	95	83	76

At the 0.05 level of significance, is there evidence of a significant relationship between the age group and where people primarily get their news? If so, explain the relationship.

11.26 PwC takes a closer look at what CEOs are looking for and are finding as new sources of value in their businesses and industries. The results of the 2014 Global CEO survey, summarized in the table below, classified CEOs by the main opportunity that they identified for business growth in their companies as well as their geographic region.

IDENTIFIED MAIN OPPORTUNITY	GEOGRAPHIC REGION				
	U.S.	China & Hong Kong	Japan	Germany	Total
Product or service innovation	58	58	45	21	182
Increased share in existing markets	60	30	31	15	136
Mergers and acquisitions	23	10	12	4	49
New geographic markets	16	18	31	2	67
New joint ventures and/or strategic alliances	5	18	8	3	34
Total	162	134	127	45	468

Source: *17th Annual Global CEO Survey*, **pwc.com/gx/en/ceo-survey/index .jhtml**.

At the 0.05 level of significance, is there evidence of a significant relationship between the identified main opportunity and geographic region?

Avoiding Guesswork About Resort Guests, Revisited

Maturos1812/Shutterstock

In the Using Statistics scenario, you were the manager of T.C. Resort Properties, a collection of five upscale hotels located on two tropical islands. To assess the quality of services being provided by your hotels, guests are encouraged to complete a satisfaction survey when they check out or via email after they check out. You analyzed the data from these surveys to determine the overall satisfaction with the services provided, the likelihood that the guests will return to the hotel, and the reasons given by some guests for not wanting to return.

On one island, T.C. Resort Properties operates the Beachcomber and Windsurfer hotels. You performed a chi-square test for the difference in two proportions and concluded that a greater proportion of guests are willing to return to the Beachcomber Hotel than to the Windsurfer. On the other island, T.C. Resort Properties operates the Golden Palm, Palm Royale, and Palm Princess hotels. To see if guest satisfaction was the same among the three hotels, you performed a chi-square test for the differences among more than two proportions. The test confirmed that the three proportions are not equal, and guests seem to be most likely to return to the Palm Royale and least likely to return to the Golden Palm.

In addition, you investigated whether the reasons given for not returning to the Golden Palm, Palm Royale, and Palm Princess were unique to a certain hotel or common to all three hotels. By performing a chi-square test of independence, you determined that the reasons given for wanting to return or not depended on the hotel where the guests had been staying. By examining the observed and expected frequencies, you concluded that guests were more satisfied with the price at the Golden Palm and were much more satisfied with the location of the Palm Princess. Guest satisfaction with room accommodations was not significantly different among the three hotels.

SUMMARY

Figure 11.10 presents a roadmap for this chapter. First, you used hypothesis testing for analyzing categorical data from two independent samples and from more than two independent samples. In addition, the rules of probability from Section 4.2 were extended to the hypothesis of independence in the joint responses to two categorical variables.

FIGURE 11.10
Roadmap of Chapter 11

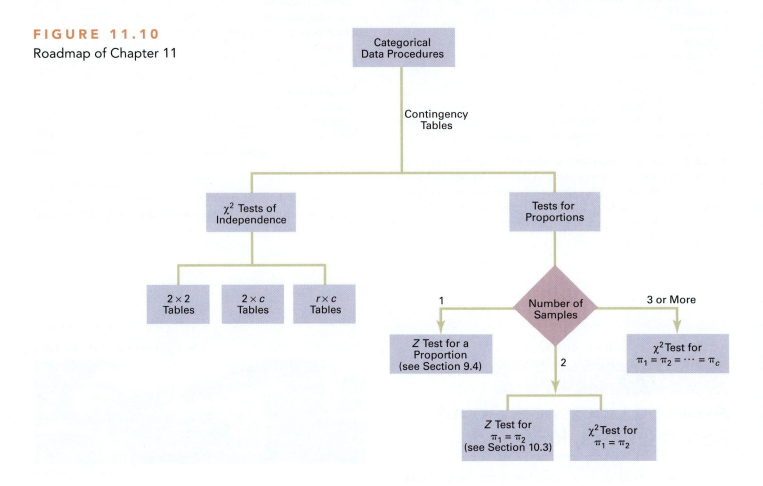

REFERENCES

1. Conover, W. J. *Practical Nonparametric Statistics*, 3rd ed. New York: Wiley, 2000.
2. Daniel, W. W. *Applied Nonparametric Statistics*, 2nd ed. Boston: PWS Kent, 1990.
3. Dixon, W. J., and F. J. Massey, Jr. *Introduction to Statistical Analysis*, 4th ed. New York: McGraw-Hill, 1983.
4. Hollander, M., and D. A. Wolfe. *Nonparametric Statistical Methods*, 2nd ed. New York: Wiley, 1999.
5. Lewontin, R. C., and J. Felsenstein. "Robustness of Homogeneity Tests in 2 × *n* Tables," *Biometrics*, 21 (March 1965): 19–33.
6. Marascuilo, L. A., and M. McSweeney. *Nonparametric and Distribution-Free Methods for the Social Sciences*. Monterey, CA: Brooks/Cole, 1977.
7. *Microsoft Excel 2013*. Redmond, WA: Microsoft Corp., 2012.
8. *Minitab Release 16*. State College, PA: Minitab Inc., 2010.

KEY EQUATIONS

χ^2 Test for the Difference Between Two Proportions

$$\chi^2_{STAT} = \sum_{all\ cells} \frac{(f_o - f_e)^2}{f_e} \qquad (11.1)$$

Computing the Estimated Overall Proportion for Two Groups

$$\bar{p} = \frac{X_1 + X_2}{n_1 + n_2} = \frac{X}{n} \qquad (11.2)$$

Computing the Estimated Overall Proportion for c Groups

$$\bar{p} = \frac{X_1 + X_2 + \cdots + X_c}{n_1 + n_2 + \cdots + n_c} = \frac{X}{n} \qquad (11.3)$$

Computing the Expected Frequency

$$f_e = \frac{\text{Row total} \times \text{Column total}}{n} \qquad (11.4)$$

KEY TERMS

chi-square (χ^2) distribution 390
chi-square (χ^2) test for the difference between two proportions 389

chi-square (χ^2) test of independence 400
expected frequency (f_e) 389
observed frequency (f_o) 389

$2 \times c$ contingency table 395
2×2 contingency table 388
two-way contingency table 388

CHECKING YOUR UNDERSTANDING

11.27 Under what conditions should you use the χ^2 test to determine whether there is a difference between the proportions of two independent populations?

11.28 Under what conditions should you use the χ^2 test to determine whether there is a difference among the proportions of more than two independent populations?

11.29 Under what conditions should you use the χ^2 test of independence?

CHAPTER REVIEW PROBLEMS

11.30 Undergraduate students at Miami University in Oxford, Ohio, were surveyed in order to evaluate the effect of gender and price on purchasing a pizza from Pizza Hut. Students were told to suppose that they were planning to have a large two-topping pizza delivered to their residence that evening. The students had to decide between ordering from Pizza Hut at a reduced price of $8.49 (the regular price for a large two-topping pizza from the Oxford Pizza Hut at the time was $11.49) and ordering a pizza from a different pizzeria. The results from this question are summarized in the following contingency table:

	PIZZERIA		
GENDER	**Pizza Hut**	**Other**	**Total**
Female	4	13	17
Male	6	12	18
Total	10	25	35

a. Using a 0.05 level of significance, is there evidence of a difference between males and females in their pizzeria selection?
b. What is your answer to (a) if nine of the male students selected Pizza Hut and nine selected another pizzeria?

A subsequent survey evaluated purchase decisions at other prices. These results are summarized in the following contingency table:

	PRICE			
PIZZERIA	**$8.49**	**$11.49**	**$14.49**	**Total**
Pizza Hut	10	5	2	17
Other	25	23	27	75
Total	35	28	29	92

c. Using a 0.05 level of significance and using the data in the second contingency table, is there evidence of a difference in pizzeria selection based on price?
d. Determine the p-value in (c) and interpret its meaning.

11.31 What social media tools do marketers commonly use? *Social Media Examiner* surveyed B2B and B2C marketers who commonly use an indicated social media tool. (B2B marketers are marketers that focus primarily on attracting businesses. B2C marketers are marketers that primarily target consumers.) Suppose the survey was based on 500 B2B marketers and 500 B2C marketers and yielded the results in the following table. (Data extracted from *2014 Social Media Marketing Industry Report*, available from **socialmediaexaminer.com**.)

SOCIAL MEDIA TOOL	BUSINESS FOCUS	
	B2B	**B2C**
Facebook	89%	97%
Twitter	86%	81%
LinkedIn	88%	59%
YouTube	52%	60%

For *each social media tool*, at the 0.05 level of significance, determine whether there is a difference between B2B marketers and B2C marketers in the proportion who used each social media tool.

11.32 A company is considering an organizational change involving the use of self-managed work teams. To assess the attitudes of employees of the company toward this change, a sample of 400 employees is selected and asked whether they favor the institution of self-managed work teams in the organization. Three responses are permitted: favor, neutral, or oppose. The results of the survey, cross-classified by type of job and attitude toward self-managed work teams, are summarized as follows:

TYPE OF JOB	SELF-MANAGED WORK TEAMS			
	Favor	**Neutral**	**Oppose**	**Total**
Hourly worker	108	46	71	225
Supervisor	18	12	30	60
Middle management	35	14	26	75
Upper management	24	7	9	40
Total	185	79	136	400

a. At the 0.05 level of significance, is there evidence of a relationship between attitude toward self-managed work teams and type of job?

The survey also asked respondents about their attitudes toward instituting a policy whereby an employee could take one additional vacation day per month without pay. The results, cross-classified by type of job, are as follows:

TYPE OF JOB	VACATION TIME WITHOUT PAY			
	Favor	**Neutral**	**Oppose**	**Total**
Hourly worker	135	23	67	225
Supervisor	39	7	14	60
Middle management	47	6	22	75
Upper management	26	6	8	40
Total	247	42	111	400

b. At the 0.05 level of significance, is there evidence of a relationship between attitude toward vacation time without pay and type of job?

11.33 Do Americans trust advertisements? The following table summarizes the results of a YouGov.com survey that asked Americans who see advertisements at least once a month how honest advertisements are.

HONEST?	GEOGRAPHIC REGION				
	Northeast	**Midwest**	**South**	**West**	**Total**
Yes	102	118	220	115	555
No	74	93	135	130	432
Total	176	211	355	245	987

Source: "Truth in advertising: 50% don't trust what they see, read and hear," **bit.ly/1jPXYc4**.

a. At the 0.05 level of significance, is there evidence of a difference in the proportion of Americans who say advertisements are honest on the basis of geographic region?

YouGov.com also asked Americans who see advertisements at least once a month whether they trust the advertisements that they see, read, and hear. The following table summarizes the results of this second survey.

TRUST?	GEOGRAPHIC REGION				
	Northeast	**Midwest**	**South**	**West**	**Total**
Yes	88	108	202	93	491
No	88	103	153	152	496
Total	176	211	355	245	987

Source: "Truth in advertising: 50% don't trust what they see, read and hear," **bit.ly/1ivIlLX**.

b. At the 0.05 level of significance is there evidence of a difference in the proportion of Americans who say they trust advertisements on the basis of geographic region?

CASES FOR CHAPTER 11

Managing Ashland MultiComm Services

PHASE 1

Reviewing the results of its research, the marketing department team concluded that a segment of Ashland households might be interested in a discounted trial subscription to the AMS *3-For-All* cable/phone/Internet service. The team decided to test various discounts before determining the type of discount to offer during the trial period. It decided to conduct an experiment using three types of discounts plus a plan that offered no discount during the trial period:

1. No discount for the *3-For-All* cable/phone/Internet service. Subscribers would pay $24.99 per week for the *3-For-All* cable/phone/Internet service during the 90-day trial period.

2. Moderate discount for the *3-For-All* cable/phone/Internet service. Subscribers would pay $19.99 per week for the *3-For-All* cable/phone/Internet service during the 90-day trial period.

3. Substantial discount for the *3-For-All* cable/phone/Internet service. Subscribers would pay $14.99 per week for the *3-For-All* cable/phone/Internet service during the 90-day trial period.

4. Discount restaurant card. Subscribers would be given a special card providing a discount of 15% at selected restaurants in Ashland during the trial period.

Each participant in the experiment was randomly assigned to a discount plan. A random sample of 100 subscribers to each plan during the trial period was tracked to determine how many would continue to subscribe to the *3-For-All* service after the trial period. The following table summarizes the results.

CONTINUE SUBSCRIPTIONS AFTER TRIAL PERIOD	DISCOUNT PLANS				
	No Discount	Moderate Discount	Substantial Discount	Restaurant Card	Total
Yes	24	30	38	51	143
No	76	70	62	49	257
Total	100	100	100	100	400

1. Analyze the results of the experiment. Write a report to the team that includes your recommendation for which discount plan to use. Be prepared to discuss the limitations and assumptions of the experiment.

PHASE 2

The marketing department team discussed the results of the survey presented in Chapter 8, on pages 277 and 278. The team realized that the evaluation of individual questions was providing only limited information. In order to further understand the market for the *3-For-All* cable/phone/Internet service, the data were organized in the following contingency tables:

HAS AMS TELEPHONE SERVICE	HAS AMS INTERNET SERVICE		
	Yes	No	Total
Yes	55	28	83
No	207	128	335
Total	262	156	418

TYPE OF SERVICE	DISCOUNT TRIAL		
	Yes	No	Total
Basic	8	156	164
Enhanced	32	222	254
Total	40	378	418

TYPE OF SERVICE	WATCHES PREMIUM OR ON-DEMAND SERVICES				
	Almost Every Day	Several Times a Week	Almost Never	Never	Total
Basic	2	5	127	30	164
Enhanced	12	30	186	26	254
Total	14	35	313	56	418

DISCOUNT	WATCHES PREMIUM OR ON-DEMAND SERVICES				
	Almost Every Day	Several Times a Week	Almost Never	Never	Total
Yes	4	5	27	4	40
No	10	30	286	52	378
Total	14	35	313	56	418

| DISCOUNT | METHOD FOR CURRENT SUBSCRIPTION | | | | | |
	Toll-Free Phone	AMS Website	Direct Mail Reply Card	Good Tunes & More	Other	Total
Yes	11	21	5	1	2	40
No	219	85	41	9	24	378
Total	230	106	46	10	26	418

| GOLD CARD | METHOD FOR CURRENT SUBSCRIPTION | | | | | |
	Toll-Free Phone	AMS Website	Direct Mail Reply Card	Good Tunes & More	Other	Total
Yes	10	20	5	1	2	38
No	220	86	41	9	24	380
Total	230	106	46	10	26	418

2. Analyze the results of the contingency tables. Write a report for the marketing department team, discussing the marketing implications of the results for Ashland MultiComm Services.

Digital Case

Apply your knowledge of testing for the difference between two proportions in this Digital Case, which extends the T.C. Resort Properties Using Statistics scenario of this chapter.

As T.C. Resort Properties seeks to improve its customer service, the company faces new competition from SunLow Resorts. SunLow has recently opened resort hotels on the islands where T.C. Resort Properties has its five hotels. SunLow is currently advertising that a random survey of 300 customers revealed that about 60% of the customers preferred its "Concierge Class" travel reward program over the T.C. Resorts "TCRewards Plus" program.

Open and review **ConciergeClass.pdf**, an electronic brochure that describes the Concierge Class program and compares it to the T.C. Resorts program. Then answer the following questions:

1. Are the claims made by SunLow valid?

2. What analyses of the survey data would lead to a more favorable impression about T.C. Resort Properties?

3. Perform one of the analyses identified in your answer to step 2.

4. Review the data about the T.C. Resort Properties customers presented in this chapter. Are there any other questions that you might include in a future survey of travel reward programs? Explain.

CardioGood Fitness

Return to the CardioGood Fitness case first presented on page 25. The data for this case are stored in CardioGood Fitness.

1. Determine whether differences exist in the relationship status (single or partnered), and the self-rated fitness based on the product purchased (TM195, TM498, TM798).

2. Write a report to be presented to the management of CardioGood Fitness, detailing your findings.

Clear Mountain State Student Surveys

1. The Student News Service at Clear Mountain State University (CMSU) has decided to gather data about the undergraduate students that attend CMSU. It creates and distributes a survey of 14 questions and receives responses from 62 undergraduates, which it stores in `UndergradSurvey`.

Construct contingency tables using gender, major, plans to go to graduate school, and employment status. (You need to construct six tables, taking two variables at a time.) Analyze the data at the 0.05 level of significance to determine whether any significant relationships exist among these variables.

2. The dean of students at CMSU has learned about the undergraduate survey and has decided to undertake a similar survey for graduate students at CMSU. She creates and distributes a survey of 14 questions and receives responses from 44 graduate students, which she stores in `GradSurvey`. For these data, at the 0.05 level of significance:

Construct contingency tables using gender, undergraduate major, graduate major, and employment status. (You need to construct six tables, taking two variables at a time.) Analyze the data to determine whether any significant relationships exist among these variables.

CHAPTER 11 EXCEL GUIDE

EG11.1 CHI-SQUARE TEST for the DIFFERENCE BETWEEN TWO PROPORTIONS

Key Technique Use the **CHISQ.INV.RT**(*level of significance, degrees of freedom*) function to compute the critical value and use the **CHISQ.DIST.RT**(*chi-square test statistic, degrees of freedom*) function to compute the *p*-value.

Example Perform this chi-square test for the two-hotel guest satisfaction data shown in Figure 11.3 on page 392.

PHStat Use **Chi-Square Test for Differences in Two Proportions**.
For the example, select **PHStat → Two-Sample Tests (Summarized Data) → Chi-Square Test for Differences in Two Proportions**. In the procedure's dialog box, enter **0.05** as the **Level of Significance**, enter a **Title**, and click **OK**. In the new worksheet:

1. Read the yellow note about entering values and then press the **Delete** key to delete the note.
2. Enter **Hotel** in cell **B4** and **Choose Again?** in cell **A5**.
3. Enter **Beachcomber** in cell **B5** and **Windsurfer** in cell **C5**.
4. Enter **Yes** in cell **A6** and **No** in cell **A7**.
5. Enter **163**, **64**, **154**, and **108** in cells **B6**, **B7**, **C6**, and **C7**, respectively.

In-Depth Excel Use the **COMPUTE worksheet** of the **Chi-Square workbook** as a template.
The worksheet already contains the Table 11.2 two-hotel guest satisfaction data. For other problems, change the **Observed Frequencies** cell counts and row and column labels in rows 4 through 7.

Read the SHORT TAKES for Chapter 11 for an explanation of the formulas found in the COMPUTE worksheet (shown in the **COMPUTE_FORMULAS worksheet**). If you are using an older Excel version, use the COMPUTE_OLDER worksheet.

EG11.2 CHI-SQUARE TEST for DIFFERENCES AMONG MORE THAN TWO PROPORTIONS

Key Technique Use the **CHISQ.INV.RT** and **CHISQ.DIST.RT** functions to compute the critical value and the *p*-value, respectively.

Example Perform this chi-square test for the three-hotel guest satisfaction data shown in Figure 11.6 on page 398.

PHStat Use **Chi-Square Test**.
For the example, select **PHStat → Multiple-Sample Tests → Chi-Square Test**. In the procedure's dialog box (shown in right column):

1. Enter **0.05** as the **Level of Significance**.
2. Enter **2** as the **Number of Rows**.

3. Enter **3** as the **Number of Columns**.
4. Enter a **Title** and click **OK**.

In the new worksheet:

5. Read the yellow note instructions about entering values and then press the **Delete** key to delete the note.
6. Enter the Table 11.6 data (see page 396), including row and column labels, in rows 4 through 7. The **#DIV/0!** error messages will disappear when you finish entering all the table data.

In-Depth Excel Use the **ChiSquare2x3 worksheet** of the **Chi-Square Worksheets workbook** as a model.
The worksheet already contains the Table 11.6 guest satisfaction data (see page 396). For other 2 × 3 problems, change the **Observed Frequencies** cell counts and row and column labels in rows 4 through 7. For 2 × 4 problems, use the **ChiSquare2x4 worksheet** and change the **Observed Frequencies** cell counts and row and column labels in that worksheet. For 2 × 5 problems, use the **ChiSquare2x5 worksheet** and change the **Observed Frequencies** cell counts and row and column labels in that worksheet.

The formulas that are found in the ChiSquare2x3 workbook (shown in the **ChiSquare2x3_FORMULAS worksheet**) are similar to the formulas found in the COMPUTE worksheet of the Chi-Square workbook (see the previous section). If you use an Excel version older than Excel 2010, use the ChiSquare2x3_OLDER worksheet.

EG11.3 CHI-SQUARE TEST of INDEPENDENCE

Key Technique Use the **CHISQ.INV.RT** and **CHISQ.DIST.RT** functions to compute the critical value and the *p*-value, respectively.

Example Perform this chi-square test for the primary reason for not returning to hotel data that is shown in Figure 11.9 on page 403.

PHStat Use **Chi-Square Test**.
For the example, select **PHStat → Multiple-Sample Tests → Chi-Square Test**. In the procedure's dialog box (shown on page 413):

1. Enter **0.05** as the **Level of Significance**.
2. Enter **4** as the **Number of Rows**.
3. Enter **3** as the **Number of Columns**.

4. Enter a **Title** and click **OK**.

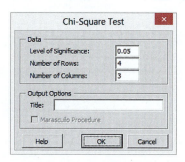

In the new worksheet:

5. Read the yellow note about entering values and then press the **Delete** key to delete the note.

6. Enter the Table 11.9 data on page 401, including row and column labels, in rows 4 through 9. The **#DIV/0!** error messages will disappear when you finish entering all of the table data.

In-Depth Excel Use the **ChiSquare4x3 worksheet** of the **Chi-Square Worksheets workbook** as a model.

The worksheet already contains the Table 11.9 primary reason for not returning to hotel data (see page 401). For other 4 × 3 problems, change the **Observed Frequencies** cell counts and row and column labels in rows 4 through 9. For 3 × 4 problems, use the **ChiSquare3x4 worksheet.** For 4 × 3 problems, use the **ChiSquare4x3 worksheet**. For 7 × 3 problems, use the **ChiSquare7x3 worksheet**. For 8 × 3 problems, use the **ChiSquare8x3 worksheet**. For each of these other worksheets, enter the contingency table data for the problem in the Observed Frequencies area.

Read the SHORT TAKES for Chapter 11 to the Calculations area in columns G through I (not shown in Figure 11.9). The formulas found in the COMPUTE worksheet (shown in the **COMPUTE_FORMULAS worksheet**) are similar to those in the other chi-square worksheets discussed in this Excel Guide.

If you use an Excel version older th an Excel 2010, use the ChiSquare4x3_OLDER worksheet.

CHAPTER 11 MINITAB GUIDE

MG11.1 CHI-SQUARE TEST for the DIFFERENCE BETWEEN TWO PROPORTIONS

Use **Chi-Square Test (Two-Way Table in Worksheet)** (requires summarized data). (In Minitab 17, select **Chi-Square Test for Association**.)

For example, to perform the Figure 11.3 test for the two-hotel guest satisfaction data on page 392, open to the **Two-Hotel Survey worksheet**. Select **Stat → Tables → Chi-Square Test (Two-Way Table in Worksheet)** (in Minitab 17, select **Chi-Square Test for Association**). In the Chi-Square Test dialog box (shown below):

1. Double-click **C2 Beachcomber** in the variables list to add **Beachcomber** to the **Columns containing the table** box. (If using in Minitab 17, first select **Summarized data in a two-way table** from the pull-down list.)

2. Double-click **C3 Windsurfer** in the variables list to add **Windsurfer** to the **Columns containing the table** box.

3. Click **OK**.

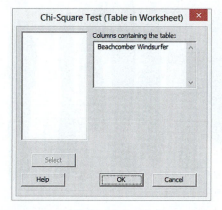

To perform this test using unsummarized data, select **Raw data (categorical variables)** in Minitab 17. For other Minitab

versions, use the Section MG2.1 instructions for using **Cross Tabulation and Chi-Square** to create contingency tables (see page 92), replacing step 4 with these steps 4 through 7:

4. Click **Chi-Square**.

In the Cross Tabulation - Chi-Square dialog box:

5. Select **Chi-Square analysis**, **Expected cell counts**, and **Each cell's contribution to the Chi-Square statistic**.

6. Click **OK**.

7. Back in the original dialog box, click **OK**.

MG11.2 CHI-SQUARE TEST for DIFFERENCES AMONG MORE THAN TWO PROPORTIONS

Use **Chi-Square Test (Two-Way Table in Worksheet)** (requires summarized data). (In Minitab 17, select **Chi-Square Test for Association.**)

Use the instructions for using unsummarized data in the previous section.

To perform the Figure 11.6 test for the three-hotel guest satisfaction data on page 398, open to the **Three-Hotel Survey worksheet**, select **Stat → Tables → Chi-Square Test (Two-Way Table in Worksheet)** (or **Chi-Square Test for Association**). In the Chi-Square Test (Table in Worksheet) dialog box, enter the names of columns 2 through 4 in the **Columns containing the table** box and click **OK**.

MG11.3 CHI-SQUARE TEST of INDEPENDENCE

Use the Section MG2.1 instructions for either **Chi-Square Test (Two-Way Table in Worksheet)** (or **Chi-Square Test for Association**) for summarized data or the (modified) **Cross Tabulation and Chi-Square** for unsummarized data to perform this test.

Simple Linear Regression

OBJECTIVES

Learn to use regression analysis to
predict the value of a dependent
variable based on the value of an
independent variable

Understand the meaning of the
regression coefficients b_0 and b_1

Learn to evaluate the assumptions of
regression analysis and what to do
if the assumptions are violated

Make inferences about the slope
and correlation coefficient

Estimate mean values and predict
individual values

USING STATISTICS

Knowing Customers at Sunflowers Apparel

Having survived recent economic slowdowns that have diminished their competitors, Sunflowers Apparel, a chain of upscale fashion stores for women, is in the midst of a companywide review that includes researching the factors that make their stores successful. Until recently, Sunflowers managers did not use data analysis to help select where to open stores, relying instead on subjective factors, such as the availability of an inexpensive lease or the perception that a particular location seemed ideal for one of their stores.

As the new director of planning, you have already consulted with marketing data firms that specialize in identifying and classifying groups of consumers. Based on such preliminary analyses, you have already tentatively discovered that the profile of Sunflowers shoppers may not only be the upper middle class long suspected of being the chain's clientele but may also include younger, aspirational families with young children, and, surprisingly, urban hipsters that set trends and are mostly single.

You seek to develop a systematic approach that will lead to making better decisions during the site-selection process. As a starting point, you have asked one marketing data firm to collect and organize data for the number of people in the identified groups of interest who live within a fixed radius of each store. You believe that the greater numbers of profiled customers contribute to store sales, and you want to explore the possible use of this relationship in the decision-making process. How can you use statistics so that you can forecast the annual sales of a proposed store based on the number of profiled customers that reside within a fixed radius of a Sunflowers store?

Fotolia

I n this chapter and the next chapter, you learn **regression analysis** techniques that help uncover relationships between variables. Regression analysis leads to selection of a **model** that expresses how one or more **independent variables** can be used to predict the value of another variable, called the **dependent variable**. Regression models identify the type of mathematical relationship that exists between a dependent variable and an independent variable, thereby enabling you to quantify the effect that a change in the independent variable has on the dependent variable. Models also help you identify unusual values that may be outliers (see references 2, 3, and 4).

This chapter discusses **simple linear regression** models that use a single numerical independent variable, X, to predict the numerical dependent variable, Y. (Chapter 13 discusses *multiple* regression models that use several independent variables to predict the dependent variable.) In the Sunflowers scenario, your initial belief reflects a possible simple linear regression model in which the number of profiled customers is the single numerical independent variable, X, being used to predict the annual sales of the store, the dependent variable, Y.

12.1 Types of Regression Models

Using a **scatter plot** (also known as **scatter diagram**) to visualize the X and Y variables, a technique introduced in Section 2.5 on page 60, can help suggest a starting point for regression analysis. The scatter plots in Figure 12.1 illustrates six possible relationships between an X and Y variable.

FIGURE 12.1

Six types of relationships found in scatter plots

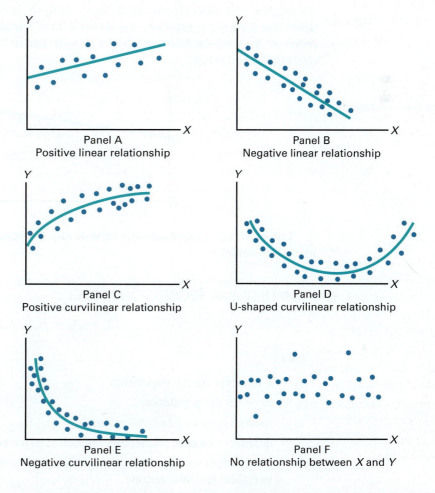

Panel A
Positive linear relationship

Panel B
Negative linear relationship

Panel C
Positive curvilinear relationship

Panel D
U-shaped curvilinear relationship

Panel E
Negative curvilinear relationship

Panel F
No relationship between X and Y

In Panel A, values of Y are generally increasing linearly as X increases. This panel is similar to Figure 12.3 on page 417, which illustrates the positive relationship between the number of profiled customers of the store and the store's annual sales for the Sunflowers Apparel women's clothing store chain.

Panel B is an example of a negative linear relationship. As X increases, the values of Y are generally decreasing. An example of this type of relationship might be the price of a particular product and the amount of sales. As the price charged for the product increases, the amount of sales may tend to decrease.

Panel C shows a positive curvilinear relationship between X and Y. The values of Y increase as X increases, but this increase tapers off beyond certain values of X. An example of a positive curvilinear relationship might be the age and maintenance cost of a machine. As a machine gets older, the maintenance cost may rise rapidly at first but then level off beyond a certain number of years.

Panel D shows a U-shaped relationship between X and Y. As X increases, at first Y generally decreases; but as X continues to increase, Y not only stops decreasing but actually increases above its minimum value. An example of this type of relationship might be entrepreneurial activity and levels of economic development as measured by GDP per capita. Entrepreneurial activity occurs more in the least and most developed countries.

Panel E illustrates an exponential relationship between X and Y. In this case, Y decreases very rapidly as X first increases, but then it decreases much less rapidly as X increases further. An example of an exponential relationship could be the value of an automobile and its age. The value drops drastically from its original price in the first year, but it decreases much less rapidly in subsequent years.

Finally, Panel F shows a set of data in which there is very little or no relationship between X and Y. High and low values of Y appear at each value of X.

Simple Linear Regression Models

Although scatter plots provide preliminary analysis, more sophisticated statistical procedures determine the most appropriate model for a set of variables. Simple linear regression models represent the simplest relationship of a straight-line or **linear relationship**. Figure 12.2 illustrates this relationship.

FIGURE 12.2

A straight-line relationship

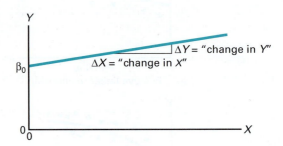

Equation (12.1) expresses this relationship mathematically by defining the simple linear regression model.

SIMPLE LINEAR REGRESSION MODEL

$$Y_i = \beta_0 + \beta_1 X_i + \varepsilon_i \tag{12.1}$$

where

$\beta_0 = Y$ intercept for the population

$\beta_1 = $ slope for the population

$\varepsilon_i = $ random error in Y for observation i

$Y_i = $ dependent variable (sometimes referred to as the **response variable**) for observation i

$X_i = $ independent variable (sometimes referred to as the predictor, or **explanatory variable**) for observation i

The $Y_i = \beta_0 + \beta_1 X_i$ portion of the simple linear regression model expressed in Equation (12.1) is a straight line. The **slope** of the line, β_1, represents the expected change in Y per unit change in X. It represents the mean amount that Y changes (either positively or negatively) for a one-unit change in X. The **Y intercept**, β_0, represents the mean value of Y when X equals 0. The last component of the model, ε_i, represents the random error in Y for each observation, i. In other words, ε_i is the vertical distance of the actual value of Y_i above or below the expected value of Y_i on the line.

12.2 Determining the Simple Linear Regression Equation

In the Sunflowers Apparel scenario on page 414, the business objective of the director of planning is to forecast annual sales for all new stores, based on the number of profiled customers who live no more than 30 minutes from a Sunflowers store. To examine the relationship between the number of profiled customers (in millions) who live within a fixed radius from a Sunflowers store and its annual sales ($millions), data were collected from a sample of 14 stores. Table 12.1 shows the organized data, which are stored in SiteSelection.

TABLE 12.1

Number of Profiled Customers (in millions) and Annual Sales (in $millions) for a Sample of 14 Sunflowers Apparel Stores

Store	Profiled Customers (millions)	Annual Sales ($millions)	Store	Profiled Customers (millions)	Annual Sales ($millions)
1	3.7	5.7	8	3.1	4.7
2	3.6	5.9	9	3.2	6.1
3	2.8	6.7	10	3.5	4.9
4	5.6	9.5	11	5.2	10.7
5	3.3	5.4	12	4.6	7.6
6	2.2	3.5	13	5.8	11.8
7	3.3	6.2	14	3.0	4.1

Figure 12.3 displays the scatter plot for the data in Table 12.1. Observe the increasing relationship between profiled customers (X) and annual sales (Y). As the number of profiled customers increases, annual sales increase approximately as a straight line (superimposed on the scatter plot). Thus, you can assume that a straight line provides a useful mathematical model of this relationship. Now you need to determine the specific straight line that is the *best* fit to these data.

FIGURE 12.3

Scatter plot for the Sunflowers Apparel data

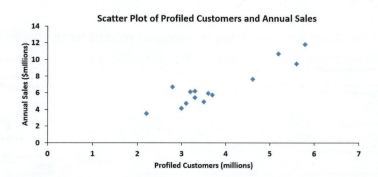

The Least-Squares Method

In the preceding section, a statistical model is hypothesized to represent the relationship between two variables—number of profiled customers and sales—in the entire population of Sunflowers Apparel stores. However, as shown in Table 12.1, the data are collected from a random sample of stores. If certain assumptions are valid (see Section 12.4), you can use the sample Y intercept, b_0, and the sample slope, b_1, as estimates of the respective population parameters, β_0 and β_1. Equation (12.2) uses these estimates to form the **simple linear regression equation**. This straight line is often referred to as the **prediction line**.

SIMPLE LINEAR REGRESSION EQUATION: THE PREDICTION LINE

The predicted value of Y equals the Y intercept plus the slope multiplied by the value of X.

$$\hat{Y}_i = b_0 + b_1 X_i \tag{12.2}$$

where

$$\hat{Y}_i = \text{predicted value of } Y \text{ for observation } i$$
$$X_i = \text{value of } X \text{ for observation } i$$
$$b_0 = \text{sample } Y \text{ intercept}$$
$$b_1 = \text{sample slope}$$

Equation (12.2) requires you to determine two **regression coefficients**—b_0 (the sample Y intercept) and b_1 (the sample slope). The most common approach to finding b_0 and b_1 is using the least-squares method. This method minimizes the sum of the squared differences between the actual values (Y_i) and the predicted values ($\hat{Y}_i$), using the simple linear regression equation [i.e., the prediction line; see Equation (12.2)]. This sum of squared differences is equal to

$$\sum_{i=1}^{n}(Y_i - \hat{Y}_i)^2$$

Because $\hat{Y}_i = b_0 + b_1 X_i$,

$$\sum_{i=1}^{n}(Y_i - \hat{Y}_i)^2 = \sum_{i=1}^{n}[Y_i - (b_0 + b_1 X_i)]^2$$

Because this equation has two unknowns, b_0 and b_1, the sum of squared differences depends on the sample Y intercept, b_0, and the sample slope, b_1. The **least-squares method** determines the values of b_0 and b_1 that minimize the sum of squared differences around the prediction line. Any values for b_0 and b_1 other than those determined by the least-squares method result in a greater sum of squared differences between the actual values (Y_i) and the predicted values ($\hat{Y}_i$).

Figure 12.4 presents results for the simple linear regression model for the Sunflowers Apparel data. Excel labels b_0 as Intercept and Minitab labels b_0 as Constant and they both label b_1 as Profiled Customers. Minitab 17 output is similar.

FIGURE 12.4

Excel and Minitab (16 or less) simple linear regression models for the Sunflowers Apparel data

	A	B	C	D	E	F	G
1	Simple Linear Regression						
2							
3	*Regression Statistics*						
4	Multiple R	0.9208					
5	R Square	0.8479					
6	Adjusted R Square	0.8352					
7	Standard Error	0.9993					
8	Observations	14					
9							
10	ANOVA						
11		*df*	*SS*	*MS*	*F*	*Significance F*	
12	Regression	1	66.7854	66.7854	66.8792	0.0000	
13	Residual	12	11.9832	0.9986			
14	Total	13	78.7686				
15							
16		Coefficients	Standard Error	t Stat	P-value	Lower 95%	Upper 95%
17	Intercept	-1.2088	0.9949	-1.2151	0.2477	-3.3765	0.9588
18	Profiled Customers	2.0742	0.2536	8.1780	0.0000	1.5216	2.6268

Regression Analysis: Annual Sales versus Profiled Customers

```
The regression equation is
Annual Sales = - 1.21 + 2.07 Profiled Customers

Predictor            Coef   SE Coef      T      P
Constant          -1.2088    0.9949  -1.22  0.248
Profiled Customers 2.0742    0.2536   8.18  0.000

S = 0.999298   R-Sq = 84.8%   R-Sq(adj) = 83.5%

Analysis of Variance
Source          DF      SS      MS      F      P
Regression       1  66.785  66.785  66.88  0.000
Residual Error  12  11.983   0.999
Total           13  78.769

Unusual Observations
              Profiled   Annual
Obs          Customers    Sales     Fit  SE Fit  Residual  St Resid
  3               2.80    6.700   4.599   0.365     2.101     2.26R
R denotes an observation with a large standardized
residual.

Predicted Values for New Observations
New Obs    Fit  SE Fit        95% CI           95% PI
  1      7.088   0.273  (6.493, 7.682)   (4.831, 9.345)

Values of Predictors for New Observations
              Profiled
New Obs      Customers
  1              4.00
```

In Figure 12.4, observe that $b_0 = -1.2088$ and $b_1 = 2.0742$. Using Equation (12.2) on page 418, the prediction line for these data is

$$\hat{Y}_i = -1.2088 + 2.0742X_i$$

The slope, b_1, is $+2.0742$. This means that for each increase of 1 unit in X, the predicted mean value of Y is estimated to increase by 2.0742 units. In other words, for each increase of 1.0 million profiled customers within 30 minutes of the store, the predicted mean annual sales are estimated to increase by $2.0742 million. Thus, the slope represents the portion of the annual sales that are estimated to vary according to the number of profiled customers.

The Y intercept, b_0, is -1.2088. The Y intercept represents the predicted value of Y when X equals 0. Because the number of profiled customers of the store cannot be 0, this Y intercept has little or no practical interpretation. Also, the Y intercept for this example is outside the range of the observed values of the X variable, and therefore interpretations of the value of b_0 should be made cautiously. Figure 12.5 displays the actual values and the prediction line.

FIGURE 12.5

Scatter plot and prediction line for Sunflowers Apparel data

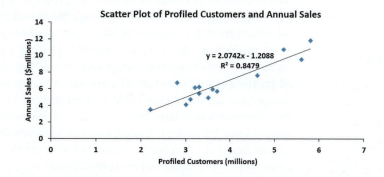

Example 12.1 illustrates a situation in which there is a direct interpretation for the Y intercept, b_0.

EXAMPLE 12.1

Interpreting the Y Intercept, b_0, and the Slope, b_1

A statistics professor wants to use the number of hours a student studies for a statistics final exam (X) to predict the final exam score (Y). A regression model is fit based on data collected from a class during the previous semester, with the following results:

$$\hat{Y}_i = 35.0 + 3X_i$$

What is the interpretation of the Y intercept, b_0, and the slope, b_1?

SOLUTION The Y intercept $b_0 = 35.0$ indicates that when the student does not study for the final exam, the predicted mean final exam score is 35.0. The slope $b_1 = 3$ indicates that for each increase of one hour in studying time, the predicted change in the mean final exam score is $+3.0$. In other words, the final exam score is predicted to increase by a mean of 3 points for each one-hour increase in studying time.

Return to the Sunflowers Apparel scenario on page 414. Example 12.2 illustrates how you use the prediction line to predict the annual sales.

EXAMPLE 12.2

Predicting Annual Sales Based on Number of Profiled Customers

Use the prediction line to predict the annual sales for a store with 4 million profiled customers.

SOLUTION You can determine the predicted value of annual sales by substituting $X = 4$ (millions of profiled customers) into the simple linear regression equation:

$$\hat{Y}_i = -1.2088 + 2.0742X_i$$
$$\hat{Y}_i = -1.2088 + 2.0742(4) = 7.0879 \text{ or } \$7,087,900$$

Thus, a store with 4 million profiled customers has predicted mean annual sales of $7,087,900.

Predictions in Regression Analysis: Interpolation Versus Extrapolation

When using a regression model for prediction purposes, you should consider only the **relevant range** of the independent variable in making predictions. This relevant range includes all values from the smallest to the largest X used in developing the regression model. Hence, when predicting Y for a given value of X, you can interpolate within this relevant range of the X values, but you should not extrapolate beyond the range of X values. When you use the number of profiled customers to predict annual sales, the number of profiled customers (in millions) varies from 2.2 to 5.8 (see Table 12.1 on page 417). Therefore, you should predict annual sales *only* for stores that have between 2.2 and 5.8 million profiled customers. Any prediction of annual sales for stores outside this range assumes that the observed relationship between sales and the number of profiled customers for stores that have between 2.2 and 5.8 million profiled customers is the same as for stores outside this range. For example, you cannot extrapolate the linear relationship beyond 5.8 million profiled customers in Example 12.2. It would be improper to use the prediction line to forecast the sales for a new store that has 8 million profiled customers because the relationship between sales and the number of profiled customers may have a point of diminishing returns. If that is true, as the number of profiled customers increases beyond 5.8 million, the effect on sales may become smaller and smaller.

Computing the Y Intercept, b_0, and the Slope, b_1

For small data sets, you can use a hand calculator to compute the least-squares regression coefficients. Equations (12.3) and (12.4) give the values of b_0 and b_1, which minimize

$$\sum_{i=1}^{n}(Y_i - \hat{Y}_i)^2 = \sum_{i=1}^{n}[Y_i - (b_0 + b_1X_i)]^2$$

COMPUTATIONAL FORMULA FOR THE SLOPE, b_1

$$b_1 = \frac{SSXY}{SSX} \tag{12.3}$$

where

$$SSXY = \sum_{i=1}^{n}(X_i - \overline{X})(Y_i - \overline{Y}) = \sum_{i=1}^{n}X_iY_i - \frac{\left(\sum_{i=1}^{n}X_i\right)\left(\sum_{i=1}^{n}Y_i\right)}{n}$$

$$SSX = \sum_{i=1}^{n}(X_i - \overline{X})^2 = \sum_{i=1}^{n}X_i^2 - \frac{\left(\sum_{i=1}^{n}X_i\right)^2}{n}$$

(continued)

COMPUTATIONAL FORMULA FOR THE Y INTERCEPT, b_0

$$b_0 = \overline{Y} - b_1 \overline{X} \tag{12.4}$$

where

$$\overline{Y} = \frac{\sum\limits_{i=1}^{n} Y_i}{n}$$

$$\overline{X} = \frac{\sum\limits_{i=1}^{n} X_i}{n}$$

EXAMPLE 12.3

Computing the Y Intercept, b_0, and the Slope, b_1

Compute the Y intercept, b_0, and the slope, b_1, for the Sunflowers Apparel data.

SOLUTION In Equations (12.3) and (12.4), five quantities need to be computed to determine b_1 and b_0. These are n, the sample size; $\sum\limits_{i=1}^{n} X_i$, the sum of the X values; $\sum\limits_{i=1}^{n} Y_i$, the sum of the Y values; $\sum\limits_{i=1}^{n} X_i^2$, the sum of the squared X values; and $\sum\limits_{i=1}^{n} X_i Y_i$, the sum of the product of X and Y. For the Sunflowers Apparel data, the number of profiled customers (X) is used to predict the annual sales (Y) in a store. Table 12.2 presents the computations of the sums needed for the site selection problem. The table also includes $\sum\limits_{i=1}^{n} Y_i^2$, the sum of the squared Y values that will be used to compute SST in Section 12.3.

TABLE 12.2

Computations for the Sunflowers Apparel Data

Store	Profiled Customers (X)	Annual Sales (Y)	X^2	Y^2	XY
1	3.7	5.7	13.69	32.49	21.09
2	3.6	5.9	12.96	34.81	21.24
3	2.8	6.7	7.84	44.89	18.76
4	5.6	9.5	31.36	90.25	53.20
5	3.3	5.4	10.89	29.16	17.82
6	2.2	3.5	4.84	12.25	7.70
7	3.3	6.2	10.89	38.44	20.46
8	3.1	4.7	9.61	22.09	14.57
9	3.2	6.1	10.24	37.21	19.52
10	3.5	4.9	12.25	24.01	17.15
11	5.2	10.7	27.04	114.49	55.64
12	4.6	7.6	21.16	57.76	34.96
13	5.8	11.8	33.64	139.24	68.44
14	3.0	4.1	9.00	16.81	12.30
Totals	52.9	92.8	215.41	693.90	382.85

Using Equations (12.3) and (12.4), you can compute b_0 and b_1:

$$SSXY = \sum_{i=1}^{n}(X_i - \overline{X})(Y_i - \overline{Y}) = \sum_{i=1}^{n}X_iY_i - \frac{\left(\sum_{i=1}^{n}X_i\right)\left(\sum_{i=1}^{n}Y_i\right)}{n}$$

$$= 382.85 - \frac{(52.9)(92.8)}{14}$$

$$= 382.85 - 350.65142$$

$$= 32.19858$$

$$SSX = \sum_{i=1}^{n}(X_i - \overline{X})^2 = \sum_{i=1}^{n}X_i^2 - \frac{\left(\sum_{i=1}^{n}X_i\right)^2}{n}$$

$$= 215.41 - \frac{(52.9)^2}{14}$$

$$= 215.41 - 199.88642$$

$$= 15.52358$$

With these values, compute b_1:

$$b_1 = \frac{SSXY}{SSX}$$

$$= \frac{32.19858}{15.52358}$$

$$= 2.07417$$

and:

$$\overline{Y} = \frac{\sum_{i=1}^{n}Y_i}{n} = \frac{92.8}{14} = 6.62857$$

$$\overline{X} = \frac{\sum_{i=1}^{n}X_i}{n} = \frac{52.9}{14} = 3.77857$$

With these values, compute b_0:

$$b_0 = \overline{Y} - b_1\overline{X}$$

$$= 6.62857 - 2.07417(3.77857)$$

$$= -1.2088265$$

VISUAL EXPLORATIONS

Exploring Simple Linear Regression Coefficients

Open the **VE-Simple Linear Regression add-in workbook** to explore the coefficients. (See Appendix C to learn more about using this workbook.) When this workbook opens properly, it adds a **Simple Linear Regression** menu in either the Add-ins tab (Microsoft Windows) or the Apple menu bar (OS X).

To explore the effects of changing the simple linear regression coefficients, select **Simple Linear Regression → Explore Coefficients**. In the Explore Coefficients floating control panel (shown inset below), click the spinner buttons for b_1 **slope** (the slope of the prediction line) and b_0 **intercept** (the Y intercept of the prediction line) to change the prediction line. Using the visual feedback of the chart, try to create a prediction line that is as close as possible to the prediction line defined by the least-squares estimates. In other words, try to make the **Difference from Target SSE** value as small as possible. (See page 427 for an explanation of SSE.)

At any time, click **Reset** to reset the b_1 and b_0 values or **Solution** to reveal the prediction line defined by the least-squares method. Click **Finish** when you are finished with this exercise.

Using Your Own Regression Data

Select **Simple Linear Regression using your worksheet data** from the **Simple Linear Regression** menu to explore the simple linear regression coefficients using data you supply from a worksheet. In the procedure's dialog box, enter the cell range of your Y variable as the **Y Variable Cell Range** and the cell range of your X variable as the **X Variable Cell Range**. Click **First cells in both ranges contain a label**, enter a **Title**, and click **OK**. After the scatter plot appears onscreen, continue with the Explore Coefficients floating control panel as described in the left column.

Exploring Simple Linear Regression Coefficients

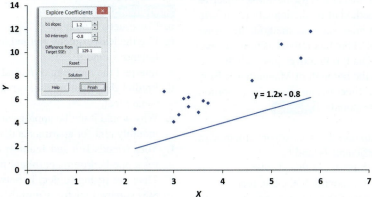

Problems for Section 12.2

LEARNING THE BASICS

12.1 Fitting a straight line to a set of data yields the following prediction line:

$$\hat{Y}_i = 2 + 5X_i$$

a. Interpret the meaning of the Y intercept, b_0.
b. Interpret the meaning of the slope, b_1.
c. Predict the value of Y for $X = 3$.

12.2 If the values of X in Problem 12.1 range from 2 to 25, should you use this model to predict the mean value of Y when X equals
a. 3?   **b.** −3?   **c.** 0?   **d.** 24?

12.3 Fitting a straight line to a set of data yields the following prediction line:

$$\hat{Y}_i = 16 - 0.5X_i$$

a. Interpret the meaning of the Y intercept, b_0.
b. Interpret the meaning of the slope, b_1.
c. Predict the value of Y for $X = 6$.

APPLYING THE CONCEPTS

✓ SELF Test **12.4** The production of wine is a multibillion-dollar worldwide industry. In an attempt to develop a model of wine quality as judged by wine experts, data was collected from red wine variants of Portuguese "Vinho Verde" wine. (Data extracted from P. Cortez, Cerdeira, A., Almeida, F., Matos, T., and Reis, J., "Modeling Wine Preferences by Data Mining from Physiochemical Properties," *Decision Support Systems*, 47, 2009, pp. 547–553 and **bit.ly/9xKlEa**.) A sample of 50 wines is stored in **VinhoVerde**. Develop a simple linear regression model to predict wine quality, measured on a scale from 0 (very bad) to 10 (excellent), based on alcohol content (%).
a. Construct a scatter plot.
    For these data, $b_0 = -0.3529$ and $b_1 = 0.5624$.
b. Interpret the meaning of the slope, b_1, in this problem.
c. Predict the mean wine quality for wines with a 10% alcohol content.
d. What conclusion can you reach based on the results of (a)–(c)?

12.5 Zagat's publishes restaurant ratings for various locations in the United States. The file Restaurants contains the Zagat rating for food, décor, service, and the cost per person for a sample of 100 restaurants located in New York City and in a suburb of New York City. Develop a regression model to predict the cost per person, based on a variable that represents the sum of the ratings for food, décor, and service.

Sources: Extracted from *Zagat Survey 2013, New York City Restaurants*; and *Zagat Survey 2012–2013, Long Island Restaurants.*

a. Construct a scatter plot.
For these data, $b_0 = -46.7718$ and $b_1 = 1.4963$.
b. Assuming a linear relationship, use the least-squares method to compute the regression coefficients b_0 and b_1.
c. Interpret the meaning of the Y intercept, b_0, and the slope, b_1, in this problem.
d. Predict the mean cost per person for a restaurant with a summated rating of 50.
e. What should you tell the owner of a group of restaurants in this geographical area about the relationship between the summated rating and the cost of a meal?

12.6 The owner of a moving company typically has his most experienced manager predict the total number of labor hours that will be required to complete an upcoming move. This approach has proved useful in the past, but the owner has the business objective of developing a more accurate method of predicting labor hours. In a preliminary effort to provide a more accurate method, the owner has decided to use the number of cubic feet moved as the independent variable and has collected data for 36 moves in which the origin and destination were within the borough of Manhattan in New York City and in which the travel time was an insignificant portion of the hours worked. The data are stored in Moving.
a. Construct a scatter plot.
b. Assuming a linear relationship, use the least-squares method to determine the regression coefficients b_0 and b_1.
c. Interpret the meaning of the slope, b_1, in this problem.
d. Predict the mean labor hours for moving 500 cubic feet.
e. What should you tell the owner of the moving company about the relationship between cubic feet moved and labor hours?

12.7 Starbucks Coffee Co. uses a data-based approach to improving the quality and customer satisfaction of its products. When survey data indicated that Starbucks needed to improve its package-sealing process, an experiment was conducted to determine the factors in the bag-sealing equipment that might be affecting the ease of opening the bag without tearing the inner liner of the bag. (Data extracted from L. Johnson and S. Burrows, "For Starbucks, It's in the Bag," *Quality Progress*, March 2011, pp. 17–23.) One factor that could affect the rating of the ability of the bag to resist tears was the plate gap on the bag-sealing equipment. Data were collected on 19 bags in which the plate gap was varied. The results are stored in Starbucks.
a. Construct a scatter plot.
b. Assuming a linear relationship, use the least-squares method to determine the regression coefficients b_0 and b_1.
c. Interpret the meaning of the slope, b_1, in this problem.
d. Predict the mean tear rating when the plate gap is equal to 0.
e. What should you tell management of Starbucks about the relationship between the plate gap and the tear rating?

12.8 The value of a sports franchise is directly related to the amount of revenue that a franchise can generate. The file BBValues represents the value in 2014 (in $millions) and the annual revenue (in $millions) for the 30 Major League Baseball franchises. (Data extracted from www.forbes.com/mlb-valuations/list.) Suppose you want to develop a simple linear regression model to predict franchise value based on annual revenue generated.
a. Construct a scatter plot.
b. Use the least-squares method to determine the regression coefficients b_0 and b_1.
c. Interpret the meaning of b_0 and b_1 in this problem.
d. Predict the mean value of a baseball franchise that generates $250 million of annual revenue.
e. What would you tell a group considering an investment in a major league baseball team about the relationship between revenue and the value of a team?

12.9 An agent for a residential real estate company in a suburb located outside of Washington, DC, has the business objective of developing more accurate estimates of the monthly rental cost for apartments. Toward that goal, the agent would like to use the size of an apartment, as defined by square footage to predict the monthly rental cost. The agent selects a sample of 48 one-bedroom apartments and collects and stores the data in RentSilverSpring.
a. Construct a scatter plot.
b. Use the least-squares method to determine the regression coefficients b_0 and b_1.
c. Interpret the meaning of b_0 and b_1 in this problem.
d. Predict the mean monthly rent for an apartment that has 800 square feet.
e. Why would it not be appropriate to use the model to predict the monthly rent for apartments that have 1,500 square feet?
f. Your friends Jim and Jennifer are considering signing a lease for a one-bedroom apartment in this residential neighborhood. They are trying to decide between two apartments, one with 800 square feet for a monthly rent of $1,130 and the other with 830 square feet for a monthly rent of $1,410. Based on (a) through (d), which apartment do you think is a better deal?

12.10 A company that holds the DVD distribution rights to movies previously released only in theaters has the business objective of developing estimates of the sales revenue of DVDs. Toward this goal, a company analyst plans to use box office gross to predict DVD sales revenue. For 26 movies, the analyst collects the box office gross (in $millions) in the year that they were released and the DVD revenue (in $millions) in the following year and stores these data in Movie. (Data extracted from "Annual Movie Chart–2012," bit.ly/1kVJIF3 and "Top-Selling DVDs in the United States 2013," bit.ly/UpTep9.)

For these data,
a. Construct a scatter plot.
b. Assuming a linear relationship, use the least-squares method to determine the regression coefficients b_0 and b_1.
c. Interpret the meaning of the slope, b_1, in this problem.
d. Predict the mean sales revenue for a movie DVD that had a box office gross of $100 million.
e. What conclusions can you reach about predicting DVD revenue from movie gross?

12.3 Measures of Variation

When using the least-squares method to determine the regression coefficients you need to compute three measures of variation. The first measure, the **total sum of squares (*SST*)**, is a measure of variation of the Y_i values around their mean, $\overline{Y}$. The **total variation**, or total sum of squares, is subdivided into **explained variation** and **unexplained variation**. The explained variation, or **regression sum of squares (*SSR*)**, represents variation that is explained by the relationship between X and Y, and the unexplained variation, or **error sum of squares (*SSE*)**, represents variation due to factors other than the relationship between X and Y. Figure 12.6 shows the different measures of variation for a single Y_i value.

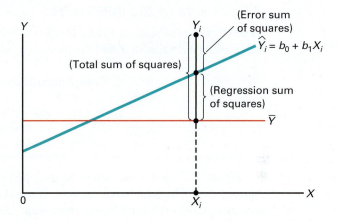

Computing the Sum of Squares

The regression sum of squares (*SSR*) is based on the difference between $\hat{Y}_i$ (the predicted value of Y from the prediction line) and $\overline{Y}$ (the mean value of Y). The error sum of squares (*SSE*) represents the part of the variation in Y that is not explained by the regression. It is based on the difference between Y_i and $\hat{Y}_i$. The total sum of squares (*SST*) is equal to the regression sum of squares (*SSR*) plus the error sum of squares (*SSE*). Equations (12.5), (12.6), (12.7), and (12.8) define these measures of variation and the total sum of squares (*SST*).

MEASURES OF VARIATION IN REGRESSION

The total sum of squares (*SST*) is equal to the regression sum of squares (*SSR*) plus the error sum of squares (*SSE*).

$$SST = SSR + SSE \tag{12.5}$$

TOTAL SUM OF SQUARES (*SST*)

The total sum of squares (*SST*) is equal to the sum of the squared differences between each observed value of Y and the mean value of Y.

$$SST = \text{Total sum of squares}$$

$$= \sum_{i=1}^{n}(Y_i - \overline{Y})^2 \tag{12.6}$$

REGRESSION SUM OF SQUARES (*SSR*)

The regression sum of squares (*SSR*) is equal to the sum of the squared differences between each predicted value of *Y* and the mean value of *Y*.

$$SSR = \text{Explained variation or regression sum of squares}$$

$$= \sum_{i=1}^{n} (\hat{Y}_i - \overline{Y})^2 \tag{12.7}$$

ERROR SUM OF SQUARES (*SSE*)

The error sum of squares (*SSE*) is equal to the sum of the squared differences between each observed value of *Y* and the predicted value of *Y*.

$$SSE = \text{Unexplained variation or error sum of squares}$$

$$= \sum_{i=1}^{n} (Y_i - \hat{Y}_i)^2 \tag{12.8}$$

Figure 12.7 shows the sum of squares portion of the Figure 12.4 results for the Sunflowers Apparel data. The total variation, *SST*, is equal to 78.7686. This amount is subdivided into the sum of squares explained by the regression (*SSR*), equal to 66.7854, and the sum of squares unexplained by the regression (*SSE*), equal to 11.9832. From Equation (12.5) on page 425:

$$SST = SSR + SSE$$
$$78.7686 = 66.7854 + 11.9832$$

FIGURE 12.7
Excel and Minitab sum of squares portion for the Sunflowers Apparel data

The Coefficient of Determination

By themselves, *SSR*, *SSE*, and *SST* provide little information. However, the ratio of the regression sum of squares (*SSR*) to the total sum of squares (*SST*) measures the proportion of variation in *Y* that is explained by the linear relationship of the independent variable *X* with the dependent variable *Y* in the regression model. This ratio, called the coefficient of determination, r^2, is defined in Equation (12.9).

COEFFICIENT OF DETERMINATION

The coefficient of determination is equal to the regression sum of squares (i.e., explained variation) divided by the total sum of squares (i.e., total variation).

$$r^2 = \frac{\text{Regression sum of squares}}{\text{Total sum of squares}} = \frac{SSR}{SST} \tag{12.9}$$

Student Tip
r^2 must be a value between 0 and 1. It cannot be negative.

The **coefficient of determination** measures the proportion of variation in Y that is explained by the variation in the independent variable X in the regression model.

For the Sunflowers Apparel data, with $SSR = 66.7854$, $SSE = 11.9832$, and $SST = 78.7686$,

$$r^2 = \frac{66.7854}{78.7686} = 0.8479$$

Therefore, 84.79% of the variation in annual sales is explained by the variability in the number of profiled customers. This large r^2 indicates a strong linear relationship between these two variables because the regression model has explained 84.79% of the variability in predicting annual sales. Only 15.21% of the sample variability in annual sales is due to factors other than what is accounted for by the linear regression model that uses the number of profiled customers.

Figure 12.8 presents the regression statistics table portion of the Figure 12.4 results for the Sunflowers Apparel data. This table contains the coefficient of determination.

FIGURE 12.8

Excel and Minitab regression statistics for the Sunflowers Apparel data

	A	B
3	**Regression Statistics**	
4	Multiple R	0.9208
5	R Square	0.8479
6	Adjusted R Square	0.8352
7	Standard Error	0.9993
8	Observations	14

Predictor	Coef	SE Coef	T	P
Constant	-1.2088	0.9949	-1.22	0.248
Profiled Customers	2.0742	0.2536	8.18	0.000

S = 0.999298   R-Sq = 84.8%   R-Sq(adj) = 83.5%

EXAMPLE 12.4

Computing the Coefficient of Determination

Compute the coefficient of determination, r^2, for the Sunflowers Apparel data.

SOLUTION You can compute SST, SSR, and SSE, which are defined in Equations (12.6), (12.7), and (12.8) on pages 425 and 426, by using Equations (12.10), (12.11), and (12.12).

COMPUTATIONAL FORMULA FOR SST

$$SST = \sum_{i=1}^{n}(Y_i - \bar{Y})^2 = \sum_{i=1}^{n} Y_i^2 - \frac{\left(\sum_{i=1}^{n} Y_i\right)^2}{n} \tag{12.10}$$

COMPUTATIONAL FORMULA FOR SSR

$$SSR = \sum_{i=1}^{n}(\hat{Y}_i - \bar{Y})^2$$

$$= b_0 \sum_{i=1}^{n} Y_i + b_1 \sum_{i=1}^{n} X_i Y_i - \frac{\left(\sum_{i=1}^{n} Y_i\right)^2}{n} \tag{12.11}$$

COMPUTATIONAL FORMULA FOR SSE

$$SSE = \sum_{i=1}^{n}(Y_i - \hat{Y}_i)^2 = \sum_{i=1}^{n} Y_i^2 - b_0 \sum_{i=1}^{n} Y_i - b_1 \sum_{i=1}^{n} X_i Y_i \tag{12.12}$$

Using the summary results from Table 12.2 on page 421,

$$SST = \sum_{i=1}^{n}(Y_i - \bar{Y})^2 = \sum_{i=1}^{n} Y_i^2 - \frac{\left(\sum_{i=1}^{n} Y_i\right)^2}{n}$$

$$= 693.9 - \frac{(92.8)^2}{14}$$

$$= 693.9 - 615.13142$$

$$= 78.76858$$

$$SSR = \sum_{i=1}^{n} (\hat{Y}_i - \bar{Y})^2$$

$$= b_0 \sum_{i=1}^{n} Y_i + b_1 \sum_{i=1}^{n} X_i Y_i - \frac{\left(\sum_{i=1}^{n} Y_i\right)^2}{n}$$

$$= (-1.2088265)(92.8) + (2.07417)(382.85) - \frac{(92.8)^2}{14}$$

$$= 66.7854$$

$$SSE = \sum_{i=1}^{n} (Y_i - \hat{Y}_i)^2$$

$$= \sum_{i=1}^{n} Y_i^2 - b_0 \sum_{i=1}^{n} Y_i - b_1 \sum_{i=1}^{n} X_i Y_i$$

$$= 693.9 - (-1.2088265)(92.8) - (2.07417)(382.85)$$

$$= 11.9832$$

> **Student Tip**
> Coefficients computed manually with the assistance of handheld calculators may differ slightly.

Therefore,

$$r^2 = \frac{66.7854}{78.7686} = 0.8479$$

Standard Error of the Estimate

Although the least-squares method produces the line that fits the data with the minimum amount of prediction error, unless all the observed data points fall on a straight line, the prediction line is not a perfect predictor. Just as all data values cannot be expected to be exactly equal to their mean, neither can all the values in a regression analysis be expected to be located exactly on the prediction line. Figure 12.5 on page 419 illustrates the variability around the prediction line for the Sunflowers Apparel data. Notice that many of the observed values of Y fall near the prediction line, but none of the values are exactly on the line.

The **standard error of the estimate** measures the variability of the observed Y values from the predicted Y values in the same way that the standard deviation in Chapter 3 measures the variability of each value around the sample mean. In other words, the standard error of the estimate is the standard deviation *around* the prediction line, whereas the standard deviation in Chapter 3 is the standard deviation *around* the sample mean. Equation (12.13) defines the standard error of the estimate, represented by the symbol S_{YX}.

STANDARD ERROR OF THE ESTIMATE

$$S_{YX} = \sqrt{\frac{SSE}{n-2}} = \sqrt{\frac{\sum_{i=1}^{n}(Y_i - \hat{Y}_i)^2}{n-2}} \tag{12.13}$$

where

$$Y_i = \text{actual value of } Y \text{ for a given } X_i$$
$$\hat{Y}_i = \text{predicted value of } Y \text{ for a given } X_i$$
$$SSE = \text{error sum of squares}$$

From Equation (12.8) and Figure 12.4 or Figure 12.7 on pages 418 or 426, $SSE = 11.9832$. Thus,

$$S_{YX} = \sqrt{\frac{11.9832}{14 - 2}} = 0.9993$$

This standard error of the estimate, equal to 0.9993 millions of dollars (i.e., $999,300), is labeled Standard Error in the Figure 12.8 Excel results and S in the Minitab results. The standard error of the estimate represents a measure of the variation around the prediction line. It is measured in the same units as the dependent variable Y. The interpretation of the standard error of the estimate is similar to that of the standard deviation. Just as the standard deviation measures variability around the mean, the standard error of the estimate measures variability around the prediction line. For Sunflowers Apparel, the typical difference between actual annual sales at a store and the predicted annual sales using the regression equation is approximately $999,300.

Problems for Section 12.3

LEARNING THE BASICS

12.11 How do you interpret a coefficient of determination, r^2, equal to 0.80?

12.12 If $SSR = 36$ and $SSE = 4$, determine SST and then compute the coefficient of determination, r^2, and interpret its meaning.

12.13 If $SSR = 66$ and $SST = 88$, compute the coefficient of determination, r^2, and interpret its meaning.

12.14 If $SSE = 10$ and $SSR = 30$, compute the coefficient of determination, r^2, and interpret its meaning.

12.15 If $SSR = 120$, why is it impossible for SST to equal 110?

APPLYING THE CONCEPTS

✓ SELF Test **12.16** In Problem 12.4 on page 423, the percentage of alcohol was used to predict wine quality (stored in **VinhoVerde**). For those data, $SSR = 21.8677$ and $SST = 64.0000$.
a. Determine the coefficient of determination, r^2, and interpret its meaning.
b. Determine the standard error of the estimate.
c. How useful do you think this regression model is for predicting sales?

12.17 In Problem 12.5 on page 424, you used the summated rating to predict the cost of a restaurant meal (stored in **Restaurants**). For those data, $SSR = 9,740.0629$ and $SST = 17,844.75$.
a. Determine the coefficient of determination, r^2, and interpret its meaning.
b. Determine the standard error of the estimate.
c. How useful do you think this regression model is for predicting the cost of a restaurant meal?

12.18 In Problem 12.6 on page 424, an owner of a moving company wanted to predict labor hours, based on the cubic feet moved (stored in **Moving**). Using the results of that problem,
a. determine the coefficient of determination, r^2, and interpret its meaning.
b. determine the standard error of the estimate.
c. How useful do you think this regression model is for predicting labor hours?

12.19 In Problem 12.7 on page 424, you used the plate gap on the bag-sealing equipment to predict the tear rating of a bag of coffee (stored in **Starbucks**). Using the results of that problem,
a. determine the coefficient of determination, r^2, and interpret its meaning.
b. determine the standard error of the estimate.
c. How useful do you think this regression model is for predicting the tear rating based on the plate gap in the bag-sealing equipment?

12.20 In Problem 12.8 on page 424, you used annual revenues to predict the value of a baseball franchise (stored in **BBValues**). Using the results of that problem,
a. determine the coefficient of determination, r^2, and interpret its meaning.
b. determine the standard error of the estimate.
c. How useful do you think this regression model is for predicting the value of a baseball franchise?

12.21 In Problem 12.9 on page 424, an agent for a real estate company wanted to predict the monthly rent for one-bedroom apartments, based on the size of the apartment (stored in **Rent-SilverSpring**). Using the results of that problem,
a. determine the coefficient of determination, r^2, and interpret its meaning.
b. determine the standard error of the estimate.
c. How useful do you think this regression model is for predicting the monthly rent?
d. Can you think of other variables that might explain the variation in monthly rent?

12.22 In Problem 12.10 on page 424, you used box office gross to predict DVD revenue (stored in **Movie**). Using the results of that problem,
a. determine the coefficient of determination, r^2, and interpret its meaning.
b. determine the standard error of the estimate.
c. How useful do you think this regression model is for predicting DVD revenue?
d. Can you think of other variables that might explain the variation in DVD revenue?

12.4 Assumptions of Regression

When hypothesis testing and the analysis of variance were discussed in Chapters 9 through 11, the importance of the assumptions to the validity of any conclusions reached was emphasized. The assumptions necessary for regression are similar to those of the analysis of variance because both are part of the general category of *linear models* (reference 4).

The four **assumptions of regression** (known by the acronym LINE) are:

- Linearity
- Independence of errors
- Normality of error
- Equal variance

The first assumption, **linearity**, states that the relationship between variables is linear. Relationships between variables that are not linear are discussed in reference 4.

The second assumption, **independence of errors**, requires that the errors (ε_i) be independent of one another. This assumption is particularly important when data are collected over a period of time. In such situations, the errors in a specific time period are sometimes correlated with those of the previous time period.

The third assumption, **normality**, requires that the errors (ε_i) be normally distributed at each value of X. Like the t test and the ANOVA F test, regression analysis is fairly robust against departures from the normality assumption. As long as the distribution of the errors at each level of X is not extremely different from a normal distribution, inferences about β_0 and β_1 are not seriously affected.

The fourth assumption, **equal variance**, or **homoscedasticity**, requires that the variance of the errors (ε_i) be constant for all values of X. In other words, the variability of Y values is the same when X is a low value as when X is a high value. The equal-variance assumption is important when making inferences about β_0 and β_1. If there are serious departures from this assumption, you can use either data transformations or weighted least-squares methods (see reference 4).

12.5 Residual Analysis

Sections 12.2 and 12.3 developed a regression model using the least-squares method for the Sunflowers Apparel data. Is this the correct model for these data? Are the assumptions presented in Section 12.4 valid? **Residual analysis** visually evaluates these assumptions and helps you determine whether the regression model that has been selected is appropriate.

The **residual**, or estimated error value, e_i, is the difference between the observed (Y_i) and predicted ($\hat{Y}_i$) values of the dependent variable for a given value of X_i. A residual appears on a scatter plot as the vertical distance between an observed value of Y and the prediction line. Equation (12.14) defines the residual.

> RESIDUAL
>
> The residual is equal to the difference between the observed value of Y and the predicted value of Y.
>
> $$e_i = Y_i - \hat{Y}_i \tag{12.14}$$

Evaluating the Assumptions

Recall from Section 12.4 that the four assumptions of regression (known by the acronym LINE) are linearity, independence, normality, and equal variance.

Linearity To evaluate linearity, you plot the residuals on the vertical axis against the corresponding X_i values of the independent variable on the horizontal axis. If the linear model is appropriate for the data, you will not see any apparent pattern in the plot. However, if the linear model is not appropriate, in the residual plot, there will be a relationship between the X_i values and the residuals, e_i.

You can see such a pattern in the residuals in Figure 12.9. Panel A shows a situation in which, although there is an increasing trend in Y as X increases, the relationship seems curvilinear because the upward trend decreases for increasing values of X. This effect is even more apparent in Panel B, where there is a clear relationship between X_i and e_i. By removing the linear trend of X with Y, the residual plot has exposed the lack of fit in the simple linear model more clearly than the scatter plot in Panel A. For these data, a quadratic or curvilinear model (see reference 4) is a better fit and should be used instead of the simple linear model.

FIGURE 12.9

Studying the appropriateness of the simple linear regression model

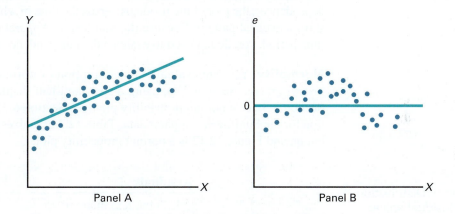

To determine whether the simple linear regression model for the Sunflowers Apparel data is appropriate, you need to determine the residuals. Figure 12.10 displays the predicted annual sales values and residuals for the Sunflowers Apparel data.

FIGURE 12.10

Table of residuals for the Sunflowers Apparel data

Store	Profiled Customers	Predicted Annual Sales	Annual Sales	Residuals
1	3.7	6.4656	5.7	-0.7656
2	3.6	6.2582	5.9	-0.3582
3	2.8	4.5988	6.7	2.1012
4	5.6	10.4065	9.5	-0.9065
5	3.3	5.6359	5.4	-0.2359
6	2.2	3.3543	3.5	0.1457
7	3.3	5.6359	6.2	0.5641
8	3.1	5.2211	4.7	-0.5211
9	3.2	5.4285	6.1	0.6715
10	3.5	6.0508	4.9	-1.1508
11	5.2	9.5769	10.7	1.1231
12	4.6	8.3324	7.6	-0.7324
13	5.8	10.8214	11.8	0.9786
14	3	5.0137	4.1	-0.9137

To assess linearity, you plot the residuals against the independent variable (number of profiled customers, in millions) in Figure 12.11. Although there is widespread scatter in the residual plot, there is no clear pattern or relationship between the residuals and X_i. The residuals appear to be evenly spread above and below 0 for different values of X. You can conclude that the linear model is appropriate for the Sunflowers Apparel data.

FIGURE 12.11

Plot of residuals against the profiled customers of a store for the Sunflowers Apparel data

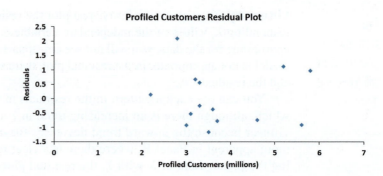

Independence You can evaluate the assumption of independence of the errors by plotting the residuals in the order or sequence in which the data were collected. If the values of Y are part of a time series (see Section 2.5), a residual may sometimes be related to the residual that precedes it. If this relationship exists between consecutive residuals (which violates the assumption of independence), the plot of the residuals versus the time in which the data were collected will often show a cyclical pattern. Because the Sunflowers Apparel data were collected during the same time period, you do not need to evaluate the independence assumption for these data.

Normality You can evaluate the assumption of normality in the errors by constructing a histogram (see Section 2.4), using a stem-and-leaf display (see Section 2.4), a boxplot (see Section 3.3), or a normal probability plot (see Section 6.3). To evaluate the normality assumption for the Sunflowers Apparel data, Table 12.3 organizes the residuals into a frequency distribution and Figure 12.12 is a normal probability plot.

TABLE 12.3

Frequency Distribution of 14 Residual Values for the Sunflowers Apparel Data

Residuals	Frequency
−1.25 but less than −0.75	4
−0.75 but less than −0.25	3
−0.25 but less than +0.25	2
+0.25 but less than +0.75	2
+0.75 but less than +1.25	2
+1.25 but less than +1.75	0
+1.75 but less than +2.25	1
	14

Although the small sample size makes it difficult to evaluate normality, from the normal probability plot of the residuals in Figure 12.12, the data do not appear to depart substantially from a normal distribution. The robustness of regression analysis with modest departures from normality enables you to conclude that you should not be overly concerned about departures from this normality assumption in the Sunflowers Apparel data.

FIGURE 12.12

Excel and Minitab normal probability plots of the residuals for the Sunflowers Apparel data

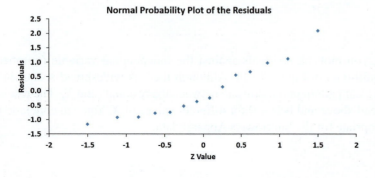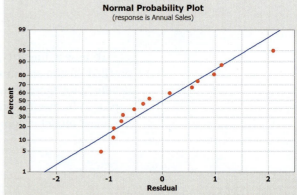

Equal Variance   You can evaluate the assumption of equal variance from a plot of the residuals with X_i. You examine the plot to see if there is approximately the same amount of variation in the residuals at each value of X. For the Sunflowers Apparel data of Figure 12.11 on page 432, there do not appear to be major differences in the variability of the residuals for different X_i values. Thus, you can conclude that there is no apparent violation in the assumption of equal variance at each level of X.

To examine a case in which the equal-variance assumption is violated, observe Figure 12.13, which is a plot of the residuals with X_i for a hypothetical set of data. This plot is fan shaped because the variability of the residuals increases dramatically as X increases. Because this plot shows unequal variances of the residuals at different levels of X, the equal-variance assumption is invalid.

FIGURE 12.13

Violation of equal variance

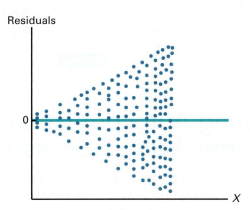

Problems for Section 12.5

LEARNING THE BASICS

12.23 The following results provide the X values, residuals, and a residual plot from a regression analysis:

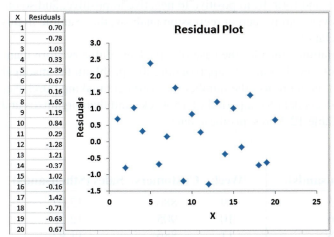

X	Residuals
1	0.70
2	-0.78
3	1.03
4	0.33
5	2.39
6	-0.67
7	0.16
8	1.65
9	-1.19
10	0.84
11	0.29
12	-1.28
13	1.21
14	-0.37
15	1.02
16	-0.16
17	1.42
18	-0.71
19	-0.63
20	0.67

Is there any evidence of a pattern in the residuals? Explain.

12.24 The following results show the X values, residuals, and a residual plot from a regression analysis:

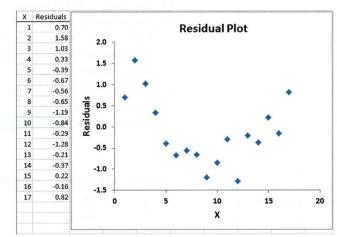

X	Residuals
1	0.70
2	1.58
3	1.03
4	0.33
5	-0.39
6	-0.67
7	-0.56
8	-0.65
9	-1.19
10	-0.84
11	-0.29
12	-1.28
13	-0.21
14	-0.37
15	0.22
16	-0.16
17	0.82

Is there any evidence of a pattern in the residuals? Explain.

costs and the number of orders received have been collected over the past 24 months and are stored in `Warecost`.

a. Assuming a linear relationship, use the least-squares method to find the regression coefficients b_0 and b_1.

b. Predict the monthly warehouse distribution costs when the number of orders is 4,500.

c. Plot the residuals versus the time period.

d. Compute the Durbin-Watson statistic. At the 0.05 level of significance, is there evidence of positive autocorrelation among the residuals?

e. Based on the results of (c) and (d), is there reason to question the validity of the model?

f. What conclusions can you reach concerning the factors that affect distribution costs?

12.37 A freshly brewed shot of espresso has three distinct components: the heart, body, and crema. The separation of these three components typically lasts only 10 to 20 seconds. To use the espresso shot in making a latte, a cappuccino, or another drink, the shot must be poured into the beverage during the separation of the heart, body, and crema. If the shot is used after the separation occurs, the drink becomes excessively bitter and acidic, ruining the final drink. Thus, a longer separation time allows the drink-maker more time to pour the shot and ensure that the beverage will meet expectations. An employee at a coffee shop hypothesized that the harder the espresso grounds were tamped down into the portafilter before brewing, the longer the separation time would be. An experiment using 24 observations was conducted to test this relationship. The independent variable Tamp measures the distance, in inches, between the espresso grounds and the top of the portafilter (i.e., the harder the tamp, the greater the distance). The dependent variable Time is the number of seconds the heart, body, and crema are separated (i.e., the amount of time after the shot is poured before it must be used for the customer's beverage). The data are stored in `Espresso`.

a. Use the least-squares method to develop a simple regression equation with Time as the dependent variable and Tamp as the independent variable.

b. Predict the separation time for a tamp distance of 0.50 inch.

c. Plot the residuals versus the time order of experimentation. Are there any noticeable patterns?

d. Compute the Durbin-Watson statistic. At the 0.05 level of significance, is there evidence of positive autocorrelation among the residuals?

e. Based on the results of (c) and (d), is there reason to question the validity of the model?

f. What conclusions can you reach concerning the effect of tamping on the time of separation?

12.38 The owners of a chain of ice cream stores have the business objective of improving the forecast of daily sales so that staffing shortages can be minimized during the summer season. As a starting point, the owners decide to develop a simple linear regression model to predict daily sales based on atmospheric temperature. They select a sample of 21 consecutive days and store the results in `IceCream`. (Hint: Determine which are the independent and dependent variables.)

a. Assuming a linear relationship, use the least-squares method to compute the regression coefficients b_0 and b_1.

b. Predict the sales for a day in which the temperature is 83°F.

c. Plot the residuals versus the time period.

d. Compute the Durbin-Watson statistic. At the 0.05 level of significance, is there evidence of positive autocorrelation among the residuals?

e. Based on the results of (c) and (d), is there reason to question the validity of the model?

f. What conclusions can you reach concerning the relationship between sales and atmospheric temperature?

12.7 Inferences About the Slope and Correlation Coefficient

In Sections 12.1 through 12.3, regression was used solely for descriptive purposes. You learned how to determine the regression coefficients using the least-squares method and how to predict Y for a given value of X. In addition, you learned how to compute and interpret the standard error of the estimate and the coefficient of determination.

When residual analysis, as discussed in Section 12.5, indicates that the assumptions of a least-squares regression model are not seriously violated and that the straight-line model is appropriate, you can make inferences about the linear relationship between the variables in the population.

t Test for the Slope

To determine the existence of a significant linear relationship between the X and Y variables, you test whether β_1 (the population slope) is equal to 0. The null and alternative hypotheses are as follows:

$$H_0: \beta_1 = 0 \, [\text{There is no linear relationship (the slope is zero).}]$$
$$H_1: \beta_1 \neq 0 \, [\text{There is a linear relationship (the slope is not zero).}]$$

If you reject the null hypothesis, you conclude that there is evidence of a linear relationship. Equation (12.16) defines the test statistic for the slope, which is based on the sampling distribution of the slope.

TESTING A HYPOTHESIS FOR A POPULATION SLOPE, β_1, USING THE t TEST

The t_{STAT} test statistic equals the difference between the sample slope and hypothesized value of the population slope divided by S_{b_1}, the standard error of the slope.

$$t_{STAT} = \frac{b_1 - \beta_1}{S_{b_1}} \tag{12.16}$$

where

$$S_{b_1} = \frac{S_{YX}}{\sqrt{SSX}}$$

$$SSX = \sum_{i=1}^{n}(X_i - \overline{X})^2$$

The t_{STAT} test statistic follows a t distribution with $n - 2$ degrees of freedom.

Return to the Sunflowers Apparel scenario on page 414. To test whether there is a significant linear relationship between the number of profiled customers and the annual sales at the 0.05 level of significance, refer to the t test results shown in Figure 12.17.

FIGURE 12.17

Excel and Minitab t test for the slope results for the Sunflowers Apparel data

	A	B	C	D	E	F	G
16		Coefficients	Standard Error	t Stat	P-value	Lower 95%	Upper 95%
17	Intercept	-1.2088	0.9949	-1.1251	0.2477	-3.3765	0.9588
18	Profiled Customers	2.0742	0.2536	8.1780	0.0000	1.5216	2.6268

Predictor	Coef	SE Coef	T	P
Constant	-1.2088	0.9949	-1.22	0.248
Profiled Customers	2.0742	0.2536	8.18	0.000

From Figure 12.4 or Figure 12.17,

$$b_1 = +2.0742 \quad n = 14 \quad S_{b_1} = 0.2536$$

and

$$t_{STAT} = \frac{b_1 - \beta_1}{S_{b_1}}$$

$$= \frac{2.0742 - 0}{0.2536} = 8.178$$

Using the 0.05 level of significance, the critical value of t with $n - 2 = 12$ degrees of freedom is 2.1788. Because $t_{STAT} = 8.178 > 2.1788$ or because the p-value is 0.0000, which is less than $\alpha = 0.05$, you reject H_0 (see Figure 12.18). Hence, you can conclude that there is a significant linear relationship between mean annual sales and the number of profiled customers.

FIGURE 12.18

Testing a hypothesis about the population slope at the 0.05 level of significance, with 12 degrees of freedom

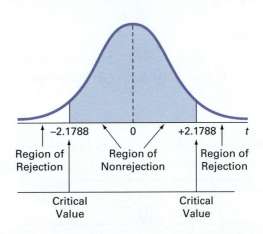

F Test for the Slope

As an alternative to the *t* test, in simple linear regression, you can use an *F* test to determine whether the slope is statistically significant. In Section 10.4, you used the *F* distribution to test the ratio of two variances. Equation (12.17) defines the *F* test for the slope as the ratio of the variance that is due to the regression (*MSR*) divided by the error variance ($MSE = S_{YX}^2$).

TESTING A HYPOTHESIS FOR A POPULATION SLOPE, β_1, USING THE *F* TEST

The F_{STAT} test statistic is equal to the regression mean square (*MSR*) divided by the mean square error (*MSE*).

$$F_{STAT} = \frac{MSR}{MSE} \qquad (12.17)$$

where

$$MSR = \frac{SSR}{1} = SSR$$

$$MSE = \frac{SSE}{n-2}$$

The F_{STAT} test statistic follows an *F* distribution with 1 and $n - 2$ degrees of freedom.

Using a level of significance α, the decision rule is

$$\text{Reject } H_0 \text{ if } F_{STAT} > F_\alpha;$$

$$\text{otherwise, do not reject } H_0.$$

Table 12.6 organizes the complete set of results into an analysis of variance (ANOVA) table.

TABLE 12.6

ANOVA Table for Testing the Significance of a Regression Coefficient

Source	df	Sum of Squares	Mean Square (variance)	F
Regression	1	SSR	$MSR = \dfrac{SSR}{1} = SSR$	$F_{STAT} = \dfrac{MSR}{MSE}$
Error	$n-2$	SSE	$MSE = \dfrac{SSE}{n-2}$	
Total	$n-1$	SST		

Figure 12.19, a completed ANOVA table for the Sunflowers sales data (extracted from Figure 12.4), shows that the computed F_{STAT} test statistic is 66.8792 and the *p*-value is 0.0000.

FIGURE 12.19

Excel and Minitab *F* test results for the Sunflowers Apparel data

	A	B	C	D	E	F
10	ANOVA					
11		df	SS	MS	F	Significance F
12	Regression	1	66.7854	66.7854	66.8792	0.0000
13	Residual	12	11.9832	0.9986		
14	Total	13	78.7686			

```
Analysis of Variance
Source          DF      SS      MS     F      P
Regression       1  66.785  66.785  66.88  0.000
Residual Error  12  11.983   0.999
Total           13  78.769
```

In simple linear regression,
$t^2 = F$.

Using a level of significance of 0.05, from Table E.5, the critical value of the F distribution, with 1 and 12 degrees of freedom, is 4.75 (see Figure 12.20). Because $F_{STAT} = 66.8792 > 4.75$ or because the p-value $= 0.0000 < 0.05$, you reject H_0 and conclude that there is a significant linear relationship between the number of profiled customers and annual sales. Because the F test in Equation (12.17) on page 440 is equivalent to the t test in Equation (12.16) on page 439, you reach the same conclusion.

FIGURE 12.20

Regions of rejection and nonrejection when testing for the significance of the slope at the 0.05 level of significance, with 1 and 12 degrees of freedom

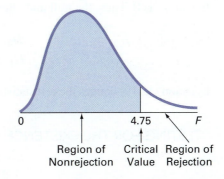

| 0 | 4.75 | F |
| Region of Nonrejection | Critical Value | Region of Rejection |

Confidence Interval Estimate for the Slope

As an alternative to testing for the existence of a linear relationship between the variables, you can construct a confidence interval estimate of β_1 using Equation (12.18).

CONFIDENCE INTERVAL ESTIMATE OF THE SLOPE, β_1

The confidence interval estimate for the population slope can be constructed by taking the sample slope, b_1, and adding and subtracting the critical t value multiplied by the standard error of the slope.

$$b_1 \pm t_{\alpha/2}S_{b_1}$$

$$b_1 - t_{\alpha/2}S_{b_1} \leq \beta_1 \leq b_1 + t_{\alpha/2}S_{b_1} \qquad \textbf{(12.18)}$$

where

$t_{\alpha/2}$ = critical value corresponding to an upper-tail probability of $\alpha/2$ from the t distribution with $n - 2$ degrees of freedom (i.e., a cumulative area of $1 - \alpha/2$)

From the Figure 12.17 results on page 440,

$$b_1 = 2.0742 \quad n = 14 \quad S_{b_1} = 0.2536$$

To construct a 95% confidence interval estimate, $\alpha/2 = 0.025$, and from Table E.3, $t_{\alpha/2} = 2.1788$. Thus,

$$b_1 \pm t_{\alpha/2}S_{b_1} = 2.0742 \pm (2.1788)(0.2536)$$
$$= 2.0742 \pm 0.5526$$
$$1.5216 \leq \beta_1 \leq 2.6268$$

Therefore, you have 95% confidence that the estimated population slope is between 1.5216 and 2.6268. The confidence interval indicates that for each increase of 1 million profiled customers, predicted annual sales are estimated to increase by at least $1,521,600 but no more than $2,626,800. Because both of these values are above 0, you have evidence of a significant linear relationship between annual sales and the number of profiled customers. Had the interval included 0, you would have concluded that there is no evidence of a significant relationship between the variables.

t Test for the Correlation Coefficient

In Section 3.5 on page 126, the strength of the relationship between two numerical variables was measured using the **correlation coefficient**, r. The values of the coefficient of correlation range from -1 for a perfect negative correlation to $+1$ for a perfect positive correlation. You can use the correlation coefficient to determine whether there is a statistically significant linear relationship between X and Y. To do so, you hypothesize that the population correlation coefficient, ρ, is 0. Thus, the null and alternative hypotheses are

$$H_0: \rho = 0 \ \ (\text{no correlation})$$
$$H_1: \rho \neq 0 \ \ (\text{correlation})$$

Equation (12.19) defines the test statistic for determining the existence of a significant correlation.

TESTING FOR THE EXISTENCE OF CORRELATION

$$t_{STAT} = \frac{r - \rho}{\sqrt{\dfrac{1 - r^2}{n - 2}}} \tag{12.19a}$$

where

$$r = +\sqrt{r^2} \ \ \text{if} \ \ b_1 > 0$$
$$r = -\sqrt{r^2} \ \ \text{if} \ \ b_1 < 0$$

The t_{STAT} test statistic follows a t distribution with $n - 2$ degrees of freedom. r is calculated as in Equation (3.15) on page 126:

$$r = \frac{\text{cov}(X, Y)}{S_X S_Y} \tag{12.19b}$$

where

$$\text{cov}(X, Y) = \frac{\sum\limits_{i=1}^{n}(X_i - \overline{X})(Y_i - \overline{Y})}{n - 1}$$

$$S_X = \sqrt{\frac{\sum\limits_{i=1}^{n}(X_i - \overline{X})^2}{n - 1}}$$

$$S_Y = \sqrt{\frac{\sum\limits_{i=1}^{n}(Y_i - \overline{Y})^2}{n - 1}}$$

In the Sunflowers Apparel problem, $r^2 = 0.8479$ and $b_1 = +2.0742$ (see Figure 12.4 on page 418). Because $b_1 > 0$, the correlation coefficient for annual sales and profiled customers is the positive square root of r^2—that is, $r = +\sqrt{0.8479} = +0.9208$. You use Equation (12.19a) to test the null hypothesis that there is no correlation between these two variables. This results in the following t_{STAT} statistic:

$$t_{STAT} = \frac{r - 0}{\sqrt{\dfrac{1 - r^2}{n - 2}}}$$

$$= \frac{0.9208 - 0}{\sqrt{\dfrac{1 - (0.9208)^2}{14 - 2}}} = 8.178$$

Using the 0.05 level of significance, because $t_{STAT} = 8.178 > 2.1788$, you reject the null hypothesis. You conclude that there is a significant association between annual sales and the number of profiled customers. This t_{STAT} test statistic is equivalent to the t_{STAT} test statistic found when testing whether the population slope, β_1, is equal to zero.

Problems for Section 12.7

LEARNING THE BASICS

12.39 You are testing the null hypothesis that there is no linear relationship between two variables, X and Y. From your sample of $n = 10$, you determine that $r = 0.80$.
a. What is the value of the t test statistic t_{STAT}?
b. At the $\alpha = 0.05$ level of significance, what are the critical values?
c. Based on your answers to (a) and (b), what statistical decision should you make?

12.40 You are testing the null hypothesis that there is no linear relationship between two variables, X and Y. From your sample of $n = 18$, you determine that $b_1 = +4.5$ and $S_{b_1} = 1.5$.
a. What is the value of t_{STAT}?
b. At the $\alpha = 0.05$ level of significance, what are the critical values?
c. Based on your answers to (a) and (b), what statistical decision should you make?
d. Construct a 95% confidence interval estimate of the population slope, β_1.

12.41 You are testing the null hypothesis that there is no linear relationship between two variables, X and Y. From your sample of $n = 20$, you determine that $SSR = 60$ and $SSE = 40$.
a. What is the value of F_{STAT}?
b. At the $\alpha = 0.05$ level of significance, what is the critical value?
c. Based on your answers to (a) and (b), what statistical decision should you make?
d. Compute the correlation coefficient by first computing r^2 and assuming that b_1 is negative.
e. At the 0.05 level of significance, is there a significant correlation between X and Y?

APPLYING THE CONCEPTS

✓ **SELF** **12.42** In Problem 12.4 on page 423, you used the percentage of alcohol to predict wine quality. The data are stored in **VinhoVerde**. From the results of that problem, $b_1 = 0.5624$ and $S_{b_1} = 0.1127$.
a. At the 0.05 level of significance, is there evidence of a linear relationship between the percentage of alcohol and wine quality?
b. Construct a 95% confidence interval estimate of the population slope, β_1.

12.43 In Problem 12.5 on page 424, you used the summated rating of a restaurant to predict the cost of a meal. The data are stored in **Restaurants**. Using the results of that problem, $b_1 = 1.4963$ and $S_{b_1} = 0.1379$.

a. At the 0.05 level of significance, is there evidence of a linear relationship between the summated rating of a restaurant and the cost of a meal?
b. Construct a 95% confidence interval estimate of the population slope, β_1.

12.44 In Problem 12.6 on page 424, the owner of a moving company wanted to predict labor hours, based on the number of cubic feet moved. The data are stored in **Moving**. Use the results of that problem.
a. At the 0.05 level of significance, is there evidence of a linear relationship between the number of cubic feet moved and labor hours?
b. Construct a 95% confidence interval estimate of the population slope, β_1.

12.45 In Problem 12.7 on page 424, you used the plate gap in the bag-sealing equipment to predict the tear rating of a bag of coffee. The data are stored in **Starbucks**. Use the results of that problem.
a. At the 0.05 level of significance, is there evidence of a linear relationship between the plate gap of the bag-sealing machine and the tear rating of a bag of coffee?
b. Construct a 95% confidence interval estimate of the population slope, β_1.

12.46 In Problem 12.8 on page 424, you used annual revenues to predict the value of a baseball franchise. The data are stored in **BBValues**. Use the results of that problem.
a. At the 0.05 level of significance, is there evidence of a linear relationship between annual revenue and franchise value?
b. Construct a 95% confidence interval estimate of the population slope, β_1.

12.47 In Problem 12.9 on page 424, an agent for a real estate company wanted to predict the monthly rent for one-bedroom apartments, based on the size of the apartment. The data are stored in **RentSilverSpring**. Use the results of that problem.
a. At the 0.05 level of significance, is there evidence of a linear relationship between the size of the apartment and the monthly rent?
b. Construct a 95% confidence interval estimate of the population slope, β_1.

12.48 In Problem 12.10 on page 424, you used box office gross to predict DVD revenue. The data are stored in **Movie**. Use the results of that problem.
a. At the 0.05 level of significance, is there evidence of a linear relationship between box office gross and DVD revenue?
b. Construct a 95% confidence interval estimate of the population slope, β_1.

12.49 The volatility of a stock is often measured by its beta value. You can estimate the beta value of a stock by developing a simple linear regression model, using the percentage weekly change in the stock as the dependent variable and the percentage weekly change in a market index as the independent variable. The S&P 500 Index is a common index to use. For example, if you wanted to estimate the beta value for Disney, you could use the following model, which is sometimes referred to as a *market model*:

$$(\% \text{ weekly change in Disney}) = \beta_0$$
$$+ \beta_1 (\% \text{ weekly change in S \& P 500 index}) + \varepsilon$$

The least-squares regression estimate of the slope b_1 is the estimate of the beta value for Disney. A stock with a beta value of 1.0 tends to move the same as the overall market. A stock with a beta value of 1.5 tends to move 50% more than the overall market, and a stock with a beta value of 0.6 tends to move only 60% as much as the overall market. Stocks with negative beta values tend to move in the opposite direction of the overall market. The following table gives some beta values for some widely held stocks as of June 8, 2014:

Company	Ticker Symbol	Beta
Apple	AAPL	0.74
Disney	DIS	1.32
Dr. Pepper Snapple Group	DPS	0.22
Marriott	MAR	1.34
Microsoft	MSFT	0.68
Procter & Gamble	PG	0.40

Source: Data extracted from finance.yahoo.com, June 8, 2014.

a. For each of the six companies, interpret the beta value.
b. How can investors use the beta value as a guide for investing?

12.50 Index funds are mutual funds that try to mimic the movement of leading indexes, such as the S&P 500 or the Russell 2000. The beta values (as described in Problem 12.49) for these funds are therefore approximately 1.0, and the estimated market models for these funds are approximately

$$(\% \text{ weekly change in index fund}) = 0.0 + 1.0$$
$$(\% \text{ weekly change in the index})$$

Leveraged index funds are designed to magnify the movement of major indexes. Direxion Funds is a leading provider of leveraged index and other alternative-class mutual fund products for investment advisors and sophisticated investors. Two of the company's funds are shown in the following table:

Name	Ticker Symbol	Description
Daily Small Cap Bull 3x Fund	TNA	300% of the Russell 2000 Index
Monthly S&P Bear 2x Fund	DXSSX	200% of the S&P 500 Index

Source: Data extracted from www.direxionfunds.com.

The estimated market models for these funds are approximately

$$(\% \text{ weekly change in TNA}) = 0.0 + 3.0$$
$$(\% \text{ weekly change in the Russell 2000})$$
$$(\% \text{ weekly change in DXSSX}) = 0.0 + 2.0$$
$$(\% \text{ weekly change in the S\&P 500 Index})$$

Thus, if the Russell 2000 Index gains 10% over a period of time, the leveraged mutual fund TNA gains approximately 30%. On the downside, if the same index loses 20%, TNA loses approximately 60%.

a. The objective of the Direxion Funds Bull 3x Fund, SPXL, is 300% of the performance of the S&P 500 Index. What is its approximate market model?
b. If the S&P 500 Index gains 10% in a year, what return do you expect SPXL to have?
c. If the S&P 500 Index loses 20% in a year, what return do you expect SPXL to have?
d. What type of investors should be attracted to leveraged index funds? What type of investors should stay away from these funds?

12.51 The file Cereals contains the calories and sugar, in grams, in one serving of seven breakfast cereals:

Cereal	Calories	Sugar
Kellogg's All Bran	80	6
Kellogg's Corn Flakes	100	2
Wheaties	100	4
Nature's Path Organic Multigrain Flakes	110	4
Kellogg's Rice Krispies	130	4
Post Shredded Wheat Vanilla Almond	190	11
Kellogg's Mini Wheats	200	10

a. Compute and interpret the coefficient of correlation, r.
b. At the 0.05 level of significance, is there a significant linear relationship between calories and sugar?

12.52 Movie companies need to predict the gross receipts of an individual movie once the movie has debuted. The following results (stored in PotterMovies) are the first weekend gross, the U.S. gross, and the worldwide gross (in $millions) of the eight Harry Potter movies that debuted from 2001 to 2011:

Title	First Weekend	U.S. Gross	Worldwide Gross
Sorcerer's Stone	90.295	317.558	976.458
Chamber of Secrets	88.357	261.988	878.988
Prisoner of Azkaban	93.687	249.539	795.539
Goblet of Fire	102.335	290.013	896.013
Order of the Phoenix	77.108	292.005	938.469
Half-Blood Prince	77.836	301.460	934.601
Deathly Hallows Part I	125.017	295.001	955.417
Deathly Hallows Part II	169.189	381.001	1,328.11

Source: Data extracted from **www.the-numbers.com/interactive/comp-Harry-Potter.php**.

a. Compute the coefficient of correlation between first weekend gross and U.S. gross, first weekend gross and worldwide gross, and U.S. gross and worldwide gross.

b. At the 0.05 level of significance, is there a significant linear relationship between first weekend gross and U.S. gross, first weekend gross and worldwide gross, and U.S. gross and worldwide gross?

12.53 College football is big business, with coaches' salaries, revenues, and expenses in millions of dollars. The file College Football contains the coaches' pay and revenue for college football at 105 of the 124 schools that are part of the Division I Football Bowl Subdivision. (Data extracted from "College Football Coaches Continue to See Salary Explosion," *USA Today*, November 20, 2012, p. 8C.)

a. Compute and interpret the coefficient of correlation, r.

b. At the 0.05 level of significance, is there a significant linear relationship between a coach's pay and revenue?

12.54 A survey by the Pew Research Center found that social networking is popular in many nations around the world. The file GlobalSocialMedia contains the level of social media networking (measured as the percent of individuals polled who use social networking sites) and the GDP per capita based on purchasing power parity (PPP) for each of 24 selected countries. (Data extracted from "Emerging Nations Embrace Internet, Mobile Technology," **bit.ly/1hL6JKA**.)

a. Compute and interpret the coefficient of correlation, r.

b. At the 0.05 level of significance, is there a significant linear relationship between GDP and social media usage?

c. What conclusions can you reach about the relationship between GDP and social media usage?

12.8 Estimation of Mean Values and Prediction of Individual Values

In Chapter 8, you studied the concept of the confidence interval estimate of the population mean. In Example 12.2 on page 420, you used the prediction line to predict the mean value of Y for a given X. The mean annual sales for stores that had 4 million profiled customers within a fixed radius was predicted to be 7.0879 millions of dollars ($\$7,087,900$). This estimate, however, is a *point estimate* of the population mean. This section presents methods to develop a confidence interval estimate for the mean response for a given X and for developing a prediction interval for an individual response, Y, for a given value of X.

The Confidence Interval Estimate for the Mean Response

Equation (12.20) defines the **confidence interval estimate for the mean response** for a given X.

CONFIDENCE INTERVAL ESTIMATE FOR THE MEAN OF Y

$$\hat{Y}_i \pm t_{\alpha/2} S_{YX} \sqrt{h_i}$$

$$\hat{Y}_i - t_{\alpha/2} S_{YX} \sqrt{h_i} \le \mu_{Y|X=X_i} \le \hat{Y}_i + t_{\alpha/2} S_{YX} \sqrt{h_i} \qquad (12.20)$$

where

$$h_i = \frac{1}{n} + \frac{(X_i - \bar{X})^2}{SSX}$$

$\hat{Y}_i = $ predicted value of Y; $\hat{Y}_i = b_0 + b_1 X_i$

$S_{YX} = $ standard error of the estimate

$n = $ sample size

$X_i = $ given value of X

$\mu_{Y|X=X_i} = $ mean value of Y when $X = X_i$

$$SSX = \sum_{i=1}^{n} (X_i - \bar{X})^2$$

$t_{\alpha/2} = $ critical value corresponding to an upper-tail probability of $\alpha/2$ from the t distribution with $n - 2$ degrees of freedom (i.e., a cumulative area of $1 - \alpha/2$)

The width of the confidence interval in Equation (12.20) depends on several factors. Increased variation around the prediction line, as measured by the standard error of the estimate, results in a wider interval. As you would expect, increased sample size reduces the width of the interval. In addition, the width of the interval varies at different values of X. When you predict Y for values of X close to $\overline{X}$, the interval is narrower than for predictions for X values farther away from $\overline{X}$.

In the Sunflowers Apparel example, suppose you want to construct a 95% confidence interval estimate of the mean annual sales for the entire population of stores that have 4 million profiled customers $(X = 4)$. Using the simple linear regression equation,

$$\hat{Y}_i = -1.2088 + 2.0742X_i$$
$$= -1.2088 + 2.0742(4) = 7.0879 \text{ (millions of dollars)}$$

Also, given the following:

$$\overline{X} = 3.7786 \quad S_{YX} = 0.9993$$

$$SSX = \sum_{i=1}^{n}(X_i - \overline{X})^2 = 15.5236$$

From Table E.3, $t_{\alpha/2} = 2.1788$. Thus,

$$\hat{Y}_i \pm t_{\alpha/2}S_{YX}\sqrt{h_i}$$

where

$$h_i = \frac{1}{n} + \frac{(X_i - \overline{X})^2}{SSX}$$

so that

$$\hat{Y}_i \pm t_{\alpha/2}S_{YX}\sqrt{\frac{1}{n} + \frac{(X_i - \overline{X})^2}{SSX}}$$

$$= 7.0879 \pm (2.1788)(0.9993)\sqrt{\frac{1}{14} + \frac{(4 - 3.7786)^2}{15.5236}}$$

$$= 7.0879 \pm 0.5946$$

so

$$6.4932 \le \mu_{Y|X=4} \le 7.6825$$

Therefore, the 95% confidence interval estimate is that the population mean annual sales are between $6,493,200 and $7,682,500 for stores with 4 million profiled customers.

The Prediction Interval for an Individual Response

In addition to constructing a confidence interval for the mean value of Y, you can also construct a prediction interval for an individual value of Y. Although the form of this interval is similar to that of the confidence interval estimate of Equation (12.20), the prediction interval is predicting an individual value, not estimating a mean. Equation (12.21) defines the **prediction interval for an individual response**, Y, at a given value, X_i, denoted by $Y_{X=X_i}$.

PREDICTION INTERVAL FOR AN INDIVIDUAL RESPONSE, Y

$$\hat{Y}_i \pm t_{\alpha/2}S_{YX}\sqrt{1 + h_i} \tag{12.21}$$

$$\hat{Y}_i - t_{\alpha/2}S_{YX}\sqrt{1 + h_i} \le Y_{X=X_i} \le \hat{Y}_i + t_{\alpha/2}S_{YX}\sqrt{1 + h_i}$$

(continued)

where

$$Y_{X=X_i} = \text{future value of } Y \text{ when } X = X_i$$

$t_{\alpha/2} =$ critical value corresponding to an upper-tail probability of $\alpha/2$ from the t distribution with $n - 2$ degrees of freedom (i.e., a cumulative area of $1 - \alpha/2$)

In addition, h_i, $\hat{Y}_i$, S_{YX}, n, and X_i are defined as in Equation (12.20) on page 445.

To construct a 95% prediction interval of the annual sales for an individual store that has 4 million profiled customers ($X = 4$), you first compute $\hat{Y}_i$. Using the prediction line:

$$\hat{Y}_i = -1.2088 + 2.0742X_i$$
$$= -1.2088 + 2.0742(4)$$
$$= 7.0879 \text{ (millions of dollars)}$$

Also, given the following:

$$\overline{X} = 3.7786 \quad S_{YX} = 0.9993$$

$$SSX = \sum_{i=1}^{n} (X_i - \overline{X})^2 = 15.5236$$

From Table E.3, $t_{\alpha/2} = 2.1788$. Thus,

$$\hat{Y}_i \pm t_{\alpha/2} S_{YX} \sqrt{1 + h_i}$$

where

$$h_i = \frac{1}{n} + \frac{(X_i - \overline{X})^2}{\sum_{i=1}^{n} (X_i - \overline{X})^2}$$

so that

$$\hat{Y}_i \pm t_{\alpha/2} S_{YX} \sqrt{1 + \frac{1}{n} + \frac{(X_i - \overline{X})^2}{SSX}}$$

$$= 7.0879 \pm (2.1788)(0.9993) \sqrt{1 + \frac{1}{14} + \frac{(4 - 3.7786)^2}{15.5236}}$$

$$= 7.0879 \pm 2.2570$$

so

$$4.8308 \leq Y_{X=4} \leq 9.3449$$

Therefore, with 95% confidence, you predict that the annual sales for an individual store with 4 million profiled customers is between \$4,830,800 and \$9,344,900.

Figure 12.21 presents Excel and Minitab results for the confidence interval estimate and the prediction interval for the Sunflowers Apparel data. If you compare the results of the confidence interval estimate and the prediction interval, you see that the width of the prediction interval for an individual store is much wider than the confidence interval estimate for the mean. Remember that there is much more variation in predicting an individual value than in estimating a mean value.

FIGURE 12.21

Excel and Minitab confidence interval estimate and prediction interval worksheets for the Sunflowers Apparel data

	A	B
1	Confidence Interval Estimate and Prediction Interval	
2		
3	Data	
4	X Value	4
5	Confidence Level	95%
6		
7	Intermediate Calculations	
8	Sample Size	14 =COUNT(SLRData!A:A)
9	Degrees of Freedom	12 =B8 - 2
10	t Value	2.1788 =T.INV.2T(1 - B5, B9)
11	Sample Mean	3.7786 =AVERAGE(SLRData!A:A)
12	Sum of Squared Difference	15.5236 =DEVSQ(SLRData!A:A)
13	Standard Error of the Estimate	0.9993 =COMPUTE!B7
14	h Statistic	0.0746 =1/B8 + (B4 - B11)^2/B12
15	Predicted Y (YHat)	7.0879 =TREND(SLRData!B2:B15, SLRData!A2:A15, B4)
16		
17	For Average Y	
18	Interval Half Width	0.5946 =B10 * B13 * SQRT(B14)
19	Confidence Interval Lower Limit	6.4932 =B15 - B18
20	Confidence Interval Upper Limit	7.6825 =B15 + B18
21		
22	For Individual Response Y	
23	Interval Half Width	2.2570 =B10 * B13 * SQRT(1 + B14)
24	Prediction Interval Lower Limit	4.8308 =B15 - B23
25	Prediction Interval Upper Limit	9.3449 =B15 + B23

```
Predicted Values for New Observations
New Obs    Fit   SE Fit      95% CI          95% PI
      1  7.088   0.273   (6.493, 7.682)  (4.831, 9.345)

Values of Predictors for New Observations
                Profiled
New Obs    Customers
      1       4.00
```

Problems for Section 12.8

LEARNING THE BASICS

12.55 Based on a sample of $n = 20$, the least-squares method was used to develop the following prediction line: $\hat{Y}_i = 5 + 3X_i$. In addition,

$$S_{YX} = 1.0 \quad \overline{X} = 2 \quad \sum_{i=1}^{n}(X_i - \overline{X})^2 = 20$$

a. Construct a 95% confidence interval estimate of the population mean response for $X = 2$.
b. Construct a 95% prediction interval of an individual response for $X = 2$.

12.56 Based on a sample of $n = 20$, the least-squares method was used to develop the following prediction line: $\hat{Y}_i = 5 + 3X_i$. In addition,

$$S_{YX} = 1.0 \quad \overline{X} = 2 \quad \sum_{i=1}^{n}(X_i - \overline{X})^2 = 20$$

a. Construct a 95% confidence interval estimate of the population mean response for $X = 4$.
b. Construct a 95% prediction interval of an individual response for $X = 4$.
c. Compare the results of (a) and (b) with those of Problem 12.55 (a) and (b). Which intervals are wider? Why?

APPLYING THE CONCEPTS

12.57 In Problem 12.5 on page 424, you used the summated rating of a restaurant to predict the cost of a meal. The data are stored in **Restaurants**. For these data, $S_{YX} = 9.094$ and $h_i = 0.046319$ when $X = 50$.

a. Construct a 95% confidence interval estimate of the mean cost of a meal for restaurants that have a summated rating of 50.
b. Construct a 95% prediction interval of the cost of a meal for an individual restaurant that has a summated rating of 50.
c. Explain the difference in the results in (a) and (b).

✓ SELF Test **12.58** In Problem 12.4 on page 423, you used the percentage of alcohol to predict wine quality. The data are stored in **VinhoVerde**. For these data, $S_{YX} = 0.9369$ and $h_i = 0.024934$ when $X = 10$.

a. Construct a 95% confidence interval estimate of the mean wine quality rating for all wines that have 10% alcohol.
b. Construct a 95% prediction interval of the wine quality rating of an individual wine that has 10% alcohol.
c. Explain the difference in the results in (a) and (b).

12.59 In Problem 12.7 on page 424, you used the plate gap on the bag-sealing equipment to predict the tear rating of a bag of coffee. The data are stored in **Starbucks**.

a. Construct a 95% confidence interval estimate of the mean tear rating for all bags of coffee when the plate gap is 0.
b. Construct a 95% prediction interval of the tear rating for an individual bag of coffee when the plate gap is 0.
c. Why is the interval in (a) narrower than the interval in (b)?

12.60 In Problem 12.6 on page 424, the owner of a moving company wanted to predict labor hours based on the number of cubic feet moved. The data are stored in **Moving**.

a. Construct a 95% confidence interval estimate of the mean labor hours for all moves of 500 cubic feet.
b. Construct a 95% prediction interval of the labor hours of an individual move that has 500 cubic feet.
c. Why is the interval in (a) narrower than the interval in (b)?

12.61 In Problem 12.9 on page 424, an agent for a real estate company wanted to predict the monthly rent for one-bedroom apartments, based on the size of an apartment. The data are stored in `RentSilverSpring`.

a. Construct a 95% confidence interval estimate of the mean monthly rental for all one-bedroom apartments that are 800 square feet in size.

b. Construct a 95% prediction interval of the monthly rental for an individual one-bedroom apartment that is 800 square feet in size.

c. Explain the difference in the results in (a) and (b).

12.62 In Problem 12.8 on page 424, you predicted the value of a baseball franchise, based on current revenue. The data are stored in `BBValues`.

a. Construct a 95% confidence interval estimate of the mean value of all baseball franchises that generate $250 million of annual revenue.

b. Construct a 95% prediction interval of the value of an individual baseball franchise that generates $250 million of annual revenue.

c. Explain the difference in the results in (a) and (b).

12.63 In Problem 12.10 on page 424, you used box office gross to predict DVD revenue. The data are stored in `Movie`. The company is about to release a movie on DVD that had a box office gross of $100 million.

a. What is the predicted DVD revenue?

b. Which interval is more useful here, the confidence interval estimate of the mean or the prediction interval for an individual response? Explain.

c. Construct and interpret the interval you selected in (b).

12.9 Potential Pitfalls in Regression

When using regression analysis, some of the potential pitfalls are:

- Lacking awareness of the assumptions of least-squares regression
- Not knowing how to evaluate the assumptions of least-squares regression
- Not knowing what the alternatives are to least-squares regression if a particular assumption is violated
- Using a regression model without knowledge of the subject matter
- Extrapolating outside the relevant range
- Concluding that a significant relationship identified in an observational study is due to a cause-and-effect relationship

The widespread availability of spreadsheet and statistical applications has made regression analysis much more feasible today than it once was. However, many users who have access to such applications do not understand how to use regression analysis properly. Someone who is not familiar with either the assumptions of regression or how to evaluate the assumptions cannot be expected to know what the alternatives to least-squares regression are if a particular assumption is violated.

The data in Table 12.7 (stored in `Anscombe`) illustrate the importance of using scatter plots and residual analysis to go beyond the basic number crunching of computing the Y intercept, the slope, and r^2.

TABLE 12.7

Four Sets of Artificial Data

Data Set A		Data Set B		Data Set C		Data Set D	
X_i	Y_i	X_i	Y_i	X_i	Y_i	X_i	Y_i
10	8.04	10	9.14	10	7.46	8	6.58
14	9.96	14	8.10	14	8.84	8	5.76
5	5.68	5	4.74	5	5.73	8	7.71
8	6.95	8	8.14	8	6.77	8	8.84
9	8.81	9	8.77	9	7.11	8	8.47
12	10.84	12	9.13	12	8.15	8	7.04
4	4.26	4	3.10	4	5.39	8	5.25
7	4.82	7	7.26	7	6.42	19	12.50
11	8.33	11	9.26	11	7.81	8	5.56
13	7.58	13	8.74	13	12.74	8	7.91
6	7.24	6	6.13	6	6.08	8	6.89

Source: Data extracted from F. J. Anscombe, "Graphs in Statistical Analysis," *The American Statistician*, 27 (1973), pp. 17–21.

Anscombe (reference 1) showed that all four data sets given in Table 12.7 have the following identical results:

$$\hat{Y}_i = 3.0 + 0.5X_i$$
$$S_{YX} = 1.237$$
$$S_{b_1} = 0.118$$
$$r^2 = 0.667$$

$$SSR = \text{Explained variation} = \sum_{i=1}^{n}(\hat{Y}_i - \overline{Y})^2 = 27.51$$

$$SSE = \text{Unexplained variation} = \sum_{i=1}^{n}(Y_i - \hat{Y}_i)^2 = 13.76$$

$$SST = \text{Total variation} = \sum_{i=1}^{n}(Y_i - \overline{Y})^2 = 41.27$$

If you stopped the analysis at this point, you would fail to observe the important differences among the four data sets that scatter plots and residual plots can reveal.

From the scatter plots and the residual plots of Figure 12.22, you see how different the data sets are. Each has a different relationship between X and Y. The only data set that seems to approximately follow a straight line is data set A. The residual plot for data set A does not show any obvious patterns or outlying residuals. This is certainly not true for data sets B, C, and D. The scatter plot for data set B shows that a curvilinear regression model is more appropriate. This conclusion is reinforced by the residual plot for data set B. The scatter plot and the residual plot for data set C clearly show an outlying observation. In this case, one approach used is to remove the outlier and reestimate the regression model (see reference 4). The scatter plot for data set D represents a situation in which the model is heavily dependent on the outcome of a single data point ($X_8 = 19$ and $Y_8 = 12.50$). Any regression model with this characteristic should be used with caution.

FIGURE 12.22

Scatter plots and residual plots for the data sets A, B, C, and D

Scatter plots

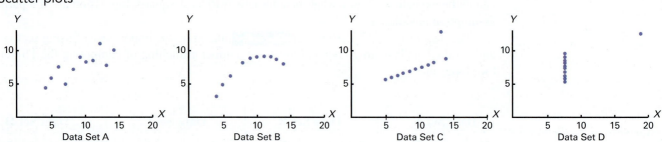

Residual plots

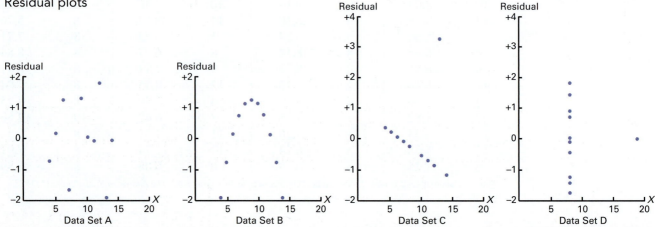

Six Steps for Avoiding the Potential Pitfalls

Apply the following six-step strategy to avoid the potential pitfalls in the regression analyses you undertake.

Step 1 Construct a scatter plot to observe the possible relationship between X and Y.

Step 2 Perform a residual analysis to check the assumptions of regression (linearity, independence, normality, equal variance):

   a. Plot the residuals versus the independent variable to determine whether the linear model is appropriate and to check for equal variance.
   b. Construct a histogram, stem-and-leaf display, boxplot, or normal probability plot of the residuals to check for normality.
   c. Plot the residuals versus time to check for independence. (This step is necessary only if the data are collected over time.)

Step 3 If there are violations of the assumptions, use alternative methods to least-squares regression or alternative least-squares models (see reference 4).

Step 4 If there are no violations of the assumptions, carry out tests for the significance of the regression coefficients and develop confidence and prediction intervals.

Step 5 Refrain from making predictions and forecasts outside the relevant range of the independent variable.

Step 6 Remember that the relationships identified in observational studies may or may not be due to cause-and-effect relationships. (While causation implies correlation, correlation does not imply causation.)

SUMMARY

As you can see from the chapter roadmap in Figure 12.23, this chapter develops the simple linear regression model and discusses the assumptions and how to evaluate them. Once you are assured that the model is appropriate, you can predict values by using the prediction line and test for the significance of the slope. Chapter 13 extends regression analysis to situations in which more than one independent variable is used to predict the value of a dependent variable.

FIGURE 12.23
Roadmap for simple linear regression

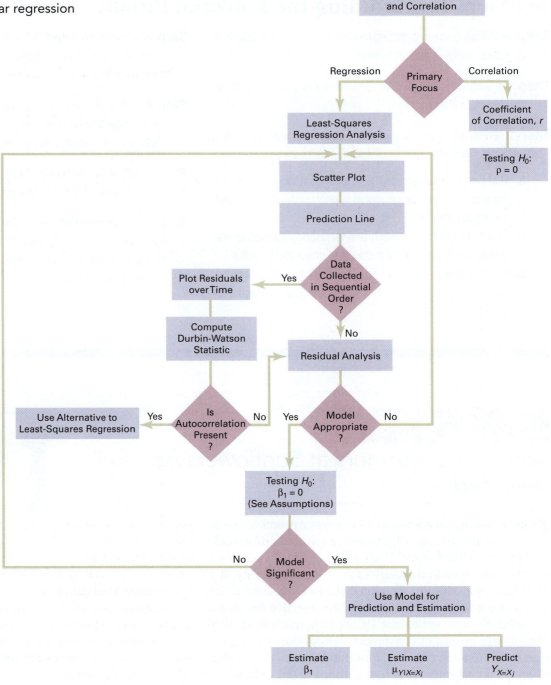

REFERENCES

1. Anscombe, F. J. "Graphs in Statistical Analysis." *The American Statistician*, 27(1973): 17–21.
2. Hoaglin, D. C., and R. Welsch. "The Hat Matrix in Regression and ANOVA." *The American Statistician*, 32(1978): 17–22.
3. Hocking, R. R. "Developments in Linear Regression Methodology: 1959–1982." *Technometrics*, 25(1983): 219–250.
4. Kutner, M. H., C. J. Nachtsheim, J. Neter, and W. Li. *Applied Linear Statistical Models*, 5th ed. New York: McGraw-Hill/Irwin, 2005.
5. *Microsoft Excel 2013*. Redmond, WA: Microsoft Corp., 2012.
6. *Minitab Release 16*. State College, PA: Minitab Inc., 2010.

KEY EQUATIONS

Simple Linear Regression Model

$$Y_i = \beta_0 + \beta_1 X_i + \varepsilon_i \tag{12.1}$$

Simple Linear Regression Equation:
The Prediction Line

$$\hat{Y}_i = b_0 + b_1 X_i \tag{12.2}$$

Computational Formula for the Slope, b_1

$$b_1 = \frac{SSXY}{SSX} \tag{12.3}$$

Computational Formula for the Y Intercept, b_0

$$b_0 = \bar{Y} - b_1 \bar{X} \tag{12.4}$$

Measures of Variation in Regression

$$SST = SSR + SSE \tag{12.5}$$

Total Sum of Squares (SST)

$$SST = \text{Total sum of squares} = \sum_{i=1}^{n} (Y_i - \bar{Y})^2 \tag{12.6}$$

Regression Sum of Squares (SSR)

$SSR = $ Explained variation or regression sum of squares

$$= \sum_{i=1}^{n} (\hat{Y}_i - \bar{Y})^2 \tag{12.7}$$

Error Sum of Squares (SSE)

$SSE = $ Unexplained variation or error sum of squares

$$= \sum_{i=1}^{n} (Y_i - \hat{Y}_i)^2 \tag{12.8}$$

Coefficient of Determination

$$r^2 = \frac{\text{Regression sum of squares}}{\text{Total sum of squares}} = \frac{SSR}{SST} \tag{12.9}$$

Computational Formula for SST

$$SST = \sum_{i=1}^{n} (Y_i - \bar{Y})^2 = \sum_{i=1}^{n} Y_i^2 - \frac{\left(\sum_{i=1}^{n} Y_i \right)^2}{n} \tag{12.10}$$

Computational Formula for SSR

$$SSR = \sum_{i=1}^{n} (\hat{Y}_i - \bar{Y})^2$$

$$= b_0 \sum_{i=1}^{n} Y_i + b_1 \sum_{i=1}^{n} X_i Y_i - \frac{\left(\sum_{i=1}^{n} Y_i \right)^2}{n} \tag{12.11}$$

Computational Formula for SSE

$$SSE = \sum_{i=1}^{n} (Y_i - \hat{Y}_i)^2 = \sum_{i=1}^{n} Y_i^2 - b_0 \sum_{i=1}^{n} Y_i - b_1 \sum_{i=1}^{n} X_i Y_i \tag{12.12}$$

Standard Error of the Estimate

$$S_{YX} = \sqrt{\frac{SSE}{n-2}} = \sqrt{\frac{\sum_{i=1}^{n} (Y_i - \hat{Y}_i)^2}{n-2}} \tag{12.13}$$

Residual

$$e_i = Y_i - \hat{Y}_i \tag{12.14}$$

Durbin-Watson Statistic

$$D = \frac{\sum_{i=2}^{n} (e_i - e_{i-1})^2}{\sum_{i=1}^{n} e_i^2} \tag{12.15}$$

Testing a Hypothesis for a Population Slope, β_1, Using the t Test

$$t_{STAT} = \frac{b_1 - \beta_1}{S_{b_1}} \tag{12.16}$$

Testing a Hypothesis for a Population Slope, β_1, Using the F Test

$$F_{STAT} = \frac{MSR}{MSE} \tag{12.17}$$

Confidence Interval Estimate of the Slope, β_1

$$b_1 \pm t_{\alpha/2} S_{b_1}$$
$$b_1 - t_{\alpha/2} S_{b_1} \le \beta_1 \le b_1 + t_{\alpha/2} S_{b_1} \tag{12.18}$$

Testing for the Existence of Correlation

$$t_{STAT} = \frac{r - \rho}{\sqrt{\frac{1 - r^2}{n - 2}}} \tag{12.19a}$$

$$r = \frac{\text{cov}(X, Y)}{S_X S_Y} \tag{12.19b}$$

Confidence Interval Estimate for the Mean of Y

$$\hat{Y}_i \pm t_{\alpha/2} S_{YX} \sqrt{h_i}$$
$$\hat{Y}_i - t_{\alpha/2} S_{YX} \sqrt{h_i} \le \mu_{Y|X=X_i} \le \hat{Y}_i + t_{\alpha/2} S_{YX} \sqrt{h_i} \tag{12.20}$$

Prediction Interval for an Individual Response, Y

$$\hat{Y}_i \pm t_{\alpha/2} S_{YX} \sqrt{1 + h_i}$$

$$\hat{Y}_i - t_{\alpha/2} S_{YX} \sqrt{1 + h_i} \le Y_{X=X_i} \le \hat{Y}_i + t_{\alpha/2} S_{YX} \sqrt{1 + h_i} \tag{12.21}$$

KEY TERMS

assumptions of regression 430
autocorrelation 434
coefficient of determination 427
confidence interval estimate for the mean response 445
correlation coefficient 442
dependent variable 415
Durbin-Watson statistic 435
equal variance 430
error sum of squares (*SSE*) 425
explained variation 425
explanatory variable 416
homoscedasticity 430
independence of errors 430

independent variable 415
least-squares method 418
linearity 430
linear relationship 416
model 415
normality 430
prediction interval for an individual response, *Y* 446
prediction line 417
regression analysis 415
regression coefficient 418
regression sum of squares (*SSR*) 425
relevant range 420
residual 430

residual analysis 430
response variable 416
scatter diagram 415
scatter plot 415
simple linear regression 415
simple linear regression equation 417
slope 417
standard error of the estimate 428
total sum of squares (*SST*) 425
total variation 425
unexplained variation 425
Y intercept 417

CHECKING YOUR UNDERSTANDING

12.64 What is the interpretation of the Y intercept and the slope in the simple linear regression equation?

12.65 What is the interpretation of the coefficient of determination?

12.66 When is the unexplained variation (i.e., error sum of squares) equal to 0?

12.67 When is the explained variation (i.e., regression sum of squares) equal to 0?

12.68 Why should you always carry out a residual analysis as part of a regression model?

12.69 What are the assumptions of regression analysis?

12.70 How do you evaluate the assumptions of regression analysis?

12.71 When and how do you use the Durbin-Watson statistic?

12.72 What is the difference between a confidence interval estimate of the mean response, $\mu_{Y|X=X_i}$, and a prediction interval of $Y_{X=X_i}$?

CHAPTER REVIEW PROBLEMS

12.73 Can you use Twitter activity to forecast box office receipts on the opening weekend? The following data (stored in `Twitter-Movies`) indicate the Twitter activity ("want to see") and the receipts ($) per theater on the weekend a movie opened for seven movies:

Movie	Twitter Activity	Receipts ($)
The Devil Inside	219,509	14,763
The Dictator	6,405	5,796
Paranormal Activity 3	165,128	15,829
The Hunger Games	579,288	36,871
Bridesmaids	6,564	8,995
Red Tails	11,104	7,477
Act of Valor	9,152	8,054

Source: R. Dodes, "Twitter Goes to the Movies," *The Wall Street Journal*, August 3, 2012, pp. D1–D12.

a. Use the least-squares method to compute the regression coefficients b_0 and b_1.
b. Interpret the meaning of b_0 and b_1 in this problem.
c. Predict the mean receipts for a movie that has a Twitter activity of 100,000.

d. Should you use the model to predict the receipts for a movie that has a Twitter activity of 1,000,000? Why or why not?
e. Determine the coefficient of determination, r^2, and explain its meaning in this problem.
f. Perform a residual analysis. Is there any evidence of a pattern in the residuals? Explain.
g. At the 0.05 level of significance, is there evidence of a linear relationship between Twitter activity and receipts?
h. Construct a 95% confidence interval estimate of the mean receipts for a movie that has a Twitter activity of 100,000 and a 95% prediction interval of the receipts for a single movie that has a Twitter activity of 100,000.
i. Based on the results of (a)–(h), do you think that Twitter activity is a useful predictor of receipts on the first weekend a movie opens? What issues about these data might make you hesitant to use Twitter activity to predict receipts?

12.74 Management of a soft-drink bottling company has the business objective of developing a method for allocating delivery costs to customers. Although one cost clearly relates to travel time within a particular route, another variable cost reflects the time required to unload the cases of soft drink at the delivery point. To begin, management decided to develop a regression model to predict delivery time based on the number of cases delivered. A sample of 20 deliveries within a territory was selected. The delivery times and the number of cases delivered were organized in the following table and stored in `Delivery` .

Customer	Number of Cases	Delivery Time (minutes)	Customer	Number of Cases	Delivery Time (minutes)
1	52	32.1	11	161	43.0
2	64	34.8	12	184	49.4
3	73	36.2	13	202	57.2
4	85	37.8	14	218	56.8
5	95	37.8	15	243	60.6
6	103	39.7	16	254	61.2
7	116	38.5	17	267	58.2
8	121	41.9	18	275	63.1
9	143	44.2	19	287	65.6
10	157	47.1	20	298	67.3

a. Use the least-squares method to compute the regression coefficients b_0 and b_1.
b. Interpret the meaning of b_0 and b_1 in this problem.
c. Predict the mean delivery time for 150 cases of soft drink.
d. Should you use the model to predict the delivery time for a customer who is receiving 500 cases of soft drink? Why or why not?
e. Determine the coefficient of determination, r^2, and explain its meaning in this problem.
f. Perform a residual analysis. Is there any evidence of a pattern in the residuals? Explain.
g. At the 0.05 level of significance, is there evidence of a linear relationship between delivery time and the number of cases delivered?
h. Construct a 95% confidence interval estimate of the mean delivery time for 150 cases of soft drink and a 95% prediction interval of the delivery time for a single delivery of 150 cases of soft drink.
i. What conclusions can you reach from (a) through (h) about the relationship between the number of cases and delivery time?

12.75 Measuring the height of a California redwood tree is very difficult because these trees grow to heights of over 300 feet. People familiar with these trees understand that the height of a California redwood tree is related to other characteristics of the tree, including the diameter of the tree at the breast height of a person. The data in `Redwood` represent the height (in feet) and diameter (in inches) at the breast height of a person for a sample of 21 California redwood trees.
a. Assuming a linear relationship, use the least-squares method to compute the regression coefficients b_0 and b_1. State the regression equation that predicts the height of a tree based on the tree's diameter at breast height of a person.
b. Interpret the meaning of the slope in this equation.
c. Predict the mean height for a tree that has a breast height diameter of 25 inches.
d. Interpret the meaning of the coefficient of determination in this problem.

e. Perform a residual analysis on the results and determine the adequacy of the model.
f. Determine whether there is a significant relationship between the height of redwood trees and the breast height diameter at the 0.05 level of significance.
g. Construct a 95% confidence interval estimate of the population slope between the height of the redwood trees and breast height diameter.
h. What conclusions can you reach about the relationship of the diameter of the tree and its height?

12.76 You want to develop a model to predict the assessed value of homes based on their size. A sample of 30 single-family houses listed for sale in Silver Spring, Maryland, a suburb of Washington, DC, is selected to study the relationship between assessed value (in $thousands) and size (in thousands of square feet), and the data is collected and stored in `SilverSpring`. (Hint: First determine which are the independent and dependent variables.)
a. Construct a scatter plot and, assuming a linear relationship, use the least-squares method to compute the regression coefficients b_0 and b_1.
b. Interpret the meaning of the Y intercept, b_0, and the slope, b_1, in this problem.
c. Use the prediction line developed in (a) to predict the mean assessed value for a house whose size is 2,000 square feet.
d. Determine the coefficient of determination, r^2, and interpret its meaning in this problem.
e. Perform a residual analysis on your results and evaluate the regression assumptions.
f. At the 0.05 level of significance, is there evidence of a linear relationship between assessed value and size?
g. Construct a 95% confidence interval estimate of the population slope.
h. What conclusions can you reach about the relationship between the size of the house and its assessed value?

12.77 You want to develop a model to predict the taxes of houses, based on assessed value. A sample of 30 single-family houses listed for sale in Silver Spring, Maryland, a suburb of Washington, DC, is selected. The taxes (in $) and the assessed value of the houses (in $thousands) are recorded and stored in `SilverSpring`. (Hint: First determine which are the independent and dependent variables.)
a. Construct a scatter plot and, assuming a linear relationship, use the least-squares method to compute the regression coefficients b_0 and b_1.
b. Interpret the meaning of the Y intercept, b_0, and the slope, b_1, in this problem.
c. Use the prediction line developed in (a) to predict the mean taxes for a house whose assessed value is $400,000.
d. Determine the coefficient of determination, r^2, and interpret its meaning in this problem.
e. Perform a residual analysis on your results and evaluate the regression assumptions.
f. At the 0.05 level of significance, is there evidence of a linear relationship between taxes and assessed value?
g. What conclusions can you reach concerning the relationship between taxes and assessed value?

12.78 The director of graduate studies at a large college of business has the objective of predicting the grade point average (GPA) of students in an MBA program. The director begins by using the Graduate Management Admission Test (GMAT) score. A sample of 20 students who have completed two years in the program is selected and stored in GPIGMAT .

a. Construct a scatter plot and, assuming a linear relationship, use the least-squares method to compute the regression coefficients b_0 and b_1.
b. Interpret the meaning of the Y intercept, b_0, and the slope, b_1, in this problem.
c. Use the prediction line developed in (a) to predict the mean GPA for a student with a GMAT score of 600.
d. Determine the coefficient of determination, r^2, and interpret its meaning in this problem.
e. Perform a residual analysis on your results and evaluate the regression assumptions.
f. At the 0.05 level of significance, is there evidence of a linear relationship between GMAT score and GPA?
g. Construct a 95% confidence interval estimate of the mean GPA of students with a GMAT score of 600 and a 95% prediction interval of the GPA for a particular student with a GMAT score of 600.
h. Construct a 95% confidence interval estimate of the population slope.
i. What conclusions can you reach concerning the relationship between GMAT score and GPA?

12.79 An accountant for a large department store has the business objective of developing a model to predict the amount of time it takes to process invoices. Data are collected from the past 32 working days, and the number of invoices processed and completion time (in hours) are stored in Invoice . (Hint: First determine which are the independent and dependent variables.)

a. Assuming a linear relationship, use the least-squares method to compute the regression coefficients b_0 and b_1.
b. Interpret the meaning of the Y intercept, b_0, and the slope, b_1, in this problem.
c. Use the prediction line developed in (a) to predict the mean amount of time it would take to process 150 invoices.
d. Determine the coefficient of determination, r^2, and interpret its meaning.
e. Plot the residuals against the number of invoices processed and also against time.
f. Based on the plots in (e), does the model seem appropriate?
g. Based on the results in (e) and (f), what conclusions can you reach about the validity of the prediction made in (c)?
h. What conclusions can you reach about the relationship between the number of invoices and the completion time?

12.80 On January 28, 1986, the space shuttle *Challenger* exploded, and seven astronauts were killed. Prior to the launch, the predicted atmospheric temperature was for freezing weather at the launch site. Engineers for Morton Thiokol (the manufacturer of the rocket motor) prepared charts to make the case that the launch should not take place due to the cold weather. These arguments were rejected, and the launch tragically took place. Upon investigation after the tragedy, experts agreed that the disaster occurred because of leaky rubber O-rings that did not seal properly due to the cold temperature. Data indicating

the atmospheric temperature at the time of 23 previous launches and the O-ring damage index are stored in O-Ring .

Note: Data from flight 4 is omitted due to unknown O-ring condition.

Sources: Data extracted from *Report of the Presidential Commission on the Space Shuttle Challenger Accident*, Washington, DC, 1986, Vol. II (H1–H3) and Vol. IV (664); and *Post-Challenger Evaluation of Space Shuttle Risk Assessment and Management*, Washington, DC, 1988, pp. 135–136.

a. Construct a scatter plot for the seven flights in which there was O-ring damage (O-ring damage index $\neq$ 0). What conclusions, if any, can you reach about the relationship between atmospheric temperature and O-ring damage?
b. Construct a scatter plot for all 23 flights.
c. Explain any differences in the interpretation of the relationship between atmospheric temperature and O-ring damage in (a) and (b).
d. Based on the scatter plot in (b), provide reasons why a prediction should not be made for an atmospheric temperature of 31°F, the temperature on the morning of the launch of the *Challenger*.
e. Although the assumption of a linear relationship may not be valid for the set of 23 flights, fit a simple linear regression model to predict O-ring damage, based on atmospheric temperature.
f. Include the prediction line found in (e) on the scatter plot developed in (b).
g. Based on the results in (f), do you think a linear model is appropriate for these data? Explain.
h. Perform a residual analysis. What conclusions do you reach?

12.81 A baseball analyst would like to study various team statistics for a recent season to determine which variables might be useful in predicting the number of wins achieved by teams during the season. He begins by using a team's earned run average (ERA), a measure of pitching performance, to predict the number of wins. He collects the team ERA and team wins for each of the 30 Major League Baseball teams and stores these data in Baseball . (Hint: First determine which are the independent and dependent variables.)

a. Assuming a linear relationship, use the least-squares method to compute the regression coefficients b_0 and b_1.
b. Interpret the meaning of the Y intercept, b_0, and the slope, b_1, in this problem.
c. Use the prediction line developed in (a) to predict the mean number of wins for a team with an ERA of 4.50.
d. Compute the coefficient of determination, r^2, and interpret its meaning.
e. Perform a residual analysis on your results and determine the adequacy of the fit of the model.
f. At the 0.05 level of significance, is there evidence of a linear relationship between the number of wins and the ERA?
g. Construct a 95% confidence interval estimate of the mean number of wins expected for teams with an ERA of 4.50.
h. Construct a 95% prediction interval of the number of wins for an individual team that has an ERA of 4.50.
i. Construct a 95% confidence interval estimate of the population slope.

j. The 30 teams constitute a population. In order to use statistical inference, as in (f) through (i), the data must be assumed to represent a random sample. What "population" would this sample be drawing conclusions about?

k. What other independent variables might you consider for inclusion in the model?

l. What conclusions can you reach concerning the relationship between ERA and wins?

12.82 Can you use the annual revenues generated by National Basketball Association (NBA) franchises to predict franchise values? Figure 2.14 on page 61 shows a scatter plot of revenue with franchise value, and Figure 3.9 on page 164, shows the correlation coefficient. Now, you want to develop a simple linear regression model to predict franchise values based on revenues. (Franchise values and revenues are stored in NBAValues .)

a. Assuming a linear relationship, use the least-squares method to compute the regression coefficients b_0 and b_1.

b. Interpret the meaning of the Y intercept, b_0, and the slope, b_1, in this problem.

c. Predict the mean value of an NBA franchise that generates $150 million of annual revenue.

d. Compute the coefficient of determination, r^2, and interpret its meaning.

e. Perform a residual analysis on your results and evaluate the regression assumptions.

f. At the 0.05 level of significance, is there evidence of a linear relationship between the annual revenues generated and the value of an NBA franchise?

g. Construct a 95% confidence interval estimate of the mean value of all NBA franchises that generate $150 million of annual revenue.

h. Construct a 95% prediction interval of the value of an individual NBA franchise that generates $150 million of annual revenue.

i. Compare the results of (a) through (h) to those of baseball franchises in Problems 12.8, 12.20, 12.30, 12.46, and 12.62 and European soccer teams in Problem 12.83.

12.83 In Problem 12.82 you used annual revenue to develop a model to predict the franchise value of National Basketball Association (NBA) teams. Can you also use the annual revenues generated by European soccer teams to predict franchise values? (European soccer team values and revenues are stored in SoccerValues2014 .)

a. Repeat Problem 12.82 (a) through (h) for the European soccer teams.

b. Compare the results of (a) to those of baseball franchises in Problems 12.8, 12.20, 12.30, 12.46, and 12.62 and NBA franchises in Problem 12.82.

12.84 During the fall harvest season in the United States, pumpkins are sold in large quantities at farm stands. Often, instead of weighing the pumpkins prior to sale, the farm stand operator will just place the pumpkin in the appropriate circular cutout on the counter. When asked why this was done, one farmer replied, "I can tell the weight of the pumpkin from its circumference." To determine whether this was really true, the circumference and weight of each pumpkin from a sample of 23 pumpkins were determined and the results stored in Pumpkin .

a. Assuming a linear relationship, use the least-squares method to compute the regression coefficients b_0 and b_1.

b. Interpret the meaning of the slope, b_1, in this problem.

c. Predict the mean weight for a pumpkin that is 60 centimeters in circumference.

d. Do you think it is a good idea for the farmer to sell pumpkins by circumference instead of weight? Explain.

e. Determine the coefficient of determination, r^2, and interpret its meaning.

f. Perform a residual analysis for these data and evaluate the regression assumptions.

g. At the 0.05 level of significance, is there evidence of a linear relationship between the circumference and weight of a pumpkin?

h. Construct a 95% confidence interval estimate of the population slope, β_1.

12.85 Refer to the discussion of beta values and market models in Problem 12.49 on page 444. The S&P 500 Index tracks the overall movement of the stock market by considering the stock prices of 500 large corporations. The file StockPrices2013 contains 2013 weekly data for the S&P 500 and three companies. The following variables are included:

WEEK—Week ending on date given
S&P—Weekly closing value for the S&P 500 Index
GE—Weekly closing stock price for General Electric
DISCA—Weekly closing stock price for Discovery Communications
GOOG—Weekly closing stock price for Google

Source: Data extracted from finance.yahoo.com, June 6, 2014.

a. Estimate the market model for GE. (Hint: Use the percentage change in the S&P 500 Index as the independent variable and the percentage change in GE's stock price as the dependent variable.)

b. Interpret the beta value for GE.

c. Repeat (a) and (b) for Discovery Communications.

d. Repeat (a) and (b) for Google.

e. Write a brief summary of your findings.

12.86 The file CEO-Compensation2013 includes the total compensation (in $millions) for CEOs of 200 Standard & Poor's 500 companies and the investment return in 2013. (Data extracted from "Millions by millions, CEO pay goes up," **usat.ly/1jhbypL**.)

a. Compute the correlation coefficient between compensation and the investment return in 2013.

b. At the 0.05 level of significance, is the correlation between compensation and the investment return in 2013 statistically significant?

c. Write a short summary of your findings in (a) and (b). Do the results surprise you?

REPORT WRITING EXERCISE

12.87 In Problems 12.8, 12.20, 12.30, 12.46, 12.62, 12.82, and 12.83, you developed regression models to predict franchise value of major league baseball, NBA basketball, and soccer teams. Now, write a report based on the models you developed. Append to your report all appropriate charts and statistical information.

CASES FOR CHAPTER 12

Managing Ashland MultiComm Services

To ensure that as many trial subscriptions to the *3-For-All* service as possible are converted to regular subscriptions, the marketing department works closely with the customer support department to accomplish a smooth initial process for the trial subscription customers. To assist in this effort, the marketing department needs to accurately forecast the monthly total of new regular subscriptions.

A team consisting of managers from the marketing and customer support departments was convened to develop a better method of forecasting new subscriptions. Previously, after examining new subscription data for the prior three months, a group of three managers would develop a subjective forecast of the number of new subscriptions. Livia Salvador, who was recently hired by the company to provide expertise in quantitative forecasting methods, suggested that the department look for factors that might help in predicting new subscriptions.

Members of the team found that the forecasts in the past year had been particularly inaccurate because in some months, much more time was spent on telemarketing than in other months. Livia collected data (stored in **AMS12**) for the number of new subscriptions and hours spent on telemarketing for each month for the past two years.

1. What criticism can you make concerning the method of forecasting that involved taking the new subscriptions data for the prior three months as the basis for future projections?

2. What factors other than number of telemarketing hours spent might be useful in predicting the number of new subscriptions? Explain.

3. a. Analyze the data and develop a regression model to predict the number of new subscriptions for a month, based on the number of hours spent on telemarketing for new subscriptions.

   b. If you expect to spend 1,200 hours on telemarketing per month, estimate the number of new subscriptions for the month. Indicate the assumptions on which this prediction is based. Do you think these assumptions are valid? Explain.

   c. What would be the danger of predicting the number of new subscriptions for a month in which 2,000 hours were spent on telemarketing?

Digital Case

Apply your knowledge of simple linear regression in this Digital Case, which extends the Sunflowers Apparel Using Statistics scenario from this chapter.

Leasing agents from the Triangle Mall Management Corporation have suggested that Sunflowers consider several locations in some of Triangle's newly renovated lifestyle malls that cater to shoppers with higher-than-mean disposable income. Although the locations are smaller than the typical Sunflowers location, the leasing agents argue that higher-than-mean disposable income in the surrounding community is a better predictor of higher sales than profiled customers. The leasing agents maintain that sample data from 14 Sunflowers stores prove that this is true.

Open **Triangle_Sunflower.pdf** and review the leasing agents' proposal and supporting documents. Then answer the following questions:

1. Should mean disposable income be used to predict sales based on the sample of 14 Sunflowers stores?

2. Should the management of Sunflowers accept the claims of Triangle's leasing agents? Why or why not?

3. Is it possible that the mean disposable income of the surrounding area is not an important factor in leasing new locations? Explain.

4. Are there any other factors not mentioned by the leasing agents that might be relevant to the store leasing decision?

Brynne Packaging

Brynne Packaging is a large packaging company, offering its customers the highest standards in innovative packaging solutions and reliable service. About 25% of the employees at Brynne Packaging are machine operators. The human resources department has suggested that the company consider using the Wesman Personnel Classification Test (WPCT), a measure of reasoning ability, to screen applicants for the machine operator job. In order to assess the WPCT as a predictor of future job performance, 25 recent applicants were tested using the WPCT; all were hired, regardless of their WPCT score. At a later time, supervisors were asked to rate the quality of the job performance of these 25 employees, using a 1-to-10 rating scale (where 1 = very low and 10 = very high). Factors considered in the ratings included the employee's output, defect rate, ability to implement continuous quality procedures, and contributions to team problem-solving efforts. The file BrynnePackaging contains the WPCT scores (WPCT) and job performance ratings (Ratings) for the 25 employees.

1. Assess the significance and importance of WPCT score as a predictor of job performance. Defend your answer.

2. Predict the mean job performance rating for all employees with a WPCT score of 6. Give a point prediction as well as a 95% confidence interval. Do you have any concerns using the regression model for predicting mean job performance rating given the WPCT score of 6?

3. Evaluate whether the assumptions of regression have been seriously violated.

CHAPTER 12 EXCEL GUIDE

EG12.1 TYPES of REGRESSION MODELS

There are no Excel Guide instructions for this section.

EG12.2 DETERMINING the SIMPLE LINEAR REGRESSION EQUATION

Key Technique Use the **LINEST**(*cell range of Y variable*, *cell range of X variable*, **True, True**) array function to compute the b_1 and b_0 coefficients, the b_1 and b_0 standard errors, r^2 and the standard error of the estimate, the *F* test statistic and error *df*, and *SSR* and *SSE*.

Example Perform the Figure 12.4 analysis of the Sunflowers Apparel data on page 418.

PHStat Use **Simple Linear Regression**.
For the example, open to the **DATA worksheet** of the **SiteSelection workbook**. Select **PHStat → Regression → Simple Linear Regression**. In the procedure's dialog box (shown below):

1. Enter **C1:C15** as the **Y Variable Cell Range**.
2. Enter **B1:B15** as the **X Variable Cell Range**.
3. Check **First cells in both ranges contain label**.
4. Enter **95** as the **Confidence level for regression coefficients.**
5. Check **Regression Statistics Table** and **ANOVA and Coefficients Table**.
6. Enter a **Title** and click **OK**.

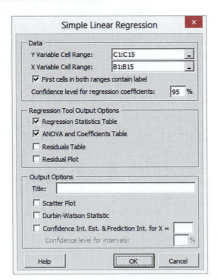

The procedure creates a worksheet that contains a copy of your data as well as the worksheet shown in Figure 12.4. For more information about these worksheets, read the following *In-Depth Excel* section.

To create a scatter plot that contains a prediction line and regression equation similar to Figure 12.5 on page 419, modify step 6 by checking **Scatter Plot** before clicking **OK**.

In-Depth Excel Use the **COMPUTE worksheet** of the **Simple Linear Regression workbook** as a template. (Use the **Simple Linear Regression 2007 workbook** if you use an Excel version that is older than Excel 2010.) For the example, the worksheet uses the regression data already in the **SLRDATA worksheet** to perform the regression analysis.

Figure 12.4 does not show the Calculations area in columns K through M. This area contains an array formula in the cell range L2:M6 that contains the expression **LINEST**(*cell range of Y variable*, *cell range of X variable*, **True, True**) to compute the b_1 and b_0 coefficients in cells L2 and M2, the b_1 and b_0 standard errors in cells L3 and M3, r^2 and the standard error of the estimate in cells L4 and M4, the *F* test statistic and error *df* in cells L5 and M5, and *SSR* and *SSE* in cells L6 and M6. In cell L9, the expression **T.INV.2T**(**1 − confidence level**, **Error degrees of freedom**) computes the critical value for the *t* test. Open the **COMPUTE_FORMULAS worksheet** to examine all the formulas in the worksheet, some of which are discussed in later sections in this Excel Guide.

To perform simple linear regression for other data, paste the regression data into the SLRDATA worksheet. Paste the values for the *X* variable into column A and the values for the *Y* variable into column B. Then, open to the COMPUTE worksheet. Enter the confidence level in cell L8 and edit the array formula in the cell range L2:M6. To edit the array formula, first select L2:M6, next make changes to the array formula, and then, while holding down the **Control** and **Shift** keys (or the **Command** key on a Mac), press the **Enter** key.

To create a scatter plot that contains a prediction line and regression equation similar to Figure 12.5 on page 419, first use the Section EG2.5 *In-Depth Excel* scatter plot instructions with the Table 12.1 Sunflowers Apparel data to create a scatter plot. Then select the chart and:

1. Select **Design → Add Chart Element → Trendline → More Trendline Options**.

In the Format Trendline pane (parts of which are shown in the next two illustrations):

2. Click **Linear** (shown below).

3. Check the **Display Equation on chart** and **Display R-squared value on chart** check boxes near the bottom of the pane (shown below).

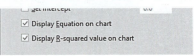

If you use an Excel version that is older than Excel 2010, use the following instructions after selecting the chart:

1. Select **Layout → Trendline → More Trendline Options**.

In the Format Trendline dialog box (similar to the Format Trendline pane):

2. Click **Trendline Options** in the left pane. In the Trendline Options right pane, click **Linear**, check **Display Equation on chart**, check **Display R-squared value on chart**, and then click **Close**.

For scatter plots of other data, if the *X* axis does not appear at the bottom of the plot, right-click the *Y* axis and click **Format Axis** from the shortcut menu. In the Format Axis dialog box, click **Axis Options** in the left pane. In the **Axis Options** pane on the right, click **Axis value** and in its box enter the value shown in the dimmed **Minimum** box at the top of the pane. Then click **Close**.

Analysis ToolPak Use **Regression**.
For the example, open to the **DATA worksheet** of the **SiteSelection workbook** and:

1. Select **Data → Data Analysis**.
2. In the Data Analysis dialog box, select **Regression** from the **Analysis** Tools list and then click **OK**.

In the Regression dialog box (shown below):

3. Enter **C1:C15** as the **Input Y Range** and enter **B1:B15** as the **Input X Range**.
4. Check **Labels** and check **Confidence Level** and enter **95** in its box.
5. Click **New Worksheet Ply** and then click **OK**.

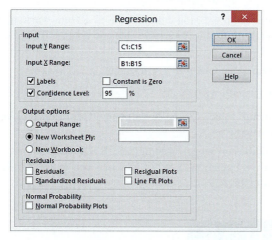

EG12.3 MEASURES of VARIATION

The measures of variation are computed as part of creating the simple linear regression worksheet using the Section EG12.2 instructions.

If you use either Section EG12.2 *PHStat* or *In-Depth Excel* instructions, formulas used to compute these measures are in the **COMPUTE worksheet** that is created. Formulas in cells B5, B7,

B13, C12, C13, D12, and E12 copy values computed by the array formula in cell range L2:M6. In cell F12, the **F.DIST.RT(*F test statistic*, *regression degrees of freedom*, *error degrees of freedom*)**, function computes the *p*-value for the *F* test for the slope, discussed in Section 12.7. (The similar FDIST function is used in the COMPUTE worksheet of the Simple Linear Regression 2007 workbook.)

EG12.4 ASSUMPTIONS of REGRESSION

There are no Excel Guide instructions for this section.

EG12.5 RESIDUAL ANALYSIS

Key Technique Use arithmetic formulas to compute the residuals. To evaluate assumptions, use the Section EG2.5 scatter plot instructions for constructing residual plots and the Section EG6.3 instructions for constructing normal probability plots.

Example Compute the residuals for the Table 12.1 Sunflowers Apparel data on page 417.

PHStat Use the Section EG12.2 *PHStat* instructions. Modify step 5 by checking **Residuals Table** and **Residual Plot** in addition to checking **Regression Statistics Table** and **ANOVA and Coefficients Table**. To construct a normal probability plot, follow the Section EG6.3 *PHStat* instructions using the cell range of the residuals as the **Variable Cell Range** in step 1.

In-Depth Excel Use the **RESIDUALS worksheet** of the **Simple Linear Regression workbook** as a template.

This worksheet already computes the residuals for the example. Column C formulas compute the predicted *Y* values (labeled Predicted Annual Sales in Figure 12.10 on page 431) by first multiplying the *X* values by the b_1 coefficient in cell B18 of the COMPUTE worksheet and then adding the b_0 coefficient (in cell B17 of COMPUTE). Column E formulas compute residuals by subtracting the predicted *Y* values from the *Y* values (labeled Annual Sales in Figure 12.10).

For other problems, modify this worksheet by pasting the *X* values into column B and the *Y* values into column D. Then, for sample sizes smaller than 14, delete the extra rows. For sample sizes greater than 14, copy the column C and E formulas down through the row containing the last pair and *X* and *Y* values and add the new observation numbers in column A.

To construct a residual plot similar to Figure 12.11 on page 432, use the original *X* variable and the residuals (plotted as the *Y* variable) as the chart data and follow the Section EG2.5 scatter plot instructions. To construct a normal probability plot, follow the Section EG6.3 *In-Depth Excel* instructions, using the cell range of the residuals as the **Variable Cell Range**.

Analysis ToolPak Use the Section EG12.2 *Analysis ToolPak* instructions.

Modify step 5 by checking **Residuals** and **Residual Plots** before clicking **New Worksheet Ply** and then **OK**. To construct a residual plot or normal probability plot, use the *In-Depth Excel* instructions.

EG12.6 MEASURING AUTOCORRELATION: the DURBIN-WATSON STATISTIC

Key Technique Use the **SUMXMY2(***cell range of the second through last residual, cell range of the first through the second-to-last residual***)** function to compute the sum of squared difference of the residuals, the numerator in Equation (12.15) on page 436, and use the **SUMSQ(***cell range of the residuals***)** function to compute the sum of squared residuals, the denominator in Equation (12.15).

Example Compute the Durbin-Watson statistic for the package delivery data on page 434.

PHStat Use the *PHStat* instructions at the beginning of Section EG12.2. Modify step 6 by checking the **Durbin-Watson Statistic** output option before clicking **OK**.

In-Depth Excel Use the **DURBIN_WATSON worksheet** of the **Simple Linear Regression** workbook as a template. The worksheet uses the SUMXMY2 function in cell B3 and the SUMSQ function in cell B4.

The **DURBIN_WATSON worksheet** of the **Package Delivery workbook** computes the statistic for the Figure 12.16 package delivery store example on page 436. (This workbook also uses the COMPUTE and RESIDUALS worksheet templates from the Simple Linear Regression workbook.)

To compute the Durbin-Watson statistic for other problems, first create the simple linear regression model and the residuals for the problem, using the Sections EG12.2 and EG12.5 *In-Depth Excel* instructions. Then open the DURBIN_WATSON worksheet and edit the formulas in cell B3 and B4 to point to the proper cell ranges of the new residuals.

EG12.7 INFERENCES ABOUT the SLOPE and CORRELATION COEFFICIENT

The *t* test for the slope and *F* test for the slope are included in the worksheet created by using the Section EG12.2 instructions. The *t* test computations in the worksheets created by using the *PHStat* and *In-Depth Excel* instructions are discussed in Section EG12.2. The *F* test computations are discussed in Section EG12.3.

EG12.8 ESTIMATION of MEAN VALUES and PREDICTION of INDIVIDUAL VALUES

Key Technique Use the **TREND(***Y variable cell range, X variable cell range, X value***)** function to compute the predicted *Y* value for the *X* value and use the **DEVSQ(***X variable cell range***)** function to compute the *SSX* value.

Example Compute the Figure 12.21 confidence interval estimate and prediction interval for the Sunflowers Apparel data that is shown on page 417.

PHStat Use the Section EG12.2 *PHStat* instructions but replace step 6 with these steps 6 and 7:

1. Check **Confidence Int. Est. & Prediction Int. for** $X =$ and enter **4** in its box. Enter **95** as the percentage for **Confidence level for intervals**.

2. Enter a **Title** and click **OK**.

The additional worksheet created is discussed in the following *In-Depth Excel* instructions.

In-Depth Excel Use the **CIEandPI worksheet** of the **Simple Linear Regression workbook**, as a template.

The worksheet already contains the data and formulas for the example. The worksheet uses the **T.INV.2T (1 –** *confidence level, degrees of freedom***)** function to compute the *t* critical value in cell B10 and the TREND function to compute the predicted *Y* value for the *X* value in cell B15. In cell B12, the function **DEVSQ(SLRData!A:A)** computes the *SSX* value that is used, in turn, to help compute the *h* statistic in cell B14.

To compute a confidence interval estimate and prediction interval for other problems:

1. Paste the regression data into the **SLRData worksheet**. Use column A for the *X* variable data and column B for the *Y* variable data.

2. Open to the **CIEandPI worksheet**.

In the CIEandPI worksheet:

3. Change values for the **X Value** and **Confidence Level**, as is necessary.

4. Edit the cell ranges used in the cell B15 formula that uses the TREND function to refer to the new cell ranges for the *Y* and *X* variables.

CHAPTER 12 MINITAB GUIDE

MG12.1 TYPES of REGRESSION MODELS

There are no Minitab Guide instructions for this section.

MG12.2 DETERMINING the SIMPLE LINEAR REGRESSION EQUATION

Use **Regression** to perform a simple linear regression analysis. For example, to perform the Figure 12.4 analysis of the Sunflowers Apparel data on page 418, open to the **SiteSelection worksheet**.

Select **Stat → Regression → Regression**. (and **Fit Regression Model** in Minitab 17.) In the Regression dialog box (shown on the next page):

1. Double-click **C3 Annual Sales** in the variables list to add **'Annual Sales'** to the **Response** box (**Responses** box in Minitab 17).

2. Double-click **C2 Profiled Customers** in the variables list to add **'Profiled Customers'** to the **Predictors** (or **Continuous predictors**) box.

3. Click **Graphs**.

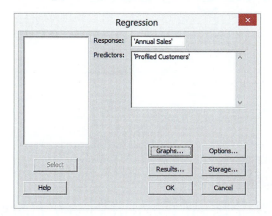

In the Regression - Graphs dialog box (shown below):

4. Click (select in Minitab 17) **Regular** in Residuals for Plots. Click **Individual Plots** in Residual Plots.

5. Check **Histogram of residuals, Normal plot of residuals, Residuals versus fits**, and **Residuals versus order** and then press **Tab**.

6. Double-click **C2 Profiled Customers** in the variables list to add **'Profiled Customers'** in the **Residuals versus the variables** box.

7. Click **OK**.

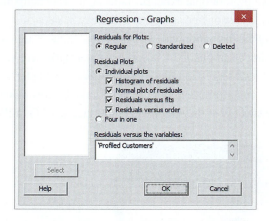

8. Back in the Regression dialog box, click **Results**.

In the Regression - Results dialog box (not shown):

9. Click **Regression equation, table of coefficients, s, R-squared, and basic analysis of variance** and then click **OK**. (In Minitab 17, check the first 6 check boxes.)

10. Back in the Regression dialog box, click **Options**.

In the Regression - Options dialog box (shown in next column):

11. Check **Fit Intercept**.

12. Clear all the **Display** and **Lack of Fit Test** check boxes.

13. Enter **4** in the **Prediction intervals for new observations** box.

14. Enter **95** in the **Confidence level** box.

15. Click **OK**. (In Minitab 17, ignore steps 11 through 14.)

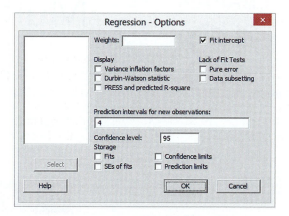

16. Back in the Regression dialog box, click **OK**.

To create a scatter plot that contains a prediction line and regression equation similar to Figure 12.5 on page 419, use the Section MG2.6 scatter plot instructions with the Table 12.1 Sunflowers Apparel data.

MG12.3 MEASURES of VARIATION

The measures of variation are computed in the Analysis of Variance table that is part of the simple linear regression results created using the Section MG12.2 instructions.

MG12.4 ASSUMPTIONS

There are no Minitab Guide instructions for this section.

MG12.5 RESIDUAL ANALYSIS

Selections in step 5 of the Section MG12.2 instructions create the residual plots and normal probability plots necessary for residual analysis. To create the list of residual values similar to the last column in Figure 12.10 on page 431, replace step 15 of the Section MG12.2 instructions with these steps 15 through 17:

15. Click **Storage**.

16. In the Regression - Storage dialog box, check **Residuals** and then click **OK**.

17. Back in the Regression dialog box, click **OK**.

MG12.6 MEASURING AUTOCORRELATION: THE DURBIN-WATSON STATISTIC

To compute the Durbin-Watson statistic, use the Section MG12.2 instructions but check **Durbin-Watson statistic** (in the Regression - Options dialog box) as part of step 12.

MG12.7 INFERENCES ABOUT the SLOPE AND CORRELATION COEFFICIENT

The *t* test for the slope and *F* test for the slope are included in the results created by using the Section MG12.2 instructions.

MG12.8 ESTIMATION of MEAN VALUES and PREDICTION of INDIVIDUAL VALUES

The confidence interval estimate and prediction interval are included in the results created by using the Section MG12.2 instructions.

Multiple Regression

CONTENTS

OBJECTIVES

Develop a multiple regression model

Interpret the regression coefficients

Determine which independent variables to include in a regression model

How to use categorical independent variables in a regression model

USING STATISTICS

The Multiple Effects of OmniPower Bars

You are a marketing manager for OmniFoods, with oversight for nutrition bars and similar snack items. You seek to revive the sales of OmniPower, the company's primary product in this category. Originally marketed as a high-energy bar to runners, mountain climbers, and other athletes, OmniPower reached its greatest sales in an earlier time, when high-energy bars were most popular with consumers. Now, you seek to remarket the product as a nutrition bar to benefit from the booming market for such bars.

Because the marketplace already contains several successful nutrition bars, you need to develop an effective marketing strategy. In particular, you need to determine the effect that price and in-store promotional expenses (special in-store coupons, signs, and displays as well as the cost of free samples) will have on sales of OmniPower. Before marketing the bar nationwide, you plan to conduct a test-market study of OmniPower sales, using a sample of 34 stores in a supermarket chain.

How can you extend the linear regression methods discussed in Chapter 12 to incorporate the effects of price *and* promotion into the same model? How can you use this model to improve the success of the nationwide introduction of OmniPower?

Ariwasabi/Shutterstock

C hapter 12 discusses simple linear regression models that use *one* numerical independent variable, *X*, to predict the value of a numerical dependent variable, *Y*. Often you can make better predictions by using *more than one* independent variable. This chapter introduces you to **multiple regression models** that use two or more independent variables to predict the value of a dependent variable.

13.1 Developing a Multiple Regression Model

In the OmniPower Bars scenario, your business objective, to determine the effect that price and in-store promotional expenses will have on sales, calls for examining a multiple regression model in which the price of an OmniPower bar in cents (X_1) and the monthly budget for in-store promotional expenditures in dollars (X_2) are the independent variables and the number of OmniPower bars sold in a month (Y) is the dependent variable.

To develop this model, you collect data from a sample of 34 stores in a supermarket chain selected for a test-market study of OmniPower. You choose stores in a way to ensure that they all have approximately the same monthly sales volume. You organize and store the data collected in OmniPower . Table 13.1 presents these data.

TABLE 13.1

Monthly OmniPower Sales, Price, and Promotional Expenditures

Store	Sales	Price	Promotion	Store	Sales	Price	Promotion
1	4,141	59	200	18	2,730	79	400
2	3,842	59	200	19	2,618	79	400
3	3,056	59	200	20	4,421	79	400
4	3,519	59	200	21	4,113	79	600
5	4,226	59	400	22	3,746	79	600
6	4,630	59	400	23	3,532	79	600
7	3,507	59	400	24	3,825	79	600
8	3,754	59	400	25	1,096	99	200
9	5,000	59	600	26	761	99	200
10	5,120	59	600	27	2,088	99	200
11	4,011	59	600	28	820	99	200
12	5,015	59	600	29	2,114	99	400
13	1,916	79	200	30	1,882	99	400
14	675	79	200	31	2,159	99	400
15	3,636	79	200	32	1,602	99	400
16	3,224	79	200	33	3,354	99	600
17	2,295	79	400	34	2,927	99	600

When there are two independent variables in the multiple regression model, using a three-dimensional (3D) scatter plot can help suggest a starting point for analysis. Figure 13.1 on page 466 presents a 3D scatter plot of the OmniPower data. In this figure, points are plotted at a height equal to their sales and have drop lines down to their corresponding price and promotion expense values. Rotating 3D plots can sometimes reveal patterns. One rotated view (Figure 13.1 right) suggests a negative linear relationship between sales and price (sales decrease as price increases) and a positive linear relationship between sales and promotional expenses (sales increase as those expenses increase). These relationships are not easily seen in the original orientation of the scatter plot.

FIGURE 13.1

Original (left) and rotated (right) Minitab 3D scatter plot of the monthly OmniPower sales, price, and promotional expenses

3D Scatterplot of Sales vs Price vs Promotional Expenses

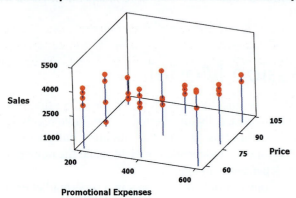

3D Scatterplot of Sales vs Price vs Promotional Expenses

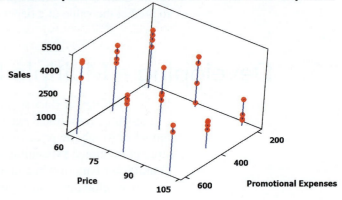

Excel does not include the capability to construct 3D scatter plots

Interpreting the Regression Coefficients

When there are several independent variables, you can extend the simple linear regression model of Equation (12.1) on page 416 by assuming a linear relationship between each independent variable and the dependent variable. For example, with k independent variables, the multiple regression model is expressed in Equation (13.1).

MULTIPLE REGRESSION MODEL WITH k INDEPENDENT VARIABLES

$$Y_i = \beta_0 + \beta_1 X_{1i} + \beta_2 X_{2i} + \beta_3 X_{3i} + \cdots + \beta_k X_{ki} + \varepsilon_i \tag{13.1}$$

where

$\beta_0 = Y$ intercept

$\beta_1 = $ slope of Y with variable X_1, holding variables $X_2, X_3, \ldots, X_k$ constant

$\beta_2 = $ slope of Y with variable X_2, holding variables $X_1, X_3, \ldots, X_k$ constant

$\beta_3 = $ slope of Y with variable X_3, holding variables $X_1, X_2, \ldots, X_k$ constant

$\vdots$

$\beta_k = $ slope of Y with variable X_k holding variables $X_1, X_2, X_3, \ldots, X_{k-1}$ constant

$\varepsilon_i = $ random error in Y for observation i

Equation (13.2) defines the multiple regression model with two independent variables.

MULTIPLE REGRESSION MODEL WITH TWO INDEPENDENT VARIABLES

$$Y_i = \beta_0 + \beta_1 X_{1i} + \beta_2 X_{2i} + \varepsilon_i \tag{13.2}$$

where

$\beta_0 = $ intercept

$\beta_1 = $ slope of Y with variable X_1, holding variable X_2 constant

$\beta_2 = $ slope of Y with variable X_2, holding variable X_1 constant

$\varepsilon_i = $ random error in Y for observation i

Compare the multiple regression model to the simple linear regression model [Equation (12.1) on page 416]:

$$Y_i = \beta_0 + \beta_1 X_i + \varepsilon_i$$

In the simple linear regression model, the slope, β_1, represents the change in the mean of Y per unit change in X and does not take into account any other variables. In the multiple regression model with two independent variables [Equation (13.2)], the slope, β_1, represents the change in the mean of Y per unit change in X_1, taking into account the effect of X_2.

As in the case of simple linear regression, you use the least-squares method to compute the sample regression coefficients b_0, b_1, and b_2 as estimates of the population parameters β_0, β_1, and β_2. Equation (13.3) defines the regression equation for a multiple regression model with two independent variables.

> **Student Tip**
> Because multiple regression computations are more complex than computations for simple linear regression, always use a computerized method to obtain multiple regression results.

MULTIPLE REGRESSION EQUATION WITH TWO INDEPENDENT VARIABLES

$$\hat{Y}_i = b_0 + b_1 X_{1i} + b_2 X_{2i} \tag{13.3}$$

Figure 13.2 shows Excel and Minitab results for the OmniPower sales data multiple regression model. In these results, the b_0 coefficient is labeled Intercept by Excel and Constant by Minitab.

FIGURE 13.2
Excel and Minitab results for the OmniPower sales multiple regression model

	A	B	C	D	E	F	G
1	OmniPower Sales Multiple Regression Model						
2							
3	*Regression Statistics*						
4	Multiple R	0.8705					
5	R Square	0.7577					
6	Adjusted R Square	0.7421					
7	Standard Error	638.0653					
8	Observations	34					
9							
10	ANOVA						
11		*df*	*SS*	*MS*	*F*	*Significance F*	
12	Regression	2	39472730.7730	19736365.3865	48.4771	0.0000	
13	Residual	31	12620946.6682	407127.3119			
14	Total	33	52093677.4412				
15							
16		*Coefficients*	*Standard Error*	*t Stat*	*P-value*	*Lower 95%*	*Upper 95%*
17	Intercept	5837.5208	628.1502	9.2932	0.0000	4556.3999	7118.6416
18	Price	-53.2173	6.8522	-7.7664	0.0000	-67.1925	-39.2421
19	Promotional Expenses	3.6131	0.6852	5.2728	0.0000	2.2155	5.0106

```
Regression Analysis: Sales versus Price, Promotion
The regression equation is
Sales = 5838 - 53.2 Price + 3.61 Promotion

Predictor     Coef    SE Coef      T      P
Constant    5837.5      628.2   9.29  0.000
Price      -53.217      6.852  -7.77  0.000
Promotion   3.6131     0.6852   5.27  0.000

S = 638.065   R-Sq = 75.8%   R-Sq(adj) = 74.2%

Analysis of Variance
Source          DF        SS        MS      F      P
Regression       2  39472731  19736365  48.48  0.000
Residual Error  31  12620947    407127
Total           33  52093677
```

From Figure 13.2, the computed values of the three regression coefficients are

$$b_0 = 5{,}837.5208 \quad b_1 = -53.2173 \quad b_2 = 3.6131$$

Therefore, the multiple regression equation is

$$\hat{Y}_i = 5{,}837.5208 - 53.2173 X_{1i} + 3.6131 X_{2i}$$

where

$$\hat{Y}_i = \text{predicted monthly sales of OmniPower bars for store } i$$
$$X_{1i} = \text{price of OmniPower bar (in cents) for store } i$$
$$X_{2i} = \text{monthly in-store promotional expenditures (in \$) for store } i$$

The sample Y intercept ($b_0 = 5,837.5208$) estimates the number of OmniPower bars sold in a month if the price is \$0.00 and the total amount spent on promotional expenditures is also \$0.00. Because these values of price and promotion are outside the range of price and promotion used in the test-market study, and because they make no sense in the context of the problem, the value of b_0 has little or no practical interpretation.

The slope of price with OmniPower sales ($b_1 = -53.2173$) indicates that, for a given amount of monthly promotional expenditures, the predicted mean sales of OmniPower are estimated to decrease by 53.2173 bars per month for each 1-cent increase in the price. The slope of monthly promotional expenditures with OmniPower sales ($b_2 = 3.6131$) indicates that, for a given price, the predicted mean sales of OmniPower are estimated to increase by 3.6131 bars for each additional \$1 spent on promotions. These estimates allow you to better understand the likely effect that price and promotion decisions will have in the marketplace. For example, a 10-cent decrease in price is predicted to increase mean sales by 532.173 bars, with a fixed amount of monthly promotional expenditures. A \$100 increase in promotional expenditures is predicted to increase mean sales by 361.31 bars for a given price.

Regression coefficients in multiple regression are called **net regression coefficients**, and they estimate the predicted mean change in Y per unit change in a particular X, *holding constant the effect of the other X variables*. For example, in the study of OmniPower bar sales, for a store with a given amount of promotional expenditures, the mean sales are predicted to decrease by 53.2173 bars per month for each 1-cent increase in the price of an OmniPower bar. Another way to interpret this "net effect" is to think of two stores with an equal amount of promotional expenditures. If the first store charges 1 cent more than the other store, the net effect of this difference is that the first store is predicted to sell a mean of 53.2173 fewer bars per month than the second store. To interpret the net effect of promotional expenditures, you can consider two stores that are charging the same price. If the first store spends \$1 more on promotional expenditures, the net effect of this difference is that the first store is predicted to sell a mean of 3.6131 more bars per month than the second store.

Student Tip
Remember that in multiple regression, the regression coefficients are conditional on holding constant the other independent variables. The slope of b_1 holds constant the effect of variable X_2. The slope of b_2 holds constant the effect of variable X_1.

Predicting the Dependent Variable Y

You can use the multiple regression equation to predict values of the dependent variable. For example, what are the predicted mean sales for a store charging 79 cents during a month in which promotional expenditures are \$400? Using the multiple regression equation,

$$\hat{Y}_i = 5,837.5208 - 53.2173X_{1i} + 3.6131X_{2i}$$

with $X_{1i} = 79$ and $X_{2i} = 400$,

$$\hat{Y}_i = 5,837.5208 - 53.2173(79) + 3.6131(400)$$
$$= 3,078.57$$

Student Tip
You should only predict within the range of the values of all the independent variables.

Thus, you predict that stores charging 79 cents and spending \$400 in promotional expenditures will sell a mean of 3,078.57 OmniPower bars per month.

After you have developed the regression equation, done a residual analysis (see Section 13.3), and determined the significance of the overall fitted model (see Section 13.2), you can construct a confidence interval estimate of the mean value and a prediction interval for an individual value. Figure 13.3 presents Excel and Minitab results that compute a confidence interval estimate and a prediction interval for the OmniPower sales data.

FIGURE 13.3

Excel confidence interval estimate and prediction interval worksheet for the OmniPower sales data

	A	B	C	D
1	Confidence Interval Estimate and Prediction Interval			
2				
3	Data			
4	Confidence Level	95%		
5		1		
6	Price given value	79		
7	Promotion given value	400		
8				
9	X'X	34	2646	13200
10		2646	214674	1018800
11		13200	1018800	6000000
12				
13	Inverse of X'X	0.9692	-0.0094	-0.0005
14		-0.0094	0.0001	0.0000
15		-0.0005	0.0000	0.0000
16				
17	X'G times Inverse of X'X	0.0121	0.0001	0.0000
18				
19	[X'G times Inverse of X'X] times XG	0.0298		
20	t Statistic	2.0395		
21	Predicted Y (YHat)	3078.57		
22				
23	For Average Predicted Y (YHat)			
24	Interval Half Width	224.50		
25	Confidence Interval Lower Limit	2854.07		
26	Confidence Interval Upper Limit	3303.08		
27				
28	For Individual Response Y			
29	Interval Half Width	1320.57		
30	Prediction Interval Lower Limit	1758.01		
31	Prediction Interval Upper Limit	4399.14		

```
Predicted Values for New Observations
New Obs   Fit  SE Fit      95% CI          95% PI
    1    3079    110   (2854, 3303)   (1758, 4399)

Values of Predictors for New Observations
New Obs  Price  Promotion
    1     79.0     400
```

The 95% confidence interval estimate of the mean OmniPower sales for all stores charging 79 cents and spending $400 in promotional expenditures is 2,854.07 to 3,303.08 bars. The prediction interval for an individual store is 1,758.01 to 4,399.14 bars.

Problems for Section 13.1

LEARNING THE BASICS

13.1 For this problem, use the following multiple regression equation:

$$\hat{Y}_i = 10 + 5X_{1i} + 3X_{2i}$$

a. Interpret the meaning of the slopes.
b. Interpret the meaning of the Y intercept.

13.2 For this problem, use the following multiple regression equation:

$$\hat{Y}_i = 50 - 2X_{1i} + 7X_{2i}$$

a. Interpret the meaning of the slopes.
b. Interpret the meaning of the Y intercept.

APPLYING THE CONCEPTS

13.3 A small business analyst seeks to determine which variables should be used to predict small-business mean annual revenue for U.S. metropolitan areas. The analyst decides to consider the independent variables age, the mean age (in months) of small businesses in the metropolitan area; and BizAnalyzer, the mean BizAnalyzer score of small businesses in the metropolitan area. (The BizAnalyzer score measures on a scale of 1 to100 the level of risk that the small businesses in the metropolitan area present to potential lenders.) The dependent variable, revenue, is mean annual revenue. Using data collected from a sample of 25 metropolitan areas, the regression results are:

Variable	Coefficients	Standard Error	t Statistic	p-Value
Intercept	−680.2357	1,313.5154	−0.52	0.6097
Age	1.7454	7.8519	0.22	0.8261
BizAnalyzer	20.5265	29.1859	0.70	0.4885

a. State the multiple regression equation.
b. Interpret the meaning of the slopes, b_1 and b_2, in this problem.
c. What conclusions can you reach concerning mean annual revenue?

✓SELF Test **13.4** Profitability remains a challenge for banks and thrifts with less than $2 billion of assets. The business problem facing a bank analyst relates to the factors that affect return on assets (ROA), an indicator of how profitable a company is relative to its total assets. Data collected from a sample of 200 community banks and stored in **CommunityBanks** include the ROA (%), the efficiency ratio (%), as a measure of bank productivity (the lower the efficiency ratio, the better), and total risk-based capital (%), as a measure of capital adequacy. (Data extracted from "Rising Tide: The Top 200 Community Banks," **bit.ly/1ldN8gC**.)
a. State the multiple regression equation.
b. Interpret the meaning of the slopes, b_1 and b_2, in this problem.
c. Predict the mean ROA when the efficiency ratio is 60% and the total risk-based capital is 15%.
d. Construct a 95% confidence interval estimate for the mean ROA when the efficiency ratio is 60% and the total risk-based capital is 15%.

e. Construct a 95% prediction interval for the ROA for a particular community bank when the efficiency ratio is 60% and the total risk-based capital is 15%.

f. Explain why the interval in (d) is narrower than the interval in (e).

g. What conclusions can you reach concerning ROA?

13.5 The production of wine is a multibillion-dollar worldwide industry. In an attempt to develop a model of wine quality as judged by wine experts, data was collected from red wine variants of Portuguese "Vinho Verde" wine. A sample of 50 wines is stored in VinhoVerde . (Data extracted from P. Cortez, A. Cerdeira, F. Almeida, T. Matos, and J. Reis, "Modeling Wine Preferences by Data Mining from Physiochemical Properties," *Decision Support Systems*, 47, 2009, pp. 547–553 and **bit.ly/ 9xKlEa**.) Develop a multiple linear regression model to predict wine quality, measured on a scale from 0 (very bad) to 10 (excellent) based on alcohol content (%) and the amount of chlorides.

a. State the multiple regression equation.

b. Interpret the meaning of the slopes, b_1 and b_2, in this problem.

c. Explain why the regression coefficient, b_0, has no practical meaning in the context of this problem.

d. Predict the mean wine quality rating for wines that have 10% alcohol and chlorides of 0.08.

e. Construct a 95% confidence interval estimate for the mean wine quality rating for wines that have 10% alcohol and chlorides of 0.08.

f. Construct a 95% prediction interval for the wine quality rating for an individual wine that has 10% alcohol and chlorides of 0.08.

g. What conclusions can you reach concerning this regression model?

13.6 The business problem facing a human resource manager is to assess the impact of factors on full-time job growth. Specifically, the human resource manager is interested in the impact of total worldwide revenues and full-time voluntary turnover on the number of full-time jobs added in a year. Data were collected from a sample of 96 "best companies to work for." The total number of full-time jobs added in the past year, total worldwide revenue (in $millions) and the full-time voluntary turnover (%) are recorded and stored in BestCompanies . (Data extracted from *Best Companies to Work For 2014*, available at **fortune.com/best-companies/google-1/**.)

a. State the multiple regression equation.

b. Interpret the meaning of the slopes, b_1 and b_2, in this problem.

c. Interpret the meaning of the regression coefficient, b_0.

d. What conclusions can you reach concerning full-time jobs added?

13.7 The business problem facing the director of broadcasting operations for a television station was the issue of standby hours (i.e., hours in which unionized graphic artists at the station are paid but are not actually involved in any activity) and what factors were related to standby hours. The study included the following variables:

> Standby hours (Y)—Total number of standby hours in a week
> Total staff present (X_1)—Weekly total of people-days
> Remote hours (X_2)—Total number of hours worked by employees at locations away from the central plant

Data were collected for 26 weeks; these data are organized and stored in Standby .

a. State the multiple regression equation.

b. Interpret the meaning of the slopes, b_1 and b_2, in this problem.

c. Explain why the regression coefficient, b_0, has no practical meaning in the context of this problem.

d. Predict the mean standby hours for a week in which the total staff present have 310 people-days and the remote hours total 400.

e. Construct a 95% confidence interval estimate for the mean standby hours for weeks in which the total staff present have 310 people-days and remote hours total 400.

f. Construct a 95% prediction interval for the standby hours for a single week in which the total staff present have 310 people-days and the remote hours total 400.

g. What conclusions can you reach concerning standby hours?

13.8 Nassau County is located approximately 25 miles east of New York City. The data organized and stored in GlenCove include the fair market value (in $thousands), land area of the property in acres, and age, in years, for a sample of 30 single-family homes located in Glen Cove, a small city in Nassau County. Develop a multiple linear regression model to predict the fair market value based on land area of the property and age, in years.

a. State the multiple regression equation.

b. Interpret the meaning of the slopes, b_1 and b_2, in this problem.

c. Explain why the regression coefficient, b_0, has no practical meaning in the context of this problem.

d. Predict the mean fair market value for a house that has a land area of 0.25 acre and is 55 years old.

e. Construct a 95% confidence interval estimate for the mean fair market value for houses that have a land area of 0.25 acre and are 55 years old.

f. Construct a 95% prediction interval estimate for the fair market value for an individual house that has a land area of 0.25 acre and is 55 years old.

13.2 r^2, Adjusted r^2, and the Overall F Test

This section discusses three methods you can use to evaluate the overall multiple regression model: the coefficient of multiple determination, r^2, the adjusted r^2, and the overall F test.

Coefficient of Multiple Determination

Recall from Section 12.3 that the coefficient of determination, r^2, measures the proportion of the variation in Y that is explained by the independent variable X in the simple linear regression model. In multiple regression, the **coefficient of multiple determination** represents the proportion of the variation in Y that is explained by all the independent variables. Equation (13.4) defines the coefficient of multiple determination for a multiple regression model with two or more independent variables.

COEFFICIENT OF MULTIPLE DETERMINATION

The coefficient of multiple determination is equal to the regression sum of squares (SSR) divided by the total sum of squares (SST).

$$r^2 = \frac{\text{Regression sum of squares}}{\text{Total sum of squares}} = \frac{SSR}{SST} \qquad (13.4)$$

In the OmniPower example, from Figure 13.2 on page 467, $SSR = 39{,}472{,}730.77$ and $SST = 52{,}093{,}677.44$. Thus,

$$r^2 = \frac{SSR}{SST} = \frac{39{,}472{,}730.77}{52{,}093{,}677.44} = 0.7577$$

> **Student Tip**
>
> Remember that r^2 in multiple regression represents the proportion of the variation in the dependent variable Y that is explained by all the independent X variables included in the model.

The coefficient of multiple determination ($r^2 = 0.7577$) indicates that 75.77% of the variation in sales is explained by the variation in the price and in the promotional expenditures. The coefficient of multiple determination also appears in the Figure 13.2 results on page 467, labeled R Square in the Excel results and R-Sq in the Minitab results.

Adjusted r^2

When considering multiple regression models, some statisticians suggest that you should use the **adjusted r^2** to take into account both the number of independent variables in the model and the sample size. Reporting the adjusted r^2 is extremely important when you are comparing two or more regression models that predict the same dependent variable but have a different number of independent variables. Equation (13.5) defines the adjusted r^2.

ADJUSTED r^2

$$r^2_{\text{adj}} = 1 - \left[(1 - r^2) \frac{n - 1}{n - k - 1} \right] \qquad (13.5)$$

where k is the number of independent variables in the regression equation.

Thus, for the OmniPower data, because $r^2 = 0.7577$, $n = 34$, and $k = 2$,

$$r^2_{\text{adj}} = 1 - \left[(1 - 0.7577) \frac{34 - 1}{34 - 2 - 1} \right]$$

$$= 1 - \left[(0.2423) \frac{33}{31} \right]$$

$$= 1 - 0.2579$$

$$= 0.7421$$

Therefore, 74.21% of the variation in sales is explained by the multiple regression model—adjusted for the number of independent variables and sample size. The adjusted r^2 also appears in the Figure 13.2 results on page 467, labeled Adjusted R Square in the Excel results and R Sq(adj) in the Minitab results.

Test for the Significance of the Overall Multiple Regression Model

You use the **overall F test** to determine whether there is a significant relationship between the dependent variable and the entire set of independent variables (the overall multiple regression model). Because there is more than one independent variable, you use the following null and alternative hypotheses:

$H_0: \beta_1 = \beta_2 = \cdots = \beta_k = 0$ (There is no linear relationship between the dependent variable and the independent variables.)

$H_1:$ At least one $\beta_j \neq 0, j = 1, 2, \ldots, k$ (There is a linear relationship between the dependent variable and at least one of the independent variables.)

Equation (13.6) defines the overall F test statistic. Table 13.2 presents the ANOVA summary table.

OVERALL F TEST

The F_{STAT} test statistic is equal to the regression mean square (MSR) divided by the mean square error (MSE).

$$F_{STAT} = \frac{MSR}{MSE} \qquad (13.6)$$

where

k = number of independent variables in the regression model

The F_{STAT} test statistic follows an F distribution with k and $n - k - 1$ degrees of freedom.

TABLE 13.2

ANOVA Summary Table for the Overall F Test

Source	Degrees of Freedom	Sum of Squares	Mean Squares (Variance)	F
Regression	k	SSR	$MSR = \dfrac{SSR}{k}$	$F_{STAT} = \dfrac{MSR}{MSE}$
Error	$n - k - 1$	SSE	$MSE = \dfrac{SSE}{n - k - 1}$	
Total	$n - 1$	SST		

The decision rule is

Reject H_0 at the α level of significance if $F_{STAT} > F_\alpha$;
otherwise, do not reject H_0.

Using a 0.05 level of significance, the critical value of the F distribution with 2 and 31 degrees of freedom found in Table E.5 is approximately 3.32 (see Figure 13.4 on page 473). From Figure 13.2 on page 467, the F_{STAT} test statistic given in the ANOVA summary table is 48.4771. Because $48.4771 > 3.32$, or because the p-value $= 0.000 < 0.05$, you reject H_0 and conclude that at least one of the independent variables (price and/or promotional expenditures) is related to sales.

FIGURE 13.4
Testing for the
significance of a set of
regression coefficients
at the 0.05 level of
significance, with 2 and
31 degrees of freedom

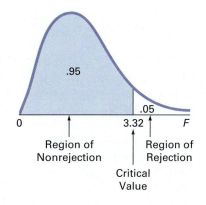

Problems for Section 13.2

LEARNING THE BASICS

13.9 The following ANOVA summary table is for a multiple regression model with two independent variables:

Source	Degrees of Freedom	Sum of Squares	Mean Squares	F
Regression	2	60		
Error	18	120		
Total	20	180		

a. Determine the regression mean square (MSR) and the mean square error (MSE).
b. Compute the overall F_{STAT} test statistic.
c. Determine whether there is a significant relationship between Y and the two independent variables at the 0.05 level of significance.
d. Compute the coefficient of multiple determination, r^2, and interpret its meaning.
e. Compute the adjusted r^2.

13.10 The following ANOVA summary table is for a multiple regression model with two independent variables:

Source	Degrees of Freedom	Sum of Squares	Mean Squares	F
Regression	2	30		
Error	10	120		
Total	12	150		

a. Determine the regression mean square (MSR) and the mean square error (MSE).
b. Compute the overall F_{STAT} test statistic.
c. Determine whether there is a significant relationship between Y and the two independent variables at the 0.05 level of significance.
d. Compute the coefficient of multiple determination, r^2, and interpret its meaning.
e. Compute the adjusted r^2.

APPLYING THE CONCEPTS

13.11 A financial analyst engaged in business valuation obtained financial data on 53 drug companies (Industry Group

SIC 3 code: 283). The file **BusinessValuation** contains the following variables:

COMPANY—Drug Company name
PB fye—Price-to-book-value ratio (fiscal year ending)
ROE—Return on equity
SGROWTH—Growth (GS5)

a. Develop a regression model to predict price-to-book-value ratio based on return on equity.
b. Develop a regression model to predict price-to-book-value ratio based on growth.
c. Develop a regression model to predict price-to-book-value ratio based on return on equity and growth.
d. Compute and interpret the adjusted r^2 for each of the three models.
e. Which of these three models do you think is the best predictor of price-to-book-value ratio?

13.12 In Problem 13.3 on page 469, you predicted the mean annual revenue for U.S. metropolitan areas, based on the mean age (Age) and mean BizAnalyzer score (BizAnalyzer) for a sample of 25 small business metropolitan areas. The regression analysis resulted in the following ANOVA summary table:

Source	Degrees of Freedom	Sum of Squares	Mean Squares	F	p-Value
Regression	2	96,655.1	48,327.6	0.6531	0.5302
Error	22	1,627,941.1	73,997.3		
Total	24	1,724,596.2			

a. Determine whether there is a significant relationship between mean annual revenue and the two independent variables at the 0.05 level of significance.
b. Interpret the meaning of the p-value.
c. Compute the coefficient of multiple determination, r^2, and interpret its meaning.

13.13 In Problem 13.5 on page 470, you used the percentage of alcohol and chlorides to predict wine quality (stored in **VinhoVerde**). Use the results from that problem to do the following:
a. Determine whether there is a significant relationship between wine quality and the two independent variables (percentage of alcohol and chlorides) at the 0.05 level of significance.

b. Interpret the meaning of the *p*-value.
c. Compute the coefficient of multiple determination, r^2, and interpret its meaning.
d. Compute the adjusted r^2.

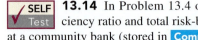 **13.14** In Problem 13.4 on page 469, you used efficiency ratio and total risk-based capital to predict ROA at a community bank (stored in CommunityBanks). Using the results from that problem,
a. determine whether there is a significant relationship between ROA and the two independent variables (used efficiency ratio and total risk-based capital) at the 0.05 level of significance.
b. interpret the meaning of the *p*-value.
c. compute the coefficient of multiple determination, r^2, and interpret its meaning.
d. compute the adjusted r^2.

13.15 In Problem 13.7 on page 470, you used the total staff present and remote hours to predict standby hours (stored in Standby). Using the results from that problem,
a. determine whether there is a significant relationship between standby hours and the two independent variables (total staff present and remote hours) at the 0.05 level of significance.
b. interpret the meaning of the *p*-value.
c. compute the coefficient of multiple determination, r^2, and interpret its meaning.
d. compute the adjusted r^2.

13.16 In Problem 13.6 on page 470, you used the total worldwide revenue ($millions), and full-time voluntary turnover (%) data stored in BestCompanies to predict the number of full-time jobs added. Using the results from that problem,
a. determine whether there is a significant relationship at the 0.05 level of significance between the number of full-time jobs added and the two independent variables, total worldwide revenue ($millions) and full-time voluntary turnover (%).
b. interpret the meaning of the *p*-value.
c. compute the coefficient of multiple determination, r^2, and interpret its meaning.
d. compute the adjusted r^2.

13.17 In Problem 13.8 on page 470, you used the land area of a property and the age of a house to predict the fair market value (stored in GlenCove). Using the results from that problem,
a. determine whether there is a significant relationship between fair market value and the two independent variables (land area of a property and age of a house) at the 0.05 level of significance.
b. interpret the meaning of the *p*-value.
c. compute the coefficient of multiple determination, r^2, and interpret its meaning.
d. compute the adjusted r^2.

13.3 Residual Analysis for the Multiple Regression Model

In Section 12.5, you used residual analysis to evaluate the fit of the simple linear regression model. For the multiple regression model with two independent variables, you need to construct and analyze the following residual plots:

- Residuals versus $\hat{Y}_i$
- Residuals versus X_{1i}
- Residuals versus X_{2i}
- Residuals versus time

> **Student Tip**
> As is the case with simple linear regression, a residual plot that does not contain any apparent patterns will look like a random scattering of points.

The first residual plot examines the pattern of residuals versus the predicted values of *Y*. If the residuals show a pattern for the predicted values of *Y*, there is evidence of a possible curvilinear effect in at least one independent variable, a possible violation of the assumption of equal variance (see Figure 12.13 on page 433), and/or the need to transform the *Y* variable.

The second and third residual plots involve the independent variables. Patterns in the plot of the residuals versus an independent variable may indicate the existence of a curvilinear effect and, therefore, the need to add a curvilinear independent variable to the multiple regression model (see reference 7).

The fourth plot is used to investigate patterns in the residuals in order to validate the independence assumption when the data are collected in time order. Associated with this residual plot, as in Section 12.6, you can compute the Durbin-Watson statistic to determine the existence of positive autocorrelation among the residuals.

Figure 13.5 presents the residual plots for the OmniPower sales example. There is very little or no pattern in the relationship between the residuals and the predicted value of *Y*, the value of X_1 (price), or the value of X_2 (promotional expenditures). Thus, you can conclude that the multiple regression model is appropriate for predicting sales. There is no need to plot the residuals versus time because the data were not collected in time order.

FIGURE 13.5

Residual plots for the OmniPower sales data: residuals versus predicted Y, residuals versus price, and residuals versus promotional expenditures

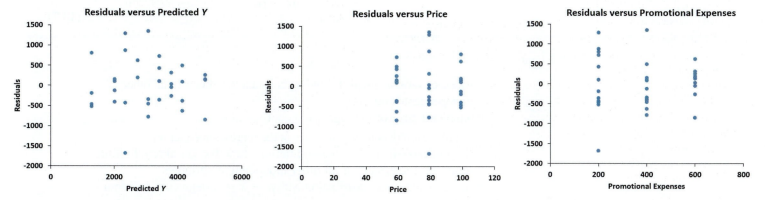

Problems for Section 13.3

APPLYING THE CONCEPTS

13.18 In Problem 13.4 on page 469, you used the efficiency ratio and total risk-based capital data stored in CommunityBanks to predict ROA at a community bank.
a. Plot the residuals versus $\hat{Y}_i$.
b. Plot the residuals versus X_{1i}.
c. Plot the residuals versus X_{2i}.
d. Plot the residuals versus time.
e. In the residual plots created in (a) through (d), is there any evidence of a violation of the regression assumptions? Explain.

13.19 In Problem 13.5 on page 470, you used the percentage of alcohol and chlorides to predict wine quality (stored in VinhoVerde).
a. Plot the residuals versus $\hat{Y}_i$
b. Plot the residuals versus X_{1i}.
c. Plot the residuals versus X_{2i}.
d. In the residual plots created in (a) through (c), is there any evidence of a violation of the regression assumptions? Explain.
e. Should you compute the Durbin-Watson statistic for these data? Explain.

13.20 In Problem 13.6 on page 470, you used the total worldwide revenue ($millions) and full-time voluntary turnover (%) stored in BestCompanies to predict the number of full-time jobs added.
a. Perform a residual analysis on your results.
b. If appropriate, perform the Durbin-Watson test, using $\alpha = 0.05$.
c. Are the regression assumptions valid for these data?

13.21 In Problem 13.7 on page 470, you used the total staff present and remote hours to predict standby hours (stored in Standby).
a. Perform a residual analysis on your results.
b. If appropriate, perform the Durbin-Watson test, using $\alpha = 0.05$.
c. Are the regression assumptions valid for these data?

13.22 In Problem 13.8 on page 470, you used the land area of a property and the age of a house to predict the fair market value (stored in GlenCove).
a. Perform a residual analysis on your results.
b. If appropriate, perform the Durbin-Watson test, using $\alpha = 0.05$.
c. Are the regression assumptions valid for these data?

13.4 Inferences Concerning the Population Regression Coefficients

In Section 12.7, you tested the slope in a simple linear regression model to determine the significance of the relationship between X and Y. In addition, you constructed a confidence interval estimate of the population slope. This section extends those procedures to multiple regression.

Tests of Hypothesis

In a simple linear regression model, to test a hypothesis concerning the population slope, β_1, you used Equation (12.16) on page 439:

$$t_{STAT} = \frac{b_1 - \beta_1}{S_{b_1}}$$

Equation (13.7) generalizes this equation for multiple regression.

TESTING FOR THE SLOPE IN MULTIPLE REGRESSION

$$t_{STAT} = \frac{b_j - \beta_j}{S_{b_j}}$$ (13.7)

where

b_j = slope of variable j with Y, holding constant the effects of all other independent variables

S_{b_j} = standard error of the regression coefficient b_j

k = number of independent variables in the regression equation

β_j = hypothesized value of the population slope for variable j, holding constant the effects of all other independent variables

t_{STAT} = test statistic for a t distribution with $n - k - 1$ degrees of freedom

To determine whether variable X_2 (amount of promotional expenditures) has a significant effect on sales, taking into account the price of OmniPower bars, the null and alternative hypotheses are

$$H_0: \beta_2 = 0$$

$$H_1: \beta_2 \neq 0$$

From Equation (13.7) and Figure 13.2 on page 467,

$$t_{STAT} = \frac{b_2 - \beta_2}{S_{b_2}}$$

$$= \frac{3.6131 - 0}{0.6852} = 5.2728$$

If you select a level of significance of 0.05, the critical values of t for 31 degrees of freedom from Table E.3 are -2.0395 and $+2.0395$ (see Figure 13.6).

FIGURE 13.6

Testing for significance of a regression coefficient at the 0.05 level of significance, with 31 degrees of freedom

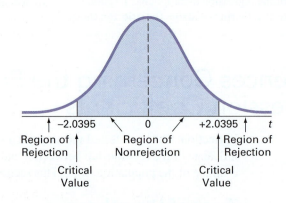

From Figure 13.2 on page 467, observe that the computed t_{STAT} test statistic is 5.2728. Because $t_{STAT} = 5.2728 > 2.0395$ or because the p-value is 0.0000, you reject H_0 and conclude that there is a significant relationship between the variable X_2 (promotional expenditures) and sales, taking into account the price, X_1. The extremely small p-value allows you to strongly reject the null hypothesis that there is no linear relationship between sales and promotional expenditures. Example 13.1 presents the test for the significance of β_1, the slope of sales with price.

EXAMPLE 13.1

Testing for the Significance of the Slope of Sales with Price

At the 0.05 level of significance, is there evidence that the slope of sales with price is different from zero?

SOLUTION From Figure 13.2 on page 467, $t_{STAT} = -7.7664 < -2.0395$ (the critical value for $\alpha = 0.05$) or the p-value $= 0.0000 < 0.05$. Thus, there is a significant relationship between price, X_1, and sales, taking into account the promotional expenditures, X_2.

As shown with these two independent variables, the test of significance for a specific regression coefficient in multiple regression is a test for the significance of adding that variable into a regression model, given that the other variable is included. In other words, the t test for the regression coefficient is actually a test for the contribution of each independent variable.

Confidence Interval Estimation

Instead of testing the significance of a population slope, you may want to estimate the value of a population slope. Equation (13.8) defines the confidence interval estimate for a population slope in multiple regression.

CONFIDENCE INTERVAL ESTIMATE FOR THE SLOPE

$$b_j \pm t_{\alpha/2}S_{b_j} \tag{13.8}$$

where

$t_{\alpha/2}$ = critical value corresponding to an upper-tail probability of $\alpha/2$ from the t distribution with $n - k - 1$ degrees of freedom (i.e., a cumulative area of $1 - \alpha/2$)

k = number of independent variables

To construct a 95% confidence interval estimate of the population slope, β_1 (the effect of price, X_1, on sales, Y, holding constant the effect of promotional expenditures, X_2), the critical value of t at the 95% confidence level with 31 degrees of freedom is 2.0395 (see Table E.3). Then, using Equation (13.8) and Figure 13.2 on page 467,

$$b_1 \pm t_{\alpha/2}S_{b_1}$$
$$-53.2173 \pm (2.0395)(6.8522)$$
$$-53.2173 \pm 13.9752$$
$$-67.1925 \le \beta_1 \le -39.2421$$

Taking into account the effect of promotional expenditures, the estimated effect of a 1-cent increase in price is to reduce mean sales by approximately 39.2 to 67.2 bars. You have 95% confidence that this interval correctly estimates the relationship between these variables. From a hypothesis-testing viewpoint, because this confidence interval does not include 0, you conclude that the regression coefficient, β_1, has a significant effect.

Example 13.2 constructs and interprets a confidence interval estimate for the slope of sales with promotional expenditures.

EXAMPLE 13.2

Constructing a Confidence Interval Estimate for the Slope of Sales with Promotional Expenditures

Construct a 95% confidence interval estimate of the population slope of sales with promotional expenditures.

SOLUTION The critical value of t at the 95% confidence level, with 31 degrees of freedom, is 2.0395 (see Table E.3). Using Equation (13.8) and Figure 13.2 on page 467,

$$b_2 \pm t_{\alpha/2}S_{b_2}$$
$$3.6131 \pm (2.0395)(0.6852)$$
$$3.6131 \pm 1.3975$$
$$2.2156 \le \beta_2 \le 5.0106$$

Thus, taking into account the effect of price, the estimated effect of each additional dollar of promotional expenditures is to increase mean sales by approximately 2.22 to 5.01 bars. You have 95% confidence that this interval correctly estimates the relationship between these variables. From a hypothesis-testing viewpoint, because this confidence interval does not include 0, you can conclude that the regression coefficient, β_2, has a significant effect.

Problems for Section 13.4

LEARNING THE BASICS

13.23 Use the following information from a multiple regression model:

$$n = 25 \quad b_1 = 5 \quad b_2 = 10 \quad S_{b_1} = 2 \quad S_{b_2} = 8$$

a. Which variable has the largest slope, in units of a t statistic?
b. Construct a 95% confidence interval estimate of the population slope, β_1.
c. At the 0.05 level of significance, determine whether each independent variable makes a significant contribution to the regression model. On the basis of these results, indicate the independent variables to include in this model.

13.24 Use the following information from a multiple regression model:

$$n = 20 \quad b_1 = 4 \quad b_2 = 3 \quad S_{b_1} = 1.2 \quad S_{b_2} = 0.8$$

a. Which variable has the largest slope, in units of a t statistic?
b. Construct a 95% confidence interval estimate of the population slope, β_1.
c. At the 0.05 level of significance, determine whether each independent variable makes a significant contribution to the regression model. On the basis of these results, indicate the independent variables to include in this model.

APPLYING THE CONCEPTS

13.25 In Problem 13.3 on page 469, you predicted the mean annual revenue for metropolitan areas in the United States, based on the mean age (Age) and mean BizAnalyzer score (Biz-Analyzer) for a sample of 25 small business metropolitan areas. Use the following results:

Variable	Coefficient	Standard Error	t Statistic	p-Value
Intercept	−680.2357	1,313.5154	−0.52	0.6097
Age	1.74539	7.85185	0.22	0.8261
BizAnalyzer	20.5265	29.18594	0.70	0.4885

a. Construct a 95% confidence interval estimate of the population slope between mean revenue and mean age.
b. At the 0.05 level of significance, determine whether each independent variable makes a significant contribution to the regression model. On the basis of these results, indicate the independent variables to include in this model.

SELF Test **13.26** In Problem 13.4 on page 469, you used efficiency ratio and total risk-based capital stored in **CommunityBanks** to predict ROA at a community bank. Using the results from that problem,
a. construct a 95% confidence interval estimate of the population slope between ROA and efficiency ratio.
b. at the 0.05 level of significance, determine whether each independent variable makes a significant contribution to the regression model. On the basis of these results, indicate the independent variables to include in this model.

13.27 In Problem 13.5 on page 470, you used the percentage of alcohol and chlorides to predict wine quality (stored in **VinhoVerde**). Using the results from that problem,
a. construct a 95% confidence interval estimate of the population slope between wine quality and the percentage of alcohol.

b. at the 0.05 level of significance, determine whether each independent variable makes a significant contribution to the regression model. On the basis of these results, indicate the independent variables to include in this model.

13.28 In Problem 13.6 on page 470, you used the total worldwide revenue ($millions) and full-time voluntary turnover (%) data stored in BestCompanies to predict the number of full-time jobs added. Using the results from that problem,
a. construct a 95% confidence interval estimate of the population slope between the number of full-time jobs added and total worldwide revenue.
b. at the 0.05 level of significance, determine whether each independent variable makes a significant contribution to the regression model. On the basis of these results, indicate the independent variables to include in this model.

13.29 In Problem 13.7 on page 470, you used the total number of staff present and remote hours to predict standby hours (stored in Standby). Using the results from that problem,

a. construct a 95% confidence interval estimate of the population slope between standby hours and total number of staff present.
b. at the 0.05 level of significance, determine whether each independent variable makes a significant contribution to the regression model. On the basis of these results, indicate the independent variables to include in this model.

13.30 In Problem 13.8 on page 470, you used land area of a property and age of a house to predict the fair market value (stored in GlenCove). Using the results from that problem,
a. construct a 95% confidence interval estimate of the population slope between fair market value and land area of a property.
b. at the 0.05 level of significance, determine whether each independent variable makes a significant contribution to the regression model. On the basis of these results, indicate the independent variables to include in this model.

13.5 Using Dummy Variables and Interaction Terms in Regression Models

The multiple regression models discussed in Sections 13.1 through 13.4 assumed that each independent variable is a numerical variable. For example, in Section 13.1, you used price and promotional expenditures, two numerical independent variables, to predict the monthly sales of OmniPower nutrition bars. However, for some models, you need to include the effect of a categorical independent variable. For example, to predict the monthly sales of the OmniPower bars, you might include the categorical variable end-cap location in the model to explore the possible effect on sales caused by displaying the OmniPower bars in the two different end-cap display locations, produce or beverage, used in the North Fork Beverages scenario in Chapter 10.

Dummy Variables

You use a **dummy variable** to include a categorical independent variable in a regression model. A dummy variable X_d recodes the categories of a categorical variable using the numeric values 0 and 1. In the special case of a categorical independent variable that has only two categories, you define one dummy variable, X_d, and use the values 0 and 1 to represent the two categories. For example, for the categorical variable end-cap location discussed in the Chapter 10 Using Statistics scenario, the dummy variable, X_d, would have these values:

$$X_d = 0 \text{ if the observation is in first category (produce end-cap)}$$
$$X_d = 1 \text{ if the observation is in second category (beverage end-cap)}$$

To illustrate using dummy variables in regression, consider the business problem that involves developing a model for predicting the assessed value ($thousands) of houses in Silver Spring, Maryland, based on house size (in thousands of square feet) and whether the house has a fireplace. To include the categorical variable for the presence of a fireplace, the dummy variable X_2 is defined as

$$X_2 = 0 \text{ if the house does not have a fireplace}$$
$$X_2 = 1 \text{ if the house has a fireplace}$$

Assuming that the slope of assessed value with the size of the house is the same for houses that have and do not have a fireplace, the multiple regression model is

$$Y_i = \beta_0 + \beta_1 X_{1i} + \beta_2 X_{2i} + \varepsilon_i$$

where

Y_i = assessed value, in thousands of dollars, for house i

β_0 = Y intercept

X_{1i} = house size, in thousands of square feet, for house i

β_1 = slope of assessed value with house size, holding constant the presence or absence of a fireplace

X_{2i} = dummy variable that represents the absence or presence of a fireplace for house i

β_2 = net effect of the presence of a fireplace on assessed value, holding constant the house size

ε_i = random error in Y for house i

Figure 13.7 presents the regression results for this model, using a sample of 30 Silver Spring houses listed for sale that was extracted from **trulia.com** and stored in SilverSpring . In these results, the dummy variable X_2 is labeled as FireplaceCoded (Excel) or Fireplace Coded (Minitab).

FIGURE 13.7

Excel and Minitab results for the regression model that includes size of house and presence of fireplace

	A	B	C	D	E	F	G
1	Assessed Value Analysis						
2							
3	*Regression Statistics*						
4	Multiple R	0.5765					
5	R Square	0.3323					
6	Adjusted R Square	0.2829					
7	Standard Error	61.8788					
8	Observations	30					
9							
10	ANOVA						
11		*df*	*SS*	*MS*	*F*	*Significance F*	
12	Regression	2	51462.3960	25731.1980	6.7201	0.0043	
13	Residual	27	103382.7120	3828.9893			
14	Total	29	154845.1080				
15							
16		*Coefficients*	*Standard Error*	*t Stat*	*P-value*	*Lower 95%*	*Upper 95%*
17	Intercept	269.4185	33.5699	8.0256	0.0000	200.5388	338.2981
18	Size	49.8215	14.1326	3.5253	0.0015	20.8239	78.8191
19	FireplaceCoded	12.1623	27.0351	0.4499	0.6564	-43.3092	67.6339

Regression Analysis: Assessed Value versus Size, Fireplace Coded
The regression equation is
Assessed Value = 269 + 49.8 Size + 12.2 Fireplace Coded

Predictor	Coef	SE Coef	T	P
Constant	269.42	33.57	8.03	0.000
Size	49.82	14.13	3.53	0.002
Fireplace Coded	12.16	27.04	0.45	0.656

S = 61.8788   R-Sq = 33.2%   R-Sq(adj) = 28.3%

Analysis of Variance

Source	DF	SS	MS	F	P
Regression	2	51462	25731	6.72	0.004
Residual Error	27	103383	3829		
Total	29	154845			

From Figure 13.7, the regression equation is

$$\hat{Y}_i = 269.4185 + 49.8215X_{1i} + 12.1623X_{2i}$$

For houses without a fireplace, you substitute $X_2 = 0$ into the regression equation:

$$\hat{Y}_i = 269.4185 + 49.8215X_{1i} + 12.1623X_{2i}$$
$$= 269.4185 + 49.8215X_{1i} + 12.1623(0)$$
$$= 269.4185 + 49.8215X_{1i}$$

For houses with a fireplace, you substitute $X_2 = 1$ into the regression equation:

$$\hat{Y}_i = 269.4185 + 49.8215X_{1i} + 12.1623X_{2i}$$
$$= 269.4185 + 49.8215X_{1i} + 12.1623(1)$$
$$= 281.5807 + 49.8215X_{1i}$$

In this model, the regression coefficients are interpreted as follows:

- Holding constant whether a house has a fireplace, for each increase of 1.0 thousand square feet in house size, the predicted mean assessed value is estimated to increase by 49.8215 thousand dollars (i.e., $49,821.50).
- Holding constant the house size, the presence of a fireplace is estimated to increase the predicted mean assessed value of the house by 12.1623 thousand dollars (i.e., $12,162.30).

Student Tip

Remember that an independent variable does not always make a significant contribution to a regression model.

In Figure 13.7, the t_{STAT} test statistic for the slope of house size with assessed value is 3.5253, and the p-value is 0.015; the t_{STAT} test statistic for presence of a fireplace is 0.4499, and the p-value is 0.6564. Thus, using the 0.05 level of significance, since $0.0015 < 0.05$, the size of the house makes a significant contribution to the model. However, since $0.6564 > 0.05$, the presence of a fireplace does not make a significant contribution to the model. In addition, from Figure 13.7, observe that the coefficient of multiple determination indicates that 33.23% of the variation in assessed value is explained by variation in house size and whether the house has a fireplace. Thus, the variable fireplace does not make a significant contribution and should not be included in the model.

Interactions

In the regression models discussed so far, the effect an independent variable has on the dependent variable has been assumed to be independent of the other independent variables in the model. An **interaction** occurs if the effect of an independent variable on the dependent variable changes according to the *value* of a second independent variable. For example, it is possible that advertising will have a large effect on the sales of a product when the price of a product is low. However, if the price of the product is too high, increases in advertising will not dramatically change sales. In this case, price and advertising are said to interact. In other words, you cannot make general statements about the effect of advertising on sales. The effect that advertising has on sales is *dependent* on the price. You use an **interaction term** (sometimes referred to as a **cross-product term**) to model an interaction effect in a regression model.

To illustrate the concept of interaction and use of an interaction term, return to the example concerning the assessed values of homes discussed on pages 479–480. In the regression model, you assumed that the effect that house size has on the assessed value is independent of whether the house has a fireplace. In other words, you assumed that the slope of assessed value with house size is the same for all houses, regardless of whether the house contains a fireplace. If these two slopes are different, an interaction exists between the house size and the presence or absence of a fireplace.

To evaluate whether an interaction exists, you first define an interaction term that is the product of the independent variable X_1 (house size) and the dummy variable X_2 (Fireplace-Coded). You then test whether this interaction variable makes a significant contribution to the regression model. If the interaction is significant, you cannot use the original model for prediction. For these data you define the following:

$$X_3 = X_1 \times X_2$$

Figure 13.8 presents regression results for the model that includes the house size, X_1, the presence of a fireplace, X_2, and the interaction of X_1 and X_2 (defined as X_3 and labeled Size*Fireplace).

To test for the existence of an interaction, you use the null hypothesis:

$$H_0: \beta_3 = 0$$

versus the alternative hypothesis:

Student Tip

The interaction between two independent variables can be significant even if one of the independent variables is not significant.

$$H_1: \beta_3 \neq 0.$$

In Figure 13.8, the t_{STAT} test statistic for the interaction of size and fireplace is -0.7474. Because $t_{STAT} = -0.7474 > -2.201$ or the p-value $= 0.4615 > 0.05$, you do not reject the null hypothesis. Therefore, the interaction does not make a significant contribution to the model, given that house size and presence of a fireplace are already included. You can conclude that the slope of assessed value with size is the same for houses with fireplaces and houses without fireplaces.

FIGURE 13.8

Excel and Minitab results for the regression model that includes house size, presence of fireplace, and interaction of house size and fireplace

	A	B	C	D	E	F	G
1	Assessed Value Analysis						
2							
3	*Regression Statistics*						
4	Multiple R	0.5885					
5	R Square	0.3464					
6	Adjusted R Square	0.2710					
7	Standard Error	62.3909					
8	Observations	30					
9							
10	ANOVA						
11		*df*	*SS*	*MS*	*F*	*Significance F*	
12	Regression	3	53636.8541	17878.9514	4.5930	0.0104	
13	Residual	26	101208.2539	3892.6252			
14	Total	29	154845.1080				
15							
16		*Coefficients*	*Standard Error*	*t Stat*	*P-value*	*Lower 95%*	*Upper 95%*
17	Intercept	226.8573	66.2454	3.4245	0.0021	90.6881	363.0266
18	Size	74.7987	36.3298	2.0589	0.0497	0.1216	149.4757
19	FireplaceCoded	63.8028	74.2760	0.8590	0.3982	-88.8737	216.4793
20	Size*Fireplace	-29.5183	39.4946	-0.7474	0.4615	-110.7006	51.6640

Regression Analysis: Assessed Value versus Size, Fireplace Coded, ...

```
The regression equation is
Assessed Value = 227 + 74.8 Size + 63.8 Fireplace Coded
                  - 29.5 Size*Fireplace

Predictor          Coef  SE Coef      T      P
Constant         226.86    66.25   3.42  0.002
Size              74.80    36.33   2.06  0.050
Fireplace Coded   63.80    74.28   0.86  0.398
Size*Fireplace   -29.52    39.49  -0.75  0.462

S = 62.3909   R-Sq = 34.6%   R-Sq(adj) = 27.1%

Analysis of Variance
Source          DF      SS     MS     F     P
Regression       3   53637  17879  4.59  0.010
Residual Error  26  101208   3893
Total           29  154845
```

Problems for Section 13.5

LEARNING THE BASICS

13.31 Suppose X_1 is a numerical variable and X_2 is a dummy variable with two categories and the regression equation for a sample of $n = 20$ is

$$\hat{Y}_i = 6 + 4X_{1i} + 2X_{2i}$$

a. Interpret the regression coefficient associated with variable X_1.
b. Interpret the regression coefficient associated with variable X_2.

13.32 Suppose that in Problem 13.31, t_{STAT} for testing the contribution of X_2 is 3.27. At the 0.05 level of significance, is there evidence that X_2 makes a significant contribution to the model?

APPLYING THE CONCEPTS

13.33 The chair of the accounting department plans to develop a regression model to predict the grade point average in accounting for those students who are graduating and have completed the accounting major, based on a student's SAT score and whether the student received a grade of B or higher in the introductory statistics course ($0 =$ no and $1 =$ yes).
a. Explain the steps involved in developing a regression model for these data. Be sure to indicate the particular models you need to evaluate and compare.
b. Suppose the regression coefficient for the variable whether the student received a grade of B or higher in the introductory statistics course is +0.30. How do you interpret this result?

13.34 A real estate association in a suburban community would like to study the relationship between the size of a single-family house (as measured by the number of rooms) and the selling price of the house (in $thousands). Two different neighborhoods are included in the study, one on the east side of the community ($=0$) and the other on the west side ($=1$). A random sample of 20

houses was selected, with the results stored in **Neighbor** . For (a) through (j), do not include an interaction term.
a. State the multiple regression equation that predicts the selling price, based on the number of rooms and the neighborhood.
b. Interpret the regression coefficients in (a).
c. Predict the mean selling price for a house with nine rooms that is located in an east-side neighborhood. Construct a 95% confidence interval estimate and a 95% prediction interval.
d. Perform a residual analysis on the results and determine whether the regression assumptions are valid.
e. Is there a significant relationship between selling price and the two independent variables (rooms and neighborhood) at the 0.05 level of significance?
f. At the 0.05 level of significance, determine whether each independent variable makes a contribution to the regression model. Indicate the most appropriate regression model for this set of data.
g. Construct and interpret a 95% confidence interval estimate of the population slope for the relationship between selling price and number of rooms.
h. Construct and interpret a 95% confidence interval estimate of the population slope for the relationship between selling price and neighborhood.
i. Compute and interpret the adjusted r^2.
j. What assumption do you need to make about the slope of selling price with number of rooms?
k. Add an interaction term to the model and, at the 0.05 level of significance, determine whether it makes a significant contribution to the model.
l. On the basis of the results of (f) and (k), which model is most appropriate? Explain.
m. What conclusions can the real estate association reach about the effect of the number of rooms and neighborhood on the selling price of homes?

13.35 In Problem 13.5 on page 470, you developed a multiple regression model to predict wine quality for red wines. Now, you wish to determine whether there is an effect on wine quality due to whether the wine is white (0) or red (1). These data are organized and stored in RedandWhite. Develop a multiple regression model to predict wine quality based on the percentage of alcohol and the type of wine.

For (a) through (l), do not include an interaction term.
a. State the multiple regression equation that predicts wine quality based on the percentage of alcohol and the type of wine.
b. Interpret the regression coefficients in (a).
c. Predict the mean quality for a red wine that has 10% alcohol. Construct a 95% confidence interval estimate and a 95% prediction interval.
d. Perform a residual analysis on the results and determine whether the regression assumptions are valid.
e. Is there a significant relationship between wine quality and the two independent variables (percentage of alcohol and the type of wine) at the 0.05 level of significance?
f. At the 0.05 level of significance, determine whether each independent variable makes a contribution to the regression model. Indicate the most appropriate regression model for this set of data.
g. Construct and interpret 95% confidence interval estimates of the population slope for the relationship between wine quality and the percentage of alcohol and between wine quality and the type of wine.
h. Compare the slope in (b) with the slope for the simple linear regression model of Problem 12.4 on page 423. Explain the difference in the results.
i. Compute and interpret the meaning of the coefficient of multiple determination, r^2.
j. Compute and interpret the adjusted r^2.
k. Compare r^2 with the r^2 value computed in Problem 12.16 (a) on page 429.
l. What assumption about the slope of type of wine with wine quality do you need to make in this problem?
m. Add an interaction term to the model and, at the 0.05 level of significance, determine whether it makes a significant contribution to the model.
n. On the basis of the results of (f) and (m), which model is most appropriate? Explain.
o. What conclusions can you reach concerning the effect of alcohol percentage and type of wine on wine quality?

13.36 In mining engineering, holes are often drilled through rock, using drill bits. As a drill hole gets deeper, additional rods are added to the drill bit to enable additional drilling to take place. It is expected that drilling time increases with depth. This increased drilling time could be caused by several factors, including the mass of the drill rods that are strung together. The business problem relates to whether drilling is faster using dry drilling holes or wet drilling holes. Using dry drilling holes involves forcing compressed air down the drill rods to flush the cuttings and drive the hammer. Using wet drilling holes involves forcing water rather than air down the hole. Data have been collected from a sample of

50 drill holes that contains measurements of the time to drill each additional 5 feet (in minutes), the depth (in feet), and whether the hole was a dry drilling hole or a wet drilling hole. The data are organized and stored in Drill. (Data extracted from R. Penner and D. G. Watts, "Mining Information," *The American Statistician*, 45, 1991, pp. 4–9.) Develop a model to predict additional drilling time, based on depth and type of drilling hole (dry or wet). For (a) through (j) do not include an interaction term.
a. State the multiple regression equation.
b. Interpret the regression coefficients in (a).
c. Predict the mean additional drilling time for a dry drilling hole at a depth of 100 feet. Construct a 95% confidence interval estimate and a 95% prediction interval.
d. Perform a residual analysis on the results and determine whether the regression assumptions are valid.
e. Is there a significant relationship between additional drilling time and the two independent variables (depth and type of drilling hole) at the 0.05 level of significance?
f. At the 0.05 level of significance, determine whether each independent variable makes a contribution to the regression model. Indicate the most appropriate regression model for this set of data.
g. Construct a 95% confidence interval estimate of the population slope for the relationship between additional drilling time and depth.
h. Construct a 95% confidence interval estimate of the population slope for the relationship between additional drilling time and the type of hole drilled.
i. Compute and interpret the adjusted r^2.
j. What assumption do you need to make about the slope of additional drilling time with depth?
k. Add an interaction term to the model and, at the 0.05 level of significance, determine whether it makes a significant contribution to the model.
l. On the basis of the results of (f) and (k), which model is most appropriate? Explain.
m. What conclusions can you reach concerning the effect of depth and type of drilling hole on drilling time?

13.37 The owner of a moving company typically has his most experienced manager predict the total number of labor hours that will be required to complete an upcoming move. This approach has proved useful in the past, but the owner has the business objective of developing a more accurate method of predicting labor hours. In a preliminary effort to provide a more accurate method, the owner has decided to use the number of cubic feet moved and whether there is an elevator in the apartment building as the independent variables and has collected data for 36 moves in which the origin and destination were within the borough of Manhattan in New York City and the travel time was an insignificant portion of the hours worked. The data are organized and stored in Moving. For (a) through (j), do not include an interaction term.
a. State the multiple regression equation for predicting labor hours, using the number of cubic feet moved and whether there is an elevator.
b. Interpret the regression coefficients in (a).

c. Predict the mean labor hours for moving 500 cubic feet in an apartment building that has an elevator and construct a 95% confidence interval estimate and a 95% prediction interval.

d. Perform a residual analysis on the results and determine whether the regression assumptions are valid.

e. Is there a significant relationship between labor hours and the two independent variables (cubic feet moved and whether there is an elevator in the apartment building) at the 0.05 level of significance?

f. At the 0.05 level of significance, determine whether each independent variable makes a contribution to the regression model. Indicate the most appropriate regression model for this set of data.

g. Construct a 95% confidence interval estimate of the population slope for the relationship between labor hours and cubic feet moved.

h. Construct a 95% confidence interval estimate for the relationship between labor hours and the presence of an elevator.

i. Compute and interpret the adjusted r^2.

j. What assumption do you need to make about the slope of labor hours with cubic feet moved?

k. Add an interaction term to the model, and at the 0.05 level of significance, determine whether it makes a significant contribution to the model.

l. On the basis of the results of (f) and (k), which model is most appropriate? Explain.

m. What conclusions can you reach concerning the effect of the number of cubic feet moved and whether there is an elevator on labor hours?

SELF Test **13.38** In Problem 13.4 on page 469, you used efficiency ratio and total risk-based capital stored in **CommunityBanks** to predict ROA at a community bank. Develop a regression model to predict ROA that includes efficiency ratio, total risk-based capital, and the interaction of efficiency ratio and total risk-based capital.

a. At the 0.05 level of significance, is there evidence that the interaction term makes a significant contribution to the model?

b. Which regression model is more appropriate, the one used in (a) or the one used in Problem 13.4? Explain.

13.39 Zagat's publishes restaurant ratings for various locations in the United States. The file **Restaurants** contains the Zagat rating for food, décor, service, and cost per person for a sample of 50 restaurants located in a city and 50 restaurants located in a suburb. (Data extracted from *Zagat Survey 2013, New York City Restaurants*; and *Zagat Survey 2012–2013, Long Island Restaurants*.) Develop a regression model to predict the cost per person, based on a variable that represents the sum of the ratings for food, décor, and service and a dummy variable concerning location (city versus suburban). For (a) through (l), do not include an interaction term.

a. State the multiple regression equation.

b. Interpret the regression coefficients in (a).

c. Predict the mean cost at a restaurant with a summated rating of 60 that is located in a city and construct a 95% confidence interval estimate and a 95% prediction interval.

d. Perform a residual analysis on the results and determine whether the regression assumptions are satisfied.

e. Is there a significant relationship between price and the two independent variables (summated rating and location) at the 0.05 level of significance?

f. At the 0.05 level of significance, determine whether each independent variable makes a contribution to the regression model. Indicate the most appropriate regression model for this set of data.

g. Construct a 95% confidence interval estimate of the population slope for the relationship between cost and summated rating.

h. Compare the slope in (b) with the slope for the simple linear regression model of Problem 12.5 on page 424. Explain the difference in the results.

i. Compute and interpret the meaning of the coefficient of multiple determination.

j. Compute and interpret the adjusted r^2.

k. Compare r^2 with the r^2 value computed in Problem 12.17 (b) on page 429.

l. What assumption about the slope of cost with summated rating do you need to make in this problem?

m. Add an interaction term to the model and, at the 0.05 level of significance, determine whether it makes a significant contribution to the model.

n. On the basis of the results of (f) and (m), which model is most appropriate? Explain.

o. What conclusions can you reach about the effect of the summated rating and the location of the restaurant on the cost of a meal?

13.40 In Problem 13.6 on page 470, you used the total worldwide revenue ($millions) and full-time voluntary turnover (%) data stored in **BestCompanies** to predict number of full-time jobs added. Develop a regression model to predict the number of full-time jobs added that includes full-time voluntary turnover, total worldwide revenue, and the interaction of full-time voluntary turnover and total worldwide revenue.

a. At the 0.05 level of significance, is there evidence that the interaction term makes a significant contribution to the model?

b. Which regression model is more appropriate, the one used in this problem or the one used in Problem 13.6? Explain.

13.41 In Problem 13.5 on page 470, the percentage of alcohol and chlorides were used to predict the quality of red wines (stored in **VinhoVerde**). Develop a regression model that includes the percentage of alcohol, the chlorides, and the interaction of the percentage of alcohol and the chlorides to predict wine quality.

a. At the 0.05 level of significance, is there evidence that the interaction term makes a significant contribution to the model?

b. Which regression model is more appropriate, the one used in this problem or the one used in Problem 13.5? Explain.

13.42 In Problem 13.7 on page 470, you used the total staff present and remote hours to predict standby hours stored in **Standby**. Develop a regression model to predict standby hours that includes total staff present, remote hours, and the interaction of total staff present and remote hours.

a. At the 0.05 level of significance, is there evidence that the interaction term makes a significant contribution to the model?

b. Which regression model is more appropriate, the one used in this problem or the one used in Problem 13.7? Explain.

USING STATISTICS

The Multiple Effects of OmniPower Bars, Revisited

Ariwasabi/Shutterstock

In the Using Statistics scenario, you were a marketing manager for OmniFoods, responsible for nutrition bars and similar snack items. You needed to determine the effect that price and in-store promotions would have on sales of OmniPower nutrition bars in order to develop an effective marketing strategy. A sample of 34 stores in a supermarket chain was selected for a test-market study. The stores charged between 59 and 99 cents per bar and were given an in-store promotion budget between $200 and $600.

At the end of the one-month test-market study, you performed a multiple regression analysis on the data. Two independent variables were considered: the price of an OmniPower bar and the monthly budget for in-store promotional expenditures. The dependent variable was the number of OmniPower bars sold in a month. The coefficient of determination indicated that 75.8% of the variation in sales was explained by knowing the price charged and the amount spent on in-store promotions. The model indicated that the predicted sales of OmniPower are estimated to decrease by 532 bars per month for each 10-cent increase in the price, and the predicted sales are estimated to increase by 361 bars for each additional $100 spent on promotions.

After studying the relative effects of price and promotion, OmniFoods needs to set price and promotion standards for a nationwide introduction (obviously, lower prices and higher promotion budgets lead to more sales, but they do so at a lower profit margin). You determined that if stores spend $400 a month for in-store promotions and charge 79 cents, the 95% confidence interval estimate of the mean monthly sales is 2,854 to 3,303 bars. OmniFoods can multiply the lower and upper bounds of this confidence interval by the number of stores included in the nationwide introduction to estimate total monthly sales. For example, if 1,000 stores are in the nationwide introduction, then total monthly sales should be between 2.854 million and 3.308 million bars.

SUMMARY

Figure 13.9 presents a roadmap of this chapter. In this chapter, you learned how to develop and fit multiple regression models that use two or more independent variables to predict the value of a dependent variable. You also learned how to include categorical independent variables and interaction terms in regression models.

REFERENCES

1. Andrews, D. F., and D. Pregibon. "Finding the Outliers that Matter." *Journal of the Royal Statistical Society* 40 (Ser. B., 1978): 85–93.
2. Atkinson, A. C. "Robust and Diagnostic Regression Analysis." *Communications in Statistics* 11 (1982): 2559–2572.
3. Belsley, D. A., E. Kuh, and R. Welsch. *Regression Diagnostics: Identifying Influential Data and Sources of Collinearity.* New York: Wiley, 1980.
4. Cook, R. D., and S. Weisberg. *Residuals and Influence in Regression.* New York: Chapman and Hall, 1982.
5. Hosmer, D. W., and S. Lemeshow. *Applied Logistic Regression*, 3rd ed. New York: Wiley, 2013.
6. Hoaglin, D. C., and R. Welsch. "The Hat Matrix in Regression and ANOVA," *The American Statistician*, 32, (1978), 17–22.
7. Kutner, M., C. Nachtsheim, J. Neter, and W. Li. *Applied Linear Statistical Models*, 5th ed. New York: McGraw-Hill/Irwin, 2005.
8. *Microsoft Excel 2013*. Redmond, WA: Microsoft Corp., 2012.
9. *Minitab Release 16*. State College, PA: Minitab, Inc., 2010.

FIGURE 13.9
Roadmap for multiple regression

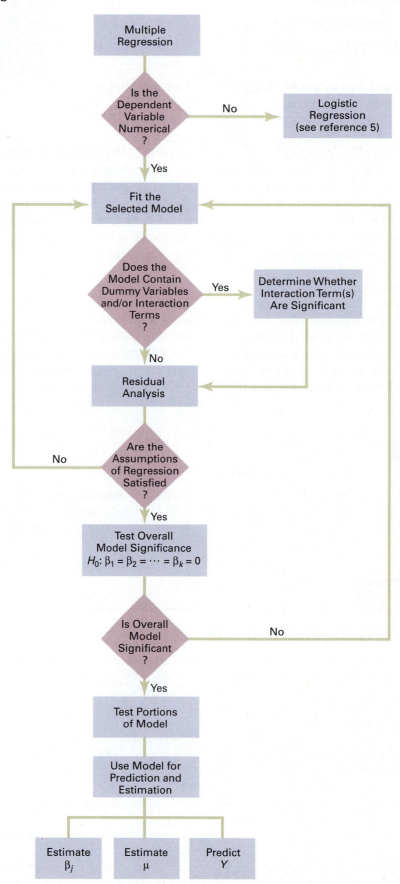

KEY EQUATIONS

Multiple Regression Model with k Independent Variables

$$Y_i = \beta_0 + \beta_1 X_{1i} + \beta_2 X_{2i} + \beta_3 X_{3i} + \cdots + \beta_k X_{ki} + \varepsilon_i \tag{13.1}$$

Multiple Regression Model with Two Independent Variables

$$Y_i = \beta_0 + \beta_1 X_{1i} + \beta_2 X_{2i} + \varepsilon_i \tag{13.2}$$

Multiple Regression Equation with Two Independent Variables

$$\hat{Y}_i = b_0 + b_1 X_{1i} + b_2 X_{2i} \tag{13.3}$$

Coefficient of Multiple Determination

$$r^2 = \frac{\text{Regression sum of squares}}{\text{Total sum of squares}} = \frac{SSR}{SST} \tag{13.4}$$

Adjusted r^2

$$r^2_{\text{adj}} = 1 - \left[(1 - r^2) \frac{n - 1}{n - k - 1} \right] \tag{13.5}$$

Overall F Test

$$F_{STAT} = \frac{MSR}{MSE} \tag{13.6}$$

Testing for the Slope in Multiple Regression

$$t_{STAT} = \frac{b_j - \beta_j}{S_{b_j}} \tag{13.7}$$

Confidence Interval Estimate for the Slope

$$b_j \pm t_{\alpha/2} S_{b_j} \tag{13.8}$$

KEY TERMS

adjusted r^2 471
coefficient of multiple determination 470
cross-product term 481

dummy variable 479
interaction 481
interaction term 481

multiple regression model 465
net regression coefficient 468
overall F test 472

CHECKING YOUR UNDERSTANDING

13.43 What is the difference between r^2 and adjusted r^2?

13.44 How does the interpretation of the regression coefficients differ in multiple regression and simple linear regression?

13.45 Why and how do you use dummy variables?

13.46 How can you evaluate whether the slope of the dependent variable with an independent variable is the same for each level of the dummy variable?

13.47 Under what circumstances do you include an interaction term in a regression model?

13.48 When a dummy variable is included in a regression model that has one numerical independent variable, what assumption do you need to make concerning the slope between the dependent variable, Y, and the numerical independent variable, X?

CHAPTER REVIEW PROBLEMS

13.49 Increasing customer satisfaction typically results in increased purchase behavior. For many products, there is more than one measure of customer satisfaction. In many, purchase behavior can increase dramatically with an increase in just one of the customer satisfaction measures. Gunst and Barry ("One Way to Moderate Ceiling Effects," *Quality Progress*, October 2003, pp. 83–85) consider a product with two satisfaction measures, X_1 and X_2, that range from the lowest level of satisfaction, 1, to the highest level of satisfaction, 7. The dependent variable, Y, is a measure of purchase behavior, with the highest value generating the most sales. Consider the regression equation:

$$\hat{Y}_i = -3.888 + 1.449 X_{1i} + 1.462 X_{2i} - 0.190 X_{1i} X_{2i}$$

Suppose that X_1 is the perceived quality of the product and X_2 is the perceived value of the product. (Note: If the customer thinks the product is overpriced, he or she perceives it to be of low value and vice versa.)

a. What is the predicted purchase behavior when $X_1 = 2$ and $X_2 = 2$?

b. What is the predicted purchase behavior when $X_1 = 2$ and $X_2 = 7$?

c. What is the predicted purchase behavior when $X_1 = 7$ and $X_2 = 2$?

d. What is the predicted purchase behavior when $X_1 = 7$ and $X_2 = 7$?

e. What is the regression equation when $X_2 = 2$? What is the slope for X_1 now?

f. What is the regression equation when $X_2 = 7$? What is the slope for X_1 now?

g. What is the regression equation when $X_1 = 2$? What is the slope for X_2 now?

h. What is the regression equation when $X_1 = 7$? What is the slope for X_2 now?

i. Discuss the implications of (a) through (h) in the context of increasing sales for this product with two customer satisfaction measures.

13.50 The owner of a moving company typically has his most experienced manager predict the total number of labor hours that will be required to complete an upcoming move. This approach has proved useful in the past, but the owner has the business objective of developing a more accurate method of predicting labor hours. In a preliminary effort to provide a more accurate method, the owner has decided to use the number of cubic feet moved and the number of pieces of large furniture as the independent variables and has collected data for 36 moves in which the origin and destination were within the borough of Manhattan in New York City and the travel time was an insignificant portion of the hours worked. The data are organized and stored in **Moving** .

a. State the multiple regression equation.

b. Interpret the meaning of the slopes in this equation.

c. Predict the mean labor hours for moving 500 cubic feet with two large pieces of furniture.

d. Perform a residual analysis on your results and determine whether the regression assumptions are valid.

e. Determine whether there is a significant relationship between labor hours and the two independent variables (the number of cubic feet moved and the number of pieces of large furniture) at the 0.05 level of significance.

f. Determine the p-value in (e) and interpret its meaning.

g. Interpret the meaning of the coefficient of multiple determination in this problem.

h. Determine the adjusted r^2.

i. At the 0.05 level of significance, determine whether each independent variable makes a significant contribution to the regression model. Indicate the most appropriate regression model for this set of data.

j. Determine the p-values in (i) and interpret their meaning.

k. Construct a 95% confidence interval estimate of the population slope between labor hours and the number of cubic feet moved. How does the interpretation of the slope here differ from that in Problem 12.44 on page 443?

l. What conclusions can you reach concerning labor hours?

13.51 Professional basketball has truly become a sport that generates interest among fans around the world. More and more players come from outside the United States to play in the National Basketball Association (NBA). You want to develop a regression model to predict the number of wins achieved by each NBA team, based on field goal (shots made) percentage and three-point field goal percentage for the team. The data are stored in **NBA** .

a. State the multiple regression equation.

b. Interpret the meaning of the slopes in this equation.

c. Predict the mean number of wins for a team that has a field goal percentage of 45% and a three-point field goal percentage of 37%.

d. Perform a residual analysis on your results and determine whether the regression assumptions are valid.

e. Is there a significant relationship between number of wins and the two independent variables (field goal percentage and three-point field goal percentage for the team) at the 0.05 level of significance?

f. Determine the p-value in (e) and interpret its meaning.

g. Interpret the meaning of the coefficient of multiple determination in this problem.

h. Determine the adjusted r^2.

i. At the 0.05 level of significance, determine whether each independent variable makes a significant contribution to the regression model. Indicate the most appropriate regression model for this set of data.

j. Determine the p-values in (i) and interpret their meaning.

k. What conclusions can you reach concerning field goal percentage and three-point field goal percentage in predicting the number of wins?

13.52 A sample of 30 houses recently listed for sale in Silver Spring, Maryland, was selected with the objective of developing a model to predict the assessed value (in $thousands), using the size of the house (in thousands of square feet) and age (in years). The results are stored in **Silver Spring** .

a. Fit a multiple regression model.

b. Interpret the meaning of the slopes in this model.

c. Predict the mean assessed value for a house that has 2,000 square feet and is 55 years old.

d. Perform a residual analysis on your results and determine whether the regression assumptions are valid.

e. Determine whether there is a significant relationship between assessed value and the two independent variables (house size and age) at the 0.05 level of significance.

f. Determine the p-value in (e) and interpret its meaning.

g. Interpret the meaning of the coefficient of multiple determination in this problem.

h. Determine the adjusted r^2.

i. At the 0.05 level of significance, determine whether each independent variable makes a significant contribution to the regression model. Indicate the most appropriate regression model for this set of data.

j. Determine the p-values in (i) and interpret their meaning.

k. Construct a 95% confidence interval estimate of the population slope between assessed value and the size of the house. How does the interpretation of the slope here differ from that in Problem 12.76 on page 455?

l. What conclusions can you reach about the assessed value?

13.53 Measuring the height of a California redwood tree is very difficult because these trees grow to heights over 300 feet. People familiar with these trees understand that the height of a California redwood tree is related to other characteristics of the tree, including the diameter of the tree at the breast height of a person (in inches) and the thickness of the bark of the tree (in inches). The file **Redwood** contains the height, diameter at breast height of a person, and bark thickness for a sample of 21 California redwood trees.

a. State the multiple regression equation that predicts the height of a tree, based on the tree's diameter at breast height and the thickness of the bark.

b. Interpret the meaning of the slopes in this equation.

c. Predict the mean height for a tree that has a breast height diameter of 25 inches and a bark thickness of 2 inches.

d. Interpret the meaning of the coefficient of multiple determination in this problem.

e. Perform a residual analysis on the results and determine whether the regression assumptions are valid.

f. Determine whether there is a significant relationship between the height of redwood trees and the two independent variables (breast-height diameter and bark thickness) at the 0.05 level of significance.

g. Construct a 95% confidence interval estimate of the population slope between the height of redwood trees and breast-height diameter and between the height of redwood trees and the bark thickness.

h. At the 0.05 level of significance, determine whether each independent variable makes a significant contribution to the regression model. Indicate the independent variables to include in this model.

i. Construct a 95% confidence interval estimate of the mean height for trees that have a breast-height diameter of 25 inches and a bark thickness of 2 inches, along with a prediction interval for an individual tree.

j. What conclusions can you reach concerning the effect of the diameter of the tree and the thickness of the bark on the height of the tree?

13.54 A sample of 30 houses recently listed for sale in Silver Spring, Maryland, was selected with the objective of developing a model to predict the taxes (in $) based on the assessed value of houses (in $thousands) and the age of the houses (in years) (stored in `SilverSpring`):

a. State the multiple regression equation.

b. Interpret the meaning of the slopes in this equation.

c. Predict the mean taxes for a house that has an assessed value of $400,000 and is 50 years old.

d. Perform a residual analysis on the results and determine whether the regression assumptions are valid.

e. Determine whether there is a significant relationship between taxes and the two independent variables (assessed value and age) at the 0.05 level of significance.

f. Determine the p-value in (e) and interpret its meaning.

g. Interpret the meaning of the coefficient of multiple determination in this problem.

h. Determine the adjusted r^2.

i. At the 0.05 level of significance, determine whether each independent variable makes a significant contribution to the regression model. Indicate the most appropriate regression model for this set of data.

j. Determine the p-values in (i) and interpret their meaning.

k. Construct a 95% confidence interval estimate of the population slope between taxes and assessed value. How does the interpretation of the slope here differ from that of Problem 12.77 on page 455?

l. The real estate assessor's office has been publicly quoted as saying that the age of a house has no bearing on its taxes. Based on your answers to (a) through (k), do you agree with this statement? Explain.

13.55 A baseball analytics specialist wants to determine which variables are important in predicting a team's wins in a given season. He has collected data related to wins, earned run average (ERA), and runs scored per game in a recent season (stored in `Baseball`). Develop a model to predict the number of wins based on ERA and runs scored per game.

a. State the multiple regression equation.

b. Interpret the meaning of the slopes in this equation.

c. Predict the mean number of wins for a team that has an ERA of 4.00 and has scored 4.0 runs per game.

d. Perform a residual analysis on the results and determine whether the regression assumptions are valid.

e. Is there a significant relationship between the number of wins and the two independent variables (ERA and runs scored per game) at the 0.05 level of significance?

f. Determine the p-value in (e) and interpret its meaning.

g. Interpret the meaning of the coefficient of multiple determination in this problem.

h. Determine the adjusted r^2.

i. At the 0.05 level of significance, determine whether each independent variable makes a significant contribution to the regression model. Indicate the most appropriate regression model for this set of data.

j. Determine the p-values in (i) and interpret their meaning.

k. Construct a 95% confidence interval estimate of the population slope between wins and ERA.

l. Which is more important in predicting wins—pitching, as measured by ERA, or offense, as measured by runs scored per game? Explain.

13.56 Referring to Problem 13.55, suppose that in addition to using ERA to predict the number of wins, the analytics specialist wants to include the league (0 = American, 1 = National) as an independent variable. Develop a model to predict wins based on ERA and league. For (a) through (j), do not include an interaction term.

a. State the multiple regression equation.

b. Interpret the slopes in (a).

c. Predict the mean number of wins for a team with an ERA of 4.00 in the American League. Construct a 95% confidence interval estimate for all teams and a 95% prediction interval for an individual team.

d. Perform a residual analysis on the results and determine whether the regression assumptions are valid.

e. Is there a significant relationship between wins and the two independent variables (ERA and league) at the 0.05 level of significance?

f. At the 0.05 level of significance, determine whether each independent variable makes a contribution to the regression model. Indicate the most appropriate regression model for this set of data.

g. Construct a 95% confidence interval estimate of the population slope for the relationship between wins and ERA.

h. Construct a 95% confidence interval estimate of the population slope for the relationship between wins and league.

i. Compute and interpret the adjusted r^2.

j. What assumption do you have to make about the slope of wins with ERA?

k. Add an interaction term to the model and, at the 0.05 level of significance, determine whether it makes a significant contribution to the model.

l. On the basis of the results of (f) and (k), which model is most appropriate? Explain.

13.57 You are a real estate broker who wants to compare property values in Glen Cove and Roslyn (which are located approximately 8 miles apart). In order to do so, you will analyze the data in `GCRoslyn`, a file that includes samples of houses from Glen Cove and Roslyn. Making sure to include the dummy variable for location (Glen Cove or Roslyn), develop a regression model to predict fair market value, based on the land area of a property, the age of a house, and location. Be sure to determine whether any interaction terms need to be included in the model.

13.58 The list of Best Small Companies in America features a group with strong earnings growth across industries. A business analyst wishes to determine the relationship between earnings per share growth (%) and sales growth (%) and return on equity (%). Data were collected on 100 small companies and stored in SmallBusinesses . (Data extracted from "America's Best Small Companies," **forbes.com/best-small-companies/list/**.)

Develop a multiple regression model that uses sales growth and return on equity to predict earnings per share growth. Be sure to perform a thorough residual analysis.

13.59 Starbucks Coffee Co. uses a data-based approach to improving the quality and customer satisfaction of its products. When survey data indicated that Starbucks needed to improve its package-sealing process, an experiment was conducted to determine the factors in the bag-sealing equipment that might be affecting the ease of opening the bag without tearing the inner liner of the bag. (Data extracted from L. Johnson and S. Burrows, "For Starbucks, It's in the Bag," *Quality Progress*, March 2011, pp. 17–23.) Among the factors that could affect the rating of the ability of the bag to resist tears were the viscosity, pressure, and plate gap on the bag-sealing equipment. Data were collected on 19 bags in

which the plate gap was varied. The results are stored in Starbucks . Develop a multiple regression model that uses the viscosity, pressure, and plate gap on the bag-sealing equipment to predict the tear rating of the bag. Be sure to perform a thorough residual analysis. Do you think that you need to use all three independent variables in the model? Explain.

13.60 An experiment was conducted to study the extrusion process of biodegradable packaging foam. Among the factors considered for their effect on the unit density (mg/ml) were the die temperature (145°C versus 155°C) and the die diameter (3 mm versus 4 mm). The results were stored in PackagingFoam3 . (Data extracted from W. Y. Koh, K. M. Eskridge, and M. A. Hanna, "Supersaturated Split-Plot Designs," *Journal of Quality Technology*, 45, January 2013, pp. 61–72.) Develop a multiple regression model that uses die temperature and die diameter to predict the unit density (mg/ml). Be sure to perform a thorough residual analysis. Do you think that you need to use both independent variables in the model? Explain.

13.61 Referring to Problem 13.60, instead of predicting the unit density, you now wish to predict the foam diameter from results stored in PackagingFoam4 . Develop a multiple regression model that uses die temperature and die diameter to predict the foam diameter (mg/ml). Be sure to perform a thorough residual analysis. Do you think that you need to use both independent variables in the model? Explain.

CASES FOR CHAPTER 13

Managing Ashland MultiComm Services

In its continuing study of the *3-For-All* subscription solicitation process, a marketing department team wants to test the effects of two types of structured sales presentations (personal formal and personal informal) and the number of hours spent on telemarketing on the number of new subscriptions. The staff has recorded these data for the past 24 weeks in AMS13 .

Analyze these data and develop a multiple regression model to predict the number of new subscriptions for a week, based on the number of hours spent on telemarketing and the sales presentation type. Write a report, giving detailed findings concerning the regression model used.

Digital Case

Apply your knowledge of multiple regression models in this Digital Case, which extends the OmniFoods Using Statistics scenario from this chapter.

To ensure a successful test marketing of its OmniPower energy bars, the OmniFoods marketing department has contracted with In-Store Placements Group (ISPG), a merchandising consulting firm. ISPG will work with the grocery store chain that is conducting the test-market study. Using the same 34-store sample used in the test-market study, ISPG claims that the choice of shelf location and the presence of in-store OmniPower coupon dispensers both increase sales of the energy bars.

Open **Omni_ISPGMemo.pdf** to review the ISPG claims and supporting data. Then answer the following questions:

1. Are the supporting data consistent with ISPG's claims? Perform an appropriate statistical analysis to confirm (or discredit) the stated relationship between sales and the two independent variables of product shelf location and the presence of in-store OmniPower coupon dispensers.

2. If you were advising OmniFoods, would you recommend using a specific shelf location and in-store coupon dispensers to sell OmniPower bars?

3. What additional data would you advise collecting in order to determine the effectiveness of the sales promotion techniques used by ISPG?

CHAPTER 13 EXCEL GUIDE

EG13.1 DEVELOPING a MULTIPLE REGRESSION MODEL

Interpreting the Regression Coefficients

Key Technique Use the **LINEST**(*cell range of Y variable, cell range of X variables,* **True**, **True**) function to compute the regression coefficients and other values related to a multiple regression analysis.

Example Develop the Figure 13.2 multiple regression model for the OmniPower sales data shown on page 467.

PHStat Use **Multiple Regression**.
For the example, open to the **DATA worksheet** of the **OmniPower workbook**. Select **PHStat → Regression → Multiple Regression**, and in the procedure's dialog box (shown below):

1. Enter **A1:A35** as the **Y Variable Cell Range**.
2. Enter **B1:C35** as the **X Variables Cell Range**.
3. Check **First cells in both ranges contain label**.
4. Enter **95** as the **Confidence level for regression coefficients**.
5. Check **Regression Statistics Table** and **ANOVA and Coefficients Table**.
6. Enter a **Title** and click **OK**.

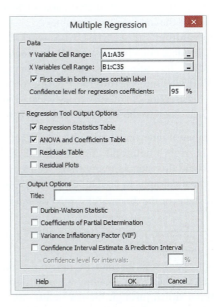

The procedure creates a worksheet that contains a copy of your data in addition to the Figure 13.2 worksheet. For more information about these worksheets, read the following *In-Depth Excel* section.

In-Depth Excel Use the **COMPUTE worksheet** of the **Multiple Regression workbook** as a template.
For the example, the COMPUTE worksheet uses the OmniPower sales data already in the **MRData worksheet** to perform the regression analysis. To perform multiple regression analyses for other data, paste the regression data into the MRData worksheet.

Figure 13.2 does not show the Calculations area in columns K through N. In the cell range L2:N6, an array formula uses the LINEST function to compute intercepts, standard error values, and other regression statistics. The Calculations area also contains the user-supplied confidence level and formulas to compute the critical value of the *t* statistic and half-widths.

To perform a multiple regression analysis with other data, first paste the regression data into the MRData worksheet. Paste the values for the *Y* variable into column A and the values for the *X* variables into consecutive columns, starting with column B. Then, open to the COMPUTE worksheet. Enter the confidence level in cell L8 and edit the five-row-by-three-column array formula that starts with cell L2 (the cell range L2:N6). If you have more than two independent variables, select the wider range that adds a column for each independent variable in excess of two.

For example, with three independent variables, select the cell range L2:O6. Then, edit the array formula to reflect the data you pasted into the MRData worksheet. Your cell ranges should start with row 2 so as to exclude the row 1 variable names (an exception to the usual practice in this book). Remember to press the **Enter key** while holding down the **Control** and **Shift keys** (or the **Command key** on a Mac) to enter the array formula as discussed in Appendix Section B.3.

Read the SHORT TAKES for Chapter 13 for an explanation of the formulas found in the COMPUTE worksheet (shown in the **COMPUTE_FORMULAS worksheet**). If you use an Excel version that is older than Excel 2010, use the same-name worksheets in the **Multiple Regression 2007 workbook**.

Analysis ToolPak Use **Regression**.
For the example, open to the **DATA worksheet** of the **OmniPower workbook** and:

1. Select **Data → Data Analysis**.
2. In the Data Analysis dialog box, select **Regression** from the **Analysis Tools** list and then click **OK**.

In the Regression dialog box (shown on page 492):

3. Enter **A1:A35** as the **Input Y Range** and enter **B1:C35** as the **Input X Range**.
4. Check **Labels** and check **Confidence Level** and enter **95** in its box.
5. Click **New Worksheet Ply**.
6. Click **OK**.

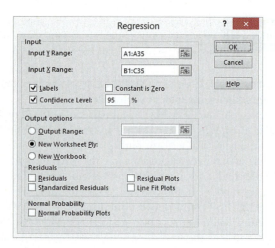

Predicting the Dependent Variable Y

Key Technique Use the **MMULT** array function and the **T.INV.2T** function to help compute intermediate values that determine the confidence interval estimate and prediction interval.

Example Compute the Figure 13.3 confidence interval estimate and prediction interval for the OmniPower sales data shown on page 469.

PHStat Use the *PHStat* "Interpreting the Regression Coefficients" instructions but replace step 6 with the following steps 6 through 8:

6. Check **Confidence Interval Estimate & Prediction Interval** and enter **95** as the percentage for **Confidence level for intervals**.
7. Enter a **Title** and click **OK**.
8. In the new worksheet, enter **79** in cell **B6** and enter **400** in cell **B7**.

These steps create a new worksheet that is discussed in the following *In-Depth Excel* instructions.

In-Depth Excel Use the **CIEandPI worksheet** of the **Multiple Regression workbook** as a template.
The worksheet already contains the data and formulas for the example. The worksheet uses the **MMULT** function (see Appendix Section F.4) in several array formulas that perform matrix operations.

Modifying this worksheet for other models with more than two independent variables requires knowledge that is beyond the scope of this book. For other models with two independent variables, first paste the data for those variables into columns B and C of the **MRArray worksheet** and adjust the number of entries in column A (all of which are **1**). Then, adjust the COMPUTE worksheet to reflect the new regression data, using the *In-Depth Excel* "Interpreting the Regression Coefficients" instructions. Finally, open to the CIEandPI worksheet and edit the array formula in cell range B9:D11 and the labels in cells A6 and A7.

Read the SHORT TAKES for Chapter 13 for an explanation of the formulas found in the CIEandPI worksheet (shown in the **CIEandPI_FORMULAS worksheet**). If you use an Excel version that is older than Excel 2010, use the CIEandPI worksheet in the **Multiple Regression 2007 workbook**.

EG13.2 r^2, ADJUSTED r^2, and the OVERALL F TEST

The coefficient of multiple determination, r^2, the adjusted r^2, and the overall F test are all computed as part of creating the multiple regression results worksheet using the Section EG13.1 instructions. If you use either the *PHStat* or *In-Depth Excel* instructions, formulas are used to compute these results in the **COMPUTE worksheet**. Formulas in cells B5, B7, B13, C12, C13, D12, and E12 copy values computed by the array formula in cell range L2:N6. In cell F12, the expression **F.DIST.RT(*F test statistic*, 1, *error degrees of freedom*)** computes the *p*-value for the overall F test.

EG13.3 RESIDUAL ANALYSIS for the MULTIPLE REGRESSION MODEL

Key Technique Use arithmetic formulas and some results from the multiple regression COMPUTE worksheet to compute residuals.

Example Perform the residual analysis for the OmniPower sales data discussed in Section 13.3, starting on page 474.

PHStat Use the Section EG13.1 "Interpreting the Regression Coefficients" *PHStat* instructions. Modify step 5 by checking **Residuals Table** and **Residual Plots** in addition to checking **Regression Statistics Table** and **ANOVA and Coefficients Table**.

In-Depth Excel Use the **RESIDUALS worksheet** of the **Multiple Regression workbook** as a template. Then construct residual plots for the residuals and the predicted value of Y and for the residuals and each of the independent variables.

For the example, the RESIDUALS worksheet uses the OmniPower sales data already in the **MRData worksheet** to compute the residuals. To compute residuals for other data, first use the Section EG13.1 "Interpreting the Regression Coefficients" *In-Depth Excel* instructions to modify the MRData and COMPUTE worksheets. Then, open to the **RESIDUALS worksheet** and:

1. If the number of independent variables is greater than 2, select column D, right-click, and click **Insert** from the shortcut menu. Repeat this step as many times as necessary to create the additional columns to hold all the X variables.
2. Paste the data for the X variables into columns, starting with column B.
3. Paste Y values in column E (or in the second-to-last column if there are more than two X variables).
4. For sample sizes smaller than 34, delete the extra rows. For sample sizes greater than 34, copy the predicted Y and residuals formulas down through the row containing the last pair of X and Y values. Also, add the new observation numbers in column A.

To construct the residual plots, open to the RESIDUALS worksheet and select pairs of columns and then use the Section EG2.5 *In-Depth Excel* "The Scatter Plot" instructions. (If you forgot to select the columns, Excel will construct a meaningless plot of all of the data in the RESIDUALS worksheet.) For example, to construct the residual plot for the residuals and the predicted value of Y, select columns D and F. (See Appendix Section B.7 for help in selecting a non-contiguous cell range.)

Read the SHORT TAKES for Chapter 13 for an explanation of the formulas found in the RESIDUALS worksheet (shown in the **RESIDUALS_FORMULAS worksheet**).

Analysis ToolPak Use the Section EG13.1 *Analysis ToolPak* instructions. Modify step 5 by checking **Residuals** and **Residual Plots** before clicking **New Worksheet Ply** and then **OK**. The **Residuals Plots** option constructs residual plots only for each independent variable. To construct a plot of the residuals and the predicted value of *Y*, select the predicted and residuals cells (in the RESIDUAL OUTPUT area of the regression results worksheet) and then apply the Section EG2.5 *In-Depth Excel* "The Scatter Plot" instructions.

EG13.4 INFERENCES CONCERNING the POPULATION REGRESSION COEFFICIENTS

The regression results worksheets created by using the Section EG13.1 instructions include the information needed to make the inferences discussed in Section 13.4.

EG13.5 USING DUMMY VARIABLES and INTERACTION TERMS in REGRESSION MODELS

Dummy Variables

Key Technique Use **Find and Replace** to create a dummy variable from a two-level categorical variable. Before using **Find and Replace**, copy and paste the categorical values to another column in order to preserve the original values.

Example From the two-level categorical variable Fireplace, create the dummy variable named FireplaceCoded that is used in the Figure 13.7 regression model on page 480.

In-Depth Excel For the example, open to the **DATA worksheet** of the **SilverSpring workbook** and:

1. Copy and paste the **Fireplace** values in column **I** to **column J** (the first empty column). Enter **FireplaceCoded** in **cell J1**.
2. Select **column J**.
3. Press **Ctrl+H** (the keyboard shortcut for **Find and Replace**).

In the Find and Replace dialog box:

4. Enter **Yes** in the **Find what** box and enter **1** in the **Replace with** box.
5. Click **Replace All**. If a message box to confirm the replacement appears, click **OK** to continue.
6. Enter **No** in the **Find what** box and enter **0** in the **Replace with** box.
7. Click **Replace All**. If a message box to confirm the replacement appears, click **OK** to continue.
8. Click **Close**.

Interactions

To create an interaction term, add a column of formulas that multiply one independent variable by another. For example, if the first independent variable appeared in column B and the second independent variable appeared in column C, enter the formula **=B2 * C2** in the row 2 cell of an empty new column and then copy the formula down through all rows of data to create the interaction.

CHAPTER 13 MINITAB GUIDE

MG13.1 DEVELOPING a MULTIPLE REGRESSION MODEL

Use **3D Scatterplot** to create a three-dimensional plot for the special case of a regression model that contains two independent variables. For example, to create the Figure 13.1 plot on page 466 for the OmniPower sales data, open the **OmniPower worksheet**. Select **Graph ➔ 3D Scatterplot**. In the 3D Scatterplots dialog box, click **Simple** and then click **OK**. In the 3D Scatterplot - Simple dialog box (shown in right column):

1. Double-click **C1 Sales** in the variables list to add **Sales** to the **Z variable** box.
2. Double-click **C2 Price** in the variables list to add **Price** to the **Y variable** box.
3. Double-click **C3 Promotional Expenses** in the variables list to add **'Promotional Expenses'** to the **X variable** box.
4. Click **Data View**.

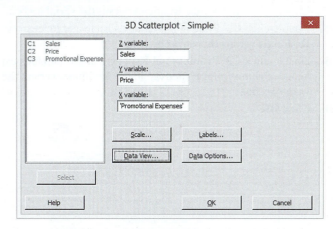

In the 3D Scatterplot - Data View dialog box:

5. Check **Symbols** and **Project lines**.
6. Click **OK**.
7. Back in the 3D Scatterplot - Simple dialog box, click **OK**.

Rotate the scatter plot using the icons to rotate the *X*, *Y*, and *Z* axes in the 3D Graph Tools toolbar. Select **Tools ➔ Toolbars ➔ 3D Graph Tools** if this toolbar is not visible in the Minitab window.

The right scatter plot in Figure 13.1 was rotated clockwise about 90 degrees around the Z axis and was slightly rotated about the two other axes.

Interpreting the Regression coefficients

Use **Regression** to perform a multiple regression analysis. For example, to perform the Figure 13.2 analysis of the OmniPower sales data on page 467, open to the **OmniPower worksheet**. Select **Stat → Regression → Regression (Fit Regression Model** in Minitab 17). In the Regression dialog box (shown below):

1. Double-click **C1 Sales** in the variables list to add **Sales** to the **Response** box.
2. Double-click **C2 Price** in the variables list to add **Price** to the **Predictors** box.
3. Double-click **C3 Promotional Expenses** in the variables list to add **'Promotional Expenses'** to the **Predictors** box.
4. Click **Graphs**.

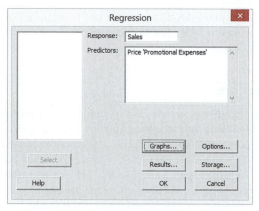

In the Regression - Graphs dialog box (shown below):

5. Click **Regular** and **Individual Plots**.
6. Check **Histogram of residuals** and **Residuals versus fits** and clear the other check boxes.
7. Click anywhere inside the **Residuals versus the variables** box.
8. Double-click **C2 Price** in the variables list to add **Price** in the **Residuals versus the variables** box.
9. Double-click **C3 Promotional Expenses** in the variables list to add **'Promotional Expenses'** in the **Residuals versus the variables** box.
10. Click **OK**.

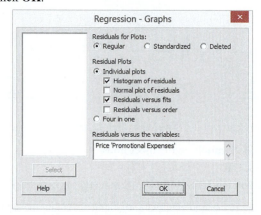

11. Back in the Regression dialog box, click **Results**.

In the Regression - Results dialog box (not shown):

12. Click **In addition, the full table of fits and residuals** and then click **OK**.
13. Back in the Regression dialog box, click **Options**.

In the Regression - Options dialog box (shown below):

14. Check **Fit Intercept**.
15. Clear all the **Display** and **Lack of Fit Test** check boxes.
16. Enter **79** and **400** in the **Prediction intervals for new observations** box.
17. Enter **95** in the **Confidence level** box.
18. Click **OK**.

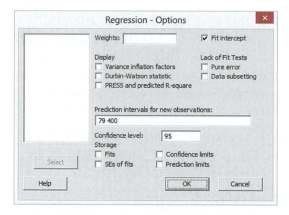

19. Back in the Regression dialog box, click **OK**.

The results in the Session Window will include additional items that are not shown in Figure 13.2.

Predicting the Dependent Variable Y

The regression results created by using the Section MG13.1 instructions include the confidence interval estimation and prediction interval. Figure 13.3 on page 469 shows these items for the OmniPower sales data.

MG13.2 r^2, ADJUSTED r^2, and the OVERALL F TEST

The coefficient of multiple determination, r^2, the adjusted r^2, and the overall F test are all computed as part of creating the multiple regression results using the Section MG13.1 instructions.

MG13.3 RESIDUAL ANALYSIS for the MULTIPLE REGRESSION MODEL

The regression results created by using the MG13.1 instructions include a residual analysis.

MG13.4 INFERENCES CONCERNING the POPULATION REGRESSION COEFFICIENTS

The regression results created by using the MG13.1 instructions include the information needed to make the inferences discussed in Section 13.4.

MG13.5 USING DUMMY VARIABLES and INTERACTION TERMS in REGRESSION MODELS

Dummy Variables

Use **Text to Numeric** to create a dummy variable. For example, to create from the categorical variable Fireplace the dummy variable named Fireplace Coded that is used in the Figure 13.7 regression model on page 480, open to the **SilverSpring worksheet**. Select **Data → Code → Text to Numeric**. In the Code - Text to Numeric dialog box (shown below):

1. Double-click **C9 Fireplace** in the variables list to add **Fireplace** to the **Code data from columns** box and press **Tab**.
2. Enter **C10** in the **Store coded data in columns** box and press **Tab**. (Column C10 is the first empty column in the worksheet.)
3. In the first row, enter **Yes** in the **Original values (eg, red "light blue")** box and enter **1** in the **New** box.
4. In the second row, enter **No** in the **Original values (eg, red "light blue")** box and enter **0** in the **New** box.
5. Click **OK**.

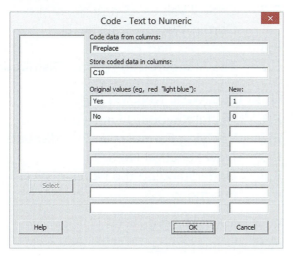

6. Enter **Fireplace Coded** as the name of column **C10**.

Interactions

Use **Calculator** to add a new column that contains the product of multiplying one independent variable by another to create an interaction term. For example, to create an interaction term of size and the dummy variable FireplaceCoded that is used in the Figure 13.8 regression model on page 482, open to the **SilverSpring worksheet**. Use the "Dummy Variables" instructions in the preceding part to create the **Fireplace Coded** column in the worksheet. Select **Calc → Calculator**. In the Calculator dialog box (shown below):

1. Enter **C11** in the **Store result in variable** box and press **Tab**.
2. Enter **Size * 'Fireplace Coded'** in the **Expression** box.
3. Click **OK**.

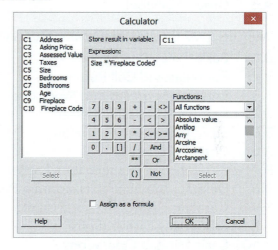

4. Enter **Size*Fireplace** as the name for column **C11**.

Appendices

Basic Math Concepts and Symbols

A.1 Rules for Arithmetic Operations

RULE	EXAMPLE
1. $a + b = c$ and $b + a = c$	$2 + 1 = 3$ and $1 + 2 = 3$
2. $a + (b + c) = (a + b) + c$	$5 + (7 + 4) = (5 + 7) + 4 = 16$
3. $a - b = c$ but $b - a \neq c$	$9 - 7 = 2$ but $7 - 9 \neq 2$
4. $(a)(b) = (b)(a)$	$(7)(6) = (6)(7) = 42$
5. $(a)(b + c) = ab + ac$	$(2)(3 + 5) = (2)(3) + (2)(5) = 16$
6. $a \div b \neq b \div a$	$12 \div 3 \neq 3 \div 12$
7. $\dfrac{a + b}{c} = \dfrac{a}{c} + \dfrac{b}{c}$	$\dfrac{7 + 3}{2} = \dfrac{7}{2} + \dfrac{3}{2} = 5$
8. $\dfrac{a}{b + c} \neq \dfrac{a}{b} + \dfrac{a}{c}$	$\dfrac{3}{4 + 5} \neq \dfrac{3}{4} + \dfrac{3}{5}$
9. $\dfrac{1}{a} + \dfrac{1}{b} = \dfrac{b + a}{ab}$	$\dfrac{1}{3} + \dfrac{1}{5} = \dfrac{5 + 3}{(3)(5)} = \dfrac{8}{15}$
10. $\left(\dfrac{a}{b}\right)\left(\dfrac{c}{d}\right) = \left(\dfrac{ac}{bd}\right)$	$\left(\dfrac{2}{3}\right)\left(\dfrac{6}{7}\right) = \left(\dfrac{(2)(6)}{(3)(7)}\right) = \dfrac{12}{21}$
11. $\dfrac{a}{b} \div \dfrac{c}{d} = \dfrac{ad}{bc}$	$\dfrac{5}{8} \div \dfrac{3}{7} = \left(\dfrac{(5)(7)}{(8)(3)}\right) = \dfrac{35}{24}$

A.2 Rules for Algebra: Exponents and Square Roots

RULE	EXAMPLE
1. $(X^a)(X^b) = X^{a+b}$	$(4^2)(4^3) = 4^5$
2. $(X^a)^b = X^{ab}$	$(2^2)^3 = 2^6$
3. $(X^a / X^b) = X^{a-b}$	$\dfrac{3^5}{3^3} = 3^2$
4. $\dfrac{X^a}{X^a} = X^0 = 1$	$\dfrac{3^4}{3^4} = 3^0 = 1$
5. $\sqrt{XY} = \sqrt{X}\sqrt{Y}$	$\sqrt{(25)(4)} = \sqrt{25}\sqrt{4} = 10$
6. $\sqrt{\dfrac{X}{Y}} = \dfrac{\sqrt{X}}{\sqrt{Y}}$	$\sqrt{\dfrac{16}{100}} = \dfrac{\sqrt{16}}{\sqrt{100}} = 0.40$

A.3 Rules for Logarithms

Base 10

Log is the symbol used for base-10 logarithms:

RULE	EXAMPLE
1. $\log(10^a) = a$	$\log(100) = \log(10^2) = 2$
2. If $\log(a) = b$, then $a = 10^b$	If $\log(a) = 2$, then $a = 10^2 = 100$
3. $\log(ab) = \log(a) + \log(b)$	$\log(100) = \log[(10)(10)] = \log(10) + \log(10)$ $= 1 + 1 = 2$
4. $\log(a^b) = (b)\log(a)$	$\log(1{,}000) = \log(10^3) = (3)\log(10) = (3)(1) = 3$
5. $\log(a/b) = \log(a) - \log(b)$	$\log(100) = \log(1{,}000/10) = \log(1{,}000) - \log(10)$ $= 3 - 1 = 2$

EXAMPLE

Take the base-10 logarithm of each side of the following equation:

$$Y = \beta_0 \beta_1^X \varepsilon$$

SOLUTION: Apply rules 3 and 4:

$$\log(Y) = \log(\beta_0 \beta_1^X \varepsilon)$$
$$= \log(\beta_0) + \log(\beta_1^X) + \log(\varepsilon)$$
$$= \log(\beta_0) + X \log(\beta_1) + \log(\varepsilon)$$

Base e

ln is the symbol used for base e logarithms, commonly referred to as natural logarithms. e is Euler's number, and $e \cong 2.718282$:

RULE	EXAMPLE
1. $\ln(e^a) = a$	$\ln(7.389056) = \ln(e^2) = 2$
2. If $\ln(a) = b$, then $a = e^b$	If $\ln(a) = 2$, then $a = e^2 = 7.389056$
3. $\ln(ab) = \ln(a) + \ln(b)$	$\ln(100) = \ln[(10)(10)]$ $= \ln(10) + \ln(10) = 2.302585 + 2.302585 = 4.605170$
4. $\ln(a^b) = (b)\ln(a)$	$\ln(1{,}000) = \ln(10^3) = 3\ln(10) = 3(2.302585) = 6.907755$
5. $\ln(a/b) = \ln(a) - \ln(b)$	$\ln(100) = \ln(1{,}000/10) = \ln(1{,}000) - \ln(10)$ $= 6.907755 - 2.302585 = 4.605170$

EXAMPLE

Take the base e logarithm of each side of the following equation:

$$Y = \beta_0 \beta_1^X \varepsilon$$

SOLUTION: Apply rules 3 and 4:

$$
\begin{aligned}
\ln(Y) &= \ln(\beta_0 \beta_1^X \varepsilon) \\
&= \ln(\beta_0) + \ln(\beta_1^X) + \ln(\varepsilon) \\
&= \ln(\beta_0) + X \ln(\beta_1) + \ln(\varepsilon)
\end{aligned}
$$

A.4 Summation Notation

The symbol Σ, the Greek capital letter sigma, represents "taking the sum of." Consider a set of n values for variable X. The expression $\sum_{i=1}^{n} X_i$ means to take the sum of the n values for variable X. Thus:

$$\sum_{i=1}^{n} X_i = X_1 + X_2 + X_3 + \cdots + X_n$$

The following problem illustrates the use of the symbol Σ. Consider five values of a variable X: $X_1 = 2, X_2 = 0, X_3 = -1, X_4 = 5,$ and $X_5 = 7$. Thus:

$$\sum_{i=1}^{5} X_i = X_1 + X_2 + X_3 + X_4 + X_5 = 2 + 0 + (-1) + 5 + 7 = 13$$

In statistics, the squared values of a variable are often summed. Thus:

$$\sum_{i=1}^{n} X_i^2 = X_1^2 + X_2^2 + X_3^2 + \cdots + X_n^2$$

and, in the example above:

$$
\begin{aligned}
\sum_{i=1}^{5} X_i^2 &= X_1^2 + X_2^2 + X_3^2 + X_4^2 + X_5^2 \\
&= 2^2 + 0^2 + (-1)^2 + 5^2 + 7^2 \\
&= 4 + 0 + 1 + 25 + 49 \\
&= 79
\end{aligned}
$$

$\sum_{i=1}^{n} X_i^2$, the summation of the squares, is *not* the same as $\left(\sum_{i=1}^{n} X_i \right)^2$, the square of the sum:

$$\sum_{i=1}^{n} X_i^2 \neq \left(\sum_{i=1}^{n} X_i \right)^2$$

In the example given above, the summation of squares is equal to 79. This is not equal to the square of the sum, which is $13^2 = 169$.

Another frequently used operation involves the summation of the product. Consider two variables, X and Y, each having n values. Then:

$$\sum_{i=1}^{n} X_i Y_i = X_1 Y_1 + X_2 Y_2 + X_3 Y_3 + \cdots + X_n Y_n$$

Continuing with the previous example, suppose there is a second variable, Y, whose five values are $Y_1 = 1$, $Y_2 = 3$, $Y_3 = -2$, $Y_4 = 4$, and $Y_5 = 3$. Then,

$$\sum_{i=1}^{n} X_i Y_i = X_1 Y_1 + X_2 Y_2 + X_3 Y_3 + X_4 Y_4 + X_5 Y_5$$

$$= (2)(1) + (0)(3) + (-1)(-2) + (5)(4) + (7)(3)$$

$$= 2 + 0 + 2 + 20 + 21$$

$$= 45$$

In computing $\sum_{i=1}^{n} X_i Y_i$, you need to realize that the first value of X is multiplied by the first value of Y, the second value of X is multiplied by the second value of Y, and so on. These products are then summed in order to compute the desired result. However, the summation of products is *not* equal to the product of the individual sums:

$$\sum_{i=1}^{n} X_i Y_i \neq \left(\sum_{i=1}^{n} X_i \right) \left(\sum_{i=1}^{n} Y_i \right)$$

In this example,

$$\sum_{i=1}^{5} X_i = 13$$

and

$$\sum_{i=1}^{5} Y_i = 1 + 3 + (-2) + 4 + 3 = 9$$

so that

$$\left(\sum_{i=1}^{5} X_i \right) \left(\sum_{i=1}^{5} Y_i \right) = (13)(9) = 117$$

However,

$$\sum_{i=1}^{5} X_i Y_i = 45$$

The following table summarizes these results:

VALUE	X_i	Y_i	$X_i Y_i$
1	2	1	2
2	0	3	0
3	−1	−2	2
4	5	4	20
5	7	3	21
	$\sum_{i=1}^{5} X_i = 13$	$\sum_{i=1}^{5} Y_i = 9$	$\sum_{i=1}^{5} X_i Y_i = 45$

Rule 1   The summation of the values of two variables is equal to the sum of the values of each summed variable:

$$\sum_{i=1}^{n} (X_i + Y_i) = \sum_{i=1}^{n} X_i + \sum_{i=1}^{n} Y_i$$

Thus,

$$\sum_{i=1}^{5}(X_i + Y_i) = (2 + 1) + (0 + 3) + (-1 + (-2)) + (5 + 4) + (7 + 3)$$

$$= 3 + 3 + (-3) + 9 + 10$$

$$= 22$$

$$\sum_{i=1}^{5}X_i + \sum_{i=1}^{5}Y_i = 13 + 9 = 22$$

Rule 2 The summation of a difference between the values of two variables is equal to the difference between the summed values of the variables:

$$\sum_{i=1}^{n}(X_i - Y_i) = \sum_{i=1}^{n}X_i - \sum_{i=1}^{n}Y_i$$

Thus,

$$\sum_{i=1}^{5}(X_i - Y_i) = (2 - 1) + (0 - 3) + (-1 - (-2)) + (5 - 4) + (7 - 3)$$

$$= 1 + (-3) + 1 + 1 + 4$$

$$= 4$$

$$\sum_{i=1}^{5}X_i - \sum_{i=1}^{5}Y_i = 13 - 9 = 4$$

Rule 3 The sum of a constant times a variable is equal to that constant times the sum of the values of the variable:

$$\sum_{i=1}^{n}cX_i = c\sum_{i=1}^{n}X_i$$

where c is a constant. Thus, if $c = 2$,

$$\sum_{i=1}^{5}cX_i = \sum_{i=1}^{5}2X_i = (2)(2) + (2)(0) + (2)(-1) + (2)(5) + (2)(7)$$

$$= 4 + 0 + (-2) + 10 + 14$$

$$= 26$$

$$c\sum_{i=1}^{5}X_i = 2\sum_{i=1}^{5}X_i = (2)(13) = 26$$

Rule 4 A constant summed n times will be equal to n times the value of the constant.

$$\sum_{i=1}^{n}c = nc$$

where c is a constant. Thus, if the constant $c = 2$ is summed 5 times,

$$\sum_{i=1}^{5}c = 2 + 2 + 2 + 2 + 2 = 10$$

$$nc = (5)(2) = 10$$

EXAMPLE

Suppose there are six values for the variables X and Y, such that $X_1 = 2, X_2 = 1, X_3 = 5, X_4 = -3, X_5 = 1, X_6 = -2$ and $Y_1 = 4, Y_2 = 0, Y_3 = -1, Y_4 = 2, Y_5 = 7$, and $Y_6 = -3$. Compute each of the following:

(a) $\sum_{i=1}^{6}X_i$

(b) $\sum_{i=1}^{6}Y_i$

(*continued*)

(c) $\sum_{i=1}^{6} X_i^2$

(g) $\sum_{i=1}^{6} (X_i - Y_i)$

(d) $\sum_{i=1}^{6} Y_i^2$

(h) $\sum_{i=1}^{6} (X_i - 3Y_i + 2X_i^2)$

(e) $\sum_{i=1}^{6} X_i Y_i$

(i) $\sum_{i=1}^{6} (cX_i)$, where $c = -1$

(f) $\sum_{i=1}^{6} (X_i + Y_i)$

(j) $\sum_{i=1}^{6} (X_i - 3Y_i + c)$, where $c = +3$

Answers

(a) 4 (b) 9 (c) 44 (d) 79 (e) 10 (f) (13) (g) −5 (h) 65 (i) −4 (j) −5

REFERENCES

1. Bashaw, W. L. *Mathematics for Statistics.* New York: Wiley, 1969.
2. Lanzer, P. *Basic Math: Fractions, Decimals, Percents.* Hicksville, NY: Video Aided Instruction, 2006.
3. Levine, D. and A. Brandwein *The MBA Primer: Business Statistics*, 3rd ed. Cincinnati, OH: Cengage Publishing, 2011.
4. Levine, D. *Statistics.* Hicksville, NY: Video Aided Instruction, 2006.
5. Shane, H. *Algebra 1.* Hicksville, NY: Video Aided Instruction, 2006.

A.5 Statistical Symbols

+	add	×	multiply
−	subtract	÷	divide
=	equal to	≠	not equal to
≅	approximately equal to	<	less than
>	greater than	≤	less than or equal to
≥	greater than or equal to		

A.6 Greek Alphabet

GREEK LETTER		LETTER NAME	ENGLISH EQUIVALENT	GREEK LETTER		LETTER NAME	ENGLISH EQUIVALENT
A	α	Alpha	a	N	ν	Nu	n
B	β	Beta	b	Ξ	ξ	Xi	x
Γ	γ	Gamma	g	O	o	Omicron	ŏ
Δ	δ	Delta	d	Π	π	Pi	p
E	ε	Epsilon	ĕ	P	ρ	Rho	r
Z	ζ	Zeta	z	Σ	σ	Sigma	s
H	η	Eta	ē	T	τ	Tau	t
Θ	θ	Theta	th	Y	υ	Upsilon	u
I	ι	Iota	i	Φ	ϕ	Phi	ph
K	κ	Kappa	k	X	χ	Chi	ch
Λ	λ	Lambda	l	Ψ	ψ	Psi	ps
M	μ	Mu	m	Ω	ω	Omega	ō

B.1 Basic Excel Operations
Open or Save Workbooks

Use **File → Open** or **File → Save As**.

You open or save a workbook by first selecting the folder that stores the workbook and then specifying the file name of the workbook. Open and Save As display nearly identical dialog boxes that vary only slightly among the different Excel versions. Shown below is part of the Excel 2013 Save As dialog box. Besides displaying a list of files in the folder selected, the Save As dialog box allows you to save your file in alternate formats for programs that cannot open Excel workbooks (defined as the **.xlsx** format). Formats you might use include a simple text file with values delimited with tab characters, **Text (Tab delimited) (*.txt)**; simple text with values delimited with commas, **CSV (Comma delimited) (*.csv)**; or the older Excel workbook format, **Excel 97–2003 Workbook (.xls)**. In OS X Excel, these alternatives are known as **Tab Delimited Text (.txt), Windows Comma Separated (.csv),** and **Excel 97–2004 Workbook (.xls)**, respectively.

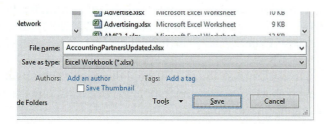

When opening files, you can specify a type of file to display or ask for all files in a folder to be listed by selecting the file type **All Files (*.*)** (Microsoft Windows Excels) or **All Files** (OS X Excel). Excel 2007 users click the **Office Button** in lieu of selecting **File**.

Insert or Copy Worksheets

To alter the contents of a workbook, by adding, deleting, or copying worksheets, you right-click a sheet tab and select **Insert, Delete,** or **Move or Copy** from the shortcut menu that appears. Selecting Insert displays the Insert dialog box in which you click **Worksheet** and then click **OK**. Selecting Move or Copy displays the Move or Copy dialog box in which you select the workbook and the position in the workbook for the worksheet being moved or copied. (To copy a worksheet, check the **Create a copy** check box.) These menu selections also work with chart sheets.

File → New (in OS X Excel, **File → New Workbook**) creates a new *workbook* with new, blank worksheets for cases in which you want to start from scratch.

Print Worksheets

Use **File → Print**.

The Print command displays a preview of what will be printed. If acceptable, click **Print**, otherwise press **Esc** (in OS X Excel, click **Cancel**) to cancel the printing processing. You can adjust print formatting while in print preview by clicking **Page Setup** to display the Page Setup dialog box. Checking the **Gridlines** and **Row and column** checkboxes in the **Sheet** tab of this dialog box creates a printed worksheet that contains gridlines and numbered row and lettered column headings (similar to the appearance of the worksheet onscreen). Excel 2007 users click the **Office Button** in lieu of selecting **File** and will experience minor differences in the printing process, including not being able to display the Page Setup dialog box from within the print preview.

B.2 Formulas and Cell References

In Excel, **formulas** are instructions that perform a calculation or some other computing task such as logical decision making. Formulas are typically found in worksheets that you use to present intermediate calculations or the results of an analysis. In some cases, formulas create or prepare new data to be analyzed.

Formulas typically use values found in other cells to compute a result that is displayed in the cell that stores the formula. This means that when you see that a particular worksheet cell is displaying a value, say, 5, you cannot determine from inspection if the cells contains the digit 5 or a formula that results in the display of the value 5. This trait of worksheets means you should always carefully review the contents of each worksheet you use. In this book, each worksheet with formulas is accompanied by a "formulas" worksheet that presents the worksheet in a mode that allows you to see all the formulas that have been entered in the worksheet.

Cell References

Most formulas use values that have been entered into other cells. To refer to those cells, Excel uses a referencing system that is based on the tabular nature of a worksheet. Columns are designated with letters and rows are designated with numbers such that the cell in the first row and first column is called A1, the cell in the third row and first column is called A3, and the cell in the third column and first row is C1. To refer to a cell in a formula, you use a cell reference in the form *WorksheetName!ColumnRow*. For example, Data!A2 refers to the cell in the Data worksheet that is in column A and row 2.

You can use only the *ColumnRow* portion of a full address—for example, A2—as a shorthand way to refer to a cell that is on the same worksheet as the one into which you are entering a formula. (Excel calls the worksheet into which you are making entries the **current worksheet**.) If the worksheet name contains spaces or special characters, such as **CITY DATA_1.2**, you must enclose the sheet name in a pair of single quotes, as in 'CITY DATA_1.2'!A2.

Use a **cell range** to refer to a group of cells, such as the cells of a column that store the data for a particular variable. A cell range names the upper-left cell and the lower-right cell of the group, using the form *Worksheet Name!UpperLeftCell:LowerRightCell*. For example, DATA!A1:A11 identifies the first 11 cells in the first column of the DATA worksheet and the cell range DATA!A1:D11 refers to the first 11 cells in the first 4 columns of the worksheet. Cell ranges in the form *Column:Column* (or *Row:Row*) that refer to all cells in a column (or row) are also allowed.

As with single cell references, you can skip the *WorksheetName!* part of the reference if you are entering a cell range on the current worksheet. As this book explains when necessary, in some Excel dialog boxes you *must* include the worksheet name as part of the cell reference in order to get the proper results.

Although not used in this book, cell references can include a workbook name in the form *'[WorkbookName] WorksheetName'!ColumnRow* or *'[WorkbookName] WorksheetName'!UpperLeftCell:LowerRightCell*. You may see such references if you copy certain worksheets or chart sheets from one workbook to another.

Recalculation

When you use formulas that refer to other cells, the result displayed by the formulas automatically changes as the values in the cells to which the formula refers change. This process is called **recalculation**.

Recalculation forms the basis for constructing worksheet *templates* and *models*. **Templates** are worksheets in which you only need to enter values to get results. Templates can be reused by entering different sets of values. Many of the worksheets illustrated in this book are templates and contain changeable data cells that are tinted a light turquoise color. **Models** are similar to templates but require the editing of certain formulas as new values are entered into a worksheet. In this book, worksheet models have been designed to simplify such editing tasks when no generalized template can be provided.

Worksheets that use formulas capable of recalculation are sometimes called "live" worksheets to distinguish them from worksheets that contain only text and numeric entries ("dead" worksheets). A novel feature of the PHStat add-in that you can use with this book is that most worksheets the add-in constructs are "live" worksheets, identical to the templates and models that the book features.

Absolute and Relative Cell References

To avoid the drudgery of typing many similar formulas, you can copy a formula and paste it into all the cells in a selected cell range. For example, to copy a formula that has been entered in cell C2 down the column through row 12:

1. Right-click cell C2 and press **Ctrl+C** to copy the formula. A movie marquee–like highlight appears around cell C2.
2. Select the cell range **C3:C12**.
3. With the cell range highlighted, press **Ctrl+V** to paste the formula into the cells of the cell range.

When you perform this copy-and-paste operation, Excel adjusts these **relative cell references** in formulas so that copying the formula =**A2** + **B2** from cell C2 to cell C3 results in the formula =**A3** + **B3** being pasted into cell C3, the formula =**A4** + **B4** being pasted into cell C4, and so on.

There are circumstances in which you do not want Excel to adjust all or part of a formula. For example, if you were copying the cell C2 formula =**(A2** + **B2)/B15**, and cell B15 contained the divisor to be used in all formulas, you would not want to see pasted into cell C3 the formula =**(A3** + **B3)/B16**. To prevent Excel from adjusting a cell reference, you use **absolute cell references** by inserting dollar signs ($) before the column and row references of a relative cell reference. For example, the absolute cell reference **$B$15** in the copied cell C2 formula =**(A2** + **B2)/$B$15** will cause Excel to paste the formula =**(A3** + **B3)/$B$15** into cell C3.

Do not confuse the use of the dollar sign symbol with the worksheet formatting operation that displays numbers as dollar currency amounts.

B.3 Entering Formulas into Worksheets

To enter a formula into a cell, first select the cell and then begin the entry by typing the equal sign (=). What follows the equal sign can be a combination of mathematical and data-processing operations and cell references that is terminated by pressing **Enter**. For simple formulas, you use the symbols +, −, *, /, and ^ for the operations addition, subtraction, multiplication, division, and exponentiation (a number raised to a power), respectively. For example, the formula =**A2** + **B2** adds the contents of cells A2 and B2 displays the sum as the value in the cell containing the formula. To revise a formula, either retype the formula or edit it in the formula bar.

You should always review and verify any formula you enter before you use its worksheet to get results. One way to view all the formulas in a worksheet is to press **Ctrl+`** (grave accent). After your formula review, you can press **Ctrl+`** a second time to restore the normal display of values.

Functions

You can use worksheet functions in formulas to simplify certain arithmetic formulas or to gain access to advanced processing or statistical functions. For example, instead of typing $=A2 + A3 + A4 + A5 + A6$, you could use the **SUM** function to enter the equivalent, and shorter, formula $=\textbf{SUM}(\textbf{A2:A6})$. Functions are entered by typing their names followed by a pair of parentheses. For almost all functions, you need to make at least one entry inside the pair of parentheses. For functions that require two or more entries, you separate entries with commas.

To use a worksheet function in a formula, either type the function as shown in the instructions in this book or select a function from one of the galleries in the Function Library group of the Formulas tab. For example, to enter the formula $=\textbf{AVERAGE}(\textbf{A:A})$ in cell C2, you could either type these 13 characters into the cell or select cell C2 and then select **Formulas → More Functions → Statistical** and click **AVERAGE** from the drop-down list and then enter **A:A** in the **Number 1** box in the Function Arguments dialog box and click **OK**.

Entering Array Formulas

An **array formula** is a formula that you enter just once but that applies to all of the cells in a selected cell range (the "array"). To enter an array formula, first select the cell range and then type the formula, and then, while holding down the **Ctrl** and **Shift** keys, press **Enter** to enter the array formula into all of the cells of the cell range. (In OS X Excel, you can also press **Command+Enter** to enter an array formula.)

To edit an array formula, you must first select the entire cell range that contains the array formula, then edit the formula and then press **Enter** while holding down **Ctrl+Shift** (or press **Command+Enter**). When you select a cell that contains an array formula, Excel adds a pair of curly braces {} to the display of the formula in the formula bar to indicate that the formula is an array formula. These curly braces disappear when you start to edit the formula. (You never type the curly braces when you enter an array formula.)

B.4 Pasting with Paste Special

While the keyboard shortcuts **Ctrl+C** and **Ctrl+V** to copy and paste cell contents will often suffice, pasting data from one worksheet to another can sometimes cause unexpected side effects. When the two worksheets are in different workbooks, a simple paste creates an external link to the original workbook that can lead to possible errors at a later time. Even pasting between worksheets in the same workbook can lead to problems if what is being pasted is a cell range of formulas. You can use **Paste Special** to avoid these complications.

To use this operation, copy the source cell range using **Ctrl+C** and then right-click the cell (or cell range) that is the target of the paste and click **Paste Special** from the shortcut menu.

In the Paste Special dialog box (shown below), click **Values** and then click **OK**. Paste Special Values pastes the current values of the cells in the first workbook and not formulas that use cell references to the first workbook.

Paste Special can paste other types of information, including cell formatting information. In some copying contexts, placing the mouse pointer over Paste Special in the shortcut menu will reveal a gallery of shortcuts to the choices presented in the Paste Special dialog box.

If you use PHStat and have data for a procedure in the form of formulas, copy your data and then use Paste Special to paste columns of equivalent *values*. (Click **Values** in the Paste Special dialog box to create the values.) PHStat will not work properly if the data for a procedure are in the form of formulas.

B.5 Basic Worksheet Cell Formatting

You format cells either by making entries in the Format Cells dialog box or by clicking shortcut buttons in the Home tab at the top of the Excel window.

To use the Format Cells dialog box, right-click a cell (or cell range) and click **Format Cells** in the shortcut menu. Excel displays the Number tab of the dialog box (partially shown below).

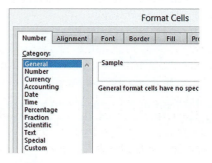

Clicking a **Category** changes the panel to the right of the list. For example, clicking **Number** displays a panel (partially shown below) in which you can set the number of decimal places.

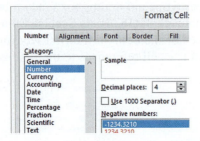

When you click the **Alignment** tab of the Format Cells dialog box (shown below), you display a panel in which you can control such things as whether cell contents get displayed centered or top- or bottom-anchored in a cell, whether cell contents are horizontally centered or left or right justified, and whether the cell contents can be wrapped to a second line if the contents are longer than the width of the cell. (many of these choices in this panel are duplicated in the Alignment group of the Home tab.)

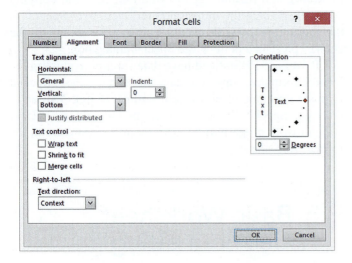

Home Tab Shortcuts

Use the Font group shortcuts (shown below) to change the formatting of the contents of a cell, including the typeface, point size, styling such as bold or italic, and the color. (The **Font** tab of the Format Cells dialog box offers equivalent choices.)

Use the **fill icon** in the same group to change the background color for a cell (shown as yellow in the illustration

below). Click the drop-down button to the right of the fill icon to display a gallery of colors (shown below) from which you can select a color or click **More Colors** for even more choices. The **A icon** and its drop-down button offer similar choices for changing the color of the text being displayed (shown as red in the illustrations below).

Click the various buttons of the **Number** group in the Home tab (shown below) to change the formatting of numeric values.

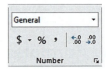

To adjust the width of a column to an optimal size, select the column and then select **Format → Autofit Column Width** in the Cells group (shown below). Excel will adjust the width of the column to accommodate the length of all the values in the column.

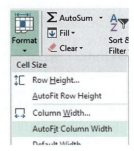

Many Home tab shortcuts, such as **Merge & Center**, have an associated drop-down list that you display by clicking the drop-down arrow at the right. For Merge & Center, this drop-down displays a gallery of similar choices (shown below).

B.6 Chart Formatting

Many of the *In-Depth Excel* instructions that involve charts refer you to this section so that you can correct the formatting of a chart that was just constructed. To apply any of the following corrections, you must first select the chart that is to be corrected. (If Chart Tools or PivotChart Tools appears above the Ribbon tabs, you have selected a chart.)

If, when you open to a chart sheet, the chart is either too large to be fully seen or too small and surrounded by a frame mat that is too large, click **Zoom Out** or **Zoom In**, located in the lower-right portion of the Excel window frame, to adjust the chart display.

In the following, instructions preceded with (**2013**) apply only to Excel 2013.

Changes You Most Commonly Make

To relocate a chart to its own chart sheet:

1. Click the chart background and click **Move Chart** from the shortcut menu.
2. In the Move Chart dialog box, click **New Sheet**, enter a name for the new chart sheet, and click **OK**.

To turn off the improper horizontal gridlines:

> (**2013**) **Design → Add Chart Element → Gridlines → Primary Major Horizontal**

> **Layout → Gridlines → Primary Horizontal Gridlines → None**

To turn off the improper vertical gridlines:

> (**2013**) **Design → Add Chart Element → Gridlines → Primary Major Vertical**

> **Layout → Gridlines → Primary Vertical Gridlines → None**

To turn off the chart legend:

> (**2013**) **Design → Add Chart Element → Legend → None**

> **Layout → Legend → None**

If you use Excel 2007, you will also need to apply these changes:

> **Layout → Data Labels → None**

> **Layout → Data Table → None**

These two apply *only* to Excel 2007.

Chart and Axis Titles

To add a chart title to a chart missing a title:

1. In Excel 2013, select **Design → Add Chart Element → Chart Title → Above Chart**. Otherwise, click on the chart and then select **Layout → Chart Title → Above Chart**.

2. In the box that is added to the chart, select the words "Chart Title" and enter an appropriate title.

To add a title to a horizontal axis missing a title:

1. In Excel 2013, select **Design → Add Chart Element → Axis Titles → Primary Horizontal.** Otherwise, click on the chart and then select **Layout → Axis Titles → Primary Horizontal Axis Title → Title Below Axis**.
2. In the box that is added to the chart, select the words "Axis Title" and enter an appropriate title.

To add a title to a vertical axis missing a title:

1. In Excel 2013, select **Design → Add Chart Element → Axis Titles → Primary Vertical.** Otherwise, click on the chart and then select **Layout → Axis Titles → Primary Vertical Axis Title → Rotated Title**.
2. In the box that is added to the chart, select the words "Axis Title" and enter an appropriate title.

Chart Axes

To turn on the display of the X axis, if not already shown:

> (**2013**) **Design → Add Chart Element → Axes → Primary Horizontal**

> **Layout → Axes → Primary Horizontal Axis → Show Left to Right Axis** (or **Show Default Axis**, if listed)

To turn on the display of the Y axis, if not already shown:

> (**2013**) **Design → Add Chart Element → Axes → Primary Vertical**

> **Layout → Axes → Primary Vertical Axis → Show Default Axis**

For a chart that contains secondary axes, to turn off the secondary horizontal axis title:

> (**2013**) **Design → Add Chart Element → Axis Titles → Secondary Horizontal**

> **Layout → Axis Titles → Secondary Horizontal → Axis Title → None**

For a chart that contains secondary axes, to turn on the secondary vertical axis title:

> (**2013**) **Design → Add Chart Element → Axis Titles → Secondary Vertical**

> **Layout → Axis Titles → Secondary Vertical Axis Title → Rotated Title**

Correcting the Display of the X Axis

In scatter plots and related line charts, Microsoft Excel displays the X axis at the Y axis origin ($Y = 0$). When plots have negative values, this causes the X axis not to appear at the bottom of the chart. To relocate the *X* axis to the bottom of a scatter plot or line chart, open to the chart sheet that contains the chart, right-click the **Y axis**, and click **Format Axis** from the shortcut menu. In Excel 2013, click **Axis value** and in its box, enter the value shown in the **Minimum box** in the same pane. For older Excels, click **Axis Options** in the left pane. In the Axis Options pane on the right, click **Axis value** and in its box enter the value shown in the dimmed **Minimum box** and then click **Close**.

Emphasizing Histogram Bars

To better emphasize each bar in a histogram, open to the chart sheet containing the histogram, right-click over one of the histogram bars, and click **Format Data Series** in the shortcut menu. In Excel 2013, in the Format Data Series pane, click the bucket icon. In the BORDER group, click **Solid line**. From the **Color drop-down list**, select the darkest color in the same column as the currently selected (highlighted) color. Then, enter **3** (for 3 pt) as the **Width**.

In older Excels, in the Format Data Series dialog box, click **Border Color** in the left pane. In the Border Color right pane, click **Solid line**. From the **Color drop-down list**, select the darkest color in the same column as the currently selected (highlighted) color. Then, click **Border Styles** in the left pane. In the Border Styles right pane, enter **3** (for 3 pt) as the **Width** and then click **OK**.

B.7 Selecting Cell Ranges for Charts

As a general rule, you either type that cell range or select the cell range by using the mouse pointer to enter a cell range in a Microsoft Excel dialog box. You are free to choose to enter the cell range either using relative or absolute references (see Section B.2). The Axis Labels and Edit Series dialog boxes, associated with chart labels and data series, are two exceptions. These dialog boxes and their contents for the Pareto chart sheet of the Pareto workbook are shown below.

To enter a cell range into these two dialog boxes, you must enter the cell range as a *formula* that uses absolute cell references in the form *WorksheetName!UpperLeftCell:LowerRightCell*. This is best done using the mouse-pointer method to enter these cell ranges. Typing the cell range, as you might normally do, will often be frustrating, as keys such as the cursor keys will not function as they do in other dialog boxes.

Selecting Non-contiguous Cell Ranges

Typically, you enter a non-contiguous cell range such as the cells A1:A11 and C1:C11 by typing the cell range of each group of cells, separated by commas—for example, **A1:A11, C1:C11**. In the dialog boxes discussed in the preceding section, you will need to select a non-contiguous cell range using the mouse pointer method. To use the mouse-pointer method with such ranges, first, select the cell range of the first group of cells and then, while holding down **Ctrl**, select the cell range of the other groups of cells that form the non-contiguous cell range.

B.8 Deleting the "Extra" Histogram Bar

As explained in "Classes and Excel Bins" on page 40, you use bins to approximate classes. One result of this approximation is that you will always create an "extra" bin that will have a frequency of zero. To delete the histogram bar associated with this extra bin, edit the cell range that Excel uses to construct the histogram.

Right-click the histogram background and click **Select Data**. In the Select Data Source Data dialog box, first click **Edit** under the **Legend Entries (Series)** heading. In the Edit Series dialog box, edit the **Series values** cell range formula to begin with the second cell of the original cell range and click **OK**. Then click **Edit** under the **Horizontal (Categories) Axis Labels** heading. In the Axis Labels dialog box, edit the **Axis label range** to begin with the second cell of the original cell range and click **OK**.

B.9 Creating Histograms for Discrete Probability Distributions

You can create a histogram for a discrete probability distribution based on a discrete probabilities table. For example, to create the Figure 5.3 histogram of the binomial probability distribution on page 185, open to the **COMPUTE worksheet** of the **Binomial workbook**. Select the cell range **B14:B18**, the probabilities in the Binomial Probabilities Table, and:

1. Select **Insert → Column** and select the first **2-D Column** gallery choice (**Clustered Column**).
2. Right-click the chart background and click **Select Data**.

In the Select Data Source dialog box:

3. Click **Edit** under the **Horizontal (Categories) Axis Labels** heading.
4. In the Axis Labels dialog box, enter the cell range *formula* **= COMPUTE!A14:A18** as the **Axis label range**. (See Section B.7 to learn how to best enter this cell range formula.) Click **OK** to return to the Select Data Source dialog box.
5. Back in the Select Data Source dialog box, click **OK**.

In the chart:

6. Right-click inside a bar and click **Format Data Series** in the shortcut menu.

In the Format Data Series dialog box:

7. Click **Series Options** in the left pane. In the Series Options right pane, change the **Gap Width** slider to **Large Gap**. Click **Close**.

Relocate the chart to a chart sheet and adjust the chart formatting by using the instructions in Section B.6.

B.10 Basic Minitab Operations

Open or Save Files

Use **File → Open Worksheet** or **File → Open Project** and **File → Save Current Worksheet** or **File → Save Project As**.

In Minitab, you can open and save individual worksheets or various open or save dialog boxes, you select the storage folder by using the drop-down list at the top of either dialog box and enter, or select from the list, name for the file. To save data in a form readable by Excel, select **Excel** from the **Save as type drop-down list** before you click Save. Other formats you might use include a simple text file, **Text**, or simple text with values delimited with commas, **CSV**.

In Minitab, you can also open and save individual graphs and a project's session window, although these operations are never used in this book.

Insert or Copy Worksheets

Use **File → New** or **File → Open Worksheet**.

To insert a new worksheet, select **File → New** and in the New dialog box click **Minitab Worksheet** and then click **OK**. To insert a copy of a worksheet, select **File → Open Worksheet** and select the *project* that contains the worksheet to be copied. Selecting a project (and not a worksheet) displays a second dialog box in which you can select the worksheet to be copied.

Print Worksheets

Use **File → Print Worksheet** (or **Print Graph** or **Print Session Window**).

Selecting Print Worksheet displays the Data Window Print Options dialog box. In this dialog box, you specify the formatting options for printing (the default selections should be fine) and enter a title for the printout. Selecting Print Graph or Print Session Window displays the Print dialog box that allows you to change the default printer settings.

If you need to change the paper size or paper orientation of your printout, first select **File → Print Setup** and make the appropriate selections in the Print dialog box before you select the Print command.

APPENDIX C Online Resources

C.1 About the Online Resources for This Book

Online resources support your study of business statistics and your use of this book. Online resources are available from the student download web page or MyStatLab course for this book. Some resources are packaged as a zip archive files. The online resources for this book are:

- **Excel and Minitab Data files**   The files that contain the data used in chapter examples, named in problems, or used in the end-of-chapter cases. Section C.3 includes a complete listing of these files and their contents.
- **Excel Guide Workbooks**   Excel workbooks that contain templates or model solutions for applying Excel to a particular statistical method. Section C.3 includes a complete listing of these files.
- **Files for the Digital Cases**   The set of PDF files that support the end-of-chapter Digital Cases. Some of the Digital Case PDF files contain attached files as well.
- **Online Topics**   The set of PDF format files that present additional statistical topics. This set includes the full text of two chapters, "Statistical Applications in Quality Management" and "Decision Making."
- **Short Takes**   The set of PDF files that extend the discussion of specific concepts or further document the results presented in the book.
- **Visual Explorations Workbooks**   The workbooks that interactively demonstrate various key statistical concepts. See *Visual Explorations* in Section C.3 for additional information.

If you plan to use PHStat, the Pearson Education statistics add-in for Microsoft Excel, see Section C.4.

C.2 Accessing the Online Resources

Online resources for this book are available either on the student download page for this book or inside the MyStatLab course for this book (see Section C.3). To access resources from the student download page for this book:

1. Visit **www.pearsonhighered.com/levine**.
2. In that web page, find the entries for this book, *Business Statistics: A First Course*, seventh edition, and click the student download page link.
3. In the download page, click the link for the desired items. Most items will cause the web browser to prompt

you to save the (zip archive) that you can save and later unzip. Some download links may require an access code (see Section C.2).

To access resources from the MyStatLab course for this book, log into the course and in the left panel of the course page for this book, click **Tools for Success**. On that page, click the link for one of the online resource categories listed in Section C.1.

Using MyStatLab requires an access code. An access code may have been packaged with this book. If your book did not come with an access code, you can obtain one at **mypearson.com**.

C.3 Details of Downloadable Files

Data Files

Throughout this book, the names of data workbooks appear in a special inverted color typeface—for example, `Retirement Funds`. Data files are stored as worksheets in both the **.xlsx** Excel workbook and the **.mtw** Minitab worksheet file formats. (For files that contain more than one worksheet, Minitab versions are stored as **.mpj** Minitab project files.)

In the following alphabetical list, the variables for each data file are presented in the order of their appearance, starting with first column (A in Excel and C1 in Minitab). Chapter references indicate the chapter or chapters that use the data file in an example or problem. A trailing (E) notes a file exclusive to Excel. A trailing (M) notes a file exclusive to Minitab.

311CALLCENTER Day and abandonment rate (%) (Chapter 3)

ACCOUNTINGPARTNERS Firm and number of partners (Chapter 3)

ACCOUNTINGPARTNERS2 Region and number of partners (Chapter 10)

ACCOUNTINGPARTNERS4 Region and number of partners (Chapter 10)

ADINDEX Respondent, cola A Adindex, and cola B Adindex (Chapter 10)

AMS2-1 Types of errors and frequency, types of errors and cost, types of wrong billing errors and cost (as three separate worksheets) (Chapter 2)

AMS2-2 Days and number of calls (Chapter 2)

AMS8 Rate willing to pay ($) (Chapter 8)

AMS9 Upload speed (Chapter 9)

AMS10-1 Update times for email interface 1 and email interface 2 (Chapter 10)

AMS10-2 Update times for system 1, system 2, and system 3 (Chapter 10)

AMS12 Number of hours spent telemarketing and number of new subscriptions (Chapter 12)

AMS13 Week, number of new subscriptions, hours spent telemarketing, and type of presentation (formal or informal) (Chapter 13)

ANSCOMBE Data sets A, B, C, and D, each with 11 pairs of *X* and *Y* values (Chapter 12)

ATM TRANSACTIONS Cause, frequency, and percentage (Chapter 2)

AUDITS Year and number of audits (Chapter 2)

AUTOMAKER1 Automaker and number of complaints (Chapter 2)

AUTOMAKER2 Category and number of complaints (Chapter 2)

AUTOSALES Manufacturer, sales, and change percentage (Chapter 2)

BANK1 Waiting time (in minutes) of 15 customers at a bank located in a commercial district (Chapters 3, 9, and 10)

BANK2 Waiting time (in minutes) of 15 customers at a bank located in a residential area (Chapters 3 and 10)

BASEBALL Team, E.R.A, runs scored per game, league (0 = American, 1 = National), wins (Chapters 12 and 13)

BBCOST2012 Team and fan cost index (Chapter 2)

BESTFUNDS1 Fund type (short-term or long-term), 1-year return, and 3-year return (Chapter 10)

BESTFUNDS2 Fund type (short-term, long-term, or world), 1-year return, and 3-year return (Chapter 10)

BESTFUNDS3 Fund type (small, mid-cap, or large), 1-year return, and 3-year return (Chapter 10)

BOOKPRICES Author, title, bookstore price, and online price ($) (Chapter 10)

BRANDZTECHFIN Brand, brand value in 2014 ($millions), % change in brand value from 2013, region, and sector (Chapter 10)

BRYNNEPACKAGING WPCT score and rating (Chapter 12)

BULBS Manufacturer (1 = A, 2 = B) and length of life (hours) (Chapters 2 and 10)

BUNDLE Restaurant, bundle score, and typical cost ($) (Chapter 2)

BUSINESSVALUATION Drug company name, price to book value ratio, return on equity (ROE), and growth% (Chapter 13)

CAFFEINE Caffeine per fluid ounce (mg/oz) (Chapter 2)

CARDIOGOODFITNESS Product purchased (TM195, TM498, TM798), age in years, gender (Male or Female), education in years, relationship status (Single or Partnered), average number of times the customer plans to use the treadmill each week, self-rated fitness on a 1-to-5 ordinal scale (1 = poor to 5 = excellent), annual household income ($), and average number of miles the customer expects to walk/run each week (Chapters 2, 3, 6, 8, 10, and 11)

CATFOOD Ounces eaten of kidney, shrimp, chicken liver, salmon, and beef cat food (Chapter 10)

CDRATE Bank, 1-year CD rate, and 5-year CD rate (Chapters 2, 3, 6, and 8)

CEO-COMPENSATION Company, CEO compensation ($millions), and return in 2012 (Chapter 2)

CEO-COMPENSATION2013 Company, CEO compensation ($millions), and return in 2013 ($millions) (Chapter 12)

CEREALS Cereal, calories, carbohydrates, and sugar (Chapters 2, 3, and 12)

CHALLENGING Data and charts for Figure 2.19 (Chapter 2)

CIGARETTETAX State and cigarette tax ($) (Chapters 2 and 3)

COFFEE Expert and rating of coffees by brand A, B, C, and D (Chapter 10)

COFFEESALES Coffee sales at $0.59, $0.69, $0.79, and $0.89 (Chapter 10)

COLA Beverage end-cap sales and produce end-cap sales (Chapter 10)

COLLEGE FOOTBALL Head coach, school, conference, school pay of head coach, other pay, total pay, max bonus, and football net revenue (Chapters 2, 3, and 12)

COMMUNITYBANKS Institution, location, return on investment (ROI%), efficiency ratio (%), total risk based capital (%) (Chapter 13)

CONCRETE1 Sample number and compressive strength after two days and seven days (Chapter 10)

CONGESTION City, annual time waiting in traffic (hours), and cost of waiting in traffic ($) (Chapters 2 and 3)

CREDIT SCORES City, state, and average credit score (Chapters 2 and 3)

CURRENCY Year, coded year, and exchange rates (against the U.S. dollar) for the Canadian dollar, Japanese yen, and English pound sterling (Chapter 2)

DELIVERY Customer, number of cases, and delivery time (Chapter 12)

DOINGBUSINESS Region, country name, 2012 GDP per capita, Internet users 2011 (per 100 people), and mobile cellular subscriptions 2011 (per 100 people) (Chapter 2)

DOMESTICBEER Brand, alcohol percentage, calories, and carbohydrates (Chapters 2, 3, and 6)

DOWDOGS Stock and one-year return (Chapter 3)

DOWMARKETCAP Company and market capitalization ($billions) (Chapters 3 and 6)

DOWNLOADSPEED Country and download speed in Mbps (Chapter 3)

DRILL Depth, time to drill additional 5 feet, and type of hole (dry or wet) (Chapter 13)

DRINK Amount of soft drink filled in 2-liter bottles (Chapters 2 and 9)

ENERGY State and per capita kilowatt hour use (Chapter 3)

ERWAITING Emergency room waiting time (in minutes) at the main facility and at satellite 1, satellite 2, and satellite 3 (Chapter 10)

ESPRESSO Tamp (inches) and time (seconds) (Chapter 12)

FASTFOOD Amount spent on fast food ($) (Chapters 2, 8, and 9)

FASTFOODCHAIN Mean sales per unit for burger, chicken, sandwich, and pizza segments (Chapter 10)

FIFTEENWEEKS Week number, number of customers, and sales ($thousands) over a period of 15 consecutive weeks (Chapter 12)

FIVEYEARCDRATE Five-year CD rates in New York and Los Angeles (Chapter 10)

FORCE Force required to break an insulator (Chapters 2, 3, 8, and 9)

FOREIGNMARKET Country, level of development (Emerging or Developed), and time required to start a business (days) (Chapter 10)

FOREIGNMARKET2 Country, region, cost to export container (US$), cost to import container (US$) (Chapter 10)

FTGLOBAL500 Sector (Automobiles & parts, Financial services, Health care equipment & services, or Software & computer services), country, company, market cap ($billions), and 52-week change (%) (Chapter 2)

FURNITURE Days between receipt and resolution of complaints regarding purchased furniture (Chapters 2, 3, 8, and 9)

GCROSLYN Address, location (Glen Cove or Roslyn), fair market value ($thousands), property size (acres), age, house size (sq. ft.), number of rooms, number of bathrooms, and number of cars that can be parked in the garage (Chapter 13)

GLENCOVE Address, fair market value ($thousands), property size (acres), age, house size (sq. ft.), number of rooms, number of bathrooms, and number of cars that can be parked in the garage (Chapter 13)

GLOBALSOCIALMEDIA Country, GDP, and social media usage (%) (Chapters 2, 3, and 12)

GOLFBALL Distance for designs 1, 2, 3, and 4 (Chapter 10)

GPIGMAT GMAT scores and GPA (Chapter 12)

GRADSURVEY ID, gender (Female or Male), age (as of last birthday), graduate major (Accounting, CIS, Economics/Finance, International Business, Management, Retailing/Marketing, or Other), current graduate GPA, undergraduate major (Biological Sciences, Business, Engineering, or Other), undergraduate GPA, current employment status (Full-Time, Part-Time, or Unemployed), number of different full-time jobs held in the past 10 years, expected salary upon completion of MBA ($thousands), amount spent for books and supplies this semester ($), advisory rating, type of computer owned (Desktop or Laptop), text messages per week, wealth accumulated to feel rich (Chapters 1, 2, 3, 4, 6, 8, 10, and 11)

GRANULE Granule loss in Boston and Vermont shingles (Chapters 3, 8, and 9)

HOTELAWAY nationality and price (US$) (Chapter 3)

HOTELPRICES City and average price (US$) of a hotel room at a 2-star price, 3-star price, and 4-star hotel (Chapters 2 and 3)

ICECREAM Daily temperature (in degrees Fahrenheit) and sales ($thousands) for 21 days (Chapter 12)

INSURANCE Processing time in days for insurance policies (Chapters 3, 8, and 9)

INSURANCECLAIMS Claims, buildup (0 = buildup not indicated, 1 = buildup indicated), excess payment ($) (Chapter 8)

INTERNETMOBILETIME Time spent per day accessing the Internet via mobile device (minutes) (Chapter 9)

INTERNETMOBILETIME2 Gender (F or M), time spent per day accessing the Internet via mobile device (minutes) (Chapter 10)

INVOICES Amount recorded (in dollars) from sales invoices (Chapter 9)

LUGGAGE Delivery time (in minutes) for luggage in Wing A and Wing B of a hotel (Chapter 10)

MARKET PENETRATION Country and Facebook penetration (in percentage) (Chapters 3 and 8)

MOBILE ELECTRONICS In-aisle sales, front sales, kiosk sales, and expert area sales (Chapter 10) (E)

MOBILE ELECTRONICS STACKED Stacked version of Mobile Electronics (Chapter 10) (M)

MOISTURE Moisture content of Boston shingles and Vermont shingles (Chapter 9)

MOTIVATION Factor, mean rating by global employees, and mean rating by U.S. employees (Chapter 10)

MOVIE Title, box office gross ($millions), and DVD revenue ($millions) (Chapter 12)

MOVIE ATTENDANCE Year and movie attendance (billions) (Chapter 2)

MOVIE REVENUES Year and revenue ($billions) (Chapter 2)

MOVING Labor hours, cubic feet, number of large pieces of furniture, and availability of an elevator (Chapters 12 and 13)

MYELOMA Patient, before transplant measurement, after transplant measurement (Chapter 10)

NATURAL GAS Month, wellhead price ($/thousands cu. ft.), and residential price ($/thousands cu. ft.) (Chapter 2)

NBA Team, team code, wins, field goal %, three-point field goal % (Chapter 13)

NBACOST2013 Team, fan cost index ($) (Chapters 2 and 6)

NBAVALUES Team, team code, annual revenue ($millions), and value ($millions) and 1-year change in value (%) (Chapters 2, 3, and 12)

NEEDS Need and frequency (Chapter 2)

NEIGHBOR Selling price ($thousands), number of rooms, neighborhood location (0 = east, 1 = west) (Chapter 13)

NEWHOMESALES Month, sales in thousands, and mean price ($thousands) (Chapter 2)

OIL&GASOLINE Week, price of a gallon of gasoline ($), and price of oil per barrel, ($) (Chapter 12)

OMNIPOWER Bars sold, price (cents), and promotion expenses ($) (Chapter 13)

ONLINE SHOPPING Main reason and percentage (Chapter 2)

ORDER Time in minutes to fill orders for a population of 200 (Chapter 8)

PACKAGINGFOAM3 Die temperature, die diameter, and foam density (Chapter 13)

PACKAGINGFOAM4 Die temperature, die diameter, and foam diameter (Chapter 13)

PALLET Weight of Boston shingles and weight of Vermont shingles (Chapters 2, 8, 9, and 10)

PEN Ad and product rating (Chapter 10)

PHONE Time (in minutes) to clear telephone line problems and location (1 = I, 2 = II) (Chapter 10)

PIZZATIME Time period, delivery time for local restaurant, and delivery time for national chain (Chapter 10)

POTTERMOVIES Title, first weekend gross ($millions), U.S. gross ($millions), and worldwide gross ($millions) (Chapters 2, 3, and 12)

PROPERTYTAXES State and property taxes per capita ($) (Chapters 2, 3, and 6)

PROTEIN Type of food, calories (in grams), protein, percentage of calories from fat, percentage of calories from saturated fat, and cholesterol (mg) (Chapters 2 and 3)

PUMPKIN Circumference and weight of pumpkins (Chapter 12)

RADIOSHACK State and number of stores (Chapters 3)

REDANDWHITE Fixed acidity, volatile acidity, citric acid, residual sugar, chlorides, free sulfur dioxide, total sulfur dioxide, density, pH, sulphates, alcohol, wine type coded (0 = White, 1 = Red), wine type (Red or White), quality (Chapter 13)

REDWOOD Height (ft.), breast height diameter (in.), and bark thickness (in.) (Chapters 12 and 13)

RENTSILVERSPRING Apartment size (sq. ft.) and monthly rental cost ($) (Chapter 12)

RESTAURANTS Location (City or Suburban), food rating, decor rating, service rating, summated rating, coded location (0 = City, 1 = Suburban), and cost of a meal (Chapters 2, 3, 10, 12, and 13)

RETIREMENT FUNDS Fund number, market cap (Small, Mid-Cap, or Large), type (Growth or Value), assets ($millions), turnover ratio, beta (measure of the volatility of a stock), standard deviation (measure of returns relative to 36-month average), risk (Low, Average, or High), 1-year return, 3-year return, 5-year return, 10-year return, expense ratio, star rating (Chapters 2, 3, 4, 6, 8, 10, and 11)

SEDANS Miles per gallon for 2014 midsized sedans (Chapters 3 and 8)

SILVERSPRING Address, asking price ($000), assessed value ($000), taxes ($), size (thousands sq. ft.) fireplace coded (0 = no, 1 = yes), number of bedrooms, number of bathrooms, age (years), fireplace (No or Yes) (Chapters 12 and 13)

SITESELECTION Store number, profiled customers, and sales ($millions) (Chapter 12)

SMALLBUSINESSES Company, earnings per share growth (%), sales growth (%), and return on equity (%) (Chapter 10)

SMARTPHONES Price ($) (Chapter 3)

SMARTPHONE SALES Type and market share percentage for the years 2011 through 2013 (Chapter 2)

SOCCERVALUES2014 Team, revenues ($millions), and value ($millions) (Chapter 12)

STANDBY Standby hours, total staff present, remote hours, Dubner hours, and total labor hours (Chapter 13)

STARBUCKS Tear, viscosity, pressure, plate gap (Chapters 12 and 13)

STEEL Error in actual length and specified length (Chapters 2, 6, 8, and 9)

STOCK PERFORMANCE Decade and stock performance (%) (Chapter 2)

STOCKPRICES2013 Date, S&P 500 value, and closing weekly stock price for GE, Discovery Communications, and Google (Chapter 12)

STUDYTIME Gender and study time in hours (Chapter 10)

SUV Miles per gallon for 2014 small SUVs (Chapters 3, 6, and 8)

TABLE_5.1 X and $P(X)$ (Chapter 5) (M)

TABLETS Battery life (hours) for WiFi-only and 3G/4G/WiFi tablets (Chapter 10)

TARGETWALMART Shopping item, Target price ($), and Walmart price ($) (Chapter 10)

TEABAGS Weight of tea bags in ounces (Chapters 3, 8, and 9)

TELECOM Provider, TV rating, and Phone rating (Chapter 10)

THREE-HOTEL SURVEY Choose again? (No or Yes) and Golden Palm, Palm Royale, and Palm Princess tallies (Chapter 12) (M)

TIMES Get-ready times (Chapter 3)

TROUGH Width of trough (Chapters 2, 3, 8, and 9)

TWITTERMOVIES Movie, Twitter activity, and receipts ($) (Chapter 12)

TWO-HOTEL SURVEY Choose again? (No or Yes) and Beachcomber and Windsurfer tallies (Chapter 12) (M)

UNDERGRADSURVEY ID, gender (Female or Male), age (as of last birthday), class designation (Sophomore, Junior, or Senior), major (Accounting, CIS, Economics/Finance, International Business, Management, Retail/Marketing, Other, or Undecided), graduate school intention (No, Yes, or Undecided), cumulative GPA, current employment status (Full-Time, Part-Time, or Unemployed), expected starting salary ($thousands), number of social networking sites registered for, satisfaction with student advisement services on campus, amount spent on books and supplies this semester, type of computer preferred (Desktop, Laptop, or Tablet), text messages per week, wealth accumulated to feel rich (Chapters 1, 2, 3, 4, 6, 8, 10, and 11)

UNSTACKED 1YRRETURN One-year return percentage for growth funds and one-year return percentage for value funds (Chapter 2) (M)

UTILITY Utilities charges ($) for 50 one-bedroom apartments (Chapters 2 and 6)

VB Time to complete program (Chapter 10)

VINHOVERDE Fixed acidity, volatile acidity, citric acid, residual sugar, chlorides, free sulfur dioxide, total sulfur dioxide, density, pH, sulphates, alcohol, and quality (Chapters 12 and 13)

WAIT Waiting time and seating time (Chapter 6)

WARECOST Distribution cost ($thousands), sales ($thousands), and number of orders (Chapter 12)

Excel Guide Workbooks

Excel Guide workbooks contain templates or model solutions for applying Excel to a particular statistical method. Chapter examples and the *In-Depth Excel* instructions of the Excel Guides feature worksheets from these workbooks and PHStat constructs many of the worksheets from these workbooks for you.

Workbooks are stored in the **.xlsx** Excel workbook format. Most contain a **COMPUTE worksheet** (often shown in this book) that presents results as well as a **COMPUTE_FORMULAS worksheet** that allows you to examine all of the formulas used in the worksheet. The Excel Guide workbooks (with the number of the chapter in which each is first mentioned) are:

Recoded (1)	**NPP (6)**
Random (1)	**SDS (7)**
Data Cleaning (1)	**CIE sigma known (8)**
Summary Table (2)	**CIE sigma unknown (8)**
Contingency Table (2)	**CIE Proportion (8)**
Distributions (2)	**Sample Size Mean (8)**
Pareto (2)	**Sample Size Proportion (8)**
Stem-and-leaf (2)	**Z Mean workbook (9)**
Histogram (2)	**T mean workbook (9)**
Polygons (2)	**Z Proportion (9)**
Scatter Plot (2)	**Pooled-Variance T (10)**
Time Series (2)	**Separate-Variance T (10)**
MCT (2)	**Paired T (10)**
Descriptive(3)	**F Two Variances (10)**
Quartiles (3)	**Z Two Proportions (10)**
Boxplot (3)	**One-Way ANOVA (10)**
Parameters (3)	**Levene (10)**
Covariance (3)	**Chi-Square (11)**
Probabilities (4)	**Chi-Square Worksheets (11)**
Bayes (4)	**Simple Linear Regression (12)**
Discrete Variable (5)	
Binomial (5)	**Package Delivery (12)**
Poisson (5)	**Multiple Regression (13)**
Normal (6)	

Digital Cases, Online Topics, and Short Takes

These files use the Portable Document Format (PDF) that are best viewed using the latest version of Adobe Reader (**get.adobe.com/reader/**).

Visual Explorations

Visual Explorations are workbooks that interactively demonstrate various key statistical concepts. Three workbooks are add-in workbooks that are stored in the **.xlam** Excel add-in format. Using these add-in workbooks with Microsoft Windows Excels requires the security settings discussed in Appendix Section D.3. The Visual Explorations workbooks are:

> **VE-Normal Distribution (add-in)**
> **VE-Sampling Distribution (add-in)**
> **VE-Simple Linear Regression (add-in)**
> **VE-Variability**

C.4 PHStat

PHStat is the Pearson Education statistics add-in for Microsoft Excel that simplifies the task of using Excel as you learn business statistics. PHStat comes packaged as a zip file archive that you download and unzip to the folder of your choice. The archive contains:

PHStat.xlam, the actual add-in workbook that is further discussed in Appendix Sections D.2 and G.1, and these four supporting files:

PHStat readme.pdf Explains the technical requirements, and setup and troubleshooting procedures for PHStat (PDF format).

PHStatHelp.chm The integrated help system for users of Microsoft Windows Excel.

PHStatHelp.pdf The help system as a PDF format file.

PHStatHelp.epub The help system in Open Publication Structure eBook format.

PHStat is available for download with an access code. If your book was packaged with an access code, download PHStat from **www.pearsonhighered.com/phstat**. Click the download link and follow the instructions for entering the access code. If your book was not packaged with an access code, visit **myPearsonStore.com** to purchase a PHStat access code.

This appendix seeks to eliminate the common types of technical problems that could complicate your use of Microsoft Excel as you learn business statistics with this book. Not all sections of this appendix apply to all readers. Sections with the code (WIN) apply to you if you use Microsoft Excel with Microsoft Windows, while sections with the code (OS X) apply to you if you use Microsoft Excel with OS X (formerly, Mac OS X). Some sections apply to all readers (ALL). (If you use Minitab, there are no configuration issues that you need to address.)

D.1 Getting Microsoft Excel Ready for Use (ALL)

You must have an up-to-date, properly licensed copy of Microsoft Excel in order to work through the examples and solve the problems in this book as well as to take advantage of the Excel-related workbooks and add-ins described in Appendix C. To get Microsoft Excel ready for use, check and apply Microsoft-supplied updates to Microsoft Excel and Microsoft Office.

If you need to install a new copy of Microsoft Excel on a Microsoft Windows computer system, choose the 32-bit version and not the 64-bit version *even if you have a 64-bit version of a Microsoft Windows operating system*. Many people mistakenly believe that the 64-bit version is somehow "better," not realizing that the OS X Excel 2011 is a 32-bit version and that Microsoft advises you to choose the 32-bit version for reasons the company details on its website. (The 64-bit WIN version can process Excel workbooks that are greater than 2GB in size—in other words, *big data*, as defined in Section GS.3.)

Checking For and Applying Updates

Microsoft Excel updates require Internet access and the process to check for and apply updates differs among Excel versions. If you use a Microsoft Windows version of Excel and use Windows 7 or 8, checking for updates is done by the Windows Update service. If you use an older version of Microsoft Windows, you may have to upgrade to this service. (Visit the Microsoft Download Center, **www.microsoft.com/download/default.aspx**, for further details.)

Windows Update can automatically apply any updates it finds, although many users prefer to set Windows Update to *notify* when updates are available and then select and apply updates manually.

In OS X Excel versions and some Microsoft Windows versions, you can manually check for updates. In Excel 2011 (OS X), select **Help → Check for Updates** and in the dialog box that appears, click **Check for Updates**. In Excel 2007 (WIN), first click the **Office Button** and then **Excel Options** at the bottom of the Office Button window. In the Excel Options dialog box, click **Resources** in the left pane and then in the right pane click **Check for Updates** and follow the instructions that appear on the web page that is displayed.

You normally do not manually check for updates in either Excel 2010 (WIN) or Excel 2013 (WIN). However, in some installations of these versions, you can select **File → Account → Update Options** (2013) or **File → Help → Check for Updates** (2010) and select options or follow instructions to manually check for updates.

If all else fails, you can open a web browser and go to the Microsoft Office part of the Microsoft Download Center at **www.microsoft.com/download/office.aspx?q=office** and manually select and download updates. On the web page displayed, filter the downloadable files by specifying the Excel version you discover by these means:

In Excel 2013 (WIN), select **File → Account** and then click **About Microsoft Excel**. In the dialog box that appears note the numbers and codes that follow the phrase "Microsoft Excel 2013."

In Excel 2010 (WIN), select **File → Help**. Under the heading "About Microsoft Excel" click **Additional Version and Copyright Information** and in the dialog box that appears note the numbers and codes that follow "Microsoft Excel 2010."

In Excel 2011 (OS X), click **Excel → About Excel**. The dialog box that appears displays the **Version** and **Latest Installed Update**.

In Excel 2007 (WIN), first click the **Office Button** and then click **Excel Options**. In the Excel options dialog box, click **Resources** in the left pane. In the right pane note the numbers and codes that follow Microsoft Office Excel 2007 under the "about Microsoft Office Excel 2007" heading.

Special Note for Office 365 Users

If you use Office 365, you are using the most current version of Excel for your system. At the time of publication, the most current version for Microsoft Windows systems was Excel 2013. For OS X, the most current version was Excel 2011.

D.2 Getting PHStat Ready for Use (ALL)

If you plan to use PHStat, the Pearson Education add-in workbook that simplifies the use of Microsoft Excel with this book (see Section EG.1 on page 8), you must first download PHStat using an access code as discussed in Section C.4. The PHStat download is a zip file archive that you unzip to the folder of your choice.

PHStat is fully compatible with these Excel versions: Excel 2007 (WIN), Excel 2010 (WIN), Excel 2011 (OS X), and Excel 2013 (WIN). PHStat is not compatible with Excel 2008 (OS X), an Excel version that did not include the capability of running add-in workbooks. If you are using Microsoft Excel with Microsoft Windows (any version), then you must first configure the security settings as discussed in Section D.3. If you are using Microsoft Excel with OS X, no additional steps are required.

D.3 Configuring Excel Security for Add-In Usage (WIN)

The Microsoft Excel security settings can prevent add-ins such as PHStat and the Visual Explorations add-in workbooks from opening or functioning properly. To configure these security settings to permit proper PHStat functioning:

1. In Excel 2010 and Excel 2013, select **File → Options**. In Excel 2007, first click the **Office Button** and then click **Excel Options**.

In the Excel Options dialog box (shown below):

2. Click **Trust Center** in the left pane and then click **Trust Center Settings** in the right pane.

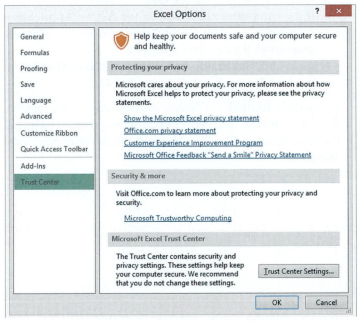

In the Trust Center dialog box:

3. Click **Add-ins** in the next left pane, and in the Add-ins right pane clear all of the checkboxes (shown below).

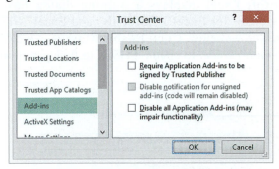

4. Click **Macro Settings** in the left pane, and in the Macro Settings right pane click **Disable all macros with notification** and check **Trust access to the VBA object model** (shown below).

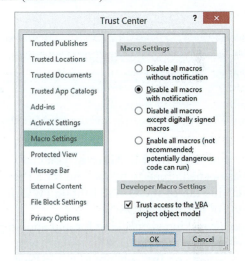

5. Click **OK** to close the Trust Center dialog box.

Back in the Excel Options dialog box:

6. Click **OK** to finish.

On some systems that have stringent security settings, you might need to modify step 4. For such systems, in step 4, also click **Trusted Locations** in the left pane and then, in the Trusted Locations right pane, click **Add new location** to add the folder path that you chose to store the PHStat files.

D.4 Opening PHStat (ALL)

When you open the **PHStat.xlam** file to use PHStat, Microsoft Excel displays a warning dialog box. The dialog boxes for Excel 2013 (WIN) and Excel 2011 (OS X) are shown below. Click **Enable Macros**, *which is not the default choice*, to enable PHStat to function properly.

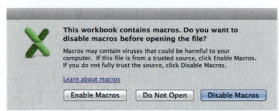

After you click **Enable Macros**, you can verify that PHStat has opened properly by looking for a PHStat menu in the Add-Ins tab of the Office Ribbon (WIN) or in the menu at top of the display (OS X).

If you have skipped checking for and applying necessary Excel updates, or if some of the updates were unable to be applied, when you first attempt to use PHStat, you may see a "Compile Error" message that talks about a "hidden module." If this occurs, repeat the process of checking for and applying updates to Excel. Review the PHStat FAQs in Appendix G for additional assistance, if necessary, and occasionally check for PHStat updates by revisiting the page from which you originally downloaded the PHStat files.

D.5 Using a Visual Explorations Add-In Workbook (ALL)

To use any of the Visual Explorations add-in workbooks, you must first download them using one of the methods discussed in Appendix Section C.1. If your download is packaged as a zip archive file, you must unzip that archive and store the add-in workbook files together in a folder of your choosing. Then apply the Section D.3 instructions, if necessary. When you open a Visual Explorations add-in workbook, you will see the same type of warning dialog box that Section D.4 describes. Click **Enable Macros** to enable the workbook to function properly.

D.6 Checking for the Presence of the Analysis ToolPak (ALL)

If you choose to use the *Analysis ToolPak* Excel Guide instructions, you will need to ensure that the Microsoft Excel Analysis ToolPak add-in has been installed. (This add-in is not available if you use Microsoft Excel with OS X.)

To check for the presence of the Analysis ToolPak add-in, if you use Microsoft Excel with Microsoft Windows:

1. Select **File → Options**. (In Excel 2007, click the **Office Button** and then click **Excel Options**.)

In the Excel Options dialog box:

2. Click **Add-Ins** in the left pane and look for the entry **Analysis ToolPak** in the right pane, under **Active Application Add-ins**.
3. If the entry appears, click **OK**.
4. If the entry does not appear in the **Active Application Add-ins** list, select **Excel Add-ins** from the **Manage** drop-down list and then click **Go**.
5. In the Add-Ins dialog box, check **Analysis ToolPak** in the **Add-Ins available** list and click **OK**.

If Analysis ToolPak (or Solver Add-in) does not appear in the list, rerun the Microsoft Office setup program to install this component, if you use Microsoft Excel with Microsoft Windows.

APPENDIX E Tables

Row	00000 12345	00001 67890	11111 12345	11112 67890	22222 12345	22223 67890	33333 12345	33334 67890
01	49280	88924	35779	00283	81163	07275	89863	02348
02	61870	41657	07468	08612	98083	97349	20775	45091
03	43898	65923	25078	86129	78496	97653	91550	08078
04	62993	93912	30454	84598	56095	20664	12872	64647
05	33850	58555	51438	85507	71865	79488	76783	31708
06	97340	03364	88472	04334	63919	36394	11095	92470
07	70543	29776	10087	10072	55980	64688	68239	20461
08	89382	93809	00796	95945	34101	81277	66090	88872
09	37818	72142	67140	50785	22380	16703	53362	44940
10	60430	22834	14130	96593	23298	56203	92671	15925
11	82975	66158	84731	19436	55790	69229	28661	13675
12	30987	71938	40355	54324	08401	26299	49420	59208
13	55700	24586	93247	32596	11865	63397	44251	43189
14	14756	23997	78643	75912	83832	32768	18928	57070
15	32166	53251	70654	92827	63491	04233	33825	69662
16	23236	73751	31888	81718	06546	83246	47651	04877
17	45794	26926	15130	82455	78305	55058	52551	47182
18	09893	20505	14225	68514	47427	56788	96297	78822
19	54382	74598	91499	14523	68479	27686	46162	83554
20	94750	89923	37089	20048	80336	94598	26940	36858
21	70297	34135	53140	33340	42050	82341	44104	82949
22	85157	47954	32979	26575	57600	40881	12250	73742
23	11100	02340	12860	74697	96644	89439	28707	25815
24	36871	50775	30592	57143	17381	68856	25853	35041
25	23913	48357	63308	16090	51690	54607	72407	55538
26	79348	36085	27973	65157	07456	22255	25626	57054
27	92074	54641	53673	54421	18130	60103	69593	49464
28	06873	21440	75593	41373	49502	17972	82578	16364
29	12478	37622	99659	31065	83613	69889	58869	29571
30	57175	55564	65411	42547	70457	03426	72937	83792
31	91616	11075	80103	07831	59309	13276	26710	73000
32	78025	73539	14621	39044	47450	03197	12787	47709
33	27587	67228	80145	10175	12822	86687	65530	49325
34	16690	20427	04251	64477	73709	73945	92396	68263
35	70183	58065	65489	31833	82093	16747	10386	59293
36	90730	35385	15679	99742	50866	78028	75573	67257
37	10934	93242	13431	24590	02770	48582	00906	58595
38	82462	30166	79613	47416	13389	80268	05085	96666
39	27463	10433	07606	16285	93699	60912	94532	95632
40	02979	52997	09079	92709	90110	47506	53693	49892
41	46888	69929	75233	52507	32097	37594	10067	67327
42	53638	83161	08289	12639	08141	12640	28437	09268
43	82433	61427	17239	89160	19666	08814	37841	12847
44	35766	31672	50082	22795	66948	65581	84393	15890
45	10853	42581	08792	13257	61973	24450	52351	16602
46	20341	27398	72906	63955	17276	10646	74692	48438
47	54458	90542	77563	51839	52901	53355	83281	19177
48	26337	66530	16687	35179	46560	00123	44546	79896
49	34314	23729	85264	05575	96855	23820	11091	79821
50	28603	10708	68933	34189	92166	15181	66628	58599

	Column							
Row	00000 12345	00001 67890	11111 12345	11112 67890	22222 12345	22223 67890	33333 12345	33334 67890
51	66194	28926	99547	16625	45515	67953	12108	57846
52	78240	43195	24837	32511	70880	22070	52622	61881
53	00833	88000	67299	68215	11274	55624	32991	17436
54	12111	86683	61270	58036	64192	90611	15145	01748
55	47189	99951	05755	03834	43782	90599	40282	51417
56	76396	72486	62423	27618	84184	78922	73561	52818
57	46409	17469	32483	09083	76175	19985	26309	91536
58	74626	22111	87286	46772	42243	68046	44250	42439
59	34450	81974	93723	49023	58432	67083	36876	93391
60	36327	72135	33005	28701	34710	49359	50693	89311
61	74185	77536	84825	09934	99103	09325	67389	45869
62	12296	41623	62873	37943	25584	09609	63360	47270
63	90822	60280	88925	99610	42772	60561	76873	04117
64	72121	79152	96591	90305	10189	79778	68016	13747
65	95268	41377	25684	08151	61816	58555	54305	86189
66	92603	09091	75884	93424	72586	88903	30061	14457
67	18813	90291	05275	01223	79607	95426	34900	09778
68	38840	26903	28624	67157	51986	42865	14508	49315
69	05959	33836	53758	16562	41081	38012	41230	20528
70	85141	21155	99212	32685	51403	31926	69813	58781
71	75047	59643	31074	38172	03718	32119	69506	67143
72	30752	95260	68032	62871	58781	34143	68790	69766
73	22986	82575	42187	62295	84295	30634	66562	31442
74	99439	86692	90348	66036	48399	73451	26698	39437
75	20389	93029	11881	71685	65452	89047	63669	02656
76	39249	05173	68256	36359	20250	68686	05947	09335
77	96777	33605	29481	20063	09398	01843	35139	61344
78	04860	32918	10798	50492	52655	33359	94713	28393
79	41613	42375	00403	03656	77580	87772	86877	57085
80	17930	00794	53836	53692	67135	98102	61912	11246
81	24649	31845	25736	75231	83808	98917	93829	99430
82	79899	34061	54308	59358	56462	58166	97302	86828
83	76801	49594	81002	30397	52728	15101	72070	33706
84	36239	63636	38140	65731	39788	06872	38971	53363
85	07392	64449	17886	63632	53995	17574	22247	62607
86	67133	04181	33874	98835	67453	59734	76381	63455
87	77759	31504	32832	70861	15152	29733	75371	39174
88	85992	72268	42920	20810	29361	51423	90306	73574
89	79553	75952	54116	65553	47139	60579	09165	85490
90	41101	17336	48951	53674	17880	45260	08575	49321
91	36191	17095	32123	91576	84221	78902	82010	30847
92	62329	63898	23268	74283	26091	68409	69704	82267
93	14751	13151	93115	01437	56945	89661	67680	79790
94	48462	59278	44185	29616	76537	19589	83139	28454
95	29435	88105	59651	44391	74588	55114	80834	85686
96	28340	29285	12965	14821	80425	16602	44653	70467
97	02167	58940	27149	80242	10587	79786	34959	75339
98	17864	00991	39557	54981	23588	81914	37609	13128
99	79675	80605	60059	35862	00254	36546	21545	78179
100	72335	82037	92003	34100	29879	46613	89720	13274

Source: Partially extracted from the Rand Corporation, *A Million Random Digits with 100,000 Normal Deviates* (Glencoe, IL, The Free Press, 1955).

TABLE E.2

The Cumulative Standardized Normal Distribution

Entry represents area under the cumulative standardized
normal distribution from $-\infty$ to Z

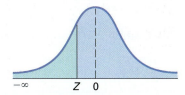

				Cumulative Probabilities						
Z	0.00	0.01	0.02	0.03	0.04	0.05	0.06	0.07	0.08	0.09
−6.0	0.000000001									
−5.5	0.000000019									
−5.0	0.000000287									
−4.5	0.000003398									
−4.0	0.000031671									
−3.9	0.00005	0.00005	0.00004	0.00004	0.00004	0.00004	0.00004	0.00004	0.00003	0.00003
−3.8	0.00007	0.00007	0.00007	0.00006	0.00006	0.00006	0.00006	0.00005	0.00005	0.00005
−3.7	0.00011	0.00010	0.00010	0.00010	0.00009	0.00009	0.00008	0.00008	0.00008	0.00008
−3.6	0.00016	0.00015	0.00015	0.00014	0.00014	0.00013	0.00013	0.00012	0.00012	0.00011
−3.5	0.00023	0.00022	0.00022	0.00021	0.00020	0.00019	0.00019	0.00018	0.00017	0.00017
−3.4	0.00034	0.00032	0.00031	0.00030	0.00029	0.00028	0.00027	0.00026	0.00025	0.00024
−3.3	0.00048	0.00047	0.00045	0.00043	0.00042	0.00040	0.00039	0.00038	0.00036	0.00035
−3.2	0.00069	0.00066	0.00064	0.00062	0.00060	0.00058	0.00056	0.00054	0.00052	0.00050
−3.1	0.00097	0.00094	0.00090	0.00087	0.00084	0.00082	0.00079	0.00076	0.00074	0.00071
−3.0	0.00135	0.00131	0.00126	0.00122	0.00118	0.00114	0.00111	0.00107	0.00103	0.00100
−2.9	0.0019	0.0018	0.0018	0.0017	0.0016	0.0016	0.0015	0.0015	0.0014	0.0014
−2.8	0.0026	0.0025	0.0024	0.0023	0.0023	0.0022	0.0021	0.0021	0.0020	0.0019
−2.7	0.0035	0.0034	0.0033	0.0032	0.0031	0.0030	0.0029	0.0028	0.0027	0.0026
−2.6	0.0047	0.0045	0.0044	0.0043	0.0041	0.0040	0.0039	0.0038	0.0037	0.0036
−2.5	0.0062	0.0060	0.0059	0.0057	0.0055	0.0054	0.0052	0.0051	0.0049	0.0048
−2.4	0.0082	0.0080	0.0078	0.0075	0.0073	0.0071	0.0069	0.0068	0.0066	0.0064
−2.3	0.0107	0.0104	0.0102	0.0099	0.0096	0.0094	0.0091	0.0089	0.0087	0.0084
−2.2	0.0139	0.0136	0.0132	0.0129	0.0125	0.0122	0.0119	0.0116	0.0113	0.0110
−2.1	0.0179	0.0174	0.0170	0.0166	0.0162	0.0158	0.0154	0.0150	0.0146	0.0143
−2.0	0.0228	0.0222	0.0217	0.0212	0.0207	0.0202	0.0197	0.0192	0.0188	0.0183
−1.9	0.0287	0.0281	0.0274	0.0268	0.0262	0.0256	0.0250	0.0244	0.0239	0.0233
−1.8	0.0359	0.0351	0.0344	0.0336	0.0329	0.0322	0.0314	0.0307	0.0301	0.0294
−1.7	0.0446	0.0436	0.0427	0.0418	0.0409	0.0401	0.0392	0.0384	0.0375	0.0367
−1.6	0.0548	0.0537	0.0526	0.0516	0.0505	0.0495	0.0485	0.0475	0.0465	0.0455
−1.5	0.0668	0.0655	0.0643	0.0630	0.0618	0.0606	0.0594	0.0582	0.0571	0.0559
−1.4	0.0808	0.0793	0.0778	0.0764	0.0749	0.0735	0.0721	0.0708	0.0694	0.0681
−1.3	0.0968	0.0951	0.0934	0.0918	0.0901	0.0885	0.0869	0.0853	0.0838	0.0823
−1.2	0.1151	0.1131	0.1112	0.1093	0.1075	0.1056	0.1038	0.1020	0.1003	0.0985
−1.1	0.1357	0.1335	0.1314	0.1292	0.1271	0.1251	0.1230	0.1210	0.1190	0.1170
−1.0	0.1587	0.1562	0.1539	0.1515	0.1492	0.1469	0.1446	0.1423	0.1401	0.1379
−0.9	0.1841	0.1814	0.1788	0.1762	0.1736	0.1711	0.1685	0.1660	0.1635	0.1611
−0.8	0.2119	0.2090	0.2061	0.2033	0.2005	0.1977	0.1949	0.1922	0.1894	0.1867
−0.7	0.2420	0.2388	0.2358	0.2327	0.2296	0.2266	0.2236	0.2206	0.2177	0.2148
−0.6	0.2743	0.2709	0.2676	0.2643	0.2611	0.2578	0.2546	0.2514	0.2482	0.2451
−0.5	0.3085	0.3050	0.3015	0.2981	0.2946	0.2912	0.2877	0.2843	0.2810	0.2776
−0.4	0.3446	0.3409	0.3372	0.3336	0.3300	0.3264	0.3228	0.3192	0.3156	0.3121
−0.3	0.3821	0.3783	0.3745	0.3707	0.3669	0.3632	0.3594	0.3557	0.3520	0.3483
−0.2	0.4207	0.4168	0.4129	0.4090	0.4052	0.4013	0.3974	0.3936	0.3897	0.3859
−0.1	0.4602	0.4562	0.4522	0.4483	0.4443	0.4404	0.4364	0.4325	0.4286	0.4247
−0.0	0.5000	0.4960	0.4920	0.4880	0.4840	0.4801	0.4761	0.4721	0.4681	0.4641

TABLE E.2

The Cumulative Standardized Normal Distribution (*continued*)

Entry represents area under the cumulative standardized
normal distribution from $-\infty$ to Z

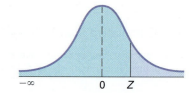

				Cumulative Probabilities					
Z	0.00	0.01	0.02	0.03	0.04	0.05	0.06	0.07	0.08	0.09
0.0	0.5000	0.5040	0.5080	0.5120	0.5160	0.5199	0.5239	0.5279	0.5319	0.5359
0.1	0.5398	0.5438	0.5478	0.5517	0.5557	0.5596	0.5636	0.5675	0.5714	0.5753
0.2	0.5793	0.5832	0.5871	0.5910	0.5948	0.5987	0.6026	0.6064	0.6103	0.6141
0.3	0.6179	0.6217	0.6255	0.6293	0.6331	0.6368	0.6406	0.6443	0.6480	0.6517
0.4	0.6554	0.6591	0.6628	0.6664	0.6700	0.6736	0.6772	0.6808	0.6844	0.6879
0.5	0.6915	0.6950	0.6985	0.7019	0.7054	0.7088	0.7123	0.7157	0.7190	0.7224
0.6	0.7257	0.7291	0.7324	0.7357	0.7389	0.7422	0.7454	0.7486	0.7518	0.7549
0.7	0.7580	0.7612	0.7642	0.7673	0.7704	0.7734	0.7764	0.7794	0.7823	0.7852
0.8	0.7881	0.7910	0.7939	0.7967	0.7995	0.8023	0.8051	0.8078	0.8106	0.8133
0.9	0.8159	0.8186	0.8212	0.8238	0.8264	0.8289	0.8315	0.8340	0.8365	0.8389
1.0	0.8413	0.8438	0.8461	0.8485	0.8508	0.8531	0.8554	0.8577	0.8599	0.8621
1.1	0.8643	0.8665	0.8686	0.8708	0.8729	0.8749	0.8770	0.8790	0.8810	0.8830
1.2	0.8849	0.8869	0.8888	0.8907	0.8925	0.8944	0.8962	0.8980	0.8997	0.9015
1.3	0.9032	0.9049	0.9066	0.9082	0.9099	0.9115	0.9131	0.9147	0.9162	0.9177
1.4	0.9192	0.9207	0.9222	0.9236	0.9251	0.9265	0.9279	0.9292	0.9306	0.9319
1.5	0.9332	0.9345	0.9357	0.9370	0.9382	0.9394	0.9406	0.9418	0.9429	0.9441
1.6	0.9452	0.9463	0.9474	0.9484	0.9495	0.9505	0.9515	0.9525	0.9535	0.9545
1.7	0.9554	0.9564	0.9573	0.9582	0.9591	0.9599	0.9608	0.9616	0.9625	0.9633
1.8	0.9641	0.9649	0.9656	0.9664	0.9671	0.9678	0.9686	0.9693	0.9699	0.9706
1.9	0.9713	0.9719	0.9726	0.9732	0.9738	0.9744	0.9750	0.9756	0.9761	0.9767
2.0	0.9772	0.9778	0.9783	0.9788	0.9793	0.9798	0.9803	0.9808	0.9812	0.9817
2.1	0.9821	0.9826	0.9830	0.9834	0.9838	0.9842	0.9846	0.9850	0.9854	0.9857
2.2	0.9861	0.9864	0.9868	0.9871	0.9875	0.9878	0.9881	0.9884	0.9887	0.9890
2.3	0.9893	0.9896	0.9898	0.9901	0.9904	0.9906	0.9909	0.9911	0.9913	0.9916
2.4	0.9918	0.9920	0.9922	0.9925	0.9927	0.9929	0.9931	0.9932	0.9934	0.9936
2.5	0.9938	0.9940	0.9941	0.9943	0.9945	0.9946	0.9948	0.9949	0.9951	0.9952
2.6	0.9953	0.9955	0.9956	0.9957	0.9959	0.9960	0.9961	0.9962	0.9963	0.9964
2.7	0.9965	0.9966	0.9967	0.9968	0.9969	0.9970	0.9971	0.9972	0.9973	0.9974
2.8	0.9974	0.9975	0.9976	0.9977	0.9977	0.9978	0.9979	0.9979	0.9980	0.9981
2.9	0.9981	0.9982	0.9982	0.9983	0.9984	0.9984	0.9985	0.9985	0.9986	0.9986
3.0	0.99865	0.99869	0.99874	0.99878	0.99882	0.99886	0.99889	0.99893	0.99897	0.99900
3.1	0.99903	0.99906	0.99910	0.99913	0.99916	0.99918	0.99921	0.99924	0.99926	0.99929
3.2	0.99931	0.99934	0.99936	0.99938	0.99940	0.99942	0.99944	0.99946	0.99948	0.99950
3.3	0.99952	0.99953	0.99955	0.99957	0.99958	0.99960	0.99961	0.99962	0.99964	0.99965
3.4	0.99966	0.99968	0.99969	0.99970	0.99971	0.99972	0.99973	0.99974	0.99975	0.99976
3.5	0.99977	0.99978	0.99978	0.99979	0.99980	0.99981	0.99981	0.99982	0.99983	0.99983
3.6	0.99984	0.99985	0.99985	0.99986	0.99986	0.99987	0.99987	0.99988	0.99988	0.99989
3.7	0.99989	0.99990	0.99990	0.99990	0.99991	0.99991	0.99992	0.99992	0.99992	0.99992
3.8	0.99993	0.99993	0.99993	0.99994	0.99994	0.99994	0.99994	0.99995	0.99995	0.99995
3.9	0.99995	0.99995	0.99996	0.99996	0.99996	0.99996	0.99996	0.99996	0.99997	0.99997
4.0	0.999968329									
4.5	0.999996602									
5.0	0.999999713									
5.5	0.999999981									
6.0	0.999999999									

TABLE E.3

Critical Values of *t*

For a particular number of degrees of freedom, entry represents the critical value of *t* corresponding to the cumulative probability $(1 - \alpha)$ and a specified upper-tail area (α).

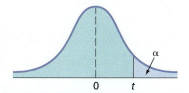

Degrees of Freedom	Cumulative Probabilities					
	0.75	0.90	0.95	0.975	0.99	0.995
	Upper-Tail Areas					
	0.25	0.10	0.05	0.025	0.01	0.005
1	1.0000	3.0777	6.3138	12.7062	31.8207	63.6574
2	0.8165	1.8856	2.9200	4.3027	6.9646	9.9248
3	0.7649	1.6377	2.3534	3.1824	4.5407	5.8409
4	0.7407	1.5332	2.1318	2.7764	3.7469	4.6041
5	0.7267	1.4759	2.0150	2.5706	3.3649	4.0322
6	0.7176	1.4398	1.9432	2.4469	3.1427	3.7074
7	0.7111	1.4149	1.8946	2.3646	2.9980	3.4995
8	0.7064	1.3968	1.8595	2.3060	2.8965	3.3554
9	0.7027	1.3830	1.8331	2.2622	2.8214	3.2498
10	0.6998	1.3722	1.8125	2.2281	2.7638	3.1693
11	0.6974	1.3634	1.7959	2.2010	2.7181	3.1058
12	0.6955	1.3562	1.7823	2.1788	2.6810	3.0545
13	0.6938	1.3502	1.7709	2.1604	2.6503	3.0123
14	0.6924	1.3450	1.7613	2.1448	2.6245	2.9768
15	0.6912	1.3406	1.7531	2.1315	2.6025	2.9467
16	0.6901	1.3368	1.7459	2.1199	2.5835	2.9208
17	0.6892	1.3334	1.7396	2.1098	2.5669	2.8982
18	0.6884	1.3304	1.7341	2.1009	2.5524	2.8784
19	0.6876	1.3277	1.7291	2.0930	2.5395	2.8609
20	0.6870	1.3253	1.7247	2.0860	2.5280	2.8453
21	0.6864	1.3232	1.7207	2.0796	2.5177	2.8314
22	0.6858	1.3212	1.7171	2.0739	2.5083	2.8188
23	0.6853	1.3195	1.7139	2.0687	2.4999	2.8073
24	0.6848	1.3178	1.7109	2.0639	2.4922	2.7969
25	0.6844	1.3163	1.7081	2.0595	2.4851	2.7874
26	0.6840	1.3150	1.7056	2.0555	2.4786	2.7787
27	0.6837	1.3137	1.7033	2.0518	2.4727	2.7707
28	0.6834	1.3125	1.7011	2.0484	2.4671	2.7633
29	0.6830	1.3114	1.6991	2.0452	2.4620	2.7564
30	0.6828	1.3104	1.6973	2.0423	2.4573	2.7500
31	0.6825	1.3095	1.6955	2.0395	2.4528	2.7440
32	0.6822	1.3086	1.6939	2.0369	2.4487	2.7385
33	0.6820	1.3077	1.6924	2.0345	2.4448	2.7333
34	0.6818	1.3070	1.6909	2.0322	2.4411	2.7284
35	0.6816	1.3062	1.6896	2.0301	2.4377	2.7238
36	0.6814	1.3055	1.6883	2.0281	2.4345	2.7195
37	0.6812	1.3049	1.6871	2.0262	2.4314	2.7154
38	0.6810	1.3042	1.6860	2.0244	2.4286	2.7116
39	0.6808	1.3036	1.6849	2.0227	2.4258	2.7079
40	0.6807	1.3031	1.6839	2.0211	2.4233	2.7045
41	0.6805	1.3025	1.6829	2.0195	2.4208	2.7012
42	0.6804	1.3020	1.6820	2.0181	2.4185	2.6981
43	0.6802	1.3016	1.6811	2.0167	2.4163	2.6951
44	0.6801	1.3011	1.6802	2.0154	2.4141	2.6923
45	0.6800	1.3006	1.6794	2.0141	2.4121	2.6896
46	0.6799	1.3002	1.6787	2.0129	2.4102	2.6870
47	0.6797	1.2998	1.6779	2.0117	2.4083	2.6846
48	0.6796	1.2994	1.6772	2.0106	2.4066	2.6822
49	0.6795	1.2991	1.6766	2.0096	2.4049	2.6800
50	0.6794	1.2987	1.6759	2.0086	2.4033	2.6778

TABLE E.3

Critical Values of t (*continued*)

For a particular number of degrees of freedom, entry represents the critical value of t corresponding to the cumulative probability $(1 - \alpha)$ and a specified upper-tail area (α).

Degrees of Freedom	Cumulative Probabilities					
	0.75	0.90	0.95	0.975	0.99	0.995
	Upper-Tail Areas					
	0.25	0.10	0.05	0.025	0.01	0.005
51	0.6793	1.2984	1.6753	2.0076	2.4017	2.6757
52	0.6792	1.2980	1.6747	2.0066	2.4002	2.6737
53	0.6791	1.2977	1.6741	2.0057	2.3988	2.6718
54	0.6791	1.2974	1.6736	2.0049	2.3974	2.6700
55	0.6790	1.2971	1.6730	2.0040	2.3961	2.6682
56	0.6789	1.2969	1.6725	2.0032	2.3948	2.6665
57	0.6788	1.2966	1.6720	2.0025	2.3936	2.6649
58	0.6787	1.2963	1.6716	2.0017	2.3924	2.6633
59	0.6787	1.2961	1.6711	2.0010	2.3912	2.6618
60	0.6786	1.2958	1.6706	2.0003	2.3901	2.6603
61	0.6785	1.2956	1.6702	1.9996	2.3890	2.6589
62	0.6785	1.2954	1.6698	1.9990	2.3880	2.6575
63	0.6784	1.2951	1.6694	1.9983	2.3870	2.6561
64	0.6783	1.2949	1.6690	1.9977	2.3860	2.6549
65	0.6783	1.2947	1.6686	1.9971	2.3851	2.6536
66	0.6782	1.2945	1.6683	1.9966	2.3842	2.6524
67	0.6782	1.2943	1.6679	1.9960	2.3833	2.6512
68	0.6781	1.2941	1.6676	1.9955	2.3824	2.6501
69	0.6781	1.2939	1.6672	1.9949	2.3816	2.6490
70	0.6780	1.2938	1.6669	1.9944	2.3808	2.6479
71	0.6780	1.2936	1.6666	1.9939	2.3800	2.6469
72	0.6779	1.2934	1.6663	1.9935	2.3793	2.6459
73	0.6779	1.2933	1.6660	1.9930	2.3785	2.6449
74	0.6778	1.2931	1.6657	1.9925	2.3778	2.6439
75	0.6778	1.2929	1.6654	1.9921	2.3771	2.6430
76	0.6777	1.2928	1.6652	1.9917	2.3764	2.6421
77	0.6777	1.2926	1.6649	1.9913	2.3758	2.6412
78	0.6776	1.2925	1.6646	1.9908	2.3751	2.6403
79	0.6776	1.2924	1.6644	1.9905	2.3745	2.6395
80	0.6776	1.2922	1.6641	1.9901	2.3739	2.6387
81	0.6775	1.2921	1.6639	1.9897	2.3733	2.6379
82	0.6775	1.2920	1.6636	1.9893	2.3727	2.6371
83	0.6775	1.2918	1.6634	1.9890	2.3721	2.6364
84	0.6774	1.2917	1.6632	1.9886	2.3716	2.6356
85	0.6774	1.2916	1.6630	1.9883	2.3710	2.6349
86	0.6774	1.2915	1.6628	1.9879	2.3705	2.6342
87	0.6773	1.2914	1.6626	1.9876	2.3700	2.6335
88	0.6773	1.2912	1.6624	1.9873	2.3695	2.6329
89	0.6773	1.2911	1.6622	1.9870	2.3690	2.6322
90	0.6772	1.2910	1.6620	1.9867	2.3685	2.6316
91	0.6772	1.2909	1.6618	1.9864	2.3680	2.6309
92	0.6772	1.2908	1.6616	1.9861	2.3676	2.6303
93	0.6771	1.2907	1.6614	1.9858	2.3671	2.6297
94	0.6771	1.2906	1.6612	1.9855	2.3667	2.6291
95	0.6771	1.2905	1.6611	1.9853	2.3662	2.6286
96	0.6771	1.2904	1.6609	1.9850	2.3658	2.6280
97	0.6770	1.2903	1.6607	1.9847	2.3654	2.6275
98	0.6770	1.2902	1.6606	1.9845	2.3650	2.6269
99	0.6770	1.2902	1.6604	1.9842	2.3646	2.6264
100	0.6770	1.2901	1.6602	1.9840	2.3642	2.6259
110	0.6767	1.2893	1.6588	1.9818	2.3607	2.6213
120	0.6765	1.2886	1.6577	1.9799	2.3578	2.6174
∞	0.6745	1.2816	1.6449	1.9600	2.3263	2.5758

TABLE E.4

Critical Values of χ^2

For a particular number of degrees of freedom, entry represents the critical value of χ^2
corresponding to the cumulative probability $(1 - \alpha)$ and a specified upper-tail area (α).

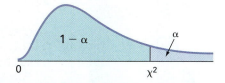

Degrees of Freedom	**Cumulative Probabilities**											
	0.005	0.01	0.025	0.05	0.10	0.25	0.75	0.90	0.95	0.975	0.99	0.995
	Upper-Tail Areas (α)											
	0.995	0.99	0.975	0.95	0.90	0.75	0.25	0.10	0.05	0.025	0.01	0.005
1			0.001	0.004	0.016	0.102	1.323	2.706	3.841	5.024	6.635	7.879
2	0.010	0.020	0.051	0.103	0.211	0.575	2.773	4.605	5.991	7.378	9.210	10.597
3	0.072	0.115	0.216	0.352	0.584	1.213	4.108	6.251	7.815	9.348	11.345	12.838
4	0.207	0.297	0.484	0.711	1.064	1.923	5.385	7.779	9.488	11.143	13.277	14.860
5	0.412	0.554	0.831	1.145	1.610	2.675	6.626	9.236	11.071	12.833	15.086	16.750
6	0.676	0.872	1.237	1.635	2.204	3.455	7.841	10.645	12.592	14.449	16.812	18.548
7	0.989	1.239	1.690	2.167	2.833	4.255	9.037	12.017	14.067	16.013	18.475	20.278
8	1.344	1.646	2.180	2.733	3.490	5.071	10.219	13.362	15.507	17.535	20.090	21.955
9	1.735	2.088	2.700	3.325	4.168	5.899	11.389	14.684	16.919	19.023	21.666	23.589
10	2.156	2.558	3.247	3.940	4.865	6.737	12.549	15.987	18.307	20.483	23.209	25.188
11	2.603	3.053	3.816	4.575	5.578	7.584	13.701	17.275	19.675	21.920	24.725	26.757
12	3.074	3.571	4.404	5.226	6.304	8.438	14.845	18.549	21.026	23.337	26.217	28.299
13	3.565	4.107	5.009	5.892	7.042	9.299	15.984	19.812	22.362	24.736	27.688	29.819
14	4.075	4.660	5.629	6.571	7.790	10.165	17.117	21.064	23.685	26.119	29.141	31.319
15	4.601	5.229	6.262	7.261	8.547	11.037	18.245	22.307	24.996	27.488	30.578	32.801
16	5.142	5.812	6.908	7.962	9.312	11.912	19.369	23.542	26.296	28.845	32.000	34.267
17	5.697	6.408	7.564	8.672	10.085	12.792	20.489	24.769	27.587	30.191	33.409	35.718
18	6.265	7.015	8.231	9.390	10.865	13.675	21.605	25.989	28.869	31.526	34.805	37.156
19	6.844	7.633	8.907	10.117	11.651	14.562	22.718	27.204	30.144	32.852	36.191	38.582
20	7.434	8.260	9.591	10.851	12.443	15.452	23.828	28.412	31.410	34.170	37.566	39.997
21	8.034	8.897	10.283	11.591	13.240	16.344	24.935	29.615	32.671	35.479	38.932	41.401
22	8.643	9.542	10.982	12.338	14.042	17.240	26.039	30.813	33.924	36.781	40.289	42.796
23	9.260	10.196	11.689	13.091	14.848	18.137	27.141	32.007	35.172	38.076	41.638	44.181
24	9.886	10.856	12.401	13.848	15.659	19.037	28.241	33.196	36.415	39.364	42.980	45.559
25	10.520	11.524	13.120	14.611	16.473	19.939	29.339	34.382	37.652	40.646	44.314	46.928
26	11.160	12.198	13.844	15.379	17.292	20.843	30.435	35.563	38.885	41.923	45.642	48.290
27	11.808	12.879	14.573	16.151	18.114	21.749	31.528	36.741	40.113	43.194	46.963	49.645
28	12.461	13.565	15.308	16.928	18.939	22.657	32.620	37.916	41.337	44.461	48.278	50.993
29	13.121	14.257	16.047	17.708	19.768	23.567	33.711	39.087	42.557	45.722	49.588	52.336
30	13.787	14.954	16.791	18.493	20.599	24.478	34.800	40.256	43.773	46.979	50.892	53.672

For larger values of degrees of freedom (df) the expression $Z = \sqrt{2\chi^2} - \sqrt{2(df) - 1}$ may be used and the resulting upper-tail area can be found
from the cumulative standardized normal distribution (Table E.2).

TABLE E.5

Critical Values of F

For a particular combination of numerator and denominator degrees of freedom, entry represents the critical values of F corresponding to the cumulative probability $(1 - \alpha)$ and a specified upper-tail area (α).

Cumulative Probabilities = 0.95

Upper-Tail Areas = 0.05

Numerator, df_1

Denominator, df_2	1	2	3	4	5	6	7	8	9	10	12	15	20	24	30	40	60	120	∞
1	161.40	199.50	215.70	224.60	230.20	234.00	236.80	238.90	240.50	241.90	243.90	245.90	248.00	249.10	250.10	251.10	252.20	253.30	254.30
2	18.51	19.00	19.16	19.25	19.30	19.33	19.35	19.37	19.38	19.40	19.41	19.43	19.45	19.45	19.46	19.47	19.48	19.49	19.50
3	10.13	9.55	9.28	9.12	9.01	8.94	8.89	8.85	8.81	8.79	8.74	8.70	8.66	8.64	8.62	8.59	8.57	8.55	8.53
4	7.71	6.94	6.59	6.39	6.26	6.16	6.09	6.04	6.00	5.96	5.91	5.86	5.80	5.77	5.75	5.72	5.69	5.66	5.63
5	6.61	5.79	5.41	5.19	5.05	4.95	4.88	4.82	4.77	4.74	4.68	4.62	4.56	4.53	4.50	4.46	4.43	4.40	4.36
6	5.99	5.14	4.76	4.53	4.39	4.28	4.21	4.15	4.10	4.06	4.00	3.94	3.87	3.84	3.81	3.77	3.74	3.70	3.67
7	5.59	4.74	4.35	4.12	3.97	3.87	3.79	3.73	3.68	3.64	3.57	3.51	3.44	3.41	3.38	3.34	3.30	3.27	3.23
8	5.32	4.46	4.07	3.84	3.69	3.58	3.50	3.44	3.39	3.35	3.28	3.22	3.15	3.12	3.08	3.04	3.01	2.97	2.93
9	5.12	4.26	3.86	3.63	3.48	3.37	3.29	3.23	3.18	3.14	3.07	3.01	2.94	2.90	2.86	2.83	2.79	2.75	2.71
10	4.96	4.10	3.71	3.48	3.33	3.22	3.14	3.07	3.02	2.98	2.91	2.85	2.77	2.74	2.70	2.66	2.62	2.58	2.54
11	4.84	3.98	3.59	3.36	3.20	3.09	3.01	2.95	2.90	2.85	2.79	2.72	2.65	2.61	2.57	2.53	2.49	2.45	2.40
12	4.75	3.89	3.49	3.26	3.11	3.00	2.91	2.85	2.80	2.75	2.69	2.62	2.54	2.51	2.47	2.43	2.38	2.34	2.30
13	4.67	3.81	3.41	3.18	3.03	2.92	2.83	2.77	2.71	2.67	2.60	2.53	2.46	2.42	2.38	2.34	2.30	2.25	2.21
14	4.60	3.74	3.34	3.11	2.96	2.85	2.76	2.70	2.65	2.60	2.53	2.46	2.39	2.35	2.31	2.27	2.22	2.18	2.13
15	4.54	3.68	3.29	3.06	2.90	2.79	2.71	2.64	2.59	2.54	2.48	2.40	2.33	2.29	2.25	2.20	2.16	2.11	2.07
16	4.49	3.63	3.24	3.01	2.85	2.74	2.66	2.59	2.54	2.49	2.42	2.35	2.28	2.24	2.19	2.15	2.11	2.06	2.01
17	4.45	3.59	3.20	2.96	2.81	2.70	2.61	2.55	2.49	2.45	2.38	2.31	2.23	2.19	2.15	2.10	2.06	2.01	1.96
18	4.41	3.55	3.16	2.93	2.77	2.66	2.58	2.51	2.46	2.41	2.34	2.27	2.19	2.15	2.11	2.06	2.02	1.97	1.92
19	4.38	3.52	3.13	2.90	2.74	2.63	2.54	2.48	2.42	2.38	2.31	2.23	2.16	2.11	2.07	2.03	1.98	1.93	1.88
20	4.35	3.49	3.10	2.87	2.71	2.60	2.51	2.45	2.39	2.35	2.28	2.20	2.12	2.08	2.04	1.99	1.95	1.90	1.84
21	4.32	3.47	3.07	2.84	2.68	2.57	2.49	2.42	2.37	2.32	2.25	2.18	2.10	2.05	2.01	1.96	1.92	1.87	1.81
22	4.30	3.44	3.05	2.82	2.66	2.55	2.46	2.40	2.34	2.30	2.23	2.15	2.07	2.03	1.98	1.91	1.89	1.84	1.78
23	4.28	3.42	3.03	2.80	2.64	2.53	2.44	2.37	2.32	2.27	2.20	2.13	2.05	2.01	1.96	1.91	1.86	1.81	1.76
24	4.26	3.40	3.01	2.78	2.62	2.51	2.42	2.36	2.30	2.25	2.18	2.11	2.03	1.98	1.94	1.89	1.84	1.79	1.73
25	4.24	3.39	2.99	2.76	2.60	2.49	2.40	2.34	2.28	2.24	2.16	2.09	2.01	1.96	1.92	1.87	1.82	1.77	1.71
26	4.23	3.37	2.98	2.74	2.59	2.47	2.39	2.32	2.27	2.22	2.15	2.07	1.99	1.95	1.90	1.85	1.80	1.75	1.69
27	4.21	3.35	2.96	2.73	2.57	2.46	2.37	2.31	2.25	2.20	2.13	2.06	1.97	1.93	1.88	1.84	1.79	1.73	1.67
28	4.20	3.34	2.95	2.71	2.56	2.45	2.36	2.29	2.24	2.19	2.12	2.04	1.96	1.91	1.87	1.82	1.77	1.71	1.65
29	4.18	3.33	2.93	2.70	2.55	2.43	2.35	2.28	2.22	2.18	2.10	2.03	1.94	1.90	1.85	1.81	1.75	1.70	1.64
30	4.17	3.32	2.92	2.69	2.53	2.42	2.33	2.27	2.21	2.16	2.09	2.01	1.93	1.89	1.84	1.79	1.74	1.68	1.62
40	4.08	3.23	2.84	2.61	2.45	2.34	2.25	2.18	2.12	2.08	2.00	1.92	1.84	1.79	1.74	1.69	1.64	1.58	1.51
60	4.00	3.15	2.76	2.53	2.37	2.25	2.17	2.10	2.04	1.99	1.92	1.84	1.75	1.70	1.65	1.59	1.53	1.47	1.39
120	3.92	3.07	2.68	2.45	2.29	2.17	2.09	2.02	1.96	1.91	1.83	1.75	1.66	1.61	1.55	1.50	1.43	1.35	1.25
∞	3.84	3.00	2.60	2.37	2.21	2.10	2.01	1.94	1.88	1.83	1.75	1.67	1.57	1.52	1.46	1.39	1.32	1.22	1.00

(continued)

Critical Values of F (continued)

For a particular combination of numerator and denominator degrees of freedom, entry represents the critical values of F corresponding to the cumulative probability $(1 - \alpha)$ and a specified upper-tail area (α).

$\alpha = 0.025$

Cumulative Probabilities = 0.975

Upper-Tail Areas = 0.025

Denominator, df_2	Numerator, df_1																		
	1	2	3	4	5	6	7	8	9	10	12	15	20	24	30	40	60	120	∞
1	647.80	799.50	864.20	899.60	921.80	937.10	948.20	956.70	963.30	968.60	976.70	984.90	993.10	997.20	1,001.00	1,006.00	1,010.00	1,014.00	1,018.00
2	38.51	39.00	39.17	39.25	39.30	39.33	39.36	39.39	39.39	39.40	39.41	39.43	39.45	39.46	39.46	39.47	39.48	39.49	39.50
3	17.44	16.04	15.44	15.10	14.88	14.73	14.62	14.54	14.47	14.42	14.34	14.25	14.17	14.12	14.08	14.04	13.99	13.95	13.90
4	12.22	10.65	9.98	9.60	9.36	9.20	9.07	8.98	8.90	8.84	8.75	8.66	8.56	8.51	8.46	8.41	8.36	8.31	8.26
5	10.01	8.43	7.76	7.39	7.15	6.98	6.85	6.76	6.68	6.62	6.52	6.43	6.33	6.28	6.23	6.18	6.12	6.07	6.02
6	8.81	7.26	6.60	6.23	5.99	5.82	5.70	5.60	5.52	5.46	5.37	5.27	5.17	5.12	5.07	5.01	4.96	4.90	4.85
7	8.07	6.54	5.89	5.52	5.29	5.12	4.99	4.90	4.82	4.76	4.67	4.57	4.47	4.42	4.36	4.31	4.25	4.20	4.14
8	7.57	6.06	5.42	5.05	4.82	4.65	4.53	4.43	4.36	4.30	4.20	4.10	4.00	3.95	3.89	3.84	3.78	3.73	3.67
9	7.21	5.71	5.08	4.72	4.48	4.32	4.20	4.10	4.03	3.96	3.87	3.77	3.67	3.61	3.56	3.51	3.45	3.39	3.33
10	6.94	5.46	4.83	4.47	4.24	4.07	3.95	3.85	3.78	3.72	3.62	3.52	3.42	3.37	3.31	3.26	3.20	3.14	3.08
11	6.72	5.26	4.63	4.28	4.04	3.88	3.76	3.66	3.59	3.53	3.43	3.33	3.23	3.17	3.12	3.06	3.00	2.94	2.88
12	6.55	5.10	4.47	4.12	3.89	3.73	3.61	3.51	3.44	3.37	3.28	3.18	3.07	3.02	2.96	2.91	2.85	2.79	2.72
13	6.41	4.97	4.35	4.00	3.77	3.60	3.48	3.39	3.31	3.25	3.15	3.05	2.95	2.89	2.84	2.78	2.72	2.66	2.60
14	6.30	4.86	4.24	3.89	3.66	3.50	3.38	3.29	3.21	3.15	3.05	2.95	2.84	2.79	2.73	2.67	2.61	2.55	2.49
15	6.20	4.77	4.15	3.80	3.58	3.41	3.29	3.20	3.12	3.06	2.96	2.86	2.76	2.70	2.64	2.59	2.52	2.46	2.40
16	6.12	4.69	4.08	3.73	3.50	3.34	3.22	3.12	3.05	2.99	2.89	2.79	2.68	2.63	2.57	2.51	2.45	2.38	2.32
17	6.04	4.62	4.01	3.66	3.44	3.28	3.16	3.06	2.98	2.92	2.82	2.72	2.62	2.56	2.50	2.44	2.38	2.32	2.25
18	5.98	4.56	3.95	3.61	3.38	3.22	3.10	3.01	2.93	2.87	2.77	2.67	2.56	2.50	2.44	2.38	2.32	2.26	2.19
19	5.92	4.51	3.90	3.56	3.33	3.17	3.05	2.96	2.88	2.82	2.72	2.62	2.51	2.45	2.39	2.33	2.27	2.20	2.13
20	5.87	4.46	3.86	3.51	3.29	3.13	3.01	2.91	2.84	2.77	2.68	2.57	2.46	2.41	2.35	2.29	2.22	2.16	2.09
21	5.83	4.42	3.82	3.48	3.25	3.09	2.97	2.87	2.80	2.73	2.64	2.53	2.42	2.37	2.31	2.25	2.18	2.11	2.04
22	5.79	4.38	3.78	3.44	3.22	3.05	2.93	2.84	2.76	2.70	2.60	2.50	2.39	2.33	2.27	2.21	2.14	2.08	2.00
23	5.75	4.35	3.75	3.41	3.18	3.02	2.90	2.81	2.73	2.67	2.57	2.47	2.36	2.30	2.24	2.18	2.11	2.04	1.97
24	5.72	4.32	3.72	3.38	3.15	2.99	2.87	2.78	2.70	2.64	2.54	2.44	2.33	2.27	2.21	2.15	2.08	2.01	1.94
25	5.69	4.29	3.69	3.35	3.13	2.97	2.85	2.75	2.68	2.61	2.51	2.41	2.30	2.24	2.18	2.12	2.05	1.98	1.91
26	5.66	4.27	3.67	3.33	3.10	2.94	2.82	2.73	2.65	2.59	2.49	2.39	2.28	2.22	2.16	2.09	2.03	1.95	1.88
27	5.63	4.24	3.65	3.31	3.08	2.92	2.80	2.71	2.63	2.57	2.47	2.36	2.25	2.19	2.13	2.07	2.00	1.93	1.85
28	5.61	4.22	3.63	3.29	3.06	2.90	2.78	2.69	2.61	2.55	2.45	2.34	2.23	2.17	2.11	2.05	1.98	1.91	1.83
29	5.59	4.20	3.61	3.27	3.04	2.88	2.76	2.67	2.59	2.53	2.43	2.32	2.21	2.15	2.09	2.03	1.96	1.89	1.81
30	5.57	4.18	3.59	3.25	3.03	2.87	2.75	2.65	2.57	2.51	2.41	2.31	2.20	2.14	2.07	2.01	1.94	1.87	1.79
40	5.42	4.05	3.46	3.13	2.90	2.74	2.62	2.53	2.45	2.39	2.29	2.18	2.07	2.01	1.94	1.88	1.80	1.72	1.64
60	5.29	3.93	3.34	3.01	2.79	2.63	2.51	2.41	2.33	2.27	2.17	2.06	1.94	1.88	1.82	1.74	1.67	1.58	1.48
120	5.15	3.80	3.23	2.89	2.67	2.52	2.39	2.30	2.22	2.16	2.05	1.94	1.82	1.76	1.69	1.61	1.53	1.43	1.31
∞	5.02	3.69	3.12	2.79	2.57	2.41	2.29	2.19	2.11	2.05	1.94	1.83	1.71	1.64	1.57	1.48	1.39	1.27	1.00

TABLE E.5

Critical Values of F (continued)

For a particular combination of numerator and denominator degrees of freedom, entry represents the critical values of F corresponding to the cumulative probability $(1 - \alpha)$ and a specified upper-tail area (α).

$\alpha = 0.01$

Cumulative Probabilities = 0.99

Upper-Tail Areas = 0.01

Denominator, df_2	Numerator, df_1																		
	1	2	3	4	5	6	7	8	9	10	12	15	20	24	30	40	60	120	∞
1	4,052.00	4,999.50	5,403.00	5,625.00	5,764.00	5,859.00	5,928.00	5,982.00	6,022.00	6,056.00	6,106.00	6,157.00	6,209.00	6,235.00	6,261.00	6,287.00	6,313.00	6,339.00	6,366.00
2	98.50	99.00	99.17	99.25	99.30	99.33	99.36	99.37	99.39	99.40	99.42	99.43	44.45	99.46	99.47	99.47	99.48	99.49	99.50
3	34.12	30.82	29.46	28.71	28.24	27.91	27.67	27.49	27.35	27.23	27.05	26.87	26.69	26.60	26.50	26.41	26.32	26.22	26.13
4	21.20	18.00	16.69	15.98	15.52	15.21	14.98	14.80	14.66	14.55	14.37	14.20	14.02	13.93	13.84	13.75	13.65	13.56	13.46
5	16.26	13.27	12.06	11.39	10.97	10.67	10.46	10.29	10.16	10.05	9.89	9.72	9.55	9.47	9.38	9.29	9.20	9.11	9.02
6	13.75	10.92	9.78	9.15	8.75	8.47	8.26	8.10	7.98	7.87	7.72	7.56	7.40	7.31	7.23	7.14	7.06	6.97	6.88
7	12.25	9.55	8.45	7.85	7.46	7.19	6.99	6.84	6.72	6.62	6.47	6.31	6.16	6.07	5.99	5.91	5.82	5.74	5.65
8	11.26	8.65	7.59	7.01	6.63	6.37	6.18	6.03	5.91	5.81	5.67	5.52	5.36	5.28	5.20	5.12	5.03	4.95	4.86
9	10.56	8.02	6.99	6.42	6.06	5.80	5.61	5.47	5.35	5.26	5.11	4.96	4.81	4.73	4.65	4.57	4.48	4.40	4.31
10	10.04	7.56	6.55	5.99	5.64	5.39	5.20	5.06	4.94	4.85	4.71	4.56	4.41	4.33	4.25	4.17	4.08	4.00	3.91
11	9.65	7.21	6.22	5.67	5.32	5.07	4.89	4.74	4.63	4.54	4.40	4.25	4.10	4.02	3.94	3.86	3.78	3.69	3.60
12	9.33	6.93	5.95	5.41	5.06	4.82	4.64	4.50	4.39	4.30	4.16	4.01	3.86	3.78	3.70	3.62	3.54	3.45	3.36
13	9.07	6.70	5.74	5.21	4.86	4.62	4.44	4.30	4.19	4.10	3.96	3.82	3.66	3.59	3.51	3.43	3.34	3.25	3.17
14	8.86	6.51	5.56	5.04	4.69	4.46	4.28	4.14	4.03	3.94	3.80	3.66	3.51	3.43	3.35	3.27	3.18	3.09	3.00
15	8.68	6.36	5.42	4.89	4.56	4.32	4.14	4.00	3.89	3.80	3.67	3.52	3.37	3.29	3.21	3.13	3.05	2.96	2.87
16	8.53	6.23	5.29	4.77	4.44	4.20	4.03	3.89	3.78	3.69	3.55	3.41	3.26	3.18	3.10	3.02	2.93	2.81	2.75
17	8.40	6.11	5.18	4.67	4.34	4.10	3.93	3.79	3.68	3.59	3.46	3.31	3.16	3.08	3.00	2.92	2.83	2.75	2.65
18	8.29	6.01	5.09	4.58	4.25	4.01	3.84	3.71	3.60	3.51	3.37	3.23	3.08	3.00	2.92	2.84	2.75	2.66	2.57
19	8.18	5.93	5.01	4.50	4.17	3.94	3.77	3.63	3.52	3.43	3.30	3.15	3.00	2.92	2.84	2.76	2.67	2.58	2.49
20	8.10	5.85	4.94	4.43	4.10	3.87	3.70	3.56	3.46	3.37	3.23	3.09	2.94	2.86	2.78	2.69	2.61	2.52	2.42
21	8.02	5.78	4.87	4.37	4.04	3.81	3.64	3.51	3.40	3.31	3.17	3.03	2.88	2.80	2.72	2.64	2.55	2.46	2.36
22	7.95	5.72	4.82	4.31	3.99	3.76	3.59	3.45	3.35	3.26	3.12	2.98	2.83	2.75	2.67	2.58	2.50	2.40	2.31
23	7.88	5.66	4.76	4.26	3.94	3.71	3.54	3.41	3.30	3.21	3.07	2.93	2.78	2.70	2.62	2.54	2.45	2.35	2.26
24	7.82	5.61	4.72	4.22	3.90	3.67	3.50	3.36	3.26	3.17	3.03	2.89	2.74	2.66	2.58	2.49	2.40	2.31	2.21
25	7.77	5.57	4.68	4.18	3.85	3.63	3.46	3.32	3.22	3.13	2.99	2.85	2.70	2.62	2.54	2.45	2.36	2.27	2.17
26	7.72	5.53	4.64	4.14	3.82	3.59	3.42	3.29	3.18	3.09	2.96	2.81	2.66	2.58	2.50	2.42	2.33	2.23	2.13
27	7.68	5.49	4.60	4.11	3.78	3.56	3.39	3.26	3.15	3.06	2.93	2.78	2.63	2.55	2.47	2.38	2.29	2.20	2.10
28	7.64	5.45	4.57	4.07	3.75	3.53	3.36	3.23	3.12	3.03	2.90	2.75	2.60	2.52	2.44	2.35	2.26	2.17	2.06
29	7.60	5.42	4.54	4.04	3.73	3.50	3.33	3.20	3.09	3.00	2.87	2.73	2.57	2.49	2.41	2.33	2.23	2.14	2.03
30	7.56	5.39	4.51	4.02	3.70	3.47	3.30	3.17	3.07	2.98	2.84	2.70	2.55	2.47	2.39	2.30	2.21	2.11	2.01
40	7.31	5.18	4.31	3.83	3.51	3.29	3.12	2.99	2.89	2.80	2.66	2.52	2.37	2.29	2.20	2.11	2.02	1.92	1.80
60	7.08	4.98	4.13	3.65	3.34	3.12	2.95	2.82	2.72	2.63	2.50	2.35	2.20	2.12	2.03	1.94	1.84	1.73	1.60
120	6.85	4.79	3.95	3.48	3.17	2.96	2.79	2.66	2.56	2.47	2.34	2.19	2.03	1.95	1.86	1.76	1.66	1.53	1.38
∞	6.63	4.61	3.78	3.32	3.02	2.80	2.64	2.51	2.41	2.32	2.18	2.04	1.88	1.79	1.70	1.59	1.47	1.32	1.00

(continued)

TABLE E.5

Critical Values of F (continued)

For a particular combination of numerator and denominator degrees of freedom, entry represents the critical values of F corresponding to the cumulative probability $(1 - \alpha)$ and a specified upper-tail area (α).

$\alpha = 0.005$

Cumulative Probabilities = 0.995

Upper – Tail Areas = 0.005

Numerator, df_1

Denominator, df_2	1	2	3	4	5	6	7	8	9	10	12	15	20	24	30	40	60	120	∞
1	16,211.00	20,000.00	21,615.00	22,500.00	23,056.00	23,437.00	23,715.00	23,925.00	24,091.00	24,224.00	24,426.00	24,630.00	24,836.00	24,910.00	25,044.00	25,148.00	25,253.00	25,359.00	25,465.00
2	198.50	199.00	199.20	199.20	199.30	199.30	199.40	199.40	199.40	199.40	199.40	199.40	199.40	199.50	199.50	199.50	199.50	199.50	199.50
3	55.55	49.80	47.47	46.19	45.39	44.84	44.43	44.13	43.88	43.69	43.39	43.08	42.78	42.62	42.47	42.31	42.15	41.99	41.83
4	31.33	26.28	24.26	23.15	22.46	21.97	21.62	21.35	21.14	20.97	20.70	20.44	20.17	20.03	19.89	19.75	19.61	19.47	19.32
5	22.78	18.31	16.53	15.56	14.94	14.51	14.20	13.96	13.77	13.62	13.38	13.15	12.90	12.78	12.66	12.53	12.40	12.27	12.11
6	18.63	14.54	12.92	12.03	11.46	11.07	10.79	10.57	10.39	10.25	10.03	9.81	9.59	9.47	9.36	9.24	9.12	9.00	8.88
7	16.24	12.40	10.88	10.05	9.52	9.16	8.89	8.68	8.51	8.38	8.18	7.97	7.75	7.65	7.53	7.42	7.31	7.19	7.08
8	14.69	11.04	9.60	8.81	8.30	7.95	7.69	7.50	7.34	7.21	7.01	6.81	6.61	6.50	6.40	6.29	6.18	6.06	5.95
9	13.61	10.11	8.72	7.96	7.47	7.13	6.88	6.69	6.54	6.42	6.23	6.03	5.83	5.73	5.62	5.52	5.41	5.30	5.19
10	12.83	9.43	8.08	7.34	6.87	6.54	6.30	6.12	5.97	5.85	5.66	5.47	5.27	5.17	5.07	4.97	4.86	4.75	4.61
11	12.23	8.91	7.60	6.88	6.42	6.10	5.86	5.68	5.54	5.42	5.24	5.05	4.86	4.75	4.65	4.55	4.44	4.34	4.23
12	11.75	8.51	7.23	6.52	6.07	5.76	5.52	5.35	5.20	5.09	4.91	4.72	4.53	4.43	4.33	4.23	4.12	4.01	3.90
13	11.37	8.19	6.93	6.23	5.79	5.48	5.25	5.08	4.94	4.82	4.64	4.46	4.27	4.17	4.07	3.97	3.87	3.76	3.65
14	11.06	7.92	6.68	6.00	5.56	5.26	5.03	4.86	4.72	4.60	4.43	4.25	4.06	3.96	3.86	3.76	3.66	3.55	3.41
15	10.80	7.70	6.48	5.80	5.37	5.07	4.85	4.67	4.54	4.42	4.25	4.07	3.88	3.79	3.69	3.58	3.48	3.37	3.26
16	10.58	7.51	6.30	5.64	5.21	4.91	4.69	4.52	4.38	4.27	4.10	3.92	3.73	3.64	3.54	3.44	3.33	3.22	3.11
17	10.38	7.35	6.16	5.50	5.07	4.78	4.56	4.39	4.25	4.14	3.97	3.79	3.61	3.51	3.41	3.31	3.21	3.10	2.98
18	10.22	7.21	6.03	5.37	4.96	4.66	4.44	4.28	4.14	4.03	3.86	3.68	3.50	3.40	3.30	3.20	3.10	2.99	2.87
19	10.07	7.09	5.92	5.27	4.85	4.56	4.34	4.18	4.04	3.93	3.76	3.59	3.40	3.31	3.21	3.11	3.00	2.89	2.78
20	9.94	6.99	5.82	5.17	4.76	4.47	4.26	4.09	3.96	3.85	3.68	3.50	3.32	3.22	3.12	3.02	2.92	2.81	2.69
21	9.83	6.89	5.73	5.09	4.68	4.39	4.18	4.02	3.88	3.77	3.60	3.43	3.24	3.15	3.05	2.95	2.84	2.73	2.61
22	9.73	6.81	5.65	5.02	4.61	4.32	4.11	3.94	3.81	3.70	3.54	3.36	3.18	3.08	2.98	2.88	2.77	2.66	2.55
23	9.63	6.73	5.58	4.95	4.54	4.26	4.05	3.88	3.75	3.64	3.47	3.30	3.12	3.02	2.92	2.82	2.71	2.60	2.48
24	9.55	6.66	5.52	4.89	4.49	4.20	3.99	3.83	3.69	3.59	3.42	3.25	3.06	2.97	2.87	2.77	2.66	2.55	2.43
25	9.48	6.60	5.46	4.84	4.43	4.15	3.94	3.78	3.64	3.54	3.37	3.20	3.01	2.92	2.82	2.72	2.61	2.50	2.38
26	9.41	6.54	5.41	4.79	4.38	4.10	3.89	3.73	3.60	3.49	3.33	3.15	2.97	2.87	2.77	2.67	2.56	2.45	2.33
27	9.34	6.49	5.36	4.74	4.34	4.06	3.85	3.69	3.56	3.45	3.28	3.11	2.93	2.83	2.73	2.63	2.52	2.41	2.29
28	9.28	6.44	5.32	4.70	4.30	4.02	3.81	3.65	3.52	3.41	3.25	3.07	2.89	2.79	2.69	2.59	2.48	2.37	2.25
29	9.23	6.40	5.28	4.66	4.26	3.98	3.77	3.61	3.48	3.38	3.21	3.04	2.86	2.76	2.66	2.56	2.45	2.33	2.21
30	9.18	6.35	5.24	4.62	4.23	3.95	3.74	3.58	3.45	3.34	3.18	3.01	2.82	2.73	2.63	2.52	2.42	2.30	2.18
40	8.83	6.07	4.98	4.37	3.99	3.71	3.51	3.35	3.22	3.12	2.95	2.78	2.60	2.50	2.40	2.30	2.18	2.06	1.93
60	8.49	5.79	4.73	4.14	3.76	3.49	3.29	3.13	3.01	2.90	2.74	2.57	2.39	2.29	2.19	2.08	1.96	1.83	1.69
120	8.18	5.54	4.50	3.92	3.55	3.28	3.09	2.93	2.81	2.71	2.54	2.37	2.19	2.09	1.98	1.87	1.75	1.61	1.43
∞	7.88	5.30	4.28	3.72	3.35	3.09	2.90	2.74	2.62	2.52	2.36	2.19	2.00	1.90	1.79	1.67	1.53	1.36	1.00

TABLE E.6

Critical Values of the Studentized Range, Q

Upper 5% Points ($\alpha = 0.05$)

Denominator, df									Numerator, df										
	2	3	4	5	6	7	8	9	10	11	12	13	14	15	16	17	18	19	20
1	18.00	27.00	32.80	37.10	40.40	43.10	45.40	47.40	49.10	50.60	52.00	53.20	54.30	55.40	56.30	57.20	58.00	58.80	59.60
2	6.09	8.30	9.80	10.90	11.70	12.40	13.00	13.50	14.00	14.40	14.70	15.10	15.40	15.70	15.90	16.10	16.40	16.60	16.80
3	4.50	5.91	6.82	7.50	8.04	8.48	8.85	9.18	9.46	9.72	9.95	10.15	10.35	10.52	10.69	10.84	10.98	11.11	11.24
4	3.93	5.04	5.76	6.29	6.71	7.05	7.35	7.60	7.83	8.03	8.21	8.37	8.52	8.66	8.79	8.91	9.03	9.13	9.23
5	3.64	4.60	5.22	5.67	6.03	6.33	6.58	6.80	6.99	7.17	7.32	7.47	7.60	7.72	7.83	7.93	8.03	8.12	8.21
6	3.46	4.34	4.90	5.31	5.63	5.89	6.12	6.32	6.49	6.65	6.79	6.92	7.03	7.14	7.24	7.34	7.43	7.51	7.59
7	3.34	4.16	4.68	5.06	5.36	5.61	5.82	6.00	6.16	6.30	6.43	6.55	6.66	6.76	6.85	6.94	7.02	7.09	7.17
8	3.26	4.04	4.53	4.89	5.17	5.40	5.60	5.77	5.92	6.05	6.18	6.29	6.39	6.48	6.57	6.65	6.73	6.80	6.87
9	3.20	3.95	4.42	4.76	5.02	5.24	5.43	5.60	5.74	5.87	5.98	6.09	6.19	6.28	6.36	6.44	6.51	6.58	6.64
10	3.15	3.88	4.33	4.65	4.91	5.12	5.30	5.46	5.60	5.72	5.83	5.93	6.03	6.11	6.20	6.27	6.34	6.40	6.47
11	3.11	3.82	4.26	4.57	4.82	5.03	5.20	5.35	5.49	5.61	5.71	5.81	5.90	5.99	6.06	6.14	6.20	6.26	6.33
12	3.08	3.77	4.20	4.51	4.75	4.95	5.12	5.27	5.40	5.51	5.62	5.71	5.80	5.88	5.95	6.03	6.09	6.15	6.21
13	3.06	3.73	4.15	4.45	4.69	4.88	5.05	5.19	5.32	5.43	5.53	5.63	5.71	5.79	5.86	5.93	6.00	6.05	6.11
14	3.03	3.70	4.11	4.41	4.64	4.83	4.99	5.13	5.25	5.36	5.46	5.55	5.64	5.72	5.79	5.85	5.92	5.97	6.03
15	3.01	3.67	4.08	4.37	4.60	4.78	4.94	5.08	5.20	5.31	5.40	5.49	5.58	5.65	5.72	5.79	5.85	5.90	5.96
16	3.00	3.65	4.05	4.33	4.56	4.74	4.90	5.03	5.15	5.26	5.35	5.44	5.52	5.59	5.66	5.72	5.79	5.84	5.90
17	2.98	3.63	4.02	4.30	4.52	4.71	4.86	4.99	5.11	5.21	5.31	5.39	5.47	5.55	5.61	5.68	5.74	5.79	5.84
18	2.97	3.61	4.00	4.28	4.49	4.67	4.82	4.96	5.07	5.17	5.27	5.35	5.43	5.50	5.57	5.63	5.69	5.74	5.79
19	2.96	3.59	3.98	4.25	4.47	4.65	4.79	4.92	5.04	5.14	5.23	5.32	5.39	5.46	5.53	5.59	5.65	5.70	5.75
20	2.95	3.58	3.96	4.23	4.45	4.62	4.77	4.90	5.01	5.11	5.20	5.28	5.36	5.43	5.49	5.55	5.61	5.66	5.71
24	2.92	3.53	3.90	4.17	4.37	4.54	4.68	4.81	4.92	5.01	5.10	5.18	5.25	5.32	5.38	5.44	5.50	5.54	5.59
30	2.89	3.49	3.84	4.10	4.30	4.46	4.60	4.72	4.83	4.92	5.00	5.08	5.15	5.21	5.27	5.33	5.38	5.43	5.48
40	2.86	3.44	3.79	4.04	4.23	4.39	4.52	4.63	4.74	4.82	4.91	4.98	5.05	5.11	5.16	5.22	5.27	5.31	5.36
60	2.83	3.40	3.74	3.98	4.16	4.31	4.44	4.55	4.65	4.73	4.81	4.88	4.94	5.00	5.06	5.11	5.16	5.20	5.24
120	2.80	3.36	3.69	3.92	4.10	4.24	4.36	4.48	4.56	4.64	4.72	4.78	4.84	4.90	4.95	5.00	5.05	5.09	5.13
∞	2.77	3.31	3.63	3.86	4.03	4.17	4.29	4.39	4.47	4.55	4.62	4.68	4.74	4.80	4.85	4.89	4.93	4.97	5.01

TABLE E.6

Critical Values of the Studentized Range, Q (continued)

Upper 1% Points ($\alpha = 0.01$)

Denominator, df	\multicolumn{19}{c}{Numerator, df}																		
	2	3	4	5	6	7	8	9	10	11	12	13	14	15	16	17	18	19	20
1	90.03	135.00	164.30	185.60	202.20	215.80	227.20	237.00	245.60	253.20	260.00	266.20	271.80	277.00	281.80	286.30	290.40	294.30	298.00
2	14.04	19.02	22.29	24.72	26.63	28.20	29.53	30.68	31.69	32.59	33.40	34.13	34.81	35.43	36.00	36.53	37.03	37.50	37.95
3	8.26	10.62	12.17	13.33	14.24	15.00	15.64	16.20	16.69	17.13	17.53	17.89	18.22	18.52	18.81	19.07	19.32	19.55	19.77
4	6.51	8.12	9.17	9.96	10.58	11.10	11.55	11.93	12.27	12.57	12.84	13.09	13.32	13.53	13.73	13.91	14.08	14.24	14.40
5	5.70	6.98	7.80	8.42	8.91	9.32	9.67	9.97	10.24	10.48	10.70	10.89	11.08	11.24	11.40	11.55	11.68	11.81	11.93
6	5.24	6.33	7.03	7.56	7.97	8.32	8.61	8.87	9.10	9.30	9.49	9.65	9.81	9.95	10.08	10.21	10.32	10.43	10.54
7	4.95	5.92	6.54	7.01	7.37	7.68	7.94	8.17	8.37	8.55	8.71	8.86	9.00	9.12	9.24	9.35	9.46	9.55	9.65
8	4.75	5.64	6.20	6.63	6.96	7.24	7.47	7.68	7.86	8.03	8.18	8.31	8.44	8.55	8.66	8.76	8.85	8.94	9.03
9	4.60	5.43	5.96	6.35	6.66	6.92	7.13	7.32	7.50	7.65	7.78	7.91	8.03	8.13	8.23	8.33	8.41	8.50	8.57
10	4.48	5.27	5.77	6.14	6.43	6.67	6.87	7.06	7.21	7.36	7.49	7.60	7.71	7.81	7.91	7.99	8.08	8.15	8.23
11	4.39	5.15	5.62	5.97	6.25	6.48	6.67	6.84	6.99	7.13	7.25	7.36	7.47	7.56	7.65	7.73	7.81	7.88	7.95
12	4.32	5.04	5.50	5.84	6.10	6.32	6.51	6.67	6.81	6.94	7.06	7.17	7.26	7.36	7.44	7.52	7.59	7.66	7.73
13	4.26	4.96	5.40	5.73	5.98	6.19	6.37	6.53	6.67	6.79	6.90	7.01	7.10	7.19	7.27	7.35	7.42	7.49	7.55
14	4.21	4.90	5.32	5.63	5.88	6.09	6.26	6.41	6.54	6.66	6.77	6.87	6.96	7.05	7.13	7.20	7.27	7.33	7.40
15	4.17	4.84	5.25	5.56	5.80	5.99	6.16	6.31	6.44	6.56	6.66	6.76	6.85	6.93	7.00	7.07	7.14	7.20	7.26
16	4.13	4.79	5.19	5.49	5.72	5.92	6.08	6.22	6.35	6.46	6.56	6.66	6.74	6.82	6.90	6.97	7.03	7.09	7.15
17	4.10	4.74	5.14	5.43	5.66	5.85	6.01	6.15	6.27	6.38	6.48	6.57	6.66	6.73	6.81	6.87	6.94	7.00	7.05
18	4.07	4.70	5.09	5.38	5.60	5.79	5.94	6.08	6.20	6.31	6.41	6.50	6.58	6.66	6.73	6.79	6.85	6.91	6.97
19	4.05	4.67	5.05	5.33	5.55	5.74	5.89	6.02	6.14	6.25	6.34	6.43	6.51	6.59	6.65	6.72	6.78	6.84	6.89
20	4.02	4.64	5.02	5.29	5.51	5.69	5.84	5.97	6.09	6.19	6.29	6.37	6.45	6.52	6.59	6.65	6.71	6.77	6.82
24	3.96	4.55	4.91	5.17	5.37	5.54	5.69	5.81	5.92	6.02	6.11	6.19	6.26	6.33	6.39	6.45	6.51	6.56	6.61
30	3.89	4.46	4.80	5.05	5.24	5.40	5.54	5.65	5.76	5.85	5.93	6.01	6.08	6.14	6.20	6.26	6.31	6.36	6.41
40	3.83	4.37	4.70	4.93	5.11	5.27	5.39	5.50	5.60	5.69	5.76	5.84	5.90	5.96	6.02	6.07	6.12	6.17	6.21
60	3.76	4.28	4.60	4.82	4.99	5.13	5.25	5.36	5.45	5.53	5.60	5.67	5.73	5.79	5.84	5.89	5.93	5.97	6.02
120	3.70	4.20	4.50	4.71	4.87	5.01	5.12	5.21	5.30	5.38	5.44	5.51	5.56	5.61	5.66	5.71	5.75	5.79	5.83
∞	3.64	4.12	4.40	4.60	4.76	4.88	4.99	5.08	5.16	5.23	5.29	5.35	5.40	5.45	5.49	5.54	5.57	5.61	5.65

Source: Extracted from H. L. Harter and D. S. Clemm, "The Probability Integrals of the Range and of the Studentized Range—Probability Integral, Percentage Points, and Moments of the Range," *Wright Air Development Technical Report 58–484*, Vol. 1, 1959.

TABLE E.7

Critical Values, d_L and d_U, of the Durbin-Watson Statistic, D (Critical Values Are One-Sided)[a]

| | $\alpha = 0.05$ | | | | | | | | | | $\alpha = 0.01$ | | | | | | | | | |
| | $k=1$ | | $k=2$ | | $k=3$ | | $k=4$ | | $k=5$ | | $k=1$ | | $k=2$ | | $k=3$ | | $k=4$ | | $k=5$ | |
n	d_L	d_U	d_L	d_U	d_L	d_U	d_L	d_U	d_L	d_U	d_L	d_U	d_L	d_U	d_L	d_U	d_L	d_U	d_L	d_U
15	1.08	1.36	.95	1.54	.82	1.75	.69	1.97	.56	2.21	.81	1.07	.70	1.25	.59	1.46	.49	1.70	.39	1.96
16	1.10	1.37	.98	1.54	.86	1.73	.74	1.93	.62	2.15	.84	1.09	.74	1.25	.63	1.44	.53	1.66	.44	1.90
17	1.13	1.38	1.02	1.54	.90	1.71	.78	1.90	.67	2.10	.87	1.10	.77	1.25	.67	1.43	.57	1.63	.48	1.85
18	1.16	1.39	1.05	1.53	.93	1.69	.82	1.87	.71	2.06	.90	1.12	.80	1.26	.71	1.42	.61	1.60	.52	1.80
19	1.18	1.40	1.08	1.53	.97	1.68	.86	1.85	.75	2.02	.93	1.13	.83	1.26	.74	1.41	.65	1.58	.56	1.77
20	1.20	1.41	1.10	1.54	1.00	1.68	.90	1.83	.79	1.99	.95	1.15	.86	1.27	.77	1.41	.68	1.57	.60	1.74
21	1.22	1.42	1.13	1.54	1.03	1.67	.93	1.81	.83	1.96	.97	1.16	.89	1.27	.80	1.41	.72	1.55	.63	1.71
22	1.24	1.43	1.15	1.54	1.05	1.66	.96	1.80	.86	1.94	1.00	1.17	.91	1.28	.83	1.40	.75	1.54	.66	1.69
23	1.26	1.44	1.17	1.54	1.08	1.66	.99	1.79	.90	1.92	1.02	1.19	.94	1.29	.86	1.40	.77	1.53	.70	1.67
24	1.27	1.45	1.19	1.55	1.10	1.66	1.01	1.78	.93	1.90	1.04	1.20	.96	1.30	.88	1.41	.80	1.53	.72	1.66
25	1.29	1.45	1.21	1.55	1.12	1.66	1.04	1.77	.95	1.89	1.05	1.21	.98	1.30	.90	1.41	.83	1.52	.75	1.65
26	1.30	1.46	1.22	1.55	1.14	1.65	1.06	1.76	.98	1.88	1.07	1.22	1.00	1.31	.93	1.41	.85	1.52	.78	1.64
27	1.32	1.47	1.24	1.56	1.16	1.65	1.08	1.76	1.01	1.86	1.09	1.23	1.02	1.32	.95	1.41	.88	1.51	.81	1.63
28	1.33	1.48	1.26	1.56	1.18	1.65	1.10	1.75	1.03	1.85	1.10	1.24	1.04	1.32	.97	1.41	.90	1.51	.83	1.62
29	1.34	1.48	1.27	1.56	1.20	1.65	1.12	1.74	1.05	1.84	1.12	1.25	1.05	1.33	.99	1.42	.92	1.51	.85	1.61
30	1.35	1.49	1.28	1.57	1.21	1.65	1.14	1.74	1.07	1.83	1.13	1.26	1.07	1.34	1.01	1.42	.94	1.51	.88	1.61
31	1.36	1.50	1.30	1.57	1.23	1.65	1.16	1.74	1.09	1.83	1.15	1.27	1.08	1.34	1.02	1.42	.96	1.51	.90	1.60
32	1.37	1.50	1.31	1.57	1.24	1.65	1.18	1.73	1.11	1.82	1.16	1.28	1.10	1.35	1.04	1.43	.98	1.51	.92	1.60
33	1.38	1.51	1.32	1.58	1.26	1.65	1.19	1.73	1.13	1.81	1.17	1.29	1.11	1.36	1.05	1.43	1.00	1.51	.94	1.59
34	1.39	1.51	1.33	1.58	1.27	1.65	1.21	1.73	1.15	1.81	1.18	1.30	1.13	1.36	1.07	1.43	1.01	1.51	.95	1.59
35	1.40	1.52	1.34	1.58	1.28	1.65	1.22	1.73	1.16	1.80	1.19	1.31	1.14	1.37	1.08	1.44	1.03	1.51	.97	1.59
36	1.41	1.52	1.35	1.59	1.29	1.65	1.24	1.73	1.18	1.80	1.21	1.32	1.15	1.38	1.10	1.44	1.04	1.51	.99	1.59
37	1.42	1.53	1.36	1.59	1.31	1.66	1.25	1.72	1.19	1.80	1.22	1.32	1.16	1.38	1.11	1.45	1.06	1.51	1.00	1.59
38	1.43	1.54	1.37	1.59	1.32	1.66	1.26	1.72	1.21	1.79	1.23	1.33	1.18	1.39	1.12	1.45	1.07	1.52	1.02	1.58
39	1.43	1.54	1.38	1.60	1.33	1.66	1.27	1.72	1.22	1.79	1.24	1.34	1.19	1.39	1.14	1.45	1.09	1.52	1.03	1.58
40	1.44	1.54	1.39	1.60	1.34	1.66	1.29	1.72	1.23	1.79	1.25	1.34	1.20	1.40	1.15	1.46	1.10	1.52	1.05	1.58
45	1.48	1.57	1.43	1.62	1.38	1.67	1.34	1.72	1.29	1.78	1.29	1.38	1.24	1.42	1.20	1.48	1.16	1.53	1.11	1.58
50	1.50	1.59	1.46	1.63	1.42	1.67	1.38	1.72	1.34	1.77	1.32	1.40	1.28	1.45	1.24	1.49	1.20	1.54	1.16	1.59
55	1.53	1.60	1.49	1.64	1.45	1.68	1.41	1.72	1.38	1.77	1.36	1.43	1.32	1.47	1.28	1.51	1.25	1.55	1.21	1.59
60	1.55	1.62	1.51	1.65	1.48	1.69	1.44	1.73	1.41	1.77	1.38	1.45	1.35	1.48	1.32	1.52	1.28	1.56	1.25	1.60
65	1.57	1.63	1.54	1.66	1.50	1.70	1.47	1.73	1.44	1.77	1.41	1.47	1.38	1.50	1.35	1.53	1.31	1.57	1.28	1.61
70	1.58	1.64	1.55	1.67	1.52	1.70	1.49	1.74	1.46	1.77	1.43	1.49	1.40	1.52	1.37	1.55	1.34	1.58	1.31	1.61
75	1.60	1.65	1.57	1.68	1.54	1.71	1.51	1.74	1.49	1.77	1.45	1.50	1.42	1.53	1.39	1.56	1.37	1.59	1.34	1.62
80	1.61	1.66	1.59	1.69	1.56	1.72	1.53	1.74	1.51	1.77	1.47	1.52	1.44	1.54	1.42	1.57	1.39	1.60	1.36	1.62
85	1.62	1.67	1.60	1.70	1.57	1.72	1.55	1.75	1.52	1.77	1.48	1.53	1.46	1.55	1.43	1.58	1.41	1.60	1.39	1.63
90	1.63	1.68	1.61	1.70	1.59	1.73	1.57	1.75	1.54	1.78	1.50	1.54	1.47	1.56	1.45	1.59	1.43	1.61	1.41	1.64
95	1.64	1.69	1.62	1.71	1.60	1.73	1.58	1.75	1.56	1.78	1.51	1.55	1.49	1.57	1.47	1.60	1.45	1.62	1.42	1.64
100	1.65	1.69	1.63	1.72	1.61	1.74	1.59	1.76	1.57	1.78	1.52	1.56	1.50	1.58	1.48	1.60	1.46	1.63	1.44	1.65

[a] n = number of observations; k = number of independent variables.

Source: Computed from TSP 4.5 based on R. W. Farebrother, "A Remark on Algorithms AS106, AS153, and AS155: The Distribution of a Linear Combination of Chi-Square Random Variables," *Journal of the Royal Statistical Society*, Series C (Applied Statistics), 29 (1984): 323–333.

TABLE E.8

Control Chart Factors

Number of Observations in Sample/Subgroup (n)	d_2	d_3	D_3	D_4	A_2
2	1.128	0.853	0	3.267	1.880
3	1.693	0.888	0	2.575	1.023
4	2.059	0.880	0	2.282	0.729
5	2.326	0.864	0	2.114	0.577
6	2.534	0.848	0	2.004	0.483
7	2.704	0.833	0.076	1.924	0.419
8	2.847	0.820	0.136	1.864	0.373
9	2.970	0.808	0.184	1.816	0.337
10	3.078	0.797	0.223	1.777	0.308
11	3.173	0.787	0.256	1.744	0.285
12	3.258	0.778	0.283	1.717	0.266
13	3.336	0.770	0.307	1.693	0.249
14	3.407	0.763	0.328	1.672	0.235
15	3.472	0.756	0.347	1.653	0.223
16	3.532	0.750	0.363	1.637	0.212
17	3.588	0.744	0.378	1.622	0.203
18	3.640	0.739	0.391	1.609	0.194
19	3.689	0.733	0.404	1.596	0.187
20	3.735	0.729	0.415	1.585	0.180
21	3.778	0.724	0.425	1.575	0.173
22	3.819	0.720	0.435	1.565	0.167
23	3.858	0.716	0.443	1.557	0.162
24	3.895	0.712	0.452	1.548	0.157
25	3.931	0.708	0.459	1.541	0.153

Source: Reprinted from *ASTM-STP 15D* by kind permission of the American Society for Testing and Materials. Copyright ASTM International, 100 Barr Harbor Drive, Conshohocken, PA 19428.

TABLE E.9

The Standardized Normal Distribution

Entry represents area under the standardized normal
distribution from the mean to Z

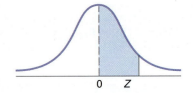

Z	.00	.01	.02	.03	.04	.05	.06	.07	.08	.09
0.0	.0000	.0040	.0080	.0120	.0160	.0199	.0239	.0279	.0319	.0359
0.1	.0398	.0438	.0478	.0517	.0557	.0596	.0636	.0675	.0714	.0753
0.2	.0793	.0832	.0871	.0910	.0948	.0987	.1026	.1064	.1103	.1141
0.3	.1179	.1217	.1255	.1293	.1331	.1368	.1406	.1443	.1480	.1517
0.4	.1554	.1591	.1628	.1664	.1700	.1736	.1772	.1808	.1844	.1879
0.5	.1915	.1950	.1985	.2019	.2054	.2088	.2123	.2157	.2190	.2224
0.6	.2257	.2291	.2324	.2357	.2389	.2422	.2454	.2486	.2518	.2549
0.7	.2580	.2612	.2642	.2673	.2704	.2734	.2764	.2794	.2823	.2852
0.8	.2881	.2910	.2939	.2967	.2995	.3023	.3051	.3078	.3106	.3133
0.9	.3159	.3186	.3212	.3238	.3264	.3289	.3315	.3340	.3365	.3389
1.0	.3413	.3438	.3461	.3485	.3508	.3531	.3554	.3577	.3599	.3621
1.1	.3643	.3665	.3686	.3708	.3729	.3749	.3770	.3790	.3810	.3830
1.2	.3849	.3869	.3888	.3907	.3925	.3944	.3962	.3980	.3997	.4015
1.3	.4032	.4049	.4066	.4082	.4099	.4115	.4131	.4147	.4162	.4177
1.4	.4192	.4207	.4222	.4236	.4251	.4265	.4279	.4292	.4306	.4319
1.5	.4332	.4345	.4357	.4370	.4382	.4394	.4406	.4418	.4429	.4441
1.6	.4452	.4463	.4474	.4484	.4495	.4505	.4515	.4525	.4535	.4545
1.7	.4554	.4564	.4573	.4582	.4591	.4599	.4608	.4616	.4625	.4633
1.8	.4641	.4649	.4656	.4664	.4671	.4678	.4686	.4693	.4699	.4706
1.9	.4713	.4719	.4726	.4732	.4738	.4744	.4750	.4756	.4761	.4767
2.0	.4772	.4778	.4783	.4788	.4793	.4798	.4803	.4808	.4812	.4817
2.1	.4821	.4826	.4830	.4834	.4838	.4842	.4846	.4850	.4854	.4857
2.2	.4861	.4864	.4868	.4871	.4875	.4878	.4881	.4884	.4887	.4890
2.3	.4893	.4896	.4898	.4901	.4904	.4906	.4909	.4911	.4913	.4916
2.4	.4918	.4920	.4922	.4925	.4927	.4929	.4931	.4932	.4934	.4936
2.5	.4938	.4940	.4941	.4943	.4945	.4946	.4948	.4949	.4951	.4952
2.6	.4953	.4955	.4956	.4957	.4959	.4960	.4961	.4962	.4963	.4964
2.7	.4965	.4966	.4967	.4968	.4969	.4970	.4971	.4972	.4973	.4974
2.8	.4974	.4975	.4976	.4977	.4977	.4978	.4979	.4979	.4980	.4981
2.9	.4981	.4982	.4982	.4983	.4984	.4984	.4985	.4985	.4986	.4986
3.0	.49865	.49869	.49874	.49878	.49882	.49886	.49889	.49893	.49897	.49900
3.1	.49903	.49906	.49910	.49913	.49916	.49918	.49921	.49924	.49926	.49929
3.2	.49931	.49934	.49936	.49938	.49940	.49942	.49944	.49946	.49948	.49950
3.3	.49952	.49953	.49955	.49957	.49958	.49960	.49961	.49962	.49964	.49965
3.4	.49966	.49968	.49969	.49970	.49971	.49972	.49973	.49974	.49975	.49976
3.5	.49977	.49978	.49978	.49979	.49980	.49981	.49981	.49982	.49983	.49983
3.6	.49984	.49985	.49985	.49986	.49986	.49987	.49987	.49988	.49988	.49989
3.7	.49989	.49990	.49990	.49990	.49991	.49991	.49992	.49992	.49992	.49992
3.8	.49993	.49993	.49993	.49994	.49994	.49994	.49994	.49995	.49995	.49995
3.9	.49995	.49995	.49996	.49996	.49996	.49996	.49996	.49996	.49997	.49997

This appendix reviews knowledge that you will find useful if you plan to be more than a casual user of Microsoft Excel. If you are using a version of Excel that is older than Excel 2010, you will need to be familiar with Section F.3 so that you can modify the names of functions used in worksheet templates and models as necessary.

Section F.4 presents an enhanced explanation of some the statistical worksheet functions that recur in two or more chapters. This section also discusses functions that either serve programming purposes or are used in novel ways to compute intermediate results. If you have a particular interest in developing your own worksheet solutions, you should be familiar with the contents of this section.

This appendix assumes that you have mastered the basic concepts presented in Appendix B. If you are a first-time user of Excel, do not make the mistake of trying to comprehend the contents of this appendix before you gain experience using Excel and familiarity with Appendix B.

F.1 Useful Keyboard Shortcuts

In Microsoft Office programs including Microsoft Excel, certain individual keys or combinations of keys held down as you press another key are shortcuts that allow you to execute common operations without having to select choices from menus or click in the Ribbon. As first explained in Section GS.4, in this book, keystroke combinations are shown using plus signs; for example, **Ctrl+C** means "while holding down the **Ctrl** key, press the **C** key."

Editing Shortcuts

Pressing **Backspace** erases typed characters to the left of the current position, one character at a time. Pressing **Delete** erases characters to the right of the cursor, one character at a time.

Ctrl+C copies a worksheet entry, and **Ctrl+V** pastes that entry into the place that the editing cursor or worksheet cell highlight indicates. Pressing **Ctrl+X** cuts the currently selected entry or object so that you can paste it somewhere else. **Ctrl+C** and **Ctrl+V** (or **Ctrl+X** and **Ctrl+V**) can also be used to copy (or cut) and paste certain workbook objects such as charts. (Using copy and paste to copy formulas from one worksheet cell to another is subject to the adjustment discussed in Appendix Section B.2.)

Pressing **Ctrl+Z** undoes the last operation, and **Ctrl+Y** redoes the last operation. Pressing **Enter** or **Tab** finalizes an entry typed into a worksheet cell. Pressing either key is implied by the use of the verb *enter* in the Excel Guides.

Formatting & Utility Shortcuts

Pressing **Ctrl+B** toggles on (or off) boldface text style for the currently selected object. Pressing **Ctrl+I** toggles on (or off) italic text style for the currently selected object. Pressing **Ctrl+Shift+%** formats numeric values as a percentage with no decimal places.

Pressing **Ctrl+F** finds a **Find what** value, and pressing **Ctrl+H** replaces a **Find what** value with the **Replace with** value. Pressing **Ctrl+A** selects the entire current worksheet (useful as part of a worksheet copy or format operation). Pressing **Esc** cancels an action or a dialog box. Pressing **F1** displays the Microsoft Excel help system.

F.2 Verifying Formulas and Worksheets

If you use formulas in your worksheets, you should review and verify formulas before you use their results. To view the formulas in a worksheet, press **Ctrl+`** (grave accent key). To restore the original view, the results of the formulas, press **Ctrl+`** a second time.

As you create and use more complicated worksheets, you might want to visually examine the relationships among a formula and the cells it uses (called the *precedents*) and the cells that use the results of the formula (the *dependents*). Select **Formulas → Trace Precedents** (or **Trace Dependents**) to examine relationships. When you are finished, clear all trace arrows by selecting **Formulas → Remove Arrows**.

After verifying formulas, you should test, using simple numbers, any worksheet that you have modified or constructed from scratch.

F.3 New Function Names

Beginning in Excel 2010, Microsoft renamed many statistical functions and reprogrammed a number of functions to improve their accuracy. Generally, this book uses the new function names in worksheet cell formulas. Table F.1 lists the new function names used in this book, along with the place of first mention in this book and their corresponding older function names.

TABLE F.1

New and Older Function Names

New Name	First Mention	Older Name
BINOM.DIST	EG5.3	BINOMDIST
CHISQ.DIST.RT	EG11.1	CHIDIST
CHISQ.INV.RT	EG11.1	CHIINV
CONFIDENCE.NORM	EG8.1	CONFIDENCE
COVARIANCE.S	EG3.5	none*
F.DIST.RT	EG10.4	FDIST
F.INV.RT	EG10.4	FINV
NORM.DIST	EG6.2	NORMDIST
NORM.INV	EG6.2	NORMINV
NORM.S.DIST	EG9.1	NORMSDIST
NORM.S.INV	EG6.2	NORMSINV
POISSON.DIST	EG5.4	POISSON
STDEV.S	EG3.2	STDEV
STDEV.P	EG3.2	STDEVP
T.DIST.RT	EG9.3	TDIST
T.DIST.2T	EG9.2	TDIST
T.INV.2T	EG8.2	TINV
VAR.S	EG3.2	VAR
VAR.P	EG3.2	VARP

COVARIANCE.S is a function that was new to Excel 2010. The COVARIANCE.P function (not used in this book) replaces the older COVAR function.

Alternative Worksheets

If a worksheet in an Excel Guide workbook uses one or more of the new function names, the workbook contains an alternative worksheet for use with Excel versions that are older than Excel 2010. Three exceptions to the rule are the **Simple Linear Regression 2007**, **Multiple Regression 2007**, and **Exponential Trend 2007** *workbooks*. Alternative worksheets and workbooks work best in Excel 2007.

The following Excel Guide workbooks contain an alternative worksheet named COMPUTE_OLDER. Numbers that appear in parentheses are the chapters in which these workbooks are first mentioned.

Parameters (3)	**CIE Proportion (8)**	**Separate-Variance T (10)**
Covariance (3)	**Z Mean workbook (9)**	**Paired T (10)**
Normal (6)	**T mean workbook (9)**	**One-Way ANOVA (10)**
CIE sigma known (8)	**Z Proportion (9)**	**Chi-Square (11)**
CIE sigma unknown (8)	**Pooled-Variance T (10)**	

The following Excel Guide workbooks have alternative worksheets with various names:

Descriptive (3)	CompleteStatistics_OLDER
Binomial (5)	CUMULATIVE_OLDER
Poisson (5)	CUMULATIVE_OLDER
NPP (6)	PLOT_OLDER and NORMAL_PLOT_OLDER
One-Way ANOVA (10)	TK4_OLDER
Chi-Square Worksheets (11)	ChiSquare2x3_OLDER and others

Quartile Function

In this book, you will see the older QUARTILE function and not the newer QUARTILE.EXC function. In Microsoft's *Function Improvements in Microsoft Office Excel 2010* (available at **bit.ly/RkoFIf**), QUARTILE.EXC is explained as being "consistent with industry best practices, assuming percentile is a value between 0 and 1, exclusive." Because there are several established but different ways of computing quartiles, there is no way of knowing exactly how the new function works.

Because of this lack of specifics, this book uses the older QUARTILE function, whose programming and limitations are well known, and not the new QUARTILE.EXC function or QUARTILE.INC function, which is the QUARTILES function renamed for consistency with QUARTILES.EXC. As noted in Section EG3.3, none of the three functions compute quartiles using the rules presented in Section 3.3, which are properly computed in the COMPUTE worksheet of the Quartiles workbook that uses the older QUARTILE function. If you are using Excel 2010 or a newer version of Excel, the COMPARE worksheet illustrates the results using the three forms of QUARTILES for the data found in column A of the DATA worksheet.

F.4 Understanding the Nonstatistical Functions

Selected Excel Guide and PHStat worksheets use a number of nonstatistical functions that either compute an intermediate result or perform a mathematical or programming operation. These functions are explained in the following alphabetical list:

CEILING(*cell, round-to value*) takes the numeric value in *cell* and rounds it to the next multiple of the *round-to value*. For example, if the *round-to value* is **0.5**, as it is in several column B formulas in the COMPUTE worksheet of the Quartiles workbook, then the numeric value will be rounded either to an integer or a number that contains a half such as 1.5.

COUNT(*cell range*) counts the number of cells in a cell range that contain a numeric value. This function is often used to compute the sample size, n, for example, in cell B9 of the COMPUTE worksheet of the Correlation workbook. When seen in the worksheets presented in this book, the *cell range* will typically be the cell range of variable column, such as **DATA!A:A**. This will result in a proper count of the sample size of that variable if you follow the Getting Started Chapter rules for entering data.

COUNTIF(*cell range for all values, value to be matched*) counts the number of occurrences of a value in a cell range. For example, the COMPUTE worksheet of the Wilcoxon workbook uses **COUNTIF(SortedRanks!A2:A21, "Beverage")** in cell B7 to compute the sample size of the Population 1 Sample by counting the number of occurrences of the sample name Beverage in column A of the SortedRanks worksheet.

DEVSQ(*variable cell range*) computes the sum of the squares of the differences between a variable value and the mean of that variable.

FLOOR(*cell*, 1) takes the numeric value in *cell* and rounds down the value to the nearest integer.

IF(*logical comparison, **what to display if comparison holds, what to display if comparison is false***) uses the *logical comparison* to make a choice between two alternatives. In the worksheets shown in this book, the IF function typically chooses from two text values, such as **Reject the null hypothesis** and **Do not reject the null hypothesis**, to display.

MMULT(*cell range* **1**, *cell range* **2**) treats both *cell range* **1** and *cell range* **2** as matrices and computes the matrix product of the two matrices. When each of the two cell ranges is either a single row or a single column, MMULT can be used as part of a regular formula. If the cell ranges each represent rows and columns, then MMULT must be used as part of an array formula (see Appendix Section B.3).

ROUND(*cell*, **0**) takes the numeric value in *cell* and rounds to the nearest whole number.

SMALL(*cell range*, *k*) selects the *k*th smallest value in *cell range*.

SQRT(*value*) computes the square root of *value*, where *value* is either a cell reference or an arithmetic expression.

SUMIF(*cell range for all values, value to be matched, cell range in which to select cells for summing*) sums only those rows in *cell range in which to select cells for summing* in which the value in *cell range for all values* matches the *value to be matched*. SUMIF provides a convenient way to compute the sum of ranks for a sample in a worksheet that contains stacked data.

SUMPRODUCT(*cell range* **1**, *cell range* **2**) multiplies each cell in *cell range* **1** by the corresponding cell in *cell range* **2** and then sums those products. If *cell range* **1** contains a column of differences between an *X* value and the mean of the variable *X*, and *cell range* **2** contains a column of differences between a *Y* value and the mean of the variable *Y*, then this function would compute the value of the numerator in Equation (3.16) that defines the sample covariance.

TRANSPOSE(*horizontal or vertical cell range*) takes the *cell range*, which must be either a horizontal cell range (cells all in the same row) or a vertical cell range (cells all in the same column) and transposes, or rearranges, the cell in the other orientation such that a horizontal cell range becomes a vertical cell range and vice versa. When used inside another function, Excel considers the results of this function to be an *array*, not a cell range.

VLOOKUP(*lookup value cell, table of lookup values, table column to use*) function displays a value that has been looked up in a *table of lookup values*, a rectangular cell range. In the ADVANCED worksheet of the Recoded workbook, the function uses the values in the second column of *table of lookup values* (an example of which is shown below) to look up the Honors values based on the GPA of a student (the *lookup value cell*). Numbers in the first column of *table of lookup values* are implied ranges such that No Honors is the value displayed if the GPA is at least 0, but less than 3; Honor Roll is the value displayed if the GPA is at least 3, but less than 3.3; and so on:

0	No Honors
3	Honor Roll
3.3	Dean's List
3.7	President's List

APPENDIX G Software FAQs

G.1 PHStat FAQs

What is PHStat?

PHStat is the macro-enabled workbook that you use with Excel to help build solutions to statistical problems. With PHStat, you fill in simple-to-use dialog boxes and watch as PHStat creates a worksheet solution for you. PHStat allows you to use the Microsoft Excel statistical functions without having to first learn advanced Excel techniques or worrying about building worksheets from scratch. As a student studying statistics, you can focus mainly on learning statistics and not worry about having to fully master Excel as well.

PHStat executes for you the low-level menu selection and worksheet entry tasks that are associated with implementing statistical analysis in Microsoft Excel. PHStat creates worksheets and chart sheets that are identical to the ones featured in this book. From these sheets, you can learn real Excel techniques at your leisure and give yourself the ability to use Excel effectively outside your introductory statistics course. (Other add-ins that appear similar to PHStat report results as a series of text labels, hiding the details of using Microsoft Excel and leaving you with no basis for learning to use Excel effectively.)

Which versions of Excel are compatible with PHStat?

PHStat works best with Microsoft Windows Excel 2010 and Excel 2013 and with OS X Excel 2011. PHStat is also compatible with Excel 2007 (WIN), although the accuracy of some Excel statistical functions PHStat uses varies from Excel 2010 and can lead to (minor) changes in the results reported.

PHStat is partially compatible with Excel 2003 (WIN). When you open PHStat in Excel 2003, you will see a file conversion dialog box as Excel translates the .xlam file into a format that can be used in Excel 2003. After this file conversion completes, you will be able to see the PHStat menu and use many of the PHStat procedures. As documented in the PHStat help system, some advanced procedures construct worksheets that use Excel functions that were added after Excel 2003 was published. In those cases, the worksheets will contain cells that display the #NAME? error message instead of results.

PHStat is not compatible with Excel 2008 (OS X), which did include the capability of running add-in workbooks.

How do I get PHStat ready for use?

Section D.2 explains how to get PHStat ready for use. You should also review the PHStat readme file (available for download as discussed in Appendix C) for any late-breaking news or changes that might affect this process.

When I open PHStat, I get a Microsoft Excel error message that mentions a "compile error" or "hidden workbook." What is wrong?

Most likely, you have not applied the Microsoft-supplied updates to your copy of Microsoft Excel (see Section D.1). If you are certain that your copy of Microsoft Excel is fully up to date, verify that your copy is properly licensed and undamaged. (If necessary, you can rerun the Microsoft Office setup program to repair the installation of Excel.)

When I use a particular PHStat procedure, I get an error message that includes the words "unexpected error." What should I do?

"Unexpected error" messages are typically caused by improperly prepared data. Review your data to ensure that you have organized your data according to the conventions PHStat expects, as explained in the PHStat help system.

Where can I get further news and information about PHStat? Where can I get further assistance about using PHStat?

Several websites can provide you with news and information or provide you with assistance that supplements the readme file and help system included with PHStat.

www.pearsonhighered.com/phstat is Pearson Education's official web page for PHStat. From this page, you can download PHStat (requires an access code as explained in Section C.4) or contact Pearson 24/7 Technical Support. You can also email statistics@pearson.com.

phstat.davidlevinestatistics.com is a website maintained by the authors of this book that contains general news and information about PHStat.

phstatcommunity.org is a new website organized by PHStat users and endorsed by the developers of PHStat. You can click **News** on the home page to display the latest news and developments about PHStat. Other content on the website explains some of the "behind-the-scenes" technical workings of PHStat.

How can I make sure that my version of PHStat is up to date? How can I get updates to PHStat when they become available?

PHStat is subject to continuous improvement. When enhancements are made, a new PHStat zip archive is posted on the PHStat home page (see Section C.4) and, if you hold a valid access code, you can download that archive and overwrite your older version. To discover the version number of your copy of PHStat, select **About PHStat** from the PHStat menu. (The version number for the PHStat version supplied for use with this book will always be a number that begins with 4.)

G.2 Microsoft Excel FAQs

Do all Microsoft Excel versions contain the same features and functionality? Which Microsoft Excel version should I use?

Unfortunately, features and functionality vary across versions still in use (including versions no longer supported by Microsoft). This book works best with Microsoft Windows versions Excel 2010 and Excel 2013 and OS X version Excel 2011. However, even among these current versions there are variations in features. For example, PivotTables have subtle differences across versions, none of which affect the instructions and examples in this book, and PivotCharts, not discussed in this book, are not included in Excel 2011.

This book identifies differences among versions when they are significant. In particular, this book supplies, when necessary, special instructions and alternative worksheets (discussed in Appendix Section F.3) designed for versions that are both older than Excel 2010 and currently supported by Microsoft. If you plan to use Microsoft Windows Excel 2007, an upgrade will give you access to the newest features and provide a version with significantly increased statistical accuracy.

If you use OS X Excel 2008, you *must* upgrade to use PHStat or any of the other add-in workbooks mentioned in this book. Even if you plan to avoid using any add-ins, you should consider upgrading to OS X Excel 2011 for the same reasons that Excel 2003 and Excel 2007 face.

What does "Compatibility Mode" in the title bar mean?

Excel displays "Compatibility Mode" when you open and use a workbook that has been previously stored using the older **.xls** Excel workbook file format. Compatibility Mode does not affect Excel functionality but will cause Excel to review your workbook for exclusive-to-xlsx formatting properties and Excel will question you with a dialog box should you go to save the workbook in this format.

To convert a **.xls** workbook to the **.xlsx** format, select **File → Save As** and select **Excel Workbook (*.xlsx)** from the **Save as type** (WIN) or the **Format** (OS X) drop-down list in Excel 2010, 2011, or 2013. To do so in Excel 2007, click the **Office Button**, move the mouse pointer over **Save As**, and, in the Save As gallery, click **Excel Workbook** to save the workbook in the **.xlsx** file format.

One quirk in Microsoft Excel is that when you convert a workbook by using **Save As**, the newly converted .xlsx workbook stays temporarily in Compatibility Mode. To avoid possible complications and errors, close the newly converted workbook and then reopen it.

Using Compatibility Mode can cause minor differences in the objects such as charts and PivotTables that Excel creates and can cause problems when you seek to transfer data from other workbooks. Unless you need to open a workbook in a version of Excel that is older than Excel 2007, you should avoid using Compatibility Mode.

What Excel security settings will allow the PHStat or a Visual Explorations add-in workbook to function properly when using a Microsoft Windows version of Microsoft Excel?

The security settings are explained in the Appendix Section D.3 instructions. (These settings do not apply to OS X Excel.)

What is a PivotChart? Why doesn't this book discuss PivotCharts?

PivotCharts are charts that Microsoft Excel creates automatically from a PivotTable. This type of chart is not discussed in this book because Excel will typically create a "wrong" chart that takes more effort to fix than the effort needed to create a proper chart and because PivotChart functionality varies very significantly among the current Excel versions—and is missing from OS X Excel 2011.

The special instructions for selecting a PivotTable cell or cell range that appear in selected Section EG2.3 *In-Depth Excel* instructions help you avoid creating an unwanted PivotChart. (PHStat never creates a PivotChart.)

What is Microsoft OneDrive?

Microsoft OneDrive is an Internet-based service that offers you online storage that enables you to access and share your files anytime and anywhere there is an Internet connection available. In Excel 2013, you will see **OneDrive** listed as a choice along with **Computer** in the Open, Save, and Save As panels. In Excel 2011, you use the Document Connection to access OneDrive files and select **File → Share → Open OneDrive** to save to a OneDrive folder.

You must sign in to the OneDrive service using a "Microsoft account," formerly known as a "Windows Live ID." If you use Office online or certain other special versions of Excel, you *may* need to sign into the OneDrive service to use Excel itself.

What is Office 365?

Office 365 is a subscription-based service that supplies you with the latest version of Microsoft Office programs for your system. Office 365 requires you to be signed in using a Microsoft account in the same way as you would sign in to use OneDrive (see previous answer). Using Office 365 gives you access to the latest version of Microsoft Excel, which, at the time of publication of this book, is Excel 2013 for Microsoft Windows systems and Excel 2011 for OS X systems. If you use Office 365, use either the Excel 2013 or Excel 2011 instructions, as appropriate.

G.3 FAQs for New Users of Microsoft Excel 2013

When I open Excel 2013, I see a screen that shows panels that represent different workbooks and not the Ribbon interface. What do I do?

Press **Esc**. That screen, called the **Start screen**, will disappear and a screen that contains an Excel window similar to the ones in Excel 2010 and Excel 2011 will appear. For a more permanent solution, select **File → Options** and in the General panel of the Excel Options dialog box that appears clear **Show the Start screen when this application starts** and then click **OK**.

Are there any significant differences between Excel 2013 and its immediate predecessor, Excel 2010?
There are no significant differences, but several File tab commands present restyled panes (with the same or similar information), and opening and saving files differs slightly, as described in the Excel Guide for the Let's Get Started chapter.

The Excel 2013 Ribbon, featured in a number of Appendix B illustrations, looks slightly different than the Excel 2010 Ribbon. However, these differences are so slight that the Excel 2013 Ribbon illustrations in Appendix B will be recognizable to you if you choose to use Excel 2010.

In the Insert tab, what are Recommended PivotTables and Recommended Charts? Should I use these features?
Recommended PivotTables and **Recommended Charts** display one or more "recommended" PivotTables or charts as shortcuts. Unfortunately, the recommended PivotTables can include statistical errors such as treating the categories of a categorical variable as zero values of a numerical variable and the recommended charts often do not conform to best practices (see Appendix Section B.6).

As programmed in Excel 2013, you should ignore and not use these features as they will likely cause you to spend more time correcting errors and formatting mistakes than the little time that you might otherwise save.

G.4 Minitab FAQs

Can I use Minitab Student 14 or Release 14 or 15 with this book?
Yes, you can use the Minitab Guide instructions with Minitab Student 14 or Release 14 or 15. For certain methods, there may be minor differences in labeling of dialog box elements. Any difference that is not minor is noted in the instructions.

Can I save my Minitab worksheets or projects for use with Minitab Student 14 or Release 14 or 15?
Yes. Select either **Minitab14** or **Minitab 15** (for a worksheet) or **Minitab 14 Project (*.MPJ)** or **Minitab 15 Project (*.MPJ)** (for a project) from the **Save as type** drop-down list in the save as dialog box. (See Appendix Section B.10 for more information.)

Can I use Minitab 17 with this book?
Yes, you can use the Minitab Guide instructions, which feature Minitab 16, with Minitab 17. For certain methods, there may be minor differences in labeling of dialog box elements and some outputs will appear formatted slightly differently than the Minitab 16 outputs shown in this book. Significant differences, such as changes in menu selection sequences, are noted in the instructions. If you plan to use Minitab 17 extensively, download the *Using Minitab 17* supplement available on the student download page for this book or inside the MyStatLab course for this book. (See Appendix Section C.2 for more information.)

Self-Test Solutions and Answers to Selected Even-Numbered Problems

The following sections present worked-out solutions to Self-Test Problems and brief answers to most of the even-numbered problems in the text. For more detailed solutions, including explanations, interpretations, and Excel and Minitab results, see the *Student Solutions Manual*.

CHAPTER 1

1.2 Small, medium, and large sizes represent different sizes.

1.4 (a) The number of cellphones is a numerical variable that is discrete because the outcome is a count. **(b)** Monthly data usage is a numerical variable that is continuous because any value within a range of values can occur. **(c)** Number of text messages exchanged per month is a numerical variable that is discrete because the outcome is a count. **(d)** Voice usage per month is a numerical variable that is continuous because any value within a range of values can occur. **(e)** Whether a cellphone is used for email is a categorical variable because the answer can be only yes or no.

1.6 (a) Categorical **(b)** Numerical, continuous **(c)** Categorical **(d)** Numerical, discrete **(e)** Categorical.

1.8 (a) Numerical, continuous **(b)** Numerical, discrete **(c)** Numerical, continuous **(d)** Categorical.

1.10 The underlying variable, ability of the students, may be continuous, but the measuring device, the test, does not have enough precision to distinguish between the two students.

1.18 Sample without replacement: Read from left to right in three-digit sequences and continue unfinished sequences from the end of the row to the beginning of the next row:
Row 05: 338 505 855 551 438 855 077 186 579 488 767 833 170
Rows 05–06: 897
Row 06: 340 033 648 847 204 334 639 193 639 411 095 924
Rows 06–07: 707
Row 07: 054 329 776 100 871 007 255 980 646 886 823 920 461
Row 08: 893 829 380 900 796 959 453 410 181 277 660 908 887
Rows 08–09: 237
Row 09: 818 721 426 714 050 785 223 801 670 353 362 449
Rows 09–10: 406
Note: All sequences above 902 and duplicates are discarded.

1.20 A simple random sample would be less practical for personal interviews because of travel costs (unless interviewees are paid to go to a central interviewing location).

1.22 Here all members of the population are equally likely to be selected, and the sample selection mechanism is based on chance. But selection of two elements is not independent; for example, if A is in the sample, we know that B is also and that C and D are not.

1.24 (a)

Row 16: 2323 6737 5131 8888 1718 0654 6832 4647 6510 4877
Row 17: 4579 4269 2615 1308 2455 7830 5550 5852 5514 7182
Row 18: 0989 3205 0514 2256 8514 4642 7567 8896 2977 8822
Row 19: 5438 2745 9891 4991 4523 6847 9276 8646 1628 3554

Row 20: 9475 0899 2337 0892 0048 8033 6945 9826 9403 6858
Row 21: 7029 7341 3553 1403 3340 4205 0823 4144 1048 2949
Row 22: 8515 7479 5432 9792 6575 5760 0408 8112 2507 3742
Row 23: 1110 0023 4012 8607 4697 9664 4894 3928 7072 5815
Row 24: 3687 1507 7530 5925 7143 1738 1688 5625 8533 5041
Row 25: 2391 3483 5763 3081 6090 5169 0546
Note: All sequences above 5,000 are discarded. There were no repeating sequences.

(b)

089	189	289	389	489	589	689	789	889	989
1089	1189	1289	1389	1489	1589	1689	1789	1889	1989
2089	2189	2289	2389	2489	2589	2689	2789	2889	2989
3089	3189	3289	3389	3489	3589	3689	3789	3889	3989
4089	4189	4289	4389	4489	4589	4689	4789	4889	4989

(c) With the single exception of invoice 0989, the invoices selected in the simple random sample are not the same as those selected in the systematic sample. It would be highly unlikely that a simple random sample would select the same units as a systematic sample.

1.26 Before accepting the results of a survey of college students, you might want to know, for example: Who funded the survey? Why was it conducted? What was the population from which the sample was selected? What sampling design was used? What mode of response was used: a personal interview, a telephone interview, or a mail survey? Were interviewers trained? Were survey questions field-tested? What questions were asked? Were the questions clear, accurate, unbiased, and valid? What operational definition of "vast majority" was used? What was the response rate? What was the sample size?

1.28 The results are based on an online survey. If the frame is supposed to be smartphone and tablet users, how is the population defined? This is a self-selecting sample of people who responded online, so there is an undefined nonresponse error. Sampling error cannot be determined since this is not a random sample.

1.30 Before accepting the results of the survey, you might want to know, for example: Who funded the study? Why was it conducted? What was the population from which the sample was selected? What sampling design was used? What mode of response was used: a personal interview, a telephone interview, or a mail survey? Were interviewers trained? Were survey questions field-tested? What other questions were asked? Were the questions clear, accurate, unbiased, and valid? What was the response rate? What was the margin of error? What was the sample size? What frame was used?

1.42 (a) All benefitted employees at the university. **(b)** The 3,095 employees who responded to the survey. **(c)** Gender and marital status are categorical. Age (years), education level (years completed), and household income ($) are numerical.

CHAPTER 2

2.2 (a) Table of frequencies for all student responses:

	STUDENT MAJOR CATEGORIES			
GENDER	A	C	M	Totals
Male	14	9	2	25
Female	6	6	3	15
Totals	20	15	5	40

(b) Table based on total percentages:

	STUDENT MAJOR CATEGORIES			
GENDER	A	C	M	Totals
Male	35.0%	22.5%	5.0%	62.5%
Female	15.0%	15.0%	7.5%	37.5%
Totals	50.0%	37.5%	12.5%	100.0%

Table based on row percentages:

	STUDENT MAJOR CATEGORIES			
GENDER	A	C	M	Totals
Male	56.0%	36.0%	8.0%	100.0%
Female	40.0%	40.0%	20.0%	100.0%
Totals	50.0%	37.5%	12.5%	100.0%

Table based on column percentages:

	STUDENT MAJOR CATEGORIES			
GENDER	A	C	M	Totals
Male	70.0%	60.0%	40.0%	62.5%
Female	30.0%	40.0%	60.0%	37.5%
Totals	100.0%	100.0%	100.0%	100.0%

2.4 (a) The percentage of complaints for each automaker:

Automaker	Frequency	Percentage	Cumulative Pct.
General Motors	551	18.91%	18.91%
Other	516	17.71%	36.62%
Nissan Motors Corporation	467	16.03%	52.64%
Ford Motor Company	440	15.10%	67.74%
Chrysler LLC	439	15.07%	82.81%
Toyota Motor Sales	332	11.39%	94.20%
American Honda	169	5.80%	100.00%

(b) General Motors has the most complaints, followed by Other, Nissan Motors Corporation, Ford Motor Company, Chrysler LLC, Toyota Motor Sales and American Honda.

(c) The percentage of complaints for each category:

Category	Frequency	Percentage	Cumulative Pct.
Powertrain	1148	42.82%	42.82%
Steering	397	14.81%	57.63%
Interior Electronics/Hardware	279	10.41%	68.03%
Fuel/Emission/Exhaust System	240	8.95%	76.99%
Airbags and Seatbelts	201	7.50%	84.48%
Body and Glass	182	6.79%	91.27%
Brakes	163	6.08%	97.35%
Tires and Wheels	71	2.65%	100.00%

(d) Powertrain has the most complaints, followed by steering, interior electronics/hardware, fuel/emission/exhaust system, airbags and seatbelts, body and glass, brakes, and, finally, tires and wheels.

2.6 (a) The percentages are 3.273, 11.656, 21.815, and 63.256. **(b)** More than 60% of the oil produced is from non-OPEC countries. More than 20% is produced by OPEC countries other than Iran and Saudi Arabia.

2.8 (a) Table of row percentages:

ENJOY SHOPPING FOR CLOTHING	GENDER		
	Male	Female	Total
Yes	46%	54%	100%
No	53%	47%	100%
Total	50%	50%	100%

Table of column percentages:

ENJOY SHOPPING FOR CLOTHING	GENDER		
	Male	Female	Total
Yes	44%	51%	47%
No	56%	49%	53%
Total	100%	100%	100%

Table of total percentages:

ENJOY SHOPPING FOR CLOTHING	GENDER		
	Male	Female	Total
Yes	22%	25%	47%
No	28%	25%	53%
Total	50%	50%	100%

(b) A higher percentage of females enjoy shopping for clothing.

2.10 Social recommendations had very little impact on correct recall. Those who arrived at the link from a recommendation had a correct recall of 73.07% as compared to those who arrived at the link from browsing who had a correct recall of 67.96%.

2.12 73 78 78 78 85 88 91.

2.14 (a) 0 but less than 5 million, 5 million but less than 10 million, 10 million but less than 15 million, 15 million but less than 20 million, 20 million but less than 25 million, 25 million but less than 30 million. **(b)** 5 million. **(c)** 2.5 million, 7.5 million, 12.5 million, 17.5 million, 22.5 million, and 27.5 million.

2.16 (a)

Electricity Costs	Frequency	Percentage
$80 but less than $100	4	8%
$100 but less than $120	7	14%
$120 but less than $140	9	18%
$140 but less than $160	13	26%
$160 but less than $180	9	18%
$180 but less than $200	5	10%
$200 but less than $220	3	6%

(b)

Electricity Costs	Frequency	Percentage	Cumulative %
$ 99	4	8.00%	8.00%
$119	7	14.00%	22.00%
$139	9	18.00%	40.00%
$159	13	26.00%	66.00%
$179	9	18.00%	84.00%
$199	5	10.00%	94.00%
$219	3	6.00%	100.00%

(c) The majority of utility charges are clustered between $120 and $180.

2.18 (a), (b)

Credit Score	Frequency	Percentage	Cumulative %
695 but less than 705	3	2.10%	2.10%
705 but less than 715	12	8.39%	10.49%
715 but less than 725	12	8.39%	18.88%
715 but less than 735	19	13.29%	32.17%
735 but less than 745	18	12.59%	44.76%
745 but less than 755	24	16.78%	61.54%
755 but less than 765	22	15.38%	76.92%
765 but less than 775	20	13.99%	90.91%
775 but less than 785	10	6.99%	97.90%
795 but less than 795	3	2.10%	100.00%

(c) The average credit scores are concentrated around 750.

2.20 (a)

Width	Frequency	Percentage
8.310 but less than 8.330	3	6.12%
8.330 but less than 8.350	2	4.08%
8.350 but less than 8.370	1	2.04%
8.370 but less than 8.390	4	8.16%
8.390 but less than 8.410	5	10.20%
8.410 but less than 8.430	16	32.65%
8.430 but less than 8.450	5	10.20%
8.450 but less than 8.470	5	10.20%
8.470 but less than 8.490	6	12.24%
8.490 but less than 8.510	2	4.08%

(b)

Width	Percentage Less Than
8.310	0
8.330	6.12
8.350	10.20
8.370	12.24
8.390	20.40
8.410	30.60
8.430	63.25
8.450	73.45
8.470	83.65
8.490	95.89
8.51	100.00

(c) All the troughs will meet the company's requirements of between 8.31 and 8.61 inches wide.

2.22 (a)

Bulb Life (hours)	Percentage, Mfgr A	Percentage, Mfgr B
6,500 but less than 7,500	7.5%	0.0%
7,500 but less than 8,500	12.5%	5.0%
8,500 but less than 9,500	50.0%	20.0%
9,500 but less than 10,500	22.5%	40.0%
10,500 but less than 11,500	7.5%	22.5%
11,500 but less than 12,500	0.0%	12.5%

(b)

% Less Than	Percentage Less Than, Mfgr A	Percentage Less Than, Mfgr B
7,500	7.5%	0.0%
8,500	20.0%	5.0%
9,500	70.0%	25.0%
10,500	92.5%	65.0%
11,500	100.0%	87.5%
12,500	100.0%	100.0%

(c) Manufacturer B produces bulbs with longer lives than Manufacturer A. The cumulative percentage for Manufacturer B shows that 65% of its bulbs lasted less than 10,500 hours, contrasted with 92.5% of Manufacturer A's bulbs. None of Manufacturer A's bulbs lasted at least 11,500 hours, but 12.5% of Manufacturer B's bulbs lasted at least 11,500 hours. At the same time, 7.5% of Manufacturer A's bulbs lasted less than 7,500 hours, whereas none of Manufacturer B's bulbs lasted less than 7,500 hours.

2.24 (b) The Pareto chart is best for portraying these data because it not only sorts the frequencies in descending order but also provides the cumulative line on the same chart. **(c)** You can conclude that "improved regulation and oversight of global systemic risk" and "improved transparency of of financial reporting and and other financial disclosures account for 50% of the most needed action to improve investor trust and market integrity.

2.26 (b) 85%. **(d)** The Pareto chart allows you to see which sources account for most of the electricity.

2.28 (b) Since energy use is spread over many types of appliances, a bar chart may be best in showing which types of appliances used the most energy. **(c)** Heating, water heating, and cooling accounted for 40% of the residential energy use in the United States.

2.30 (b) A higher percentage of females enjoy shopping for clothing.

2.32 (b) Social recommendations had very little impact on correct recall.

2.34 50 74 74 76 81 89 92.

2.36 (a)

Stem Unit	100
1	0 1 1 3 4 5 6 6 7 7 7
2	7 8
3	0 1 1 2 2 2 2 4 4 4 8
4	0 3 6 7
5	4
6	6

(b) The results are concentrated between $200 and $380.

2.38 (c) The majority of utility charges are clustered between $120 and $180.

2.40 Property taxes seem concentrated between $1,000 and $1,500 and also between $500 and $1,000 per capita. There were more states with property taxes per capita below $1,500 than above $1,500.

2.42 The average credit scores are concentrated around 750.

2.44 (c) All the troughs will meet the company's requirements of between 8.31 and 8.61 inches wide.

2.46 (c) Manufacturer B produces bulbs with longer lives than Manufacturer A.

2.48 (b) Yes, there is a strong positive relationship between X and Y. As X increases, so does Y.

2.50 (c) There appears to be a linear relationship between the first weekend gross and either the U.S. gross or the worldwide gross of Harry Potter movies. However, this relationship is greatly affected by the results of the last movie, *Deathly Hallows, Part II*.

2.52 (a), (c) There appears to be a positive relationship between the coaches' total pay and revenue. Yes, this is borne out by the data.

2.54 (b) There is a great deal of variation in the returns from decade to decade. Most of the returns are between 5% and 15%. The 1950s, 1980s, and 1990s had exceptionally high returns, and only the 1930s and 2000s had negative returns.

2.56 (b) There was a decline in movie attendance between 2001 and 2013. During that time, movie attendance increased from 2002 to 2004 but then decreased to a level below that in 2001.

2.58 (a) Pivot table of tallies in terms of counts:

	Five	Four	One	Three	Two	Grand Total
Growth	**18**	**76**	**16**	**74**	**43**	**227**
Large	9	31	5	37	21	103
Mid-Cap	7	28	4	20	13	72
Small	2	17	7	17	9	52
Value	**5**	**22**	**7**	**36**	**19**	**89**
Large	2	13	5	21	9	50
Mid-Cap	1	4		9	5	19
Small	2	5	2	6	5	20
Grand Total	**23**	**98**	**23**	**110**	**62**	**316**

Pivot table in terms of % of total

	Five	Four	One	Three	Two	Grand Total
Growth	**5.70%**	**24.05%**	**5.06%**	**23.42%**	**13.61%**	**71.84%**
Large	2.85%	9.81%	1.58%	11.71%	6.65%	32.59%
Mid-Cap	2.22%	8.86%	1.27%	6.33%	4.11%	22.78%
Small	0.63%	5.38%	2.22%	5.38%	2.85%	16.46%
Value	**1.58%**	**6.96%**	**2.22%**	**11.39%**	**6.01%**	**28.16%**
Large	0.63%	4.11%	1.58%	6.65%	2.85%	15.82%
Mid-Cap	0.32%	1.27%	0.00%	2.85%	1.58%	6.01%
Small	0.63%	1.58%	0.63%	1.90%	1.58%	6.33%
Grand Total	**7.28%**	**31.01%**	**7.28%**	**34.81%**	**19.62%**	**100.00%**

(b) Patterns of star rating conditioned on market cap:

For the growth funds as a group, most are rated as four-star, followed by three-star, two-star, five-star, and one-star. The pattern of star rating is the same across the different market caps within the growth funds with most of the funds receiving a four-star rating, followed by three-star, two-star, five-star, and one-star with the exception of small-cap funds with most of the funds receiving a four-star or three-star rating, followed by two-star, one-star, and five-star.

For the value funds as a group, most are rated as three-star, followed by four-star, two-star, one-star, and five-star. Within the value funds, the large-cap funds follow the same pattern as the value funds as a group. Most of the mid-cap funds are rated as three-star, followed by two-star, four-star, five-star, and one-star while most of the small-cap funds are rated as three-star, followed by either two-star or four-star, and either one-star or five star.

Patterns of market cap conditioned on star rating:

Most of the growth funds are large-cap, followed by mid-cap and small-cap. The pattern is similar among the five-star, four-star, three-star, and two-star growth funds, but among the one-star growth funds, most are small-cap, followed by large-cap and mid-cap.

The largest share of the value funds is large-cap, followed by small-cap and mid-cap. The pattern is similar among the four-star and one-star value funds. Among the three-star value funds, most are large-cap, followed by mid-cap and then small-cap while most are large-cap, followed by equal portions of mid-cap and small-cap among the two-star value funds and most are either large-cap or small-cap followed by mid-cap among the five-star value funds.

2.60 (a) Pivot table of tallies in terms of counts:

	Five	Four	One	Three	Two	Grand Total
Growth	**18**	**76**	**16**	**74**	**43**	**227**
Average	3	15	6	28	22	74
High		1	5	1	3	10
Low	15	60	5	45	18	143
Value	**5**	**22**	**7**	**36**	**19**	**89**
Average	1		3	7	6	17
High			2		1	3
Low	4	22	2	29	12	69
Grand Total	**23**	**98**	**23**	**110**	**62**	**316**

Pivot table of tallies in terms of percentage of grand total:

	Five	Four	One	Three	Two	Grand Total
Growth	**5.70%**	**24.05%**	**5.06%**	**23.42%**	**13.61%**	**71.84%**
Average	0.95%	4.75%	1.90%	8.86%	6.96%	23.42%
High	0.00%	0.32%	1.58%	0.32%	0.95%	3.16%
Low	4.75%	18.99%	1.58%	14.24%	5.70%	45.25%
Value	**1.58%**	**6.96%**	**2.22%**	**11.39%**	**6.01%**	**28.16%**
Average	0.32%	0.00%	0.95%	2.22%	1.90%	5.38%
High	0.00%	0.00%	0.63%	0.00%	0.32%	0.95%
Low	1.27%	6.96%	0.63%	9.18%	3.80%	21.84%
Grand Total	**7.28%**	**31.01%**	**7.28%**	**34.81%**	**19.62%**	**100.00%**

(b) Patterns of star rating conditioned on risk:

For the growth funds as a group, most are rated as four-star, followed by three-star, two-star, five-star, and one-star. The pattern of star rating is the same among the low-risk growth funds. The pattern is different among the high-risk and average-risk growth funds. Among the high-risk growth funds, most are rated as one-star, followed by two-star, equal portions of three-star and four-star, with no five-star. Among the average-risk growth funds, most are rated as three-star, followed by two-star, four-star, one-star, and five-star.

For the value funds as a group, most are rated as three-star, followed by four-star, two-star, one-star and five-star. Among the average-risk value funds, most are three-star, followed by two-star, five-star, and one-star with no four-star. Among the high-risk value funds, most are one-star, followed by two-star with no three-star, four-star, or five-star. Among the low-risk value funds, most are three-star, followed by four-star, two-star, five-star, and one-star. Patterns of risk conditioned on star rating:

Most of the growth funds are rated as low-risk, followed by average-risk and then high-risk. The pattern is the same among the three-star, four-star, and five-star growth funds. Among the one-star growth funds, most are average-risk, followed by equal portions of high-risk and low-risk. Among the two-star growth funds, most are average-risk, followed by low-risk and high-risk.

Most of the value funds are rated as low-risk, followed by average-risk and then high-risk. The pattern is the same among the two-star, three-star, and five-star value funds. Among the one-star value funds, most are average-risk, followed by equal portions of high-risk and low-risk. Among the four-star value funds, all are low-risk with no average-risk or high-risk.

2.62 (b) The values of the teams varied from $405 million for the Milwaukee Bucks to $1,400 million for the New York Knicks. The change in values was not consistent across the teams. The Brooklyn Nets had the largest increase of 47% in value probably due to their move to a new arena in Brooklyn. Two moderately valued teams, the Houston Rockets had increases in value of 36% and 35%, respectively, perhaps due to their improved performance.

2.64 (c) Almost all the countries that had lower GDP had lower Internet use except for the Republic of Korea. The pattern of mobile cellular subscriptions does not seem to depend on the GDP of the country.

2.66 (b) There are 37 funds.

2.68 (b) There is only one fund.

2.88 (c) The publisher gets the largest portion (64.8%) of the revenue. About half (32.3%) of the revenue received by the publisher covers manufacturing costs. The publisher's marketing and promotion account for the next largest share of the revenue, at 15.4%. Author, bookstore employee salaries and benefits, and publisher administrative costs and taxes each account for around 10% of the revenue, whereas the publisher after-tax profit, bookstore operations, bookstore pretax profit, and freight constitute the "trivial few" allocations of the revenue. Yes, the bookstore gets twice the revenue of the authors.

2.90 (b) The pie chart may be best since with only five categories, it enables you to see the portion of the whole in each category. **(d)** The pie chart may be best since, with only three categories it enables you to see the portion of the whole in each category. **(e)** Marketers mostly find out about new marketing agencies from calls/emails from agencies and referrals from friends and colleagues. Almost 90% believe that it is important for a marketing agency to specialize in the marketer's industry.

2.92 (a)

DESSERT ORDERED	GENDER Male	Female	Total
Yes	34%	66%	100%
No	52%	48%	100%
Total	48%	52%	100%

DESSERT ORDERED	GENDER Male	Female	Total
Yes	17%	29%	23%
No	83%	71%	77%
Total	100%	100%	100%

DESSERT ORDERED	GENDER Male	Female	Total
Yes	8%	15%	23%
No	40%	37%	77%
Total	48%	52%	100%

DESSERT ORDERED	BEEF ENTRÉE Yes	No	Total
Yes	52%	48%	100%
No	25%	75%	100%
Total	31%	69%	100%

DESSERT ORDERED	BEEF ENTRÉE Yes	No	Total
Yes	38%	16%	23%
No	62%	84%	77%
Total	100%	100%	100%

DESSERT ORDERED	BEEF ENTRÉE Yes	No	Total
Yes	11.75%	10.79%	22.54%
No	19.52%	57.94%	77.46%
Total	31.27%	68.73%	100%

(b) If the owner is interested in finding out the percentage of males and females who order dessert or the percentage of those who order a beef entrée and a dessert among all patrons, the table of total percentages is most informative. If the owner is interested in the effect of gender on ordering of dessert or the effect of ordering a beef entrée on the ordering of dessert, the table of column percentages will be most informative. Because dessert is usually ordered after the main entrée, and the owner has no direct control over the gender of patrons, the table of row percentages is not very useful here. **(c)** 17% of the men ordered desserts, compared to 29% of the women; women are almost twice as likely to order dessert as women. Almost 38% of the patrons ordering a beef entrée ordered dessert, compared to 16% of patrons ordering all other entrées. Patrons ordering beef are more than 2.3 times as likely to order dessert as patrons ordering any other entrée.

2.94 (a) Most of the complaints were against the airlines. **(c)** Most of the complaints against U.S. airlines were about flight problems, followed by baggage. **(d)** Most of the complaints against foreign airlines were about baggage, then reservations/ticketing/boarding, flight problems, and customer service.

Complaint Category	Complaints Against U.S. Airlines	Complaints Against Foreign Airlines
Flight Problems	263	41
Oversales	38	5
Reservation/Ticketing/Boarding	98	41
Fares	23	4
Refunds	48	24
Baggage	147	56
Customer Service	92	30
Disability	38	8
Advertising	8	0
Discrimination	6	3
Animals	0	0
Other	14	5
Total	775	217

2.96 (c) The alcohol percentage is concentrated between 4% and 6%, with more between 4% and 5%. The calories are concentrated between 140 and 160. The carbohydrates are concentrated between 12 and 15. There are outliers in the percentage of alcohol in both tails. The outlier in the lower tail is due to the non-alcoholic beer O'Doul's, with only a 0.4% alcohol content. There are a few beers with alcohol content as high as around 11.5%. There are a few beers with calorie content as high as around 327.5 and carbohydrates as high as 31.5. There is a strong positive relationship between percentage of alcohol and calories and between calories and carbohydrates, and there is a moderately positive relationship between percentage alcohol and carbohydrates.

2.98 (c) There appears to be a moderate positive relationship between the yield of the one-year CD and the five-year CD.

2.100 (a)

Frequency (Boston)

Weight (Boston)	Frequency	Percentage
3,015 but less than 3,050	2	0.54%
3,050 but less than 3,085	44	11.96%
3,085 but less than 3,120	122	33.15%
3,120 but less than 3,155	131	35.60%
3,155 but less than 3,190	58	15.76%
3,190 but less than 3,225	7	1.90%
3,225 but less than 3,260	3	0.82%
3,260 but less than 3,295	1	0.27%

(b)

Frequency (Vermont)

Weight (Vermont)	Frequency	Percentage
3,550 but less than 3,600	4	1.21%
3,600 but less than 3,650	31	9.39%
3,650 but less than 3,700	115	34.85%
3,700 but less than 3,750	131	39.70%
3,750 but less than 3,800	36	10.91%
3,800 but less than 3,850	12	3.64%
3,850 but less than 3,900	1	0.30%

(d) 0.54% of the Boston shingles pallets are underweight and 0.27% are overweight. 1.21% of the Vermont shingles pallets are underweight and 3.94% are overweight.

2.102 (c)

Calories	Frequency	Percentage	Limit	Percentage Less Than
50 but less than 100	3	12%	100	12%
100 but less than 150	3	12%	150	24%
150 but less than 200	9	36%	200	60%
200 but less than 250	6	24%	250	84%
250 but less than 300	3	12%	300	96%
300 but less than 350	0	0%	350	96%
350 but less than 400	1	4%	400	100%

Cholesterol	Frequency	Percentage	Limit	Percentage Less Than
0 but less than 50	2	8%	50	8%
50 but less than 100	17	68%	100	76%
100 but less than 150	4	16%	150	92%
150 but less than 200	1	4%	200	96%
200 but less than 250	0	0%	250	96%
250 but less than 300	0	0%	300	96%
300 but less than 350	0	0%	350	96%
350 but less than 400	0	0%	400	96%
400 but less than 450	0	0%	450	96%
450 but less than 500	1	4%	500	100%

The sampled fresh red meats, poultry, and fish vary from 98 to 397 calories per serving, with the highest concentration between 150 and 200 calories. One protein source, spareribs, with 397 calories, is more than 100 calories above the next-highest-caloric food. The protein content of the sampled foods varies from 16 to 33 grams, with 68% of the values falling between 24 and 32 grams. Spareribs and fried liver are both very different from other foods sampled—the former on calories and the latter on cholesterol content.

2.104 (b) There is a downward trend in the amount filled. **(c)** The amount filled in the next bottle will most likely be below 1.894 liters. **(d)** The scatter plot of the amount of soft drink filled against time reveals the trend of the data, whereas a histogram only provides information on the distribution of the data.

2.106 (a) The percentage of downloads is 9.64% for the Original Call to Action Button and 9.64% for the New Call to Action Button. **(c)** The New Call to Action Button has a higher percentage of downloads at 13.64% when compared to the Original Call to Action Button with a 9.64% of downloads. **(d)** The percentage of downloads is 8.90% for the Original web design and 9.41% for the New web design. **(f)** The New web design has only a slightly higher percentage of downloads at 9.41% when compared to the Original web design with an 8.90% of downloads. **(g)** The New web design is only slightly more successful than the Original web design while the New Call to Action Button is much more successful than the Original Call to Action Button with about 41% higher percentage of downloads.

(h)

Call to Action Button	Web Design	Percentage of Downloads
Old	Old	8.30%
New	Old	13.70%
Old	New	9.50%
New	New	17.00%

(i) Call to Action Button and the Original web design. **(j)** The New web design is only slightly more successful than the Original web design while the New Call to Action Button is much more successful than the Original Call to Action Button with about 41% higher percentage of downloads. However, the combination of the New Call to Action Button and the New web design results in more than twice as high a percentage of downloads than the combination of the Original Call to Action Button and the Origuinal web design.

CHAPTER 3

3.2 (a) Mean $= 7$, median $= 7$, mode $= 7$. **(b)** Range $= 9, S^2 = 10.8$, $S = 3.286, CV = 46.948\%$. **(c)** Z scores: 0, -0.913, 0.609, 0, -1.217, 1.522. None of the Z scores are larger than 3.0 or smaller than -3.0. There is no outlier. **(d)** Symmetric because mean $=$ median.

3.4 (a) Mean $= 2$, median $= 7$, mode $= 7$. **(b)** Range $= 17, S^2 = 62$ $S = 7.874, CV = 393.7\%$. **(c)** 0.635, -0.889, -1.270, 0.635, 0.889. There are no outliers. **(d)** Left-skewed because mean $<$ median.

3.6 (a)

	Grade X	Grade Y
Mean	575	575.4
Median	575	575
Standard deviation	6.40	2.07

(b) If quality is measured by central tendency, Grade X tires provide slightly better quality because X's mean and median are both equal to the expected value, 575 mm. If, however, quality is measured by consistency, Grade Y provides better quality because, even though Y's mean is only slightly larger than the mean for Grade X, Y's standard deviation is much smaller. The range in values for Grade Y is 5 mm compared to the range in values for Grade X, which is 16 mm.

(c)

	Grade X	Grade Y, Altered
Mean	575	577.4
Median	575	575
Standard deviation	6.40	6.11

When the fifth Y tire measures 588 mm rather than 578 mm, Y's mean inner diameter becomes 577.4 mm, which is larger than X's mean inner diameter, and Y's standard deviation increases from 2.07 mm to 6.11 mm. In this case, X's tires are providing better quality in terms of the mean inner diameter, with only slightly more variation among the tires than Y's.

3.8 (a), (b)

Spend ($)

Mean	56.40
Median	55.35
Minimum	22.90
Maximum	108.25
Range	85.35
Variance	380.4062
Standard Deviation	19.5040
Coefficient of Variation	34.58%
Skewness	1.1078
Kurtosis	3.0651
Count	15

(c) The mean is greater than the median and the skewness statistic is positive, so the amount spent is right- or positive-skewed. **(d)** The mean amount spent is $56.40 and half the customers spent more than $55.35. The amount spent is right-skewed since there are some amounts spent that are high. The average scatter around the mean is $19.50. The difference between the largest amount spent and the smallest amount spent is $85.35.

3.10 (a), (b)

MPG

Mean	22.85
Median	22
Minimum	21
Maximum	26
Range	5
Variance	2.6605
Standard Deviation	1.6311
Coeff. of Variation	7.14%
Skewness	0.7521
Kurtosis	−0.5423
Count	20

MPG	Z Score	MPG	Z Score
26	1.9312	21	−1.1342
22	−0.5211	21	−1.1342
23	0.0920	22	−0.5211
21	−1.1342	22	−0.5211
25	1.3181	23	0.0920
24	0.7050	24	0.7050
22	−0.5211	23	0.0920
26	1.9312	22	−0.5211
25	−1.3181	21	−1.1342
22	−0.5211	22	−0.5211

(c) Since the mean MPG is greater than the median and the skewness statistic is positive, the distribution of MPG is right- or positive-skewed. **(d)** The mean miles per gallon of small SUVs is 22.85 and half the small SUVs achieve at least 22 miles per gallon. There are no outliers in the data as the largest Z score is 1.9312 and the smallest Z score is −1.1342. The average scatter around the mean is 1.6311 mpg. The lowest mpg is 21 and the highest is 26. The mpg of mid-sized sedans is much higher than for small SUVs. The mean miles per gallon of mid-sized sedans is 27.7727 and half the mid-sized sedans achieve at least 26 miles per gallon. The average scatter around the mean is 5.1263 mpg. The lowest mpg of mid-sized sedans is 22 and the highest is 39.

3.12 (a), (b)

Facebook Penetration (%)

Mean	39.4091
Median	42
Minimum	6
Maximum	80
Range	74
Variance	340.6342
Standard Deviation	18.4563
Coefficient of Variation	46.83%
Skewness	0.0126
Kurtosis	−0.1492
Count	22

Country	Facebook Penetration (%)	Z Score
Argentina	56	0.8989
Australia	57	0.9531
Brazil	43	0.1946
Canada	55	0.8447
France	42	0.1404
Germany	35	−0.2389
India	7	−1.7560
Indonesia	25	−0.7807
Italy	42	0.1404
Japan	17	−1.2142
Mexico	43	0.1946
Nigeria	6	−1.8102
Poland	31	−0.4556
Saudi Arabia	28	−0.6182
Singapore	59	1.0615
South Africa	20	−1.0516
South Korea	27	−0.6724
Thailand	36	−0.1847
Turkey	45	0.3029
United Arab Republic	80	2.1993
United Kingdom	57	0.9531
United States	56	0.8989

The highest Z score is 2.1993 and the lowest Z score is −1.8102, so there are no extreme values. **(c)** The mean is less than the median, so Facebook penetration is left-skewed. **(d)** The mean Facebook penetration is 39.4901% and half the countries have Facebook penetration greater than or equal to 42%. The average scatter around the mean is 18.4563%. The lowest Facebook penetration is 6% in Nigeria and the highest Facebook penetration is 80% in the United Arab Republic.

3.14 (a), (b)

Price (USD)	
Mean	164.375
Median	168.5
Range	36
Variance	164.2679
Standard Deviation	12.8167

(c) The mean room price is $164.375 and half the room prices are greater than or equal to $168.50, so room price is left-skewed. The average scatter around the mean is 12.8167. The lowest room price is $143 in France and the highest room price is $179 in the United States.

3.16 (a) Mean = 7.11, median = 6.68. **(b)** Variance = 4.336, standard deviation = 2.082, range = 6.67, $CV = 29.27\%$.

Waiting Time	Z Score
9.66	1.222431
5.90	−0.58336
8.02	0.434799
5.79	−0.63619
8.73	0.775786
3.82	−1.58231
8.01	0.429996
8.35	0.593286
10.49	1.62105
6.68	−0.20875
5.64	−0.70823
4.08	−1.45744
6.17	−0.45369
9.91	1.342497
5.47	−0.78987

(c) Because the mean is greater than the median, the distribution is right-skewed. **(d)** The mean and median are both greater than five minutes. The distribution is right-skewed, meaning that there are some unusually high values. Further, 13 of the 15 bank customers sampled (or 86.7%) had waiting times greater than five minutes. So the customer is likely to experience a waiting time in excess of five minutes. The manager overstated the bank's service record in responding that the customer would "almost certainly" not wait longer than five minutes for service.

3.18 (a)

Average of 1YrReturn%	Star Rating					
Type	Five	Four	One	Three	Two	Grand Total
Growth	16.5544	15.2193	10.3575	13.9957	13.6058	14.2780
Large	18.0756	15.4971	12.3320	14.8743	17.1257	15.6771
Mid-Cap	15.5200	15.0400	10.0875	13.4140	8.7046	13.2160
Small	13.3300	15.0082	9.1014	12.7676	12.4722	12.9771
Value	17.2820	12.7295	13.4957	15.3603	15.4863	14.6982
Large	16.4150	11.7515	12.1120	14.5648	14.1633	13.5898
Mid-Cap	16.4400	16.1625		16.7267	17.4680	16.7879
Small	18.5700	12.5260	16.9550	16.0950	15.8860	15.4840
Grand Total	16.7126	14.6604	11.3126	14.4423	14.1821	14.3963

(b)

StdDev of 1YrReturn%	Star Rating					
Type	Five	Four	One	Three	Two	Grand Total
Growth	4.0813	3.6946	5.0187	3.8308	7.6709	5.0041
Large	4.3119	4.1374	4.6690	2.7064	7.4925	4.7615
Mid-Cap	3.3099	3.1017	8.7458	4.8023	7.6199	5.4705
Small	4.4265	3.9244	2.2479	4.3906	2.9127	4.0854
Value	6.9822	4.5679	4.3343	4.1815	3.6530	4.4651
Large	1.1384	3.6990	4.3732	4.5739	2.5803	4.0592
Mid-Cap	#DIV/0!	4.1910		3.1676	4.5127	3.4837
Small	13.7179	6.3546	1.6476	3.9994	4.1620	5.4861
Grand Total	4.6722	4.0202	4.9474	3.9820	6.7243	4.8551

(c) The mean one-year return of small-cap value funds is higher than that of the small-cap growth funds across the different star ratings with the exception of those rated as four-star. On the other hand, the mean one-year return of large-cap value funds is lower than that of the growth funds across the different star ratings, but the mid-cap value funds are higher across the different star ratings.

The standard deviation of the one-year return of growth funds is generally higher than that of the value funds across all the star ratings and market caps with the exception of the large-cap and three-star, mid-cap and five-star, mid-cap and four-star, mid-cap and one-star, small-cap and five-star, small-cap and four-star, and small-cap and two-star.

3.20 (a)

Average of 1YrReturn%	Star Rating					
Type	Five	Four	One	Three	Two	Grand Total
Growth	16.5544	15.2193	10.3575	13.9957	13.6058	14.2780
Average	16.5333	16.2233	11.6467	13.0514	10.8005	13.0524
High		14.6100	9.3620	14.5900	33.7200	17.7170
Low	16.5587	14.9785	9.8060	14.5700	13.6822	14.6717
Value	17.2820	12.7295	13.4957	15.3603	15.4863	14.6982
Average	28.2700		13.9800	16.4786	17.5267	17.1012
High		12.0500			22.1400	15.4133
Low	14.5350	12.7295	14.2150	15.0903	13.9117	14.0751
Grand Total	16.7126	14.6604	11.3126	14.4423	14.1821	14.3963

(b)

StdDev of 1YrReturn%	Star Rating					
Type	Five	Four	One	Three	Two	Grand Total
Growth	4.0813	3.6946	5.0187	3.8308	7.6709	5.0041
Average	3.0735	4.9524	7.6948	4.9654	6.9272	6.0163
High		#DIV/0!	2.6945	#DIV/0!	0.2946	11.3821
Low	4.3448	3.3483	3.0114	2.8818	2.1220	3.3562
Value	6.9822	4.5679	4.3343	4.1815	3.6530	4.4651
Average	#DIV/0!		4.0506	2.9673	3.8277	4.4488
High		8.5843			#DIV/0!	8.4131
Low	3.8335	4.5679	0.5445	4.4251	2.4852	4.1475
Grand Total	4.6722	4.0202	4.9474	3.9820	6.7243	4.8551

(c) In general, the mean one-year return of the five-star rated growth funds is highest, followed by that of the four-star, three-star, two-star, and one-star rated growth funds across the various risk levels. However, a similar pattern does not hold through among the value funds.

There is no obvious pattern in the standard deviation of the one-year return.

3.22 (a) 4, 9, 5. **(b)** 3, 4, 7, 9, 12. **(c)** The distances between the median and the extremes are close, 4 and 5, but the differences in the tails are different (1 on the left and 3 on the right), so this distribution is slightly right-skewed. **(d)** In Problem 3.2 (d), because mean = median, the distribution is symmetric. The box part of the graph is symmetric, but the tails show right-skewness.

3.24 (a) $-6.5, 8, 14.5$. **(b)** $-8, -6.5, 7, 8, 9$. **(c)** The shape is left-skewed. **(d)** This is consistent with the answer in Problem 3.4 (d).

3.26 (a), (b) What is given is the five-number summary Minimum $= 6$ $Q_1 = 27$ Median $= 42$ $Q_3 = 56$ Maximum $= 80$ Interquartile range $= 29$ **(c)** the boxplot is approximately symmetric.

3.28 (a), (b) What is given is the five-number summary Minimum $= 21$ $Q_1 = 22$ Median $= 22$ $Q_3 = 24$ Maximum $= 26$ Interquartile range $= 2$

3.30 (a) Commercial district five-number summary: 0.38 3.2 4.5 5.55 6.46. Residential area five-number summary: 3.82 5.64 6.68 8.73 10.49. **(b)** Commercial district: The distribution is left-skewed. Residential area: The distribution is slightly right-skewed. **(c)** The central tendency of the waiting times for the bank branch located in the commercial district of a city is lower than that of the branch located in the residential area. There are a few long waiting times for the branch located in the residential area, whereas there are a few exceptionally short waiting times for the branch located in the commercial area.

3.32 (a) Population mean, $\mu = 6$. **(b)** Population standard deviation, $\sigma = 1.673$, population variance, $\sigma^2 = 2.8$.

3.34 (a) 68%. **(b)** 95%. **(c)** Not calculable, 75%, 88.89%. **(d)** $\mu - 4\sigma$ to $\mu + 4\sigma$ or -2.8 to 19.2.

3.36 (a)

$$\text{Mean} = \frac{662,960}{51} = 12,999.22, \text{ variance} = \frac{762,944,726.6}{51} = 14,959,700.52,$$

standard deviation $= \sqrt{14,959,700.52} = 3,867.78$. **(b)** 64.71%, 98.04%, and 100% of these states have mean per capita energy consumption within 1, 2, and 3 standard deviations of the mean, respectively. **(c)** This is consistent with 68%, 95%, and 99.7%,

according to the empirical rule. **(d) (a)** Mean $= \dfrac{642,887}{50} = 12,857.74,$

variance $= \dfrac{711,905,533.6}{50} = 14,238,110.67,$ standard deviation

$= \sqrt{14,238,110.67} = 3,773.34$. **(b)** 66%, 98%, and 100% of these states have a mean per capita energy consumption within 1, 2, and 3 standard deviations of the mean, respectively. **(c)** This is consistent with 68%, 95%, and 99.7%, according to the empirical rule.

3.38 (a) Covariance $= 65.2909$, **(b)** $r = +1.0$.

3.40 (a) $\text{cov}(X, Y) = \dfrac{\sum_{i=1}^{n}(X_i - \bar{X})(Y_i - \bar{Y})}{n-1} = \dfrac{800}{6} = 133.3333.$

(b) $r = \dfrac{\text{cov}(X, Y)}{S_X S_Y} = \dfrac{133.3333}{(46.9042)(3.3877)} = 0.8391.$

(c) The correlation coefficient is more valuable for expressing the relationship between calories and sugar because it does not depend on the units used to measure calories and sugar. **(d)** There is a strong positive linear relationship between calories and sugar.

3.42 (a) $\text{cov}(X, Y) = 1.4115 \times 10^{13}$ **(b)** $r = 0.7752$ **(c)** There is a positive linear relationship between the coaches' total pay and revenue.

3.58 (a) Mean $= 43.89$, median $= 45$, 1st quartile $= 18$, 3rd quartile $= 63$. **(b)** Range $= 76$, interquartile range $= 45$, variance $= 639.2564$, standard deviation $= 25.28$, $CV = 57.61\%$. **(c)** The distribution is right-skewed because there are a few policies that require an exceptionally long period to be approved. **(d)** The mean approval process takes 43.89 days, with 50% of the policies being approved in less than 45 days. 50% of the applications are approved between 18 and 63 days. About 67% of the applications are approved between 18.6 and 69.2 days.

3.60 (a) Mean $= 8.421$, median $= 8.42$, range $= 0.186$, $S = 0.0461$. The mean and median width are both 8.42 inches. The range of the widths is 0.186 inch, and the average scatter around the mean is 0.0461 inch. **(b)** 8.312, 8.404, 8.42, 8.459, 8.498. **(c)** Even though the mean = median, the left tail is slightly longer, so the distribution is slightly left-skewed. **(d)** All the troughs in this sample meet the specifications.

3.62 (a), (b)

	Bundle Score	Typical Cost ($)
Mean	54.775	24.175
Standard Error	4.3673	2.8662
Median	62	20
Mode	75	8
Standard Deviation	27.6215	328.6096
Sample Variance	762.9481	18.1276
Kurtosis	−0.8454	2.7664
Skewness	−0.4804	1.5412
Range	98	83
Minimum	2	5
Maximum	100	88
Sum	2,191	967
Count	40	40
First Quartile	34	9
Third Quartile	75	31
Interquartile Range	41	22
CV	50.43%	74.98%

(c) The typical cost is right-skewed, while the bundle score is left-skewed. **(d)** $r = 0.3465$. **(e)** The mean typical cost is $24.18, with an average spread around the mean equaling $18.13. The spread between the lowest and highest costs is $83. The middle 50% of the typical cost fall over a range of $22 from $9 to $31, while half of the typical cost is below $20. The mean bundle score is 54.775, with an average spread around the mean equaling 27.6215. The spread between the lowest and highest scores is 98. The middle 50% of the scores fall over a range of 41 from 34 to 75, while half of the scores are below 62. The typical cost is right-skewed, while the bundle score is left-skewed. There is a weak positive linear relationship between typical cost and bundle score.

3.64 (a) Boston: 0.04, 0.17, 0.23, 0.32, 0.98; Vermont: 0.02, 0.13, 0.20, 0.28, 0.83. **(b)** Both distributions are right-skewed. **(c)** Both sets of shingles did quite well in achieving a granule loss of 0.8 gram or less. Only two Boston shingles had a granule loss greater than 0.8 gram. The next highest to these was 0.6 gram. These two values can be considered outliers. Only 1.176% of the shingles failed the specification. Only one of the Vermont shingles had a granule loss greater than 0.8 gram. The next highest was 0.58 gram. Thus, only 0.714% of the shingles failed to meet the specification.

3.66 (a) The correlation between calories and protein is 0.4644. **(b)** The correlation between calories and cholesterol is 0.1777. **(c)** The correlation between protein and cholesterol is 0.1417. **(d)** There is a weak positive linear relationship between calories and protein, with a correlation coefficient of 0.46. The positive linear relationships between calories and cholesterol and between protein and cholesterol are very weak.

3.68 (a), (b)

Property Taxes per Capita ($)

Mean	1,332.2353
Median	1,230
Standard deviation	577.8308
Sample variance	333,888.4235
Range	2,479
First quartile	867
Third quartile	1,633
Interquartile range	766
Coefficient of variation	43.37%

(c), (d) The distribution of the property taxes per capita is right-skewed, with a mean value of $1,332.24, a median of $1,230, and an average spread around the mean of $577.83. There is an outlier in the right tail at $2,985, while the standard deviation is about 43.37% of the mean. Twenty-five percent of the states have property tax that falls below $867 per capita, and 25% have property taxes that are higher than $1,633 per capita.

3.70 (a), (b)

	Abandonment Rate in % (7:00AM–3:00PM)
Mean	13.8636
Standard Error	1.6254
Median	10
Mode	9
Standard Deviation	7.6239
Sample Variance	58.1233
Kurtosis	0.7236
Skewness	1.1807
Range	29
Minimum	5
Maximum	34
Sum	305
Count	22
First Quartile	9
Third Quartile	20
Interquartile Range	11
CV	54.99%

(c) The data are right-skewed.

(d) $r = 0.7575$

(e) The mean abandonment rate is 13.86%. Half of the abandonment rates are less than 10%. One-quarter of the abandonment rates are less than 9% while another one-quarter are more than 20%. The overall spread of the abandonment rates is 29%. The middle 50% of the abandonment rates are spread over 11%. The average spread of abandonment rates around the mean is 7.62%. The abandonment rates are right-skewed.

3.72 (a), (b)

Average Credit Score	
Mean	746.2238
Standard Error	1.821
Median	749
Mode	760
Standard Deviation	21.780
Sample Variance	474.4003
Kurtosis	–0.8304
Skewness	–0.229
Range	89
Minimum	700
Maximum	789
Sum	106,710
Count	143
First Quartile	730
Third Quartile	763
Interquartile Range	33
CV	2.92%

(c) The data are symmetrical. **(d)** The mean of the average credit scores is 746.2238. Half of the average credit scores are less than 749. One-quarter of the average credit scores are less than 730 while another one-quarter is more than 763. The overall spread of average credit scores is 89. The middle 50% of the average credit scores spread over 33. The average spread of average credit scores around the mean is 21.7807.

CHAPTER 4

4.2 (a) Simple events include selecting a red ball. **(b)** Selecting a white ball. **(c)** The sample space consists of the 12 red balls and the 8 white balls.

4.4 (a) $60/100 = 3/5 = 0.6$. **(b)** $10/100 = 1/10 = 0.1$. **(c)** $35/100 = 7/20 = 0.35$. **(d)** $9/10 = 0.9$.

4.6 (a) Mutually exclusive, not collectively exhaustive. **(b)** Not mutually exclusive, not collectively exhaustive. **(c)** Mutually exclusive, not collectively exhaustive. **(d)** Mutually exclusive, collectively exhaustive.

4.8 (a) Is a male.
(b) Is a male and feels tense or stressed out at work.
(c) Does not feel tense or stressed out at work.
(d) Is a male and feels tense or stressed out at work is a joint event because it consists of two characteristics.

4.10 (a) A marketer who plans to increase use of LinkedIn. **(b)** A B2B marketer who plans to increase use of LinkedIn. **(c)** A marketer who does not plan to increase use of LinkedIn. **(d)** A marketer who plans to increase use of LinkedIn and is a B2C marketer is a joint event because it consists of two characteristics, plans to increase use of LinkedIn and is a B2C marketer.

4.12 (a) $8,007/14,074 = 0.5689$. **(b)** $6,264/14,074 = 0.4451$. **(c)** $8,007/14,074 + 6,264/14,074 - 3,633/14,074 = 0.7559$ **(d)** The probability of saying that analyzing data is critical *or* is a manager includes the probability of saying that analyzing data is critical plus the probability of being a manager minus the joint probability of saying that analyzing data is critical *and* is a manager.

4.14 (a) 514/1,085. **(b)** 276/1,085. **(c)** 781/1,085.
(d) 1,085/1,085 = 1.00.

4.16 (a) 10/30 = 1/3 = 0.33. **(b)** 20/60 = 1/3 = 0.33.
(c) 40/60 = 2/3 = 0.67. **(d)** Because $P(A|B) = P(A) = 1/3$, events A
and B are independent.

4.18 $\frac{1}{2}$ = 0.5.

4.20 Because $P(A \text{ and } B) = 0.20$ and $P(A)P(B) = 0.12$, events A and B
are not independent.

4.22 (a) 1,038/1,331 = 0.7799. **(b)** 915/1,694 = 0.5401.
(c) $P(\text{Increased use of LinkedIn}) = 1,953/3,025 = 0.6456$, which is
not equal to $P(\text{Increased use of LinkedIn}|\text{B2B}) = 0.7799$. Therefore,
increased use of LinkedIn and business focus are not independent.

4.24 (a) 4,374/7,810 = 0.5601. **(b)** 3,436/7,810 = 0.4399.
(c) 3,633/6,264 = 0.5800. **(d)** 2,631/6,264 = 0.4200.

4.26 (a) 0.025/0.6 = 0.0417. **(b)** 0.015/0.4 = 0.0375. **(c)** Because
$P(\text{Needs warranty repair} \mid \text{Manufacturer based in the United States}) =$
0.0417 and $P(\text{Needs warranty repair}) = 0.04$, the two events are not
independent.

4.28 (a) 0.0045. **(b)** 0.012. **(c)** 0.0059. **(d)** 0.0483.

4.30 0.095.

4.32 (a) 0.736. **(b)** 0.997.

4.34 (a) $P(B'|O) = \dfrac{(0.5)(0.3)}{(0.5)(0.3) + (0.25)(0.7)} = 0.4615.$
(b) $P(O) = 0.175 + 0.15 = 0.325.$

4.36 (a) $P(\text{Huge success} \mid \text{Favorable review}) = 0.099/0.459 = 0.2157;$
$P(\text{Moderate success} \mid \text{Favorable review}) = 0.14/0.459 = 0.3050;$
$P(\text{Break-even} \mid \text{Favorable review}) = 0.16/0.459 = 0.3486;$
$P(\text{Loser} \mid \text{Favorable review}) = 0.06/0.459 = 0.1307.$
(b) $P(\text{Favorable review}) = 0.459.$

4.38 $3^{10} = 59{,}049.$

4.40 (a) $2^7 = 128.$ **(b)** $6^7 = 279{,}936.$ **(c)** There are two mutually exclusive and collectively exhaustive outcomes in (a) and six in (b).

4.42 $(5)(7)(4)(5) = 700.$

4.44 $5! = (5)(4)(3)(2)(1) = 120.$ Not all the orders are equally likely
because the teams have a different probability of finishing first through
fifth.

4.46 $6! = 720.$

4.48 $\dfrac{10!}{4!6!} = 210.$

4.50 4,950.

4.60 (a)

SHARE HEALTH INFORMATION	AGE 18–24	45–64	Total
Yes	400	225	625
No	100	275	375
Total	500	500	1,000

(b) Simple event: "Shares health information through social media."
Joint event: "Shares health information through social media and
is between 18 and 24 years old." **(c)** $P(\text{Shares health information}$
$\text{through social media}) = 675/1,000 = 0.675.$ **(d)** $P(\text{Shares health}$
information through social media and is in the 45- to 64-year-old
group) $= 225/1,000 = 0.225.$ **(e)** Not independent.

4.62 (a) 84/200. **(b)** 126/200. **(c)** 141/200. **(d)** 33/200. **(f)** 16/100.

4.64 (a) $202/447 = 0.4519.$ **(b)** $95/237 = 0.4008.$ **(c)** $107/210 =$
$0.5095.$ **(d)** $217/447 = 0.4855.$ **(e)** $122/237 = 0.5148.$ **(f)** $95/210$
$= 0.4524.$ **(g)** IT executives were more likely to identify big data as critical while marketing executives were more likely to identify functional
silos as an issue.

CHAPTER 5

5.2 (a)
$$\mu = 0(0.10) + 1(0.20) + 2(0.45) + 3(0.15) + 4(0.05) + 5(0.05) = 2.0.$$
(b) $\sigma = \sqrt{\begin{array}{l}(0-2)^2(0.10) + (1-2)^2(0.20) + (2-2)^2(0.45) + \\ (3-2)^2(0.15) + (4-2)^2(0.05) + (5-2)^2(0.05)\end{array}} = 1.183.$

5.4 (a)

X	P(X)
$ − 1	21/36
$ + 1	15/36

(b)

X	P(X)
$ − 1	21/36
$ + 1	15/36

(c)

X	P(X)
$ − 1	30/36
$ + 1	6/36

(d) −$0.167 for each method of play.

5.6 (a) 2.1058. **(b)** 1.4671.

5.8 (a) $E(X) = \$66.20;$ $E(Y) = \$63.01.$ **(b)** $\sigma_X = \$57.22;$ $\sigma_Y =$
$\$195.22.$ **(c)** Based on the expected value criteria, you would choose the
common stock fund. However, the common stock fund also has a standard deviation more than three times higher than that for the corporate
bond fund. An investor should carefully weigh the increased risk. **(d)** If
you chose the common stock fund, you would need to assess your reaction to the small possibility that you could lose virtually all of your entire
investment.

5.10 (a) 0.40, 0.60. **(b)** 1.60, 0.98. **(c)** 4.0, 0.894. **(d)** 1.50, 0.866.

5.12 (a) 0.2153. **(b)** 0.0122. **(c)** 0.3070. **(d)** $\mu = 2.88,$ $\sigma = 1.2238.$
(e) That each 18- to 29-year-old in the United States owns a tablet or does
not own a tablet and that each person is independent of all other persons.

5.14 (a) 0.5987. **(b)** 0.3151. **(c)** 0.9885. **(d)** 0.0115.

5.16 (a) 0.5574. **(b)** 0.0055. **(c)** 0.9171. **(d)** $\mu = 2.469,$ $\sigma = 0.6611.$

5.18 (a) 0.2565. **(b)** 0.1396. **(c)** 0.3033. **(d)** 0.0247.

5.20 (a) 0.0337. **(b)** 0.0067. **(c)** 0.9596. **(d)** 0.0404.

5.22 (a)

$$P(X < 5) = P(X = 0) + P(X = 1) + P(x = 2) + P(X = 3) \\ \quad + P(X = 4)$$

$$= \frac{e^{-6}(6)^0}{0!} + \frac{e^{-6}(6)^1}{1!} + \frac{e^{-6}(6)^2}{2!} + \frac{e^{-6}(6)^3}{3!} + \frac{e^{-6}(6)^4}{4!}$$

$$= 0.002479 + 0.014873 + 0.044618 + 0.089235 \\ \quad + 0.133853$$

$$= 0.2851.$$

(b) $P(X = 5) = \dfrac{e^{-6}(6)^5}{5!} = 0.1606.$

(c) $P(X \geq 5) = 1 - P(X < 5) = 1 - 0.2851 = 0.7149.$

(d) $P(X = 4 \text{ or } X = 5) = P(X = 4) + P(X = 5) = \dfrac{e^{-6}(6)^4}{4!} + \dfrac{e^{-6}(6)^5}{5!}$
$$= 0.2945.$$

5.24 (a) 0.2122. **(b)** 0.7878. **(c)** 0.4588.

5.26 (a) 0.0672. **(b)** 0.1815. **(c)** 0.7513. **(d)** 0.2487.

5.28 (a) 0.3263. **(b)** 0.8964. **(c)** Because Ford had a higher mean rate of problems per car than Toyota, the probability of a randomly selected Ford having zero problems and the probability of no more than two problems are both lower than for Toyota.

5.30 (a) 0.3198 **(b)** 0.8922. **(c)** Because Toyota had a slightly higher mean rate of problems per car in 2011 compared to 2010, the probability of a randomly selected Toyota having zero problems and the probability of no more than two problems are both slightly lower in 2011 than in 2010.

5.36 (a) 0.66. **(b)** 0.66. **(c)** 0.3226. **(d)** 0.0045. **(e)** The assumption of independence may not be true.

5.38 (a) If $\pi = 0.50$ and $n = 13$, $P(X \geq 10) = 0.0461$.
(b) If $\pi = 0.75$ and $n = 13$, $P(X \geq 10) = 0.5843$.

5.40 (a) 0.0060. **(b)** 0.2007. **(c)** 0.1662. **(d)** Mean = 4.0, standard deviation = 1.5492. **(e)** Since the percentage of bills containing an error is lower in this problem, the probability is higher in (a) and (b) of this problem and lower in (c).

5.42 (a) $\mu = n\pi = 9.0$ **(b)** $\sigma = \sqrt{n\pi(1 - \pi)} = 2.2248$.
(c) $P(X = 10) = 0.1593$. **(d)** $P(X \leq 5) = 0.0553$.
(e) $P(X \geq 5) = 0.9811$.

5.44 (a) If $\pi = 0.50$ and $n = 41$, $P(X \geq 36) = 0.000000392$.
(b) If $\pi = 0.70$ and $n = 41$, $P(X \geq 36) = 0.0068$. **(c)** If $\pi = 0.90$ and $n = 41$, $P(X \geq 36) = 0.777256$. **(d)** Based on the results in (a)–(c), the probability that the Standard & Poor's 500 Index will increase if there is an early gain in the first five trading days of the year is very likely to be close to 0.90 because that yields a probability of 77.73% that at least 36 of the 41 years the Standard & Poor's 500 Index will increase the entire year.

5.46 (a) The assumptions needed are (i) the probability that a questionable claim is referred by an investigator is constant, (ii) the probability that a questionable claim is referred by an investigator approaches 0 as the interval gets smaller, and (iii) the probability that a questionable claim is referred by an investigator is independent from interval to interval.
(b) 0.1277. **(c)** 0.9015. **(d)** 0.0985.

CHAPTER 6

6.2 (a) 0.9089. **(b)** 0.0911. **(c)** +1.96. **(d)** −1.00 and +1.00.

6.4 (a) 0.1401. **(b)** 0.4168. **(c)** 0.3918. **(d)** +1.00.

6.6 (a) 0.9599. **(b)** 0.0228. **(c)** 43.42. **(d)** 46.64 and 53.36.

6.8 (a) $P(34 < X < 50) = P(-1.33 < Z < 0) = 0.4082$.
(b) $P(X < 30) + P(X > 60) = P(Z < -1.67) + P(Z > 0.83)$
$= 0.0475 + (1.0 - 0.7967) = 0.2508$. **(c)** $P(Z < -0.84) \cong 0.20$,
$Z = -0.84 = \dfrac{X - 50}{12}$, $X = 50 - 0.84(12) = 39.92$ thousand miles, or
39,920 miles. **(d)** The smaller standard deviation makes the absolute
Z values larger. **(a)** $P(34 < X < 50) = P(-1.60 < Z < 0)$
$= 0.4452$. **(b)** $P(X < 30) + P(X > 60) = P(Z < -2.00)$
$+ P(Z > 1.00) = 0.0228 + (1.0 - 0.8413) = 0.1815$.
(c) $X = 50 - 0.84(10) = 41.6$ thousand miles, or 41,600 miles.

6.10 (a) 0.9878. **(b)** 0.8185. **(c)** 86.16%. **(d)** Option 1: Because your score of 81% on this exam represents a Z score of 1.00, which is below the minimum Z score of 1.28, you will not earn an A grade on the exam under this grading option. Option 2: Because your score of 68% on this exam represents a Z score of 2.00, which is well above the minimum Z score of 1.28, you will earn an A grade on the exam under this grading option. You should prefer Option 2.

6.12 (a) 0.0855. **(b)** 0.1558. **(c)** 0.0182. **(d)** 72.4425.

6.14 With 39 values, the smallest of the standard normal quantile values covers an area under the normal curve of 0.025. The corresponding Z value is −1.96. The middle (20th) value has a cumulative area of 0.50 and a corresponding Z value of 0.0. The largest of the standard normal quantile values covers an area under the normal curve of 0.975, and its corresponding Z value is +1.96.

6.16 (a) Mean = 22.85, median = 22, S = 1.6311, range = 5, 6S = 6(1.6311) = 9.7866, interquartile range = 2.0, 1.33(1.6311) = 2.1694. The mean is slightly more than the median. The range is much less than 6S, and the interquartile range is less than 1.33S. **(b)** The normal probability plot appears to be slightly right skewed. The skewness statistic is 0.7523 The kurtosis is −0.5423, indicating some departure from a normal distribution.

6.18 (a) Mean = 1,332.2353, median = 1,230, S = 577.8308, range = 2,479, 6S = 6(577.8308) = 3,466.9848, interquartile range = 766, 1.33(577.8308) = 768.5150. The mean is greater than the median. The range is much less than 6S, and the interquartile range is approximately equal to 1.33S. **(b)** The normal probability plot appears to be right skewed. The skewness statistic is 0.9183 The kurtosis is 0.5395, indicating some departure from a normal distribution.

6.20 (a) Interquartile range = 0.0025, S = 0.0017, range = 0.008, 1.33(S) = 0.0023, 6(S) = 0.0102. Because the interquartile range is close to 1.33S and the range is also close to 6S, the data appear to be approximately normally distributed. **(b)** The normal probability plot suggests that the data appear to be approximately normally distributed.

6.22 (a) Five-number summary: 82 127 148.5 168 213; mean = 147.06, mode = 130, range = 131, interquartile range = 41, standard deviation = 31.69. The mean is very close to the median. The five-number summary suggests that the distribution is approximately symmetric around the median. The interquartile range is very close to 1.33S. The range is about $50 below 6S. In general, the distribution of the data appears to closely resemble a normal distribution. **(b)** The normal probability plot confirms that the data appear to be approximately normally distributed.

6.30 (a) 0.4772. **(b)** 0.9544. **(c)** 0.0456. **(d)** 1.8835. **(e)** 1.8710 and 2.1290.

6.32 (a) 0.1405. **(b)** 0.0256. **(c)** $2,179.78. **(d)** $898.22 to $2,179.78.

6.34 (a) Waiting time will more closely resemble an exponential distribution. **(b)** Seating time will more closely resemble a normal distribution. **(c)** Both the histogram and normal probability plot suggest that waiting time more closely resembles an exponential distribution. **(d)** Both the histogram and normal probability plot suggest that seating time more closely resembles a normal distribution.

6.36 (a) 0.3557. **(b)** 0.3596. **(c)** 0.0838. **(d)** $3,717.46. **(e)** $3,864.01 and $5,431.99.

CHAPTER 7

7.2 (a) Virtually 0. **(b)** 0.1587. **(c)** 0.0139. **(d)** 50.195.

7.4 (a) Both means are equal to 6. This property is called unbiasedness. **(c)** The distribution for $n = 3$ has less variability. The larger sample size has resulted in sample means being closer to μ.

7.6 (a) When $n = 4$, because the mean is larger than the median, the distribution of the sales price of new houses is skewed to the right, and so is the sampling distribution of $\overline{X}$ although it will be less skewed than the population. **(b)** If you select samples of $n = 100$, the shape of the sampling distribution of the sample mean will be very close to a normal distribution, with a mean of $322,100 and a standard deviation of $9,000. **(c)** 0.9960. **(d)** 0.3145.

7.8 (a) $P(\overline{X} > 26) = P(Z > -1.00) = 1.0 - 0.1587 = 0.8413.$ **(b)** $P(Z < 1.04) = 0.85; \overline{X} = 27 + 1.04(1.0) = 28.04.$ **(c)** To be able to use the standardized normal distribution as an approximation for the area under the curve, you must assume that the population is approximately symmetrical. **(d)** $P(Z < 1.04) = 0.85;$ $\overline{X} = 27 + 1.04(0.50) = 27.52.$

7.10 (a) 0.40. **(b)** 0.0704.

7.12 (a) $\pi = 0.501, \sigma_p = \sqrt{\dfrac{\pi(1-\pi)}{n}} = \sqrt{\dfrac{0.501(1-0.501)}{100}} = 0.05$

$P(p > 0.55) = P(Z > 0.98) = 1.0 - 0.8365 = 0.1635.$

(b) $\pi = 0.60, \sigma_p = \sqrt{\dfrac{\pi(1-\pi)}{n}} = \sqrt{\dfrac{0.6(1-0.6)}{100}} = 0.04899$

$P(p > 0.55) = P(Z > -1.021) = 1.0 - 0.1539 = 0.8461.$

(c) $\pi = 0.49, \sigma_p = \sqrt{\dfrac{\pi(1-\pi)}{n}} = \sqrt{\dfrac{0.49(1-0.49)}{100}} = 0.05$

$P(p > 0.55) = P(Z > 1.20) = 1.0 - 0.8849 = 0.1151.$

(d) Increasing the sample size by a factor of 4 decreases the standard error by a factor of 2.
(a) $P(p > 0.55) = P(Z > 1.96) = 1.0 - 0.9750 = 0.0250.$

(b) $P(p > 0.55) = P(Z > -2.04) = 1.0 - 0.0207 = 0.9793.$

(c) $P(p > 0.55) = P(Z > 2.40) = 1.0 - 0.9918 = 0.0082.$

7.14 (a) 0.8944. **(b)** 0.7887. **(c)** 0.3085. **(d) (a)** 0.9938. **(b)** 0.9876. **(c)** 0.1587.

7.16 (a) 0.7661. **(b)** The probability is 90% that the sample percentage will be contained between 0.1085 to 0.1915. **(c)** The probability is 95% that the sample percentage will be contained between 0.1005 and 0.1995.

7.18 (a) 0.1056. **(b)** 0.0062. **(c)** Increasing the sample size by a factor of 4 decreases the standard error by a factor of 2. The sampling distribution of the proportion becomes more concentrated around the true proportion of 0.36 and, hence, the probability in (b) becomes smaller than that in (a).

7.24 (a) 0.4999. **(b)** 0.00009. **(c)** 0. **(d)** 0. **(e)** 0.7518.

7.26 (a) 0.8944. **(b)** 4.617; 4.783. **(c)** 4.641.

7.28 (a) 0.0012. **(b)** 0.1478. **(c)** 0.8522.

CHAPTER 8

8.2 $114.68 \leq \mu \leq 135.32.$

8.4 Yes, it is true because 5% of intervals will not include the population mean.

8.6 (a) You would compute the mean first because you need the mean to compute the standard deviation. If you had a sample, you would compute the sample mean. If you had the population mean, you would compute the population standard deviation. **(b)** If you have a sample, you are computing the sample standard deviation, not the population standard deviation needed in Equation (8.1). If you have a population and have computed the population mean and population standard deviation, you don't need a confidence interval estimate of the population mean because you already know the mean.

8.8 Equation (8.1) assumes that you know the population standard deviation. Because you are selecting a sample of 100 from the population, you are computing a sample standard deviation, not the population standard deviation.

8.10 (a) $\overline{X} \pm Z \cdot \dfrac{\sigma}{\sqrt{n}} = 7,500 \pm 1.96 \cdot \dfrac{1,000}{\sqrt{64}}; 7,255 \leq \mu \leq 7,745.$

(b) No, since the confidence interval does not include 8,000 hours the manufacturer cannot support a claim that the bulbs have a mean of 8,000 hours. **(c)** No. Because σ is known and $n = 64$, from the Central Limit Theorem, you know that the sampling distribution of $\overline{X}$ is approximately normal. **(d)** The confidence interval is narrower, based on a population standard deviation of 800 hours rather than the original standard deviation of 1,000 hours. $\overline{X} \pm Z \times \dfrac{\sigma}{\sqrt{n}} = 7,500 \pm 1.96 \times \dfrac{800}{\sqrt{64}},$ $7.304 \leq \mu \leq 7,696.$ No, since the confidence interval does not include 8,000 the manufacturer cannot support a claim that the bulbs have a mean life of 8,000 hours.

8.12 (a) 2.2622. **(b)** 3.2498. **(c)** 2.0395. **(d)** 1.9977. **(e)** 1.7531.

8.14 $-0.12 \leq \mu \leq 11.84, 2.00 \leq \mu \leq 6.00.$ The presence of the outlier increases the sample mean and greatly inflates the sample standard deviation.

8.16 (a) $75 \pm (2.0049)(9)/\sqrt{55}; 72.57 \leq \mu \leq 77.43.$ **(b)** You can be 95% confident that the population mean amount of one-time gift is between $72.57 and $77.43.

8.18 (a) $6.31 \leq \mu \leq 7.87.$ **(b)** You can be 95% confident that the population mean amount spent for lunch at a fast-food restaurant is between $6.31 and $7.87.

8.20 (a) $22.09 \leq \mu \leq 23.61.$ **(b)** You can be 95% confident that the population mean miles per gallon of 2014 small SUVs is between 22.09 and 23.61. **(c)** Because the 95% confidence interval for population mean miles per gallon of 2014 small SUVs does not overlap with that for the population mean miles per gallon of 2014 family sedans, you can conclude that the population mean miles per gallon of 2014 small SUVs is lower than that of 2014 family sedans.

8.22 (a) $31.12 \le \mu \le 54.96$. **(b)** The number of days is approximately normally distributed. **(c)** No, the outliers skew the data. **(d)** Because the sample size is fairly large, at $n = 50$, the use of the t distribution is appropriate.

8.24 (a) $31.23 \le \mu \le 47.59$. **(b)** That the population distribution is normally distributed. **(c)** The boxplot and the skewness and kurtosis statistics indicate an approximately normal distribution although the normal probability plot does not clearly show that.

8.26 $0.19 \le \pi \le 0.31$.

8.28 (a) $p = \dfrac{X}{n} = \dfrac{135}{500} = 0.27, p \pm Z\sqrt{\dfrac{p(1-p)}{n}} = 0.27 \pm$
$2.58\sqrt{\dfrac{0.27(0.73)}{500}}; 0.2189 \le \pi \le 0.3211$. **(b)** The manager in charge of promotional programs can infer that the proportion of households that would upgrade to an improved cellphone if it were made available at a substantially reduced cost is somewhere between 0.22 and 0.32, with 99% confidence.

8.30 (a) $0.2328 \le \pi \le 0.2872$. **(b)** No, you cannot because the interval estimate includes 0.25 (25%). **(c)** $0.2514 \le \pi \le 0.2686$. Yes, you can, because the interval is above 0.25 (25%). **(d)** The larger the sample size, the narrower the confidence interval, holding everything else constant.

8.32 (a) $0.4393 \le \pi \le 0.5024$. **(b)** $0.2811 \le \pi \le 0.3397$. **(c)** More people use Facebook to see photos and videos than keeping up with news and current events.

8.34 $n = 35$.

8.36 $n = 1,041$.

8.38 (a) $n = \dfrac{Z^2\sigma^2}{e^2} = \dfrac{(1.96)^2(400)^2}{50^2} = 245.86$. Use $n = 246$.
(b) $n = \dfrac{Z^2\sigma^2}{e^2} = \dfrac{(1.96)^2(400)^2}{25^2} = 983.41$. Use $n = 984$.

8.40 $n = 97$.

8.42 (a) $n = 107$. **(b)** $n = 62$.

8.44 (a) $n = 246$. **(b)** $n = 385$. **(c)** $n = 554$. **(d)** When there is more variability in the population, a larger sample is needed to accurately estimate the mean.

8.46 (a) $0.2198 \le \pi \le 0.3202$. **(b)** $0.1639 \le \pi \le 0.2561$. **(c)** $0.0661 \le \pi \le 0.1339$. **(d) (a)** $n = 1,893$, **(b)** $n = 1,594$, **(c)** $n = 865$.

8.48 (a) If you conducted a follow-up study to estimate the population proportion of financial institutions that use churn rate to gauge the effectiveness of their marketing efforts, you would use $\pi = 0.68$ in the sample size formula because it is based on past information on the proportion. **(b)** $n = 929$.

8.54 (a)   Cellphone: $p = 0.9006; 0.8821 \le \pi \le 0.9191$.
              Smartphone: $p = 0.5805; 0.5500 \le \pi \le 0.6110$.
                  E-reader: $p = 0.3201; 0.2913 \le \pi \le 0.3489$.
         Tablet computer: $p = 0.4205; 0.3900 \le \pi \le 0.4510$.
(b) Most adults have a cellphone. Many adults have a smartphone. Some adults have an e reader or a tablet computer.

8.56 (a) $39.88 \le \mu \le 42.12$. **(b)** $0.6158 \le \pi \le 0.8842$. **(c)** $n = 25$. **(d)** $n = 267$. **(e)** If a single sample were to be selected for both purposes, the larger of the two sample sizes ($n = 267$) should be used.

8.58 (a) $3.19 \le \mu \le 9.21$. **(b)** $0.3242 \le \pi \le 0.7158$. **(c)** $n = 110$. **(d)** $n = 121$. **(e)** If a single sample were to be selected for both purposes, the larger of the two sample sizes ($n = 121$) should be used.

8.60 (a) $0.2459 \le \pi \le 0.3741$. **(b)** $3.22 \le \mu \le \$3.78$. **(c)** $\$17,581.68 \le \mu \le \$18,418.32$.

8.62 (a) $\$36.66 \le \mu \le \$40.42$. **(b)** $0.2027 \le \pi \le 0.3973$. **(c)** $n = 110$. **(d)** $n = 423$. **(e)** If a single sample were to be selected for both purposes, the larger of the two sample sizes ($n = 423$) should be used.

8.64 (a) $0.4643 \le \pi \le 0.6690$. **(b)** $\$136.28 \le \mu \le \$502.21$.

8.66 (a) $8.41 \le \mu \le 8.43$. **(b)** With 95% confidence, the population mean width of troughs is somewhere between 8.41 and 8.43 inches. **(c)** The assumption is valid as the width of the troughs is approximately normally distributed.

8.68 (a) $0.2425 \le \mu \le 0.2856$. **(b)** $0.1975 \le \mu \le 0.2385$. **(c)** The amounts of granule loss for both brands are skewed to the right, but the sample sizes are large enough. **(d)** Because the two confidence intervals do not overlap, you can conclude that the mean granule loss of Boston shingles is higher than that of Vermont shingles.

CHAPTER 9

9.2 Because $Z_{STAT} = +2.21 > 1.96$, reject H_0.

9.4 Reject H_0 if $Z_{STAT} < -2.58$ or if $Z_{STAT} > 2.58$.

9.6 p-value $= 0.0456$.

9.8 p-value $= 0.1676$.

9.10 H_0: Defendant is guilty; H_1: Defendant is innocent. A Type I error would be not convicting a guilty person. A Type II error would be convicting an innocent person.

9.12 H_0: $\mu = 20$ minutes. 20 minutes is adequate travel time between classes. H_1: $\mu \ne 20$ minutes. 20 minutes is not adequate travel time between classes.

9.14 (a) $Z_{STAT} = \dfrac{7,250 - 7,500}{\dfrac{1,000}{\sqrt{64}}} = -2.0$. Because $Z_{STAT} = -2.00$
< -1.96, reject H_0. **(b)** p-value $= 0.0456$. **(c)** $7,005 \le \mu \le 7,495$. **(d)** The conclusions are the same.

9.16 (a) Because $-2.58 < Z_{STAT} = -1.7678 < 2.58$, do not reject H_0. **(b)** p-value $= 0.0771$. **(c)** $0.9877 \le \mu \le 1.0023$. **(d)** The conclusions are the same.

9.18 $t_{STAT} = 2.00$.

9.20 ± 2.1315.

9.22 No, you should not use a t test because the original population is left-skewed, and the sample size is not large enough for the t test to be valid.

9.24 (a) $t_{STAT} = (3.57 - 3.70)/0.8/\sqrt{64} = -1.30$. Because $-1.9983 < t_{STAT} = -1.30 < 1.9983$ and p-value $= 0.1984 > 0.05$, there is no evidence that the population mean waiting time is different from 3.7 minutes. **(b)** Because $n = 64$, the sampling distribution of the t test statistic is approximately normal. In general, the t test is appropriate for this sample size except for the case where the population is extremely skewed or bimodal.

9.26 (a) $-1.9842 < t_{STAT} = 1.4545 < 1.9842$. There is no evidence that the population mean savings for all showroomers is different from \$50. **(b)** p-value $= 0.1490 > 0.05$. The probability of getting a t_{STAT} statistic greater than $+1.4545$ or less than -1.4545, given that the null hypothesis is true, is 0.1490.

9.28 (a) Because $-2.1448 < t_{STAT} = 1.6344 < 2.1448$, do not reject H_0. There is not enough evidence to conclude that the mean amount spent for lunch at a fast-food restaurant, is different from \$6.50. **(b)** The p-value is 0.1245. If the population mean is \$6.50, the probability of observing a sample of nine customers that will result in a sample mean farther away from the hypothesized value than this sample is 0.1245. **(c)** The distribution of the amount spent is normally distributed. **(d)** With a sample size of 15, it is difficult to evaluate the assumption of normality. However, the distribution may be fairly symmetric because the mean and the median are close in value. Also, the boxplot appears only slightly skewed so the normality assumption does not appear to be seriously violated.

9.30 (a) Because $-2.0096 < t_{STAT} = 0.114 < 2.0096$, do not reject H_0. There is no evidence that the mean amount is different from 2 liters. **(b)** p-value $= 0.9095$. **(d)** Yes, the data appear to have met the normality assumption. **(e)** The amount of fill is decreasing over time so the values are not independent. Therefore, the t test is invalid.

9.32 (a) Because $t_{STAT} = -5.9355 < -2.0106$, reject H_0. There is enough evidence to conclude that mean widths of the troughs is different from 8.46 inches. **(b)** The population distribution is normal. **(c)** Although the distribution of the widths is left-skewed, the large sample size means that the validity of the t test is not seriously affected. The large sample size allows you to use the t distribution.

9.34 (a) Because $-2.68 < t_{STAT} = 0.094 < 2.68$, do not reject H_0. There is no evidence that the mean amount is different from 5.5 grams. **(b)** $5.462 \leq \mu \leq 5.542$. **(c)** The conclusions are the same.

9.36 p-value $= 0.0228$.

9.38 p-value $= 0.0838$.

9.40 p-value $= 0.9162$.

9.42 $t_{STAT} = 2.7638$.

9.44 $t_{STAT} = -2.5280$.

9.46 (a) $t_{STAT} = 2.7273 > 1.6604$. There is evidence that the population mean bus miles is greater than 3,900 miles. **(b)** p-value $= 0.0038 < 0.05$. The probability of getting a t_{STAT} statistic greater than 2.7273 given that the null hypothesis is true, is 0.0038.

9.48 (a) $t_{STAT} = (23.05 - 25)/16.83/\sqrt{355} = -2.1831$. Because $t_{STAT} = -2.1831 > -2.3369$, do not reject H_0. p-value $= 0.0148 > 0.01$, do not reject H_0. **(b)** The probability of getting a sample mean of 23.05 minutes or less if the population mean is 25 minutes is 0.0148.

9.50 (a) $t_{STAT} = 4.1201 > 2.3974$. There is evidence that the population mean one-time gift donation is greater than \$70. **(b)** The probability of getting a sample mean of \$75 or more if the population mean is \$70 is 0.0001.

9.52 $p = 0.22$.

9.54 Do not reject H_0.

9.56 (a) $Z_{STAT} = 1.3311$, p-value $= 0.0916$. Because $Z_{STAT} = 1.3311 < 1.645$ or $0.0916 > 0.05$, do not reject H_0. There is no evidence to show that more than 17% of students at your university use the Mozilla Firefox web browser. **(b)** $Z_{STAT} = 2.6622$, p-value $= 0.0039$. Because $Z_{STAT} = 2.6622 > 1.645$, reject H_0. There is evidence to show that more than 17% of students at your university use the Mozilla Firefox web browser. **(c)** The sample size had a major effect on being able to reject the null hypothesis. **(d)** You would be very unlikely to reject the null hypothesis with a sample of 20.

9.58 H_0: $\pi = 0.52$; H_1: $\pi \neq 0.52$. Decision rule: If $Z_{STAT} > 1.96$ or $Z_{STAT} < -1.96$, reject H_0.

$$p = \frac{543}{935} = 0.5807$$

Test statistic:

$$Z_{STAT} = \frac{p - \pi}{\sqrt{\dfrac{\pi(1 - \pi)}{n}}} = \frac{0.5807 - 0.52}{\sqrt{\dfrac{0.52(1 - 0.52)}{935}}} = 3.7181.$$

Because $Z_{STAT} = 3.7181 > 1.96$ or p-value $= 0.0002 < 0.05$, reject H_0 and conclude that there is evidence that the proportion of all LinkedIn members who engaged in professional networking within the last month is different from 52%.

9.60 (a) H_0: $\pi \geq 0.37$. The proportion who respond that the organization has a coherent business strategy that they stick to and effectively communicate is greater than or equal to 0.37. H_1: $\pi < 0.37$. The proportion who respond that the organization has a coherent business strategy that they stick to and effectively communicate is less than 0.37. **(b)** $Z_{STAT} = -0.6214 > -1.645$; p-value $= 0.2672$. Because $Z_{STAT} = -0.6214 > -1.645$ or p-value $= 0.2672 > 0.05$, do not reject H_0. There is insufficient evidence that the proportion who respond that the organization has a coherent business strategy that they stick to and effectively communicate is less than 0.37.

9.70 (a) Concluding that a firm will go bankrupt when it will not. **(b)** Concluding that a firm will not go bankrupt when it will go bankrupt. **(c)** Type I. **(d)** If the revised model results in more moderate or large Z scores, the probability of committing a Type I error will increase. Many more of the firms will be predicted to go bankrupt than will go bankrupt. On the other hand, the revised model that results in more moderate or large Z scores will lower the probability of committing a Type II error because few firms will be predicted to go bankrupt than will actually go bankrupt.

9.72 (a) Because $t_{STAT} = 3.3197 > 2.0010$, reject H_0. **(b)** p-value $= 0.0015$. **(c)** Because $Z_{STAT} = 0.2582 < 1.645$, do not reject H_0. **(d)** Because $-2.0010 < t_{STAT} = -1.1066 < 2.0010$, do not reject H_0. **(e)** Because $Z_{STAT} = 2.3238 > 1.645$, reject H_0.

9.74 (a) Because $t_{STAT} = -1.69 > -1.7613$, do not reject H_0. **(b)** The data are from a population that is normally distributed. **(d)** With the exception of one extreme value, the data are approximately normally distributed. **(e)** There is insufficient evidence to state that the waiting time is less than five minutes.

9.76 (a) Because $t_{STAT} = -1.47 > -1.6896$, do not reject H_0. **(b)** p-value $= 0.0748$. If the null hypothesis is true, the probability of obtaining a t_{STAT} of -1.47 or more extreme is 0.0748. **(c)** Because $t_{STAT} = -3.10 < -1.6973$, reject H_0. **(d)** p-value $= 0.0021$. If the null hypothesis is true, the probability of obtaining a t_{STAT} of -3.10 or more extreme is 0.0021. **(e)** The data in the population are assumed to be normally distributed. **(g)** Both boxplots suggest that the data are skewed slightly to the right, more so for the Boston shingles. However, the very large sample sizes mean that the results of the t test are relatively insensitive to the departure from normality.

9.78 (a) $t_{STAT} = -3.2912$, reject H_0. **(b)** p-value $= 0.0012$. **(c)** $t_{STAT} = -7.9075$, reject H_0. **(d)** p-value $= 0.0000$. **(e)** Because of the large sample sizes, you do not need to be concerned with the normality assumption.

CHAPTER 10

10.2 (a) $t = 3.8959$. **(b)** $df = 21$. **(c)** 2.5177. **(d)** Because $t_{STAT} = t_{STAT} = 3.8959 > 2.5177$, reject H_0.

10.4 $3.73 \leq \mu_1 - \mu_2 \leq 12.27$.

10.6 Because $t_{STAT} = 2.6762 < 2.9979$ or p-value $= 0.0158 > 0.01$, do not reject H_0. There is no evidence of a difference in the means of the two populations.

10.8 (a) Because $t_{STAT} = 2.8990 > 1.6620$ or p-value $= 0.0024 < 0.05$, reject H_0. There is evidence that the mean amount of Walker Crisps eaten by children who watched a commercial featuring a long-standing sports celebrity endorser is higher than for those who watched a commercial for an alternative food snack. **(b)** $3.4616 \leq \mu_1 - \mu_2 \leq 18.5384$. **(c)** The results cannot be compared because (a) is a one-tail test and (b) is a confidence interval that is comparable only to the results of a two-tail test.

10.10 (a) $H_0: \mu_1 = \mu_2$, where Populations: $1 =$ Southeast, $2 =$ Gulf Coast. $H_1: \mu_1 \neq \mu_2$. Decision rule: $df = 28$. If $t_{STAT} < -2.0484$ or $t_{STAT} > 2.0484$, reject H_0.

Test statistic:

$$S_p^2 = \frac{(n_1 - 1)(S_1^2) + (n_2 - 1)(S_2^2)}{(n_1 - 1) + (n_2 - 1)}$$

$$= \frac{(12)(42.5927^2) + (16)(36.1970^2)}{12 + 16} = 1,526.1865$$

$$t_{STAT} = \frac{(\bar{X}_1 - \bar{X}_2) - (\mu_1 - \mu_2)}{\sqrt{S_p^2 \left(\frac{1}{n_1} + \frac{1}{n_2}\right)}}$$

$$= \frac{(43.1538 - 29.7059) - 0}{\sqrt{1,526.1865 \left(\frac{1}{13} + \frac{1}{17}\right)}} = 0.9343.$$

Decision: Because $-2.0484 < t_{STAT} = 0.9343 < 2.0484$, do not reject H_0. There is not enough evidence to conclude that the mean number of partners between the Southeast and Gulf Coast is different. **(b)** p-value $= 0.3581$. **(c)** In order to use the pooled-variance t test, you need to assume that the populations are normally distributed with equal variances.

10.12 (a) Because $t_{STAT} = -4.1343 < -2.0484$, reject H_0. **(b)** p-value $= 0.0003$. **(c)** The populations of waiting times are approximately normally distributed. **(d)** $-4.2292 \leq \mu_1 - \mu_2 \leq -1.4268$.

10.14 (a) Because $t_{STAT} = -1.4458 > -2.0484$, do not reject H_0. There is insufficient evidence of a difference in the mean time to start a business between developed and emerging countries. **(b)** p-value $= 0.1593$. The probability that two samples have a mean difference of 10.0667 or more is 0.1593 if there is no difference in the mean time to start a business between developed and emerging countries. **(c)** You need to assume that the population distribution of the time to start a busi-

ness of both developed and emerging countries is normally distributed. **(d)** $-24.3286 \leq \mu_1 - \mu_2 \leq 4.1953$.

10.16 (a) Because $t_{STAT} = -2.1554 < -2.0017$ or p-value $= 0.0353 < 0.05$, reject H_0. There is evidence of a difference in the mean time per day accessing the Internet via a mobile device between males and females. **(b)** You must assume that each of the two independent populations is normally distributed.

10.18 $df = 19$.

10.20 (a) $t_{STAT} = (-1.5566)/(1.424)/\sqrt{9} = -3.2772$. Because $t_{STAT} = -3.2772 < -2.306$ or p-value $= 0.0112 < 0.05$, reject H_0. There is enough evidence of a difference in the mean summated ratings between the two brands. **(b)** You must assume that the distribution of the differences between the two ratings is approximately normal. **(c)** p-value $= 0.0112$. The probability of obtaining a mean difference in ratings that results in a test statistic that deviates from 0 by 3.2772 or more in either direction is 0.0112 if there is no difference in the mean summated ratings between the two brands. **(d)** $-2.6501 \leq \mu_D \leq -0.4610$. You are 95% confident that the mean difference in summated ratings between brand A and brand B is somewhere between -2.6501 and -0.4610.

10.22 (a) Because $t_{STAT} = 1.7948 > 1.6939$ reject H_0. There is evidence to conclude that the mean at Super Target is higher than at Walmart. **(b)** You must assume that the distribution of the differences between the prices is approximately normal. **(c)** p-value $= 0.0411$. The likelihood that you will obtain a t_{STAT} statistic greater than 1.7948 if the mean price at Super Target is not greater than Walmart is 0.0411.

10.24 (a) Because $t_{STAT} = 1.8425 < 1.943$, do not reject H_0. There is not enough evidence to conclude that the mean bone marrow microvessel density is higher before the stem cell transplant than after the stem cell transplant. **(b)** p-value $= 0.0575$. The probability that the t statistic for the mean difference in microvessel density is 1.8425 or more is 5.75% if the mean density is not higher before the stem cell transplant than after the stem cell transplant. **(c)** $-28.26 \leq \mu_D \leq 200.55$. You are 95% confident that the mean difference in bone marrow microvessel density before and after the stem cell transplant is somewhere between -28.26 and 200.55. **(d)** That the distribution of the difference before and after the stem cell transplant is normally distributed.

10.26 (a) Because $t_{STAT} = -9.3721 < -2.4258$, reject H_0. There is evidence that the mean strength is lower at two days than at seven days. **(b)** The population of differences in strength is approximately normally distributed. **(c)** $p = 0.000$.

10.28 (a) Because $-2.58 \leq Z_{STAT} = -0.58 \leq 2.58$, do not reject H_0. **(b)** $-0.273 \leq \pi_1 - \pi_2 \leq 0.173$.

10.30 (a) $H_0: \pi_1 \leq \pi_2. H_1: \pi_1 > \pi_2$. Populations: $1 =$ social media recommendation, $2 =$ web browsing. **(b)** Because $Z_{STAT} = 1.5507 < 1.6449$ or p-value $= 0.0605 > 0.05$, do not reject H_0. There is insufficient evidence to conclude that the population proportion of those who recalled the brand is greater for those who had a social media recommendation than for those who did web browsing. **(c)** No, the result in (b) makes it inappropriate to claim that the population proportion of those who recalled the brand is greater for those who had a social media recommendation than for those who did web browsing.

10.32 (a) $H_0: \pi_1 = \pi_2. H_1: \pi_1 \neq \pi_2$. Decision rule: If $|Z_{STAT}| > 2.58$, reject H_0.

Test statistic: $\bar{p} = \dfrac{X_1 + X_2}{n_1 + n_2} = \dfrac{930 + 230}{1,000 + 1,000} = 0.58$

$$Z_{STAT} = \frac{(p_1 - p_2) - (\pi_2 - \pi_2)}{\sqrt{\bar{p}(1 - \bar{p})\left(\frac{1}{n_1} + \frac{1}{n_2}\right)}} = \frac{(0.93 - 0.23) - 0}{\sqrt{0.58(1 - 0.58)\left(\frac{1}{1,000} + \frac{1}{1,000}\right)}}.$$

$Z_{STAT} = 31.7135 > 2.58$, reject H_0. There is evidence of a difference in the proportion of Superbanked and Unbanked with respect to the proportion that use credit cards. **(b)** p-value $= 0.0001$. The probability of obtaining a difference in proportions that gives rise to a test statistic below -31.7135 or above $+31.7135$ is 0.0000 if there is no difference in the proportion of Superbanked and Unbanked who use credit cards. **(c)** $0.6599 \le (\pi_1 - \pi_2) \le 0.7401$. You are 99% confident that the difference in the proportion of Superbanked and Unbanked who use credit cards is between 0.6599 and 0.7401.

10.34 (a) Because $Z_{STAT} = 4.4662 > 1.96$, reject H_0. There is evidence of a difference in the proportion of co-browsing organizations and non-co-browsing organizations that use skills-based routing to match the caller with the *right* agent. **(b)** p-value $= 0.0000$. The probability of obtaining a difference in proportions that is 0.2586 or more in either direction is 0.0000 if there is no difference between the proportion of co-browsing organizations and non-co-browsing organizations that use skills-based routing to match the caller with the *right* agent.

10.36 (a) 2.20. **(b)** 2.57. **(c)** 3.50.

10.38 (a) Population B: $S^2 = 25$. **(b)** 1.5625.

10.40 $df_{numerator} = 24$, $df_{denominator} = 24$.

10.42 Because $F_{STAT} = 1.2109 < 2.27$, do not reject H_0.

10.44 (a) Because $F_{STAT} = 1.2995 < 3.18$, do not reject H_0. **(b)** Because $F_{STAT} = 1.2995 < 2.62$, do not reject H_0.

10.46 (a) $H_0: \sigma_1^2 = \sigma_2^2$. $H_1: \sigma_1^2 \ne \sigma_2^2$.

Decision rule: If $F_{STAT} > 2.8890$, reject H_0.

Test statistic: $F_{STAT} = \dfrac{S_1^2}{S_2^2} = \dfrac{(42.5927)^2}{(36.1970)^2} = 1.3846$.

Decision: Because $F_{STAT} = 1.3846 < 2.8890$, do not reject H_0. There is insufficient evidence to conclude that the two population variances are different. **(b)** p-value $= 0.5346$. **(c)** The test assumes that each of the two populations is normally distributed. **(d)** Based on (a) and (b), a pooled-variance t test should be used.

10.48 (a) Because $F_{STAT} = 1.9078 < 5.4098$ or p-value $= 0.4417 > 0.05$, do not reject H_0. There is no evidence of a difference in the variability of the battery life between the two types of tablets. **(b)** p-value $= 0.4417$. The probability of obtaining a sample that yields a test statistic more extreme than 1.9078 is 0.4417 if there is no difference in the two population variances. **(c)** The test assumes that each of the two populations are normally distributed. The boxplots appear left-skewed especially the 3G/4G/WiFi tablets. The skewness and kurtosis statistics for the 3G/4G/WiFi tablets are very different from 0. Thus, the 3G/4G/WiFi tablets appear to be substantially different from a normal distribution. **(d)** Based on (a) and (b), a pooled-variance t test should be used. However, because of the skewness and kurtosis in the 3G/4G/WiFi tablets, the validity of either a pooled-variance or separate-variance t test is in doubt.

10.50 Because $F_{STAT} = 1.2908 < 4.8232$, or p-value $= 0.75 > 0.05$, do not reject H_0. There is insufficient evidence of a difference in the variance of the yield in the two cities.

10.52 (a) $SSW = 150$. **(b)** $MSA = 15$. **(c)** $MSW = 5$. **(d)** $F_{STAT} = 3$.

10.54 (a) 2. **(b)** 18. **(c)** 20.

10.56 (a) Reject H_0 if $F_{STAT} > 2.95$; otherwise, do not reject H_0. **(b)** Because $F_{STAT} = 4 > 2.95$, reject H_0. **(c)** The table does not have 28 degrees of freedom in the denominator, so use the next larger critical value, $Q_\alpha = 3.90$. **(d)** Critical range $= 6.166$.

10.58 (a) $H_0: \mu_A = \mu_B = \mu_C = \mu_D$ and H_1: At least one mean is different.

$$MSA = \frac{SSA}{c - 1} = \frac{8,812,582.2}{3} = 2,937,527.4.$$

$$MSW = \frac{SSW}{n - c} = \frac{17,231,437.4}{36} = 478,651.0389.$$

$$F_{STAT} = \frac{MSA}{MSW} = \frac{2,937,527.4}{478,651.0389} = 6.1371.$$

$$F_{0.05,3,36} = 2.8663.$$

Because the p-value is 0.0018 and $F_{STAT} = 6.1371 > 2.8663$, reject H_0. There is sufficient evidence of a difference in the mean import cost across the four global regions. **(b)** Critical range $= Q_\alpha \sqrt{\dfrac{MSW}{2}\left(\dfrac{1}{n_j} + \dfrac{1}{n_{j'}}\right)}$

$$= 3.79 \sqrt{\frac{478,651.0389}{2}\left(\frac{1}{10} + \frac{1}{10}\right)} = 829.2.$$

From the Tukey-Kramer procedure, there is a difference in the mean import cost between the East Asia and Pacific region and each of the other regions. None of the other regions are different. **(c)** ANOVA output for Levene's test for homogeneity of variance:

$$MSA = \frac{SSA}{c - 1} = \frac{1,620,045}{3} = 540,015$$

$$MSW = \frac{SSW}{n - c} = \frac{9,545,488.5}{36} = 265,152.4583$$

$$F_{STAT} = \frac{MSA}{MSW} = \frac{540,015}{265,152.4583} = 2.0366$$

$$F_{0.05,3,36} = 2.8663$$

Because p-value $= 0.1261 > 0.05$ and $F_{STAT} = 2.0366 < 2.8663$, do not reject H_0. There is insufficient evidence to conclude that the variances in the import cost are different. **(d)** From the results in (a) and (b), the mean import cost for the East Asia and Pacific region is lower than for the other regions.

10.60 (a) Because $F_{STAT} = 12.56 > 2.76$, reject H_0. **(b)** Critical range $= 4.67$. Advertisements A and B are different from Advertisements C and D. Advertisement E is only different from Advertisement D. **(c)** Because $F_{STAT} = 1.927 < 2.76$, do not reject H_0. There is no evidence of a significant difference in the variation in the ratings among the five advertisements. **(d)** The advertisements underselling the pen's characteristics had the highest mean ratings, and the advertisements overselling the pen's characteristics had the lowest mean ratings. Therefore, use an advertisement that undersells the pen's characteristics and avoid advertisements that oversell the pen's characteristics.

10.62 (a)

Source	Degrees of Freedom	Sum of Squares	Mean Squares	F
Among groups	2	1.879	0.9395	8.7558
Within groups	297	31.865	0.1073	
Total	299	33.744		

(b) Since $F_{STAT} = 8.7558 > 3.00$, reject H_0. There is evidence of a difference in the mean soft-skill score of the different groups. **(c)** Group 1 versus group 2: $0.072 <$ Critical range $= 0.1092$; group 1 versus group 3: $0.181 > 0.1056$; group 2 versus group 3: $0.109 < 0.1108$. There is evidence of a difference in the mean soft-skill score between those who had no coursework in leadership and those who had a degree in leadership.

10.64 (a) Because $F_{STAT} = 53.03 > 2.92$, reject H_0. **(b)** Critical range $= 5.27$ (using 30 degrees of freedom). Designs 3 and 4 are different from designs 1 and 2. Designs 1 and 2 are different from each other. **(c)** The assumptions are that the samples are randomly and independently selected (or randomly assigned), the original populations of distances are approximately normally distributed, and the variances are equal. **(d)** Because $F_{STAT} = 2.093 < 2.92$, do not reject H_0. There is sufficient evidence of a difference in the variation in the distance among the four designs. **(e)** The manager should choose design 3 or 4.

10.76 (a) Because $F_{STAT} = 1.0041 < 1.6195$, or p-value $= 0.9501 > 0.05$, do not reject H_0. There is not enough evidence of a difference in the variance of the salary of Black Belts and Green Belts. **(b)** The pooled-variance t test. **(c)** Because $t_{STAT} = 5.1766 > 1.6541$ or p-value $= 0.0000 < 0.05$, reject H_0. There is evidence that the mean salary of Black Belts is greater than the mean salary of Green Belts.

10.78 (a) Because $F_{STAT} = 1.5625 < F_\alpha = 1.6854$, do not reject H_0. There is not enough evidence to conclude that there is a difference between the variances in the talking time per month between women and men. **(b)** It is more appropriate to use a pooled-variance t test. Using the pooled-variance t test, because $t_{STAT} = 11.1196 > 2.6009$, reject H_0. There is enough evidence of a difference in the mean talking time per month between women and men. **(c)** Because $F_{STAT} = 1.44 < 1.6854$, do not reject H_0. There is not enough evidence to conclude that there is a difference between the variances in the number of text messages sent per month between women and men. **(d)** Using the pooled-variance t test, because $t_{STAT} = 8.2456 > 2.6009$, reject H_0. There is enough evidence of a difference in the mean number of text messages sent per month between women and men.

10.80 (a) Because $t_{STAT} = 3.3282 > 1.8595$, reject H_0. There is enough evidence to conclude that the introductory computer students required more than a mean of 10 minutes to write and run a program in VB.NET **(b)** Because $t_{STAT} = 1.3636 < 1.8595$, do not reject H_0. There is not enough evidence to conclude that the introductory computer students required more than a mean of 10 minutes to write and run a program in VB.NET **(c)** Although the mean time necessary to complete the assignment increased from 12 to 16 minutes as a result of the increase in one data value, the standard deviation went from 1.8 to 13.2, which reduced the value of t statistic. **(d)** Because $F_{STAT} = 1.2308 < 3.8549$, do not reject H_0. There is not enough evidence to conclude that the population variances are different for the Introduction to Computers students and computer majors. Hence, the pooled-variance t test is a valid test to determine whether computer majors can write a VB.NET program in less time than introductory students, assuming that the distributions of the time needed to write a VB.NET program for both the Introduction to Computers students and the computer majors are approximately normally distributed. Because $t_{STAT} = 4.0666 > 1.7341$, reject H_0. There is enough evidence that the mean time is higher for Introduction to Computers students than for computer majors. **(e)** p-value $= 0.000362$. If the true population mean amount of time needed for Introduction to Computer students to write a VB.NET program is no more than 10 minutes, the probability of observing a sample mean greater than the 12 minutes in the current sample is 0.0362%. Hence, at a 5% level of significance, you can conclude that the population mean amount of time needed for Introduction to Computer students to write a VB.NET program is more than 10 minutes. As illustrated in (d), in which there is not enough evidence to conclude that the population variances are different for the Introduction to Computers students and computer majors, the pooled-variance t test performed is a valid test to determine whether computer majors can write a VB.NET program in less time than introductory students, assuming that the distribution of the time needed to write a VB.NET program for both the Introduction to Computers students and the computer majors are approximately normally distributed.

10.82 From the boxplot and the summary statistics, both distributions are approximately normally distributed. $F_{STAT} = 1.056 < 1.89$. There is insufficient evidence to conclude that the two population variances are significantly different at the 5% level of significance. $t_{STAT} = -5.084 < -1.99$. At the 5% level of significance, there is sufficient evidence to reject the null

hypothesis of no difference in the mean life of the bulbs between the two manufacturers. You can conclude that there is a significant difference in the mean life of the bulbs between the two manufacturers.

10.84 (a) Because $Z_{STAT} = -3.6911 < -1.96$, reject H_0. There is enough evidence to conclude that there is a difference in the proportion of men and women who order dessert. **(b)** Because $Z_{STAT} = 6.0873 > 1.96$, reject H_0. There is enough evidence to conclude that there is a difference in the proportion of people who order dessert based on whether they ordered a beef entree.

10.86 The normal probability plots suggest that the two populations are not normally distributed. An F test is inappropriate for testing the difference in the two variances. The sample variances for Boston and Vermont shingles are 0.0203 and 0.015, respectively. Because $t_{STAT} = 3.015 > 1.967$ or p-value $= 0.0028 < \alpha = 0.05$, reject H_0. There is sufficient evidence to conclude that there is a difference in the mean granule loss of Boston and Vermont shingles.

10.88 Population 1 = short term 2 = long term, 3 = world; One-year return: Levene test: Since the p-value $0.4621 > 0.05$ do not reject H_0. There is insufficient evidence to show a difference in the variance of the return among the three different types of bond funds at a 5% level of significance. Since the p-value is $0.4202 > 0.05$, do not, reject H_0. There is insufficient evidence to show a difference in the mean one-year returns among the three different types of bond funds at a 5% level of significance.

CHAPTER 11

11.2 (a) For $df = 1$ and $\alpha = 0.05$, $\chi_\alpha^2 = 3.841$. **(b)** For $df = 1$ and $\alpha = 0.025$, $\chi^2 = 5.024$. **(c)** For $df = 1$ and $\alpha = 0.01$, $\chi_\alpha^2 = 6.635$.

11.4 (a) All $f_e = 25$. **(b)** Because $\chi_{STAT}^2 = 4.00 > 3.841$, reject H_0.

11.6 (a) $H_0: \pi_1 = \pi_2$. $H_1: \pi_1 \neq \pi_2$. **(b)** Because $\chi_{STAT}^2 = 2.4045 < 3.841$, do not reject H_0. There is insufficient evidence to conclude that the population proportion of those who recalled the brand is different for those who had a social media recommendation than for those who did web browsing. p-value $= 0.1210$. The probability of obtaining a test statistic of 2.4045 or larger when the null hypothesis is true is 0.1210. **(c)** You should not compare the results in (a) to those of Problem 10.30 (b) because that was a one-tail test.

11.8 (a) $H_0: \pi_1 = \pi_2$. $H_1: \pi_1 \neq \pi_2$. Because $\chi_{STAT}^2 = (930 - 580)^2/580 + (70 - 420)^2/420 + (230 - 580)^2/580 + (770 - 420)^2 = 1,005.7471 > 6.635$, reject H_0. There is evidence of a difference in the proportion of Superbanked and Unbanked with respect to the proportion that use credit cards. **(b)** p-value $= 0.0000$. The probability of obtaining a difference in proportions that gives rise to a test statistic above 1,005.7471 is 0.0000 if there is no difference in the proportion of Superbanked and Unbanked who use credit cards. **(c)** The results of (a) and (b) are exactly the same as those of Problem 10.32. The χ^2 in (a) and the Z in Problem 10.32 (a) satisfy the relationship that $\chi^2 = 1,005.7471 = Z^2 = (31.7135)^2$, and the p-value in (b) is exactly the same as the p-value computed in Problem 10.32 (b).

11.10 (b) Since $\chi_{STAT}^2 = 19.9467 > 3.841$, reject H_0. There is evidence that there is a significant difference between the proportion of co-browsing organizations and non-co-browsing organizations that use skills-based routing to match the caller with the *right* agent. **(c)** p-value is virtually zero. The probability of obtaining a test statistic of 19.9467 or larger when the null hypothesis is true is 0.0000. **(d)** The results are identical since $(4.4662)^2 = 19.9467$.

11.12 (a) The expected frequencies for the first row are 20, 30, and 40. The expected frequencies for the second row are 30, 45, and 60. **(b)** Because $\chi_{STAT}^2 = 12.5 > 5.991$, reject H_0.

11.14 (a) Since the calculated test statistic 5.3863 is less than the critical value of 7.8147, you do not reject H_0 and conclude that there is no evidence of a difference among the age groups in the proportion who have had important personal information stolen. (b) p-value $= 0.1456$. The probability of obtaining a data set that gives rise to a test statistic of 5.3863 or more is 0.1456 if there is no difference in the proportion who have had important personal information stolen.

11.16 (a) H_0: $\pi_1 = \pi_2 = \pi_3$. H_1: At least one proportion differs where population 1 = small, 2 = medium, 3 = large.

PHStat output:

Observed Frequencies

Deployed	Column Variable			Total
	Small	Medium	Large	
Yes	18	74	52	144
No	182	126	148	456
Total	200	200	200	600

Expected Frequencies

Deployed	Column Variable			Total
	Small	Medium	Large	
Yes	48	48	48	144
No	152	152	152	456
Total	200	200	200	600

Data

Level of Significance	0.05
Number of Rows	2
Number of Columns	3
Degrees of Freedom	2

Results

Critical Value	5.991465
Chi-Square Test Statistic	43.64035
p-Value	3.34E-10
Reject the Null Hypothesis	

Decision rule: $df = (c - 1) = (3 - 1) = 2$. If $\chi^2_{STAT} > 5.9915$, reject H_0.

Test statistic: $\chi^2_{STAT} \sum_{all\ cells} \frac{(f_o - f_e)^2}{f_e} = 43.64035$

Decision: Since $\chi^2_{STAT} = 43.64035$ is greater than the upper critical value of 5.9915, reject H_0. There is evidence of a difference among the groups with respect to the proportion of companies that have already deployed Big Data projects. (b) p-value $= 0.0000$. The probability of obtaining a sample that gives rise to a test statistic that is equal to or more than 43.64035 is 0.0000 if there is no difference among the groups with respect to the proportion of companies that have already deployed Big Data projects.

11.18 (a) Since the calculated test statistic 28.0506 is greater than the critical value of 7.8147, you reject H_0 and conclude that there is evidence of a significant difference among the companies of different sizes with respect to the proportion that are working simultaneously with five or more vendors. **(b)** p-value $= 0.0000$. The probability of obtaining a data set that gives rise to a test statistic of 28.0506 or more is 0.0000 if there is no difference among the companies of different sizes with respect to the proportion that are working simultaneously with five or more vendors.

11.20 $df = (r - 1)(c - 1) = (3 - 1)(4 - 1) = 6$.

11.22 $\chi^2_{STAT} = 92.1028 > 16.919$, reject H_0 and conclude that there is evidence of a relationship between the type of dessert ordered and the type of entrée ordered.

11.24 H_0: There is no relationship between number of airline loyalty programs and age.
H_1: There is a relationship between number of airline loyalty programs and age.
PHStat output:

Observed Frequencies

Number of Loyalty Programs	Age						Total
	18–22	23–29	30–39	40–49	50–64	65+	
0	78	113	79	74	88	88	520
1	36	50	41	48	69	82	326
3-Feb	12	34	36	48	52	85	267
5-Apr	4	4	6	7	13	25	59
6	0	0	3	0	2	3	8
Total	130	201	165	177	224	283	1,180

Expected Frequencies

Number of Loyalty Programs	Age						Total
	18–22	23–29	30–39	40–49	50–64	65+	
0	57.28814	88.57627	72.71186	78	98.71186	124.7119	520
1	35.91525	55.53051	45.58475	48.9	61.88475	78.18475	326
41,673	29.41525	45.48051	37.33475	40.05	50.68475	64.03475	267
41,734	6.5	10.05	8.25	8.85	11.2	14.15	59
6	0.881356	1.362712	1.118644	1.2	1.518644	1.918644	8
Total	130	201	165	177	224	283	1,180

Calculations

$$f_o - f_e$$

20.71186	24.42373	6.288136	−4	−10.7119	−36.7119
0.084746	−5.53051	−4.58475	−0.9	7.115254	3.815254
−17.4153	−11.4805	−1.33475	7.95	1.315254	20.96525
−2.5	−6.05	−2.25	−1.85	1.8	10.85
−0.88136	−1.36271	1.881356	−1.2	0.481356	1.081356

$$(f_o - f_e)^2/f_e$$

7.488136	6.734518	0.543799	0.205128	1.162414	10.807
0.0002	0.550806	0.461117	0.016564	0.818083	0.186177
10.31067	2.89799	0.047718	1.57809	0.03413	6.864115
0.961538	3.64204	0.613636	0.386723	0.289286	8.319611
0.881356	1.362712	3.164099	1.2	0.152573	0.609457

Data

Level of Significance	0.01
Number of Rows	5
Number of Columns	6
Degrees of Freedom	20

Results

Critical Value	37.56623
Chi-Square Test Statistic	72.28969
p-Value	7.67E-08

Reject the Null Hypothesis

Decision rule: If $\chi^2_{STAT} >$, reject H_0.

Test statistic: $\chi^2_{STAT} \sum\limits_{all\ cells} \dfrac{(f_o - f_e)^2}{f_e} = 72.2897$

Decision: Since $\chi^2_{STAT} = 72.2897 > 37.5662$, reject H_0. There is evidence to conclude there is a relationship between number of airline loyalty programs and age.

11.26 Because $\chi^2_{STAT} = 38.021 > 21.0261$ reject H_0. There is evidence of a relationship between identified main opportunity and geographic region.

11.30 (a) Because $\chi^2_{STAT} = 0.412 < 3.841$, do not reject H_0. There is insufficient evidence to conclude that there is a relationship between a student's gender and pizzeria selection. **(b)** Because $\chi^2_{STAT} = 2.624 < 3.841$, do not reject H_0. There is insufficient evidence to conclude that there is a relationship between a student's gender and pizzeria selection. **(c)** Because $\chi^2_{STAT} = 4.956 < 5.991$, do not reject H_0. There is insufficient evidence to conclude that there is a relationship between price and pizzeria selection. **(d)** *p*-value = 0.0839. The probability of a sample that gives a test statistic equal to or greater than 4.956 is 8.39% if the null hypothesis of no relationship between price and pizzeria selection is true.

11.32 (a) Because $\chi^2_{STAT} = 11.895 < 12.592$, do not reject H_0. There is not enough evidence to conclude that there is a relationship between the attitudes of employees toward the use of self-managed work teams and employee job classification. **(b)** Because $\chi^2_{STAT} = 3.294 < 12.592$, do not reject H_0. There is insufficient evidence to conclude that there is a relationship between the attitudes of employees toward vacation time without pay and employee job classification.

CHAPTER 12

12.2 (a) Yes. **(b)** No. **(c)** No. **(d)** Yes.

12.4 (a) The scatter plot shows a positive linear relationship. **(b)** For each increase in alcohol percentage of 1.0, mean predicted mean wine quality is estimated to increase by 0.5624. **(c)** $\hat{Y} = -0.3529 + 0.5624X = -0.3529 + 0.5624(10) = 5.2715$. **(d)** Wine quality appears to be affected by the alcohol percentage. Each increase of 1% in alcohol leads to a mean increase in wine quality of a little more than half a unit.

12.6 (b) $b_0 = -2.37, b_1 = 0.0501$. **(c)** For every cubic foot increase in the amount moved, predicted mean labor hours are estimated to increase by 0.0501. **(d)** 22.67 labor hours. **(e)** That as expected, the labor hours are affected by the amount to be moved.

12.8 (b) $b_0 = -748.1752, b_1 = 6.5988$. **(c)** For each additional million-dollar increase in revenue, the mean value is predicted to increase by an estimated \$6.5988 million. Literal interpretation of b_0 is not meaningful because an operating franchise cannot have zero revenue. **(d)** \$901.5234 million. **(e)** That the value of the franchise can be expected to increase as revenue increases.

12.10 (b) $b_0 = 11.9081, b_1 = 0.1303$. **(c)** For each increase of \$1 million of box office gross, the predicted DVD revenue is estimated to increase by \$0.1303 million. **(d)** \$24.937 million. **(e)** You can conclude that the mean predicted increase in DVD sales is \$130,300 for each million-dollar increase in movie gross.

12.12 $r^2 = 0.90$. 90% of the variation in the dependent variable can be explained by the variation in the independent variable.

12.14 $r^2 = 0.75$. 75% of the variation in the dependent variable can be explained by the variation in the independent variable.

12.16 (a) $r^2 = \dfrac{SSR}{SST} = \dfrac{21.8677}{64.0000} = 0.3417$, 34.17% of the variation in wine quality can be explained by the variation in the percentage of alcohol.

(b) $S_{YX} = \sqrt{\dfrac{SSE}{n-2}} = \sqrt{\dfrac{\sum\limits_{i=1}^{n}(Y_i - \hat{Y}_i)^2}{n-2}} = \sqrt{\dfrac{42.1323}{48}} = 0.9369$.

(c) Based on (a) and (b), the model should be somewhat useful for predicting wine quality.

12.18 (a) $r^2 = 0.8892$. 88.92% of the variation in labor hours can be explained by the variation in cubic feet moved. **(b)** $S_{YX} = 5.0314$. **(c)** Based on (a) and (b), the model should be very useful for predicting the labor hours.

12.20 (a) $r^2 = 0.7997$, 79.97% of the variation in the value of a baseball franchise can be explained by the variation in its annual revenue. **(b)** $S_{YX} = 206.9141$. **(c)** Based on (a) and (b), the model should be useful for predicting the value of a baseball franchise.

12.22 (a) $r^2 = 0.4524$, 45.24% of the variation in DVD revenue can be explained by the variation in box office gross. **(b)** $S_{YX} = 12.1366$. The variation of DVD revenue around the prediction line is \$12.1366 million. The typical difference between actual DVD revenue and the predicted DVD revenue using the regression equation is approximately \$12.1366 million. **(c)** Based on (a) and (b), the model may only be somewhat useful for predicting DVD revenue. **(d)** Other variables that might explain the variation in DVD revenue could be the amount spent on advertising, the timing of the release of the DVDs, and the type of movie.

12.24 A residual analysis of the data indicates a pattern, with sizable clusters of consecutive residuals that are either all positive or all negative. This pattern indicates a violation of the assumption of linearity. A curvilinear model should be investigated.

12.26 There does not appear to be a pattern in the residual plot. The assumptions of regression do not appear to be seriously violated.

12.28 Based on the residual plot, there does not appear to be a curvilinear pattern in the residuals. The assumptions of normality and equal variance do not appear to be seriously violated.

12.30 Based on the residual plot, there appears to be an outlier in the residuals, but no evidence of a pattern. The outlier is the Los Angeles Dodgers whose value has increased drastically due to a recent long term cable TV deal.

12.32 (a) An increasing linear relationship exists. **(b)** There is evidence of a strong positive autocorrelation among the residuals.

12.34 (a) No, because the data were not collected over time. **(b)** If data were collected at a single store had been selected and studied over a period of time, you would compute the Durbin-Watson statistic.

12.36 (a)

$$b_1 = \frac{SSXY}{SSX} = \frac{201,399.05}{12,495,626} = 0.0161$$

$$b_0 = \bar{Y} - b_1\bar{X} = 71.2621 - 0.0161\,(4,393) = 0.458.$$

(b) $\hat{Y} = 0.458 + 0.0161X = 0.458 + 0.0161(4,500) = 72.908$, or $72,908. **(c)** There is no evidence of a pattern in the residuals over time.

(d) $D = \dfrac{\sum\limits_{i=2}^{n} (e_i - e_{i-1})^2}{\sum\limits_{i=1}^{n} e_i^2} = \dfrac{1,243.2244}{599.0683} = 2.08 > 1.45$. There is no

evidence of positive autocorrelation among the residuals. **(e)** Based on a residual analysis, the model appears to be adequate.

12.38 (a) $b_0 = -2.535$, $b_1 = 0.06073$. **(b)** $2,505.40. **(d)** $D = 1.64 > d_U = 1.42$, so there is no evidence of positive autocorrelation among the residuals. **(e)** The plot shows some nonlinear pattern, suggesting that a nonlinear model might be better. Otherwise, the model appears to be adequate.

12.40 (a) 3.00. **(b)** ± 2.1199. **(c)** Reject H_0. There is evidence that the fitted linear regression model is useful. **(d)** $1.32 \leq \beta_1 \leq 7.68$.

12.42 (a) $t_{STAT} = \dfrac{b_1 - \beta_1}{S_{b_1}} = \dfrac{0.5624}{0.1127} = 4.9913 > 2.0106$. Reject H_0.

There is evidence of a linear relationship between the percentage of alcohol and wine quality.
(b) $b_1 \pm t_{\alpha/2}S_{b_1} = 0.5624 \pm 2.0106(0.1127)\; 0.3359 \leq \beta_1 \leq 0.7890.$

12.44 (a) $t_{STAT} = 16.52 > 2.0322$; reject H_0. There is evidence of a linear relationship between the number of cubic feet moved and labor hours. **(b)** $0.0439 \leq \beta_1 \leq 0.0562.$

12.46 (a) $t_{STAT} = 10.5744 > 2.0484$ or because the p-value is 0.0000, reject H_0 at the 5% level of significance. There is evidence of a linear relationship between annual revenue and franchise value. **(b)** $5.3205 \leq \beta_1 \leq 7.8771.$

12.48 (a) $t_{STAT} = 4.4532 > 2.0639$ or because the p-value $= 0.0002 < 0.05$; reject H_0. There is evidence of a linear relationship between box office gross and sales of DVDs. **(b)** $0.0699 \leq \beta_1 \leq 0.1907.$

12.50 (a) (% daily change in SPXL) $= b_0 + 3.0$ (% daily change in S&P 500 index). **(b)** If the S&P 500 gains 10% in a year, SPXL is expected to gain an estimated 30%. **(c)** If the S&P 500 loses 20% in a year, SPXL is expected to lose an estimated 60%. **(d)** Risk takers will be attracted to leveraged funds, and risk-averse investors will stay away.

12.52 (a), (b) First weekend and U.S. gross: $r = 0.7264$, $t_{STAT} = 2.5893 > 2.4469$, p-value $= 0.0413 < 0.05$. reject H_0. At the 0.05 level of significance, there is evidence of a linear relationship between first weekend sales and U.S. gross. First weekend and worldwide gross: $r = 0.8234$, $t_{STAT} = 3.5549 > 2.4469$, p-value $= 0.0120 < 0.05$. reject H_0. At the 0.05 level of significance, there is evidence of a linear relationship between first weekend sales and worldwide gross. U.S. gross and worldwide gross: $r = 0.9629$, $t_{STAT} = 8.7456 > 2.4469$, p-value $= 0.0001 < 0.05$. Reject H_0. At the 0.05 level of significance, there is evidence of a linear relationship between U.S. gross and worldwide gross.

12.54 (a) $r = 0.8009$. There appears to be a strong positive linear relationship between social media networking and the GDP per capita. **(b)** $t_{STAT} = 6.2744$, p-value $= 0.0000 < 0.05$. Reject H_0. At the 0.05 level of significance, there is a significant linear relationship between social media networking and the GDP per capita. **(c)** There appears to be a strong relationship.

12.56 (a) $15.95 \leq \mu_{Y|X=4} \leq 18.05$. **(b)** $14.651 \leq Y_{X=4} \leq 19.349.$

12.58 (a) $\hat{Y} = -0.3529 + (0.5624)(10) = 5.2715$ $\hat{Y} \pm t_{\alpha/2}S_{YX}\sqrt{h_i}$

$$= 5.2715 \pm 2.0106(0.9369)\sqrt{0.0249}$$
$$4.9741 \leq \mu_{Y|X=10} \leq 5.5690.$$

(b) $\hat{Y} \pm t_{\alpha/2}S_{YX}\sqrt{1 + h_i}$

$$= 5.2715 \pm 2.0106(9,369)\sqrt{1 + 0.0249}$$
$$3.3645 \leq Y_{X=10} \leq 7.1786.$$

(c) Part (b) provides a prediction interval for the individual response given a specific value of the independent variable, and part (a) provides an interval estimate for the mean value, given a specific value of the independent variable. Because there is much more variation in predicting an individual value than in estimating a mean value, a prediction interval is wider than a confidence interval estimate.

12.60 (a) $20.799 \leq \mu_{Y|X=500} \leq 24.542$. **(b)** $12.276 \leq Y_{X=500} \leq 33.065$. **(c)** You can estimate a mean more precisely than you can predict a single observation.

12.62 (a) $822.1742 \leq \mu_{Y|X=250} \leq 980.8727$. **(b)** $470.3155 \leq Y_{X=250} \leq 1,332.731$. **(c)** Part (b) provides a prediction interval for an individual response given a specific value of X, and part (a) provides a confidence interval estimate for the mean value, given a specific value of X. Because there is much more variation in predicting an individual value than in estimating a mean, the prediction interval is wider than the confidence interval.

12.74 (a) $b_0 = 24.84$, $b_1 = 0.14$. **(b)** For each additional case, the predicted delivery time is estimated to increase by 0.14 minute. **(c)** 45.84. **(d)** No, 500 is outside the relevant range of the data used to fit the regression equation. **(e)** $r^2 = 0.972$. **(f)** There is no obvious pattern in the residuals, so the assumptions of regression are met. The model appears to be adequate. **(g)** $t_{STAT} = 24.88 > 2.1009$; reject H_0. **(h)** $44.88 \leq \mu_{Y|X=150} \leq 46.80$. $41.56 \leq Y_{X=150} \leq 50.12$. **(i)** The number of cases explains almost all of the variation in delivery time.

12.76 (a) $b_0 = 276.848$, $b_1 = 50.8031$. **(b)** For each additional 1,000 square feet in the size of the house, the mean assessed value is predicted to increase by $50,803.10. The estimated selling price of a house with a 0 size is $276,848 thousand. However, this interpretation is not meaningful because the size of the house cannot be 0. **(c)** $\hat{Y} = 276.848 + 50.8031(2) = 378.4542$ thousand dollars. **(d)** $r^2 = 0.3273$. So 32.73% of the variation in assessed value be explained by the variation in size. **(e)** Neither the residual plot nor the normal probability plot reveals any potential violation of the linearity, equal variance, and normality assumptions. **(f)** $t_{STAT} = 3.6913 > 2.0484$, p-value is 0.0009. Because p-value < 0.05, reject H_0. There is evidence of a linear relationship between assessed value and size. **(g)** $22.6113 \le \beta_1 \le 78.9949$. **(h)** The size of the house is somewhat useful in predicting the assessed value, but since only 32.73% of the variation in assessed value is explained by variation in size, other variables should be considered.

12.78 (a) $b_0 = 0.30$, $b_1 = 0.00487$. **(b)** For each additional point on the GMAT score, the predicted GPA is estimated to increase by 0.00487. Because a GMAT score of 0 is not possible, the Y intercept does not have a practical interpretation. **(c)** 3.222. **(d)** $r^2 = 0.798$. **(e)** There is no obvious pattern in the residuals, so the assumptions of regression are met. The model appears to be adequate. **(f)** $t_{STAT} = 8.43 > 2.1009$; reject H_0. **(g)** $3.144 \le \mu_{Y|X=600} \le 3.301$, $2.866 \le Y_{X=600} \le 3.559$. **(h)** $.00366 \le \beta_1 \le .00608$. **(i)** Most of the variation in GPA can be explained by variation in the GMAT score.

12.80 (a) There is no clear relationship shown on the scatter plot. **(c)** Looking at all 23 flights, when the temperature is lower, there is likely to be some O-ring damage, particularly if the temperature is below 60 degrees. **(d)** 31 degrees is outside the relevant range, so a prediction should not be made. **(e)** Predicted $Y = 18.036 - 0.240X$, where $X =$ temperature and $Y =$ O-ring damage. **(g)** A nonlinear model would be more appropriate. **(h)** The appearance on the residual plot of a nonlinear pattern indicates that a nonlinear model would be better. It also appears that the normality assumption is invalid.

12.82 (a) $b_0 = -177.4298$, $b_1 = 5.3450$. **(b)** For each additional million-dollar increase in revenue, the franchise value will increase by an estimated $5.3450 million. Literal interpretation of b_0 is not meaningful because an operating franchise cannot have zero revenue. **(c)** $624.3226 million. **(d)** $r^2 = 0.9331$. 93.31% of the variation in the value of an NBA franchise can be explained by the variation in its annual revenue. **(e)** There does not appear to be a pattern in the residual plot. The assumptions of regression do not appear to be seriously violated. **(f)** $t_{STAT} = 19.764 > 2.0484$ or because the p-value is 0.0000, reject H_0 at the 5% level of significance. There is evidence of a linear relationship between annual revenue and franchise value. **(g)** $599.5015 \le \mu_{Y|X=150} \le 649.1438$. **(h)** $486.2403 \le Y_{X=150} \le 762.405$. **(i)** The strength of the relationship between revenue and value is higher for NBA franchises than for European soccer teams and Major League Baseball teams.

12.84 (a) $b_0 = -2,629.222$, $b_1 = 82.472$. **(b)** For each additional centimeter in circumference, the weight is estimated to increase by 82.472 grams. **(c)** 2,319.08 grams. **(d)** Yes, since circumference is a very strong predictor of weight. **(e)** $r^2 = 0.937$. **(f)** There appears to be a nonlinear relationship between circumference and weight. **(g)** p-value is virtually $0 < 0.05$; reject H_0. **(h)** $72.7875 \le \beta_1 \le 92.156$.

12.86 (a) The correlation between compensation and stock performance is 0.1854. **(b)** $t_{STAT} = 2.6543$; p-value $= 0.0086 < 0.05$. The correlation between compensation and stock performance is significant, but only 3.44% of the variation in compensation can be explained by return. **(c)** The small correlation between compensation and stock performance was surprising (or maybe it shouldn't have been!).

CHAPTER 13

13.2 (a) For each one-unit increase in X_1, you estimate that the mean of Y will decrease 2 units, holding X_2 constant. For each one-unit increase in X_2, you estimate that the mean of Y will increase 7 units, holding X_1 constant. **(b)** The Y intercept, equal to 50, estimates the value of Y when both X_1 and X_2 are 0.

13.4 (a) $\hat{Y} = -0.2245 + 0.0111X_1 + 0.0445X_2$. **(b)** For a given total risk-based capital (%), each increase of 1% in the efficiency ratio is estimated to result in a mean increase in ROA of 0.0111%. For a given efficiency ratio, each increase of 1% in the total risk-based capital (%) is estimated to result in a mean increase in ROA of 0.0445%. **(c)** The interpretation of b_0 has no practical meaning here because it would have been the estimated mean ROA when the efficiency ratio and the total risk-based capital are each zero. **(d)** $\hat{Y}_i = -0.2245 + 0.0111(60) + 0.0445(15) = 1.1123$ or $69,878. **(e)** $0.9888 \le \mu_{Y|X} \le 1.2357$. **(f)** $-0.4268 \le Y_X \le 2.6513$. **(g)** Since there is much more variation in predicting an individual value than in estimating a mean value, a prediction interval is wider than a confidence interval estimate holding everything else fixed.

13.6 (a) $\hat{Y} = -186.5501 + 0.0333X_1 + 50.8778X_2$. **(b)** For a given amount of voluntary turnover, each increase of $1 million in total worldwide revenue is estimated to result in a mean increase in the number of full-time jobs added in a year by 0.0333. For a given amount of total worldwide revenue, each increase of 1% in voluntary turnover is estimated to result in the mean increase in the number of full-time jobs added in a year of 50.8778. **(c)** The Y intercept of -186.5501 has no direct interpretation since it represents the value of the mean increase in the number of full-time jobs added in a year when there is no worldwide revenue and no voluntary turnover. **(d)** The number of full-time jobs added seems to be affected by the amount of worldwide revenue and the voluntary turnover.

13.8 (a) $\hat{Y} = 532.2883 + 407.1346X_1 - 2.8257X_2$, where $X_1 =$ land area, $X_2 =$ age. **(b)** For a given age, each increase by one acre in land area is estimated to result in an increase in the mean fair market value by $407.1346 thousands. For a given land area, each increase of one year in age is estimated to result in a decrease in the mean fair market value by $2.8257 thousands. **(c)** The interpretation of b_0 has no practical meaning here because it would represent the estimated fair market value of a new house that has no land area. **(d)** $\hat{Y} = 5,332.2883 + 407.1346(0.25) - 2.8257(55) = 478.6577 thousands. **(e)** $446.8367 \le \mu_{Y|X} \le 510.4788$. **(f)** $307.2577 \le Y_X \le 650.0577$.

13.10 (a) $MSR = 15$, $MSE = 12$. **(b)** 1.25. **(c)** $F_{STAT} = 1.25 < 4.10$; do not reject H_0. **(d)** 0.20. **(e)** 0.04.

13.12 (a) $F_{STAT} = 0.6531 < 3.44$. Do not reject H_0. There is insufficient evidence of a significant linear relationship with at least one of the independent variables. **(b)** p-value $= 0.5302$. The probability of obtaining an F test statistic of 0.6531 or larger is 0.5302 if H_0 is true. **(c)** $r^2_{Y.12} = SSR/SST = 96,655.1/1,724,596.2 = 0.056$. So, 5.6% of the variation in the mean annual revenue can be explained by variation in the mean age and mean BizAnalyzer score.

13.14 (a) $MSR = SSR/k = 7.5929/2 = 3.7964$
$MSE = SSE/(n - k - 1) = 119.2044/197 = 0.6051$
$F_{STAT} = MSR/MSE = 3.7964/0.6051 = 6.2741$
$F_{STAT} = 6.2741 > 3.0$. Reject H_0. There is evidence of a significant linear relationship. **(b)** p-value $= 0.0023$. The probability of obtaining an F test statistic of 6.2741 or larger is 0.0023 if H_0 is true. **(c)** $r^2_{Y.12} = SSR/SST = 7.5929/126.7973 = 0.0599$. So, 5.99% of the

variation in ROA can be explained by variation in used efficiency ratio and total risk-based capital.

(d) $r_{adj}^2 = 1 - \left[(1 - r_{Y.12}^2)\dfrac{n-1}{n-k-1}\right] =$

$1 - \left[(1 - 0.0599)\dfrac{200-1}{200-2-1}\right] = 0.0503$

13.16 (a) $MSR = SSR/k = 19,534,514.2835/2 = 9,767,257.1417$
$MSE = SSE/(n-k-1) = 115,096,077.0499/93 = 1,237,592.2263$
$F_{STAT} = MSR/MSE = 9,767,257.1417/1,237,592.2263 = 7.8921$
$F_{STAT} = 7.8921 > 3.0943$. Reject H_0. There is evidence of a significant linear relationship. **(b)** p-value <0.0007. The probability of obtaining an F test statistic of 7.8921 or larger is less than 0.0007 if H_0 is true.
(c) $r_{Y.12}^2 = SSR/SST = 19,534,514.2835/134,630,591.3333 = 0.1451$.
So, 14.51% of the variation in the number of full-time jobs added can be explained by variation in the total worldwide revenue ($millions), and full-time voluntary turnover (%). **(d)** $r_{adj}^2 = 0.1267$

13.18 Since the data were not collected over time, there is no reason to plot the residuals over time. **(c)** There appears to be a departure in the equal variance assumption in the plot of the residuals versus the efficiency ratio. Therefore, a data transformation should be considered.

13.20 Based on a residual analysis, there is evidence of a violation of the assumptions of equal variance and normality. **(b)** Since the data were not collected over time, the Durbin-Watson test is not appropriate. **(c)** No.

13.22 (a) The residual analysis reveals no patterns. **(b)** Since the data are not collected over time, the Durbin-Watson test is not appropriate. **(c)** There are no apparent violations in the assumptions.

13.24 (a) Variable X_2 has a larger slope in terms of the t statistic of 3.75 than variable X_1, which has a smaller slope in terms of the t statistic of 3.33. **(b)** $1.46824 \le \beta_1 \le 6.53176$. **(c)** For X_1: $t_{STAT} = 4/1.2 = 3.33 > 2.1098$, with 17 degrees of freedom for $\alpha = 0.05$. Reject H_0. There is evidence that X_1 contributes to a model already containing X_2. For X_2: $t_{STAT} = 3/0.8 = 3.75 > 2.1098$, with 17 degrees of freedom for $\alpha = 0.05$. Reject H_0. There is evidence that X_2 contributes to a model already containing X_1. Both X_1 and X_2 should be included in the model.

13.26 (a) 95% confidence interval on β_1: $b_1 \pm t_{n-k-1}s_{b_1}$, $0.0111 \pm 1.9721(0.0051)$ $0.0011 \le \beta_1 \le 0.0212$.
(b) For X_1: $t_{STAT} = b_1/s_{b_1} = 0.0111/0.0051 = 2.1881 > 1.9721$ with 197 degrees of freedom for $\alpha = 0.05$. Reject H_0. There is evidence that the variable X_1 contributes to a model already containing X_2.
For X_2: $t_{STAT} = b_2/s_{b_2} = 0.0445/0.0145 = 3.065 > 1.9721$ with 197 degrees of freedom for $\alpha = 0.05$. Reject H_0. There is evidence that the variable X_2 contributes to a model already containing X_1. Both variables X_1 and X_2 should be included in the model.

13.28 (a) $0.0333 \pm 1.9858(0.0092)$ $0.0151 \le \beta_1 \le 0.0515$.
(b) For X_1: $t_{STAT} = b_1/s_{b_1} = 0.0333/0.0092 = 3.639 > 1.9858$ with 93 degrees of freedom for $\alpha = 0.05$. Reject H_0. There is evidence that the variable X_1 contributes to a model already containing X_2.
For X_2: $t_{STAT} = b_2/s_{b_2} = 50.8778/23.7425 = 2.1429 > 1.9858$ with 93 degrees of freedom for $\alpha = 0.05$. Reject H_0. There is evidence that the variable X_2 contributes to a model already containing X_1. Both variables X_1 and X_2 should be included in the model.

13.30 (a) $274.1702 \le \beta_1 \le 540.0990$. **(b)** For X_1: $t_{STAT} = 6.2827$ and p-value $= 0.0000$. Because p-value < 0.05, reject H_0. There is evidence that X_1 contributes to a model already containing X_2. For X_2: $t_{STAT} = -4.1475$ and p-value $= 0.0003$. Because p-value < 0.05 reject H_0. There is evidence that X_2 contributes to a model already

containing X_1: $F_{STAT} = 30.4533$ p-value $= 0.0000$. Both X_1 (land area) and X_2 (age) should be included in the model.

13.32 Because $t_{STAT} = 3.27 > 2.1098$, reject H_0. X_2 makes a significant contribution to the model.

13.34 (a) $\hat{Y} = 243.7371 + 9.2189X_1 + 12.6967X_2$, where $X_1 =$ number of rooms and $X_2 =$ neighborhood (east $= 0$).
(b) Holding constant the effect of neighborhood, for each additional room, the mean selling price is estimated to increase by 9.2189 thousands of dollars, or $9,218.9. For a given number of rooms, a west neighborhood is estimated to increase the mean selling price over an east neighborhood by 12.6967 thousands of dollars, or $12,696.7.
(c) $\hat{Y} = 243.7371 + 9.2189(9) + 12.6967(0) = 326.7076$, or $326,707.6. $309,560.04 \le Y_X \le 343,855.1$. $321,471.44 \le \mu_{Y|X} \le 331,943.71$. **(d)** Based on a residual analysis, the model appears to be adequate. **(e)** $F_{STAT} = 55.39$, the p-value is virtually 0. Because p-value < 0.05, reject H_0. There is evidence of a significant relationship between selling price and the two independent variables (rooms and neighborhood). **(f)** For X_1: $t_{STAT} = 8.9537$, the p-value is virtually 0. Reject H_0. Number of rooms makes a significant contribution and should be included in the model. For X_2: $t_{STAT} = 3.5913$, p-value $= 0.0023 < 0.05$. Reject H_0. Neighborhood makes a significant contribution and should be included in the model. Based on these results, the regression model with the two independent variables should be used. **(g)** $7.0466 \le \beta_1 \le 11.3913$.
(h) $5.2378 \le \beta_2 \le 20.1557$. **(i)** $r_{adj}^2 = 0.851$. **(j)** The slope of selling price with number of rooms is the same, regardless of whether the house is located in an east or west neighborhood.
(k) $\hat{Y} = 253.95 + 8.032X_1 - 5.90X_2 + 2.089X_1X_2$. For X_1X_2, p-value $= 0.330$. Do not reject H_0. There is no evidence that the interaction term makes a contribution to the model. **(l)** The model in (b) should be used. **(m)** The number of rooms and the neighborhood both significantly affect the selling price, but the number of rooms has a greater effect.

13.36 (a) Predicted time $= 8.01 + 0.00523$ Depth $- 2.105$ Dry.
(b) Holding constant the effect of type of drilling, for each foot increase in depth of the hole, the mean drilling time is estimated to increase by 0.00523 minutes. For a given depth, a dry drilling hole is estimated to reduce the drilling time over wet drilling by a mean of 2.1052 minutes.
(c) 6.428 minutes, $6.210 \le \mu_{Y|X} \le 6.646$, $4.923 \le Y_X \le 7.932$.
(d) The model appears to be adequate. **(e)** $F_{STAT} = 111.11 > 3.09$; reject H_0. **(f)** $t_{STAT} = 5.03 > 1.9847$; reject H_0. $t_{STAT} = -14.03 < -1.9847$; reject H_0. Include both variables. **(g)** $0.0032 \le \beta_1 \le 0.0073$.
(h) $-2.403 \le \beta_2 \le -1.808$. **(i)** 69.0%. **(j)** The slope of the additional drilling time with the depth of the hole is the same, regardless of the type of drilling method used. **(k)** The p-value of the interaction term $= 0.462 > 0.05$, so the term is not significant and should not be included in the model. **(l)** The model in part (b) should be used. Both variables affect the drilling time. Dry drilling holes should be used to reduce the drilling time.

13.38 (a) $\hat{Y} = 2.5213 - 0.0313X_1 - 0.1131X_2 + 0.0024X_3$, where $X_1 =$ efficiency ratio, $X_2 =$ total risk-based capital, $X_3 = X_1X_2$. For X_1X_2: the p-value is $0.0297 < 0.05$. Reject H_0. There is evidence that the interaction term makes a contribution to the model. **(b)** Since there is evidence of an interaction effect between efficiency ratio and total risk-based capital, the model in (a) should be used.

13.40 (a) $\hat{Y} = 85.1106 + 0.0033X_1 + 15.8856X_2 + 0.0045X_3$, where $X_1 =$ total worldwide revenue ($millions), $X_2 =$ full-time voluntary turnover (%), $X_3 = X_1X_2$. For X_1X_2: the p-value is $0.0396 < 0.05$. Reject H_0. There is evidence that the interaction term makes a contribution to the model. **(b)** Since there is evidence of an interaction effect between total worldwide revenue ($millions) and full-time voluntary turnover, the model in (a) should be used.

13.42 (a) For $X_1 X_2$, p-value $= 0.2353 > 0.05$. Do not reject H_0. There is insufficient evidence that the interaction term makes a contribution to the model. **(b)** Because there is not enough evidence of an interaction effect between total staff present and remote hours, the model in Problem 13.7 should be used.

13.50 (a) $\hat{Y} = -3.9152 + 0.0319X_1 + 4.2228X_2$, where $X_1 =$ number cubic feet moved and $X_2 =$ number of pieces of large furniture. **(b)** Holding constant the number of pieces of large furniture, for each additional cubic foot moved, the mean labor hours are estimated to increase by 0.0319. Holding constant the amount of cubic feet moved, for each additional piece of large furniture, the mean labor hours are estimated to increase by 4.2228. **(c)** $\hat{Y} = -3.9152 + 0.0319$ $(500) + 4.2228 (2) = 20.4926$. **(d)** Based on a residual analysis, the errors appear to be normally distributed. The equal-variance assumption might be violated because the variances appear to be larger around the center region of both independent variables. There might also be violation of the linearity assumption. A model with quadratic terms for both independent variables might be fitted. **(e)** $F_{STAT} = 228.80$, p-value is virtually 0. Because p-value < 0.05, reject H_0. There is evidence of a significant relationship between labor hours and the two independent variables (the amount of cubic feet moved and the number of pieces of large furniture). **(f)** The p-value is virtually 0. The probability of obtaining a test statistic of 228.80 or greater is virtually 0 if there is no significant relationship between labor hours and the two independent variables (the amount of cubic feet moved and the number of pieces of large furniture). **(g)** $r^2 = 0.9327$. 93.27% of the variation in labor hours can be explained by variation in the number of cubic feet moved and the number of pieces of large furniture. **(h)** $r^2_{adj} = 0.9287$. **(i)** For X_1: $t_{STAT} = 6.9339$, the p-value is virtually 0. Reject H_0. The number of cubic feet moved makes a significant contribution and should be included in the model. For X_2: $t_{STAT} = 4.6192$, the p-value is virtually 0. Reject H_0. The number of pieces of large furniture makes a significant contribution and should be included in the model. Based on these results, the regression model with the two independent variables should be used. **(j)** For X_1: $t_{STAT} = 6.9339$, the p-value is virtually 0. The probability of obtaining a sample that will yield a test statistic farther away than 6.9339 is virtually 0 if the number of cubic feet moved does not make a significant contribution, holding the effect of the number of pieces of large furniture constant. For X_2: $t_{STAT} = 4.6192$, the p-value is virtually 0. The probability of obtaining a sample that will yield a test statistic farther away than 4.6192 is virtually 0 if the number of pieces of large furniture does not make a significant contribution, holding the effect of the amount of cubic feet moved constant. **(k)** $0.0226 \le \beta_1 \le 0.0413$. You are 95% confident that the mean labor hours will increase by between 0.0226 and 0.0413 for each additional cubic foot moved, holding constant the number of pieces of large furniture. In Problem 12.44, you are 95% confident that the labor hours will increase by between 0.0439 and 0.0562 for each additional cubic foot moved, regardless of the number of pieces of large furniture. **(l)** Both the number of cubic feet moved and the number of large pieces of furniture are useful in predicting the labor hours, but the cubic feet removed is more important.

13.52 (a) $\hat{Y} = 257.9033 + 53.3606X_1 + 0.2521X_2$, where $X_1 =$ house size and $X_2 =$ age. **(b)** Holding constant the age, for each additional thousand square feet in the size of the house, the mean assessed value is estimated to increase by 53.3606 thousand dollars. Holding constant the size of the house, for each additional year in age, the assessed value is estimated to increase by 0.2521 thousand dollars. **(c)** $\hat{Y} = 257.9033 + 53.3606(2) + 0.2521(55) = 378.4093$ thousand dollars. **(d)** Based on a residual analysis, the model appears to

be adequate. **(e)** $F_{STAT} = 6.6459$, the p-value $= 0.0045$. Because p-value < 0.05, reject H_0. There is evidence of a significant relationship between assessed value and the two independent variables (size of the house and age). **(f)** The p-value is 0.0045. The probability of obtaining a test statistic of 6.6459 or greater is virtually 0 if there is no significant relationship between assessed value and the two independent variables (size of the house and age). **(g)** $r^2 = 0.3299$. 32.99% of the variation in assessed value can be explained by variation in the size of the house and age. **(h)** $r^2_{adj} = 0.2803$. **(i)** For X_1: $t_{STAT} = 3.3128$, the p-value is 0.0026. Reject H_0. The size of the house makes a significant contribution and should be included in the model. For X_2: $t_{STAT} = 0.3203$, p-value $= 0.7512 > 0.05$. Do not reject H_0. Age does not make a significant contribution and should not be included in the model. Based on these results, the regression model with only the size of the house should be used. **(j)** For X_1: $t_{STAT} = 3.3128$, the p-value is virtually 0. The probability of obtaining a sample that will yield a test statistic farther away than 3.3128 is 0.0026 if the house size does not make a significant contribution, holding age constant. For X_2: $t_{STAT} = 0.3203$, the p-value is 0.7512. The probability of obtaining a sample that will yield a test statistic farther away than 0.3203 is 0.7512 if the age does not make a significant contribution holding the effect of the house size constant. **(k)** $20.3109 \le \beta_1 \le 86.4104$. You are 95% confident that the assessed value will increase by an amount somewhere between $20.3109 thousand and $86.4104 thousand for each additional thousand square foot increase in house size, holding constant the age of the house. In Problem 12.76, you are 95% confident that the assessed value will increase by an amount somewhere between $22.6113 thousand and $78.9949 thousand for each additional 1,000 square foot increase in house size, regardless of the age of the house. **(l)** Only size of the house should be included in the model.

13.54 (a) $\hat{Y} = 694.9557 + 8.6059X_1 + 2069X_2$, where $X_1 =$ assessed value and $X_2 =$ age. **(b)** Holding age constant, for each additional $1,000, the taxes are estimated to increase by a mean of $8.61 thousand. Holding assessed value constant, for each additional year, the taxes are estimated to increase by $2.069 **(c)** $\hat{Y} = 694.9557 + 8.6059(400) + 2.069(50) = 4,240.542$ dollars. **(d)** Based on a residual analysis, the errors appear to be normally distributed. The equal-variance assumption appears to be valid. **(e)** $F_{STAT} = 22.0699$, p-value $= 0.0000$. Because p-value $= 0.0000 < 0.05$, reject H_0. There is evidence of a significant relationship between taxes and the two independent variables (assessed value and age). **(f)** p-value $= 0.0000$. The probability of obtaining an F_{STAT} test statistic of 22.0699 or greater is virtually 0 if there is no significant relationship between taxes and the two independent variables (assessed value and age). **(g)** $r^2 = 0.6205$. 62.05% of the variation in taxes can be explained by variation in assessed value and age. **(h)** $r^2_{adj} = 0.5924$. **(i)** For X_1: $t_{STAT} = 6.5271$, p-value $= 0.0000 < 0.05$. Reject H_0. The assessed value makes a significant contribution and should be included in the model. For X_2: $t_{STAT} = 0.3617$, p-value $= 0.7204 > 0.05$. Do not reject H_0. The age of a house does not make a significant contribution and should not be included in the model. Based on these results, the regression model with only assessed value should be used. **(j)** For X_1: p-value $= 0.0000$. The probability of obtaining a sample that will yield a test statistic farther away than 6.5271 is 0.0000 if the assessed value does not make a significant contribution, holding age constant. For X_2: p-value $= 0.7204$. The probability of obtaining a sample that will yield a test statistic farther away than 0.3617 is 0.7204 if the age of a house does not make a significant contribution, holding the effect of the assessed value constant. **(k)** $5.9005 \le \beta_1 \le 11.3112$. You are 95% confident that the mean taxes will increase by an amount somewhere between $5.90 and $11.31 for each additional $1,000 increase in the assessed value, holding constant the age. In Problem 12.77, you are 95% confident that the mean taxes will increase by an amount somewhere between $5.91

and $11.07 for each additional $thousand increase in assessed value, regardless of the age. **(l)** Based on your answers to (b) through (k), the age of a house does not have an effect on its taxes.

13.56 (a) $\hat{Y} = 183.1738 - 25.5406X_1 - 6.9866X_2$, where $X_1 = $ ERA and $X_2 = $ League (American $= 0$, National $= 1$). **(b)** Holding constant the effect of the league, for each additional ERA, the number of wins is estimated to decrease by a mean of 25.5406. For a given ERA, a team in the National League is estimated to have a mean of 6.9866 fewer wins than a team in the American League. **(c)** $\hat{Y} = 183.1738 - 25.5406(4.0) - 6.9866(0) = 81.0113$ wins $= 81$ wins. **(d)** Based on a residual analysis, there is no pattern in the errors. There is no apparent violation of other assumptions. **(e)** $F_{STAT} = 23.4629$, p-value $= 0.0000$. Since p-value < 0.05, reject H_0. There is evidence of a significant relationship between wins and the two independent variables (ERA and league). **(f)** For X_1: $t_{STAT} = -6.8476$, p-value $= 0.0000 < 0.05$. Reject H_0. ERA makes a significant contribution and should be included in the model. For X_2: $t_{STAT} = -2.368$, p-value $= 0.0253 < 0.05$. Reject H_0. The league makes a significant contribution and should be included in the model. Based on these results, the regression model with ERA and league as the independent variables should be used. **(g)** $-33.1937 \le \beta_1 \le -17.8876$ **(h)** $-13.0404 \le \beta_2 \le -0.9328$ **(i)** $r_{adj}^2 = 0.6077$. So 60.77% of the variation in wins can be explained by the variation in ERA and league after adjusting for number of independent variables and sample size. **(j)** The slope of the number of wins with ERA is the same regardless of whether the team belongs to the American or the National League. **(k)** For X_1X_2: the p-value is $0.3024 > 0.05$. Do not reject H_0. There is no evidence that the interaction term makes a contribution to the model. **(l)** The regression model with ERA and league as the independent variables should be used.

13.58 The r^2 of the multiple regression is 0.1996. 19.96% of the variation in earnings per share growth can be explained by the variation of sales growth (%) and return on equity (%). The F test statistic for the combined significance of sales growth (%) and return on equity (%) is 12.0965 with a p-value of 0.0000. Hence, at a 5% level of significance, there is evidence to conclude sales growth (%) and/or return on equity (%) affect earnings per share growth. The p-value of the t test for the significance of sales growth is $0.0002 < 0.05$. Hence, there is sufficient evidence to conclude that sales growth affects earnings per share growth holding constant the effect of return on equity. The p-value of the t test for the significance of return on equity is $0.0037 < 0.05$. There is evidence to conclude that return on equity affects earnings per share growth holding constant the effect of sales growth. There do not appear to be any obvious patterns in the residual plots. Hence, both sales growth (%) and return on equity (%) should be used in a regression model to predict earnings per share growth.

13.60 $b_0 = 18.2892$ (die temperature), $b_1 = 0.5976$, (die diameter), $b_2 = -13.5108$. The r^2 of the multiple regression is 0.3257 so 32.57% of the variation in unit density can be explained by the variation of die temperature and die diameter. The F test statistic for the combined significance of die temperature and die diameter is 5.0718 with a p-value of 0.0160. Hence, at a 5% level of significance, there is enough evidence to conclude that die temperature and die diameter affect unit density. The p-value of the t test for the significance of die temperature is 0.2117, which is greater than 5%. Hence, there is insufficient evidence to conclude that die temperature affects unit density holding constant the effect of die diameter. The p-value of the t test for the significance of die diameter is 0.0083, which is less than 5%. There is enough evidence to conclude that die diameter affects unit density at the 5% level of significance holding constant the effect of die temperature. After removing die temperature from the model, $b_0 = 107.9267$ (die diameter), $b_1 = -13.5108$. The r^2 of the multiple regression is 0.2724. So 27.24% of the variation in unit density can be explained by the variation of die diameter. The p-value of the t test for the significance of die diameter is 0.0087, which is less than 5%. There is enough evidence to conclude that die diameter affects unit density at the 5% level of significance. There is some lack of equality in the residuals and some departure from normality.

Index

The Cumulative Standardized Normal Distribution

Entry represents area under the cumulative standardized
normal distribution from $-\infty$ to Z

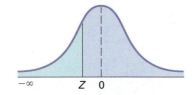

					Cumulative Probabilities					
Z	0.00	0.01	0.02	0.03	0.04	0.05	0.06	0.07	0.08	0.09
−6.0	0.000000001									
−5.5	0.000000019									
−5.0	0.000000287									
−4.5	0.000003398									
−4.0	0.000031671									
−3.9	0.00005	0.00005	0.00004	0.00004	0.00004	0.00004	0.00004	0.00004	0.00003	0.00003
−3.8	0.00007	0.00007	0.00007	0.00006	0.00006	0.00006	0.00006	0.00005	0.00005	0.00005
−3.7	0.00011	0.00010	0.00010	0.00010	0.00009	0.00009	0.00008	0.00008	0.00008	0.00008
−3.6	0.00016	0.00015	0.00015	0.00014	0.00014	0.00013	0.00013	0.00012	0.00012	0.00011
−3.5	0.00023	0.00022	0.00022	0.00021	0.00020	0.00019	0.00019	0.00018	0.00017	0.00017
−3.4	0.00034	0.00032	0.00031	0.00030	0.00029	0.00028	0.00027	0.00026	0.00025	0.00024
−3.3	0.00048	0.00047	0.00045	0.00043	0.00042	0.00040	0.00039	0.00038	0.00036	0.00035
−3.2	0.00069	0.00066	0.00064	0.00062	0.00060	0.00058	0.00056	0.00054	0.00052	0.00050
−3.1	0.00097	0.00094	0.00090	0.00087	0.00084	0.00082	0.00079	0.00076	0.00074	0.00071
−3.0	0.00135	0.00131	0.00126	0.00122	0.00118	0.00114	0.00111	0.00107	0.00103	0.00100
−2.9	0.0019	0.0018	0.0018	0.0017	0.0016	0.0016	0.0015	0.0015	0.0014	0.0014
−2.8	0.0026	0.0025	0.0024	0.0023	0.0023	0.0022	0.0021	0.0021	0.0020	0.0019
−2.7	0.0035	0.0034	0.0033	0.0032	0.0031	0.0030	0.0029	0.0028	0.0027	0.0026
−2.6	0.0047	0.0045	0.0044	0.0043	0.0041	0.0040	0.0039	0.0038	0.0037	0.0036
−2.5	0.0062	0.0060	0.0059	0.0057	0.0055	0.0054	0.0052	0.0051	0.0049	0.0048
−2.4	0.0082	0.0080	0.0078	0.0075	0.0073	0.0071	0.0069	0.0068	0.0066	0.0064
−2.3	0.0107	0.0104	0.0102	0.0099	0.0096	0.0094	0.0091	0.0089	0.0087	0.0084
−2.2	0.0139	0.0136	0.0132	0.0129	0.0125	0.0122	0.0119	0.0116	0.0113	0.0110
−2.1	0.0179	0.0174	0.0170	0.0166	0.0162	0.0158	0.0154	0.0150	0.0146	0.0143
−2.0	0.0228	0.0222	0.0217	0.0212	0.0207	0.0202	0.0197	0.0192	0.0188	0.0183
−1.9	0.0287	0.0281	0.0274	0.0268	0.0262	0.0256	0.0250	0.0244	0.0239	0.0233
−1.8	0.0359	0.0351	0.0344	0.0336	0.0329	0.0322	0.0314	0.0307	0.0301	0.0294
−1.7	0.0446	0.0436	0.0427	0.0418	0.0409	0.0401	0.0392	0.0384	0.0375	0.0367
−1.6	0.0548	0.0537	0.0526	0.0516	0.0505	0.0495	0.0485	0.0475	0.0465	0.0455
−1.5	0.0668	0.0655	0.0643	0.0630	0.0618	0.0606	0.0594	0.0582	0.0571	0.0559
−1.4	0.0808	0.0793	0.0778	0.0764	0.0749	0.0735	0.0721	0.0708	0.0694	0.0681
−1.3	0.0968	0.0951	0.0934	0.0918	0.0901	0.0885	0.0869	0.0853	0.0838	0.0823
−1.2	0.1151	0.1131	0.1112	0.1093	0.1075	0.1056	0.1038	0.1020	0.1003	0.0985
−1.1	0.1357	0.1335	0.1314	0.1292	0.1271	0.1251	0.1230	0.1210	0.1190	0.1170
−1.0	0.1587	0.1562	0.1539	0.1515	0.1492	0.1469	0.1446	0.1423	0.1401	0.1379
−0.9	0.1841	0.1814	0.1788	0.1762	0.1736	0.1711	0.1685	0.1660	0.1635	0.1611
−0.8	0.2119	0.2090	0.2061	0.2033	0.2005	0.1977	0.1949	0.1922	0.1894	0.1867
−0.7	0.2420	0.2388	0.2358	0.2327	0.2296	0.2266	0.2236	0.2206	0.2177	0.2148
−0.6	0.2743	0.2709	0.2676	0.2643	0.2611	0.2578	0.2546	0.2514	0.2482	0.2451
−0.5	0.3085	0.3050	0.3015	0.2981	0.2946	0.2912	0.2877	0.2843	0.2810	0.2776
−0.4	0.3446	0.3409	0.3372	0.3336	0.3300	0.3264	0.3228	0.3192	0.3156	0.3121
−0.3	0.3821	0.3783	0.3745	0.3707	0.3669	0.3632	0.3594	0.3557	0.3520	0.3483
−0.2	0.4207	0.4168	0.4129	0.4090	0.4052	0.4013	0.3974	0.3936	0.3897	0.3859
−0.1	0.4602	0.4562	0.4522	0.4483	0.4443	0.4404	0.4364	0.4325	0.4286	0.4247
−0.0	0.5000	0.4960	0.4920	0.4880	0.4840	0.4801	0.4761	0.4721	0.4681	0.4641